GO! with Microsoft® Office: Introductory

Now with:
GO! with Basic Computer Concepts: Getting Started
GO! with Windows® XP: Getting Started
CD included

Custom Edition for HACC, Central PA's Community College

CIS 105

Shelley Gaskin, Robert L. Ferrett, Alicia Vargas, Carolyn McLellan

Taken from:

GO! with Microsoft® Office 2007: Introductory, Third Edition
by Shelley Gaskin, Robert L. Ferrett, Alicia Vargas and Carolyn McLellan
GO! with Basic Computer Concepts: Getting Started
by Shelley Gaskin and Diane M. Coyle
GO! with Windows® XP: Getting Started
by Shelley Gaskin, Robert L. Ferrett, John Preston and Sally Preston

Custom Publishing

New York   Boston   San Francisco
London   Toronto   Sydney   Tokyo   Singapore   Madrid
Mexico City   Munich   Paris   Cape Town   Hong Kong   Montreal

Cover art: Courtesy of Photodisc/Getty Images and Brand X Pictures

Taken from:

GO! with Microsoft® Office 2007: Introductory, Third Edition
by Shelley Gaskin, Robert L. Ferrett, Alicia Vargas and Carolyn McLellan
Copyright © 2010, 2009, 2008 by Pearson Education, Inc.
Published by Prentice Hall
Upper Saddle River, New Jersey 07458

GO! with Basic Computer Concepts: Getting Started
by Shelley Gaskin and Diane M. Coyle
Copyright © 2008 by Pearson Education, Inc.
Published by Prentice Hall
Upper Saddle River, New Jersey 07458

GO! with Windows® XP: Getting Started
by Shelley Gaskin, Robert L. Ferrett, John Preston and Sally Preston
Copyright © 2008 by Pearson Education, Inc.
Published by Prentice Hall
Upper Saddle River, New Jersey 07458

This special edition published in cooperation with Pearson Custom Publishing.

The information, illustrations, and/or software contained in this book, and regarding the above-mentioned programs, are provided "As Is," without warranty of any kind, express or implied, including without limitation any warranty concerning the accuracy, adequacy, or completeness of such information. Neither the publisher, the authors, nor the copyright holders shall be responsible for any claims attributable to errors, omissions, or other inaccuracies contained in this book. Nor shall they be liable for direct, indirect, special, incidental, or consequential damages arising out of the use of such information or material.

All trademarks, service marks, registered trademarks, and registered service marks are the property of their respective owners and are used herein for identification purposes only.

Printed in the United States of America

10 9 8 7 6 5 4 3

2009820036

AM

Pearson
Custom Publishing
is a division of

www.pearsonhighered.com

ISBN 10: 0-558-31197-0
ISBN 13: 978-0-558-31197-1

Taken from: *GO! with Computer Concepts: Getting Started*
by Shelley Gaskin and Diane M. Coyle

Table of Contents

Taken from *GO! with Microsoft Windows XP: Getting Started* by Shelley Gaskin, Robert L. Ferrett, John Preston and Sally Preston

Table of Contents

Taken from *GO! with Microsoft Office 2007: Introductory,* **Third Edition**
by **Shelley Gaskin, Robert L. Ferrett, Alicia Vargas and Carolyn McLellan**

Table of Contents

Taken from: *GO! with Computer Concepts: Getting Started*
by Shelley Gaskin and Diane M. Coyle

Table of Contents

Letter from the Editor

Dear Instructors and Students,

The primary goal of the *GO!* Series is two-fold. The first goal is to help instructors teach the course they want in less time. The second goal is to provide students with the skills to solve business problems using the computer as a tool, for both themselves and the organization for which they might be employed.

The *GO!* Series was originally created by Series Editor Shelley Gaskin and published with the release of Microsoft Office 2003. Her ideas came from years of using textbooks that didn't meet all the needs of today's diverse classroom and that were too confusing for students. Shelley continues to enhance the series by ensuring we stay true to our vision of developing quality instruction and useful classroom tools.

But we also need your input and ideas.

Over time, the *GO!* Series has evolved based on direct feedback from instructors and students using the series. *We are the publisher that listens.* To publish a textbook that works for you, it's critical that we continue to listen to this feedback. It's important to me to talk with you and hear your stories about using *GO!* Your voice can make a difference.

My hope is that this letter will inspire you to write me an e-mail and share your thoughts on using the *GO!* Series.

Stephanie Wall
Executive Editor, *GO!* Series
stephanie_wall@prenhall.com

GO! System Contributors

We thank the following people for their hard work and support in making the GO! System all that it is!

Additional Author Support

Coyle, Diane	Montgomery County Community College
Fry, Susan	Boise State
Townsend, Kris	Spokane Falls Community College
Stroup, Tracey	Amgen Corporation

Instructor Resource Authors

Amer, Beverly	Northern Arizona University	Paterson, Jim	Paradise Valley Community College
Boito, Nancy	Harrisburg Area Community College	Prince, Lisa	Missouri State
Coyle, Diane	Montgomery County Community College	Rodgers, Gwen	Southern Nazarene University
Dawson, Tamara	Southern Nazarene University	Ruymann, Amy	Burlington Community College
Driskel, Loretta	Niagara County Community College	Ryan, Bob	Montgomery County Community College
Elliott, Melissa	Odessa College		
Fry, Susan	Boise State	Smith, Diane	Henry Ford College
Geoghan, Debra	Bucks County Community College	Spangler, Candice	Columbus State Community College
Hearn, Barbara	Community College of Philadelphia	Thompson, Joyce	Lehigh Carbon Community College
Jones, Stephanie	South Plains College	Tiffany, Janine	Reading Area Community College
Madsen, Donna	Kirkwood Community College	Watt, Adrienne	Douglas College
Meck, Kari	Harrisburg Area Community College	Weaver, Paul	Bossier Parish Community College
Miller, Cindy	Ivy Tech	Weber, Sandy	Gateway Technical College
Nowakowski, Tony	Buffalo State	Wood, Dawn	
Pace, Phyllis	Queensborough Community College	Weissman, Jonathan	Finger Lakes Community College

Super Reviewers

Brotherton, Cathy	Riverside Community College	Maurer, Trina	Odessa College
Cates, Wally	Central New Mexico Community College	Meck, Kari	Harrisburg Area Community College
		Miller, Cindy	Ivy Tech Community College
Cone, Bill	Northern Arizona University	Nielson, Phil	Salt Lake Community College
Coverdale, John	Riverside Community College	Rodgers, Gwen	Southern Nazarene University
Foster, Nancy	Baker College	Smolenski, Robert	Delaware Community College
Helfand, Terri	Chaffey College	Spangler, Candice	Columbus State Community College
Hibbert, Marilyn	Salt Lake Community College	Thompson, Joyce	Lehigh Carbon Community College
Holliday, Mardi	Community College of Philadelphia	Weber, Sandy	Gateway Technical College
Jerry, Gina	Santa Monica College	Wells, Lorna	Salt Lake Community College
Martin, Carol	Harrisburg Area Community College	Zaboski, Maureen	University of Scranton

Technical Editors

Janice Snyder
Joyce Nielsen
Colette Eisele
Janet Pickard
Mara Zebest
Lindsey Allen
William Daley

Student Reviewers

Allen, John	Asheville-Buncombe Tech Community College	Erickson, Mike	Ball State University
		Gadomski, Amanda	Northern Michigan University
Alexander, Steven	St. Johns River Community College	Gyselinck, Craig	Central Washington University
Alexander, Melissa	Tulsa Community College	Harrison, Margo	Central Washington University
Bolz, Stephanie	Northern Michigan University	Heacox, Kate	Central Washington University
Berner, Ashley	Central Washington University	Hill, Cheretta	Northwestern State University
Boomer, Michelle	Northern Michigan University	Innis, Tim	Tulsa Community College
Busse, Brennan	Northern Michigan University	Jarboe, Aaron	Central Washington University
Butkey, Maura	Central Washington University	Klein, Colleen	Northern Michigan University
Christensen, Kaylie	Northern Michigan University	Moeller, Jeffrey	Northern Michigan University
Connally, Brianna	Central Washington University	Nicholson, Regina	Athens Tech College
Davis, Brandon	Northern Michigan University	Niehaus, Kristina	Northern Michigan University
Davis, Christen	Central Washington University	Nisa, Zaibun	Santa Rosa Community College
Den Boer, Lance	Central Washington University	Nunez, Nohelia	Santa Rosa Community College
Dix, Jessica	Central Washington University	Oak, Samantha	Central Washington University
Moeller, Jeffrey	Northern Michigan University	Oertii, Monica	Central Washington University
Downs, Elizabeth	Central Washington University	Palenshus, Juliet	Central Washington University

Contributors continued

Pohl, Amanda	Northern Michigan University
Presnell, Randy	Central Washington University
Ritner, April	Northern Michigan University
Rodriguez, Flavia	Northwestern State University
Roberts, Corey	Tulsa Community College
Rossi, Jessica Ann	Central Washington University
Shafapay, Natasha	Central Washington University
Shanahan, Megan	Northern Michigan University
Teska, Erika	Hawaii Pacific University
Traub, Amy	Northern Michigan University
Underwood, Katie	Central Washington University
Walters, Kim	Central Washington University
Wilson, Kelsie	Central Washington University
Wilson, Amanda	Green River Community College

Series Reviewers

Abraham, Reni	Houston Community College
Agatston, Ann	Agatston Consulting Technical College
Alexander, Melody	Ball Sate University
Alejandro, Manuel	Southwest Texas Junior College
Ali, Farha	Lander University
Amici, Penny	Harrisburg Area Community College
Anderson, Patty A.	Lake City Community College
Andrews, Wilma	Virginia Commonwealth College, Nebraska University
Anik, Mazhar	Tiffin University
Armstrong, Gary	Shippensburg University
Atkins, Bonnie	Delaware Technical Community College
Bachand, LaDonna	Santa Rosa Community College
Bagui, Sikha	University of West Florida
Beecroft, Anita	Kwantlen University College
Bell, Paula	Lock Haven College
Belton, Linda	Springfield Tech. Community College
Bennett, Judith	Sam Houston State University
Bhatia, Sai	Riverside Community College
Bishop, Frances	DeVry Institute—Alpharetta (ATL)
Blaszkiewicz, Holly	Ivy Tech Community College/Region 1
Branigan, Dave	DeVry University
Bray, Patricia	Allegany College of Maryland
Brotherton, Cathy	Riverside Community College
Buehler, Lesley	Ohlone College
Buell, C	Central Oregon Community College
Byars, Pat	Brookhaven College
Byrd, Lynn	Delta State University, Cleveland, Mississippi
Cacace, Richard N.	Pensacola Junior College
Cadenhead, Charles	Brookhaven College
Calhoun, Ric	Gordon College
Cameron, Eric	Passaic Community College
Carriker, Sandra	North Shore Community College
Cannamore, Madie	Kennedy King
Carreon, Cleda	Indiana University—Purdue University, Indianapolis
Chaffin, Catherine	Shawnee State University
Chauvin, Marg	Palm Beach Community College, Boca Raton
Challa, Chandrashekar	Virginia State University
Chamlou, Afsaneh	NOVA Alexandria
Chapman, Pam	Wabaunsee Community College
Christensen, Dan	Iowa Western Community College
Clay, Betty	Southeastern Oklahoma State University
Collins, Linda D.	Mesa Community College
Conroy-Link, Janet	Holy Family College
Cosgrove, Janet	Northwestern CT Community
Courtney, Kevin	Hillsborough Community College
Cox, Rollie	Madison Area Technical College
Crawford, Hiram	Olive Harvey College
Crawford, Thomasina	Miami-Dade College, Kendall Campus
Credico, Grace	Lethbridge Community College
Crenshaw, Richard	Miami Dade Community College, North
Crespo, Beverly	Mt. San Antonio College
Crossley, Connie	Cincinnati State Technical Community College
Curik, Mary	Central New Mexico Community College
De Arazoza, Ralph	Miami Dade Community College
Danno, John	DeVry University/Keller Graduate School
Davis, Phillip	Del Mar College
DeHerrera, Laurie	Pikes Peak Community College
Delk, Dr. K. Kay	Seminole Community College
Doroshow, Mike	Eastfield College
Douglas, Gretchen	SUNYCortland
Dove, Carol	Community College of Allegheny
Driskel, Loretta	Niagara Community College
Duckwiler, Carol	Wabaunsee Community College
Duncan, Mimi	University of Missouri-St. Louis
Duthie, Judy	Green River Community College
Duvall, Annette	Central New Mexico Community College
Ecklund, Paula	Duke University
Eng, Bernice	Brookdale Community College
Evans, Billie	Vance-Granville Community College
Feuerbach, Lisa	Ivy Tech East Chicago
Fisher, Fred	Florida State University
Foster, Penny L.	Anne Arundel Community College
Foszcz, Russ	McHenry County College
Fry, Susan	Boise State University
Fustos, Janos	Metro State
Gallup, Jeanette	Blinn College
Gelb, Janet	Grossmont College
Gentry, Barb	Parkland College
Gerace, Karin	St. Angela Merici School
Gerace, Tom	Tulane University
Ghajar, Homa	Oklahoma State University
Gifford, Steve	Northwest Iowa Community College
Glazer, Ellen	Broward Community College
Gordon, Robert	Hofstra University
Gramlich, Steven	Pasco-Hernando Community College
Graviett, Nancy M.	St. Charles Community College, St. Peters, Missouri
Greene, Rich	Community College of Allegheny County
Gregoryk, Kerry	Virginia Commonwealth State
Griggs, Debra	Bellevue Community College
Grimm, Carol	Palm Beach Community College
Hahn, Norm	Thomas Nelson Community College
Hammerschlag, Dr. Bill	Brookhaven College
Hansen, Michelle	Davenport University
Hayden, Nancy	Indiana University—Purdue University, Indianapolis

Hayes, Theresa — Broward Community College
Helfand, Terri — Chaffey College
Helms, Liz — Columbus State Community College
Hernandez, Leticia — TCI College of Technology
Hibbert, Marilyn — Salt Lake Community College
Hoffman, Joan — Milwaukee Area Technical College
Hogan, Pat — Cape Fear Community College
Holland, Susan — Southeast Community College
Hopson, Bonnie — Athens Technical College
Horvath, Carrie — Albertus Magnus College
Horwitz, Steve — Community College of Philadelphia
Hotta, Barbara — Leeward Community College
Howard, Bunny — St. Johns River Community
Howard, Chris — DeVry University
Huckabay, Jamie — Austin Community College
Hudgins, Susan — East Central University
Hulett, Michelle J. — Missouri State University
Hunt, Darla A. — Morehead State University, Morehead, Kentucky
Hunt, Laura — Tulsa Community College
Jacob, Sherry — Jefferson Community College
Jacobs, Duane — Salt Lake Community College
Jauken, Barb — Southeastern Community
Johnson, Kathy — Wright College
Johnson, Mary — Kingwood College
Johnson, Mary — Mt. San Antonio College
Jones, Stacey — Benedict College
Jones, Warren — University of Alabama, Birmingham
Jordan, Cheryl — San Juan College
Kapoor, Bhushan — California State University, Fullerton
Kasai, Susumu — Salt Lake Community College
Kates, Hazel — Miami Dade Community College, Kendall
Keen, Debby — University of Kentucky
Keeter, Sandy — Seminole Community College
Kern-Blystone, Dorothy Jean — Bowling Green State
Keskin, Ilknur — The University of South Dakota
Kirk, Colleen — Mercy College
Kleckner, Michelle — Elon University
Kliston, Linda — Broward Community College, North Campus
Kochis, Dennis — Suffolk County Community College
Kramer, Ed — Northern Virginia Community College
Laird, Jeff — Northeast State Community College
Lamoureaux, Jackie — Central New Mexico Community College
Lange, David — Grand Valley State
LaPointe, Deb — Central New Mexico Community College
Larson, Donna — Louisville Technical Institute
Laspina, Kathy — Vance-Granville Community College
Le Grand, Dr. Kate — Broward Community College
Lenhart, Sheryl — Terra Community College
Letavec, Chris — University of Cincinnati
Liefert, Jane — Everett Community College
Lindaman, Linda — Black Hawk Community College
Lindberg, Martha — Minnesota State University
Lightner, Renee — Broward Community College
Lindberg, Martha — Minnesota State University
Linge, Richard — Arizona Western College
Logan, Mary G. — Delgado Community College
Loizeaux, Barbara — Westchester Community College
Lopez, Don — Clovis-State Center Community College District

Lord, Alexandria — Asheville Buncombe Tech
Lowe, Rita — Harold Washington College
Low, Willy Hui — Joliet Junior College
Lucas, Vickie — Broward Community College
Lynam, Linda — Central Missouri State University
Lyon, Lynne — Durham College
Lyon, Pat Rajski — Tomball College
MacKinnon, Ruth — Georgia Southern University
Macon, Lisa — Valencia Community College, West Campus
Machuca, Wayne — College of the Sequoias
Madison, Dana — Clarion University
Maguire, Trish — Eastern New Mexico University
Malkan, Rajiv — Montgomery College
Manning, David — Northern Kentucky University
Marcus, Jacquie — Niagara Community College
Marghitu, Daniela — Auburn University
Marks, Suzanne — Bellevue Community College
Marquez, Juanita — El Centro College
Marquez, Juan — Mesa Community College
Martyn, Margie — Baldwin-Wallace College
Marucco, Toni — Lincoln Land Community College
Mason, Lynn — Lubbock Christian University
Matutis, Audrone — Houston Community College
Matkin, Marie — University of Lethbridge
McCain, Evelynn — Boise State University
McCannon, Melinda — Gordon College
McCarthy, Marguerite — Northwestern Business College
McCaskill, Matt L. — Brevard Community College
McClellan, Carolyn — Tidewater Community College
McClure, Darlean — College of Sequoias
McCrory, Sue A. — Missouri State University
McCue, Stacy — Harrisburg Area Community College
McEntire-Orbach, Teresa — Middlesex County College
McLeod, Todd — Fresno City College
McManus, Illyana — Grossmont College
McPherson, Dori — Schoolcraft College
Meiklejohn, Nancy — Pikes Peak Community College
Menking, Rick — Hardin-Simmons University
Meredith, Mary — University of Louisiana at Lafayette
Mermelstein, Lisa — Baruch College
Metos, Linda — Salt Lake Community College
Meurer, Daniel — University of Cincinnati
Meyer, Marian — Central New Mexico Community College
Miller, Cindy — Ivy Tech Community College, Lafayette, Indiana
Mitchell, Susan — Davenport University
Mohle, Dennis — Fresno Community College
Monk, Ellen — University of Delaware
Moore, Rodney — Holland College
Morris, Mike — Southeastern Oklahoma State University
Morris, Nancy — Hudson Valley Community College
Moseler, Dan — Harrisburg Area Community College
Nabors, Brent — Reedley College, Clovis Center
Nadas, Erika — Wright College
Nadelman, Cindi — New England College
Nademlynsky, Lisa — Johnson & Wales University
Ncube, Cathy — University of West Florida
Nagengast, Joseph — Florida Career College
Newsome, Eloise — Northern Virginia Community College Woodbridge
Nicholls, Doreen — Mohawk Valley Community College
Nunan, Karen — Northeast State Technical Community College

Contributors continued

Odegard, Teri	Edmonds Community College	Sterling, Janet	Houston Community College
Ogle, Gregory	North Community College	Stoughton, Catherine	Laramie County Community College
Orr, Dr. Claudia	Northern Michigan University South	Sullivan, Angela	Joliet Junior College
Otieno, Derek	DeVry University	Szurek, Joseph	University of Pittsburgh at Greensburg
Otton, Diana Hill	Chesapeake College		
Oxendale, Lucia	West Virginia Institute of Technology	Tarver, Mary Beth	Northwestern State University
		Taylor, Michael	Seattle Central Community College
Paiano, Frank	Southwestern College	Thangiah, Sam	Slippery Rock University
Patrick, Tanya	Clackamas Community College	Thompson-Sellers, Ingrid	Georgia Perimeter College
Peairs, Deb	Clark State Community College	Tomasi, Erik	Baruch College
Prince, Lisa	Missouri State University-Springfield Campus	Toreson, Karen	Shoreline Community College
		Trifiletti, John J.	Florida Community College at Jacksonville
Proietti, Kathleen	Northern Essex Community College		
Pusins, Delores	HCCC	Trivedi, Charulata	Quinsigamond Community College, Woodbridge
Raghuraman, Ram	Joliet Junior College		
Reasoner, Ted Allen	Indiana University—Purdue	Tucker, William	Austin Community College
Reeves, Karen	High Point University	Turgeon, Cheryl	Asnuntuck Community College
Remillard, Debbie	New Hampshire Technical Institute	Turpen, Linda	Central New Mexico Community College
Rhue, Shelly	DeVry University		
Richards, Karen	Maplewoods Community College	Upshaw, Susan	Del Mar College
Richardson, Mary	Albany Technical College	Unruh, Angela	Central Washington University
Rodgers, Gwen	Southern Nazarene University	Vanderhoof, Dr. Glenna	Missouri State University-Springfield Campus
Roselli, Diane	Harrisburg Area Community College		
Ross, Dianne	University of Louisiana in Lafayette	Vargas, Tony	El Paso Community College
Rousseau, Mary	Broward Community College, South	Vicars, Mitzi	Hampton University
Samson, Dolly	Hawaii Pacific University	Villarreal, Kathleen	Fresno
Sams, Todd	University of Cincinnati	Vitrano, Mary Ellen	Palm Beach Community College
Sandoval, Everett	Reedley College	Volker, Bonita	Tidewater Community College
Sardone, Nancy	Seton Hall University	Wahila, Lori (Mindy)	Tompkins Cortland Community College
Scafide, Jean	Mississippi Gulf Coast Community College		
		Waswick, Kim	Southeast Community College, Nebraska
Scheeren, Judy	Westmoreland County Community College		
		Wavle, Sharon	Tompkins Cortland Community College
Schneider, Sol	Sam Houston State University		
Scroggins, Michael	Southwest Missouri State University	Webb, Nancy	City College of San Francisco
Sever, Suzanne	Northwest Arkansas Community College	Wells, Barbara E.	Central Carolina Technical College
		Wells, Lorna	Salt Lake Community College
Sheridan, Rick	California State University-Chico	Welsh, Jean	Lansing Community College Nebraska
Silvers, Pamela	Asheville Buncombe Tech		
Singer, Steven A.	University of Hawai'i, Kapi'olani Community College	White, Bruce	Quinnipiac University
		Willer, Ann	Solano Community College
Sinha, Atin	Albany State University	Williams, Mark	Lane Community College
Skolnick, Martin	Florida Atlantic University	Wilson, Kit	Red River College
Smith, T. Michael	Austin Community College	Wilson, Roger	Fairmont State University
Smith, Tammy	Tompkins Cortland Community Collge	Wimberly, Leanne	International Academy of Design and Technology
Smolenski, Bob	Delaware County Community College		
		Worthington, Paula	Northern Virginia Community College
Spangler, Candice	Columbus State		
Stedham, Vicki	St. Petersburg College, Clearwater	Yauney, Annette	Herkimer County Community College
Stefanelli, Greg	Carroll Community College		
Steiner, Ester	New Mexico State University	Yip, Thomas	Passaic Community College
Stenlund, Neal	Northern Virginia Community College, Alexandria	Zavala, Ben	Webster Tech
		Zlotow, Mary Ann	College of DuPage
St. John, Steve	Tulsa Community College	Zudeck, Steve	Broward Community College, North

About the Author

Shelley Gaskin, Series Editor, is a professor of business and computer technology at Pasadena City College in Pasadena, California. She holds a master's degree in business education from Northern Illinois University and a doctorate in adult and community education from Ball State University. Dr. Gaskin has 15 years of experience in the computer industry with several Fortune 500 companies and has developed and written training materials for custom systems applications in both the public and private sector. She is also the author of books on Microsoft Outlook and word processing.

Diane M. Coyle is an adjunct instructor and full-time administrator at Montgomery County Community College in Blue Bell, Pennsylvania, where she has been teaching computer literacy, office applications, and Web design classes for more than six years. Her work in the fields of marketing and project management helps her to present a balanced and practical focus to the information she shares with her students.

Visual Walk-Through of the *GO!* System

The *GO!* System is designed for ease of implementation on the instructor side and ease of understanding on the student. It has been completely developed based on professor and student feedback.

The *GO!* System is divided into three categories that reflect how you might organize your course— **Prepare**, **Teach**, and **Assess**.

Prepare

NEW

Transition Guide

New to *GO!*—We've made it quick and easy to plan the format and activities for your class.

GO!

Because the GO! System was designed and written by instructors like yourself, it includes the tools that allow you to Prepare, Teach, and Assess in your course. We have organized the GO! System into these three categories that match how you work through your course and thus, it's even easier for you to implement.

To help you get started, here is an outline of the first activities you may want to do in order to conduct your course.

There are several other tools not listed here that are available in the GO! System so please refer to your GO! Guide for a complete listing of all the tools.

Prepare
1. Prepare the course syllabus
2. Plan the course assignments
3. Organize the student resources

Teach
4. Conduct demonstrations and lectures

Assess
5. Assign and grade assignments, quizzes, tests, and assessments

PREPARE

1. Prepare the course syllabus
A syllabus template is provided on the IRCD in the **go07_syllabus_template** folder of the main directory. It includes a course calendar planner for 8-week, 12-week, and 16-week formats. Depending on your term (summer or regular semester) you can modify one of these according to your course plan, and then add information pertinent to your course and institution.

2. Plan course assignments
For each chapter, an Assignment Sheet listing every in-chapter and end-of-chapter project is located on the IRCD within the **go001_goloffice2007intro_instructor_resources_by_chapter** folder. From there, navigate to the specific chapter folder. These sheets are Word tables, so you can delete rows for the projects that you choose not to assign or add rows for your own assignments—if any. There is a column to add the number of points you want to assign to each project depending on your grading scheme. At the top of the sheet, you can fill in the course information.

Transitioning to GO! Office 2007   Page 1 of 1

Syllabus Template

Includes course calendar planner for 8-,12-, and 16-week formats.

GO! with Microsoft Office 2007 Introductory
SAMPLE SYLLABUS (16 weeks)

I. COURSE INFORMATION

Course No.:	Semester:
Course Title:	Credits:
Course Hours:	
Instructor:	Office:
Office Hours:	
Email:	Phone:

II. TEXT AND MATERIALS
Before starting the course, you will need the following:

- GO! with Microsoft Office 2007 Introductory by Shelley Gaskin, Robert L. Ferrett, Alicia Vargas, Suzanne Marks ©2007, published by Pearson Prentice Hall. ISBN 0-13-167990-6
- Storage device for saving files (any of the following: multiple diskettes, CD-RW, flash drive, etc.)

III. WHAT YOU WILL LEARN IN THIS COURSE
This is a hands-on course where you will learn to use a computer to practice the most commonly used Microsoft programs including the Windows operating system, Internet Explorer for navigating the Internet, Outlook for managing your personal information and the four most popular programs within the Microsoft Office Suite (Word, Excel, PowerPoint and Access). You will also practice the basics of using a computer, mouse and keyboard. You will learn to be an intermediate level user of the Microsoft Office Suite.

Within the Microsoft Office Suite, you will use Word, Excel, PowerPoint, and Access. Microsoft Word is a word processing program with which you can create common business and personal documents. Microsoft Excel is a spreadsheet program that organizes and calculates accounting-type information. Microsoft PowerPoint is a presentation graphics program with which you can develop slides to accompany an oral presentation. Finally, Microsoft Access is a database program that organizes large amounts of information in a useful manner.

Assignment Sheet

One per chapter. Lists all possible assignments; add to and delete from this simple Word table according to your course plan.

GO! with Microsoft Office 2007 Introductory

Assignment Sheet for GO! with Microsoft Office 2007 Introductory
Chapter 5

Instructor Name: _____
Course Information: _____

Do This (✓ when done)	Then Hand In This Check each Project for the elements listed on the Assignment Tag. Attach the Tag to your Project.	Submit Printed Formulas	By This Date	Possible Points	Your Points
Study the text and perform the steps for Activities 5.1 – 5.11	Project 5A Application Letter				
Study the text and perform the steps for Activities 5.12 – 5.29	Project 5B Company Overview				
End-of-Chapter Assessments					
Complete the Matching and Fill-in-the-Blank questions	As directed by your instructor				
Complete Project 5C	Project 5C Receipt Letter				
Complete Project 5D	Project 5D Marketing				
Complete Project 5E	Project 5E School Tour				
Complete Project 5F	Project 5F Scouting Trip				
Complete Project 5G	Project 5G Contract				
Complete Project 5H	Project 5H Invitation				
Complete Project 5I	Project 5I Fax Cover				
Complete Project 5J	Project 5J Business Running Case				
Complete Project 5K	Project 5K Services				
Complete Project 5L	Project 5L Survey Form				
Complete Project 5M	Project 5M Press Release				

Copyright © 2006 Pearson Prentice Hall   Page 1 of 1

File Guide to the GO! Supplements

Tabular listing of all supplements and their file names.

GO! with Microsoft Office Office 2003
Supplements File Guide - Assess & Grade

(tabular listing of supplement file names)

Assignment Planning Guide

Description of GO! assignments with recommendations based on class size, delivery mode, and student needs. Includes examples from fellow instructors.

GO! with Microsoft Office 2007 Introductory
Assignment Planning Guide

Planning the Course Assignments

For each chapter in GO!, an Assignment Sheet listing every in-chapter and end-of-chapter project is located on the IRCD. These sheets are Word tables, so you can delete rows for the projects that you will not assign, and then add rows for any of your own assignments that you may have developed. There is a column to add the number of points you want to assign to each project—depending on your grading scheme. At the top of the sheet, you can fill in your course information.

Additionally, for each chapter, student Assignment Tags are provided for every project (including Problem Solving projects)—also located on the IRCD. These are small scoring checklists on which you can check off errors made by the student, and with which the student can verify that all project elements are complete. For campus classes, the student can attach the tags to his or her paper submissions. For online classes, many GO! instructors have the student include these with the electronic submission.

Deciding What to Assign

Front Portion of the Chapter—Instructional Projects: The projects in the front portion of the chapter, which are listed on the first page of each chapter, are the instructional projects. Most instructors assign all of these projects, because this is where the student receives the instruction and engages in the active learning.

End-of-Chapter—Practice and Critical Thinking Projects: In the back portion of the chapter (the gray pages), you can assign on a prescriptive basis; that is, for students who were challenged by the instructional projects, you might assign one or more projects from the two *Skills Reviews*, which provide maximum prompting and a thorough review of the entire chapter. For students who have previous software knowledge and who completed the instructional projects easily, you might assign only the *Mastery Projects*.

You can also assign prescriptively by Objective, because each end-of-chapter project indicates the Objectives covered. So you might assign, on a student-by-student basis, only the projects that cover the Objectives with which the student seemed to have difficulty in the instructional projects.

The five Problem Solving projects and the You and GO! project are the authentic assessments that pull together the student's learning. Here the student is presented with a "messy real-life situation" and then uses his or her knowledge and skill to solve a problem, produce a product, give a presentation, or demonstrate a procedure. You might assign one or more of the Problem

GO! Assignment Planning Guide   Page 1 of 1

Student Data Files

Music School Records discovers, launches, and and develops the careers of young artists in classical, jazz, and contemporary music. Our philosophy is to not only shape, distribute, and sell a music product, but to help artists create a career that can lats a lifetime. too often in the music industry, artists are forced to fit their music to a trend that is short-lived. Music School Records doesn't just follow trends, we take a long-term view of the music industry and help our artists develop a style and repertiore that is fluid and flexible and that will appeal to audiences for years and even decades.

The music industry is constantly changing, but over the last decade the changes have been enormous. New forms of entertainment such as DVDs, video games, and the Internet mean there are more competition for the leisure dollar in the market. New technologies give consmers more options for buying and listening to music, and they are demaning high quality recordings. Young consumers are comfortable with technology and want the music they love when and where they want it, no matter where they are or what they are doing.

Music School Records embraces new technologies and the sophisticated market of young music lovers. We believe that providing high quality recordings of truly talented artists make for more discerning listeners who will cherish the gift of music for the rest of their lives. The expertise of Music School Records includes:

- Insight into our target market and the ability to reach the desired audience
- The ability to access all current sources of music income
- A management team with years of experience in music commerce
- Innovative business strategies and artist development plans
- Investment in technology infrastructure for high quality recordings and business services
- Initiative and proactive management of artist careers

Online Study Guide for Students

Interactive objective-style questions based on chapter content.

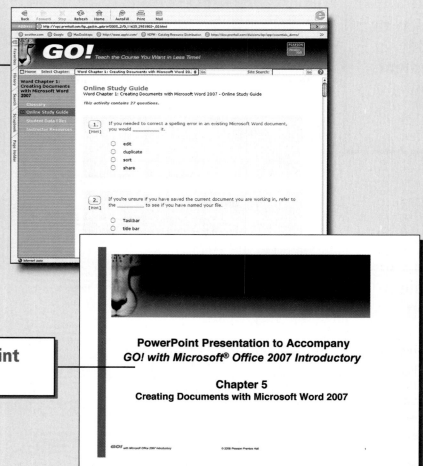

PowerPoint Slides

PowerPoint Presentation to Accompany
GO! with Microsoft® Office 2007 Introductory

Chapter 5
Creating Documents with Microsoft Word 2007

Teach

Student Textbook

Learning Objectives and Student Outcomes

Objectives are clustered around projects that result in student outcomes. They help students learn how to solve problems, not just learn software features.

Word 2007

5 chapterfive

Creating Documents with Microsoft Word 2007

OBJECTIVES
At the end of this chapter you will be able to:

OUTCOMES
Mastering these objectives will enable you to:

1. Create and Save a New Document
2. Edit Text
3. Select, Delete, and Format Text
4. Print a Document

PROJECT 5A
Create, Edit, Save, and Print a Document

5. Navigate the Word Window
6. Add a Graphic to a Document
7. Use the Spelling and Grammar Checker
8. Preview and Print Documents, Close a Document, and Close Word
9. Use the Microsoft Help System

PROJECT 5B
Navigate the Word Window and Check Your Work

Word 237

Project-Based Instruction

Students do not practice features of the application; they create real projects that they will need in the real world. Projects are color coded for easy reference and are named to reflect skills the students will be practicing.

NEW

A and B Projects

Each chapter contains two instructional projects—A and B.

Music School Records

Music School Records was created to launch young musical artists with undiscovered talent in jazz, classical, and contemporary music. The creative management team searches internationally for talented young people, and has a reputation for mentoring and developing the skills of its artists. The company's music is tailored to an audience that is young, knowledgeable about music, and demands the highest quality recordings. Music School Records releases are available in CD format as well as digital downloads.

Getting Started with Microsoft Office Word 2007

A word processor is the most common program found on personal computers and one that almost everyone has a reason to use. When you learn word processing you are also learning skills and techniques that you need to work efficiently on a personal computer. You can use Microsoft Word to perform basic word processing tasks such as writing a memo, a report, or a letter. You can also use Word to complete complex word processing tasks, such as those that include sophisticated tables, embedded graphics, and links to other documents and the Internet. Word is a program that you can learn gradually, and then add more advanced skills one at a time.

Each chapter opens with a story that sets the stage for the projects the student will create; the instruction does not force the student to pretend to be someone or make up a scenario.

Each chapter has an introductory paragraph that briefs students on what is important.

Visual Summary
Shows students upfront what their projects will look like when they are done.

Project Summary
Stated clearly and quickly in one paragraph.

NEW

File Guide
Clearly shows students which files are needed for the project and the names they will use to save their documents.

Objective
The skills the student will learn are clearly stated at the beginning of each project and color coded to match projects listed on the chapter opener page.

Teachable Moment
Expository text is woven into the steps—at the moment students need to know it—not chunked together in a block of text that will go unread.

KEY FEATURE **GO!**

NEW

Screen Shots
Larger screen shots.

5A

Project 5A Application Letter

In Activities 5.1 through 5.11, you will create and make changes to a letter from John Diamond, Vice President of Creative Development, to William Hawken, an artist interested in becoming a client of Music School Records. Your completed document will look similar to Figure 5.1.

For Project 5A, you will need the following file:

New blank Word document

You will save your document as
5A_Application_Letter_Firstname_Lastname

Figure 5.1
Project 5A—Application Letter

Objective 1
Create and Save a New Document

With a word processing program, you can type, *edit*—make changes to—move, and delete text or change the appearance of text. Because the documents that you create are stored electronically, they can be duplicated, printed, copied, and shared with others. In this project, you will become

Project 5A: Application Letter | **Word** 239

---

familiar with the parts of the Word window. Then you will create a document, edit and format text, and save your work.

Activity 5.1 Starting Word and Identifying Parts of the Word Window

Note — Comparing Your Screen With the Figures in This Textbook

Your screen will match the figures shown in this textbook if you set your screen resolution to 1024 × 768. At other resolutions, your screen will closely resemble, but not match, the figures shown. To view your screen's resolution, on the Windows desktop, right-click in a blank area, click Properties, and then click the Settings tab.

1. On the left side of the Windows taskbar, point to, and then click the **Start** button.

2. From the displayed **Start** menu, locate the **Word** program, and then click **Microsoft Office Word 2007**.
   The Word program may be located under All Programs or Microsoft Office or on the main Start menu.
   Print Layout view is the ideal view to use when you are learning Microsoft Word 2007 because you can see the document exactly the way it will look when it is printed.

3. If necessary, on the right side of the status bar, click the **Print Layout** button. If the ruler does not display, click the View tab, and then in the Show/Hide group, click the Ruler check box. Take a moment to study the parts of the Word screen shown in Figure 5.2 and described in the table in Figure 5.3.

Figure 5.2

240 **Word** | Chapter 5: Creating Documents with Microsoft Word 2007

Steps

Color coded to the current project, easy to read, and not too many to confuse the student or too few to be meaningless.

Sequential Pagination

No more confusing letters and abbreviations.

End-of-Project Icon

All projects in the *GO! Series* have clearly identifiable end points, useful in self-paced or on-line environments.

Microsoft Procedural Syntax

All steps are written in Microsoft Procedural Syntax to put the student in the right place at the right time.

Press [Enter] two more times.

In a business letter, insert two blank lines between the date and the inside address, which is the same as the address you would use on an envelope.

Type **Mr. William Hawken** and then press [Enter].

The wavy red line under the proper name *Hawken* indicates that the word has been flagged as misspelled because it is a word not contained in the Word dictionary.

On two lines, type the following address, but do not press [Enter] at the end of the second line:

123 Eighth Street
Harrisville, MI 48740

Note — Typing the Address

Include a comma after the city name in an inside address. However, for mailing addresses on envelopes, eliminate the comma after the city name.

On the **Home tab**, in the **Styles group**, click the **Normal** button.

The Normal style is applied to the text in the rest of the document. Recall that the Normal style adds extra space between paragraphs; it also adds slightly more space between lines in a paragraph.

Press [Enter]. Type **Dear William:** and then press [Enter].

This salutation is the line that greets the person receiving the letter.

Type **Subject: Your Application to Music School Records** and press [Enter]. Notice the light dots between words, which indicate spaces and display when formatting marks are displayed. Also, notice the extra space after each paragraph, and then compare your screen with Figure 5.6.

The subject line is optional, but you should include a subject line in most letters to identify the topic. Depending on your Word settings, a wavy green line may display in the subject line, indicating a potential grammar error.

Note — Space Between Lines in Your Printed Document

The Cambria font, and many others, uses a slightly larger space between the lines than more traditional fonts like Times New Roman. As you progress in your study of Word, you will use many different fonts and also adjust the spacing between lines.

From the **Office** menu, click **Close**, saving any changes if prompted to do so. Leave Word open for the next project.

Another Way

To Print a Document

To Print a document:

• From the Office menu, click Print to display the Print dialog box (to be covered later), from which you can choose a variety of different options, such as printing multiple copies, printing on a different printer, and printing some but not all pages.

• Hold down [Ctrl] and then press [P]. This is an alternative to the Office menu command, and opens the Print dialog box.

• Hold down [Alt], press [F], and then press [P]. This opens the Print dialog box.

End You have completed Project 5A

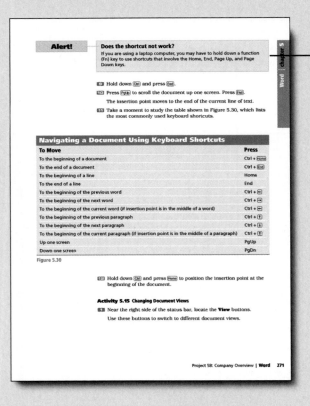

Alert box
Draws students' attention to make sure they aren't getting too far off course.

Another Way box
Shows students other ways of doing tasks.

More Knowledge box
Expands on a topic by going deeper into the material.

Note box
Points out important items to remember.

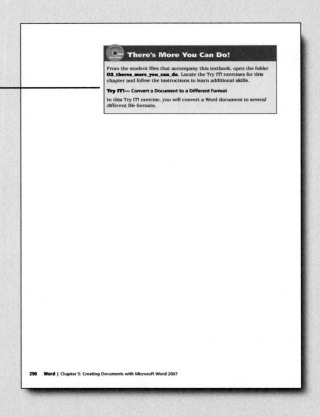

NEW

There's More You Can Do!
Try IT! exercises that teach students additional skills.

End-of-Chapter Material

Take your pick! Content-based or Outcomes-based projects to choose from. Below is a table outlining the various types of projects that fit into these two categories.

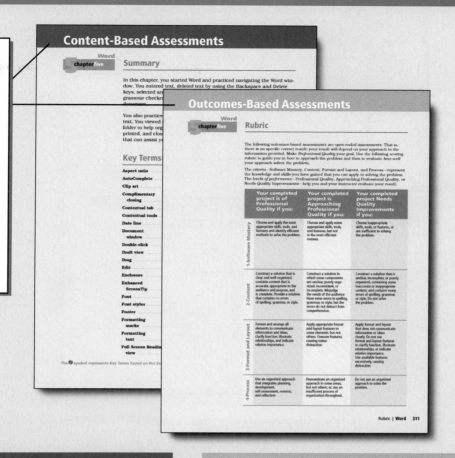

Content-Based Assessments
(Defined solutions with solution files provided for grading)

Project Letter	Name	Objectives Covered
N/A	Summary and Key Terms	
N/A	Multiple Choice	
N/A	Fill-in-the-blank	
C	Skills Review	Covers A Objectives
D	Skills Review	Covers B Objectives
E	Mastering Excel	Covers A Objectives
F	Mastering Excel	Covers B Objectives
G	Mastering Excel	Covers any combination of A and B Objectives
H	Mastering Excel	Covers any combination of A and B Objectives
I	Mastering Excel	Covers all A and B Objectives
J	Business Running Case	Covers all A and B Objectives

Outcomes-Based Assessments
(Open solutions that require a rubric for grading)

Project Letter	Name	Objectives Covered
N/A	Rubric	
K	Problem Solving	Covers as many Objectives from A and B as possible
L	Problem Solving	Covers as many Objectives from A and B as possible.
M	Problem Solving	Covers as many Objectives from A and B as possible.
N	Problem Solving	Covers as many Objectives from A and B as possible.
O	Problem Solving	Covers as many Objectives from A and B as possible.
P	You and GO!	Covers as many Objectives from A and B as possible
Q	GO! Help	Not tied to specific objectives
R	* Group Business Running Case	Covers A and B Objectives

* This project is provided only with the *GO! with Microsoft Office 2007 Introductory* book.

Teach (continued)

Objectives List

Most projects in the end-of-chapter section begin with a list of the objectives covered.

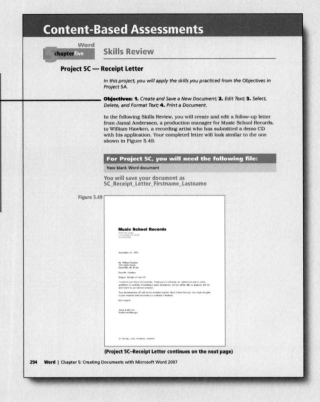

End of Each Project Clearly Marked

Clearly identified end points help separate the end-of-chapter projects.

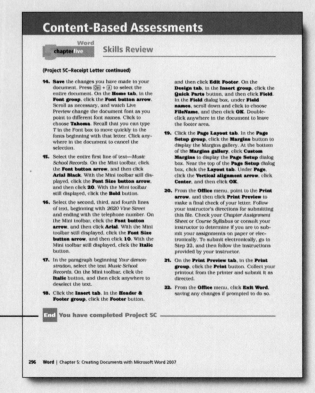

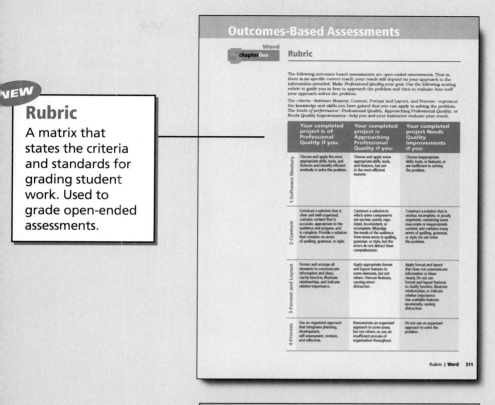

NEW

Rubric

A matrix that states the criteria and standards for grading student work. Used to grade open-ended assessments.

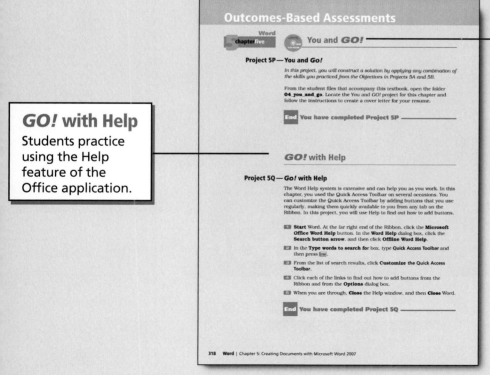

NEW

You and *GO!*

A project in which students use information from their own lives and apply the skills from the chapter to a personal task.

GO! with Help

Students practice using the Help feature of the Office application.

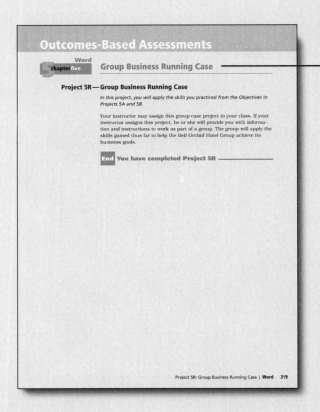

NEW

Group Business Running Case

A continuing project developed for groups that spans the chapters within each application.

Student CD includes:

- Student Data Files
- There's More You Can Do!
- Business Running Case
- You and *GO!*

Companion Web site

An interactive Web site to further student leaning.

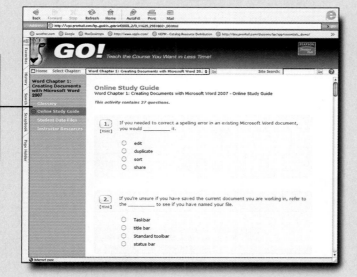

Online Study Guide

Interactive objective-style questions to help students study.

Annotated Instructor Edition

The Annotated Instructor Edition contains a full version of the student textbook that includes tips, supplement references, and pointers on teaching with the *GO!* instructional system.

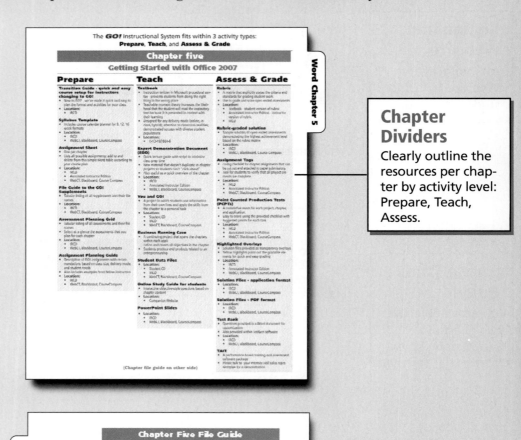

Chapter Dividers

Clearly outline the resources per chapter by activity level: Prepare, Teach, Assess.

Instructor File Guide

Complete list of all Student Data Files and instructor Solution Files needed for the chapter.

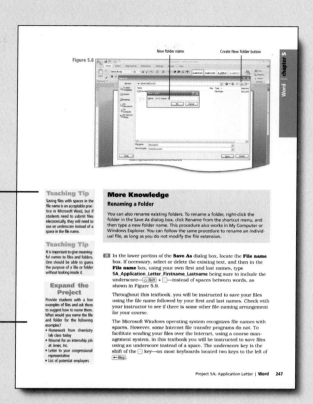

Helpful Hints, Teaching Tips, Expand the Project

References correspond to what is being taught in the student textbook.

NEW

Full-Size Textbook Pages

An instructor copy of the textbook with traditional Instructor Manual content incorporated.

End-of-Chapter Concepts Assessments

contain the answers for quick reference.

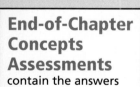

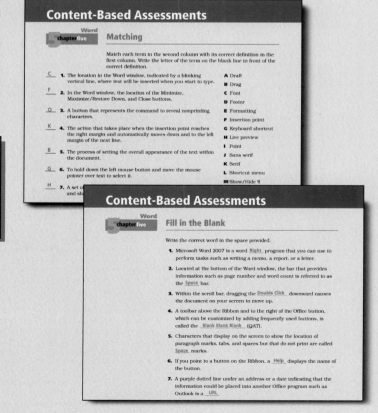

NEW

Rubric

A matrix to guide the student on how they will be assessed is reprinted in the Annotated Instructor Edition with suggested weights for each of the criteria and levels of performance. Instructors can modify the weights to suit their needs.

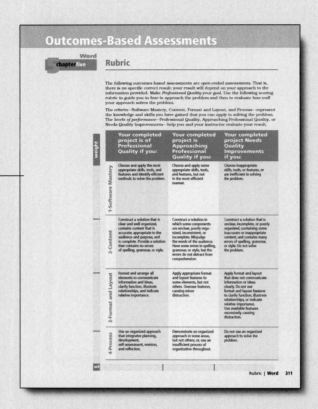

Assess

Assignment Tags

Scoring checklist for assignments. Now also available for Problem-Solving projects.

NEW

GO! with Microsoft® Office 2007

Assignment Tags for GO! with Office 2007
Word Chapter 5

Name:	Project:	5A
Professor:	Course:	

Task	Points	Your Score
Center text vertically on page	2	
Delete the word "really"	1	
Delete the words "try to"	1	
Replace "last" with "first"	1	
Insert the word "potential"	1	
Replace "John W. Diamond" with "Lucy Burrows"	2	
Change entire document to the Cambria font	2	
Change the first line of text to Arial Black 20 pt. font	2	
Bold the first line of text	2	
Change the 2nd through 4th lines to Arial 10 pt.	2	
Italicize the 2nd through 4th lines of text	2	
Correct/Add footer as instructed	2	
Circled information is incorrect or formatted incorrectly		
Total Points	**20**	**0**

Name:	Project:	5B
Professor:	Course:	

Task	Points	Your Score
Insert the file w05B_Music_School_Records	4	
Insert the Music Logo	4	
Remove duplicate "and"	2	
Change spelling and grammar errors (4)	8	
Correct/Add footer as instructed	2	
Circled information is incorrect or formatted incorrectly		
Total Points	**20**	**0**

Name:	Project:	5C
Professor:	Course:	

Task	Points	Your Score
Add four line letterhead	2	
Insert today's date	1	
Add address block, subject line, and greeting	2	
Add two-paragraph body of letter	2	
Add closing, name, and title	2	
In subject line, capitalize "receipt"	1	
Change "standards" to "guidelines"	1	
Insert "quite"	1	
Insert "all"	1	
Change the first line of text to Arial Black 20 pt. font	2	
Bold the first line of text		
Change the 2nd through 4th lines to Arial 10 pt.	1	
Italicize the 2nd through 4th lines of text	1	
Correct/add footer as instructed	2	
Circled information is incorrect or formatted incorrectly		
Total Points	**20**	**0**

Name:	Project:	5D
Professor:	Course:	

Task	Points	Your Score
Insert the file w05D_Marketing	4	
Bold the first two title lines	2	
Correct spelling of "Marketting"	2	
Correct spelling of "geners"	2	
Correct all misspellings of "already"	2	
Correct grammar error "are" to "is"	2	
Insert the Piano image	4	
Correct/add footer as instructed	2	
Circled information is incorrect or formatted incorrectly		
Total Points	**20**	**0**

Highlighted Overlays

Solution files provided as transparency overlays. Yellow highlights point out the gradable elements for quick and easy grading.

Music School Records

← 20 point Arial Black, bold and underline

2620 Vine Street
Los Angeles, CA 90028 ← 10 point Arial, italic
323-555-0028

September 12, 2009

Mr. William Hawken
123 Eighth Street
Harrisville, MI 48740

Text vertically centered on page

Body of document changed to Cambria font, 11 point

Dear William:

Subject: Your Application to Music School Records

Thank you for submitting your application to Music School Records. Our talent scout for Northern Michigan, Catherine McDonald, is very enthusiastic about your music, and the demo CD you submitted certainly confirms her opinion.   Word "really" deleted

We discuss our applications from potential clients during the first week of each month. We will have a decision for you by the second week of October.

Words "try to" deleted

Yours Truly,

Lucy Burroughs

Point-Counted Production Tests (PCPTs)

A cumulative exam for each **project**, **chapter**, and **application**. Easy to score using the provided checklist with suggested points for each task.

GO! with Microsoft® Office 2007 Introductory

Point-Counted Production Test—Project for GO! with Microsoft® Office 2007 Introductory Project 5A

Instructor Name: _____
Course Information: _____

1. Start Word 2007 to begin a new blank document. Save your document as 5A_Cover_Letter_Firstname_Lastname Remember to save your file frequently as you work.

2. If necessary, display the formatting marks. With the insertion point blinking in the upper left corner of the document to the left of the default first paragraph mark, type the current date (you can use AutoComplete).

3. Press Enter three times and type the inside address:

   Music School Records
   2620 Vine Street
   Los Angeles, CA 90028

4. Press Enter three times, and type Dear Ms. Burroughs:

   Press Enter twice, and type Subject: Application to Music School Records

   Press Enter twice, and type the following text (skipping one line between paragraphs):

   I read about Music School Records in Con Brio magazine and I would like to inquire about the possibility of being represented by your company.

   I am very interested in a career in jazz and am planning to relocate to the Los Angeles area in the very near future. I would be interested in learning more about the company and about available opportunities.

   I was a member of my high school jazz band for three years. In addition, I have been playing in the local coffee shop for the last two years. My demo CD, which is enclosed, contains three of my most requested songs.

   I would appreciate the opportunity to speak with you. Thank you for your time and consideration. I look forward to speaking with you about this exciting opportunity.

5. Press Enter three times, and type the closing Sincerely, Press enter four times, and type your name.

6. Insert a footer that contains the file name.

7. Delete the first instance of the word *very* in the second body paragraph, and insert the word modern in front of *jazz*.

Copyright © 2008 Pearson Prentice Hall   Page 1 of 1

Test Bank

Available as TestGen Software or as a Word document for customization.

Chapter 5: Creating Documents with Microsoft Word 2007

Multiple Choice:

1. With word processing programs, how are documents stored?

   A. On a network

   B. On the computer

   C. Electronically

   D. On the floppy disk

   Answer: C   **Reference:** Objective 1: Create and Save a New Document   **Difficulty:** Moderate

2. Because you will see the document as it will print, _____ view is the ideal view to use when learning Microsoft Word 2007.

   A. Reading

   B. Normal

   C. Print Layout

   D. Outline

   Answer: C   **Reference:** Objective 1: Create and Save a New Document   **Difficulty:** Moderate

3. The blinking vertical line where text or graphics will be inserted is called the:

   A. cursor.

   B. insertion point.

   C. blinking line.

   D. I-beam.

   Answer: B   **Reference:** Objective 1: Create and Save a New Document   **Difficulty:** Easy

---

Music School Records

Music School Records discovers, launches, and develops the careers of young artists in classical, jazz, and contemporary music. Our philosophy is to not only shape, distribute, and sell a music product, but to help artists create a career that can last a lifetime. Too often in the music industry, artists are forced to fit their music to a trend that is short-lived. Music School Records does not just follow trends, we take a long-term view of the music industry and help our artists develop a style and repertoire that is fluid and flexible and that will appeal to audiences for years and even decades.

The music industry is constantly changing, but over the last decade, the changes have been enormous. New forms of entertainment such as DVDs, video games, and the Internet mean there is more competition for the leisure dollar in the market. New technologies give consumers more options for buying and listening to music, and they are demanding high quality recordings. Young consumers are comfortable with technology and want the music they love when and where they want it, no matter where they are or what they are doing.

Music School Records embraces new technologies and the sophisticated market of young music lovers. We believe that providing high quality recordings of truly talented artists make for more discerning listeners who will cherish the gift of music for the rest of their lives. The expertise of Music School Records includes:

- Insight into our target market and the ability to reach the desired audience
- The ability to access all current sources of music income
- A management team with years of experience in music commerce
- Innovative business strategies and artist development plans
- Investment in technology infrastructure for high quality recordings and business services

pagexxxix_top.docx

Solution Files– Application and PDF format

Online Assessment and Training

my**it**lab is Prentice Hall's new performance-based solution that allows you to easily deliver outcomes-based courses on Microsoft Office 2007, with customized training and defensible assessment. Key features of my**it**lab include:

A *true* "system" approach: my**it**lab content is the same as in your textbook.
Project-based *and* skills-based: Students complete real-life assignments.
Advanced reporting *and* gradebook: These include student click stream data.
***No* installation required:** my**it**lab is completely Web-based. You just need an Internet connection, small plug-in, and Adobe Flash Player.

Ask your Prentice Hall sales representative for a demonstration or visit:

www.prenhall.com/myitlab

chapterone

Basic Computer Concepts

OBJECTIVES

At the end of this chapter you will be able to:

1. Define Computer and Identify the Four Basic Computing Functions
2. Identify the Different Types of Computers
3. Describe Hardware Devices and Their Uses
4. Identify Types of Software and Their Uses
5. Describe Networks and Define Network Terms
6. Identify Safe Computing Practices

Introduction

Computers are an integral part of our lives. They are found in homes, offices, stores, hospitals, libraries, and many other places. Computers are part of cars and phones, and they enable you to access bank accounts from home, shop online, and quickly communicate with people around the world by means of e-mail and the Internet. It is difficult to find a business or occupation that doesn't rely on computers. Whether it's a truck driver who keeps an electronic travel log or a high-powered stockbroker who needs up-to-the-second market information, computers make these tasks easier, more efficient, and more accurate.

Computers are all around us, which makes it important to learn basic computing skills and gain the knowledge to be a responsible computer user. Knowing how to use a computer makes you ***computer fluent***.

This chapter looks at different types of computers and their functions. It discusses computer hardware and software and the benefits of networking. In addition, this chapter also discusses the importance of safe computing practices and the ways that you can protect your computer from various threats.

Objective 1
Define Computer and Identify the Four Basic Computing Functions

What are the benefits of using computers? Becoming computer fluent can benefit you in several ways. The most practical advantage of being computer fluent is that it makes employees more attractive to potential employers. In fact, many employers expect employees to have basic computer skills when they are hired. If you are knowledgeable about computers and their uses, it also makes you a better consumer. It is easier to select and purchase the right computer for your needs if you understand computer terminology and the components of a computer. In addition, if you have a basic understanding of today's technology, you can better understand and use *new* technologies.

What are the basic functions of a computer? A ***computer*** is a programmable electronic device that can input, process, output, and store data. A computer takes ***data*** and converts it into ***information***. Many people use the words *data* and *information* interchangeably; however, they are different in computing and it is important to understand the distinction. Each piece of data entered into a computer represents a single fact or idea. Data can be a word, a number, a sound, or a picture.

Information is data that has been processed so that it can be presented in an organized and meaningful way. You might also think of data as pieces of a jigsaw puzzle and information as the finished puzzle. Putting the pieces of the puzzle together gives you the overall picture. For example, CIS 110, the letter B, and the names Amy and Stevens are pieces of data. Individually, these pieces of data seem meaningless. However, when processed, this data becomes the information on a grade report that indicates Amy Stevens received a grade of B in her CIS 110 class.

The four basic computer functions are also known as the ***information processing cycle***. The functions are

- ***Input***—The computer gathers data or allows a user to add data.
- ***Process***—Data is converted into information.
- ***Output***—The processed results are retrieved from the computer.
- ***Storage***—Data or information is stored for future use.

In the grade report, the instructor used a computer to enter, or input, the students' grades into the school's computerized grading system. A computer then processed this data along with data for other classes the students might have taken. In the example, the student, Amy, then received a written record of her grade or she accessed it online. Either way, the grade report was output by the computer. In addition, her grades remain stored in the system so they can be used to generate her transcript or to determine her future grade point average as she continues to take classes.

Objective 2
Identify the Different Types of Computers

What are the different types of computers and what are they used for? Although computers come in a variety of sizes and shapes, the basic components required to complete the information-processing cycle must be present in them. In addition to microcomputers—the desktop and notebook computers and mobile devices that many of us are familiar with—there are also specialty computers, including servers, mainframes, supercomputers, and embedded computers.

Microcomputers

What are microcomputers? **Microcomputers** are classified as small, inexpensive computers designed for personal use and are the computers that most people typically use. Computers in this category range in size from large desktop systems to handheld devices that fit in your pocket. Some of the most common types of microcomputers include the following:

- ***Desktop computers*** are computers that sit on the desk, floor, table, or another flat surface and have a detachable keyboard, mouse, monitor, and possibly other pieces of equipment.

  Desktop computers generally fall into two main categories: PCs or Macs. The PC, or personal computer—originally referred to as the IBM personal computer—is now manufactured by a variety of companies including Hewlett-Packard, Dell, and Gateway. The Apple Macintosh computer, now known as Mac, can perform the same functions as the PC.

  Computer users have been in a long-running argument about which is better—PC or Mac? There are pros and cons to both types of computers, but in reality, both are good systems and the choice usually comes down to personal preference. The primary differences between the PC and the Mac relate to the different microprocessors and operating systems each one uses. The PC is typically used in a Microsoft Windows operating environment, and the Mac uses the Mac operating system. Although the PC and the Mac each process information differently, both can perform the same types of tasks. The PC has a larger market share among general computer users and in business settings, whereas the Mac is popular with graphic design professionals.

- ***Notebook computers*** give users the ability to take their computers with them, making their information portable or mobile. Originally referred to as "laptops," this term is slowly being phased out in favor of the more accurate notebook designation. Although smaller than a desktop computer, notebook computers are not meant to be used on your lap, due to the amount of heat they generate. Notebooks are designed to be portable and include a rechargeable battery to provide power, permitting them to be used in a variety of places. Averaging about 6 pounds, a notebook's size and weight can also limit its computing power. Notebooks typically have a built-in display screen, a keyboard, and a pointing device, although it is possible to connect them to detachable devices for more comfortable desktop use.

- **Tablet computers** might seem similar to notebooks; however, they have some special features that set them apart. Tablet computers weigh less than notebooks, averaging about 3 pounds. They also have a convertible screen that swivels, allowing the tablet to be used like a standard notebook computer in one position or like a clipboard in the second position. This "clipboard" aspect is how the tablet got its name. When used in the tablet configuration, the user can actually write directly on the screen using a special pen known as a **stylus**. Tablets use advanced handwriting-recognition technology to convert handwriting to digital text. Many also use speech-recognition technology, which enables the user to record discussions or lectures, for example, or to control the computer using voice commands.

- **Mobile devices** include items such as **personal digital assistants (PDAs)**, **handheld computers**, and **smartphones**. These devices originally varied in size and purpose, but they are all ultra-lightweight and portable. PDAs were initially designed to provide a convenient resource for maintaining an organized calendar and list of business and personal associates. Handheld computers enabled users to access personal productivity software and send e-mail over the Internet, while smartphones added Internet capability to the wireless communication aspects of cell phones.

The newest mobile devices, often referred to simply as "handhelds," combine the best features of each of these devices. Many handheld devices now include personal productivity software and enable the user to play music, take photos, make phone calls, and access the Internet. PDAs and handheld computers often use a stylus, which is a pointed device used to input information and access various features. However, it is not uncommon for these devices to use a small detachable keyboard for text and data entry. As the features of mobile devices continue to converge, permitting them to perform similar tasks, it becomes more difficult to differentiate between these handheld devices. Figure 1.1 identifies four different types of microcomputers.

Figure 1.1

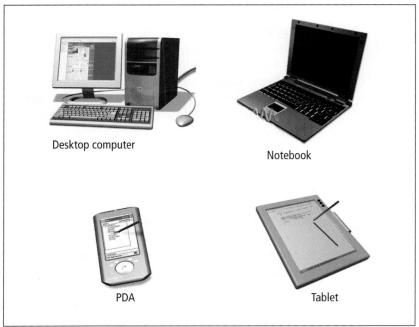

Desktop computer

Notebook

PDA

Tablet

Servers

What are servers? **Servers** are an important component of computer networks. These specialized computers manage network resources through the use of administrative software, and they provide desktop computers with access to the network. Servers can handle a variety of resources or may be assigned to just one particular type of task. Thus, within the same company, you may find a Web server that processes requests for the organization's Web pages and a file server that handles the storage and retrieval tasks for all of the company's files stored on the network.

Mainframe Computers

What are mainframe computers? **Mainframe computers** are large computers often found in businesses and colleges, where thousands of people are able to simultaneously use the computer to process data. Mainframe computers **multitask**; that is, they can perform more than one task at a time. Mainframes can store vast amounts of data using a variety of storage devices. Early mainframe computers were very large and required separate rooms to house them. Today's mainframe computers are significantly smaller.

Supercomputers

What are supercomputers? **Supercomputers** are large, powerful computers that perform specialized tasks. You might have heard of Deep Blue, the IBM supercomputer that challenged champion chess players to chess matches—and beat them! Supercomputers are the fastest and most expensive computers. Unlike a mainframe computer that can handle a number of programs simultaneously, the supercomputer is designed to run fewer programs at one time, but to do so as quickly as possible. They perform sophisticated mathematical calculations, track weather patterns, monitor satellites, and perform other complex, dedicated tasks.

Embedded Computers

What are embedded computers? **Embedded computers** are components of larger products that usually have a digital interface. These computers use a specially programmed microprocessor to perform a set of predefined tasks, and may require little or no input from the user. Microwave ovens, digital cameras, programmable thermostats, and airbags and antilock braking systems for cars are just a few examples of products that use embedded computers.

Objective 3
Describe Hardware Devices and Their Uses

What is computer hardware? **Hardware** is the computer and any equipment connected to it. Hardware devices are the physical components of the computer. Items such as the monitor, keyboard, mouse, and printer are also known as **peripherals** because they attach to the computer.

The computer itself is known as the **system unit**, and it contains many of the critical hardware and electrical components. The system unit is sometimes referred to as the tower, box, or console. When the system unit is combined with the appropriate peripheral devices, the system can perform the four basic computer functions: input, process, output, and storage. Peripheral devices are used to input and output data and information, and the system unit processes and stores the data. Figure 1.2 shows a standard computer system and identifies the function each piece of hardware performs.

Figure 1.2

Output devices — Storage devices — Main computer unit houses the processor — Input devices

System Unit

What is inside the system unit? If you remove the cover from the system unit, you find several key components inside. One of the most essential components is the ***microprocessor chip***, also known as the ***central processing unit (CPU)***. The CPU is located on the ***motherboard***, a large printed circuit board to which all the other circuit boards in the computer are connected. Figure 1.3 displays a standard motherboard and identifies its components. The table in Figure 1.4 identifies and explains each of the components.

Figure 1.3

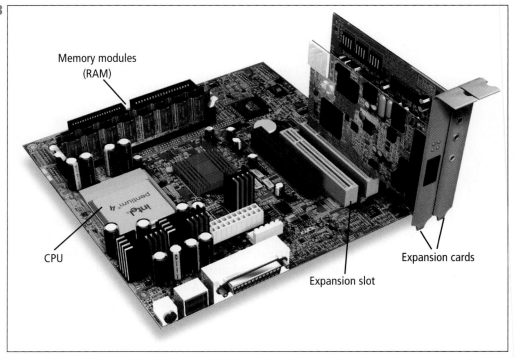

Memory modules (RAM) — CPU — Expansion cards — Expansion slot

Motherboard Features

Component	Description
Motherboard/System board	The main computer circuit board that connects all computer components.
CPU	The central processing unit that gets data from memory and performs mathematical or logical operations to process the data.
Memory (RAM) chips	The temporary holding area inside the computer where data is stored electronically to make it accessible for processing. Data must be stored in memory, so the processor can access and process it. RAM stands for Random Access Memory.
Memory (RAM) slots	The slots on the motherboard used to hold memory (RAM) chips.
Expansion cards	Removable circuit boards used to add new peripherals or increase computer capabilities.
Expansion slots	The slots used to hold expansion cards.

Figure 1.4

What does the CPU do?   The CPU is the brain of the computer, and is responsible for controlling the commands and tasks that the computer performs. It has two main parts—the ***control unit*** and the ***arithmetic logic unit (ALU)***. The control unit is responsible for obtaining instructions from the computer's memory. It then interprets these instructions and executes them, thereby coordinating the activities of all the other computer components. The arithmetic logic unit, or ALU, performs all the arithmetic and logic functions for the computer. The ALU handles addition, subtraction, multiplication, and division, and also makes logical and comparison decisions. This enables the CPU to perform tasks such as sorting data alphabetically or numerically and filtering data to locate specific criteria.

As important as the CPU is to your computer, you might expect it to take up a large amount of space in the console. However, the CPU is actually rather small. Over the years, manufacturers have successfully attempted to reduce the size of microprocessor chips while continuing to increase their computing power. In fact, Moore's law (formulated in 1965 by Gordon Moore, cofounder of Intel) addresses this increase in computing power, observing that current production methods allow CPU capacity to double every 18 months!

Are there different brands of CPUs?   The most well-known chip manufacturers include Intel, Advanced Micro Devices (AMD), and Motorola. Chip manufacturers often produce several different models of chips. Some of the chips that Intel makes include Core Duo, Pentium, Celeron, and Centrino. AMD manufactures chips such as the Athlon, Sempron, and Turion. Intel and AMD chips are the mainstays for PCs. For many years, Apple relied on Motorola to provide the PowerPC processor, the only CPUs the Macintosh used. However, in 2006, Apple stopped producing PowerPC-based systems and began using Intel chips, such as the Core Duo, in its computers.

How is a CPU's processing power measured? One indicator of a CPU's processing power is its ***clock speed***. Clock speed measures the speed at which a CPU processes data and is measured in ***megahertz (MHz)*** or ***gigahertz (GHz)***, depending on the age of the CPU. Early computers had CPUs that processed at speeds of less than 5 MHz, whereas modern processors can operate at over 3 GHz (the equivalent of 3,000 MHz) and newer processors continue to surpass these numbers.

Are there other factors that affect a CPU's processing power? CPUs may use different technologies to enhance their processing performance. Some Intel chips use ***hyperthreading*** technology, which enables the microprocessor to act as if it were two processors, resulting in faster processing and improved processing power. ***Dual-core*** or ***multicore*** processors are manufactured by Intel and AMD. These CPUs have more than one processor (two for a dual-core, more for a multicore) on a single chip. Using multiple processors has several advantages over a single processor CPU, including improved multitasking capabilities and system performance, lower power consumption, reduced usage of system resources, and lower heat emissions.

What types of memory does a computer have and what are they used for? Memory is another critical computer component found within the system unit. There are two basic types of memory: ROM and RAM. ***ROM***, or ***Read Only Memory***, is prerecorded on a chip. As the name implies, the computer can read this memory, although that's all it can do. The information on a ROM chip can't be changed, removed, or rewritten and is generally inaccessible to the computer user. ROM is also known as ***nonvolatile*** memory because it retains its contents even if the computer is turned off. ROM is used to store critical information, such as the program used to start up, or ***boot***, the computer.

The second type of memory is ***RAM***, which stands for ***Random Access Memory***. RAM acts as the computer's short-term memory and stores data temporarily as it is being processed. RAM is considered to be ***volatile*** because this memory is erased when the computer is turned off. The more tasks your computer performs at the same time, the more memory is used.

Why is it important to have enough RAM? Your computer's RAM is like the juggler for your system. When you first start your computer, it's as if a juggler is tossing bean bags. As you open more programs, or use a memory-intensive program such as a video editor, the level of difficulty for the juggler increases. Soon RAM is trying to juggle the equivalent of bowling balls! If you don't have a sufficient amount of memory in your system, you might notice your computer slows down or even stops responding if you try to do too much at one time. Computer users often think this means they have too much information saved on their computer's hard drive. It really means that they are running out of memory, not storage space. To fix this problem, you can reduce the number of programs running at the same time or you can add more RAM to your system.

Installing new memory is one of the cheapest and easiest upgrades you can do for your computer and often results in noticeable performance improvements. RAM is usually measured in **megabytes (MB)** or **gigabytes (GB)**. For newer systems, a minimum of 512 MB to 1 GB is recommended. If you are thinking of purchasing a new computer, experts recommend you buy one with as much RAM as possible.

Storage Devices

What are storage devices?   Storage devices are used to store the data and information used by or created with the computer. Such storage is often referred to as **permanent memory** because, unlike data that is in RAM, data saved to a storage device remains there until the user deletes or overwrites it. Data can be stored within internal hardware devices located within the system unit or in removable external units. Additionally, storage can be fixed or portable, depending on whether the data saved remains within the system unit or is saved on removable units and accessed elsewhere.

How is data stored?   Before discussing specific storage devices, it is helpful to understand the different technologies used to store data. Data is generally saved using one of three forms of storage medium: magnetic, optical, or flash memory.

- **Magnetic** storage uses tape or film covered in a thin, magnetic coating that enables data to be saved as magnetic particles. It works in much the same fashion as an audiocassette or videotape works. Hard disks, floppy disks, Zip disks, and backup tape are all forms of magnetic media. Magnetic disks are divided into **tracks** and **sectors**. Just like an old vinyl record, tracks form rings around the circumference of the media. Sectors divide the tracks into pie-shaped wedges extending from the center to the outer edge of the disk. Data is stored magnetically within the sectors. Magnetic media has read/write capability, which means it is possible to use it over and over again, enabling you to delete or revise existing data and save new data.

- **Optical** storage uses flat plastic discs coated in a special reflective material. Data is saved by using a laser beam to burn tiny pits into the storage medium. The laser is also used to read the saved data. The saved data is organized using tracks and sectors, similar to those used in magnetic media. Compact discs (CDs) and digital video discs (DVDs) are examples of optical media. Unlike magnetic media, not all optical storage is read/write capable. CD-ROMs and DVD-ROMs are considered read-only media (ROM); the information contained on them can be read, but not changed or deleted, and it is not possible to save new data to them. If you purchase new software, music, or a movie, it is most likely on a CD-ROM or DVD-ROM. A record-only disc, or CD-R, allows you to record, or **burn**, information to the disc one time only; information saved this way cannot be deleted or rewritten. A rewritable disc, known as a CD-RW, allows information to be recorded, revised, or deleted, and new data can also be written to the disc, just as with magnetic media. The same possibilities are available in DVDs. However, there are currently two competing formats—DVD-R/RW, known as "DVD dash," and DVD+R/RW, known as "DVD plus." The R/RW suffix indicates the DVD can be used to record and can also be rewritten. Although most DVD players can play either format, if you want to record to a DVD, you need to know which format the DVD recorder requires.

- **Flash memory** uses solid-state technology. It is completely electronic and has no moving mechanical parts. Flash memory is a quick and easy form of rewritable storage, capable of exceeding the storage capacity of magnetic or optical media. Flash memory cards are often used in mobile devices such as PDAs, digital cameras, and MP3 players. Depending on the manufacturer, flash memory cards may be called Memory Stick, CompactFlash, Secure Digital, or MultiMediaCard. Typically, a device can use only one style of memory card; however, a computer equipped with the appropriate card reader can read any of them. Small, removable storage devices known as flash drives also use flash technology and have become increasingly popular.

The table in Figure 1.5 lists the various types of storage media and their capacities.

Figure 1.5

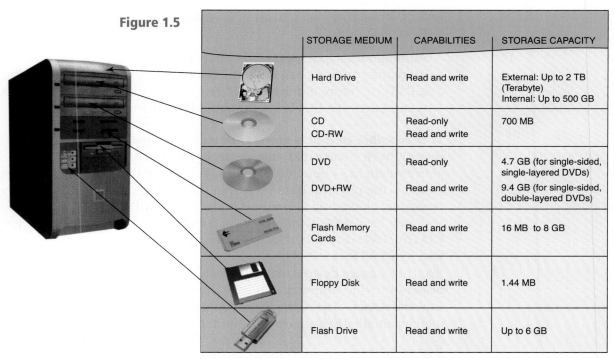

STORAGE MEDIUM	CAPABILITIES	STORAGE CAPACITY
Hard Drive	Read and write	External: Up to 2 TB (Terabyte) Internal: Up to 500 GB
CD CD-RW	Read-only Read and write	700 MB
DVD DVD+RW	Read-only Read and write	4.7 GB (for single-sided, single-layered DVDs) 9.4 GB (for single-sided, double-layered DVDs)
Flash Memory Cards	Read and write	16 MB to 8 GB
Floppy Disk	Read and write	1.44 MB
Flash Drive	Read and write	Up to 6 GB

What are the main types of storage devices? Depending on the age and type of computer you have, you might find some or all of the following internal storage options:

- **Hard disk drive**—A hard disk drive is the computer's largest internal storage device. Also referred to as a hard drive, its storage space is usually measured in gigabytes (GB), with newer computers ranging in size from 40 GB to 500 GB, although it is possible to find some specialized, high-end computers with storage space measuring up to 2 terabytes (TB). As with everything else in computing, these numbers tend to increase with each new model. Hard drives are traditionally permanent storage devices fixed inside the system unit.

- **Floppy disk drive**—The floppy disk drive was the original storage device for microcomputers. Floppy disks are magnetic media capable of holding up to 1.44 megabytes (MB) of data, and are an example of portable storage. Although floppy disks are still a viable storage method for small, text-based files, their limited capacity makes them ill-suited for larger graphics or multimedia files. They can be useful for saving and transporting small files, or backing up individual files for safekeeping. Floppy drives are considered legacy technology and many newer computers no longer include them as standard equipment, primarily because other higher-capacity storage methods are beginning to replace this old standby. If you can't live without one, it might be possible to special order a floppy drive if you purchase a customized computer or to install one after the fact.

- **CD and/or DVD drives**—Your computer may have one, two, or none of these optical drives. As a general rule, new computers come equipped with at least a CD drive to provide an option for portable storage. It's important to know whether this drive is a simple CD-ROM drive, which can only read CDs, or if it is a CD-RW drive, also known as a CD burner. A **CD burner** gives you the ability to save, or burn, files to a CD. You might also have a separate drive that can read and/or write DVDs. Another configuration is to have only one optical drive: a CD-RW/DVD drive.

  Although CDs and DVDs look alike, DVDs are capable of holding much more information than CDs. A CD can hold up to 700 MB of data, but a DVD can store almost 10 GB! Because of their differences, a CD drive is unable to read DVDs, although a DVD drive can read CDs.

Is it possible to add a storage device to a system? If your system doesn't have a particular storage device, it may be possible to add it—if your system has enough room for it. You would need an available drive bay, which is the physical location within the system unit, or you might consider removing an existing device and replacing it with another. For instance, if you only have a CD-ROM drive you could remove that and replace it with a CD-RW/DVD drive, thereby giving you the ability to read and burn CDs and play DVDs too. It is also possible to purchase many of these units as external storage devices. An external storage device is a peripheral that attaches to the computer and performs the same tasks as its corresponding internal device. One of the most popular of these is the external hard drive, which can greatly increase a computer's storage capacity.

Are there other types of storage devices? Other storage devices you might be familiar with include ***flash drives***, a newer form of data storage, as well as two older, legacy drives—***Zip drives*** and ***backup tape drives***.

- **Flash drives** are removable storage devices that use flash memory and connect to the computer by a USB port. Flash drives are also known as thumb drives, universal serial bus (USB) drives, and jump drives. The flash drive is typically a device small enough to fit on a keychain or in a pocket and, because of its solid-state circuitry and lack of moving parts, it is extremely durable. Available in several storage sizes ranging from 16 MB to 64 GB, a flash drive is a quick and easy way to save and transport files. As an example, a 64-MB flash drive, which is relatively small, holds the equivalent of almost 45 floppy disks! To use one of these devices, you simply plug it into a computer's USB port. The computer recognizes the new device and enables the user to save or retrieve files from the flash drive.

- **Zip drives** are magnetic storage devices that save data to Zip disks. Zip disks appear similar to floppy disks but are capable of holding 100 MB, 250 MB, or 750 MB of information. Some older computers may include an internal Zip drive, but they are more often found as external storage devices. Zip drives were popular in earlier computers, but they are rarely found in newer models because they have been replaced by the more efficient and affordable optical and flash drives.

- **Backup tape drives** are storage devices that resemble audiocassette tape recorders and save data to magnetic tape. Although they are rarely used for home computers anymore, many businesses and organizations still rely on tape backup systems to safeguard their data on a daily basis.

The capacity of the components found in your system unit is measured in terms of storage size or speed. Computer systems continue to increase in storage capacity and computing speed, while decreasing in size. Generally, higher measurements indicate a system that is quicker and more powerful than a system with lower measurements. However, it is important to balance size and speed with financial considerations too. Although it is tempting to consider buying a computer with the most power possible, a lesser computer may be more reasonably priced and still be sufficient for the typical user's needs. Recall that CPU speed is measured in megahertz (MHz) or gigahertz (GHz). The amount of RAM in a computer is generally measured in megabytes (MB), while storage space is usually measured in megabytes or gigabytes (GB), depending on the device. Figure 1.6 illustrates an explanation of the various measurements and how they relate to each other.

Evaluating Your System

Now that you have seen some of the items you can find in a computer, you might wonder about your computer's features. If you're new to computers, you might not know all the details about your computer, especially if you didn't buy it brand new. If you did buy a new computer, the easiest way is to check your paperwork—all the basic information should be there. However, if your computer isn't new or you didn't keep the paperwork, there are some ways to determine exactly what is in your system.

What kind of computer do you have?   This is one of the easiest questions to answer. Like almost every other appliance you've used, you can probably find the manufacturer's name and a brand name or model number on the case of the computer. If not, check the back of the unit; there should be a metal tag that will include the manufacturer name, model number, and serial number.

What operating system does the computer use?   If you watch carefully as a computer boots up, you can often determine the operating system. If the computer uses Microsoft Windows, you will usually see a splash screen display for a few moments, showing the version of Windows that is running (for example, Windows 95, Windows 98, Windows Me, Windows XP, Windows Vista, and so on).

How much memory is in the computer?   What is the type and speed of the CPU?   To determine how much memory or RAM is

How Much Is a Byte?

Name	Abbreviation	Number of Bytes	Relative Size
Byte	B	1 byte	Can hold one character of data.
Kilobyte	KB	1,024 bytes	Can hold 1,024 characters or about half of a typewritten page double-spaced.
Megabyte	MB	1,048,576 bytes	A floppy disk holds approximately 1.4 MB of data, or approximately 768 pages of typed text.
Gigabyte	GB	1,073,741,824 bytes	Approximately 786,432 pages of text. Because 500 sheets of paper is approximately 2 inches, this represents a stack of paper 262 feet high.
Terabyte	TB	1,099,511,627,776 bytes	This represents a stack of typewritten pages almost 51 miles high.
Petabyte	PB	1,125,899,906,842,624 bytes	The stack of pages is now 52,000 miles high, or about one-fourth the distance from the Earth to the moon.

Figure 1.6

installed, or which model and type of CPU is in the system, locate the My Computer icon on your desktop and right-click it. Select Properties from the resulting shortcut menu. As you see in Figure 1.7, the General tab of the System Properties dialog box provides a lot of information about your system. This view shows you the operating system used on the computer, which is helpful if you didn't see the splash screen at startup, and also to whom the system is registered. Additionally, you can determine the computer manufacturer and model name, the type of CPU and its chip speed, and the amount of memory or RAM that is installed.

In Figure 1.7, the computer shown is running Windows XP Home Edition with Service Pack 2 installed. It has an Intel Pentium 4 chip, with a speed of 1,600 MHz, which is equivalent to 1.60 GHz. In addition, this system has 512 MB of RAM.

Figure 1.7

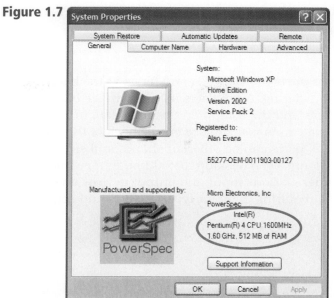

How do you determine what drives are on the system and how much storage space is available? It's important to know how much information you can store on your computer and how much room you have left. Is there enough storage space or is the computer getting full? Use My Computer to find the answers. Double-click the My Computer icon on the desktop to open a dialog box that displays your hard disk drive (or drives), in addition to all the removable storage devices attached to your system. For more information about your hard drive (or any other storage device), choose the drive you want to look at, and then right-click. Click Properties from the resulting menu. A new dialog box displays, similar to the one shown in Figure 1.8. The pie chart displayed on

Figure 1.8

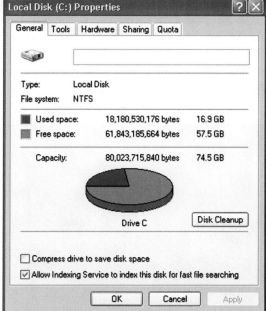

the General tab is a good visual tool that shows the size of your hard drive and how much space is in use.

Ports

What are ports? The wires and plugs at the back of a computer can seem intimidating. A ***port*** acts as an interface between a system's peripheral devices and the computer, enabling data to be exchanged once they are connected. As you can see on the back of the notebook shown in Figure 1.9, ports can be different shapes and sizes. The same ports are typically found on a desktop too, although they might be arranged in a different order. Various input and output devices use different data exchange methods, requiring different types of ports and connectors (or plugs).

Figure 1.9

USB ports
FireWire port
Modem port or RJ-11 port
DVI port
Monitor port
Parallel port
S-video
Speaker port
Microphone port
Ethernet port

How do you determine which port a peripheral device needs? Manufacturers have attempted to make the process of connecting peripheral devices less complicated on newer computers. Rather than trying to match the size and shape of a connector to its port, many manufacturers now use a color-coding system that coordinates the colors of the connectors with their corresponding ports. Additionally, many newer desktop computers include ports, such as USB and audio ports, on the front panel of the system unit to provide easier access to them, as shown in Figure 1.10. Locating these ports on the front panel makes it a simple process to connect and disconnect devices that are used only occasionally, such as digital cameras or MP3 players. Peripherals that are rarely disconnected, such as a keyboard or printer, are generally plugged into the ports on the back of the computer.

Figure 1.10

Audio ports
FireWire port
USB ports

What are the different ports used for? Serial and parallel ports are two of the oldest types of ports found on a computer. ***Serial ports*** are ports that can send data only one bit at a time, so the data exchange rate is slow compared to newer technology. The maximum rate at which a standard serial port can transfer data is 115 kilobits per second (Kbps). The mouse and modem are examples of devices that might use a serial port. A ***parallel port*** is a port that sends data in groups of bits, at transfer rates of up to 500 Kbps, so it is a considerably faster method of transferring data than the serial port. Older printers were often connected to a computer through a parallel port.

Are there faster ports? Over the years, newer ports have come into existence. One of these is the ***universal serial bus (USB) port***. This type of port is able to interface with several different peripheral devices, which reduces the need for individual, dedicated ports. USB ports are also able to transfer data at extremely high rates of speed. Original USB ports, known as USB 1.1, are capable of speeds of 12 megabits per second (Mbps). The newest version, USB 2.0, can attain a rate of 480 Mbps—40 times faster than USB 1.1 technology and over 400 times faster than a serial port! USB 2.0 ports are backwards compatible, which means that older USB devices work with them, however, data will only transfer at the slower USB 1.1 speed. The higher data transfer capabilities of USB ports, coupled with their capability to work with multiple devices, have made the older serial and parallel ports obsolete. Because of the USB port's speedy data transfer rate and its ability to be used with numerous devices, new computers often include four or more USB ports. Devices using USB ports include keyboards, mice, printers, MP3 players, and PDAs. In general, it's a good idea to get a computer with as many USB ports as possible.

The ***FireWire port***, developed by Apple and also known as IEEE 1394, is another means of transferring data quickly. The FireWire 400 has a data transfer rate of 400 Mbps, while the newer FireWire 800 transfers data at a blazing 800 Mbps! This port is typically used to connect devices that need to transfer huge amounts of data to a computer quickly, such as digital cameras or digital video recorders, or external hard drives. FireWire ports are standard on many Apple products, but are usually found only on higher-end Windows PCs and peripheral devices. Some peripheral devices offer users a choice of connecting using a USB port or a FireWire port.

What kind of port is used to connect to another computer? ***Connectivity ports***, such as Ethernet and modem ports, are used to connect a computer to a local network or to the Internet. An ***Ethernet port***, also known as an RJ-45 jack, resembles a standard phone jack, but is slightly larger. The Ethernet port is used for network access and can also be used to connect a cable modem or router for Internet access. A ***modem port*** is the same size and shape as a phone jack and is used to connect the modem to a phone system, enabling dial-up Internet access. The maximum data transfer rate for a modem is 56 Kbps, while the most common Ethernet standard, Fast Ethernet, transfers data at the rate of 100 Mbps. However, Gigabit Ethernet, with a potential transfer rate of 1,000 Mbps, is becoming an option on higher-end systems, and is standard on many Mac systems.

Even faster Ethernet technologies, such as 10 Gigabit Ethernet or 10GbE, exist, but they are currently used for network backbones and enterprise network infrastructures, rather than home users. The table in Figure 1.11 lists some of the different types of ports and the devices that use them.

Ports and Their Uses

Port Name	Port Shape	Connector Shape	Data Transfer Speed	Typical Devices Attached to Port
Legacy Technologies				
Serial			115 Kbps	Mice External modems
Parallel			500 Kbps	Printers External Zip drives
USB 1.1			12 Mbps	Mice Keyboards External Zip drives Printers Scanners Game controllers
New Technologies				
USB 2.0			480 Mbps	Same as USB 1.1, but at faster transfer rates Also suitable for camcorders and digital cameras Maintains backward compatibility with USB 1.1
FireWire/ FireWire 800			400 Mbps/ 800 Mbps	Digital video camcorders Digital cameras
Ethernet/ Gigabit Ethernet			Up to 100 Mbps/ Up to 1,000 Mbps	Network connections Cable modems

Figure 1.11

Are there special purpose ports? Despite the prevalence of USB ports, which can be used for a variety of peripherals, there are still some devices that require special ports. These ports include Musical Instrument Digital Interface (MIDI), IrDA, Bluetooth, video, and audio ports:

- **MIDI ports** are used to connect electronic musical devices, such as keyboards and synthesizers, to a computer, enabling musicians to create digital music files.

- The **IrDA port** is used to allow devices such as PDAs, keyboards, mice, and printers to transmit data wirelessly to another device by using infrared light waves. In order to transmit information, each of the devices must have an IrDA port, as well as a clear line of sight, with no other objects blocking the transmission.

- **Bluetooth** is another type of wireless technology that relies on radio wave transmission and doesn't require a clear line of sight. Bluetooth-enabled devices such as PDAs or other mobile devices can only communicate with each other over short distances, typically less than 30 feet.

- Video ports include standard monitor ports, DVI ports, and S-video ports. A **monitor port** is used to connect the monitor to the graphics processing unit, which is usually located on the motherboard or on a video card. However, to get the best results from a flat panel (LCD) monitor, the **Digital Video Interface (DVI) port** should be used instead. The DVI port transmits a pure digital signal, eliminating the need for digital-to-analog conversion and resulting in a higher quality transmission and a clearer picture on the monitor. The **S-video port** is typically used to connect other video sources, such as a television, projector, or digital recorder, to the computer.

- Similar to video ports, **audio ports** connect audio devices, such as speakers, headphones, and microphones, to the computer's sound card. These jacks will probably be very familiar to anyone who is accustomed to using standard stereo components.

Input Devices

The system unit and its storage devices process and store data. However, before that can happen, you need to get the data into the system. You also need a way to get the processed data back out of the system. **Input** and **output devices** are used to enter and retrieve the data in a useful format.

The two most familiar input devices are the keyboard and the mouse, but they aren't the only ones. This section discusses each of these devices, in addition to some other useful devices used to get data into the computer.

Keyboards

Are there different types of keyboards? The **keyboard** is the primary input device for computers. There are actually several different kinds of keyboards. The QWERTY keyboard is the one most people are familiar with. It is based on the original typewriter keyboard and is named for the arrangement of the letters on the top-left alphabetic row of keys. Another style is the Dvorak keyboard, which arranges the letters and numbers in a different pattern for increased typing speed. Some ergonomic keyboards use a split keyboard arrangement, offsetting each half at an angle to reduce the incidence of repetitive stress injuries such as carpal tunnel syndrome.

Keyboard size and layout on notebook and tablet computers can differ slightly from a standard desktop keyboard. Keyboards usually send information to the computer through a cable connected to a USB port; however, wireless or remote keyboards are gaining in popularity. A wireless keyboard communicates with the computer by infrared or radio frequency technology and also requires batteries.

What are all these other keys used for? In addition to the standard alphanumeric keys originally found on typewriters, computer keyboards have a variety of keys that provide additional functionality. Many of these keys are shown in Figure 1.12 and include

- ***Control keys***, such as the Ctrl, Alt, and Windows keys, often provide shortcuts or increased functionality to the keyboard when used in combination with another key. If you press the Shift key and a letter, the result is an uppercase, rather than a lowercase, letter. In the same way, using one of the control keys enables the standard keys to be used for additional purposes. For example, pressing Ctrl and the letter P opens the Print dialog box. Another example of a control key is the Esc key, which can often be used to stop, or *escape*, from a currently running task. A unique control key that is found only on Windows-based keyboards is the Windows key.

- The ***numeric keypad***, located at the right of the keyboard, provides an alternate method of quickly entering numbers. This is useful for individuals who are accustomed to using an adding machine or calculator.

- ***Function keys*** are located above the standard row of number keys. Numbered F1 through F12, these keys are generally associated with certain software-specific commands. Pressing the F1 key will usually open the Help menu for a program; however, pressing one of the other function keys can produce different results, depending on the software program running.

- ***Arrow keys*** are the keys located at the bottom of the keyboard between the standard keys and the numeric keypad. These keys enable the user to move the insertion point around the window one space at a time.

- ***Toggle and other keys***, which are located just above the arrow keys, are used for various purposes, including navigation and editing. The Insert, Num Lock, and Caps Lock keys are all examples of toggle keys. A toggle key works just like a light switch—press it once and the feature is turned on, press it again and it is turned off. If you've ever accidentally pressed the Caps Lock key and typed a long string of all capital letters, you've seen this feature in action. Pressing the Caps Lock key again allows you to return to normal keyboarding mode.

- ***Multimedia and Internet control keys*** are typically found at the top edge of the keyboard. The precise placement and function of these keys usually depends on the keyboard manufacturer. However, most modern keyboards have at least a few keys or buttons that can be used for such tasks as muting or adjusting speaker volume, opening a Web browser, and sending an e-mail. Generally, each button has an icon that indicates its function.

Figure 1.12

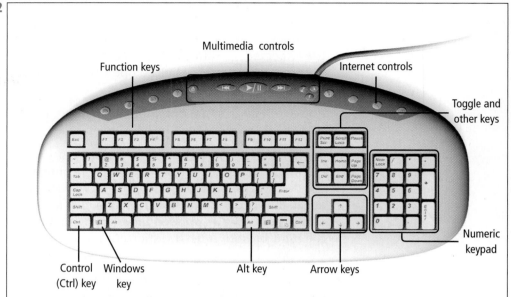

The Mouse

Is there an easier way to control cursor movement? The ***mouse*** became an essential input device with the introduction of graphical user interfaces, such as Microsoft Windows. This point-and-click device is useful for positioning the insertion point by translating hand movements into corresponding actions on the screen. If the mouse has a rollerball on the bottom, you also need a mousepad to create the friction necessary for the mouse to track properly. Optical mice use a laser beam, instead of a rollerball, to control the pointer movement. Because the bottom of an optical mouse is sealed, dirt and debris are less likely to get inside and interfere with the mouse's internal mechanisms. Such mice don't require mousepads, although many people continue to use one. Just as with keyboards, mice can be wired or wireless. Notebook and tablet computers can use mice, or they may use a built-in touchpad, trackball, or track-point to move the insertion point.

How can the mouse be used more efficiently? Although there are different kinds of mice, the traditional mouse has two buttons and a scroll wheel. The palm of your hand should rest comfortably over the mouse. For the best and most accurate results when you click the mouse, simply press the button with your finger. Often, people who are new to computing think they need to lift their finger and press hard to click a mouse button. This can actually create problems by causing the mouse to move suddenly, making clicking inaccurate. The following provides a brief description of some of the ways the mouse can be used:

• ***Click***—By default, the left mouse button is considered the primary button. When instructed to click the mouse, it is understood this means that the left mouse button should be pressed one time. Clicking is done to position the insertion point or to select an object on the screen.

- **Double-click**—Double-clicking is performed by pressing the left mouse button two times in rapid succession. It is important that the mouse does not move while double-clicking or the command will not produce the expected results. Double-clicking is done to activate an object; for example, you double-click to open a file or start a program.

- **Drag**—To carry out this action, press the left mouse button and continue to hold it while dragging, or moving, the mouse. This action can be used to select large blocks of text.

- **Right-click**—Pressing the right mouse button one time will open a shortcut menu. Shortcut menus are usually context-sensitive, which means they will vary depending on what you've clicked and what program you are using. The right mouse button is also known as the secondary button and is not typically pressed more than one time—no double-clicking for the right button. After the shortcut menu has been opened, you select the appropriate choice by clicking it with the left mouse button.

- **Scroll wheel**—If your mouse is equipped with a scroll wheel, it can be used to quickly move a page up or down in a window. It is an easy way to navigate through lengthy documents or Web sites.

Are there other input devices? Although the keyboard and mouse are the two most common input devices, there are many other input devices. **Scanners** are similar to copy machines, but instead of producing a paper copy, they convert documents or photos to digital files that can then be saved on your computer. **Microphones** are used to digitally record sounds. Game controls such as **joysticks** are used to control movement within games. **Digital cameras** and **digital video recorders** enable you to transfer digital images of photos and movies directly to your computer.

Output Devices

Output devices help you retrieve data that has been entered, processed, and stored in your system and present it in a useful format. This format can be text, graphics, audio, or video. Monitors and printers are the two most common output devices.

Monitors

What are monitors? **Monitors**, also known as **display screens**, are an essential component of the computer system. Text, video, and graphics are displayed on a monitor. When a monitor outputs data or information, it is called **soft copy**—you can view it, but you can't touch it.

What is the difference between a CRT monitor and an LCD monitor? Monitors come in a variety of sizes and styles, but, as shown in Figure 1.13, there are just two main categories: **cathode-ray tube (CRT)** and **liquid crystal display (LCD)**. A CRT monitor resembles a traditional television set and uses a cathode-ray tube to produce the picture on the screen. The glass screen of a CRT monitor can be curved or flat (sometimes called a **flat screen** monitor). The flat screen generally has less glare. It is important not to confuse a flat screen monitor with a flat panel monitor. **Flat panel** or LCD monitors use a liquid crystal display and are much thinner and lighter than CRT monitors. They are also more expensive than CRTs, although they have become more affordable in recent years.

Figure 1.13

What factors determine a monitor's display quality? A monitor's display is made up of millions of tiny dots, known as *pixels*. Each pixel, which is short for picture element, represents a single point on a display screen or in a graphic image. The number of pixels on the screen determines a monitor's sharpness and clarity, also known as its *resolution*. A higher number of pixels results in a clearer and sharper monitor resolution. A standard screen resolution might be expressed as 1024 x 768, which means there are 1,024 columns, each containing 768 pixels, for a total of more than 786,000 pixels on the screen.

Dot pitch is another display characteristic and refers to the diagonal distance between two pixels of the same color. Dot pitch is measured in millimeters with smaller measurements resulting in a crisper viewing image because there is less blank space between the pixels. For best viewing, monitors should have a dot pitch measurement of .28 mm or less. CRT monitors use an electric beam to light up the pixels. The electric beam quickly passes back and forth across the back of the screen, relighting the pixels and redrawing the screen image. LCD monitors use an electric current to illuminate the pixels. The speed at which the pixels are reilluminated is called the *refresh rate*, which is measured in cycles per second, expressed as hertz (Hz). Refresh rates generally average between 75 and 85 Hz, which means the screen image is redrawn 75 to 85 times per second. Higher refresh rates result in less screen flicker and less eye strain.

How are a monitor's color settings and display size determined? Although monochrome monitors were the standard in the early days of computers, color monitors are more common now. Modern monitors can display at least 256 colors and most can display up to 16.8 million colors. Monitor sizes range from 14 to 40 inches or larger. Desktop computers use CRT or LCD monitors, whereas notebook and tablet computers use LCD screens. Popular desktop sizes include 17-inch, 19-inch, and 21-inch monitors. Notebooks tend to have slightly smaller LCD screens, which range from 12 to 17 inches. Monitor sizes are determined by measuring them diagonally. However, the measurement for a CRT monitor includes the outer housing, which makes the actual viewing area of the monitor smaller than the size indicated. LCD monitor measurements do not include the bezel, or edge, of the screen. Because of these different measurement methods, a 17-inch LCD monitor has virtually the same viewing area as a 19-inch CRT monitor.

Which type of monitor is best? Consider some of the following questions to help make your decision. How much can you afford to spend? Do you have the room for a CRT monitor or is your workspace limited? How important is color accuracy to you or your work?

There are advantages and disadvantages to both types of monitors, and the ultimate decision should be based on which one will work best for you. CRT monitors are cheaper and tend to display colors better; however, LCD monitors are becoming less expensive. LCD monitors are also smaller and lighter weight, with a larger display screen than similarly sized CRTs. Figure 1.14 compares the advantages for both CRT and LCD monitors to help you decide which style best suits your needs.

CRT Monitors Versus LCD Monitors

CRT Monitor Advantages	LCD Monitor Advantages
Images viewable from all angles (LCD monitors often have a limited viewing angle).	Take up less space and weigh less.
Resolution can be adjusted more completely.	Cause less eye strain than CRT monitors.
Better color accuracy and clarity.	Are more environmentally friendly than CRT monitors.
Better for gaming and watching DVDs due to quicker pixel response time and higher color accuracy than LCD monitors.	Larger viewable area compared with similar sized CRT (17-inch viewable area on 17-inch monitor compared with 15-inch viewable area on a 17-inch CRT monitor).

Figure 1.14

Printers

Using a monitor is a good way to view the information on your computer, but sometimes a soft copy isn't sufficient for your needs. The ability to generate a **hard copy**—a permanent record of your work—is the primary benefit of a **printer**.

What types of printers are available? There are two categories of printers: impact and nonimpact. **Impact** printers have small keys, similar to a typewriter's, that strike an ink ribbon against paper, leaving behind an image of the character on the key. The **dot matrix** printer is an impact printer. One of the earliest printers, the dot matrix printer has been almost completely phased out by newer types of printers. Despite this, the dot matrix printer can still be found in some business settings because it is useful for printing multipage forms such as invoices or purchase orders.

How does a nonimpact printer work? **Nonimpact** printers do not actually touch the paper when printing. There are a variety of nonimpact printers, but the two most commonly used with home computers are the ink-jet printer and the laser printer. Figure 1.15 shows a typical example of each of these printers. The ***ink-jet*** printer uses a special nozzle and ink cartridges to spray ink in small droplets onto the surface of the paper. Ink-jet printers are able to easily print in color and in black and white, produce good quality copy, and are relatively inexpensive to buy. ***Laser*** printers use the same process as photocopiers to produce their output. They use a special cylinder known as a drum, dry ink or toner, and a laser. Static electricity attracts toner to the surface of the drum and the laser distributes the toner in the correct pattern. The drum transfers the toner to the paper and heat is used to permanently fuse the toner to the paper. Laser printers are generally more expensive to purchase than ink-jet printers, although they often print more quickly and are more cost-effective. Lower-end laser printers print only in black and white; however, more expensive printers can produce color copies.

Figure 1.15

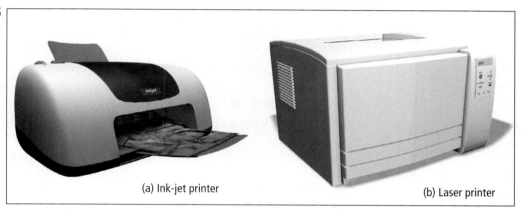

(a) Ink-jet printer

(b) Laser printer

How do you assess a printer's capabilities? When you select a printer, there are some key characteristics to consider. The first of these is print speed, often described as pages per minute (ppm). Print speed can vary depending on the manufacturer and model, and is also affected by whether the page is text-only or if it also includes graphics. Just as with monitors, resolution is also important to print quality. For printing purposes, resolution is expressed as ***dots per inch*** or ***dpi***. The higher the dpi, the better the print quality. Print qualities of 300 to 600 dpi are typical of most printers, although special photo printers can offer resolutions up to 1,200 dpi. Professional printers can reach even higher values. Color output and its related cost is another important consideration. Ink-jet printers offer four- or six-color options. Many ink-jet printers use one cartridge for black ink and another for color. When available, printers that offer a separate cartridge for each color are a practical choice because you only need to replace one color at a time as the cartridges run out. Laser printers use separate toner cartridges for each color.

Speakers and Multimedia Projectors

Are there other output devices? ***Speakers*** and ***multimedia projectors*** are also examples of output devices. Many computers include small speakers to allow the user to listen to CDs or DVDs and hear any auditory signals the computer sends. However, if you're serious about multimedia, you will probably want to invest in a better set of speakers for improved performance. Multimedia projectors are used to conduct presentations and training sessions. Imagine how difficult it would be to have a room full of students or conference attendees crowd around a single monitor to view a presentation. A multimedia projector allows information to be projected onto a larger screen so it can easily be viewed by a group.

Multifunction Devices

Some devices, known as **multifunction devices (MFDs)**, combine input and output capabilities. A good example of such a device is the telephone, which allows you to both speak (output) and listen (input) to another person. Other examples include the touchscreen monitor at a convenience store or ATM or the "all-in-one" printer, which combines a printer with a scanner, copier, and fax machine. In each instance, you can use the device to input information by touching the screen to make your selection or by using the device's scanning capability. At the same time, each of these devices displays information on the screen or generates printed copies to output information.

Objective 4
Identify Types of Software and Their Uses

Computer hardware consists of the physical components of the system. However, without software, the computer would just be a collection of mechanical parts. Software provides the instructions that tell the computer what to do. To perform various tasks, the computer requires a set of instructions, called **programs**. These programs enable individuals to use the computer without the need for special programming skills. There are two categories of computer software: system software and application software. Both types of software are required to work effectively with your computer.

System Software

System software provides the instructions that the computer needs to run. It contains the directions needed to start up the computer (known as the **boot process**), checks to ensure everything is in good working order, and enables you to interface with the computer and its peripheral devices so that you can use them. System software consists of two main types of programs: the operating system and utility programs.

Operating Systems

What is the operating system? The **operating system (OS)** is a special computer program that is present on every desktop or notebook computer, in addition to many others ranging from mainframes to PDAs. The operating system controls the way the computer works from the time it is turned on until it is shut down. As shown in Figure 1.16, the operating system manages the various hardware components, including the CPU, memory, storage devices, and peripheral devices. It also coordinates with the various software applications that might be running.

Is it possible to communicate with the operating system?   Although the operating system communicates with the computer and its peripherals, it also includes a *user interface* that you can use to interact with the computer. Early operating systems used a DOS-based interface, which required knowledge of special commands that had to be typed accurately to achieve the desired results. As you can imagine, this type of system was not very user-friendly. Most current operating systems use a point-and-click format known as a *graphical user interface (GUI)*. GUIs are more user-friendly and intuitive than DOS systems. Rather than typing specific commands, you can use a mouse to point to and click on an *icon* (a graphical depiction of an object such as a file or program) or a *menu* (a list of commands) to perform a task. GUI operating systems display information on the monitor in the form of rectangular boxes called *screens* or *windows*.

Figure 1.16

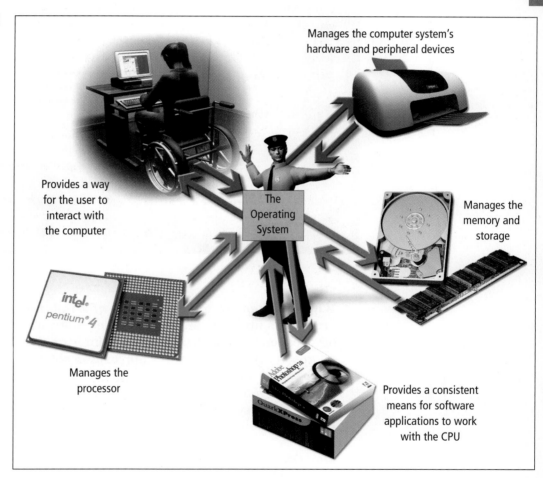

Manages the computer system's hardware and peripheral devices

Provides a way for the user to interact with the computer

The Operating System

Manages the memory and storage

Manages the processor

Provides a consistent means for software applications to work with the CPU

Do all computers need an operating system?   The operating system is a critical part of a computer system. Without an OS to provide specific instructions, the computer would be unable to fulfill its four main functions. However, different computers require different types of operating systems. There are several popular operating systems available for home computers. They include Microsoft Windows, Mac OS, and Linux.

Microsoft Windows has the largest market share of the three main operating systems and is found on most of today's desktop and notebook computers. There have been many versions of Microsoft Windows, including Windows 3.0, Windows 95, Windows 98, Windows ME, and Windows Vista. Although a previous version of Windows might be found on an older computer, Windows Vista is the current version installed on most computers. A sample Windows XP desktop is displayed in Figure 1.17.

Figure 1.17

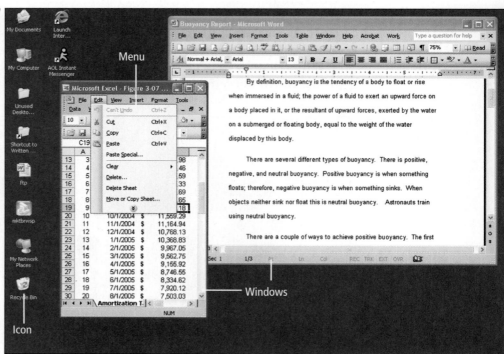

Why are there so many versions of Windows?   Software developers are always updating and refining their software to adapt to new technology, respond to vulnerabilities, and improve their product. Because Microsoft also manufactures application software, some of its products have similar names and users can become confused. It's important to note that even though your computer might use Microsoft Windows for its operating system, it may not have Microsoft Office (an application software suite) installed.

Mac OS is an operating system designed specifically for Apple's Macintosh computers. The current version is Mac OS X Tiger. As you can see in Figure 1.18, the Mac OS appears similar to Windows, because it also uses a GUI. In fact, Apple was the first company to introduce a GUI operating system for commercial sale. But, because of the overwhelming popularity of the Windows-based PC, Mac OS has a much smaller market share. There are also significant differences in the way the Mac OS performs. Mac users tend to be very loyal and believe their system is far superior to the Windows system, although there are many Windows users who disagree.

Figure 1.18

Files

Icons

Windows

Icons on the "Dock"
can launch programs

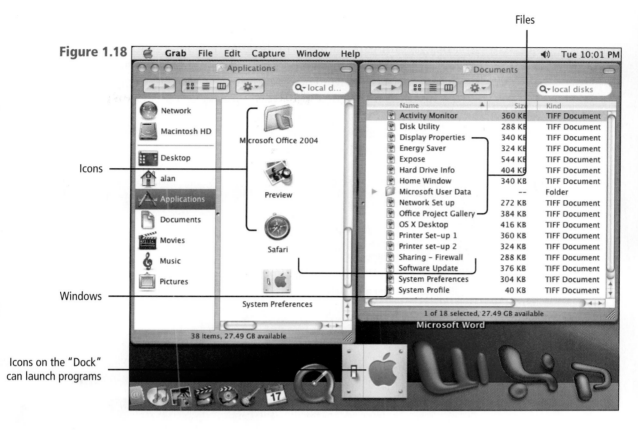

Can Windows run on an Apple computer? Until recently, the Mac OS could not run on a PC, and the Windows OS could not run on a Mac. This was primarily due to the differences in CPUs used by each system. However, now that Apple is also using Intel chips, the concept of a ***dual-boot*** computer (one that can run more than one operating system) running both Mac and Windows operating systems on the same computer has become a reality. Apple has developed Boot Camp, a utility program that will allow Windows XP to be installed on a Mac. While this may appeal to some users—especially those who want to use a Mac but have some applications that will only run on Windows—it is still in the early stages and may not be a good option for everyone.

Linux is an alternative operating system. Based on the UNIX operating system developed for mainframe computers, it also has a dedicated group of users. Linux is an ***open-source*** operating system, which means it is not owned by a single company and some versions are available at no cost.

How is open-source software different from other types of software? Open-source software makes its source code, essentially the program instructions, available to anyone who would like to see it. Programmers are encouraged to work with and change the code as they see fit, in the hope that having many "eyes" looking at the code will streamline and improve it. Proprietary software, such as Microsoft Windows, keeps this code secret and inaccessible to programmers who are not authorized by the software development company.

Why is Linux used? Linux is rarely used by novice computer users, although it is popular among developers and other technologically advanced individuals who prefer to use an alternative operating system.

Some people appreciate the opportunity to work in this more "open" programming environment. However, one of the disadvantages of Linux is that, because no single company is responsible for it, technical support is not easily found. Users might find help from various resources such as user groups and Internet communities. Alternatively, some software companies have chosen to develop and sell a version of Linux that includes a warranty and technical support as a way of alleviating user concerns. Figure 1.19 shows an example of one version of the Linux operating system.

Figure 1.19

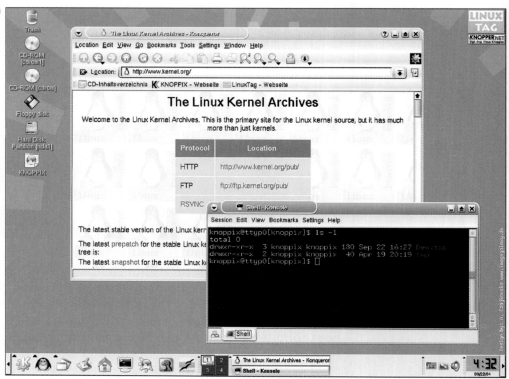

Utility Programs

What are utility programs? Operating system software is the most critical software on the computer, because nothing can run without it. However, **utility programs** are another important component of system software. These small applications handle many important tasks involved with the management and maintenance of your system. Utility programs can be used to help back up important files, remove unwanted files or programs from your system, and schedule various tasks to keep your system running smoothly. Some of these utilities are included with the operating system, whereas others are stand-alone versions that you can purchase or download for free. Figure 1.20 displays a variety of utility programs that ship with the Windows operating system and compares them with similar stand-alone products, describing the function of each utility.

Utility Programs Available within Windows and as Stand-Alone Programs

Windows Utility Program	Off-the-Shelf (Stand-Alone) Utility Program	Function
File Management		
Add/Remove Programs	Aladdin Systems Easy Uninstall	Properly installs/uninstalls software
Windows Explorer File Compression	Win Zip	Reduces file size
Windows System Maintenance and Diagnostics		
Backup	Norton Ghost	Backs up important information
Disk Cleanup	Ontrack System Suite	Removes unnecessary files from hard drive
Disk Defragmenter	Norton SystemWorks	Arranges files on hard drive in sequential order
Error-checking (previously ScanDisk)	Norton CleanSweep	Checks hard drive for unnecessary or damaged files
System Restore	FarStone RestoreIT!	Restores system to a previously established set point
Task Manager		Displays performance measures for processes; provides information on programs and processes running on computer
Task Scheduler		Schedules programs to run automatically at prescribed times

Figure 1.20

Application Software

Although you interact with system software every time you use the computer, in some ways you don't really notice it. **Application software**, on the other hand, is comprised of programs that enable you to accomplish tasks and use the computer in a productive manner.

How do system software and application software work together?
System software is a bit like breathing—you need to do it to live; however, you don't usually think much about it unless something goes wrong. Application software might be compared to a musical instrument like a flute. When a musician combines each of these—her breath and her flute—the result may be a beautiful melody (if she has practiced, of course!). Computer software works together similarly—the system software acts as the "breath," while the application software provides the "instrument," enabling you to create something too.

There are many different kinds of application software, although they often fall into one of several general categories, each of which has a different purpose. These categories include financial and business-related software, graphics and multimedia software, educational and reference software, entertainment software, and communication software. You might be most familiar with productivity software, which includes the following applications:

- **Word processing software**—Used to create, edit, format, and save documents and other text-based files. Word processing software enables you to create or edit letters, reports, memos, and many other types of written documents and print them out. Revisions to existing documents can be made quickly and easily, without having to re-create the entire document. Documents created with this type of software can also include graphics, charts, and other graphic elements. Microsoft Word, Lotus Word Pro, and Corel WordPerfect are all examples of word processing programs. A document created using Microsoft Word 2007 is shown in Figure 1.21. Notice that the document contains a graphic element as well as text.

Figure 1.21

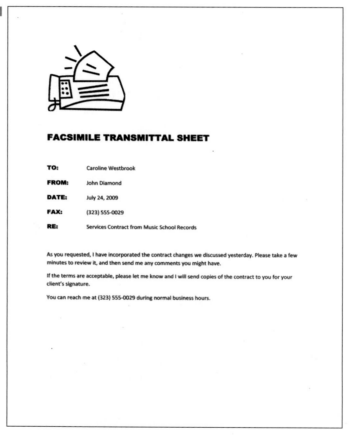

FACSIMILE TRANSMITTAL SHEET

TO:	Caroline Westbrook
FROM:	John Diamond
DATE:	July 24, 2009
FAX:	(323) 555-0029
RE:	Services Contract from Music School Records

As you requested, I have incorporated the contract changes we discussed yesterday. Please take a few minutes to review it, and then send me any comments you might have.

If the terms are acceptable, please let me know and I will send copies of the contract to you for your client's signature.

You can reach me at (323) 555-0029 during normal business hours.

- **Spreadsheet software**—Spreadsheet software enables you to perform calculations and other mathematical tasks. Similar to the documents used by accountants, spreadsheets contain data entered in columns and rows and enable you to perform calculations, create scenarios, perform "what-if" analyses, chart and graph data, and format the worksheet layout. A key advantage of spreadsheet software is its capability to recalculate spreadsheets without user intervention. When data used in a calculation or formula is changed, the spreadsheet software automatically updates the worksheet with the correct result. Microsoft Excel, Lotus 1-2-3, and Corel Quattro Pro are examples of spreadsheet programs. Figure 1.22 shows a worksheet created in Microsoft Excel 2007.

Figure 1.22

Rio Rancho Auto Gallery
February Tire Sales

Store Name	Standard Tires	Performance Tires	Total Standard Sales	Total Performance Sales	Total Tire Sales	Percent of Total Sales
Diamond Valley	42	38	$ 5,250	$ 8,930	$ 14,180	28.71%
Sierra Vista	26	37	3,250	8,695	11,945	24.19%
Tire Factory	27	26	3,375	6,110	9,485	19.21%
Tread Works	35	40	4,375	9,400	13,775	27.89%
Total	130	141	$ 16,250	$ 33,135	$ 49,385	

Standard Price	$	125
Performance Price	$	235

- **Database software**—Databases are used to store and organize large amounts of data. Typically, database software can be used to manage various types of information, such as that found in large mailing lists, inventories, order histories, and invoicing. Databases help you to enter, store, sort, filter, retrieve, and summarize the information they contain and then generate meaningful reports. Common database programs include Microsoft Access, Lotus Approach, and Corel Paradox. Figure 1.23 shows a database table created in Microsoft Access 2007.

Figure 1.23

Scholarship ID	Scholarship Name	Amount	Sport	Team	Award Date	Student ID
S-01	Southern States Jump Ball Award	$300	Basketball	Men's	09/22/09	STU-1018
S-02	Tech Corridor Sportsmanship Award	$100	Swimming	Men's	05/23/09	STU-1018
S-03	Bay Sports Fellowship Award	$500	Football	Men's	05/01/09	STU-1224
S-04	Golden Sands Country Club Award	$300	Golf	Men's	05/23/09	STU-1231
S-05	Bay Sports Fellowship Award	$500	Basketball	Men's	02/15/09	STU-1264
S-06	Ocean Surf Protection Foundation Award	$750	Swimming	Women's	03/22/09	STU-1510
S-07	Palm Beach Country Club Award	$200	Golf	Women's	06/25/09	STU-1571
S-08	Florida State Baseball Association	$500	Baseball	Men's	01/16/09	STU-1581
S-09	Florida State Baseball Association	$300	Baseball	Men's	10/30/09	STU-1018
S-10	Ocean Bay Volleyball Club Leadership Award	$200	Tennis	Women's	05/06/09	STU-1510
S-11	June Claudino Walters Memorial Award	$200	Volleyball	Women's	11/04/09	STU-1715
S-12	Florida Sportswomen Foundation Award	$300	Basketball	Women's	05/06/09	STU-1111
S-13	Home Run Foundation Award	$200	Baseball	Men's	08/04/09	STU-1888
S-14	Florida Port Science Achievement Award	$750	Football	Men's	11/12/09	STU-1810
S-15	Roundball Academic Achievement Award	$500	Basketball	Men's	01/25/09	STU-1859
S-16	Florida Port Country Club Foundation Award	$400	Swimming	Women's	05/23/09	STU-1868
S-17	Go To The Net Award	$200	Tennis	Men's	07/29/09	STU-1888
S-18	Pinellas Academic Achievement Award	$250	Volleyball	Women's	05/21/09	STU-1125
S-19	Florida Port Country Club Foundation Award	$200	Golf	Men's	12/06/09	STU-1167
S-20	Lee Henry Foundation Award	$400	Tennis	Women's	04/14/09	STU-1111
S-21	Silver Helmet Award	$100	Football	Men's	07/12/09	STU-1921
S-22	Spike It Award	$200	Volleyball	Women's	02/02/09	STU-1977
S-23	Bay Town Sports Award	$500	Basketball	Men's	09/15/09	STU-1112
S-24	Bay Sports Fellowship Award	$500	Basketball	Women's	04/10/09	STU-1990
S-25	Hoops National Winner Award	$400	Basketball	Women's	12/22/09	STU-1125

- **Presentation software**—Because of presentation software, lecturers no longer need to rely on flip charts, slide projectors, or overhead transparencies for their presentations. This software is used to create graphic presentations, known as slide shows, that can be shown to large groups by means of an overhead projector or displayed on the Web. Presentation software is also used to create audience handouts, speaker notes, and other materials that can be used during an oral presentation or for distribution to an audience. Microsoft PowerPoint, Lotus Freelance Graphics, and Corel Presentations are examples of presentation software programs. Figure 1.24 shows a presentation created with Microsoft PowerPoint 2007.

Figure 1.24

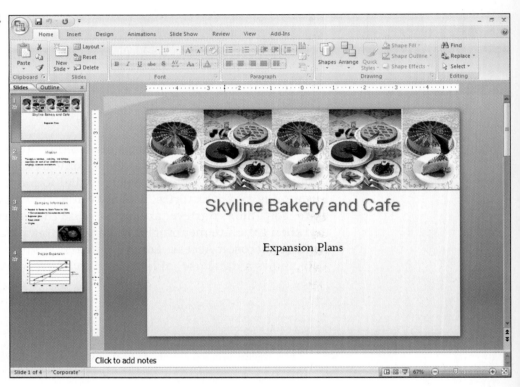

- **Communication and organizational software**—Communication software can cover a broad range of tasks including videoconferencing and telephony. However, applications within the productivity category are most often used to send and receive e-mail. These applications typically include an address book, a calendar, and task functions, which help users organize their personal and professional responsibilities. Microsoft Outlook, Lotus Notes, and Corel WordPerfect Mail are examples of communication and organizational software. Figure 1.25 shows an example of a calendar in Microsoft Outlook 2007.

Figure 1.25

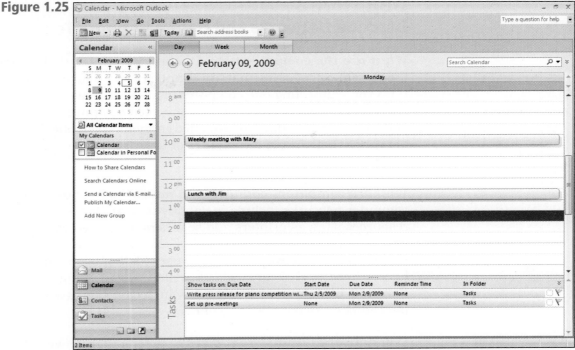

What is a software suite? Although it is possible to buy any of the previous applications separately, most software manufacturers, including Microsoft, Corel, and Lotus, also group applications together into a package called a *suite*. This can be an economical way to purchase software if you need some or all of the programs in the suite. The cost of a suite is usually less than the total cost of purchasing each of the applications individually. Additionally, because products from the same company have many common elements, such as basic window design and layout, toolbars containing similar tools, dictionaries, and media galleries, many users find this familiarity makes it easier to switch between the programs in a suite. Examples of suites include Microsoft Office, Corel WordPerfect Office, and Lotus SmartSuite.

What are some other common software applications? As mentioned earlier, there are many different types of application software besides productivity software, each one with a specific function. You might use Microsoft Publisher or QuarkXPress to create a newsletter or brochure. Bookkeepers rely on special accounting packages such as Peachtree Accounting or QuickBooks to balance the books and handle other accounting functions. Graphic designers turn to packages like Adobe Photoshop or Adobe Illustrator to develop creative artwork. You might use Microsoft FrontPage or Macromedia Dreamweaver to create your own Web site. To identify other software programs and their uses, visit a home electronics or discount store to see which programs they stock, or browse the shelves of your local bookstore for some of the latest "how-to" information.

Objective 5
Describe Networks and Define Network Terms

What are the components of a network? Recall that computers and the various peripherals that are connected to them are called hardware. However, connecting one computer to another creates a **network**. Networks consist of two or more connected computers plus the various peripheral devices that are attached to them. Each object connected to a network, whether it is a computer or a peripheral device, is known as a **node**.

Why are computers connected to networks? Some of the benefits of computer networks include the ability to share software applications and resources such as printers and scanners. Improved communication and data sharing are additional benefits. Computers can be connected to a network in several ways. They can use existing telephone wires or power lines, or use coaxial, unshielded twisted pair (UTP), or fiber-optic cable. Networks can also be **wireless**, in which case they use radio waves instead of wires or cables to connect.

Can networks be different sizes? A computer network that connects computers reasonably close together, such as within a home or in a small office or business, is called a **local area network (LAN).** Usually these networks are contained within a single building or group of adjacent buildings. If the network begins to cover a larger geographic area or begins to include other networks, it becomes a **wide area network (WAN).** An example of this is the network used by Penn State University. Penn State has many campuses located across the state of Pennsylvania. Because the different campuses are connected through a WAN, students and teachers are able to use a computer in one location and access files or resources located at any of the other campuses, wherever they might be located. Both LANs and WANs can be wired or wireless. Wired LANs might use phone lines or cable connections, while wired WANs might use phone lines, satellites, or special leased lines, known as T-1 or T-3 lines, for high-speed communication. In fact, the Internet is actually the largest network of all because it connects computers around the world.

How are networks configured? Networks can be configured in several ways. There are two main categories: peer-to-peer and client/server. **Peer-to-peer** or **P2P networks** are most commonly found in homes and small businesses. In a peer-to-peer network, each node on the network can communicate with every other node. Peer-to-peer networks are relatively easy to set up, but tend to be rather small. This makes them ideal for home use, although not as desirable in the workplace. If a network has more than ten nodes, it is generally best to use the **client/server network** instead. Remember that a node can be a computer, printer, scanner, modem, or any other peripheral device that can be connected to a computer. Therefore, it isn't difficult to find more than ten nodes in an office or business setting.

How is a client/server network different from a P2P network?
Client/server networks typically have two different types of computers.

The **client** is the computer used at your desk or workstation to write letters, send e-mail, produce invoices, or perform any of the many tasks that can be accomplished with a computer. The client computer is the one most people directly interact with. In contrast, the **server** computer is typically kept in a secure location and is used to manage network resources. If a server is assigned to handle only specific tasks, it is known as a **dedicated server.** For instance, a Web server is used to deliver Web pages, a file server is used to store and archive files, and a print server manages the printing resources for the network. Each of these is a dedicated server.

Network topology describes the different types of network architecture used for client/server networks. Just as there are different sizes and styles of buildings that are designed for different purposes, networks are designed to be physically configured and connected in different ways.

Which topologies are used most often? The three most common layouts are explained in the following list:

- **Bus topology** connects each node to a single, central high-speed line known as a bus. No server is used, and although it is possible for each node to communicate with all the others, they can only do so one at a time. If one computer or device is sending over the network, all the others must wait until the transmission is complete before they can begin. Because this is an inexpensive and easy way to connect, this topology is often found in peer-to-peer networks.

- **Ring topology**, sometimes known as **token-ring topology**, connects each node to the next, forming a loop or a circle. The data that's sent is passed from node to node, traveling around the circle in only one direction. A token travels around the ring until one of the nodes is ready to send a transmission. The node then holds the token until the transmission is finished, preventing any of the other devices from sending until the token is released to make its way around the circle again. This type of topology gives each device an equal chance of being able to send data and prevents one node from doing all the communicating.

- **Star topology** is the most frequent networking style used for businesses. It offers a high degree of flexibility. Each node is connected to a special device known as a switch, which is centrally located. Each node must go through the switch to communicate with the others. If something happens to one node, the others are still able to communicate.

Figure 1.26 shows an example of each of these layouts, and Figure 1.27 discusses the advantages and disadvantages of each of these topographies.

Figure 1.26

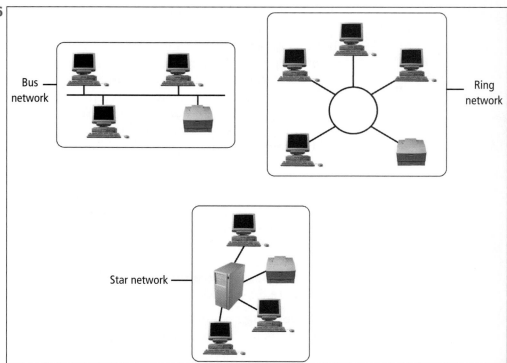

Bus network

Ring network

Star network

Advantages and Disadvantages of Bus, Ring, and Star Topologies

Topology	Advantages	Disadvantages
Bus	Uses a minimal amount of cabling. Easy, reliable, and inexpensive to install.	Breaks in the cable can disable the network. Large numbers of users will greatly decrease performance because of high volumes of data traffic.
Ring	Allocates access to the network fairly. Performance remains acceptable even with large numbers of users.	Adding or removing nodes disables the network. Failure of one computer can bring down the entire network. Problems in data transmission can sometimes be difficult to find.
Star	Failure of one computer does not affect other computers on the network. Centralized design simplifies trouble-shooting and repairs. Easy to add additional computers or network segments as needed (high scalability). Performance remains acceptable even with large numbers of users.	Requires more cable and is often more expensive than a bus or ring topology. The switch is a central point of failure. If it fails, all computers connected to that switch are affected.

Figure 1.27

Objective 6
Identify Safe Computing Practices

Being computer fluent implies you are a responsible computer user. This means more than just understanding the key components of a computer or the differences between hardware and software. Responsible computer users also know how to properly maintain their computers, back up necessary data, and protect themselves and others from security breaches and attacks.

Computer Maintenance

The first step to protect your computer and the valuable information it contains is to establish a regular maintenance routine. Backup utility programs, which may be part of your system software or purchased separately, enable you to back up your files. You can back up everything on your computer, just one or two important files, or anything in between. People often think that the computer is the most expensive item to replace if their hard drive fails. In reality, it is usually all the lost information that was contained on the hard drive that is the most costly to replace, if it is even possible to do so. Think about the types of files you might have on your own computer—financial records, resumes, homework or school projects, your CD collection and purchased music files, and family photos—then imagine how you would re-create these files if they were irretrievably damaged. Would you be able to find them again? If you back up files on a regular basis and store the backups in a secure location, you lessen the impact that a mechanical failure or security breach will have on your data.

What other types of maintenance tasks should be performed? In addition to backing up files, regular file maintenance also helps to maintain order in your system. Several useful Windows utilities can be accessed from the System Tools folder. You can access the System Tools folder by clicking Start, clicking All Programs, and then clicking Accessories. Disk Cleanup scans the hard drive and removes unnecessary files such as those found in the Recycle Bin, in addition to temporary Internet files and other temporary files created by various programs. It is possible to adjust the settings and select which files to delete and which files to retain.

Similarly, the Disk Defragmenter scans the hard drive. However, rather than removing files, it attempts to reallocate files so they use the available hard drive space more efficiently. Recall that data is stored on hard drives in sectors and tracks. As file sizes change, they can outgrow their original location. When that happens, the remaining portion of the file may be stored elsewhere. If a file size decreases, or a file is deleted, this can create a blank area on the hard drive. Defragmenting a hard drive enables scattered portions of files to be regrouped and open spaces to be rearranged. This results in faster and more efficient file access, which improves the response time of the hard drive.

Is there a way to automate these maintenance tasks? Running these programs can be time consuming, especially when you want to use your computer for other tasks. It is also easy to forget to do these things on a regular basis. That is why newer versions of Windows include a Scheduled Task Wizard. This utility, listed as Scheduled Tasks in the System Tools folder, enables you to select the best time for each task to run, in addition to how often, which makes the whole process automatic. Figure 1.28 shows the Scheduled Task Wizard being used to set up the Disk Cleanup task.

Figure 1.28

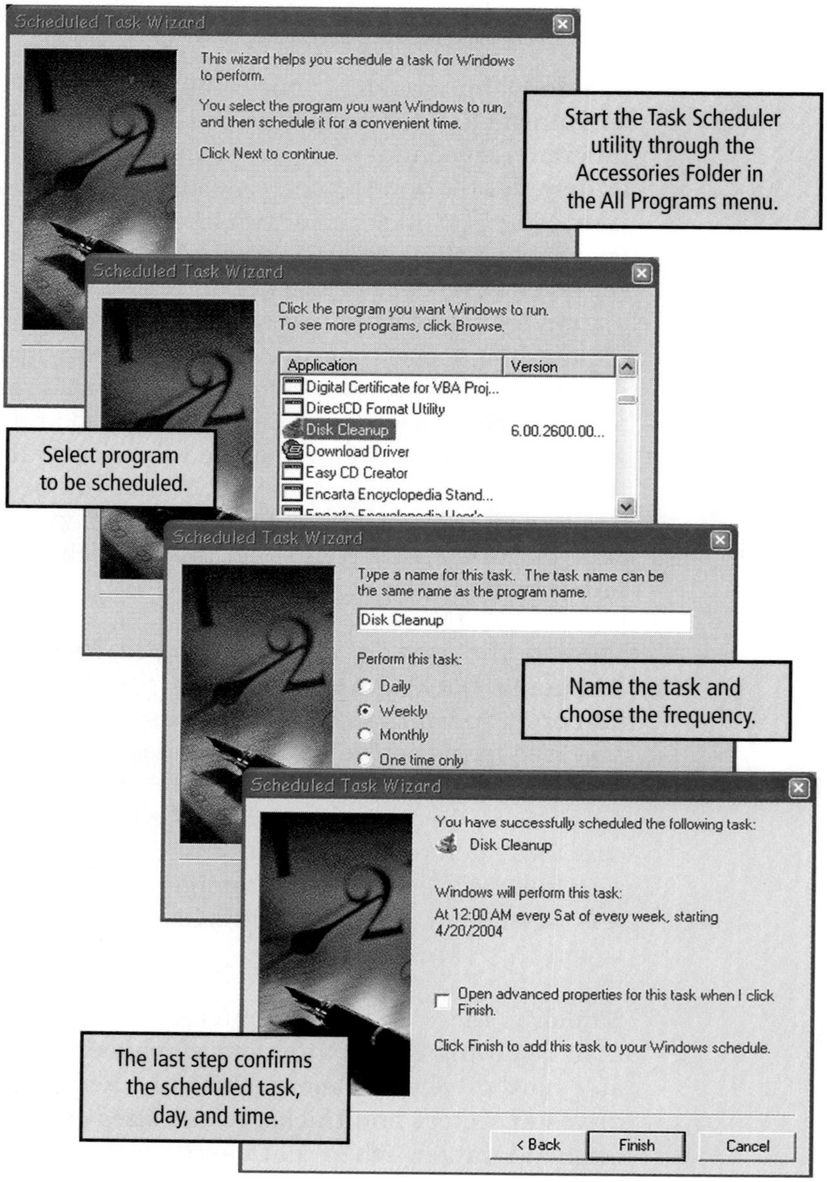

Start the Task Scheduler utility through the Accessories Folder in the All Programs menu.

Select program to be scheduled.

Name the task and choose the frequency.

The last step confirms the scheduled task, day, and time.

Can changes to my system be undone? Sometimes when new software is installed on a computer, the results are not what you anticipated. Instead of playing a new game, you find your system stops responding each time you start it. Or, you might find the new driver you installed for your printer is causing conflicts. Even though you've tried to uninstall the software, the system is still not right.

Fortunately, if you are running a newer version of Windows the System Restore utility (also found in the System Tools folder) can come to the rescue. Periodically, Windows creates a **restore point**, which records all the settings for your system. It's similar to taking a picture of how everything is currently set up. See System Restore in action in Figure 1.29.

It is also possible to set manual restore points, and it is highly recommended that you set one before installing new software or hardware, or when making any major changes to your system. If you experience a problem with your system after the new software is installed, you can roll your system back to an earlier restore point when the system was working correctly. Think of it as an Undo button for your operating system. The good news is, returning to an earlier restore point affects only your system settings—it does not delete any of the data files you may have created during the interval.

Figure 1.29

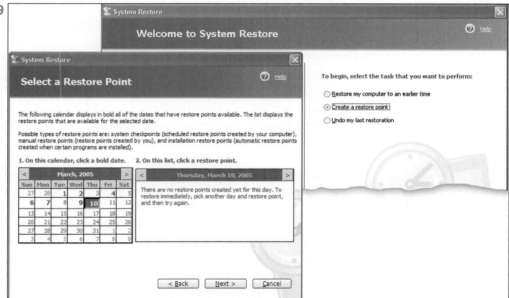

Viruses

Establishing the habit of performing regular maintenance on your computer is one way to protect it, and yourself, from data loss. But there are many other dangers you need to be aware of too. Viruses, spyware, and hackers are all out there waiting to pounce on the unwary computer user.

What are viruses and how do they get on the computer? Computer **viruses** are malicious codes or programs that are usually installed on your computer without your knowledge and against your wishes. The severity of a virus can vary. Some viruses merely seem to be nuisances or might not even be obvious to the user; some cause files to be corrupted or erased; and others are capable of shutting down a computer and erasing the entire hard drive. Viruses infect a system and then attach themselves to a program or file to spread to other users.

Viruses can be distributed in several ways. In the early days of computers, viruses were spread by sharing infected floppy disks. Now, due to the ease in which files can be shared over the Internet, viruses are able to spread much more quickly. One of the most common ways to send a virus is through e-mail attachments. Security experts recommend that you never open an e-mail attachment unless you have first scanned it with antivirus software to determine that it is virus-free. Experts also recommend that unless you know the sender and have been expecting the e-mail attachment, it is best to delete the attachment without ever opening it. File-sharing services are another source for these types of problems.

Are viruses and worms the same thing? **Worms** are similar to viruses because they are also malicious programs that spread from computer to computer; however, unlike viruses, worms are able to do this without any human interaction and are able to replicate themselves so numerous copies can be sent. Worms can burrow into your e-mail address book, or locate e-mail addresses on files saved on your hard drive, then send themselves out without any help from you. When it reaches the e-mail recipient, it does the same thing to the recipient's Address Book. Also, because worms can quickly replicate themselves, they can repeat this scenario over and over. Just the sheer amount of traffic they cause on a network can be enough to bring an entire company to a grinding halt. Worms can also open a "back door" to your system, which enables hackers access to it and gives them the ability to control your computer remotely. Sasser, Blaster, NetSky, and MyDoom are all worms that have created a great deal of trouble in recent years.

Trojan horses are not truly viruses because they do not duplicate themselves or infect other files; however, they can be just as problematic. At first glance, a Trojan horse often appears to be a desirable software program. Perhaps it is a free screensaver program or a set of animated cursors. Unfortunately, these programs come with an unwanted and hidden agenda. After the software is installed, the effects can be similar to those that viruses or worms cause. Before you install new software, it is important to scan the program files with antivirus software to ensure there are no Trojan horses lurking there. And, as with unknown e-mail attachments, it is important to be skeptical about free software—it's not often that you really get something for nothing!

Spyware

How is spyware different from viruses? **Spyware** is software designed to capture personal and confidential information that resides on your system and send it elsewhere. It has quickly become as large a problem as viruses. Spyware's primary threat is to your privacy and confidentiality. Although spyware is not usually intended to harm your system, it can sometimes have that effect on it. **Adware** is spyware that tracks your Internet browsing and can install malicious cookies on your computer. A **cookie** is a small text file that contains information that can identify you to a Web site. Cookies are not necessarily bad. They are useful when they are used to help personalize your Web browsing experience, but cookies can threaten your privacy if they are used to reveal too much information.

How can you tell if spyware is on a computer? One symptom that indicates adware is on a computer is an increase in the number of pop-up ads the user receives, some of which might even address the user by name! Adware can generate pop-up ads even when you're not online. Some types of adware can also reset a Web browser's home page to a page of its choosing and take control of the search engine, directing you to Web sites that have been predetermined by the adware.

Are there other privacy threats? **Key loggers** are another type of spyware. In this case, a software program records every keystroke made on the computer. Key loggers can capture all sorts of confidential information this way—passwords, credit card numbers, bank account numbers, and so on—and then relay this information elsewhere. Entire e-mail messages and instant messaging conversations can be recorded this way too. Some key loggers are hardware, rather than software, although they perform the same devious function. Such hardware devices can be attached between the keyboard and the computer. The information stolen through the use of key loggers can easily make you a victim of identity theft. Trojan horses can be used to distribute key loggers and other types of spyware just as easily as they deliver viruses.

How can you avoid being a victim? To minimize the risk of having spyware installed on your computer, there are some practical precautions you can take. One of the most prevalent methods of spreading spyware is through file-sharing services, such as Morpheus or Kazaa. Not only can the file-sharing software include spyware, but often the files you think you are downloading for free are infected too. Although it's tempting to get the newest song or video for free from such a site, don't risk it!

This problem can be avoided if you use one of the legitimate, pay-as-you-go file-sharing services such as iTunes or the reincarnated Napster. Additionally, be cautious when you download and install freeware or shareware software. Make sure you deal with a reputable software publisher, scan the downloaded software for viruses and spyware, and read the licensing agreement. Some licensing agreements actually include information about additional software that will be automatically installed if you accept it.

Another way to prevent spyware is to avoid pop-up and banner ads whenever possible. You should never click on them. Often the "No Thanks" button is just a ruse to get you to click it and enable the spyware installation. Close pop-up ads by clicking the Close button in the top right corner. Even better, installing pop-up blocking software can help to eliminate this risk almost entirely.

If you are running the most recent version of Windows you already have a pop-up blocker available to you. You can view the pop-up blocker settings for Windows XP in Figure 1.30 and access this dialog box through Internet Explorer's Tools menu. Many popular search engines, such as Google and Yahoo!, also include pop-up blocking features in their toolbars, which you can download at no charge. It is also wise to avoid questionable Web sites, because some of them can install spyware on your system just by visiting the site.

Figure 1.30

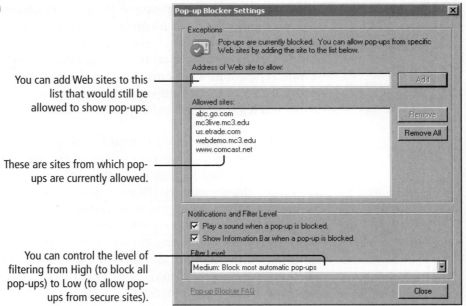

You can add Web sites to this list that would still be allowed to show pop-ups.

These are sites from which pop-ups are currently allowed.

You can control the level of filtering from High (to block all pop-ups) to Low (to allow pop-ups from secure sites).

Protecting Yourself and Your Computer

In addition to being cautious in your Internet travels, there are some proactive measures you can take to protect yourself and your computer from viruses and spyware. These include

- **Software updates and patches**—Keeping your operating system and software up-to-date is critical. Software manufacturers are constantly on the lookout for security threats, and they issue updates and patches to help protect your system. Check for these and install them regularly. Software manufacturers have begun to implement automated procedures to check and install such updates. If your computer has this capability, it's a good idea to use this feature. Figure 1.31 shows the Windows XP System Properties dialog box, with the Automatic Updates tab open.

Figure 1.31

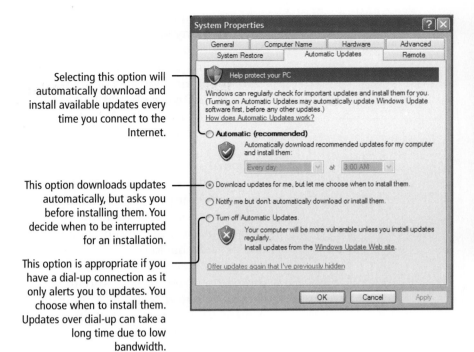

Selecting this option will automatically download and install available updates every time you connect to the Internet.

This option downloads updates automatically, but asks you before installing them. You decide when to be interrupted for an installation.

This option is appropriate if you have a dial-up connection as it only alerts you to updates. You choose when to install them. Updates over dial-up can take a long time due to low bandwidth.

- *Antivirus and antispyware software—Antivirus software* is a utility program used to search your hard drive and files for viruses, and remove those that are found. *Antispyware software* works in a similar fashion, but searches for spyware rather than viruses. No computer should be without this protection. Many users erroneously think that because they aren't regularly online or use only a slow dial-up connection, they aren't a target. Nothing could be further from the truth! Recent studies show more than two-thirds of all computer users have some form of virus or spyware on their system.

There are a variety of antivirus and antispyware products available. Unfortunately, there are also a lot of dishonest companies purporting to offer these products. Too often, these are really scams that will actually install spyware or viruses on your system! To avoid being scammed or downloading something malicious, you should never respond to offers that are received in a pop-up ad or unsolicited e-mail. To obtain legitimate products, it is best to purchase them from the manufacturer's Web site or from a local retailer. Additionally, some Internet Service Providers are beginning to provide some of these products as part of their services.

Some well-known antivirus products include Norton AntiVirus (*www.symantec.com*), McAfee VirusScan (*www.mcafee.com*), and AVG Anti-Virus (*www.grisoft.com*). Antispyware products include eTrust PestPatrol (*www.pestpatrol.com*), Ad-Aware (*www.lavasoft.com*), and Spybot Search & Destroy (*www.safer-networking.org*). You can search for other products at popular download sites such as Download.com (*www.download.com*) or Tucows (*www.tucows.com*) but you should be sure to read the software reviews and evaluate their usefulness before downloading or installing them.

It is best to use only one antivirus product, because running more than one can cause conflicts between the programs. However, because there are so many different types of spyware, antispyware products may address these problems in different ways. Experts recommend running at least two different antispyware applications in order to catch as many spyware programs as possible. It's not enough to install antivirus and antispyware software on your system; you need to update it frequently—at least once a week. Doing so will protect you against any new viruses or spyware created since the last time you checked. Software should be set to scan incoming data—files, e-mail, and so on—but regular full-system scans should be conducted on a weekly basis as well.

- **Personal firewalls**—Firewalls may be software programs or hardware devices, although their purpose is the same—to prevent unauthorized access to your computer. When a firewall is installed properly, it can make your computer invisible to hackers and other invaders. Not only can a good firewall help prevent infections and identity theft; it can also prevent hackers from accessing your computer and turning it into a **zombie**. A zombie computer is one that can be controlled remotely and can be used to help spread viruses, spyware, or junk e-mail known as **spam**. Zombie computers can also be used in **denial of service (DoS)** attacks. DoS attacks occur when a large number of computers try to access a Web site at the same time, effectively overloading it and causing it to shut down. If you are using Windows XP or Windows Vista you already have a firewall available to you.

Figure 1.32 shows the Windows XP Firewall dialog box. You can access the firewall settings by clicking Start, and then clicking Control Panel and clicking Windows Security Center. Click Windows Firewall from the Security Center. Note that you can also access Windows Update from this area too.

Figure 1.32

Unless you have another firewall installed, choose this option to activate the Windows firewall.

When connecting your laptop to a public wireless network, checking this option will provide you with additional security.

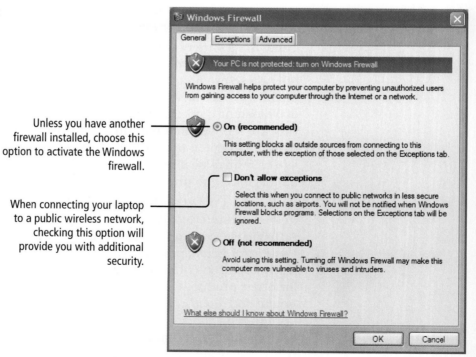

What else should I look out for?   It might sound simple, but when online, do not give out personal information unless it is for legitimate purposes. It is important to avoid spam e-mail and *phishing* attacks— e-mails that masquerade as authentic entities such as banks and credit card companies and ask for confidential information. Legitimate organizations will not ask for passwords, bank account numbers, or credit card details through e-mail. It is also possible to check for hoaxes and scams at a variety of Web sites, including many of the antivirus and antispyware sites. When in doubt, do some research to see if the request you've received is legitimate. If necessary, make a telephone call to the agency in question. Viewing such requests with a critical eye can help you avoid online scams and hoaxes.

Content-Based Assessments

Summary

In this chapter, you examined the benefits of computer fluency and identified the four basic functions of computing. You explored the various types of computers and their components, including CPUs, RAM, and storage devices. This chapter also discussed how to evaluate a computer system and understand the terminology used to measure storage capacity, memory, and microprocessor speed. Various hardware and peripheral devices were reviewed, including input and output devices, and different types of storage media. You explored the basic types of computer software—system software and application software—and the different uses for each type. You identified various types of networks and the different ways networks can be configured. You also reviewed ways to maintain your computer and keep it safe from various threats, including viruses and spyware.

Key Terms

Content-Based Assessments

Key Terms

Content-Based Assessments

Key Terms

Content-Based Assessments

Matching

Match each term in the second column with its correct definition in the first column. Write the letter of the term on the blank line in front of the correct definition.

_____ **1.** Computer programs.

_____ **2.** Programs that enable you to accomplish tasks and use the computer in a productive manner.

_____ **3.** Two or more computers connected together to enable resource sharing.

_____ **4.** Used to manage network resources, this type of computer can be dedicated to a specific task.

_____ **5.** Floppy disks use this type of storage media.

_____ **6.** The layout or design/arrangement of computers connected to a network.

_____ **7.** A peripheral device uses this to attach to the computer.

_____ **8.** An electronic system that contains input, processing, output, and storage units.

_____ **9.** The physical components of a computer system.

_____ **10.** Hardware connected outside the main computer system unit.

_____ **11.** The hardware unit that contains the CPU, memory, hard disk, and power supply.

_____ **12.** The unit that contains the circuitry that enables a computer system to operate.

_____ **13.** The temporary storage available inside the computer.

_____ **14.** The processing unit.

_____ **15.** This type of program threatens a user's privacy.

A Application software

B Computer

C Computer network

D Console/system unit

E CPU

F Hardware

G Magnetic

H Memory (RAM)

I Motherboard/system board

J Peripherals

K Port

L Server

M Software

N Spyware

O Topology

Content-Based Assessments

Computer Concepts

chapterone

Fill in the Blank

Write the correct word in the space provided.

1. Used to perform complex, dedicated tasks, the _____ is the fastest and most expensive computer.

2. The four basic functions of a computer are _____, _____, _____, and _____.

3. Someone with the basic skills and knowledge of a responsible computer user is considered to be computer _____.

4. Personal digital assistants (PDAs) are also known as _____ computers.

5. _____ is data that has been processed and presented in an organized format.

6. The control unit and the arithmetic logic unit are located in the _____.

7. _____ measures how quickly the CPU processes data.

8. An object connected to a network is known as a(n) _____.

9. A(n) _____ network is often found in homes and allows each node to communicate with all the others.

10. A(n) _____ records system settings and can be used to roll back a system to an earlier date in case a software installation has unexpected results.

11. When information is displayed on a monitor it is known as _____ copy.

12. The number of pixels displayed on the screen determines a monitor's _____.

13. _____ printers use a drum and toner in the printing process.

14. The quality of a printed page is measured in dpi, which is an acronym for _____.

15. The point-and-click format that modern operating systems use is called a(n) _____.

Content-Based Assessments

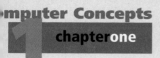

Multiple Choice

Circle the letter of the item that correctly answers the question.

1. Which of the following requires one byte of storage?

   a. Page

   b. Paragraph

   c. Sentence

   d. Character

2. Which of the following terms represents the fastest CPU speed?

   a. 733 MHz

   b. 286 MHz

   c. 2 GHz

   d. 2 GB

3. Which of the following is not an input device?

   a. Keyboard

   b. Speaker

   c. Mouse

   d. Stylus

4. Which of the following is an example of optical storage?

   a. Disk drive

   b. Flash card

   c. Memory

   d. Compact disc

5. Which of the following is not a type of computer?

   a. Mainframe

   b. Multitask

   c. Server

   d. Supercomputer

6. Before a computer can process data, where must data be stored?

   a. On a disk

   b. In computer memory

   c. In the control unit

   d. On the monitor

Content-Based Assessments

Multiple Choice

7. What term, related to computers, means billions?

  a. Byte

  b. Mega

  c. Giga

  d. Hertz

8. Which of the following is not a type of microcomputer?

  a. Desktop

  b. Notebook

  c. Personal digital assistant

  d. Microprocessor

9. Which of the following can make a computer invisible to hackers?

  a. Disk defragmenter

  b. Antivirus software

  c. Firewall

  d. Key logger

10. Which of the following is capable of opening a "back door" on a computer and is able to spread without human interaction?

  a. Trojan horse

  b. Worm

  c. Adware

  d. Zombie

Glossary

Adware Spyware that tracks a user's Internet browsing and installs malicious cookies.

Antispyware software A program that protects a computer from malicious software designed to threaten privacy and confidentiality.

Antivirus software A program that protects a computer from malicious codes such as viruses, worms, and Trojan horses.

Application software Programs with which you accomplish tasks such as word processing, photo editing, or sending e-mail, and use the computer in a productive manner.

Arithmetic logic unit (ALU) Part of the CPU that performs all the arithmetic and logic functions for the computer; handles addition, subtraction, multiplication, and division, and also makes logical and comparison decisions.

Arrow keys The arrow keys found at the bottom center section of the keyboard, used to move the insertion point within the program window.

Audio port A port that connects audio equipment to the sound card of a computer to facilitate the exchange of data.

Backup tape drive A storage device used to save data to tapes resembling audiocassettes.

Bluetooth Wireless technology that uses radio waves to transmit data over short distances, and often used with mobile devices.

Boot The process of starting up a computer.

Boot process See Boot.

Burn The process of recording data to optical media such as a CD or DVD.

Bus topology A networking configuration in which all devices are connected to a central high-speed cable called the bus or backbone.

Cathode-ray tube (CRT) A picture tube device used in a monitor, similar to a television.

CD burner An optical storage device capable of reading data from and writing data to a CD.

CD drive A storage device used to read and, possibly, write data to CD.

Central processing unit (CPU) The part of the computer responsible for controlling all the commands and tasks the computer performs, acting as the brain of the computer.

Click To press the left (or primary) mouse button once.

Client In a client/server network, this is the computer most people interact with to request information from the server and to perform many of the tasks that can be accomplished with a computer.

Client/server network A network consisting of client and server computers; often used in businesses.

Clock speed A measurement of how quickly a CPU processes data, an indication of a CPU's processing power.

Communication or organizational software A program such as Microsoft Outlook, used to send and retrieve e-mail and manage day-to-day tasks.

Computer A programmable electronic device that can input, process, output, and store data.

Computer fluent The term used to describe a person who understands the capabilities and limitations of computers and knows how to use computer technology to accomplish tasks.

Connectivity port A port that enables a computer to be connected to other devices or systems, such as networks, modems, and the Internet.

Control keys Special keys, such as Ctrl, Alt, or Esc, used to increase keyboard functionality or provide shortcuts.

Control unit The part of the CPU responsible for obtaining instructions from the computer's memory; the control unit interprets the instructions and executes them, thereby coordinating the activities of all the other computer components.

Cookie A small text file containing information that identifies a visitor to a Web site.

CPU See Central processing unit.

CRT See Cathode-ray tube.

Data Words, numbers, sounds, or pictures that represent facts about people, events, things, or ideas.

Database software Programs, such as Microsoft Access, used to store and organize large amounts of data and perform complex tasks such as sorting and querying to generate specialized reports.

Dedicated server A computer that is assigned to handle one specific task on a network.

Denial of service (DoS) An attack caused when a large number of computers attempt to access a Web site at the same time, effectively overloading it and causing it to shut down.

Desktop computer A class of microcomputer, such as a PC or a Mac.

Digital camera A type of camera that saves photographs in a digital format rather than on film.

Digital Video Interface (DVI) port A port used to connect an LCD monitor to a computer in order to use a pure digital signal.

Digital video recorder A device used to record video in digital format directly to a hard drive, without the need for videotape.

Display screen See Monitor.

Dot matrix An impact printer, useful for printing multi-page forms.

Dot pitch The diagonal distance between adjacent pixels, measured in millimeters and that is used to determine image quality for monitors.

Dots per inch (dpi) A measurement of printer resolution.

Double-click The action of clicking the left mouse button twice in rapid succession while keeping the mouse still.

Drag The action of moving something from one location on the screen to another; the action of dragging includes releasing the mouse button at the desired time or location.

Dual-boot A system with two different operating systems installed, giving the user the option to boot the computer using either one.

Dual-core A CPU that includes two microprocessors on a single integrated circuit. See also Multicore.

DVD drive A storage device used to read and, possibly, write data to DVD.

DVI port See Digital Video Interface (DVI) port.

Embedded computers Components of larger products, devices that perform pre-defined tasks using specially programmed processors.

Ethernet port A port, slightly larger than a telephone jack, that can transmit data at speeds up to 1,000 megabits per second (Mbps) and is usually used to connect to a cable modem or a network.

Firewall See Personal firewall.

FireWire port A port used to send data at rates up to 800 megabits per second (Mbps), frequently used for digital cameras or digital video recorders.

Flash drive A small, portable, digital storage device that connects to a computer's USB port; also called a thumb drive, jump drive, or USB drive.

Flash memory Portable, nonvolatile memory, that uses electronic, solid-state circuitry.

Flat panel See Liquid crystal display.

Flat screen A type of screen used in CRT monitors, and which differs from flat panel monitors.

Floppy disk drive (or floppy drive) The original storage device for a microcomputer, which enables portable, permanent storage on floppy disks.

Function key The keys, numbered F1 through F12, located above the numeric keys on a keyboard that have different functions depending upon the software program in use.

Gigabyte (GB) Approximately one billion bytes; a unit of measure for memory and storage space.

Gigahertz (GHz) One billion hertz; hertz is the unit of measure for processor speed.

Graphical user interface (GUI) A computer interface with which you interact with the computer through the use of graphics and point-and-click technology; GUIs show documents as they will look in their final form.

GUI See Graphical user interface.

Handheld computers See Personal digital assistant.

Hard copy Data or information retrieved from a computer and printed.

Hard disk drive (or hard drive) Permanent storage device, located within the system unit, that holds all permanently stored software and data.

Hardware The physical components of the computer and any equipment connected to it.

Hyperthreading Technology that allows a CPU to emulate multiple processors, improving processing power and speed.

Icon A graphic representation of an object that you can click to open that object.

Impact A type of printer that resembles a typewriter; a key and ink ribbon are used to imprint a character on paper.

Information Data that has been organized in a useful manner.

Information processing cycle The cycle composed of the four basic computer functions: input, process, output, and storage.

Ink-jet Type of printer that uses a special nozzle and ink cartridges to distribute liquid ink on the surface of the paper.

Input The act of entering data into a computer.

Input devices Computer hardware used to enter data and instructions into a computer; examples include the keyboard, mouse, stylus, scanner, microphone, and digital camera.

Internet control key Usually found at the top of a keyboard, this type of key can be used for various Internet-related activities including opening a Web browser and sending e-mail.

IrDA port A port enabling data transmission through the use of infrared light waves; the devices sharing data require a clear line of site with no visual obstructions.

Joysticks Input devices used to control actions and movement within computer games.

Key logger A software program or hardware device that records every keystroke made on the computer.

Keyboard The hardware device used to input typed data and commands into a computer.

LAN See Local area network.

Laser A type of printer that uses a drum, static electricity, and a laser to distribute dry ink or toner on the surface of the paper.

LCD See Liquid crystal display.

Linux An open-source operating system based on the UNIX operating system developed for mainframe computers.

Liquid crystal display (LCD) Technology used in flat panel monitors, resulting in thinner and lighter monitors.

Local area network (LAN) A network in which the nodes are located within a small geographic area.

Mac OS The operating system designed specifically for Apple's Mac computers.

Magnetic A type of storage process using magnetized film to store data; used by media such as floppy disks or Zip disks.

Mainframe A large computer capable of performing more than one task at the same time and supporting many users simultaneously.

Megabyte (MB) Approximately one million bytes; a unit of measure for memory and storage space.

Megahertz (MHz) One million hertz; hertz is the unit of measure for processor speed.

Menu A list of commands within a category.

MFD See Multifunction device.

Microcomputer The computer most users are familiar with, ranging in size from large desktop systems to handheld devices.

Microphones Input devices used to digitally record sound.

Microprocessor chip See Central processing unit.

Microsoft Windows The operating system found on most microcomputers.

MIDI port Musical Instrument Digital Interface port used to connect electronic musical instruments to a system.

Mobile devices Lightweight, portable computing devices such as PDAs, smartphones, and handheld computers.

Modem port A port that connects to a standard telephone line, usually used to connect to the Internet or a local network, with a maximum speed of 56 kilobits per second (Kbps).

Monitor (or display screen) A common output device that displays text, graphics, and video.

Monitor port A port used to connect a monitor to a computer's graphic processing unit, located on the motherboard or video card.

Motherboard A large printed circuit board located in the system unit to which all other boards are connected; the motherboard contains the central processing unit (CPU), the memory (RAM) chips, and expansion card slots.

Mouse An input device used to enter commands and user responses into a computer.

Multicore A CPU that includes more than two microprocessors on a single integrated circuit. See also Dual-core.

Multifunction device (MFD) A device that has more than one purpose, often combining input and output capabilities.

Multimedia control key Usually found at the top of a keyboard, this type of key can be used to control or mute speaker volume.

Multimedia projectors Output devices used to display information on a screen for viewing by an audience.

Multitask The action of performing more than one task at the same time.

Network A group of two or more computers (or nodes) connected to share information and resources.

Network topology The layout and structure of a computer network.

Node Any object connected to a network—may be a computer or a peripheral device.

Nonimpact A type of printer that does not actually touch the paper.

Nonvolatile Permanent storage, as in read only memory (ROM); data remains even when power is shut down.

Notebook computer Also known as a laptop, this microcomputer is smaller than a desktop and designed to be portable.

Numeric keypad A bank of keys on a keyboard with which you can input numbers, it is located on the right side of a keyboard and is similar to an adding machine or calculator.

Open-source Software whose code is made available for developers to modify and use as they wish, usually available at no cost.

Operating system (OS) System software that controls the way in which a computer system functions, including the management of hardware, peripherals, and software; Microsoft Windows XP is an operating system.

Optical A type of storage process using a laser to read and write data; used by media such as CDs and DVDs.

OS See Operating system.

Output To retrieve data or information from a computer.

Output devices Computer hardware used to retrieve processed data and information from a computer; examples include the monitor, printer, and speakers.

P2P network See Peer-to-peer network.

PDA See Personal digital assistant.

Peer-to-peer (P2P) network A network in which each node can communicate directly with every other node, and which is often used for home and small business networks.

Peripheral A hardware device connected to a computer, but not located within the system unit, such as a monitor, printer, or mouse.

Permanent memory Memory used by storage devices to retain data and information.

Personal digital assistant (PDA) Also known as a handheld computer, a small device that enables a user to carry digital information.

Personal firewall A software program or hardware device designed to prevent unauthorized access to a computer.

Phishing Email that masquerades as an authentic entity such as a bank or credit card company, requesting confidential information.

Pixel An abbreviated name for picture element.

Port An interface through which external devices are connected to the computer.

Presentation software A program used to create dynamic slideshows and generate speaker notes and audience handouts.

Printer An output device used to generate hard copy.

Process The term used to describe the action of a computer when it converts data into information.

Program A set of instructions used by a computer to perform certain tasks.

RAM See Random access memory.

Random Access Memory (RAM) A computer's temporary storage space or short-term memory and stored on chips located on the motherboard; measured in megabytes (MB) and gigabytes (GB). Known as volatile memory.

Read Only Memory (ROM) A set of memory chips located on the motherboard that stores data and instructions that cannot be changed or erased; it holds all the instructions the computer needs to start up. Also known as nonvolatile memory.

Refresh rate The speed at which the pixels are reilluminated, measured in cycles per second and expressed as hertz (Hz).

Resolution The measurement used to assess the clarity of an image on a monitor; determined by pixel density.

Restore point A record created by Windows XP for all of a computer's system settings.

Right-click The action of clicking the right mouse button.

Ring (or token-ring) topology A networking configuration in which all devices are set up in a circular layout; data flows in a circular fashion, in one direction only.

ROM See Read only memory.

S-video port A port used to connect ancillary video equipment, such as a television or projector to a computer.

Scanners Input devices used to convert hard copy documents or images into digital files.

Screen (or window) In a graphical user interface, the rectangular box that contains the program displayed on the monitor.

Scroll wheel A feature on some mouse pointing devices; rolling the wheel enables you to quickly move a page up or down within a window.

Sectors Wedge-shaped sections of a hard disk drive, each measured from the center point to the outer edge.

Serial port A type of port that sends data one bit at a time at speeds of up to 115 kilobits per second (Kbps). A mouse or modem may use a serial port to connect to a computer.

Server In a client/server network, the computer that manages shared network resources and provides access to the client computer when requested.

Smartphones Cell phones with additional computing capabilities or the ability to access the Internet.

Soft copy Data or information displayed on a monitor.

Software patches Quick software fixes provided to resolve an error found in program code until a software update can be issued.

Software updates Small, downloadable software modules that repair errors identified in commercial program code.

Spam Junk or unsolicited e-mail.

Speakers Output devices that allow the user to hear any auditory signals the computer sends.

Spreadsheet software A program with which you perform calculations and numerical analyses.

Spyware Software designed to capture personal and confidential information that resides on a computer and then send it elsewhere.

Star topology A flexible and frequently used network configuration for businesses, in which nodes connect to a central communication device known as a switch.

Storage To retain data or information for future use.

Stylus An input device used to write on a tablet computer or PDA.

Suite A collection of application software programs developed by the same manufacturer, bundled together and sold at a price that is usually less than the cost of purchasing each program individually.

Supercomputer A large, powerful computer typically devoted to specialized tasks. It is able to perform complex calculations quickly.

System software The set of programs that enables a computer's hardware devices and program software to work together; it includes the operating system and utility programs.

System unit The tower, box, or console that contains the critical hardware and electrical components of a computer.

Tablet computer A portable computer that features a screen that swivels and can be written on using advanced handwriting recognition software.

Toggle key A keyboard key that switches on or off each time it is pressed.

Token-ring topology See Ring topology.

Topology See Network topology.

Tracks Concentric circles on a hard disk drive.

Trojan horse A program that appears to be useful or desirable, but acts maliciously in the background after installation.

Universal serial bus (USB) port A versatile port used to connect a wide array of peripheral devices to a computer. USB 1.1 ports can send data at speeds of up to 12 megabits per second (Mbps). USB 2.0 ports can attain a rate of 480 Mbps.

User interface The features of a computer operating system that enable you to interact with the computer.

Utility program A component of system software, typically a small program used to perform routine maintenance and housekeeping tasks for the computer.

Virus Malicious code or program, usually installed on a computer without the user's knowledge or permission.

Volatile Temporary storage, as in random access memory (RAM); data is erased when power is shut down.

WAN See Wide area network.

Wide area network (WAN) A network composed of local area networks connected over long distances.

Window A box or screen that displays information or a program. Windows usually consist of title bars, toolbars, menu bars, and status bars. A window will always have a Minimize button.

Windows See Microsoft Windows.

Wireless network A network that connects using radio waves instead of wires or cable.

Word processing software A program used to create and edit written documents such as papers, letters, and resumes.

Worm A program that is able to replicate and spread from computer to computer without human interaction.

Zip drive A magnetic storage device used to save and retrieve data on Zip disks.

Zombie A computer that is controlled remotely and can be used to help spread viruses, spyware, and spam.

Index

R

RAM (Random Access Memory), 9–10
refresh rate, 23
resolution, screen, 23
restore point, 41
right-click, 22
ring topology, 37–38
ROM (Read Only Memory), 9

S

S-video port, 19
safe practices
    antivirus and antispyware software, 45–46
    maintenance, 39–41
    personal firewalls, 46–47
    spyware, 42–44
    updates and patches, 44
    viruses, 41–42
scanners, 22
Scheduled Task Wizard, 40
screens, 27
scroll wheel, 22, 49
sectors, 10
serial ports, 17, 18
servers, 6
slots, memory (RAM), 8
smartphones, 5
soft copy, 22
software
    application, 31–35
    operating system (OS), 26–30
    unanticipated changes caused by
        installation of, 40–41
    updates and patches, 44
    utility programs, 30–31
software suite, 35
spam, 46
speakers, 25–26
spreadsheet software, 32–33
spyware, 42–44

T

star topology, 37–38
storage, 3
storage devices, 10–13
stylus, tablet computer, 5
System Restore utility, 31
system unit, 6–7, 6–10

tablet computers, 5
Task Manager utility, 31
Task Scheduler utility, 31
terabyte (TB), 11, 14
toggle keys, 20
token-ring topology, 37–38
tracks, 10
Trojan horses, 42

U

universal serial bus (USB) port, 17, 18
updates and patches, 44
user interface, 27
utility programs, 30–31

V

viruses, 41–42

W

Windows Security Center, 46–47
Windows System Maintenance and
    Diagnostics utility programs, 31
Windows XP restore point, 41
Windows, prevalence of, 27–28
wireless networks, 36
word processing software, 32
worms, 42

Z

zip drives, 13
zombie, 46

Taken from: *GO! with Microsoft Windows XP: Getting Started*
by Shelley Gaskin, Robert L. Ferrett, John Preston and Sally Preston

Students
How to Find the Student Data Files
to Complete the Projects in This Book

Projects in this book begin either with a new blank file or from a student data file that has already been started for you.

The student data files can be accessed from the enclosed CD-ROM or from the *GO!* Web site.

 *Files from the CD-ROM*

As specifically directed in each project, navigate to the CD-ROM, and then save and rename the file according to the instructions in the project.

Files from
www.prenhall.com/go

1 Decide where you want to store your student data files.

* If you are storing on the hard drive of your computer or on a network drive, you may want to create a folder with an appropriate name on that drive.

* If you are storing on a removable storage device such as a USB flash drive, Zip disk, or floppy disk, insert the device now.

2 From your Web browser, go to **www.prenhall.com/go**

3 From the list of books provided, point to the title of this book, click the active link and then follow the instructions as specified on the Web site.

Table of Contents

Letter from the Editor

Dear Instructors and Students,

The primary goal of the *GO!* Series is two-fold. The first goal is to help instructors teach the course they want in less time. The second goal is to provide students with the skills to solve business problems using the computer as a tool, for both themselves and the organization for which they might be employed.

The *GO!* Series was originally created by Series Editor Shelley Gaskin and published with the release of Microsoft Office 2003. Her ideas came from years of using textbooks that didn't meet all the needs of today's diverse classroom and that were too confusing for students. Shelley continues to enhance the series by ensuring we stay true to our vision of developing quality instruction and useful classroom tools.

But we also need your input and ideas.

Over time, the *GO!* Series has evolved based on direct feedback from instructors and students using the series. *We are the publisher that listens.* To publish a textbook that works for you, it's critical that we continue to listen to this feedback. It's important to me to talk with you and hear your stories about using *GO!* Your voice can make a difference.

My hope is that this letter will inspire you to write me an e-mail and share your thoughts on using the *GO!* Series.

Stephanie Wall
Executive Editor, *GO!* Series
stephanie_wall@prenhall.com

GO! System Contributors

We thank the following people for their hard work and support in making the GO! System all that it is!

Additional Author Support

Coyle, Diane	Montgomery County Community College
Fry, Susan	Boise State
Townsend, Kris	Spokane Falls Community College
Stroup, Tracey	Amgen Corporation

Instructor Resource Authors

Amer, Beverly	Northern Arizona University	Paterson, Jim	Paradise Valley Community College
Boito, Nancy	Harrisburg Area Community College	Prince, Lisa	Missouri State
Coyle, Diane	Montgomery County Community College	Rodgers, Gwen	Southern Nazarene University
Dawson, Tamara	Southern Nazarene University	Ruymann, Amy	Burlington Community College
Driskel, Loretta	Niagara County Community College	Ryan, Bob	Montgomery County Community College
Elliott, Melissa	Odessa College		
Fry, Susan	Boise State	Smith, Diane	Henry Ford College
Geoghan, Debra	Bucks County Community College	Spangler, Candice	Columbus State Community College
Hearn, Barbara	Community College of Philadelphia	Thompson, Joyce	Lehigh Carbon Community College
Jones, Stephanie	South Plains College	Tiffany, Janine	Reading Area Community College
Madsen, Donna	Kirkwood Community College	Watt, Adrienne	Douglas College
Meck, Kari	Harrisburg Area Community College	Weaver, Paul	Bossier Parish Community College
Miller, Cindy	Ivy Tech	Weber, Sandy	Gateway Technical College
Nowakowski, Tony	Buffalo State	Wood, Dawn	
Pace, Phyllis	Queensborough Community College	Weissman, Jonathan	Finger Lakes Community College

Super Reviewers

Brotherton, Cathy	Riverside Community College	Maurer, Trina	Odessa College
Cates, Wally	Central New Mexico Community College	Meck, Kari	Harrisburg Area Community College
		Miller, Cindy	Ivy Tech Community College
Cone, Bill	Northern Arizona University	Nielson, Phil	Salt Lake Community College
Coverdale, John	Riverside Community College	Rodgers, Gwen	Southern Nazarene University
Foster, Nancy	Baker College	Smolenski, Robert	Delaware Community College
Helfand, Terri	Chaffey College	Spangler, Candice	Columbus State Community College
Hibbert, Marilyn	Salt Lake Community College	Thompson, Joyce	Lehigh Carbon Community College
Holliday, Mardi	Community College of Philadelphia	Weber, Sandy	Gateway Technical College
Jerry, Gina	Santa Monica College	Wells, Lorna	Salt Lake Community College
Martin, Carol	Harrisburg Area Community College	Zaboski, Maureen	University of Scranton

Technical Editors

Janice Snyder
Joyce Nielsen
Colette Eisele
Janet Pickard
Mara Zebest
Lindsey Allen
William Daley

Student Reviewers

Allen, John	Asheville-Buncombe Tech Community College	Erickson, Mike	Ball State University
		Gadomski, Amanda	Northern Michigan University
Alexander, Steven	St. Johns River Community College	Gyselinck, Craig	Central Washington University
Alexander, Melissa	Tulsa Community College	Harrison, Margo	Central Washington University
Bolz, Stephanie	Northern Michigan University	Heacox, Kate	Central Washington University
Berner, Ashley	Central Washington University	Hill, Cheretta	Northwestern State University
Boomer, Michelle	Northern Michigan University	Innis, Tim	Tulsa Community College
Busse, Brennan	Northern Michigan University	Jarboe, Aaron	Central Washington University
Butkey, Maura	Central Washington University	Klein, Colleen	Northern Michigan University
Christensen, Kaylie	Northern Michigan University	Moeller, Jeffrey	Northern Michigan University
Connally, Brianna	Central Washington University	Nicholson, Regina	Athens Tech College
Davis, Brandon	Northern Michigan University	Niehaus, Kristina	Northern Michigan University
Davis, Christen	Central Washington University	Nisa, Zaibun	Santa Rosa Community College
Den Boer, Lance	Central Washington University	Nunez, Nohelia	Santa Rosa Community College
Dix, Jessica	Central Washington University	Oak, Samantha	Central Washington University
Moeller, Jeffrey	Northern Michigan University	Oertii, Monica	Central Washington University
Downs, Elizabeth	Central Washington University	Palenshus, Juliet	Central Washington University

Pohl, Amanda	Northern Michigan University	Shanahan, Megan	Northern Michigan University
Presnell, Randy	Central Washington University	Teska, Erika	Hawaii Pacific University
Ritner, April	Northern Michigan University	Traub, Amy	Northern Michigan University
Rodriguez, Flavia	Northwestern State University	Underwood, Katie	Central Washington University
Roberts, Corey	Tulsa Community College	Walters, Kim	Central Washington University
Rossi, Jessica Ann	Central Washington University	Wilson, Kelsie	Central Washington University
Shafapay, Natasha	Central Washington University	Wilson, Amanda	Green River Community College

Series Reviewers

Abraham, Reni	Houston Community College	Crawford, Thomasina	Miami-Dade College, Kendall Campus
Agatston, Ann	Agatston Consulting Technical College	Credico, Grace	Lethbridge Community College
		Crenshaw, Richard	Miami Dade Community College, North
Alexander, Melody	Ball Sate University		
Alejandro, Manuel	Southwest Texas Junior College	Crespo, Beverly	Mt. San Antonio College
Ali, Farha	Lander University	Crossley, Connie	Cincinnati State Technical Community College
Amici, Penny	Harrisburg Area Community College		
Anderson, Patty A.	Lake City Community College	Curik, Mary	Central New Mexico Community College
Andrews, Wilma	Virginia Commonwealth College, Nebraska University		
		De Arazoza, Ralph	Miami Dade Community College
Anik, Mazhar	Tiffin University	Danno, John	DeVry University/Keller Graduate School
Armstrong, Gary	Shippensburg University		
Atkins, Bonnie	Delaware Technical Community College	Davis, Phillip	Del Mar College
		DeHerrera, Laurie	Pikes Peak Community College
Bachand, LaDonna	Santa Rosa Community College	Delk, Dr. K. Kay	Seminole Community College
Bagui, Sikha	University of West Florida	Doroshow, Mike	Eastfield College
Beecroft, Anita	Kwantlen University College	Douglas, Gretchen	SUNYCortland
Bell, Paula	Lock Haven College	Dove, Carol	Community College of Allegheny
Belton, Linda	Springfield Tech. Community College	Driskel, Loretta	Niagara Community College
		Duckwiler, Carol	Wabaunsee Community College
Bennett, Judith	Sam Houston State University	Duncan, Mimi	University of Missouri-St. Louis
Bhatia, Sai	Riverside Community College	Duthie, Judy	Green River Community College
Bishop, Frances	DeVry Institute—Alpharetta (ATL)	Duvall, Annette	Central New Mexico Community College
Blaszkiewicz, Holly	Ivy Tech Community College/Region 1		
Branigan, Dave	DeVry University	Ecklund, Paula	Duke University
Bray, Patricia	Allegany College of Maryland	Eng, Bernice	Brookdale Community College
Brotherton, Cathy	Riverside Community College	Evans, Billie	Vance-Granville Community College
Buehler, Lesley	Ohlone College	Feuerbach, Lisa	Ivy Tech East Chicago
Buell, C	Central Oregon Community College	Fisher, Fred	Florida State University
Byars, Pat	Brookhaven College	Foster, Penny L.	Anne Arundel Community College
Byrd, Lynn	Delta State University, Cleveland, Mississippi	Foszcz, Russ	McHenry County College
		Fry, Susan	Boise State University
Cacace, Richard N.	Pensacola Junior College	Fustos, Janos	Metro State
Cadenhead, Charles	Brookhaven College	Gallup, Jeanette	Blinn College
Calhoun, Ric	Gordon College	Gelb, Janet	Grossmont College
Cameron, Eric	Passaic Community College	Gentry, Barb	Parkland College
Carriker, Sandra	North Shore Community College	Gerace, Karin	St. Angela Merici School
Cannamore, Madie	Kennedy King	Gerace, Tom	Tulane University
Carreon, Cleda	Indiana University—Purdue University, Indianapolis	Ghajar, Homa	Oklahoma State University
		Gifford, Steve	Northwest Iowa Community College
Chaffin, Catherine	Shawnee State University	Glazer, Ellen	Broward Community College
Chauvin, Marg	Palm Beach Community College, Boca Raton	Gordon, Robert	Hofstra University
		Gramlich, Steven	Pasco-Hernando Community College
Challa, Chandrashekar	Virginia State University	Graviett, Nancy M.	St. Charles Community College, St. Peters, Missouri
Chamlou, Afsaneh	NOVA Alexandria		
Chapman, Pam	Wabaunsee Community College	Greene, Rich	Community College of Allegheny County
Christensen, Dan	Iowa Western Community College		
Clay, Betty	Southeastern Oklahoma State University	Gregoryk, Kerry	Virginia Commonwealth State
		Griggs, Debra	Bellevue Community College
Collins, Linda D.	Mesa Community College	Grimm, Carol	Palm Beach Community College
Conroy-Link, Janet	Holy Family College	Hahn, Norm	Thomas Nelson Community College
Cosgrove, Janet	Northwestern CT Community	Hammerschlag, Dr. Bill	Brookhaven College
Courtney, Kevin	Hillsborough Community College	Hansen, Michelle	Davenport University
Cox, Rollie	Madison Area Technical College	Hayden, Nancy	Indiana University—Purdue University, Indianapolis
Crawford, Hiram	Olive Harvey College		

Hayes, Theresa	Broward Community College	Lord, Alexandria	Asheville Buncombe Tech
Helfand, Terri	Chaffey College	Lowe, Rita	Harold Washington College
Helms, Liz	Columbus State Community College	Low, Willy Hui	Joliet Junior College
Hernandez, Leticia	TCI College of Technology	Lucas, Vickie	Broward Community College
Hibbert, Marilyn	Salt Lake Community College	Lynam, Linda	Central Missouri State University
Hoffman, Joan	Milwaukee Area Technical College	Lyon, Lynne	Durham College
Hogan, Pat	Cape Fear Community College	Lyon, Pat Rajski	Tomball College
Holland, Susan	Southeast Community College	MacKinnon, Ruth	Georgia Southern University
Hopson, Bonnie	Athens Technical College	Macon, Lisa	Valencia Community College, West Campus
Horvath, Carrie	Albertus Magnus College		
Horwitz, Steve	Community College of Philadelphia	Machuca, Wayne	College of the Sequoias
Hotta, Barbara	Leeward Community College	Madison, Dana	Clarion University
Howard, Bunny	St. Johns River Community	Maguire, Trish	Eastern New Mexico University
Howard, Chris	DeVry University	Malkan, Rajiv	Montgomery College
Huckabay, Jamie	Austin Community College	Manning, David	Northern Kentucky University
Hudgins, Susan	East Central University	Marcus, Jacquie	Niagara Community College
Hulett, Michelle J.	Missouri State University	Marghitu, Daniela	Auburn University
Hunt, Darla A.	Morehead State University, Morehead, Kentucky	Marks, Suzanne	Bellevue Community College
		Marquez, Juanita	El Centro College
Hunt, Laura	Tulsa Community College	Marquez, Juan	Mesa Community College
Jacob, Sherry	Jefferson Community College	Martyn, Margie	Baldwin-Wallace College
Jacobs, Duane	Salt Lake Community College	Marucco, Toni	Lincoln Land Community College
Jauken, Barb	Southeastern Community	Mason, Lynn	Lubbock Christian University
Johnson, Kathy	Wright College	Matutis, Audrone	Houston Community College
Johnson, Mary	Kingwood College	Matkin, Marie	University of Lethbridge
Johnson, Mary	Mt. San Antonio College	McCain, Evelynn	Boise State University
Jones, Stacey	Benedict College	McCannon, Melinda	Gordon College
Jones, Warren	University of Alabama, Birmingham	McCarthy, Marguerite	Northwestern Business College
Jordan, Cheryl	San Juan College	McCaskill, Matt L.	Brevard Community College
Kapoor, Bhushan	California State University, Fullerton	McClellan, Carolyn	Tidewater Community College
Kasai, Susumu	Salt Lake Community College	McClure, Darlean	College of Sequoias
Kates, Hazel	Miami Dade Community College, Kendall	McCrory, Sue A.	Missouri State University
		McCue, Stacy	Harrisburg Area Community College
Keen, Debby	University of Kentucky	McEntire-Orbach, Teresa	Middlesex County College
Keeter, Sandy	Seminole Community College	McLeod, Todd	Fresno City College
Kern-Blystone, Dorothy Jean	Bowling Green State	McManus, Illyana	Grossmont College
		McPherson, Dori	Schoolcraft College
Keskin, Ilknur	The University of South Dakota	Meiklejohn, Nancy	Pikes Peak Community College
Kirk, Colleen	Mercy College	Menking, Rick	Hardin-Simmons University
Kleckner, Michelle	Elon University	Meredith, Mary	University of Louisiana at Lafayette
Kliston, Linda	Broward Community College, North Campus	Mermelstein, Lisa	Baruch College
		Metos, Linda	Salt Lake Community College
Kochis, Dennis	Suffolk County Community College	Meurer, Daniel	University of Cincinnati
Kramer, Ed	Northern Virginia Community College	Meyer, Marian	Central New Mexico Community College
Laird, Jeff	Northeast State Community College	Miller, Cindy	Ivy Tech Community College, Lafayette, Indiana
Lamoureaux, Jackie	Central New Mexico Community College		
		Mitchell, Susan	Davenport University
Lange, David	Grand Valley State	Mohle, Dennis	Fresno Community College
LaPointe, Deb	Central New Mexico Community College	Monk, Ellen	University of Delaware
		Moore, Rodney	Holland College
Larson, Donna	Louisville Technical Institute	Morris, Mike	Southeastern Oklahoma State University
Laspina, Kathy	Vance-Granville Community College		
Le Grand, Dr. Kate	Broward Community College	Morris, Nancy	Hudson Valley Community College
Lenhart, Sheryl	Terra Community College	Moseler, Dan	Harrisburg Area Community College
Letavec, Chris	University of Cincinnati	Nabors, Brent	Reedley College, Clovis Center
Liefert, Jane	Everett Community College	Nadas, Erika	Wright College
Lindaman, Linda	Black Hawk Community College	Nadelman, Cindi	New England College
Lindberg, Martha	Minnesota State University	Nademlynsky, Lisa	Johnson & Wales University
Lightner, Renee	Broward Community College	Ncube, Cathy	University of West Florida
Lindberg, Martha	Minnesota State University	Nagengast, Joseph	Florida Career College
Linge, Richard	Arizona Western College	Newsome, Eloise	Northern Virginia Community College Woodbridge
Logan, Mary G.	Delgado Community College		
Loizeaux, Barbara	Westchester Community College	Nicholls, Doreen	Mohawk Valley Community College
Lopez, Don	Clovis-State Center Community College District	Nunan, Karen	Northeast State Technical Community College

Odegard, Teri	Edmonds Community College
Ogle, Gregory	North Community College
Orr, Dr. Claudia	Northern Michigan University South
Otieno, Derek	DeVry University
Otton, Diana Hill	Chesapeake College
Oxendale, Lucia	West Virginia Institute of Technology
Paiano, Frank	Southwestern College
Patrick, Tanya	Clackamas Community College
Peairs, Deb	Clark State Community College
Prince, Lisa	Missouri State University-Springfield Campus
Proietti, Kathleen	Northern Essex Community College
Pusins, Delores	HCCC
Raghuraman, Ram	Joliet Junior College
Reasoner, Ted Allen	Indiana University—Purdue
Reeves, Karen	High Point University
Remillard, Debbie	New Hampshire Technical Institute
Rhue, Shelly	DeVry University
Richards, Karen	Maplewoods Community College
Richardson, Mary	Albany Technical College
Rodgers, Gwen	Southern Nazarene University
Roselli, Diane	Harrisburg Area Community College
Ross, Dianne	University of Louisiana in Lafayette
Rousseau, Mary	Broward Community College, South
Samson, Dolly	Hawaii Pacific University
Sams, Todd	University of Cincinnati
Sandoval, Everett	Reedley College
Sardone, Nancy	Seton Hall University
Scafide, Jean	Mississippi Gulf Coast Community College
Scheeren, Judy	Westmoreland County Community College
Schneider, Sol	Sam Houston State University
Scroggins, Michael	Southwest Missouri State University
Sever, Suzanne	Northwest Arkansas Community College
Sheridan, Rick	California State University-Chico
Silvers, Pamela	Asheville Buncombe Tech
Singer, Steven A.	University of Hawai'i, Kapi'olani Community College
Sinha, Atin	Albany State University
Skolnick, Martin	Florida Atlantic University
Smith, T. Michael	Austin Community College
Smith, Tammy	Tompkins Cortland Community Collge
Smolenski, Bob	Delaware County Community College
Spangler, Candice	Columbus State
Stedham, Vicki	St. Petersburg College, Clearwater
Stefanelli, Greg	Carroll Community College
Steiner, Ester	New Mexico State University
Stenlund, Neal	Northern Virginia Community College, Alexandria
St. John, Steve	Tulsa Community College

Sterling, Janet	Houston Community College
Stoughton, Catherine	Laramie County Community College
Sullivan, Angela	Joliet Junior College
Szurek, Joseph	University of Pittsburgh at Greensburg
Tarver, Mary Beth	Northwestern State University
Taylor, Michael	Seattle Central Community College
Thangiah, Sam	Slippery Rock University
Thompson-Sellers, Ingrid	Georgia Perimeter College
Tomasi, Erik	Baruch College
Toreson, Karen	Shoreline Community College
Trifiletti, John J.	Florida Community College at Jacksonville
Trivedi, Charulata	Quinsigamond Community College, Woodbridge
Tucker, William	Austin Community College
Turgeon, Cheryl	Asnuntuck Community College
Turpen, Linda	Central New Mexico Community College
Upshaw, Susan	Del Mar College
Unruh, Angela	Central Washington University
Vanderhoof, Dr. Glenna	Missouri State University-Springfield Campus
Vargas, Tony	El Paso Community College
Vicars, Mitzi	Hampton University
Villarreal, Kathleen	Fresno
Vitrano, Mary Ellen	Palm Beach Community College
Volker, Bonita	Tidewater Community College
Wahila, Lori (Mindy)	Tompkins Cortland Community College
Waswick, Kim	Southeast Community College, Nebraska
Wavle, Sharon	Tompkins Cortland Community College
Webb, Nancy	City College of San Francisco
Wells, Barbara E.	Central Carolina Technical College
Wells, Lorna	Salt Lake Community College
Welsh, Jean	Lansing Community College Nebraska
White, Bruce	Quinnipiac University
Willer, Ann	Solano Community College
Williams, Mark	Lane Community College
Wilson, Kit	Red River College
Wilson, Roger	Fairmont State University
Wimberly, Leanne	International Academy of Design and Technology
Worthington, Paula	Northern Virginia Community College
Yauney, Annette	Herkimer County Community College
Yip, Thomas	Passaic Community College
Zavala, Ben	Webster Tech
Zlotow, Mary Ann	College of DuPage
Zudeck, Steve	Broward Community College, North

About the Authors

Shelley Gaskin, Series Editor, is a professor of business and computer technology at Pasadena City College in Pasadena, California. She holds a master's degree in business education from Northern Illinois University and a doctorate in adult and community education from Ball State University. Dr. Gaskin has 15 years of experience in the computer industry with several Fortune 500 companies and has developed and written training materials for custom systems applications in both the public and private sector. She is also the author of books on Microsoft Outlook and word processing.

Robert L. Ferrett recently retired as the director of the Center for Instructional Computing at Eastern Michigan University, where he provided computer training and support to faculty. He has authored or co-authored more than 70 books on Access, PowerPoint, Excel, Publisher, WordPerfect, and Word. Before writing for the *GO! Series*, Bob was a series editor and author for the *Learn Series*. He has a bachelor's degree in psychology, a master's degree in geography, and a master's degree in interdisciplinary technology from Eastern Michigan University. Bob's doctoral studies were in instructional technology at Wayne State University. For fun, Bob teaches a four-week computers and genealogy class and has written genealogy and local history books.

John Preston is an Associate Professor at Eastern Michigan University in the College of Technology, where he teaches microcomputer application courses at the undergraduate and graduate levels. He has been teaching, writing, and designing computer training courses since the advent of PCs and has authored and co-authored over 70 books on Microsoft Word, Excel, Access, and PowerPoint. He is a series editor for the Learn 97, Learn 2000, and Learn XP books. Two books on Microsoft Access that he co-authored with Robert Ferrett have been translated into Greek and Chinese. He has received grants from the Detroit Edison Institute and the Department of Energy to develop Web sites for energy education and alternative fuels. He has also developed one of the first Internet-based microcomputer applications courses at an accredited university. He has a bachelor's degree from the University of Michigan in Physics, Mathematics, and Education and a master's degree from Eastern Michigan University in Physics Education. His doctoral studies were in Instructional Technology at Wayne State University.

Sally Preston is president of Preston & Associates, which provides software consulting and training. She currently teaches computing in a variety of settings, which gives her ample opportunity to observe how people learn, what works best, and what challenges are present when learning a new software program. This diverse experience provides a complementary set of skills and knowledge that blends into her writing. Prior to writing for the *GO! Series*, Sally was a co-author on the *Learn* series since its inception and has authored books for the *Essentials* and *Microsoft Office User Specialist (MOUS) Essentials* series. Sally has a master's in business administration from Eastern Michigan University. When away from her computer, she is often found planting flowers in her garden.

Visual Walk-Through of the *GO!* System

The *GO!* System is designed for ease of implementation on the instructor side and ease of understanding on the student. It has been completely developed based on professor and student feedback.

The *GO!* System is divided into three categories that reflect how you might organize your course— **Prepare**, **Teach**, and **Assess**.

Prepare

GO!

Because the GO! System was designed and written by instructors like yourself, it includes the tools that allow you to Prepare, Teach, and Assess in your course. We have organized the GO! System into these three categories that match how you work through your course and thus, it's even easier for you to implement.

To help you get started, here is an outline of the first activities you may want to do in order to conduct your course.

There are several other tools not listed here that are available in the GO! System so please refer to your GO! Guide for a complete listing of all the tools.

Prepare
1. Prepare the course syllabus
2. Plan the course assignments
3. Organize the student resources

Teach
4. Conduct demonstrations and lectures

Assess
5. Assign and grade assignments, quizzes, tests, and assessments

PREPARE

1. Prepare the course syllabus
A syllabus template is provided on the IRCD in the **go07_syllabus_template** folder of the main directory. It includes a course calendar planner for 8-week, 12-week, and 16-week formats. Depending on your term (summer or regular semester) you can modify one of these according to your course plan, and then add information pertinent to your course and institution.

2. Plan course assignments
For each chapter, an Assignment Sheet listing every in-chapter and end-of-chapter project is located on the IRCD within the **go01_gotoffice2007intro_instructor_resources_by_chapter** folder. From there, navigate to the specific chapter folder. These sheets are Word tables, so you can delete rows for the projects that you choose not to assign or add rows for your own assignments—if any. There is a column to add the number of points you want to assign to each project depending on your grading scheme. At the top of the sheet, you can fill in the course information.

Transitioning to GO! Office 2007 — Page 1 of 1

NEW

Transition Guide

New to *GO!*—We've made it quick and easy to plan the format and activities for your class.

GO! with Microsoft Office 2007 Introductory
SAMPLE SYLLABUS (16 weeks)

I. COURSE INFORMATION

Course No.:	Semester:
Course Title:	Credits:
Course Hours:	
Instructor:	Office:
Office Hours:	
Email:	Phone:

II. TEXT AND MATERIALS
Before starting the course, you will need the following:

> GO! with Microsoft Office 2007 Introductory by Shelley Gaskin, Robert L. Ferrett, Alicia Vargas, Suzanne Marks ©2007, published by Pearson Prentice Hall. ISBN 0-13-167990-6

> Storage device for saving files (any of the following: multiple diskettes, CD-RW, flash drive, etc.)

III. WHAT YOU WILL LEARN IN THIS COURSE
This is a hands-on course where you will learn to use a computer to practice the most commonly used Microsoft programs including the Windows operating system, Internet Explorer for navigating the Internet, Outlook for managing your personal information and the four most popular programs within the Microsoft Office Suite (Word, Excel, PowerPoint and Access). You will also practice the basics of using a computer, mouse and keyboard. You will learn to be an intermediate level user of the Microsoft Office Suite.

Within the Microsoft Office Suite, you will use Word, Excel, PowerPoint, and Access. Microsoft Word is a word processing program with which you can create common business and personal documents. Microsoft Excel is a spreadsheet program that organizes and calculates accounting-type information. Microsoft PowerPoint is a presentation graphics program with which you can develop slides to accompany an oral presentation. Finally, Microsoft Access is a database program that organizes large amounts of information in a useful manner.

Syllabus Template

Includes course calendar planner for 8-,12-, and 16-week formats.

Assignment Sheet

One per chapter. Lists all possible assignments; add to and delete from this simple Word table according to your course plan.

File Guide to the *GO!* Supplements

Tabular listing of all supplements and their file names.

Assignment Planning Guide

Description of *GO!* assignments with recommendations based on class size, delivery mode, and student needs. Includes examples from fellow instructors.

GO! with Microsoft Office 2007 Introductory
Assignment Planning Guide

Planning the Course Assignments

For each chapter in GO!, an Assignment Sheet listing every in-chapter and end-of-chapter project is located on the IRCD. These sheets are Word tables, so you can delete rows for the projects that you will not assign, and then add rows for any of your own assignments that you may have developed. There is a column to add the number of points you want to assign to each project—depending on your grading scheme. At the top of the sheet, you can fill in your course information.

Additionally, for each chapter, student Assignment Tags are provided for every project (including Problem Solving projects)—also located on the IRCD. These are small scoring checklists on which you can check off errors made by the student, and with which the student can verify that all project elements are complete. For campus classes, the student can attach the tags to his or her paper submissions. For online classes, many GO! instructors have the student include these with the electronic submission.

Deciding What to Assign

Front Portion of the Chapter—Instructional Projects: The projects in the front portion of the chapter, which are listed on the first page of each chapter, are the instructional projects. Most instructors assign all of these projects, because this is where the student receives the instruction and engages in the active learning.

End-of-Chapter—Practice and Critical Thinking Projects: In the back portion of the chapter (the gray pages), you can assign on a prescriptive basis; that is, for students who were challenged by the instructional projects, you might assign one or more projects from the two *Skills Reviews*, which provide maximum prompting and a thorough review of the entire chapter. For students who have previous software knowledge and who completed the instructional projects easily, you might assign only the *Mastery Projects*.

You can also assign prescriptively by Objective, because each end-of-chapter project indicates the Objectives covered. So you might assign, on a student-by-student basis, only the projects that cover the Objectives with which the student seemed to have difficulty in the instructional projects.

The five Problem Solving projects and the You and GO! project are the authentic assessments that pull together the student's learning. Here the student is presented with a "messy real-life situation" and then uses his or her knowledge and skill to solve a problem, produce a product, give a presentation, or demonstrate a procedure. You might assign one or more of the Problem

GO! Assignment Planning Guide   Page 1 of 1

Student Data Files

Music School Records discovers, launches, and and develops the careers of young artists in classical, jazz, and contemporary music. Our philosophy is to not only shape, distribute, and sell a music product, but to help artists create a career that can lats a lifetime. too often in the music industry, artists are forced to fit their music to a trend that is short-lived. Music School Records doesn't just follow trends, we take a long-term view of the music industry and help our artists develop a style and repertiore that is fluid and flexible and that will appeal to audiences for years and even decades.

The music industry is constantly changing, but over the last decade the changes have been enormous. New forms of entertainment such as DVDs, video games, and the Internet mean there are more competition for the leisure dollar in the market. New technologies give consomers more options for buying and listening to music, and they are demaning high quality recordings. Young consomers are comfortable with technology and want the music they love when and where they want it, no matter where they are or what they are doing.

Music School Records embraces new technologies and the sophisticated market of young music lovers. We believe that providing high quality recordings of truly talented artists make for more discerning listeners who will cherish the gift of music for the rest of their lives. The expertise of Music School Records includes:

- Insight into our target market and the ability to reach the desired audience
- The ability to access all current sources of music income
- A management team with years of experience in music commerce
- Innovative business strategies and artist development plans
- Investment in technology infrastructure for high quality recordings and business services
- Initiative and proactive management of artist careers

Online Study Guide for Students

Interactive objective-style questions based on chapter content.

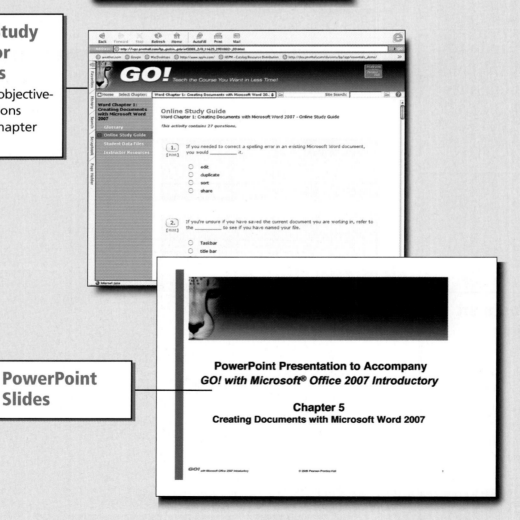

PowerPoint Slides

Teach

Student Textbook

Learning Objectives and Student Outcomes

Objectives are clustered around projects that result in student outcomes. They help students learn how to solve problems, not just learn software features.

Word 2007

chapterfive

Creating Documents with Microsoft Word 2007

OBJECTIVES
At the end of this chapter you will be able to:

OUTCOMES
Mastering these objectives will enable you to:

1. Create and Save a New Document
2. Edit Text
3. Select, Delete, and Format Text
4. Print a Document

PROJECT 5A
Create, Edit, Save, and Print a Document

5. Navigate the Word Window
6. Add a Graphic to a Document
7. Use the Spelling and Grammar Checker
8. Preview and Print Documents, Close a Document, and Close Word
9. Use the Microsoft Help System

PROJECT 5B
Navigate the Word Window and Check Your Work

NEW

Word   237

Project-Based Instruction

Students do not practice features of the application; they create real projects that they will need in the real world. Projects are color coded for easy reference and are named to reflect skills the students will be practicing.

A and B Projects

Each chapter contains two instructional projects—A and B.

Each chapter opens with a story that sets the stage for the projects the student will create; the instruction does not force the student to pretend to be someone or make up a scenario.

Music School Records

Music School Records was created to launch young musical artists with undiscovered talent in jazz, classical, and contemporary music. The creative management team searches internationally for talented young people, and has a reputation for mentoring and developing the skills of its artists. The company's music is tailored to an audience that is young, knowledgeable about music, and demands the highest quality recordings. Music School Records releases are available in CD format as well as digital downloads.

Getting Started with Microsoft Office Word 2007

A word processor is the most common program found on personal computers and one that almost everyone has a reason to use. When you learn word processing you are also learning skills and techniques that you need to work efficiently on a personal computer. You can use Microsoft Word to perform basic word processing tasks such as writing a memo, a report, or a letter. You can also use Word to complete complex word processing tasks, such as those that include sophisticated tables, embedded graphics, and links to other documents and the Internet. Word is a program that you can learn gradually, and then add more advanced skills one at a time.

Each chapter has an introductory paragraph that briefs students on what is important.

Visual Summary

Shows students upfront what their projects will look like when they are done.

Objective

The skills the student will learn are clearly stated at the beginning of each project and color coded to match projects listed on the chapter opener page.

Screen Shots

Larger screen shots.

Project 5A Application Letter

In Activities 5.1 through 5.11, you will create and make changes to a letter from John Diamond, Vice President of Creative Development, to William Hawken, an artist interested in becoming a client of Music School Records. Your completed document will look similar to Figure 5.1.

For Project 5A, you will need the following file:

New blank Word document

You will save your document as
5A_Application_Letter_Firstname_Lastname

Music School Records

Figure 5.1
Project 5A—Application Letter

Objective 1
Create and Save a New Document

With a word processing program, you can type, *edit*—make changes to—move, and delete text or change the appearance of text. Because the documents that you create are stored electronically, they can be duplicated, printed, copied, and shared with others. In this project, you will become

Project 5A: Application Letter | **Word**   239

---

familiar with the parts of the Word window. Then you will create a document, edit and format text, and save your work.

Activity 5.1 Starting Word and Identifying Parts of the Word Window

Note — Comparing Your Screen With the Figures in This Textbook

Your screen will match the figures shown in this textbook if you set your screen resolution to 1024 × 768. At other resolutions, your screen will closely resemble, but not match, the figures shown. To view your screen's resolution, on the Windows desktop, right-click in a blank area, click Properties, and then click the Settings tab.

On the left side of the Windows taskbar, point to, and then click the **Start** button.

From the displayed **Start** menu, locate the **Word** program, and then click **Microsoft Office Word 2007**.
The Word program may be located under All Programs or Microsoft Office or on the main Start menu.
Print Layout view is the ideal view to use when you are learning Microsoft Word 2007 because you can see the document exactly the way it will look when it is printed.

If necessary, on the right side of the status bar, click the **Print Layout** button. If the ruler does not display, click the View tab, and then in the Show/Hide group, click the Ruler check box. Take a moment to study the parts of the Word screen shown in Figure 5.2 and described in the table in Figure 5.3.

Figure 5.2

240   **Word** | Chapter 5: Creating Documents with Microsoft Word 2007

Project Summary

Stated clearly and quickly in one paragraph.

File Guide

NEW

Clearly shows students which files are needed for the project and the names they will use to save their documents.

Teachable Moment

GO! KEY FEATURE

Expository text is woven into the steps—at the moment students need to know it—not chunked together in a block of text that will go unread.

Steps

Color coded to the current project, easy to read, and not too many to confuse the student or too few to be meaningless.

Sequential Pagination

No more confusing letters and abbreviations.

End-of-Project Icon

All projects in the *GO! Series* have clearly identifiable end points, useful in self-paced or on-line environments.

Microsoft Procedural Syntax

All steps are written in Microsoft Procedural Syntax to put the student in the right place at the right time.

Press [Enter] two more times.

In a business letter, insert two blank lines between the date and the inside address, which is the same as the address you would use on an envelope.

Type Mr. William Hawken and then press [Enter].

The wavy red line under the proper name *Hawken* indicates that the word has been flagged as misspelled because it is a word not contained in the Word dictionary.

On two lines, type the following address, but do not press [Enter] **at the end of the second line:**

123 Eighth Street
Harrisville, MI 48740

Note — Typing the Address

Include a comma after the city name in an inside address. However, for mailing addresses on envelopes, eliminate the comma after the city name.

On the Home tab, in the **Styles group**, click the **Normal** button.

The Normal style is applied to the text in the rest of the document. Recall that the Normal style adds extra space between paragraphs; it also adds slightly more space between lines in a paragraph.

Press [Enter]. **Type Dear William:** and then press [Enter].

This salutation is the line that greets the person receiving the letter.

Type Subject: Your Application to Music School Records and press [Enter]. Notice the light dots between words, which indicate spaces and display when formatting marks are displayed. Also, notice the extra space after each paragraph, and then compare your screen with Figure 5.6.

The subject line is optional, but you should include a subject line in most letters to identify the topic. Depending on your Word settings, a wavy green line may display in the subject line, indicating a potential grammar error.

Note — Space Between Lines in Your Printed Document

The Cambria font, and many others, uses a slightly larger space between the lines than more traditional fonts like Times New Roman. As you progress in your study of Word, you will use many different fonts and also adjust the spacing between lines.

From the Office menu click **Close**, saving any changes if prompted to do so. Leave Word open for the next project.

Another Way

To Print a Document

To Print a document:

- From the Office menu, click Print to display the Print dialog box (to be covered later), from which you can choose a variety of different options, such as printing multiple copies, printing on a different printer, and printing some but not all pages.
- Hold down [Ctrl] and then press [P]. This is an alternative to the Office menu command, and opens the Print dialog box.
- Hold down [Alt], press [F], and then press [P]. This opens the Print dialog box.

End You have completed Project 5A

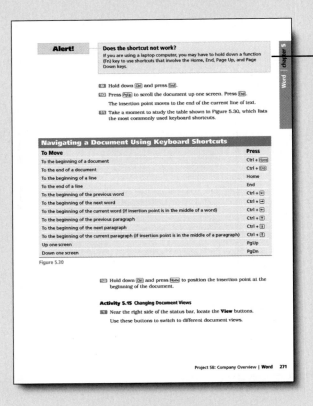

Alert box
Draws students' attention to make sure they aren't getting too far off course.

Another Way box
Shows students other ways of doing tasks.

More Knowledge box
Expands on a topic by going deeper into the material.

Note box
Points out important items to remember.

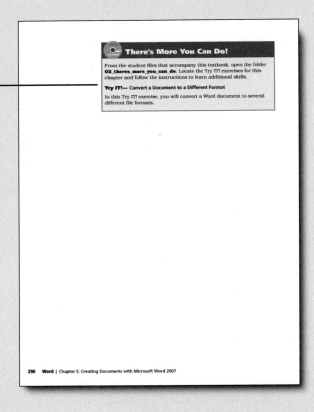

NEW

There's More You Can Do!
Try IT! exercises that teach students additional skills.

End-of-Chapter Material

Take your pick! Content-based or Outcomes-based projects to choose from. Below is a table outlining the various types of projects that fit into these two categories.

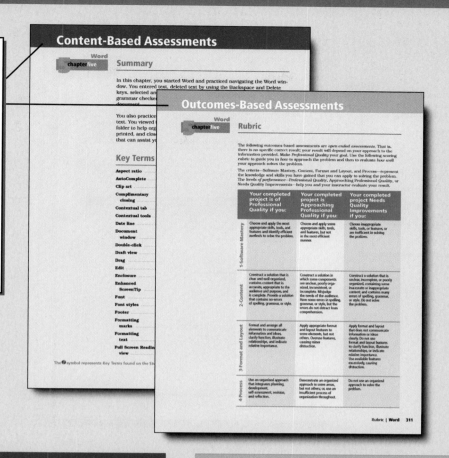

Content-Based Assessments

(Defined solutions with solution files provided for grading)

Project Letter	Name	Objectives Covered
N/A	Summary and Key Terms	
N/A	Multiple Choice	
N/A	Fill-in-the-blank	
C	Skills Review	Covers A Objectives
D	Skills Review	Covers B Objectives
E	Mastering Excel	Covers A Objectives
F	Mastering Excel	Covers B Objectives
G	Mastering Excel	Covers any combination of A and B Objectives
H	Mastering Excel	Covers any combination of A and B Objectives
I	Mastering Excel	Covers all A and B Objectives
J	Business Running Case	Covers all A and B Objectives

Outcomes-Based Assessments

(Open solutions that require a rubric for grading)

Project Letter	Name	Objectives Covered
N/A	Rubric	
K	Problem Solving	Covers as many Objectives from A and B as possible
L	Problem Solving	Covers as many Objectives from A and B as possible.
M	Problem Solving	Covers as many Objectives from A and B as possible.
N	Problem Solving	Covers as many Objectives from A and B as possible.
O	Problem Solving	Covers as many Objectives from A and B as possible.
P	You and GO!	Covers as many Objectives from A and B as possible
Q	GO! Help	Not tied to specific objectives
R	* Group Business Running Case	Covers A and B Objectives

* This project is provided only with the *GO! with Microsoft Office 2007 Introductory* book.

Objectives List

Most projects in the end-of-chapter section begin with a list of the objectives covered.

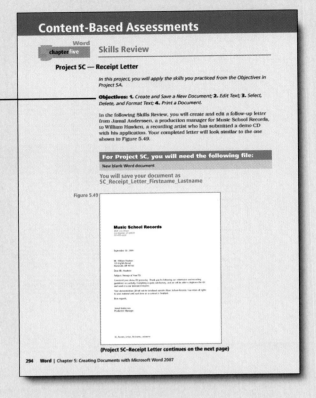

End of Each Project Clearly Marked

Clearly identified end points help separate the end-of-chapter projects.

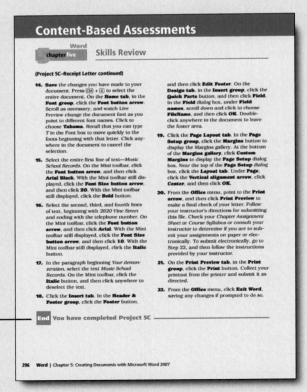

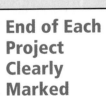

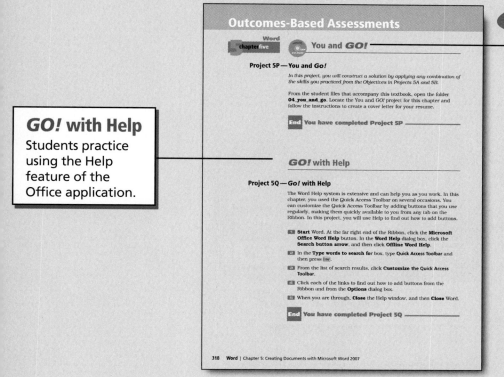

NEW

Rubric

A matrix that states the criteria and standards for grading student work. Used to grade open-ended assessments.

NEW

You and *GO!*

A project in which students use information from their own lives and apply the skills from the chapter to a personal task.

GO! with Help

Students practice using the Help feature of the Office application.

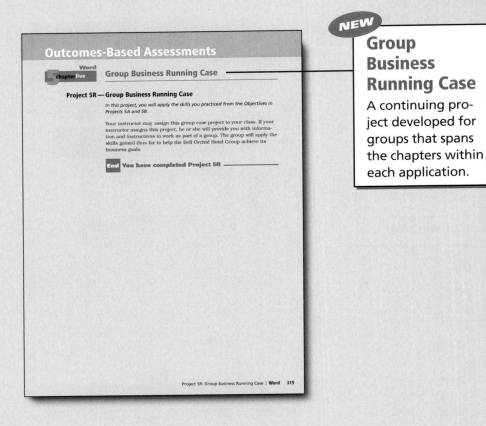

NEW

Group Business Running Case

A continuing project developed for groups that spans the chapters within each application.

Student CD includes:

- Student Data Files
- There's More You Can Do!
- Business Running Case
- You and *GO!*

Companion Web site

An interactive Web site to further student leaning.

Online Study Guide

Interactive objective-style questions to help students study.

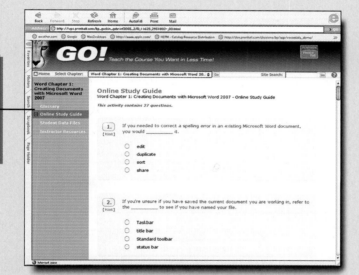

Annotated Instructor Edition

The Annotated Instructor Edition contains a full version of the student textbook that includes tips, supplement references, and pointers on teaching with the *GO!* instructional system.

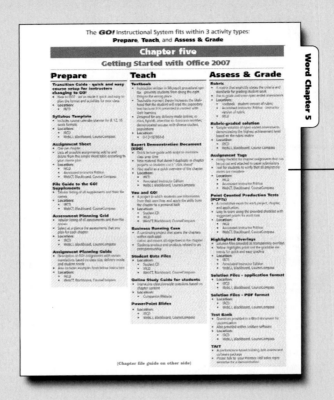

Chapter Dividers

Clearly outline the resources per chapter by activity level: Prepare, Teach, Assess.

Instructor File Guide

Complete list of all Student Data Files and instructor Solution Files needed for the chapter.

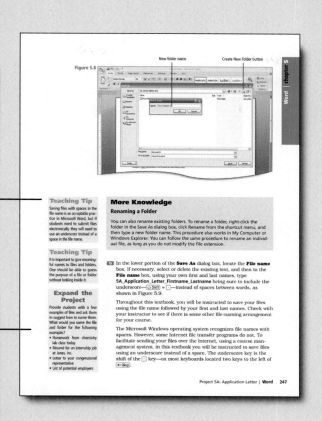

Figure 5.8

New folder name   Create New Folder button

Helpful Hints, Teaching Tips, Expand the Project

References correspond to what is being taught in the student textbook.

Full-Size Textbook Pages

An instructor copy of the textbook with traditional Instructor Manual content incorporated.

Teaching Tip

Saving files with spaces in the file name is an acceptable practice in Microsoft Word, but if students need to submit files electronically, they will need to use an underscore instead of a space in the file name.

Teaching Tip

It is important to give meaningful names to files and folders. One should be able to guess the purpose of a file or folder without looking inside it.

Expand the Project

Provide students with a few examples of files and ask them to suggest how to name them. What would you name the file and folder for the following examples?

- Homework from chemistry lab class today
- Résumé for an internship job at Jones, Inc.
- Letter to your congressional representative
- List of potential employers

More Knowledge
Renaming a Folder

You can also rename existing folders. To rename a folder, right-click the folder in the Save As dialog box, click Rename from the shortcut menu, and then type a new folder name. This procedure also works in My Computer or Windows Explorer. You can follow the same procedure to rename an individual file, as long as you do not modify the file extension.

In the lower portion of the **Save As** dialog box, locate the **File name** box. If necessary, select or delete the existing text, and then in the **File name** box, using your own first and last names, type **5A_Application_Letter_Firstname_Lastname** being sure to include the underscore—(Shift) + (_)—instead of spaces between words, as shown in Figure 5.9.

Throughout this textbook, you will be instructed to save your files using the file name followed by your first and last names. Check with your instructor to see if there is some other file-naming arrangement for your course.

The Microsoft Windows operating system recognizes file names with spaces. However, some Internet file transfer programs do not. To facilitate sending your files over the Internet, using a course management system, in this textbook you will be instructed to save files using an underscore instead of a space. The underscore key is the shift of the (-) key—on most keyboards located two keys to the left of (Bksp).

Project 5A: Application Letter | **Word** 247

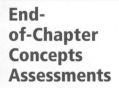

End-of-Chapter Concepts Assessments

contain the answers for quick reference.

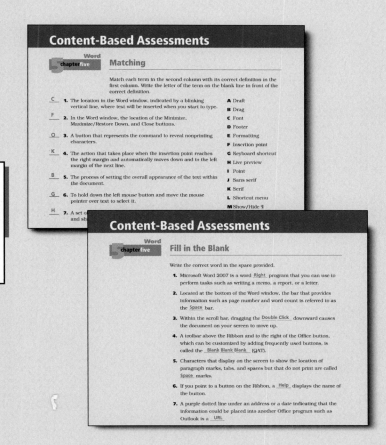

Content-Based Assessments

Word
chapter five

Matching

Match each term in the second column with its correct definition in the first column. Write the letter of the term on the blank line in front of the correct definition.

_C_ **1.** The location in the Word window, indicated by a blinking vertical line, where text will be inserted when you start to type.

_F_ **2.** In the Word window, the location of the Minimize, Maximize/Restore Down, and Close buttons.

_Q_ **3.** A button that represents the command to reveal nonprinting characters.

_K_ **4.** The action that takes place when the insertion point reaches the right margin and automatically moves down and to the left margin of the next line.

_B_ **5.** The process of setting the overall appearance of the text within the document.

_G_ **6.** To hold down the left mouse button and move the mouse pointer over text to select it.

_H_ **7.** A set of and sh

A Draft
B Drag
C Font
D Footer
E Formatting
F Insertion point
G Keyboard shortcut
H Live preview
I Point
J Sans serif
K Serif
L Shortcut menu
M Show/Hide ¶

Content-Based Assessments

Word
chapter five

Fill in the Blank

Write the correct word in the space provided.

1. Microsoft Word 2007 is a word _Right_ program that you can use to perform tasks such as writing a memo, a report, or a letter.

2. Located at the bottom of the Word window, the bar that provides information such as page number and word count is referred to as the _Space_ bar.

3. Within the scroll bar, dragging the _Double Click_ downward causes the document on your screen to move up.

4. A toolbar above the Ribbon and to the right of the Office button, which can be customized by adding frequently used buttons, is called the _Blank Blank Blank_ (QAT).

5. Characters that display on the screen to show the location of paragraph marks, tabs, and spaces but that do not print are called _Space_ marks.

6. If you point to a button on the Ribbon, a _Help_ displays the name of the button.

7. A purple dotted line under an address or a date indicating that the information could be placed into another Office program such as Outlook is a _URL_

NEW

Rubric

A matrix to guide the student on how they will be assessed is reprinted in the Annotated Instructor Edition with suggested weights for each of the criteria and levels of performance. Instructors can modify the weights to suit their needs.

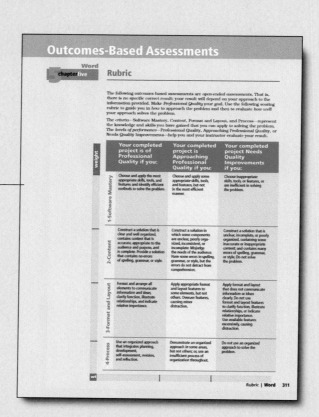

Assignment Tags

NEW

Scoring checklist for assignments. Now also available for Problem-Solving projects.

GO! with Microsoft® Office 2007

Assignment Tags for GO! with Office 2007
Word Chapter 5

Name:	Project:	5A
Professor:	Course:	

Task	Points	Your Score
Center text vertically on page	2	
Delete the word "really"	1	
Delete the words "try to"	1	
Replace "last" with "first"	1	
Insert the word "potential"	1	
Replace "John W. Diamond" with "Lucy Burrows"	2	
Change entire document to the Cambria font	2	
Change the first line of text to Arial Black 20 pt. font	2	
Bold the first line of text	2	
Change the 2nd through 4th lines to Arial 10 pt.	2	
Italicize the 2nd through 4th lines of text	2	
Correct/Add footer as instructed	2	
Circled information is incorrect or formatted incorrectly		
Total Points	**20**	**0**

Name:	Project:	5B
Professor:	Course:	

Task	Points	Your Score
Insert the file w05B_Music_School_Records	4	
Insert the Music Logo	4	
Remove duplicate "and"	2	
Change spelling and grammar errors (4)	8	
Correct/Add footer as instructed	2	
Circled information is incorrect or formatted incorrectly		
Total Points	**20**	**0**

Name:	Project:	5C
Professor:	Course:	

Task	Points	Your Score
Add four line letterhead	2	
Insert today's date	1	
Add address block, subject line, and greeting	2	
Add two-paragraph body of letter	2	
Add closing, name, and title	2	
In subject line, capitalize "receipt"	1	
Change "standards" to "guidelines"	1	
Insert "quite"	1	
Insert "all"	1	
Change the first line of text to Arial Black 20 pt. font	2	
Bold the first line of text	1	
Change the 2nd through 4th lines to Arial 10 pt.	1	
Italicize the 2nd through 4th lines of text	1	
Correct/add footer as instructed	2	
Circled information is incorrect or formatted incorrectly		
Total Points	**20**	**0**

Name:	Project:	5D
Professor:	Course:	

Task	Points	Your Score
Insert the file w05D_Marketing	4	
Bold the first two title lines	2	
Correct spelling of "Marketting"	2	
Correct spelling of "geners"	2	
Correct all misspellings of "allready"	2	
Correct grammar error "are" to "is"	2	
Insert the Piano image	4	
Correct/add footer as instructed	2	
Circled information is incorrect or formatted incorrectly		
Total Points	**20**	**0**

Highlighted Overlays

Solution files provided as transparency overlays. Yellow highlights point out the gradable elements for quick and easy grading.

Music School Records

— 20 point Arial Black, bold and underline

2620 Vine Street
Los Angeles, CA 90028
323-555-0028

— 10 point Arial, italic

September 12, 2009

Mr. William Hawken
123 Eighth Street
Harrisville, MI 48740

— Text vertically centered on page

— Body of document changed to Cambria font, 11 point

Dear William:

Subject: Your Application to Music School Records

Thank you for submitting your application to Music School Records. Our talent scout for Northern Michigan, Catherine McDonald, is very enthusiastic about your music, and the demo CD you submitted certainly confirms her opinion.

— Word "really" deleted

We discuss our applications from potential clients during the first week of each month. We will have a decision for you by the second week of October.

— Words "try to" deleted

Yours Truly,

Lucy Burroughs

Point-Counted Production Tests (PCPTs)

A cumulative exam for each **project**, **chapter**, and **application**. Easy to score using the provided checklist with suggested points for each task.

GO! with Microsoft® Office 2007 Introductory

Point-Counted Production Test—Project for GO! with Microsoft® Office 2007 Introductory Project 5A

Instructor Name: _____
Course Information: _____

1. Start Word 2007 to begin a new blank document. Save your document as 5A_Cover_Letter_Firstname_Lastname Remember to save your file frequently as you work.

2. If necessary, display the formatting marks. With the insertion point blinking in the upper left corner of the document to the left of the default first paragraph mark, type the current date (you can use AutoComplete).

3. Press Enter three times and type the inside address:

   Music School Records
   2620 Vine Street
   Los Angeles, CA 90028

4. Press Enter three times, and type Dear Ms. Burroughs:

   Press Enter twice, and type Subject: Application to Music School Records

   Press Enter twice, and type the following text (skipping one line between paragraphs):

   I read about Music School Records in Con Brio magazine and I would like to inquire about the possibility of being represented by your company.

   I am very interested in a career in jazz and am planning to relocate to the Los Angeles area in the very near future. I would be interested in learning more about the company and about available opportunities.

   I was a member of my high school jazz band for three years. In addition, I have been playing in the local coffee shop for the last two years. My demo CD, which is enclosed, contains three of my most requested songs.

   I would appreciate the opportunity to speak with you. Thank you for your time and consideration. I look forward to speaking with you about this exciting opportunity.

5. Press Enter three times, and type the closing Sincerely, Press enter four times, and type your name.

6. Insert a footer that contains the file name.

7. Delete the first instance of the word *very* in the second body paragraph, and insert the word modern in front of *jazz*.

Page 1 of 1

Test Bank

Available as TestGen Software or as a Word document for customization.

Chapter 5: Creating Documents with Microsoft Word 2007

Multiple Choice:

1. With word processing programs, how are documents stored?

   A. On a network

   B. On the computer

   C. Electronically

   D. On the floppy disk

   Answer: C   **Reference:** Objective 1: Create and Save a New Document   **Difficulty:** Moderate

2. Because you will see the document as it will print, _____ view is the ideal view to use when learning Microsoft Word 2007.

   A. Reading

   B. Normal

   C. Print Layout

   D. Outline

   Answer: C   **Reference:** Objective 1: Create and Save a New Document   **Difficulty:** Moderate

3. The blinking vertical line where text or graphics will be inserted is called the:

   A. cursor.

   B. insertion point.

   C. blinking line.

   D. I-beam.

   Answer: B   **Reference:** Objective 1: Create and Save a New Document   **Difficulty:** Easy

Solution Files– Application and PDF format

Online Assessment and Training

my**it**lab is Prentice Hall's new performance-based solution that allows you to easily deliver outcomes-based courses on Microsoft Office 2007, with customized training and defensible assessment. Key features of my**it**lab include:

A *true* "system" approach: my**it**lab content is the same as in your textbook.

Project-based *and* skills-based: Students complete real-life assignments.

Advanced reporting *and* gradebook: These include student click stream data.

***No* installation required:** my**it**lab is completely Web-based. You just need an Internet connection, small plug-in, and Adobe Flash Player.

Ask your Prentice Hall sales representative for a demonstration or visit:

www.prenhall.com/myitlab

1 chapterone

Getting Started with Windows XP

OBJECTIVES

At the end of this chapter you will be able to:

1. Get Started with Windows XP
2. Resize, Move, and Scroll Windows
3. Maximize, Restore, Minimize, and Close Windows
4. Create a New Folder
5. Copy, Move, Rename, and Delete Files
6. Find Files and Folders
7. Compress Files

OUTCOMES

Mastering these objectives will enable you to:

PROJECT 1A
Start Windows XP and Work with Windows, Folders, and Files

Windows XP is the software that coordinates the activities of your computer's hardware. Windows XP controls how your screen is displayed, how you open and close programs, and the startup, shutdown, and navigation procedures for your computer. It is useful to become familiar with the basic features of the Microsoft Windows operating system, especially working with the Start button and taskbar; opening, closing, moving, and resizing windows; and saving and managing files.

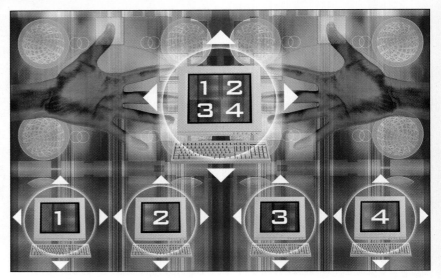

Getting Started with Windows XP

Project 1A **Start Windows XP and Work with Windows, Folders, and Files**

In Activities 1.1 through 1.9, you will practice navigating Windows XP. You will manage files and folders and compress and decompress files for easy file transfer. You will also capture an image of your screen, which will look similar to Figure 1.1.

For Project 1A, you will need the following files:

Flower.wmf

Plant.wmf

Roller Coaster.wmf

Golfer.wmf

Artist Picture.wmf

Lightning.docx

LSS-Charlotte NY Station.jpg

LSS-Crew Pulling Lifeboat.bmp

Volunteers.pptx

New blank Word document

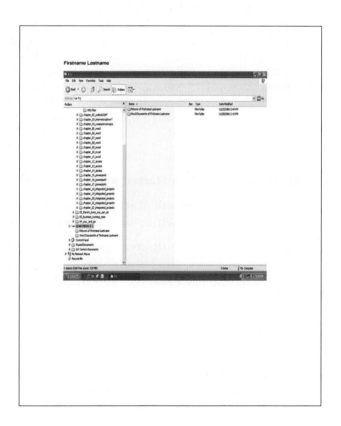

Figure 1.1
Project 1A—Windows XP

Objective 1
Get Started with Windows XP

Windows XP is an *operating system*—software that controls the hardware attached to your computer including its memory, disk drive space, attached devices such as printers and scanners, and the central processing unit. Windows XP and earlier versions of Windows are similar; they use a *graphical user interface (GUI)*. A GUI uses graphics or pictures to represent commands and actions and lets you see document formatting on the screen as it will look when printed on paper. *Windows*, when spelled with a capital W, refers to the operating system that runs your computer.

Starting Windows is an automatic procedure; you turn on your computer, and after a few moments the version of Windows installed on your computer displays. Some versions require that you log in, and some do not. If you are using a different version of Windows, some procedures used in this chapter may work differently. Windows XP is available in two versions: a Professional Edition and a Home Edition. For basic tasks, the two versions work the same. The Professional version includes security and other features necessary in large organizations.

Alert!

Does your screen differ?

This chapter uses Windows XP Home Edition. When you see the word Windows, it will often be accompanied by the version, such as Windows 98, Windows NT, Windows 2000, or Windows XP, which is the version introduced in this chapter. These operating systems are similar and use graphics or pictures to represent commands and actions. Different versions may result in screens that differ from those shown in this chapter. Your screen may also differ because of the setting options that have been selected for your computer.

Activity 1.1 Getting Started with Windows XP

In Activity 1.1, you will start Windows, use the mouse, and use the Start button to open the Windows Calculator program.

1 Turn on your computer and wait for the **Windows** program to display, or follow the log-on instructions required for the computer you are using. For example, you may have to click a name on a Welcome screen, or enter a user ID or password. If this is your home computer and you are the only user, it is likely that you need do nothing except wait for a few moments.

The Windows *desktop*, which is the working area of the Windows XP screen, displays. The working area is called a desktop because on it you can place electronic versions of things you have on your regular desk. The screen look will vary, depending on which version of Windows you are using and what you have on your own desktop.

2 Compare your Windows desktop with Figure 1.2 and then take a moment to study the Windows elements identified in the table in Figure 1.3.

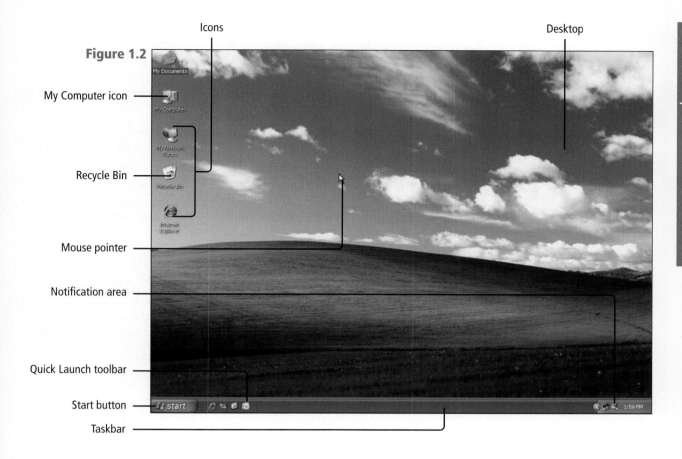

Figure 1.2

Icons

Desktop

My Computer icon

Recycle Bin

Mouse pointer

Notification area

Quick Launch toolbar

Start button

Taskbar

Windows Screen Elements

Element	Description
Desktop	The working area of the Windows XP screen consisting of program icons, a taskbar, and a Start button.
Icon	A graphic representation of an object that you can select and open, such as a drive, a disk, a folder, a document, or a program.
Mouse pointer	The arrow, I-beam, or other symbol that moves when you move the mouse or other pointing device, and that indicates a location or position on your screen—also called the *pointer*.
My Computer icon	An icon that represents the computer on which you are working, and that provides access to the drives, folders, and files on your computer.
Quick Launch toolbar	An area to the right of the Start button that contains shortcut icons for commonly used programs.

(*Continued*)

Element	Description
Recycle Bin	A temporary storage area for files that you have deleted. Files can be either recovered or permanently removed from the Recycle Bin.
Taskbar	Displays the Start button and the name of any open documents. The taskbar may also display shortcut buttons for other programs.
Notification area	The area on the right side of the taskbar, formerly called the *system tray* or *status area*, where the clock and system notifications display. These notifications keep you informed about processes that are occurring in the background, such as antivirus software checking, network connections, and other utility programs. Some notifications display only temporarily.
Start button	The button on the left side of the taskbar that is used to start programs, change system settings, find Windows help, or shut down the computer.

Figure 1.3

3 Move the mouse across a flat surface to move the pointer on your screen. On the desktop, position the tip of the pointer in the center of the **My Computer** icon—referred to as *pointing*. *Double-click*—press the left mouse button two times in rapid succession—using caution not to move the mouse. If the My Computer icon is not visible, click the **Start** button ![start], and then from the displayed **Start** menu, click **My Computer**. Compare your screen with Figure 1.4 and then take a moment to study the My Computer window elements in Figure 1.5.

The My Computer window displays. A *window*—spelled with a lowercase *w*—is a rectangular box that displays information or a program. When a window is open, the name of the window is displayed both in the title bar and in a button on the taskbar at the bottom of the desktop.

Figure 1.4

Window name in title bar

Title bar

Close button

Menu bar

Toolbar

Address bar

Left pane

Window name in taskbar

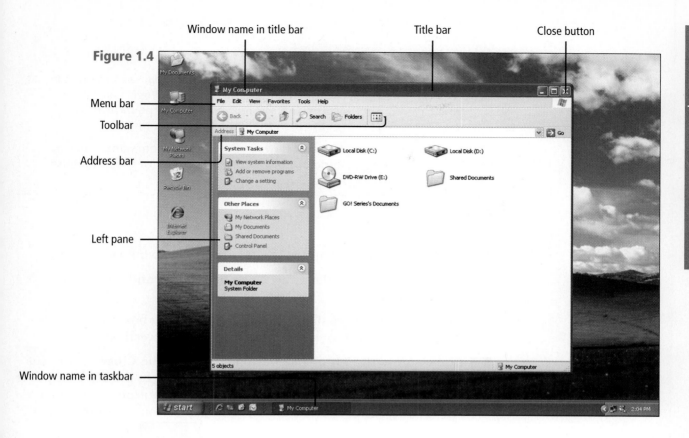

Parts of a Window

Screen Element	Description
Address bar	A toolbar that displays the organizational path to the active file, folder, or window.
Close button	A shortcut button in a title bar that closes a window or a program.
Left pane	In the My Computer window, a pane that displays information and commonly used tools.
Menu	A list of commands within a category.
Menu bar	The bar beneath the title bar that lists the names of menu categories, for example, *File*, *Edit*, *View*, and so on.
ScreenTip	A small box, activated by pointing to a button or other screen object, that displays the name of or further information about the screen element.
Status bar	A horizontal bar at the bottom of the document window that provides information about the current state of what you are viewing in the window, for example, the page number of a document.

(*Continued*)

Continued

Screen Element	Description
Title bar	Displays the program icon, the name of the document, and the name of the program. The Minimize, Maximize/Restore Down, and Close buttons are grouped on the right side of the title bar.
Toolbar	A row of buttons that activate commands, such as Undo or Bold, with a single click of the left mouse button.

Figure 1.5

4 In the upper right corner of the **My Computer** window title bar, point to, but do not click, the **Close** button ⊠ and notice the ScreenTip *Close*.

A ***ScreenTip*** is a small note, usually in a yellow box, that provides the name of a button, or information about a screen element.

5 ***Click***—press the left mouse button one time—the **Close** button ⊠ to close the **My Computer** window. Then, point to the **My Computer** icon on the desktop and click the right mouse button—this action is known as a ***right-click***. If the **My Computer** icon does not display on your desktop, click the **Start** button � start ⎸, and then right-click **My Computer**. Compare your screen with Figure 1.6.

A shortcut menu displays. ***Shortcut menus*** list commands that are ***context-sensitive***—commands commonly used when working with the selected object. On this shortcut menu, the Open command is displayed in bold because it is the default action that occurs when you double-click this icon.

Shortcut menu

Figure 1.6

Command in bold is the default action

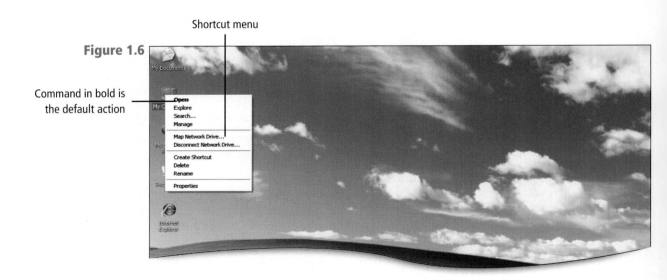

6 In the displayed shortcut menu, point to **Open** to highlight—select—the command, and then click. In the displayed **My Computer** window, point to and then click the disk drive labeled **Local Disk (C:)**, and then in the left pane, notice the lower panel. Compare your screen with Figure 1.7.

The specifications of the *Local disk*—the large disk drive inside your computer system also referred to as the *hard drive*—are displayed in the Details panel of the left pane. A *drive* is an area of storage that is formatted with the Windows file system and that has a drive letter such as C, D, E, and so on. If the Details panel does not display any information, click the expand/hide arrow next to Details to expand this panel of the task pane.

Window title   Drive C: selected   Close button

Figure 1.7

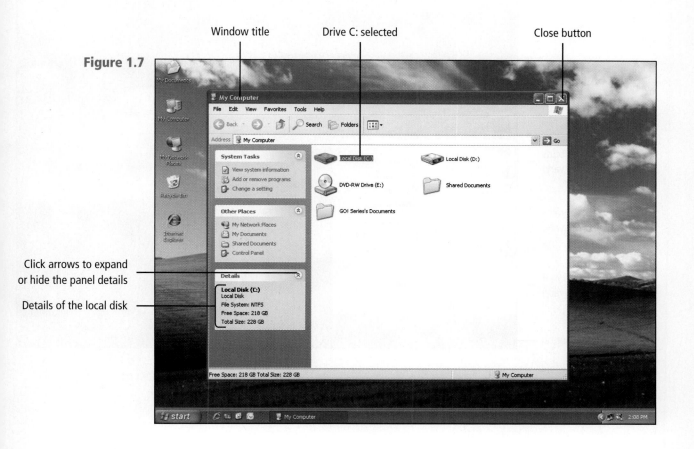

Click arrows to expand
or hide the panel details

Details of the local disk

7 In the **My Computer** window title bar, click the **Close** button ⊠. In the lower left corner of the screen, point to, and then click the **Start** button ⏣ start . Compare your screen with Figure 1.8.

Commands in the displayed Start menu that have arrows on the right indicate that a submenu is available for a command. A *submenu* is a second-level menu. You can customize the Start menu to include shortcuts to programs and files you use often.

Current user
(yours will differ)

Arrows indicate submenus
are available

Figure 1.8

Customized shortcuts
(yours will vary)

Recently used programs
(yours will vary)

Start menu (your
list will vary)

Start button

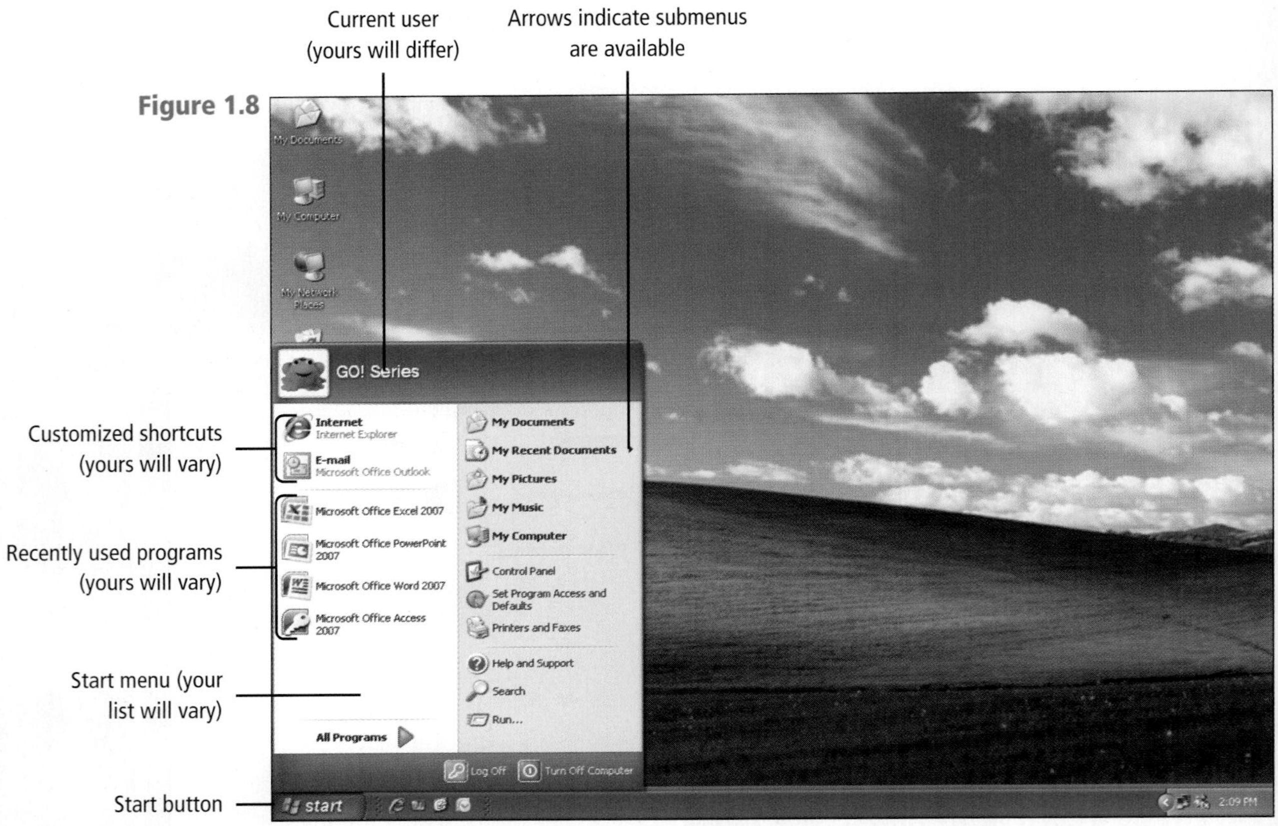

8 On the **Start** menu, point to, but do not click, the **All Programs** command.

The All Programs submenu displays. Your menu will differ from the one shown in Figure 1.9 because your computer will have different programs installed. Folders in the menu contain more programs, or more folders, or some of each. A small arrow to the right of a folder indicates that the folder contains other folders or zipped— compressed—files.

9 On the **All Programs** menu, point to, but do not click, **Accessories**.

Accessories   Folders that contain programs

Figure 1.9

All Programs menu

All Programs command

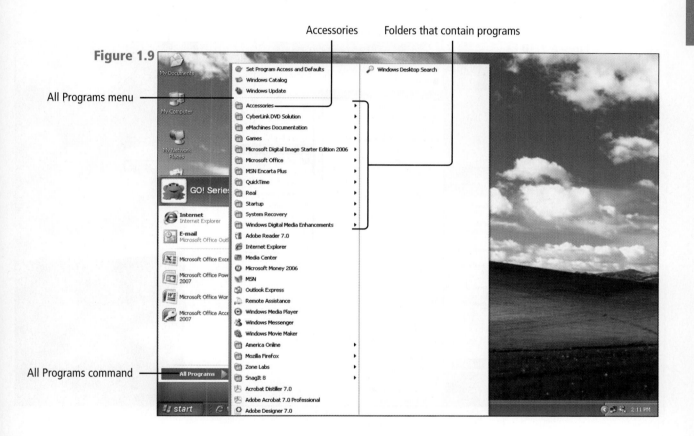

10 In the displayed **Accessories** submenu, point to **Calculator** as shown in Figure 1.10, and notice the displayed ScreenTip, *Performs basic arithmetic tasks with an on-screen calculator.*

You can access the Accessories programs from the Start menu and use them while you are using other Office programs. For example, you may want to make a quick calculation while you are typing a document in Microsoft Word. You can open the calculator, make the calculation, and then place the result in your Word document without closing Word.

Calculator   ScreenTip

Figure 1.10

Accessories submenu

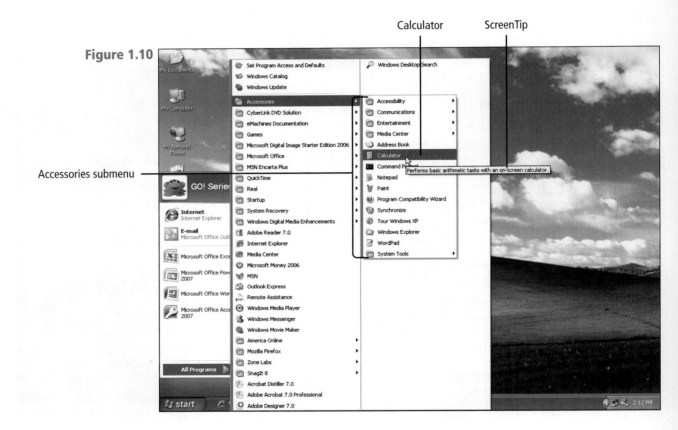

11 Click the **Calculator** command to open the Calculator window and close the **Start** menu. Then, practice using the calculator, which is shown in Figure 1.11. Point to click numbers and keys exactly as you would press keys on a calculator.

Close button

Figure 1.11

Calculator program icon and name

Calculator button on the taskbar

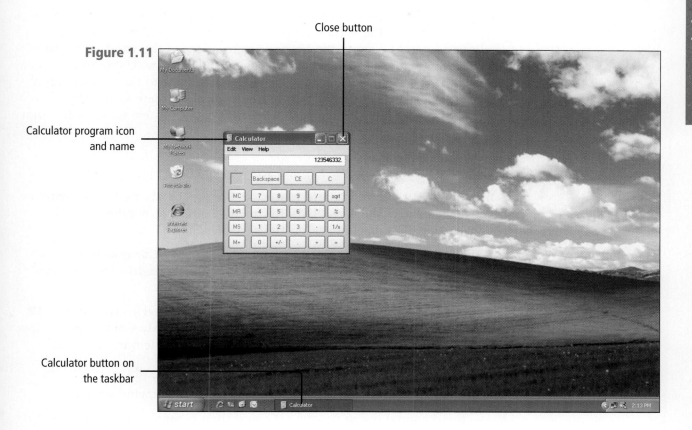

12 On the **Calculator** title bar, click the **Close** button.

Objective 2
Resize, Move, and Scroll Windows

When a window opens on your screen, it generally opens in the same size and shape as it was when last used. If you are using more than one window at a time, you can increase or decrease the size of a window, or move a window so that you can see the information you need.

As you work within a program, the information you create will often grow larger than the screen can display. When the information in a window extends beyond the lower or right edges of the window, scroll bars display at the lower and right side of the window. Using the *horizontal scroll bar*, you can move left and right to view information that extends beyond the left or right edge of the screen. Using the *vertical scroll bar*, you can move up and down to view information that extends beyond the top or bottom of the screen.

Activity 1.2 Resizing, Moving, and Scrolling Windows

In Activity 1.2, you will open, resize, and move the My Computer window. You will also use the scroll bars in the My Computer window to view information that does not fit on the screen.

1 On the **Windows** desktop, double-click the **My Computer** icon to open the **My Computer** window. Alternatively, right-click the icon and click Open.

2 Check to see if the **My Computer** window opened as shown in 1.12, or if it opened and fills the entire screen. If the My Computer window fills the entire screen, on the right side of the title bar, click the

Restore Down button ⬚.

3 Move the pointer to the lower right corner of the window to display the diagonal resize pointer ⬚, and then compare your screen with Figure 1.12.

When the mouse pointer is in this shape, you can use it to change the size and shape of a window.

Figure 1.12

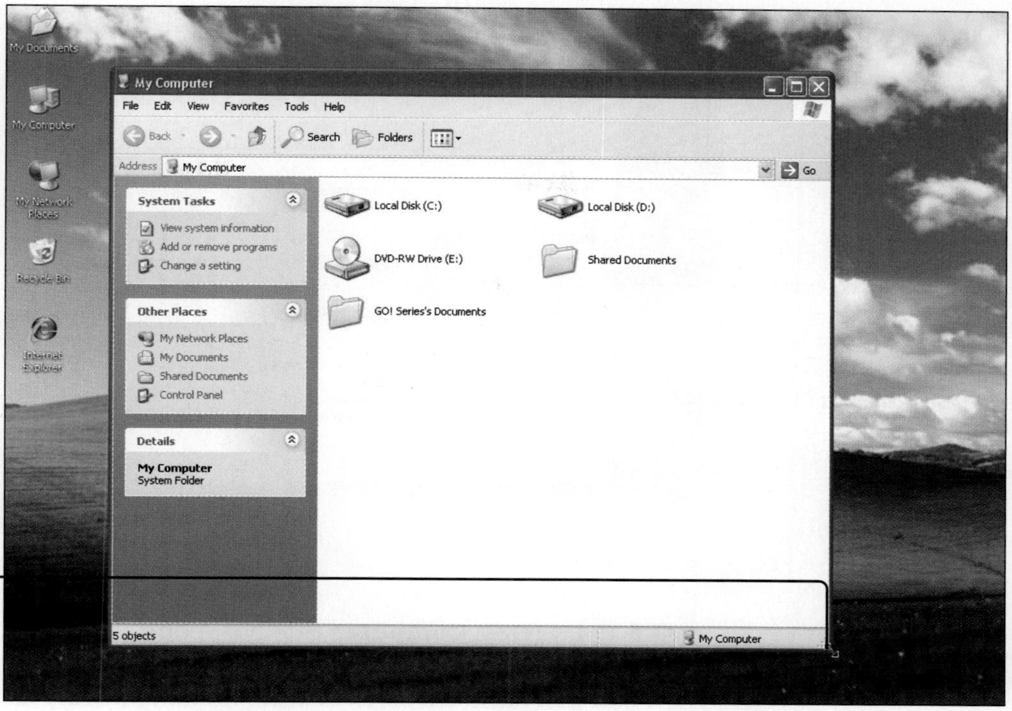

Diagonal resize pointer —

4 Hold down the left mouse button, **_drag_**—move the mouse while holding down the left mouse button, and then release at the appropriate time—diagonally up and to the left until you see a scroll bar at both the bottom and right sides. Adjust as necessary so that the My Computer window is the approximate size of the one shown in Figure 1.13. Adjust as necessary to be sure that scroll bars display.

Scroll bars display on the right side and at the bottom of the window. A scroll bar is added to the window whenever the window contains more than it can display.

Vertical scroll bar

Figure 1.13

The window is smaller

Horizontal scroll bar

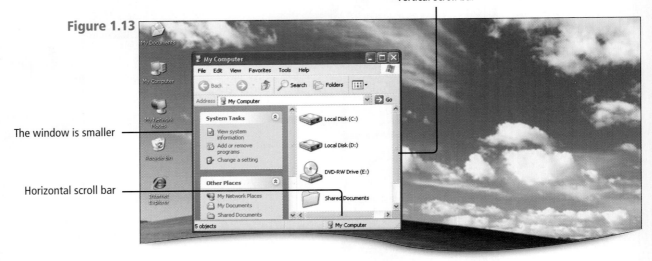

5   On the **My Computer** title bar, point to a blank area. Hold down the left mouse button, drag—hold down the left mouse button, move the mouse, and then release the mouse button—down approximately 2 inches and to the right approximately 2 inches. Compare your screen with Figure 1.14.

When you release the mouse button, the window drops into the new location. Use this technique to move an open window on your screen.

Window moved to a
different location on the screen

Title bar

Figure 1.14

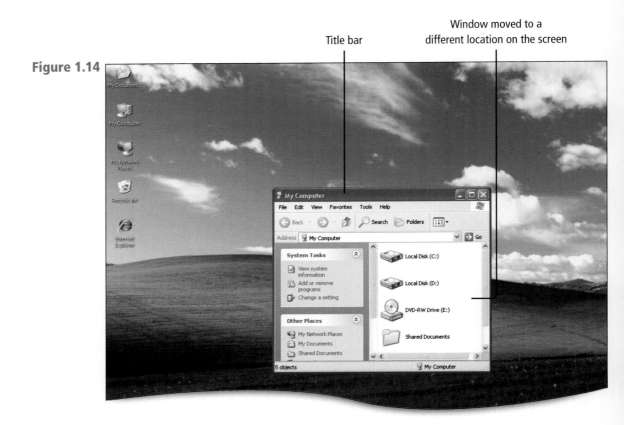

6 At the bottom of the vertical scroll bar, point to the **down arrow** and click, and notice that information at the bottom of the window scrolls up so that you can see the folders and icons that were not visible before, as shown in Figure 1.15.

Up arrow

Figure 1.15

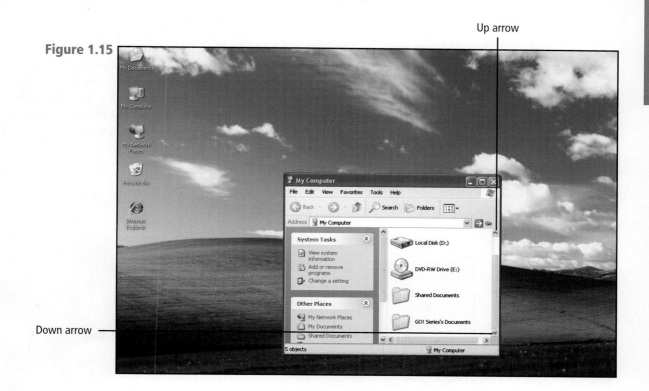

Down arrow

7 Point to the **up arrow** on the same scroll bar, and then click and hold down the left mouse button.

The list scrolls up until the first item is displayed. You can click and hold down the left mouse button on the up or down scroll arrow to scroll rapidly through a long list of information.

8 Point to the scroll box, as shown in Figure 1.16, and then drag it downward.

The **_scroll box_** displays within the vertical and horizontal scroll bars and provides a visual indication of your location within the information displayed. It can also be used with the mouse to reposition the information on the screen. The size of the scroll box varies to indicate the relative size of the information. Moving the scroll box gives you more control as you scroll because you can see the information as it moves up or down in the window.

You can move up or down a screen at a time by clicking in the area above or below the vertical scroll box. You can also move left or right a screen at a time by clicking in the area to the left or right of the horizontal scroll box. The size of the scroll box indicates the relative size of the display to the whole document. If the scroll box is small, it means that the display is a small portion of the whole document.

Figure 1.16

Scroll box —

9 Move the pointer to the upper edge of the **My Computer** window to display the vertical resize pointer ⬍. Drag the top edge of the window to approximately 1 inch below the top of the screen.

10 Move the pointer to the left edge of the **My Computer** window to display the horizontal resize pointer ⬌. Drag the left side of the window to within approximately 1 inch of the left side of the screen.

You can see that by resizing the corners and sides of a window, and by dragging the window to different positions on the screen by the title bar, you have plenty of freedom to move and size any window to make it easier to use.

Objective 3
Maximize, Restore, Minimize, and Close Windows

You can *maximize* a window, which enlarges the window to occupy the entire screen, and you can *restore* a window, which reduces the window to the size it was before being maximized. You can also *minimize* a window, which reduces the window to a button on the taskbar, removing it from the screen entirely without actually closing it. When you need to view the window again, you can click the taskbar button to bring it back into view.

Activity 1.3 Maximizing, Restoring, Minimizing, and Closing a Window

In Activity 1.3, you will maximize, restore, minimize, and close the My Computer window.

1 In the upper right corner of the **My Computer** window, on the **My Computer** title bar, point to the **Maximize** button ◻, and then compare your screen with Figure 1.17.

The Maximize button is the middle button in the group of three. When you point to it, a ScreenTip displays. Recall that a ScreenTip describes a button or screen element.

Figure 1.17

Minimize button

Maximize button   Close button

ScreenTip

2 Click the **Maximize** button ▢ , and then compare your screen with Figure 1.18. Alternatively, maximize or restore a window by double-clicking anywhere in the window's title bar.

The My Computer window occupies the entire screen. The Maximize button is replaced by the Restore Down button, which has a different icon.

Figure 1.18

Minimize button

Restore Down button

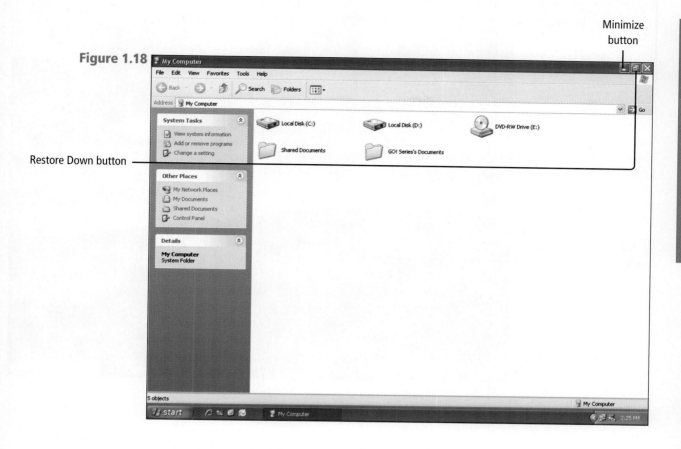

3 On the **My Computer** title bar, click the **Restore Down** button to return the window to the size it was before it was maximized.

4 On the **My Computer** title bar, click the **Minimize** button , and then compare your screen with Figure 1.19.

The My Computer program is still running but the window is minimized. It is represented by a button on the taskbar at the bottom of the screen. The window is not closed, only temporarily hidden from view.

Figure 1.19

My Computer window
minimized to a button on
the taskbar

5 On the taskbar, click the **My Computer** button.

The window redisplays in the same size and location it occupied when you clicked the Minimize button.

6 On the taskbar, click the **Start** button ![start], point to **All Programs**, point to **Accessories**, and then click **Calculator**. Point to the **Calculator** window title bar and drag the Calculator window near the left side of the screen. Notice that both open programs display on the taskbar.

My Computer is a program that helps you manage and organize the space on drives attached to your computer. Calculator is a program that performs basic arithmetic. Both programs occupy their own window, with the Calculator program in front of the My Computer window. Calculator becomes the *active window*. When two or more windows are open, the active window is the window in which the insertion point movements, commands, or text entry occur.

7 Click anywhere on the **My Computer** window, and notice that the **My Computer** window moves to the front, as shown in Figure 1.20.

Figure 1.20

Darker title bar indicates the active program

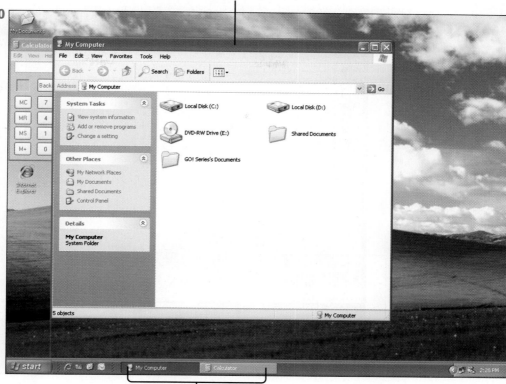

Two programs are
running at the same time

8 On the taskbar, click the **Calculator** button to move the calculator window to the front. On the taskbar, click the **Start** button

start, point to **All Programs**, point to **Accessories**, and then click **Paint**. Notice that all three open programs display on the taskbar, as shown in Figure 1.21.

Paint, a program that comes with Windows XP, creates and edits drawings and displays and edits scanned photos. The Calculator program window is still open, but it is likely hidden behind the other windows.

Figure 1.21

Paint button in the taskbar

Calculator button in the taskbar

My Computer button in the taskbar

9 On the **Paint** title bar, click the **Close** button ⊠. On the **Calculator** title bar, click the **Close** button ⊠. On the **My Computer** window title bar, click the **Close** button ⊠.

More Knowledge
Keeping More Than One Program Window Open at a Time

The ability to keep more than one window open at a time will become more useful as you become more familiar with Microsoft Office. For example, if you want to take information from two word processing documents to create a third document, you can open all three documents and use the taskbar to move among them, copying and pasting text from one document to another. Or, you could copy a chart from Excel and paste it into Word or take a table of data and paste it into PowerPoint. You can even have the same document open in two windows.

Objective 4
Create a New Folder

Information you create in a computer program is stored in the computer's memory, which is a temporary storage location. This data will be lost if the computer is turned off. To keep the information you create, you must save it as a file on one of the drives available to you. For example, a five-page term paper that you create in a word processing program such as Microsoft Word, when saved, is a *file*. Files can be stored directly on a drive, but more commonly are stored in a folder on the drive. A *folder* is a container for programs and files and is represented on the screen by a picture of a common paper file folder.

Use folders to organize the location of your programs and files so that you can easily locate them for later use. Folders and files must be created and stored on one of the drives attached to your computer. Your available drives fall into three categories: 1) the nonremovable hard drive, also called the local disk, inside the computer; 2) removable drives that you insert into the computer such as a $3\frac{1}{2}$ inch floppy disk, a ZIP disk, a flash drive, or a writable CD; or 3) a shared network drive connected to your computer through a computer network, such as the network at your college.

Activity 1.4 Creating a New Folder

In Activity 1.4, you will create a folder on one of the three types of drives available to you—the local disk (hard drive), a removable drive (USB flash drive, ZIP disk, $3\frac{1}{2}$ inch floppy disk, or some other type of removable drive), or a network drive. If you are using a computer in a college lab, you may have space assigned to you on a shared network drive. You can create these folders on any drive that is available to you. The following activity assumes that you are saving your file to a USB flash drive.

1 Insert your USB flash drive or other removable drive. If an action dialog box displays asking what you want Windows to do, click

Cancel. On the taskbar, click the **Start** button [*start*], and then click **My Computer** to open the **My Computer** window. In the **My**

Computer title bar, click the **Maximize** button [▣] if the window is not already maximized.

A *dialog box* is a window that displays and that asks you to make a decision about an individual object or topic.

2 On the Standard Buttons toolbar, click the **Folders** button ▦, and then compare your screen to Figure 1.22. If you do not see a list of drives, in the left pane, click **My Computer**.

The left pane changes to the Folders task pane. A ***task pane*** is an area within an Office program that provides commonly used commands. Its location and small size enable you to use these commands while still working on your files. The Folders task pane displays the drives and folders on your computer. This task pane is useful when navigating among the drives and folders on your computer. A flash drive, labeled F: (your drive letter may be different) is visible in both the Folders task pane on the left and in the pane on the right. You can display the contents of a flash drive, which is used in this instruction, using either icon.

Standard
Buttons toolbar   Folders button   My Documents folder   Right pane

Figure 1.22

The left pane changed
to the Folders task pane

Hard drive

DVD drive

Flash drive

My Network Places

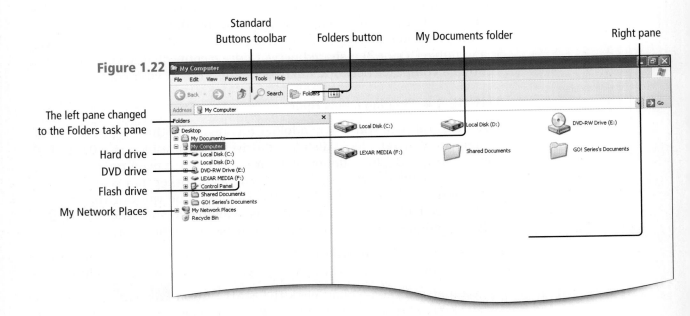

3 On the Standard Buttons toolbar, click the **Views** button ▦ ▾, and then, if necessary, click **Tiles** to select this view option. Notice that icons and a brief description display in the right pane.

4 On the Standard Buttons toolbar, click the **Views** button ▦ ▾, and then click **Details**.

Views button   Detail view

Figure 1.23

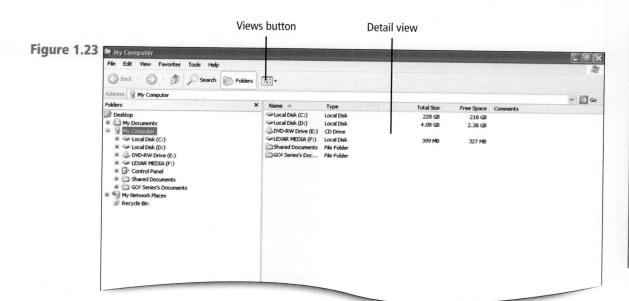

The drives and folders display in a list format, with more information about the hard drive(s), as shown in Figure 1.23. The columns displayed on your computer may be different and may also be numbered differently.

5️⃣ In the **Folders** task pane, click the **USB flash drive** (or other removable media that you have inserted). For purposes of this instruction, the examples will indicate a USB flash drive, called LEXAR MEDIA (F:).

The contents of the drive are displayed in the right pane—in Figure 1.23, the drive is empty; your drive may contain files and folders. Your drive letter may also differ.

6️⃣ In the right pane, right-click in a blank area. In the displayed short-cut menu, point to the **New** command, and then compare your screen with Figure 1.24. Alternatively, from the **File** menu, click **New**.

A submenu displays, showing the various items that can be created using the New command.

Folder command

Figure 1.24

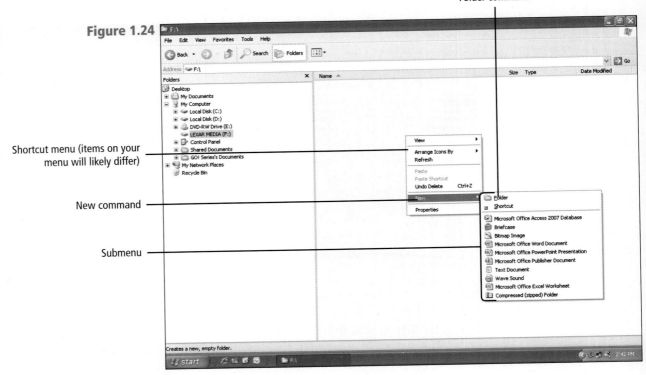

Shortcut menu (items on your
menu will likely differ)

New command

Submenu

7 Click the **Folder** command, and then compare your screen with
Figure 1.25.

A new folder—named *New Folder*—is created with the name of the
folder displayed in the *edit mode*. Edit mode enables you to change the
name of a file or folder, and works the same in all Windows programs.

Box around folder name
indicates it is ready to be edited

Figure 1.25

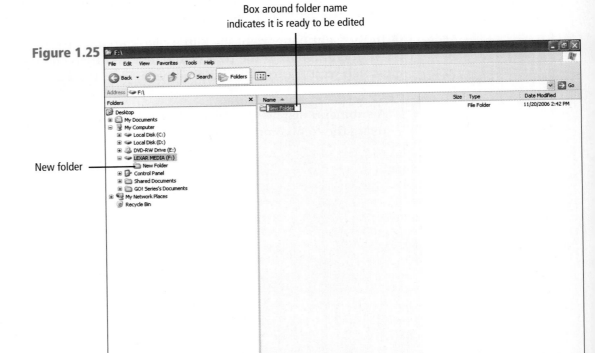

New folder

8 With **New Folder** selected in blue, substituting your name where indicated, type **Word Documents of Firstname Lastname** and press Enter. Then, click anywhere in the blank area of the right pane to deselect the new folder and then compare your screen with Figure 1.26.

Renamed folder

Figure 1.26

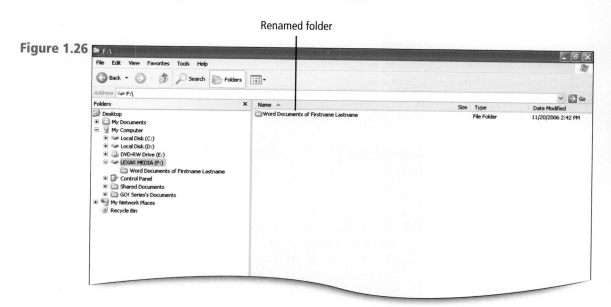

<table>
<tr><td colspan="3">File Edit View Favorites Tools Help</td></tr>
</table>

Name ▲	Size	Type	Date Modified
Word Documents of Firstname Lastname		File Folder	11/20/2006 2:42 PM

Folders
- Desktop
  - My Documents
  - My Computer
    - Local Disk (C:)
    - Local Disk (D:)
    - DVD-RW Drive (E:)
    - LEXAR MEDIA (F:)
      - Word Documents of Firstname Lastname
    - Control Panel
    - Shared Documents
    - GO! Series's Documents
  - My Network Places
  - Recycle Bin

Another Way — **To Rename a Folder**

If you accidentally press Enter before you have a chance to name the folder, you can still rename it. Right-click the folder, click Rename from the shortcut menu, type a new name, and then press Enter. Alternatively, you can click the folder once, pause, and then click the folder again.

---

9 From the **File** menu, point to **New**, and then click **Folder**. Substituting your name where indicated, type **Pictures of Firstname Lastname** and press Enter. Compare your screen to Figure 1.27.

Two new folders have been created in your storage location. The folders are currently in the Details view. Notice the order in which the folders display.

Figure 1.27

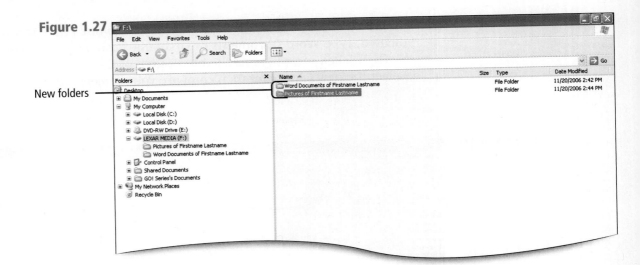

New folders

10 In the right pane, click the **Name** column heading several times to sort the folders and file names from *a* to *z* and from *z* to *a*. Notice that the arrow in the Name column heading points up when the folders are displayed in ascending (*a* to *z*) order, and points down when the folders are displayed in descending (*z* to *a*) order. Stop when the folders are sorted in descending alphabetical order—from *z* to *a*—as shown in Figure 1.28.

Name column heading with arrow indicating sort order

Figure 1.28

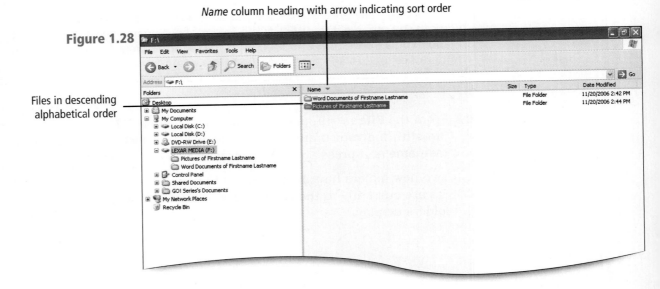

Files in descending alphabetical order

11 In the right pane, move the pointer to the line at the right of the **Name** column heading to display the **resize pointer** , as shown in Figure 1.29.

Column resize pointer

Figure 1.29

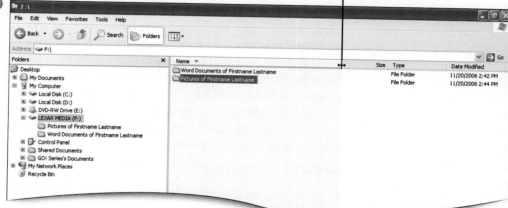

12 Drag the resize pointer to the left about **1 inch**.

The column width is resized. You can resize all the columns in the right pane using the resize pointer.

More Knowledge

Computer Storage Devices

The hard drive (local disk) is usually identified on your computer by the notation C:\ (and sometimes D:\, E:\, and so on for additional drives). A *floppy disk drive* provides storage on a floppy disk and is generally identified on your computer by the notation $3\frac{1}{2}$ Floppy (A:). Floppy disk drives are becoming outdated—many computers no longer come with a floppy drive. A Zip drive also uses a removable disk that holds more information than a floppy disk. *Flash drives*—also known as *USB drives* or *thumb drives*—are small storage devices that plug into a computer's Universal Serial Bus (USB) port, a connection between a computer's and a peripheral device such as a printer, a mouse, a keyboard, or a USB drive.

You may also have access to files on another type of storage device, a *CD-ROM* disc. CD-ROM stands for Compact Disc-Read Only Memory. If you are using files stored on a CD-ROM, you will need to open a file from the disc, and then save it to a writable drive or copy a file from the CD-ROM disc to another disk and then open it. CD drives can store information on one of two types of CDs—a CD that can be written to but not erased—*CD-R*—or a CD that can be written to and erased many times—*CD-RW*.

Objective 5
Copy, Move, Rename, and Delete Files

Recall that Windows manages your data files because your files are stored on the drives attached to your computer. Copying files from one folder to another is a frequent data management task. For example, you may want to make a backup copy of important information, copy a file from a CD to a local disk, or copy information from your local disk drive to a removable drive. Copying files and folders works the same regardless of the type of drive—removable drive, local disk drive, or shared network drive.

Performing other operations on files, such as deleting them or moving them, also works the same regardless of the type of drive. As you accumulate files, you will likely need to delete some to reduce clutter on your hard drive. You may also want to move documents into other folders on another drive to **archive** them—place them somewhere for long-term storage. Finally, you may want to change the names of files or folders to make the names more descriptive. All of these tasks are functions of your Windows operating system.

Activity 1.5 Copying Files and Folders

In Activity 1.5, you will copy files onto your removable drive and into the folders you created in Activity 1.4.

1 Be sure the **My Computer** window is displayed, and that the **Folders** button on the toolbar is selected and the **Folders** task pane is displayed on the left. Place the student CD that came with this book in the CD drive. In the **Folders** task pane, click the **expand button (+)** to the left of the **CD drive** to display the contents of the drive. If a go2007_intro1e dialog box opens, click Cancel.

The folders and files in the CD drive display, and the expand button changes to a **collapse button** (-). Expanded items are in view and collapsed items are hidden from view. The **expand button** indicates that additional items are available but hidden from view.

Note — If Your Student Files Are in a Different Location

Some instructors will place the student files in a folder on a shared network drive, or in a file-sharing folder in a course Web site. If you are instructed to use files from another source, follow the instructions below, substituting your file location for the CD drive.

2 In the **Folders** task pane, click the **expand button (+)** to the left of the **go2007_intro1e** folder, click the **expand button (+)** to the left of the **01_student_data_files** folder, and then click the **chapter_ 01_windowsxp** folder. If necessary, on the Standard

Buttons toolbar, click the Views button ▦ ▾, and then click Details. Compare your screen with Figure 1.30.

The subfolders in the *chapter_01_windowsxp* folder display in the Folders task pane on the left, and the subfolders and files in the *chapter_01_windowsxp* folder display in the right pane. The files you see may display four letters following the file name, such as *.docx*. These are ***file extensions***, and most files have these extensions—although they may or may not display on your system. Files created by Microsoft Office programs have a standard set of extensions that identify the type of program used to create the file. For example, Microsoft Word documents end in *.doc* or *.docx*, Excel worksheets end in *.xls* or *.xlsx*, PowerPoint presentations end with *.ppt* or *.pptx*, and so on.

Subfolders in the
chapter_01_windowsxp folder

Files in the
chapter_01_windowsxp folder

Figure 1.30

CD containing the data files
for this book (if you are
using the CD)

Indicates that the folder has
been expanded

Indicates that there are
subfolders in this folder

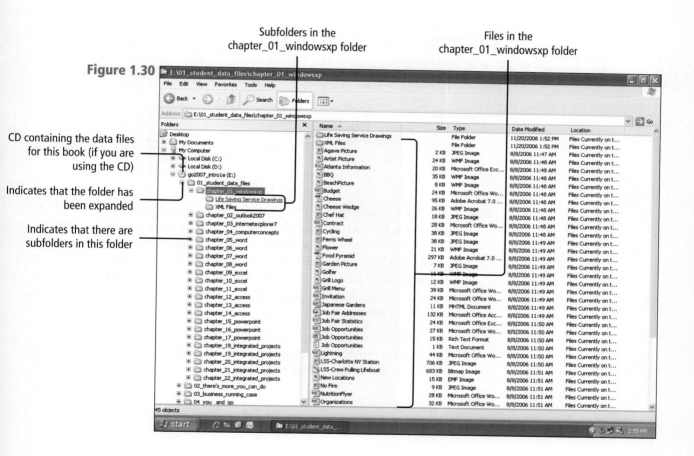

3 On the menu bar, click **Tools**, and then from the displayed menu, click **Folder Options**. Near the top of the **Folder Options** dialog box, click the **View tab**. Under **Advanced settings**, locate the **Hide extensions for known file types** check box. If the check box is selected (there is a check mark in it), click to clear the check box, and then compare your screen with Figure 1.31.

In this chapter, from this point on, it is assumed that the file extensions are turned on and will display.

View tab

Figure 1.31

Clear this check box to display file extensions

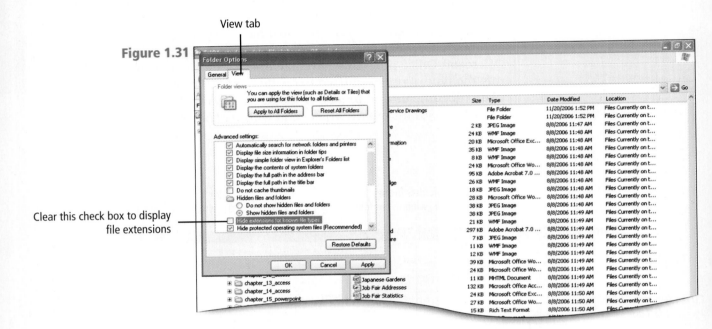

4 Click **OK** to close the **Folder Options** dialog box. In the **Folders** task pane, click the removable drive you used to create the *Pictures of Firstname Lastname* and *Word Documents of Firstname Lastname* folders. Click the **chapter_01_windowsxp** folder, which refreshes the window and re-displays the file names with their file extensions. In the right pane, click the **Type** column heading. Be sure you can see all of the WMF files.

When you click the Type column heading, the files display by file type in *a*-to-*z* order. The displayed WMF files are images that come with Microsoft Office 2007.

5 In the **Name** column, click to select the **Flower.wmf** file. In the **Folders** task pane, scroll as necessary until you can see your removable drive. Watch the shape of the pointer and begin to drag the **Flower.wmf** file over to the **Pictures of Firstname Lastname** folder that you created on your removable drive.

The Pictures folder on your removable drive is selected, and the file name is attached to the pointer, as shown in Figure 1.32. When you release the mouse button, the file will be copied. Files are copied when dragged to a different drive, and moved when dragged to a different location in the same drive.

6 Release the mouse button to copy the file to the **Pictures of Firstname Lastname** folder.

7 In the **Name** column, click to select the **Plant.wmf** file. From the **Edit** menu, click **Copy**.

The file is copied to a temporary storage area called the *Clipboard*. The Clipboard stores the most recent item that was copied.

Shows file that is being copied   File being copied

Figure 1.32

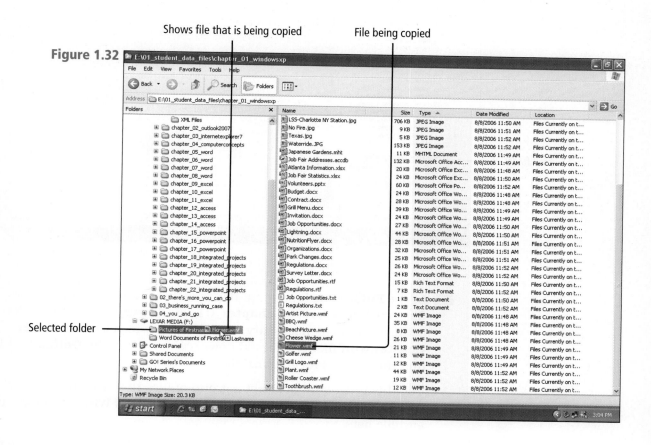

Selected folder

8 In the **Folders** task pane, click to select the **Pictures of Firstname Lastname** folder. From the **Edit** menu, click **Paste**. Compare your screen to Figure 1.33.

The file is copied to the selected folder, and the folder contains two files—the file you dragged to the folder and the file you pasted into the folder. You can see that there are various ways in which you can copy a file from one location to another.

Two files copied to the folder

Figure 1.33

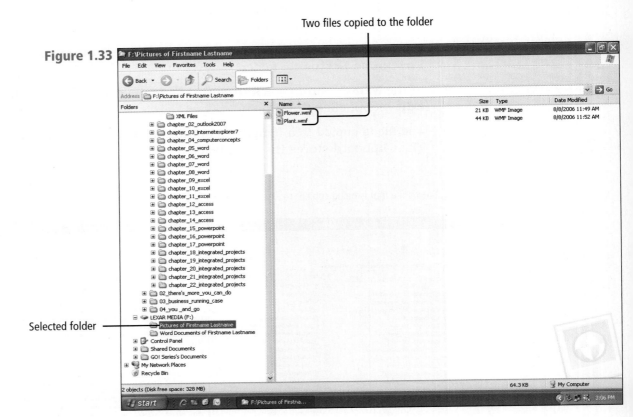

Selected folder

9 In the **Folders** task pane, under the **CD** containing your student files, click to select the **chapter_01_windowsxp** folder. In the **Name** column, scroll as necessary, and then click to select the **Roller Coaster.wmf** file. Then, hold down Ctrl and click the **Golfer.wmf** file and the **Artist Picture.wmf** file.

Use this technique to select a group of files that are not adjacent to (next to) each other. This technique works in all Windows programs and file lists.

10 From the **File** menu, point to **Send To**, and then click the name of your removable disk drive.

The files are copied to your removable drive. This copy option enables you to send a file or files to the drive of your choice, but does not permit you to specify a folder on that drive.

11 In the right pane, click the **Name** column heading, and then scroll to the top of the list of folders and files. In the **Folders** task pane, scroll down if necessary to see your removable drive. Drag the **XML Files** folder over the name of your removable drive until it is selected, and then release the mouse button. Compare your screen with Figure 1.34.

The folder and all of the files in the folder are copied to your removable drive.

Folder copied from the CD

Figure 1.34

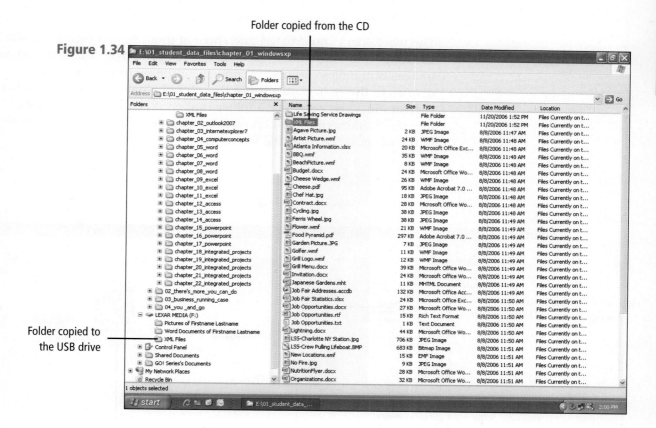

Folder copied to the USB drive

Activity 1.6 Moving, Renaming, and Deleting Files

In Activity 1.6, you will move files from one location on your removable drive to another location on the same drive. You will also rename and delete files.

1 In the **Folders** task pane, scroll down if necessary and then click the removable drive you are using to store your files. In the right pane, click the **Name** column as necessary to display the files in alphabetical order. Click the **Views button arrow** and then click **Thumbnails**. Compare your screen with Figure 1.35.

The two folders you created and three of the files you copied—along with the XML Files folder—display in the right pane. Small *thumbnail* images of the files—miniature images of the pictures in the files—display in the right pane. These thumbnails make it easy to select the correct file when you have a folder that contains a large number of images. Folders that contain pictures display thumbnails of up to four of the images in a large file folder icon.

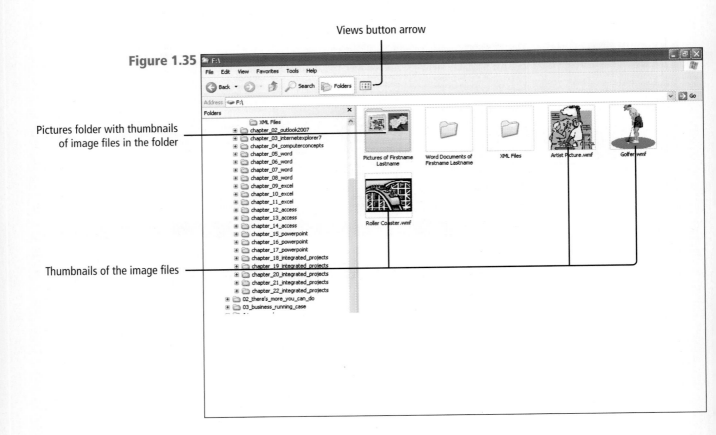

Figure 1.35

Views button arrow

Pictures folder with thumbnails of image files in the folder

Thumbnails of the image files

2 In the right pane, click the **Artist Picture.wmf** file. Hold down the mouse button, drag the file to the **Pictures of Firstname Lastname** folder that you created, and then release the mouse button.

When you drag a file from one folder to another in the same drive, the file is moved, rather than copied.

3 Drag the **Golfer.wmf** file to the **Pictures** folder, and then drag the **Roller Coaster.wmf** file to the **Pictures** folder.

4 In the **Folders** task pane, click the **Pictures of Firstname Lastname** folder in your removable drive. On the Standard Buttons toolbar, click the **Views** button [image], and then click **Thumbnails**. Compare your screen with Figure 1.36.

Figure 1.36

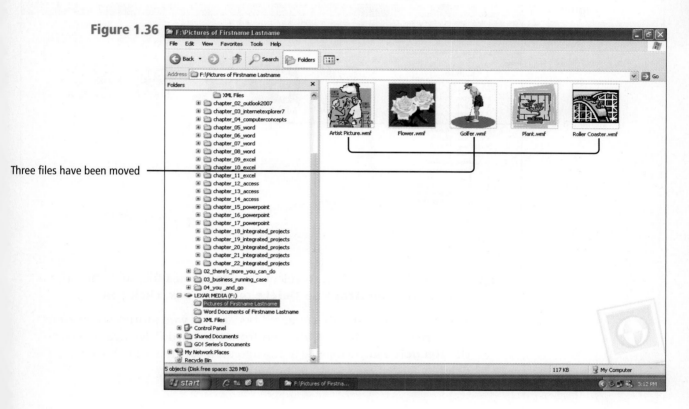

Three files have been moved

5 In the right pane, right-click the **Flower.wmf** file. Then, from the displayed shortcut menu, click the **Rename** command. Click to position the insertion point at the beginning of the file name, type **Water** and then press [Spacebar]. Press [Enter] to change the file name to *Water Flower.wmf.* Compare your screen with Figure 1.37.

When the file extensions are displayed, you need to include the extension when you rename the file. There are several restrictions for naming files or folders. A file name can contain up to 255 characters, including spaces, although the file name cannot begin with a space. It also cannot contain the following characters: \ / : * ? " < > |

Figure 1.37

Renamed file

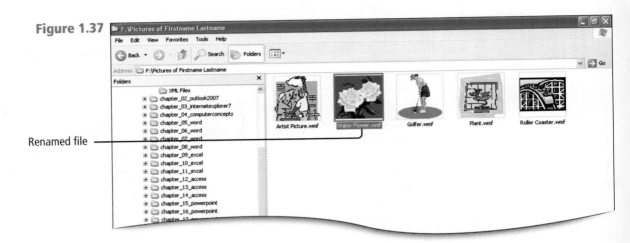

6 In the right pane, click to select the **Plant.wmf** file, and then press [Delete]. In the **Confirm File Delete** message box, click **Yes**.

The file is permanently removed because it was stored on a removable drive. Files that are deleted from the hard drive are moved to the **Recycle Bin**, which is a storage area for files that have been deleted.

Note — If You Cannot Delete a File

Sometimes you will try to delete a file and a message displays indicating that the file cannot be deleted. This usually means that the file is open. You must close a file before you can delete it.

7 In the **Folders** task pane, click to select your removable disk. In the right pane, select the **XML Files** folder, and then press (Delete).

8 In the **Confirm Folder Delete** dialog box, click **Yes** to delete the folder.

The folder and all of the files and folders it contains are deleted.

More Knowledge

Recovering Deleted Files

If you accidentally delete a file from the hard disk drive that you want to keep, there is a good chance you can recover it. Windows temporarily stores files deleted from your hard drive in a Recycle Bin, which you can find on the desktop or in the My Computer Folders pane. You can open the Recycle Bin in the same way you open a file folder. If the discarded files have not been permanently removed, right-click the file name in the Contents pane, and then click Restore in the shortcut menu.

Activity 1.7 Capturing an Image of a Screen

Windows includes a screen capture utility that enables you to capture an image of your screen and then print it or save it as a file.

1 On your keyboard, locate and press (PrtScr).

The Print Screen key on your keyboard is commonly located near the right side of the top row of keys. This key captures an image of the entire screen and places it in a temporary storage area called the Clipboard. Items in the Clipboard can be placed in a document using the Paste command.

2 Click the **Start** button ![start], point to **All Programs**, point to **Accessories**, and then click **WordPad**. If necessary, maximize the WordPad window.

WordPad is a simple word-processing program that comes with Windows XP.

3 In the WordPad window, type **Firstname Lastname** using your own name. Press (Enter) two times.

4 From the WordPad menu bar, click **Edit**, and then click **Paste**. Compare your screen with Figure 1.38.

The captured screen is pasted at the insertion point. The image is larger than the WordPad page.

Captured screen

Figure 1.38

Sizing handle —

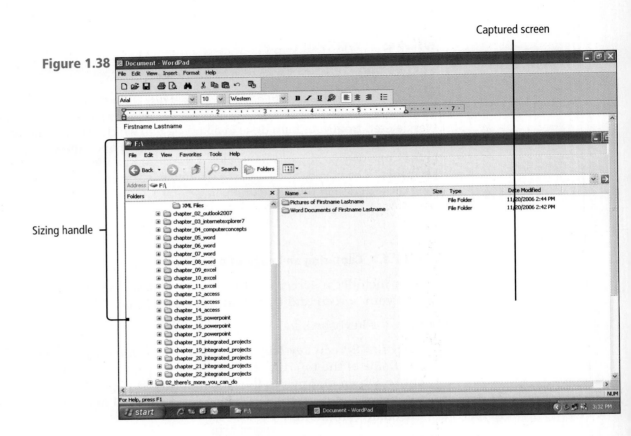

5 If necessary, use the vertical and horizontal scroll bars to display the sizing handle in the lower right corner of the pasted image. In the lower right corner of the image, move the pointer over the sizing handle—the little box in the corner—to display the diagonal

resize pointer.

When an image is selected, **sizing handles** display in all four corners and in the middle of the side and top borders. Use handles to resize the image in a manner similar to the way you resized a window.

6 With the diagonal size pointer, drag up and to the left of **6 inches** on the ruler. Compare your screen with Figure 1.39.

Recall that to drag an object, you need to point, click, and move the mouse to the desired location. Use the ruler as a guide.

Six inches mark   Diagonal resize pointer

Figure 1.39

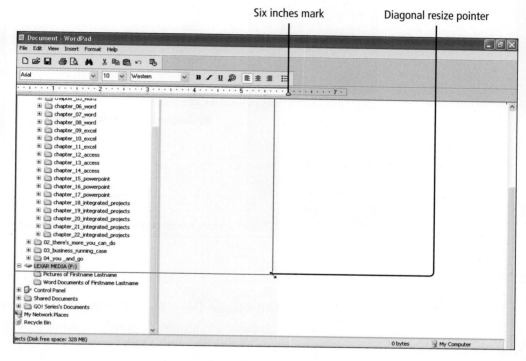

7 Release the mouse button, and then from the File menu click **Print Preview** to display the Print Preview window. Compare your screen to Figure 1.40.

8 In the **Print Preview** title bar, click the **Close** button. Alternatively, click the **Close** button on the Print Preview toolbar.

9 Check your Course Syllabus or Chapter Assignment Sheet, or ask your instructor, to determine if you are to submit a printed or electronic copy of this file. To print, from the WordPad toolbar, click the **Print** button. To submit electronically using your college's course management system, consult your instructor's directions for saving and submitting the file.

10 From the **File** menu, click **Exit**. When prompted to save your work, click **No**.

Close button

Figure 1.40

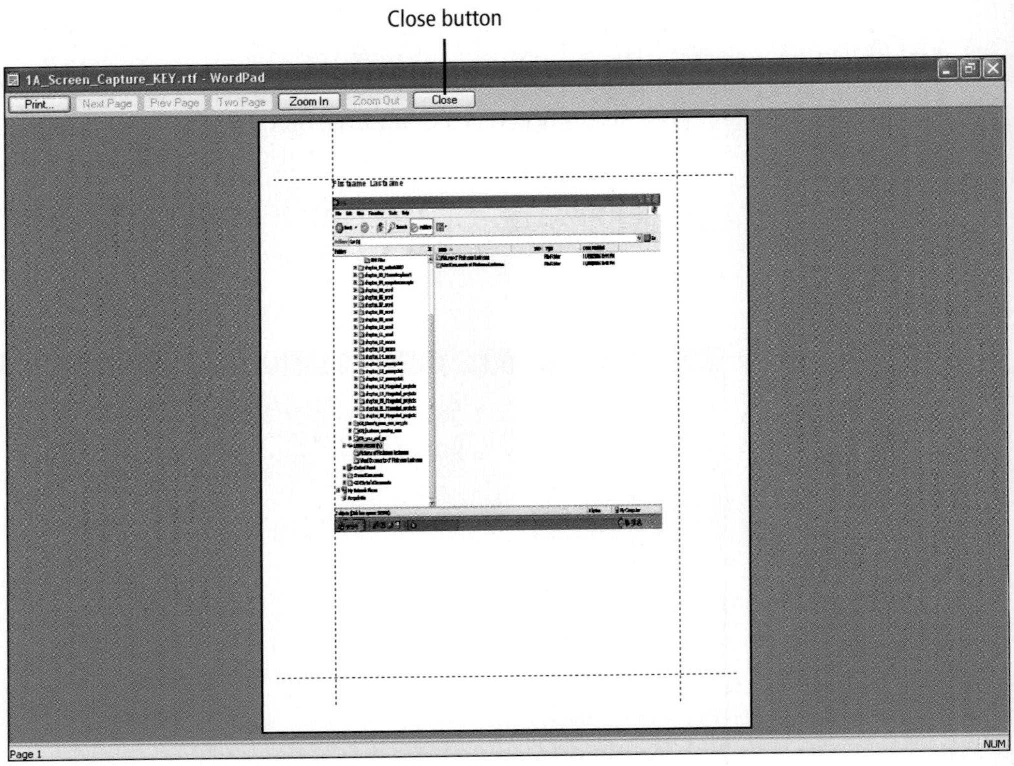

Alert!

What If the Image Does Not Display in Print Preview?

On some computers, if the image is larger than the page, the image will not display. If you cannot see your pasted image, close the Print Preview window and use the sizing handle to reduce the size of the image again. Repeat this procedure until you can see the image in Print Preview.

Objective 6
Find Files and Folders

As you use a computer, you will likely accumulate a large number of files and folders. It's easy to forget where you stored a file, or what you named it. Windows XP provides a search function that enables you to find files and folders.

Activity 1.8 Finding Files and Folders

In Activity 1.8, you will use several different methods to search for files and folders.

1 In the **Folders** task pane, click **My Computer**. On the Standard Buttons toolbar, click the **Search** button 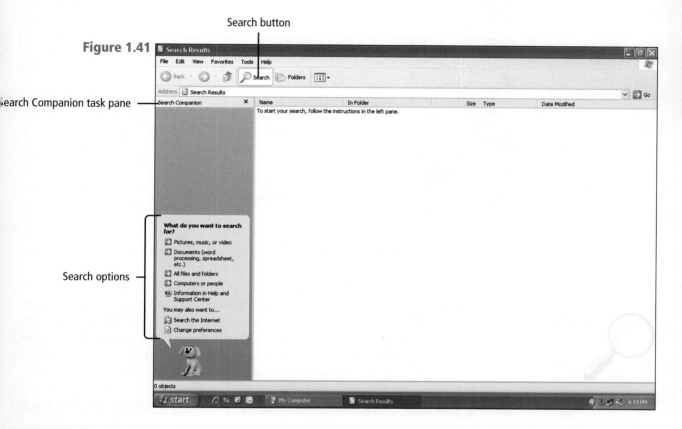, and then compare your screen with Figure 1.41.

The Search Companion task pane displays on the left. Here you can search for specific file types or you can search through all the files and folders.

Search button

Figure 1.41

Search Companion task pane

Search options

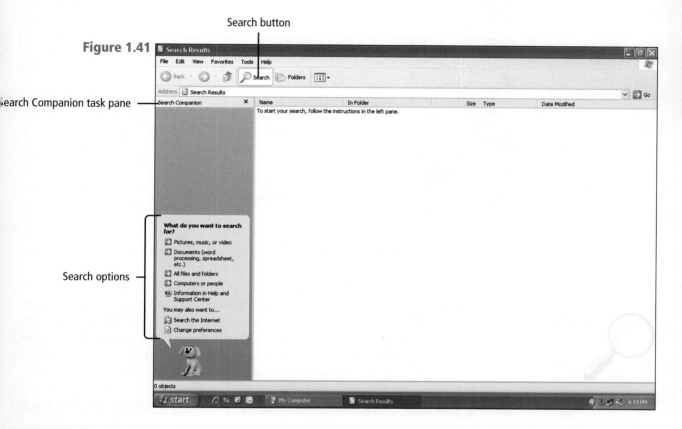

Alert!

What If Windows Desktop Search starts instead of the Search Companion?

At the bottom of the Windows Desktop Search pane, click the link to the Search Companion. Maximize the Search Results window and complete the rest of Activity 1.8 as directed. When you are done with Activity 1.8, close both the Search Results window and the Windows Desktop Search pane.

2 In the **Search Companion** task pane, click the **All files and folders** option.

A search dialog box displays. Here you can specify the file name (or part of a file name) or text contained in the file. You can also narrow the search by specifying the search location.

3 In the **All or part of the file name** box, type **coaster**, If necessary, click the **Look in down arrow**, and then click **My Computer**. Compare your screen with Figure 1.42.

The actual file name is capitalized, but this search option is not case sensitive.

Figure 1.42

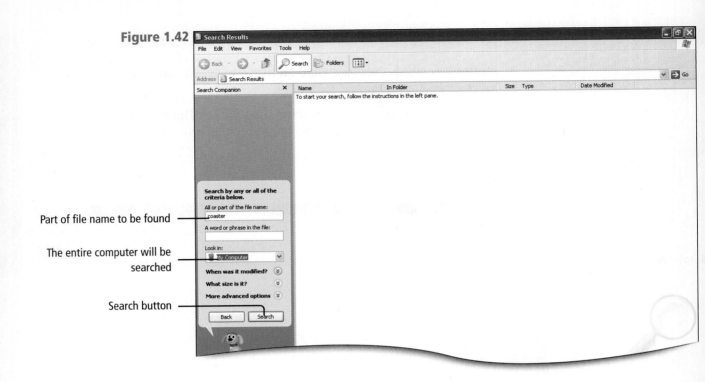

Part of file name to be found

The entire computer will be searched

Search button

---

4 At the bottom of the task pane, click the **Search** button, and then compare your screen with Figure 1.43.

The search begins. Notice that a couple of files display rather quickly, but the search program goes on and on. (You may see only one file, depending on the way your computer has been set up.) This is because you did not specify a location, so the program is checking all storage locations on the computer. You can click the Stop button at any time if the procedure seems to be taking too long.

Figure 1.43

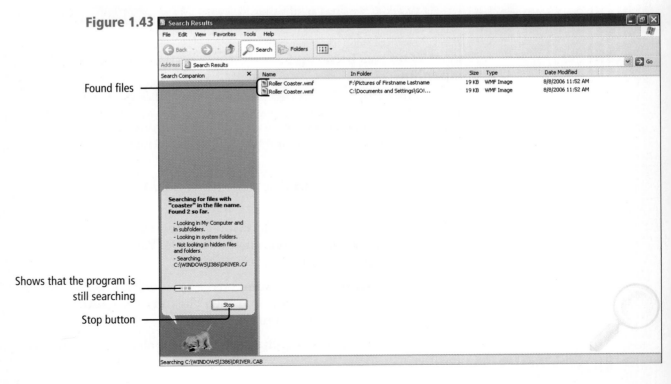

Found files

Shows that the program is still searching

Stop button

5 Click **Stop** to stop the current search. Click **Start a new search**, and then click **Pictures, music, or video**. Click to select the **Pictures and Photos** check box. In the **All or part of the file name** box, type surf

This is part of several file names in the Life Saving Service Drawings folder on your student CD.

6 In the **Search Companion** task pane, click the **Use advanced search options** check box to add more search options. At the right of the **Look in** box, click the arrow. From the location list, click your student **CD** and then compare your screen with Figure 1.44. If you are not using the CD, select the location where your student files are stored.

Figure 1.44

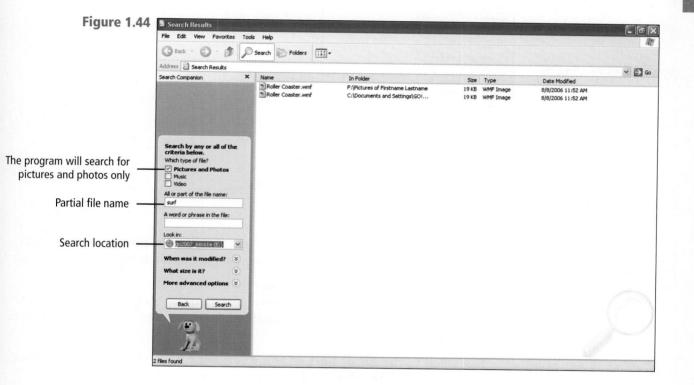

The program will search for pictures and photos only

Partial file name

Search location

7 At the bottom of the task pane, click the **Search** button. Compare your screen with Figure 1.45.

Three files are found. This time, the search only took a few seconds.

Figure 1.45

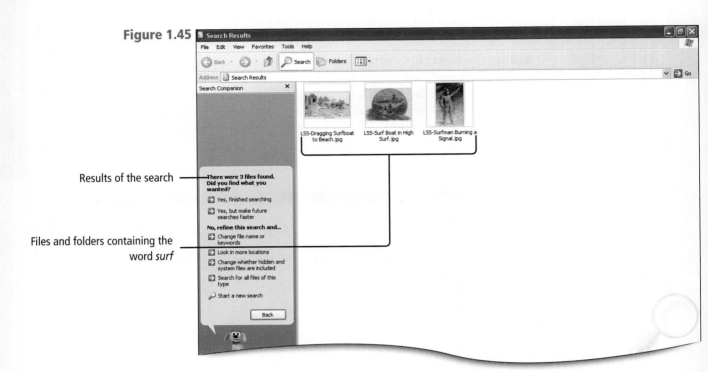

Results of the search

Files and folders containing the word *surf*

8 Scroll down, if necessary, and click the **Start a new search** option. Click the **Documents (word processing, spreadsheet, etc.)** option.

This dialog box gives you greater control over the search. You can search for documents that have specified file extensions, or you can search for documents last modified during a certain time period. You can even combine the two.

9 Click in the **All or part of the document name** box and type ***.docx** Click the **Use advanced search options** check box to add more search options. At the right of the **Look in** box, click the arrow. From the location list, click your student **CD** or other student file location. Click the **Search** button and view the results.

This restricts the search to Word 2007 documents, which have the *.docx* extension. The asterisk is called a ***wildcard*** and means that you will be searching for anything that has the *.docx* extension. This is very helpful when you cannot remember the file name or where you put it.

10 In the **Search Companion** task pane, click the **Look in arrow** again, and then click **Local Disk (C:)**—or **Local Hard Drives**. Click the **Search** button. Compare your screen with Figure 1.46.

The right pane displays the files that have the *.docx* extension. The list may be quite long.

11 On the **Search Companion** task pane, click the **Stop** button.

Figure 1.46

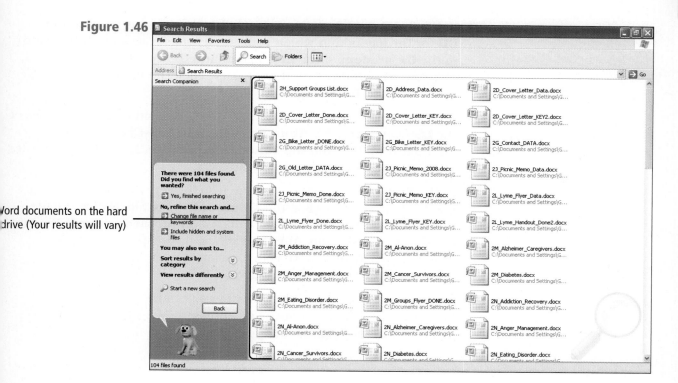

Word documents on the hard drive (Your results will vary)

Objective 7
Compress Files

Some files may be too large to send quickly as an e-mail attachment. For example, files containing graphics tend to be quite large. Windows XP includes a feature with which you can ***compress***—reduce the file size of—one or more files into a single file that uses a *.zip* file extension. These files can then be unzipped for editing on any other computer running Windows XP.

Activity 1.9 Compressing Files

In Activity 1.9, you will compress a single file and then compress several files at the same time.

1 On the Standard Buttons toolbar, click the **Folders** button [Folders]. In the Folders task pane, click **My Computer**.

Note — To Work with Third-Party Zip Programs

If you are using a third-party zip program, such as WinZip™ or PKZIP™, you will need to use that program to complete this task—the procedure listed below will not work.

---

2 In the **Folders** task pane, click the drive containing your student **CD**, or the location in which your student files are stored. Navigate to the **01_student_data_files** folder, and then click **chapter_01_windowsxp**. If necessary, click the **Views** button [▦▾], and then click **Details**.

3 Click the **Lightning.docx** file. Hold down [Ctrl] and then click to select the **LSS-Charlotte NY Station.jpg** file, the **LSS-Crew Pulling Lifeboat.bmp** file, and the **Volunteers.pptx** file. Drag these four files to copy them to your removable drive.

4 In the **Folders** task pane, click the icon for your removable disk. In the right pane, right-click the **Volunteers.pptx** file. Notice the file size. Point to **Send To**, and then click **Compressed (zipped) Folder**. If a **Compressed (zipped) Folder** dialog box displays, click **Yes** to designate the Windows XP compression feature to zip your file. Compare your screen with Figure 1.47.

A compressed version of the Volunteers.pptx file displays as Volunteers.zip. Notice that the compressed folder is reduced in size compared to the original file.

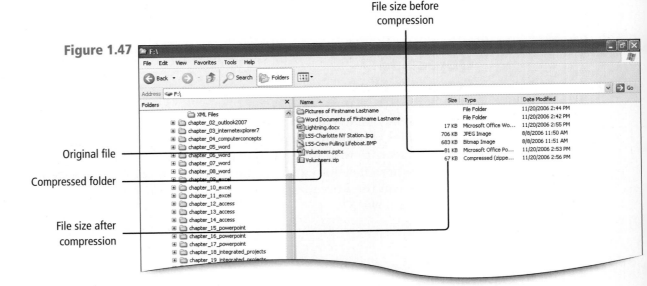

Figure 1.47

File size before compression

Original file

Compressed folder

File size after compression

5 Repeat the procedure you used in Step 4 to compress the other three files you just copied to your removable drive—**Lightning.docx**, **LSS-Charlotte NY Station.jpg**, and **LSS-Crew Pulling Lifeboat.bmp**. Compare your screen with Figure 1.48.

Notice that the amount of compression depends on the type of file being compressed. Word files can often be reduced by 10 to 20 percent, while files that use compression features when the files are saved—such as *.jpg* or *.pdf* files—do not benefit much from further compression.

Figure 1.48

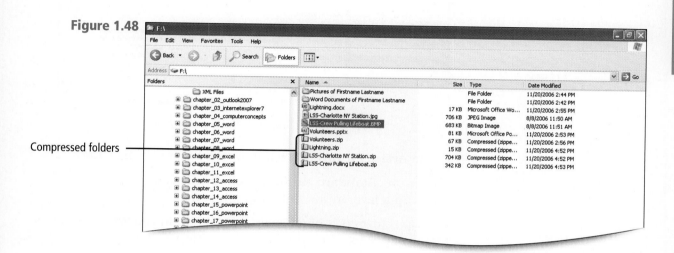

Compressed folders

6 Click the **Lightning.docx** file. Hold down Ctrl and then click to select the **LSS-Charlotte NY Station.jpg** file, the **LSS-Crew Pulling Lifeboat.bmp** file, and the **Volunteers.pptx** file. Press Delete to remove the original files, and then click **Yes** when prompted.

7 In the **Folders** task pane, click the **Pictures of Firstname Lastname** folder. From the **Edit** menu, click **Select All** to select all the files in the folder. Alternatively, hold down Ctrl and press A.

8 Right-click the **Artist Picture.wmf** file, click **Send To**, and then click **Compressed (zipped) Folder**.

All four files are compressed into one folder, called *Artist Picture.zip*. The compressed folder takes the name of whichever file you right-click when you compress more than one file at a time.

9 Double-click the **Artist Picture.zip** folder to display the contents of the compressed folder. Compare your screen with Figure 1.49.

Figure 1.49

Compressed folder name in Window title bar

Files in the compressed folder

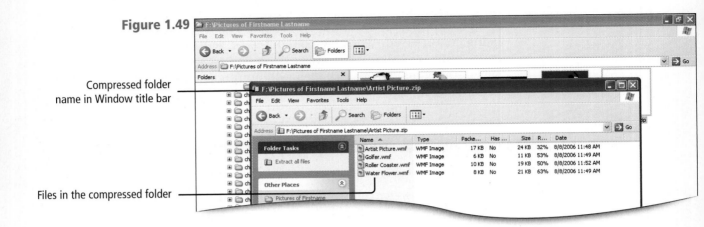

10 In the **Artist Picture.zip** window title bar, click the **Close** button. In the Standard Buttons toolbar, click the **Up** button to move up a level in the **Folders** task pane.

The Up button is a handy way to move up in the Windows folder hierarchy—each time you click the button, you move up one folder level.

11 Double-click the **Lightning.zip** compressed folder. In the left pane, click **Extract all files** to start the Extraction Wizard. Compare your screen with Figure 1.50.

Extraction Wizard

Figure 1.50

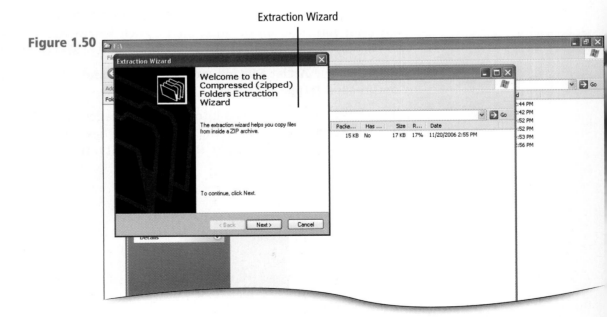

12 Click **Next** to display the second **Extraction Wizard** dialog box, which enables you to change the location of the file.

If you do not change the file location, the file will be extracted to the folder that contains the zipped file.

13 In the **Extraction Wizard** dialog box, click the **Next** button to accept the default location.

14 In the **Extraction Wizard** dialog box, clear the **Show extracted files** check box, and then click **Finish**. Close the Lightning.zip window.

The Show extracted files option is useful when you are sending files to a different location and want to move to that location when the Extraction Wizard closes.

The file is extracted and placed in a folder along with the compressed file, as shown in Figure 1.51.

Figure 1.51

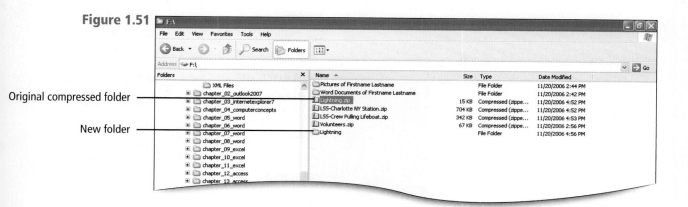

Original compressed folder

New folder

15 On the menu bar, click **Tools**, and then from the displayed menu, click **Folder Options**. Near the top of the **Folder Options** dialog box, click the **View tab**. Under **Advanced settings**, locate the **Hide extensions for known file types** check box. Click to select the check box. Click **OK** to turn off the file extensions.

16 Close the **Removable Media** window.

More Knowledge

File Associations and Compression Programs

You may see a dialog box when you click the Compressed (zipped) Folder command. Because every file type needs to be associated with a program, your computer may already associate files that have the *.zip* extension with a third-party program such as WinZip. The dialog box will ask whether you want to designate Compressed (zipped) Folders as the program for handling ZIP files (compressed files that have a *.zip* extension). If you are working in a lab, ask the lab manager how to answer this question. If you are working at home, click Yes, unless you want to use another program to compress your files.

Content-Based Assessments

Windows XP
chapter one

Summary

You will find that a working knowledge of Windows functions is useful as you create files in various programs like those in Microsoft Office. In this chapter, you practiced setting up, organizing, and navigating the Windows desktop. You adjusted window size and moved windows. You created folders to store your documents and then copied, moved, renamed, and deleted files. Finally, you compressed files to save space.

Key Terms

Content-Based Assessments

Matching

Match each term in the second column with its correct definition in the first column. Write the letter of the term on the blank line in front of the correct definition.

_____ **1.** A bar that contains the Start button, buttons representing open programs, and other buttons that will activate programs.

_____ **2.** The arrow, I-beam, or other symbol that moves when you move the mouse or other pointing device, and that indicates a location or position on your screen.

_____ **3.** A box that displays information and usually consists of a title bar, menu bar, status bar, and toolbars, and that always has a Minimize button.

_____ **4.** The area at the top of a window that displays the file name and also contains the Minimize, Maximize/Restore Down, and Close buttons.

_____ **5.** A list of context-sensitive commands—commands that are commonly used when working on the selected object—usually activated by right-clicking a screen item.

_____ **6.** An area to the right of the Start button that contains shortcut icons for commonly used programs.

_____ **7.** The area on the right side of the taskbar where the clock and system notifications display, and where notifications display that keep you informed about processes that are occurring in the background, such as antivirus software checking, network connections, and other utility programs.

A CD-RW

B Compress

C File extension

D Folder

E Mouse pointer

F Notification area

G Quick Launch tool-bar

H Scroll bar

I Shortcut menu

J Status bar

K Taskbar

L Thumbnail

M Title bar

N Wildcard

O Window

_____ **8.** A horizontal bar at the bottom of the document window that provides information about the current state of what you are viewing in the window, for example the page number of a document.

_____ **9.** The Windows feature that enables you to view text that extends beyond the edges of the screen.

_____ **10.** A Windows object used to keep related files stored together in one location.

_____ **11.** A compact disc that can be used over and over again to read and save files.

_____ **12.** The three- or four-letter ending to a file—that may or may not display—and that identifies the file type.

_____ **13.** The term given to an asterisk (*) or other character used to substitute for several characters in a file search.

_____ **14.** A miniature representation of the contents of a picture file, used in one of the file views in My Computer.

_____ **15.** To reduce the size of a file.

Content-Based Assessments

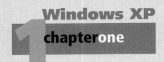
Fill in the Blank

Write the correct word in the space provided.

1. A(n) _____ is a graphic representation that enables you to run a program or use a program function.

2. Windows XP is an example of a(n) _____, which coordinates the activities of a computer.

3. The _____ button on the left end of the taskbar is used to run programs, change system settings, or find help.

4. When more than one document or program is open at the same time, you can switch back and forth between them by clicking the appropriate button in the _____.

5. A(n) _____ is a second-level menu that is accessed using a menu command.

6. When you delete a file, it is stored in a temporary area called the _____, from which it can often be recovered.

7. A box that asks you to make a decision about an individual object or topic is called a(n) _____ box.

8. The arrow, I-beam, or other symbol that shows the location or position of the mouse on your screen is called a mouse _____.

9. When you right-click an object, a(n) _____ menu displays.

10. The bar that usually displays under the menu bar, and that uses buttons to activate commands, is call a(n) _____.

11. To make a window fill the screen, use the _____ button from the title bar.

12. You can hide a program or document without closing it by clicking the _____ button.

13. In My Computer, you can sort file names alphabetically by clicking the _____ column heading.

Content-Based Assessments

Fill in the Blank

14. The main storage device on your computer is the _____ disk drive.

15. A file _____, which consists of the last three or four characters of a file name, indicates which program was used to create the file.

Glossary

Active window The window in which the mouse pointer movements, commands, or text entry occur when two or more windows are open.

Address bar Displays the path of the current file or folder; also, in Internet Explorer, displays the address of the active Web page.

Archive To back up files and store them somewhere other than the main hard drive.

CD-R Another name for a CD-ROM disc.

CD-ROM The acronym for Compact Disc-Read Only Memory; an optical storage device used to permanently store data and from which you can read and open files.

CD-RW A compact disc that can be reused to read and save files.

Click To press the left (or primary) mouse button once.

Clipboard A temporary storage area in Windows that stores the most recently copied item.

Close button The button in a title bar that closes a window or a program.

Collapse button A small minus (−) button to the left of a folder that you click to hide the items in that folder.

Compress A process to reduce the size of a file.

Context-sensitive command A command associated with activities in which you are engaged; often activated by right-clicking a screen item.

Desktop The basic screen from which Windows and programs are run, and which consists of program icons, a taskbar, a Start button, and a mouse pointer.

Dialog box A box that asks you to make a decision about an individual object or topic. Dialog boxes do not have Minimize buttons.

Double-click The action of clicking the left mouse button twice in rapid succession while keeping the mouse still.

Drag The action of moving something from one location on the screen to another; the action of dragging includes releasing the mouse button at the desired time or location.

Drive An area of storage that is formatted with the Windows file system and that has a drive letter such as C.

Edit mode A Windows mode that enables you to change the name of a file or folder, and works the same in all Windows programs.

Expand button A small plus (+) button to the left of a folder that you click to display the items in that folder.

File Data that you save and store on a drive, such as a Word document or a PowerPoint presentation.

File extension The characters to the right of the period in a file name, and that tell the computer the program to use to open the file; extensions can be displayed or hidden.

Flash drive A small, portable, digital storage device that connects to a computer's USB port; also called a thumb drive, jump drive, or USB drive.

Floppy disk drive (or floppy drive) The original storage device for a microcomputer, which enables portable, permanent storage on floppy disks.

Folder A storage area, represented on the screen by a picture of a paper file folder, used to store files or other folders.

Graphical user interface (GUI) A computer interface with which you interact with the computer through the use of graphics and point-and-click technology; GUIs show documents as they will look in their final form.

Hard drive A large disk drive inside your computer, also referred to as a Local Disk.

Horizontal scroll bar The bar at the bottom of a window that enables you to move left and right to view information that extends beyond the left and right edges of the screen.

Icon A graphic representation of an object that you can click to open that object.

Left pane In the My Computer window, a pane at the left that displays information and commonly used tools.

Local Disk A large disk drive inside your computer, also referred to as a hard disk.

Maximize To increase the size of a window to fill the screen.

Menu A list of commands within a category.

Menu bar The bar beneath the title bar that lists the names of menu categories.

Minimize Removing the window from the screen without closing it; minimized windows can be reopened by clicking the associated button in the taskbar.

Mouse pointer The arrow, I-beam, or other symbol that shows the location or position of the mouse on your screen; also called the pointer.

My Computer A window that gives you access to the files and folders on your computer.

Notification area The area on the right side of the taskbar that keeps you informed about processes that are occurring in the background, such as antivirus software, network connections, and other utility programs; also displays the time.

Operating system A set of instructions that coordinates the activities of your computer; Microsoft Windows XP is an operating system.

Paint A Windows program in which graphics are created or edited.

Pointer See mouse pointer.

Pointing Positioning the tip of the pointer in the center of an icon or other screen object.

Quick Launch toolbar An area to the right of the Start button that contains shortcut icons for commonly used programs.

Recycle Bin A storage area for files that have been deleted; files can be recovered from the Recycle Bin or permanently removed.

Restore Using the Restore Down button to return a window to the size it was before it was maximized.

Right-click The action of clicking the right mouse button.

ScreenTip A small box that displays useful information when you perform various mouse actions such as pointing to screen elements or dragging.

Scroll box The box in the vertical and horizontal scroll bars that can be dragged to reposition the document on the screen.

Shortcut menu A context-sensitive menu that displays commands and options relevant to the selected object.

Sizing handle A small square or circle in the corners and the middle of the sides of a graphic that can be used to increase or decrease the size of the graphic.

Start button The button on the left side of the taskbar that is used to start programs, change system settings, find Windows help, or shut down the computer.

Status area Another name for the notification area on the right side of the taskbar.

Submenu A second-level menu activated by selecting a menu option.

System tray Another name for the notification area on the right side of the taskbar.

Task pane A pane that opens on the side of a window that is used to display commonly used tools.

Taskbar The area of the screen that displays the Start button and the name of any open documents. The taskbar may also display shortcut buttons for other programs.

Thumb drive A small storage device that plugs into a computer USB port; also called a USB drive or a flash drive.

Thumbnail A miniature representation of the contents of a picture file.

Title bar Displays the program icon, the name of the document, and the name of the program. The Minimize, Maximize/Restore Down, and Close buttons are grouped on the right side of the title bar.

Toolbars Rows of buttons, usually located under a menu bar, from which you can perform commands using a single click.

USB drive A small storage device that plugs into a computer USB port; also called a thumb drive or a flash drive.

Vertical scroll bar The bar at the right side of a window that enables you to move up and down to view information that extends beyond the top and bottom of the screen.

Wildcard A character, such as an asterisk, that can be used to match any number of characters in a file search.

Window A box or screen that displays information or a program. Windows usually consist of title bars, toolbars, menu bars, and status bars. A window will always have a Minimize button and a Close button.

Windows When spelled with a capital *W*, refers to the operating system that runs your computer.

Wordpad A simple word processing program that comes with Windows XP.

Index

SINGLE PC LICENSE AGREEMENT AND LIMITED WARRANTY

READ THIS LICENSE CAREFULLY BEFORE OPENING THIS PACKAGE. BY OPENING THIS PACKAGE, YOU ARE AGREEING TO THE TERMS AND CONDITIONS OF THIS LICENSE. IF YOU DO NOT AGREE, DO NOT OPEN THE PACKAGE. PROMPTLY RETURN THE UNOPENED PACKAGE AND ALL ACCOMPANYING ITEMS TO THE PLACE YOU OBTAINED THEM. *THESE TERMS APPLY TO ALL LICENSED SOFTWARE ON THE DISK EXCEPT THAT THE TERMS FOR USE OF ANY SHAREWARE OR FREEWARE ON THE DISKETTES ARE AS SET FORTH IN THE ELECTRONIC LICENSE LOCATED ON THE DISK:*

1. GRANT OF LICENSE and OWNERSHIP: The enclosed computer programs ("Software") are licensed, not sold, to you by Prentice-Hall, Inc. ("We" or the "Company") and in consideration of your purchase or adoption of the accompanying Company textbooks and/or other materials, and your agreement to these terms. We reserve any rights not granted to you. You own only the disk(s) but we and/or our licensors own the Software itself. This license allows you to use and display your copy of the Software on a single computer (i.e., with a single CPU) at a single location for academic use only, so long as you comply with the terms of this Agreement. You may make one copy for back up, or transfer your copy to another CPU, provided that the Software is usable on only one computer.

2. RESTRICTIONS: You may not transfer or distribute the Software or documentation to anyone else. Except for backup, you may not copy the documentation or the Software. You may not network the Software or otherwise use it on more than one computer or computer terminal at the same time. You may not reverse engineer, disassemble, decompile, modify, adapt, translate, or create derivative works based on the Software or the Documentation. You may be held legally responsible for any copying or copyright infringement which is caused by your failure to abide by the terms of these restrictions.

3. TERMINATION: This license is effective until terminated. This license will terminate automatically without notice from the Company if you fail to comply with any provisions or limitations of this license. Upon termination, you shall destroy the Documentation and all copies of the Software. All provisions of this Agreement as to limitation and disclaimer of warranties, limitation of liability, remedies or damages, and our ownership rights shall survive termination.

4. DISCLAIMER OF WARRANTY: THE COMPANY AND ITS LICENSORS MAKE NO WARRANTIES ABOUT THE SOFTWARE, WHICH IS PROVIDED "AS-IS." IF THE DISK IS DEFECTIVE IN MATERIALS OR WORKMANSHIP, YOUR ONLY REMEDY IS TO RETURN IT TO THE COMPANY WITHIN 30 DAYS FOR REPLACEMENT UNLESS THE COMPANY DETERMINES IN GOOD FAITH THAT THE DISK HAS BEEN MISUSED OR IMPROPERLY INSTALLED, REPAIRED, ALTERED OR DAMAGED. THE COMPANY DISCLAIMS ALL WARRANTIES, EXPRESS OR IMPLIED, INCLUDING WITHOUT LIMITATION, THE IMPLIED WARRANTIES OF MERCHANTABILITY AND FITNESS FOR A PARTICULAR PURPOSE. THE COMPANY DOES NOT WARRANT, GUARANTEE OR MAKE ANY REPRESENTATION REGARDING THE ACCURACY, RELIABILITY, CURRENTNESS, USE, OR RESULTS OF USE, OF THE SOFTWARE.

5. LIMITATION OF REMEDIES AND DAMAGES: IN NO EVENT, SHALL THE COMPANY OR ITS EMPLOYEES, AGENTS, LICENSORS OR CONTRACTORS BE LIABLE FOR ANY INCIDENTAL, INDIRECT, SPECIAL OR CONSEQUENTIAL DAMAGES ARISING OUT OF OR IN CONNECTION WITH THIS LICENSE OR THE SOFTWARE, INCLUDING, WITHOUT LIMITATION, LOSS OF USE, LOSS OF DATA, LOSS OF INCOME OR PROFIT, OR OTHER LOSSES SUSTAINED AS A RESULT OF INJURY TO ANY PERSON, OR LOSS OF OR DAMAGE TO PROPERTY, OR CLAIMS OF THIRD PARTIES, EVEN IF THE COMPANY OR AN AUTHORIZED REPRESENTATIVE OF THE COMPANY HAS BEEN ADVISED OF THE POSSIBILITY OF SUCH DAMAGES. SOME JURISDICTIONS DO NOT ALLOW THE LIMITATION OF DAMAGES IN CERTAIN CIRCUMSTANCES, SO THE ABOVE LIMITATIONS MAY NOT ALWAYS APPLY.

6. GENERAL: THIS AGREEMENT SHALL BE CONSTRUED IN ACCORDANCE WITH THE LAWS OF THE UNITED STATES OF AMERICA AND THE STATE OF NEW YORK, APPLICABLE TO CONTRACTS MADE IN NEW YORK, AND SHALL BENEFIT THE COMPANY, ITS AFFILIATES AND ASSIGNEES. This Agreement is the complete and exclusive statement of the agreement between you and the Company and supersedes all proposals, prior agreements, oral or written, and any other communications between you and the company or any of its representatives relating to the subject matter. If you are a U.S. Government user, this Software is licensed with "restricted rights" as set forth in subparagraphs (a)-(d) of the Commercial Computer-Restricted Rights clause at FAR 52.227-19 or in subparagraphs (c)(1)(ii) of the Rights in Technical Data and Computer Software clause at DFARS 252.227-7013, and similar clauses, as applicable.

Should you have any questions concerning this agreement or if you wish to contact the Company for any reason, please contact in writing:

Multimedia Production
Higher Education Division
Prentice-Hall, Inc.
1 Lake Street
Upper Saddle River NJ 07458

Contents in Brief

Table of Contents

Excel 2007

Access 2007

Letter from the Editor

Dear Instructors and Students,

The primary goal of the *GO!* Series is two-fold. The first goal is to help instructors teach the course they want in less time. The second goal is to provide students with the skills to solve business problems using the computer as a tool, for both themselves and the organization for which they might be employed.

The *GO!* Series was originally created by Series Editor Shelley Gaskin and published with the release of Microsoft Office 2003. Her ideas came from years of using textbooks that didn't meet all the needs of today's diverse classroom and that were too confusing for students. Shelley continues to enhance the series by ensuring we stay true to our vision of developing quality instruction and useful classroom tools.

But we also need your input and ideas.

Over time, the *GO!* Series has evolved based on direct feedback from instructors and students using the series. *We are the publisher that listens.* To publish a textbook that works for you, it's critical that we continue to listen to this feedback. It's important to me to talk with you and hear your stories about using *GO!* Your voice can make a difference.

My hope is that this letter will inspire you to write me an e-mail and share your thoughts on using the *GO!* Series.

Stephanie Wall
Executive Editor, *GO!* Series
stephanie_wall@prenhall.com

GO! System Contributors

We thank the following people for their hard work and support in making the *GO!* System all that it is!

Additional Author Support

Bell, Susan	Mendocino College
Coyle, Diane	Montgomery County Community College
Fry, Susan	Boise State
Townsend, Kris	Spokane Falls Community College
Stroup, Tracey	Amgen Corporation

Instructor Resource Authors

Amer, Beverly	Northern Arizona University	Paterson, Jim	Paradise Valley Community College
Boito, Nancy	Harrisburg Area Community College	Prince, Lisa	Missouri State
Coyle, Diane	Montgomery County Community College	Rodgers, Gwen	Southern Nazarene University
Dawson, Tamara	Southern Nazarene University	Ruymann, Amy	Burlington Community College
Driskel, Loretta	Niagara County Community College	Ryan, Bob	Montgomery County Community College
Elliott, Melissa	Odessa College		
Fry, Susan	Boise State	Smith, Diane	Henry Ford Community College
Geoghan, Debra	Bucks County Community College	Spangler, Candice	Columbus State Community College
Hearn, Barbara	Community College of Philadelphia	Thompson, Joyce	Lehigh Carbon Community College
Jones, Stephanie	South Plains College	Tiffany, Janine	Reading Area Community College
Madsen, Donna	Kirkwood Community College	Watt, Adrienne	Douglas College
Meck, Kari	Harrisburg Area Community College	Weaver, Paul	Bossier Parish Community College
Miller, Cindy	Ivy Tech	Weber, Sandy	Gateway Technical College
Nowakowski, Tony	Buffalo State	Wood, Dawn	
Pace, Phyllis	Queensborough Community College	Weissman, Jonathan	Finger Lakes Community College

Super Reviewers

Brotherton, Cathy	Riverside Community College	Maurer, Trina	Odessa College
Cates, Wally	Central New Mexico Community College	Meck, Kari	Harrisburg Area Community College
		Miller, Cindy	Ivy Tech Community College
Cone, Bill	Northern Arizona University	Nielson, Phil	Salt Lake Community College
Coverdale, John	Riverside Community College	Rodgers, Gwen	Southern Nazarene University
Foster, Nancy	Baker College	Smolenski, Robert	Delaware Community College
Helfand, Terri	Chaffey College	Spangler, Candice	Columbus State Community College
Hibbert, Marilyn	Salt Lake Community College	Thompson, Joyce	Lehigh Carbon Community College
Holliday, Mardi	Community College of Philadelphia	Weber, Sandy	Gateway Technical College
Jerry, Gina	Santa Monica College	Wells, Lorna	Salt Lake Community College
Martin, Carol	Harrisburg Area Community College	Zaboski, Maureen	University of Scranton

Technical Editors

Janice Snyder
Joyce Nielsen
Colette Eisele
Janet Pickard
Mara Zebest
Lindsey Allen
William Daley
LeeAnn Bates

Student Reviewers

Allen, John	Asheville-Buncombe Tech Community College	Erickson, Mike	Ball State University
		Gadomski, Amanda	Northern Michigan University
Alexander, Steven	St. Johns River Community College	Gyselinck, Craig	Central Washington University
Alexander, Melissa	Tulsa Community College	Harrison, Margo	Central Washington University
Bolz, Stephanie	Northern Michigan University	Heacox, Kate	Central Washington University
Berner, Ashley	Central Washington University	Hill, Cheretta	Northwestern State University
Boomer, Michelle	Northern Michigan University	Innis, Tim	Tulsa Community College
Busse, Brennan	Northern Michigan University	Jarboe, Aaron	Central Washington University
Butkey, Maura	Central Washington University	Klein, Colleen	Northern Michigan University
Christensen, Kaylie	Northern Michigan University	Moeller, Jeffrey	Northern Michigan University
Connally, Brianna	Central Washington University	Nicholson, Regina	Athens Tech College
Davis, Brandon	Northern Michigan University	Niehaus, Kristina	Northern Michigan University
Davis, Christen	Central Washington University	Nisa, Zaibun	Santa Rosa Community College
Den Boer, Lance	Central Washington University	Nunez, Nohelia	Santa Rosa Community College
Dix, Jessica	Central Washington University	Oak, Samantha	Central Washington University
Moeller, Jeffrey	Northern Michigan University	Oertii, Monica	Central Washington University
Downs, Elizabeth	Central Washington University	Palenshus, Juliet	Central Washington University

Contributors continued

Pohl, Amanda	Northern Michigan University
Presnell, Randy	Central Washington University
Ritner, April	Northern Michigan University
Rodriguez, Flavia	Northwestern State University
Roberts, Corey	Tulsa Community College
Rossi, Jessica Ann	Central Washington University
Shafapay, Natasha	Central Washington University
Shanahan, Megan	Northern Michigan University
Teska, Erika	Hawaii Pacific University
Traub, Amy	Northern Michigan University
Underwood, Katie	Central Washington University
Walters, Kim	Central Washington University
Wilson, Kelsie	Central Washington University
Wilson, Amanda	Green River Community College

Series Reviewers

Abraham, Reni	Houston Community College
Agatston, Ann	Agatston Consulting Technical College
Alexander, Melody	Ball Sate University
Alejandro, Manuel	Southwest Texas Junior College
Ali, Farha	Lander University
Amici, Penny	Harrisburg Area Community College
Anderson, Patty A.	Lake City Community College
Andrews, Wilma	Virginia Commonwealth College, Nebraska University
Anik, Mazhar	Tiffin University
Armstrong, Gary	Shippensburg University
Atkins, Bonnie	Delaware Technical Community College
Bachand, LaDonna	Santa Rosa Community College
Bagui, Sikha	University of West Florida
Beecroft, Anita	Kwantlen University College
Bell, Paula	Lock Haven College
Belton, Linda	Springfield Tech. Community College
Bennett, Judith	Sam Houston State University
Bhatia, Sai	Riverside Community College
Bishop, Frances	DeVry Institute—Alpharetta (ATL)
Blaszkiewicz, Holly	Ivy Tech Community College/Region 1
Branigan, Dave	DeVry University
Bray, Patricia	Allegany College of Maryland
Brotherton, Cathy	Riverside Community College
Buehler, Lesley	Ohlone College
Buell, C	Central Oregon Community College
Byars, Pat	Brookhaven College
Byrd, Lynn	Delta State University, Cleveland, Mississippi
Cacace, Richard N.	Pensacola Junior College
Cadenhead, Charles	Brookhaven College
Calhoun, Ric	Gordon College
Cameron, Eric	Passaic Community College
Carriker, Sandra	North Shore Community College
Cannamore, Madie	Kennedy King
Carreon, Cleda	Indiana University—Purdue University, Indianapolis
Chaffin, Catherine	Shawnee State University
Chauvin, Marg	Palm Beach Community College, Boca Raton
Challa, Chandrashekar	Virginia State University
Chamlou, Afsaneh	NOVA Alexandria
Chapman, Pam	Wabaunsee Community College
Christensen, Dan	Iowa Western Community College
Clay, Betty	Southeastern Oklahoma State University
Collins, Linda D.	Mesa Community College
Conroy-Link, Janet	Holy Family College
Cosgrove, Janet	Northwestern CT Community
Courtney, Kevin	Hillsborough Community College
Cox, Rollie	Madison Area Technical College
Crawford, Hiram	Olive Harvey College
Crawford, Thomasina	Miami-Dade College, Kendall Campus
Credico, Grace	Lethbridge Community College
Crenshaw, Richard	Miami Dade Community College, North
Crespo, Beverly	Mt. San Antonio College
Crossley, Connie	Cincinnati State Technical Community College
Curik, Mary	Central New Mexico Community College
De Arazoza, Ralph	Miami Dade Community College
Danno, John	DeVry University/Keller Graduate School
Davis, Phillip	Del Mar College
DeHerrera, Laurie	Pikes Peak Community College
Delk, Dr. K. Kay	Seminole Community College
Doroshow, Mike	Eastfield College
Douglas, Gretchen	SUNYCortland
Dove, Carol	Community College of Allegheny
Driskel, Loretta	Niagara Community College
Duckwiler, Carol	Wabaunsee Community College
Duncan, Mimi	University of Missouri-St. Louis
Duthie, Judy	Green River Community College
Duvall, Annette	Central New Mexico Community College
Ecklund, Paula	Duke University
Eng, Bernice	Brookdale Community College
Evans, Billie	Vance-Granville Community College
Feuerbach, Lisa	Ivy Tech East Chicago
Fisher, Fred	Florida State University
Foster, Penny L.	Anne Arundel Community College
Foszcz, Russ	McHenry County College
Fry, Susan	Boise State University
Fustos, Janos	Metro State
Gallup, Jeanette	Blinn College
Gelb, Janet	Grossmont College
Gentry, Barb	Parkland College
Gerace, Karin	St. Angela Merici School
Gerace, Tom	Tulane University
Ghajar, Homa	Oklahoma State University
Gifford, Steve	Northwest Iowa Community College
Glazer, Ellen	Broward Community College
Gordon, Robert	Hofstra University
Gramlich, Steven	Pasco-Hernando Community College
Graviett, Nancy M.	St. Charles Community College, St. Peters, Missouri
Greene, Rich	Community College of Allegheny County
Gregoryk, Kerry	Virginia Commonwealth State
Griggs, Debra	Bellevue Community College
Grimm, Carol	Palm Beach Community College
Hahn, Norm	Thomas Nelson Community College
Hammerschlag, Dr. Bill	Brookhaven College
Hansen, Michelle	Davenport University
Hayden, Nancy	Indiana University—Purdue University, Indianapolis

Hayes, Theresa	Broward Community College	Lord, Alexandria	Asheville Buncombe Tech
Helfand, Terri	Chaffey College	Lowe, Rita	Harold Washington College
Helms, Liz	Columbus State Community College	Low, Willy Hui	Joliet Junior College
Hernandez, Leticia	TCI College of Technology	Lucas, Vickie	Broward Community College
Hibbert, Marilyn	Salt Lake Community College	Lynam, Linda	Central Missouri State University
Hoffman, Joan	Milwaukee Area Technical College	Lyon, Lynne	Durham College
Hogan, Pat	Cape Fear Community College	Lyon, Pat Rajski	Tomball College
Holland, Susan	Southeast Community College	MacKinnon, Ruth	Georgia Southern University
Hopson, Bonnie	Athens Technical College	Macon, Lisa	Valencia Community College, West Campus
Horvath, Carrie	Albertus Magnus College		
Horwitz, Steve	Community College of Philadelphia	Machuca, Wayne	College of the Sequoias
Hotta, Barbara	Leeward Community College	Madison, Dana	Clarion University
Howard, Bunny	St. Johns River Community	Maguire, Trish	Eastern New Mexico University
Howard, Chris	DeVry University	Malkan, Rajiv	Montgomery College
Huckabay, Jamie	Austin Community College	Manning, David	Northern Kentucky University
Hudgins, Susan	East Central University	Marcus, Jacquie	Niagara Community College
Hulett, Michelle J.	Missouri State University	Marghitu, Daniela	Auburn University
Hunt, Darla A.	Morehead State University, Morehead, Kentucky	Marks, Suzanne	Bellevue Community College
		Marquez, Juanita	El Centro College
Hunt, Laura	Tulsa Community College	Marquez, Juan	Mesa Community College
Jacob, Sherry	Jefferson Community College	Martyn, Margie	Baldwin-Wallace College
Jacobs, Duane	Salt Lake Community College	Marucco, Toni	Lincoln Land Community College
Jauken, Barb	Southeastern Community	Mason, Lynn	Lubbock Christian University
Johnson, Kathy	Wright College	Matutis, Audrone	Houston Community College
Johnson, Mary	Kingwood College	Matkin, Marie	University of Lethbridge
Johnson, Mary	Mt. San Antonio College	McCain, Evelynn	Boise State University
Jones, Stacey	Benedict College	McCannon, Melinda	Gordon College
Jones, Warren	University of Alabama, Birmingham	McCarthy, Marguerite	Northwestern Business College
Jordan, Cheryl	San Juan College	McCaskill, Matt L.	Brevard Community College
Kapoor, Bhushan	California State University, Fullerton	McClellan, Carolyn	Tidewater Community College
Kasai, Susumu	Salt Lake Community College	McClure, Darlean	College of Sequoias
Kates, Hazel	Miami Dade Community College, Kendall	McCrory, Sue A.	Missouri State University
		McCue, Stacy	Harrisburg Area Community College
Keen, Debby	University of Kentucky	McEntire-Orbach, Teresa	Middlesex County College
Keeter, Sandy	Seminole Community College	McLeod, Todd	Fresno City College
Kern-Blystone, Dorothy Jean	Bowling Green State	McManus, Illyana	Grossmont College
		McPherson, Dori	Schoolcraft College
Keskin, Ilknur	The University of South Dakota	Meiklejohn, Nancy	Pikes Peak Community College
Kirk, Colleen	Mercy College	Menking, Rick	Hardin-Simmons University
Kleckner, Michelle	Elon University	Meredith, Mary	University of Louisiana at Lafayette
Kliston, Linda	Broward Community College, North Campus	Mermelstein, Lisa	Baruch College
		Metos, Linda	Salt Lake Community College
Kochis, Dennis	Suffolk County Community College	Meurer, Daniel	University of Cincinnati
Kramer, Ed	Northern Virginia Community College	Meyer, Marian	Central New Mexico Community College
Laird, Jeff	Northeast State Community College	Miller, Cindy	Ivy Tech Community College, Lafayette, Indiana
Lamoureaux, Jackie	Central New Mexico Community College		
		Mitchell, Susan	Davenport University
Lange, David	Grand Valley State	Mohle, Dennis	Fresno Community College
LaPointe, Deb	Central New Mexico Community College	Monk, Ellen	University of Delaware
		Moore, Rodney	Holland College
Larson, Donna	Louisville Technical Institute	Morris, Mike	Southeastern Oklahoma State University
Laspina, Kathy	Vance-Granville Community College		
Le Grand, Dr. Kate	Broward Community College	Morris, Nancy	Hudson Valley Community College
Lenhart, Sheryl	Terra Community College	Moseler, Dan	Harrisburg Area Community College
Letavec, Chris	University of Cincinnati	Nabors, Brent	Reedley College, Clovis Center
Liefert, Jane	Everett Community College	Nadas, Erika	Wright College
Lindaman, Linda	Black Hawk Community College	Nadelman, Cindi	New England College
Lindberg, Martha	Minnesota State University	Nademlynsky, Lisa	Johnson & Wales University
Lightner, Renee	Broward Community College	Ncube, Cathy	University of West Florida
Lindberg, Martha	Minnesota State University	Nagengast, Joseph	Florida Career College
Linge, Richard	Arizona Western College	Newsome, Eloise	Northern Virginia Community College Woodbridge
Logan, Mary G.	Delgado Community College		
Loizeaux, Barbara	Westchester Community College	Nicholls, Doreen	Mohawk Valley Community College
Lopez, Don	Clovis-State Center Community College District	Nunan, Karen	Northeast State Technical Community College

Odegard, Teri	Edmonds Community College
Ogle, Gregory	North Community College
Orr, Dr. Claudia	Northern Michigan University South
Otieno, Derek	DeVry University
Otton, Diana Hill	Chesapeake College
Oxendale, Lucia	West Virginia Institute of Technology
Paiano, Frank	Southwestern College
Patrick, Tanya	Clackamas Community College
Peairs, Deb	Clark State Community College
Prince, Lisa	Missouri State University-Springfield Campus
Proietti, Kathleen	Northern Essex Community College
Pusins, Delores	HCCC
Raghuraman, Ram	Joliet Junior College
Reasoner, Ted Allen	Indiana University—Purdue
Reeves, Karen	High Point University
Remillard, Debbie	New Hampshire Technical Institute
Rhue, Shelly	DeVry University
Richards, Karen	Maplewoods Community College
Richardson, Mary	Albany Technical College
Rodgers, Gwen	Southern Nazarene University
Roselli, Diane	Harrisburg Area Community College
Ross, Dianne	University of Louisiana in Lafayette
Rousseau, Mary	Broward Community College, South
Samson, Dolly	Hawaii Pacific University
Sams, Todd	University of Cincinnati
Sandoval, Everett	Reedley College
Sardone, Nancy	Seton Hall University
Scafide, Jean	Mississippi Gulf Coast Community College
Scheeren, Judy	Westmoreland County Community College
Schneider, Sol	Sam Houston State University
Scroggins, Michael	Southwest Missouri State University
Sever, Suzanne	Northwest Arkansas Community College
Sheridan, Rick	California State University-Chico
Silvers, Pamela	Asheville Buncombe Tech
Singer, Steven A.	University of Hawai'i, Kapi'olani Community College
Sinha, Atin	Albany State University
Skolnick, Martin	Florida Atlantic University
Smith, T. Michael	Austin Community College
Smith, Tammy	Tompkins Cortland Community Collge
Smolenski, Bob	Delaware County Community College
Spangler, Candice	Columbus State
Stedham, Vicki	St. Petersburg College, Clearwater
Stefanelli, Greg	Carroll Community College
Steiner, Ester	New Mexico State University
Stenlund, Neal	Northern Virginia Community College, Alexandria
St. John, Steve	Tulsa Community College

Sterling, Janet	Houston Community College
Stoughton, Catherine	Laramie County Community College
Sullivan, Angela	Joliet Junior College
Szurek, Joseph	University of Pittsburgh at Greensburg
Tarver, Mary Beth	Northwestern State University
Taylor, Michael	Seattle Central Community College
Thangiah, Sam	Slippery Rock University
Thompson-Sellers, Ingrid	Georgia Perimeter College
Tomasi, Erik	Baruch College
Toreson, Karen	Shoreline Community College
Trifiletti, John J.	Florida Community College at Jacksonville
Trivedi, Charulata	Quinsigamond Community College, Woodbridge
Tucker, William	Austin Community College
Turgeon, Cheryl	Asnuntuck Community College
Turpen, Linda	Central New Mexico Community College
Upshaw, Susan	Del Mar College
Unruh, Angela	Central Washington University
Vanderhoof, Dr. Glenna	Missouri State University-Springfield Campus
Vargas, Tony	El Paso Community College
Vicars, Mitzi	Hampton University
Villarreal, Kathleen	Fresno
Vitrano, Mary Ellen	Palm Beach Community College
Volker, Bonita	Tidewater Community College
Wahila, Lori (Mindy)	Tompkins Cortland Community College
Waswick, Kim	Southeast Community College, Nebraska
Wavle, Sharon	Tompkins Cortland Community College
Webb, Nancy	City College of San Francisco
Wells, Barbara E.	Central Carolina Technical College
Wells, Lorna	Salt Lake Community College
Welsh, Jean	Lansing Community College Nebraska
White, Bruce	Quinnipiac University
Willer, Ann	Solano Community College
Williams, Mark	Lane Community College
Wilson, Kit	Red River College
Wilson, Roger	Fairmont State University
Wimberly, Leanne	International Academy of Design and Technology
Worthington, Paula	Northern Virginia Community College
Yauney, Annette	Herkimer County Community College
Yip, Thomas	Passaic Community College
Zavala, Ben	Webster Tech
Zlotow, Mary Ann	College of DuPage
Zudeck, Steve	Broward Community College, North

About the Authors

Shelley Gaskin, Series Editor, is a professor of business and computer technology at Pasadena City College in Pasadena, California. She holds a master's degree in business education from Northern Illinois University and a doctorate in adult and community education from Ball State University. Dr. Gaskin has 15 years of experience in the computer industry with several Fortune 500 companies and has developed and written training materials for custom systems applications in both the public and private sector. She is also the author of books on Microsoft Outlook and word processing.

Robert L. Ferrett recently retired as the director of the Center for Instructional Computing at Eastern Michigan University, where he provided computer training and support to faculty. He has authored or co-authored more than 70 books on Access, PowerPoint, Excel, Publisher, WordPerfect, and Word. Before writing for the GO! Series, Bob was a series editor and author for the Learn Series. He has a bachelor's degree in psychology, a master's degree in geography, and a master's degree in interdisciplinary technology from Eastern Michigan University. Bob's doctoral studies were in instructional technology at Wayne State University. For fun, Bob teaches a four-week computers and genealogy class and has written genealogy and local history books.

Alicia Vargas is a faculty member in Business Information Technology at Pasadena City College. She holds a master's and a bachelor's degree in business education from California State University, Los Angeles, and has authored several textbooks and training manuals on Microsoft Word, Microsoft Excel, and Microsoft PowerPoint.

Carolyn McLellan is the Dean of the Division of Information Technology and Business at Tidewater Community College in Virginia Beach, Virginia. She has an M.A. degree in Secondary Education from Regent University and a B.S. degree in Business Education from Old Dominion University. She taught for Norfolk Public Schools for 17 years in Business Education and served as a faculty member at Tidewater Community College for eight years teaching networking, where she developed over 23 new courses and earned the Microsoft Certified Trainer and Microsoft Certified System Engineer industry certifications. In addition to teaching, Carolyn loves to play volleyball, boogie board at the beach, bicycle, crochet, cook, and read.

Visual Walk-Through of the *GO!* System

The *GO!* System is designed for ease of implementation on the instructor side and ease of understanding on the student. It has been completely developed based on professor and student feedback.

The *GO!* System is divided into three categories that reflect how you might organize your course—**Prepare**, **Teach**, and **Assess**.

Prepare

Syllabus Template

Includes course calendar planner for 8-, 12-, and 16-week formats.

GO! with Microsoft® Office 2007 Introductory, 3e

GO! with Microsoft® Office 2007 Introductory, 3e
SAMPLE SYLLABUS (8 weeks)

I. COURSE INFORMATION

Course No.:	Semester:
Course Title:	Credits:
Course Hours:	
Instructor:	Office:
Office Hours:	
Email:	Phone:

II. TEXT AND MATERIALS

Before starting the course, you will need the following:

> *GO!* with Microsoft® Office 2007 Introductory, 3e by Shelley Gaskin, Robert L. Ferrett, Alicia Vargas, and Suzanne Marks ©2010, published by Pearson Prentice Hall. ISBN 0-13-505923-2

> Storage device for saving files (any of the following: multiple diskettes, CD-RW, flash drive, etc.)

III. WHAT YOU WILL LEARN IN THIS COURSE

This is a hands-on course in which you will learn to use a computer to practice the four most popular programs within the Microsoft Office Suite (Word, Excel, Access, and PowerPoint). You will learn to be an intermediate level user of the Microsoft Office Suite.

Within the Microsoft Office Suite, you will use Word, Excel, Access, and PowerPoint. Microsoft Word is a word processing program with which you can create common business and personal documents. Microsoft Excel is a spreadsheet program that organizes and calculates accounting-type information. Microsoft Access is a database program that organizes large amounts of information in a useful manner. Finally, Microsoft PowerPoint is a presentation graphics program with which you can develop slides to accompany an oral presentation.

Assignment Sheet

One per chapter. Lists all possible assignments; add to and delete from this simple Word table according to your course plan.

GO! with Microsoft® Office 2007 Introductory, 3e

Assignment Sheet for GO! with Microsoft® Office 2007 Introductory, 3e
Chapter 5 Word

Instructor Name: _____
Course Information: _____

Do This (✓ when done)	Then Hand in This Check each Project for the elements listed on the Assignment Tag. Attach the Tag to your Project.	By This Date	Possible Points	Your Points
Study the text and perform the steps for Activities 5.1 – 5.11	Project 5A Application Letter			
Study the text and perform the steps for Activities 5.12 – 5.23	Project 5B Company Overview			
End-of-Chapter Assessments				
Complete the Matching and Fill-in-the-Blank questions	As directed by your instructor			
Complete Project 5C	Project 5C Receipt Letter			
Complete Project 5D	Project 5D Marketing			
Complete Project 5E	Project 5E Contract			
Complete Project 5F	Project 5F Invitation			
Complete Project 5G	Project 5G Fax Cover			
Complete Project 5H	Project 5H Approval Letter			
Complete Project 5I	Project 5I Services			
Complete Project 5J	Project 5J Survey Form			
Complete Project 5K	Project 5K Holidays			
Complete Project 5L	Project 5L School Tour			
Complete Project 5M	Project 5M Scouting Trip			

Copyright © 2010 Pearson Education, Inc. Publishing as Prentice Hall   Page 1 of 1

Student Data Files

Music School Records discovers, launches, and and develops the careers of young artists in classical, jazz, and contemporary music. Our philosophy is to not only shape, distribute, and sell a music product, but to help artists create a career that can lats a lifetime. too often in the music industry, artists are forced to fit their music to a trend that is short-lived. Music School Records doesn't just follow trends, we take a long-term view of the music industry and help our artists develop a style and repertiore that is fluid and flexible and that will appeal to audiences for years and even decades.

The music industry is constantly changing, but over the last decade the changes have been enormous. New forms of entertainment such as DVDs, video games, and the Internet mean there are more competition for the leisure dollar in the market. New technologies give consomers more options for buying and listening to music, and they are demanding high quality recordings. Young consomers are comfortable with technology and want the music they love when and where they want it, no matter where they are or what they are doing.

Music School Records embraces new technologies and the sophisticated market of young music lovers. We believe that providing high quality recordings of truly talented artists make for more discerning listeners who will cherish the gift of music for the rest of their lives. The expertise of Music School Records includes:

- Insight into our target market and the ability to reach the desired audience
- The ability to access all current sources of music income
- A management team with years of experience in music commerce
- Innovative business strategies and artist development plans
- Investment in technology infrastructure for high quality recordings and business services
- Initiative and proactive management of artist careers

PowerPoint Slides

PowerPoint Presentation to Accompany
GO! with Microsoft® Office 2007
Introductory, 3e

Chapter 5
Creating Documents with Microsoft Word 2007

Teach

Student Textbook

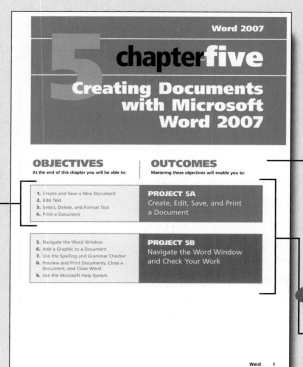

Word 2007

5 chapterfive

Creating Documents with Microsoft Word 2007

OBJECTIVES
At the end of this chapter you will be able to:

1. Create and Save a New Document
2. Edit Text
3. Select, Delete, and Format Text
4. Print a Document

5. Navigate the Word Window
6. Add a Graphic to a Document
7. Use the Spelling and Grammar Checker
8. Preview and Print Documents, Close a Document, and Close Word
9. Use the Microsoft Help System

OUTCOMES
Mastering these objectives will enable you to:

PROJECT 5A
Create, Edit, Save, and Print a Document

PROJECT 5B
Navigate the Word Window and Check Your Work

Word   1

Learning Objectives and Student Outcomes
Objectives are clustered around projects that result in student outcomes. They help students learn how to solve problems, not just learn software features.

Project-Based Instruction
Students do not practice features of the application; they create real projects that they will need in the real world. Projects are color coded for easy reference and are named to reflect skills the students will be practicing.

NEW

A and B Projects
Each chapter contains two instructional projects—A and B.

Music School Records

Music School Records was created to launch young musical artists with undiscovered talent in jazz, classical, and contemporary music. The creative management team searches internationally for talented young people, and has a reputation for mentoring and developing the skills of its artists. The company's music is tailored to an audience that is young, knowledgeable about music, and demands the highest quality recordings. Music School Records releases are available in CD format as well as digital downloads.

© Steve Mercer / Getty Images, Inc.—Taxi

Getting Started with Microsoft Office Word 2007

A word processor is the most common program found on personal computers and one that almost everyone has a reason to use. When you learn word processing you are also learning skills and techniques that you need to work efficiently on a personal computer. You can use Microsoft Word to perform basic word processing tasks such as writing a memo, a report, or a letter. You can also use Word to complete complex word processing tasks, such as creating sophisticated tables, embedding graphics, and linking to other documents and the Internet. Word is a program that you can learn gradually, and then add more advanced skills one at a time.

Each chapter opens with a story that sets the stage for the projects the student will create; the instruction does not force the student to pretend to be someone or make up a scenario.

Each chapter has an introductory paragraph that briefs students on what is important.

Visual Summary

Shows students upfront what their projects will look like when they are done.

Project Summary

Stated clearly and quickly in one paragraph.

NEW

File Guide

Clearly shows students which files are needed for the project and the names they will use to save their documents.

Objective

The skills the student will learn are clearly stated at the beginning of each project and color coded to match projects listed on the chapter opener page.

Teachable Moment

Expository text is woven into the steps—at the moment students need to know it—not chunked together in a block of text that will go unread.

NEW

Screen Shots

Larger screen shots.

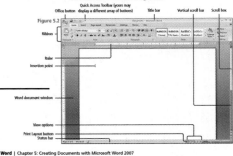

Steps

Color coded to the current project, easy to read, and not too many to confuse the student or too few to be meaningless.

GO! Sequential Pagination

No more confusing letters and abbreviations.

GO! Microsoft Procedural Syntax

All steps are written in Microsoft Procedural Syntax to put the student in the right place at the right time.

End-of-Project Icon

All projects in the *GO! Series* have clearly identifiable end points, useful in self-paced or on-line environments.

---

[8] Press **Enter** two more times.

In a business letter, insert two blank lines between the date and the inside address, which is the same as the address you would use on an envelope.

[9] Type **Mr. William Hawken** and then press **Enter**.

The wavy red line under the proper name *Hawken* indicates that the word has been flagged as misspelled because it is a word not contained in the Word dictionary.

[10] On two lines, type the following address, but do not press **Enter** at the end of the second line:

123 Eighth Street
Harrisville, MI 48740

Note — Typing the Address

Include a comma after the city name in an inside address. However, for mailing addresses on envelopes, eliminate the comma after the city name.

[11] On the **Home tab**, in the **Styles group**, click the **Normal** button.

The Normal style is applied to the text in the rest of the document. Recall that the Normal style adds extra space between paragraphs; it also adds slightly more space between lines in a paragraph.

[12] Press **Enter**. Type **Dear William:** and then press **Enter**.

This salutation is the line that greets the person receiving the letter.

[13] Type **Subject: Your Application to Music School Records** and press **Enter**.

Notice the light dots between words, which indicate spaces and display when formatting marks are displayed. Also, notice the extra space after each paragraph, and then compare your screen with Figure 5.6.

The subject line is optional, but you should include a subject line in most letters to identify the topic. Depending on your Word settings, a wavy green line may display in the subject line, indicating a potential grammar error.

Note — Space Between Lines in Your Printed Document

The Cambria font, and many others, uses a slightly larger space between the lines than more traditional fonts like Times New Roman. As you progress in your study of Word, you will use many different fonts and also adjust the spacing between lines.

[14] From the **Office** menu, click **Close**, saving any changes if prompted to do so. Leave Word open for the next project.

Another Way — **To Print a Document**

To Print a document:

- From the Office menu, click Print to display the Print dialog box (to be covered later), from which you can choose a variety of different options, such as printing multiple copies, printing on a different printer, and printing some but not all pages.
- Hold down **Ctrl** and then press **P**. This is an alternative to the Office menu command, and opens the Print dialog box.
- Hold down **Alt**, press **F**, and then press **P**. This opens the Print dialog box.

End You have completed Project 5A

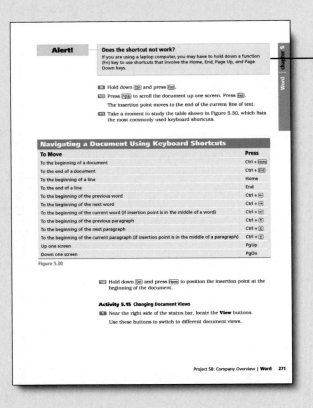

Alert box

Draws students' attention to make sure they aren't getting too far off course.

Another Way box

Shows students other ways of doing tasks.

More Knowledge box

Expands on a topic by going deeper into the material.

Note box

Points out important items to remember.

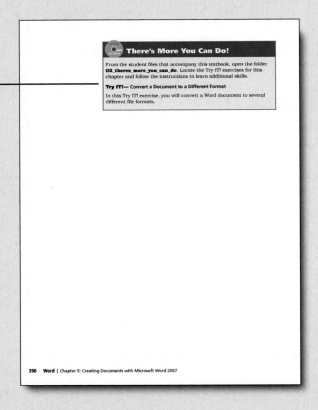

NEW

There's More You Can Do!

Try IT! exercises that teach students additional skills.

End-of-Chapter Material

Take your pick! Content-based or Outcomes-based projects to choose from. Below is a table outlining the various types of projects that fit into these two categories.

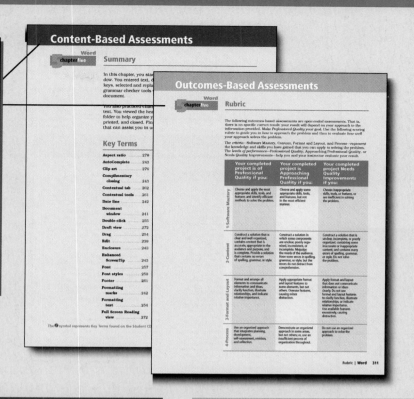

Content-Based Assessments

(Defined solutions with solution files provided for grading)

Project Letter	Name	Objectives Covered
N/A	Summary and Key Terms	
N/A	Multiple Choice	
N/A	Fill-in-the-blank	
C	Skills Review	Covers A Objectives
D	Skills Review	Covers B Objectives
E	Mastering Excel	Covers any combination of A and B Objectives
F	Mastering Excel	Covers any combination of A and B Objectives
G	Mastering Excel A and B Objectives	Covers any combination of
H	GO! Fix It A and B Objectives	Covers any combination of

Outcomes-Based Assessments

(Open solutions that require a rubric for grading)

Project Letter	Name	Objectives Covered
N/A	Rubric	
I	Problem Solving from A and B as possible	Covers as many Objectives
J	Problem Solving from A and B as possible.	Covers as many Objectives
K	Problem Solving from A and B as possible.	Covers as many Objectives

More on your Student CD

Project Letter	Name	Objectives Covered
Content-Based Assessments		
L	Mastering Excel	Covers A Objectives
M	Mastering Excel	Covers B Objectives
N	Business Running Case	Covers all A and B Objectives
Outcomes-Based Assessments		
O	Problem Solving	Covers as many Objectives from A and B as possible
P	Problem Solving	Covers as many Objectives from A and B as possible
Q	You and GO!	Covers as many Objectives from A and B as possible
R	GO! with Help	Not tied to specific Objectives
S	* Group Business Running Case	Covers A and B Objectives

* This project is provided only with the *GO! with Microsoft Office 2007 Introductory* book.

Objectives List

Most projects in the end-of-chapter section begin with a list of the objectives covered.

End of Each Project Clearly Marked

Clearly identified end points help separate the end-of-chapter projects.

NEW

Rubric

A matrix that states the criteria and standards for grading student work. Used to grade open-ended assessments.

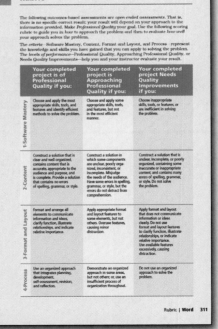

Content-Based Assessments

chapter five — Skills Review

Project 5C — Receipt Letter

In this project, you will apply the skills you practiced from the Objectives in Project 5A.

Objectives: 1. Create and Save a New Document; **2.** Edit Text; **3.** Select, Delete, and Format Text; **4.** Print a Document.

In this Skills Review, you will create and edit a follow-up letter ...erssen, a production manager for Music School Records, ...en, a recording artist who has submitted a demo CD ...on. Your completed letter will look similar to the one 5.49.

5C, you will need the following file:

...document

...ter_Firstname_Lastname

Content-Based Assessments

chapter five — Skills Review

(Project 5C—Receipt Letter continued)

14. Save the changes you have made to your document. Press Ctrl + A to select the entire document. On the **Home tab**, in the **Font group**, click the **Font button arrow**. Scroll as necessary, and watch Live Preview change the document font as you point to different font names. Click to choose **Tahoma**. Recall that you can type *T* in the Font box to move quickly to the fonts beginning with that letter. Click anywhere in the document to cancel the selection.

15. Select the entire first line of text—*Music School Records*. On the Mini toolbar, click the **Font button arrow**, and then click **Arial Black**. With the Mini toolbar still displayed, click the **Font Size button arrow**, and then click **20**. With the Mini toolbar still displayed, click the **Bold** button.

16. Select the second, third, and fourth lines of text, beginning with *2620 Vine Street* and ending with the telephone number. On the Mini toolbar, click the **Font Size button arrow**, and then click **Arial**. With the Mini toolbar still displayed, click the **Font Size button arrow**, and then click **10**. With the Mini toolbar still displayed, click the **Italic** button.

17. In the paragraph beginning *Your demonstration*, select the text *Music School Records*. On the Mini toolbar, click the **Italic** button, and then click anywhere to deselect the text.

18. Click the **Insert tab**. In the **Header & Footer group**, click the **Footer** button,

and then click **Edit Footer**. On the **Design tab**, in the **Insert group**, click the **Quick Parts** button, and then click **Field**. In the **Field** dialog box, under **Field names**, scroll down and click to choose **FileName**, and then click **OK**. Double-click anywhere in the document to leave the footer area.

19. Click the **Page Layout tab**. In the **Page Setup group**, click the **Margins** button to display the Margins gallery. At the bottom of the **Margins gallery**, click **Custom Margins** to display the **Page Setup** dialog box. Near the top of the **Page Setup** dialog box, click the **Layout tab**. Under **Page**, click the **Vertical alignment arrow**, click **Center**, and then click **OK**.

20. From the **Office** menu, point to the **Print arrow**, and then click **Print Preview** to make a final check of your letter. Follow your instructor's directions for submitting this file. Check your *Chapter Assignment Sheet* or *Course Syllabus* or consult your instructor to determine if you are to submit your assignments on paper or electronically. To submit electronically, go to Step 22, and then follow the instructions provided by your instructor.

21. On the **Print Preview tab**, in the **Print group**, click the **Print** button. Collect your printout from the printer and submit it as directed.

22. From the **Office** menu, click **Exit Word**, saving any changes if prompted to do so.

End You have completed Project 5C ——————

(...ript Letter continues on the next page)

...osoft Word 2007

Outcomes-Based Assessments

chapter five — Rubric

The following outcomes-based assessments are *open-ended assessments*. That is, there is no specific correct result; your result will depend on your approach to the information provided. Make *Professional Quality* your goal. Use the following scoring rubric to guide you in how to approach the problem and then to evaluate how well your approach solves the problem.

The *criteria*—Software Mastery, Content, Format and Layout, and Process—represent the knowledge and skills you have gained that you can apply to solving the problem. The *levels of performance*—Professional Quality, Approaching Professional Quality, or Needs Quality Improvements—help you and your instructor evaluate your result.

	Your completed project is of Professional Quality if you:	Your completed project is Approaching Professional Quality if you:	Your completed project Needs Quality Improvements if you:
1-Software Mastery	Choose and apply the most appropriate skills, tools, and features and identify efficient methods to solve the problem.	Choose and apply some appropriate skills, tools, and features, but not in the most efficient manner.	Choose inappropriate skills, tools, or features, or are inefficient in solving the problem.
2-Content	Construct a solution that is clear and well organized, contains content that is accurate, appropriate to the audience and purpose, and is complete. Provide a solution that contains no errors of spelling, grammar, or style.	Construct a solution in which some components are unclear, poorly organized, inconsistent, or incomplete. Misjudge the needs of the audience. Have some errors in spelling, grammar, or style, but the errors do not detract from comprehension.	Construct a solution that is unclear, incomplete, or poorly organized, containing some inaccurate or inappropriate content, and contains many errors of spelling, grammar, or style. Do not solve the problem.
3-Format and Layout	Format and arrange all elements to communicate information and ideas, clarify function, illustrate relationships, and indicate relative importance.	Apply appropriate format and layout features to some elements, but not others. Overuse features, causing minor distraction.	Apply format and layout that does not communicate information or ideas clearly. Do not use format and layout features to clarify function, illustrate relationships, or indicate relative importance. Use available features excessively, causing distraction.
4-Process	Use an organized approach that integrates planning, development, self-assessment, revision, and reflection.	Demonstrate an organized approach in some areas, but not others; or use an insufficient process of organization throughout.	Do not use an organized approach to solve the problem.

Student CD includes:

- Student Data Files
- There's More You Can Do!
- Additional End-of-Chapter Pages

NEW

Podcasts

Videos that reinforce some of the more difficult topics in Microsoft Office 2007.

Companion Web site

An interactive Web site to further student leaning. Contains objective-style questions to help students study.

Annotated Instructor Edition

The Annotated Instructor Edition contains a full version of the student textbook that includes tips, supplement references, and pointers on teaching with the *GO!* instructional system.

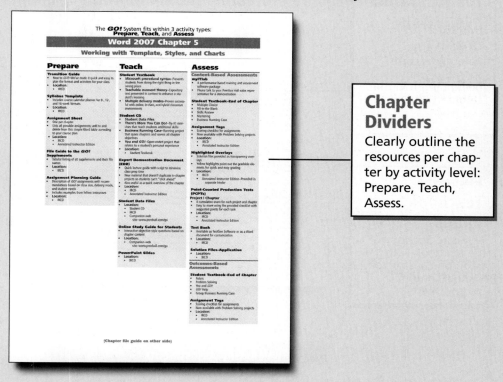

Chapter Dividers

Clearly outline the resources per chapter by activity level: Prepare, Teach, Assess.

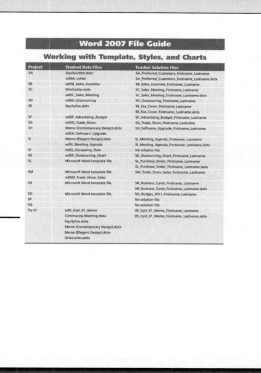

Instructor File Guide

Complete list of all Student Data Files and instructor Solution Files needed for the chapter.

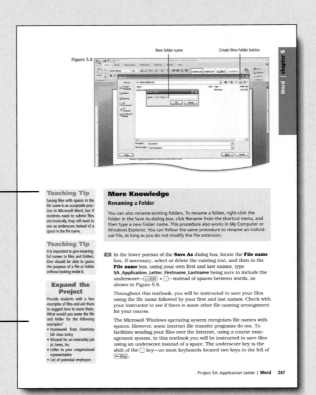

Helpful Hints, Teaching Tips, Expand the Project

References correspond to what is being taught in the student textbook.

NEW

Full-Size Textbook Pages

An instructor copy of the textbook with traditional Instructor Manual content incorporated.

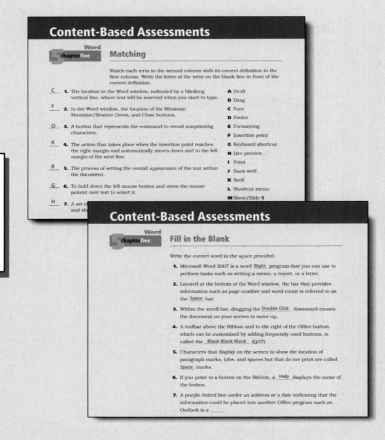

End-of-Chapter Concepts Assessments

contain the answers for quick reference.

Assignment Tags

Scoring checklist for assignments. Now also available for Problem-Solving projects.

NEW

GO! with Microsoft® Office 2007

Assignment Tags for GO! with Office 2007
Word Chapter 5

Name:	Course:		
Professor:			
Project: 5A_Application_Letter			
Task	**Points**	**Your Score**	
Center text vertically on page	2		
Delete the word "really"	1		
Delete the words "try to"	1		
Replace "last" with "first"	1		
Insert the word "potential"	1		
Replace "John W. Diamond" with "Lucy Burroughs"	2		
Change entire document to the Cambria font	2		
Change the first line of text to Arial Black 20 pt. font	2		
Bold and underline the first line of text	2		
Change the 2nd through 4th lines to Arial 10 pt.	2		
Italicize the 2nd through 4th lines of text	2		
Correct/Add footer as instructed	2		
Total Points	**20**	**0**	

Name:		Project:	5B
Professor:		Course:	
Task		**Points**	**Your Score**
Insert the file w05B_Music_School_Records		4	
Insert the Music Logo		4	
Remove duplicate "and"		2	
Change spelling and grammar errors (4)		8	
Correct/Add footer as instructed		2	
Circled information is incorrect or formatted incorrectly			
Total Points		**20**	**0**

Name:		Project:	5C
Professor:		Course:	
Task		**Points**	**Your Score**
Add four line letterhead		2	
Insert today's date		1	
Add address block, subject line, and greeting		2	
Add two-paragraph body of letter		2	
Add closing, name, and title		2	
In subject line, capitalize "receipt"		1	
Change "standards" to "guidelines"		1	
Insert "quite"		1	
Insert "all"		1	
Change the first line of text to Arial Black 20 pt. font		2	
Bold the first line of text		1	
Change the 2nd through 4th lines to Arial 10 pt.		1	
Italicize the 2nd through 4th lines of text		1	
Correct/add footer as instructed		2	
Circled information is incorrect or formatted incorrectly			
Total Points		**20**	**0**

Name:		Project:	5D
Professor:		Course:	
Task		**Points**	**Your Score**
Insert the file w05D_Marketing		4	
Bold the first two title lines		2	
Correct spelling of "Marketting"		2	
Correct spelling of "geners"		2	
Correct all misspellings of "allready"		2	
Correct grammar error "are" to "is"		2	
Insert the Piano image		4	
Correct/add footer as instructed		2	
Circled information is incorrect or formatted incorrectly			
Total Points		**20**	**0**

Highlighted Overlays

Solution files provided as electronic files. Yellow highlights point out the gradable elements for quick and easy grading.

Music School Records

20 point Arial Black, bold and underline

2620 Vine Street
Los Angeles, CA 90028
323-555-0028

10 point Arial, italic

September 12, 2009

Mr. William Hawken
123 Eighth Street
Harrisville, MI 48740

Text vertically centered on page

Body of document changed to Cambria font, 11 point

Dear William:

Subject: Your Application to Music School Records

Thank you for submitting your application to Music School Records. Our talent scout for Northern Michigan, Catherine McDonald, is very enthusiastic about your music, and the demo CD you submitted certainly confirms her opinion.

Word "really" deleted

We discuss our applications from potential clients during the first week of each month. We will have a decision for you by the second week of October.

Words "try to" deleted

Yours Truly,

Lucy Burroughs

Point-Counted Production Tests (PCPTs)

A cumulative exam for each **project**, **chapter**, and **application**. Easy to score using the provided checklist with suggested points for each task.

GO! with Microsoft® Office 2007 Introductory, 3e

Point-Counted Production Test—Project
for GO! with Microsoft® Office 2007 Introductory, 3e
Project 5A Word

Instructor Name: _____
Course Information: _____

1. Start Word 2007 to begin a new, blank document. Save your document as 5A_Cover_Letter_Firstname_Lastname. Remember to save your file frequently as you work.

2. If necessary, display the formatting marks. With the insertion point blinking in the upper left corner of the document to the left of the default first paragraph mark, type the current date (you can use AutoComplete).

3. Skip two lines, then type the inside address block (single-spaced):

   Music School Records
   2620 Vine Street
   Los Angeles, CA 90028

4. Skip two lines, then type Dear Ms. Burroughs:

   Skip one line, then type Subject: Application to Music School Records

   Skip one line, then type the following text:

   I read about Music School Records in Con Brio magazine and I would like to inquire about the possibility of being represented by your company.

   I am very interested in a career in jazz and am planning to relocate to the Los Angeles area in the very near future. I would be interested in learning more about the company and about available opportunities.

   I was a member of my high school jazz band for three years. In addition, I have been playing in the local coffee shop for the last two years. My demo CD, which is enclosed, contains three of my most requested songs.

   I would appreciate the opportunity to speak with you. Thank you for your time and consideration. I look forward to speaking with you about this exciting opportunity.

5. Skip two lines, then type the closing Sincerely, Skip three lines and type your name.

6. Insert a footer that contains the file name.

7. Delete the first instance of the word very in the second body paragraph, and insert the word modern in front of jazz.

Copyright © 2010 Pearson Education, Inc. Publishing as Prentice Hall   Page 1 of 1

Test Bank

Available as TestGen Software or as a Word document for customization.

Chapter 5: Creating Documents with Microsoft Word 2007

Multiple Choice:

1. With word processing programs, how are documents stored?

   A. On a network

   B. On the computer

   C. Electronically

   D. On the floppy disk

Answer: C   **Reference:** Objective 1: Create and Save a New Document   **Difficulty:** Moderate

2. Because you will see the document as it will print, _____ view is the ideal view to use when learning Microsoft Word 2007.

   A. Reading

   B. Normal

   C. Print Layout

   D. Outline

Answer: C   **Reference:** Objective 1: Create and Save a New Document   **Difficulty:** Moderate

3. The blinking vertical line where text or graphics will be inserted is called the:

   A. cursor.

   B. insertion point.

   C. blinking line.

   D. I-beam.

Answer: B   **Reference:** Objective 1: Create and Save a New Document   **Difficulty:** Easy

**Solution Files–
Application
and PDF
format**

Music School Records

Music School Records discovers, launches, and develops the careers of young artists in classical, jazz,
and contemporary music. Our philosophy is to not only shape, distribute, and sell a music product, but
to help artists create a career that can last a lifetime. Too often in the music industry, artists are forced
to fit their music to a trend that is short-lived. Music School Records does not just follow trends, we take
a long-term view of the music industry and help our artists develop a style and repertoire that is fluid
and flexible and that will appeal to audiences for years and even decades.

The music industry is constantly changing, but over the last decade, the changes have been
enormous. New forms of entertainment such as DVDs, video games, and the Internet mean there is
more competition for the leisure dollar in the market. New technologies give consumers more options
for buying and listening to music, and they are demanding high quality recordings. Young consumers are
comfortable with technology and want the music they love when and where they want it, no matter
where they are or what they are doing.

Music School Records embraces new technologies and the sophisticated market of young music
lovers. We believe that providing high quality recordings of truly talented artists make for more
discerning listeners who will cherish the gift of music for the rest of their lives. The expertise of Music
School Records includes:

- Insight into our target market and the ability to reach the desired audience
- The ability to access all current sources of music income
- A management team with years of experience in music commerce
- Innovative business strategies and artist development plans
- Investment in technology infrastructure for high quality recordings and business services

pagexxxix_top.docx

Online Assessment and Training

my**it**lab is Prentice Hall's new performance-based solution that allows you
to easily deliver outcomes-based courses on Microsoft Office 2007, with
customized training and defensible assessment. Key features of my**it**lab
include:

A *true* "system" approach: my**it**lab content is the same as in your
textbook.
Project-based *and* skills-based: Students complete real-life assignments.
Advanced reporting *and* gradebook: These include student click
stream data.
***No* installation required:** my**it**lab is completely Web-based. You just need
an Internet connection, small plug-in, and Adobe Flash Player.

Ask your Prentice Hall sales representative for a demonstration or visit:

www.prenhall.com/myitlab

Students and Instructors – **To better meet your needs, we have removed Chapters 1–4 (identified below) from this textbook and have made them available as individual textbooks.**

For this reason, this textbook starts with Chapter 5.

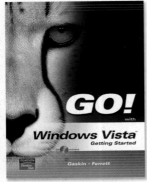

GO! with Windows Vista™ Getting Started
978-0-13-614097-9

GO! with Microsoft® Outlook 2007 Getting Started
978-0-13-225617-9

GO! with Internet Explorer® 7.0 Getting Started
978-0-13-157244-7

GO! with Basic Computer Concepts Getting Started
978-0-13-232793-0

5

chapterfive

Creating Documents with Microsoft Word 2007

OBJECTIVES

At the end of this chapter you will be able to:

1. Create and Save a New Document
2. Edit Text
3. Select, Delete, and Format Text
4. Print a Document

5. Navigate the Word Window
6. Add a Graphic to a Document
7. Use the Spelling and Grammar Checker
8. Preview and Print Documents, Close a Document, and Close Word
9. Use the Microsoft Help System

OUTCOMES

Mastering these objectives will enable you to:

PROJECT 5A
Create, Edit, Save, and Print a Document

PROJECT 5B
Navigate the Word Window and Check Your Work

Music School Records

Music School Records was created to launch young musical artists with undiscovered talent in jazz, classical, and contemporary music. The creative management team searches internationally for talented young people, and has a reputation for mentoring and developing the skills of its artists. The company's music is tailored to an audience that is young, knowledgeable about music, and demands the highest quality recordings. Music School Records releases are available in CD format as well as digital downloads.

© Steve Mercer / Getty Images, Inc.—Taxi

Getting Started with Microsoft Office Word 2007

A word processor is the most common program found on personal computers and one that almost everyone has a reason to use. When you learn word processing you are also learning skills and techniques that you need to work efficiently on a personal computer. You can use Microsoft Word to perform basic word processing tasks such as writing a memo, a report, or a letter. You can also use Word to complete complex word processing tasks, such as creating sophisticated tables, embedding graphics, and linking to other documents and the Internet. Word is a program that you can learn gradually, and then add more advanced skills one at a time.

Project 5A **Application Letter**

In Activities 5.01 through 5.11, you will create and make changes to a letter from Lucy Burroughs, Vice President of Creative Development, to William Hawken, an artist interested in becoming a client of Music School Records. Your completed document will look similar to Figure 5.1.

For Project 5A, you will need the following file:

New blank Word document

You will save your document as
5A_Application_Letter_Firstname_Lastname

Music School Records
2620 Vine Street
Los Angeles, CA 90028
323-555-0028

September 12, 2009

Mr. William Hawken
123 Eighth Street
Harrisville, MI 48740

Dear William:

Subject: Your Application to Music School Records

Thank you for submitting your application to Music School Records. Our talent scout for Northern Michigan, Catherine McDonald, is very enthusiastic about your music, and the demo CD you submitted certainly confirms her opinion.

We discuss our applications from potential clients during the first week of each month. We will have a decision for you by the second week of October.

Yours truly,

Lucy Burroughs

5A_Application_Letter_Firstname_Lastname

Figure 5.1
Project 5A—Application Letter

Objective 1
Create and Save a New Document

With a word processing program, you can type, *edit*—make changes to—move, and delete text or change the appearance of text. Because the documents that you create are stored electronically, they can be duplicated, printed, copied, and shared with others. In this project, you will become familiar with the parts of the Word window. Then you will create a document, edit and format text, and save your document.

Activity 5.01 Starting Word and Identifying Parts of the Word Window

1 On the left side of the Windows taskbar, point to, and then click the **Start** button ⊕.

2 From the **Start** menu, locate the **Word** program, and then click **Microsoft Office Word 2007**.

> The Word program may be located under All Programs or Microsoft Office or on the main Start menu.

3 If necessary, on the right side of the status bar, click the Print Layout button 🔲. If the ruler does not display, click the View tab, and then in the Show/Hide group, select the Ruler check box. Take a moment to study the parts of the Word screen shown in Figure 5.2 and described in the table in Figure 5.3.

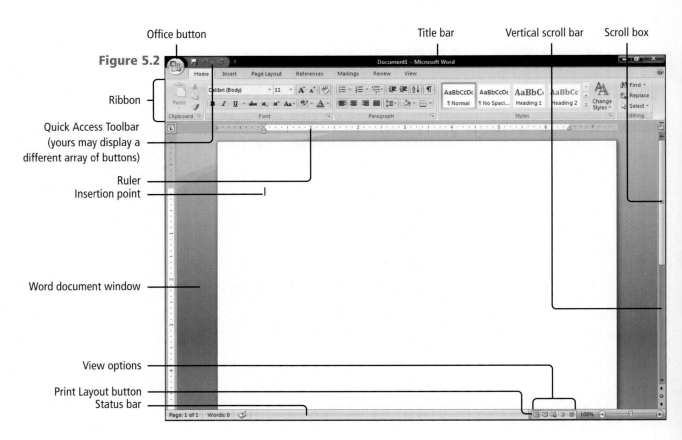

Figure 5.2

Office button · Title bar · Vertical scroll bar · Scroll box · Ribbon · Quick Access Toolbar (yours may display a different array of buttons) · Ruler · Insertion point · Word document window · View options · Print Layout button · Status bar

Microsoft Word Screen Elements

Screen Element	Description
Insertion point	Indicates, with a blinking vertical line, where text or graphics will be inserted.
Office button	Displays a list of commands related to things you can do *with* a document, such as opening, saving, printing, or sharing.
Quick Access Toolbar	Displays buttons to perform frequently used commands with a single click.
Ribbon	Organizes commands on tabs, and then groups the commands by topic for performing related document tasks.
Ruler	Displays the location of margins, indents, columns, and tab stops for the selected paragraph(s).
Scroll box	Provides a visual indication of your location in a document. It can also be used with the mouse to drag a document up and down to reposition the document.
Status bar	Displays, on the left side, the page number, word count, and the Proof button. On the right side, displays buttons to control the look of the window.
Title bar	Displays the name of the document and the name of the program. The Minimize, Maximize/Restore Down, and Close buttons are grouped on the right side of the title bar.
Vertical scroll bar	Enables you to move up and down in a document to display text that is not visible.
View options	Contains buttons for viewing the document in Print Layout, Full Screen Reading, Web Layout, Outline, or Draft views, and also displays controls to Zoom Out and Zoom In.
Word document window	Displays the active document.

Figure 5.3

Alert!

Does your screen differ?

The appearance of the screen can vary, depending on various settings that were established when Office 2007 was installed. Additionally, the Quick Access Toolbar can display any combination of buttons.

Activity 5.02 Beginning a New Document and Displaying Formatting Marks

When you start Word, you need only start typing to create a new document.

Note — Comparing Your Screen with the Figures in This Textbook

Your screen will match the figures shown in this textbook if you set your screen resolution to 1024 × 768. At other resolutions, your screen will closely resemble, but not match, the figures shown. To view your screen's resolution, on the Windows desktop, right-click in a blank area, click Personalize, and then click Display Settings.

1 On the title bar, notice that *Document1* displays.

Word displays the file name of a document in both the title bar at the top of the screen and on a button in the Windows taskbar at the lower edge of the screen. New unsaved documents display *Document* followed by a number.

2 In the displayed blank document, determine if a paragraph symbol (¶) displays in the upper left corner of the document, as shown in Figure 5.4. If you do *not* see the paragraph symbol, on the Ribbon, on the Home tab, in the Paragraph group, click the Show/Hide ¶ button **¶** .

> When you press Enter, Spacebar, or Tab on your keyboard, characters display in your document to represent these keystrokes. These characters do not print and are referred to as ***formatting marks*** or ***nonprinting characters***. These marks will display throughout this instruction.

Figure 5.4

Default document name

Show/Hide ¶ button

Paragraph symbol

No Spacing style button

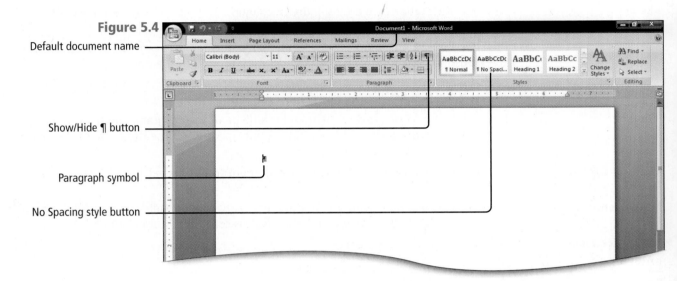

3 Click the **Show/Hide ¶** button **¶** to turn off the display of nonprinting characters. Then, click the **Show/Hide ¶** button **¶** one more time to turn it on again.

> The Show/Hide ¶ button is referred to as a ***toggle button***—you can click the button one time to turn it on and click it again to turn it off.

4 On the **Home tab**, in the **Styles group**, click the **No Spacing** style button.

> By default, Word adds spacing after each paragraph. The No Spacing button applies a style to the text that removes extra spacing. A ***style*** is a set of formatting characteristics—such as line spacing, space after paragraphs, font, and font style—that can be applied to text, paragraphs, tables, or lists.

Activity 5.03 Entering Text and Inserting Blank Lines

Business letters follow a standard format and contain the following parts: the current date—the ***date line***; the name and address of the person receiving the letter—the ***inside address***; a greeting—the ***salutation***; an optional subject—the ***subject line***; the body of the letter; a closing line— the ***complimentary closing***; and the ***writer's identification***, which includes the name or job title (or both) of the writer. Some letters also include the initials of the person who prepared the letter, and a list of ***enclosures***—documents included with the letter.

1 With the insertion point blinking in the upper left corner of the document, to the left of the default first paragraph mark, type **Music School Records** and then press [Enter].

> The first paragraph is complete and the insertion point is positioned at the beginning of the next line. A paragraph is created when you press [Enter]. Thus, a paragraph can be a single line or a blank line.

2 Type the following and press [Enter] after each line:

> **2620 Vine Street**
> **Los Angeles, CA 90028**
> **323-555-0028**

3 Press [Enter] five times, type **Sept** and then compare your screen with Figure 5.5.

> A ScreenTip displays *September (Press ENTER to Insert)*. This feature, called ***AutoComplete***, assists you in typing. After you type the first few characters, AutoComplete suggests commonly used words and phrases to enter. A ***ScreenTip*** is a small note, activated by pointing to a button or other screen object, which displays information about a screen element.

Figure 5.5

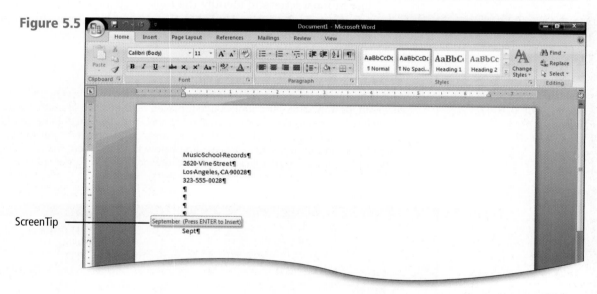

ScreenTip

4 To finish the word *September*, press [Enter]. Press [Spacebar], type **12, 2009** and then press [Enter]. If you are completing this activity during the month of September, AutoComplete may offer to fill in the current date. To ignore the suggestion, continue typing as indicated.

5 Press [Enter] two times.

6 Type **Mr. William Hawken** and then press [Enter].

> The wavy red line under the proper name *Hawken* indicates that the word has been flagged as misspelled because it is a word not contained in the Word dictionary.

7 On two lines, type the following address, but do not press [Enter] at the end of the second line:

> **123 Eighth Street**
> **Harrisville, MI 48740**

8 On the **Home tab**, in the **Styles group**, click the **Normal** button.

> Word applies the Normal style to the text in the remainder of the document. Recall that the Normal style adds extra space between paragraphs; it also adds slightly more space between lines in a paragraph.

9 Press Enter. Type the salutation **Dear William:** and then press Enter.

10 Type **Subject: Your Application to Music School Records** and press Enter. Notice the light dots between words, which indicate spaces and display when formatting marks are displayed. Also, notice the extra space below each paragraph, and then compare your screen with Figure 5.6.

> The subject line is optional, but it is good practice to include a subject line in most letters to identify the topic. Depending on your Word settings, a wavy green line may display in the subject line, indicating a potential grammar error.

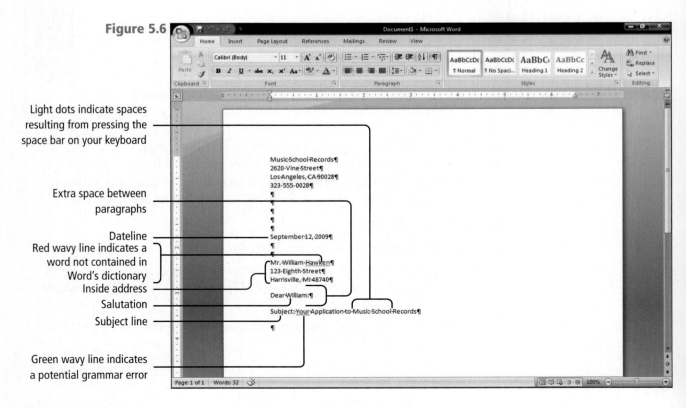

Figure 5.6

Light dots indicate spaces resulting from pressing the space bar on your keyboard

Extra space between paragraphs

Dateline

Red wavy line indicates a word not contained in Word's dictionary

Inside address

Salutation

Subject line

Green wavy line indicates a potential grammar error

Activity 5.04 Creating Folders for Document Storage and Saving a Document

In the same way that you use file folders to organize your paper documents, Windows uses a hierarchy of electronic folders to keep your electronic files organized. Changes that you make to existing documents, such as changing text or typing in new text, are not permanently saved until you perform a Save operation.

1 In the upper left corner of your screen, click the **Office** button , and from the menu, point to the words **Save As**—not the Save As arrow—and click.

2 In the **Save As** dialog box, in the **Navigation** pane, click **Computer** to view a list of available drives, as shown in Figure 5.7. If you are saving your files on your hard drive, in the Navigation pane, click Documents.

Figure 5.7

Your list of available drives will differ

New Folder button

Displays documents on the hard drive

Displays a list of storage devices

Navigation pane

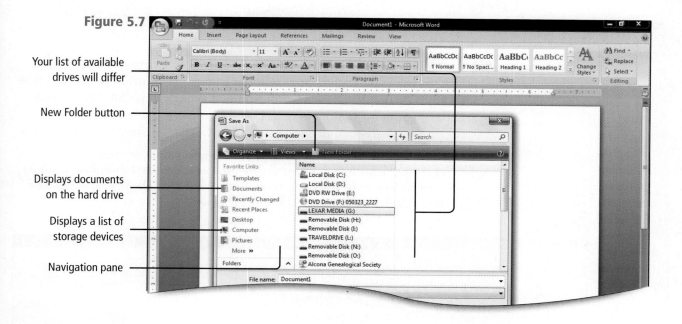

3 Navigate to the location in which you will be storing your folders and projects for this chapter—for example, a USB flash drive, a shared drive on a network, the Documents folder on your computer's hard drive, or the drive designated by your instructor or lab coordinator.

4 In the **Save As** dialog box, on the toolbar, click the **New Folder** button. With **New Folder** displayed in edit mode, type **Word Chapter 5** as shown in Figure 5.8, and then press Enter. If the new folder is not displayed in edit mode, right-click the words *New Folder*, and then from the shortcut menu, click Rename and type the new folder name.

A ***shortcut menu*** is a context-sensitive menu that displays commands relevant to the selected object. The new folder name displays in the Address bar, indicating that the folder is open and ready to store your document. The folder is currently empty.

Figure 5.8

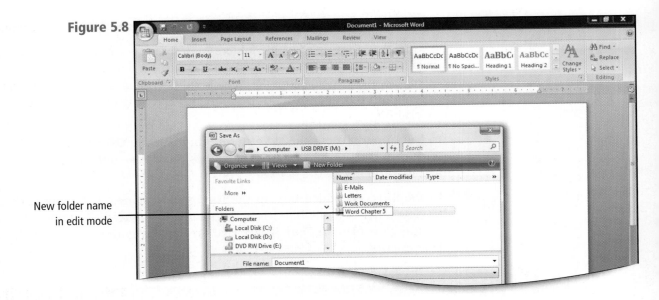

New folder name
in edit mode

5 In the lower portion of the **Save As** dialog box, locate the **File name** box. If necessary, select or delete the existing text, and then in the **File name** box, using your own first and last names, type **5A_Application_ Letter_Firstname_Lastname** being sure to include the underscore— `⇧ Shift` + `-`—instead of spaces between words, as shown in Figure 5.9.

The Microsoft Windows operating system recognizes file names with spaces. However, some Internet file transfer programs do not. To facilitate sending your files over the Internet, in this textbook you will be instructed to save files using an underscore instead of a space.

Figure 5.9

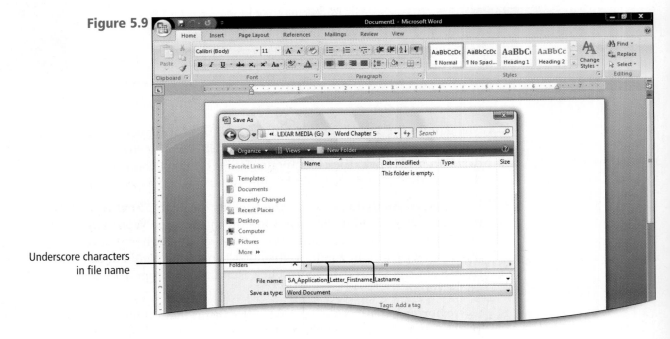

Underscore characters
in file name

6 In the lower portion of the **Save As** dialog box, click the **Save** button. The file extension *.docx* may or may not display, depending on your Word settings.

Word saves your file on the storage device that you selected in the *Word Chapter 5* folder with the new file name. The new file name also displays in the title bar.

7 As you type the following text, press ⎵Spacebar only one time at the end of a sentence: **Thank you for submitting your application to Music School Records. Our talent scout for Northern Michigan, Catherine McDonald, is really very enthusiastic about your music, and the demo CD you submitted certainly confirms her opinion.** Press Enter.

As you type, the insertion point moves to the right, and when it approaches the right margin, Word determines whether or not the next word in the line will fit within the established right margin. If the word does not fit, Word will move the whole word down to the next line. This feature, called **wordwrap**, enables you to type without having to press Enter to end a line. Press Enter *only* when you reach the end of a paragraph.

> **Note** — **Spacing Between Sentences**
>
> Although you may have learned to press ⎵Spacebar two times at the end of a sentence, now it is common practice to space only one time between sentences.

8 Type **We discuss our applications from clients during the last week of each month. We will try to have a decision for you by the second week of October.**

9 Press Enter. Type **Yours truly,** and then press Enter two times.

10 Type **John W. Diamond** and then compare your screen with Figure 5.10.

As you reach the bottom of the screen, the page scrolls up to enable you to read what you are typing.

Figure 5.10

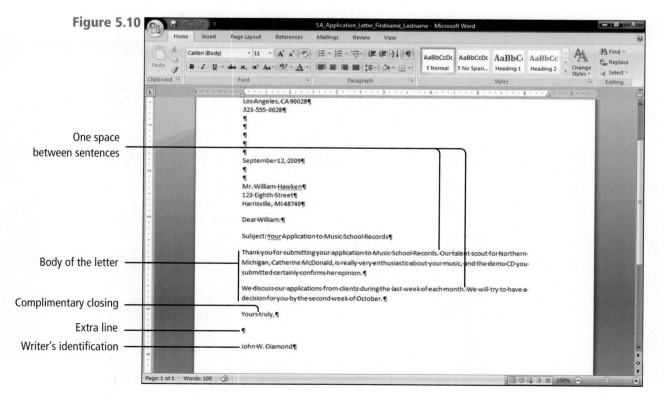

One space between sentences

Body of the letter

Complimentary closing

Extra line

Writer's identification

11 On the Ribbon, click the **Page Layout tab**. In the **Page Setup group**, click the **Margins** button to display the Margins gallery, as shown in Figure 5.11.

A *gallery* displays a list of potential results.

Figure 5.11

Margins button ——

Margins gallery ——

Custom Margins ——

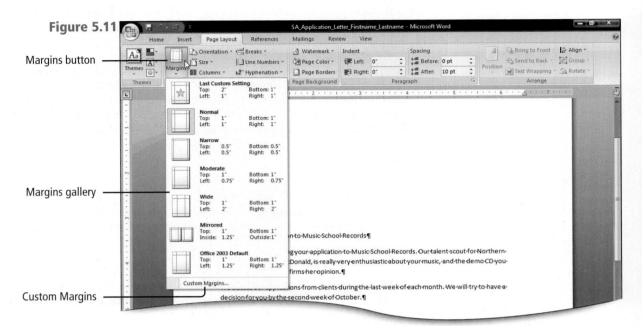

12 At the bottom of the **Margins gallery**, click **Custom Margins** to display the **Page Setup** dialog box.

13 Near the top of the **Page Setup** dialog box, click the **Layout tab**. Under **Page**, click the **Vertical alignment arrow**, and then click **Center**. Compare your dialog box with Figure 5.12.

Figure 5.12

Layout tab ——

Center ——

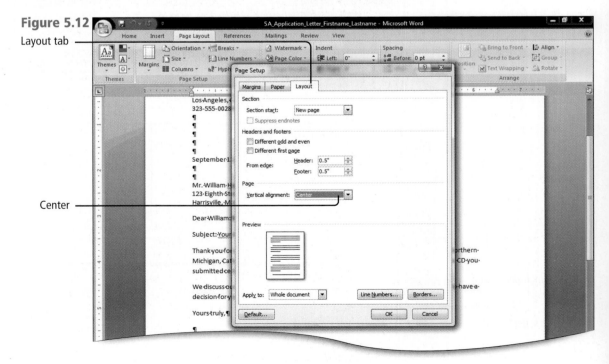

14 In the lower right corner of the **Page Setup** dialog box, click **OK**. Notice that the text is centered vertically on the page, which makes the letter more visually appealing.

15 On the **Quick Access Toolbar**, click the **Save** button 💾 to save the changes you have made to the letter since your last save operation.

More Knowledge — **Letter Placement**

According to *The Gregg Reference Manual*, Tenth Edition, a one-page letter typed on blank stationery may be centered vertically in this manner. If you are using letterhead stationery, leave at least a 0.5-inch space between the letterhead and the first element typed. Always consult trusted references when deciding on the proper formats for your personal and professional documents.

Objective 2
Edit Text

When you change text or formatting in a document, you are editing the text. Two commonly used editing tools are the Delete key and the Backspace key. The Backspace and Delete keys on your keyboard remove text from the screen one character at a time. Backspace removes a character to the left of the insertion point; Delete removes a character to the right of the insertion point.

Activity 5.05 Editing Text with the Delete and Backspace Keys

1 Using the vertical scroll bar, scroll as necessary to view the paragraph beginning *Thank you*. In the middle of the second line of the paragraph, click to position your insertion point to the left of the *v* in the word *very* and then press ⟵Bksp. Compare your screen with Figure 5.13.

Word removes the space between the words *really* and *very*.

Figure 5.13

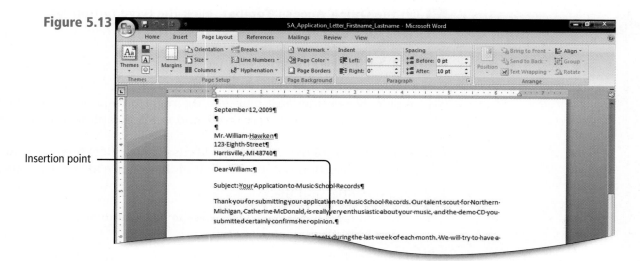

Insertion point

2 With the insertion point between the two words, press ←Bksp six times.

> The word *really* is removed. Be sure there is only one dot—recall that dots are the formatting marks that indicate spaces—between *is* and *very*. You can see that when editing text, it is useful to display formatting marks.

3 In the paragraph beginning *We discuss*, in the first line, locate the phrase *try to* and then click to position the insertion point to the left of the word *to*.

4 Press ←Bksp four times to remove the word *try* and the extra space. Press Delete three times, and then compare your screen with Figure 5.14.

> The word *to* at the right of the insertion point is removed, along with the space following the word. Be sure there is only one dot (space) between *will* and *have*.

Figure 5.14

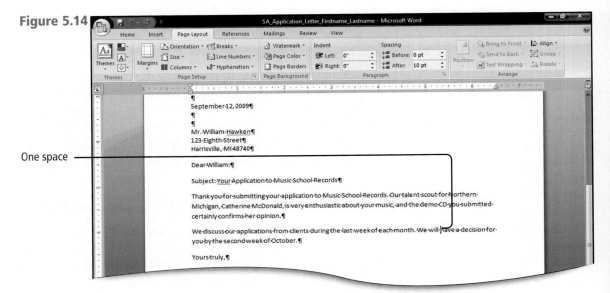

One space

5 On the **Quick Access Toolbar**, click the **Save** button.

Activity 5.06 Inserting New Text

When you place the insertion point in the middle of a word or sentence and start typing, the existing text moves to the right to make space for your new keystrokes. This is called **insert mode** and is the default setting in Word.

1 In the paragraph beginning *We discuss*, in the first line, click to place the insertion point to the left of the letter *c* in the word *clients*.

2 Type **potential** and then press Spacebar.

> As you type, the existing text moves to the right to make space for your new keystrokes.

3 In the last line of the document, click to place the insertion point to the left of *John W. Diamond*.

4 Type **Lucy Burroughs** and then press Delete until the name *John W. Diamond* is removed. Compare your screen with Figure 5.15.

Figure 5.15

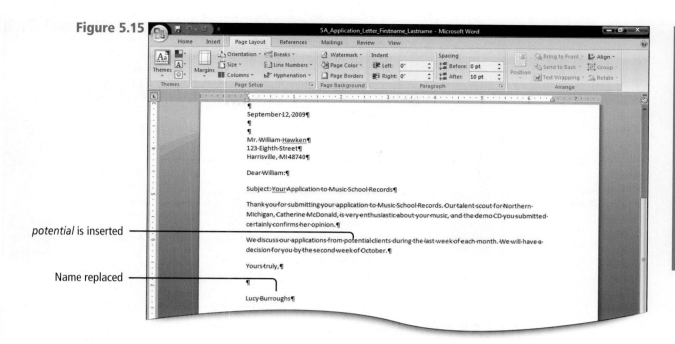

potential is inserted

Name replaced

5 **Save** 🔲 the changes you have made to your document.

Objective 3
Select, Delete, and Format Text

Selecting text refers to highlighting, by dragging with your mouse, areas of text so that the text can be edited, formatted, copied, or moved. Word recognizes a selected area of text as one unit, to which you can make changes. ***Formatting text*** is the process of setting the overall appearance of text by changing the text layout, color, shading, emphasis, or font characteristics.

Activity 5.07 Selecting and Deleting Text

1 In the paragraph beginning *Thank you*, position the I pointer to the left of *Thank*, hold down the left mouse button, and then drag to the right to select the first sentence including the ending period and its following space, as shown in Figure 5.16. Release the mouse button.

> The first sentence of the paragraph is selected, and a Mini toolbar displays above and to the right of the selected text. ***Dragging*** is the technique of holding down the left mouse button and moving over an area of text. Selected text is indicated when the background changes to a light blue or gray.

> The ***Mini toolbar*** displays buttons that are commonly used with the selected object. When you move the pointer away from the Mini toolbar, it fades from view. Selecting text may require some practice. If you are not satisfied with your result, click anywhere and begin again.

Figure 5.16

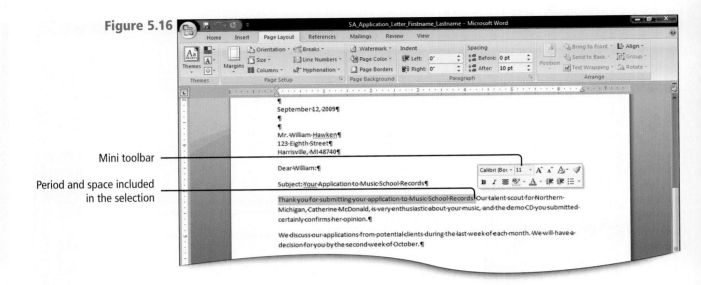

Mini toolbar

Period and space included
in the selection

2 Click anywhere in the document to deselect the sentence. Then, in the same sentence, move the pointer over the word *Music* and **double-click**—click the left mouse button two times in rapid succession.

> The entire word is selected and the Mini toolbar displays. Double-clicking takes a steady hand. The speed of the two clicks is not difficult (although you only have about a second between clicks), but you must hold the mouse perfectly still between the two clicks.

3 Click anywhere in the document to deselect the word *Music*. Then, in the paragraph that begins *We discuss*, point to the word *last* and double-click. Type **first** and notice that when you type the first letter, the selected word is deleted.

4 In the paragraph beginning *Thank you*, point to the word *Music*, and then triple-click the left mouse button.

> The entire paragraph is selected. You can triple-click anywhere in a paragraph to select the entire paragraph.

5 Hold down Ctrl and press A to select the entire document, as shown in Figure 5.17.

> Holding down Ctrl and typing a letter to perform a command is called a **keyboard shortcut**. There are many keyboard shortcuts for selecting text. Take a moment to study the shortcuts shown in the table in Figure 5.18.

Figure 5.17

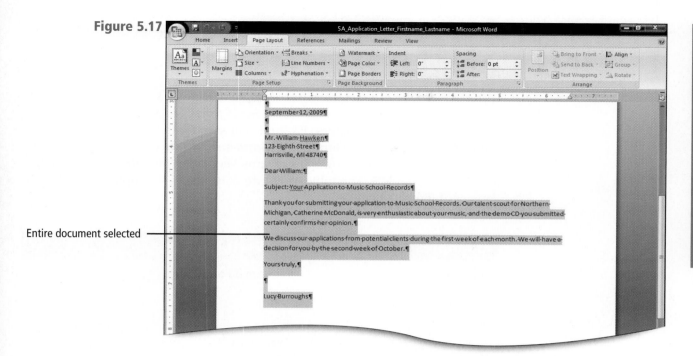

Entire document selected

Figure 5.18

Selecting Text in a Document

To Select	Do This
A portion of text	Click to position the insertion point at the beginning of the text you want to select, hold down Shift, and then click at the end of the text you want to select. Alternatively, hold down the left mouse button and drag from the beginning to the end of the text you want to select.
A word	Double-click the word.
A sentence	Hold down Ctrl and click anywhere in the sentence.
A paragraph	Triple-click anywhere in the paragraph; or, move the pointer to the left of the line, into the margin area. When the pointer displays, double-click.
A line	Move the pointer to the left of the line. When the pointer displays, click one time.
One character at a time	Position the insertion point to the left of the first character, hold down Shift, and press → or ← as many times as desired.
A string of words	Position the insertion point to the left of the first word, hold down Shift and Ctrl, and then press ← or → as many times as desired.
Consecutive lines	Position the insertion point to the left of the first word, hold down Shift and press ↑ or ↓.
Consecutive paragraphs	Position the insertion point to the left of the first word, hold down Shift and Ctrl and press ↑ or ↓.
The entire document	Hold down Ctrl and press A. Alternatively, move the pointer to the left of any line in the document. When the pointer displays, triple-click.

6 Click anywhere to cancel the text selection. **Save** 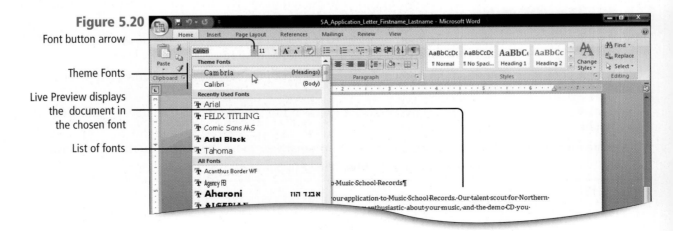 your document.

Activity 5.08 Changing Font and Font Size

A *font* is a set of characters with the same design and shape. There are two basic font types—serif and sans serif. **Serif fonts** have extensions or lines on the ends of the characters. Examples of serif fonts include Cambria, Times New Roman, and Garamond. **Sans serif fonts** do not have lines on the ends of characters. Examples of sans serif fonts include Calibri, Arial, and Comic Sans MS. The table in Figure 5.19 shows examples of serif and sans serif fonts.

Examples of Serif and Sans Serif Fonts	
Serif Fonts	**Sans Serif Fonts**
Cambria	Calibri
Times New Roman	Arial
Garamond	Comic Sans MS

Figure 5.19

1 Hold down [Ctrl] and press [A] to select the entire document.

2 Click the **Home tab**, and then in the **Font group**, click the **Font button arrow**. At the top of the **Font gallery**, under **Theme Fonts**, point to—but do not click—**Cambria**. Notice that the font in the document changes to a preview of the Cambria font, as shown in Figure 5.20.

This is an example of **Live Preview**—a technology that shows the results of applying editing or formatting changes as you point to selections in a gallery or list. Here, Live Preview changes the selected text to the Cambria font, even though you did not click the font name.

A **theme** is a predefined set of colors, fonts, lines, and fill effects that look good together and that can be applied to your entire document or to specific items—for example, to a paragraph or table. As you progress in your study of Word, you will use more theme features.

Figure 5.20
Font button arrow

Theme Fonts

Live Preview displays the document in the chosen font

List of fonts

3 Click **Cambria** to apply the font to the entire document. On the **Home tab**, in the **Font group**, click the **Font Size button arrow** 12 ▾ , click **12**, and then click anywhere to cancel the selection.

Fonts are measured in *points*, with one point equal to 1/72 of an inch. A higher point size indicates a larger font size. For large amounts of text, font sizes between 10 point and 12 point are good choices. Headings and titles are often formatted by using a larger font size. The word *point* is abbreviated as ***pt***.

4 Scroll up, and then move the pointer into the left margin area, slightly to the left of the first line of the document—*Music School Records*. When the ↗ pointer displays, click one time to select the entire first line of text.

5 On the Mini toolbar, click the **Font button arrow**, scroll down if necessary, and then click **Arial Black**.

6 With the Mini toolbar still displayed, click the **Font Size button arrow** 12 ▾ , and then click **20**.

7 Position the ↗ pointer to the left of the second line of the document— *2620 Vine Street*. Drag down to select the second, third, and fourth lines of the document, ending with the telephone number.

8 On the Mini toolbar, click the **Font button arrow**, and then click **Arial**. With the Mini toolbar still displayed, click the **Font Size button arrow** 12 ▾ , and then click **10**. Click anywhere to cancel the selection, and then compare your screen with Figure 5.21.

Figure 5.21

20 point Arial Black font

10 point Arial font

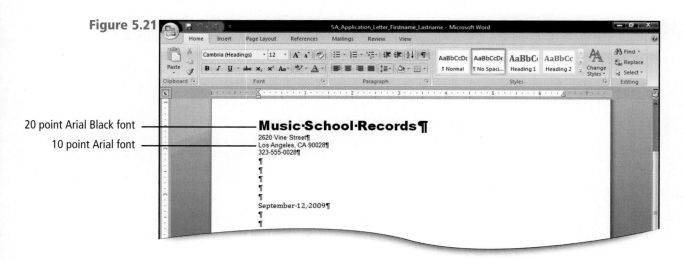

Note — Moving Quickly in a Long List

The list of available fonts is frequently very long. You can move quickly to any font by typing the first (or even first and second) letter of the font after you click the Font button arrow.

9 **Save** 💾 the changes you have made to your document.

Activity 5.09 Adding Emphasis to Text

Font styles emphasize text and are a visual cue to draw the reader's eye to important text. Font styles include bold, italic, and underline, although underline is not commonly used for emphasis.

1 Point anywhere in the first line of text—*Music School Records*—and triple-click to select the paragraph. Then, on the Mini toolbar, click the **Bold** button **B** to apply bold emphasis to the paragraph that forms the first line of the letterhead.

2 On the **Home tab**, in the **Font group**, click the **Underline** button **U ▾**.

Another Way

To Apply Font Styles

Use the keyboard shortcuts of Ctrl + B for bold, Ctrl + I for italic, or Ctrl + U for underline.

---

3 Position the pointer to the left of the second line of the document— *2620 Vine Street*. Drag down to select the second, third, and fourth lines of the document, ending with the telephone number.

4 On the Mini toolbar, click the **Italic** button *I* to apply italic emphasis to the paragraphs that form the remainder of the letterhead. Click anywhere to cancel the selection.

5 From the **Office** menu, point to **Print**, and then click **Print Preview**. Compare your screen with Figure 5.22.

> The Ribbon displays the Print Preview *program tab*, which replaces the standard set of tabs when you switch to certain authoring modes or views, including Print Preview. Print Preview displays the entire page and enables you to see what the document will look like when printed.

Note — Viewing Keyboard Shortcuts

The key combinations for Ctrl keyboard shortcuts are identified in the ScreenTip for each button. The Alt keyboard shortcuts are displayed by pressing and then releasing the Alt key.

Figure 5.22

Print Preview program tab

Close Print Preview button

Bold, underlined text

Text with italic emphasis

Document displayed
in Print Preview

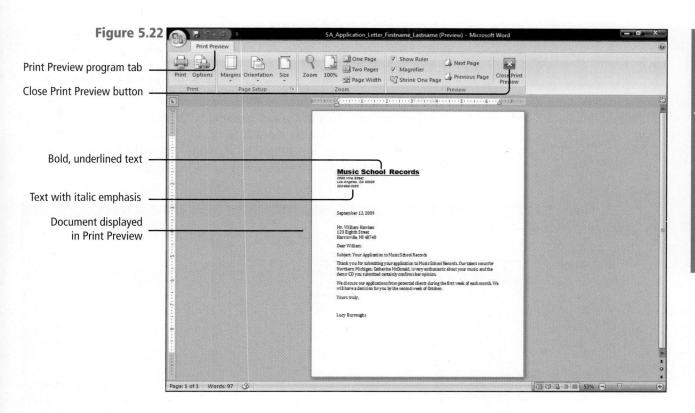

6 On the **Print Preview tab**, in the **Preview group**, click the **Close Print Preview** button, and then **Save** ▣ your changes.

Objective 4
Print a Document

Information in headers and footers helps identify a document when it is printed. A *header* is information that prints at the top of every page; a *footer* is information that prints at the bottom of every page.

Activity 5.10 Accessing Headers and Footers

1 Click the **Insert tab**, and then, in the **Header & Footer group**, click the **Footer** button.

Another Way

To Open a Footer

Scroll to the bottom of the page, right-click near the bottom edge of the page, and then click Edit Footer to open the footer area.

2 At the bottom of the **Footer gallery**, click **Edit Footer**.

The footer area displays with the insertion point blinking at the left edge of the footer area. Because the footer area is active, the contextual tools *Header & Footer Tools* display and add contextual tabs—in this instance the Design tab—next to the standard tabs on the Ribbon.

Contextual tools enable you to perform specific commands related to the active area or selected object, and display one or more **contextual tabs** that contain related **groups** of commands that you will need. Contextual tools display only when needed for a selected area or object; when you deselect the area or object, the contextual tools no longer display.

3 On the **Design tab**, in the **Insert group**, click the **Quick Parts** button, and then click **Field**. In the **Field** dialog box, under **Field names**, use the vertical scroll bar to examine the items that you can insert in a header or footer, as shown in Figure 5.23.

Figure 5.23

Quick Parts button

Header and Footer Tools Design tab

Field dialog box

Vertical scroll bar
Inserts file name

Footer area

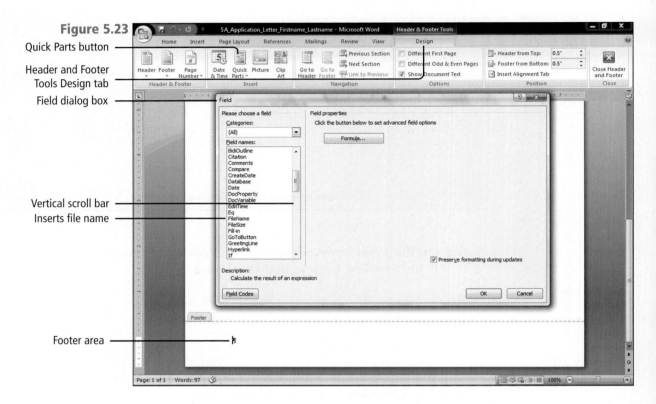

4 In the **Field names** list, scroll as necessary to locate and click **FileName**, and then click **OK**.

The file name displays in the Footer area. The file extension *.docx* may or may not display, depending on your Windows settings.

5 Double-click anywhere in the document to close the footer area. Alternatively, in the Close group, click the Close Header and Footer button. Scroll down until you can see the footer, and then compare your screen with Figure 5.24.

The footer displays in gray. Because it is a proper name and is likely not in Word's dictionary, your name in the footer may display with wavy red lines.

Figure 5.24

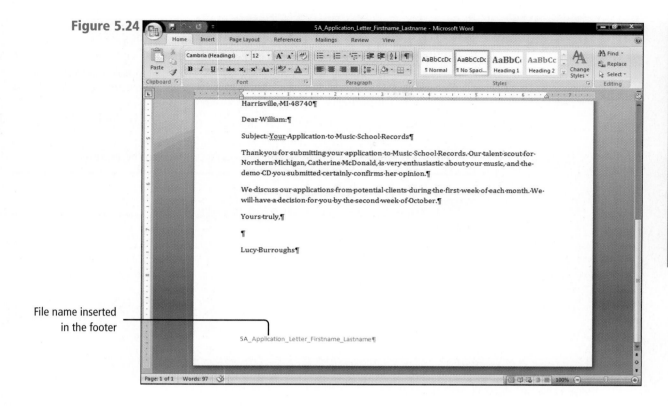

File name inserted in the footer

6 **Save** 💾 your document.

More Knowledge — Moving to the Header or Footer

To quickly edit an existing header or footer, double-click in the header or footer area. This will display the Header & Footer contextual tools and place the insertion point at the beginning of the header or footer.

Activity 5.11 Printing a Document

1 Check your *Chapter Assignment Sheet* or *Course Syllabus*, or consult your instructor, to determine if you are to submit your assignments on paper or electronically. To submit electronically, go to Step 3, and then follow the instructions provided by your instructor.

2 Click the **Office** button 🔘, point to the **Print arrow**, and then click **Quick Print**.

   One copy of your document prints on the default printer connected to your system. The formatting marks that indicate spaces and paragraphs do not print.

3 From the **Office** menu 🔘, click **Close**, saving any changes if prompted to do so. Leave Word open for the next project.

Another Way

To Print a Document

To print a document:

- From the Office menu, click Print to display the Print dialog box, from which you can choose a variety of different options, such as printing multiple copies, printing on a different printer, and printing some but not all pages.

- Hold down Ctrl, and then press P. This is an alternative to the Office menu command, and opens the Print dialog box.

- Press and release Alt, press F, and then press P to open the Print dialog box.

End **You have completed Project 5A** ————————

Project 5B **Company Overview**

In Activities 5.12 through 5.23, you will create a document that describes the mission of Music School Records. You will add a graphic image to the document, and insert text from another document. Your completed document will look similar to Figure 5.25.

For Project 5B, you will need the following files:

w05B_Music_School_Records
w05B_Music_Logo

You will save your document as
5B_Company_Overview_Firstname_Lastname

Figure 5.25
Project 5B—Company Overview

Objective 5
Navigate the Word Window

Most Word documents are longer than the Word window—some are wider than the window. Use the scroll bars to **navigate**—move around in—a document.

Activity 5.12 Opening and Closing an Existing Document

1 If necessary, **Start** 💿 Word. From the **Office** menu 🔵, click **Open**.

2 Navigate to the location where the student files for this textbook are stored, which may be on a CD that came with your textbook or in some other location designated by your instructor.

3 Locate **w05B_Music_School_Records** and click to select it. Then, in the lower right corner of the **Open** dialog box, click the **Open** button.

4 If necessary, on the Home tab, in the Paragraph group, click the Show/Hide ¶ button ⬚ to display the nonprinting characters.

> The document displays in the Word window. This text will be inserted into a new document in Activity 5.13.

5 From the **Office** menu 🔵, click **Close** to close the document and leave Word open.

Activity 5.13 Inserting Existing Text into a New Document

1 From the **Office** menu 🔵, click **New** to display the **New Document** dialog box. Notice that the *Blank document* button is selected by default. Compare your screen with Figure 5.26.

Figure 5.26

New Document dialog box ———

Blank document button ———

Create button ———

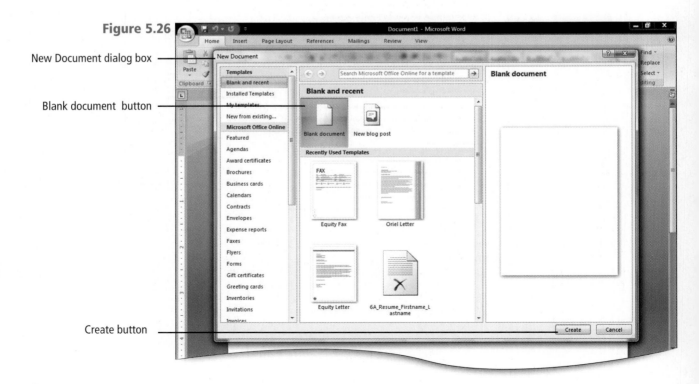

2 In the lower right corner of the **New Document** dialog box, click **Create** to create a new document. Type **Music School Records** and then press Enter.

3 Click the **Insert tab**. In the **Text group**, click the **Object button arrow**, and then click **Text from File**.

Alert!

Did the Object dialog box display?

If the Object dialog box displays, then you clicked the Object *button* instead of the Object *button arrow*. Close the Object dialog box, and then in the Text group, click the Object button arrow, as shown in Figure 5.27. Click *Text from File*, and then continue with Step 4.

4 In the **Insert File** dialog box, navigate to your student files. Locate **w05B_Music_School_Records**, click to select it, and then in the lower right corner, click the **Insert** button. Compare your screen with Figure 5.27.

A copy of the text from the w05B_Music_School_Records document is inserted into the blank document, the last page of the three-page document displays, and the insertion point displays at the end of the inserted text. The original w05B_Music_School_Records document remains intact. The page number, total number of pages in the document, and number of words in the document display in the status bar.

Figure 5.27

Object button arrow

Number of words in the document

Number of pages in the document

Current page number

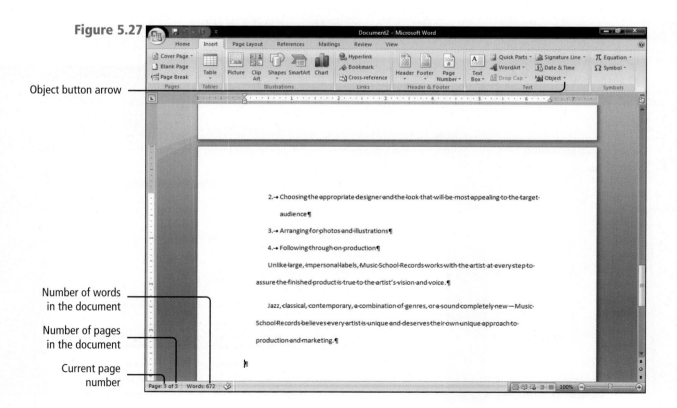

5 Press ←Bksp to delete the blank line at the end of the document. On the **Quick Access Toolbar**, click **Save** 🖫. In the **Save As** dialog box, navigate to your **Word Chapter 5** folder.

> Recall that because this is a new unnamed document—*Document2* or some other number displays in the title bar—the *Save As* dialog box displays so that you can name and designate a storage location for the document. The first line of text in the document displays in the *File name* box.

6 In the **File name** box, delete any existing text. Using your own name, type **5B_Company_Overview_Firstname_ Lastname** and then click **Save**.

7 On the **Insert tab**, in the **Header & Footer group**, click the **Footer** button. At the bottom of the **Footer gallery**, click **Edit Footer**.

8 On the **Design tab**, in the **Insert group**, click the **Quick Parts** button, and then click **Field**. In the **Field** dialog box, under **Field names**, locate and click **FileName**, and then click **OK**.

9 Double-click anywhere in the document to close the footer area. **Save** 🖫 your document.

Activity 5.14 Navigating a Document

1 At the right of your screen, in the vertical scroll bar, locate the **up scroll arrow** ▲ at the top of the scroll bar, as shown in Figure 5.28. Then, click the **up scroll arrow** ▲ five times. Notice that the document scrolls up one line at a time. Also, notice that the scroll box is near the bottom of the vertical scroll bar.

Figure 5.28

Up scroll arrow

Scroll box

Down scroll arrow

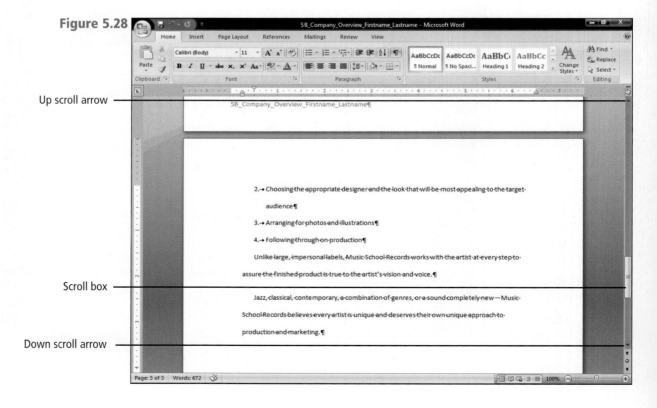

2 Point to the **up scroll arrow** ▲ again. Click and hold down the mouse button for several seconds.

The document text scrolls up continuously, one line at a time.

3 At the top of the vertical scroll bar, point to the **up scroll arrow** ▲, and then click and hold down the mouse button until you have scrolled to the beginning of the document. As you do so, notice that the scroll box moves up in the scroll bar.

4 Near the top of the vertical scroll bar, point to the **scroll box**, and then press and hold down the left mouse button. Compare your screen with Figure 5.29.

A ScreenTip displays, indicating the page number. The page number and total number of pages in the document display in the status bar—in this instance, page 1 of 3 pages.

Figure 5.29

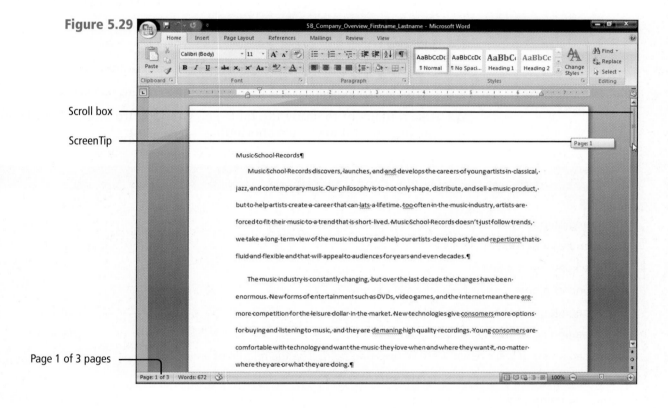

Scroll box

ScreenTip

Page 1 of 3 pages

5 Drag the **scroll box** slowly down to the bottom of the scroll bar. As you do so, notice that the ScreenTip changes as each new page reaches the top of the screen.

6 Release the mouse button, and then click in the dark area just above the scroll box.

The document scrolls up one screen. This is a quick way to scan a document.

7 Practice clicking in the area above and below the scroll box.

Another Way

To Scroll Through a Document

If your mouse has a small wheel button between the left and right mouse buttons, you can scroll up and down in the document by rotating the wheel.

8 On your keyboard, hold down Ctrl and press Home.

The beginning of the document displays, and the insertion point moves to the left of the first word in the document. In this document, Word has flagged some spelling, grammar, and contextual errors (red, green, and blue wavy lines), which you will correct in Activity 5.19.

Alert!

Does the shortcut work?

If you are using a laptop computer, you may have to hold down a function Fn key to use shortcuts that involve the Home, End, Page Up, and PgDn keys.

9 Hold down Ctrl and press End.

10 Press PgUp to scroll the document up one screen. Press End.

The insertion point moves to the end of the current line of text.

11 Take a moment to study the table shown in Figure 5.30, which lists the most useful keyboard shortcuts.

Navigating a Document Using Keyboard Shortcuts

To Move	Press
To the beginning of a document	Ctrl + Home
To the end of a document	Ctrl + End
To the beginning of a line	Home
To the end of a line	End
To the beginning of the previous word	Ctrl + ←
To the beginning of the next word	Ctrl + →
To the beginning of the current word (if insertion point is in the middle of a word)	Ctrl + ←
To the beginning of the previous paragraph	Ctrl + ↑
To the beginning of the next paragraph	Ctrl + ↓
To the beginning of the current paragraph (if insertion point is in the middle of a paragraph)	Ctrl + ↑
Up one screen	PgUp
Down one screen	PgDn

Figure 5.30

12 Hold down Ctrl and press Home to position the insertion point at the beginning of the document.

Activity 5.15 Changing Document Views

1 Near the right side of the status bar, locate the **View** buttons.

Note — Viewing Documents

There are five ways to view your document on the screen. Each view is useful in different situations.

- *Print Layout view* displays the page borders, margins, text, and graphics as they will look when you print the document. Because Word users commonly prefer this view for most tasks, it is the default view.
- *Full Screen Reading view* creates easy-to-read pages that fit on the screen to increase legibility. This view does not represent the pages as they would print. Each screen page is labeled with a screen number, rather than a page number.
- *Web Layout view* shows how the document will look when saved as a Web page and viewed in a Web browser.
- *Outline view* shows the organizational structure of your document by headings and subheadings and can be collapsed and expanded to look at individual sections of a document.
- *Draft view* simplifies the page layout for quick typing, and shows a little more text on the screen than the Print Layout view. Graphics, headers, and footers do not display.

---

2 Click the **Draft** button ▤, and then examine the document display.

3 Click the **Full Screen Reading** button 📖.

Text displays in a side-by-side format, and can be read like a book.

4 Near the upper right corner of the screen, click the **Close** button to display the document in Print Layout view.

Activity 5.16 Using the Zoom Slider

To *zoom* means to increase or decrease the viewing area of the screen. You can zoom in to look closely at a particular section of a document, and then zoom out to see an entire page on the screen. You can also zoom to view multiple pages on the screen.

1 On the right side of the status bar, just to the right of the View buttons, drag the **Zoom slider** to the right until you have zoomed to approximately 150%, as shown in Figure 5.31.

Figure 5.31

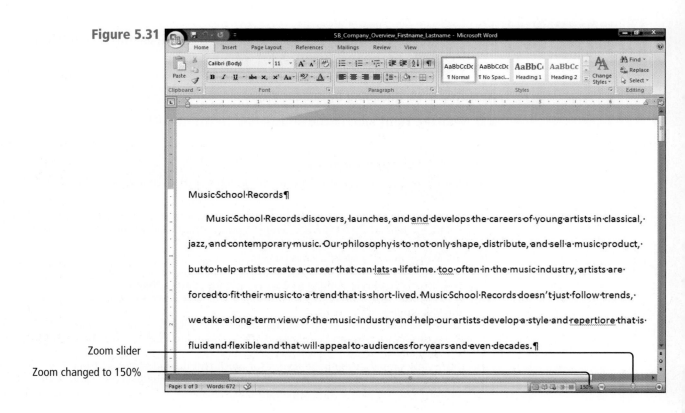

Zoom slider

Zoom changed to 150%

2 Drag the **Zoom slider** to the left until you have zoomed to approximately 40%, as shown in Figure 5.32. Notice that as the pages get smaller, multiple pages display.

Figure 5.32

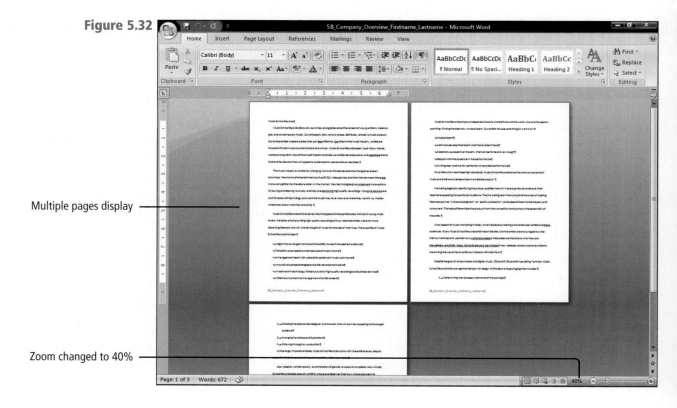

Multiple pages display

Zoom changed to 40%

3 Drag the **Zoom slider** to the right until you have zoomed to a page size with which you are comfortable—typically 100%.

As you work on various documents, adjust the zoom to best display the document.

Another Way

To Change the Zoom

You can click the page percentage label to the right of the View buttons to open the Zoom dialog box. Here you can specify the exact page percentage you want, stretch the page to the width of the screen, or display several pages at once.

Activity 5.17 Splitting Windows and Arranging Panes

You can split the Word screen so that you can look at two different parts of the same document at the same time. You can also view two documents side by side and make comparisons between the two.

1 Press Ctrl + Home to move the insertion point to the beginning of the document. Click the **View tab**, and then, in the **Window group**, click the **Split** button. Compare your screen with Figure 5.33.

A **split bar** displays near the middle of the document area, with a move pointer ✚ on the bar. The split bar indicates the location of the border between the windows.

Figure 5.33

Split button

Vertical move pointer

Split bar

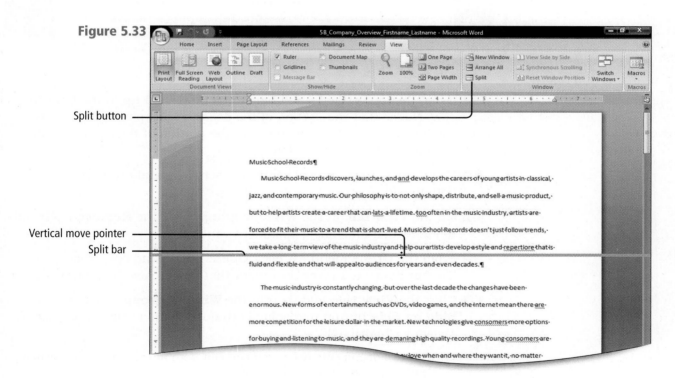

2 Drag the split bar slightly below the fifth line of text—including the title—that contains the phrase *that is short lived*, and then click to position the split bar.

3 Notice that both the top and bottom halves of the screen display rulers, and two different parts of the same document display in the two document windows, as shown in Figure 5.34. If you don't see the rulers, on the View tab, in the Show/Hide group, select the Ruler check box.

Figure 5.34

Different areas of the same document

Split bar extends across the screen

Two document windows

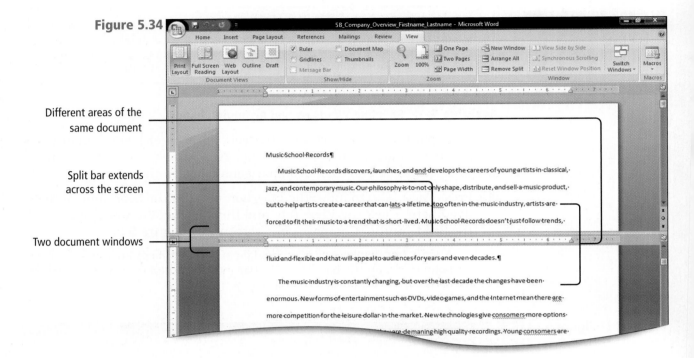

4 Using the top vertical scroll bar, scroll down and up in the top window. Notice that the portion of the document displayed in the top window moves independently from the portion of the document displayed in the bottom window.

5 Using the bottom vertical scroll bar, scroll up and down in the bottom widow.

6 On the **View tab**, in the **Window group**, click the **Remove Split** button to return to a single document window.

7 From the **Office** menu 🗔, click **Open**. Locate and open the **5A_Application_Letter** document that you created in Project 5A.

8 Click the **View tab**, and then in the **Window group**, click the **View Side by Side** button to display both documents at the same time, as shown in Figure 5.35.

> With two documents open, you can edit both at the same time, or move text or objects between the documents.

Figure 5.35

View tab ———

Different documents ———

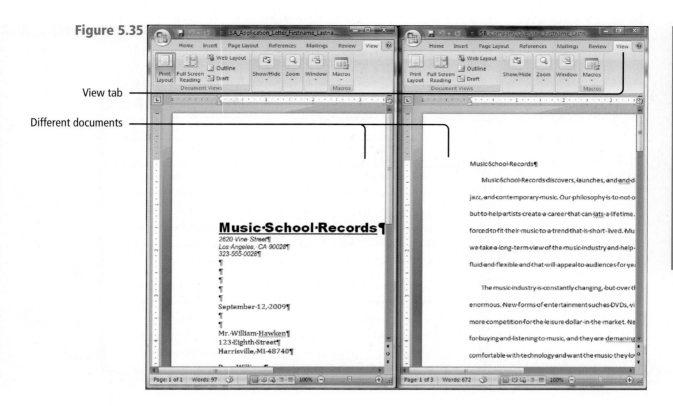

On the title bar of the document on the left, click the **Close** button to close the letter. Notice that the **5B_Company_Overview** window is maximized when the other window is closed.

Objective 6
Add a Graphic to a Document

Clip art images—predefined graphics included with Microsoft Office or downloaded from the Web—can make your document more interesting and visually appealing.

Activity 5.18 Inserting Clip Art

1 Press Ctrl + Home to move the insertion point to the beginning of the document. Press Spacebar three times, and then press ← three times to move the insertion point back to the beginning of the line.

2 Click the **Insert tab**, and then in the **Illustrations group**, click the **Clip Art** button.

3 In the **Clip Art** task pane, in the **Search for** box, type **Music** and then in the **Search in** box, be sure **All collections** is selected. Click the **Results should be arrow**, and then clear all the check boxes except **Clip Art**.

4 Click **Go**, and then compare your screen with Figure 5.36. If necessary, scroll up to view the first displayed music images.

Figure 5.36

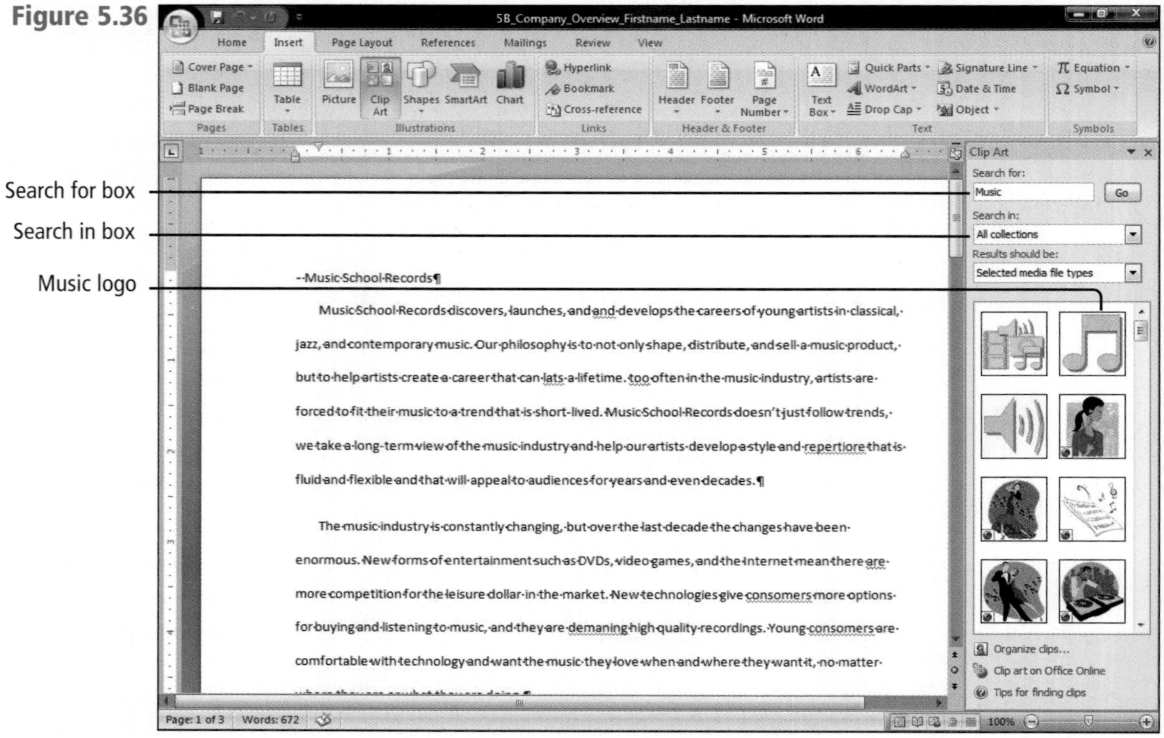

Search for box
Search in box
Music logo

5 Click the **music logo** clip art image. Notice that the image displays over the text.

6 Right-click the image, and then from the shortcut menu, click **Format AutoShape**. In the **Format AutoShape** dialog box, on the **Layout tab**, under **Wrapping style**, click **In line with text**, which will treat the clip art image as a text character.

7 In the **Format AutoShape** dialog box, click the **Size tab**. Under **Scale**, click the **Lock aspect ratio** check box. In the **Height** box, select the current value, and then type **30** to reduce the image to 30 percent of its original size. Compare your dialog box with Figure 5.37.

The ***aspect ratio*** of an object is the relationship of its height to its width. If you lock the aspect ratio, changing either the height or width of an object will resize the object proportionally.

Figure 5.37

Layout tab

Size tab

New size of object

Lock aspect ratio check box

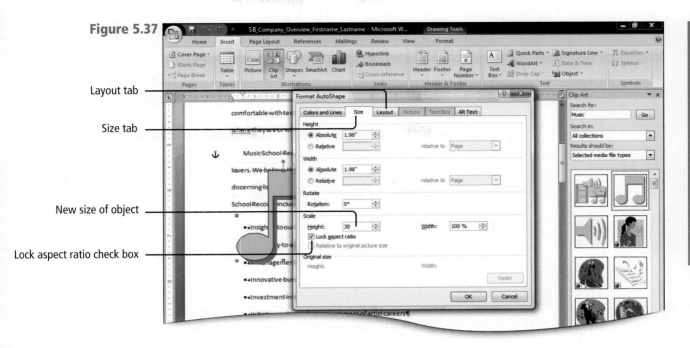

8 At the bottom of the **Format AutoShape** dialog box, click **OK**, and then click anywhere in the document to deselect the image. Compare your screen with Figure 5.38.

Figure 5.38

Task pane Close button

Inserted clip art image

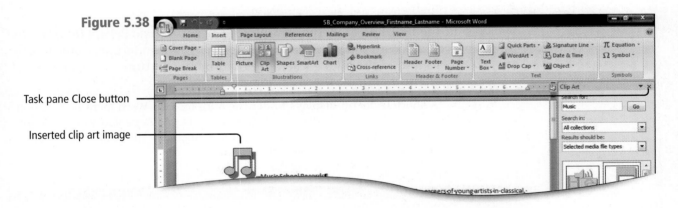

9 **Close** ☒ the **Clip Art** task pane, and then **Save** 🖫 your document.

Objective 7
Use the Spelling and Grammar Checker

Word compares your typing to words in the Word dictionary and compares your phrases and punctuation to a list of grammar rules. Words that are not in the Word dictionary are marked with a wavy red underline. Phrases and punctuation that differ from the grammar rules are marked with a wavy green underline. A list of grammar rules applied by a computer program can never be exact, and a computer dictionary cannot contain all known words and proper names; thus, you will need to check any words flagged by Word with wavy underlines.

Word also places a wavy blue underline under a word that is spelled correctly but used incorrectly, such as the misuse of *their*, *there*, and *they're*. However, Word will not flag the word *sign* as misspelled, even though you intended to type *sing a song* rather than *sign a song*, because both are legitimate words contained within Word's dictionary.

Activity 5.19 Checking Individual Spelling and Grammar Errors

One way to check spelling and grammar errors flagged by Word is to right-click the flagged word or phrase, and then from the shortcut menu, choose a suitable correction or instruction.

1 Scan the text on the screen to locate green, red, and blue wavy underlines.

> **Note — Activating Spelling and Grammar Checking**
>
> If you do not see any wavy red, green, or blue lines under words, the automatic spelling and/or grammar checking has been turned off on your system. To activate the spelling and grammar checking, display the Office menu, click Word Options, and then in the list, click Proofing. Under *When correcting spelling in Microsoft Office programs*, select the first four check boxes. Under *When correcting spelling and grammar in Word*, select the first four check boxes, and then click the Writing Style arrow and click Grammar & Style. Under *Exceptions for*, clear both check boxes. To display the flagged spelling and grammar errors, click the Recheck Document button, and then close the dialog box.

2 In the first line of the paragraph that begins *Music School Records discovers*, locate the word *and* with the wavy red underline. Point to the word and **right-click**—click the right mouse button—to display a shortcut menu, as shown in Figure 5.39.

> A shortcut menu displays under the Mini toolbar. Word identified a duplicate word, and provides two suggestions—*Delete Repeated Word* or *Ignore*. The second option is included because sometimes the same word will be correctly used two times in succession.

Figure 5.39

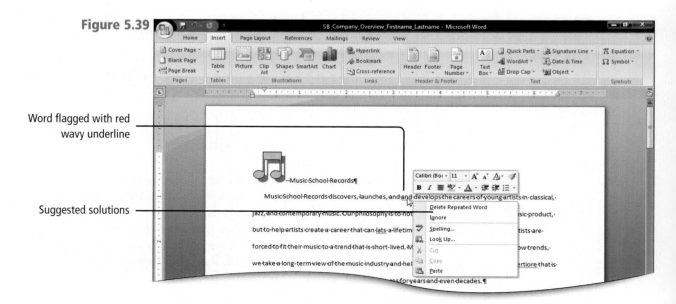

Word flagged with red wavy underline

Suggested solutions

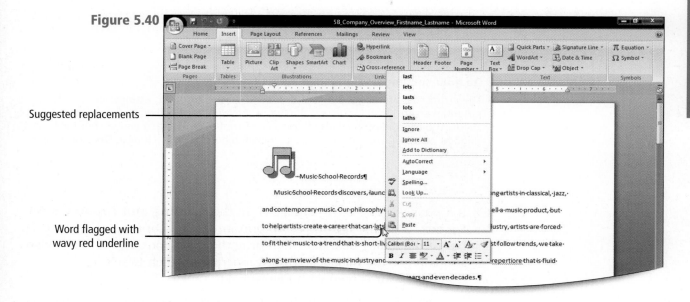

3 From the shortcut menu, click **Delete Repeated Word** to delete the duplicate word.

4 In the third line of the same paragraph, locate and right-click the mis-spelled word *lats*, and then compare your screen with Figure 5.40.

In this instance, Word identifies a misspelled word. Suggested replacements are shown at the top of the shortcut menu.

Figure 5.40

Suggested replacements

Word flagged with wavy red underline

5 At the top of the shortcut menu, click **last** to replace the mis-spelled widow.

6 In the third line of the same paragraph, locate and right-click the word *too* that has a wavy green underline.

The wavy green underline indicates a grammar error; in this instance, a word at the beginning of a sentence that should be capitalized.

7 From the shortcut menu, click **Too** to capitalize the word.

8 Scroll down to view the bottom of **Page 2**. In the paragraph beginning *A key aspect*, notice that two words have wavy blue underlines.

The wavy blue underline indicates a word that is recognized by the dic-tionary, but may be the wrong form of the word—in this instance *there* is incorrectly used instead of *their*, and *too* is used instead of *to*.

9 In the paragraph beginning *A key aspect*, right-click *there*, and then from the shortcut menu, click **their**. In the same paragraph, right-click *too*, and then from the shortcut menu, click **to**.

10 **Save** your document.

Activity 5.20 Checking Spelling and Grammar in an Entire Document

Initiating the spelling and grammar checking feature from the Ribbon displays the Spelling and Grammar dialog box, which provides more options than the shortcut menus.

1 Scan the document to locate red, green, and blue wavy underlines. Notice the ⌖ icon in the status bar, which indicates that the document contains flagged entries that need to be addressed.

2 Press Ctrl + Home to move the insertion point to the beginning of the document. Click the **Review tab**, and then in the **Proofing group**, click the **Spelling & Grammar** button to begin to check the document.

> The first suggested error may be a potential grammar error—using a passive voice.

Alert!

Do your spelling and grammar selections differ?

The errors that are flagged by Word depend on the Proofing settings. Not all of the potential errors listed in this activity may appear in your spelling and grammar check. Your document may also display errors not noted here. If you encounter flagged words or phrases that are not included here, click the Ignore Once button to move to the next potential error.

3 If a *passive voice* error is flagged, in the **Spelling and Grammar** dialog box, click the **Ignore Once** button. If necessary, point to the title bar of the dialog box, and then drag the dialog box out of the way so you can see the misspelled word *repertiore*, which is selected. Compare your screen with Figure 5.41.

> Under *Not in Dictionary*, the misspelled word displays in red, and under *Suggestions*, a suggested change is presented.

Figure 5.41

Spelling & Grammar button —

Highlighted word in document —

Word not in dictionary —

Suggested alternative —

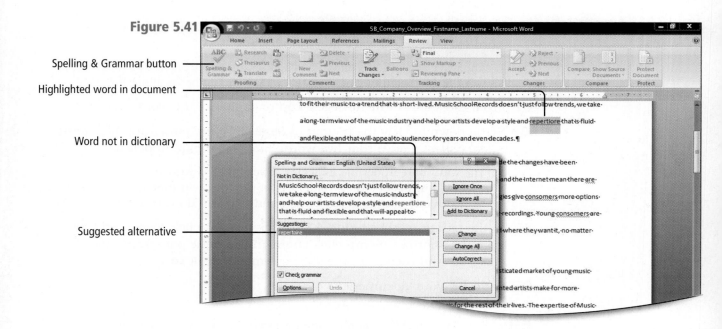

4 Take a moment to study the spelling and grammar options available in the **Spelling and Grammar** dialog box, as shown in the table in Figure 5.42.

Spelling and Grammar Dialog Box Buttons

Button	Action
Ignore Once	Ignores the identified word one time, but flags it in other locations in the document.
Ignore All	Discontinues flagging any instance of the word anywhere in the document.
Add to Dictionary	Adds the word to a custom dictionary, which can be edited. This option does not change the built-in Office dictionary.
Change	Changes the identified word to the word highlighted under Suggestions.
Change All	Changes every instance of the word in the document to the word highlighted under Suggestions.
AutoCorrect	Adds the flagged word to the AutoCorrect list, which will subsequently correct the word automatically if misspelled in any documents typed in the future.
Ignore Rule (Grammar)	Ignores the specific rule used to determine a grammar error and removes the green wavy line.
Next Sentence (Grammar)	Moves to the next identified error.
Explain (Grammar)	Displays the rule used to identify a grammar error.
Options	Displays the Proofing section of the Word Options dialog box.

Figure 5.42

5 If necessary, under **Suggestions**, select **repertoire**, and then click the **Change** button. Compare your screen with Figure 5.43.

The correction is made and the next identified error is highlighted, which is a contraction use error. Under *Contraction Use*, the entire sentence displays, with the contraction *doesn't* displayed in green. The suggested replacement—*does not*—displays in the Suggestions box.

Alert!

Did your spelling and grammar checker miss the Contraction Use error?

Recall that because of the settings on your computer, your spelling and grammar selections may differ. If you do not see a Contraction Use error, you have Grammar checking turned on, but not Style checking. When the Spelling check is done, go back and make this change manually.

Figure 5.43

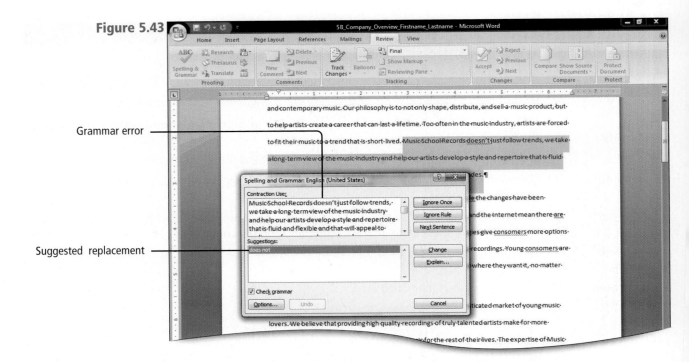

Grammar error

Suggested replacement

6 Under **Suggestions**, be sure **does not** is selected, and then click the **Change** button.

The correction is made and the next identified error is highlighted, which is a grammar error. Under *Comma Use*, the entire sentence displays. The suggested change is to add a comma.

7 Under **Suggestions**, be sure **decade** is selected, and then click the **Change** button.

The error is corrected, and the next potential error displays—a Subject-Verb Agreement grammar error.

8 Under **Suggestions**, be sure **is** is selected, and then click the **Change** button.

The error is corrected, and the next potential error displays. The word *consomers* is misspelled in two successive sentences.

9 Under **Suggestions**, be sure **consumers** is selected, and then click the **Change All** button to change all instances of the misspelled word.

10 Continue to the end of the document. Change *demaning* to **demanding**, and then click **Ignore Once** for any other marked words or phrases.

A message indicates that the spelling and grammar check is complete.

11 Click **OK** to close the dialog box, and then **Save** your changes.

Alert!

Does the Readability Statistics box display?

If, on your computer, Word is configured to display readability statistics, a Readability Statistics dialog box displays. Readability statistics include character, word, paragraph, and sentence counts, along with reading level statistics. After reviewing the information, click OK to close the dialog box.

Objective 8
Preview and Print Documents, Close a Document, and Close Word

To ensure that you are getting the result you want, it is useful to display Print Preview from time to time while creating your document. Then, before printing, make a final preview to be sure the document layout is what you intended.

Activity 5.21 Previewing and Printing a Document

1 Press [Ctrl] + [Home] to move the insertion point to the beginning of the document. From the **Office** menu 🔘, point to **Print**, and then click **Print Preview**.

> One or more pages of your document display exactly as they will print. The formatting marks, which do not print, are not displayed. The size of the preview depends on the zoom level used the last time the Print Preview window was opened.

2 In the **Print Preview** window, move the mouse pointer anywhere over the document. Notice that the pointer becomes a magnifying glass with a plus in it, indicating that you can magnify the view, as shown in Figure 5.44.

> If you are viewing multiple pages, you may have to click on a page before the magnifying glass displays.

Figure 5.44

Magnifying glass pointer —————————

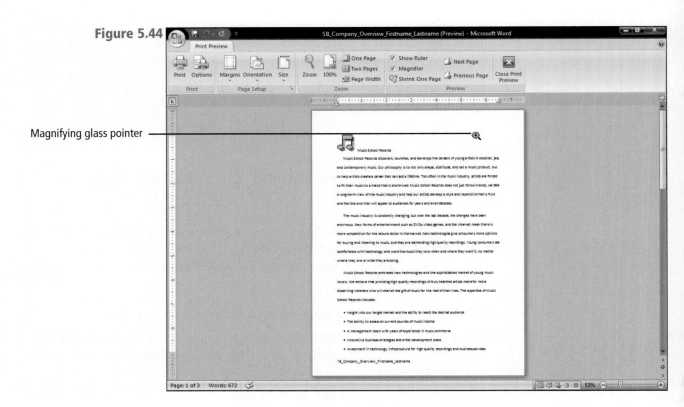

3 Move the 🔍 pointer over the upper portion of the first page of the document and click one time.

The top portion of the document magnifies, making it easier to read. The pointer changes to a magnifying glass with a minus sign.

4 Click anywhere on the document to zoom out. On the right side of the status bar, drag the **Zoom slider** to the left until you can see all three pages, as shown in Figure 5.45. Notice that the footers display on the bottom of each page.

Figure 5.45

One Page button

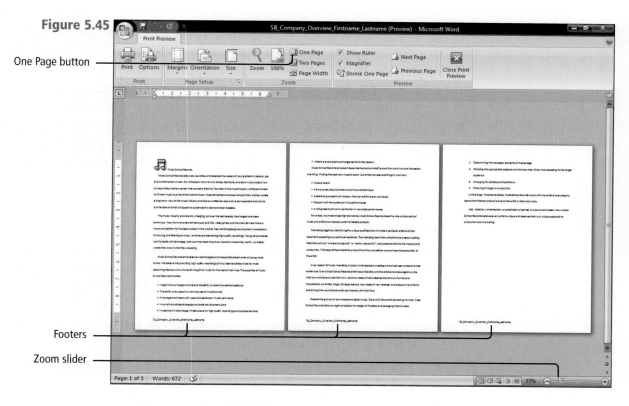

Footers

Zoom slider

5 On the **Print Preview tab**, in the **Zoom group**, click the **One Page** button to display a single page of the document.

6 In the **Preview group**, click the **Close Print Preview** button.

7 From the **Office** menu 🔘, click **Print**, and then compare your screen with Figure 5.46.

The Print dialog box displays. Here you can specify which pages to print and how many copies you want. Additional command buttons for Options and Properties provide more printing choices. The printer that displays will be the default printer that is selected for your computer.

Figure 5.46

Selected printer

Number of copies

Current page option

Pages to print

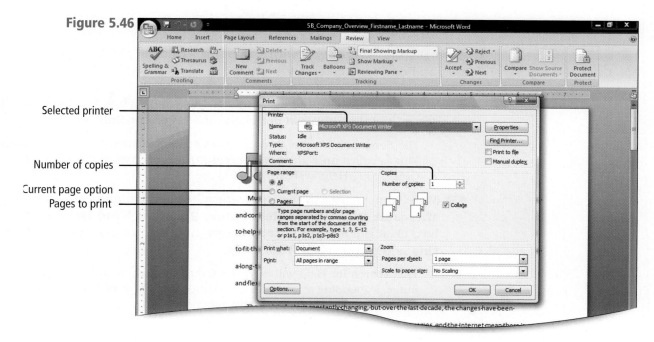

8 In the **Print** dialog box, under **Copies**, change the number of copies to *2* by typing **2** in the text box, or by clicking the **spin box up arrow**.

A **spin box** is a small box with upward- and downward-pointing arrows that enables you to move—spin—through a set of values by clicking.

9 Under **Page range**, click the **Current page** option button, and then, at the bottom of the **Print** dialog box, click **OK** if you want to print two copies of the first page. If you do not want to print, click **Cancel**.

Activity 5.22 Closing a Document and Closing Word

1 Check your *Chapter Assignment Sheet* or *Course Syllabus* or consult your instructor to determine if you are to submit your assignments on paper or electronically. To submit electronically, go to Step 3, and then follow the instructions provided by your instructor.

2 From the **Office** menu ⊙, click **Print**. At the bottom of the **Print** dialog box, click **OK**.

3 From the **Office** menu ⊙, click **Close**, saving any changes if prompted to do so.

4 At the far right of the title bar, click the **Close** button ⊠ to exit the Word program.

Objective 9
Use the Microsoft Help System

As you work with Word, you can get assistance by using the Help feature. You can type key words and phrases and Help will provide you with information and step-by-step instructions for performing tasks.

Activity 5.23 Getting Help

Word Help is available on your computer, online at the Microsoft Web site, and on your screen with enhanced ScreenTips.

1 **Start** Word. Click the **Page Layout tab**, and then in the **Page Setup group**, point to—but do not click—the **Hyphenation** button.

The ScreenTip for this button has more information than just the name. This is called an **Enhanced ScreenTip**, and is part of the Microsoft Office 2007 Help system.

2 Move your pointer to the right side of the Ribbon and click the **Microsoft Office Word Help** button ⊙. In the **Word Help** dialog box, click the **Search button arrow**, and then under **Content from this computer**, click **Word Help**.

This search for Help will be restricted to the Help installed on your computer. Depending on your Word settings, the *Table of Contents* on the left of the Word Help dialog box may not display.

3 To the left of the **Search** button, click in the **Type words to search for** box, type **save a file** and then press Enter. Notice that a list of related topics displays, as shown in Figure 5.47. Your list may differ.

Figure 5.47

Search button arrow —

Type words to search for box —

Help button —

Search results —

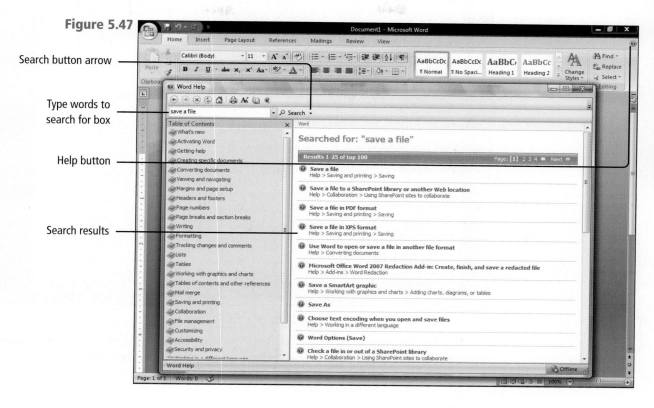

4 From the list, point to, and then click **Save a file**.

5 Under **What do you want to do?** click **Save a file to another format (Save As command)**—the wording for this topic may vary. Notice that step-by-step instructions are given, as shown in Figure 5.48.

Figure 5.48

Instructions for saving a
document under
another format

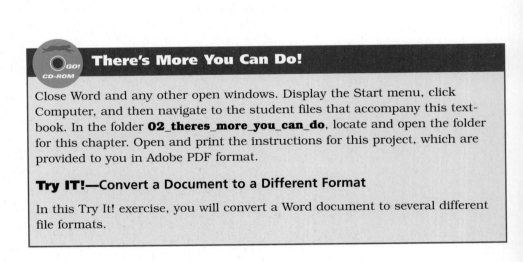

6 In the upper right corner of the Word Help window, click the **Close** button **X**. From the **Office** menu, click **Exit Word** to close the Word program.

End **You have completed Project 5B**

There's More You Can Do!

Close Word and any other open windows. Display the Start menu, click Computer, and then navigate to the student files that accompany this textbook. In the folder **02_theres_more_you_can_do**, locate and open the folder for this chapter. Open and print the instructions for this project, which are provided to you in Adobe PDF format.

Try IT!—Convert a Document to a Different Format

In this Try It! exercise, you will convert a Word document to several different file formats.

Content-Based Assessments

chapter **five**

Summary

In this chapter, you started Word and practiced navigating the Word window. You entered text, deleted text by using the Backspace and Delete keys, selected and replaced text, and inserted text. The spelling and grammar checker tools were demonstrated, and an image was added to a document.

You also practiced changing font style and size and adding emphasis to text. You viewed the header and footer areas, and created a chapter folder to help organize your files. Each document was saved, previewed, printed, and closed. Finally, the Help program was introduced as a tool that can assist you in using Word.

Key Terms

The ⊕ symbol represents Key Terms found on the Student CD in the 02_theres_more_you_can_do folder for this chapter.

Content-Based Assessments

Matching

Match each term in the second column with its correct definition in the first column. Write the letter of the term on the blank line in front of the correct definition.

_____ **1.** The location in the Word window, indicated by a blinking vertical line, where text will be inserted when you start to type.

_____ **2.** In the Word window, the location of the Minimize, Maximize/Restore Down, and Close buttons.

_____ **3.** A button that represents the command to reveal nonprinting characters.

_____ **4.** The action that takes place when the insertion point reaches the right margin and automatically moves down and to the left margin of the next line.

_____ **5.** The process of setting the overall appearance of the text within the document.

_____ **6.** To hold down the left mouse button and move the mouse pointer over text to select it.

_____ **7.** A set of characters (letters and numbers) with the same design and shape.

_____ **8.** A unit of measure to describe the size of a font.

_____ **9.** A font type, such as Calibri or Arial, that does not have lines on the ends of characters.

_____ **10.** A font type, such as Cambria or Times New Roman, that has extensions or lines on the ends of the characters.

_____ **11.** The term that refers to pressing one or more keys to navigate a window or execute commands.

_____ **12.** This feature changes the selected text when the pointer points to a button or list item to display what the text will look like if the button or list item is clicked.

_____ **13.** A reserved area for text and graphics that displays at the bottom of each page in a document or section of a document.

_____ **14.** A view that simplifies the page layout for quick typing and can show more text on a smaller screen.

_____ **15.** A context-sensitive list that displays when you click the right mouse button.

A Draft

B Drag

C Font

D Footer

E Formatting

F Insertion point

G Keyboard shortcut

H Live Preview

I Point

J Sans serif

K Serif

L Shortcut menu

M Show/Hide

N Title bar

O Wordwrap

Content-Based Assessments

Fill in the Blank

Write the correct word in the space provided.

1. Microsoft Word 2007 is a word _____ program that you can use to perform tasks such as writing a memo, a report, or a letter.

2. Located at the bottom of the Word window, the bar that provides information such as page number and word count is referred to as the _____ bar.

3. Within the scroll bar, dragging the _____ _____ downward causes the document on your screen to move up.

4. A toolbar above the Ribbon and to the right of the Office button, which can be customized by adding frequently used buttons, is called the _____ _____ _____.

5. Characters that display on the screen to show the location of paragraph marks, tabs, and spaces but that do not print are called _____ marks.

6. If you point to a button on the Ribbon, a _____ displays the name of the button.

7. In a business letter, the address of the recipient is called a _____ address.

8. When you select text, the _____ toolbar displays buttons that are commonly used with the selected object.

9. Before text can be edited, changed, formatted, copied, or moved, it must first be _____.

10. To add emphasis to text, use the _____ or _____ or _____ command, each of which has a button on the Ribbon.

11. The view that displays the page borders, margins, text, and graphics is the _____ _____ view.

12. The View buttons are located on the right side of the _____ bar.

13. To enlarge or decrease the viewing area of the document, use the _____ _____ on the status bar.

14. Graphic images, of which some are included with Word, that can be inserted in the document are called _____ art.

15. To display a shortcut menu, click the _____ mouse button.

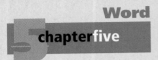

Project 5C—Receipt Letter

In this project, you will apply the skills you practiced from the Objectives in Project 5A.

Objectives: 1. *Create and Save a New Document;* **2.** *Edit Text;* **3.** *Select, Delete, and Format Text;* **4.** *Print a Document.*

In the following Skills Review, you will create and edit a follow-up letter from Jamal Anderssen, a production manager for Music School Records, to William Hawken, a recording artist who has submitted a demo CD with his application. Your completed letter will look similar to the one shown in Figure 5.49.

For Project 5C, you will need the following file:

New blank Word document

You will save your document as
5C_Receipt_Letter_Firstname_Lastname

Figure 5.49

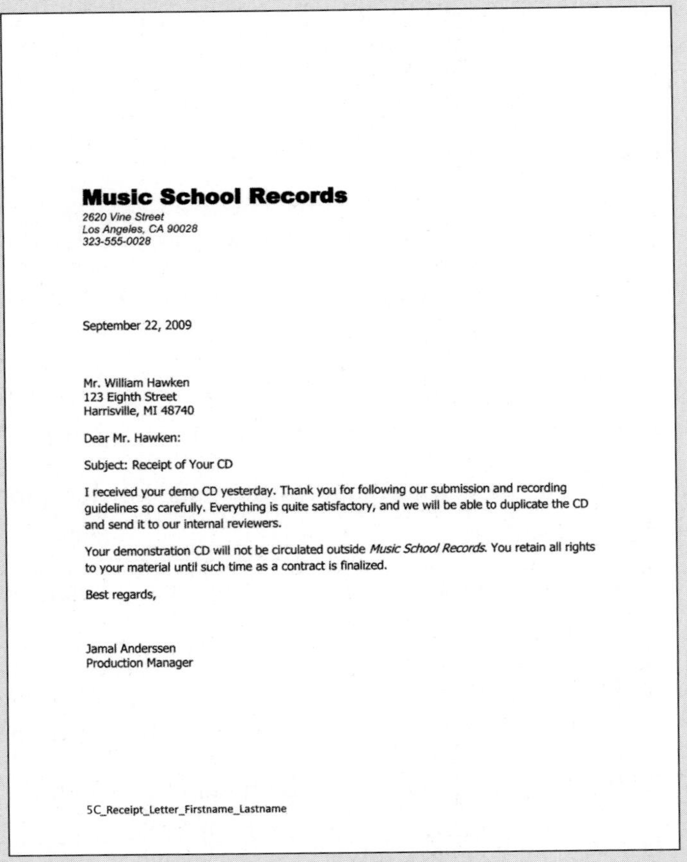

Music School Records
2620 Vine Street
Los Angeles, CA 90028
323-555-0028

September 22, 2009

Mr. William Hawken
123 Eighth Street
Harrisville, MI 48740

Dear Mr. Hawken:

Subject: Receipt of Your CD

I received your demo CD yesterday. Thank you for following our submission and recording guidelines so carefully. Everything is quite satisfactory, and we will be able to duplicate the CD and send it to our internal reviewers.

Your demonstration CD will not be circulated outside *Music School Records*. You retain all rights to your material until such time as a contract is finalized.

Best regards,

Jamal Anderssen
Production Manager

5C_Receipt_Letter_Firstname_Lastname

(Project 5C–Receipt Letter continues on the next page)

Content-Based Assessments

(Project 5C–Receipt Letter continued)

1. **Start** Word. If necessary, on the Ribbon, in the **Paragraph group**, click the **Show/Hide ¶** button to display the formatting marks. In the status bar, use the **Zoom slider** to adjust the page width to display both the left and right page edges.

2. On the **Home tab**, in the **Styles group**, click the **No Spacing** style. With the insertion point blinking in the upper left corner of the document to the left of the default first paragraph mark, type **Music School Records** and then press [Enter]. Type the following text and press [Enter] after each line:

   2620 Vine Street
   Los Angeles, CA 90028
   323-555-0028

3. Press [Enter] five more times. Begin typing today's date and let AutoComplete assist in your typing by pressing [Enter] when the ScreenTip displays. Press [Enter] four times. Type the inside address on three lines:

   Mr. William Hawken
   123 Eighth Street
   Harrisville, MI 48740

4. On the **Quick Access Toolbar**, click the **Save** button. In the **Save As** dialog box, navigate to your **Word Chapter 5** folder. In the **File name** box, using your own first and last names, type **5C_Receipt_Letter_ Firstname_Lastname** and then click **Save**.

5. On the **Home tab**, in the **Styles group**, click the **Normal** style. Press [Enter], type the salutation **Dear Mr. Hawken:** and then press [Enter].

6. Type **Subject: receipt of Your CD** and then press [Enter]. Then, using just one space following the periods at the end of sentences, type the following text:

   I received your demo CD yesterday.
   Thank you for following our submission
   and recording standards so carefully.

Everything is satisfactory, and we will be able to duplicate the CD and send it to our internal reviewers.

7. Press [Enter] to begin a new paragraph, and then type the following:

   Your demonstration CD will not be circulated outside Music School Records. You retain the rights to your material until such time as a contract is finalized.

8. Press [Enter], type the closing **Best regards,** and then press [Enter] two times.

9. On the **Quick Access Toolbar**, click the **Save** button to save your changes. On the **Home tab**, in the **Styles group**, click the **No Spacing** style. Finish the letter by typing the writer's identification on two lines:

   Jamal Anderssen
   Production Manager

10. If necessary, drag the vertical scroll box to the top of the scroll bar to view the upper portion of the document. In the *Subject* line, position the insertion point to the left of *receipt*, and then press [Del]. Type **R** to capitalize *Receipt*.

11. In the paragraph beginning *I received*, double-click the word **standards** to select it, and then type **guidelines**

12. In the same paragraph, position the insertion point to the left of the word *satisfactory*. Type **quite** and then press [Spacebar] one time.

13. In the paragraph beginning *Your demonstration*, click to position the insertion point to the left of *rights*, press [←Bksp] four times. Type **all** and then press [Spacebar] to change the phrase to *retain all rights*.

14. **Save** your changes. Press [Ctrl] + [A] to select the entire document. On the **Home**

(Project 5C–Receipt Letter continues on the next page)

(Project 5C–Receipt Letter continued)

tab, in the **Font group**, click the **Font button arrow**. Scroll as necessary, and watch Live Preview change the document font as you point to different font names. Click to choose **Tahoma**. Click anywhere in the document to cancel the selection.

15. Select the entire first line of text—*Music School Records*. On the Mini toolbar, click the **Font button arrow**, and then click **Arial Black**. With the Mini toolbar still displayed, click the **Font Size button arrow**, and then click **20**. With the Mini toolbar still displayed, click the **Bold** button.

16. Select the second, third, and fourth lines of text, beginning with *2620 Vine Street* and ending with the telephone number. On the Mini toolbar, click the **Font button arrow**, and then click **Arial**. With the Mini toolbar still displayed, click the **Font Size button arrow**, and then click **10**. With the Mini toolbar still displayed, click the **Italic** button.

17. In the paragraph beginning *Your demonstration*, select the text *Music School Records*. On the Mini toolbar, click the **Italic** button, and then click anywhere to deselect the text.

18. Click the **Insert tab**. In the **Header & Footer group**, click the **Footer** button, and then click **Edit Footer**. On the

Design tab, in the **Insert group**, click the **Quick Parts** button, and then click **Field**. In the **Field** dialog box, under **Field names**, scroll down and click to choose **FileName**, and then click **OK**. Double-click anywhere in the document to leave the footer area.

19. Click the **Page Layout tab**. In the **Page Setup group**, click the **Margins** button to display the Margins gallery. At the bottom of the **Margins gallery**, click **Custom Margins** to display the **Page Setup** dialog box. Near the top of the **Page Setup** dialog box, click the **Layout tab**. Under **Page**, click the **Vertical alignment arrow**, click **Center**, and then click **OK**.

20. From the **Office** menu, point to **Print**, and then click **Print Preview** to make a final check of your letter. Check your *Chapter Assignment Sheet* or *Course Syllabus* or consult your instructor to determine if you are to submit your assignments on paper or electronically. To submit electronically, go to Step 22, and then follow the instructions provided by your instructor.

21. On the **Print Preview tab**, in the **Print group**, click the **Print** button. Click **OK**, and then **Close Print Preview**.

22. From the **Office** menu, click **Exit Word**, saving any changes if prompted to do so.

End **You have completed Project 5C** ―――――――――――

Content-Based Assessments

Skills Review

Project 5D — Marketing

In this project, you will apply the skills you practiced from the Objectives in Project 5B.

Objectives: 5. *Navigate the Word Window;* **6.** *Add a Graphic to a Document;* **7.** *Use the Spelling and Grammar Checker;* **8.** *Preview and Print Documents, Close a Document, and Close Word;* **9.** *Use the Microsoft Help System.*

In the following Skills Review, you will edit a document that details the marketing and promotion plan for Music School Records. Your completed document will look similar to Figure 5.50.

For Project 5D, you will need the following files:

New blank Word document
w05D_Marketing
w05D_Piano

You will save your document as
5D_Marketing_Firstname_Lastname

Figure 5.50

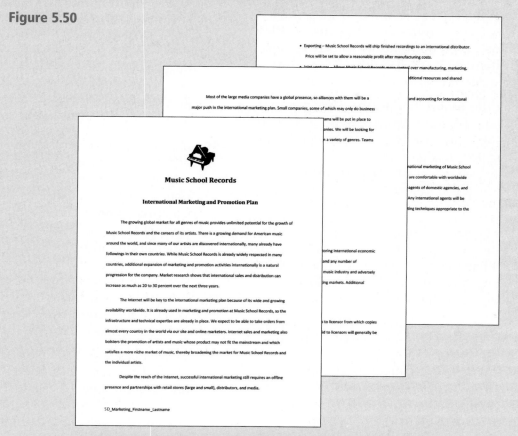

(Project 5D–Marketing continues on the next page)

Content-Based Assessments

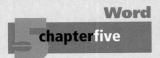

Skills Review

(Project 5D–Marketing continued)

1. **Start** Word and be sure a new blank document is displayed. If necessary, on the Ribbon, in the Paragraph group, click the Show/Hide ¶ button to display the formatting marks. In the status bar, use the Zoom slider to adjust the page width to display both the left and right page edges.

2. On the **Quick Access Toolbar**, click the **Save** button. In the **Save As** dialog box, navigate to your **Word Chapter 5** folder. In the **File name** box, using your own first and last names, type **5D_Marketing_Firstname_Lastname** and then click **Save**.

3. Click the **Insert tab**. In the **Header & Footer group**, click the **Footer** button to display the Footer gallery. At the bottom of the **Footer gallery**, click **Edit Footer**. On the **Design tab**, in the **Insert group**, click the **Quick Parts** button, and then click **Field**. In the **Field** dialog box, under **Field names**, scroll down and click **FileName**, and then click **OK**. Double-click anywhere in the document to leave the footer area.

4. Click the **Insert tab**. In the **Text group**, click the **Object button arrow**, and then click **Text from File**. In the **Insert File** dialog box, navigate to your student files. Locate and select **w05D_Marketing**, and then click the **Insert** button to insert the text.

5. Press ⟨←Bksp⟩ to remove the blank line at the end of the document. Use the vertical scroll bar to examine the document. When you are finished, press ⟨Ctrl⟩ + ⟨Home⟩ to move to the beginning of the document.

6. **Save** your document. Move the ⟨⟩ pointer into the margin area to the left of the title *Music School Records* and drag down to select the title, the blank line, and the second title that begins *International Marketting*. Be sure to include the blank

line between the two titles. On the Mini toolbar, click the **Bold** button. Click anywhere in the document to deselect the text.

7. In the second title line, notice that the word *Marketting* is marked as misspelled. Right-click *Marketting*, and from the shortcut menu, click **Marketing**. In the first line of the paragraph that begins *The growing global*, right-click *geners*, and from the shortcut menu, locate and click **genres**.

8. Click the **Review tab**, and then, in the **Proofing group**, click the **Spelling & Grammar** button to open the **Spelling and Grammar** dialog box. The first word flagged is *allready*. Notice that this word is misspelled several times in the document.

9. In the **Spelling and Grammar** dialog box, click the **Change All** button to correct all occurrences of this misspelled word. The next potential error—a subject-verb agreement problem—is highlighted. Notice that two suggested corrections are listed. If necessary, click **is a growing demand**, and then click the **Change** button.

10. If a Passive Voice error is identified next, click Ignore Once. In the paragraph that begins *The Internet will be key*, another potential grammar problem is highlighted. Click the **Ignore Once** button to leave the sentence the way it was written. Ignore other grammar errors, and then correct the spelling error for the word *Millenium*. Continue to click the **Ignore Once** button until you reach the end of the document. When a message box tells you the check is complete, click **OK**.

11. Press ⟨Ctrl⟩ + ⟨Home⟩ to move to the beginning of the document, and then press ⟨Enter⟩ to add a blank line. Click to position the insertion point in the new blank line.

(Project 5D–Marketing continues on the next page)

Word

chapterfive   Skills Review

(Project 5D–Marketing continued)

12. Click the **Microsoft Office Word Help** button. In the **Word Help** dialog box, click the **Search button arrow**, and then under **Content from this computer**, click **Word Help**. In the **Type words to search for** box, type **graphic file types** and then press ⏎. In the search results, click **Types of media files you can add** and examine the list of graphic file types that can be added to a Word document.

13. **Close** the **Word Help** window, and then click the **Insert tab**. In the **Illustrations group**, click the **Picture** button. In the **Insert Picture** dialog box, navigate to the student files that accompany this textbook, click the **w05D_Piano** file, and then click **Insert**.

14. **Save** your changes. Check your *Chapter Assignment Sheet* or *Course Syllabus* or consult your instructor to determine if you are to submit your assignments on paper or electronically. To submit electronically, go to Step 16, and then follow the instructions provided by your instructor.

15. From the **Office** menu, point to **Print**, and then click **Print Preview** to make a final check of your document. On the **Print Preview tab**, in the **Print group**, click the **Print** button, and from the **Print** dialog box, click **OK**. Then, in the **Preview group**, click the **Close Print Preview** button.

16. From the **Office** menu, click **Close**. At the right end of the title bar, click the **Close** button to close Word.

End **You have completed Project 5D** ⸺⸺⸺⸺⸺⸺⸺⸺⸺

Word
chapterfive

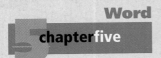

Mastering Word

Project 5E — Contract

In this project, you will apply the skills you practiced from the Objectives in Projects 5A and 5B.

Objectives: 2. *Edit Text;* **3.** *Select, Delete, and Format Text;* **4.** *Print a Document;* **5.** *Navigate the Word Window;* **7.** *Use the Spelling and Grammar Checker;* **8.** *Preview and Print Documents, Close a Document, and Close Word.*

In the following Mastering Word project, you will edit a contract between a client and Music School Records. Your completed document will look similar to Figure 5.51.

For Project 5E, you will need the following file:

w05E_Contract

You will save your document as
5E_Contract_Firstname_Lastname

Figure 5.51

The Second Party is required to present an individualized promotional plan for the Artist in the Chicago Metropolitan Area. Upon approval of the plan, Music School Records will release the above-mentioned products and allow access to the Artist. The Second Party

Contract for Services

PARTIES TO THE CONTRACT
The First Party's name is Music School Records, a Corporation.

The Second Party's name is **Evie Chardan**, an individual proprietor.

WHO HAS TO DO WHAT
Music School Records and **Evie Chardan** agree to the following:
Music School Records will provide the Second Party various marketing materials and recordings of **Evie Chardan** (the Artist) for the purposes of publicizing and promoting the Artist to music stores in the Chicago metropolitan area.

The materials provided by Music School Records may include printed brochures, promotional CDs, pre-loaded digital music players, advertising copy, Artist fact sheets, photographs, and press clips. Also available as requested will be low-value promotional items such as buttons, stickers, and other trinkets.

Music School Records will also provide, with proper notice and approval of venue, access to the Artist for press conferences, interviews, media appearances, and performances. All such personal appearances will be subject to Music School Records' contract with the Artist.

Music School Records is responsible for the accuracy of all printed materials. Music School Records is also

The Second Party will take all legally required actions and professionally appropriate care in protecting the copyrights of Music School Records and the Artist. The Second Party is responsible for the health and safety of the Artist while at appearances arranged by the Second Party. If the Artist is a minor, the Second Party will follow all applicable laws relating to care and work of a minor.

The Second Party will be responsible for writing/producing and releasing press clips (print, audio and video) following any promotional events. The Second Party is responsible for the accuracy of such releases and clips. Other promotional actions are expected to include, but are not limited to:

- Announcements and listings in local press entertainment calendars
- Arrangement of and public service announcements for charity events
- Mailings, faxes, and phone calls to local press, club owners, music store managers, etc.
- Any necessary local Web presence

5E_Contract_Firstname_Lastname

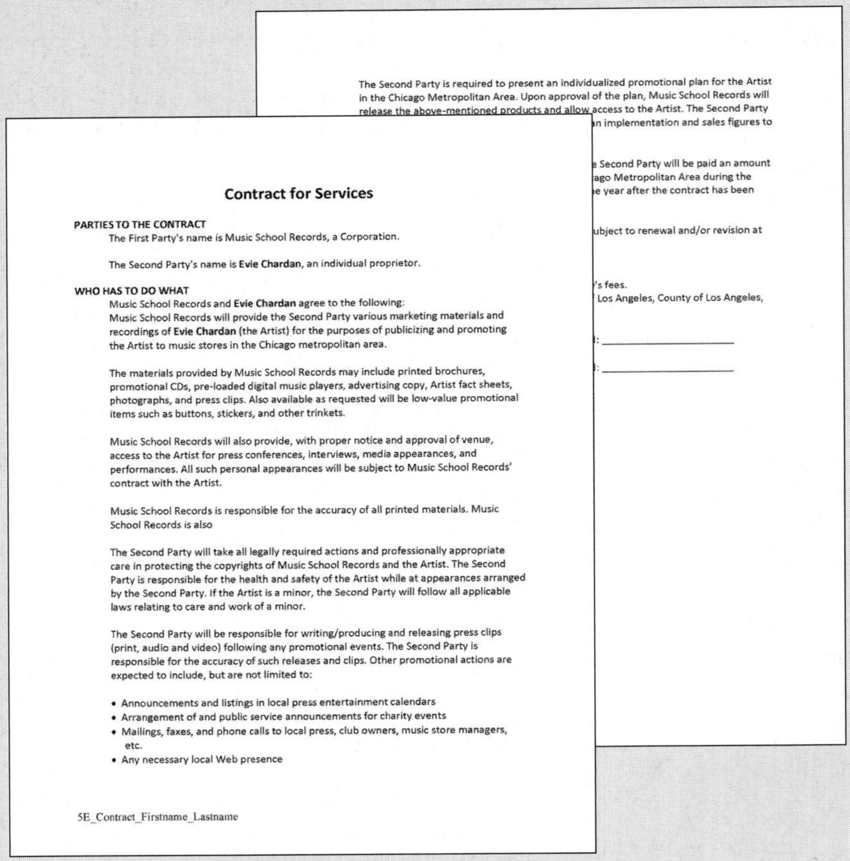

(Project 5E–Contract continues on the next page)

Content-Based Assessments

(Project 5E–Contract continued)

1. Locate and open the document **w05E_ Contract**. **Save** the document in your **Word Chapter 5** folder as **5E_Contract_ Firstname_Lastname** and then add the file name to the footer. Display formatting marks, display the ruler, and set the page width to a comfortable size for you.

2. If necessary, move to the beginning of the document, type **Contract for Services** and press Enter. Select *Contract for Services*, change the **Font Size** to **18** points, and apply **Bold** emphasis.

3. Use the **Spelling and Grammar** checker to correct the errors in the document. There are several misspellings of the word *responsibel* and a subject-verb agreement error—*are* instead of *is*. Ignore all other flagged items.

4. Locate the three headings in uppercase letters. Select each one and add **Bold** emphasis. Recall that when you select the text, the Mini toolbar displays with the Bold button on it.

5. Locate the black lines in the document that represent blanks to be filled in. In the line beginning *The Second Party's name*, select the long line, but not the comma following it. Type **Evie Chardan** and notice that as you type, your typing will be displayed in bold. On the next two long lines, use the same technique to type **Evie Chardan** again.

6. On **Page 2**, in the paragraph beginning *For services provided*, select the line and type **12** Select the line following *This agreement will be in force for*, type **2** and then delete *months/* so that the sentence reads *in force for 2 years*.

7. **Save** your changes. At the end of the contract, under *Signed*, select the text *Music School Records*, and then on the Mini toolbar, change the font size to **10** and add **Bold** emphasis. **Save** your changes. **Preview** the document and then print or submit electronically as directed by your instructor. **Close** the document, and then **Exit** Word.

End **You have completed Project 5E** ——————————————

Content-Based Assessments

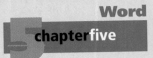
Mastering Word

Project 5F—Invitation

In this project, you will apply the skills you practiced from the Objectives in Projects 5A and 5B.

Objectives: 1. *Create and Save a New Document;* **2.** *Edit Text;* **3.** *Select, Delete, and Format Text;* **4.** *Print a Document;* **5.** *Navigate the Word Window;* **6.** *Add a Graphic to a Document;* **7.** *Use the Spelling and Grammar Checker;* **8.** *Preview and Print Documents, Close a Document, and Close Word.*

In the following Mastering Word project, you will create a new letter to a talent agent, and then insert and edit text from a file. Your completed document will look similar to Figure 5.52.

For Project 5F, you will need the following files:

New blank Word document
w05F_Invitation
w05F_Letterhead

You will save your document as
5F_Invitation_Firstname_Lastname

Figure 5.52

> **Music School Records**
>
> **2620 Vine Street**
>
> **Los Angeles, CA 90028**
>
> **323-555-0028**
>
> **Musicschoolrecords.com**
>
> September 30, 2009
>
> Ms. Caroline Westbrook
> Artists' Workshop Agency
> 249 Fifth Avenue #2700
> New York, NY 10001
>
> Dear Ms. Westbrook:
>
> Thank you for the introduction to your client, Ms. Evie Chardan. Our representatives were very impressed with the quality of Ms. Chardan's music, stage presence, and obvious rapport with the young audience for which she performed. It is certainly our pleasure to invite Ms. Chardan to consider a recording contract with **Music School Records**.
>
> Upon your approval, we will draft a standard contract for your and Ms. Chardan's attorneys' review. The contract will be subject to the laws of California and will include language outlining the term of the contract, guaranteed minimum payments per year, and obligations of the artist and **Music School Records**. As part of the standard contract we do require a period of exclusivity regarding the artist's recording, and this period is subject to negotiation.
>
> Please call me as soon as possible to confirm your client's agreement to draft the contract. We are looking forward to working with you again and playing a key role in the development of Ms. Chardan's career.
>
> Sincerely,
>
> John Diamond
> Assistant Vice President, Creative Development
>
> 5F_Invitation_Firstname_Lastname

(Project 5F–Invitation continues on the next page)

Word

chapterfive

Mastering Word

(Project 5F–Invitation continued)

1. **Start** Word and be sure a new blank document is displayed. Display formatting marks, display the ruler, and be sure your screen displays both the left and right document edges. **Save** the document in your **Word Chapter 5** folder as **5F_Invitation_Firstname_Lastname** Open the document footer and add the file name.

2. Locate and insert the file **w05F_ Letterhead**. Be sure the insertion point is positioned at the second blank line below the letterhead, and then type the current date. Using the skills you practiced in Project 5A, be sure the address style is set to **No Spacing**, and then add the following inside address:

   Ms. Caroline Westbrook
   Artists' Workshop Agency
   249 Fifth Avenue #2700
   New York, NY 10001

3. Change the style back to **Normal**, press Enter, and then type **Dear Ms. Westbrook:** Press Enter, and then locate and insert the file **w05F_Invitation**. Add the following paragraph at the end of the document:

   Please call me as soon as possible to confirm your client's agreement to draft the contract. We are looking forward to working with you again and playing a key role in the development of Ms. Chardan's career.

4. Using appropriate spacing, add the complimentary closing **Sincerely,** and then add the following writer's identification:

   John Diamond
   Assistant Vice President, Creative Development

5. **Save** your changes. Be sure grammar errors are flagged in the document. In the paragraph beginning *Thank you*, in the second sentence, correct the grammar error *was*, and then type **very** between *were* and *impressed*. In the third line of the same paragraph, add **certainly** between *It is* and *our pleasure*. In the last sentence of the same paragraph, change *sign* to **consider**

6. Use the **Spelling & Grammar** checker to correct the errors in the document. There is one error—the misspelled word *qualty*. Ignore all other flagged items.

7. At the end of the paragraph beginning *Thank you for the introduction*, locate the text *Music School Records* and add **Bold** emphasis. In the paragraph beginning *Upon your approval*, add **Bold** emphasis to *Music School Records*.

8. Select the entire document. Change the **Font** to **Cambria**. **Save** your changes.

9. **Preview** the document and then print or submit electronically as directed by your instructor. **Close** the file, and then **Exit** Word.

 End **You have completed Project 5F** ─────────────

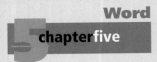

Word
chapterfive

Mastering Word

Project 5G—Fax Cover

In this project, you will apply the skills you practiced from the Objectives in Projects 5A and 5B.

Objectives: 1. *Create and Save a New Document;* **2.** *Edit Text;* **3.** *Select, Delete, and Format Text;* **4.** *Print a Document;* **5.** *Navigate the Word Window;* **6.** *Add a Graphic to a Document;* **7.** *Use the Spelling and Grammar Checker;* **8.** *Preview and Print Documents, Close a Document, and Close Word.*

In the following Mastering Word project, you will create a cover sheet for a facsimile (fax) transmission. When sending a fax, it is common practice to include a cover sheet with a note describing the pages that will follow. Your completed document will look similar to Figure 5.53.

For Project 5G, you will need the following files:

New blank Word document
w05G_Fax_Cover
w05G_Fax_Machine

**You will save your document as
5G_Fax_Cover_Firstname_Lastname**

Figure 5.53

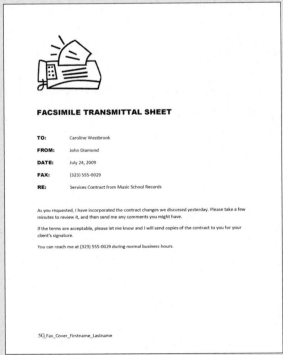

(Project 5G–Fax Cover continues on the next page)

Word

chapterfive

Mastering Word

(Project 5G–Fax Cover continued)

1. **Start** Word and be sure a new blank document is displayed. Display formatting marks and rulers, and be sure your screen displays both the left and right document edges. **Save** the document in your **Word Chapter 5** folder as **5G_Fax_Cover_Firstname_Lastname** Open the document footer and add the file name to the footer.

2. Move the insertion point to the top of the document. Press Enter two times, and then move back to the top of the document. From your student files, insert the **w05G_Fax_Machine** picture. Press Ctrl + End. Press CapsLock, type **FACSIMILE TRANSMITTAL SHEET** and then press Enter two times. Press CapsLock again.

3. Locate and insert the file **w05G_Fax_Cover**. Move to the blank line at the end of the document, and then type **You can reach me at (323) 555-0029 during normal business hours. Save** your document.

4. Select the text *FACSIMILE TRANSMITTAL SHEET*. Change the **Font Size** to **16**, and the **Font** to **Arial Black**. Change the font of the line headings *TO:, FROM:, DATE:, FAX:,* and *RE:* to **Arial Black**.

5. In the paragraph that begins *As you requested*, select and delete the text *on the telephone*. In the same paragraph, replace the phrase *look it over* with **review it** and, in the same sentence, add an **s** to *comment*.

6. There are several grammar and spelling errors that need to be corrected. Use the **Spelling & Grammar** checker to correct the duplicate or misspelled words. In the paragraph beginning *If the term are*, select the **terms are** suggested change. **Save** your changes.

7. Use Ctrl + Home to navigate to the beginning of the document. Proofread the fax cover to be sure you have made all necessary corrections.

8. **Preview** the document, and then print or submit electronically as directed by your instructor. **Close** the document, and **Exit** Word.

End **You have completed Project 5G**

Content-Based Assessments

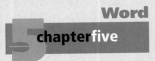
Mastering Word

Project 5H — *GO!* Fix It

In this project, you will construct a solution by applying any combination of the skills you practiced from the Objectives in Projects 5A and 5B.

For Project 5H, you will need the following files:

w05H_Approval_Letter
w05H_Music_Logo

You will save your document as
5H_Approval_Letter_Firstname_Lastname

From the student files that accompany this textbook, locate and open the file **w05H_Approval_Letter**, and then save the file in your chapter folder as **5H_Approval_Letter_Firstname_Lastname**

This document contains errors that you must find and correct. Read and examine the document, and then edit to correct the errors that you find. Types of errors could include:

- Spelling, grammar, punctuation, and usage errors such as text case, repeated text, subject-verb agreement, and meaning.

- Content errors such as missing or incorrect text.

- Paragraph formatting and positioning errors such as wordwrap, sentence spacing, missing text, or unnecessary text or blank lines.

- Page setup errors such as margins, orientation, layout, or alignment.

Things you should know to complete this project:

- Displaying formatting marks will assist in locating spacing errors.

- The name Hawken and the name HawkenDove are spelled correctly.

- Set the Word Proofing Options so that when correcting spelling and grammar in Word, Grammar & Style is selected.

- There are no errors in the fonts or font sizes.

- A logo graphic is missing in the letterhead. From your student files, insert the logo graphic **w05H_ Music_Logo** to the left of *Music School Records* followed by one space. Format the logo graphic using wrapping style In line with text. For the size, modify the scale height to 50% and select the lock aspect ratio.

- Spacing following the inside address should change to Normal style.

Save your document, add the file name to the footer, and then submit as directed.

End **You have completed Project 5H**

Rubric

The following outcomes-based assessments are *open-ended assessments*. That is, there is no specific correct result; your result will depend on your approach to the information provided. Make *Professional Quality* your goal. Use the following scoring rubric to guide you in *how* to approach the problem and then to evaluate *how well* your approach solves the problem.

The *criteria*—Software Mastery, Content, Format and Layout, and Process—represent the knowledge and skills you have gained that you can apply to solving the problem. The *levels of performance*—Professional Quality, Approaching Professional Quality, or Needs Quality Improvements—help you and your instructor evaluate your result.

	Your completed project is of Professional Quality if you:	Your completed project is Approaching Professional Quality if you:	Your completed project Needs Quality Improvements if you:
1-Software Mastery	Choose and apply the most appropriate skills, tools, and features and identify efficient methods to solve the problem.	Choose and apply some appropriate skills, tools, and features, but not in the most efficient manner.	Choose inappropriate skills, tools, or features, or are inefficient in solving the problem.
2-Content	Construct a solution that is clear and well organized, contains content that is accurate, appropriate to the audience and purpose, and is complete. Provide a solution that contains no errors of spelling, grammar, or style.	Construct a solution in which some components are unclear, poorly organized, inconsistent, or incomplete. Misjudge the needs of the audience. Have some errors in spelling, grammar, or style, but the errors do not detract from comprehension.	Construct a solution that is unclear, incomplete, or poorly organized; contains some inaccurate or inappropriate content; and contains many errors of spelling, grammar, or style. Do not solve the problem.
3-Format and Layout	Format and arrange all elements to communicate information and ideas, clarify function, illustrate relationships, and indicate relative importance.	Apply appropriate format and layout features to some elements, but not others. Overuse features, causing minor distraction.	Apply format and layout that does not communicate information or ideas clearly. Do not use format and layout features to clarify function, illustrate relationships, or indicate relative importance. Use available features excessively, causing distraction.
4-Process	Use an organized approach that integrates planning, development, self-assessment, revision, and reflection.	Demonstrate an organized approach in some areas, but not others; or, use an insufficient process of organization throughout.	Do not use an organized approach to solve the problem.

Outcomes-Based Assessments

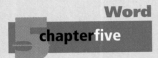
Problem Solving

Project 5I — Services

In this project, you will construct a solution by applying any combination of the skills you practiced from the Objectives in Projects 5A and 5B.

For Project 5I, you will need the following file:

New blank Word document

You will save your document as
5I_Services_Firstname_Lastname

Using the information provided, compose a form letter from Lucy Burroughs—Vice President of Creative Services—that explains the services offered by the company. Music School Records is located at 2620 Vine Street, Los Angeles, CA 90028, (323) 555-0028. The tone of the letter should be positive and sales-oriented. The letter should answer the question, *Why do I need this service?* As you write the letter, use the information in Project 5B that describes the company. The letter should contain three paragraphs—an introductory paragraph, a second paragraph describing the services offered, and a closing paragraph.

The letter should include the appropriate business letter components, and should be in the proper business format. Add the file name to the footer. Check the letter for spelling or grammar errors. Save the letter as **5I_Services_Firstname_Lastname** and submit it as directed.

End **You have completed Project 5I** ——————————————

Outcomes-Based Assessments

Word
chapter five

Problem Solving

Project 5J—Survey Form

In this project, you will construct a solution by applying any combination of the skills you practiced from the Objectives in Projects 5A and 5B.

> ### For Project 5J, you will need the following file:
>
> New blank Word document
>
> **You will save your document as**
> **5J_Survey_Form_Firstname_Lastname**

In Project 5J, you will create a brief survey form to be filled out by potential clients of Music School Records. The purpose of the survey form is to do a quick screening of applicants to be sure they are a match for the company before they talk to a field representative or send in a demo recording.

The target audience will be high school and college students, and young performers already working in their field. The form should include information that may be important to a screening committee, including the client's:

- Place of residence
- Current school (if any)
- Type of talent (instrument, voice)
- Genre of music
- Professional experience (if any)
- Awards and other types of public recognition

Include any other topics you feel would be helpful in a brief survey form. The form should list the topics down the left side of the page, and should leave three or four blank lines between each so the person filling out the form will have enough space to write.

Add the file name to the footer. Check the survey form for spelling or grammar errors. Save the document as **5J_Survey_Form_Firstname_Lastname** and submit it as directed.

End **You have completed Project 5J** ————————

Outcomes-Based Assessments

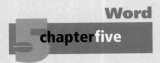

Word

chapter five

Problem Solving

Project 5K—Holidays

In this project, you will construct a solution by applying any combination of the skills you practiced from the Objectives in Projects 5A and 5B.

For Project 5K, you will need the following files:

New blank Word document
w05K_Musical_Score

**You will save your document as
5K_Holidays_Firstname_Lastname**

In Project 5K, you will write a memo to announce the days that Music School Records will be closed for holidays in the upcoming year. Use a memo format that you like. If you are unsure of what should be contained in the memo heading, search *memo format* on the Internet. Most memos have at least four lines at the top—Date, To, From, and Subject.

The memo should be from Mahadevan Ropa, Vice President for Business Development, to all employees at the Los Angeles office. Include an opening paragraph that mentions the reason for the memo, and then identify seven or eight holidays for which the office will be closed. Choose any typical holidays that you want to include. If you are not sure of the dates of holidays, or which ones to include, search the Web, using as search terms the year and the word *holidays*.

Add the file name to the footer. Check the memo for spelling or grammar errors. Add the **w05K_Musical_Score** image where appropriate. Save the document as **5K_Holidays_Firstname_Lastname** and submit it as directed.

End **You have completed Project 5K** ————————————

More on your Student CD

The instructions for the following additional end-of-chapter projects are on your student CD in the folder 03_additional_end_of_chapter_projects.

Content-Based Assessments

Project L Mastering Word	Apply the skills you practiced in Project A.
Project M Mastering Word	Apply the skills you practiced in Project B.
Project N Business Running Case	Apply the skills you practiced in Projects A and B while helping an entrepreneur with the daily tasks of running a business. In each chapter, this project focuses on applying the skills you have practiced in Projects A and B to a business. The project related to this business runs throughout the textbook. You will see how the Office applications relate to the day-to-day operation of a small business called Nelson Architectural Planning.

Outcomes-Based Assessments

Project O Problem Solving	Construct a solution by applying any combination of the skills you practiced from Projects A and B.
Project P Problem Solving	Construct a solution by applying any combination of the skills you practiced from Projects A and B.
Project Q You and GO!	Construct a solution that applies to your own life by applying any combination of the skills you practiced from Projects A and B.
Project R GO! with Help	Practice using Microsoft Office's Help Feature.
Project S Group Business Running Case	Work as part of a group to apply the skills you have gained thus far to help the Bell Orchid Hotel Group achieve its business goals.

Multimedia

The following multimedia accompany this textbook:

Companion Web site *www.prenhall.com/go*	An interactive Web site designed to reinforce and test your understanding of the skills in this chapter.
AV-EDDs	In the folder in the front of this book you will find videos that demonstrate the objectives of the A and B projects in this chapter. These may help you understand how to complete the projects in this book.
Video Podcasts	In the folder in the front of this book are videos that can be played on your iPod, MP3 player, or computer. These videos demonstrate how to complete the more challenging objectives in this textbook.

chaptersix

Formatting and Organizing Text

OBJECTIVES

At the end of this chapter you will be able to:

OUTCOMES

Mastering these objectives will enable you to:

1. Change Document and Paragraph Layout
2. Change and Reorganize Text
3. Create and Modify Lists

PROJECT 6A
Format Text and Use Lists

4. Insert and Format Headers and Footers
5. Insert Frequently Used Text
6. Insert and Format References

PROJECT 6B
Create a Research Paper

GHS Law Partners

GHS Law Partners specializes in patent and intellectual property law and government contracts, serving clients in the e-commerce, computer technology, pharmaceutical, and health care fields. The firm researches and prepares patents, litigates intellectual property infringement, handles licensing disputes, and prepares appeals. In the growing area of government contracts, the firm counsels its clients regarding United States government policymaking and prepares contracts according to government procurement policies. The firm's experienced staff of attorneys includes many who have formerly worked as prosecutors, federal court law clerks, and United States patent inspectors and procurement contract attorneys.

© Christine Balderas / Courtesy of www.istockphoto.com

Formatting and Organizing Text

Typing text is just the beginning of the process of creating an effective, professional looking document. Microsoft Word provides many tools for formatting paragraphs and documents. For example, there are tools to create shortcuts for entering commonly used text, and quick ways to copy, cut, and move text. Word also provides tools that enable you to create specialized formats, such as footnotes, bulleted and numbered lists, and indented paragraphs.

In this chapter, you will edit a seminar announcement, and then you will create and format a research paper.

Project 6A **Seminar**

In Activities 6.01 through 6.15, you will edit an announcement from GHS Law Partners about an upcoming Intellectual Property Seminar. Your completed document will look similar to Figure 6.1.

For Project 6A, you will need the following file:

w06A_Seminar

You will save your document as
6A_Seminar_Firstname_Lastname

GHS Law Partners
Intellectual Property Seminar for Business Attorneys

July 12, 2009
Atlanta, GA
Draft Announcement

GHS Law Partners will present its fifth annual Intellectual Property Seminar for Business Attorneys in Atlanta, GA, on July 12, 2009. This event is intended for attorneys who want to expand their knowledge of intellectual property in order to better serve their clients. Intellectual property law affects every kind of business and clients' rights, obligations, and strategies. GHS Law Partners believes that sharing knowledge and expertise in this area of law enhances the business climate and improves the ability of business-focused firms to serve their diverse client base.

Some states confer Continuing Legal Education credits for this seminar. Each attendee will receive a complete set of all seminar materials along with an Intellectual Property textbook written by one of our partners. Audio tapes and DVDs of selected sessions will also be available.

The three morning sessions will focus on copyrights:

1. Introduction to Copyrights
2. Copyright FAQs
3. Current Issues in Copyrights

Lunch will feature a panel discussion of GHS attorneys and other trademark experts. Among the topics discussed will be:

™ Use of trademarks
™ Trademark enforcement
™ Avoiding dilution of trademark

The four afternoon sessions will cover patents:

1. Patent Basics
2. Understanding Trade Secrets and Patent Protection
3. Current Issues in Patents
4. Business Considerations in Patents and Trademarks

Questions and discussion are encouraged at all sessions, and attendees are reminded that such discussions should be kept confidential to protect the wide array of clients represented by the group.

Registration will open on April 1, 2009, and is limited to 400 attendees. Discounted rates are available at several nearby hotels. A "dine-around" dinner will be arranged at several local restaurants for those who want to participate.

If you would like a brochure containing much more detailed information about the topics to be covered in the upcoming Intellectual Property Seminar, contact Melissa Rosella at (404) 555-0022. You can also register online at www.ghslaw.com/ipseminar.

6A_Seminar_Firstname_Lastname

Figure 6.1
Project 6A—Seminar

Objective 1
Change Document and Paragraph Layout

Document layout includes *margins*—the space between the text and the top, bottom, left, and right edges of the paper. Paragraph layout includes line spacing, indents, and tabs. In Word, the information about paragraph formats is stored in the paragraph mark at the end of a paragraph. When you press the Enter key, the new paragraph mark contains the formatting of the previous paragraph, unless you take steps to change it.

Activity 6.01 Setting Margins

You can change each of the four page margins—top, bottom, left, and right—independently.

> **Note — Comparing Your Screen with the Figures in This Textbook**
>
> Your screen will match the figures shown in this textbook if you set your screen resolution to 1024 × 768. At other resolutions, your screen will closely resemble, but not match, the figures shown. To view your screen's resolution, on the Windows desktop, right-click in a blank area, click Personalize, and then click Display Settings.

1 **Start** Word. From your student files, locate and open the document **w06A_Seminar**.

2 From the **Office** menu ⊕, display the **Save As** dialog box, and then navigate to the location where you are saving your files. On the toolbar, click the **New Folder** button. Name the new folder **Word Chapter 6** and then press Enter.

3 In the **File name** box, delete the existing text. Using your own name, type **6A_Seminar_Firstname_Lastname** and then click **Save**. If necessary, display formatting marks.

4 Click the **Page Layout tab**. In the **Page Setup group**, click the **Margins** button, and then at the bottom of the **Margins gallery**, click **Custom Margins**.

5 In the **Page Setup** dialog box, press Tab as necessary to select the value in the **Left** box, and then, with *1.25″* selected, type **1**

> This action will change the left margin to 1 inch on all pages of the document. You do not need to type the inch (″) mark.

6 Press Tab to select the measurement in the **Right** box, type **1** and then compare your screen with Figure 6.2. Notice that the new margins will be applied to the entire document.

Figure 6.2

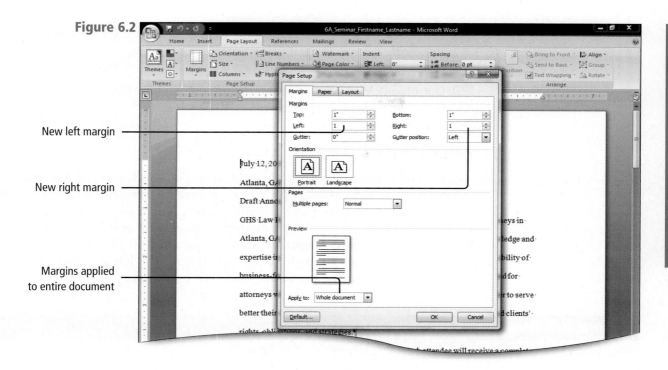

New left margin

New right margin

Margins applied
to entire document

---

7 Click **OK** to apply the new margins and close the dialog box. If the ruler below the Ribbon is not displayed, at the top of the vertical scroll bar, click the **View Ruler** button. Compare your screen with Figure 6.3.

Figure 6.3

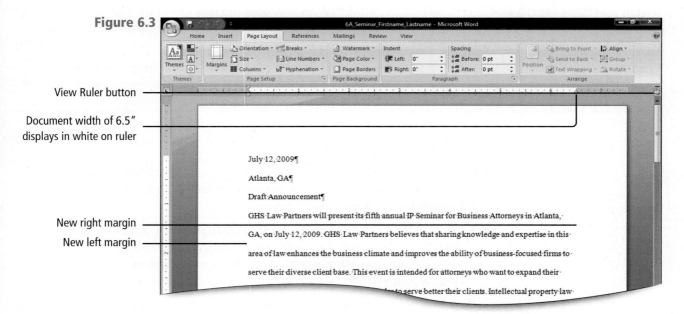

View Ruler button

Document width of 6.5"
displays in white on ruler

New right margin
New left margin

July·12,·2009¶

Atlanta,·GA¶

Draft·Announcement¶

GHS·Law·Partners·will·present·its·fifth·annual·IP·Seminar·for·Business·Attorneys·in·Atlanta,·

GA,·on·July·12,·2009.·GHS·Law·Partners·believes·that·sharing·knowledge·and·expertise·in·this·

area·of·law·enhances·the·business·climate·and·improves·the·ability·of·business-focused·firms·to·

serve·their·diverse·client·base.·This·event·is·intended·for·attorneys·who·want·to·expand·their·

to·serve·better·their·clients.·Intellectual·property·law·

---

8 Scroll to view the bottom of **Page 1**. Near the bottom edge of the page, right-click, and then click **Edit Footer** to display the footer area.

This shortcut provides a quick way to display either the footer or header area. Because the insertion point is in the footer area, *Header & Footer Tools* displays, and the Design tab is added to the standard tabs on the Ribbon.

9 On the **Design tab**, in the **Insert group**, click the **Quick Parts** button, and then click **Field**. In the **Field** dialog box, under **Field names**, locate and click **FileName**, and then click **OK**.

10 Double-click anywhere in the document to close the footer area. **Save** 🖫 your document.

Activity 6.02 Aligning Text

Alignment is the placement of paragraph text relative to the left and right margins. Most paragraph text uses *left alignment*—aligned at the left margin, leaving the right margin uneven. Three other types of paragraph alignment are available: *center alignment*—centered between the left and right margins; *right alignment*—aligned on the right margin; and *justified alignment*—text aligned on both the left and right margins. Examples are shown in the table in Figure 6.4.

Paragraph Alignment Options

Alignment	Button	Description and Example
Align Text Left	▤	Align Text Left is the default paragraph alignment in Word. Text in the paragraph aligns at the left margin, and the right margin is uneven.
Center	▤	Center alignment aligns text in the paragraph so that it is centered between the left and right margins.
Align Text Right	▤	Align Text Right is used to align text at the right margin. Using Align Text Right, the left margin, which is normally even, is uneven.
Justify	▤	The Justify alignment option adds additional space between words so that both the left and right margins are even. Justify is often used when formatting newspaper-style columns.

Figure 6.4

1 Press Ctrl + Home to place the insertion point at the beginning of the document. Type **GHS Law Partners Intellectual Property Seminar for Business Attorneys** and then press Enter.

2 Click to place the insertion point anywhere in the first line of the document—the title that you just typed that begins *GHS Law Partners*. On the **Home tab**, in the **Paragraph group**, click the **Center** button ▤.

> The first paragraph is centered. To format a paragraph, you just need to have the insertion point somewhere in the paragraph.

3 Move the mouse pointer into the left margin area to the left of the second line of text that begins *July 12* until the ◩ pointer displays. Drag down to select that line and the two lines following it, ending with *Draft Announcement*, and then on the Mini toolbar, click the **Center** button ▤. Compare your screen with Figure 6.5.

> A paragraph consists of a paragraph mark and all the text in front of it. To format multiple paragraphs, they must all be selected.

Figure 6.5

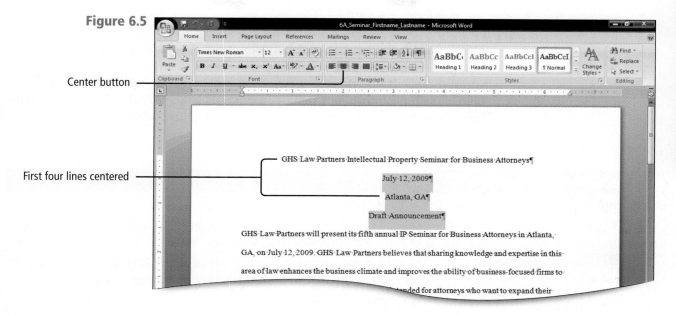

Center button

First four lines centered

4 Move the ⤢ pointer into the left margin area to the left of the fifth line of text that begins *GHS Law Partners will present*. Then, drag down to select this line of text and the next eight lines of text—including the line that ends *will also be available*.

5 In the **Paragraph group**, click the **Justify** button ▤, and then compare your screen with Figure 6.6.

> Both the left and right edges of the paragraphs are even. The other paragraphs are not affected.

Figure 6.6

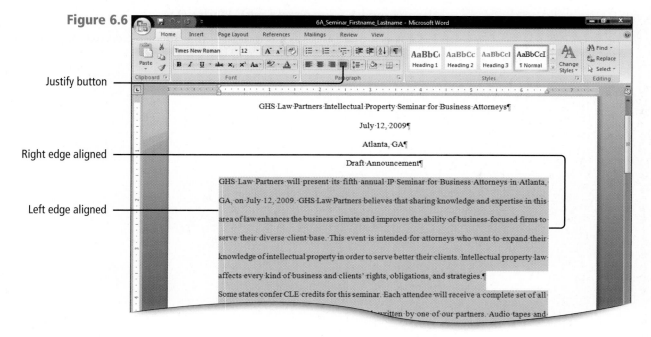

Justify button

Right edge aligned

Left edge aligned

6 Because justified text is better used in narrow columns, with the text still selected, in the **Paragraph group**, click the **Align Text Left** button ▤ . Click anywhere in the document to deselect the text. **Save** 🖫 the document.

Activity 6.03 Changing Line Spacing

Line spacing is the distance between lines of text in a paragraph. A single-spaced paragraph of 12-point text accommodates six lines in a vertical inch. If you double-space the same text, each line will be 24 points high—12 points of text, 12 points of space—and will accommodate only three lines in a vertical inch as shown in the table in Figure 6.7.

Line Spacing Options	
Spacing	**Example**
Single (1.0)	Most business documents are single-spaced. This means that the spacing between lines is just enough to separate the text.
Multiple with 1.15 line spacing	The default line spacing in Microsoft Word 2007 is 1.15, which is equivalent to single spacing with an extra 1/6 line added between lines.
Double (2.0)	Many college research papers and reports, and many draft documents that need space for notes, are double-spaced; there is space for a full line of text between each document line.

Figure 6.7

1 Press Ctrl + Home. In the left margin area, display the ▨ pointer and drag down to select the first four lines of text—the four centered title lines.

2 In the **Paragraph group**, click the **Line spacing** button ▤▾ , and then compare your screen with Figure 6.8.

A check mark next to 2.0 indicates that the selected paragraphs are double-spaced.

Figure 6.8

Line spacing button

Double-spacing

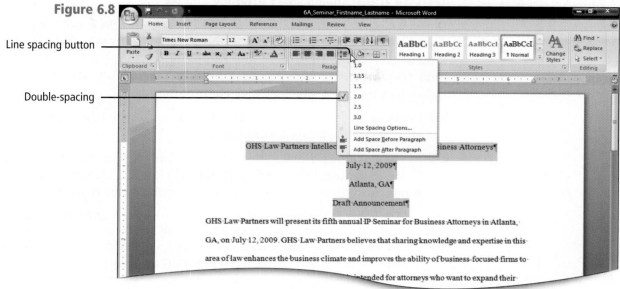

▸**3** In the **Line spacing** list, click **1.0** to change the line spacing of the first four paragraphs.

▸**4** Click to place the insertion point in the paragraph that begins *GHS Law Partners will present*. In the **Paragraph group**, click the **Line spacing** button, and then click **1.0**. Compare your screen with Figure 6.9.

The first five paragraphs of the document are single-spaced.

Figure 6.9

First five paragraphs of the document are single-spaced

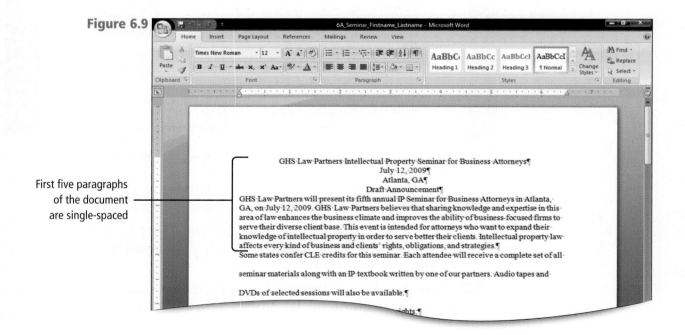

▸**5** **Save** the changes you have made to your document.

Activity 6.04 Adding Space After Paragraphs

Adjusting paragraph spacing from the Paragraph dialog box enables you to control the space before or after paragraphs using points as the unit of measure. Recall that there are 72 points per inch. The Word default adds 10-pt. spacing after each paragraph. The document you are working on has no extra spacing after each paragraph.

1 Press Ctrl + Home. In the lower right corner of the **Paragraph group**, click the **Dialog Box Launcher** 🔲.

2 In the **Paragraph** dialog box, click the **Indents and Spacing tab**. Under **Spacing**, in the **After** spin box, click the **up spin arrow** two times, and then compare your screen with Figure 6.10.

> The value in the box changes from 0 pt to 12 pt. A **spin box** is a small box with upward- and downward-pointing arrows that lets you move (spin) through a set of values by clicking. The up and down arrows, called **spin box arrows**, increment the point size by six points at a time.

Figure 6.10

Spacing after paragraph set to 12 pt

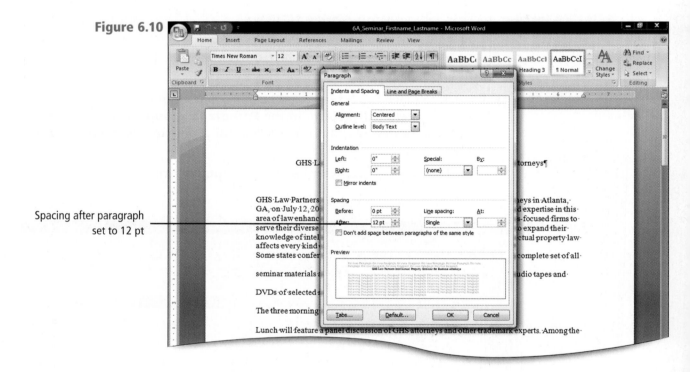

3 Click **OK** to add a 12-pt space after the first paragraph.

4 In the *Draft Announcement* paragraph, click to position the insertion point anywhere in the paragraph. In the **Paragraph group**, click the **Dialog Box Launcher** 🔲.

5 Under **Spacing**, in the **After** box, click the **up spin arrow** one time to change the value in the box from *0 pt* to **6 pt**. Click **OK**.

To Add Spacing Before and After Paragraphs
You can also change the spacing before and after paragraphs using the Ribbon. Click the Page Layout tab, and then in the Paragraph group, use the Spacing buttons.

6 In the paragraph beginning *GHS Law Partners will present*, click to position the insertion point anywhere in the paragraph. In the **Paragraph group**, display the **Paragraph** dialog box. Under **Spacing**, set **After** to **6 pt**, and then click **OK**. Compare your screen with Figure 6.11.

Figure 6.11

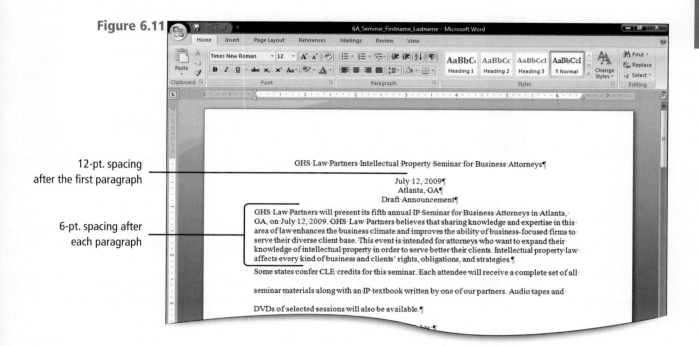

12-pt. spacing after the first paragraph

6-pt. spacing after each paragraph

7 **Save** the changes you have made to your document.

Activity 6.05 Using the Format Painter

Use the ***Format Painter*** to copy the formatting of specific text or of a paragraph and then apply it in other locations in your document.

1 Click anywhere in the paragraph that begins *GHS Law Partners will present*. On the **Home tab**, in the **Clipboard group**, click the **Format Painter** button . Position the pointer anywhere in the paragraph that begins *Some states confer*, and then compare your screen with Figure 6.12.

The pointer takes the shape of a paintbrush, and contains the formatting information from the paragraph where the insertion point is positioned. Instructions on how to turn the Format Painter off display in the status bar.

Figure 6.12

Format Painter button ——

Format Painter pointer ——

Status bar instructions ——

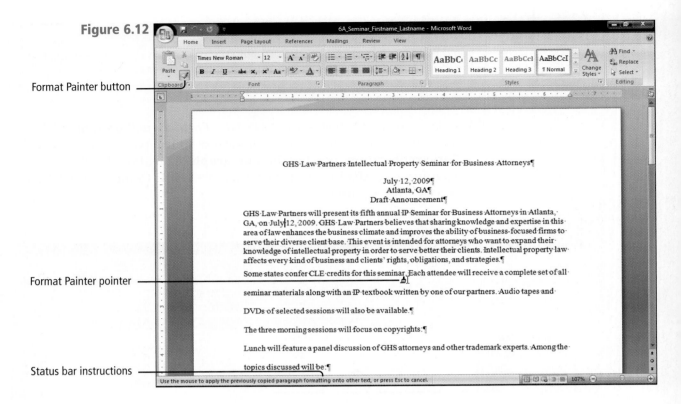

GHS·Law·Partners·Intellectual·Property·Seminar·for·Business·Attorneys¶

July·12,·2009¶
Atlanta,·GA¶
Draft·Announcement¶

GHS·Law·Partners·will·present·its·fifth·annual·IP·Seminar·for·Business·Attorneys·in·Atlanta,·GA,·on·July·12,·2009.·GHS·Law·Partners·believes·that·sharing·knowledge·and·expertise·in·this·area·of·law·enhances·the·business·climate·and·improves·the·ability·of·business-focused·firms·to·serve·their·diverse·client·base.·This·event·is·intended·for·attorneys·who·want·to·expand·their·knowledge·of·intellectual·property·in·order·to·serve·better·their·clients.·Intellectual·property·law·affects·every·kind·of·business·and·clients'·rights,·obligations,·and·strategies.¶

Some·states·confer·CLE·credits·for·this·seminar.·Each·attendee·will·receive·a·complete·set·of·all·

seminar·materials·along·with·an·IP·textbook·written·by·one·of·our·partners.·Audio·tapes·and·

DVDs·of·selected·sessions·will·also·be·available.¶

The·three·morning·sessions·will·focus·on·copyrights:¶

Lunch·will·feature·a·panel·discussion·of·GHS·attorneys·and·other·trademark·experts.·Among·the·

topics·discussed·will·be:¶

Use the mouse to apply the previously copied paragraph formatting onto other text, or press Esc to cancel.

---

2 Click the 🖌 pointer one time.

> The paragraph formatting from the original paragraph—single-spacing, 6-pt space after the paragraph—is copied to this paragraph. The Format Painter is no longer active.

3 With the insertion point in the recently formatted paragraph, double-click the **Format Painter** button 🖌 to use the Format Painter multiple times.

4 Move the 🖌 pointer to the paragraph that begins *The three morning sessions*, and then click one time.

> The paragraph formatting from the original paragraph is copied to this paragraph, and the Format Painter remains active.

5 Move the 🖌 pointer to the paragraph that begins *Lunch will feature*, and then click one time.

6 Using the **down scroll arrow**, locate and click in the paragraph that begins *The four afternoon sessions*. Use the Format Painter to change the formatting of the last three paragraphs, starting with the paragraph that begins *Registration will open*. Compare your screen with Figure 6.13.

Figure 6.13

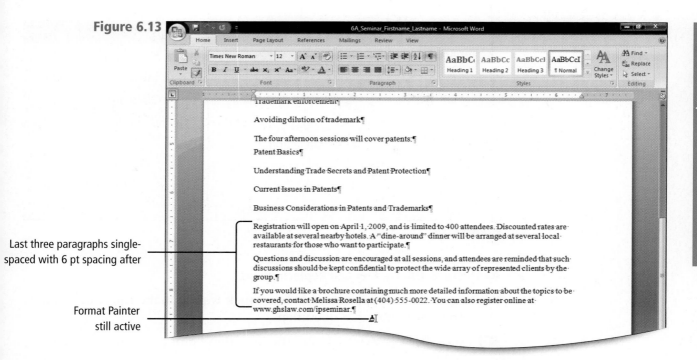

Last three paragraphs single-spaced with 6 pt spacing after

Format Painter still active

Alert!

Did you click the wrong paragraph?

If you accidentally click in one of the other paragraphs while scrolling down, click the Undo button to undo the formatting. Clicking the Undo button turns off the Format Painter, so you will need to click in the paragraph with the desired formatting again, and then turn the Format Painter on again to format the last paragraphs.

7 In the **Clipboard group**, click the **Format Painter** button to turn the command off. Alternatively, press Esc to turn off the Format Painter feature.

8 **Save** your document.

Objective 2
Change and Reorganize Text

Changing and reorganizing text is accomplished using Word features such as the Find and Replace dialog box and the ***Office Clipboard***, a temporary storage area that holds text. You can ***copy*** text to the Office Clipboard, which leaves the original text in place, or ***cut*** text, which removes it from its original location. Then, you can ***paste***—insert—the contents of the Office Clipboard in a new location. The keyboard short-cuts for these commands are shown in the table in Figure 6.14.

Keyboard Shortcut for Editing Text	
Keyboard Shortcut	**Action**
Ctrl + X	Cut text or graphic and move it to the Office Clipboard.
Ctrl + C	Copy text or graphic to the Office Clipboard.
Ctrl + V	Paste the contents of the Office Clipboard.
Ctrl + Z	Undo an action.
Ctrl + Y	Redo an action.
Ctrl + F	Find text.
Ctrl + H	Find and replace text.

Figure 6.14

Activity 6.06 Finding and Replacing Text

Finding and then replacing text is a quick way to make the same change more than one time in a document.

1 Press Ctrl + Home to position the insertion point at the beginning of the document.

> When you initiate a find operation or a find-and-replace operation, the search begins from the location of the insertion point and proceeds to the end of the document.

2 On the **Home tab**, in the **Editing group**, click the **Find** button. In the **Find and Replace** dialog box, in the **Find what** box, type **CLE** which is an acronym for *Continuing Legal Education*.

3 In the **Find and Replace** dialog box, click the **Find Next** button to select the first occurrence of *CLE*.

4 In the **Find and Replace** dialog box, click **Cancel**. Press Ctrl + Home.

5 In the **Editing group**, click the **Replace** button.

6 If necessary, in the **Find and Replace** dialog box, in the **Find what** box, type **CLE** and then in the **Replace with** box, type **Continuing Legal Education**

7 Click the **More** button to expand the dialog box, and then under **Search Options**, select the **Match case** and **Find whole words only** check boxes. Click **Find Next**, and then compare your screen with Figure 6.15.

> By searching for whole words only, you will avoid changing the search text if it occurs in the middle of a word—for example, *CLEVELAND*. By matching case, you not only instruct the program to look for text in the same case, but also to replace text using the same case as the text in the Replace with box.

Figure 6.15

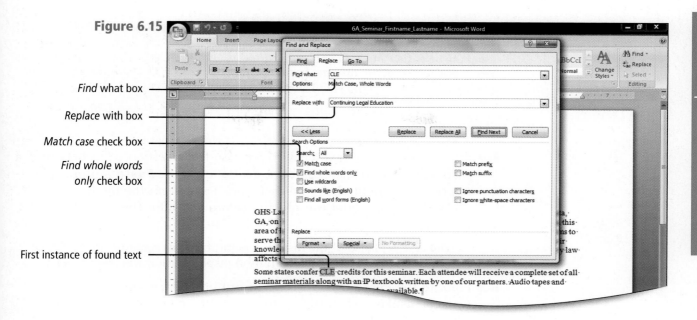

Find what box

Replace with box

Match case check box

Find whole words only check box

First instance of found text

8 In the **Find and Replace** dialog box, click the **Replace** button.

> The text is replaced, and a message indicates that Word has finished searching the document.

9 Click **OK**. In the **Find what** box, type **IP** and in the **Replace with** box, type **Intellectual Property**

10 Click **Replace All**.

> A message displays, indicating that two replacements have been made.

11 Click **OK** to close the message box. Clear the two **Search Options** check boxes, click the **Less** button, and then click **Close**. **Save** your document.

Activity 6.07 Cutting, Copying, and Pasting Text

Use the Cut command to move text out of the document to the Office Clipboard—the temporary storage location for text or graphics. Then, use the Paste command to paste the contents of the Office Clipboard to the new location. The Copy command places a copy of selected text on the Office Clipboard, which you can then paste to another location.

1 Near the end of the document, locate the paragraph that begins *Questions and discussion*, and then double-click to select the word *represented*.

2 On the **Home tab**, in the **Clipboard group**, click the **Cut** button. Alternatively, right-click the selected text and click Cut from the shortcut menu; or, press Ctrl + X.

> The selected text is removed from the document and moved to the Office Clipboard.

> **Note** — **The Difference Between Using Delete, Backspace, and Cut**
>
> When you use the Cut command to remove text, it is moved to the Office Clipboard and can be pasted into the same—or a different—document. When you use Delete or Backspace to remove text, the text is not moved to the Office Clipboard. The only way you can retrieve text removed with Delete or Backspace is by using the Undo command.

3 In the same line of text, click to position the insertion point between *clients* and *by*. In the **Clipboard group**, click the **Paste** button. Alternatively, right-click and then click Paste from the menu, or press Ctrl + V. Adjust the spacing before and after the word if necessary.

> The text is placed at the insertion point, but also remains on the Office Clipboard. The Paste Options button displays below the pasted word.

4 Point to the **Paste Options** button until its ScreenTip *Paste Options* displays, click the button, and then compare your screen with Figure 6.16.

> The displayed list provides commands related specifically to the Paste command. You can determine whether you want to format the pasted text the same as the surrounding text or retain its original formatting.

Figure 6.16

Pasted text

Paste Options button

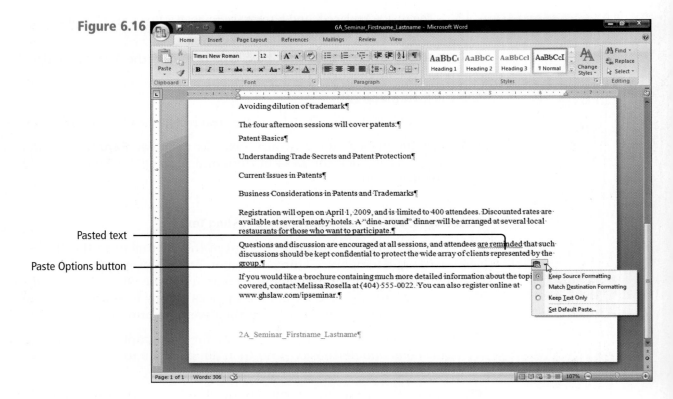

5 Click anywhere in the document to close the **Paste Options** menu and retain the same formatting. Alternatively, press [Esc] to cancel its display.

6 Position the pointer in the paragraph that begins *Registration will open*, and then triple-click to select the entire paragraph.

7 In the **Clipboard group**, click the **Cut** button [✂]. Locate the paragraph that begins *If you would like* and position the insertion point at the beginning of that paragraph. In the **Clipboard group**, click the **Paste** button to paste the text in the new location.

Alert!	**Did the Clipboard task pane open?**
	The Clipboard task pane may display on your screen depending on the options that have been set for the Office Clipboard on your computer. If the task pane opens, click the Close button on the task pane title bar.

8 Press [Ctrl] + [Home]. In the first title line, select *Intellectual Property Seminar*. In the **Clipboard group**, click the **Copy** button [📋]. Press [Ctrl] + [End] to move to the end of the document.

9 In the last paragraph, locate the word *covered* and position the insertion point between the word and the following comma. Press [Spacebar], type **in the upcoming** and then press [Spacebar]. In the **Clipboard group**, click the **Paste** button, and then compare your screen with Figure 6.17.

The copied text is inserted in the new location, but is not removed from the original location. The Paste Options button displays below the pasted text.

Figure 6.17

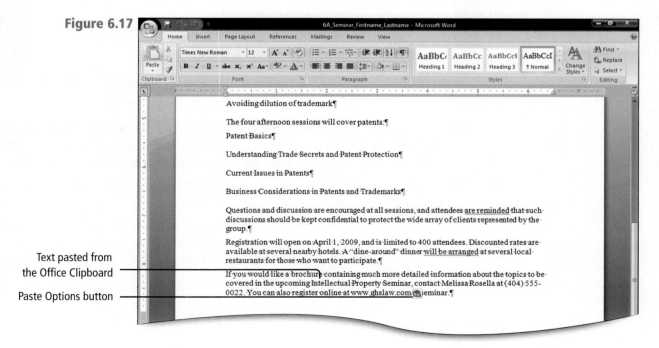

Text pasted from the Office Clipboard

Paste Options button

10 **Save** [💾] the changes you have made to your document.

Activity 6.08 Moving Text to a New Location

Another method of moving text is the ***drag and drop*** technique, which uses the mouse to drag selected text from one location to another. This method is useful if the text to be moved is on the same screen as the destination location.

1 Press Ctrl + Home. In the fifth line of the paragraph that begins *GHS Law Partners will present*, locate and select *better*.

2 Point to the selected word to display the ▷ pointer as shown in Figure 6.18.

Figure 6.18

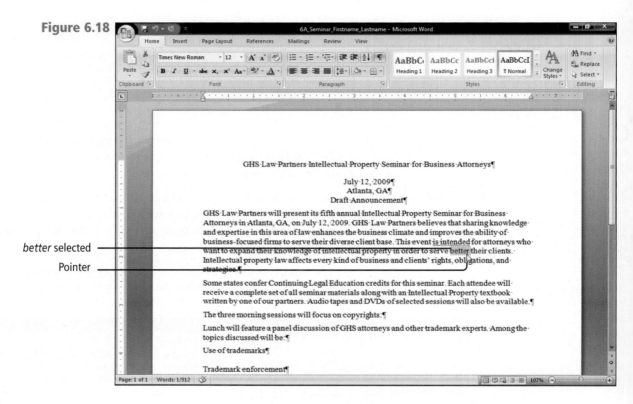

better selected

Pointer

3 Hold down the left mouse button and drag to the left until the dotted vertical line that floats next to the pointer is positioned to the left of the word *serve* in the same line, and then release the left mouse button.

4 Click anywhere to deselect the text, and then compare your screen with Figure 6.19.

> The word is moved to the insertion point location. The vertical line of the pointer assists you in dropping the moved text in the place where you want it. The small box attached to the pointer indicates that there is text attached to the pointer.

Figure 6.19

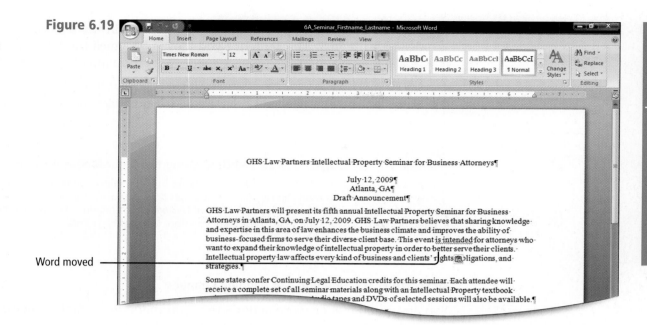

Word moved

5 In the same paragraph, point to the second sentence—the one that begins *GHS Law Partners believes*. Hold down Ctrl and click one time to select the entire sentence.

6 Point to the selected sentence to display the ⟨ pointer, and then drag down to the end of the paragraph and position the vertical line to the right of the period at the end of *obligations, and strategies*, as shown in Figure 6.20.

Figure 6.20

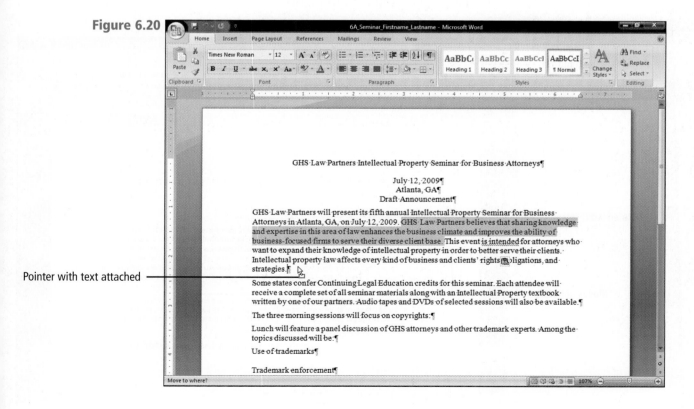

Pointer with text attached

7 Release the mouse button, and click anywhere in the document to deselect the text. The sentence you moved becomes the last sentence in the paragraph. Notice that a space was automatically added before the sentence.

8 Save 🖫 the changes you have made to your document.

More Knowledge — Drag and Drop Using the Right Mouse Button

You can also drag and drop using the right mouse button. Select the text, point to the selected text and hold the right mouse button down, and then drag to a new location. A shortcut menu displays, giving you the option of moving the text to the new location, copying the text to the new location, or creating a link.

Activity 6.09 Undoing and Redoing Changes

You can undo one or more actions that you made to an active document. An Undo action can be reversed with the Redo command.

1 In the fourth paragraph, *Draft Announcement*, double-click *Draft* to select it, and then press Delete.

2 On the **Quick Access Toolbar**, click the **Undo** button 🔙.

The word you deleted returns to its original location.

3 On the **Quick Access Toolbar**, click the **Undo** button 🔙 two times. The sentence you dragged and dropped returns to its original location, and the words *serve* and *better* are switched back to their original locations, as shown in Figure 6.21.

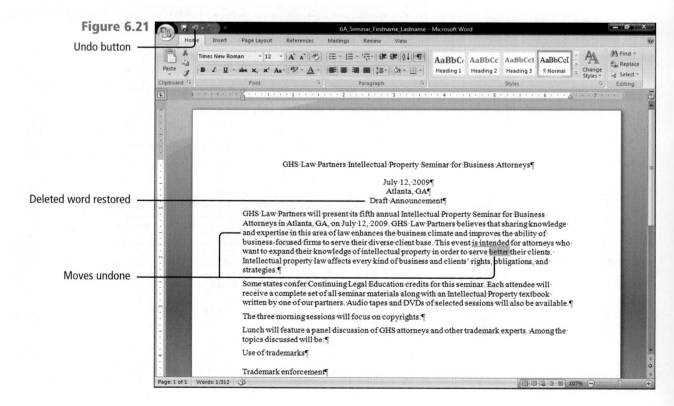

Figure 6.21
Undo button
Deleted word restored
Moves undone

4 On the **Quick Access Toolbar**, click the **Redo** button ↻ two times. The words are switched back, and the sentence moves back to the end of the paragraph. Notice that clicking the Undo and Redo buttons changes one action at a time.

5 On the **Quick Access Toolbar**, click the **Undo button arrow** ↻ ▾.

A list of changes displays showing all of the changes made since you last opened your document. From the displayed list, you can click any of the actions and undo it, but all of the changes above the one you select will also be undone.

6 Click anywhere in the document to close the Undo button list without undoing any other actions.

Activity 6.10 Inserting Nonbreaking Spaces and Hyphens

When you want to keep two words together regardless of where they fall in a paragraph, use a **nonbreaking space**, which will wrap both words even if only the second word would normally wrap to the next line. For example, if the words *Mt. McKinley* fall at the end of a line so that *Mt.* is on one line and *McKinley* moves to the next, inserting a nonbreaking space will treat the two words as one so that they are not split between two lines. Similarly, you may have a hyphenated term, such as a postal code with the four-digit extension. If you want that term to be treated as one entity, use a nonbreaking hyphen.

1 Press Ctrl + End to move to the end of the document. Locate the paragraph that begins *If you would like*, and then click to position the insertion point at the end of the second line.

2 In the telephone number, delete the hyphen. While holding down both Ctrl and ⇧ Shift, press - one time.

The hyphen is replaced with a **nonbreaking hyphen**; the telephone number will not break at the hyphen if you edit the paragraph. The nonbreaking hyphen is indicated by a slightly longer, slightly higher line than a standard hyphen, but prints as a normal hyphen.

3 At the end of the second line, after the telephone number area code, delete the space. While holding down both Ctrl and ⇧ Shift, press Spacebar one time. Compare your screen with Figure 6.22.

This combination of keys inserts a nonbreaking space. The result of inserting the nonbreaking space and nonbreaking hyphen is that the telephone number is treated as one word, so when Word applies its word-wrapping rules, the number is kept together on the same line. The nonbreaking space is indicated by an open circle rather than the dot normally used to indicate a space, but prints as a normal space.

Figure 6.22

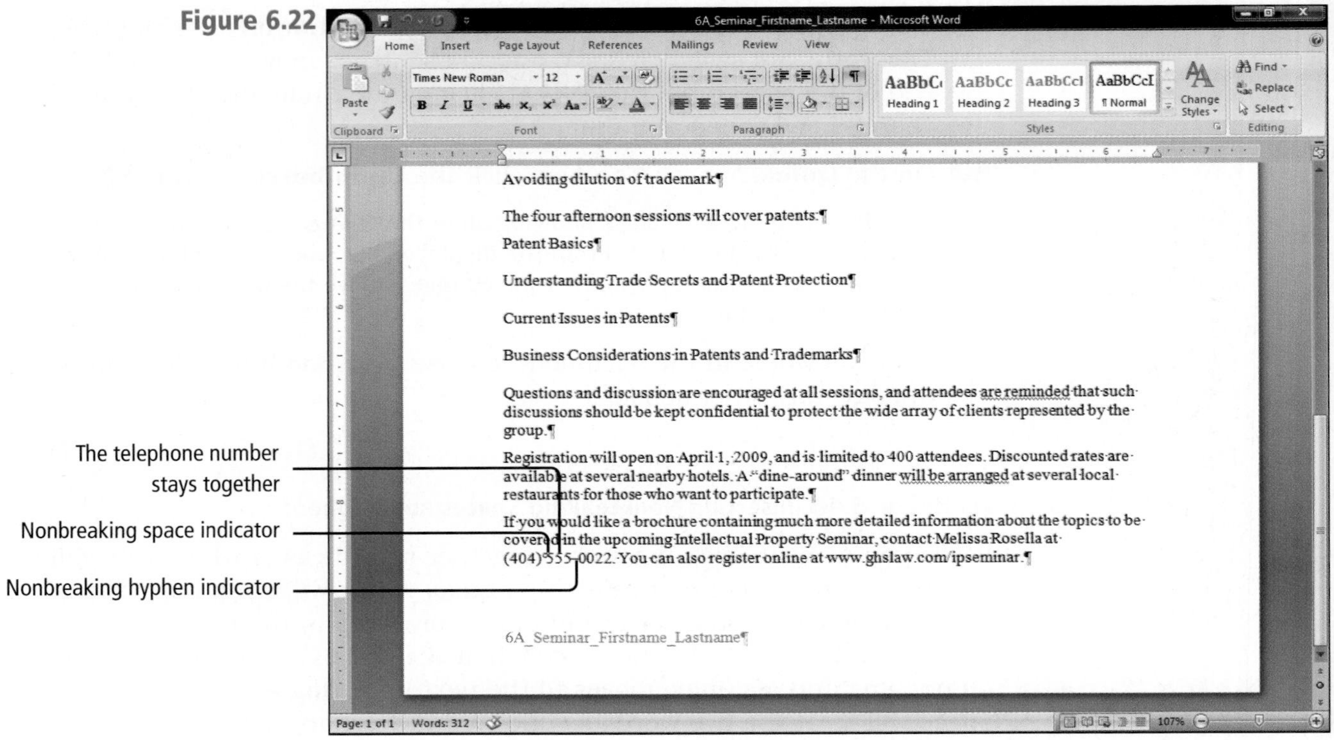

The telephone number stays together

Nonbreaking space indicator

Nonbreaking hyphen indicator

4 In the same sentence, locate and select the word *Seminar*, and then press Delete. Notice that the telephone number moves to the previous line as one word.

5 On the **Quick Access Toolbar**, click the **Undo** button to reinsert the deleted word. **Save** your changes.

Activity 6.11 Entering a Line Break

You can end a line of text with a ***manual line break***, which moves the insertion point to the next line without creating a new paragraph.

1 Press Ctrl + Home to move to the beginning of the document. Position the pointer in the left margin area, and then select the first four lines of text—the four centered title lines.

2 On the Mini toolbar, click the **Bold** button B, click the **Font Size button arrow** 12, and then click **14**.

3 In the first title line, notice the 12-point spacing after the first paragraph. Then, select the space between *Partners* and *Intellectual* and press Delete.

4 Hold down Shift, and then press Enter. Compare your screen with Figure 6.23.

By using a manual line break, the 12-pt spacing after the paragraph is not inserted because a new paragraph is not created; rather, a new line within the same paragraph is created. The bent arrow at the end of the first line indicates an inserted line break.

Figure 6.23

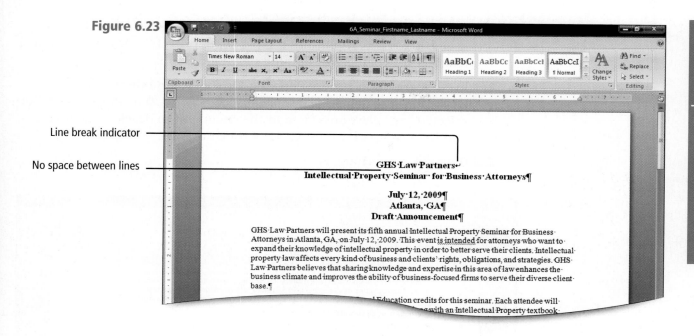

Line break indicator

No space between lines

5 **Save** 🔲 your changes.

Objective 3
Create and Modify Lists

Word displays lists of information in two ways. A ***bulleted list*** uses ***bullets***, which are text symbols such as small circles or check marks, to introduce each piece of information. ***Numbered lists*** use consecutive numbers or letters to introduce each item in a list. Use bulleted lists when the items in the list can be displayed in any order; use numbered lists for items that have definite steps, a sequence of actions, or are in chronological order.

Activity 6.12 Creating a Bulleted List

1 Locate the *Use of trademarks* paragraph, and then move the pointer into the left margin area to display the 🔎 pointer. Drag down to select this paragraph and the next two paragraphs.

2 On the Mini toolbar, click the **Bullets** button ▤ ▾. Alternatively, on the Home tab, in the Paragraph group, click the Bullets button.

> The default bullet is a large, round, black dot. Your bullet symbols may differ, depending on which bullets were most recently used on your computer.

3 With the bulleted list still selected, in the **Paragraph group**, click the **Increase Indent** button ▤ one time. Click anywhere in the document to deselect the text.

> The bulleted list indents another 0.25 inch to the right.

4 Move the pointer into the left margin area to the left of the *Use of trademarks* paragraph until the 🔏 pointer displays. Then, drag down to select this paragraph and the next paragraph.

5 In the **Paragraph group**, click the **Line spacing** button 🔲▾, and notice that the items are double-spaced. Click **1.0** to single-space the selected text, click anywhere in the document to deselect the text, and then compare your screen with Figure 6.24.

6 **Save** 🔲 your changes.

Figure 6.24

Bulleted list

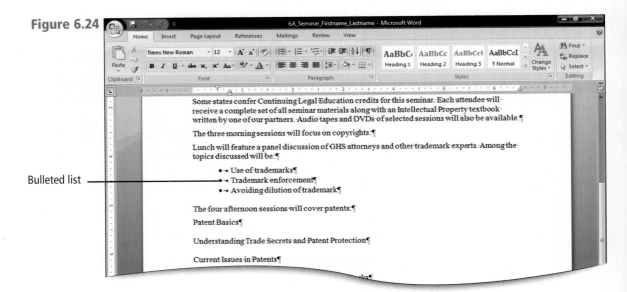

Activity 6.13 Using AutoFormat to Create a Numbered List

In the previous activity, you created a list using existing text. In this activity, you will create a new list. Because the list items are the names of sessions in sequential order, you will number the items using Word's Numbering command.

1 Locate the paragraph that begins *The three morning sessions*, and then position the insertion point at the end of that paragraph. Press Enter to create a blank line.

> Until you change it, your newly created paragraph will retain the formatting of the previous paragraph, because formatting information is stored in the paragraph mark.

2 From the **Office** menu 🔵, in the lower right corner click **Word Options**. In the list on the left side of the **Word Options** dialog box, click **Proofing**. Under **AutoCorrect options**, click the **AutoCorrect Options** button.

3 In the **AutoCorrect** dialog box, click the **AutoFormat As You Type tab**, and then compare your screen with Figure 6.25.

> ***AutoFormat As You Type*** is a Word feature that anticipates formatting based on what you type.

Figure 6.25

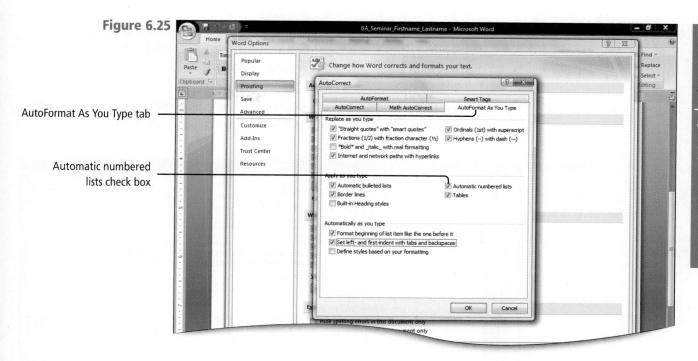

AutoFormat As You Type tab

Automatic numbered lists check box

4 Under **Apply as you type**, if it is not selected, select the **Automatic numbered lists** check box, and then click **OK**. At the bottom of the **Word Options** dialog box, click **OK**.

5 Type **1.** and press Spacebar. Be sure to type the period after the number.

Word determines that this paragraph is the first item in a numbered list and formats the new paragraph accordingly. The space after the number changes to a tab, and the AutoCorrect Options button displays to the left of the list item.

6 Click the **AutoCorrect Options** button, and then compare your screen with Figure 6.26.

From the displayed list, you can remove the automatic formatting here, or stop using the automatic numbered lists option in this document. You also have the option to open the AutoCorrect dialog box to *Control AutoFormat Options*.

Figure 6.26

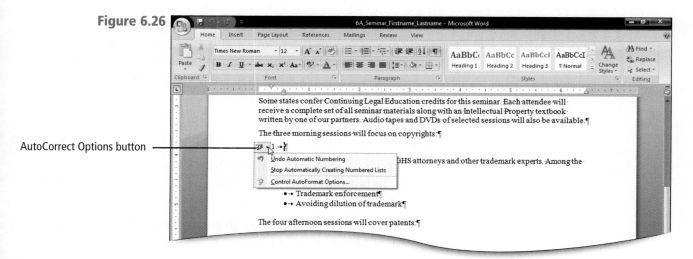

AutoCorrect Options button

7 Click the **AutoCorrect Options** button to close the menu without selecting any of the commands. Type **Introduction to Copyrights** and press ⏎Enter. Notice that the second number and a tab are added to the next line.

8 Type **Copyright FAQs** and press ⏎Enter. Type **Current Issues in Copyrights** and press ⏎Enter. Compare your screen with Figure 6.27.

Figure 6.27

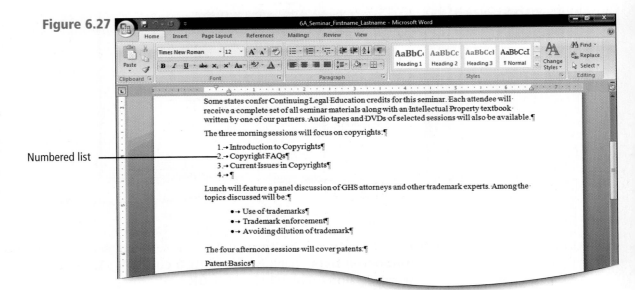

Numbered list

9 Press ←Bksp to turn off the list. Then, press ←Bksp as necessary to remove the blank line.

More Knowledge — To End a List

When you end a list and press ⏎Enter, the next line will be formatted as a list item. To turn the list off, you can press ←Bksp, click the Numbering or Bullets button, or press ⏎Enter a second time. Both list buttons—Numbering and Bullets—act as *toggle buttons*; that is, clicking the button one time turns the feature on, and clicking the button again turns the feature off.

---

10 Select all three items in the numbered list. In the **Paragraph group**, click the **Increase Indent** button one time to move the list 0.25 inch to the right.

11 **Save** your document.

Activity 6.14 Formatting Lists

Each item in a list is a separate paragraph and can be formatted in the same way other paragraphs are formatted. The Format Painter can also be used to create lists.

1 In the bulleted list, click anywhere in the last bulleted item, which begins *Avoiding dilution*. Display the **Paragraph** dialog box.

2 Under **Spacing**, click the **Line spacing arrow**, and then click **Single**. Under **Spacing**, in the **After** spin box, click the **up spin arrow** one time to add **6pt** spacing, and then click **OK**. Compare your screen with Figure 6.28.

> The last item in the bulleted list now has the same formatting as the last item in the numbered list.

Figure 6.28

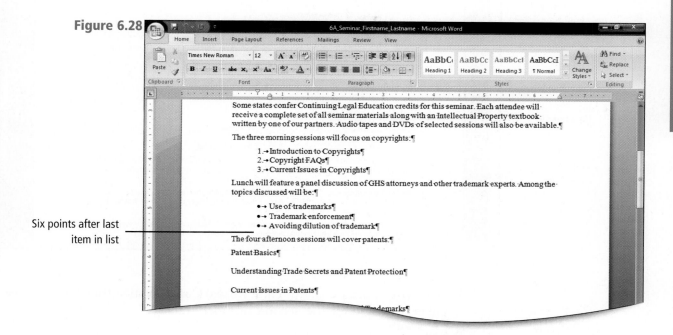

Six points after last item in list

3 In the first item of the numbered list, click anywhere to place the insertion point. In the **Clipboard group**, click the **Format Painter** button.

4 Move the pointer to the *Patent Basics* one-line paragraph, and then click one time. Notice that the *Patent Basics* paragraph takes on the formatting characteristics of the first item in the numbered list, and the numbering continues with the number 4. Also notice that the Format Painter pointer no longer displays.

5 In the **Clipboard group**, double-click the **Format Painter** button. Use the pointer to change the paragraph beginning *Understanding Trade*.

> The Format Painter pointer still displays. When you double-click the Format Painter button, it remains active until you turn it off.

6 Use the pointer to change the paragraphs that begin *Current Issues* and *Business Considerations*. Then, in the **Clipboard group**, click the **Format Painter** button to turn it off. Alternatively, press [Esc] to turn off the Format Painter.

7 Move to **item number 4** in the list—*Patent Basics*—and then right click. Notice that the shortcut menu contains list formatting commands, as shown in Figure 6.29.

Figure 6.29

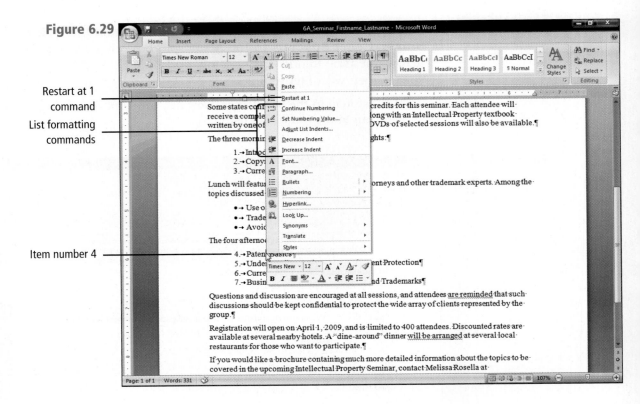

Restart at 1 command
List formatting commands
Item number 4

▣8 From the shortcut menu, click **Restart at 1**. Notice that the numbering is restarted for the second numbered list.

▣9 **Save** 🖫 your document.

More Knowledge — Using Multiple Levels in a Numbered List

If your numbered list contains two levels of information, type all of the list entries using automatic numbering. When you have completed the list, select the items that are at the lower level and click the Increase Indent button. The top level will retain the *1, 2, 3* format, while the lower level will use an *a, b, c* format.

Activity 6.15 Customizing Bullets

You can use any symbol from any font on your computer for your bullet character.

▣1 Select the three bulleted points, and then right-click anywhere in the selected text. From the shortcut menu, point to **Bullets**, and then compare your screen with Figure 6.30.

A gallery displays showing recently used bullets and a library of popular bullet shapes. The bullets that display in your gallery may differ.

Figure 6.30

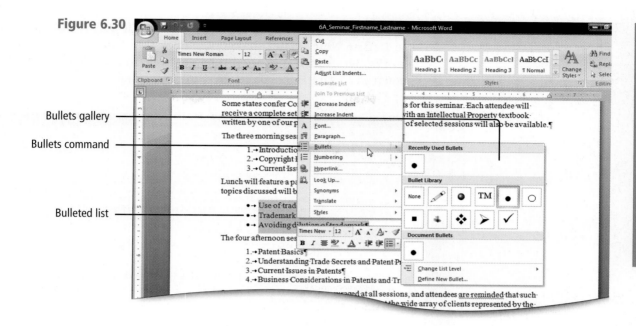

Bullets gallery

Bullets command

Bulleted list

2 At the bottom of the **Bullets gallery**, click **Define New Bullet**. In the **Define New Bullet** dialog box, click the **Symbol** button.

3 In the **Symbol** dialog box, be sure *Symbol* displays in the **Font** box. Scroll to the bottom of the list of symbols, and then in the third row from the bottom, click the trademark (TM) symbol, as shown in Figure 6.31.

Figure 6.31

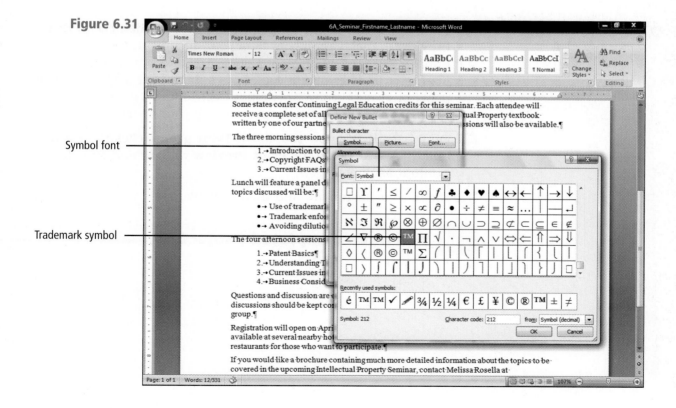

Symbol font

Trademark symbol

4 At the bottom of the **Symbol** dialog box, click **OK**. At the bottom of the **Define New Bullet** dialog box, click **OK**. Click anywhere to deselect the list. Notice that the bullets change to a trademark symbol, as shown in Figure 6.32. **Save** 🖫 your document.

Figure 6.32

New bullet symbol

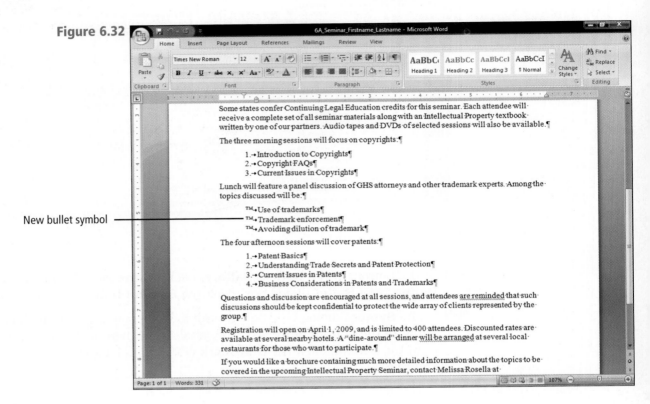

5 From the **Office** menu 🔵, point to **Print**, and then click **Print Preview** to make a final check of your document. Check your *Chapter Assignment Sheet* or *Course Syllabus* or consult your instructor to determine if you are to submit your assignments on paper or electronically. To submit electronically, go to Step 7, and then follow the instructions provided by your instructor.

6 On the **Print Preview tab**, in the **Print group**, click the **Print** button. Click **OK**, **Close** the **Print Preview** window and submit your printout as directed.

7 **Close** your document, and then **Exit** Word.

End You have completed Project 6A ―――――――――――

Project 6B **Law Overview**

In Activities 6.16 through 6.24, you will edit a research paper, which contains an overview of intellectual property law. This paper was created by a student intern of GHS Law Partners, and will later be modified for inclusion in an information packet for potential clients. Your completed document will look similar to Figure 6.33.

For Project 6B, you will need the following file:

w06B_Law_Overview

You will save your document as
6B_Law_Overview_Firstname_Lastname

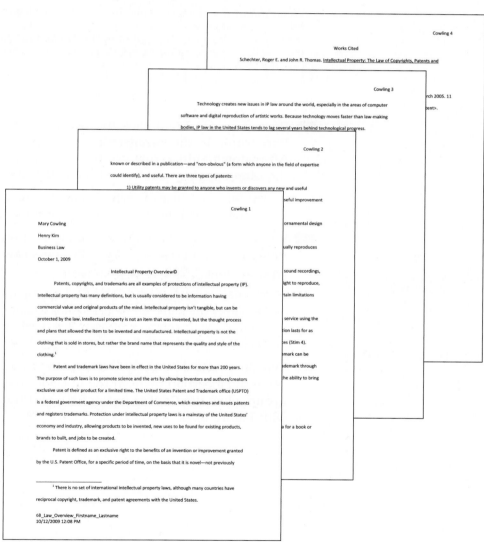

Figure 6.33
Project 6B—Law Overview

Objective 4
Insert and Format Headers and Footers

Text that you insert into a header or footer displays on every page of a document. Within a header or footer, you can add automatic page numbers, dates, times, the file name, and pictures.

Activity 6.16 Inserting and Formatting Page Numbers

1 **Start** Word. From your student files, locate and open the document **w06B_Law_Overview**. If necessary, display the formatting marks. Be sure all document margins are set to **1"**. **Save** the file in your **Word Chapter 6** folder as **6B_Law_Overview_Firstname_Lastname**

Note — Standard Styles for Research Papers

When you write a research paper or a report for college or business, you will need to follow a format prescribed by one of the standard style guides. The two most commonly used styles are those created by the *Modern Language Association (MLA)* and the *American Psychological Association (APA)*; there are several others. This project uses the MLA style.

---

2 Press Ctrl + A. Right-click the selected text, and then click **Paragraph**. In the **Paragraph** dialog box, under **Spacing**, click the **After down spin arrow** two times to set the space after to **0**. Click the **Line spacing arrow**, and then click **Double**. Click **OK**.

> The MLA style uses 1-inch margins and double spacing throughout the document, with no extra space between paragraphs.

3 Press Ctrl + Home. Type **Mary Cowling** and press Enter, and then type **Henry Kim** and press Enter. Type **Business Law** and press Enter, and then type **October 1, 2009** and press Enter.

> The first line in an MLA research paper is the name of the author; the second is the name of the person for whom the report is prepared—for example, your course professor. The third line contains the name of the class, and the fourth line contains the date.

4 Type **Intellectual Property Overview** and then press Enter. Press ↑ to place the insertion point in the line you just typed. In the **Paragraph group**, click the **Center** button ≣, and then compare your screen with Figure 6.34.

Figure 6.34

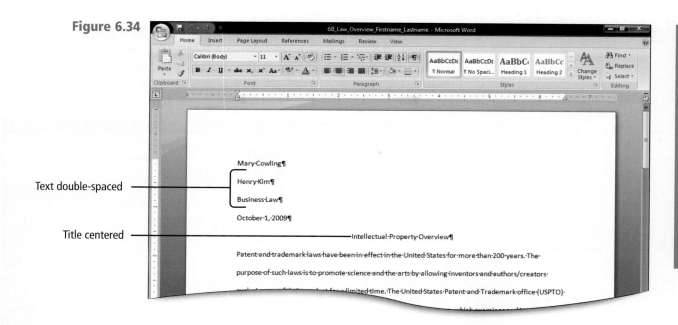

Text double-spaced

Title centered

5 Move the pointer to the top edge of **Page 1** and right-click. Click **Edit Header**, in the header area, type **Cowling** and then press Spacebar.

6 On the **Design tab**, in the **Insert group**, click the **Quick Parts** button, and then click **Field**. In the **Field** dialog box, under **Field names**, locate and click **Page**. Under **Field properties**, click the first page number style—**1, 2, 3**. Compare your screen with Figure 6.35.

Figure 6.35

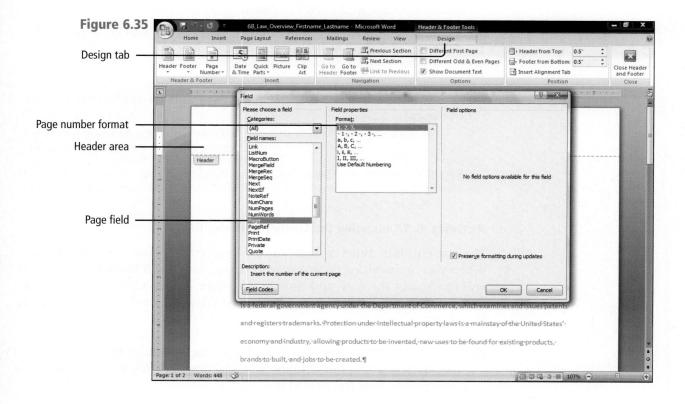

Design tab

Page number format

Header area

Page field

7 Click **OK** to place the page number at the insertion point location. Click the **Home tab**, and then in the **Paragraph group**, click the **Align Text Right** button ![align right icon]. Compare your screen with Figure 6.36.

Figure 6.36

Name and page number inserted

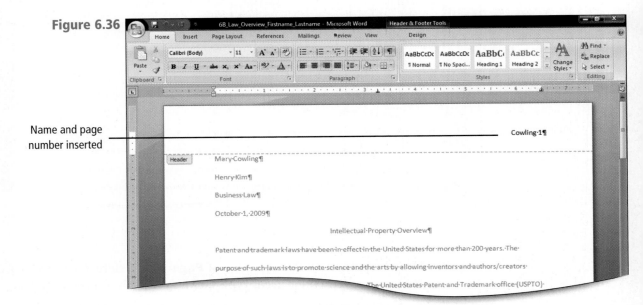

8 Click the **Design tab**, and then in the **Navigation group**, click the **Go to Footer** button. In the **Insert group**, click the **Quick Parts** button, and then click **Field**. In the **Field** dialog box, under **Field names**, locate and click **FileName**, and then click **OK**.

9 Double-click anywhere outside the footer area, and then press Ctrl + Home. **Save** ![save icon] your changes.

> **More Knowledge — Suppressing the Page Number on the First Page of a Document**
>
> Some style guidelines may require that the page number on the first page be hidden from view—suppressed. To hide the information contained in the header and footer areas on Page 1 of a document, double-click in the header or footer area. On the Design tab, in the Options group, select the Different First Page check box.

Activity 6.17 Inserting the Current Date and Time

The current date, time, or both can be inserted anywhere in a document. When you are working on a research paper, which will likely be revised several times, put the date and time in the footer to help identify the various revisions you will make. Then, remove the date and time before submitting the paper.

1 Use the vertical scroll bar to scroll to the bottom of the first page of the document to view the footer area. Double-click in the footer area, and notice that the **FileName** field is shaded in gray.

2 Click to position the insertion point to the right of the file name, and then press [Enter] to move the insertion point to the next line.

3 On the **Design tab**, in the **Insert group**, click the **Date & Time** button.

4 In the **Date and Time** dialog box, locate and click the date and time format that displays the date in a *10/01/2009 4:43 PM* (or *AM*) format, as shown in Figure 6.37.

Figure 6.37
Date & Time button

Selected format
(your date and
time will vary)

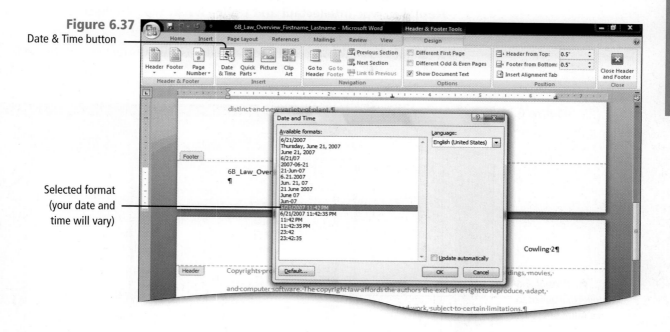

Note — Automatically Update the Date

At the bottom of the Date and Time dialog box, you can select the *Update automatically* check box to have Word update the date every time you open the document.

---

5 In the **Date and Time** dialog box, click **OK**. Double-click anywhere outside the footer area, and then press [Ctrl] + [Home].

6 **Save** your changes.

Objective 5
Insert Frequently Used Text

AutoCorrect corrects common spelling errors as you type. When you type a word incorrectly, for example *teh*, Word automatically changes it to *the*. You can add words that you frequently misspell to the AutoCorrect list. You can also add shortcuts to phrases you type often. Another type of frequently used text includes various symbols, such as the trademark symbol ™ or copyright symbol ©.

Activity 6.18 Recording AutoCorrect Entries

You can add words that you frequently misspell to the AutoCorrect list for automatic correction.

1 From the **Office** menu 🔘, click **Word Options**. In the **Word Options** list, click **Proofing**, and then under **AutoCorrect options**, click the **AutoCorrect Options** button.

2 In the **AutoCorrect** dialog box, click the **AutoCorrect tab**. Under **Replace**, type **intellectaul** and under **With**, type **intellectual** Compare your screen with Figure 6.38.

> If another student has already added this AutoCorrect entry, the Add button will change to a Replace button.

Figure 6.38

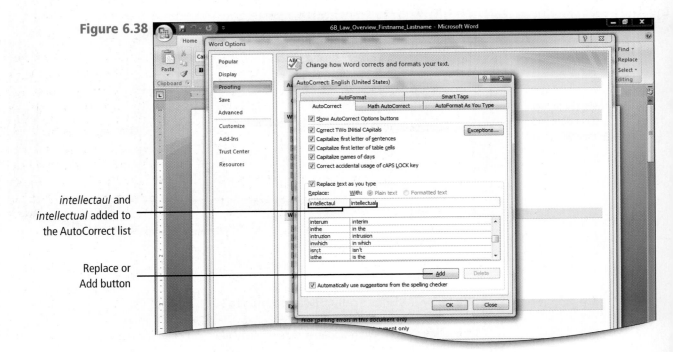

intellectaul and *intellectual* added to the AutoCorrect list

Replace or Add button

3 Click **Add**. If the entry already exists, click Replace instead, and then click Yes. Click **OK** two times to close the dialog boxes.

4 Near the top of the document, locate the paragraph beginning *Patent and trademark laws*, and then click to position the insertion point at the beginning of the paragraph. Scroll to the end of the document, hold down ⇧Shift, and then click to the right of the last paragraph mark. Scroll up to see the top of the document.

5 Right-click the selected text and click **Paragraph**. On the **Indents and Spacing tab**, under **Indentation**, click the **Special arrow**, and then click **First line**. Under **Indentation**, in the **By** box, be sure *0.5"* displays. Compare your screen with Figure 6.39.

> ***Indenting***—moving the beginning of the first line of a paragraph to the right or left of the rest of the paragraph—provides visual cues to the reader to help break the document up and make it easier to read. The MLA style uses 0.5-inch indents at the beginning of the first line of every paragraph.

Figure 6.39

Indentation will be applied to the *First line* of the paragraph

First line will be indented 0.5 (one-half) inch

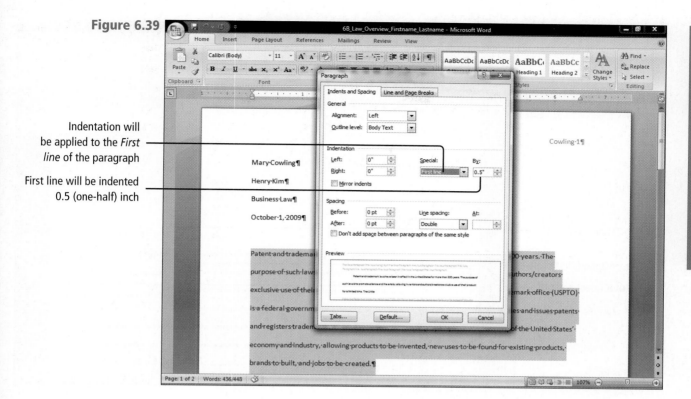

6 Click **OK**. Near the top of the document, locate the paragraph beginning *Patent and trademark laws*, and then click to position the insertion point at the beginning of the paragraph.

7 Press [Enter], and then press [↑] to place the insertion point in the blank line. Type **Patents, copyrights, and trademarks are all examples of protections of** and then press [Spacebar].

8 Type **intellectaul** and watch the screen as you press [Spacebar]. Notice that the misspelled word is automatically corrected.

9 Click in the corrected word, and then notice the blue line that displays under the word. Move the pointer over the blue line until the **AutoCorrect Options** button displays, and then click the button. Compare your screen with Figure 6.40.

Figure 6.40

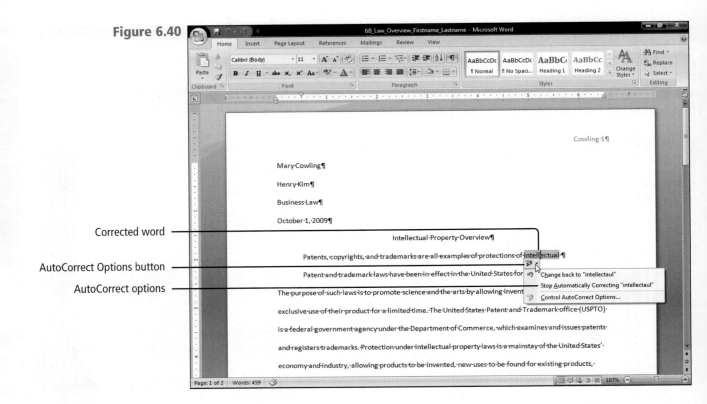

Corrected word

AutoCorrect Options button

AutoCorrect options

10 Click anywhere in the document to close the **AutoCorrect Options** menu without selecting a command. Locate the word *intellectual* that you just corrected and position the insertion point at the end of that line. Type **property (IP).** and then press Spacebar.

11 Type the remainder of the paragraph, and then compare your screen with Figure 6.41.

Intellectual property has many definitions, but is usually considered to be information having commercial value and original products of the mind. Intellectual property isn't tangible, but can be protected by the law. Intellectual property is not an item that was invented, but the thought process and plans that allowed the item to be invented and manufactured. Intellectual property is not the clothing that is sold in stores, but rather the brand name that represents the quality and style of the clothing.

Figure 6.41

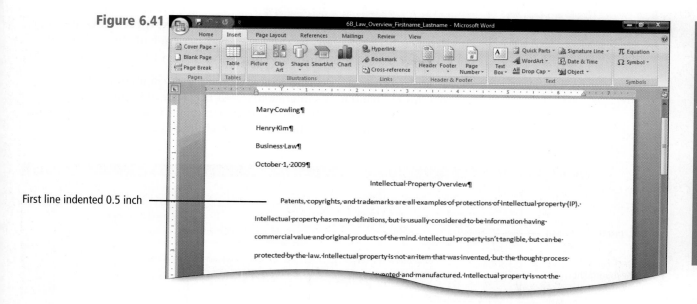

First line indented 0.5 inch

12 **Save** 📥 your changes.

More Knowledge — AutoCorrect Shortcuts

The AutoCorrect replacement is most commonly used to correct spelling errors, but it can also be used to expand shortcut text into longer words or phrases. In the Replace box, type a shortcut phrase, and type the full phrase in the With box. When setting up an AutoCorrect shortcut, it is best not to use shortcut text that is an actual word or a commonly used abbreviation. For example, if you type both *GHS* and *GHS Law Partners* frequently, you may want to add ghsx (or just ghx) as an AutoCorrect shortcut for the text *GHS Law Partners*.

Activity 6.19 Inserting Symbols

There are many symbols that are used occasionally, but not often enough to put on a standard keyboard. These symbols can be found on, and inserted from, the Symbols group on the Insert tab.

1 Use the vertical scroll bar to move down in the document to display the bottom half of **Page 1**.

2 In the paragraph that begins *Patent is defined*, in the second line, locate the word *novel*, and then place the insertion point just to the right of the word. Press [Delete] two times to remove the space and the left parenthesis.

3 Click the **Insert tab**, and then in the **Symbols group**, click the **Symbol** button. At the bottom of the **Symbol gallery**, click **More Symbols**.

4 In the **Symbol** dialog box, click the **Special Characters tab**. Be sure the **Em Dash** is selected. In the lower right corner of the dialog box, click **Insert**, and then compare your screen with Figure 6.42.

An ***em dash*** is the default symbol in the list of commonly used symbols. An em dash in a sentence marks a break in thought, similar to a comma but stronger. The keyboard shortcuts for inserting the commonly used symbols display to the right of the character name.

Figure 6.42

Inserted em dash

Keyboard shortcuts

Em dash

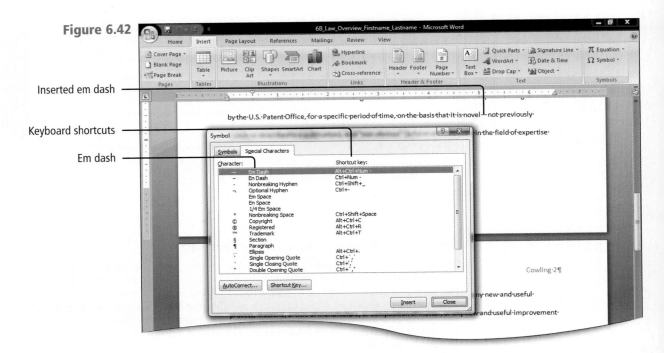

5 If necessary, drag the dialog box out of the way so you can see the third line of the same paragraph. With the **Symbol** dialog box still open, to the right of *in a publication*, remove the right parenthesis, the comma, and the space; and then click the **Insert** button again. At the bottom of the **Symbol** dialog box, click **Close**.

6 Press Ctrl + Home to move to the beginning of the document. Place the insertion point to the right of the title text *Intellectual Property Overview*, type **(c)** and then compare your document with Figure 6.43.

Your typed text *(c)* changes to the copyright symbol ©. Although this symbol is available from the Symbol gallery, it is also included in Word's AutoCorrect list. The parentheses are necessary for AutoComplete to insert a Copyright symbol. If you point to the copyright symbol, the AutoCorrect Options button displays, which enables you to remove the copyright symbol and display *(c)* instead.

Figure 6.43

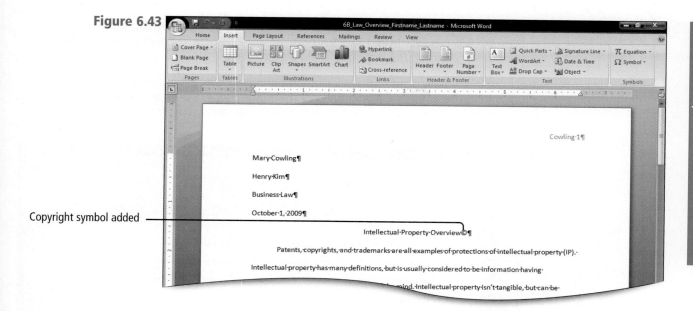

Copyright symbol added

7 **Save** your changes.

Objective 6
Insert and Format References

Reports frequently include information taken from other sources, and these must be credited. Within report text, numbers mark the location of *references*—information that has been taken from another source. The numbers refer to *footnotes*—references placed at the bottom of the page containing the reference, or *endnotes*—references placed at the end of a document or chapter. When footnotes or endnotes are included in a report, a page listing the references is included. Such a list is commonly titled *Works Cited*, *Bibliography*, *Sources*, or References.

Activity 6.20 Inserting Footnotes

Footnotes can be added as you type the document or after the document is complete. Footnotes do not need to be entered in order, and if one footnote is removed, Word renumbers the remaining footnotes automatically.

1 Scroll to view **Page 2** and locate the paragraph that begins *Copyrights protect*. At the end of the paragraph, position the insertion point following the period.

2 Click the **References tab**, and then in the **Footnotes group**, click **Insert Footnote**.

Word creates a footnote in the footnote area at the bottom of the page, and adds a footnote number to the text at the insertion point location. Footnote 1 displays at the top of the footnote area, and the insertion point moves to the right of the number. A short blank line is added just above the footnote area. You do not need to type the footnote number.

3 Type **According to the United States Copyright Office, abstractions, such as an idea for a book or movie, are not subject to copyright law.** Compare your screen with Figure 6.44.

> This is an explanatory footnote, giving additional information that does not fit well in the body of the report. The new footnote is single-spaced, even though the document text is double-spaced.

Figure 6.44

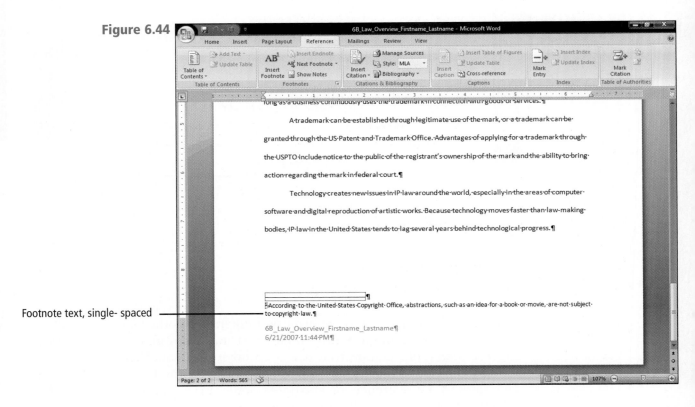

Footnote text, single- spaced

4 Press Ctrl + Home to move to the beginning of the document. Locate the paragraph that begins *Patents, copyrights.* At the end of the paragraph, position the insertion point following the period.

> This sentence refers to the *protections* of intellectual property, and the report's author wants to clarify the scope of protections by adding a reference.

5 In the **Footnotes group**, click the **Insert Footnote** button. Type **There is no set of international intellectual property laws, although many countries have reciprocal copyright, trademark, and patent agreements with the United States.** Notice that the footnote you just added is the new footnote *1*, while the other footnote is renumbered as footnote *2*.

6 **Save** 💾 your changes.

More Knowledge — Using Symbols Rather Than Numbers for Notes

Instead of using numbers to designate footnotes, you can use standard footnote symbols. The seven traditional symbols, available from the Footnote and Endnote dialog box, in order, are * (asterisk), † (dagger), ‡ (double dagger), § (section mark), ‖ (parallels), ¶ (paragraph mark), and # (number or pound sign). This sequence can be continuous (this is the default setting), or can begin anew with each page.

Activity 6.21 Modifying a Footnote Style

Microsoft Word contains built-in paragraph formats called *styles*, which can be applied to a paragraph with one command. The default style for footnote text is a single-spaced paragraph that uses a 10-point Calibri font and no indents. MLA style specifies double-spaced text in all areas of a research paper—including footnotes. According to the MLA style, footnotes must also be indented 0.5 inch.

1 Scroll to view the bottom of **Page 1** and right-click anywhere in the footnote text. From the shortcut menu, click **Style**. Compare your screen with Figure 6.45.

> The Style dialog box displays, listing the styles currently in use in the document, in addition to some of the word processing elements that come with special built-in styles. Because you right-clicked on the footnote text, the selected style is the Footnote Text paragraph style.

Figure 6.45

All styles selected

Elements with special built-in styles

Footnote Text paragraph style

Modify button

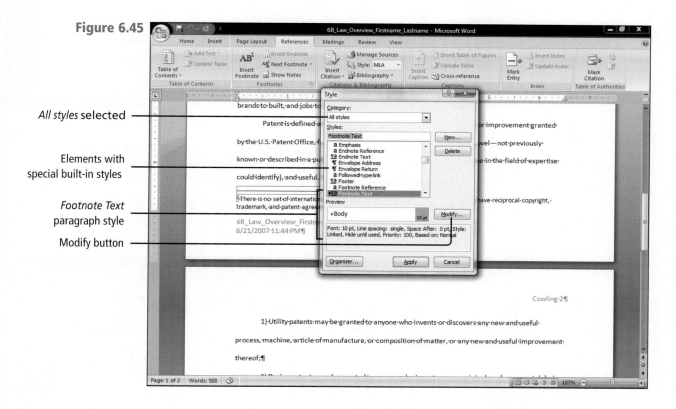

2 In the **Style** dialog box, click the **Modify** button. In the **Modify Style** dialog box, locate the small Formatting toolbar in the center of the dialog box, click the **Font Size button arrow**, click **11**, and then compare your screen with Figure 6.46.

Figure 6.46

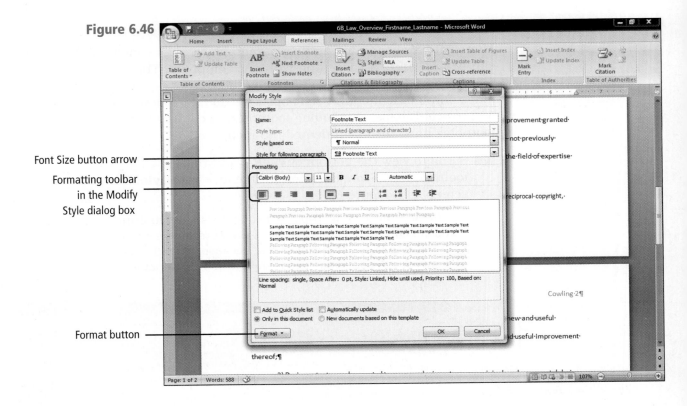

Font Size button arrow

Formatting toolbar
in the Modify
Style dialog box

Format button

3 In the lower left corner of the dialog box, click the **Format** button,
and then click **Paragraph**. In the **Paragraph** dialog box, under
Indentation, click the **Special arrow**, and then click **First line**.

4 Under **Spacing**, click the **Line spacing button arrow**, and then click
Double. Compare your dialog box with Figure 6.47.

Figure 6.47

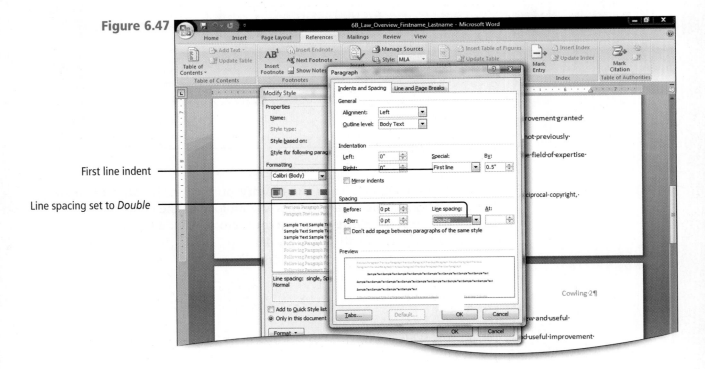

First line indent

Line spacing set to *Double*

5 Click **OK** to close the **Paragraph** dialog box, click **OK** to close the **Modify Style** dialog box, and then click **Apply** to apply the new style and close the **Style** dialog box. Compare your screen with Figure 6.48.

> Your inserted footnotes are formatted with the new Footnote Text paragraph style; any new footnotes that you insert will also use this format.

Figure 6.48

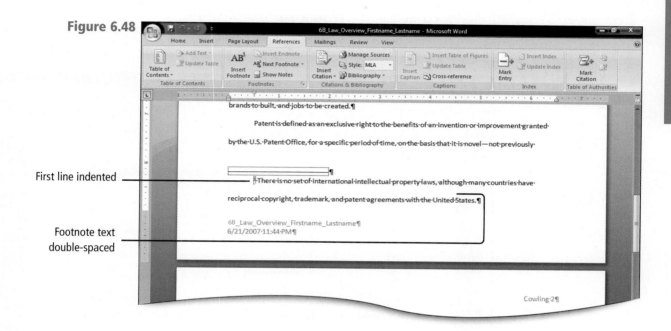

First line indented

Footnote text double-spaced

6 Scroll to view the bottom of **Page 2** to confirm that the new format was also applied to the second footnote, and then **Save** 🖫 your document.

Activity 6.22 Adding Citations

When writing a long research paper, you will likely reference numerous books, articles, and Web sites. Some of your research sources may be referenced many times, others only one time. References to sources within the text of your research paper are indicated in an *abbreviated* manner. However, as you enter a reference for the first time, you can also enter the *complete* information about the source. Then, when you have finished your paper, you will be able to automatically generate the list of sources that must be included at the end of your research paper.

1 On **Page 2** of the document, locate the paragraph that begins *Copyrights protect*, and then position the insertion point at the end of the paragraph, but before the period. Click the **References tab** to begin the process of inserting a citation.

> A ***citation*** is a list of information about a source, usually including the name of the author, the full title of the work, the year of publication, and other publication information.

2 In the **Citations & Bibliography group**, click the **Style button arrow**, and then click **MLA** to insert a reference using MLA style.

3 Click the **Insert Citation** button, and then click **Add New Source**. Be sure **Book** is selected as the **Type of Source**. Add the following information, and then compare your screen with Figure 6.49:

Author:	**Schechter, Roger E.; Thomas, John R.**
Title:	**Intellectual Property: The Law of Copyrights, Patents and Trademarks**
Year:	**2003**
City:	**St. Paul, MN**
Publisher:	**West Publishing Company**

Figure 6.49

Insert Citation button on the Ribbon

Source type

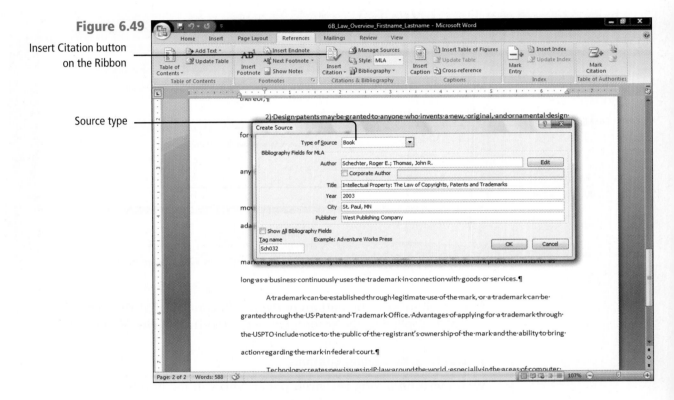

In the MLA style, references to items on the Works Cited page are placed in ***parenthetical references***—references that include the last name of the author or authors and the page number in the referenced source, which you add to the reference. No year is indicated, and there is no comma between the name and the page number.

4 Click **OK** to insert the reference. Click to select the reference, and notice that a small box surrounds the reference and an arrow displays in the lower right corner of the box. Click this **Citation Options arrow**, and then from the list of options, click **Edit Citation**.

5 In the **Edit Citation** dialog box, under **Add**, in the **Pages** box, type **2** to indicate that you are citing from page 2 of this source. Compare your screen with Figure 6.50. Notice that the citation wraps from one line to the next, so the citation box also wraps between lines.

Figure 6.50

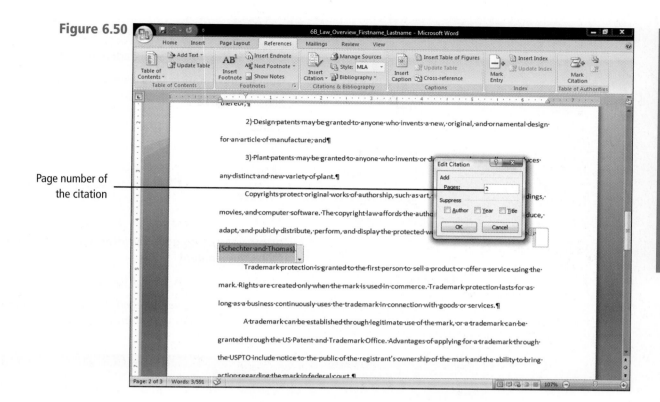

Page number of the citation

6 Click **OK** to display the page number of the citation. In the next paragraph, which begins *Trademark protection*, position the insertion point at the end of the paragraph, but before the period.

7 In the **Citations & Bibliography group**, click the **Insert Citation** button, and then click **Add New Source**. Be sure **Book** is selected as the **Type of Source**, and then add the following information:

Author:	**Stim, Richard W.**
Title:	**Trademark Law**
Year:	**2000**
City:	**Stamford, CT**
Publisher:	**Thomson Delmar Learning**

8 Click **OK**. Click to select the reference, click the **Citation Options arrow**, and then click **Edit Citation**. In the **Edit Citation** dialog box, under **Add**, in the **Pages** box, type **4** to indicate that you are citing from page 4 of this source. Click **OK**.

9 On the same page, locate the paragraph that begins *3) Plant patents*. At the end of that sentence, click to position the insertion point before the period. In the **Citations & Bibliography group**, click the **Insert Citation** button, and then click **Add New Source**. Click the **Type of Source arrow**, scroll down, and select **Web site** from the list. Under **Bibliography Fields for MLA**, click to select the **Corporate Author** check box.

10 Type the following information:

Corporate Author:	**United States Patent and Trademark Office**
Name of Web Page:	**General Information Concerning Patents**
Year:	**2005**
Month:	**March**
Day:	**22**
Year Accessed:	**2009**
Month Accessed:	**October**
Day Accessed:	**11**
URL:	**http://www.uspto.gov/web/offices/pac/doc/general/index.html#patent**

11 Click **OK**, and then compare your screen with Figure 6.51.

A parenthetical reference is added. Because the cited Web page has no page numbers, only the author name is used in the parenthetical reference.

Figure 6.51

Parenthetical references

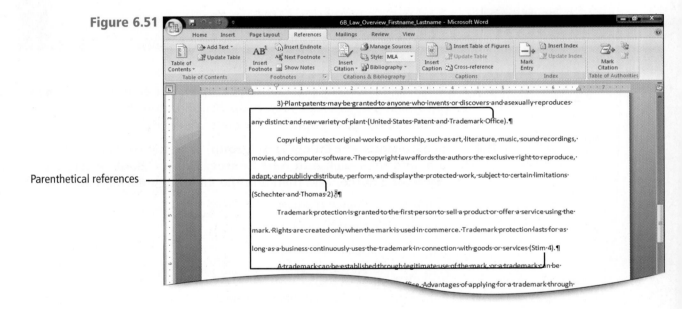

12 On the **References tab**, in the **Citations & Bibliography group**, click the **Manage Sources** button, and then compare your screen with Figure 6.52.

The Source Manager dialog box displays. You may have fewer sources, more sources, or different sources. Other citations on your computer display in the Master List box. The citations for the current document display in the Current List box. If you use the same sources regularly, you can copy sources from your Master List to the current document.

Figure 6.52

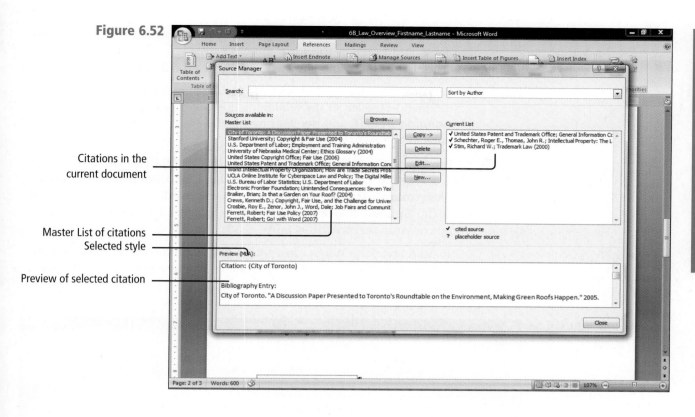

Citations in the current document

Master List of citations

Selected style

Preview of selected citation

13 At the bottom of the **Source Manager** dialog box, click **Close**. **Save** your changes.

Activity 6.23 Creating a Reference Page

It is common to include, at the end of a report, a list of each source referenced. *Works Cited* is the reference page heading used in the MLA style guidelines. Other styles may refer to this page as a *Bibliography* (Business Style) or *References* (APA Style).

1 Press Ctrl + End to move the insertion point to the end of the document. Press Ctrl + Enter to insert a manual page break.

2 Type **Works Cited** and then press Enter. On the **References tab**, in the **Citations & Bibliography group**, be sure **MLA** displays in the **Style** box.

3 In the **Citations & Bibliography group**, click the **Bibliography** button, and then click **Insert Bibliography**.

> The bibliography displays as a field, and the field links to the Source Manager for the citations. The references display alphabetically by author name.

4 In the bibliography, move the pointer to the left of the first entry— beginning *Schechter, Roger*—to display the pointer. Drag down to select all three references. Right-click the selected text, and then click **Paragraph**.

5 Under **Indentation**, click the **Special arrow**, and then click **Hanging**. Under **Spacing**, click the **Line spacing arrow**, and then click **Double**. Under **Spacing**, in the **After** box, type **0** and then click **OK**.

> The text is double-spaced, and the first line of each entry extends 0.5 inch to the left of the remaining lines of the entry. This is called a *hanging indent*, and the lines are double-spaced according to MLA guidelines.

6 At the top of the last page, right-click the *Works Cited* title, and then click **Paragraph**. In the **Paragraph** dialog box, under **General**, click the **Alignment arrow**, and then click **Centered**. Under **Indentation**, click the **Special arrow**, and then click **(none)**. Click **OK**, and then compare your screen with Figure 6.53.

> In MLA style, the *Works Cited* title is aligned and centered. The first line indent of 0.5 inch was removed to center the title between the left and right margins.

Figure 6.53

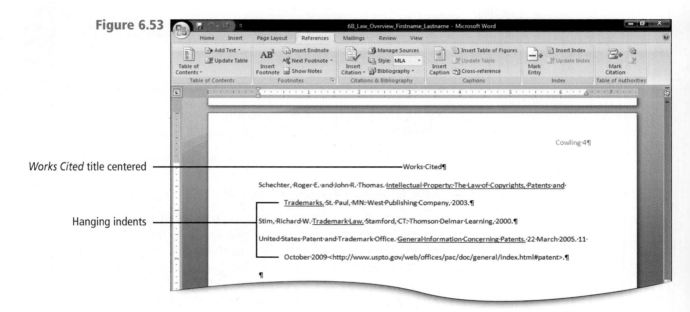

Works Cited title centered

Hanging indents

7 **Save** your document.

Activity 6.24 Managing Document Properties

Document properties refer to the detailed information about your Word document file that can help you identify or organize your electronic files. Document property information is stored in the ***Document Information Panel***, and can include the document title, the name of the author, the subject of the document, and keywords that will help you search for the document in your computer system.

1 From the **Office** menu ⊞, point to **Prepare**, and then click **Properties** to display the **Document Information Panel**.

2 In the **Author** box, type your name, if necessary.

3 In the **Title** box, type **Intellectual Property Law**

4 In the **Keywords** box, type **copyright, patent, trademark** and then compare your screen with Figure 6.54. Notice that not all boxes need to be filled in.

Figure 6.54

Close button

Author

Title

Keywords

Document Information Panel

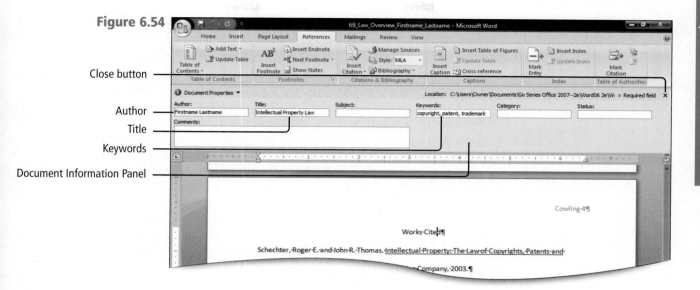

5 On the right side of the **Document Information Panel**, click the **Close** button ✕. **Save** 🖫 your document.

6 From the **Office** menu 🏣, point to **Print**, and then click **Print Preview** to make a final check of your research paper. Check your *Chapter Assignment Sheet* or *Course Syllabus* or consult your instructor to determine if you are to submit your assignments on paper or electronically. To submit electronically, go to Step 8, and then follow the instructions provided by your instructor.

7 On the **Print Preview tab**, in the **Print group**, click the **Print** button, click **OK**, and then click **Close Print Preview**.

8 From the **Office** menu 🏣, click **Exit Word**, saving any changes if prompted to do so.

End **You have completed Project 6B** ————————

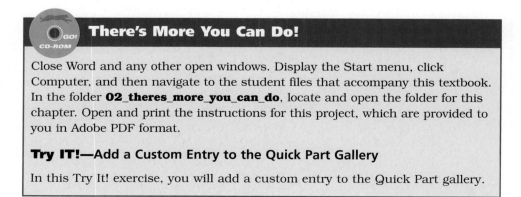

There's More You Can Do!

Close Word and any other open windows. Display the Start menu, click Computer, and then navigate to the student files that accompany this textbook. In the folder **02_theres_more_you_can_do**, locate and open the folder for this chapter. Open and print the instructions for this project, which are provided to you in Adobe PDF format.

Try IT!—Add a Custom Entry to the Quick Part Gallery

In this Try It! exercise, you will add a custom entry to the Quick Part gallery.

Content-Based Assessments

Summary

You can change the format of pages by setting different margins, and change the format of paragraphs by changing indents, line spacing, and the spacing after paragraphs. To apply formats from one paragraph to others, use the Format Painter. You can also format paragraphs by creating numbered and bulleted lists and modifying the bullets.

Use commands such as Cut and Paste, or techniques such as the drag-and-drop operation, to move and copy text. Use the Find and Replace dialog box to locate text that you want to modify. Some formatting in Word can be performed automatically using AutoCorrect and AutoComplete.

When creating reports, use the header and footer areas to add page numbers or to insert the date, time, or file name. Reports also require adding footnotes or endnotes and a reference page to list other sources of information cited within the report.

Key Terms

Alignment 76

American Psychological Association (APA) style 102

AutoCorrect 105

AutoFormat As You Type 94

AutoText .... 🖱

Bibliography 111

Building block .... 🖱

Bulleted list 93

Bullets 93

Center alignment 76

Citation 115

Copy 83

Cut 83

Document Information Panel 120

Document properties 120

Drag and drop 88

Em dash 110

Endnotes 111

Footnotes 111

Format Painter 81

Hanging indent 120

Indenting 106

Justified alignment 76

Left alignment 76

Line spacing 78

Manual line break 92

Margins 74

Modern Language Association (MLA) style 102

Nonbreaking hyphen 91

Nonbreaking space 91

Numbered list 93

Office Clipboard 83

Parenthetical reference 116

Paste 83

References 111

Right alignment 76

Sources 111

Spin box 80

Spin box arrows 80

Styles 113

Toggle button 96

Works Cited 111

The 🖱 symbol represents Key Terms found on the Student CD in the 02_theres_more_you_can_do folder for this chapter.

Content-Based Assessments

Word

chaptersix

Matching

Match each term in the second column with its correct definition in the first column by writing the letter of the term on the blank line in front of the correct definition.

_____ **1.** The most commonly used text alignment, where text is aligned at the left margin, leaving the right margin uneven.

_____ **2.** The alignment of text centered between the left and right margins.

_____ **3.** Text that is aligned on both the left and right margins.

_____ **4.** The distance between lines of text in a paragraph.

_____ **5.** A small box with upward- and downward-pointing arrows that let you move rapidly through a set of values.

_____ **6.** A Word tool with which you can copy the formatting of specific text, or of a paragraph, to text in another location in the document.

_____ **7.** A temporary storage area that holds text or graphics that have been cut or copied, and that can subsequently be placed in another location in the document or in another Office program.

_____ **8.** The action of removing selected text from a document and moving it to the Office Clipboard.

_____ **9.** A small button that displays beneath pasted text, and lets you determine how the information is pasted into your document.

_____ **10.** Text symbols such as small circles or check marks used to introduce items in a list.

_____ **11.** A Word feature that automatically corrects common typing and spelling errors as you type, such as changing _teh_ to _the_.

_____ **12.** The word processing name for a long dash in a sentence that marks a break in thought, similar to a comma but stronger.

_____ **13.** In a report or research paper, references placed at the bottom of a report page containing the source of the reference.

_____ **14.** A term used to describe a list of referenced works placed at the end of a research paper or report when using the MLA style.

_____ **15.** An indent style in which the first line of a paragraph extends to the left of the remaining lines; this indent style is commonly used for bibliographic entries.

A AutoCorrect

B Bullets

C Center alignment

D Cutting

E Em dash

F Footnotes

G Format Painter

H Hanging indent

I Justified alignment

J Left alignment

K Line spacing

L Office Clipboard

M Paste Options

N Spin box

O Works Cited

Content-Based Assessments

Fill in the Blank

Write the correct answer in the space provided.

1. The space between the text and the top, bottom, left, and right edges of the paper is known as the _____.

2. The placement of paragraph text relative to the left and right margins is known as the _____.

3. When you paste text, the text is moved from the _____ _____ and placed where the insertion point is positioned.

4. The keyboard shortcut used to copy text is Ctrl + _____.

5. When you drag text and then drop it in another location, the text is _____ from one place to another.

6. When you click the Redo button, it reverses the action of the _____ button.

7. To keep two words together as one unit, so that Word does not split them at the end of a line, insert a _____ space.

8. To move the insertion point to the next line without pressing Enter and without creating a new paragraph, insert a manual _____ _____.

9. A list of items with each item introduced by a consecutive number to indicate definite steps, a sequence of actions, or chronological order is a _____ list.

10. In a report or research paper, a reference placed at the end of a report is called an _____.

11. If you need to add ™ or ® or © to a document, display the _____ dialog box.

12. A set of formatting characteristics that can be applied to a paragraph with one shortcut command is known as a _____.

13. In the MLA report style, references placed in parentheses within the report text that includes the last name of the author or authors and the page number in the referenced source, are called _____ _____.

14. A list of information about a reference source, usually including the name of the author, the full title of the work, the year of publication, a Web address, and other publication information, is called a _____.

15. The detailed information about a document that can help you identify or organize your files, including author name, title, and keywords, is called the Document _____.

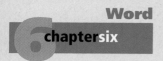

Skills Review

Project 6C — Patent Search

In this project, you will apply the skills you practiced from the Objectives in Project 6A.

Objectives: 1. *Change Document and Paragraph Layout;* **2.** *Change and Reorganize Text;* **3.** *Create and Modify Lists.*

In the following Skills Review, you will edit a document describing the patent search process performed by GHS Law Partners. Your completed document will look similar to the one shown in Figure 6.55.

For Project 6C, you will need the following file:

w06C_Patent_Search

You will save your document as
6C_Patent_Search_Firstname_Lastname

Figure 6.55

permit storage of information about large numbers of chips having complex designs.

e, CA); Hubbell; Earl (Los
alo Alto, CA); Cheung;
an Jose, CA)

ra, CA)

2000

GHS Law Partners
Patent Search Process and Procedures

GHS Law Partners conducts patent searches on behalf of its clients. Patent searches are conducted before preparing the patent application in order to discern if a similar product or process has been patented already. If a similar patent is discovered, the client's pending patent application can be abandoned before too much time or money is invested in it; or, the information in the existing patent can be used to modify the patent application or change its focus.

Patents are grouped into numerous classifications covering all areas of technology. The search process can be time consuming and expensive, but it is valuable for clients to have a search conducted by experts before investing millions of dollars in a new product or process. The number of patents granted by the United States Patent and Trademark Office is large, and has been growing every year. According to the USPTO, in 1963, 48,971 patents were granted. In 2004, 181,302 patents were granted.

GHS Law Partners conducts three main portions of the patent search:

1. Organize the search and determine whether manual searches will be needed in addition to electronic searches. Manual searches may be needed for older technologies not available in the USPTO databases.
2. Run electronic searches and/or manually search at USPTO depository libraries or the USPTO main office in Virginia.
3. Examine the patent documents.

GHS Law Partners employs experts in many fields who will examine the patent documents for their similarity to the new product or process. Patent documents consist of:

- Reference section
- Abstract – for example:

United States Patent 6,826,296

Balaban, et al. November 30, 2004

Method and system for providing a probe array chip design database

Abstract

Systems and method for organizing information relating to the design of polymer probe array chips including oligonucleotide array chips. A database model is provided which organizes information interrelating probes on a chip, genomic items investigated by the chip, and sequence information relating to the design of the chip. The model is readily translatable into database languages such as SQL. The database model scales to

to drawings and figures

of patent searches, such as infringement
can reveal whether a product already in
rches, conducted as part of large research
recent developments in a particular area.

6C_Patent_Search_Firstname_Lastname

(Project 6C–Patent Search continues on the next page)

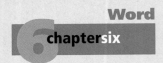

Skills Review

(Project 6C–Patent Search continued)

1. **Start** Word. Locate and open the file **w06C_Patent_Search**, and then **Save** the file in your **Word Chapter 6** folder as **6C_Patent_Search_Firstname_Lastname** Display formatting marks and rulers.

2. Click the **Page Layout tab**, click the **Margins** button, and then at the bottom of the **Margins gallery**, click **Custom Margins**. In the **Page Setup** dialog box, press Tab as necessary to select the value in the **Left** box. With *1.25"* selected, type **1** and then press Tab. In the **Right** box, change the value from *1.25"* to **1** and then click **OK**.

3. Click the **Insert tab**. In the **Header & Footer group**, click the **Footer** button, and then click **Edit Footer**. On the **Design tab**, in the **Insert group**, click the **Quick Parts** button, and then click **Field**. In the **Field** dialog box, under **Field names**, locate and click **FileName**, and then click **OK**. Double-click anywhere in the document to close the footer area. **Save** your document.

4. Select the first line of the document. On the Mini toolbar, click the **Center** button, and then click the **Bold** button.

5. Right-click anywhere in the paragraph beginning *GHS Law Partners conducts patent*, and then from the shortcut menu, click **Paragraph**. In the **Paragraph** dialog box, under **Indentation**, click the **Special arrow**, and then click **First line**. Under **Spacing**, in the **After** box, click the **up spin arrow** to change the spacing from *10 pt* to **12 pt**. Under **Spacing**, click the **Line spacing arrow**, and then click **Single**. Click **OK** to close the Paragraph dialog box.

6. With the insertion point in the paragraph beginning *GHS Law Partners conducts patent*, in the **Clipboard group**, double-click the **Format Painter** button. Move the ⌐I pointer to the paragraph beginning *The search process* and click one time. Use the **Format Painter** to format the paragraph that begins *GHS Law Partners conducts three*, the paragraph beginning *GHS Law Partners employs*, and the last paragraph in the document, beginning *GHS Law Partners can also*. In the **Clipboard group**, click the **Format Painter** button again to turn it off.

7. **Save** your changes. Press Ctrl + Home. On the right side of the **Home tab**, in the **Editing group**, click the **Replace** button. In the **Find and Replace** dialog box, in the **Find what** box, type **USPTO** and in the **Replace with** box, type **United States Patent and Trademark Office**

8. In the **Find and Replace** dialog box, click the **More** button, and then under **Search Options**, if necessary, select the **Match case** check box. Click **Find Next** to find the first instance of *USPTO*, and then click the **Replace** button. **Close** the dialog box.

9. In the fourth line of the document, double-click to select the word *already*, and then in the **Clipboard group**, click the **Cut** button. Move the pointer to the right of the next word in the sentence—*patented*—and then click the **Paste** button. In the next paragraph, beginning *The search process*, locate and select the last sentence, beginning *Patents are grouped*. In the **Clipboard group**, click the **Cut** button. Move the insertion point to the beginning of the same paragraph, and then click the **Paste** button. Adjust spacing at the end of the pasted sentence as necessary.

10. In the fifth paragraph beginning *Examine the patent*, select the entire paragraph, including the paragraph mark. Drag the

(Project 6C–Patent Search continues on the next page)

Content-Based Assessments

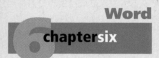
(Project 6C–Patent Search continued)

paragraph down to the beginning of the paragraph beginning *GHS Law Partners employs.* In the same paragraph, select *Examine* and replace it with **Study**

11. On the **Quick Access Toolbar**, click the **Undo** button to remove *Study* and replace it with *Examine.* Click the **Undo** button one more time to move the paragraph back to its original location, and then click the **Redo** button to move it back to its new location.

12. Near the top of **Page 2**, in the paragraph beginning *Appl. No.: 737838*, select the space before *2000.* Hold down Ctrl and ⇧Shift, and then press Spacebar to add a nonbreaking space. Use the same procedure to add a nonbreaking space between *December* and *14* to keep the date together if the line is edited.

13. Press Ctrl + Home. Right-click the title, and then click **Paragraph**. Under **Spacing**, in the **After** box, click the **up spin arrow** two times to change the value in the box from *10 pt* to **18 pt**. Click the **Line spacing arrow**, and then click **Single**. Click **OK**. In the title, click to the left of **Patent**, and then remove the space between *Partners* and *Patent.* Hold down ⇧Shift and press Enter to enter a manual line break. **Save** your document.

14. In the middle of **Page 1**, point to the left of the paragraph beginning *Organize the search*, and then drag down to select the next four lines, including the line beginning *Examine the patent.* On the **Home**

tab, in the **Paragraph group**, click the **Numbering** button.

15. Below the numbered list, select the two paragraphs that begin *Reference section* and *Abstract.* In the **Paragraph group**, click the **Bullets** button. Use the same procedure to add bullets to the four paragraphs near the end of the document beginning *Field and background* and ending with *Inventor's description.*

16. On **Page 1**, below the second bulleted point, point to the left of the paragraph beginning *United States Patent*, and then drag down to select the text through the paragraph beginning *Appl. No.*—the line above the second part of the bulleted list. In the **Paragraph group**, click the **Increase Indent** button two times. **Save** your document.

17. From the **Office** menu, point to **Print**, and then click **Print Preview** to make a final check of your document. Check your *Chapter Assignment Sheet* or *Course Syllabus* or consult your instructor to determine if you are to submit your assignments on paper or electronically. To submit electronically, go to Step 19, and then follow the instructions provided by your instructor.

18. On the **Print Preview tab**, click the **Print** button, click **OK**, and then click **Close Print Preview**.

19. From the **Office** menu, click **Exit Word**, saving any changes if prompted to do so.

End **You have completed Project 6C**

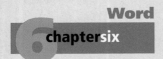

Skills Review

Project 6D — Copyright Law

In this project, you will apply the skills you practiced from the Objectives in Project 6B.

Objectives: 4. *Insert and Format Headers and Footers;* **5.** *Insert Frequently Used Text;* **6.** *Insert and Format References.*

In the following Skills Review, you will edit a short research paper about the Digital Millennium Copyright Act. This paper was written by an intern at GHS Law Partners. Your completed document will look similar to Figure 6.56.

For Project 6D, you will need the following files:

New blank Word document
w06D_Copyright_Law

**You will save your document as
6D_Copyright_Law_Firstname_Lastname**

Figure 6.56

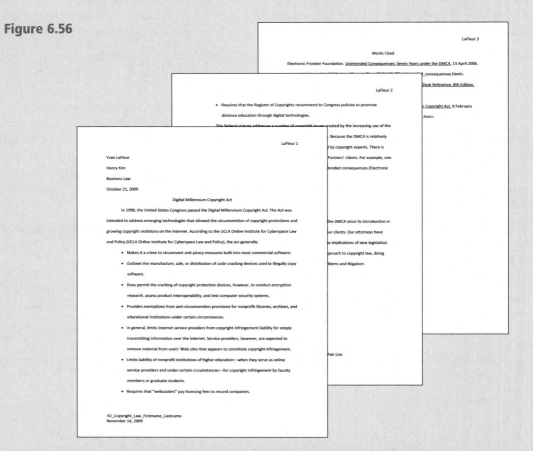

(Project 6D–Copyright Law continues on the next page)

Content-Based Assessments

Skills Review

(Project 6D—Copyright Law continued)

1. **Start** Word and be sure a new blank document is displayed. Display formatting marks and rulers. Be sure all margins are set to **1** inch.

2. On the **Quick Access Toolbar**, click the **Save** button. In the **Save As** dialog box, navigate to your **Word Chapter 6** folder. Name your file **6D_Copyright_Law_ Firstname_Lastname** and then click **Save**.

3. Type **Yvan LaFleur** and press Enter, and then type **Henry Kim** and press Enter. Type **Business Law** and press Enter, and then type **October 21, 2009** and press Enter. Click the **Home tab**, and then in the **Paragraph group**, click the **Center** button, type **Digital Millennium Copyright Act** and press Enter. Then, in the **Paragraph group**, click the **Align Text Left** button.

4. Click the **Insert tab**. In the **Header & Footer group**, click **Header**, and then click **Edit Header**. In the header area, type **LaFleur** and then press Spacebar. On the **Design tab**, in the **Insert group**, click the **Quick Parts** button, and then click **Field**. In the **Field** dialog box, under **Field names**, locate and click **Page**. Under **Field properties**, click the first page number style—**1, 2, 3**—and then click **OK**. Click the **Home tab**, and then in the **Paragraph group**, click the **Align Text Right** button.

5. Click the **Design tab**, and then in the **Navigation group**, click the **Go to Footer** button. In the **Insert group**, click the **Quick Parts** button, and then click **Field**. In the **Field** dialog box, under **Field names**, locate and click **FileName**, and then click **OK**. Press Enter to create a new line in the footer.

6. In the **Insert group**, click the **Date & Time** button. In the **Date and Time** dialog box, locate and click the date and time format that displays the date in a *November 14, 2009* format. Click **OK**. Double-click anywhere in the document to close the footer area. **Save** your changes.

7. Press Ctrl + End. Click the **Insert tab**. In the **Text group**, click the **Object button arrow**, and then click **Text from File**. Navigate to your student files, select **w06D_Copyright_Law**, and then click **Insert**. Press ←Bksp to remove the empty paragraph at the end of the document. Press Ctrl + A to select the entire document. On the **Home tab**, in the **Paragraph group**, click the **Line spacing** button, and then click **2.0**. Click the **Page Layout tab**, and then in the **Paragraph group**, click the **After down spin arrow** to set the space after to **0**. Click anywhere in the document to deselect the text.

8. From the **Office** menu, click **Word Options**. Click **Proofing**, and then under **AutoCorrect options**, click the **AutoCorrect Options** button. In the **AutoCorrect** dialog box, under **Replace**, type **intruzion** and under **With**, type **intrusion** and then click **OK** two times to close both dialog boxes.

9. Locate the last bulleted item near the end of the document, and then click to place the insertion point to the right of the space after *computer*. Watch the screen as you type **intruzion** and then press Spacebar to see the AutoCorrect feature work.

10. On **Page 1**, locate the bulleted item that begins *Limits liability*. In the first line, select the two hyphens. On the **Insert tab**, in the **Symbols group**, click the **Symbol** button, and then click **More Symbols**. In the **Symbol** dialog box, click the **Special Characters tab**. Be sure the **Em Dash** is selected, and then click **Insert**. Repeat this procedure to replace the two hyphens

(Project 6D—Copyright Law continues on the next page)

Content-Based Assessments

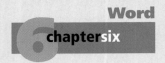
(Project 6D–Copyright Law continued)

in the second line of the same bulleted item with an em dash. **Close** the **Symbol** dialog box.

11. Scroll to view the middle of **Page 2**, locate the first bulleted item that begins *Jeopardizing,* and then position the insertion point following the last quotation mark. Click the **References tab**, and then in the **Footnotes group**, click the **Dialog Box Launcher**. In the **Footnote and Endnote** dialog box, under **Location**, be sure **Footnotes** is selected. Under **Format**, in the **Custom mark** box, type an asterisk (*) and then click **Insert**. Type **See GHS Law Partners internal memorandum** *The Changing Face of Fair Use.*

12. At the bottom of **Page 2**, right-click the footnote text, and then from the shortcut menu, click **Style**. In the **Style** dialog box, click **Modify**, change the **Font Size** to **11**, and then click **OK**. **Close** the **Style** dialog box.

13. In the middle of **Page 2**, in the paragraph that begins *This federal statute,* at the end of the first sentence, click to place the insertion point before the period. Click the **References tab**. In the **Citations & Bibliography group**, be sure **MLA** style is selected, click the **Insert Citation** button, and then click **Add New Source**. Click the **Type of Source arrow**, and then click **Book**. Add the following book citation:

Author:	**Stim, Richard W.**
Title:	**Patent, Copyright & Trademark: An Intellectual Property Desk Reference, 8th Edition**
Year:	**2006**
City:	**Berkeley, CA**
Publisher:	**NOLO**

14. Click **OK**. If prompted to Update an existing reference, click Yes. Click to select the reference, click the **Citation Options arrow**, and then click **Edit Citation**. In the **Edit Citation** dialog box, under **Add**, in the **Pages** box, type **227** and then click **OK**. **Save** your document.

15. Move to the top of the document. In the paragraph beginning *In 1998,* in the last line of the paragraph, place the insertion point after the word *Policy,* but before the comma. In the **Citations & Bibliography group**, click the **Insert Citation** button, and then click **Add New Source**. Click the **Type of Source arrow**, and then scroll down and select **Web site** from the list. Under **Bibliography Fields for MLA**, select the **Corporate Author** check box. Type the following information:

Corporate Author:	**UCLA Online Institute for Cyberspace Law and Policy**
Name of Web Page:	**The Digital Millennium Copyright Act**
Year:	**2001**
Month:	**February**
Day:	**8**
Year Accessed:	**2009**
Month Accessed:	**November**
Day Accessed:	**14**

16. Click **OK**. If you are prompted to update an existing reference, click Yes.

17. Move to **Page 2** and locate the paragraph beginning *This federal statute.* At the end of the last sentence, after *unintended consequences,* place the insertion point before the comma. In the **Citations & Bibliography group**, click the **Insert Citation** button, and then click **Add New Source**. Under **Type of Source**, be sure **Web site** is selected. Under **Bibliography Fields for MLA**, select the **Corporate**

(Project 6D–Copyright Law continues on the next page)

Content-Based Assessments

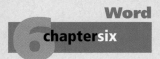
Skills Review

(Project 6D–Copyright Law continued)

Author check box. Type the following information:

Corporate Author:	**Electronic Frontier Foundation**
Name of Web Page:	**Unintended Consequences: Seven Years under the DMCA**
Year:	**2006**
Month:	**April**
Day:	**13**
Year Accessed:	**2009**
Month Accessed:	**November**
Day Accessed:	**14**
URL:	**http://www.eff.org/ IP/DMCA/?f= unintended_ consequences.html**

18. Click **OK**. If you are prompted to update an existing reference, click Yes.

19. **Save** your document. Press ⌈Ctrl⌉ + ⌈End⌉. Hold down ⌈Ctrl⌉ and press ⌈Enter⌉ to insert a manual page break. Type **Works Cited** and press ⌈Enter⌉. On the **References tab**, in the **Citations & Bibliography group**, be sure **MLA** displays in the **Style** box.

20. In the **Citations & Bibliography group**, click the **Bibliography** button, and then click **Insert Bibliography** to insert the citations you typed earlier. Select the three references, right-click the selected text, and then click **Paragraph**.

21. Under **Indentation**, click the **Special arrow**, and then click **Hanging**. Under

Spacing, click the **Line spacing button arrow**, and then click **Double**. Under **Spacing**, in the **After** box, type **0** and then click **OK**.

22. Right-click the *Works Cited* title, and then click **Paragraph**. In the **Paragraph** dialog box, under **General**, click the **Alignment arrow**, and then click **Centered**. Under **Indentation**, click the **Special arrow**, and then click **(none)**. Click **OK**.

23. From the **Office** menu, point to **Prepare**, and then click **Properties**. In the **Document Information Panel**, in the **Author** box, type your name, and in the **Title** box, type **Digital Millennium Copyright Act** On the right side of the **Document Information Panel**, click the **Close** button.

24. From the **Office** menu, point to **Print**, and then click **Print Preview** to make a final check of your document. Check your *Chapter Assignment Sheet* or *Course Syllabus* or consult your instructor to determine if you are to submit your assignments on paper or electronically. To submit electronically, go to Step 26, and then follow the instructions provided by your instructor.

25. On the **Print Preview tab**, click the **Print** button, click **OK**, and then click **Close Print Preview**.

26. From the **Office** menu, click **Exit Word**, saving any changes if prompted to do so.

End **You have completed Project 6D** ⸻

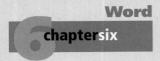

Mastering Word

Project 6E — Disputes

In this project, you will apply the skills you practiced from the Objectives in Projects 6A and 6B.

Objectives: 1. *Change Document and Paragraph Layout;* **2.** *Change and Reorganize Text;* **3.** *Create and Modify Lists;* **4.** *Insert and Format Headers and Footers;* **5.** *Insert Frequently Used Text;* **6.** *Insert and Format References.*

In the following Mastering Word project, you will edit an internal document on domain name disputes for GHS Law Partners. Your completed document will look similar to Figure 6.57.

For Project 6E, you will need the following file:

w06E_Disputes

You will save your document as 6E_Disputes_Firstname_Lastname

Figure 6.57

INTERNAL DISTRIBUTION ONLY

...ket costs directly related to the

...on both sides of domain name
...nd have relationships with other
...ts in these disputes regardless of the

INTERNAL DISTRIBUTION ONLY

GHS Law Partners and Internet Domain Name Disputes

Domain names are Web site addresses used to direct Internet users to a particular site. Companies and organizations prefer to use a domain name that is easily identifiable with their company, service, or brand. Such domain names are easy to remember and often become identified with the company itself. Because Web sites are now an accepted and important part of almost every company's operations and a huge profit-driver, the right to use a particular domain name has become an issue in intellectual property.

Domain names are registered to various owners on a first-come, first-served basis. Under current law, a company like GHS Law Partners does not have automatic right to the terms *GHS*, *law*, or *partners* in a domain name simply because that is the name of the business. Because anyone can register a domain name, registration of a domain name before someone else registers it is an important part of business strategy.

Registering a Web site name is inexpensive, but the names are highly valuable to businesses. This has resulted in what is called *cybersquatting*—registering a domain name with little intention of creating a Web site and assuming the name will be valuable enough to another entity to force them to buy it at a much greater price than was paid to register it. As WIPO, the World Intellectual Property Organization describes it, "As the holders of these registrations, cybersquatters often then put the domain names up for auction, or offer them for sale directly to the company or person involved, at prices far beyond the cost of registration. Alternatively, they often keep the registration and use the good name of the person or business associated with that domain name to attract business for their own sites."

When domain name disputes arise for GHS Law Partners' clients, we work under the Uniform Domain Name Dispute Resolution Policy (UDRP), which was developed by WIPO for domain name disputes worldwide. In cases under this policy, the following factors are considered:

1. Whether the domain name is identical or confusingly similar to a trademark or service mark in which the complainant has rights.
2. Whether the respondent has any rights or legitimate interests in the domain name (for example, the legitimate offering of goods and services under the same name).
3. Whether the domain name was registered and is being used in bad faith.[1]

The policy defines "bad faith" in part as "circumstances indicating that you have registered or you have acquired the domain name primarily for the purpose of selling, renting, or otherwise transferring the domain name registration to the complainant who is the owner of the trademark or service mark or to a competitor of that complainant, for valuable

[1] http://www.wipo.int/about-ip/en/studies/publications/domain_names.htm

6E_Disputes_Firstname_Lastname

(Project 6E–Disputes continues on the next page)

Word

chapter six

Mastering Word

(Project 6E–Disputes continued)

1. Locate and open the file **w06E_Disputes**. **Save** the file in your **Word Chapter 6** folder as **6E_Disputes_Firstname_Lastname** and then add the file name to the footer. Display formatting marks and rulers.

2. Select the document title, increase the **Font Size** to **14** points, and add **Bold** emphasis. Select all of the text in the document, change the **Font** to **Cambria**, change the **Line Spacing** to **1.0**, and then add **6 pt.** spacing after each paragraph.

3. Change the top margin to **1.5** inches and the other margins to **1** inch. Open the document header, type **INTERNAL DISTRIBUTION ONLY** and then **Center** the header. Change the header font to **Cambria**.

4. Near the top of the document, in the paragraph beginning *Because Web sites*, select the first sentence of the paragraph and move it to the end of the same paragraph.

5. In the paragraph that begins *Registering a Web site*, locate the two hyphens (--) after the word *cybersquatting*, and then replace the hyphens with an **em dash**.

6. **Save** your changes. Use the **Find and Replace** dialog box to locate the second

occurrence of *World Intellectual Property Organization,* replace it with **WIPO** and then remove the word *the* preceding WIPO.

7. Near the bottom of **Page 1**, select the three paragraphs that begin with *Whether*. Change the selected paragraphs to a numbered list, and **Increase Indent** one time.

8. At the end of the third item in the list, after the period following *bad faith,* insert the following footnote:

http://www.wipo.int/about-ip/en/studies/ publications/domain_names.htm

9. At the bottom of **Page 1**, at the end of the paragraph beginning *The policy defines,* insert the following footnote:

http://www.icann.org/udrp/udrp-policy-24oct99.htm

10. Modify the **Footnote** style to use the **Cambria** font, and **11** point font size.

11. **Save** your changes. **Preview** the document, and then **Print** it, or submit it electronically as directed. **Close** the file, and then **Exit** Word.

End **You have completed Project 6E**

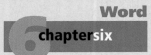

Mastering Word

Project 6F — Trademarks

In this project, you will apply the skills you practiced from the Objectives in Projects 6A and 6B.

Objectives: 1. *Change Document and Paragraph Layout;* **2.** *Change and Reorganize Text;* **3.** *Create and Modify Lists;* **4.** *Insert and Format Headers and Footers;* **5.** *Insert Frequently Used Text;* **6.** *Insert and Format References.*

In the following Mastering Word project, you will edit a handout on trademarks and commercial identifiers prepared by GHS Law Partners. Your completed document will look similar to Figure 6.58.

For Project 6F, you will need the following files:

New blank Word document
w06F_Trademarks

You will save your document as
6F_Trademarks_Firstname_Lastname

Figure 6.58

GHS LAW PARTNERS

GHS LAW PARTNERS

Trademarks and Commercial Identifiers

Trademarks—also known as commercial identifiers or marks—can be words, phrases, logos, symbols, or images. Sometimes a trademark is made up of two or more of these. You can look at just about any product and see one or more trademarks. A trademark is used to identify a product as being unique to the company that owns it, so therefore trademarks are extremely valuable to their owners. A trademark can be identified with a company to indicate quality, flavor, scent, innovation, or any number of "ideas" that a company wishes to express.

Exclusive rights to a mark are partially established through commercial use, such as:

- Entering the mark on state or county records
- Applying the mark to signs and promotional materials
- Using the mark on letterhead, business cards, and Web sites

Marks can also be registered with the United States Patent and Trademark Office (USPTO), which gives companies more leverage should a dispute arise over a mark. The mark will return a result during trademark searches, discouraging others from trying to claim the mark as their own, and registration puts the burden of proof of originality on any infringer.

A company may hold hundreds of trademarks. Microsoft provides a Web page listing its many trademarked names for games, software, fonts, brands, etc., along with information on how to cite each name. Microsoft also provides a page titled "General Microsoft Trademark Guidelines," that provides very specific instructions on referencing Microsoft trademarks and logos in any kind of publication.

Some trademarked names become so common in the language that they can become generic. This can be financially harmful to a company because the word or phrase is no longer necessarily associated with its creator. Some common name brands that have become generic include:

- ™ Jacuzzi for hot tub
- ™ Xerox for copiers
- ™ Band-Aid for adhesive
- ™ AstroTurf for artificial grass

Skilled intellectual property attorneys like those at GHS Law Partners are helpful to companies at every stage in the trademark process. In the design phase, our attorneys perform thorough searches for similar phrases or logos, preventing resources from being spent on an idea unlikely to achieve registration. Once design is complete, GHS Law Partners assists in the preparation and filing of the registration application and work with the USPTO to resolve objection and answer questions. After

6F_Trademarks_Firstname_Lastname
11/24/2009 6:00 PM

...s kept in commercial use and is not being

...usiness and intellectual property law, ...cial identifiers and their value to your ...ous types of marks and enable you to ...iness for years to come.

...and desist letters (which often end the case)

(Project 6F–Trademarks continues on the next page)

Content-Based Assessments

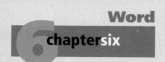
Mastering Word

(Project 6F–Trademarks continued)

1. **Start** Word and be sure a new blank document is displayed. Display formatting marks and rulers. Change the top margin to **2** inches and the other margins to **1** inch.

2. Type **Trademarks and Commercial Identifiers** and press Enter. Select the title and increase the **Font Size** to **14 pt**, add **Bold** emphasis, and **Center** the title. **Save** the file in your **Word Chapter 6** folder as **6F_Trademarks_Firstname_Lastname** and then add the file name to the footer. With the footer open, insert a blank line under the **FileName** field, and then insert the **Date** field in the format *6/26/2009 5:15 PM*. **Close** the footer.

3. Place the insertion point in the blank line below the title. Locate and insert the file **w06F_Trademarks**. Remove the blank line at the end of the document. Select all of the text in the document—including the title—change the line spacing to **1.0**, and add **18 pt** spacing after each paragraph.

4. Open the document header, type **GHS LAW PARTNERS** and then **Center** the header. Select the header text and change the font to **Arial Black**, **28 pt**.

5. Near the top of **Page 2**, at the end of the second line, position the insertion point after the word *generic*. Display the **Footnote and Endnote** dialog box, and then change the footnote mark from a number to an asterisk (*). Insert a footnote and type **If infringements or disputes arise, we handle all details from cease and desist letters (which often end the case) through litigation.**

6. **Save** your changes and move to the beginning of the document. Use the **Find and Replace** dialog box to find the word **allow** and then replace it with **enable**

7. Near the top of the document, in the paragraph beginning *Trademarks, also known as*, delete the comma and space after *Trademarks* and insert an **em dash**. In the same line, after *marks*, delete the comma and space and insert an **em dash**.

8. Near the bottom of **Page 1**, select the four lines of trademarked names, beginning with *Xerox*. Change the selected paragraphs to a bulleted list, and increase the indent one time. With the bullets still selected, right-click any of the list items, display the **Define New Bullet** dialog box, and then change the bullet type to a trademark symbol (™).

9. Near the top of **Page 1**, select the three lines beginning with *Entering the mark* and ending with *Using the mark*. Change the selected paragraphs to a bulleted list using black dots for bullets, and increase the indent one time.

10. In the bottom bulleted list, select the fourth bullet point—beginning with *Jacuzzi*—and move it up so it becomes the first bullet point.

11. **Save** your changes. **Preview** the document, and then **Print** it, or submit it electronically as directed. **Close** the file, and then **Exit** Word.

End **You have completed Project 6F**

Content-Based Assessments

Mastering Word

Project 6G — Fair Use

In this project, you will apply the skills you practiced from all the Objectives in Projects 6A and 6B.

Objectives: 1. *Change Document and Paragraph Layout;* **2.** *Change and Reorganize Text;* **3.** *Create and Modify Lists;* **4.** *Insert and Format Headers and Footers;* **5.** *Insert Frequently Used Text;* **6.** *Insert and Format References.*

In the following Mastering Word project, you will edit a report on fair use of copyrighted material, created by summer intern Clara Madison for GHS Law Partners. Your completed document will look similar to Figure 6.59.

For Project 6G, you will need the following files:

New blank Word document
w06G_Fair_Use

You will save your document as
6G_Fair_Use_Firstname_Lastname

Figure 6.59

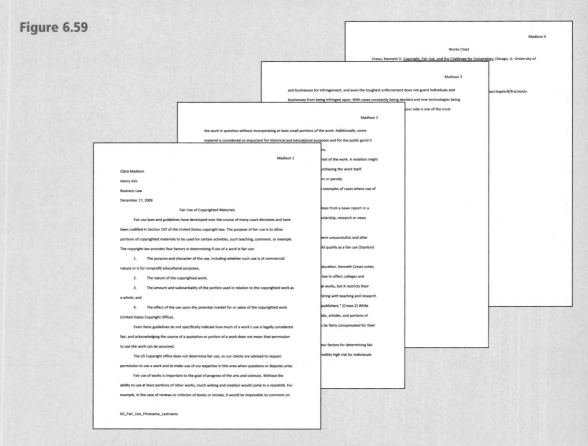

(Project 6G–Fair Use continues on the next page)

Word

chaptersix

Mastering Word

(Project 6G–Fair Use continued)

1. **Start** Word and be sure a new blank document is displayed. Display formatting marks and rulers. If necessary, change all document margins to **1** inch. **Save** the document as **6G_Fair_Use_Firstname_Lastname** Open the document footer and add the file name to the footer.

2. Move to the document header. In the header area, type **Madison** and then add a space and the page number, using the **1, 2, 3** format. Right align the header text.

3. Move to the beginning of the document. Type the following, pressing Enter after each line:

   Clara Madison
   Henry Kim
   Business Law
   December 17, 2009
   Fair Use of Copyrighted Materials

4. Center the last paragraph you typed—*Fair Use of Copyrighted Materials*. In the blank line below the centered title, insert the **w06G_Fair_Use** file. Delete the blank line at the end of the document. Select all of the document text. Set the **Line Spacing** to **2**, and the space **After** to **0**.

5. Select the inserted text, but not the five lines at the beginning of the document that you typed. Open the **Paragraph** dialog box, add a **0.5** inch first line indent.

6. Near the top of **Page 1**, select the four paragraphs, starting with the paragraph beginning *The purpose and character*. Create a numbered list from the selected paragraphs. Decrease the indent of the numbered list until it is aligned with the left margin of the document. Display the **Paragraph** dialog box, and set the **Special** indentation to **First line**. Set the **First line** indent to **0.5** inches.

7. Near the middle of **Page 2**, select the two paragraphs starting with the paragraph

   beginning *You use a very small excerpt.* Create a bulleted list from the selected paragraphs. Decrease the indent of the bulleted list until it is aligned with the left margin of the document. Modify the paragraph formatting using the procedure in Step 6.

8. Move to the end of the document. In the second-to-last paragraph, beginning with *Laws governing*, locate and select the three periods between *availability* and *many*. Display the **Symbol** dialog box, and from the **Special Characters tab**, insert an **Ellipsis** (...).

9. In the last paragraph of the document, move the first sentence—beginning with *With cases constantly*—to the end of the paragraph.

10. Display the **Find and Replace** dialog box, use it to replace **make the determinations into** with **determine** and then **Save** your document.

11. Near the top of **Page 1**, in the fourth item in the numbered list, position the insertion point to the left of the period. Insert the following **Web site** citation, using **MLA** style. Be sure to select the **Corporate Author** check box:

Corporate Author:	**United States Copyright Office**
Name of Web Page:	**Fair Use**
Year:	**2006**
Month:	**January**
Day:	**31**
Year Accessed:	**2009**
Month Accessed:	**June**
Day Accessed:	**6**
URL:	**http://www.copyright.gov/fls/fl102.html**

(Project 6G–Fair Use continues on the next page)

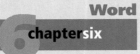

Mastering Word

(Project 6G–Fair Use continued)

12. **Save** your document. On **Page 2**, at the end of the second bullet point, use the same procedure to add the following **Web site** citation:

Corporate Author:	**Stanford University**
Name of Web Page:	**Copyright & Fair Use**
Year:	**2004**
Year Accessed:	**2009**
Month Accessed:	**June**
Day Accessed:	**8**
URL:	**http://fairuse. stanford.edu/ Copyright_and_Fair_ Use_Overview/ chapter9/9-d.html**

13. **Save** your document. At the end of the second-to-last paragraph of the document, locate the long quotation, which begins *"Copyright is among,"* and position the insertion point to the right of the second quotation mark. Add the following **Book** citation:

Author:	**Crews, Kenneth D.**
Title:	**Copyright, Fair Use, and the Challenge for Universities**

Year:	**1993**
City:	**Chicago, IL**
Publisher:	**University of Chicago Press**

14. Add the page number **2** to the citation.

15. **Save** your document. Move to the end of the document and insert a manual page break. Type **Works Cited** and press Enter. **Center** the *Works Cited* title and remove the first line indent. Position the insertion point in the blank line below *Works Cited*.

16. On the **References tab**, click the **MLA** style, and then insert a **Bibliography**. Select the bibliography field, and then display the **Paragraph** dialog box. Double-space the selected text, and then add a hanging indent.

17. **Save** your changes. **Preview** the document, and then **Print** it, or submit it electronically as directed. **Close** the file, and then **Exit** Word.

End You have completed Project 6G

Content-Based Assessments

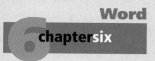

Mastering Word

Project 6H — *GO!* Fix It

In this project, you will construct a solution by applying any combination of the skills you practiced from the Objectives in Projects 6A and 6B.

For Project 6H, you will need the following file:

w06H_Garageman

You will save your document as
6H_Garageman_Firstname_Lastname

Locate and open the file **w06H_Garageman**, and then save it in your chapter folder as **6H_Garageman_Firstname_Lastname**

This short research paper, which was written for GHS Law Partners by their intern, Yvan LeFleur, contains errors that you must find and correct. Read and examine the document, and then edit to correct the errors that you find. Types of errors may include:

- Spelling, grammar, punctuation, and usage errors such as text case, repeated text, subject-verb agreement, and meaning.
- Content errors such as missing or incorrect data, text, pictures, hyperlinks, or other objects.
- Font formatting and positioning errors such as font used, style, size, color, underline style, effects, font character spacing, text effects, special characters, and styles.
- Paragraph formatting and positioning errors such as indents and spacing, tabs, line and page breaks, wordwrap, sentence spacing, missing text or unnecessary text or blank lines, or errors in footnotes or endnotes or references.
- Page setup errors such as margins, orientation, layout, or alignment.

Things you should know to complete this project:

- The research paper should conform to the MLA formatting style that was covered in Project 6B.
- The AutoFormat feature in Word may cause paragraph indents to shift position when lists are reformatted. An easy way to correct this problem is to select the text and then drag the indent marker(s) on the ruler to the correct position.
- Numbered lists are used in this project, instead of bulleted lists, to allow easier identification of individual items.
- There are no errors in the citation on the reference page.
- Save the changes you have made, add the file name to the footer, and then submit it as directed.

End **You have completed Project 6H** ————

Outcomes-Based Assessments

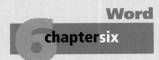

Rubric

The following outcomes-based assessments are *open-ended assessments*. That is, there is no specific correct result; your result will depend on your approach to the information provided. Make *Professional Quality* your goal. Use the following scoring rubric to guide you in *how* to approach the problem and then to evaluate *how well* your approach solves the problem.

The *criteria*—Software Mastery, Content, Format and Layout, and Process—represent the knowledge and skills you have gained that you can apply to solving the problem. The *levels of performance*—Professional Quality, Approaching Professional Quality, or Needs Quality Improvements—help you and your instructor evaluate your result.

	Your completed project is of Professional Quality if you:	Your completed project is Approaching Professional Quality if you:	Your completed project Needs Quality Improvements if you:
1-Software Mastery	Choose and apply the most appropriate skills, tools, and features and identify efficient methods to solve the problem.	Choose and apply some appropriate skills, tools, and features, but not in the most efficient manner.	Choose inappropriate skills, tools, or features, or are inefficient in solving the problem.
2-Content	Construct a solution that is clear and well organized, contains content that is accurate, appropriate to the audience and purpose, and is complete. Provide a solution that contains no errors of spelling, grammar, or style.	Construct a solution in which some components are unclear, poorly organized, inconsistent, or incomplete. Misjudge the needs of the audience. Have some errors in spelling, grammar, or style, but the errors do not detract from comprehension.	Construct a solution that is unclear, incomplete, or poorly organized; contains some inaccurate or inappropriate content; and contains many errors of spelling, grammar, or style. Do not solve the problem.
3-Format and Layout	Format and arrange all elements to communicate information and ideas, clarify function, illustrate relationships, and indicate relative importance.	Apply appropriate format and layout features to some elements, but not others. Overuse features, causing minor distraction.	Apply format and layout that does not communicate information or ideas clearly. Do not use format and layout features to clarify function, illustrate relationships, or indicate relative importance. Use available features excessively, causing distraction.
4-Process	Use an organized approach that integrates planning, development, self-assessment, revision, and reflection.	Demonstrate an organized approach in some areas, but not others; or, use an insufficient process of organization throughout.	Do not use an organized approach to solve the problem.

Outcomes-Based Assessments

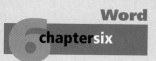
chaptersix

Problem Solving

Project 6I — Seminar

In this project, you will construct a solution by applying any combination of the skills you practiced from the Objectives in Projects 6A and 6B.

For Project 6I, you will need the following file:

New blank Word document

You will save your document as
6I_Seminar_Firstname_Lastname

College students are often asked to write research papers and presentations that involve information gathered from many sources. GHS Law Partners has been asked by the local college to conduct a seminar for faculty members that covers the topic of how students use the intellectual property of others. In this Problem Solving project, you will create a one-page document that outlines the topic.

Your document should consist of an introduction to the law firm and the topic, followed by a list of definitions of terms, including—but not limited to—*intellectual property, copyright, fair use,* and *plagiarism.* Add a footnote indicating your source for the definitions. Then, add a list of the topics to be covered in the order in which they will be presented. You might include topics such as quotations, downloaded pictures from the Web, and how to cite sources. Add a title to the document, and format the text appropriately. You may want to do some research on the Web or in your school library on such topics as copyrights, plagiarism, and citing sources to develop your topics.

Add the file name to the footer. Check your document for spelling and grammar errors. Save the document as **6I_Seminar_Firstname_Lastname** and submit it as directed.

End **You have completed Project 6I** ————————

Outcomes-Based Assessments

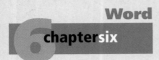
Problem Solving

Project 6J — Evaluation

In this project, you will construct a solution by applying any combination of the skills you practiced from the Objectives in Projects 6A and 6B.

For Project 6J, you will need the following file:

New blank Word document

You will save your document as
6J_Evaluation_Firstname_Lastname

In this project, you will write a letter that summarizes the categories and the criteria to be used in a job performance evaluation for summer interns. The letter should be addressed to Andrea Smith, 1884 Bullpen Dr., Black River, GA 30366, and should be from Michael Scott, the Office Manager of the law firm, GHS Law Partners.

Be sure to

- Use the letter style you practiced in Chapter 5.

- Research the topic in your library or on the Web. There are many sites that discuss the types of criteria used when rating employee performance. (Hint: Search for *employee evaluation* or *job evaluation*.)

- Divide the criteria into two or three categories. Introduce the categories, and then add a short list of criteria under each category.

- Use at least one special bullet symbol for a list.

Add the file name to the footer. Check the letter for spelling and grammar errors. Save the document as **6J_Evaluation_Firstname_Lastname** and submit it as directed.

 End **You have completed Project 6J** _____

Outcomes-Based Assessments

Word

chaptersix **Problem Solving**

Project 6K — Trademarks

In this project, you will construct a solution by applying any combination of the skills you practiced from the Objectives in Projects 6A and 6B.

For Project 6K, you will need the following file:

New blank Word document

You will save your document as
6K_Trademarks_Firstname_Lastname

When a company has a very recognizable name that is used for a product, they often get protection for that name from the U.S. Patent and Trademark Office. Microsoft, for example, has a long list of trademarks, logos, and trade names, including Microsoft Windows® and MapVision™. To view the list, use a Web browser and go to *www.microsoft.com*. At the bottom of the Microsoft home page, click **Trademarks**. Notice that some of the items use the Registered® symbol, and some use the Trademark™ symbol.

Write a 400 to 600 word research paper (about two pages long) that identifies the similarities and differences between items that are identified as *registered* and those identified as *trademarked*. Your paper should follow MLA style guidelines, or other style guidelines as directed by your instructor. Use at least two references, and include a Works Cited page. Detailed information about writing in the MLA style can be found in your college library and also online. Include at least one list, two symbols, and one informational endnote or footnote. Save the research paper as **6K_Trademarks_Firstname_Lastname** and then create a footer that contains the file name. Submit the document as directed.

End **You have completed Project 6K** ————————————

More on your Student CD

The instructions for the following additional end-of-chapter projects are on your student CD in the folder 03_additional_end_of_chapter_projects.

Content-Based Assessments

Project L Mastering Word	Apply the skills you practiced in Project A.
Project M Mastering Word	Apply the skills you practiced in Project B.
Project N Business Running Case	Apply the skills you practiced in Projects A and B while helping an entrepreneur with the daily tasks of running a business.
	In each chapter, this project focuses on applying the skills you have practiced in Projects A and B to a business. The project related to this business runs throughout the textbook. You will see how the Office applications relate to the day-to-day operation of a small business called Nelson Architectural Planning.

Outcomes-Based Assessments

Project O Problem Solving	Construct a solution by applying any combination of the skills you practiced from Projects A and B.
Project P Problem Solving	Construct a solution by applying any combination of the skills you practiced from Projects A and B.
Project Q You and GO!	Construct a solution that applies to your own life by applying any combination of the skills you practiced from Projects A and B.
Project R GO! with Help	Practice using Microsoft Office's Help Feature.
Project S Group Business Running Case	Work as part of a group to apply the skills you have gained thus far to help the Bell Orchid Hotel Group achieve its business goals.

Multimedia

The following multimedia accompany this textbook:

Companion Web site *www.prenhall.com/go*	An interactive Web site designed to reinforce and test your understanding of the skills in this chapter.
AV-EDDs	In the folder in the front of this book you will find videos that demonstrate the objectives of the A and B projects in this chapter. These may help you understand how to complete the projects in this book.
Video Podcasts	In the folder in the front of this book are videos that can be played on your iPod, MP3 player, or computer. These videos demonstrate how to complete the more challenging objectives in this textbook.

7 chapterseven

Using Graphics and Tables

OBJECTIVES

At the end of this chapter you will be able to:

1. Insert and Format Graphics
2. Set Tab Stops
3. Insert and Modify Text Boxes and Shapes

4. Create a Table
5. Format a Table

OUTCOMES

Mastering these objectives will enable you to:

PROJECT 7A
Insert and Modify Graphics and Set Tab Stops

PROJECT 7B
Create and Format a Table

Memories Old and New

Professional and amateur artists, photographers, students, teachers, and hobbyists have made Memories Old and New one of Chicago's fastest-growing art, photography, and scrapbooking supply stores. The store carries a wide variety of premium art supplies, such as paints, pencils, cutting and framing tools, and brushes. Local photographers are featured in the small gallery, and photo restoration services and supplies are offered. For scrapbookers, the store provides the newest and highest quality books, papers, stencils, and archival supplies. Scrapbooking classes are also offered to assist customers in adding principles of art and design to their projects.

© David Young-Wolff PhotoEdit Inc.

Using Graphics and Tables

Adding graphics enhances the effectiveness of documents. Digital images, such as those obtained from a digital camera or a scanner, can be inserted into documents. You can also create your own graphic objects by using the Drawing tools.

Tab stops are useful to horizontally align text and numbers. Use the Tab key to move text to specific tab stop locations on a line. You can set and specify the alignment of your own tab locations.

Tables present data effectively and efficiently. The row and column format of a table makes information easy to find and easy to read. A table also helps the reader organize and categorize the data. The Word table feature has tools with which you can format text, change column width and row height, and change the background for all or part of a table. You can also modify the table's borders and lines.

Project 7A **Photography Flyer**

In Activities 7.01 through 7.14, you will create a flyer for an upcoming exhibition of photographs by photographer Annie DeCesare at Memories Old and New. Your completed document will look similar to Figure 7.1.

For Project 7A, you will need the following files:

New blank Word document

w07A_Photography_Flyer
w07A_Machine
w07A_Ore_Cart
You will save your document as
7A_Photography_Flyer_Firstname_Lastname

Figure 7.1
Project 7A—Photography Flyer

Objective 1
Insert and Format Graphics

Graphics include pictures, clip art, charts, and **drawing objects**—shapes, diagrams, lines, and so on. You can modify drawing objects by changing their color, pattern, border, and other characteristics. Graphics that you insert in a document convey information in a way that plain text cannot. For additional visual interest, you can convert text to an attractive graphic format; add, resize, move and format pictures; and provide a finishing touch to your document by adding a page border.

Activity 7.01 Formatting Text Using WordArt

WordArt is a gallery of text styles with which you can create decorative effects, such as shadowed or mirrored text.

Note — Comparing Your Screen with the Figures in This Textbook

Your screen will match the figures shown in this textbook if you set your screen resolution to 1024 × 768. At other resolutions, your screen will closely resemble, but not match, the figures shown. To view your screen's resolution, on the Windows desktop, right-click in a blank area, click Personalize, and then click Display Settings.

---

1 **Start** Word, and display formatting marks and rulers. Display the **Page Setup** dialog box, and then set all margins to **.75″**. On the **Home tab**, in the **Styles group**, click the **No Spacing** button.

2 Type **Annie DeCesare, Photographer** and then press Enter. Notice that the last name is flagged as a spelling error. Right-click *DeCesare*, and then click **Ignore All**.

3 Without selecting the paragraph mark at the end, select the first line of text. Click the **Insert tab**. In the **Text group**, click the **WordArt** button, and then notice the ScreenTip *WordArt style 8* shown in Figure 7.2.

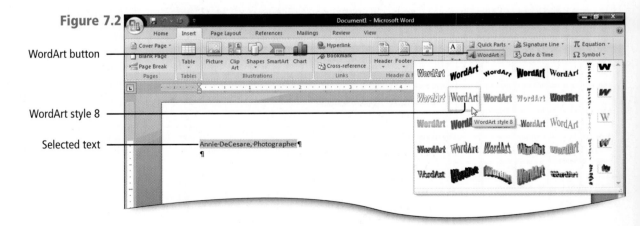

Figure 7.2

WordArt button

WordArt style 8

Selected text

4 Click **WordArt style 8**, and then compare your screen with Figure 7.3.

The Edit WordArt Text dialog box displays, and the selected text displays in the Text box. The default font size is 36 point.

Figure 7.3

Word | Chapter 7

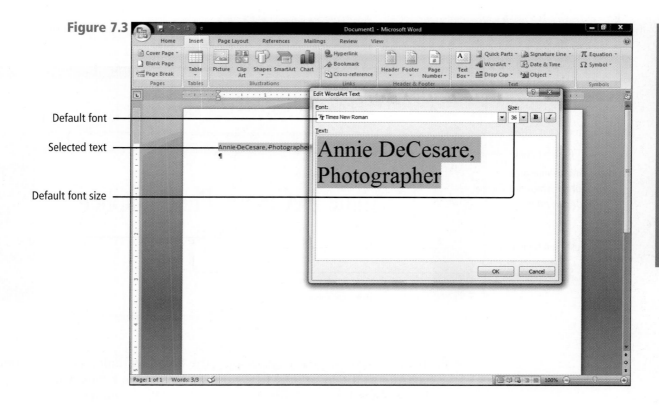

Default font

Selected text

Default font size

5 At the bottom of the **Edit WordArt Text** dialog box, click **OK**.

> The WordArt contextual tools display on the Ribbon. The WordArt object displays *sizing handles*—small dark boxes with which you can manually change its size.

6 On the **Format tab**, in the **Size group**, click the **Shape Height button up spin arrow** as necessary to change the height of the WordArt to **0.7"**. Click the **Shape Width button up spin arrow** as necessary to change the width of the WordArt to **6.5"**.

7 In the **Arrange group**, click the **Position** button, and then under **With Text Wrapping**, in the top row of the gallery, point to the second button to display the ScreenTip *Position in Top Center with Square Text Wrapping*, and then click the button. Compare your screen with Figure 7.4.

> The WordArt is centered between the left and right margins, and positioned at the top of the document. The *anchor* symbol indicates the paragraph to which the WordArt is attached and the corner sizing handles display as circles. Additionally, a *rotate handle* to rotate the WordArt and an *adjustment handle* to drag parts of the object into various positions display.

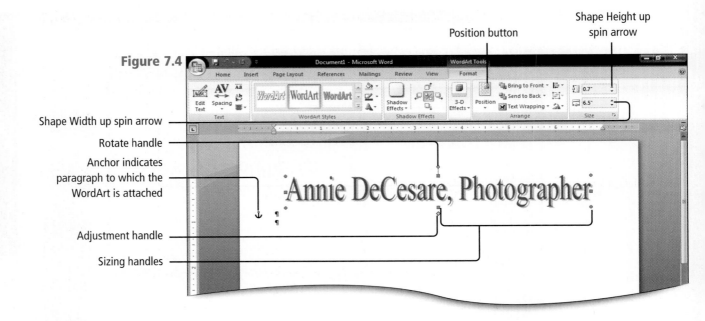

Figure 7.4

Position button

Shape Height up spin arrow

Shape Width up spin arrow

Rotate handle

Anchor indicates paragraph to which the WordArt is attached

Adjustment handle

Sizing handles

Annie DeCesare, Photographer

8 From the **Office** menu, display the **Save As** dialog box, and then navigate to the location where you are saving your files. Click the **New Folder** button. Name the new folder **Word Chapter 7**

9 In the **File name** box, using your own name, type **7A_Photography_ Flyer_Firstname_Lastname** and then click **Save**.

Activity 7.02 Inserting Pictures from Files

1 Press Ctrl + End. Click the **Insert tab**. In the **Text group**, click the **Object button arrow**, and then click **Text from File**. Locate and **Insert** the file **w07A_Photography_Flyer**.

2 Delete the blank line at the end of the document. If necessary, right-click any words flagged with wavy underlines and ignore all suggested corrections.

3 In the paragraph beginning *Memories Old and New*, click to position the insertion point at the beginning of the paragraph. On the **Insert tab**, in the **Illustrations group**, click the **Picture** button. From your student data files, **Insert** the file **w07A_Ore_Cart**. Compare your screen with Figure 7.5.

> Word inserts the picture as an ***inline object***; that is, the picture is positioned directly in the text at the insertion point, just like a character in a sentence. Sizing handles surround the picture.
>
> The round corner sizing handles resize the graphic proportionally. The square sizing handles resize a graphic vertically or horizontally only; sizing with these will distort the graphic. A rotate handle, with which you can rotate the graphic to any angle, displays above the top center sizing handle.

4 **Save** your document.

Figure 7.5

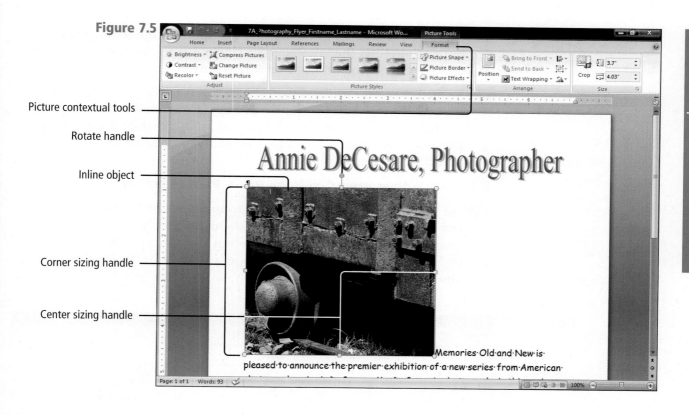

Picture contextual tools

Rotate handle

Inline object

Corner sizing handle

Center sizing handle

Activity 7.03 Resizing a Graphic

1 If necessary, click to select the ore cart picture.

2 On the lower edge of the picture, point to the center square sizing handle until the ⬍ pointer displays. Drag upward until the bottom of the graphic is aligned at approximately **2 inches on the vertical ruler**. Notice that the height of the graphic is resized, but the width remains unchanged, as shown in Figure 7.6.

Figure 7.6

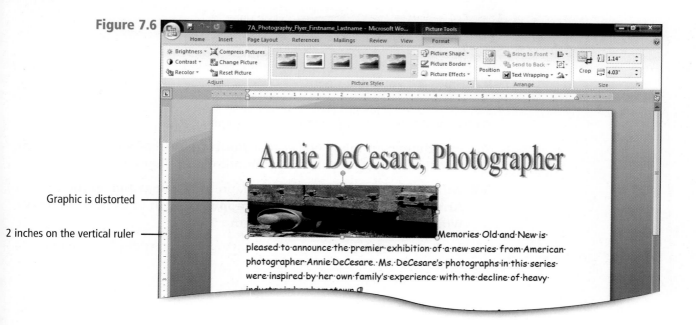

Graphic is distorted

2 inches on the vertical ruler

3 On the **Format tab**, in the **Adjust group**, click the **Reset Picture** button to return the graphic to its original size. Alternatively, on the Quick Access Toolbar, click the Undo button.

4 At the lower left corner of the picture, point to the round sizing handle until the ⤢ pointer displays. Drag upward and to the right until the bottom of the graphic is aligned at approximately **2 inches on the vertical ruler**. Notice that the graphic is resized proportionally and not distorted.

5 In the **Adjust group**, click the **Reset Picture** button.

6 On the **Format tab**, in the **Size group**, click the **Shape Height button spin box down arrow** ⬚3.5 ⬚ as necessary to change the height of the picture to **2"**. Notice that the picture resizes proportionally—the width adjusts as you change the height—as shown in Figure 7.7.

Figure 7.7

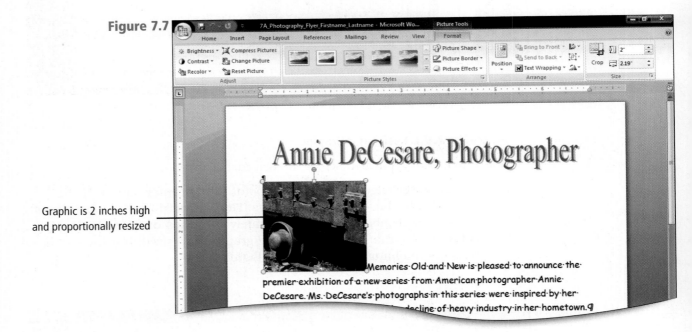

Graphic is 2 inches high and proportionally resized

7 **Save** 💾 your document.

Activity 7.04 Wrapping Text Around a Graphic

You can change an inline object to a **_floating object_**—a graphic that can be moved independently of the surrounding text characters.

1 With the **ore cart** picture selected, on the **Format tab**, in the **Arrange group**, click the **Text Wrapping** button to display the Text Wrapping gallery, as shown in Figure 7.8.

> **_Text wrapping_** refers to the manner in which text displays around an object.

Figure 7.8

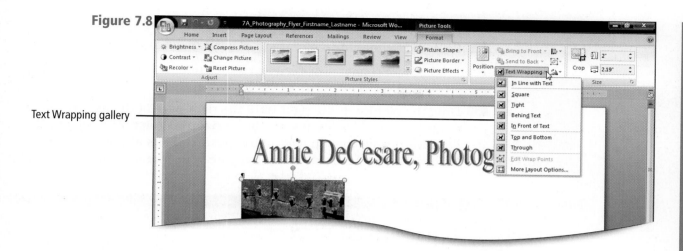

Text Wrapping gallery

2 From the **Text Wrapping gallery**, click **Square**.

Square text wrapping ensures that all four edges of the surrounding text will be straight. To wrap text around an irregularly shaped object use the Tight text wrap format.

3 Click to the left of *M* in the first line of the paragraph that begins *Memories Old and New* to deselect the picture. Click the **Insert tab**. In the **Illustrations group**, click the **Picture** button. Locate and **Insert** the file **w07A_Machine**.

The inserted picture becomes the first character in the paragraph and the text is forced down in the document.

4 On the **Format tab**, in the **Arrange group**, click the **Text Wrapping** button, and then click **Square**. Compare your screen with Figure 7.9.

The text wraps around the second graphic.

Figure 7.9

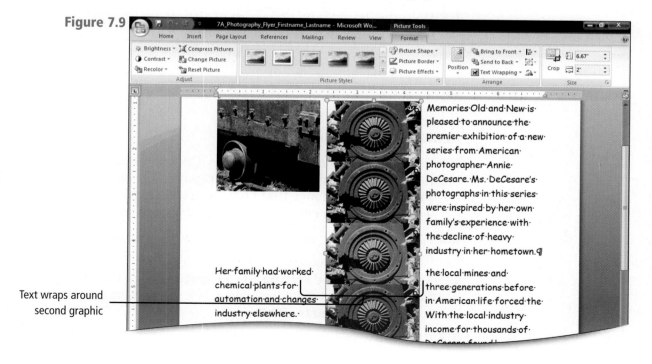

Text wraps around second graphic

5 **Save** your document.

Activity 7.05 Moving a Graphic

1 Point to the **machine** picture to display the ⚟ pointer.

> The Move pointer displays a four-way arrow, and enables you to move a floating object anywhere in the document.

2 Drag the picture to the right until the right edge of the picture aligns at approximately **7 inches on the horizontal ruler**, and then drag downward until the top edge of the picture aligns at approximately **2.5 inches on the vertical ruler**. Compare your screen with Figure 7.10.

Figure 7.10

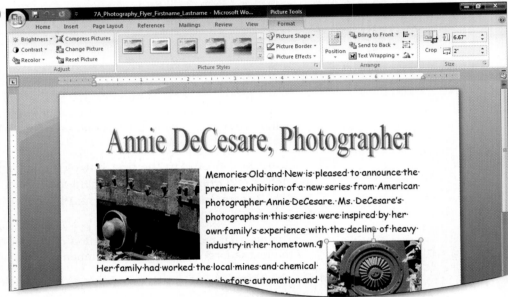

3 Move the graphics as necessary to align them in approximately the same position as those shown in Figure 7.10.

> Recall that you can nudge an object in small increments by pressing the arrow keys.

4 **Save** 🖫 your document.

Activity 7.06 Applying Picture Styles

1 Click to select the **ore cart** picture. Click the **Format tab**, and then in the **Picture Styles group**, point to the first picture style—**Simple Frame, White**. Notice that Live Preview displays the graphic as it would look if you clicked the *Simple Frame, White* button.

2 Point to the other picture styles to view some of the styles that are available.

3 To the right of the **Picture Styles gallery**, click the **More** button ⮛ to display more available styles. Click the second button in the first row—**Beveled Matte, White**.

4 Click anywhere in the document to deselect the picture, and then compare your screen with Figure 7.11.

Figure 7.11

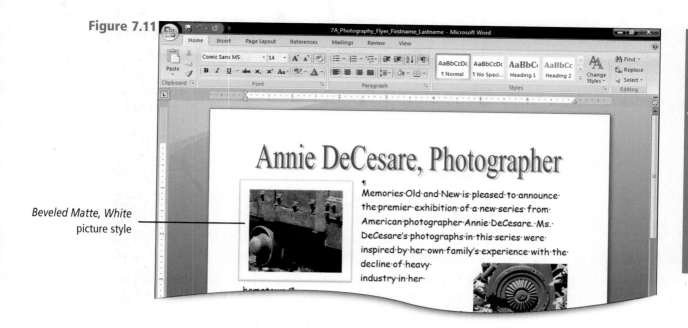

Beveled Matte, White
picture style

⑤ Click to select the **w07A_Machine** picture. On the **Format tab**, in the **Picture Styles group**, click the **Picture Effects** button. In the **Picture Effects gallery**, point to **Soft Edges**, and then click **25 Point**.

⑥ Click anywhere in the document to deselect the picture, and then compare your screen with Figure 7.12.

> The Soft Edges feature fades the edges of the picture. The number of points you choose determines how far the fade goes inward from the edges of the picture. Recall that a point is 1/72 of an inch.

Figure 7.12

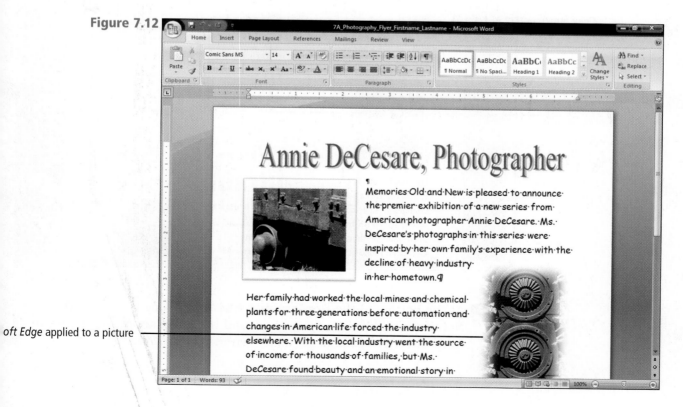

oft Edge applied to a picture

Word | Chapter 7

7 From the **Office** menu ⊙, point to the **Print button arrow**, and then click **Print Preview** to see the arrangement of your pictures in relation to the text.

8 On the **Print Preview tab**, in the **Preview group**, click the **Close Print Preview** button.

9 **Save** 🖫 your document.

Activity 7.07 Adding a Page Border

Page borders frame a page and help to focus the information on the page.

1 Click the **Page Layout tab**, and then in the **Page Background group**, click the **Page Borders** button.

2 In the **Borders and Shading** dialog box, under **Setting**, click **Box**. Under **Style**, scroll down the list about a third of the way and click the heavy outer line with the thin inner line—check the **Preview** area to be sure the heavier line is the nearest to the edges of the page.

3 Click the **Color arrow**, and then under **Theme Colors**, in the fifth column, click the first color—**Blue, Accent 1**. Compare your screen with Figure 7.13.

Figure 7.13

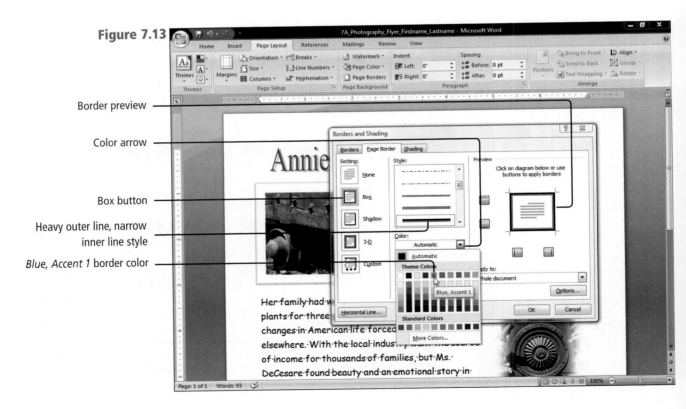

Border preview

Color arrow

Box button

Heavy outer line, narrow inner line style

Blue, Accent 1 border color

4 At the bottom of the **Borders and Shading** dialog box, click **OK**. Notice that a border is placed around the page, about 0.5 inches in from the edge of the page, as shown in Figure 7.14.

Figure 7.14

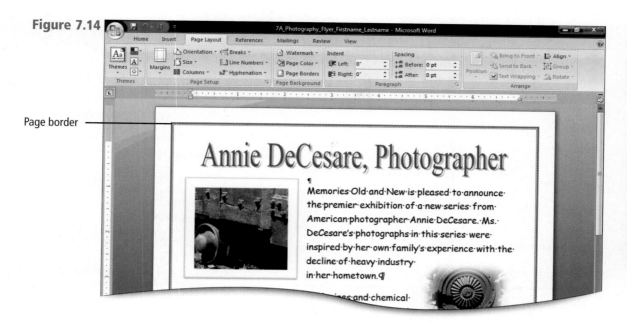

Page border —

Annie DeCesare, Photographer

¶Memories·Old·and·New·is·pleased·to·announce· the·premier·exhibition·of·a·new·series·from· American·photographer·Annie·DeCesare.·Ms.· DeCesare's·photographs·in·this·series·were· inspired·by·her·own·family's·experience·with·the· decline·of·heavy·industry· in·her·hometown.¶

⌐5 **Save** 🔲 your document.

Objective 2
Set Tab Stops

Tab stops mark specific locations on a line of text; use tab stops to indent and align text. Press Tab to move to tab stops. In the following activities, you will use tab stops to format a short table of dates and times.

Activity 7.08 Setting Tab Stops and Using Click and Type

⌐1 Take a moment to study the tab alignment options shown in Figure 7.15 and described in the table in Figure 7.16.

Figure 7.15

Left Tab   Center Tab   Right Tab   Decimal Tab   Bar Tab

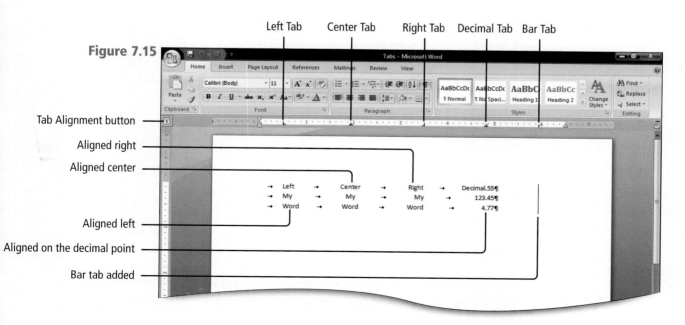

Tab Alignment button —
Aligned right —
Aligned center —

Aligned left —
Aligned on the decimal point —
Bar tab added —

→ Left → Center → Right → Decimal.55¶
→ My → My → My → 123.45¶
→ Word → Word → Word → 4.77¶

Tab Alignment Options

Type	Tab Alignment Button Displays	Description
Left	L	Text is left aligned at the tab stop and extends to the right.
Center	⊥	Text is centered around the tab stop.
Right	⌐	Text is right aligned at the tab stop and extends to the left.
Decimal	⊥	The decimal point aligns at the tab stop.
Bar	I	A vertical bar is inserted in the document at the tab stop.
First Line Indent	▽	Indents the first line of a paragraph.
Hanging Indent	⊔	Indents all lines but the first in a paragraph.

Figure 7.16

2 Scroll to the bottom of the document and click anywhere in the last paragraph. Position the pointer below the text and near the left margin to display the I≡ pointer, as shown in Figure 7.17.

This is one of several *click and type pointers*; a series of pointers with lines attached in various arrangements to depict alignment. In this instance, the pointer displays left aligned horizontal lines. The shape attached to the pointer indicates what type of formatting will be applied if you double-click at the pointer location on the page.

Figure 7.17

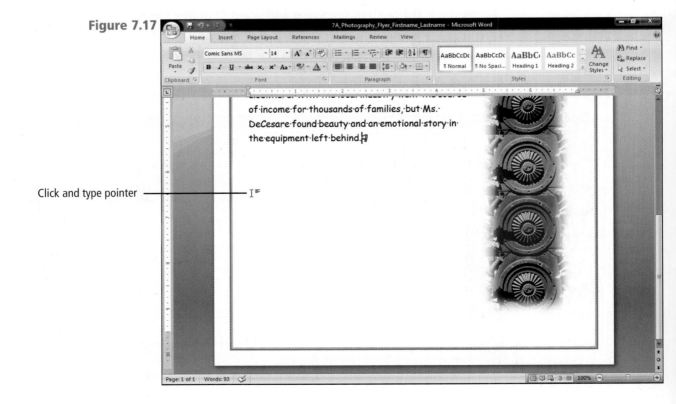

Click and type pointer

Alert!

What if the click and type pointer does not display?

If you move the pointer around the blank area of the document and do not see the click and type pointer, click the Office button, and then click Word Options. Click Advanced, and then under *Editing options*, select the *Enable click and type* check box.

3 With the I⁼ pointer displayed at approximately **7 inches on the vertical ruler** and at the left margin, double-click to place the insertion point. Notice that the insertion point is positioned at the left margin.

> Because you cannot type in a blank area of a document without some type of paragraph formatting in place, click and type inserts blank lines without having to press Enter numerous times—and uses the formatting of the nearest paragraph above.

> If you double-click the click and type pointer near the horizontal middle of the document, a center tab is inserted; if you double-click near the right margin, a right tab is inserted.

4 To the left of the horizontal ruler, point to the **Tab Alignment** button and notice the *Left Tab* ScreenTip. Click the **Tab Alignment** button L one time, move the mouse pointer away, and then point to the button again to display the next ScreenTip—*Center Tab*. Repeat this process to cycle through and view the ScreenTip for each of the types of tab stops, and then stop at the **Left Tab** button L.

5 Move the pointer into the horizontal ruler, click at **0.5 inches on the horizontal ruler**, and then compare your screen with Figure 7.18.

> A left tab stop displays on the ruler for the paragraph containing the insertion point. By default, tab stops are set every half inch, but they do not display on the ruler. When you customize a tab by clicking on the ruler, the custom tab stop overrides default tab stops that are to the left of the custom tab. A tab stop is part of a paragraph's format and thus the information about tab stops is stored in the paragraph mark.

Figure 7.18

Left alignment tab at 0.5 inch

Insertion point

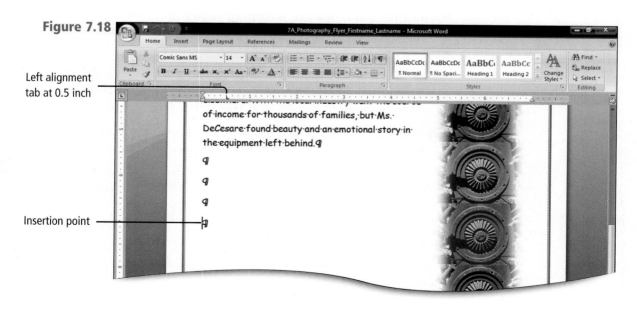

6 Click the **Tab Alignment** button ⌊L⌋ two times to display the **Right Tab** button ⌊⌋. Point to **2.25 inches on the horizontal ruler**, and then click one time to insert a right tab stop at this position in the paragraph.

7 Click the **Tab Alignment** button ⌊⌋ six times to display the **Center Tab** button ⌊⊥⌋. Click at **3.5 inches on the horizontal ruler**, and then click again at **4.5 inches**. Notice that two center tab stops display on the ruler, as shown in Figure 7.19.

Figure 7.19

Right alignment tab

Center alignment tabs

Tabs set only for the line in which the insertion point is positioned

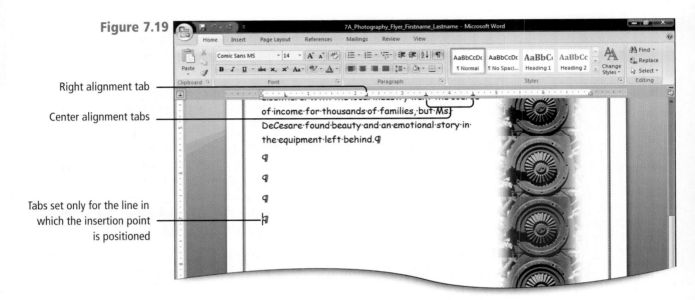

8 **Save** 💾 your document.

Activity 7.09 Formatting and Removing Tab Stops

Recall that tab stops are a form of paragraph formatting, and thus, the information about them is stored in the paragraph mark to which they were applied.

1 On the **Home tab**, in the **Paragraph group**, click the **Dialog Box Launcher** ⌐. If necessary, change the spacing *After* to 0, and the *Line Spacing* to Single, and then click **OK**.

2 Point to any of the tab markers on the ruler, double-click to display the **Tabs** dialog box, and then compare your screen with Figure 7.20.

The tabs you just added to the ruler display under *Tab stop position*. In the Tabs dialog box, you have more flexibility in adding, removing, and formatting tab stops.

Figure 7.20

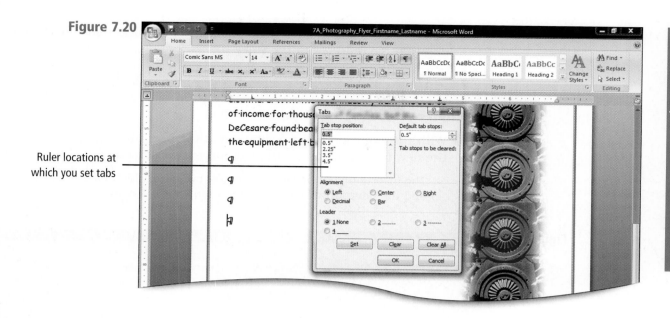

Ruler locations at
which you set tabs

3️⃣ Under **Tab stop position**, click **3.5″**, and then at the bottom of the **Tabs** dialog box, click the **Clear** button.

> The cleared tab stop will be removed when you click OK to close the dialog box.

4️⃣ If necessary, under **Tab stop position**, click **4.5″**. Under **Alignment**, click the **Right** option button. Under **Leader**, click the **2** option button. Near the bottom of the **Tabs** dialog box, click **Set**, and then compare your screen with Figure 7.21.

> The Set button saves the change. The tab stop at 4.5 inches changes to a right tab and displays a ***leader character***. Leader characters create a solid, dotted, or dashed line that fills the space to the left of a tab character. A leader character draws the reader's eyes across the page from one item to the next. When the character used for the leader is a dot, this is commonly referred to as a ***dot leader***.

Figure 7.21

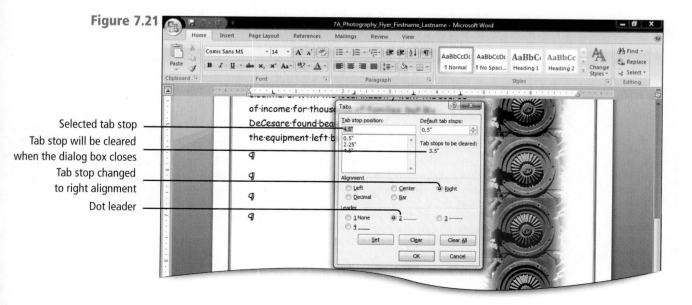

Selected tab stop
Tab stop will be cleared
when the dialog box closes
Tab stop changed
to right alignment
Dot leader

5 At the bottom of the **Tabs** dialog box, click **OK**, and notice that the changes are reflected in the ruler.

6 **Save** 🔲 your document.

Activity 7.10 Using Tab Stops to Enter Text

1 With the insertion point positioned at the beginning of the line with the new tab stops, press ⟨Tab⟩. Compare your screen with Figure 7.22.

> The insertion point moves to the first tab stop, which is at 0.5 inches, and the nonprinting character for a tab—a small arrow—displays.

Figure 7.22

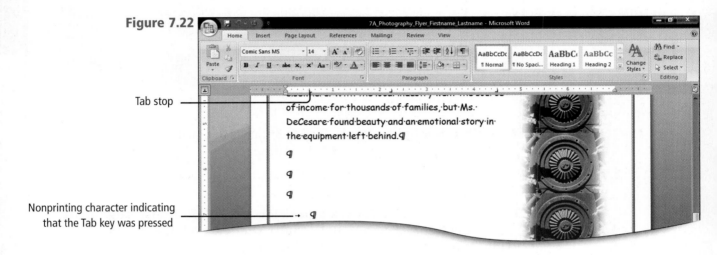

Tab stop

Nonprinting character indicating that the Tab key was pressed

2 Type **Sunday** and notice that the left edge of the text remains aligned with the tab stop. Press ⟨Tab⟩, and then type **July 30**

> The insertion point moves to the tab stop at 2.25 inches, and the text moves to the left of the right tab mark.

3 Press ⟨Tab⟩, type **Daytime 9 - 6** and then press ⟨Enter⟩. Compare your screen with Figure 7.23. Look at the ruler, and notice that the formatting of the previous paragraph, including tab stops, is copied to the new paragraph.

> A dot leader is added, helping to draw your eyes across the page to the next item. Depending on your Word settings, when you type a hyphen surrounded by spaces, the hyphen may change to a longer dash.

> **Note — Using Dot Leaders**
>
> It is sometimes tempting to hold down ⟨.⟩ on the keyboard to create a string of dots. This is not a good idea for several reasons. The periods, because of proportional spacing, may be spaced differently between rows. The periods will not line up, and, most importantly, the column on the right side of the string of periods may look lined up on the screen, but will be crooked when printed. If you need a string of dots, always insert a tab stop with a dot leader.

Figure 7.23

Tab stops included in new paragraph

Dot leader

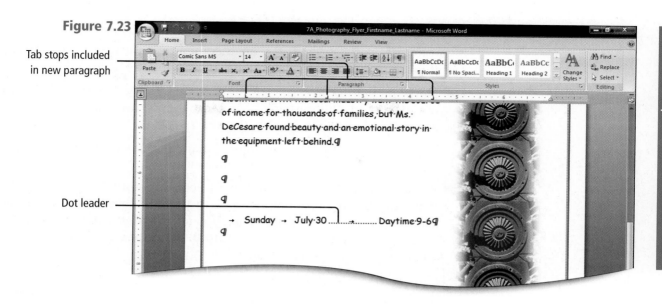

4 Type the following—first pressing Tab one time to indent each line—to complete the exhibition schedule. Click **Save** 🔲, and then compare your screen with Figure 7.24:

Monday	**July 31**	**Evening 6 - 9**
Tuesday	**August 1**	**All Day 9 - 9**

Figure 7.24

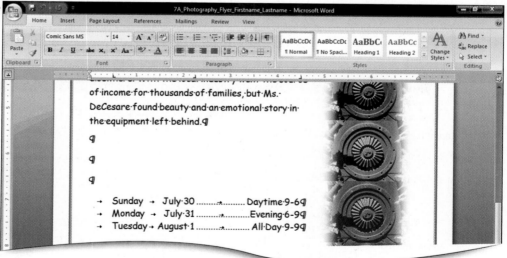

Another Way — **To Create an Indent**

If the items in the first column of a list are indented the same amount using a left-aligned tab, you can save keystrokes by indenting the paragraph instead. You can do this on the Home tab by clicking the Increase Indent button in the Paragraph group, or by setting Indentation in the Paragraph dialog box. You can also drag the Left Indent marker from the left side of the ruler and position it at the desired location. When you are finished typing the list, you can drag the marker back to the left margin position. When you use an indent at the beginning of the paragraph for a tabbed list, it is not necessary to press Tab before you type the first item in the list.

Activity 7.11 Moving Tab Stops

If you are not satisfied with the arrangement of your text after setting tab stops, you can reposition the text by moving tab stops.

1 Move the pointer into the left margin area, to the left of the first line of tabbed text. When the ▧ pointer displays, drag downward to select the three lines of tabbed text.

> By selecting all of the paragraphs, changes you make to the tab stops will change all three lines simultaneously.

2 With the three lines of tabbed text selected, point to the horizontal ruler and position the pointer so the tip of the pointer arrow is touching the **0.5-inch tab stop**. When you see the *Left Tab* ScreenTip, drag the tab stop mark to the left to **0.25 inches on the ruler**, and then release the mouse button.

Note — Selecting Tab Stop Marks

Selecting and moving tab stop marks on the horizontal ruler requires fairly exact mouse movement. The tip of the pointer must touch the tab mark. If you miss the mark by even a little, you will probably insert another tab stop. One way to tell if you are in the right position to move a tab stop on the ruler is to look for a ScreenTip showing the tab type. To remove an accidental tab stop when you are trying to select an existing one, click the Undo button and try again. Alternatively, you can drag the unwanted tab stop marker below the ruler and release the mouse button.

---

3 In the horizontal ruler, point to the **4.5-inch tab stop** until you see the *Right Tab* ScreenTip. Drag the tab stop mark to the right to **4.75 inches on the horizontal ruler**. Compare your screen with Figure 7.25.

Figure 7.25

Tab stop at 0.25 inch

Tab stop at 4.75 inches

Selected text moved

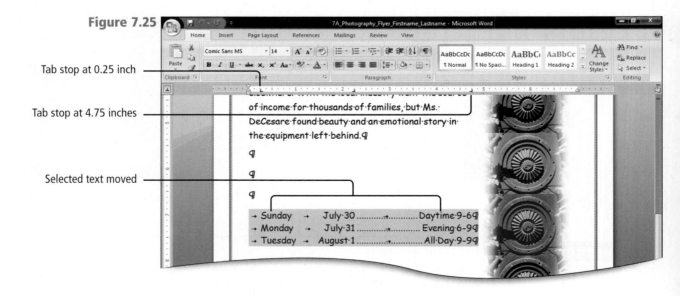

4 Click anywhere to deselect the text, and then **Save** 🖫 your document.

Objective 3
Insert and Modify Text Boxes and Shapes

In addition to graphics such as pictures and clip art you can also add predefined shapes and text boxes to documents. The ***drawing canvas*** feature provides a work area for complex drawings; however, when inserting and formatting simple drawing objects, it is not necessary to activate the drawing canvas.

Activity 7.12 Inserting a Text Box

A ***text box*** is a movable, resizable container for text or graphics. A text box is useful to give text a different orientation from other text in the document because a text box can be placed anywhere in the document in the manner of a floating object.

1 Scroll down to display the bottom edge of the document. Click the **Insert tab**, and then from the **Text group**, click the **Text Box** button. At the bottom of the **Text Box gallery**, click **Draw Text Box**.

2 Position the $\boxed{+}$ pointer at the left margin and at approximately **5.5 inches on the vertical ruler**. Drag down and to the right to create a text box approximately **1.25 inches** high and **4 inches** wide.

3 In the **Size group**, use the spin arrows to set the height and width precisely at **1.3** and **4** inches. Compare your screen with Figure 7.26. If you are not satisfied with your result, click the Undo button and try again.

Figure 7.26

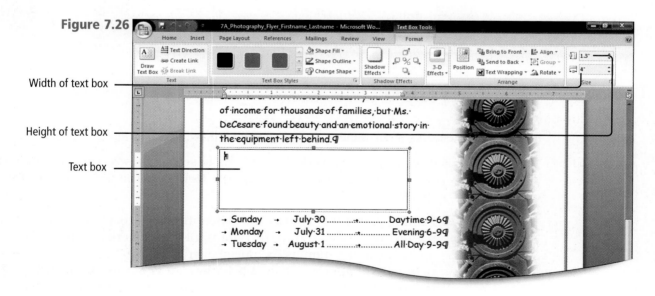

Width of text box

Height of text box

Text box

4 With the insertion point displayed in the text box, click the **Home tab**. In the **Styles group**, click the **No Spacing** style to remove the space *After* paragraphs and change the line spacing to *Single*.

5 Include the quotation marks as you type **"Annie DeCesare finds beauty where no one else thinks to look."** and then press [Enter]. Type **Chicago Arts Review**

6 In the text box, select the quote, including both quotation marks and the paragraph mark. On the Mini toolbar, click the **Font Size button arrow**, and then click **16**. With the text still selected, on the Mini toolbar, click the **Bold** button **B**.

7 In the text box, select *Chicago Arts Review*, and then on the Mini toolbar, click the **Italic** button **I**. In the **Paragraph group**, click the **Align Text Right** button. Click anywhere outside the text box, and then compare your screen with Figure 7.27.

Figure 7.27

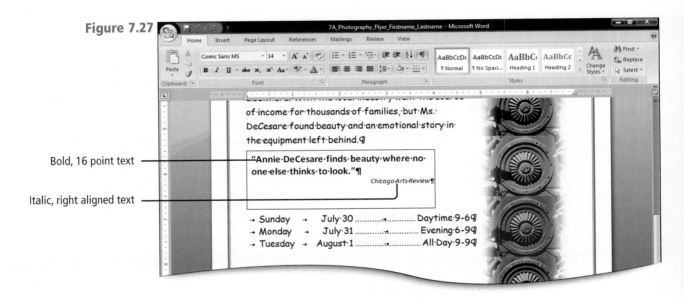

Bold, 16 point text

Italic, right aligned text

8 **Save** your document.

Activity 7.13 Moving, Resizing, and Formatting a Text Box

1 Click anywhere inside the text box to select the box. Click the **Format tab**. In the **Size group**, change the **Height** of the text box to **0.9"** and the **Width** to **3.5"**.

2 Point to one of the text box borders until the pointer displays. Drag the text box down and to the right until it is centered in the same approximate location as the one shown in Figure 7.28. Position the right edge at approximately **4.5 inches on the horizontal ruler**, and the top edge at approximately **5.75 inches on the vertical ruler**.

> Because the rulers show the size of the text box, but not the location of the text box relative to the rest of the document, you will likely need to deselect the text box, check the position, and then move the box again.

Figure 7.28

Word | Chapter 7

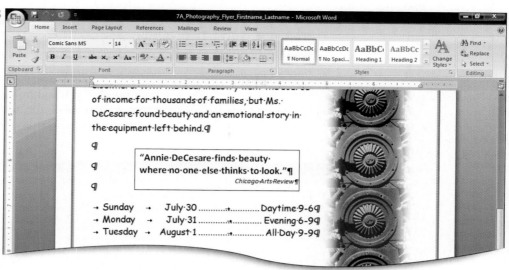

3 If necessary, select the text box. On the **Format tab**, in the **Shadow Effects group**, click the **Shadow Effects** button.

4 In the **Shadow Effects gallery**, under **Drop Shadow**, in the first row, point to the fourth shadow—**Shadow Style 4**. Notice that Live Preview displays a shadow around the text box, as shown in Figure 7.29.

Because the default shadow on the WordArt is down and to the right, it is good design to create a text box shadow in the same direction.

Figure 7.29

Shadow Effects gallery

Shadow Style 4

Live Preview displays the shadow

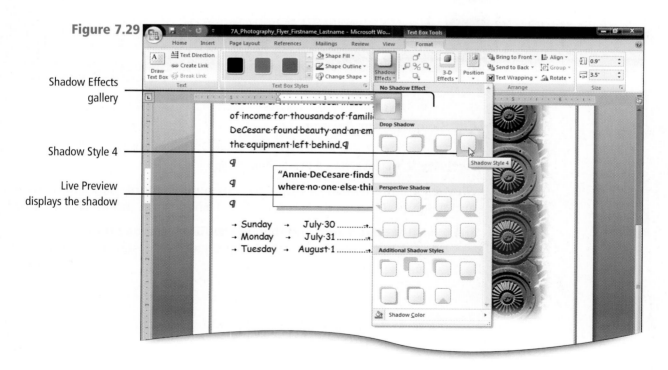

5 Click **Shadow Style 4**. In the **Shadow Effects group**, click the **Nudge Shadow Left** button ⬚ two times, and then click the **Nudge Shadow Up** ⬚ button two times. Click anywhere in the document to deselect the text box, and then compare your screen with Figure 7.30.

The Nudge Shadow buttons enable you to apply precision formatting to your shadows; in this instance you made the shadow more subtle and in proportion to the shadows on the other graphic on the page.

Figure 7.30

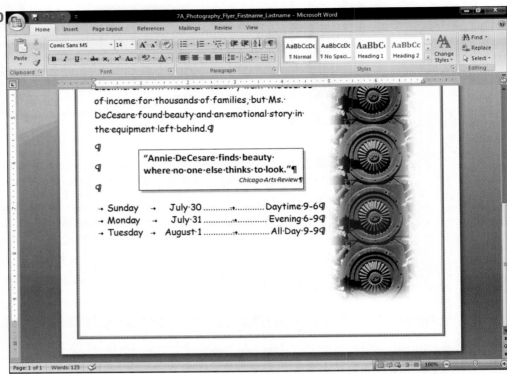

6 **Save** 💾 your document.

Activity 7.14 Inserting a Predefined Shape

Shapes are predefined drawing objects such as stars, banners, arrows, and callouts. More than 150 predefined Shapes are available with Word.

1 Click the **Insert tab**, and then in the **Illustrations group**, click the **Shapes** button to display the Shapes gallery, as shown in Figure 7.31.

Figure 7.31

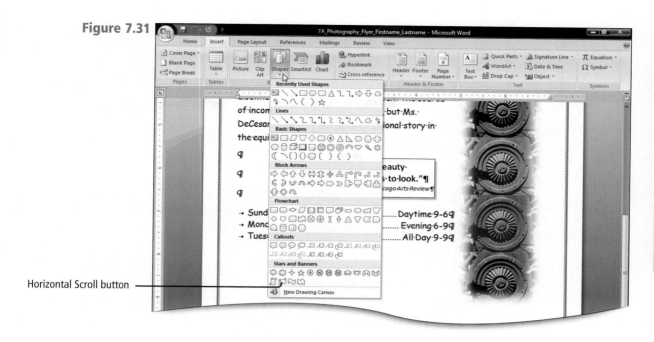

Horizontal Scroll button

2 From the **Shapes gallery**, under **Stars and Banners**, in the second row, click the second shape—**Horizontal Scroll**.

3 Move the ⊞ pointer near the left margin at approximately **8 inches on the vertical ruler**. Using both the horizontal and vertical rulers as guides, drag down and to the right to create a banner approximately **1 inch** high and **3 inches** wide.

4 In the **Size group**, use the **Shape Height** and **Shape Width spin box arrows** to set the **Height** to **1.2"** and the **Width** to **3"**. Compare your screen with Figure 7.32. If you are not satisfied with your result, undo your changes and begin again.

Figure 7.32

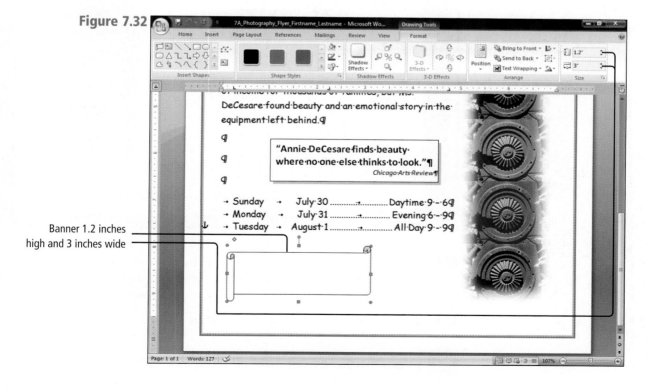

Banner 1.2 inches high and 3 inches wide

5 Right-click the banner, and then from the shortcut menu, click **Add Text**. Click the **Home tab**. In the **Styles group**, click the **No Spacing** style button to remove the space *After* paragraphs and change the line spacing to *Single*.

6 Type the following text, pressing Enter after each line except the last line:

Memories Old and New
220 West Randolph Street
Chicago, IL 60601
312-555-0023

7 In the banner, select the first line of text—*Memories Old and New*—and then on the Mini toolbar, click **Bold** B. Click the **Font Size button arrow**, and then click **14**.

8 Select all of the text in the banner, and then on the Mini toolbar, click the **Center** button ≡. If necessary, adjust the height of the banner to accommodate the text.

9 Click the **Format tab**, and then in the **Shadow Effects group**, click the **Shadow Effects** button. Use the technique you practiced with the text box to apply **Shadow Style 4**.

10 Nudge the shadow **Up** two times and to the **Left** two times. Click outside of the banner to deselect it, and then compare your screen with Figure 7.33.

Figure 7.33

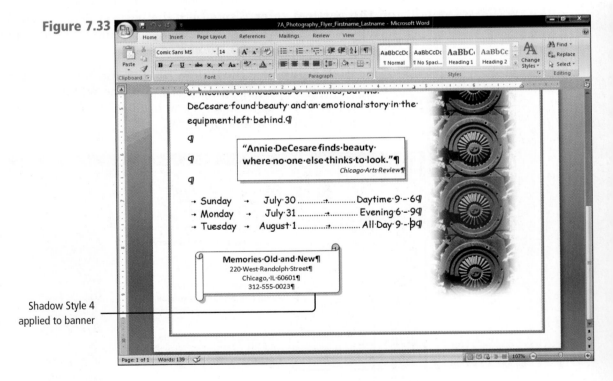

Shadow Style 4 applied to banner

11 Add the file name to the footer, and then display the **Print Preview** window to make a final check of your document. **Save** 💾 your document, and then submit the document as directed.

12 **Close** your document, and then **Exit** Word.

End You have completed Project 7A

Project 7B Price List

In Activities 7.15 through 7.24, you will create a price list for framed and unframed prints by photographer Annie DeCesare at Memories Old and New. Your completed document will look similar to Figure 7.34.

For Project 7B, you will need the following file:

w07B_Price_List

**You will save your document as
7B_Price_List_Firstname_Lastname**

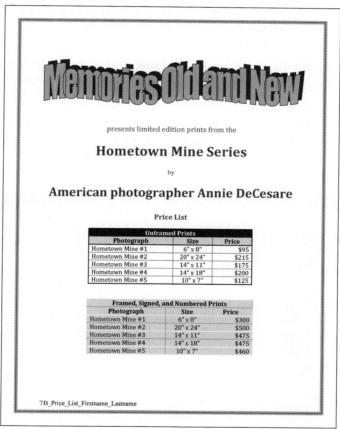

Figure 7.34
Project 7B—Price List

Objective 4
Create a Table

The table feature in Word has largely replaced the use of tabs because of its flexibility and ease of use. *Tables* contain rows and columns in which you can organize data. You can create an empty table, and then fill in the *cells*—the boxes created at the intersections of columns and rows. You can also convert existing text to a table provided the text is properly formatted.

Activity 7.15 Creating a Table and Entering Text

1 **Start** Word, display the formatting marks and rulers, and then from your student files, locate and open the file **w07B_Price_List**. From the **Office** menu 🔘, click **Save As**, and then navigate to your **Word Chapter 7** folder. In the **File name** box, type 7B_Price_List_Firstname_ Lastname and press Enter.

2 In the three blank lines under *Price List*, click in the middle blank line. Click the **Insert tab**, and then in the **Tables group**, click the **Table** button.

3 In the **Table gallery**, in the fifth row, point to the second square. Notice that the size of the table—*2x5*—displays at the top of the gallery, as shown in Figure 7.35.

Figure 7.35

Table size

Preview of inserted table

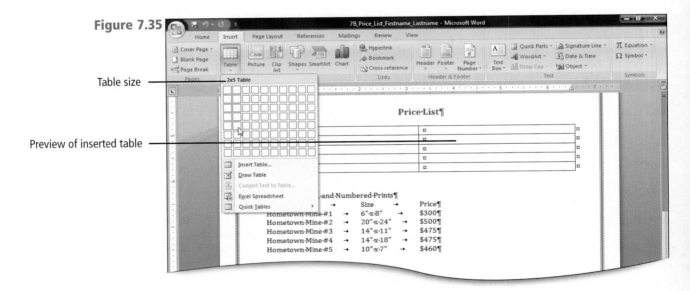

4 Click one time, and then compare your screen with Figure 7.36.

A table with five rows and two columns displays at the insertion point location, and the insertion point displays in the upper left cell. The table fills the width of the page, from the left margin to the right margin. Table Tools display on the Ribbon, and add two contextual tabs—*Design* and *Layout*.

Figure 7.36

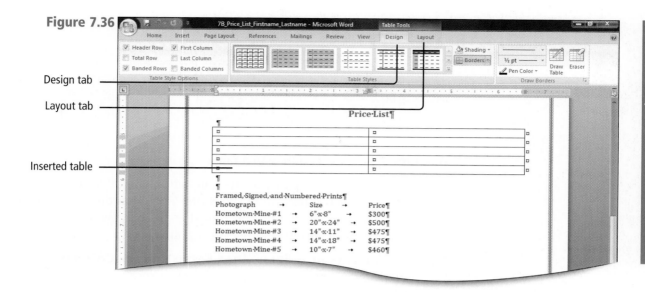

Design tab

Layout tab

Inserted table

5 Type **Unframed Prints** and then press Tab to move to the second cell in the first row of the table.

> Use Tab—rather than Enter—to move from cell to cell in a Word table. Pressing Enter creates an additional line in the same cell, similar to the way you add a new line in a document. If you press Enter by mistake, press ←Bksp to remove the extra line.

6 Press Tab again to move to the first cell in the second row. Type **Hometown Mine #1** and press Tab. Type **$95** and press Tab.

7 Type the following to complete the table, but do not press Tab after the last item. Compare your screen with Figure 7.37.

Hometown Mine #2	**$215**
Hometown Mine #3	**$175**
Hometown Mine #4	**$200**

Figure 7.37

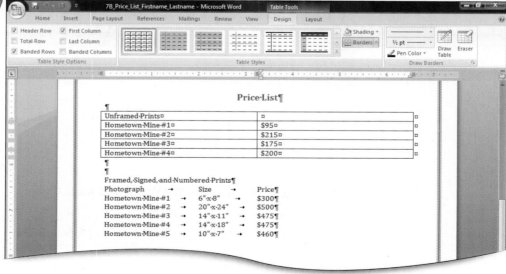

8 Save the document.

Activity 7.16 Adding a Row to a Table

1 With the insertion point in the last cell in the table, press Tab to add a new row to the bottom of the table. Type **Hometown Mine #5** and press Tab. Type **$125** and then, in the second row of the table, click anywhere to position the insertion point.

2 Click the **Layout tab**, and then in the **Rows & Columns group**, click the **Insert Above** button to insert a new row.

3 In the new row, type **Photograph** and press Tab.

  When the entire row is selected, text that you type automatically begins in the cell on the left.

4 Type **Price** and then compare your table with Figure 7.38.

Figure 7.38

New rows

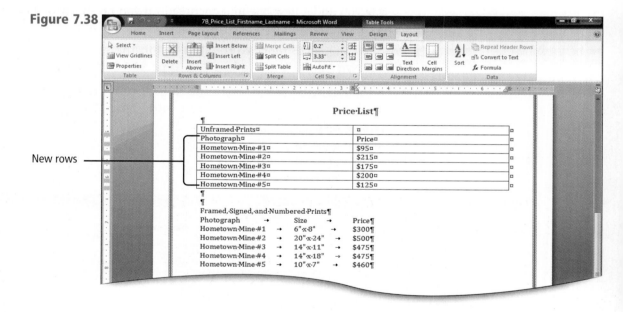

5 **Save** your document.

Activity 7.17 Changing the Width of a Table Column

1 In the first column of the table, point to the right boundary until the ⊹ pointer displays, as shown in Figure 7.39.

Figure 7.39

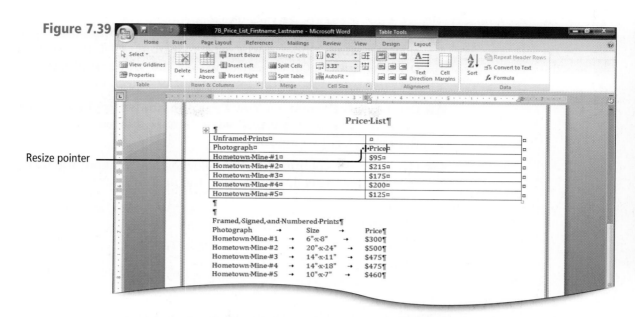

Resize pointer

2 Drag the boundary to the left until the first column's right boundary aligns at approximately **2 inches on the horizontal ruler**; use the horizontal ruler as a guide. If only one row resizes, click the Undo button and begin again.

3 Drag the right boundary of the second column to **2.75 inches on the horizontal ruler**. Compare your table with Figure 7.40.

4 **Save** your document.

Figure 7.40

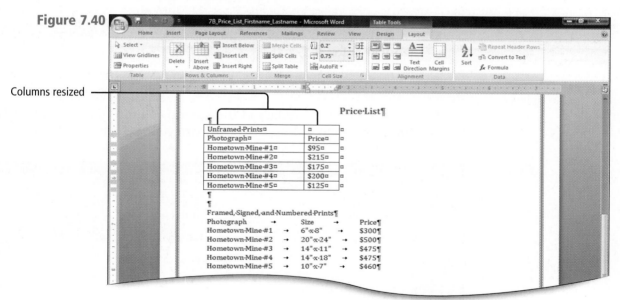

Columns resized

Activity 7.18 Adding a Column to a Table

You can add a column to a Word table in a manner similar to inserting a row.

1 In the first column of the table, click anywhere in the column to position the insertion point. On the **Layout tab**, in the **Rows & Columns group**, click the **Insert Right** button.

2 In the new column, click to place the insertion point in the second row. Type **Size** and press ↓.

3 From the **Office** menu 🔘, click the **Word Options** button, and then click **Proofing**. Under **AutoCorrect options**, click the **AutoCorrect Options** button. On the **AutoFormat tab**, under **Replace**, clear the **"Straight quotes" with "smart quotes"** check box.

4 On the **AutoFormat As You Type tab**, under **Replace as you type**, clear the **"Straight quotes" with "smart quotes"** check box, and then click **OK** two times.

5 Complete the column with the following information; the text may be too wide for the cell, and wrap to the next line in the same cell.

6" × 8"
20" × 24"
14" × 11"
14" × 18"
10" × 7"

Note — **Using Straight Quotes Versus Smart Quotes**

When you type a quotation mark in Word, one of two characters displays—a straight quote (") or a smart quote ("). *Straight quotes* consist of two straight lines, and are used for inch marks. *Smart quotes*, which have rounded sides and are more decorative, are often used for quotations. By default, when you type a quotation mark, Word's AutoCorrect feature automatically changes it to a smart quote. However, many computers will have this AutoCorrect feature turned off. The single quote mark works the same way, where a smart single quotation mark is used as an apostrophe for contractions and possessive words, while the straight single quotation mark is used for foot marks in measurements.

---

6 Drag the right boundary of the third column to **4 inches on the horizontal ruler**.

If you try to resize the middle column first, the right border of the table will remain fixed, thus decreasing the width of the column on the right.

7 Drag the right boundary of the second column to **3 inches on the horizontal ruler**, and then compare your screen with Figure 7.41.

Figure 7.41

New column inserted

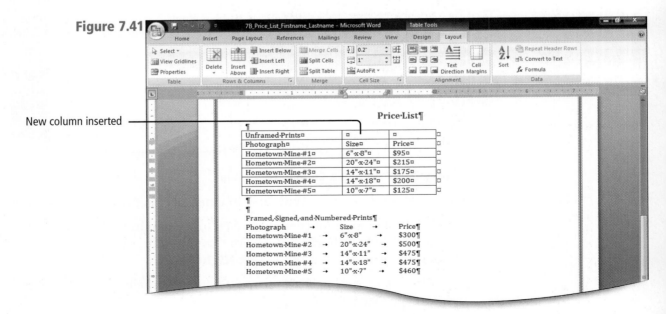

8 **Save** 💾 your document.

More Knowledge — Using Tabs in Tables

You can add tabs to a table column; doing so lets you indent items within a table cell. The easiest way to add a tab is to click on the ruler to set the location within a column. Then you can drag the tab stop indicator to change the location of the tab within the column or add the hanging indent marker so multiple lines in a list are evenly indented. To move to the tabbed location within the cell—and not to the next cell—press Ctrl + Tab.

Activity 7.19 Converting Text to Tables

The Insert Table feature is useful if you are beginning a new table, but Word also provides a tool that enables you to convert existing text to a table. The text must be marked using *separator characters*—usually tabs or commas that separate the text in each line. When you convert text to a table, you can have Word optimize the column widths at the same time.

1 Scroll as necessary to view the lower portion of the document. In the block of text at the end of the document, beginning with *Framed* and continuing to the end of the document, notice the tab marks, as shown in Figure 7.42.

> Tab marks can act as separator characters for the purpose of converting text to a table.

Figure 7.42

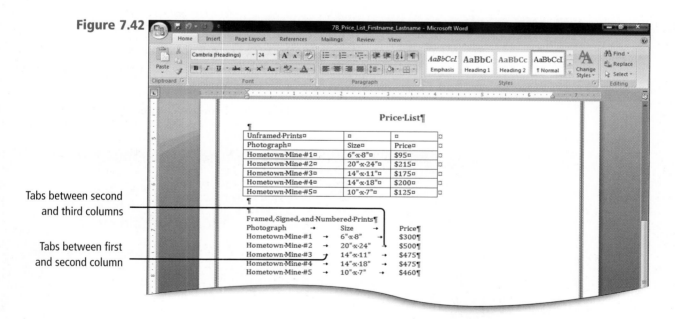

Tabs between second and third columns

Tabs between first and second column

2 Click to position the insertion point to the left of the word *Framed*, hold down ⇧Shift, and then click at the end of the last line, after *$460*. Be sure you include the paragraph mark to the right of *$460*.

3 With the text selected, click the **Insert tab**. In the **Tables group**, click the **Table** button, and then click **Convert Text to Table**.

4 In the **Convert Text to Table** dialog box, under **Table size**, click the **Number of columns up spin arrow** to change the number of columns to **3**. Then, under **AutoFit behavior**, click the **AutoFit to contents** option button.

> The AutoFit to contents option instructs Word to evaluate the contents of the columns and choose appropriate column widths for each column.

5 Under **Separate text at**, click the **Tabs** option button. Compare your dialog box with Figure 7.43.

Figure 7.43

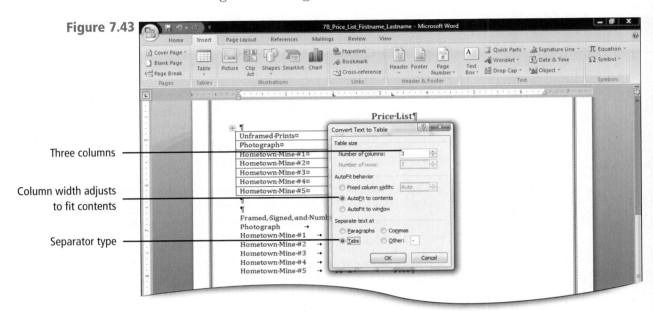

Three columns

Column width adjusts to fit contents

Separator type

6 At the bottom of the **Convert Text to Table** dialog box, click **OK**. Click anywhere in the document to deselect the table. Click **Save**, and then compare your table with Figure 7.44.

> The columns are set to the width of the widest item in each column.

Figure 7.44

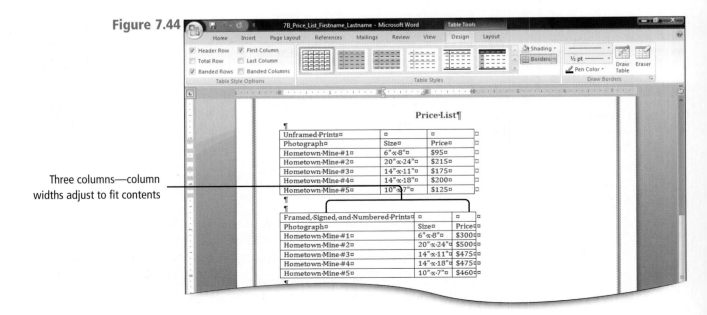

Three columns—column widths adjust to fit contents

Objective 5
Format a Table

You can format tables to make them more attractive and easier to read. When you type numbers, for example, they line up on the left of a column instead of on the right. With Word's formatting tools, you can shade cells, format the table borders and grid, align text, and center the table between the document margins. All of these features make a table more inviting to the reader.

Activity 7.20 Formatting Text in Cells and Shading Cells

1 In the upper table, click anywhere in the cell containing the word *Photograph*, hold down the left mouse button, and then drag to the right to select all three cells in the second row. On the Mini toolbar, click **Bold** **B** and **Center** ≡. Compare your screen with Figure 7.45.

Figure 7.45

Bold, centered text

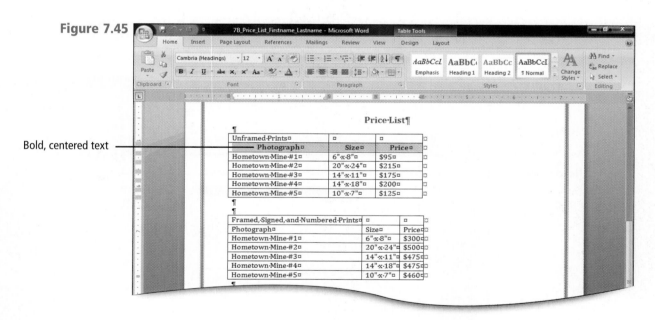

2 In the second column, click in the cell containing *6" × 8"*, and then drag down to select the third cell through the seventh cell. On the Mini toolbar, click **Center** ≡.

3 In the third column, click in the cell containing *$95*, and then drag down to select the third cell through the seventh cell. On the **Home tab**, in the **Paragraph group**, click the **Align Text Right** button ≡. Compare your screen with Figure 7.46.

Figure 7.46

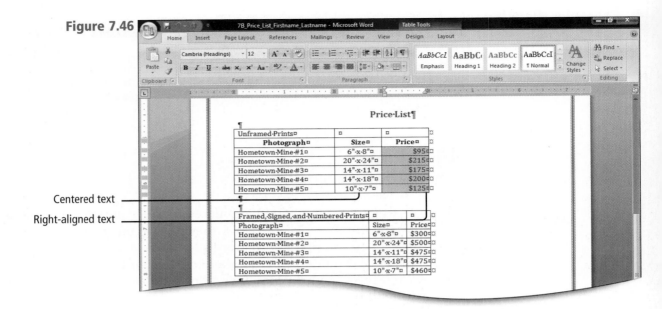

Centered text ———

Right-aligned text ———

---

4 In the upper table, click anywhere in the cell containing the *Unframed Prints*, and then drag to the right to select all three cells in the first row. Click the **Design tab**, and then in the **Table Styles group**, click the **Shading button arrow**.

5 In the **Shading gallery**, near the bottom of the fourth column, point to—but do not click—**Dark Blue, Text 2, Darker 25%**. Compare your screen with Figure 7.47.

Figure 7.47

Shading button ———

Selected shade ———

Name of shade ———

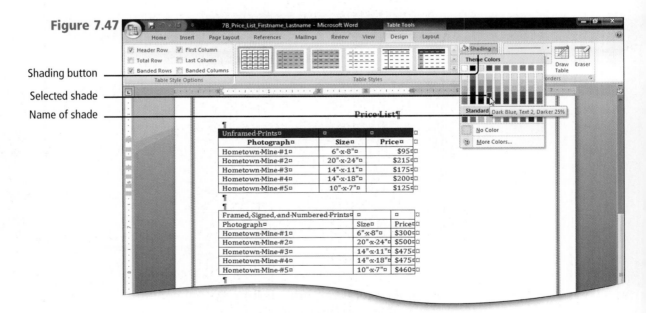

6 Click to apply *Dark Blue, Text 2, Darker 25%*.

7 In the upper table, click anywhere in the cell containing the word *Photograph*, and then drag to the right to select all three cells in the second row. On the **Design tab**, in the **Table Styles group**, click the **Shading button arrow**.

8 In the **Shading gallery**, click the second button in the fourth column—**Dark Blue, Text 2, Lighter 80%**. Click anywhere in the table to deselect the cells, and then compare your screen with Figure 7.48.

Figure 7.48

Shades applied

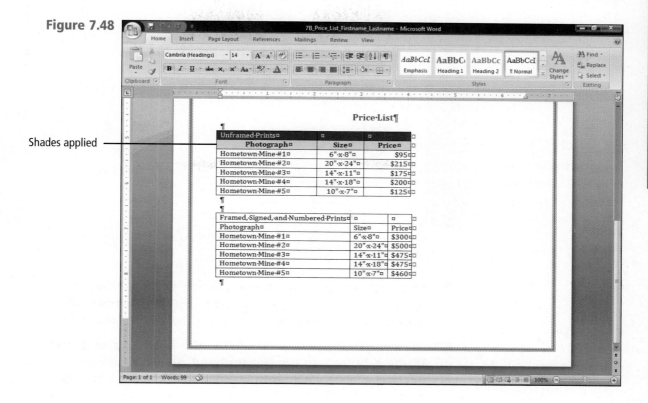

9 **Save** the document.

Activity 7.21 Changing the Table Border

You can modify or remove the border from an entire table, a selected cell, or individual boundaries of a cell.

1 In the upper table, click anywhere in the cell containing the word *Photograph*, and then drag to the right to select all three cells in the second row.

2 On the **Design tab**, in the **Table Styles group**, click the **Borders button arrow**, and then click **Borders and Shading**.

3 In the **Borders and Shading** dialog box, under **Setting**, click the **Custom** button. Click the **Width arrow**, and then click **1 1/2 pt**. In the **Preview** area, click the bottom border of the preview diagram. Notice that the Preview area displays a bottom border that is heavier than the side or top borders, as shown in Figure 7.49.

The Custom setting enables you to change the characteristics of individual border lines, rather than change all of the borders at one time.

Figure 7.49

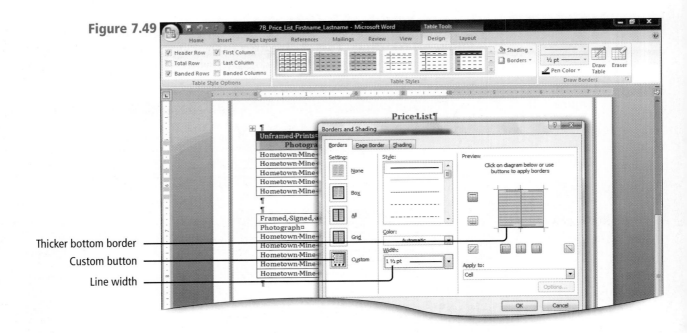

Thicker bottom border
Custom button
Line width

4 Click **OK** to change the bottom border of the selected cells. Click anywhere in the upper table, and then click the **Layout tab**. In the **Table group**, click the **Select** button, and then click **Select Table**.

5 Click the **Design tab**, and then in the **Table Styles group**, click the **Borders** button. In the **Borders and Shading** dialog box, under **Setting**, click the **Custom** button, if necessary. Click the **Width arrow**, and then click **1 1/2 pt**. In the **Preview** area, click the four outside borders, and then click **OK**.

6 Click anywhere in the document to deselect the table, and then compare your screen with Figure 7.50.

Figure 7.50

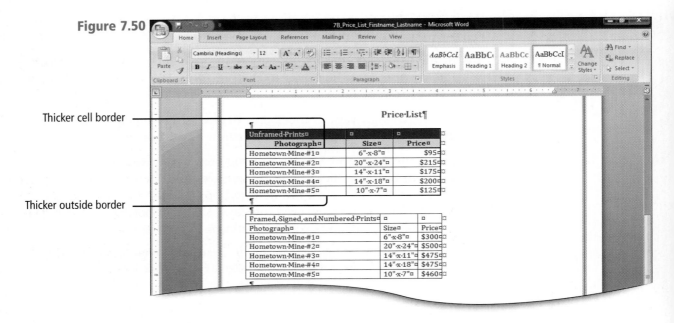

Thicker cell border

Thicker outside border

7 Save your document.

Activity 7.22 Centering a Table

1 Click anywhere in the upper table, and then click the **Layout tab**. In the **Table group**, click the **Select** button, and then click **Select Table**.

2 Click the **Home tab**, and then in the **Paragraph group**, click the **Center** button .

Another Way

To Center a Table

You can center a table without selecting the table first. Right-click anywhere in the table, and then, from the shortcut menu, click Table Properties. In the Table Properties dialog box, on the Table tab, under Alignment, click Center. The Table Properties dialog box also enables you to wrap text around a table in the same way you wrap text around a graphic.

3 Click anywhere in the document to deselect the table, and then compare your screen with Figure 7.51.

Figure 7.51

Table centered horizontally on the page

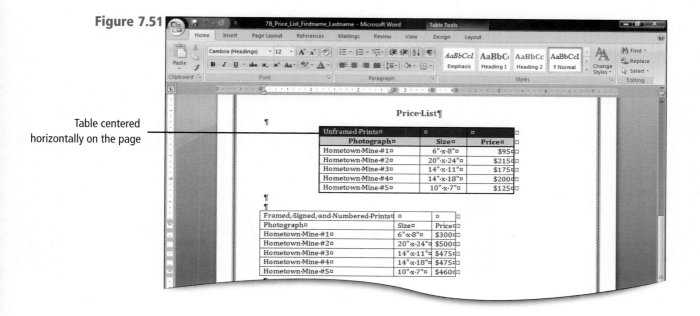

4 **Save** your document.

Activity 7.23 Merging Cells

The title of a table typically spans two or more columns. In this activity, you will merge cells so that you can position the table title across the columns.

1 In the upper table, click anywhere in the cell containing the word *Unframed Prints*, and then drag to the right to select all three cells in the first row.

2 Click the **Layout tab**, and then in the **Merge group**, click the **Merge Cells** button.

> The cells are merged, and the borders between the cells in the top row are removed.

3 Select the text in the top cell—**Unframed Prints**. On the Mini toolbar, click **Bold** **B** and **Center** ≡.

Another Way ──┤ **To Align Text in a Table**

You can use shortcut menus to align text in a table. Right-click the cell, point to Cell Alignment from the shortcut menu, and then from the Cell Alignment gallery that displays, click the alignment style you want. You can choose from both vertical and horizontal cell alignment options using the Cell Alignment gallery.

---

4 Click anywhere in the document to deselect the table, and then compare your screen with Figure 7.52.

Figure 7.52

Text is merged across three cells

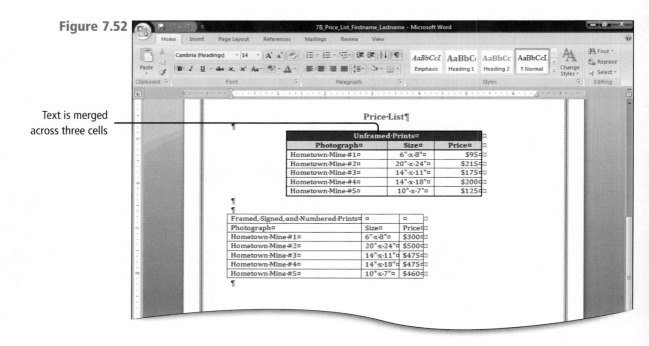

5 **Save** 🖫 your document.

Activity 7.24 Applying a Predefined Format to a Table

Word includes a number of built-in table formats with which you can quickly give your table a professional design. This is accomplished by applying a ***Table Style***—a predefined set of formatting characteristics, including font, alignment, and cell shading.

1 In the lower table, click anywhere to position the insertion point within the table—you need not select the entire table to use Table Styles.

2 Click the **Design tab**. In the **Table Styles group**, point to the second Table Style—**Table 3D effects 1**—and notice that Live Preview displays the table the way it would look if you clicked that style, as shown in Figure 7.53.

Figure 7.53

Table 3D effects 1 style

Live Preview displays the table style

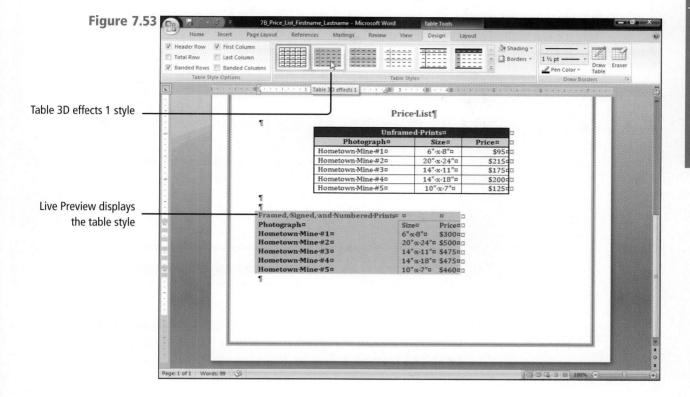

3 In the **Table Styles group**, click the **More** button. Scroll down to view the available table styles, and then point to several of the styles in the gallery. Click anywhere in the document to close the gallery.

4 In the **Table Styles group**, point to the third style—**Table 3D effects 2**—and click to apply the style. Click the **Layout tab**. In the **Table group**, click the **Select** button, and then click **Select Table**.

5 Click the **Design tab**. In the **Table Styles group**, click the **Shading button arrow**, and then in the second row, click the fourth color—**Dark Blue, Text 2, Lighter 80%**.

6 Right-click the table, and then from the shortcut menu, click **Table Properties**. In the **Table Properties** dialog box, on the **Table tab**, under **Alignment**, click **Center**.

7 Point to the **Table Properties** dialog box title bar, and then drag the dialog box up and to the right so that you can see most of the lower table. In the **Table Properties** dialog box, click the **Column tab**. Under **Size**, click the **Next Column** button to select the first column, as shown in Figure 7.54.

Figure 7.54

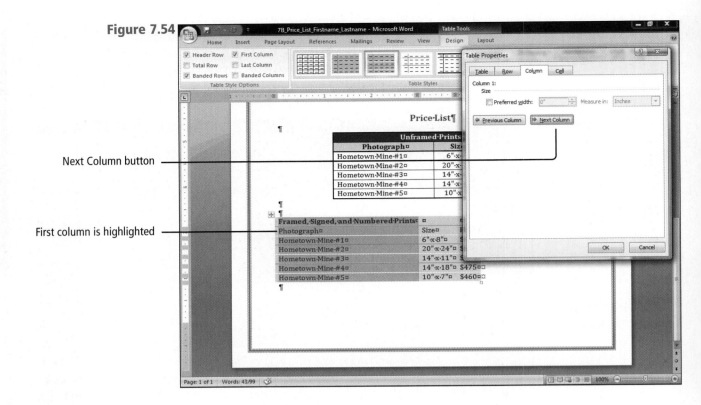

Next Column button

First column is highlighted

8 With the first column selected, select the **Preferred width** check box, select the text in the **Preferred width** box, type **2** and then click the **Next Column** button. Use the same procedure to make the second and third columns **1.1** inches wide, and then click **OK**.

9 Point to the first cell of the top row and drag to the right to select all three cells. Click the **Layout tab**. In the **Merge group**, click the **Merge Cells** button. In the **Alignment group**, click the **Align Center** button ▤.

10 In the second row of the table, select all three cells, and then on the Mini toolbar, click **Bold** Ⓑ and **Center** ▤.

11 In the second column, click in the cell containing 6" × 8", and then drag down to select the third cell through the seventh cell. On the Mini toolbar, click the **Center** button ▤.

12 In the third column, click in the cell containing $300, and then drag down to select the third cell through the seventh cell. Click the **Home tab**, and then in the **Paragraph group**, click the **Align Text Right** button ▤. Click anywhere in the document to deselect the cells, and then compare your screen with Figure 7.55.

Figure 7.55

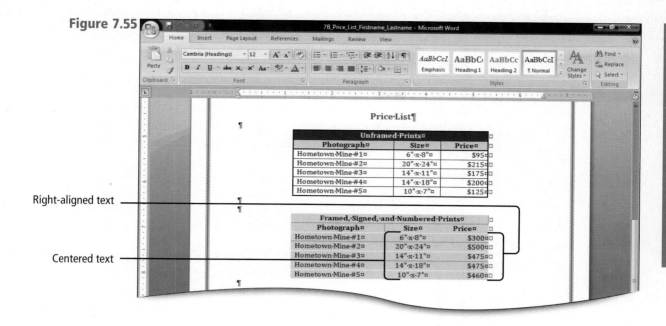

Right-aligned text

Centered text

13 From the **Office** menu 🔘, click the **Word Options** button, and then click **Proofing**. Under **AutoCorrect options**, click the **AutoCorrect Options** button. On the **AutoFormat tab**, under **Replace**, select the **"Straight quotes" with "smart quotes"** check box. Repeat this procedure on the **AutoFormat As You Type tab**, and then click **OK** two times.

14 Add the file name to the footer, and then **Save** 💾 your document. Submit the document as directed.

15 **Close** your document, and then **Exit** Word.

End You have completed Project 7B ────────────

🔘GO! There's More You Can Do!
CD-ROM

Close Word and any other open windows. Display the Start menu, click Computer, and then navigate to the student files that accompany this textbook. From the CD that came with your book, open the folder **02_theres_more_you_can_do**, locate and open the folder for this chapter. Open and print the instructions for this project, which are provided to you in Adobe PDF format.

Try IT! — Create a Chart

In this Try It! exercise, you will insert a chart into a Word document.

Content-Based Assessments

Summary

Many graphic elements can be inserted into a Word document, including clip art, pictures, and basic shapes created with Word's drawing tools. Text can also be converted into a graphic format using WordArt.

An effective way to present information is with a tabbed list or a table. A variety of tabs can be used, such as left-aligned, decimal, centered, or right-aligned. Leader characters, such as a solid, dotted, or dashed line, can be used to fill the space created by using a tab stop.

Tables present information in a format of rows and columns. Tables can be formatted to display the information in a manner that emphasizes certain parts of the table. Text in a table can be formatted using both the Table contextual tools and Table Styles. Existing text can be converted to a table format.

Key Terms

Adjustment handle 149

Anchor 149

Cell............................172

Click and type
  pointer 158

Column chart............. ●

Dot leader 161

Drawing canvas 165

Drawing object 148

Floating object 152

Graphic 148

Inline object 150

Leader character 161

Pie chart .... ●

Rotate handle 149

Separator
  character 177

Shapes 168

Sizing handle 149

Smart quote 176

Straight quote 176

Tab stop...................157

Table 172

Table Style 184

Text box 165

Text wrapping 152

WordArt 148

The ● symbol represents Key Terms found on the Student CD in the 02_theres_more_you_can_do folder for this chapter

Content-Based Assessments

Matching

Match each term in the second column with its correct definition in the first column by writing the letter of the term on the blank line in front of the correct definition.

_____ **1.** A gallery of text styles with which you can create decorative effects, such as shadowed or mirrored text.

_____ **2.** An object or graphic that can be moved independently of the surrounding text.

_____ **3.** An object or graphic inserted in a document that acts like a character in a sentence.

_____ **4.** Small circles in the corners of a selected graphic with which you can resize the graphic proportionally.

_____ **5.** A movable, resizable container for text or graphics.

_____ **6.** A handle on a selected graphic that can be dragged to rotate the graphic to any angle.

_____ **7.** The symbol that indicates the paragraph to which an object is attached.

_____ **8.** Predefined drawing shapes, such as stars, banners, arrows, and callouts, included with Microsoft Office, that can be inserted into documents.

_____ **9.** Characters that form a solid, dotted, or dashed line that fills the space used by a tab character.

_____ **10.** A character used to identify column placement in text; usually a tab or a comma.

_____ **11.** A mark on the ruler that indicates the location where the insertion point will be placed when you press the Tab key.

_____ **12.** The text select (I-beam) pointer with various attached shapes that indicate which formatting will be applied when you double-click—such as a left-aligned, centered, or right-aligned tab stop.

_____ **13.** The rectangular box in a table formed by the intersection of a row and column.

_____ **14.** Rows and columns of text or numbers used to organize data and present it effectively.

_____ **15.** A command that applies one of a number of built-in table formats—resulting in a table with a professional design.

A Anchor

B Cell

C Click and type pointer

D Corner sizing handles

E Floating object

F Inline object

G Leader characters

H Rotate handle

I Separator character

J Shapes

K Tab stop

O Table

N Table Style

L Text box

M WordArt

Content-Based Assessments

Fill in the Blank

Write the correct answer in the space provided.

1. An _____ symbol indicates the paragraph to which an object is attached.

2. When a graphic is selected, _____ _____ display around the edge of the graphic.

3. To align text to the contours of an irregularly shaped graphic, choose _____ Text Wrapping.

4. A banner is an example of a predefined _____ that can be inserted into a document.

5. Tab stops are a form of paragraph formatting and are stored in the _____ mark.

6. The tab alignment option that centers text around a tab stop is the _____ tab.

7. A series of dots following a tab that serve to guide the reader's eyes is known as a dot _____.

8. To move text aligned with tabs, select the text and drag the _____ _____ on the ruler.

9. To move from cell to cell across a table as you enter text, press _____.

10. To create a table in Word, click the _____ button on the Insert tab.

11. When you press [Tab] with the insertion point in the last cell in a table, a new _____ is added to the table.

12. On the Table Tools Design tab, click the _____ button to add gray or color to a table cell.

13. To set the alignment of a table on a page, display the Table tab of the _____ _____ dialog box.

14. A predefined set of table formatting characteristics, including font, alignment, and cell shading is called a Table _____.

15. To combine two or more cells into one cell, use the _____ _____ button on the Layout tab.

Content-Based Assessments

Skills Review

Project 7C—Creative Supplies

In this project, you will apply the skills you practiced from the Objectives in Project 7A.

Objectives: 1. *Insert and Format Graphics;* **2**. *Set Tab Stops;* **3**. *Insert and Modify Text Boxes and Shapes.*

In the following Skills Review, you will create a flyer for Memories Old and New that describes the range of products available at the store. Your completed flyer will look similar to the one shown in Figure 7.56.

For Project 7C, you will need the following files:

New blank Word document
w07C_Art_Supplies
w07C_Supplies

You will save your document as 7C_Creative_Supplies_Firstname_Lastname

Figure 7.56

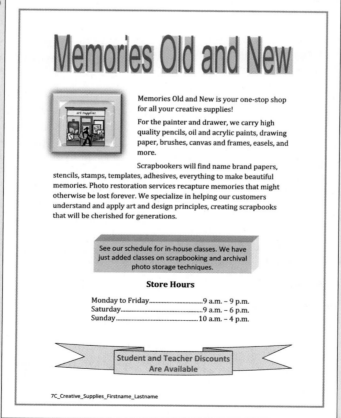

(Project 7C–Creative Supplies continues on the next page)

Content-Based Assessments

(Project 7C–Creative Supplies continued)

1. **Start** Word and display formatting marks and rulers. From the **Page Layout tab**, display the **Page Setup** dialog box, set the **Top** and **Bottom** margins to **1"**, the **Left** and **Right** margins to **1.25"**, and then click **OK**.

2. Type **Memories Old and New** and then press Enter two times. Select the text you just typed, but do not select the paragraph mark. Click the **Insert tab**. In the **Text group**, click the **WordArt** button. From the **WordArt gallery**, in the second row, click the second style—**WordArt style 8**. Click **OK**.

3. On the **Format tab**, in the **Size group**, click the **Shape Height button up spin arrow** as necessary to change the height of the WordArt to **1"**. Click the **Shape Width button up spin arrow** as necessary to change the width of the WordArt to **6"**. Display the **Save As** dialog box, navigate to your **Word Chapter 7** folder, **Save** the document as **7C_Creative_Supplies_Firstname_Lastname** and then add the file name to the footer.

4. **Close** the footer area. Press Ctrl + End. Click the **Insert tab**. From the **Text group**, click the **Object button arrow**, and then click **Text from File**. Locate and insert the file **w07C_Supplies**. In the paragraph beginning *Scrapbookers*, click to position the insertion point at the beginning of the paragraph. In the **Illustrations group**, click the **Picture** button. Locate and insert **w07C_Art_Supplies**.

5. On the **Format tab**, in the **Size group**, click the **Shape Height spin box down arrow** as necessary to change the height of the picture to **1.4"**. With the graphic still selected, on the **Format tab**, in the **Arrange group**, click the **Text Wrapping** button. From the **Text Wrapping gallery**, click **Square** to wrap the text around the graphic.

6. Point anywhere in the **w07C_Art_Supplies** graphic to display the pointer, and then drag the graphic up until the top edge of the graphic is aligned with the top edge of the paragraph beginning *Memories Old and New*. Be sure the left side of the graphic is aligned with the left side of the text.

7. With the graphic still selected, on the **Format tab**, in the **Picture Styles group**, click the third picture style—**Metal Frame**. Move the picture as necessary to match Figure 7.56.

8. Click anywhere in the document to deselect the graphic. Click the **Page Layout tab**, and then in the **Page Background group**, click the **Page Borders** button. In the **Borders and Shading** dialog box, under **Setting**, click **Box**. Click the **Color arrow**, and then in the last column of colors, click the fifth button—**Orange, Accent 6, Darker 25%**. Click the **Width arrow**, click **3 pt**, and then click **OK**. **Save** your document.

9. Scroll to display the lower half of the document on your screen, and then click in the blank line at the end of the document. Move the pointer on your screen to position it at approximately **6.5 inches on the vertical ruler** and at the left margin, double-click to place the insertion point. If necessary, change the Font to Cambria, and the Font Size to 14. Type **Store Hours** and press Enter.

10. Be sure the **Tab Alignment** button displays a **Left tab**. Click on **4 inches on the horizontal ruler**. Double-click the tab

(Project 7C–Creative Supplies continues on the next page)

(Project 7C–Creative Supplies continued)

stop you just added to the ruler. In the **Tabs** dialog box, under **Tab stop position**, click to select the lower **4"**. Under **Alignment**, click the **Right** option button. Under **Leader**, click the **2** option button to add a dot leader. Click the **Set** button, and then click **OK**.

11. Display the **Paragraph** dialog box. Under **Indentation**, click the **Left spin box up arrow** to change the left margin indent to **1"**. Under **Spacing**, click the **After down spin arrow** two times to change the spacing to **0**. Click the **Line spacing arrow**, click **Single**, and then click **OK**.

12. Type the following text, pressing Tab after the days of the week, and Enter after the time:

Monday to Friday	9 a.m. – 9 p.m.
Saturday	9 a.m. – 6 p.m.
Sunday	10 a.m. – 4 p.m.

13. Select the text *Store Hours*. On the Mini toolbar, click the **Bold** and **Center** buttons. Click the **Font Size button arrow**, and then click **16**. Select the three lines of tabbed text. Point to the horizontal ruler and position the pointer so the tip of the pointer arrow is touching the **4-inch tab stop**. When you see the *Right Tab* ScreenTip, drag the tab stop mark to the right to **5 inches on the ruler**. Click anywhere in the document to deselect the text.

14. Click the **Insert tab**, and then in the **Text group**, click the **Text Box** button. At the bottom of the **Text Box gallery**, click **Draw Text Box**. Move the ⊞ pointer to the left margin at **5 inches on the vertical ruler**. Using both the horizontal and vertical rulers as guides, drag down and to the right to create a text box approximately **1 inch** high and **3 inches** wide—then use the spin arrows in the **Size group** to size the text box precisely.

15. With the insertion point displayed in the text box, type **See our schedule for in-house classes. We have just added classes on scrapbooking and archival photo storage techniques.**

16. In the text box, select all of the text. On the Mini toolbar, click the **Font Size button arrow**, and then click **14**. If necessary, click the Font button arrow, and then click Calibri. Click the **Center** button. Display the **Paragraph** dialog box. Change the spacing **After** to **0** and the **Line spacing** to **Single**.

17. With the text box still selected, on the **Format tab**, in the **Size group**, click the **Shape Width button up spin arrow** as necessary to change the width of the text box to **4"**. Click the **Shape Height button down spin arrow** as necessary to change the height of the text box to **0.8"**.

18. Point to one of the text box borders until the ⬚ pointer displays. Drag the text box down and to the right until the left edge is at approximately **1 inch on the horizontal ruler**, and the top edge is at approximately **5.5 inches on the vertical ruler**. Use Figure 7.56 as a guide. On the **Format tab**, in the **3-D Effects group**, click the **3-D Effects** button. Under **Parallel**, click the first button—**3-D Style 1**. Click anywhere in the document to deselect the text box. **Save** your document.

19. Click the **Insert tab**, and then in the **Illustrations group**, click the **Shapes** button. In the **Shapes gallery**, under **Stars and Banners**, in the first row, click the last button—**Curved Down Ribbon**.

20. Move the ⊞ pointer to the left margin at **8 inches on the vertical ruler**. Using both the horizontal and vertical rulers as guides, drag down and to the right to

(Project 7C–Creative Supplies continues on the next page)

(Project 7C–Creative Supplies continued)

create a banner approximately **0.8 inch** high and **6 inches** wide—then use the spin box arrows in the **Size group** to size the banner precisely. Center the banner between the left and right border, and between the tabbed list and the bottom border.

21. Right-click the banner. From the shortcut menu, click **Add Text**. Type **Student and Teacher Discounts Are Available** Select the banner text. On the Mini toolbar, click the **Bold** button, and then click the **Center** button. Click the **Font Color button arrow**, and then in the last column, click the last button—click **Orange, Accent 6, Darker 50%**. Click the **Font Size button**

arrow, and then click **16**. On the **Home tab**, in the **Paragraph group**, click the **Line spacing button arrow**, and then click **1.0**.

22. On the **Format tab**, in the **Text Box Styles group**, click the **Shape Fill arrow**, and then in the last column, click the third button—**Orange, Accent 6, Lighter 60%**. Click to deselect the banner, and then **Save** your document.

23. Display the **Print Preview** to make a final check of your document. Submit your document as directed.

24. **Close** your document, and then **Exit** Word.

End **You have completed Project 7C**

Content-Based Assessments

Project 7D — Sales Figures

In this project, you will apply the skills you practiced from the Objectives in Project 7B.

Objectives: 4. *Create a Table;* **5**. *Format a Table.*

In the following Skills Review, you will edit a memo about the recent photography exhibition at Memories Old and New. You will create and format a table, convert text to a table, and then AutoFormat the table. Your completed document will look similar to Figure 7.57.

For Project 7D, you will need the following file:

w07D_Sales_Figures

You will save your document as
7D_Sales_Figures_Firstname_Lastname

Figure 7.57

To:	Henry Smith
	Bill Masterson
From:	Sharon Nguyen, Manager
Date:	March 12, 2009
Subject:	Winter Exhibition Sales Results

This year's winter photography exhibition was a big success, with attendance and sales surpassing last year's event. Extended hours and increased promotion in the store and local media ads clearly made a difference.

2009 Exhibition		
Day	Attendees	Increase
Opening Night	300	60
Saturday	250	40
Sunday	220	30
Monday	130	-10
Tuesday	90	50
Closing	270	70

Gross Photograph Sales		
Day	2009	2008
Opening Night	$20,320	$15,600
Saturday	$18,500	$10,000
Sunday	$17,680	$10,900
Monday	$5,850	$6,000
Tuesday	$4,900	$3,200
Closing	$19,700	$17,800

Planning for next year's ad buys is already under way in order to secure space and rates. At the next staff meeting I will present a plan and budget for next year's winter exhibit, including further increasing in-store promotional activities.

7D_Sales_Figures_Firstname_Lastname

(Project 7D–Sales Figures continues on the next page)

Content-Based Assessments

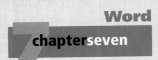
(Project 7D–Sales Figures continued)

1. **Start** Word. From your student files, locate and open the document **w07D_Sales_Figures**, and display formatting marks and rulers. In the three blank lines under the paragraph beginning *This year's winter*, click in the middle blank line. Click the **Insert tab**, and then in the **Tables group**, click the **Table** button. In the **Table gallery**, in the sixth row of squares, point to the second square, and then click to insert a **2x6** table.

2. Type **2009 Exhibition** and then press ⬇ to move to the first cell in the second row. Type **Opening Night** and press Tab. Type **300** and press Tab.

3. Type the following to complete the table, but do not press Tab after the last item.

Saturday	250
Sunday	220
Monday	130
Tuesday	90

4. From the **Office** menu, display the **Save As** dialog box, and then navigate to your **Word Chapter 7 folder**. In the **File name** box, type **7D_Sales_Figures_Firstname_Lastname** and press Enter. Add the file name to the footer area.

5. Position the insertion point in the last cell in the table, and then press Tab to add a new row to the bottom of the table. Type **Closing** and press Tab. Type **270** and then in the second row of the table, click anywhere to position the insertion point. Click the **Layout tab**, and then in the **Rows & Columns group**, click the **Insert Above** button to insert a new row. Type **Day** and press Tab. Type **Attendees**

6. In the first column of the table, move the pointer to the right boundary until the ↔ pointer displays. Drag the boundary to the left until the first column's right boundary

aligns at approximately **1.5 inches on the horizontal ruler**. If only one row resizes, click the Undo button and begin again. In the second column, drag the right boundary to **2.5 inches on the horizontal ruler**. **Save** your document.

7. In the second column of the table, click anywhere in the column to position the insertion point. On the **Layout tab**, in the **Rows & Columns group**, click the **Insert Right** button. In the new column, click to place the insertion point in the second row. Type **Increase** and press ⬇.

8. Complete the column with the following information:

60
40
30
−10
50
70

9. In the second row, click anywhere in the first cell, and then drag to the right to select all three cells in the second row. On the Mini toolbar, click the **Bold** and **Center** buttons.

10. In the second column, click in the cell containing *300*, and then drag down and to the right to select the third cell through the eighth cell of the second and third columns, ending with *70*. Click the **Home tab**, and then in the **Paragraph group**, click the **Align Text Right** button.

11. Select all three cells in the first row. Click the **Design tab**, and then in the **Table Styles group**, click the **Shading** button. Under **Theme Colors**, click the third button in the first row—**Tan, Background 2**.

12. Click the **Layout tab**, and then in the **Merge group**, click the **Merge Cells** button. Select the text in the top cell—**2009 Exhibition**. On the Mini toolbar, click the

(Project 7D–Sales Figures continues on the next page)

Word

(Project 7D–Sales Figures continued)

Bold and **Center** buttons. **Save** the document.

13. Click anywhere in the table to deselect the cells. On the **Design tab**, in the **Table Styles group**, click the **Borders button arrow**, and then click **Borders and Shading**. In the **Borders and Shading** dialog box, under **Setting**, click **Box**. Click the **Width arrow**, and then click **3 pt**. In the **Apply to** box, be sure that **Table** is indicated, and then click **OK**.

14. Click the **Layout tab**. In the **Table group**, click the **Select** button, and then click **Select Table**. Click the **Home tab**, and then in the **Paragraph group**, click the **Center** button. **Save** the document.

15. In the block of text near the end of the document, beginning with *Gross Photograph Sales*, click to position the insertion point to the left of the word *Gross*, hold down ⇧ Shift, and then click after the paragraph mark at the end of the line beginning *Closing*—after *$17,800*.

16. With the text selected, click the **Insert tab**. In the **Tables group**, click the **Table** button, and then click **Convert Text to Table**. In the **Convert Text to Table** dialog box, under **Table size**, click the **Number of columns up spin arrow** to change the number of columns to **3**.

17. Under **AutoFit behavior**, click the **AutoFit to contents** option button. Then, under **Separate text at**, click the **Tabs** option button. At the bottom of the **Convert Text to Table** dialog box, click **OK**.

18. Click anywhere to position the insertion point in the lower table. On the **Design tab**, in the **Table Styles group**, click the **More** button. Under **Built-In**, in the first row, click the fifth table style—**Table Classic 2**. Right-click the table, and then

from the shortcut menu, click **Table Properties**. In the **Table Properties** dialog box, on the **Table tab**, under **Alignment**, click **Center**.

19. Drag the dialog box so that you can see most of the lower table. In the **Table Properties** dialog box, click the **Column tab**. Under **Size**, click the **Next Column** button until the first column of the lower table is highlighted. Select the **Preferred width** check box, and then in the box to the right, click the spin box arrows as necessary to set the **Preferred width** to **1.5"**. Click the **Next Column** button. Use the same procedure to make the second and third columns **1"** wide, and then click **OK**.

20. In the lower table, point to the first cell of the top row and drag to the right to select all three cells. Click the **Layout tab**, and then in the **Merge group**, click the **Merge Cells** button. In the **Alignment group**, click the **Align Center** button.

21. In the second row of the table, select the second and third cells, and then on the Mini toolbar, click the **Bold** and **Center** buttons. In the second row, in the first cell, select the text *Day*, and then on the Mini toolbar, click the **Center** button.

22. In the second column, click in the cell containing *$20,320*, and then drag down and to the right to select the third cell of the second column through the eighth cell of the third column—*$17,800*. Click the **Home tab**, and then in the **Paragraph group**, click the **Align Text Right** button.

23. Display the **Print Preview** to make a final check of your document. **Save** your changes, and then submit your document as directed.

24. **Close** your document, and then **Exit** Word.

End **You have completed Project 7D**

Mastering Word

Project 7E—Photo Enhancement

In this project, you will apply the skills you practiced from the Objectives in Projects 7A and 7B.

Objectives: 1. *Insert and Format Graphics;* **3.** *Insert and Modify Text Boxes and Shapes;* **4.** *Create a Table;* **5.** *Format a Table.*

In the following Mastering Word project, you will create a handout that describes the photo enhancement services offered by Memories Old and New. Your completed document will look similar to Figure 7.58.

> ### For Project 7E, you will need the following files:
>
> w07E_Photo_Enhancement
> w07E_Chess
>
> **You will save your document as**
> **7E_Photo_Enhancement_Firstname_Lastname**

Figure 7.58

(Project 7E–Photo Enhancement continues on the next page)

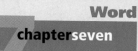
(Project 7E–Photo Enhancement continued)

1. Locate and open the file **w07E_Photo_Enhancement**. **Save** the file in your chapter folder as **7E_Photo_Enhancement_Firstname_Lastname** and then add the file name to the footer. Display formatting marks and rulers.

2. Position the insertion point at the beginning of the document. **Insert** a **Fun With Photos** vertical **WordArt** title using **WordArt style 12**—in the second row, the sixth style. Set the **Width** to **9 inches** and the **Height** to **.8 inch**. Note that with a vertical WordArt, the Width setting is actually the height.

3. Add **Square** text wrapping, and then drag the WordArt title so that the upper right corner is at **0 inches on the vertical ruler** and **6.5 inches on the horizontal ruler**.

4. Position the insertion point at the beginning of the document. **Insert** the picture **w07E_Chess**, and change the **Width** to **2.5 inches**. Change the **Text Wrapping** to **Square**, and then position left edge of the picture at **3 inches on the horizontal ruler**, and the top edge of the picture level with the top edge of the text.

5. Click to place the insertion point in the blank line at the end of the document, and then press Enter. **Insert** a **2x6 Table**, and then add the following text:

Photo Service	From
Remove people from a group	$40
Add special effects	20
Change the background	40
Remove red eyes	5
Restore old photos	50

6. Display the **Table Properties** dialog box and **Center** the table horizontally on the page. Click the **Column tab**, and then set the first column to **2.5 inches** wide, and set the width of the second column to **.6**

inch wide. In the second column of the table, format the cells that contain numbers with the **Align Text Right** command.

7. In the first row, apply **Center** and **Bold** to both cells. Select the first row of the table, display the **Shading gallery**, and the second color in the first row—**Black, Text 1** shading. **Save** your work.

8. Click to place the insertion point anywhere in the table and display the **Borders and Shading** dialog box. Click **Box**, and then change the line width to **1 1/2 pt**.

9. Press Ctrl + End. Display the **Shapes gallery**. Under **Stars and Banners**, click the first shape in the second row—**Vertical Scroll**. Starting at **7.25 inches on the vertical ruler**, and at **1 inch on the horizontal ruler**, draw a bevel that is **3 inches** wide by **1.5 inches** high. Use the **Size** buttons to make the measurements exact.

10. Right-click on the bevel, click **Add Text**, and type the following:

Memories Old and New
220 West Randolph Street
Chicago, IL 60601
312-555-0023

11. **Center** the bevel text, change the **Font** to **Calibri**, and increase the **Font Size** to **14**. If necessary, remove any spacing *After* the paragraphs, and set the *Line Spacing* to Single.

12. Select the first line of text in the bevel, apply **Bold**, and then change the **Font Size** to **16**. Display the **Shadow Effects gallery**, and then under **Additional Shadow Styles**, click **Shadow Style 16**. **Nudge Shadow Left** two clicks and **Nudge Shadow Up** two clicks.

(Project 7E–Photo Enhancement continues on the next page)

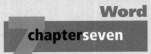

Mastering Word

(Project 7E–Photo Enhancement continued)

13. Move the bevel so that it is centered horizontally under the table, with the top edge at about **7.25 inches on the vertical ruler**. Add a **Box** page border to the document, using a **1 1/2 pt** line width and the default black color.

14. **Preview** the document, and then print it, or submit it electronically as directed. **Save** your changes. **Close** the file, and then **Exit** Word.

End **You have completed Project 7E** ————————————————

Content-Based Assessments

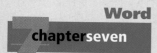
Mastering Word

Project 7F—Photo Restoration

In this project, you will apply the skills you practiced from the Objectives in Projects 7A and 7B.

Objectives: 1. *Insert and Format Graphics;* **2**. *Set Tab Stops;* **3**. *Insert and Modify Text Boxes and Shapes.*

In the following Mastering Word project, you will create a handout about photograph restoration services available at Memories Old and New. Your completed document will look similar to Figure 7.59.

For Project 7F, you will need the following files:

w07F_Original
w07F_Photo_Restoration
w07F_Quick_Restore

**You will save your document as
7F_Photo_Restoration_Firstname_Lastname**

Figure 7.59

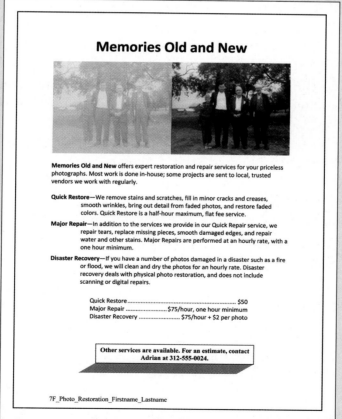

(Project 7F–Photo Restoration continues on the next page)

Content-Based Assessments

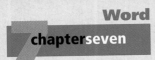

(Project 7F–Photo Restoration continued)

1. Locate and open the file **w07F_Photo_Restoration**. **Save** the file in your chapter folder as **7F_Photo_ Restoration_Firstname_Lastname** and then add the file name to the footer. Display formatting marks and rulers.

2. Position the insertion point in the blank line under the title. Locate and **Insert** the picture **w07F_Original**. Reduce the **Width** of the picture to **3 inches**, and then change the **Text Wrapping** of the picture to **Square**.

3. Click to position the insertion point in the blank line under the title, and then **Insert** the **w07F_Quick_Restore** picture. Format this second picture in the same manner you formatted the first picture. Move the second picture to the right of (and touching) the first picture—use Figure 7.59 as a guide.

4. Press Ctrl + End. Insert a **Right tab stop** at **5 inches on the horizontal ruler**. Display the **Paragraph** dialog box and set the **Left Indentation** to **1 inch**. Display the **Tabs** dialog box. Add a **dot leader** to the tab stop at **5 inches on the horizontal ruler**. Type the following text, pressing Tab between the service and the price:

Quick Restore	$50
Major Repair	$75/hour, one hour minimum
Disaster Recovery	$75/hour + $2 per photo

5. **Save** your changes. **Draw** a **Text Box** that is aligned with the left margin, with the top edge at **8 inches on the vertical ruler**. Use the **Size** buttons to change the **Width** to **4"** and the **Height** to **.5"**.

6. In the text box, type **Other services are available. For an estimate, contact Adrian at 312-555-0024.** Select all of the text in the text box, and use the Mini toolbar to **Center** the text and add **Bold** emphasis.

7. With the insertion point in the text box, display the **Shadow Effects gallery**. Under **Perspective Shadow**, add a **Shadow Style 8** shadow effect to the text box. Drag the text box to center it horizontally on the page, and position the top edge at about **7.75 inches on the vertical ruler**, as shown in Figure 7.59.

8. Add a **Box** page border, using a **1 1/2 pt** line width and the default black color.

9. **Save** your document. **Preview** the document, and then print it, or submit it electronically as directed. **Close** the file, and then **Exit** Word.

End You have completed Project 7F ——————————

Content-Based Assessments

Mastering Word

Project 7G — Student Days

In this project, you will apply the skills you practiced from all the Objectives in Projects 7A and 7B.

Objectives: 1. *Insert and Format Graphics;* **2.** *Set Tab Stops;* **3.** *Insert and Modify Text Boxes and Shapes;* **4.** *Create a Table;* **5.** *Format a Table.*

In the following Mastering Word Assessment, you will create a flyer for the Student Days celebration at Memories Old and New. Your completed document will look similar to Figure 7.60.

For Project 7G, you will need the following files:

New blank Word document
w07G_Student_Artist

You will save your document as
7G_Student_Days_Firstname_Lastname

Figure 7.60

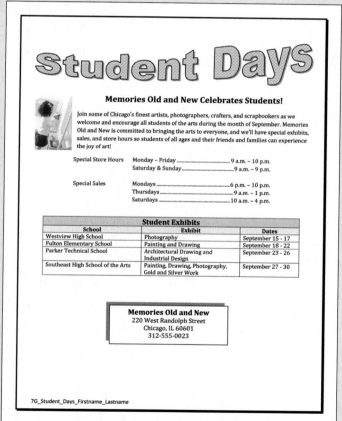

(Project 7G–Student Days continues on the next page)

Content-Based Assessments

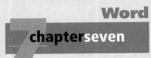
(Project 7G–Student Days continued)

1.   **Start** Word and be sure a new blank document is displayed. Display formatting marks and rulers. **Save** the document in your chapter folder as **7G_Student_Days_Firstname_Lastname** and add the file name to the footer. Change all four document margins to **.75 inch**. Change the **Font** to **Cambria** and be sure the **Font Size** is set to **11**.

2.   **Insert** a **Student Days** WordArt title, using the fifth style in the fourth row—**WordArt style 23**. Change the **WordArt** size to **7 inches** wide and **1.5 inches** high.

3.   Click to the right of the WordArt title, and then press Enter. Type **Memories Old and New Celebrates Students!** and press Enter. Select the text you just typed, **Center** the text, apply **Bold** emphasis, and then change the **Font Size** to **16**.

4.   Position the insertion point in the blank line below the title you just typed, press Enter, and then type the following text:

   Join some of Chicago's finest artists, photographers, crafters, and scrapbookers as we welcome and encourage all students of the arts during the month of September. Memories Old and New is committed to bringing the arts to everyone, and we'll have special exhibits, sales, and store hours so students of all ages and their friends and families can experience the joy of art!

5.   Press Enter. Insert a **Left tab stop** at **2.5 inches on the horizontal ruler**. Insert a **Right tab stop** at **6 inches on the horizontal ruler**. Display the **Tabs** dialog box. Add a **dot leader** to the tab stop at **6 inches**. Type the following text, pressing Tab between entries, and press Enter at the end of each line, including the last line. In the lines with no text in the first column, press Tab. Leave the third line blank:

Special Store Hours	Monday - Friday	9 a.m. - 10 p.m.
	Saturday & Sunday	9 a.m. - 9 p.m.
Special Sales	Mondays	6 p.m. - 10 p.m.
	Thursdays	9 a.m. - 1 p.m.
	Saturdays	10 a.m. - 4 p.m.

6.   Starting with the text that begins *Special Store Hours*, select the text from that point to the end of the document, but do not include the blank line at the end of the document. Display the **Paragraph** dialog box, set the **Left Indentation** to **1 inch**, and set the **Spacing After** to **0**.

7.   Press Ctrl + End, and then press Enter. Display the **Paragraph** dialog box and set the **Spacing After** to **0**. **Insert** a **3x6** table, and then add the following text:

Student Exhibits		
School	Exhibit	Dates
Westview High School	Photography	September 15 - 17
Fulton Elementary School	Painting and Drawing	September 18 - 22
Parker Technical School	Architectural Drawing and Industrial Design	September 23 - 26
Southeast High School of the Arts	Painting, Drawing, Photography, Gold and Silver Work	September 27 - 30

(Project 7G–Student Days continues on the next page)

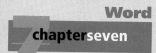

(Project 7G–Student Days continued)

8. Display the **Table Properties** dialog box and **Center** the table. Click the **Column tab**, and then set the first two columns to **2.5 inches** wide, and the third column to **1.5 inches** wide.

9. In the first row, merge the three cells, and then **Center** and **Bold** *Student Exhibits*, and change the **Font Size** to **14**. **Center** and **Bold** the text in the three cells in the second row of the table.

10. Select the first row of the table. On the **Design tab**, display the **Shading gallery**, and add the fourth color in the last column—**Orange, Accent 6, Lighter 40%** shading. Select the second row of the table, display the **Shading gallery**, and add the second shade in the last column—**Orange, Accent 6, Lighter 80%**. **Save** your work.

11. Place the insertion point to the left of the paragraph that begins *Join some of Chicago's*, and then from your student files, insert the picture **w07G_Student_Artist**. Change the **Height** of the picture to **1.4 inches**, and then apply **Square Text Wrapping**. Move the picture to the position shown in Figure 7.60 at the beginning of this project.

12. **Save** your changes. **Draw** a **Text Box** that is aligned with the left margin, with the top edge at **7.0 inches on the vertical ruler**. Use the **Size** buttons to change the **Height** to **1"** and the **Width** to **3"**. Select the paragraph mark in the text box, display the **Paragraph** dialog box, and then set the space **After** to **0** and the **Line Spacing** to **Single**. In the text box, type:

    Memories Old and New
    220 West Randolph Street
    Chicago, IL 60601
    312-555-0023

13. Select all of the text in the text box and **Center** the text. Change the **Font Size** to **12**. Select the top line of text in the text box, add **Bold** emphasis, and change the **Font Size** to **14**. Display the **Shadow Effects gallery**, and under **Drop Shadow**, click the first style—**Shadow Style 1**. Drag to center the text box under the table.

14. Add a **Shadow** page border, using a **2 1/4 pt** line width and the default black color.

15. **Preview** the document, and then print it, or submit it electronically as directed. **Save** your changes. **Close** the file, and then **Exit** Word.

End **You have completed Project 7G** ────────────────

Content-Based Assessments

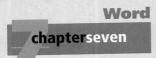

chapterseven Word

Mastering Word

Project 7H — *GO!* Fix It

In this project, you will apply the skills you practiced from the Objectives in Projects 7A and 7B.

For Project 7H, you will need the following file:

w07H_Digital_Dog_Flyer

You will save your document as
7H_Digital_Dog_Flyer_Firstname_Lastname

In this project, you will edit a flyer for a workshop on digital pet photography that is being prepared for Memories Old and New. From the student files that accompany this textbook, open the file **w07H_Digital_Dog_Flyer**, and then save the file in your chapter folder as **7H_Digital_Dog_Flyer_Firstname_Lastname**

This document contains errors that you must find and correct. Read and examine the document, and then edit to correct the errors that you find. Types of errors could include:

- Spelling, grammar, punctuation, and usage errors such as text case, repeated text, subject-verb agreement, and meaning.
- Content errors such as missing or incorrect text, pictures, or other objects.
- Font formatting and positioning errors such as font used, style, size, color, underline style, effects, font character spacing, text effects, special characters, and styles.
- Paragraph formatting and positioning errors such as indents and spacing, tabs, line and page breaks, wordwrap, sentence spacing, missing text, unnecessary text, or blank lines
- Image or object formatting and positioning errors relating to color, lines, size, scale, layout, positioning, or picture control.
- Page setup errors such as margins, orientation, layout, or alignment.

To complete the project you should:

- Be aware that there are no errors in sentence or paragraph spacing.
- Reformat the picture style of the dog image by using *Metal Frame*.
- Modify the words *Pet Photos?* in the title by applying WordArt style 9 with 36 pt font size.
- Format the Horizontal Scroll shape by applying Shadow Style 4.

(Project 7H–*GO!* Fix It continues on the next page)

Content-Based Assessments

(Project 7H–*GO!* Fix It continued)

- Modify the table by merging cells, aligning text in the first row and in the second column, and by applying Table Style *Linear Up Gradient - Dark*.

- Center the table horizontally on the page.

Save the changes you have made, add the file name to the footer, and then submit as directed.

End **You have completed Project 7H** ————————————

Outcomes-Based Assessments

Rubric

The following outcomes-based assessments are *open-ended assessments*. That is, there is no specific correct result; your result will depend on your approach to the information provided. Make *Professional Quality* your goal. Use the following scoring rubric to guide you in *how* to approach the problem, and then to evaluate *how well* your approach solves the problem.

The *criteria*—Software Mastery, Content, Format and Layout, and Process—represent the knowledge and skills you have gained that you can apply to solving the problem. The *levels of performance*—Professional Quality, Approaching Professional Quality, or Needs Quality Improvements—help you and your instructor evaluate your result.

	Your completed project is of Professional Quality if you:	Your completed project is Approaching Professional Quality if you:	Your completed project Needs Quality Improvements if you:
1-Software Mastery	Choose and apply the most appropriate skills, tools, and features and identify efficient methods to solve the problem.	Choose and apply some appropriate skills, tools, and features, but not in the most efficient manner.	Choose inappropriate skills, tools, or features, or are inefficient in solving the problem.
2-Content	Construct a solution that is clear and well organized, contains content that is accurate, appropriate to the audience and purpose, and is complete. Provide a solution that contains no errors of spelling, grammar, or style.	Construct a solution in which some components are unclear, poorly organized, inconsistent, or incomplete. Misjudge the needs of the audience. Have some errors in spelling, grammar, or style, but the errors do not detract from comprehension.	Construct a solution that is unclear, incomplete, or poorly organized; contains some inaccurate or inappropriate content; and contains many errors of spelling, grammar, or style. Do not solve the problem.
3-Format and Layout	Format and arrange all elements to communicate information and ideas, clarify function, illustrate relationships, and indicate relative importance.	Apply appropriate format and layout features to some elements, but not others. Overuse features, causing minor distraction.	Apply format and layout that does not communicate information or ideas clearly. Do not use format and layout features to clarify function, illustrate relationships, or indicate relative importance. Use available features excessively, causing distraction.
4-Process	Use an organized approach that integrates planning, development, self-assessment, revision, and reflection.	Demonstrate an organized approach in some areas, but not others; or, use an insufficient process of organization throughout.	Do not use an organized approach to solve the problem.

Outcomes-Based Assessments

Problem Solving

Project 7I — Books

In this project, you will apply the skills you practiced from the Objectives in Projects 7A and 7B.

For Project 7I, you will need the following file:

New blank Word document

You will save your document as
7I_Books_Firstname_Lastname

Memories Old and New carries an extensive line of books and periodicals for artists, photographers, students, teachers, and hobbyists. They have recently begun stocking a full line of scrapbooking books. In this project, you will create a flyer that includes a table of popular scrapbooking books for sale in the store.

To complete this assignment:

- Include a WordArt title, either with the name of the store, or the topic that is covered in the flyer.

- Write an opening paragraph introducing the topic.

- Create a table that consists of books on scrapbooking. The table should use at least three columns, including the author's name, the title of the book, and the book price. You should include at least six books in the table—use an online book dealer to search for appropriate titles.

- Format the table with a title that spans all of the columns and include a heading for each column. The title and column headings should be formatted distinctively.

- Include a text box with instructions for placing orders by phone.

- Include a shape with the name, address, and phone number of the store.

Add the file name to the footer. Check the flyer for spelling or grammar errors. Save the document as **7I_Books_Firstname_Lastname** and submit it as directed.

End **You have completed Project 7I** ——————————

Outcomes-Based Assessments

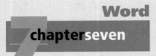
Problem Solving

Project 7J—Restoration Class

In this project, you will construct a solution by applying any combination of the skills you practiced from the Objectives in Projects 7A and 7B.

For Project 7J, you will need the following files:

New blank Word document
w07J_McArthur

You will save your document as
7J_Restoration_Class_Firstname_Lastname

Memories Old and New offers extensive photo restoration and photo recovery services. They also offer Beginner, Intermediate, and Advanced level classes on basic restoration techniques, using popular photograph manipulation software. Each level consists of two sessions that are four hours in length. Each session costs $50, and all six sessions can be taken for $250.

Create a flyer that can be handed out to customers in the store, and that contains information about the photo restoration classes. The flyer should include a decorative title, an introductory paragraph about Memories Old and New and photo restoration, and information about the classes. Format the information using a table, or using tab stops and dot leaders. You will need to include at least one text box with the name and address of the company, and one photo. If you have one or two old family photos that you would like to include, use those. Otherwise, use **w07J_McArthur**, which is included with your student files. Add a Picture Style or a Picture Effect to make the picture more visually interesting. The address information for Memories Old and New can be found in Activity 7.14.

Add the file name to the footer. Check the flyer for spelling or grammar errors. Save the document as **7J_Restoration_Class_Firstname_Lastname** and submit it as directed.

End **You have completed Project 7J** ——————

Outcomes-Based Assessments

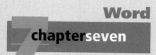

Problem Solving

Project 7K — Flower Show

In this project, you will construct a solution by applying any combination of the skills you practiced from the Objectives in Projects 7A and 7B.

For Project 7K, you will need the following files:

New blank Word document
w07K_Flower1
w07K_Flower2
w07K_Flower3
w07K_Flower4
w07K_Flower5
w07K_Flower6

**You will save your document as
7K_Flower_Show_Firstname_Lastname**

Memories Old and New is heavily involved in community activities. Every year, the neighborhood's small botanical garden—The Northwest Chicago Botanical Garden—sponsors a flower show, and solicits local businesses to participate and to help defray the expenses of the event. In return, participating companies receive good publicity. This year, Memories Old and New has agreed to create the event flyers.

In this project, you will create a flyer advertising the event. This year's event runs from May 20 to May 25. Admission is free, and the hours are from 10 a.m. until 7 p.m. on May 20–22; 10 a.m. until 5 p.m. on May 23; and Noon to 5 p.m. on May 24–25. On the flyer, the abbreviated name of the garden—NWC Botanical Garden—should display as a decorative title. One or two paragraphs are necessary to describe the details of the event, which include a flower show and flower sale, and activities for children. A table or tabbed list is necessary to convey information about dates and times. Include at least two pictures in the flyer. You can use any flower pictures you'd like, including the six that are included with your student files. Resize the pictures as necessary, and apply special effects to the pictures that enhance the overall design of the flyer. Add a banner indicating that Memories Old and New provided the flyers and that provides information about the company. Add an appropriate page border.

Save the flyer as **7K_Flower_Show_Firstname_Lastname** and then create a footer that contains file name. Submit the document as directed.

End You have completed Project 7K ————————————

More on your Student CD

The instructions for the following additional end-of-chapter projects are on your student CD in the folder 03_additional_end_of_chapter_projects.

Content-Based Assessments

Project L Mastering Word

Apply the skills you practiced in Project A.

Project M Mastering Word

Apply the skills you practiced in Project B.

Project N Business Running Case

Apply the skills you practiced in Projects A and B while helping an entrepreneur with the daily tasks of running a business.

In each chapter, this project focuses on applying the skills you have practiced in Projects A and B to a business. The project related to this business runs throughout the textbook. You will see how the Office programs relate to the day-to-day operation of a small business called Nelson Architectural Planning.

Outcomes-Based Assessments

Project O Problem Solving

Construct a solution by applying any combination of the skills you practiced from Projects A and B.

Project P Problem Solving

Construct a solution by applying any combination of the skills you practiced from Projects A and B.

Project Q You and GO!

Construct a solution that applies to your own life by applying any combination of the skills you practiced from Projects A and B.

Project R GO! with Help

Practice using Microsoft Office's Help Feature.

Project S Group Business Running Case

Work as part of a group to apply the skills you have gained thus far to help the Bell Orchid Hotel Group achieve its business goals.

Multimedia

The following multimedia accompany this textbook:

Companion Web site
www.prenhall.com/go

An interactive Web site designed to reinforce and test your understanding of the skills in this chapter.

AV-EDDs

In the folder in the front of this book you will find videos that demonstrate the objectives of the A and B projects in this chapter. These may help you understand how to complete the projects in this book.

Video Podcasts

In the folder in the front of this book are videos that can be played on your iPod, MP3 player, or computer. These videos demonstrate how to complete the more challenging objectives in this textbook.

8 chaptereight

Special Document Formats, Columns, and Mail Merge

OBJECTIVES

At the end of this chapter you will be able to:

1. Collect and Paste Text and Graphics
2. Create and Format Columns
3. Use Special Character and Paragraph Formatting
4. Create Mailing Labels by Using Mail Merge

OUTCOMES

Mastering these objectives will enable you to:

PROJECT 8A
Create a Multicolumn Newsletter and Print Mailing Labels

5. Insert Hyperlinks
6. Insert a SmartArt Graphic
7. Preview and Save a Document as a Web Page

PROJECT 8B
Create and Preview a Web Page

Georgia Gardens

Gardening and lawn care in the southern United States are year-round activities. More and more people are approaching what used to be considered a chore as a rewarding and exciting hobby. Southern Home Media produces the television show *Georgia Gardens* to present information on the proven methods, newest techniques, and hottest tools for growing healthy food and creating beautiful yards and gardens. The show's hosts also travel to interesting and lovely private and public gardens throughout the United States to provide viewers a glimpse into the many possibilities that gardening provides.

© iofoto Shutterstock

Using Special Document Formats, Columns, and Mail Merge

Creating a newsletter is usually a job reserved for desktop publishing programs, such as Microsoft Publisher. Word, however, has a number of tools that enable you to create a simple and attractive newsletter that effectively communicates your message.

Newsletters consist of a number of elements, but nearly all have a title, article headlines, articles, and graphics. The text of each article is typically split into two or three columns, which is easier to read than text formatted in a single, wide column. Newsletters are typically printed, but can also be designed to display as Web pages. A useful tool to couple with newsletters is mail merge, which enables you to print mailing labels.

Project 8A Garden Newsletter

In Activities 8.01 through 8.11, you will edit a newsletter for the *Georgia Gardens* subscribers. You will collect text and graphics from other documents, and then paste the collected information into a new document. You will change the text from one column to two columns, and then format the columns. You will use special text formatting features to change the font color and set off one of the paragraphs with a border and shading. Finally, you will create mailing labels for the newsletter. Your completed documents will look similar to Figure 8.1.

For Project 8A, you will need the following files:

New blank Word document
w08A_Tomatoes
w08A_Ornamental_Grasses
w08A_Pictures
w08A_Addresses

You will save your documents as
8A_Garden_Newsletter_Firstname_Lastname
8A_Mailing_Labels_Firstname_Lastname
8A_Addresses_Firstname_Lastname

Taylor Dunnahoo
189 Ventura Street
Rome, GA 30161

Daniel Echols
2000 St. Luke Place
Rome, GA 30165

Isabelle Riniker
8720 Natchez Trail
Rome, GA 30149

Byeong Chang
2221 S. Flowers Road
Atlanta, GA 30358

Ruth Thompson
4220 Thornewood Dr.
#320
Atlanta, GA 30317

Leland Wang
600 County Line NE
Atlanta, GA 30331

Julian Orndahl
34 Gloucester Pl.
Gainesville, GA 30504

Andrew Lau
975 Treetop Place
#G
Seneca, SC 29672

Anthony Blankenship
2820 Clairewood Terrace
Chattanooga, TN 37450

Phillip Scroggs
1518 Orchard Place West
Hunstville, AL 35806

Harriet Hasty
1875 Bullpen Dr.
Columbus, GA 31993

Georgia Gardens Newsletter

ORNAMENTAL GRASSES

As seen on *Georgia Gardens*, ornamental grasses can add new drama, texture, and color to your garden. Best of all, they tend to be very hardy and low-maintenance plants.

In the South, most ornamental grasses grow quickly in the spring and summer, bloom late in the summer and fall, and are dormant throughout the winter. They are very versatile—they can be annuals or perennials, and they can be ground covers or can reach up to 20 feet tall. Some have flowers and are brightly colored, and all have interesting textures and sway gracefully in the wind.

Ornamental grasses can be used as accent plants, but they can also be used to solve problems in your landscape. Try planting them to create a hedge, a border, or a groundcover.

Some dramatic ornamental grasses that do well in the South: Pampas Grass, which can reach up to 20 feet in height and has large silvery white flower plumes on long stems; Red Baron Japanese Blood Grass, which is about 12 to 18 inches tall and has bright red foliage in summer and fall; and Variegated Purple Moor Grass, which has purplish leaves with cream stripes.

To see more examples of how ornamental grasses can enhance your landscape, watch *Georgia Gardens.*

TOMATO TIPS

Few things taste more delicious than a freshly picked tomato from the garden in summer. With a little extra knowledge, you can help ensure a healthy tomato harvest this year.

After the last frost in your area, the soil should be warm enough to plant tomatoes. Choose a spot where the plants will receive at least six hours of sunlight each day. Due to the clay soil found in most of the South, it is recommended that you augment the soil with some peat moss or humus. You have the right mix if it crumbles when you squeeze a handful.

Be sure to dig a deep hole for the tomato plant. It should sit deeper in the ground than it does in the pot. This helps the roots grow stronger and produces a stronger plant. Add a little fertilizer to the soil before planting. Tomato plants can get very large and need extra support, so it is best to use stakes or a cage to hold them up so they won't fall over.

Water the plants well when you plant them, and then check them regularly to see if they need more water (wilted leaves are a sign that they need water). When you water, focus on the soil around the plant rather than watering the plant itself. Consider adding fertilizer after another six to eight weeks.

By following these tips, you should be able to enjoy a fruitful tomato season.

8A_Garden_Newsletter_Firstname_Lastname

Figure 8.1
Project 8A—Garden Newsletter

Objective 1
Collect and Paste Text and Graphics

When you perform the Copy command or the Cut command, the selected text or object is moved to the Office Clipboard. From the Office Clipboard storage area, you can paste the text or object into another location of your document, into a different document, or into another Office program.

You can copy and then paste a single selection of text without displaying the Clipboard task pane. However, displaying the Clipboard task pane is essential if you want to **collect and paste** information—collect a group of graphics or selected text blocks and then paste them into a document at any time. The Office Clipboard holds up to 24 items, and the Clipboard task pane displays a preview of each item.

Activity 8.01 Using Collect and Paste to Gather Images and Text

Newsletters typically contain articles written by different people and contain graphics from various sources. Use the Office Clipboard to collect all of the components of the newsletter in one place.

1 **Start** Word and display a new blank document. Display formatting marks and rulers. Display the **Save As** dialog box, navigate to your storage location, create a new folder named **Word Chapter 8** and then **Save** the document as **8A_Garden_Newsletter_Firstname_Lastname**

2 Add the file name to the footer, and then set the top, left, and right margins to **1 inch**, and the bottom margin to **0.5 inch**.

3 On the **Home tab**, in the **Clipboard group**, click the **Dialog Box Launcher** to display the **Clipboard** task pane. If any items display in the Clipboard, at the top of the task pane, click the **Clear All** button. At the bottom of the task pane, click the **Options** button, and then compare your screen with Figure 8.2.

> The options displayed in the list enable you to display the Clipboard task pane whenever you cut or copy an object, and also enable you to collect items without displaying the Clipboard task pane.

Figure 8.2

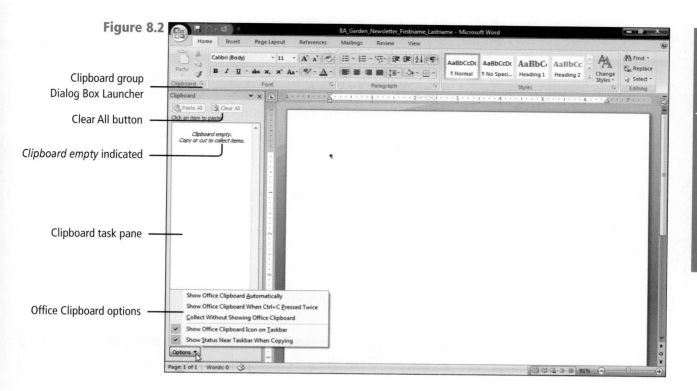

Clipboard group
Dialog Box Launcher

Clear All button

Clipboard empty indicated

Clipboard task pane

Office Clipboard options

---

4 Click anywhere in the document to close the **Options** list. Locate and open the file **w08A_Ornamental_Grasses**. Press Ctrl + A to select all of the text in the document, and then in the **Clipboard group**, click the **Copy** button. **Close** the **w08A_Ornamental_Grasses** file. Notice that the first few lines of text display in the Clipboard task pane, as shown in Figure 8.3.

Figure 8.3

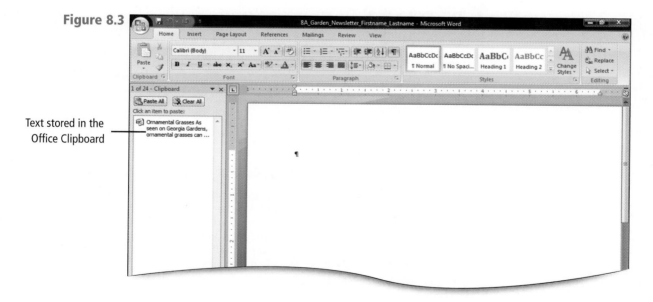

Text stored in the
Office Clipboard

5 Locate, and then **Open**, the file **w08A_Tomatoes**. Press `Ctrl` + `A` to select all of the text in the document, and then in the **Clipboard group**, click the **Copy** button 📋. **Close** ❎ the **w08A_Tomatoes** file.

> The copied text displays at the top of the Clipboard task pane.

6 Locate, and then **Open**, the file **w08A_Pictures**.

> This file contains no text; rather, the file contains three graphics— a WordArt title and two pictures. Recall that WordArt changes text into a decorative graphic.

7 Select the **Georgia Gardens Newsletter** WordArt title, and then in the **Clipboard group**, click the **Copy** button 📋 to copy it to the Office Clipboard. Use the same procedure to **Copy** 📋 the **Grass picture** on the left and the **Tomatoes picture** on the right.

8 **Close** ❎ the **w08A_Pictures** file, and notice that the Clipboard task pane contains five items, with the most recently copied item at the top of the list, as shown in Figure 8.4.

Figure 8.4

Most recently copied item at the top of the list

Five items stored in the Office Clipboard

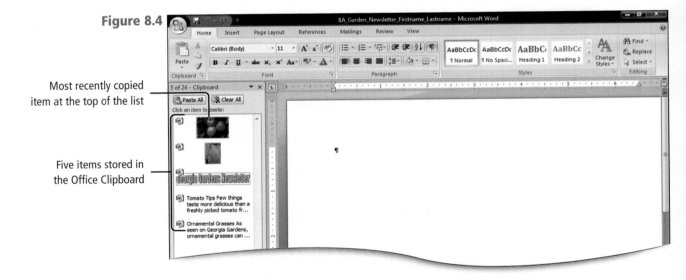

9 **Save** 💾 the document.

More Knowledge — Being Careful of Copyright Issues

You can collect and paste text and graphics from the Internet. However, nearly everything you find on the Internet is protected by *copyright* law, which protects authors of original works, including text, art, photographs, and music. If you want to use text or graphics that you find online, you will need to get permission. One of the exceptions to this law is the use of small amounts of information for educational purposes, which falls under fair use guidelines.

Copyright laws in the United States are open to different interpretations, and copyright laws can be very different in other countries. As a general rule, if you want to use someone else's material, always get permission first.

Activity 8.02 Pasting Information from the Clipboard Task Pane

1 With your **8A_Garden_Newsletter** file displayed, in the **Clipboard** task pane, locate and click the **Georgia Gardens Newsletter** WordArt title. Compare your screen with Figure 8.5.

> The WordArt title is pasted into the document at the insertion point location, and also remains available in the Office Clipboard.

Figure 8.5

WordArt title is pasted at the insertion point location

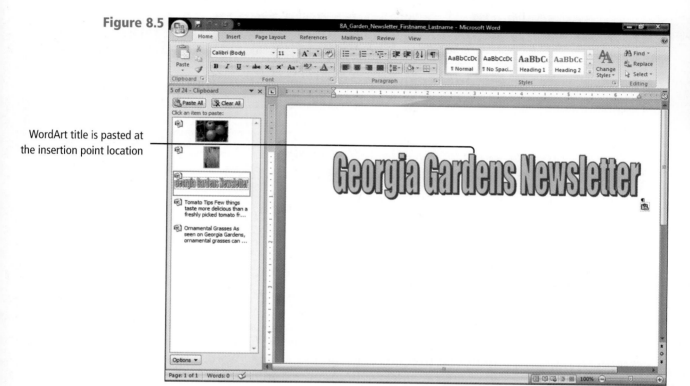

2 Press [Enter]. In the **Clipboard** task pane, click the text entry beginning *Ornamental Grasses* to paste the entire block of text at the insertion point.

3 In the **Clipboard** task pane, click the text entry beginning *Tomato Tips* to paste the entire block of text at the insertion point. Press [←Bksp] to remove the blank line at the bottom of the inserted text.

4 Select all of the text in the document except the WordArt title. Be sure to include the paragraph mark at the end of the document.

5 Right-click the selected text, and then click **Paragraph**. In the **Paragraph** dialog box, under **Spacing**, in the **After** box, click the **down spin arrow** to change the spacing to **6 pt**.

6 Under **Spacing**, click the **Line spacing arrow**, and then click **Single**. Click **OK** to close the **Paragraph** dialog box. Press [Ctrl] + [Home], and then compare your screen with Figure 8.6.

Figure 8.6

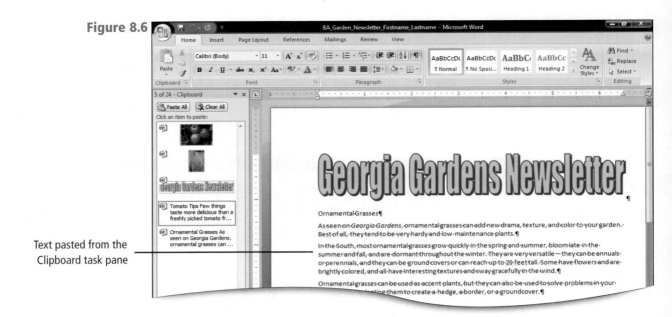

Text pasted from the Clipboard task pane

7 **Save** the document.

Objective 2
Create and Format Columns

All newspapers and most magazines and newsletters use multiple columns for articles because text in narrower columns is easier to read than text that stretches across a page. Word has a tool that enables you to change a single column of text into two or more columns, and then format the columns. If a column does not end where you want, you can end the column at a location of your choice by inserting a ***manual column break***.

Activity 8.03 Changing One Column of Text to Two Columns

Newsletters are usually two or three columns wide. When using 8.5 × 11-inch paper in portrait orientation, avoid creating four or more columns because they are so narrow that word spacing looks awkward, often resulting in one long word by itself on a line.

1 Select all of the text in the document except the WordArt title. Be sure to include the paragraph mark at the end of the document.

2 Click the **Page Layout tab**, and then in the **Page Setup group**, click the **Columns** button. From the **Columns gallery**, click **Two**, scroll to the top of the document, and then compare your screen with Figure 8.7.

> The text is divided into two columns, and a section break is inserted below the WordArt title, dividing the one-column section of the document from the two-column section of the document. Do not be concerned if your columns do not break at the same line as shown in the figure.

Figure 8.7

Word | Chapter 8

Two-column format

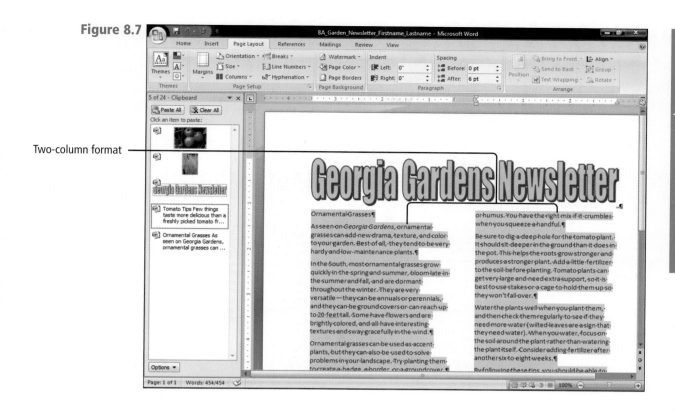

3 **Save** the document.

Activity 8.04 Formatting Multiple Columns

The uneven right edge of a single page-width column is readable. When you create narrow columns, justified text is sometimes preferable. The font you choose should also match the style of newsletter you are creating.

1 With the text still selected, click the **Home tab**. In the **Font group**, click the **Font button arrow**, scroll down the font list, and then click **Comic Sans MS**.

2 In the **Font group**, click the **Font Size button arrow**, and then click **10**.

3 In the **Paragraph group**, click the **Justify** button . Click anywhere in the document to deselect the text, and then compare your screen with Figure 8.8.

The document displays in 10 pt. Comic Sans MS font, an informal and easy-to-read font; the text is justified.

Figure 8.8

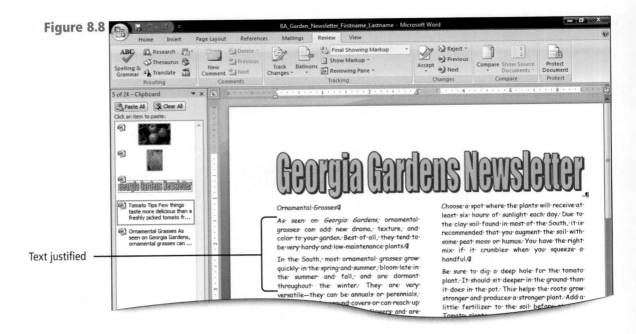

Text justified

4 **Save** 🖫 the document.

More Knowledge — Justifying Column Text

Although many magazines and newspapers still justify text in columns, there is a great deal of disagreement about whether to justify the columns, or to use left alignment and leave the right edge uneven. Justified text tends to look more formal and cleaner, but in a word processing document, it also results in uneven spacing between words. It is the opinion of some authorities that justified text is more difficult to read.

Activity 8.05 Inserting a Column Break

Insert manual column breaks to adjust columns that end or begin awkwardly, or to make space for graphics or text boxes.

1 From the **Office** menu ⓐ, point to **Print**, and then click **Print Preview**. Notice that the columns end unevenly.

2 In the **Preview group**, click the **Close Print Preview** button. Scroll down, and then near the bottom of the first column, position the insertion point to the left of *Tomato Tips*.

3 Click the **Page Layout tab**, and then in the **Page Setup group**, click the **Breaks** button to display the **Page and Section Breaks gallery**, as shown in Figure 8.9.

Figure 8.9

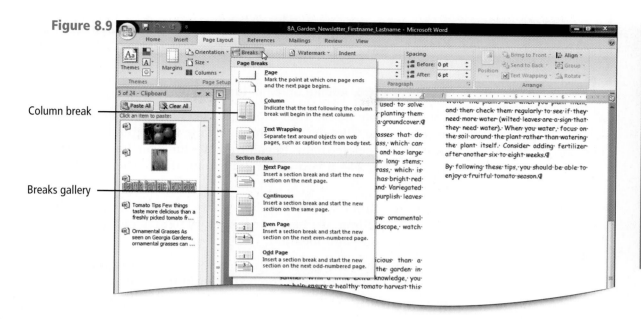

Column break

Breaks gallery

4 From the **Breaks gallery**, under **Page Breaks**, click **Column**.

The column breaks at the insertion point, and the text to the right of the insertion point moves to the top of the next column.

5 From the **Office** menu 🔵, point to **Print**, and then click **Print Preview**. Compare your screen with Figure 8.10.

The columns are more even, although they still do not align at exactly the same line. The bottom alignment will be adjusted when graphics are added to the newsletter.

Figure 8.10

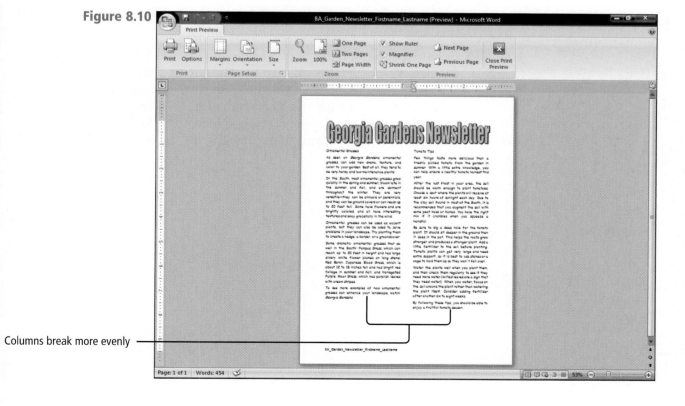

Columns break more evenly

6 In the **Preview group**, click the **Close Print Preview** button, and then **Save** 🖫 the document.

Activity 8.06 Adding Graphics to Columns

You can paste items from the Clipboard task pane at any time. Items on the Office Clipboard remain available throughout your Word session unless you delete them. Recall that the limit for items on the Office Clipboard is 24—if you add a 25th item, the earliest item added is removed.

1 In the first column, click anywhere to position the insertion point. In the **Clipboard** task pane, click the **grass** picture to paste it at the insertion point location.

2 Right-click the **grass** picture, point to **Text Wrapping**, and then click **Square** to wrap the text around the picture.

3 Right-click the **grass** picture, and then from the shortcut menu, click **Size**. In the **Size** dialog box, under **Scale**, select the **Lock aspect ratio** check box. Under **Size and rotate**, click the **Height down spin arrow** as necessary to set the picture height to **2″**.

> Recall that the aspect ratio is the ratio of the height to the width of an object. Locking the aspect ratio ensures that the proportions of the object will remain unchanged when either the height or width is changed.

4 At the bottom of the **Size** dialog box, click the **Close** button. Drag the picture to the left margin of the first column, with the top edge of the picture even with the top of the paragraph beginning *In the South*.

5 In the second column, click anywhere to position the insertion point. In the **Clipboard** task pane, click the **tomatoes** picture to paste it at the insertion point location.

6 Use the procedure you just practiced to set the **Text Wrapping** to **Square**. Proportionally change the **Height** to **1.2″**. Drag the picture to the right margin of the second column, with the top edge at approximately **5.5 inches on the vertical ruler**, as shown in Figure 8.11. Recall that you can more precisely adjust the position of the picture by holding down Ctrl and then pressing the arrow keys.

Figure 8.11

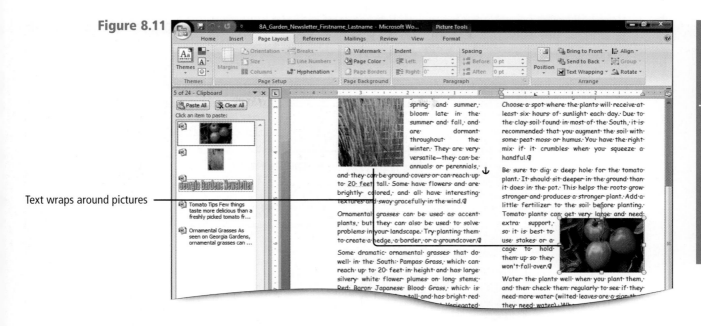

Text wraps around pictures

7 Near the top of the **Clipboard** task pane, click the **Clear All** button to remove all items from the Office Clipboard. **Close** ☒ the Clipboard task pane.

8 **Save** 🖫 the document.

Objective 3
Use Special Character and Paragraph Formatting

Special text and paragraph formatting is useful to emphasize text, and it makes your newsletter look more professional. There are various ways to call attention to specific text. One way is to place a border around a paragraph. Another is to shade a paragraph, although use caution not to make the shade too dark, because shading can make the text difficult to read.

Activity 8.07 Using Small Caps and Changing the Font Color

For headlines and titles, *small caps* is an attractive font effect. Lowercase letters are changed to uppercase letters but remain the height of lowercase letters. Titles are frequently formatted using this style.

1 Press [Ctrl] + [Home]. At the top of the first column, select the text *Ornamental Grasses*. Be sure to include the paragraph mark.

2 Right-click the selected text, and then from the shortcut menu, click **Font**. In the **Font** dialog box, click the **Font color arrow**, and then under **Theme Colors**, in the last column, click **Orange, Accent 6, Darker 50%**.

3 Under **Font style**, click **Bold**. Under **Size**, click **18**. Under **Effects**, select the **Small caps** check box. Compare your screen with Figure 8.12.

> The Font dialog box gives you more options than are available on the Ribbon, and enables you to make several changes at the same time. In the Preview box, the text displays with the selected formatting options applied.

Figure 8.12

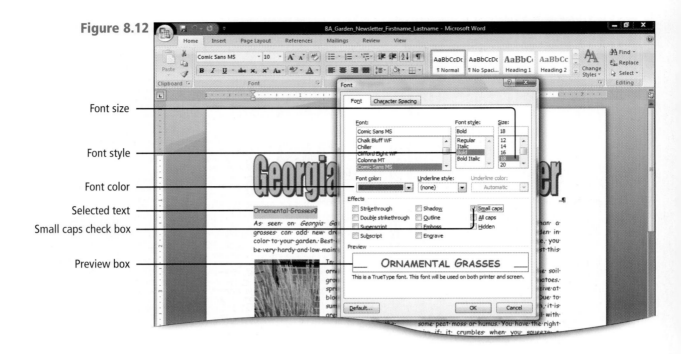

Font size ——

Font style ——

Font color ——

Selected text ——

Small caps check box ——

Preview box ——

4 At the bottom of the **Font** dialog box, click **OK**.

5 At the top of the second column, select the text *Tomato Tips*. Use the technique you just practiced to apply the same formatting that you added to the title of the first column. Click anywhere in the document to deselect the text, and then compare your screen with Figure 8.13.

Figure 8.13

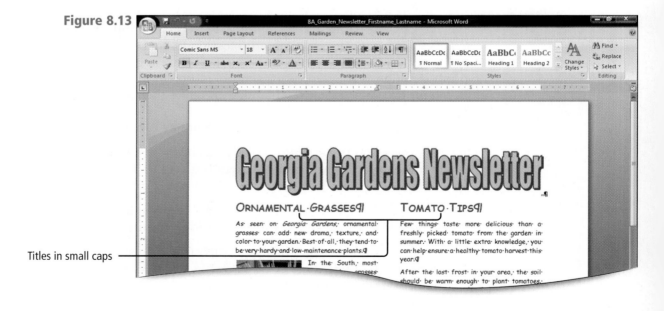

Titles in small caps ——

6 **Save** the document.

Activity 8.08 Adding a Border and Shading to a Paragraph

Paragraph borders provide strong visual cues to the reader. Shading can be used with or without borders. When used with a border, light shading can be very effective in drawing the reader's eye to the text.

1 At the bottom of the first column, in the paragraph that begins *To see more examples*, triple-click in the paragraph to select it. On the **Home tab**, in the **Paragraph group**, click the **Border button arrow**, and then click **Borders and Shading**.

2 In the **Borders and Shading** dialog box, be sure the **Borders tab** is selected. Under **Setting**, click **Box**. Click the **Width arrow**, and then click **1 1/2 pt**. Click the **Color arrow**, and then in the last column, click **Orange, Accent 6, Darker 50%**. Compare your screen with Figure 8.14.

In the lower right portion of the Borders and Shading dialog box, the *Apply to* box displays *Paragraph*. The *Apply to* box directs where the border will be applied—in this instance, the border will be applied to the selected paragraph.

Figure 8.14

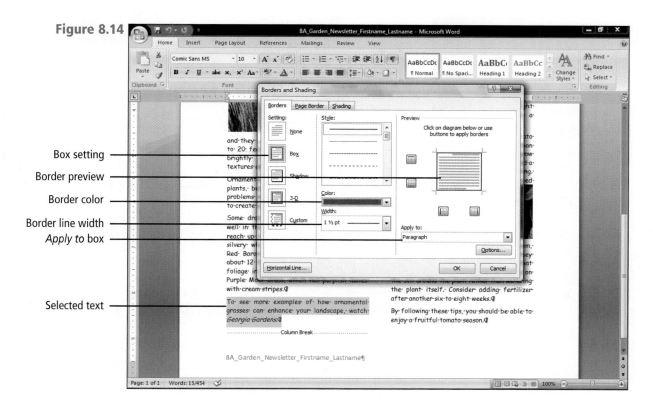

Box setting
Border preview
Border color
Border line width
Apply to box
Selected text

Note — Adding Simple Borders to Text

Simple borders and border edges can be added using the Border button in the Paragraph group. This button offers very little control, however, because line thickness and color depend on the previous thickness and color chosen from the Borders and Shading dialog box.

3 At the top of the **Borders and Shading** dialog box, click the **Shading tab**.

4 Click the **Fill arrow**, and then in the last column, click **Orange, Accent 6, Lighter 80%**. At the bottom of the **Borders and Shading** dialog box, click **OK**. Click anywhere in the document to deselect the text, and then compare your screen with Figure 8.15.

Figure 8.15

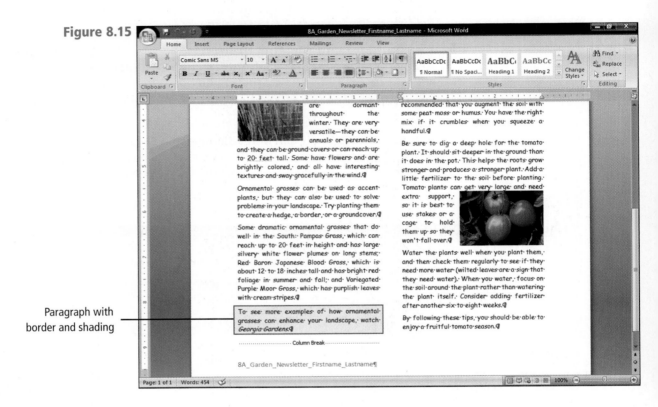

Paragraph with border and shading

5 **Save** the document, submit your file as directed, and then **Exit** Word.

Objective 4
Create Mailing Labels by Using Mail Merge

Word's *mail merge* feature joins a main document and a data source to create customized letters or labels. The *main document* contains the text or formatting that remains constant. In the case of labels, the main document contains the formatting for a specific label size. The *data source* contains information including the names and addresses of the individuals for whom the labels are being created. Names and addresses in a data source might come from a Word table, an Excel spreadsheet, or an Access database.

The easiest way to perform a mail merge is to use the Mail Merge Wizard. Recall that a wizard asks you questions and, based on your answers, walks you step-by-step through a process.

Activity 8.09 Opening the Mail Merge Wizard Template

Mail merge information can be stored in various formats and programs, including Microsoft Word tables. Such tables can be edited in the same manner as other Word tables.

1 **Start** Word and display a new blank document. Display formatting marks and rulers. **Save** the document in your **Word Chapter 8** folder as **8A_Mailing_Labels_Firstname_Lastname**

2 **Open** the file **w08A_Addresses**—be sure to use **w08A** and not one of the other address files. **Save** the address file in your **Word Chapter 8** folder as **8A_Addresses_Firstname_Lastname**

> A table of addresses displays. The first row contains the column names. The remaining rows contain addresses. This data file will be modified, but is not intended for submission to your instructor.

3 Click to position the insertion point in the last cell in the table, and then press [Tab] to create a new row. Enter the following information, and then compare your table with Figure 8.16.

First Name	**Duncan**
Last Name	**McArthur**
Address 1	**3336 S. Flowers Rd.**
Address 2	**#234**
City	**Macon**
State	**GA**
ZIP Code	**31217**

Figure 8.16

Column names

New row

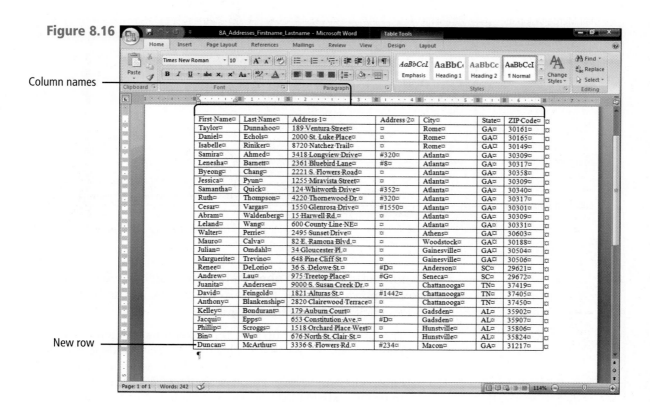

4 **Save** 💾, and then **Close** ❎ the table of addresses; be sure your **8A_Mailing_Labels** document displays.

5 Click the **Mailings tab**. In the **Start Mail Merge group**, click the **Start Mail Merge** button, and then click **Step by Step Mail Merge Wizard** to display the **Mail Merge** task pane. Under **Select document type**, click the **Labels** option button.

6 At the bottom of the task pane, click **Next: Starting document** to display **Step 2 of 6** of the Mail Merge Wizard. Under **Select starting document**, be sure **Change document layout** is selected, and then under **Change document layout**, click **Label options**.

7 In the **Label Options** dialog box, under **Printer information**, click the **Tray arrow**, and then click **Default tray (Automatically Select)**—your wording may vary—to print the labels on regular paper, rather than feeding label pages manually.

8 Under **Label information**, click the **Label vendors arrow**, and then click **Avery US Letter**. Under **Product number**, scroll about halfway down the list, and then click **5160**. Compare your screen with Figure 8.17.

> The Avery 5160 address label is a commonly used label. The precut sheets contain three columns of 10 labels each—for a total of 30 labels per sheet.

Figure 8.17

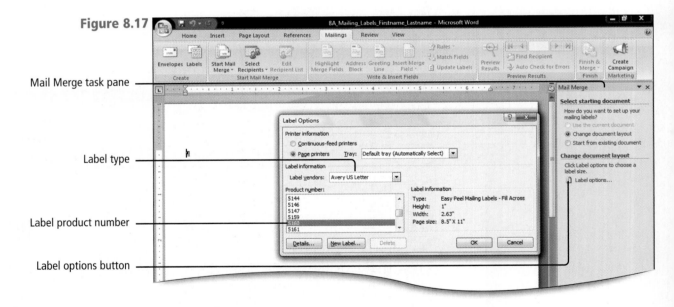

Mail Merge task pane

Label type

Label product number

Label options button

9 At the bottom of the **Label Options** dialog box, click **OK**. If a message box displays, click OK to set up the labels. At the bottom of the task pane, click **Next: Select recipients**.

> The label page is set up with three columns and ten rows. The label borders may or may not display on your screen, depending on your setup. In Step 3 of the Mail Merge Wizard, you must identify the recipients—the data source. For your recipient data source, you can choose to use an existing list—for example, a list of names and addresses that you have in an Access database, an Excel worksheet, a Word table, or

your Outlook contacts list. If you do not have an existing data source, you can type a new list at this point in the wizard.

10 Under **Select recipients**, be sure the **Use an existing list** option button is selected. Under **Use an existing list**, click **Browse**. Navigate to your **Word Chapter 8** folder, select your **8A_Addresses_Firstname_Lastname** file, and then click **Open** to display the Mail Merge Recipients dialog box, as shown in Figure 8.18.

The labels in the first row of the Word table display as the column headings in the Mail Merge Recipients dialog box. In a database or Word address table, each row of information that contains data for one person is called a **record**. The column headings—for example, *Last_Name* and *First_Name*—are referred to as **fields**. An underscore replaces the spaces between words in the field names.

Figure 8.18

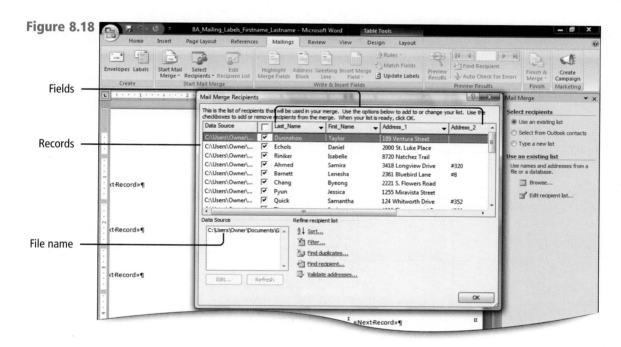

Fields

Records

File name

Activity 8.10 Completing the Mail Merge Wizard

You can add or edit names and addresses while completing the Mail Merge Wizard. You can also match your column names with preset names used in Mail Merge; for example, if the column heading for city names was *Place*, you could match that column with the *City* field to create the correct address blocks.

1 Near the bottom of the **Mail Merge Recipients** dialog box, under **Data Source**, click the file name. At the bottom of the **Mail Merge Recipients** dialog box, click **Edit**.

The Data Form dialog box displays. You can edit or delete the selected record, or use the same dialog box to add a new recipient.

2 On the right side of the **Data Form** dialog box, click **Add New**. In the blank record, type the following, pressing `Tab` to move from field to field, and then compare your **Data Form** dialog box with Figure 8.19:

First_Name	**Harriet**
Last_Name	**Hasty**
Address_1	**1875 Bullpen Dr.**
Address_2	
City	**Columbus**
State	**GA**
ZIP_Code	**31993**

Figure 8.19

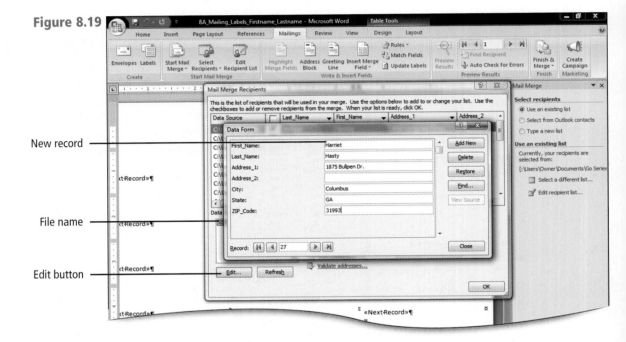

New record

File name

Edit button

3 At the bottom of the **Data Form** dialog box, click **Close**. Scroll to the end of the recipient list to confirm that the record you just added is in the list. At the bottom of the **Mail Merge Recipients** dialog box, click **OK**, and then click **Next: Arrange your labels**.

At Step 4 of the Mail Merge Wizard, Word provides various ways to arrange and add features to your labels.

4 Under **Arrange your labels**, click **Address block**. In the **Insert Address Block** dialog box, under **Specify address elements**, examine the various formats for names. If necessary, under **Insert recipient's name in this format**, select the **Joshua Randall Jr.** format. Compare your dialog box with Figure 8.20.

Figure 8.20

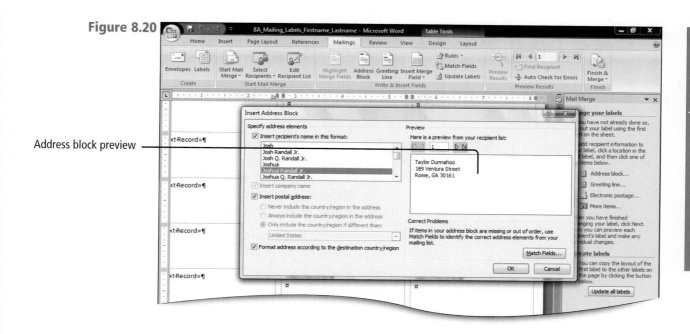

Address block preview ——

5 Near the lower right corner of the **Insert Address Block** dialog box, click **Match Fields**. Scroll down and examine the dialog box, and then compare your screen with Figure 8.21.

If your field names are descriptive, the Mail Merge program will identify them correctly, as is the case with the information in the *Required for Address Block* section. If you need to match a field, display the list to choose the correct field from your database or table.

Figure 8.21

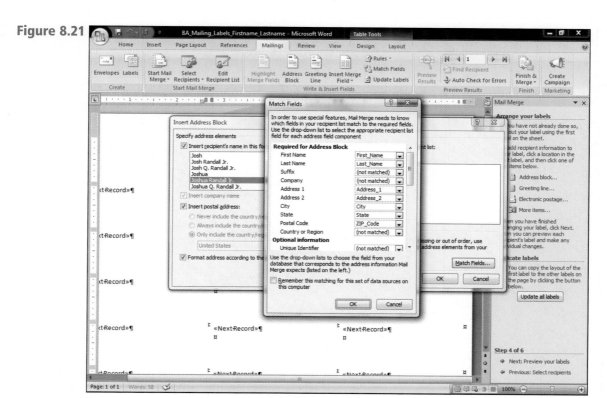

6 At the bottom of the **Match Fields** dialog box, click **OK**. At the bottom of the **Insert Address Block** dialog box, click **OK**.

> The Address block is inserted in the first label space and is surrounded by double angle brackets. The *AddressBlock* field name displays, which represents the address block you saw in the Preview area of the Insert Address Block dialog box.

7 In the upper left corner of the document, select the **<<AddressBlock>>** field. Be sure to include the paragraph mark. Click the **Page Layout tab**, and in the **Paragraph group**, under **Spacing**, use the **spin box arrows** to set the **Before** and **After** boxes to **0** to ensure that the four-line addresses will fit on the labels.

8 In the task pane, under **Replicate labels**, click **Update all labels** to insert an address block in each label space for each subsequent record.

9 Click **Next: Preview your labels**. If the address block lines are spaced too far apart and some of the text at the bottom of the labels is cut off, press ⌃ Ctrl + A to select the entire document, and then on the Home tab, in the Styles group, click the No Spacing style. If necessary, scroll to the left to view the left edge of the page, and then compare your labels with Figure 8.22.

> Some Word defaults add extra spacing after paragraphs. Changing the line spacing ensures that the address blocks will fit properly on the labels. In some cases, where there is an apartment or unit number, there are addresses on two lines. The wizard creates the lines automatically when the Address Block is inserted.

Figure 8.22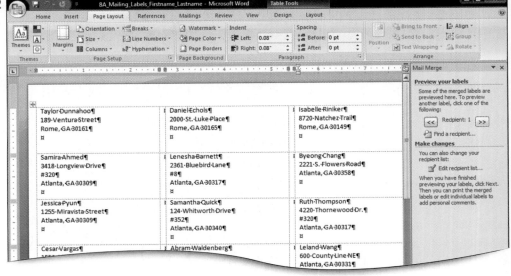

10 At the bottom of the task pane, click **Next: Complete the merge**.

> Step 6 of the Mail Merge task pane displays. At this point you can print or edit your labels, although this is done more easily in the document window.

11 **Save** 🖫 your labels, and then **Close** ☒ the **Mail Merge** task pane.

Activity 8.11 Previewing and Printing the Mail Merge Document

Before you print, preview your labels to be sure the information fits in the space reserved for each label.

1 Add the file name to the footer, and then close the footer area. From the **Office** menu 🔵, point to the **Print arrow**, and then click **Print Preview**. Position the 🔍 pointer over the labels and click one time. Compare your screen with Figure 8.23.

> Adding footer text to a label sheet replaces the last row of labels on a page with the footer text, and moves the last row of labels to the top of the next page. In this case, a blank second page is created.

Figure 8.23

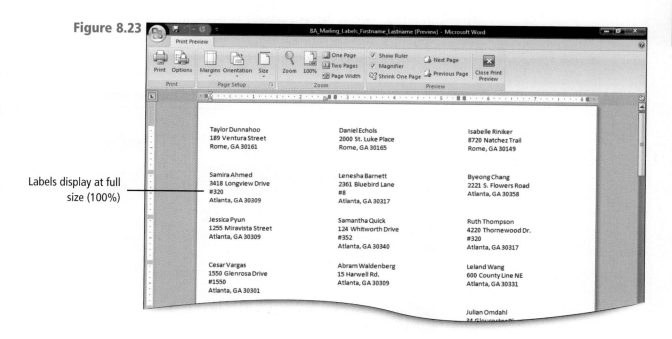

Labels display at full size (100%)

2 To submit electronically, follow your instructor's directions. Otherwise, on the **Print Preview tab**, in the **Print group**, click the **Print** button. In the **Print** dialog box, under **Page range**, click the **Current page** option button, and then click **OK**.

> The labels will print on whatever paper is in the printer. In this case, unless you have preformatted labels available, you will print your labels on a sheet of paper. Printing the labels on plain paper first enables you to proofread the labels before you print them on more expensive label sheets.

3 On the **Print Preview tab**, in the **Preview group**, click the **Close Print Preview** button.

4 **Close** the document, click **Yes** to save the data source, click **Yes** to save the labels, and then **Exit** Word.

End **You have completed Project 8A** ————————

Project 8B Television Hosts

In Activities 8.12 through 8.18, you will edit a document that introduces the hosts of the *Georgia Gardens* television show. You will add links to text and graphics, and you will add a SmartArt graphic. Finally, you will save the document as both a Word document and as a Web page. Your completed documents will look similar to Figure 8.24.

For Project 8B, you will need the following file:

w08B_Television_Hosts

You will save your documents as
8B_Television_Hosts_Firstname_Lastname
8B_Television_Hosts_Firstname_Lastname.mht

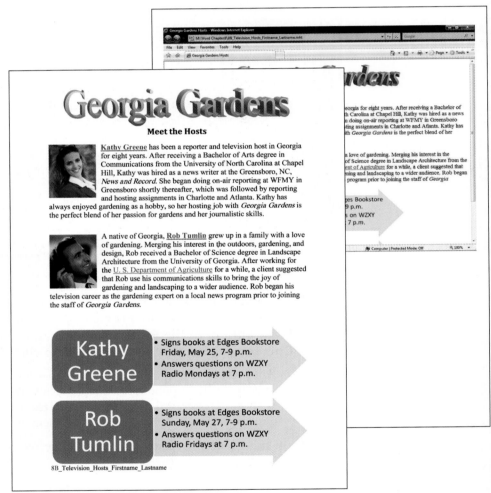

Figure 8.24
Project 8B—Television Hosts

Objective 5
Insert Hyperlinks

Organizations publish information on the Web. Microsoft Word has tools that enable the creation of Web pages directly from word processing documents. **Hyperlinks** can be added to move to related sites quickly. Hyperlinks are text or graphics that you click to move to a file, another page in a Web site, or a page in a different Web site.

Activity 8.12 Inserting Text Hyperlinks

The type of hyperlink used most frequently is one that is attached to text. Text hyperlinks usually display underlined and in blue.

1 **Start** Word. Locate and open the document **w08B_Television_Hosts**. Display formatting marks. Save the document in your **Word Chapter 8** folder as **8B_Television_Hosts_Firstname_Lastname** Add the file name to the footer.

2 In the paragraph to the right of the upper picture, select the text *Kathy Greene*. Click the **Insert tab**, and then in the **Links group**, click the **Hyperlink** button.

3 In the **Insert Hyperlink** dialog box, under **Link to**, be sure **Existing File or Web Page** is selected. In the **Address** box, type **http://www.georgiagardens.tv/hosts/greene.htm**

When you begin to type, AutoComplete may display an address in the Address box. It displays the Web address typed most recently in this dialog box or in your Web browser. The Georgia Gardens Web addresses used in this project are not live links.

4 In the upper right corner of the **Insert Hyperlink** dialog box, click **ScreenTip**. In the **Set Hyperlink ScreenTip** dialog box, under **ScreenTip text**, type **Kathy Greene Biography** and then compare your screen with Figure 8.25.

This is the ScreenTip that will display when the pointer is moved over the hyperlink.

Figure 8.25

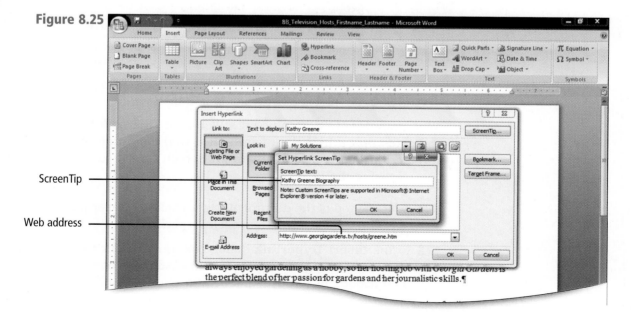

ScreenTip

Web address

5 In the **Set Hyperlink ScreenTip** dialog box, click **OK**. At the bottom of the **Insert Hyperlink** dialog box, click **OK**.

> The hyperlink is recorded, and the selected text changes to blue and is underlined.

6 In the next paragraph, in the first line, select the text *Rob Tumlin*. Using the technique you just practiced, create a hyperlink to the address **http://www.georgiagardens.tv/hosts/tumlin.htm** and then as the **ScreenTip**, type **Rob Tumlin Biography**

7 In the same paragraph, select the text *U. S. Department of Agriculture*. Using the technique you just practiced, create a hyperlink to the address **http://www.usda.gov** and then as the **ScreenTip**, type **Department of Agriculture**

8 **Save** 🖫 your document, and then compare your screen with Figure 8.26.

Figure 8.26

Inserted hyperlinks

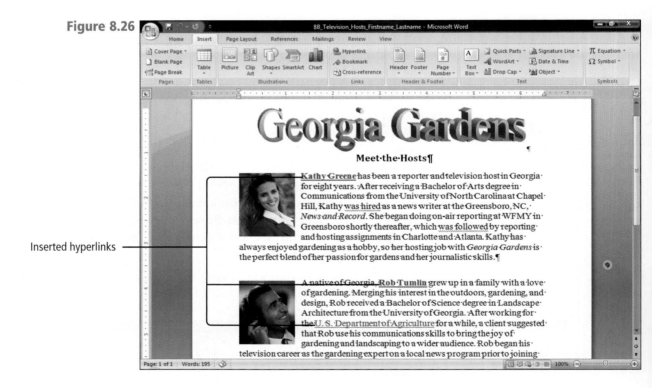

Activity 8.13 Adding a Hyperlink to a Graphic

When pointing to a graphic on a Web page, the Link Select pointer 🖑 indicates that a hyperlink is attached to the graphic. When you point to a hyperlink in a Word document, a ScreenTip displays with instructions for accessing the link.

1 Near the top of the document, right-click the upper picture—the picture of *Kathy Greene*—and then click **Hyperlink**.

2 In the **Insert Hyperlink** dialog box, under **Link to**, be sure **Existing File or Web Page** is selected. In the **Address** box, type **http://www. georgiagardens.tv/hosts/greene.htm**

This is the same address you typed for the text in the paragraph to the right of the picture. In this document, there will be two hyperlinks to the same address for each host.

3 In the upper right corner of the **Insert Hyperlink** dialog box, click **ScreenTip**. In the **Set Hyperlink ScreenTip** dialog box, under **ScreenTip text**, type **Kathy Greene Biography** and then **Close** both dialog boxes.

4 Click to deselect the picture. Point to the *Kathy Greene* picture and notice the ScreenTip and the Web address in the status bar, as shown in Figure 8.27. Use the same procedure to check the *Kathy Greene* text hyperlink.

Figure 8.27

Hyperlink ScreenTip

Web address in status bar

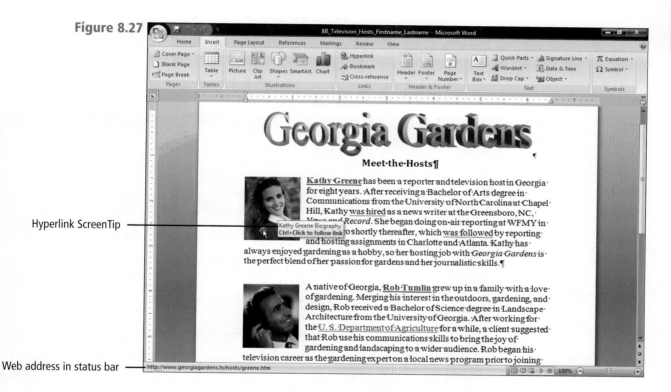

5 Right-click the lower picture—the picture of *Rob Tumlin*—and click **Hyperlink**. Using the technique you just practiced, create a hyperlink to the address **http://www.georgiagardens.tv/hosts/tumlin.htm** and then type **Rob Tumlin Biography** as the ScreenTip.

6 **Save** the document.

More Knowledge — Adding an E-Mail Hyperlink

You can also add a hyperlink to an e-mail address in a document. Select the text that you want to link to, and then display the Insert Hyperlink dialog box. Under Link to, click E-mail Address. Type the e-mail address, or select it from the *Recently used e-mail addresses* list. If desired, type a Subject line. You can also click the ScreenTip button to add a ScreenTip to the hyperlink.

Activity 8.14 Testing and Modifying Hyperlinks

1 Be sure you have an Internet connection. Point to the *U. S. Department of Agriculture* hyperlink and read the ScreenTip. Follow the ScreenTip directions to test the hyperlink.

> Your computer may be configured to click to activate a hyperlink, or you may be required to hold down Ctrl, and then click the hyperlink.

2 **Close** ⊠ your browser window and return to your Word document. Point to the *U. S. Department of Agriculture* hyperlink, right-click, and then click **Edit Hyperlink**.

3 At the bottom of the **Edit Hyperlink** dialog box, in the **Address** box, change the address to **http://www.usna.usda.gov/Gardens/collections/friend.html** Be sure to capitalize *Gardens*.

4 In the upper right corner of the **Edit Hyperlink** dialog box, click **ScreenTip**. Change the ScreenTip to **USDA Friendship Garden** and then compare your dialog box with Figure 8.28.

Figure 8.28

ScreenTip changed ——

Hyperlink address changed ——

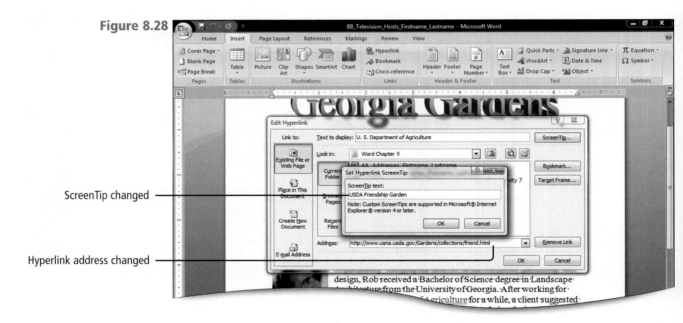

Note — If the Text Displays Automatically

When you begin typing the text in the text boxes of the Edit Hyperlink dialog box, the complete text may display after typing only a few letters. This indicates that another student used the computer to complete this project and that the AutoComplete feature is turned on.

5 Click **OK** to close both dialog boxes. Point to the *U. S. Department of Agriculture* hyperlink and read the new ScreenTip. Follow the ScreenTip directions to test the new hyperlink address. **Close** ⊠ your browser window and return to your Word document.

6 **Save** 🖫 the document.

Objective 6
Insert a SmartArt Graphic

SmartArt graphics are designer-quality visual representations of information that you can create by choosing from among many different layouts. Insert a SmartArt graphic to more effectively communicate your messages or ideas, and to add visual appeal to a document or a Web page.

Activity 8.15 Inserting a SmartArt Graphic

1 Press [Ctrl] + [End] to move to the end of the document, and then press [Enter].

2 Click the **Insert tab**, and then in the **Illustrations group**, point to the **SmartArt** button to display its ScreenTip. Read the ScreenTip, and then click the button.

3 In the **Choose a SmartArt Graphic** dialog box, use the scroll bar to examine the types of SmartArt graphics available to you.

4 After examining the SmartArt graphics, scroll to the top of the list, and then in the fifth row, click the first graphic—**Vertical Arrow List**. At the right of the dialog box, notice the preview and description of the graphic, as shown in Figure 8.29.

Figure 8.29

Preview and description

Vertical Arrow List
SmartArt graphic

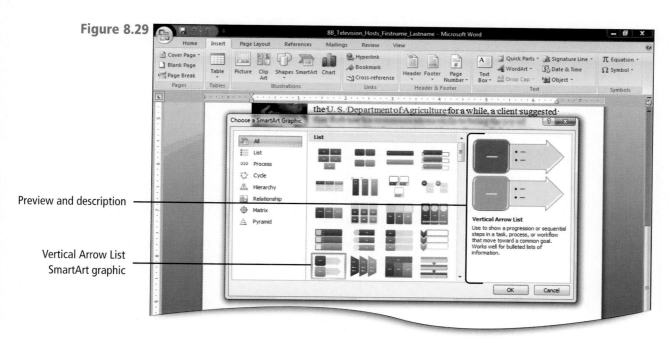

5 At the bottom of the **Choose a SmartArt Graphic** dialog box, click **OK**. If the *Type your text here* box does not display, on the Design tab, in the Create Graphic group, click the Text Pane button. Compare your screen with Figure 8.30.

The SmartArt graphic is placed at the insertion point location. The graphic consists of two parts—the graphic itself, and a *Type your text here* box, into which you can type the SmartArt graphic text in outline format. On the Ribbon, the SmartArt Tools display on two contextual tabs—the Design tab and the Format tab.

Figure 8.30

Text Pane button

SmartArt Tools

Type your text here box

Vertical Arrow List
SmartArt graphic

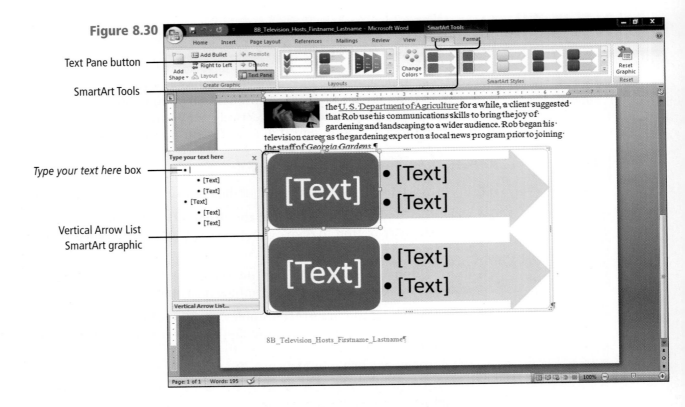

6 **Save** 💾 your document.

Activity 8.16 Adding Text to a SmartArt Graphic

1 In the **Type your text here** box, click in the first top-level bullet point. Type **Kathy Greene** and then press ⬇.

> The **top-level points** are the main points in a SmartArt graphic. **Subpoints** are second-level bullet points. The name displays in the left SmartArt box, and the insertion point moves to the first second-level bullet. If you press the Enter key, a new bullet point will be added at the same level as the previous bullet point.

2 Type **Signs books at Edges Bookstore Friday, May 25, 7-9 p.m.** and then press ⬇. Compare your screen with Figure 8.31.

Figure 8.31

First bullet point

Subpoint text

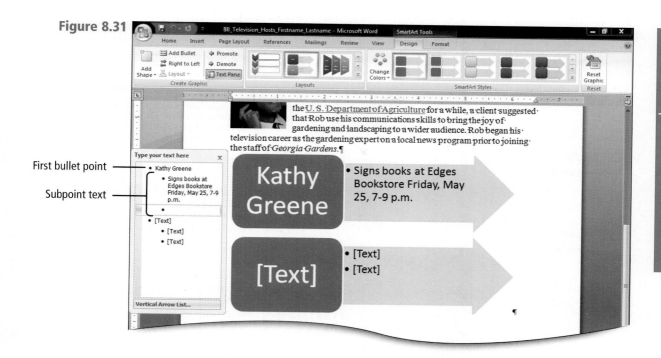

▶3 Type **Answers questions on WZXY Radio Mondays at 7 p.m.** and then press ↓.

▶4 Type **Rob Tumlin** and then press ↓. Type **Signs books at Edges Bookstore Sunday, May 27, 7-9 p.m.** and then press ↓. Type **Answers questions on WZXY Radio Fridays at 7 p.m.** and then on the **Design tab**, in the **Create Graphic group**, click the **Text Pane** button to close the *Type your text here* box.

▶5 Move the pointer to the middle of the right border of the SmartArt graphic to display the ↔ pointer, and then drag the right edge of the graphic to **6.5 inches on the horizontal ruler**.

▶6 On the Ribbon, click the **Format tab**. At the right end of the Ribbon, click the **Arrange** button, click the **Position** button, and then under **With Text Wrapping**, in the last row, click the middle button—**Position in Bottom Center with Square Text Wrapping**. Compare your screen with Figure 8.32.

Figure 8.32

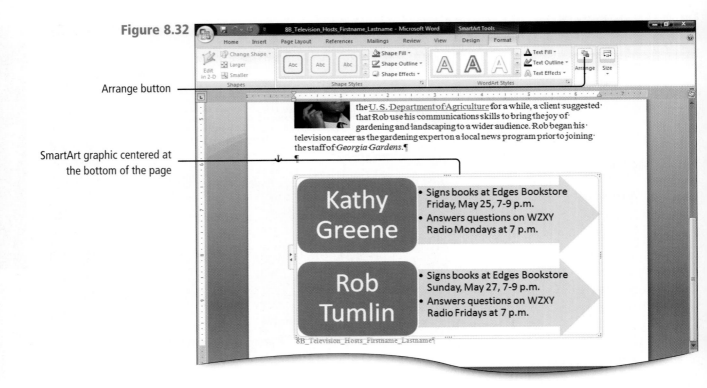

Arrange button

SmartArt graphic centered at the bottom of the page

---

7 Deselect the SmartArt graphic, and then **Save** 🖫 your document.

Objective 7
Preview and Save a Document as a Web Page

A Word document that you will publish as a Web page should be pre-viewed in a Web browser such as Internet Explorer. A **Web browser** is software that enables you to use the Web and navigate from page to page and site to site. You can adjust the image and preview it, and then save the document as a Web page.

Activity 8.17 Previewing a Document as a Web Page

1 Click the **View tab**, and then in the **Document Views group**, click the **Web Layout** button. Maximize the screen if necessary, and then scroll to the top of the page. Compare your screen with Figure 8.33.

> The document displays as a Web page, although Word does not open your Web browser. Your screen may look different from the figures shown, depending on your screen size, screen resolution, and the Web browser you use.

Figure 8.33

Click Web Layout button

Document previewed as
Web page—your
screen may vary

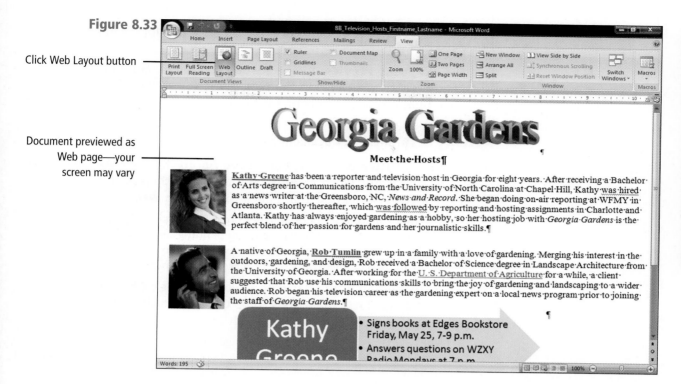

2 On the right side of the status bar, use the **Zoom slider** to zoom in and out to see what the Web page will look like on screens with lower or higher resolutions, or with the browser window not maximized.

3 Notice that the font and picture sizes increase and decrease as you zoom in and out, but the word wrapping continues, and centered text remains centered. Figure 8.34 displays the look of the screen if your screen is set to a lower resolution.

Figure 8.34

Zoom In button

Zoom Out button

Zoom increased—your
screen may vary

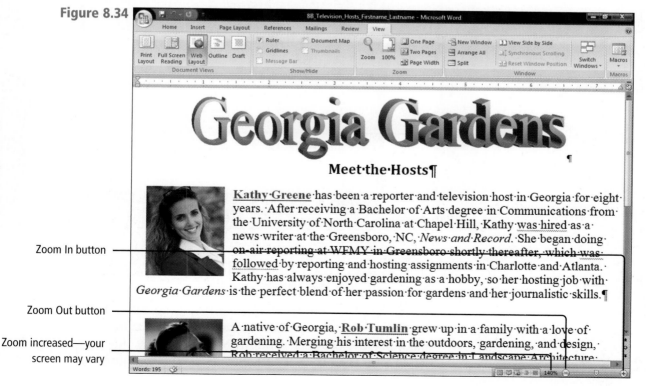

4 On the **View tab**, in the **Document Views group**, click the **Print Layout** button.

5 Display **Print Preview** to check your document. Submit the Word document as directed—in the next activity, you will create a Web page using the same document. If necessary, close the Print Preview.

Activity 8.18 Saving a Document as a Web Page

1 From the **Office** menu 🖱, click **Save As**. In the **Save As** dialog box, navigate to your **Word Chapter 8** folder, and then click the **Save as type arrow**. Scroll down and click **Single File Web Page**.

> The first line of the document—*Georgia Gardens*—may display as the default Page title for the Web page depending on your program settings. The default title is the first line of text in the document. If your system is set to display file extensions, *.mht* displays in place of *.docx.*

2 Near the bottom of the **Save As** dialog box, click **Change Title**. In the **Set Page Title** dialog box, type **Georgia Gardens Hosts** and then click **OK**. Compare your screen with Figure 8.35.

> The text that you type in the Set Page Title dialog box will become the Web page title; that is, the title that displays in the browser title bar and displays in the Web browser's history list.

Figure 8.35

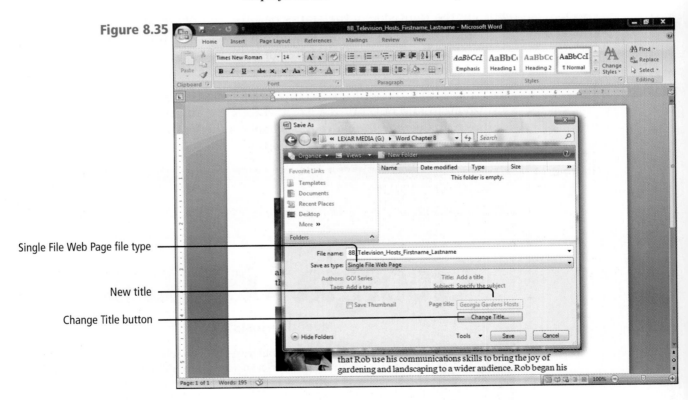

Single File Web Page file type

New title

Change Title button

3 Click **Save** to save the document as a Web page. **Close** the document, and then **Exit** Word.

4 Navigate to your **Word Chapter 8** folder. Locate and double-click your **8B_Television_Hosts_Firstname_Lastname.mht** file. If necessary, maximize the browser window. Notice that the title you changed displays in the browser title bar, as shown in Figure 8.36.

The Web page you created will have a different file extension and file type icon to distinguish it from the Word document by the same name.

Figure 8.36

Document open in browser window

New Web page title

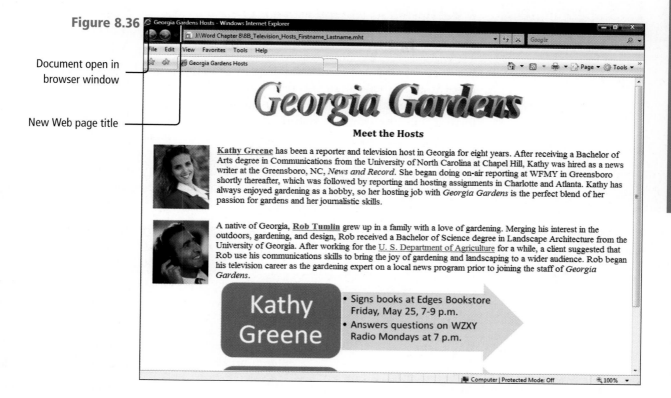

5 Submit your Web page as directed, and then **Close** ⊠ the Web browser.

End You have completed Project 8B ─────────────

There's More You Can Do!

Close Word and any other open windows. Display the Start menu, click Computer, and then navigate to the student files that accompany this textbook. From the CD that came with your book, open the folder **02_theres_more_you_ can_do**, locate and open the folder for this chapter. Open and print the instructions for this project, which are provided to you in Adobe PDF format.

Try IT! 1—Adding Comments and Tracking Changes

In this Try It! exercise, you will use Word's reviewing features to track changes made to the document and to add nonprinting comments.

Content-Based Assessments

Summary

Microsoft Word includes features you can use to create newsletters and Web pages, similar to those created by desktop publishing or Web design programs. For example, you can add borders and shading to paragraphs, and use special character formats to create distinctive headings. You can format text into multiple-column documents and add hyperlinks to a Word document and save it as a Web page. Word also assists you in creating mailing labels using the Mail Merge Wizard. Word enables you to use the collect-and-paste process to gather information from various sources and store them in the Office Clipboard. You can also create professional-looking graphics using SmartArt.

Key Terms

The 🌐 symbol represents Key Terms found on the Student CD in the 02_theres_more_you_can_do folder for this chapter.

Content-Based Assessments

Matching

Match each term in the second column with its correct definition in the first column. Write the letter of the term on the blank line in front of the correct definition.

_____ **1.** Laws that protect the rights of authors of original works, including text, art, photographs, and music.

_____ **2.** The Microsoft Office feature that enables you to place up to 24 objects on the Office Clipboard, and then paste them as needed, and in any order.

_____ **3.** A Microsoft Office feature with which you can turn text into decorative graphics.

_____ **4.** An artificial end to a column to balance columns or to provide space for the insertion of other objects.

_____ **5.** A font effect, usually used in titles, that changes lowercase text into capital (uppercase) letters using a reduced font size.

_____ **6.** A category of information stored in columns in a data table.

_____ **7.** All of the fields containing information about one topic (a person or organization) and stored in a row in a data table.

_____ **8.** A Word feature that joins a main document and a data source to create customized letters or labels.

A Collect and paste

B Copyright

C Data source

D Field

E Hyperlink

F Mail merge

G Main document

H Manual column break

I Record

J Small caps

K SmartArt

L Top-level point

M Web browser

N Web page

O WordArt

_____ **9.** The document that contains the text or formatting that remains constant in a mail merge.

_____ **10.** A list of variable information, such as names and addresses, that is merged with a main document to create customized form letters or labels.

_____ **11.** Text that you click to go to another location in a document, another document, or a Web site; the text is a different color (usually blue) than the surrounding text, and is commonly underlined.

_____ **12.** A designer-quality graphic used to create visual representations of information.

_____ **13.** The main points in a SmartArt graphic.

_____ **14.** Software that enables you to use the Web and navigate from page to page and site to site.

_____ **15.** A document that has been saved with an *.mht* extension so it can be viewed with a Web browser.

Content-Based Assessments

Fill in the Blank

Write the correct word in the space provided.

1. You can store up to _____ items in the Office Clipboard.

2. To remove the items in the Clipboard task pane, click the _____ _____ button.

3. WordArt changes text into a decorative _____.

4. Microsoft Publisher is a _____ _____ program.

5. Use a _____ _____ to change uneven columns into more equal lengths.

6. To change one column of text into two columns, use the _____ button on the Page Layout tab.

7. When you change from a one-column format to a two-column format, Word inserts a _____ _____.

8. Magazines and newspapers use narrower columns of text because they are easier to _____ than text that stretches across a page.

9. All of the information about a single person or business in a mail merge address file is known as a _____.

10. The column headings in a mail merge data source are known as _____.

11. In a SmartArt graphic, the main text points are the _____ points.

12. In a SmartArt graphic, the secondary points are the _____.

13. Internet Explorer is an example of _____ software.

14. To enable a user to click on text or a graphic to move to another file or a Web site, add a _____ to the text or graphic.

15. When you save a Word document as a Web page, the text that you type in the Set Page Title dialog box displays in the browser _____ bar.

Skills Review

Project 8C — Trellis

In this project, you will apply the skills you practiced from the Objectives in Project 8A.

Objectives: 1. *Collect and Paste Text and Graphics;* **2**. *Create and Format Columns;* **3**. *Use Special Character and Paragraph Formatting;* **4**. *Create Mailing Labels by Using Mail Merge.*

In the following Skills Review, you will use collect and paste to create a newsletter about building a trellis. You will also create mailing labels for the newsletter. Your completed documents will look similar to the ones shown in Figure 8.37.

For Project 8C, you will need the following files:

New blank Word document
w08C_Trellis_Graphics
w08C_Basic_Trellis
w08C_Rough_Trellis
w08C_Addresses

You will save your documents as
8C_Trellis_Firstname_Lastname
8C_Labels_Firstname_Lastname
8C_Addresses_Firstname_Lastname

Figure 8.37

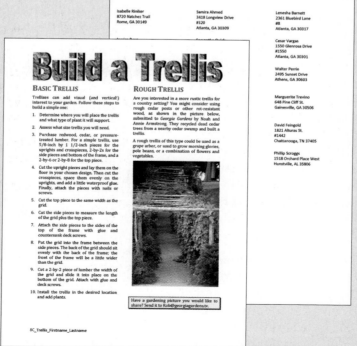

(Project 8C–Trellis continues on the next page)

Content-Based Assessments

Skills Review

(Project 8C–Trellis continued)

1. **Start** Word and display a new blank document. Display formatting marks and rulers. Set the left and right margins to **1"**, and the top and bottom margins to **0.5"**. **Save** the document in your **Word Chapter 8** folder as **8C_Trellis_Firstname_Lastname** and add the file name to the footer.

2. On the **Home tab**, in the **Clipboard group**, click the **Dialog Box Launcher** to display the **Clipboard** task pane. If any items display in the Clipboard, at the top of the task pane, click the Clear All button.

3. Locate, and then **Open t**he file **w08C_Basic_Trellis**. Select all of the text in the document, and then in the **Clipboard group**, click the **Copy** button. Locate, and then open the file **w08C_Rough_Trellis**. Select, and then **Copy** all of the text in the document. Locate, and then **Open t**he file **w08C_Trellis_Graphics**. **Copy** the WordArt title and the picture. Close the three documents from which you copied; leave your **8C_Trellis** document open.

4. In the **Clipboard** task pane, click the **Build a Trellis** WordArt title, and then press Enter. In the **Clipboard** task pane, click the text entry beginning *Basic Trellis* to paste the entire block of text at the insertion point. In the **Clipboard** task pane, click the text entry beginning *Rough Trellis* to paste the entire block of text at the insertion point. At the bottom of the text, click the **Paste Options** button, and then click **Paste List Without Merging**—this removes the numbered list from the last three paragraphs. Press ←Bksp to remove the blank line at the bottom of the inserted text.

5. Select all of the text in the document except the WordArt title. Be sure to include the paragraph mark at the end of the document. Right-click the selected text, and then click **Paragraph**. In the

displayed **Paragraph** dialog box, under **Spacing**, in the **After** box, click the **up spin arrow** to change the spacing to **6 pt**. Under **Spacing**, click the **Line spacing arrow**, and then click **Single**. Under **Spacing**, be sure the *Don't add space between paragraph of the same style* check box is cleared—you may have to click it two times to clear the check mark. Click **OK**, and then **Save** the document.

6. With the text still selected, click the **Page Layout tab**, and then in the **Page Setup group**, click the **Columns** button. From the displayed **Columns gallery**, click **Two**.

7. With the text still selected, click the **Home tab**. In the **Font group**, click the **Font button arrow**, and then click **Cambria**. In the **Font group**, click the **Font Size button arrow**, and then click **11**. In the **Paragraph group**, click the **Justify** button. Click anywhere in the document to deselect the text.

8. Click to the left of the *Rough Trellis* title, and then click the **Page Layout tab**. In the **Page Setup group**, click the **Breaks** button, and then under **Page Breaks**, click **Column**.

9. Press Ctrl + End to move to the end of the second column, and then press Enter. In the **Clipboard** task pane, click the **Trellis** picture. Right-click the picture, and then click **Size**. In the displayed **Size** dialog box under **Scale**, click the **Lock aspect ratio** check box. Under **Size and rotate**, click the **Width up spin arrow**, as necessary to set the picture width to **3"**. **Close** the dialog box.

10. Near the top of the **Clipboard** task pane, click the **Clear All** button to remove all items from the Office Clipboard. **Close** the Clipboard task pane, and then **Save** the document.

(Project 8C–Trellis continues on the next page)

Content-Based Assessments

(Project 8C–Trellis continued)

11. At the top of the first column, select the text *Basic Trellis*. Be sure to include the paragraph mark. Right-click the selected text, and then click **Font**. In the displayed **Font** dialog box, click the **Font color arrow**, and then under **Theme Colors**, in the last column, click **Orange, Accent 6, Darker 50%**. Under **Font style**, click **Bold**. Under **Size**, click **20**. Under **Effects**, select the **Small caps** check box, and then click **OK**. At the top of the second column, select **Rough Trellis**. Apply the same formatting you added to the title of the first column.

12. Press [Ctrl] + [End] to move to the end of the second column, and then press [Enter] two times. Type **Have a gardening picture you would like to share? Send it to Rob@georgiagardens.tv.** and then select the new paragraph. On the **Home tab**, in the **Paragraph group**, click the **Border button arrow**, and then click **Borders and Shading**.

13. In the **Borders and Shading** dialog box, be sure the **Borders tab** is selected. Under **Setting**, click **Shadow**. Click the **Width arrow** and then click **1 1/2 pt**. Click the **Color arrow**, and then in the last column, click **Orange, Accent 6, Darker 50%**.

14. At the top of the **Borders and Shading** dialog box, click the **Shading tab**. Click the **Fill arrow**, and then in the last column, click **Orange, Accent 6, Lighter 80%**. At the bottom of the **Borders and Shading** dialog box, click **OK**. **Save**, and then **Close** the document.

15. Submit your file as directed. Next, you will create mailing labels for a small group of subscribers.

16. **Open a** new blank document. Display the **Save As** dialog box and, in your **Word Chapter 8** folder, **Save** the document as

8C_Labels_Firstname_Lastname Locate and **Open** the file **w08C_Addresses**. Display the **Save As** dialog box, navigate to the **Word Chapter 8** folder, and then **Save** the file as **8C_Addresses_Firstname_Lastname**

17. Click to position the insertion point in the last cell in the table, and then press [Tab] to create a new row. Enter the following information:

First Name	Robert
Last Name	Hasty
Address 1	1884 Alcona Rd.
Address 2	
City	Columbus
State	GA
ZIP Code	31993

18. **Save**, and then **Close** the table of addresses; be sure your **8C_Labels** document displays. Click the **Mailings tab**. In the **Start Mail Merge group**, click the **Start Mail Merge** button, and then click **Step by Step Mail Merge Wizard** to display the **Mail Merge** task pane. Under **Select document type**, click the **Labels** option button.

19. At the bottom of the task pane, click **Next: Starting document**. Under **Select starting document**, be sure **Change document layout** is selected, and then under **Change document layout**, click **Label options**. In the **Label Options** dialog box, under **Printer information**, click the **Tray arrow**, and then click **Default tray (Automatically Select)**—your text may vary.

20. Under **Label information**, click the **Label vendors arrow**, and then click **Avery US Letter**. Under **Product number**, scroll as necessary and click **5160**. At the bottom of the **Label Options** dialog box, click **OK**, and then at the bottom of the task pane, click **Next: Select recipients**.

(Project 8C–Trellis continues on the next page)

(Project 8C–Trellis continued)

21. Under **Select recipients**, be sure the **Use an existing list** option button is selected. Under **Use an existing list**, click **Browse**. Navigate to your **Word Chapter 8** folder, select your **8C_Addresses_Firstname_Lastname** file, and then click **Open**. Click **OK**.

22. Click **Next: Arrange your labels**. Under **Arrange your labels**, click **Address block**. In the **Insert Address Block** dialog box, under **Insert recipient's name in this format**, if necessary, select the *Joshua Randall Jr.* format. Examine the **Preview** area to see how the label will look, and then click **OK**.

23. In the upper left corner of the document, select the **<<AddressBlock>>** field. Be sure to include the paragraph mark. Click the **Page Layout tab**, and in the **Paragraph**

group, use the **spin box arrows** to set the **Before** and **After** boxes to **0** to ensure that the four-line addresses will fit on the labels.

24. In the task pane, under **Replicate labels**, click **Update all labels**. Click **Next: Preview your labels**. Click **Next: Complete the merge**. Add the file name to the footer. **Save** your labels, and then **Close** the task pane.

25. To submit electronically, follow your instructor's directions. Otherwise, display **Print Preview**, and then on the **Print Preview tab**, in the **Print group**, click the **Print** button. In the **Print** dialog box, under **Page range**, click the **Current page** option button, and then click **OK**. On the **Print Preview tab**, in the **Preview group**, click the **Close Print Preview** button.

26. **Close** the document, click **Yes** to save the labels, and then **Exit** Word.

End **You have completed Project 8C**

Project 8D — Lawn Care

In this project, you will apply the skills you practiced from the Objectives in Project 8B.

Objectives: 5. *Insert Hyperlinks;* **6**. *Insert a SmartArt Graphic;* **7**. *Preview and Save a Document as a Web Page.*

In the following Skills Review, you will add hyperlinks to a lawn care document created by the *Georgia Gardens* staff, and then add a SmartArt graphic. You will also save the document as a Web page, to be posted on the show's Web site. Your completed documents will look similar to Figure 8.38.

For Project 8D, you will need the following file:

w08D_Lawn_Care

You will save your documents as
8D_Lawn_Care_Firstname_Lastname
8D_Lawn_Care_Firstname_Lastname.mht

Figure 8.38

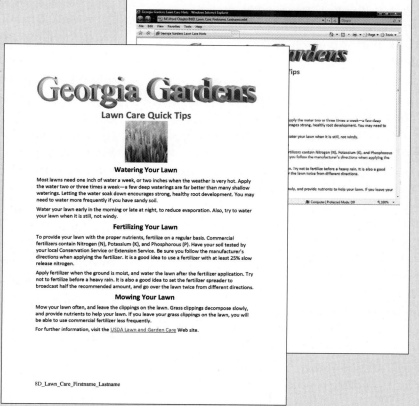

(Project 8D–Lawn Care continues on the next page)

Content-Based Assessments

(Project 8D–Lawn Care continued)

1. **Start** Word. Locate and open the document **w08D_Lawn_Care**. Display formatting marks and rulers. **Save** the document in your **Word Chapter 8** folder as **8D_Lawn_Care_Firstname_Lastname** Add the file name to the footer.

2. In the last paragraph in the document, select the text *USDA Lawn and Garden Care*. Click the **Insert tab**, and then in the **Links group**, click the **Hyperlink** button.

3. In the displayed **Insert Hyperlink** dialog box, under **Link to**, be sure **Existing File or Web Page** is selected. In the **Address** box, type **http://www.nrcs.usda.gov/feature/highlights/homegarden/lawn.html**

4. In the upper right corner of the **Insert Hyperlink** dialog box, click **ScreenTip**. In the **Set Hyperlink ScreenTip** dialog box, under **ScreenTip text**, type **Lawn Care Tips**

5. In the **Set Hyperlink ScreenTip** dialog box, click **OK**. At the bottom of the **Insert Hyperlink** dialog box, click **OK**. **Save** your document.

6. Near the top of the document, right-click the **grass** picture, and then click **Hyperlink**. Using the procedure you just practiced, add the same address and ScreenTip, and then return to the document.

7. Be sure you have an Internet connection. Point to the *USDA Lawn and Garden Care* text hyperlink and read the ScreenTip. Follow the directions to test the hyperlink. Close your browser window to return to your document, and then test the hyperlink associated with the picture. Close your browser window.

8. Display **Print Preview** to check your document. **Close** the **Print Preview** window and submit the Word document as directed.

9. Press [Ctrl] + [End] to move to the end of the document, and then press [Enter]. Click the

Insert tab. In the **Illustrations group**, click the **SmartArt** button.

10. On the left side of the displayed **Choose a SmartArt Graphic** dialog box, click **Cycle**. In the middle of the dialog box, click the first SmartArt graphic—**Basic Cycle**.

11. At the bottom of the displayed **Choose a SmartArt Graphic** dialog box, click **OK**. The graphic will display on the second page of the document. If the *Type your text here* box does not display, click one of the Text circles to select it, and then on the Design tab, in the Create Graphic group, click the Text Pane button.

12. With the SmartArt graphic displayed on your screen, in the first bullet point in the **Type your text here** box, type **Water Regularly** and then press [↓].

13. Type **Fertilize As Needed** and then press [↓]. Type **Mow Often** and then press [↓]. Type **Leave Clippings** and then press [↓].

14. With the insertion point in the fifth (blank) bullet point, press [←Bksp] to remove the fifth item.

15. **Close** the *Type your text here* box. Click the **View tab**, and then in the **Document Views group**, click the **Web Layout** button. **Maximize** the screen if necessary. Scroll to view the page.

16. From the **Office** menu, click **Save As**. In the displayed **Save As** dialog box, navigate to your **Word Chapter 8** folder. Click the **Save as type arrow**. Scroll down, and then click **Single File Web Page**.

17. Near the bottom of the **Save As** dialog box, click **Change Title**. In the displayed **Set Page Title** dialog box, type **Georgia Gardens Lawn Care Hints** and then click **OK**. At the bottom of the **Save As** dialog box, click **Save** to save the document as a Web page.

(Project 8D–Lawn Care continues on the next page)

Content-Based Assessments

(Project 8D–Lawn Care continued)

18. **Close** the document, and then **Exit** Word. Display the **My Computer** window, and then navigate to your **Word Chapter 8** folder. Locate and double-click the **8D_Lawn_Care_Firstname_Lastname .mht** file. If necessary, maximize the browser window. Notice that the title you changed displays in the browser title bar.

19. Submit your Web page as directed, and then **Close** the Web browser.

End **You have completed Project 8D** ——————————————

Content-Based Assessments

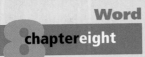
Mastering Word

Project 8E — Itinerary

In this project, you will apply the skills you practiced from the Objectives in Projects 8A and 8B.

Objectives: 1. *Collect and Paste Text and Graphics;* **3**. *Use Special Character and Paragraph Formatting;* **5**. *Insert Hyperlinks;* **7**. *Preview and Save a Document as a Web Page.*

In the following Mastering Word project, you will collect information, and then create an itinerary for Rob Tumlin. You will save it as a document, and also as a Web page for the program's internal, private Web site. Your completed documents will look similar to Figure 8.39.

For Project 8E, you will need the following files:

New blank Word document
w08E_Itinerary
w08E_Itinerary_Graphics

You will save your documents as
8E_Itinerary_Firstname_Lastname
8E_Itinerary_Firstname_Lastname.mht

Figure 8.39

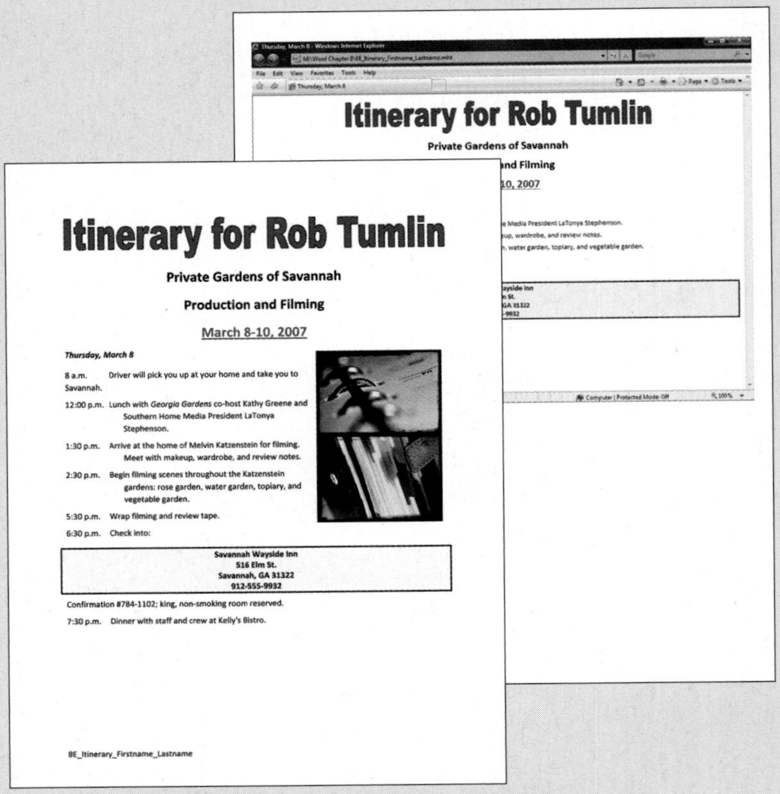

(Project 8E–Itinerary continues on the next page)

(Project 8E–Itinerary continued)

1. **Start** Word and be sure a new blank document is displayed. Display formatting marks and rulers, and be sure the document margins are all set to **1"**. **Save** the file in your **Word Chapter 8** folder as **8E_Itinerary_Firstname_Lastname** and then add the file name to the footer.

2. Display the **Clipboard** task pane, and if necessary, **Clear All** contents. Locate and open the file **w08E_Itinerary**. Select all of the text in the document, and then **Copy** the text to the **Office Clipboard**.

3. Locate, and then open the file **w08E_Itinerary_Graphics**. Select and **Copy** the **WordArt title**, and then **Copy** the **appointment book** picture. Leave the **8E_Itinerary** document open, but **Close** the other files.

4. In the **Clipboard** task pane, click the **WordArt title**, **Center** the title, and then press [Enter]. Use the **Clipboard** task pane to insert the text beginning *Private Gardens*, and then remove the blank line at the bottom of the inserted text. **Save** the document.

5. Insert the **appointment book** picture. Right-click the picture, and then display the **Size** dialog box. Select the **Lock aspect ratio** check box so that the picture is resized proportionally, and then change the **Height** to **3"**. Change the **Text Wrapping** to **Square**.

6. Align the top edge of the picture with the top edge of the paragraph *Thursday, March 8*, and align the right edge of the picture with the right document margin. **Clear All** entries in the **Clipboard** task pane, and then **Close** the task pane. Compare the size and placement of the picture with Figure 8.39.

7. Near the bottom of the document, select the lines containing the name, address, and telephone number of the Inn. Display the **Borders and Shading** dialog box. Be sure the **Borders tab** is selected.

8. Add a **Box** border to the selected text, with a **Width** of **1 1/2 pt**. If necessary, change the box Color to Black. On the **Shading tab**, fill the box using the second color in the first column—**White, Background 1, Darker 5%**.

9. With the text still selected, **Center** the text and add **Bold** emphasis. Display the **Paragraph** dialog box, and then change the **Special Indentation** to (**none**). Change the spacing **After** to **0**, and then change the **Line spacing** to **Single**.

10. Near the top of the document, select the text *March 8-10, 2007*. Insert a hyperlink to the address **http://www.georgiagardens.tv/hosts/tumlin/schedule.htm** Add a **Rob's Full Schedule** ScreenTip to the hyperlink. Move the pointer over the new hyperlink to examine the ScreenTip, but do not click the link. **Save** your document, and then submit it as directed.

11. Select, and then delete the graphic. **Save** your document as a **Single File Web Page**, and then change the page **Title** to **Thursday, March 8**

12. **Close** the document, and then **Exit** Word. Locate and double-click the **8E_Itinerary_Firstname_Lastname.mht** file. If necessary, maximize the browser window. Notice that the shape and position of the paragraph with the box border are different—your screen may vary.

13. Submit your Web page as directed, and then **Close** the Web browser.

End You have completed Project 8E

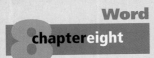
Mastering Word

Project 8F—Episode Guide

In this project, you will apply the skills you practiced from the Objectives in Project 8B.

Objectives: 6. *Insert a SmartArt Graphic;* **7**. *Preview and Save a Document as a Web Page.*

In the following Mastering Word project, you will create a *Georgia Gardens* episode guide document that will also be used as a Web page. The focus of the document will be a SmartArt graphic. Your completed documents will look similar to Figure 8.40.

For Project 8F, you will need the following file:

New blank Word document

You will save your documents as
8F_Episode_Guide_Firstname_Lastname
8F_Episode_Guide_Firstname_Lastname.mht

Figure 8.40

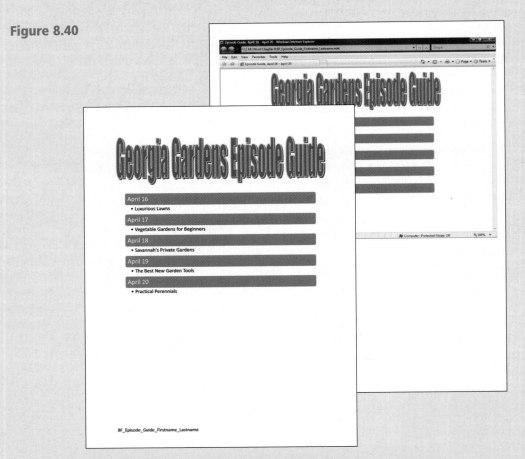

(Project 8F–Episode Guide continues on the next page)

Content-Based Assessments

(Project 8F–Episode Guide continued)

1. **Start** Word and be sure a new blank document is displayed. Display formatting marks and rulers. **Save** the document as **8F_Episode_Guide_Firstname_Lastname** Add the file name to the footer.

2. Add a **Georgia Gardens Episode Guide** WordArt title using **WordArt style 11**. Change the **Height** of the WordArt title to **1.5"** and the **Width** to **6.5"**. **Center** the WordArt title.

3. Insert a blank line below the WordArt title, and then insert a **Vertical Bullet List** SmartArt graphic—the third style in the first row of the **List** category.

4. Use the **Type your text here** box to enter the two dates and program titles shown in the following table. The dates should appear in the blue boxes, with the titles below the date in the white areas, as shown in Figure 8.40.

April 16	Luxurious Lawns
April 17	Vegetable Gardens for Beginners

5. After you have entered the first two dates and titles, on the **Design tab**, in the

Create Graphic group, click the **Add Bullet** button. Recall that you can change the bullet levels using the **Promote** and **Demote** buttons. Add the last three dates and program titles:

April 18	Savannah's Private Gardens
April 19	The Best New Garden Tools
April 20	Practical Perennials

6. **Close** the **Type your text here** box. **Save** your document, and then submit it as directed.

7. **Save** your document as a **Single File Web Page**, and then change the **Page Title** to **Episode Guide, April 16 - April 20**

8. **Close** the document, and then **Exit** Word. Locate and double-click the **8F_Episode_ Guide_Firstname_Lastname.mht** file. If necessary, maximize the browser window.

9. Submit your Web page as directed, and then **Close** the Web browser.

End **You have completed Project 8F**

Mastering Word

Project 8G — Extension Service

In this project, you will apply the skills you practiced from all of the Objectives in Projects 8A and 8B.

Objectives: 1. *Collect and Paste Text and Graphics;* **2**. *Create and Format Columns;* **3**. *Use Special Character and Paragraph Formatting;* **4**. *Create Mailing Labels by Using Mail Merge;* **5**. *Insert Hyperlinks;* **6**. *Insert a SmartArt Graphic;* **7**. *Preview and Save a Document as a Web Page.*

In the following Mastering Word project, you will create a newsletter and Web page about the Georgia Gardens Extension Service, and a set of name tags for people who have confirmed that they will attend an open house. Your completed documents will look similar to Figure 8.41.

For Project 8G, you will need the following files:

New blank Word document
w08G_Extension_Service
w08G_Extension_Service_Graphics
w08G_Addresses

You will save your documents as
8G_Extension_Service_Firstname_Lastname
8G_Extension_Service_Firstname_Lastname.mht
8G_Name_Tags_Firstname_Lastname
8G_Addresses_Firstname_Lastname

Figure 8.41

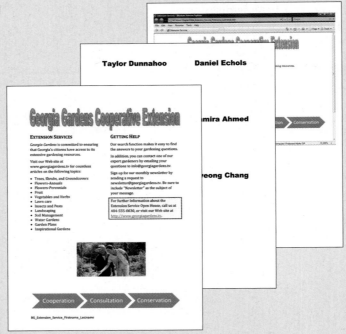

(Project 8G–Extension Service continues on the next page)

Content-Based Assessments

Mastering Word

(Project 8G–Extension Service continued)

1. **Start** Word and be sure a new blank document is displayed. Display formatting marks and rulers. **Save** the file as **8G_Extension_Service_Firstname_Lastname** and then add the file name to the footer.

2. Display the **Clipboard** task pane, and if necessary, Clear All contents. Locate and open the file **w08G_Extension_Service**. Select all of the text in the document, and then **Copy** the text to the **Office Clipboard**. Locate and **Open** the file **w08G_Extension_Service_Graphics**. Select and **Copy** the WordArt title, and then **Copy** the **gardening** picture. Leave your **8G_Extension_Service** document open, but **Close** the other files.

3. In the **Clipboard** task pane, click the **WordArt title**, and then press Enter. Use the **Clipboard** task pane to insert the text beginning *Extension Services*, and then remove the blank line at the bottom of the inserted text. Select all of the text except the WordArt title. On the **Page Layout tab**, change the number of **Columns** to **Two**. Change the **Font Size** to **12**, **Center** the WordArt title, and then **Save** the document.

4. Position the insertion point to the left of *Getting Help*. On the **Page Layout tab**, insert a **Column** break. Press Ctrl + End. Press Enter, and then type **For further information about the Extension Service Open House, call us at 404-555-0030, or visit our Web site at www.georgiagardens.tv.** and then select the new paragraph.

5. On the **Home tab**, display the **Borders and Shading** dialog box. Add a **Box** border to the selected text, with a **Width** of **1 1/2 pt**. On the **Shading tab**, fill the box using the second color in the first column—**White, Background 1, Darker 5%**.

6. Click anywhere in the document to deselect the text. In the paragraph with the border, select the text *www.georgiagardens.tv*.

Insert a hyperlink to the address **http://www.georgiagardens.tv** Add a **Georgia Gardens Home Page** ScreenTip to the hyperlink.

7. Click anywhere outside the bordered text, and then from the **Clipboard** task pane, insert the **gardening** picture. Display the **Format tab**, confirm that the **Width** is **3"**, and then change the **Text Wrapping** to **Square**. Align the top edge of the picture at **6 inches on the vertical ruler**, and center it horizontally on the page, as shown in Figure 8.41. **Clear All** items from the **Office Clipboard**, and then **Close** the **Clipboard** task pane. **Save** the document.

8. At the top of the first column, select the title *Extension Services*, and then display the **Font** dialog box. Change the **Font Size** to **16**, add **Bold** emphasis, and then change the text to **Small Caps**. Repeat this procedure with the second title—*Getting Help*.

9. Position the insertion point at the bottom of the first column. From the **Insert tab**, insert a **Basic Chevron Process** SmartArt graphic—located at the beginning of the third row of the **Process** graphics.

10. If necessary, display the Text Pane. Type **Cooperation** and then press ↓. Type **Consultation** and then press ↓. Type **Conservation**

11. With the SmartArt graphic still selected, display the **Format tab**. Change the **Position** to **Position in Bottom Center with Square Text Wrapping**—the middle button in the bottom row of the **Position gallery**. Close the **Text Pane**, and then change the **Width** to **6.5"** and the **Height** to **0.7"**. **Save** your document, and submit it as directed.

12. **Save** your document as a **Single File Web Page**, and then change the **Page Title** to

(Project 8G–Extension Service continues on the next page)

Content-Based Assessments

(Project 8G–Extension Service continued)

Extension Services If you see a message about Small Caps changing to All Caps, click Continue.

13. **Close** the document, and then **Exit** Word. Locate and double-click the **8G_Extension_Service_Firstname_Lastname.mht** file. If necessary, maximize the browser window. Notice that the graphics and columns are rearranged when displayed as a Web page.

14. **Close** the browser, and then submit the Web file as directed. Next, you will create name tags for the Extension Service open house.

15. **Start** Word and display a new blank document. Display the **Save As** dialog box, and, in your **Word Chapter 8** folder, **Save** the document as 8G_Name_Tags_Firstname_Lastname Locate and **Open** the file **w08G_Addresses**, and then save the file as 8G_Addresses_Firstname_Lastname Add the file name to the footer.

16. **Save** and **Close** the table of addresses. With the **8G_Name_Tags** document displayed, on the **Mailings tab**, start the **Step by Step Mail Merge Wizard**. Select **Labels**, click **Next**, and then click **Label options**. Select the **Default tray (Automatically Select)**—your text may differ—for the printer. Select the **Avery 5095** name badge label format.

17. Select your **8G_Addresses_Firstname_Lastname** file as the data source for the recipients. Select the **Address block** option. In the **Insert Address Block** dialog box, clear the **Insert postal address** check box. Then, **Update all labels**. **Preview** your labels, and then complete the merge.

18. Press Ctrl + A to select all of the name tags. Change the **Font** to **Arial Black**, the **Font Size** to **22**, and then **Center** the names. Add the file name to the footer, and then **Save** your labels.

19. To submit electronically, follow your instructor's directions. Otherwise, **Print** the first page of name tags. **Close** the document, click **Yes** to save the labels, and then **Exit** Word.

End **You have completed Project 8G**

Content-Based Assessments

Project 8H — *GO!* Fix It

In this project, you will construct a solution by applying any combination of the skills you practiced from the Objectives in Projects 8A and 8B.

For Project 8H, you will need the following files:

w08H_Retail_Suppliers
w08H_Addresses

You will save your documents as
8H_Retail_Suppliers_Firstname_Lastname
8H_Addresses_Firstname_Lastname
8H_Labels_Firstname_Lastname

From the student files that accompany this textbook, locate and open the files **w08H_Retail_Suppliers** and **w08H_Addresses**. Save the files in your chapter folder as **8H_Retail_Suppliers_Firstname_Lastname** and **8H_Addresses_Firstname_Lastname**

This project contains errors that you must find and correct. Read and examine the document, and then edit to correct the errors that you find. Types of errors could include:

- Spelling, grammar, punctuation, and usage errors such as text case, repeated text, subject-verb agreement, and meaning.

- Content errors such as missing or incorrect data, text, pictures, hyperlinks, or other objects.

- Font formatting and positioning errors such as font used, style, size, color, underline style, effects, font character spacing, text effects, special characters, and styles.

- Paragraph formatting and positioning errors such as indents and spacing, tabs, line and page breaks, word wrap, sentence spacing, missing text or unnecessary text or blank lines, or errors in footnotes or endnotes or references.

- Image or object formatting and positioning errors relating to color, lines, size, scale, layout, and positioning.

- Page setup errors such as margins, orientation, layout, or alignment.

To complete the project, you should make the following changes to the *Retail Suppliers* document:

- Check spelling in the non-list portion of the document.

- Reformat the WordArt title by using the font Times New Roman.

- Change the SmartArt graphic to an Isosceles Triangle.

(Project 8H–*GO!* Fix It continues on the next page)

Content-Based Assessments

(Project 8H–*GO!* Fix It continued)

- Activate the hyperlink.

- For the category headings at the beginning of each list, apply the same effects to the third category heading that are applied to the first and second.

- Be sure the size of all graphics is set to 35%.

- Format the layout of all the lists as two columns.

- In your **8K_Addresses** file, delete any duplicate records and delete any records that are *not* in a ZIP code that begins with *30*.

Create mailing labels as follows:

- Open a new blank Word document and save it in your chapter folder as **8H_Labels_Firstname_Lastname**

- Use the Mail Merge Wizard and follow the specifications and procedures described in Project 8A.

- Use your corrected **8H_Addresses_Firstname_Lastname** file for the data source.

Save the changes you have made, add the file names to the footers, and then submit as directed.

 You have completed Project 8H —————————————————

Outcomes-Based Assessments

Rubric

The following outcomes-based assessments are *open-ended assessments*. That is, there is no specific correct result; your result will depend on your approach to the information provided. Make *professional quality* your goal. Use the following scoring rubric to guide you in *how* to approach the problem and then to evaluate *how well* your approach solves the problem.

The *criteria*—Software Mastery, Content, Format and Layout, and Process—represent the knowledge and skills you have gained that you can apply to solving the problem. The *levels of performance*—Professional Quality, Approaching Professional Quality, or Needs Quality Improvements—help you and your instructor evaluate your result.

	Your completed project is of Professional Quality if you:	Your completed project is Approaching Professional Quality if you:	Your completed project Needs Quality Improvements if you:
1-Software Mastery	Choose and apply the most appropriate skills, tools, and features and identify efficient methods to solve the problem.	Choose and apply some appropriate skills, tools, and features, but not in the most efficient manner.	Choose inappropriate skills, tools, or features, or are inefficient in solving the problem.
2-Content	Construct a solution that is clear and well organized, contains content that is accurate, appropriate to the audience and purpose, and is complete. Provide a solution that contains no errors of spelling, grammar, or style.	Construct a solution in which some components are unclear, poorly organized, inconsistent, or incomplete. Misjudge the needs of the audience. Have some errors in spelling, grammar, or style, but the errors do not detract from comprehension.	Construct a solution that is unclear, incomplete, or poorly organized; contains some inaccurate or inappropriate content; and contains many errors of spelling, grammar, or style. Do not solve the problem.
3-Format and Layout	Format and arrange all elements to communicate information and ideas, clarify function, illustrate relationships, and indicate relative importance.	Apply appropriate format and layout features to some elements, but not others. Overuse features, causing minor distraction.	Apply format and layout that does not communicate information or ideas clearly. Do not use format and layout features to clarify function, illustrate relationships, or indicate relative importance. Use available features excessively, causing distraction.
4-Process	Use an organized approach that integrates planning, development, self-assessment, revision, and reflection.	Demonstrate an organized approach in some areas, but not others; or, use an insufficient process of organization throughout.	Do not use an organized approach to solve the problem.

Outcomes-Based Assessments

Problem Solving

Project 8I—Extension Classes

In this project, you will construct a solution by applying any combination of the skills you practiced from the Objectives in Projects 8A and 8B.

For Project 8I, you will need the following files:

New blank Word document
w08I_Extension_Classes

You will save your document as
8I_Extension_Classes_Firstname_Lastname

Georgia Gardens Extension Service offers classes on gardening and garden-related topics. The March and April schedule includes a wide variety of topics, ranging from *Pruning Basics* to *Attracting Butterflies to Your Garden*. All classes are single-day sessions, and are three hours long unless otherwise noted.

In this project, you will create a two-page newsletter announcing the upcoming classes and topics. Information about the classes can be found in a table in the file **w08I_Extension_Classes**. Open the Clipboard task pane and collect the information, or copy and paste the table information directly into your newsletter. Include a decorative title, information about where the classes are offered, and a link to the Georgia Gardens Extension Service Web site at **www.georgiagardens.tv/extension/classes.htm** Locate a related picture or clip art image—a garden or a classroom—and add it to the newsletter. Put the class information in a two-column format. (*Hint:* For each class, you might want to have a title that includes the date and time, followed by the title of the class, and finally, the class description.) Format the class titles from the descriptions in a distinctive manner.

Add the file name to the footer. Check the newsletter for spelling and grammar errors. Save the newsletter as **8I_Extension_Classes_Firstname_ Lastname** and submit it as directed.

End **You have completed Project 8I** ——————

Problem Solving

Project 8J—Business Cards

In this project, you will construct a solution by applying any combination of the skills you practiced from the Objectives in Projects 8A and 8B.

For Project 8J, you will need the following files:

New blank Word document
w08J_Rob_Tumlin_Address

**You will save your document as
8J_Business_Cards_Firstname_Lastname**

In this project, you will create business cards for Rob Tumlin, co-host of the *Georgia Gardens* television show. Business cards are a type of label that you can create using the Mail Merge Wizard, in much the same way you created mailing labels in Project 8A. The major difference is the data source—instead of a list of different people, the data source is a Word or Access table, in this project, an Access table—that contains one name and address, repeated over and over.

Start the Step by Step Mail Merge Wizard. Using the method you practiced in Project 8A, create a set of labels that uses the default printer tray, and the 5911 Avery US Letter business card label type. As a data source, use the **w08J_Rob_Tumlin_Address** Access file. Use the Address Block format, and be sure to insert the company name. With the address block in place, press Enter to add a new line to the business card. In the same area where you select the Address block, select More items and add the E-mail Address field. Update all labels.

Check the business cards for spelling or grammar errors. Save the document as **8J_Business_Cards_Firstname_Lastname** and add the file name to the footer. Submit it as directed. If you are to submit a printed copy, print only records 1 through 8.

End You have completed Project 8J ————————————

Outcomes-Based Assessments

Problem Solving

Project 8K—Gardening Web Sites

In this project, you will construct a solution by applying any combination of the skills you practiced from the Objectives in Projects 8A and 8B.

For Project 8K, you will need the following file:

New blank Word document

You will save your documents as
8K_Gardening_Web_Sites_Firstname_Lastname
8K_Gardening_Web_Sites_Firstname_Lastname.mht

In this project, you will create a flyer and a Web page that contains a list of gardening Web sites. To complete this project:

- Add an appropriate decorative title to the document.

- Add one or more appropriate pictures or clip art graphics.

- Include lists of gardening-related Web sites, with a link to each site, and a ScreenTip with a short description of the site.

- Include at least one SmartArt graphic. The links could all be contained in the SmartArt graphic, or the graphic could relate to a particular topic contained in one of the links.

To find the gardening sources, use a Web browser and search using terms such as *flower garden*, *vegetable garden*, *shade garden*, or some other appropriate phrase. Choose several of the sites that are of interest to you.

Save the document as **8K_Gardening_Web_Sites_Firstname_Lastname** and add the file name to the footer. Submit it as directed. Then, save the document as a Single File Web Page and test your hyperlinks. Submit the Web page as directed.

End You have completed Project 8K ——————

More on your Student CD

The instructions for the following additional end-of-chapter projects are on your student CD in the folder 03_additional_end_of_chapter_projects.

Content-Based Assessments

Project L Mastering Word   Apply the skills you practiced in Project A.

Project M Mastering Word   Apply the skills you practiced in Project B.

Project N Business Running Case   Apply the skills you practiced in Projects A and B while helping an entrepreneur with the daily tasks of running a business.

In each chapter, this project focuses on applying the skills you have practiced in Projects A and B to a business. The project related to this business runs throughout the textbook. You will see how the Office applications relate to the day-to-day operation of a small business called Nelson Architectural Planning.

Outcomes-Based Assessments

Project O Problem Solving   Construct a solution by applying any combination of the skills you practiced from Projects A and B.

Project P Problem Solving   Construct a solution by applying any combination of the skills you practiced from Projects A and B.

Project Q You and GO!   Construct a solution that applies to your own life by applying any combination of the skills you practiced from Projects A and B.

Project R GO! with Help   Practice using Microsoft Office's Help Feature.

Project S Group Business Running Case   Work as part of a group to apply the skills you have gained thus far to help the Bell Orchid Hotel Group achieve its business goals.

Multimedia

The following multimedia accompany this textbook:

Companion Web site
www.prenhall.com/go

An interactive Web site designed to reinforce and test your understanding of the skills in this chapter.

AV-EDDs

In the folder in the front of this book you will find videos that demonstrate the objectives of the A and B projects in this chapter. These may help you understand how to complete the projects in this book.

Video Podcasts

In the folder in the front of this book are videos that can be played on your iPod, MP3 player, or computer. These videos demonstrate how to complete the more challenging objectives in this textbook.

9 chapternine

Creating a Worksheet and Charting Data

OBJECTIVES

At the end of this chapter you will be able to:

1. Create, Save, and Navigate an Excel Workbook
2. Enter and Edit Data in a Worksheet
3. Construct and Copy Formulas, Use the Sum Function, and Edit Cells
4. Format Data, Cells, and Worksheets
5. Close and Reopen a Workbook
6. Chart Data
7. Use Page Layout View, Prepare a Worksheet for Printing, and Close Excel

8. Design a Worksheet
9. Construct Formulas for Mathematical Operations
10. Format Percentages and Move Formulas
11. Create a Pie Chart and a Chart Sheet
12. Use the Excel Help System

OUTCOMES

Mastering these objectives will enable you **to:**

PROJECT 9A
Create a Worksheet and Chart Data

Project 9B
Perform Calculations and Make Comparisons by Using a Pie Chart

Rio Rancho Auto Gallery

Rio Rancho Auto Gallery is a one-stop shop for car enthusiasts. The auto sales group sells a wide variety of manufacturer-certified preowned cars, cars that have passed rigorous inspection as determined by the manufacturers and that meet strict mileage and condition standards. The retail department sells automotive accessories such as custom wheels and performance parts, gadgets, gifts, books, magazines, and clothing, including branded items from major manufacturers. To complete the package, the company also offers auto financing and repairs and service.

© Jan Tyler / Courtesy of www.istockphoto.com

Creating a Worksheet and Charting Data

With Microsoft Office Excel 2007, you can create and analyze data organized into columns and rows. After you have entered data in a worksheet, you can perform calculations, analyze the data to make logical decisions, and create a visual representation of the data in the form of a chart. In addition to its worksheet capability, Excel can manage your data, sort your data, and search for specific pieces of information.

In this chapter, you will create and modify Excel workbooks. You will practice the basics of worksheet design, create a footer, enter and edit data in a worksheet, and save, preview, and print your work. You will construct formulas to perform calculations, automatically complete text, use Excel's spelling tool, create a chart, and access Excel's Help feature.

Project 9A **Auto Sales**

In Activities 9.01 through 9.17, you will construct an Excel worksheet for Sandy Cizek, the Auto Sales Manager for Rio Rancho Auto Gallery. The worksheet will display the first quarter sales of vehicle types for the current year, and will include a chart to visually represent the worksheet. Your completed worksheet will look similar to Figure 9.1.

For Project 9A, you will need the following file:

New blank Excel workbook

You will save your workbook as
9A_Auto_Sales_Firstname_Lastname

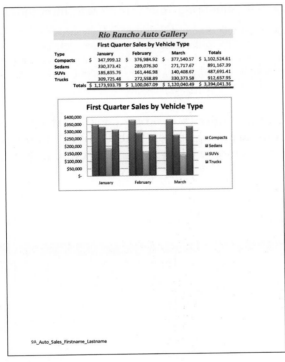

Figure 9.1
Project 9A—Auto Sales

Objective 1
Create, Save, and Navigate an Excel Workbook

When you start Excel, a new blank **workbook** displays. A workbook contains one or more pages called **worksheets**. A worksheet—also called a **spreadsheet**—is the primary document that you use in Excel to store and work with data. A worksheet is always stored in a workbook.

A worksheet is formatted as a pattern of uniformly spaced horizontal and vertical lines. This grid pattern of the worksheet forms vertical columns and horizontal rows. The intersection of a column and a row forms a small box referred to as a **cell**.

Activity 9.01 Starting Excel and Naming and Saving a Workbook

In this activity, you will start Excel and use the first worksheet in the workbook to prepare a report of quarterly auto sales.

> **Note — Comparing Your Screen with the Figures in This Textbook**
>
> Your screen will match the figures shown in this textbook if you set your screen resolution to 1024 × 768. At other resolutions, your screen will closely resemble, but not match, the figures shown. To view your screen's resolution, on the Windows desktop, right-click in a blank area, click Personalize, and then click Display Settings.

1 On the Windows taskbar, click **Start** ⊕. Locate and open Excel. Compare your screen with Figure 9.2 and study the parts of the Excel window described in the table in Figure 9.3.

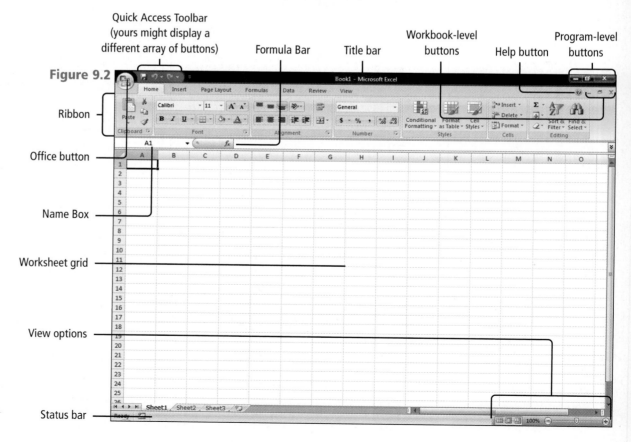

Figure 9.2

Parts of the Excel Window

Screen Part	Description
Formula Bar	Displays the value or formula contained in the active cell; also permits entry or editing of values or formulas.
Help button	Displays the Help window.
Name Box	Displays the name of the selected cell, table, chart, or object.
Office button	Displays a list of commands related to things you can do *with* a workbook, such as opening, saving, printing, or sharing.
Program-level buttons	Minimize, restore, or close the Excel program.
Quick Access Toolbar	Displays buttons to perform frequently used commands with a single click. Frequently used commands in Excel include Save, Undo, and Redo. For commands that *you* use frequently, you can add additional buttons here.
Ribbon	Groups the commands for performing related workbook tasks.
Status bar	Displays, on the left side, the current cell mode, page number, and worksheet information. On the right side, displays buttons to control how the window looks; when numerical data is selected, common calculations such as Sum and Average display.
Title bar	Indicates the name of the current workbook and the program name.
View options	Contain buttons for viewing the workbook in Normal view, Page Layout view, or Page Break Preview, and also displays controls for Zoom Out and Zoom In to increase or decrease the number of rows and columns displayed.
Workbook-level buttons	Minimize or restore the displayed workbook.
Worksheet grid	Displays the columns and rows that intersect to form the worksheet's cells.

Figure 9.3

2 In the upper left corner of your screen, click the **Office** button 🔘; on the menu, point to **Save As**. Compare your screen with Figure 9.4.

Figure 9.4

Office button

Save As command

Office menu

▣ Click **Save As**. In the **Save As** dialog box, if necessary, click Browse Folders to display the Navigation pane.

▣ In the **Navigation pane**, click **Computer** to view a list of the drives available to you, and then navigate to the drive on which you will store your folders and workbooks for this textbook—for example, a USB flash drive such as the one shown in Figure 9.5. If you are saving your files on your hard disk drive, in the Navigation pane, click Documents or the location of your choice.

Figure 9.5

Address bar displays path to your selected drive

New Folder button

Navigation pane expanded

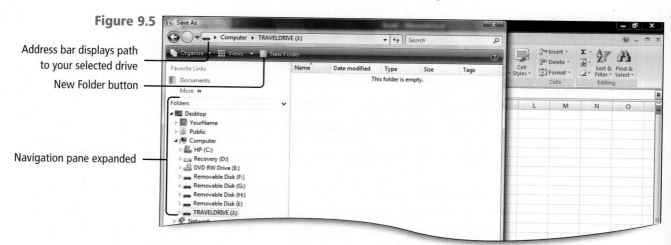

▣ On the **Save As** dialog box toolbar, click the **New Folder** button. With *New Folder* selected, type **Excel Chapter 9** and then press Enter.

Windows creates the *Excel Chapter 9* folder and makes it the active folder in the Save As dialog box. At the bottom of the Save As dialog box, in the File name box, *Book1* displays as the default file name.

▣ In the **File name** box, type **9A_Auto_Sales_Firstname_Lastname** Compare your screen with Figure 9.6.

Figure 9.6

Your folder name

File name with your name and underscores between words

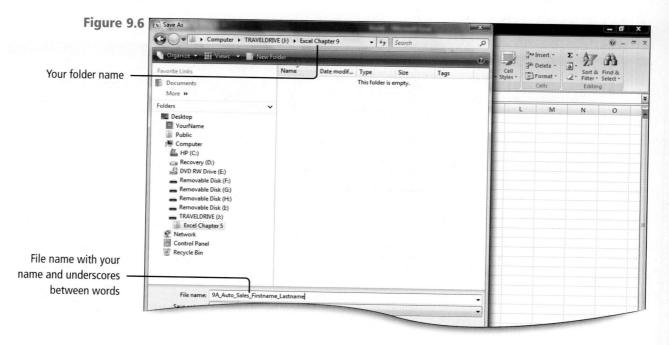

7 In the lower right corner of the **Save As** dialog box, click **Save**; or press Enter.

> Windows saves the file in the new folder with the new name. The workbook redisplays, and the new name displays in the title bar.

Activity 9.02 Navigating a Worksheet and a Workbook

1 Take a moment to study Figure 9.7 and the table in Figure 9.8 to become familiar with the Excel workbook window.

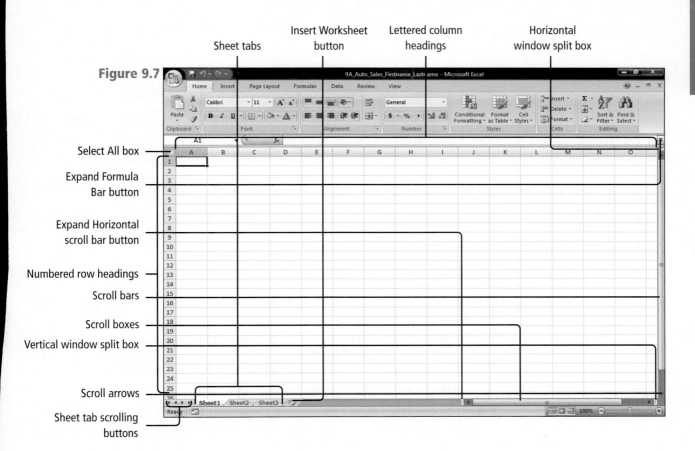

Figure 9.7

Excel Workbook Window Elements

Workbook window element	Description
Expand Formula Bar button	Increases the height of the Formula Bar to display lengthy cell content.
Expand horizontal scroll bar button	Increases the width of the horizontal scroll bar.
Horizontal window split box	Splits the worksheet into two horizontal views of the same worksheet.
Insert Worksheet button	Inserts an additional worksheet into the workbook.
Lettered column headings	Indicate the column letter.
Numbered row headings	Indicate the row number.
Scroll arrows	Scroll one column or row at a time.
Scroll bars	Scroll the Excel window up and down or left and right.
Scroll boxes	Move the position of the window up and down or left and right.
Select All box	Selects all the cells in a worksheet.
Sheet tab scrolling buttons	Display sheet tabs that are not in view; used when there are more sheet tabs than will display in the space provided.
Sheet tabs	Identify the worksheets in a workbook.
Vertical window split box	Splits the worksheet into two vertical views of the same worksheet.

Figure 9.8

2 In the horizontal scroll bar, point to, and then click the **right scroll arrow**.

> The workbook window shifts so that column A moves out of view. The number of times you click one of the arrows on the horizontal scroll bar determines the number of columns by which the window shifts—either to the left or to the right.

3 In the horizontal scroll bar, click the **right scroll arrow**, and then hold down the left mouse button until the columns begin to scroll rapidly to the right; release when you begin to see pairs of letters as the column headings.

> The workbook window moves rapidly. This technique also works for the left scroll arrow and for the two vertical scroll arrows.

4 In the horizontal scroll bar, click the **left scroll arrow** to shift one column. Then, in the horizontal scroll bar, point to the **horizontal scroll box**.

5 Hold down the left mouse button, *drag* the box to the left to display **column A**, and then notice that *ScreenTips* with the column letters display as you drag. Release the mouse button.

> You can drag to move something from one location on the screen to another; the action of dragging includes releasing the mouse button at the desired time or location. ScreenTips display useful information when you perform various mouse actions such as pointing to screen elements or dragging.

> Use the scroll boxes in this manner to move various parts of the worksheet into view. Scroll boxes change in size to indicate how the visible portion of the worksheet compares to the total amount of the worksheet in use.

6 Use the techniques you just practiced to scroll the worksheet to position **column Z** near the center of your screen.

> Column headings to the right of column Z use two letters starting with AA, AB, AC, and so on through ZZ. After that, columns begin with three letters beginning with AAA. This pattern is used to provide a total of 16,384 columns. The last column available is column XFD.

7 Near the lower left of the screen, click the **Sheet2 tab**.

> The second worksheet in the workbook displays and becomes the active worksheet. Column A displays at the left.

8 Click the **Sheet1 tab**.

> The first worksheet in the workbook becomes the active worksheet. A workbook consists of one or more worksheets. By default, new workbooks contain three worksheets. When you save a workbook, the worksheets are contained within it and do not have separate file names.

9 In the vertical scroll bar, point to, and then click the **down scroll arrow** one time.

> Row 1 moves out of view. The number of times you click the arrows on the vertical scroll bar determines the number of rows shifted either up or down. You can drag the vertical scroll box to scroll downward in a manner similar to the technique used in the horizontal scroll bar.

10 In the vertical scroll bar, point to, and then click the **up scroll arrow**.

> Row 1 comes back into view. The maximum number of rows on a single Excel worksheet is 1,048,576.

11 Use the skills you just practiced to scroll horizontally to display **column A**.

Activity 9.03 Selecting Parts of a Worksheet

In this activity, you will **select** both individual cells and groups of cells. Selecting refers to highlighting, by clicking or dragging with your mouse, one or more cells so that the selected cells can be edited, formatted, copied, or moved. Selected cells are indicated by a dark border, and Excel treats the selected **range**—two or more cells on a worksheet that are adjacent or nonadjacent—as a single unit so you can make the same change, or combination of changes, to more than one cell at a time.

In Excel, text or numbers in a cell are referred to as **data**. Before you enter data into a worksheet, you must select the location in the worksheet where you want the data to display. You can select one or more cells of data to which you can apply Excel's formatting, features, and functions.

1 In **Sheet1**, move the mouse pointer over—**point** to—the cell at the intersection of **column A** and **row 3**, and then click. Compare your screen with Figure 9.9.

A black border surrounds the cell, indicating that it is the **active cell**. The active cell is ready to receive data or be affected by the next Excel command.

A cell is identified by the intersecting column letter and row number, which forms the **cell reference**. A cell reference is also referred to as a **cell address**. The cell reference displays in the **Name Box**. You can use lowercase or uppercase letters to indicate columns; uppercase letters are commonly used.

Figure 9.9

Cell A3 is selected

Cell address displays in the Name Box

Active cell

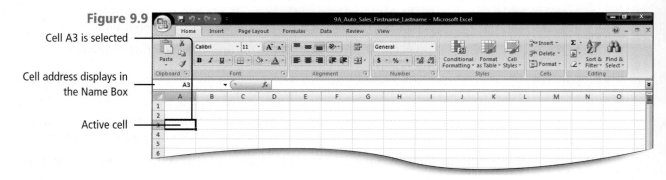

2 Press ↓ three times, and then look at the cell address in the **Name Box**.

Cell A6 becomes the active cell. Pressing one of the four direction arrow keys relocates the active cell. The cell address of the active cell always displays in the Name Box.

3 Point to cell **B2** and drag down to select cells **B2**, **B3**, **B4**, and **B5**, and then continue to drag across to cell **C5** and release the left mouse button. Alternatively, drag diagonally from cell B2 to C5. If you are not satisfied with your result, click anywhere and begin again. Compare your screen with Figure 9.10.

> The eight cells, B2 through B5 and C2 through C5 are selected. This range of cells is referred to as *B2:C5*. When you see a colon (:) between two cell references, the range includes all the cells between the two cell references.

> The cell references used to indicate the range are the upper left cell and the lower right cell—in this instance, B2 and C5. When you select a range of cells, the cells are bordered by a thick black line, and the cells change color except for the first cell in the range, which displays in the Name Box.

Selected range B2:C5

Figure 9.10

Name Box always indicates address of the first cell in range

First cell selected but not highlighted

Black border surrounds selected range

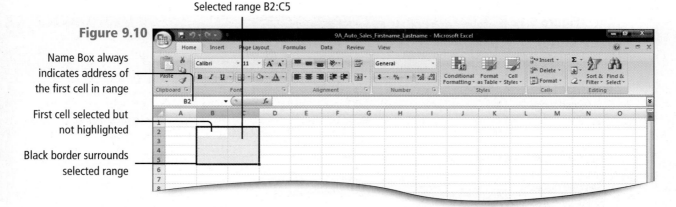

4 At the left edge of the worksheet, point to **3** to display the ➡ mouse pointer, and then click the **row 3** heading to select the entire row.

> A *row* is a horizontal group of cells in a worksheet. Beginning with number 1, a unique number identifies each row—this is the *row heading*, located at the left side of the worksheet. All the cells in the row are selected, including those that are out of view.

5 In the upper left corner of **Sheet1**, point to the letter **A** to display the ⬇ pointer, and then click one time.

> Column A is selected. A *column* is a vertical group of cells in a worksheet. Beginning with the first letter of the alphabet, A, a unique letter identifies each column—this is called the *column heading*. All the cells in the column are selected, including those that are out of view.

6 Click in the **Name Box**; notice that the cell reference *A1* moves to the left edge and is highlighted in blue.

> In any Windows program, text highlighted in blue in this manner will be replaced by your typing.

7 Type **d4:f6** and then compare your screen with Figure 9.11.

Figure 9.11

Range typed in
Name Box— OK to
type lowercase or
uppercaseletters

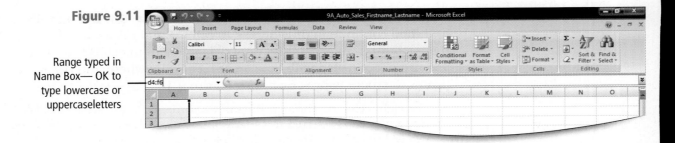

8 Press [Enter] to select the range. Then, click in the **Name Box**, type
b2:b8,e2:e8 press [Enter], and compare your screen with Figure 9.12.

Two ***nonadjacent ranges***—ranges that are not next to each other—are
selected. Ranges of cells that are not ***adjacent***—next to each other—can be
selected by typing the ranges into the Name Box separated by a comma.

Figure 9.12

Name Box displays
the first cell in the
second range

Selected ranges
B2:B8 and E2:E8

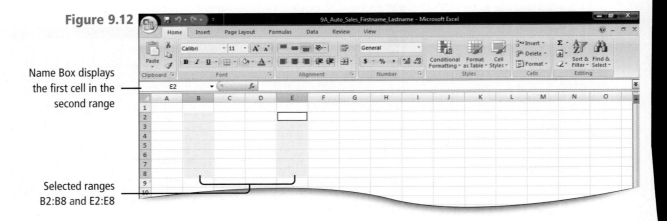

9 Select the range **C3:C5**, notice that the previously selected cells are
deselected, and then hold down [Ctrl] and select the range **E3:E5**.

Use either technique to select cells that are nonadjacent. A range of cells
can be adjacent or nonadjacent. Recall that a range of cells that is nonadjacent can be indicated by separating the ranges with a comma. In
this instance, the selected ranges can be referred to as *c3:c5,e3:e5*.

10 At the upper left corner of your worksheet, locate, and then click
the **Select All** box—the small box above **row heading 1** and to
the left of **column heading A** to select all of the cells in the worksheet. Then, point to any cell on your worksheet and click to cancel
the selection.

Objective 2
Enter and Edit Data in a Worksheet

Anything you type into a cell is *cell content*. Cell content can be one of two things—either a *constant value*—referred to simply as a *value*—or a *formula*. The most commonly used values are text values and number values, but a value can also include a date or a time of day. A formula is an equation that performs mathematical calculations on values in your worksheet.

Values in a cell can be *edited*—changed—or cleared from the cell. Text values usually provide information about number values in other worksheet cells. For example, a title such as *Quarterly Auto Sales* gives the reader an indication that the data in the worksheet relates to information about sales of autos during a three-month period.

Activity 9.04 Entering Text, Using AutoComplete, Filling a Series with Auto Fill, and Using Spelling Checker and Undo to Correct Typing Errors

To enter text in a cell, select the cell and type. In this activity, you will enter a title for the worksheet and titles for the rows and columns that will identify the types of vehicles purchased and the monthly sales amount for each vehicle type.

1 Click the **Sheet1 tab**, if necessary, so that **Sheet 1** is the active sheet. Click cell **A1**, type **Rio Rancho Auto Gallery** and then press Enter.

> After you type data in a cell, you must confirm the entry to store it in the cell. One way to do this is to press the Enter key, which typically moves the selection to the cell below to facilitate entry in a column of cells. You can also use other keyboard movements, such as Tab, or one of the arrow keys on your keyboard.

2 Look at cell **A1** and notice that the text does not fit; the text spills over and displays in cells **B1** and **C1** to the right.

> If text is too long for a cell and the cells to the right are empty, the text will display. If the cells to the right contain other data, only the text that will fit in the cell will display. Cell A2 is the active cell, as indicated by the black border surrounding it.

3 In cell **A2**, type **Monthly Sales by Vehicle Type** and then press Enter. In cell **A3**, type **Type** and then press Enter. Compare your screen with Figure 9.13.

Figure 9.13

Text too long for cell spills into adjacent cells if the adjacent cells are empty

Cell A4 active cell

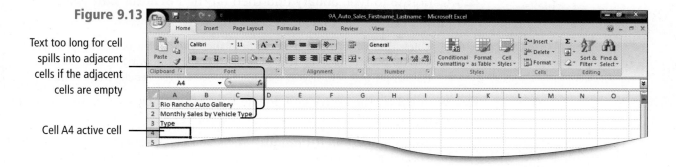

4 In cell **A4**, type **Sedans** and then press Enter.

> The text is left aligned in the cell and the selection moves to cell A5. *Left alignment*—characters align at the left edge of the cell—is the default for text values. Information about how a cell is formatted is stored with the cell.

5 In cell **A5**, type **S** and notice that the text from the previous cell displays.

> Excel assists you in typing. If the first characters you type in a cell match an existing entry in the column, Excel fills in the remaining characters for you. This feature, called *AutoComplete*, speeds your typing. AutoComplete assists only with alphabetic values; it does not assist with numeric values.

6 Continue typing the remainder of the row title, **UVs** and press Enter.

> As soon as the entry you are typing differs from the previous value, the AutoComplete suggestion is removed.

7 Without correcting the spelling error, in cell **A6**, type **Truks** and then press Enter. Then, in cell **A7**, type **Convertibles** and press Enter. In cell **A8**, type **Totals** and press Enter.

8 Click cell **B3** to make it the active cell. Type **J** and notice that when you begin to type in a cell, on the **Formula Bar**, the **Cancel** and **Enter** buttons become active, as shown in Figure 9.14.

Figure 9.14

Enter button

Cancel button

Formula Bar

Completed text
entry (SUVs)

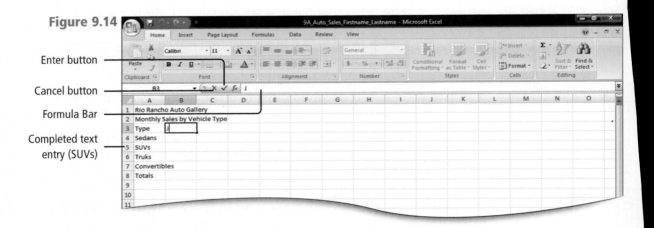

9 Continue to type **anuary** and then on the **Formula Bar**, click the **Enter** button ✓ to keep cell **B3** the active cell.

> Click this Enter button to confirm the entry and maintain the current cell as the active cell. This is convenient if you want to take further action on the cell. If you mistakenly press Enter, reselect the cell.

10 With **B3** as the active cell, locate the small black square in the lower right corner of the selected cell.

> You can drag the *fill handle*—the small black square in the lower right corner of a selected cell—to adjacent cells to fill the cells with values based on the first cell or cells in the series.

11 Point to the fill handle until the ⊞ pointer displays, hold down the left mouse button, drag to the right to cell **F3**, and as you drag notice the ScreenTips *February, March, April* and *May*. Release the left mouse button, point to the **Auto Fill Options** button that displays, and then compare your screen with Figure 9.15.

> Excel's ***Auto Fill*** feature can generate a ***series*** of values into adjacent cells, based on the value of other cells. A series is a group of things that come one after another in succession. For example, *January, February, March*, and so on, is a series. Likewise, *1st Qtr, 2nd Qtr, 3rd Qtr*, and *4th Qtr* form a series.

Figure 9.15

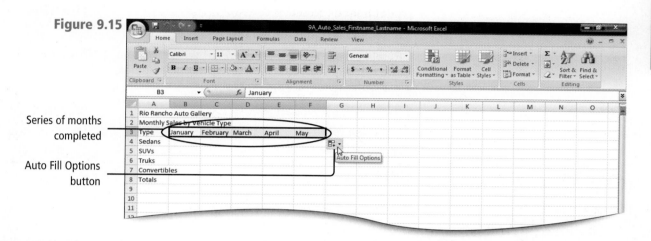

Series of months completed

Auto Fill Options button

12 To the right of and below the filled data, point to, and then click the **Auto Fill Options** button.

> The Auto Fill Options button displays just below a filled selection after you fill data in a worksheet. When you click the button, a list displays with options to fill the data. The list of options varies depending on the content you are filling, the program you are filling from, and the format of the data you are filling.

> *Fill Series* is selected, indicating the action that was taken. Because the options are related to the current task, the button is referred to as being ***context sensitive***.

13 Click in any cell to cancel the display of the Auto Fill Options list.

> The list no longer displays; the button will display until you perform some other screen action.

14 Hold down (Ctrl), and then press (Home) to make cell **A1** the active cell.

> This type of action is a ***keyboard shortcut***, which is an individual keystroke or a combination of keys pressed simultaneously to either perform an Excel command or move to another location on your screen.

15 Take a moment to study the table in Figure 9.16 to become familiar with additional keyboard shortcuts with which you can navigate the Excel worksheet.

Keyboard Shortcuts to Navigate the Excel Screen	
To Move the Location of the Active Cell:	**Press:**
Up, down, right, or left one cell	⬆, ⬇, ➡, ⬅
Down one cell	Enter
Up one cell	⇧ Shift + Enter
Up one full screen	Page Up
Down one full screen	PageDown
Left one full screen	Alt + Page Up
Right one full screen	Alt + PageDown
To column A of the current row	Home
To the last cell in the last column of the active area (the rectangle formed by all the rows and columns in a worksheet that contain entries)	Ctrl + End
To cell A1	Ctrl + Home
Right one cell	Tab
Left one cell	⇧ Shift + Tab

Figure 9.16

16 With cell **A1** active, click the **Review tab**, and then in the **Proofing group**, click the **Spelling** button. Alternatively, press F7—the keyboard shortcut for the Spelling command. Compare your screen with Figure 9.17.

Figure 9.17

Spelling dialog box

Word indicated as *Not in Dictionary*

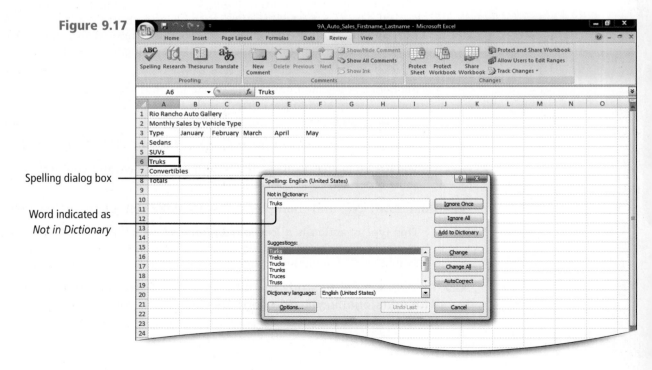

Does a message display asking if you want to continue checking at the beginning of the sheet?

If a message displays asking if you want to continue checking at the beginning of the sheet, click Yes. The Spelling command begins its checking process with the currently selected cell and moves to the right and down. Thus, if your active cell was a cell after A6, this message may display.

17 In the **Spelling** dialog box, under **Not in Dictionary**, notice the word *Truks*.

The spelling tool does not have this word in its dictionary. Under *Suggestions*, Excel provides a list of suggested spellings.

18 Under **Suggestions**, click **Trucks**, and then click the **Change** button.

Truks, a typing error, is changed to *Trucks*. A message box displays *The spelling check is complete for the entire sheet*. Because the spelling check begins its checking process starting with the currently selected cell, it is good practice to return to cell A1 before starting the Spelling command.

Note — Words Not in the Dictionary Are Not Necessarily Misspelled

Many proper nouns or less commonly used words are not in the dictionary used by Excel. If Excel indicates a correct word as *Not in Dictionary*, you can choose to ignore this word or add it to the dictionary. You may want to add proper names that you expect to use often, such as your own last name, to the dictionary.

19 Correct any other errors you may have made. When the message displays, *The spelling check is complete for the entire sheet*, click **OK**.

20 Point to cell **A5**, and then ***double-click***—click the left mouse button two times in rapid succession while keeping the mouse still. Compare your screen with Figure 9.18.

The insertion point displays in the text in cell A5, and the text also displays in the Formula Bar.

Figure 9.18

Cell content displays in the Formula Bar

Insertion point displays inside the cell

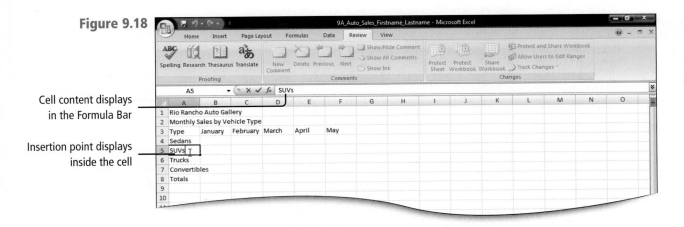

21 Move the mouse pointer away from the cell so that you have a clear view, and then using the [Del], [←Bksp], or arrow keys as necessary, edit the text and change it to **Vans** Confirm the change by pressing [Enter].

22 On the **Quick Access Toolbar**, click the **Undo** button [↶]. Alternatively, you can press [Ctrl] + [Z] on the keyboard to reverse (undo) the last action.

> *SUVs* is restored and *Vans* is deleted—your action was undone.

More Knowledge — AutoCorrect Also Assists in Your Typing

AutoCorrect assists in your typing by automatically correcting and formatting some text as you type. Excel compares your typing to a list of commonly mistyped words and when it finds a match, it substitutes the correct word. For example, if you type *monday*, Excel will automatically correct to *Monday*. To view the AutoCorrect options, display the Office menu. At the lower right, click Excel Options; on the left, click Proofing, and then click the AutoCorrect Options button.

Activity 9.05 Aligning Text and Adjusting the Size of Columns and Rows

Data in a cell can be aligned at the left, at the right, or centered. You can make columns wider or narrower and make rows taller or shorter.

1 In the **column heading area**, point to the vertical line between **column A** and **column B** to display the [↔] pointer, press and hold down the left mouse button, and then compare your screen with Figure 9.19.

> A ScreenTip displays information about the width of the column.

Figure 9.19

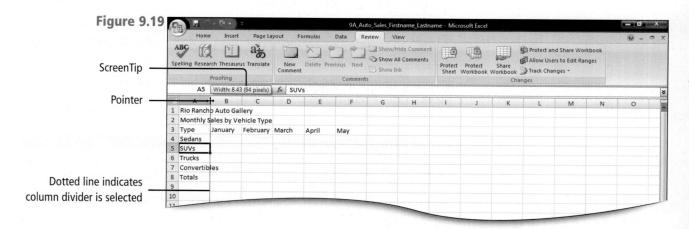

ScreenTip
Pointer
Dotted line indicates column divider is selected

2 Drag to the right and release the mouse button when the number of pixels indicated in the ScreenTip reaches **90 pixels**, which is wide enough to display the longest row title in cells A4 through A7—the worksheet title in A1 will span more than one column and still does not fit in column A. If you are not satisfied with your result, click the Undo button and begin again.

The default width of a column is 64 **pixels**. A pixel, short for **picture element**, is a point of light measured in dots per square inch on a screen. Sixty-four pixels equals 8.43 characters, which is the average number of digits that will fit in a cell using the default **font**—a set of characters with the same design, size, and shape.

The default font in Excel is Calibri, and the default **font size**—the size of characters in a font measured in **points**—is 11. There are 72 points in an inch, with 10 or 11 points being a typical font size in Excel. Point is usually abbreviated as **pt**.

3 Click cell **A8**. Click the **Home tab**, and then in the **Alignment group**, click the **Align Text Right** button [icon].

The row title aligns at the right side of the cell to distinguish it from the other row titles in the column. Text can be aligned at the center, left, or right of a cell. By default, text values align at the left.

4 Select the range **B3:F3**, and then with your pointer positioned anywhere over the selected range, **right-click**—click the right mouse button—to display a **shortcut menu** and a **Mini toolbar**—both of which display commands most commonly used in the context of selected text of this type.

5 On the Mini toolbar, click the **Center** button [icon] and notice that the shortcut menu no longer displays. Then, move the mouse slightly below the Mini toolbar and notice that the Mini toolbar fades so that you can see the result of your formatting.

6 Move the pointer back into the Mini toolbar, and then notice that it displays and once again becomes a functioning toolbar.

The column titles *January – May* align in the center of each cell. A shortcut menu offers the most commonly used commands relevant to the selected area and thus is context sensitive. You can also press [⇧ Shift] + [F10] to display a shortcut menu.

7 Click any cell to cancel the selection and close the Mini toolbar. In the **row heading area**, point to the boundary between **row 1** and **row 2** until the [+] pointer displays. Drag downward, release the mouse button when the height of **row 1** is **28 pixels**, and then compare your screen with Figure 9.20.

The row height increases. Row height is measured in points or in pixels. Points are the units in which font size is measured and pixels are units of screen display. The default height of a row is 15.00 points or 20 pixels.

Figure 9.20

Column A changed to 90 pixels wide

Row 1 changed to 28 pixels high

Text centered within the cells

Text in cell A8 right aligned

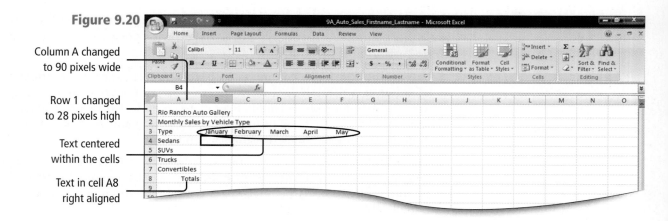

8 On the **Quick Access Toolbar**, click **Save** [icon] to save the changes you have made to your workbook; alternatively, press Ctrl + S.

Activity 9.06 Entering Numbers

To type number values, you can use either the number keys across the top of your keyboard or the number keys and Enter on the numeric keypad. Try to develop some proficiency in touch control of the numeric keypad. In this activity, you will enter the sales amounts for Rio Rancho Auto Gallery.

1 Click cell **B4**, type **330373.42** and then on the **Formula Bar**, click the **Enter** button ✓ to maintain cell **B4** as the active cell. Compare your screen with Figure 9.21.

> By default, number values align at the right edge of the cell. The default *number format*—a specific way in which Excel displays numbers—is the *general format*. The general format has no specific characteristics—whatever you type in the cell will display, with the exception that trailing zeros to the right of a decimal point will not display. For example, if you type *125.50* the cell will display *125.5* instead.
>
> Number values that are too long to fit in the cell do *not* spill over into the unoccupied cell to the right in the same manner as text values. Rather, the number is rounded. However, the entire number still exists and displays in the Formula Bar.
>
> Data that displays in a cell is referred to as the ***displayed value***. Data that displays in the Formula Bar is referred to as the ***underlying value***. The number of digits or characters that display in a cell—the displayed value—depends on the width of the column.

Figure 9.21

Cell content, in full, displays in Formula Bar

Display of number does not extend into occupied cells, number is rounded

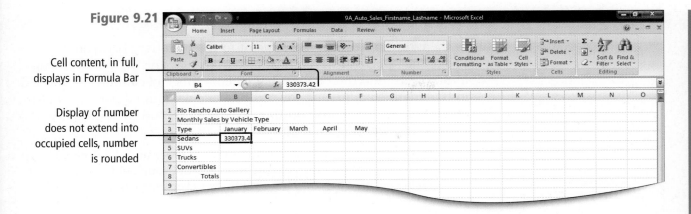

2 Enter the remaining sales figures for *Sedans* and *SUVs* in the months of January through May, as shown in the following table. Press Tab to simultaneously confirm your entry and move across the row, and then press Enter at the end of a row to move to the next row. Notice that as you type, if the column is too narrow to display all of the decimal places in a number, the display of the number will be rounded to fit the available space. When finished, compare your screen with Figure 9.22.

> *Rounding* is a procedure in which you determine which digit at the right of the number will be the last digit displayed and then increase it by one if the next digit to its right is 5, 6, 7, 8, or 9.

> Recall that trailing zeros to the right of a decimal point will not display. So for example, if you type 289076.30, the cell will display 289076.3 and if you type 297467.00, the cell will display 297467.

> Calculations performed on numbers in Excel will always be based on the underlying value, not the displayed value.

	January	February	March	April	May
Sedans	330373.42	289076.30	271717.67	326243.00	297467.00
SUVs	185835.76	163446.98	140408.67	247780.87	189756.00

Figure 9.22

Values entered for Sedans and SUVs

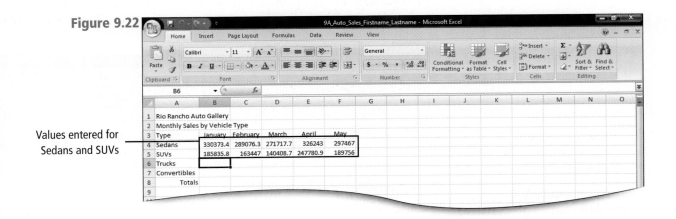

3 Click in the **Name Box**, type **b:f** and then press Enter.

4 In the **column heading area**, point to the boundary between any two of the selected column headings to display the ⊹ pointer, drag to **50** pixels, and then notice that when a range of columns is selected in this manner, adjusting the width of one column adjusts the width of all. Release the mouse button, click cell **C5**, and then compare your screen with Figure 9.23.

> In this example, as the columns become narrower and the decimal places cannot fit into the cell, the numbers are rounded further to fit the available space. The underlying value, however, is unchanged.

Figure 9.23

Cell content, in full, displays in Formula Bar; displays underlying value

Display of numbers does not extend into occupied cells; rounded to 163447

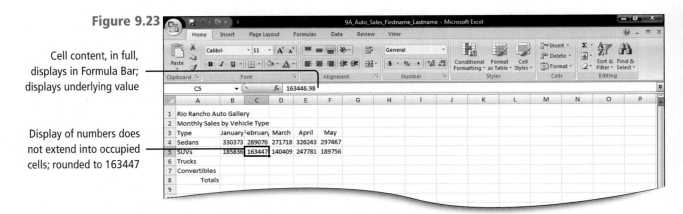

5 On the **Quick Access Toolbar**, click the **Undo** button ↺ to restore the column widths to 64 pixels. Click in any cell to deselect the columns.

6 In the **column heading area**, point to the right boundary of **column D**, and then drag the right column border to the left to set the width of **column D** to **30 pixels**. Then, click cell **D5** and compare your screen with Figure 9.24.

> If a cell width is too narrow to display the entire number, Excel displays a series of # symbols instead; displaying only a portion of a whole number would be misleading. The underlying values remain unchanged and are displayed in the Formula Bar for the selected cell. The underlying value also displays in the ScreenTip if you point to a cell containing ###.

Figure 9.24

Underlying value displays in the Formula Bar

Pound signs indicate cell is too narrow to display the number

Point to a cell containing ### to display underlying value in a ScreenTip

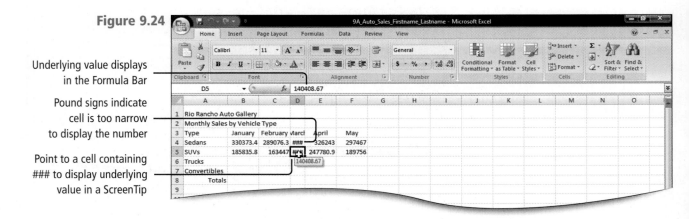

7 On the **Quick Access Toolbar**, click the **Undo** button 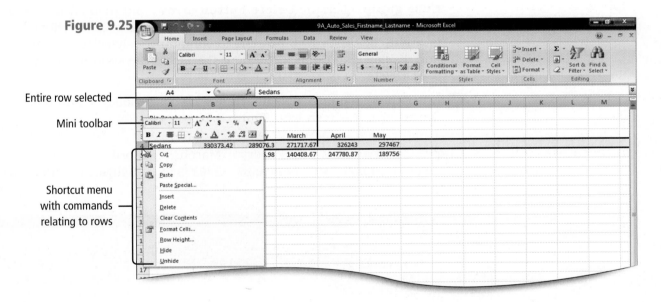 to restore **column D** to a width of 64 pixels. Select **columns B:F**. In the **column heading area**, point to the boundary between any two of the selected column headings to display the ⊞ pointer, and then drag to **85** pixels.

Recall that in the default general number format, trailing zeros to the right of a decimal point do not display regardless of the column width.

8 Click any cell to cancel the selection, and then **Save** 📄 your workbook.

Activity 9.07 Inserting and Deleting Rows and Columns, and Using the Insert Options Button

In this activity, you will insert a new row to record sales for the vehicle type *Compacts* and delete the *Convertibles* vehicle type.

1 Point to the **row 4** heading, and then right-click to simultaneously select the row and display the shortcut menu and the Mini toolbar. Compare your screen with Figure 9.25.

You can right-click row numbers or column headings to simultaneously select and display a context-sensitive shortcut menu and the Mini toolbar.

Figure 9.25

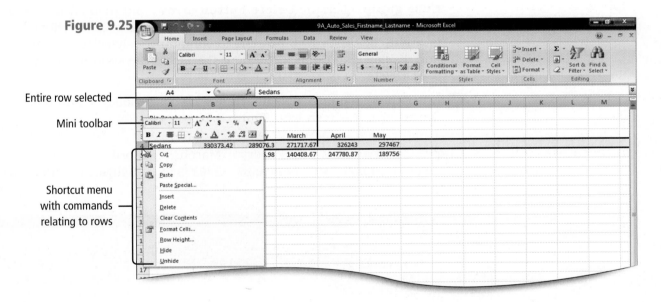

Entire row selected

Mini toolbar

Shortcut menu with commands relating to rows

2 On the shortcut menu, click **Insert**.

Excel inserts a new row 4 above the selected row, and the existing rows shift down one row. Additionally, the Insert Options button displays.

Note — Insert Columns by Using the Same Shortcut Menu Technique

Use a similar technique to insert a new column in a worksheet. That is, from the column heading area, right-click to simultaneously select the column and display the context-sensitive shortcut menu. Click Insert to insert a new column and shift the remaining columns to the right. Alternatively, select the column, and then on the Ribbon, in the Cells group, click the Insert button or the Insert button arrow for additional options.

3 Point to the **Insert Options** button to display its ScreenTip and its arrow, and then click the button to display a list of options.

From this menu, you can format the new row like the row above or the row below, or you can leave it unformatted. The default is *Format Same As Above*.

4 Click **Format Same As Below**.

The new row is formatted, using the format from the row of data *below* instead of the row of column titles above, which are centered. The Insert Options button remains visible until you perform another screen action.

5 Click cell **A4**, type **Compacts** and then press Tab. Enter the values for *Compacts* for each month, as shown in the following table. Use Tab to confirm each entry and move the active cell across the row.

Type	January	February	March	April	May
Compacts	326485.76	376984.92	367540.57	330373.58	345765.64

6 From the **row heading area**, select **row 8**. On the Ribbon, in the **Cells group**, click the **Delete button arrow**, and then click **Delete Sheet Rows**. Alternatively, click the Delete button on the Ribbon; or, right-click the row 8 heading to simultaneously select the row and display a shortcut menu, and then from the shortcut menu, click Delete.

7 Enter the remaining sales figures for *Trucks* as follows, and then compare your screen with Figure 9.26.

Type	January	February	March	April	May
Trucks	309725.48	272558.89	330373.58	289076.55	319583.61

Figure 9.26

Values entered for Compacts and Trucks

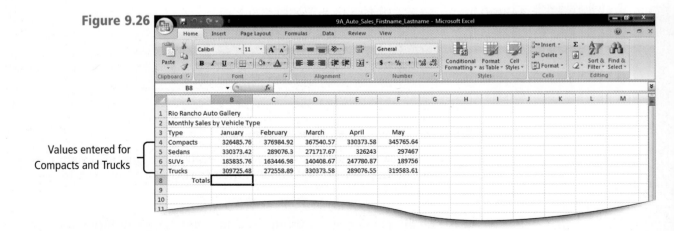

8 **Save** your workbook.

Objective 3
Construct and Copy Formulas, Use the Sum Function, and Edit Cells

Excel performs calculations on numbers; that is why you use Excel. If you make changes to the numbers, Excel automatically *re*-calculates. This is one of the most powerful and valuable features of Excel. You can arrange data in a format of columns and rows in other programs—in a word processing program, for example—and even perform simple calculations. Excel, however, performs complex calculations on numbers.

Recall that a cell contains either a constant value or a formula. Recall also that a formula is an equation that performs mathematical calculations on values in other cells, and then places the result in the cell containing the formula. You can create your own formulas, or you can use one of Excel's prewritten formulas called a ***function***. A function is a prewritten formula that takes one or more values, performs an operation, and then returns a value or values.

Activity 9.08 Constructing a Formula, Using the Sum Function, and Editing Numbers in Cells

In this activity, you will sum the sales of vehicles by month and by type and use various methods to edit numbers within a cell.

1 Click cell **B8** to make it the active cell and type **=**

> The equal sign (=) displays in the cell with the insertion point blinking, ready to accept more data.
>
> All formulas begin with the = sign, which signals Excel to begin a calculation. The Formula Bar displays the = sign, and the Formula Bar Cancel and Enter buttons display.

2 At the insertion point, type **b4** and then compare your screen with Figure 9.27.

> A list of Excel functions that begin with the letter *B* may briefly display—as you progress in your study of Excel, you will use functions of this type. A blue border with small corner boxes surrounds cell B4, which indicates that the cell is part of an active formula. The color used in the box matches the color of the cell reference in the formula.

Figure 9.27

Your typing displays in Formula Bar

Cell outlined in the same color as the cell reference in the formula

Formula started in the active cell

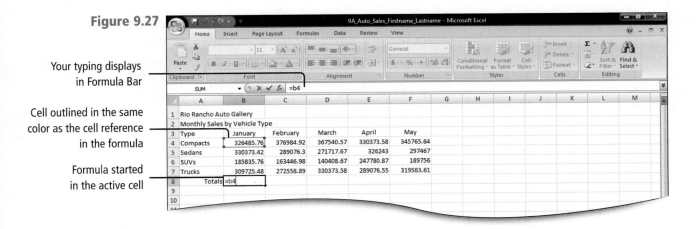

3 At the insertion point, type **+** and then type **b5** Alternatively, use the ⊞ key on your numeric keypad, which does not require the ⇧Shift key.

> A border of another color surrounds cell B5, and the color matches the color of the cell reference in the active formula. Recall that when typing cell references, it is not necessary to use uppercase letters.

4 At the insertion point, type **+b6+b7** and then press Enter.

> The result of the formula calculation—*1152420.42*—displays in the cell.

5 Click cell **B8** again to make it the active cell, and then look at the **Formula Bar**. Compare your screen with Figure 9.28.

> The formula adds the values in cells B4 through B7, and the result of adding the values in those cells displays in cell B8. Although cell B8 displays the *result* of the formula, the formula itself displays in the Formula Bar. This is referred to as the ***underlying formula***. Always view the Formula Bar to be sure of the exact content of a cell—*a displayed number may actually be a formula.*

Figure 9.28

Underlying formula displays in the Formula Bar

Result of the formula displays in the active cell

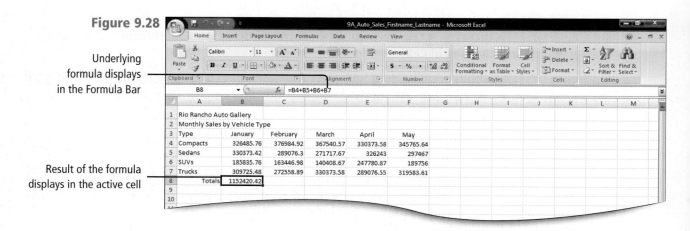

6 To change the value in cell B4, click cell **B4**, type **347999.12** and then watch cell **B8** as you press Enter.

> Excel recalculates the formula and displays *1173933.78*. Excel formulas *recalculate* if you change values in a cell that is referenced in the formula. It is not necessary to delete the old value in a cell; selecting the cell and typing a new value replaces the old value with your new typing.

7 In cell **C8**, type **=** to signal the beginning of a formula. Then, point to cell **C4**, click one time, and compare your screen with Figure 9.29.

> The reference to the cell, C4, is added to the active formula. A moving border surrounds the referenced cell, and the border color and the color of the cell reference in the formula are color-coded to match.

Figure 9.29

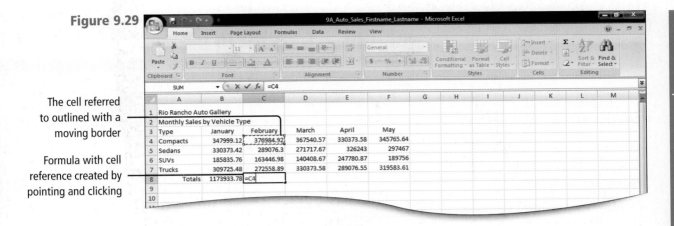

The cell referred to outlined with a moving border

Formula with cell reference created by pointing and clicking

8 At the insertion point, type **+** and then click cell **C5**. Repeat this process to complete the formula to add cells **C4** through **C7**, and then press [Enter].

The result of the formula calculation—*1102067.09*—displays in the cell. This method of constructing a formula is the ***point and click method***. Constructing a formula by using the point and click method is convenient when the referenced cells are not adjacent to one another.

9 Point to cell **C6**, and then double-click to place the insertion point within the cell. Use the arrow keys to move the insertion point to the left or right of *3*, and then use either [Del] or [←Bksp] to delete the *3* and then type **1** Watch cell **C8** as you press [Enter] and then notice the recalculation of the formula.

10 Click cell **D8**. On the **Home tab**, in the **Editing group**, click the **Sum** button [Σ ▾]. Alternatively, use the keyboard shortcut [Alt] + [=]; or, on the Formulas tab, in the Function Library group, click the AutoSum button. Compare your screen with Figure 9.30.

Sum is an Excel function—a prewritten formula. A moving border surrounds cells D4:D7, and *=SUM(D4:D7)* displays in cell D8.

The = sign signals the beginning of a formula, *SUM* indicates the type of calculation that will take place (addition), and *(D4:D7)* indicates the range of cells on which the sum operation will be performed. A ScreenTip provides additional information about the action.

Figure 9.30

Underlying formula
displays in Formula Bar

Moving border surrounds
the range selected by Sum

Formula generated by
the Sum function

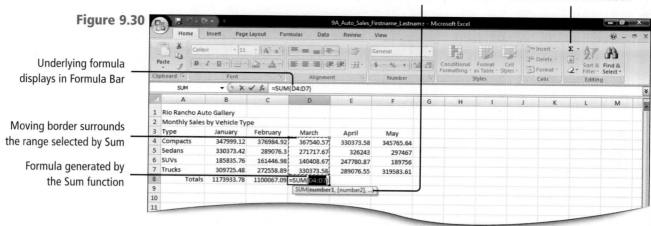

11 Look at the **Formula Bar**, and notice that the formula also displays
there. Then, look again at the cells surrounded by the moving border.

When you activate the Sum function, Excel first looks *above* the active
cell for a range of cells to sum. If no range is above the active cell, Excel
will look to the *left* for a range of cells to sum. If the proposed range is
not what you want to calculate, you can select a different group of cells.

12 Press Enter to view the sum of March sales—*1110040.49*—in cell **D8**.

Because the Sum function is frequently used, it has its own button in
the Editing group on the Ribbon. A larger version of the button also
displays on the Formulas tab in the Function Library group. As you
progress in your study of Excel, you will use additional Excel functions.
This button is also referred to as *AutoSum*.

13 Click cell **D4**, and then click in the **Formula Bar** to position the
insertion point there. Change the number *6* to **7** so that the value is
377540.57, and then press Enter to recalculate the formula.

The total for March is recalculated to *1120040.49*. You can edit cells in
the Formula Bar or inside the cell itself.

14 Select the range **E4:F8**, look at the status bar at the lower right of
your screen, and then compare your screen with Figure 9.31.

By selecting a range of cells and including the empty cells at the bottom
of each column, you can apply the Sum function to sum several
columns at once; the formula for adding each column will be placed
in the empty cells at the bottom of each column.

Additionally, when you select a range of cells containing numbers, Excel
displays the result of applying the Average, Count, or Sum functions
in the status bar. You can see that if you averaged the numbers of the
selected cells, the result would be 293255.7813; if you counted the cells
in the selection that contain values (text or numbers), the result would
be 8, and if you added the numbers in the selected cells, the total would
be 2346046.25.

Figure 9.31

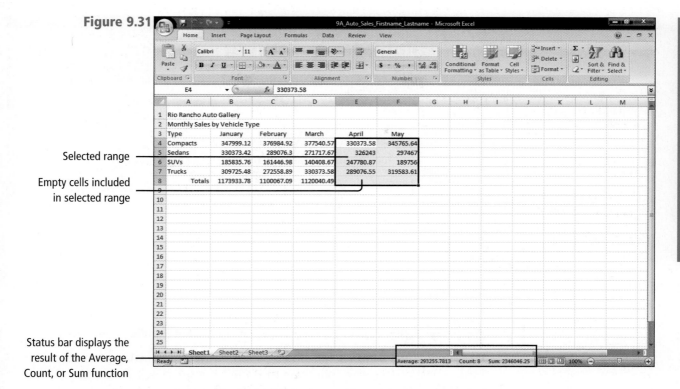

Selected range

Empty cells included in selected range

Status bar displays the result of the Average, Count, or Sum function

---

More Knowledge — Multiple Status Bar Calculations

When numerical data is selected, three calculations display in the status bar by default—Average, Count, and Sum. You can display a total of six of these calculations on the status bar by adding the Numerical Count (the number of cells within the selection that contain numbers), Minimum, and Maximum functions to the status bar. To add additional calculations, right-click the status bar and select the calculations you want to display.

---

15 In the **Editing group**, click the **Sum** button Σ ▾ or press Alt + =.

Excel places the Sum formula in cells E8 and F8 and a result displays in cells E8 and F8 indicating the sums *1193474* and *1152572.25*. Recall that in the General number format, trailing zeros do not display.

16 Click cell **E8**, and then notice the formula in the **Formula Bar**. Click cell **F8** to view the formula in the **Formula Bar**. Compare your screen with Figure 9.32.

The cells display the result of the calculated function, which is a formula that Excel has prewritten and named.

Figure 9.32

Formula indicated in Formula Bar

All monthly totals calculated

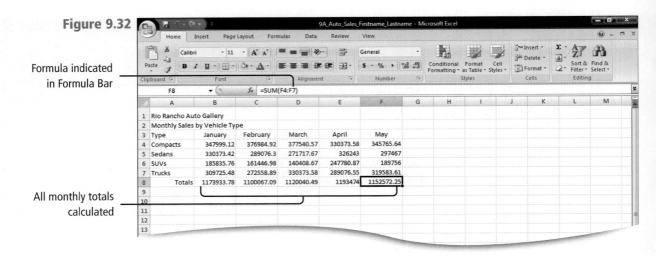

17 **Save** 💾 your workbook.

Activity 9.09 Copying a Formula by Using the Fill Handle

Excel provides a quick method—called copying formulas—to create formulas without typing, pointing and clicking, or using a command from the Ribbon. When you copy a formula from one cell to another, Excel adjusts the cell references to fit the new location of the formula. In this activity, you will delete the columns that do not relate to the first quarter, and then copy formulas.

1 From the **column heading area**, select **columns E:F**. In the **Cells group**, click the **Delete button arrow**, and then click **Delete Sheet Columns**. Alternatively, click the Delete button; or, right-click over the selected columns to display the shortcut menu and click Delete.

> Only the monthly sales for the first quarter of the year—January through March—display.

2 Click cell **E4**, hold down Alt, and then press =. Compare your screen with Figure 9.33.

> The Alt + = keyboard shortcut is the fastest way to apply the Sum function. Recall that Excel first looks above the selected cell for a proposed range of cells to sum, and if no data is detected, Excel then looks to the left and proposes a range of cells to sum.

Figure 9.33

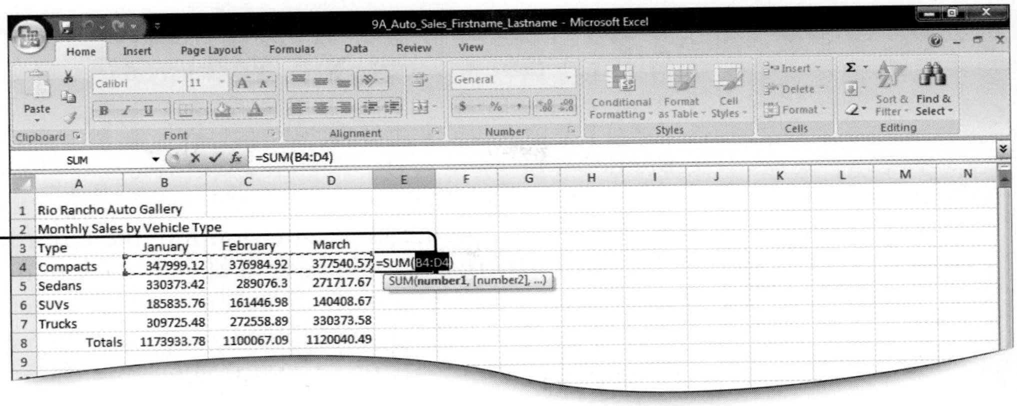

Sum function applied with proposed range of cells to sum

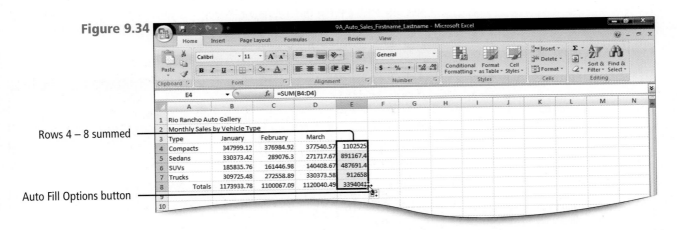

3 On the **Formula Bar**, click the **Enter** button ☑ to keep cell **E4** active.

> The total dollar amount of *Compacts* sold in the quarter is *1102525*. In cells E5:E8, you can see that you need a formula similar to the one in E4, but one that refers to the cells in row 5, row 6, and so forth.

4 With cell **E4** active, point to the fill handle in the lower right corner of the cell until the ✚ pointer displays. Then, drag downward through cell **E8**. Compare your screen with Figure 9.34.

Figure 9.34

Rows 4 – 8 summed

Auto Fill Options button

5 Click cell **E5**, look at the **Formula Bar**, and notice the formula *=SUM(B5:D5)*. Click cell **E6**, look at the **Formula Bar**, and then notice the formula *=SUM(B6:D6)*.

> In each row, Excel copied the formula but adjusted the cell references *relative to* the row number. This is called a **relative cell reference**— a cell reference based on the relative position of the cell that contains the formula and the cells referred to.

> The calculation is the same, but it is performed on the cells in that particular row. Use this quick method to insert numerous formulas into spreadsheets.

6 **Save** 🖫 your workbook.

Objective 4
Format Data, Cells, and Worksheets

Excel has many options for displaying numbers—think of percentages, fractions, or money. Recall that Excel refers to the various ways to write numbers as number formats. Some common number formats are those used for reporting financial information like monthly sales.

Formatting is the process of specifying the appearance of cells and the overall layout of a worksheet. Formatting is accomplished through various commands on the Ribbon, many of which are also available by using shortcut menus or keyboard shortcuts.

Activity 9.10 Formatting Financial Numbers, Using Column AutoFit, and Using Format Painter

The General format is the default format for a number that you type in a cell. Unless you apply a different number format to a cell, Excel will use the General format. The General format displays a number exactly as you type it—with three exceptions, as noted in the table in Figure 9.36.

1 Click cell **B4** so that a cell with a number value is selected. On the **Home tab**, in the **Number group**, point to the **Dialog Box Launcher** button ⬚ in the lower right corner, as shown in Figure 9.35.

> A ScreenTip displays what the result of clicking the button will be. A **Dialog Box Launcher** displays in some groups on the Ribbon and opens a related dialog box providing additional options and commands related to that group.

Figure 9.35

Dialog Box Launcher button

Number group on the Home tab

ScreenTip indicates what will display

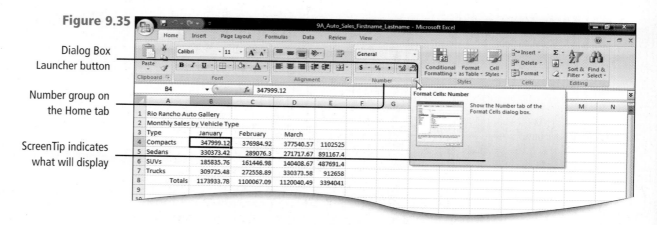

2 Click the **Dialog Box Launcher** button ⬚, and then in the **Format Cells** dialog box, on the **Number tab** under **Category**, click each category. As you do so, look at the **Sample** box to view the effect that each number format will have on the selected cell, and then take a moment to study the information about each number format in the table in Figure 9.36.

Excel Number Formats

Number Format	Description
General	The General format is the default format for a number that you type in a cell. The General format displays a number exactly as you type it—with three exceptions: 1. Extremely long numbers may be abbreviated to a shorthand version of numbers called scientific notation; Excel will still use the underlying value in any calculations. 2. Trailing zeros will not display in the General format. 3. A decimal fraction entered without a number to the left of the decimal point will display with a zero.
Number	Number format is used for the general display of non-currency numbers. The default format has two decimal places, and you may choose to check the option for using a comma as a thousand separator. Negative numbers can display in red, be preceded by a minus sign, be enclosed in parentheses, or display both in red and in parentheses.
Currency	Currency format is used for general monetary values—the U.S. dollar sign is the default symbol. The default format has two decimal places.
Accounting	Accounting format lines up the currency symbols and decimal points in a column. It is similar to Currency format with two differences—the dollar sign (or other currency symbol) always displays at the left edge of the cell, rather than flush against the first number. Thus, both dollar signs and numbers are vertically aligned in the same column. Also, Accounting format adds a blank space equal to the width of a closing parenthesis on the right side of positive values to ensure that decimal points align if a column has both positive and negative numbers. The default format has two decimal places.
Date	Date format provides many common ways to display dates. The default format is month, day, and year, separated by a slash. The year displays as four digits by default, but may be changed in the Control Panel to a two-digit display. Formats that begin with an asterisk are subject to change by regional date and time settings specified in the Control Panel.
Time	Time format provides many common ways to display time; formats are subject to change in the manner described above for dates.
Percentage	Percentage format multiplies the cell value by 100 and displays the result with a percent sign. The default format has two decimal places.
Fraction	Fraction format displays fractional amounts as actual fractions rather than as decimal values.
Scientific	Scientific format displays numbers in scientific (exponential) notation. This is useful for extremely large numbers. The default format has two decimal places.
Text	Text format treats a number as if it were text. The number is left-aligned like text.
Special	Special formats used primarily with database functions such as postal codes, telephone numbers, and taxpayer ID numbers.
Custom	Custom format is used to create your own number format.

Figure 9.36

3 In the **Format Cells** dialog box, click **Cancel**. Hold down Ctrl, select the nonadjacent ranges **B4:E4** and **B8:E8**, and then in the **Number group**, click the **Accounting Number Format** button $ ▾ . Compare your screen with Figure 9.37.

Columns B through D are not wide enough to accommodate the newly formatted numbers and thus display # symbols.

The **Accounting Number Format** button formats the number with the default Accounting format that uses the U.S. dollar sign. That is, it applies a thousand comma separator where appropriate, inserts a fixed U.S. dollar sign aligned at the left edge of the cell, applies two decimal places, and leaves a small amount of space at the right edge of the cell to accommodate a parenthesis for negative numbers.

Figure 9.37

Accounting Number Format button in Number group

Accounting Number Format applied to selected cells

Cells too narrow for newly formatted numbers display # signs

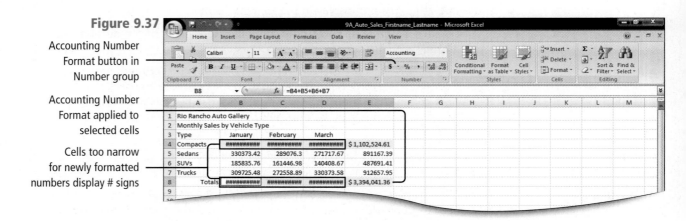

Note — Showing Fewer Decimal Places

Many financial documents do not display values with cents because either it is unnecessary to be completely precise or it not feasible to determine the exact number. To decrease the number of decimal places and round to the nearest whole dollar amount, select the cells, and then on the Home tab of the Ribbon, in the Number group, click the Decrease Decimal button two times to show a less precise value by showing fewer decimal places. Alternatively, on the Home tab, in the Styles group, click the Cell Style button, and then under Number Format, click *Currency [0]*.

---

4 Select **column B**. In the **Cells group**, click the **Format** button, and then from the menu, click **AutoFit Column Width**.

The width of the column adjusts to accommodate the longest entry, which is the formatted total in cell B8.

5 Select **columns C:E**. In the **column heading area**, point to the right boundary of any of the selected columns to display the ✛ pointer, and then double-click.

This is an alternative method to apply the AutoFit Column Width command. Each column width adjusts to accommodate the longest entry in its column.

6 Select the range **B5:B7**, and then in the **Number group**, click the **Comma Style** button ⏺.

The **Comma Style** inserts thousand comma separators where appropriate and applies two decimal places. Comma Style also leaves space at the right to accommodate a parenthesis for negative numbers.

7 Click cell **B5**. In the **Clipboard group**, click the **Format Painter** button 🖌. With the 🖱 pointer, select the range **C5:E7**, and then compare your screen with Figure 9.38.

Use **Format Painter** to copy the *formatting* of one cell to other cells—there are numerous methods to apply formatting to cells.

When preparing worksheets with financial information, the first row of dollar amounts and the total rows of dollar amounts are formatted in the Accounting Number Format; that is, with thousand comma separators, dollar signs, two decimal places, and space at the right to accommodate a parenthesis for negative numbers, if any. Rows that are not the first row or the total row should be formatted with the Comma Style.

Cells in selected range formatted with the Comma Style

Cells formatted with the Accounting Number Format

Figure 9.38

Accounting Number Format aligns dollar sign at left edge of cell

Space allowed for a parenthesis when number is negative

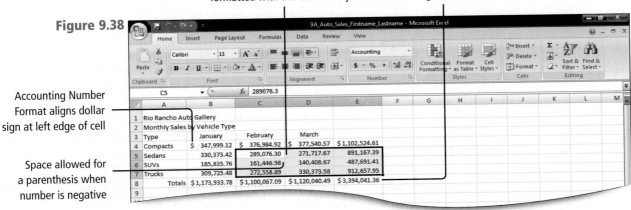

Note — Double-Click Format Painter to Copy Formatting to Multiple Selections

Double-clicking the Format Painter button causes it to remain active until you click the button again, or press [Esc], to turn it off. Use this technique to copy cell formatting to two or more cells that are not adjacent.

8 Select the range **B8:E8**. In the **Font group**, click the **Borders button arrow** 🔲 ▾ to display a gallery of commonly used border styles. Compare your screen with Figure 9.39.

A *gallery* displays a list of potential results. The Borders button displays the most recently used border style; clicking the button, rather than the arrow, applies the most recently used style as indicated by the button.

Figure 9.39

Borders arrow

Top and Double
Bottom Border

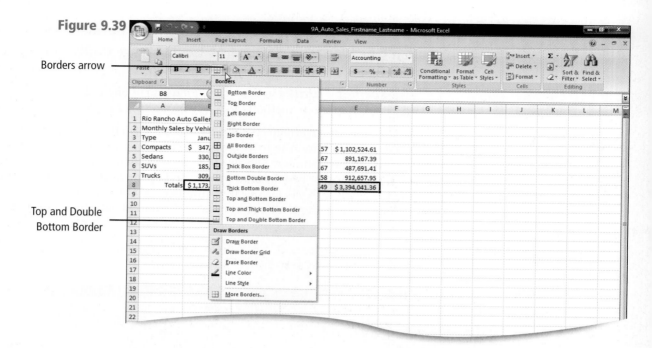

9 From the list, click **Top and Double Bottom Border**. Click any empty cell to deselect the range, and then compare your screen with Figure 9.40.

This is a common way to apply borders to financial information. The single border indicates that calculations were performed on the numbers above, and the double border indicates that the information is complete.

Figure 9.40

Top border
Double bottom border

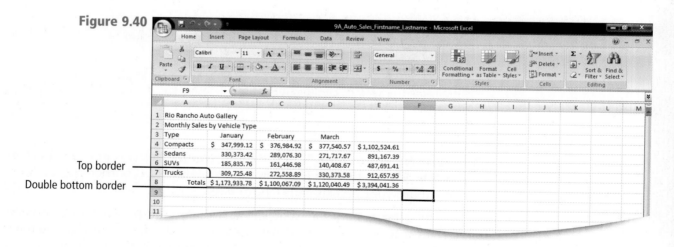

10 **Save** your workbook.

Note — Using Negative Numbers in a Worksheet

You can see a small amount of space to the right of each of the formatted number cells. The formats you applied allow this space in the event parentheses are needed to indicate negative numbers. If your worksheet contains negative numbers, display the Format Cells dialog box and select from among various formats to accommodate negative numbers. As you progress in your study of Excel, you will practice formatting negative numbers.

Activity 9.11 Formatting Text and Using Merge and Center

Use techniques similar to other Office programs to change fonts; you can add emphasis by using bold, italic, and underline, and align text in the center, or at the left or right edge of a cell. In this activity, you will format the worksheet's title and subtitle to increase their visibility and inform the reader of the worksheet's purpose.

1 Select the range **A1:E1**, and then in the **Alignment group**, click the **Merge & Center** button ⊞▾.

> The Merge & Center command joins the selected cells into one larger cell and centers the contents in the new cell; cells A1:E1 can no longer be selected individually because they are merged into cell A1.

2 Select the range **A2:E2**, right-click over the selection, and then on the Mini toolbar, click the **Merge & Center** button ⊞▾.

3 Click cell **A1**. In the **Font group**, click the **Font button arrow**.

4 At the top of the list, under **Theme Fonts**, point to **Cambria**, and notice *(Headings)* to the right.

> A *theme* is a predefined set of colors, fonts, lines, and fill effects that look good together and that can be applied to your entire workbook or to specific items—for example, to a chart or table.

> Cambria is a *serif* font—a font that includes small line extensions on the ends of the letters to guide the eye in reading from left to right. In the default theme, *Cambria* is the suggested font for headings, and *Calibri* is the suggested font for the body of the worksheet.

5 Click **Cambria** to apply the font. With cell **A1** still selected, in the **Font group**, click the **Font Size button arrow**, and then point to **14**, and then **16**, and then **18**, and notice how the text expands as you point to each size. Click **18**.

> This is *Live Preview*—a technology that shows the results of applying an editing or formatting change as you point to the items presented in the gallery or list.

6 With cell **A1** active, in the **Font group**, click **Bold** ⬚.

> The Bold *font style* is applied to your text. Font styles are used to emphasize text by using bold, italic, and underline.

7 With cell **A1** still selected, in the lower right corner of the **Font group**, click the **Dialog Box Launcher** ⬚ to display the **Font tab** of the **Format Cells** dialog box. Notice that *Cambria* is selected and that a preview of the font is also displayed under **Preview**.

8 Under **Font style**, click **Bold Italic**, and then notice that the Preview changes to reflect your selection.

9 Click the **Color arrow**. Under **Theme Colors**, in the fourth column, point to the first box to display the ScreenTip *Dark Blue, Text 2,* and then in that column of colors, click the next to last color—**Dark Blue, Text 2, Darker 25%**—as shown in Figure 9.41.

> From the Format Cells dialog box, you can apply multiple formats at one time in this manner.

Figure 9.41

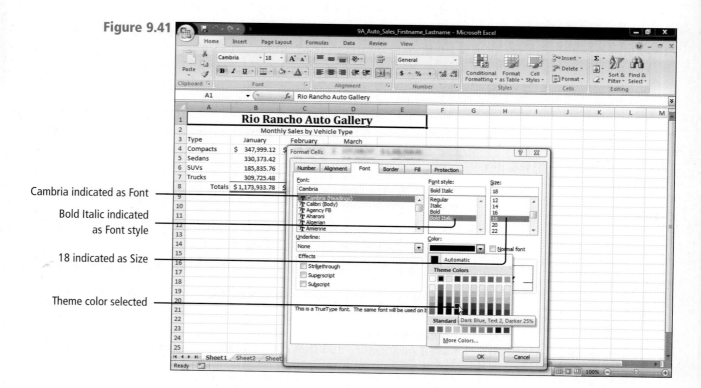

Cambria indicated as Font

Bold Italic indicated as Font style

18 indicated as Size

Theme color selected

10 Click **OK**. With cell **A1** still active, in the **Font group**, click the **Underline** button ⊔ ▾.

> From the Ribbon, you can apply some common formats such as this one. The Underline button places a single underline under the *contents* of a cell. The Bold, Italic, and Underline buttons on the Ribbon are **toggle buttons**, which means that you can click the button one time to turn the formatting on and click it again to turn it off.

11 With cell **A1** selected, in the **Font group**, click the **Underline** button ⊔ ▾ again to turn off Underline.

> The Underline font style is removed from the text, but the Bold and Italic font styles remain.

12 With cell **A1** selected, in the **Font group**, click the **Fill Color button arrow** ♦ ▾. Under **Theme Colors**, in the fourth column, click the second color—**Dark Blue, Text 2, Lighter 80%**.

> The background of the cell—its **fill color**—changes. If your printer does not print in color, the colors will print as shades of gray, so select light

colors to provide better contrast. Colors are especially distinctive if your workbook will be viewed on a screen.

13 Point to cell **A2**, right-click, on the Mini toolbar, click the **Increase Font Size** button A two times, and as you click, notice that the new Font Size number displays on both the Ribbon and the Mini toolbar. Then, on the Mini toolbar, click the **Bold** button B.

14 Move the mouse pointer slightly away so that the Mini toolbar fades, view your formatting, and then click any cell to cancel the selection and close the Mini toolbar.

15 Double-click cell **A2** and edit the word *Monthly* to change it to **First Quarter** Press Enter.

16 Select **row 2**, and in the **row heading area**, drag the lower border of **row 2** down to increase the row height to **35 pixels**.

17 Select cell **A2**, and then in the **Alignment group**, click the **Middle Align** button $\equiv$ to align the text vertically in the cell.

18 In cell **E3**, type **Totals** and then press Enter. Select the nonadjacent ranges **A3:E3** and **A4:A8** and apply **Bold** B emphasis.

19 **Save** 💾 your workbook, click any cell, and then compare your screen with Figure 9.42.

> The text in cell E3 is centered because the centered format continues from the adjacent cell. The same formatting will be applied to adjacent cells until two cells are left blank, and then the formatting is not continued.

Figure 9.42

Column title added

Monthly changed to First Quarter

Formatting applied to worksheet title and subtitle

Column and row titles in bold

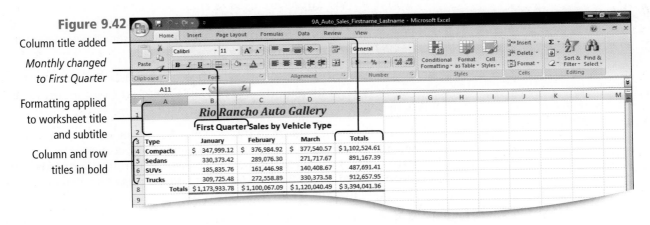

Objective 5
Close and Reopen a Workbook

You can save and close a workbook and then reopen it later to continue working. For example, at this point in this project, you may want to close the workbook and continue working later.

Activity 9.12 Closing and Reopening an Existing Workbook

1 To close the workbook, from the **Office** menu 🏛, click **Close**; if there are changes to be saved, Excel will prompt you to save before closing.

2 In the upper right corner of your screen, click the **Close** button ![X] to exit Excel. Alternatively, from the Office menu, click Exit Excel. Or, to simultaneously close your workbook and close the Excel program, from the Office menu in the lower right corner, click Exit Excel.

3 To reopen the workbook, start Excel, and then display the **Office** menu 🔘. From the list of **Recent Documents**, click your workbook name if it displays. Alternatively, click the Open button and navigate to your storage location, select your workbook, and then click Open.

Objective 6
Chart Data

A **_chart_** is a graphic representation of data in a worksheet. Data presented as a chart is easier to understand than a table of numbers.

Activity 9.13 Charting Data

In this activity, you will create a column chart showing the monthly sales of vehicles by type during the first quarter. The chart will enable Sandy Cizek, the Auto Sales Manager, to see a pattern of overall monthly sales and a pattern of monthly sales by vehicle type.

1 Select the range **A3:E8**. Click the **Insert tab**, and then in the **Charts group**, click **Column** to display a gallery of Column chart types.

> Various **_chart types_** are used to chart data in a way that is meaningful to the reader—common examples are column charts, pie charts, and line charts. A **_column chart_** is useful for illustrating comparisons among related numbers.

2 From the gallery of column chart types, under **2-D Column**, point to the first chart to display the ScreenTip _Clustered Column_, and then click to select it. Compare your screen with Figure 9.43.

> A column chart displays in the worksheet, and the charted data is bordered by colored lines. Because the chart object is selected—surrounded by a border and displaying sizing handles—**_contextual tools_** named _Chart Tools_ display and add **_contextual tabs_** next to the standard tabs on the Ribbon.

> Contextual tools display only when needed for a selected object; when you deselect the object, the contextual tools no longer display.

Figure 9.43

Cells outlined in blue represented in chart columns

Cells outlined in green represent the legend

Chart Tools indicates that tools for selected object added to the Ribbon

Chart Tools contextual tabs added to standard Ribbon tabs

Cells outlined in purple represent category labels

Clustered column chart displays in the worksheet

Border and sizing handles indicate chart is selected

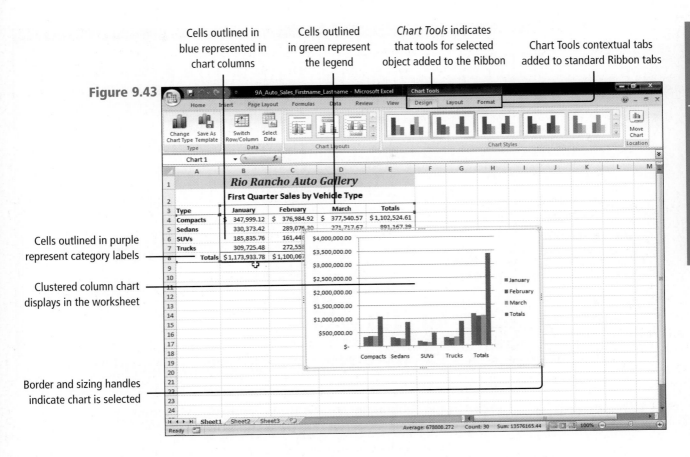

3 Point to the top border of the chart to display the 🔭 pointer, hold down the left mouse button, and then drag the upper left corner of the chart just inside the upper left corner of cell **A10**, approximately as shown in Figure 9.44.

Based on the data in your worksheet, Excel constructs a column chart and adds *category labels*—the labels that display along the bottom of the chart to identify the category of data. This area is referred to as the *category axis* or the *x-axis*. Excel uses the row titles as the category names.

On the left, Excel includes a numerical scale on which the charted data is based; this is referred to as the *value axis* or the *y-axis*. On the right, a *legend*, which identifies the patterns or colors that are assigned to the categories in the chart, displays.

Figure 9.44

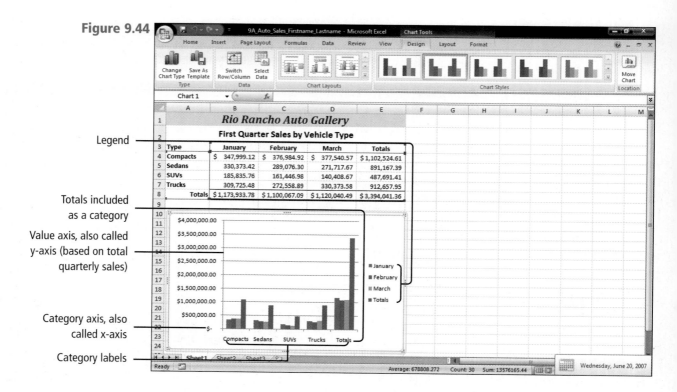

Legend

Totals included as a category

Value axis, also called y-axis (based on total quarterly sales)

Category axis, also called x-axis

Category labels

4 On the Ribbon, locate the three contextual tabs that are active under **Chart Tools—Design**, **Layout**, and **Format**.

When a chart is selected, Chart Tools become available and these three tabs—Design, Layout, and Format—provide commands for working with the chart. When the chart is not selected, the Chart Tools do not display.

5 Point to the lower right corner of cell **E8** to display the pointer, and then notice that the blue border surrounding the group of charted cells becomes thicker and brighter in color. Compare your screen with Figure 9.45.

You can adjust the chart by selecting a different group of cells to chart. On this chart, Sandy Cizek, the Auto Sales Manager, wants to see only the sales by month and not the total sales for the quarter.

When charting data, typically, you should *not* include totals—include only the comparable data.

Figure 9.45

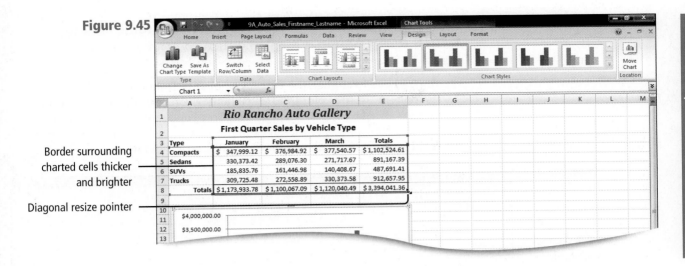

Border surrounding
charted cells thicker
and brighter

Diagonal resize pointer

6 Drag the ⬉ pointer up and to the left until only the monthly dollar amounts in the range **B4:D7** are surrounded by the blue border. Release the left mouse button and notice the changes in your chart. Compare your screen with Figure 9.46.

Each of the 12 cells bordered in blue is referred to as a ***data point***—a value that originates in a worksheet cell. Each data point is represented in the chart by a ***data marker***—a column, bar, area, dot, pie slice, or other symbol in a chart that represents a single data point.

Related data points form a ***data series***; for example, there is a data series for *January*, for *February*, and for *March*. Each data series has a unique color or pattern represented in the chart legend.

Figure 9.46

Only sales figures for January,
February, and March display

Each value in the selected
range is a data point

Totals no longer included
in the charted data

Data markers (columns)
represent each data point

Color for each data series
defined in legend

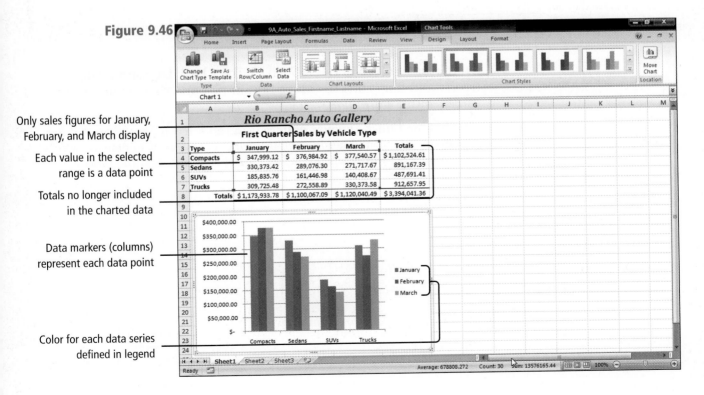

7 On the **Design tab** of the Ribbon, in the **Data group**, click the **Switch Row/Column** button, and then compare your chart with Figure 9.47.

> You can easily change the categories of data from the row titles, which is the default, to the column titles. Whether you use row or column titles as your category names depends on how you want to view your charted data. In this instance, the Sales Manager wants to see monthly sales and the breakdown of vehicle type within each month.

Figure 9.47

More button in Chart Layouts and Chart Styles

Each value in the selected range is a data point

Data series switched to row names (vehicle types) as defined in legend

Categories switched to column names (months)

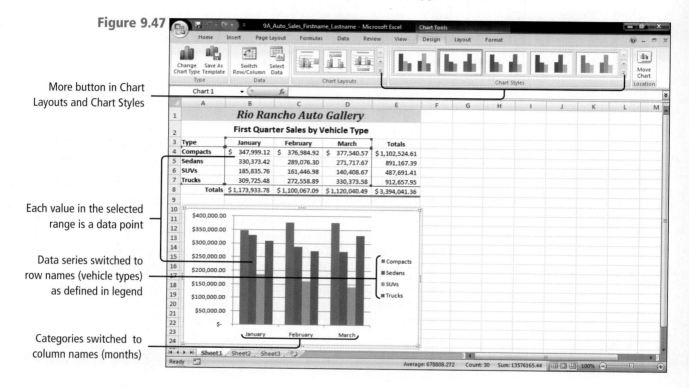

8 On the **Design tab** of the Ribbon, in the **Chart Layouts group**, locate, and then click the **More** button, and then compare your screen with Figure 9.48.

> From the *Chart Layouts gallery*, you can select a predesigned *chart layout*—the combination of chart elements you want to display, which can include a title, legend, labels for the columns, and the table of charted cells.

Figure 9.48

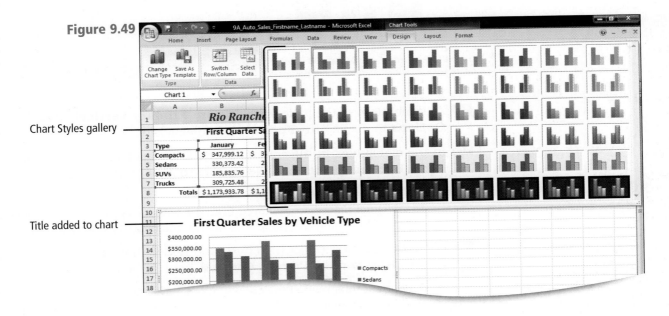

Chart Layouts gallery

Type	January	Fe...			Totals
Compacts	$ 347,999.12	$ 3...			102,524.61
Sedans	330,373.42		289,076.30	271,717.67	891,167.39
SUVs	185,835.76		161,446.98	140,408.67	487,691.41
Trucks	309,725.48		272,558.89	330,373.58	912,657.95
Totals	$1,173,933.78	$1,100,067.09	$1,120,040.49	$3,394,041.36

9 Click several different layouts to see the effect on your chart, and then using the ScreenTips as your guide, locate and click **Layout 1**.

10 In the chart, point to the text *Chart Title*, right-click, and then click **Edit Text**. Delete the text, and then type **First Quarter Sales by Vehicle Type**

11 Click in a white area *inside* the chart to deselect the chart title, but leaving the chart itself selected. On the **Design tab**, in the **Chart Styles group**, point to, and then click the **More** button ⬇, and then compare your screen with Figure 9.49.

The ***Chart Styles gallery*** displays. Here you can select from an array of predefined ***chart styles***—the overall visual look of the chart in terms of its graphic effects, colors, and backgrounds. For example, you can have flat or beveled columns, colors that are solid or transparent, and backgrounds that are dark or light.

Figure 9.49

Chart Styles gallery

Title added to chart

12 Click several different styles to see the effect on your chart, and then using the ScreenTips as your guide, locate and click **Style 26**.

> This style uses a white background, formats the columns by using theme colors, and applies a slightly beveled effect to the columns.

> With this clear visual representation of the data, Mr. Cizek can see that sales of compact cars have risen in each month of the quarter. He can also see that sales of sedans and SUVs have declined steadily in each month of the quarter. Finally, Mr. Cizek can see that truck sales declined slightly, and then rose again in March.

13 In your chart, notice that the values on the **value axis** include two decimal places. Then, on the Ribbon, click the **Layout tab**. In the **Axes group**, click the **Axes** button, point to **Primary Vertical Axis**, and then compare your screen with Figure 9.50.

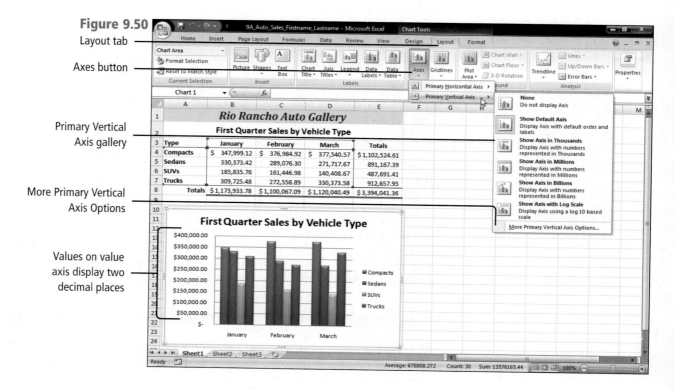

Figure 9.50
Layout tab
Axes button
Primary Vertical Axis gallery
More Primary Vertical Axis Options
Values on value axis display two decimal places

14 At the bottom of the gallery, click **More Primary Vertical Axis Options** to display the **Format Axis** dialog box.

15 In the dialog box, in the column at the left, click **Number**, and then in the **Decimal places** box, delete the existing number, type **0** and then click **Close**.

> The decimal places are removed from the value axis, resulting in a less cluttered look, and the value axis area of the chart is selected.

16 Click any cell to deselect the chart, and notice that the *Chart Tools* no longer display on the Ribbon. Compare your screen with Figure 9.51.

> Contextual tabs related to contextual tools in Office 2007 programs display when an object is selected, and then are removed from view when the object is deselected.

Figure 9.51

Chart Tools removed from view when chart not selected

Decimal places removed from value axis

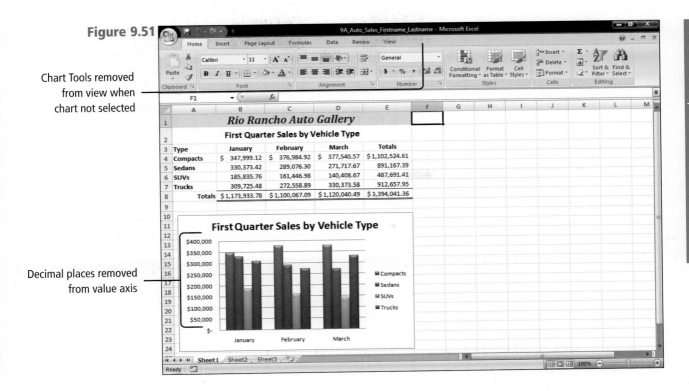

17 Save your workbook.

More Knowledge — A Chart Can Occupy a Separate Sheet in the Workbook

When a chart displays as an object within the worksheet, it is referred to as an *embedded chart*. With the chart selected, on the Design tab of the Ribbon, the last button—Move Chart—creates a new workbook sheet and places the chart on a separate workbook sheet. An embedded chart is useful when you want to view or print a chart on the same page as its source data.

Objective 7
Use Page Layout View, Prepare a Worksheet for Printing, and Close Excel

Before you print a worksheet, use *Page Layout view* and the commands on the Page Layout tab to prepare your data for printing. In Page Layout view, you can use the rulers to measure the width and height of data, set margins for printing, hide or display the numbered row headings and the lettered column headings, and change the *page orientation*—the position of data on the paper.

In *portrait orientation*, the paper is taller than it is wide. In *landscape orientation*, the paper is wider than it is tall. In Page Layout view, you can also add *headers* or *footers* which are text, page numbers, graphics, and formatting that print at the top (header) or bottom (footer) of every page of a worksheet. Finally, using Print Preview, you can see how the data and chart are centered on the page and if everything fits onto one page.

Activity 9.14 Changing Views, Creating a Footer and Using Print Preview

For each of your projects in this textbook, you will create a footer containing your name and the project name. This will make it easy for you to identify your printed documents in a shared printer environment such as a lab or classroom, or if you or your instructor view your completed work electronically.

1 On the Ribbon, click the **Insert tab**, and then in the **Text group**, click **Header & Footer** to switch to **Page Layout view** and open the **Header area**. Compare your screen with Figure 9.52.

> In this view, you can see the edges of the paper of multiple pages, the margins, and the rulers. You can also insert a header or footer by typing in the areas indicated and using the Header & Footer Tools.

Figure 9.52

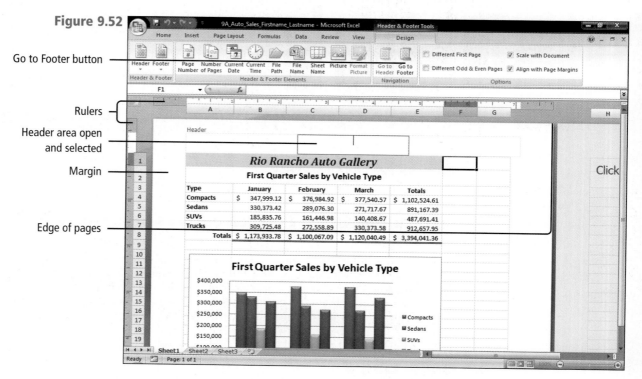

Go to Footer button

Rulers

Header area open and selected

Margin

Edge of pages

2 In the **Navigation group**, click the **Go to Footer** button to move to the bottom of the page and open the **Footer area**, and then click just above the word *Footer* to place the insertion point in the left section of the **Footer area**.

> The Header and Footer areas have three distinct sections—left, center, and right.

3 On the Ribbon, in the **Header & Footer Elements group**, click the **File Name** button to add the name of your file to the footer—&[File] displays in the left section of the **Footer area**. Then, click in a cell just above the footer to exit the **Footer area** and view your file name.

> The Header & Footer Tools are removed from view. In Page Layout vew, you can also type a header or footer directly into the areas indicated, but use this technique to automatically insert the file name.

4 Scroll up to view your chart, click the upper right corner of the chart to select it, and then check to see if the chart is centered under the data in the cells. If necessary, point to the **right resize handle** to display the ↔ pointer, as shown in Figure 9.53.

Figure 9.53

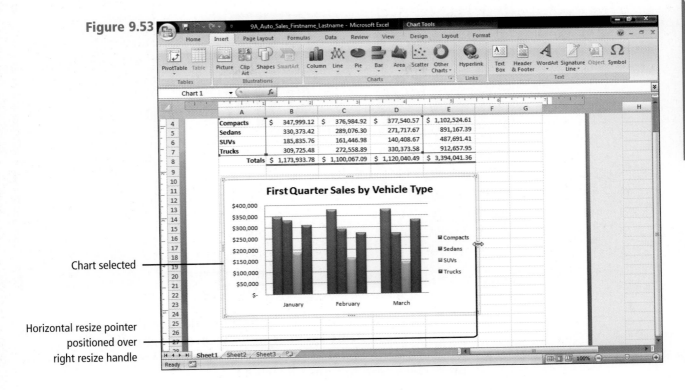

Chart selected

Horizontal resize pointer positioned over right resize handle

5 Drag the right border of the chart until it is almost even with the right border of **column E**, and then click any cell to deselect the chart. Be sure the left and right borders of the chart are just slightly inside the left border of **column A** and the right border of **column E**—adjust as necessary.

6 Click any cell to deselect the chart. Click the **Page Layout tab**, in the **Page Setup group**, click the **Margins** button, and then at the bottom of the **Margins gallery**, click **Custom Margins**. In the **Page Setup** dialog box, under **Center on page**, select the **Horizontally** check box.

This action will center the data and chart horizontally on the page, as shown in the Preview area.

7 In the lower right corner of the **Page Setup** dialog box, click **OK**. In the upper left corner of your screen, click the **Office** button 🏢, on the menu, point to the **Print button**, and then click **Print Preview**. Alternatively, press [Ctrl] + [F2] to view the Print Preview. Compare your screen with Figure 9.54.

The Ribbon displays the Print Preview program tab, which replaces the standard set of tabs when you switch to Print Preview.

Figure 9.54

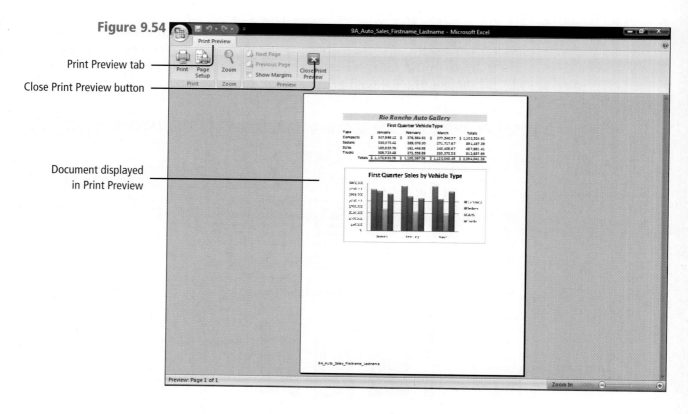

Print Preview tab

Close Print Preview button

Document displayed in Print Preview

8 Note any adjustments that need to be made, and then on the Ribbon, click the **Close Print Preview** button. On the right side of the status bar, click the **Normal** button ⊞ to return to Normal view, and then press Ctrl + Home to return to cell **A1**.

Normal view maximizes the number of cells visible on your screen and keeps the column letters and row numbers closer. The vertical dotted line between columns indicates that as currently arranged, only the columns to the left of the dotted line will print on the first page. The exact position of the vertical line will depend on your default printer setting—yours may fall elsewhere.

9 **Save** 🖫 your workbook.

Activity 9.15 Deleting Unused Sheets in a Workbook

By default, each new Excel workbook contains three blank worksheets. Although it is not necessary to delete unused sheets, doing so saves storage space and removes any doubt that additional information is in the workbook.

1 At the bottom of your worksheet, click the **Sheet2 tab** to display Sheet 2 and make it the active worksheet.

2 Hold down Ctrl, and then click the **Sheet3 tab**. With both sheets selected (tab background is white, not blue, on the selected sheets), display the **Home tab**. In the **Cells group**, click the **Delete button arrow**, and then click **Delete Sheet**. Alternatively, point to either of the selected sheet tabs, right-click, and then click Delete to delete the sheets.

Excel deletes the two unused sheets from your workbook. If you attempt to delete a worksheet with data, Excel will display a warning and permit you to cancel the deletion.

3 **Save** 🖫 your workbook.

Activity 9.16 Printing a Worksheet

1 Check your *Chapter Assignment Sheet* or *Course Syllabus*, or consult your instructor, to determine if you are to submit your assignments on paper or electronically. To submit electronically, follow the instructions provided by your instructor.

2 From the **Office** menu 🔘, click the **Print** button. In the **Print** dialog box, under **Print range**, verify that the **All** option button is selected. Under **Print what**, verify that **Active sheet(s)** is selected, and then under **Copies**, verify that the **Number of copies** is **1**. Compare your screen with Figure 9.55.

Figure 9.55

Print dialog box
Your default printer

Print all pages

Print currently active worksheet

One copy

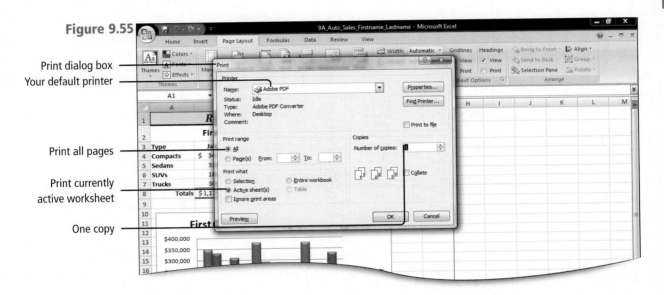

3 Click **OK** to print your worksheet, and then **Save** 🖫 your workbook.

Alert!

Is your printed result centered horizontally?

If your worksheet does not appear to be centered horizontally on the page, reduce the width of the chart by a small amount so that its borders fall slightly inside the left and right columns with which they are aligned.

Activity 9.17 Displaying, Printing, and Hiding Formulas

When you place a formula in a cell, the cell displays the results of the formula. Recall that this value is called the displayed value. You can view and print the underlying formulas in the cells. When you do so, a formula often takes more horizontal space to display than the result of the calculation. Thus, the landscape orientation is usually a better choice than portrait orientation to fit the formulas on one page. In this activity, you will print the formulas in Sheet1 in landscape orientation and then close the workbook without saving the changes.

1 Because you will make some temporary changes to your workbook, on the **Quick Access Toolbar**, click the **Save** button 🔲 to be sure that you have saved your work up to this point.

2 Hold down Ctrl, press ⌐ (usually located below Esc), and then compare your screen with Figure 9.56. Alternatively, on the Formulas tab, in the Formula Auditing group, click the Show Formulas button.

> The Ctrl + ⌐ keyboard shortcut acts like a toggle; that is, pressing the two keys once displays the formulas, and pressing the two keys again hides the formulas.

Figure 9.56

Dotted line shows
page break

Underlying formulas
displayed

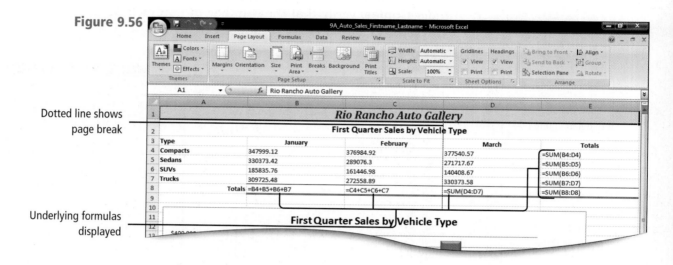

3 From the **column heading area**, select columns **A:E**. Point to the column heading boundary between any two of the selected columns and double-click to AutoFit the selected columns.

4 Display the **Page Layout tab**. In the **Page Setup group**, click the **Orientation** button, and then click **Landscape**. In the **Scale to Fit group**, click the **Dialog Box Launcher** button 🔲 to display the **Page tab** of the **Page Setup** dialog box.

5 Under **Scaling**, click the **Fit to** option button, and then in the lower right corner, click the **Print Preview** button—this is another point from which you can display the Print Preview.

> Scaling adjusts the size of the printed worksheet to fit on the page, and is convenient for printing formulas. Although it is not always the case, formulas frequently take up more space than the actual data.

6 Click **Close Print Preview**. Check your *Chapter Assignment Sheet* or *Course Syllabus*, or consult your instructor, to determine if you are to submit your printed formulas on paper or electronically. To submit electronically, follow the instructions provided by your instructor.

7 From the **Office** menu 🔘, click the **Print** button. In the **Print** dialog box, under **Print range**, verify that the **All** option button is selected. Under **Print what**, verify that **Active sheet(s)** is selected, and then under **Copies**, verify that the **Number of copies** is **1**.

8 Click **OK** to print your worksheet. From the **Office** menu , click **Close**, and when prompted, click **No** so that you do *not* save the changes you made—displaying formulas, changing column widths and orientation, and scaling—to print your formulas.

9 In the upper right corner of your screen, click the **Close** button ✕ to close Excel.

End **You have completed Project 9A** ——————————

Project 9B Safety Products

In Activities 9.18 through 9.25, you will create a workbook for Arthur Potempa, the Retail Sales Manager for Rio Rancho Auto Gallery. One of the retail areas in the Auto Gallery carries an inventory of safety products. Mr. Potempa wants to calculate the retail value of the inventory of safety products and then, using a pie chart, display how each item's retail value contributes to the total retail value. Your completed worksheet and chart will look similar to Figure 9.57.

For Project 9B, you will need the following file:

New blank Excel workbook

You will save your workbook as
9B_Safety_Products_Firstname_Lastname

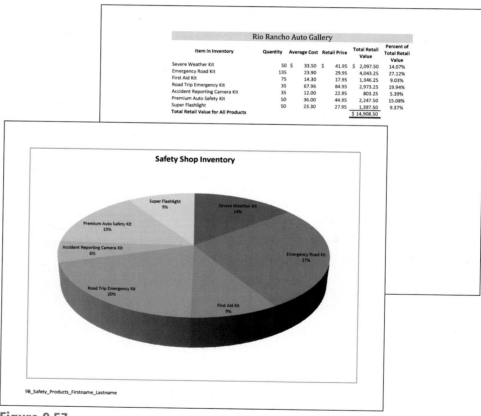

Figure 9.57
Project 9B—Safety Products

Objective 8
Design a Worksheet

Make your worksheet useful to the reader by using good design techniques, such as: use rows rather than columns for the most abundant data; consider how the worksheet will look on paper; and, arrange the data so that it is easily charted.

Activity 9.18 Setting Column Widths and Creating Row and Column Titles

The worksheet title is typically placed in the first row and centered above the columns of data.

1 **Start** 👉 **Excel**. From the **Office** menu 👉, click **Close** to close the open workbook but leave the Excel program open.

2 Display the **Office** menu 👉 again and click **New**. In the **New Workbook** dialog box, under **Blank and recent**, click **Blank Workbook**, and then in the lower right corner, click the **Create** button. Alternatively, press [Ctrl] + [N].

> With Excel open, these are techniques you can use to begin a new workbook.

3 From the **Office** menu 👉, display the **Save As** dialog box, navigate to your **Excel Chapter 9** folder, and then in the **File name** box, replace the existing text with **9B_Safety_Products_Firstname_Lastname** and then click **Save**.

4 Click cell **A2**, type **Item in Inventory** and press [Tab]. In cell **B2**, type **Quantity** and press [Tab].

5 In cell **C2**, type **Average Cost** and press [Tab]. In cell **D2**, type **Retail Price** and press [Tab].

6 In cell **E2**, type **Total Retail Value** and press [Tab]. In cell **F2**, type **Percent of Total Retail Value** and press [Enter].

7 In cell **A3**, type **Severe Weather Kit** and press [Enter]. Type the remaining row titles in cells **A4:A9**, and then compare your screen with Figure 9.58.

> **Emergency Road Kit**
>
> **First Aid Kit**
>
> **Accident Reporting Camera Kit**
>
> **Premium Auto Safety Kit**
>
> **Super Flashlight**
>
> **Total Retail Value for All Products**

Figure 9.58

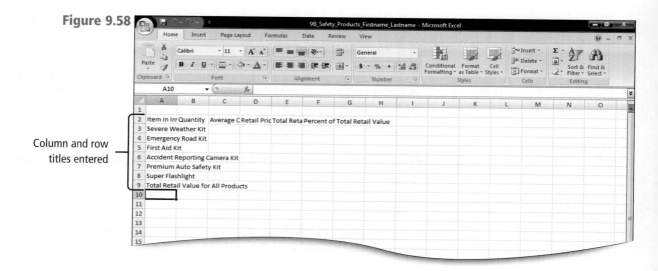

Column and row
titles entered

8 Right-click cell **A9** and on the Mini toolbar, click **Bold** [B].

9 Select **columns A:F**, position the [+] pointer over the right boundary
of any of the selected column heading letters, and then double-click
to apply **AutoFit Column Width**. Alternatively, click the Format button arrow, and then click AutoFit Column Width.

10 Click cell **A1** and type **Rio Rancho Auto Gallery** and then on the
Formula Bar, click the **Enter** button [✓]. Select the range **A1:F1**,
and then right-click over the selection.

11 On the Mini toolbar, click the **Merge & Center** button [⊞▾], change
the **Font** to **Cambria**, and then change the **Font Size** to **16**.

12 With cell **A1** selected, click the **Fill Color arrow** [◇▾]. In the seventh
column of colors, click the third color—**Olive Green, Accent 3,
Lighter 60%**.

13 Click anywhere to deselect cell **A1**, **Save** [💾] your workbook, and
then compare your screen with Figure 9.59.

> Formatting the worksheet title with a different font, font size, and fill
> color distinguishes it visually from the worksheet data.

Figure 9.59

Column widths adjusted

Worksheet title entered and formatted

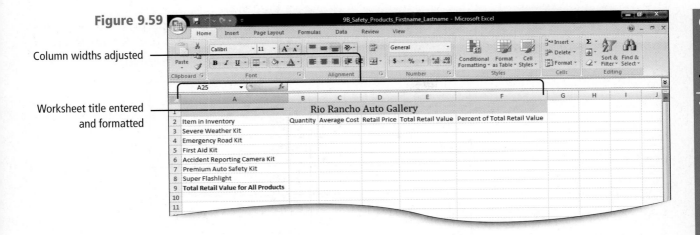

Activity 9.19 Entering Data by Range

In this activity, you will enter data by first selecting a range of cells; this is a time-saving technique, especially if you use the numeric keypad to enter the numbers.

1 Select the range **B3:D8**, type **50** and then press [Enter].

The first value displays in cell B3 and cell B4 becomes the active cell.

2 Beginning in cell **B4** and pressing [Enter] after each entry, type the following, and then compare your screen with Figure 9.60:

135

75

35

50

50

After you enter the last value and press [Enter], the active cell moves to the top of the next column within the selected range. Selecting the range in this manner—before you enter data—saves time because it confines the movement of the active cell to the selected range.

Figure 9.60

Active cell moves to the next column

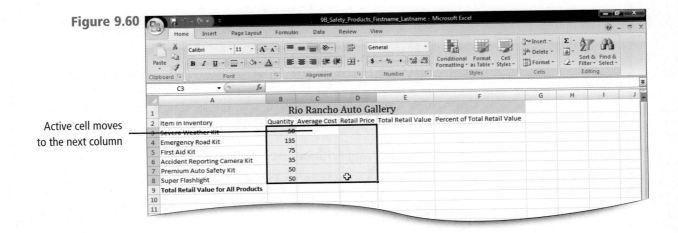

3 From the following table, beginning in cell **C3** and pressing Enter after each entry, enter the data for the **Average Cost** and **Retail Price** columns. Then compare your screen with Figure 9.61.

Average Cost	Retail Price
33.5	41.95
23.9	29.95
14.3	17.95
12	22.95
36	44.95
23.3	27.95

Recall that the default number format for cells is the *General* number format, in which numbers display exactly as you type them and trailing zeros do not display, even if you type them.

Figure 9.61

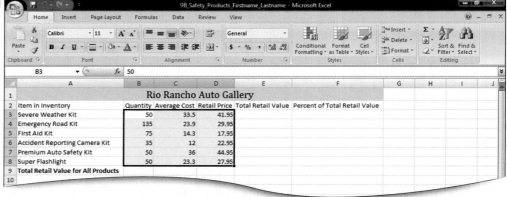

4 **Save** 💾 your workbook.

Objective 9
Construct Formulas for Mathematical Operations

Operators are symbols with which you can specify the type of calculation you want to perform in a formula.

Activity 9.20 Using Arithmetic Operators

1 In cell **E3**, type **=b3*d3** and press Enter.

The *Total Retail Value* of all *Severe Weather Kit* items in the shop—2097.5—equals the *Quantity* (50) times the *Retail Price* (selling price) of 41.95. In Excel, the asterisk (*) indicates multiplication.

2 Take a moment to study the symbols you will use to perform basic mathematical operations in Excel, as shown in the table in Figure 9.62—these are referred to as *arithmetic operators*.

Symbols Used in Excel for Arithmetic Operators	
Operator Symbol	**Operation**
+	Addition
-	Subtraction (also negation)
*	Multiplication
/	Division
%	Percent
^	Exponentiation

Figure 9.62

3 Click cell **E3**.

You can see that in cells E4:E8, you need a formula similar to the one in E3, but one that refers to the cells in row 4, row 5, and so forth. Recall that you can copy formulas and the cell references will change *relative to* the row number.

4 With cell **E3** selected, position your pointer over the fill handle in the lower right corner of the cell until the ➕ pointer displays. Then, drag down through cell **E8** to copy the formula.

5 Select the range **C3:E3**, right-click over the selection, and then on the Mini toolbar, click the **Accounting Number Format** button ⊞.

6 Select the range **C4:E8**, right-click over the selection, and then on the Mini toolbar, click the **Comma Style** button ⊞.

7 Click cell **E9**, in the **Editing group**, click the **Sum** button ⊞, and then press Enter. Click **Save** ⊞ and compare your screen with Figure 9.63.

Your result is *$11,935.25*. The Accounting Number Format is automatically applied to cell E9. The format of the cell containing the formula is the same as the format of the cells used in the formula. If the formula references a range of cells and those cells contain a mix of formats, the format from the cell in the upper left corner of the range is applied.

Figure 9.63

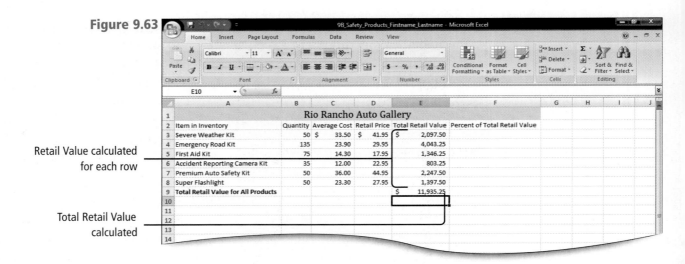

Retail Value calculated for each row

Total Retail Value calculated

Activity 9.21 Copying Formulas Containing Absolute Cell References

A relative cell reference refers to cells by their position in relation to the cell that contains the formula. An *absolute cell reference*, on the other hand, refers to a cell by its *fixed* position in the worksheet, for example, the total in cell E9.

A relative cell reference automatically adjusts when a formula is copied. An absolute cell reference does *not* adjust; rather, it remains the same when the formula is copied—and there are times when you will want to do this.

1 Click cell **F3**, type **=** and then click cell **E3**. Type **/** and then click cell **E9**.

The formula *=E3/E9* indicates that the value in cell E3 will be divided by the value in cell E9. Why? Because Mr. Potempa wants to know the percentage by which each product's Total Retail Value makes up the Total Retail Value for All Products. Arithmetically, the percentage is computed by dividing the *Total Retail Value* for each product by the *Total Retail Value for All Products*. The result will be a percentage expressed as a decimal.

Workshop

Calculate a Percentage if You Know the Total and the Amount

Using the equation *amount/total = percentage*, you can calculate the percentage by which a part makes up a total—with the percentage formatted as a decimal.

For example, if on a quiz you score 42 points correctly out of 50, your percentage of correct answers is 42/50 = 0.84 or 84%.

2 Press Enter. Click cell **F3** and notice that the formula displays in the **Formula Bar**. Then, point to cell **F3** and double-click.

> The formula, with the two referenced cells displayed in color and bordered with the same color, displays in the cell. This is the *range finder*, and is useful for verifying formulas or quickly positioning the insertion point within the cell to perform editing directly in the cell.

3 Press Enter to redisplay the result of the calculation in the cell, and notice that approximately 17% of the total retail value of the inventory is made up of Severe Weather Kits.

4 Click cell **F3** again, and drag the fill handle down through cell **F8**. Compare your screen with Figure 9.64.

> Each cell displays an error message—*#DIV/0!* and a green triangle in the upper left corner of each cell indicates an error has been found. Like a grammar checker, Excel uses rules to check for formula errors and flags them in this manner. Additionally, the Auto Fill Options button displays, from which you can select formatting options for the copied cells.

Figure 9.64

Error messages

Green triangles indicate errors

Auto Fill Options button

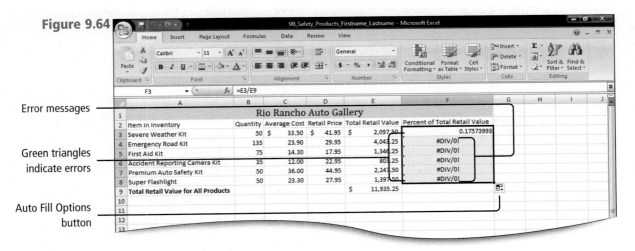

5 Click cell **F4**, and to the left of the cell, point to the **Error Checking** button to display its ScreenTip—*The formula or function used is dividing by zero or empty cells.*

> In this manner, Excel suggests the cause of an error.

6 Look at the **Formula Bar** and examine the formula.

> The formula is *=E4/E10*. The cell reference to *E4* is correct, but the cell reference following the division operator (/) is *E10*, and E10 is an *empty* cell.

7 Click cell **F5**, point to the **Error Checking** button 🔸, and in the **Formula Bar** examine the formula.

> Because the cell references are relative, Excel attempts to build the formulas by increasing the row number for each equation. In this particular calculation, however, the divisor must always be the value in cell E9—the *Total Retail Value for All Products.*

8 Point to cell **F3**, and then double-click to have the range finder display the cell's formula and place the insertion point within the cell.

9 Within the cell, be sure the insertion point is blinking to the right of *E9*, and then press F4. Alternatively, edit the formula so that it indicates *=E3/$E$9* Compare your screen with Figure 9.65.

> Dollar signs ($) display in an absolute cell reference. The use of the dollar sign to denote an absolute reference is not related in any way to whether or not the values you are working with are currency values. It is simply the symbol used by Excel to denote an absolute cell reference.

Figure 9.65

Edited formula with dollar signs denoting an absolute cell reference

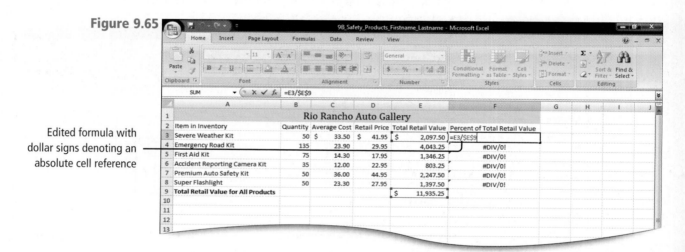

10 On the **Formula Bar**, click the **Enter** button ✔ so that **F3** is still the active cell. Then, drag the fill handle to copy the formula down through cell **F8**. Compare your screen with Figure 9.66.

Figure 9.66

Absolute cell reference

Percentages calculated for each product

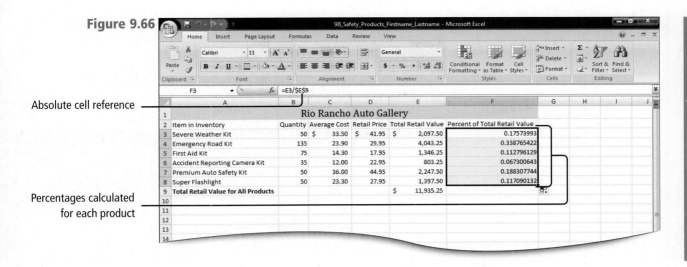

11 Click cell **F4**, examine the formula in the **Formula Bar**, and then examine the formulas for cells **F5**, **F6**, **F7**, and **F8**.

> For each formula, the cell reference for the *Total Retail Value* of each product changed relative to its row; however, the value used as the divisor—*Total Retail Value for All Products* in cell E9—remained absolute. Thus, using either relative or absolute cell references, it is easy to duplicate formulas without typing them.

12 **Save** your workbook.

Objective 10
Format Percentages and Move Formulas

A percentage is part of a whole expressed in hundredths. For example, 75 cents is the same as 75 percent of one dollar. The Percent Style button formats the selected cell as a percentage rounded to the nearest hundredth.

Excel adjusts formulas automatically if you move formulas by inserting additional rows or columns.

Activity 9.22 Formatting Cells with the Percent Style Button

1 Click cell **F3** and notice the number *0.17573993*. In the **Number group**, click the **Percent Style** button.

> Your result is 18%, which is *0.17573993* rounded up to the nearest hundredth and expressed as a percentage. Percent Style displays the value of a cell as a percentage.

2 Select the range **F3:F8**, right-click over the selection, and then on the Mini toolbar, click the **Percent Style** button, click the **Increase Decimal** button two times, and then click the **Center** button.

> Percent Style may not offer a percentage precise enough to analyze important financial information—adding additional decimal places

to a percentage makes data more precise. For example, with additional decimal places, Mr. Potempa can see a slight difference in the percentage of First Aid Kits and Super Flashlights.

3 Click any cell to cancel the selection, compare your screen with Figure 9.67, and then **Save** 💾 your workbook.

Figure 9.67

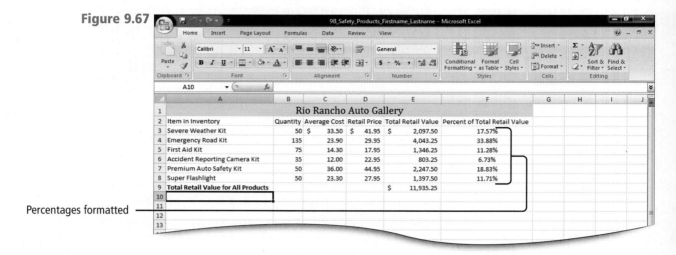

Percentages formatted

Activity 9.23 Inserting Rows in a Worksheet Containing Formulas and Wrapping Text in a Cell

You can edit formulas in the same manner as you edit text. In this activity, you will add a row for Road Trip Emergency Kits, which is another item carried by the Safety Shop, and wrap text.

1 Double-click cell **E9** and confirm that the range finder shows the formula to be the sum of cells *E3:E8*. Press Enter.

2 Click cell **E6**. On the **Home tab**, in the **Cells group**, click the **Insert button arrow**, and then from the list, click **Insert Sheet Rows**.

Another Way

To Insert Rows

Click the row heading and then in the Cells group, click the Insert button; or, right-click the cell, click Insert, and then click Entire row.

---

3 Click cell **E10**. On the **Formula Bar**, notice that the range was edited and changed to sum the newly expanded range **E3:E9**.

4 In the range **A6:D6**, type the following:

Road Trip Emergency Kit	35	67.96	84.95

5 Select the range **E5:F5** to select the two formulas above the new row, and then drag the fill handle to fill both formulas down to cells **E6** and **F6**.

6 Click cell **E10**. Move the pointer to the bottom edge of the cell until the ⬚ pointer displays, and then drag downward until cell **E11** is outlined, as shown in Figure 9.68.

Figure 9.68

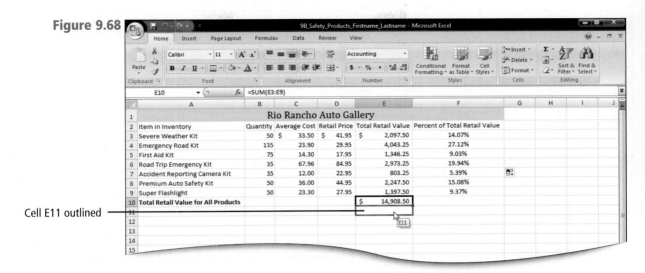

Cell E11 outlined

7 Release the mouse button, double-click cell **E11** to display the range finder, and then in cell **E11** and on the **Formula Bar**, notice that the range, **E3:E9**, did not change when you moved the formula.

If you move a formula to another cell, the cell references do not change.

8 Press [Esc] to cancel the range finder, and then on the **Quick Access Toolbar**, click **Undo** ⮌ to return the formula to cell **E10**.

9 In the **row heading area**, point to the lower boundary of **row 2** to display the ╬ pointer, and then drag downward until the row is **60 pixels** high.

10 Select **columns B:F**, and then from the **column heading area**, drag the right border of one of the selected columns to **80 pixels**.

11 Select the range **C2:F2**, and then in the **Alignment group**, click the **Wrap Text** button ⬚.

Use the Wrap Text command to display text on multiple lines within a single cell when the column is not wide enough to display all of the cell's content.

12 Select the range **A2:F2**. In the **Font group**, click the **Bold** button **B**; in the **Alignment group**, click the **Center** button ≡ and the **Middle Align** button ≡.

13 Click cell **E10**. In the **Font** group, click the **Borders button arrow** ⬚, and then from the list, click **Top and Double Bottom Border**. Click any cell to cancel the selection from cell E10.

14 **Save** 💾 your workbook, and then compare your screen with Figure 9.69.

Figure 9.69

Column widths adjusted

Row height increased

Text wrapped and centered

Percents formatted

Border added

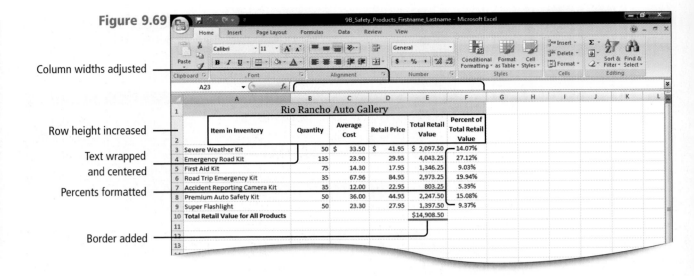

15 On the Ribbon, click the **Insert tab**, and then in the **Text group**, click **Header & Footer** to switch to **Page Layout view** and open the **Header area**. On the **Design tab**, in the **Navigation group**, click the **Go to Footer** button.

16 Click just above the word *Footer* to place your insertion point in the left section of the **Footer area**, and then in the **Header & Footer Elements group**, click the **File Name** button. Click any cell above the footer to exit the **Footer area** and view your file name.

17 Press (Ctrl) + (Home) to move to cell **A1** and display the upper portion of your worksheet. Click the **Page Layout tab**. In the **Page Setup group**, click the **Orientation** button, and then click **Landscape**.

18 In the **Page Setup group**, click the **Margins** button, and then at the bottom of the **Margins gallery**, click **Custom Margins**. In the **Page Setup** dialog box, under **Center on page**, select the **Horizontally** check box. Click **OK**, and then **Save** 🖫.

Objective 11
Create a Pie Chart and a Chart Sheet

Pie charts show the relationship of each part to a whole. To create a pie chart, you must select two ranges. One range contains the labels for each slice of the pie chart, and the other range contains the values that add up to a total. The two ranges must have the same number of cells and the range with the values should *not* include the cell with the total.

A legend can identify the slices of the pie by using colors, but it is usually more effective to place the labels within or close to each pie slice.

Activity 9.24 Creating a Pie Chart and a Chart Sheet

The purpose of the inventory worksheet is to determine how each item contributes to the total retail value of the inventory. To display the relationship of parts to a whole, use a pie chart. In the 9B_Safety_Products worksheet, you calculated the percent of the total in column F. This percentage can also be calculated by the Chart feature and added to the chart as a label.

1 In the lower right of your screen, on the status bar, click the **Normal** button ▦ to return to **Normal view**.

2 Select the range **A3:A9** and then hold down Ctrl and select the non-adjacent range **E3:E9**—the item names and the total retail value of each item.

3 Click the **Insert tab**, and then in the **Charts group**, click **Pie**. Under **3-D Pie**, click the first chart—**Pie in 3-D**—to create the chart on your worksheet.

4 On the **Design tab**, in the **Location group**, click the **Move Chart** button. In the **Move Chart** dialog box, click the **New sheet** option button. Replace the highlighted text *Chart1* by typing **Inventory Chart** and then click **OK**.

> A ***chart sheet*** is created in your workbook, which is a workbook sheet that contains only a chart and is useful when you want to view a chart separately from the worksheet data. The sheet tab indicates *Inventory Chart*.

5 On the **Design tab**, in the **Chart Layouts group**, click the first layout—**Layout 1**. Right-click over the text *Chart Title*, click **Edit Text**, delete the existing text, and then type **Safety Shop Inventory**

> In this layout, there is no legend and the category labels and the percentages—calculated by the chart feature—display on the pie slices. If you plan to print a chart sheet on a printer that does not print in color, it is better to label each pie slice individually rather than use a legend.

6 In the **Chart Styles group**, click the **More** button ⯆, and then click **Style 5**. Click anywhere in the white area of the chart to deselect the Chart Title, and then compare your screen with Figure 9.70.

> To print on paper, the paler colors will display well. To present this chart in a PowerPoint presentation, you would likely pick one of the more vibrant styles with multiple colors.

Figure 9.70

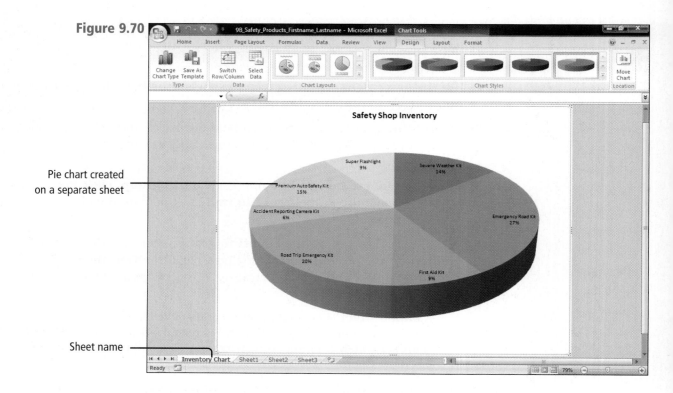

Pie chart created on a separate sheet

Sheet name

7 Click the **Insert tab**. In the **Text group**, click **Header & Footer**, and then in the **Page Setup** dialog box, click the **Custom Footer** button.

8 With the insertion point positioned in the **Left section**, click the **Insert File Name** button 📇, and then click **OK** two times.

Use the Page Setup dialog box in this manner to insert a footer on a chart sheet, which has no Page Layout view in which you can see the Header and Footer areas.

9 To delete the unused worksheets, click the **Sheet2 tab**, hold down Ctrl, and then click the **Sheet3 tab**.

10 Right-click over one of the selected sheet tabs, and then from the shortcut menu, click **Delete**. Be sure **Sheet1** is the active sheet, and then press Ctrl + Home to cancel the selections and make cell **A1** the active cell.

11 **Save** 💾 your workbook. Check your *Chapter Assignment Sheet* or *Course Syllabus*, or consult your instructor, to determine if you are to submit your assignments on paper or electronically. To submit electronically, follow the instructions provided by your instructor.

12 To print, from the **Office** menu 🔵, click **Print**. In the **Print** dialog box, under **Print what**, click the **Entire workbook** option button.

13 In the lower left corner of the dialog box, click **Preview**, and notice in the status bar, *Preview: Page 1 of 2* displays.

14 Review the preview of your chart sheet, and then in the **Preview group**, click the **Next Page** button to preview the worksheet containing your data. In the **Print group**, click **Print** to print the two pages.

15 **Save** 🖫 your workbook. If you are instructed to print your formulas on Sheet1, follow the instructions in Activity 9.17 to do so, and then redisplay the worksheet by pressing Ctrl + `.

16 From the **Office** menu 🏢, click **Close**. If prompted to save changes, click **No** so that you do not save the changes that you made to print your formulas. **Close** ❎ Excel.

Objective 12
Use the Excel Help System

Excel's Help feature provides information about all of Excel's features and displays step-by-step instructions for performing many tasks.

Activity 9.25 Using the Excel Help System

Workbooks that you create in Excel 2007 can be opened in Excel 2003. In this activity, you will use the Microsoft Help feature to learn more about this feature.

1 **Start** Excel. In the upper right corner of your screen, click the **Microsoft Office Excel Help** button ❓. Alternatively, press F1. In the displayed window, click the **Search arrow**, and then under **Content from this computer**, click **Excel Help**. In the white box on the left, type **open an Excel 2007 workbook in Excel 2003**

2 Click **Search** or press Enter. On the list of results, click **Open an Office Excel 2007 workbook in an earlier version of Excel**.

3 If you want to do so, click the **Print** button to print a copy of this information for your reference. Your name will not print.

4 On the title bar of the Excel Help window, click the **Close** button ❎ On the right side of the Microsoft Excel title bar, click the **Close** button ❎ to close Excel.

End **You have completed Project 9B**

There's More You Can Do!

Close Excel and any other open windows. Display the Start menu, click Computer, and then navigate to the student files that accompany this textbook. From the CD that came with your book, open the folder **02_theres_more_you_can_do**, locate and open the folder for this chapter. Open and print the instructions for this project, which are provided to you in Adobe PDF format.

Try IT!—Change a Chart Type

In this Try It! exercise, you will change the chart type of an existing chart from a column chart to a bar chart.

Summary

In this chapter, you used Microsoft Office Excel 2007 to create and analyze data organized into columns and rows and to chart and perform calculations on the data. By organizing your data with Excel, you will be able to make logical decisions and create visual representations of your data in the form of charts.

Key Terms

(Key Terms continues on the next page)

The ⬤ symbol represents Key Terms found on the Student CD in the 02_theres_more_you_can_do folder for this chapter

Content-Based Assessments

Key Terms

(Key Terms continued)

Content-Based Assessments

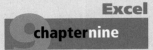
Matching

Match each term in the second column with its correct definition in the first column by writing the letter of the term on the blank line in front of the correct definition.

_____ **1.** An Excel file that contains one or more worksheets.

_____ **2.** The primary document that you use in Excel to store and work with data, and which is formatted as a pattern of uniformly spaced horizontal and vertical lines.

_____ **3.** The intersection of a row and column in an Excel worksheet.

_____ **4.** An element in the Excel window that displays the value or formula contained in the active cell, and in which you can enter or edit values or formulas.

_____ **5.** The box to the left of the Formula Bar that identifies the selected cell, table, chart, or object.

_____ **6.** The user interface in Office 2007 that groups the commands for performing related tasks on tabs across the upper portion of the program window.

_____ **7.** Buttons on the right side of the status bar for viewing in Normal, Page Layout View, or Page Break Preview; also displays controls for zoom out and zoom in.

_____ **8.** The letters at the top of an Excel worksheet that designate the columns.

_____ **9.** Two or more selected cells on a worksheet that are adjacent or nonadjacent, and treated by Excel as a single unit for the purpose of editing.

_____ **10.** The cell, surrounded by a black border, ready to receive data or be affected by the next Excel command.

_____ **11.** The identification of a specific cell by its intersecting column letter and row number.

_____ **12.** Anything typed into a cell.

_____ **13.** Numbers, text, dates, or times of day that you type into a cell.

_____ **14.** An equation that performs mathematical calculations on values in a worksheet.

_____ **15.** The small black square in the lower right corner of a selected cell.

A Active cell

B Cell

C Cell content

D Cell reference

E Column headings

F Constant value

G Fill handle

H Formula

I Formula Bar

J Name Box

K Range

L Ribbon

M View options

N Workbook

O Worksheet

Content-Based Assessments

Fill in the Blank

Write the correct answer in the space provided.

1. A set of characters with the same design, size, and shape is called a _____.

2. A specific way in which Excel displays numbers in a cell is referred to as the _____ _____.

3. The default format that Excel applies to numbers, which has no specific characteristics except that trailing zeros to the right of a decimal point will not display, is the _____ format.

4. The data that displays in the Formula Bar is referred to as the _____ _____.

5. A formula prewritten by Excel is a _____.

6. In a formula, the address of a cell based on the relative position of the cell that contains the formula and the cell referred to is a _____ cell reference.

7. The Excel number format that applies a thousand comma separator where appropriate, inserts a fixed U.S. dollar sign aligned at the left edge of the cell, applies two decimal places, and leaves a small amount of space at the right edge of the cell to accommodate a parenthesis for negative numbers is the _____ _____ format.

8. The Excel number format that inserts thousand comma separators where appropriate, applies two decimal places, and leaves space at the right to accommodate a parenthesis for negative numbers is the _____ _____.

9. The area along the bottom of a chart that identifies the categories of data, and which is also referred to as the x-axis, is the _____ axis.

10. A numerical scale on the left side of a chart that shows the range of numbers for the data points, and also referred to as the y-axis, is the _____ axis.

11. In a chart, an explanation of the patterns or colors that are assigned to a data series that represents a category is called the _____.

12. Related data points represented by data markers in a chart, each of which has a unique color or pattern represented in the chart legend, are referred to as a _____ _____.

(Fill in the Blank continues on the next page)

Fill in the Blank

(Fill in the Blank continued)

13. The combination of chart elements that can be displayed in a chart such as a title, legend, labels for the columns, and the table of charted cells is referred to as the _____ _____.

14. Symbols that specify addition, subtraction, multiplication, division, percentage, and exponentiation in an Excel formula are called _____ _____.

15. A cell reference that refers to cells by their fixed position in a worksheet and which remain the same when the formula is copied is referred to as an _____ cell reference.

Content-Based Assessments

Skills Review

Project 9C — Service

In this project, you will apply the skills you practiced from the Objectives in Project 9A.

Objectives: 1. *Create, Save, and Navigate an Excel Workbook;* **2.** *Enter and Edit Data in a Worksheet;* **3.** *Construct and Copy Formulas, Use the Sum Function, and Edit Cells;* **4.** *Format Data, Cells, and Worksheets;* **5.** *Close and Reopen a Workbook;* **6.** *Chart Data;* **7.** *Use Page Layout View, Prepare a Worksheet for Printing, and Close Excel.*

In the following Skills Review, you will create a worksheet for Ellie Rose, Service Manager at the Rio Rancho Auto Gallery, to track weekly service revenue. Your completed worksheet will look similar to the one shown in Figure 9.71.

For Project 9C, you will need the following file:

New blank Excel workbook

You will save your workbook as 9C_Service_Firstname_Lastname

Figure 9.71

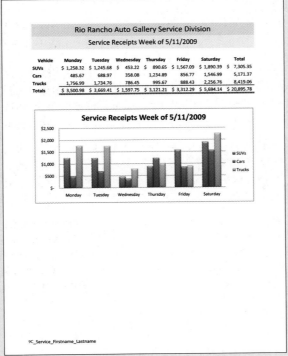

(Project 9C–Service continues on the next page)

Content-Based Assessments

(Project 9C–Service continued)

1. **Start** Excel. In cell **A1**, type **Rio Rancho Auto Gallery Service Division** and then press Enter. In cell **A2**, type **Service Receipts Week of 5/11/2009** and then press Enter. Display the **Save As** dialog box, navigate to your **Excel Chapter 9** folder, and then using your own first and last names, **Save** the workbook as 9C_Service_Firstname_Lastname

2. In cell **A3**, type **Vehicle** and then press Enter. Type **SUVs** and then press Enter. Type **Cars** and then press Enter. Type **Trucks** and then press Enter. In cell **A7**, type **Totals** and then press Enter.

3. In cell **B3**, type **Monday** and then press Enter. Click in cell **B3** again to make it the active cell. In the lower right corner of cell **B3**, point to the fill handle to display the ➕ pointer, drag the fill handle to the right to cell **G3** so that the last ScreenTip that displays is *Saturday*, and then release the mouse button to fill the days of the week. In cell **H3**, type **Total** and then press Enter.

4. Press Ctrl + Home to move to cell **A1**, and then on the Ribbon, click the **Review tab**. In the **Proofing group**, click **Spelling**, and then correct any spelling errors that you may have made while typing. Beginning in cell **B4**, type the following data:

Vehicle	Monday	Tuesday	Wednesday	Thursday	Friday	Saturday
SUVs	1258.32	1245.68	453.22	890.65	1567.09	1890.39
Cars	485.67	688.97	358.08	1234.89	856.77	1546.99
Trucks	1756.99	1734.76	786.45	995.67	888.43	2256.76

5. From the **column heading area**, select **columns A:G**, and then point to the right boundary of any of the selected column letters to display the ➕ pointer. Drag to the right until the ScreenTip indicates **75 pixels**, and then release the mouse button to resize the selected columns.

6. Point to the **row 3** heading, and then right-click to simultaneously select the row and display the shortcut menu and the Mini toolbar. From the shortcut menu, click **Insert** to insert a blank row—this will add some space between the worksheet titles and the column titles.

7. Click cell **H5**. On the **Home tab**, in the **Editing group**, click the **Sum** button, and then press Enter to enter the function—a prewritten formula. Your result is *7305.35*. Click cell **H5**, and then drag the fill handle down to cell **H7** to copy the formula. Recall that the cell references will adjust relative to their row.

8. Select the range **B5:H8**, which includes the columns to be totaled and the cells in which each total will display. Hold down Alt and then press = to enter the Sum function in cells **B8:H8**. **Save** your workbook.

9. Select the range **A1:H1**, and then on the **Home tab**, in the **Alignment group**, click the **Merge & Center** button. Select the range **A2:H2**, right-click over the selection, and then on the Mini toolbar, click the **Merge & Center** button. Both worksheet titles are centered over the worksheet.

10. Right-click cell **A1**. On the Mini toolbar, click the **Font Size arrow**, and then click **18**. Then, click the **Fill Color button arrow**, and under **Theme Colors**, in the next to last column, click the third color—**Aqua, Accent 5, Lighter 60%**.

(Project 9C–Service continues on the next page)

(Project 9C–Service continued)

11. Right-click cell **A2**. On the Mini toolbar, change the **Font Size** to **16**. Click the **Fill Color button arrow**, and then under **Theme Colors**, in the next to last column, click the second color— **Aqua, Accent 5, Lighter 80%**.

12. Select **rows 1** and **2**. Position the [↕] pointer over the lower border of either of the selected row headings, and then drag down to increase the row height of both rows to **40 pixels**. Then, in the **Alignment group**, click the **Middle Align** button to center the titles vertically in the cells. Select **rows 4:8**, and then increase the row height of all of the selected rows to **24 pixels**.

13. Select the range **A4:H4**. Then, hold down Ctrl, and select the nonadjacent range **A5:A8**, so that both the column and row titles are selected. On the **Home tab**, in the **Font group**, click the **Bold** button. Select the range **A4:H4**, and then in the **Alignment group**, click the **Center** button.

14. Select the range **B5:H5**. Then, hold down Ctrl and select the nonadjacent range **B8:H8**. In the **Number group**, click the **Accounting Number Format** button to apply the format to the selected ranges. Select the range **B6:H7**, and then in the **Number group**, click the **Comma Style** button. Select the range **B8:H8**. In the **Font group**, click the **Borders button arrow**, and then click **Top and Double Bottom Border**. **Save** your workbook.

15. To chart the week's receipts by day and vehicle type, select the range **A4:G7**. On the Ribbon, click the **Insert tab**, and then in the **Charts group**, click **Column**. Under **2-D Column**, click the first chart type—**Clustered Column**. Point to the top border of the chart to display the [↖] pointer, and then drag to position the chart so that its upper left corner is positioned inside the upper left corner of cell **A11**.

16. On the **Design tab**, in the **Chart Layouts group**, click **Layout 1**. Click in the **Chart Title**, delete the existing text, and then type **Service Receipts Week of 5/11/2009** Click in a white area slightly *inside* the chart's border to deselect the chart title, but leave the chart itself selected. On the **Design tab**, in the **Chart Styles group**, click the **More** button to display the gallery of chart styles. Click **Style 26**.

17. Click the **Layout tab**, and then, in the **Axes group**, click the **Axes** button. Point to **Primary Vertical Axis**, and then click **More Primary Vertical Axis Options**. In the **Format Axis** dialog box, in the column at the left, click **Number**. In the **Decimal places** box, change the number to **0** and then click **Close**.

18. Click any cell to deselect the chart. Click the **Insert tab**, and then in the **Text group**, click the **Header & Footer** button to switch to **Page Layout view** and open the **Header area**. In the **Navigation group**, click the **Go to Footer** button, click just above the word *Footer*, and then in the **Header & Footer Elements group**, click the **File Name** button. Click in a cell just above the footer to exit the footer area and view your file name.

19. Scroll up to view your chart. Click the chart to select it, and notice that the chart is not centered under the data in the cells. Position the pointer over the **right resize handle**, which will display the [↔] pointer, and then drag to the right so that the right border of the chart is just inside the right border of **column H**.

(Project 9C–Service continues on the next page)

Content-Based Assessments

(Project 9C–Service continued)

20. Click any cell to deselect the chart. Click the **Page Layout tab**. In the **Page Setup group**, click the **Margins** button, and then at the bottom of the **Margins gallery**, click **Custom Margins**. In the **Page Setup** dialog box, under **Center on page**, select the **Horizontally** check box. Click **OK**, and then **Save** the changes to your workbook.

21. On the status bar, click the **Normal** button to return to **Normal view**, and then press Ctrl + Home to move to the top of your worksheet. At the lower edge of the window, click to select the **Sheet2 tab**, hold down Ctrl and click the **Sheet3 tab** to select the two unused sheets. On the **Home tab**, in the **Cells group**, click the **Delete button arrow**, and then from the list, click **Delete Sheet**.

22. **Save** the changes you have made to your workbook. Check your *Chapter Assignment Sheet* or *Course Syllabus* or consult your instructor to determine if you are to submit your assignments on paper or electronically. To submit electronically, follow the instructions provided by your instructor.

23. From the **Office** menu, point to the **Print button**, and then click **Print Preview** to check the placement of your worksheet. In the **Print group**, click the **Print** button. In the **Print** dialog box, under **Print range**, verify that the **All** option button is selected. Under **Print what**, verify that **Active sheet(s)** is selected, and then under **Copies**, verify that the **Number of copies** is **1**. Click **OK** to print your worksheet. If you are directed to submit printed formulas, refer to Activity 9.17 to do so.

24. If you printed your formulas, be sure to redisplay the worksheet by pressing Ctrl + `'`. From the **Office** menu, click **Close**. If a dialog box displays asking if you want to save changes, click **No** so that you do *not* save the changes you made for printing formulas. **Exit** Excel.

End **You have completed Project 9C**

Content-Based Assessments

Skills Review

Project 9D — Tires

In this project, you will apply the skills you practiced from the Objectives in Project 9B.

Objectives: 8. *Design a Worksheet;* **9.** *Construct Formulas for Mathematical Operations;* **10.** *Format Percentages and Move Formulas;* **11.** *Create a Pie Chart and a Chart Sheet.*

In the following Skills Review, you will create a worksheet for Arthur Potempa, Retail Sales Manager of the Rio Rancho Auto Gallery, to track the sales of two different types of tires at the four subsidiary stores that sell only tires. Your completed worksheet will look similar to the one shown in Figure 9.72.

For Project 9D, you will need the following file:

New blank Excel workbook

You will save your workbook as
9D_Tires_Firstname_Lastname

Figure 9.72

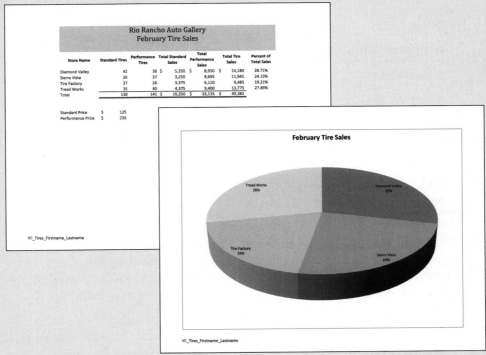

(Project 9D–Tires continues on the next page)

Content-Based Assessments

(Project 9D–Tires continued)

1. **Start** Excel and display a new blank workbook. In cell **A1**, type **Rio Rancho Auto Gallery** and then press Enter. In cell **A2**, type **February Tire Sales** and then press Enter. Select the range **A1:A2**. In the **Font group**, click the **Font arrow**, and then click **Cambria**. Click the **Font Size arrow**, and then click **18**. Display the **Save As** dialog box, navigate to your **Excel Chapter 9** folder, and then using your own first and last names, **Save** the workbook as **9D_Tires_ Firstname_Lastname**

2. In cell **A3**, type **Store Name** and then press Tab. In cell **B3**, type **Standard Tires** and then press Tab. In cell **C3**, type **Performance Tires** and then press Tab. In cell **D3**, type **Total Standard Sales** and then press Tab. In cell **E3**, type **Total Performance Sales** and then press Tab. In **F3**, type **Total Tire Sales** and then press Tab. In cell **G3**, type **Percent of Total Sales** and then press Enter.

3. In the **column heading area**, point to the right boundary of **column A** to display the ⊹ pointer, and then drag to the right to widen the column to **120 pixels**. Select the range **A3:G3**, and then in the **Font group**, click the **Bold** button. In the **Alignment group**, click the **Wrap Text** button, click the **Center** button, and then click the **Middle Align** button. Select **columns B:G**. In the **column heading area**, point to the right boundary of any of the selected columns to display the ⊹ pointer, and then drag to the right to increase the column width to **90 pixels**.

4. Select the range **A4:C6**, and then type the following data, pressing Enter to move from cell to cell within the selected range.

Store Name	Standard Tires	Performance Tires
Diamond Valley	42	38
Sierra Vista	26	37
Tread Works	35	40

5. In the range **A10:B11**, type the following:

Standard Price	125
Performance Price	235

6. Click cell **D4** and type = to begin a formula. Click cell **B4**, type * and then click cell **B10** to construct a formula that will multiply the number of Standard Tires sold at the Diamond Valley store by the Standard Price, which is 125. Then, press F4 to make the reference to cell **B10** absolute so that your formula indicates =B4*$B$10.

Because you will copy the formula down for the other two stores, the first cell reference should change relative to each row, but the price, located in cell B10, should remain the same for each formula.

(Project 9D–Tires continues on the next page)

(Project 9D–Tires continued)

7. Press Enter; your result is *5250*. Select cell **D4** again, and then drag the fill handle down through cell **D6**. Check each formula to be sure that the first cell reference changed relative to the row and that the second cell reference remained absolute—in each formula referring to the price in cell **B10**.

8. In cell **E4**, construct a similar formula to calculate the total sales of Performance Tires at Diamond Valley, using the Performance Price in cell **B11**. Then, copy the formula down through cell **E6** to compute the sales of Performance Tires for the other locations.

9. In cell **F4**, type = and then use the point and click method to construct a formula to add the Total Standard Sales and the Total Performance Sales at the Diamond Valley store; your formula should indicate *=D4+E4*, and then click the **Enter** button on the **Formula Bar**. Your result is *14180*. With cell **F4** still selected, use the fill handle to copy the formula down to compute the Total Tire Sales for the Sierra Vista store and the Tread Works store.

10. In cell **A7**, type **Total** and then press Enter. Select the range **B4:F7**. On the **Home tab**, in the **Editing group**, click the **Sum** button to calculate totals for each column. Click any cell to deselect. Select the range **D4:F4**, and then hold down Ctrl and select the nonadjacent ranges **D7:F7** and **B10:B11**. On the **Home tab**, in the **Number group**, click **Accounting Number Format**, and then click the **Decrease Decimal** button two times to format the numbers with zero decimal places.

11. Select the range **D5:F6**, in the **Number group**, click **Comma Style**, and then click the **Decrease Decimal** button two times to format the numbers with comma separators and zero decimal places. Select the range **B7:F7**. In the **Font group**, click the **Borders button arrow**, and then from the list, click **Top and Double Bottom Border**.

12. Point to the **row 6** heading and right-click to select the row and display the shortcut menu. Click **Insert** to insert a blank row, and as you type the following data in **A6:C6**, notice that the Total in cell **B8** and cell **C8** recalculates:

Tire Factory	27	26

13. Select the range **D5:F5**, and then drag the fill handle down to fill the three formulas to the range **D6:F6**, which will calculate the sales for the Tire Factory store and recalculate the column totals.

14. Click in cell **G4**, type = click cell **F4**, type / click cell **F8**, and then press F4. Your formula *=F4/$F$8* will calculate the percentage by which Diamond Valley's sales contributes to the Rio Rancho Auto Gallery's total tire sales. Press Enter; your result is *0.28713172* or approximately 29 percent. Click cell **G4**, and then use the fill handle to copy the formula down through cell **G7**. In each formula, the first cell reference will change relative to its row, and the second cell reference will remain absolute—referring to the total in cell **F8**.

15. If necessary, select the range **G4:G7**. Right-click over the selection, on the Mini toolbar, click the **Percent Style** button, click the **Center** button, and then click the **Increase Decimal** button two times. Recall that for precise information, you can increase the decimal places in a percentage.

(Project 9D–Tires continues on the next page)

(Project 9D–Tires continued)

16. Select the range **A1:G1**, and then on the **Home tab**, in the **Alignment group**, click **Merge & Center**. Repeat this formatting for cells **A2:G2**. Select the range **A1:A2**, click the **Fill Color arrow**, and then under **Theme Colors**, in the last column, click **Orange**, **Accent 6**, **Lighter 40%**. Right-click the **row 3** heading and insert a blank row to create space between the worksheet titles and the column titles—recall that the formulas will be moved and adjusted accordingly. On the **Insert tab**, in the **Text group**, click the **Header & Footer** button. In the **Navigation group**, click the **Go to Footer** button. Click just above the word *Footer* in the left section of the **Footer area**, and then in the **Header & Footer Elements group**, click the **File Name** button. Click any cell just above the **Footer area** to deselect the footer and view your file name, and then press Ctrl + Home to move to the top of your worksheet.

17. Click the **Page Layout tab**. In the **Page Setup group**, click the **Orientation** button, and then click **Landscape**. Click the **Margins** button, and then at the bottom of the **Margins gallery**, click **Custom Margins**. In the **Page Setup** dialog box, under **Center on page**, select the **Horizontally** check box. Click **OK**.

18. **Save** the changes you have made. On the right edge of the status bar, click the **Normal** button to return to **Normal view**. Select the range **A4:A8**, hold down Ctrl, and then select the range **F4:F8**. Click the **Insert tab**. In the **Charts group**, click **Pie**, and then under **3-D Pie**, click the first chart—**Pie in 3-D**. On the **Design tab**, in the **Location group**, click the **Move Chart** button. In the **Move Chart** dialog box, click the **New sheet** option button and replace the highlighted text *Chart1* by typing **Tire Sales Chart** Click **OK** to move the pie chart to a separate chart sheet in the workbook.

19. On the **Design tab**, in the **Chart Layouts group**, click **Layout 1**. Click the text *Total Tire Sales*, and then edit to indicate **February Tire Sales** Click inside the white area of the chart to deselect the title. In the **Chart Styles group**, click the **More** button, and then click **Style 8**.

20. To create a footer on your chart sheet, click the **Insert tab**. In the **Text group**, click the **Header & Footer** button, and then in the **Page Setup dialog box**, click the **Custom Footer** button. With the insertion point positioned in the **Left section**, click the seventh button—**Insert File Name**, and then click **OK** two times.

21. Click the **Sheet1 tab** and press Ctrl + Home to cancel the selections. Click the **Sheet2 tab**, hold down Ctrl and click the **Sheet3 tab**, right-click over the selected sheet tabs, and then click **Delete**.

22. **Save** your workbook. Check your *Chapter Assignment Sheet* or *Course Syllabus* or consult your instructor to determine if you are to submit your assignments on paper or electronically. To submit electronically, follow the instructions provided by your instructor.

23. To print, from the **Office** menu, click the **Print** button. In the **Print** dialog box, under **Print what**, click the **Entire workbook** option button. In the lower left corner of the dialog box, click **Preview**, and notice in the status bar, *Preview: Page 1 of 2* displays. Check the preview, in the **Preview group**, click the **Next Page** button, and then in the **Print group**, click **Print** to print the two pages. If you are directed to submit printed formulas, refer to Activity 9.17 to do so.

24. If you printed your formulas, be sure to redisplay the worksheet by pressing Ctrl + ` . From the **Office** menu, click **Close**. If a dialog box displays asking if you want to save changes, click **No** so that you do *not* save the changes you made for printing formulas. **Exit** Excel.

End **You have completed Project 9D**

Content-Based Assessments

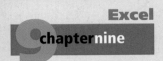
Mastering Excel

Project 9E — Compensation

In this project, you will apply the skills you practiced from the Objectives in Projects 9A and 9B.

Objectives: 1. *Create, Save, and Navigate an Excel Workbook;* **2.** *Enter and Edit Data in a Worksheet;* **3.** *Construct and Copy Formulas, Use the Sum Function, and Edit Cells;* **4.** *Format Data, Cells, and Worksheets;* **7.** *Use Page Layout View, Prepare a Worksheet for Printing, and Close Excel;* **9.** *Construct Formulas for Mathematical Operations;* **10.** *Format Percentages and Move Formulas;* **11.** *Create a Pie Chart and a Chart Sheet.*

In the following Mastering Excel project, you will create a worksheet for Clint Williams, Truck Sales Manager of Rio Rancho Auto Gallery. Members of the sales staff are paid a 5 percent commission on their total sales and also receive a small expense allowance to purchase promotional items like mugs, license plate holders, and key chains to give to customers. Your completed worksheet will look similar to Figure 9.73.

For Project 9E, you will need the following file:

New blank Excel workbook

You will save your workbook as
9E_Compensation_Firstname_Lastname

Figure 9.73

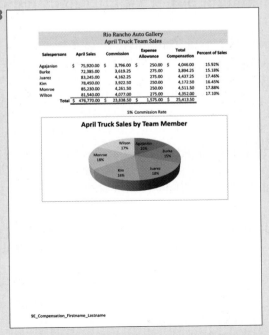

(Project 9E–Compensation continues on the next page)

Content-Based Assessments

(Project 9E–Compensation continued)

1. **Start** Excel and display a new blank workbook. In cell **A1**, type **Rio Rancho Auto Gallery** and in cell **A2**, type **April Truck Team Sales** In cell **A3**, type **Salespersons** and then press Tab. In cell **B3**, type **April Sales** In cell **C3**, type **Commission** In cell **D3**, type **Expense Allowance** In cell **E3**, type **Total Compensation** In cell **F3**, type **Percent of Sales** In your **Excel Chapter 9** folder, **Save** the workbook as **9E_Compensation_Firstname_Lastname**

2. Beginning in cell **A4**, enter the following data:

Salespersons	April Sales	Commission	Expense Allowance
Agajanian	75920		250
Burke	72385		275
Juarez	83245		275
Kim	78450		250
Monroe	85230		250
Wilson	81540		275

3. Apply the **Wrap Text** command to the range **D3:F3**. Widen all the columns to approximately **95 pixels**, and then select the column titles and apply **Bold**, **Center**, and **Middle Align**. **Merge and Center** cells **A1** and **A2** over the column titles. Select the two worksheet titles and change the **Font** to **Cambria**, the **Font Size** to **14**, and apply a **Fill Color** of **Olive Green, Accent 3, Lighter 60%**.

4. In cell **C12**, type **5%** and in cell **D12**, type **Commission Rate** In cell **C4**, construct a formula to calculate the Commission for Agajanian—April Sales times the 5% rate in cell **C12**, using absolute cell references where necessary so that you can copy the formula down. Your result is *3796*. Copy the formula down for the remaining salespersons. In cell **E4**, construct a formula to calculate Agajanian's Total Compensation by adding the Commission plus the Expense Allowance. Your result is *4046*. Copy the formula down for the remaining salespersons.

5. In cell **A10**, type **Total** Then, **Align Text Right** and apply **Bold**. Calculate totals for each of the four columns. Using financial formatting for the appropriate numbers, first apply **Comma Style**, next apply **Accounting Number Format**, and then apply a **Top and Double Bottom Border** to the total row.

6. In cell **F4**, construct a formula to calculate Agajanian's Percent of Sales by dividing Agajanian's April Sales in **B4** by Total April Sales in **B10**, using absolute cell references as necessary so that you copy the formula. Your result is *0.159238207*. Apply **Percent Style**, increase the decimal places to two, and then **Center** the percentage. Fill the formula down for the remaining salespersons.

(Project 9E–Compensation continues on the next page)

Content-Based Assessments

(Project 9E–Compensation continued)

7. Select the range of data containing the name of each salesperson and each salesperson's April Sales. **Insert** a **Pie** chart, using the **Pie in 3-D** chart type. Position the upper left corner of the chart just inside the upper left corner of cell **A13**. Apply **Chart Layout 1**, **Chart Style 5**, and as the **Chart Title**, type **April Truck Sales by Team Member**

8. **Save** your workbook. Click any cell to deselect the chart. On the **Insert tab**, in the **Text group**, click **Header & Footer** to switch to **Page Layout view** and open the **Header area**. In the **Navigation group**, click the **Go to Footer** button, click just above the word *Footer*, and then in the **Header & Footer Elements group**, click the **File Name** button. Click in a cell just above the footer to deselect the **Footer area** and view your file name.

9. Scroll up to view your chart. Select the chart, and then using the pointer, drag the right sizing handle of the chart as necessary to widen the chart so that the right border of the chart is just inside the right border of **column F**. Deselect the chart. On the **Page Layout tab**, in the **Page Setup group**, click the **Margins** button, and then at the bottom of the **Margins gallery**, click **Custom Margins**. Under **Center on page**, select the **Horizontally** check box, click **OK**, and then **Save** your workbook. Return to **Normal view** and scroll up as necessary to view the top of your worksheet. Select and delete **Sheet2** and **Sheet3**.

10. **Save** the changes to your workbook. To submit electronically, follow the instructions provided by your instructor. To print on paper, from the **Office** menu, preview and then print your worksheet. If you are directed to submit printed formulas, refer to Activity 9.17 to do so. If you printed your formulas, be sure to redisplay the worksheet by pressing Ctrl + ' . **Close** your workbook. If a dialog box displays asking if you want to save changes, click **No** so that you do *not* save the changes you made for printing formulas. **Exit** Excel.

End **You have completed Project 9E**

Content-Based Assessments

Mastering Excel

Project 9F—Warranties

In this project, you will apply the skills you practiced from the Objectives in Projects 9A and 9B.

Objectives: 1. *Create, Save, and Navigate an Excel Workbook;* **2.** *Enter and Edit Data in a Worksheet;* **3.** *Construct and Copy Formulas, Use the Sum Function, and Edit Cells;* **4.** *Format Data, Cells, and Worksheets;* **7.** *Use Page Layout View, Prepare a Worksheet for Printing, and Close Excel;* **8.** *Design a Worksheet;* **9.** *Construct Formulas for Mathematical Operations;* **11.** *Create a Pie Chart and a Chart Sheet.*

In the following Mastering Excel project, you will create a workbook for Sandy Cizek, the Auto Sales Manager, which summarizes both the sales of vehicle warranties and the commissions paid on the warranties that were sold. Your completed worksheets will look similar to Figure 9.74.

For Project 9F, you will need the following file:

New blank Excel workbook

You will save your workbook as
9F_Warranties_Firstname_Lastname

Figure 9.74

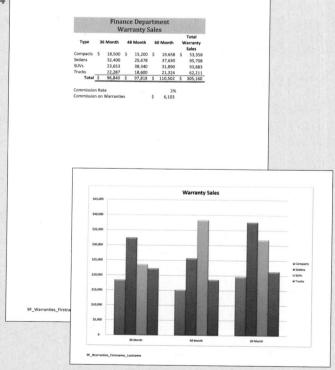

(Project 9F–Warranties continues on the next page)

Content-Based Assessments

(Project 9F–Warranties continued)

1. **Start** Excel and display a new blank workbook. In cell **A1**, type **Finance Department** and in cell **A2**, type **Warranty Sales** In cell **A3**, type **Type** and press Tab. In cell **B3**, type **36 Month** In cell **C3**, type **48 Month** In cell **D3**, type **60 Month** In cell **E3**, type **Total Warranty Sales** In your **Excel Chapter 9** folder, **Save** the workbook as 9F_Warranties_Firstname_Lastname

2. In the range **A4:D7**, type the following data; if you want to do so, select the range first and use Enter to confine the movement of the active cell within the range.

Type	36 Month	48 Month	60 Month
Compacts	18500	15200	19658
Sedans	32400	25678	37630
SUVs	23653	38340	31890
Trucks	22287	18600	21324

3. Apply the **Wrap Text** command to cell **E3**. Format all the column titles in **row 3** with **Center**, **Middle Align**, and **Bold**. Adjust the width of **columns B:E** to **80 pixels. Merge and Center** the two worksheet titles over columns **A:E**, and then select and format the two titles by changing the **Font** to **Cambria**, the **Font Size** to **16**, and the **Fill Color** to **Red, Accent 2, Lighter 60%**.

4. In cell **E4**, **Sum** all the warranties sold for Compacts, and then copy the formula down for the remaining vehicle types. **Sum** the columns. In cell **A8**, type **Total** and apply **Bold** and **Align Text Right**. Using financial formatting for the appropriate numbers, first apply **Comma Style** with zero decimals, next apply **Accounting Number Format** with zero decimals, and then apply a **Top and Double Bottom Border** to the total row.

5. In cell **A10**, type **Commission Rate** and in cell **D10**, type **2%** In cell **A11**, type **Commission on Warranties** In cell **D11**, construct a formula that multiplies the Total Warranty Sales in cell **E8** by the Commission Rate in **D10**, and then apply **Accounting Number Format** with zero decimals.

6. On the **Insert tab**, in the **Text group**, click **Header & Footer** to switch to **Page Layout view**. In the **Navigation group**, click the **Go to Footer** button, click just above the word *Footer*, and then in the **Header & Footer Elements group**, click the **File Name** button. Click a cell just above the footer to deselect the **Footer area** and view your file name. On the **Page Layout tab**, display the **Margins gallery**, click **Custom Margins**, and then under **Center on page**, select the **Horizontally** check box.

7. Switch to **Normal view** and scroll to the top of your worksheet. Select the range of data that represents the types of vehicles and the warranty sales for each of the three types, including the column titles. **Insert** a **Column** chart, using the **2-D Clustered Column** chart type. Move the chart to a new sheet and name the sheet **Warranty Sales Chart** On the **Design tab**, in the **Data group**, click the **Switch Row/Column** button to display the warranty periods as the

(Project 9F–Warranties continues on the next page)

(Project 9F–Warranties continued)

categories. Apply **Chart Layout 1**, **Chart Style 26**, and change the **Chart Title** to **Warranty Sales** Deselect the chart by clicking in an area outside of the chart. To create a footer on the chart sheet, on the **Insert tab**, click the **Header & Footer** button, create a **Custom Footer** with the file name in the **Left section**.

8. Click the **Sheet1 tab** and press Ctrl + Home to cancel the selections. Select and delete **Sheet2** and **Sheet3**.

9. **Save** your workbook. To submit electronically, follow the instructions provided by your instructor. To print, from the **Office** menu, click the **Print** button. In the **Print** dialog box, under **Print what**, click the **Entire workbook** option button. In the lower left corner of the dialog box, click **Preview**, and notice in the status bar, *Preview: Page 1 of 2* displays. Check the preview, in the **Preview group**, click the **Next Page** button, and then in the **Print group**, click **Print** to print the two pages. If you are directed to submit printed formulas, refer to Activity 9.17 to do so.

10. If you printed your formulas, be sure to redisplay the worksheet by pressing Ctrl + `. From the **Office** menu, click **Close**. If a dialog box displays asking if you want to save changes, click **No** so that you do *not* save the changes you made for printing formulas. **Exit** Excel.

End **You have completed Project 9F** ─────────────────────

Mastering Excel

Project 9G—Team Comparison

In this project, you will apply the skills you practiced from all the Objectives in Projects 9A and 9B.

In the following Mastering Excel project, you will create a workbook for Sandy Cizek, Auto Sales Manager, which summarizes the monthly team sales for one of the three auto sales teams at Rio Rancho Auto Gallery. Your completed worksheet will look similar to Figure 9.75.

For Project 9G, you will need the following file:

New blank Excel workbook

**You will save your workbook as
9G_Team_Comparison_Firstname_Lastname**

Figure 9.75

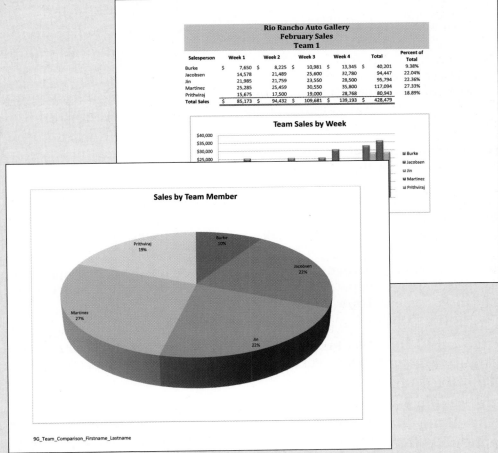

(Project 9G–Team Comparison continues on the next page)

(Project 9G–Team Comparison continued)

1. **Start** Excel and display a new blank workbook. In cell **A1**, type **Rio Rancho Auto Gallery** In cell **A2**, type **February Sales** In cell **A3**, type **Team 1** In cell **A4**, type **Salesperson** and then press [Tab]. In cell **B4**, type **Week 1** Select cell **B4**, and then use the fill handle to create a series in the range **B4:E4** so that *Week 2* and *Week 3* and *Week 4* display in the cells. In cell **F4**, type **Total** and then in cell **G4**, type **Percent of Total** In your **Excel Chapter 9** folder, **Save** the workbook as **9G_Team_Comparison_Firstname_Lastname**

2. In the range **A5:E8**, type the following data; if you want to do so, select the range first and use [Enter] to confine the movement of the active cell within the range.

Salesperson	Week 1	Week 2	Week 3	Week 4
Burke	7650	8225	10981	13345
Jacobsen	14578	21489	25600	32780
Jin	21985	21759	23550	28500
Prithviraj	15675	17500	19000	28768

3. Apply the **Wrap Text** command to cell **G4**. To all the column titles in **row 4**, apply the **Bold**, **Center**, and **Middle Align** commands. Adjust the width of **columns A:G** to **90 pixels**. **Merge & Center** the three worksheet titles over columns **A:G**, and then format the three titles by changing the **Font** to **Cambria**, the **Font Size** to **16**, the **Fill Color** to **Aqua, Accent 5, Lighter 40%** and applying **Bold**.

4. In cell **A9**, type **Total Sales** and format the cell with **Bold**. **Sum** the rows for each salesperson, and then **Sum** the columns for each week and for the Total. Insert a row above *Prithviraj* and enter the following data—recall that Excel will move and adjust formulas when rows are inserted. After you enter the data, use the fill handle to copy the formula from **F7** to **F8**.

Martinez	25285	25459	30550	35800

5. Using financial formatting for the appropriate numbers, first apply **Comma Style** with zero decimals, next apply **Accounting Number Format** with zero decimals, and then apply a **Top and Double Bottom Border** to the total row.

6. In cell **G5**, construct a formula to calculate the percentage by which Burke's total sales makes up the Total in cell **F10**. Use [F4] to apply absolute cell referencing where necessary. Apply **Percent Style** formatting with two decimals, and then fill the formula down to cell **G9**. **Center** the percentages.

7. Select the range of data that represents the names and each week's sales of each salesperson including the column titles. **Insert** a **2-D Clustered Column** chart, and then click the **Switch Row/Column** button so that the chart displays the weeks on the category axis and the salespersons as the data points. Position the upper left corner of the chart in the upper left corner of cell **A12**.

(Project 9G–Team Comparison continues on the next page)

Content-Based Assessments

(Project 9G–Team Comparison continued)

8. Click any cell to deselect the chart. On the **Insert tab**, click the **Header & Footer** button to switch to **Page Layout view**. Click the **Go to Footer** button, click just above the word *Footer*, and then click the **File Name** button. Click a cell just above the footer to deselect the **Footer area** and view your file name. On the **Page Layout tab**, change the **Orientation** to **Landscape**. Display the **Margins gallery**, click **Custom Margins**, and then under **Center on page**, select the **Horizontally** check box.

9. Scroll up, and then use the ⟷ pointer to resize the chart so that its right edge is even with the right side of the data. Format the chart, using **Chart Layout 1**, **Chart Style 26**, and then change the **Chart Title** to Team Sales by Week

10. **Save** your workbook, click any cell to deselect the chart, switch to **Normal view**, and then press Ctrl + Home to move to the top of your worksheet. Select the ranges of data that represent each salesperson's name and his or her Total for the month. **Insert** a **Pie** chart, using the **Pie in 3-D** chart type. Move the chart to a new sheet, and then name the sheet **Team Chart** Apply **Chart Layout 1**, **Chart Style 7**, and then change the **Chart Title** to Sales by Team Member Deselect the chart by clicking outside of the chart. To create a footer on the chart sheet, on the **Insert tab**, click the **Header & Footer** button, and then create a **Custom Footer** with the file name in the **Left section**.

11. Click the **Sheet1 tab**, and press Ctrl + Home to cancel the selections. Select and delete **Sheet2** and **Sheet3**. **Save** your workbook. Check your *Chapter Assignment Sheet* or *Course Syllabus* or consult your instructor to determine if you are to submit your assignments on paper or electronically. To submit electronically, follow the instructions provided by your instructor.

12. To print, from the **Office** menu, click the **Print** button. In the **Print** dialog box, under **Print what**, click the **Entire workbook** option button. In the lower left corner of the dialog box, click **Preview**, and notice in the status bar, *Preview: Page 1 of 2* displays. Check the preview, in the **Preview group**, click the **Next Page** button, and then in the **Print group**, click **Print** to print the two pages. If you are directed to submit printed formulas, refer to Activity 9.17 to do so.

13. If you printed your formulas, be sure to redisplay the worksheet by pressing Ctrl + `. From the **Office** menu, click **Close**. If a dialog box displays asking if you want to save changes, click **No** so that you do *not* save the changes you made for printing formulas. **Exit** Excel.

End **You have completed Project 9G**

Mastering Excel

Project 9H — *GO!* Fix It

In this project, you will construct a solution by applying any combination of the skills you practiced from the Objectives in Projects 9A and 9B.

For Project 9H, you will need the following file:

e09H_Accessories

**You will save your workbook as
9H_Accessories_Firstname_Lastname**

From the student files that accompany this textbook, locate and open the file **e09H_Accessories**, and then save the file in your chapter folder as **9H_Accessories_Firstname_Lastname**

In this project, you will edit the first draft of an Excel workbook that contains information about sales of automotive electronic accessories. The workbook was prepared for Arthur Potempa, Retail Accessories Manager of Rio Rancho Auto Gallery.

This workbook contains **ten errors** that you must find and correct. Read and examine the workbook and then edit to correct the errors that you find. Types of errors could include:

- Spelling, grammar, and punctuation errors in cells, charts, worksheet tabs, or file names.

- Errors in data entry and workbook layout. Formatting errors in text, numbers, alignment, indents and spacing, tabs, wrapping, merge and center, text direction and orientation, fonts, borders, patterns, protection, AutoFormat, conditional formatting, data sort, filter, and validation.

- Formula and function errors such as incorrect and missing formulas, error indicators and values, relative versus absolute cell referencing, What-If Analysis, Paste Special, function arguments, and Goal Seek.

- Errors in object design, layout, and formatting; for example, chart type, location, data source, elements, size, scale, positioning, pictures, and hyperlinks.

- Row and column formatting errors such as height, width, and AutoFit.

- Worksheet, tab design, and formatting errors such as missing or blank worksheets, worksheet tab colors, and locations.

- Page setup errors such as page orientation and scaling, margins and centering, headers and footers, sheet gridlines, and row and column headings.

(Project 9H–*GO!* Fix It continues on the next page)

(Project 9H–*GO!* Fix It continued)

To complete the project you should know that in this workbook:

- Formula errors in a *range* of cells count as a *single* error.
- Cell A2 should be centered horizontally and vertically.
- Chart design should be Style 3.
- Chart title should be changed to February Sales Chart.

Save the changes you have made, add the file name to the worksheet footers, and then submit as directed.

End You have completed Project 9H ⎯⎯⎯⎯⎯⎯⎯⎯⎯⎯

Outcomes-Based Assessments

Rubric

The following outcomes-based assessments are *open-ended assessments*. That is, there is no specific correct result; your result will depend on your approach to the information provided. Make *Professional Quality* your goal. Use the following scoring rubric to guide you in *how* to approach the problem and then to evaluate *how well* your approach solves the problem.

The *criteria*—Software Mastery, Content, Format and Layout, and Process—represent the knowledge and skills you have gained that you can apply to solving the problem. The *levels of performance*—Professional Quality, Approaching Professional Quality, or Needs Quality Improvements—help you and your instructor evaluate your result.

	Your completed project is of Professional Quality if you:	Your completed project is Approaching Professional Quality if you:	Your completed project Needs Quality Improvements if you:
1-Software Mastery	Choose and apply the most appropriate skills, tools, and features and identify efficient methods to solve the problem.	Choose and apply some appropriate skills, tools, and features, but not in the most efficient manner.	Choose inappropriate skills, tools, or features, or are inefficient in solving the problem.
2-Content	Construct a solution that is clear and well organized, contains content that is accurate, appropriate to the audience and purpose, and is complete. Provide a solution that contains no errors of spelling, grammar, or style.	Construct a solution in which some components are unclear, poorly organized, inconsistent, or incomplete. Misjudge the needs of the audience. Have some errors in spelling, grammar, or style, but the errors do not detract from comprehension.	Construct a solution that is unclear, incomplete, or poorly organized; contains some inaccurate or inappropriate content; and contains many errors of spelling, grammar, or style. Do not solve the problem.
3-Format and Layout	Format and arrange all elements to communicate information and ideas, clarify function, illustrate relationships, and indicate relative importance.	Apply appropriate format and layout features to some elements, but not others. Overuse features, causing minor distraction.	Apply format and layout that does not communicate information or ideas clearly. Do not use format and layout features to clarify function, illustrate relationships, or indicate relative importance. Use available features excessively, causing distraction.
4-Process	Use an organized approach that integrates planning, development, self-assessment, revision, and reflection.	Demonstrate an organized approach in some areas, but not others; or, use an insufficient process of organization throughout.	Do not use an organized approach to solve the problem.

Outcomes-Based Assessments

Problem Solving

Project 9I — Rims

In this project, you will construct a solution by applying any combination of the skills you practiced from the Objectives in Projects 9A and 9B.

> **For Project 9I, you will need the following file:**
>
> New blank Excel workbook

You will save your workbook as
9I_Rims_Firstname_Lastname

Rio Rancho Auto Gallery stocks one brand of tire rims and in January sold 10 16-inch rims priced at $150 each, 20 18-inch rims priced at $225 each, 32 20-inch rims priced at $375 each, and 16 22-inch rims priced at $500 each. The installation fee for all rims is $50 each.

Create a spreadsheet detailing this information and include a column that calculates the Installed Price for each rim size (Price + Installation Fee) and the Total Sales for each rim size (Installed Price times Number Sold). Total the columns to calculate the total number of rims sold and the Total Sales of all rims. Add an additional column in which you create a formula that calculates the Percent of Sales that each rim size is of the Total Sales of all rim sales. Create a 3-D pie chart that compares the Total Sales generated by each rim size. Position the pie chart below the data on the worksheet.

Create a title that identifies the worksheet and apply appropriate formats to the data and the pie chart. Use borders, fill colors, and font styles and font sizes to format a professional worksheet. Add a footer that includes the file name, and center the worksheet on the page. Save the workbook as **9I_Rims_Firstname_Lastname** and submit it as directed.

End **You have completed Project 9I** ——————

Problem Solving

Project 9J—Finance

In this project, you will construct a solution by applying any combination of the skills you practiced from the Objectives in Projects 9A and 9B.

For Project 9J, you will need the following file:

New blank Excel workbook

**You will save your workbook as
9J_Finance_Firstname_Lastname**

In this project, you will create a worksheet for Tony Konecki, President of Rio Rancho Auto Gallery, which specifies, by quarter, the amount of credit extended to customers on vehicle purchases during the past fiscal year. The data is organized according to customer credit scores—overall, more credit was given to customers with higher credit scores. Create a worksheet with appropriate titles, and then enter the following data for Quarters 1 through 4.

Credit Score	Quarter 1	Quarter 2	Quarter 3	Quarter 4
750 or Above	350190	322489	368700	385644
700- 749	425654	496451	485200	501780
650- 699	328976	298560	316789	335679
600- 649	489561	462312	475232	490520
550- 599	182597	215600	202450	228600
Under 550	162487	175800	186532	188423

Calculate totals for each quarter and for each credit score, and then create a column chart that compares the amounts for each quarter by credit score. A chart layout that places the legend at the bottom of the chart will allow more space for the columns. Use formatting and editing techniques so that the worksheet and chart are professional and accurate. Add the file name to the footer and save the workbook as **9J_Finance_Firstname_Lastname** Submit the project as directed.

End **You have completed Project 9J** ───────────────

Outcomes-Based Assessments

Excel

chapternine

Problem Solving

Project 9K — Service

In this project, you will construct a solution by applying any combination of the skills you practiced from the Objectives in Projects 9A and 9B.

For Project 9K, you will need the following file:

New blank Excel workbook

You will save your workbook as
9K_Service_Firstname_Lastname

In this project, you will create a worksheet for the service department to analyze the labor costs associated with different types of repairs during the current month. Create an appropriate worksheet title and then enter the following data and column headings.

Service	Hours to Complete Service	Cost for Service at Standard Rate	Number Completed During June	Total Labor Cost
Valve replacement	8		13	
Head gasket	12		12	
Transmission	15		10	
Engine replacement	15		11	
Total Labor Cost				

Two rows below the Total Labor Cost row, in column A, type **Standard Labor Rate** and in column B, type **35.75** In the Cost for Service at Standard Rate column, construct a formula to calculate the cost to complete each type of service at the standard rate. In the Total Labor Cost column, construct a formula to calculate the total labor cost for each of the services completed during the month.

Add a column to the worksheet with the column heading **Percent of Total Labor Cost** and calculate the percent that each service is of the Total Labor Cost. Create a pie chart on a separate chart sheet that compares the Total Labor Costs by Service. Add the file name to the footer in both sheets and check for spelling errors. Save the workbook as **9K_Service_Firstname_Lastname** and submit it as directed.

End **You have completed Project 9K**

More on your Student CD

The instructions for the following additional end-of-chapter projects are on your student CD in the folder 03_additional_end_of_chapter_projects.

Content-Based Assessments

Project L Mastering Excel

Apply the skills you practiced in Project A.

Project M Mastering Excel

Apply the skills you practiced in Project B.

Project N Business Running Case

Apply the skills you practiced in Projects A and B while helping an entrepreneur with the daily tasks of running a business.

In each chapter, this project focuses on applying the skills you have practiced in Projects A and B to a business. The project related to this business runs throughout the textbook. You will see how the Office applications relate to the day-to-day operation of a small business called Nelson Architectural Planning.

Outcomes-Based Assessments

Project O Problem Solving

Construct a solution by applying any combination of the skills you practiced from Projects A and B.

Project P Problem Solving

Construct a solution by applying any combination of the skills you practiced from Projects A and B.

Project Q You and GO!

Construct a solution that applies to your own life by applying any combination of the skills you practiced from Projects A and B.

Project R GO! with Help

Practice using Microsoft Office's Help Feature.

Project S Group Business Running Case

Work as part of a group to apply the skills you have gained thus far to help the Bell Orchid Hotel Group achieve its business goals.

Multimedia

The following multimedia accompany this textbook:

Companion Web site
www.prenhall.com/go

An interactive Web site designed to reinforce and test your understanding of the skills in this chapter.

AV-EDDs

In the folder in the front of this book you will find videos that demonstrate the objectives in the A and B projects in this chapter. These may help you understand how to complete the projects in this book.

Video Podcasts

In the folder in the front of this book are videos that can be played on your iPod, MP3 player, or computer. These videos demonstrate how to complete the more challenging objectives in this textbook.

10 chapterten

Managing Workbooks and Analyzing Data

OBJECTIVES

At the end of this chapter you will be able to:

1. Create and Save a Workbook from an Existing Workbook
2. Navigate a Workbook and Rename Worksheets
3. Enter Dates, Clear Contents, and Clear Formats
4. Move, Copy, and Paste Cell Contents
5. Edit and Format Multiple Worksheets at the Same Time
6. Create a Summary Sheet
7. Format and Print Multiple Worksheets in a Workbook

8. Design a Worksheet for What-If Analysis
9. Perform What-If Analysis
10. Compare Data with a Line Chart

OUTCOMES

Mastering these objectives will enable you to:

PROJECT 10A
Create a Summary Sheet from Multiple Worksheets

PROJECT 10B
Make Projections Using What-If Analysis

The City of Golden Grove

Golden Grove is a California city located between Los Angeles and San Diego, about 20 miles from the Pacific shore. Ten years ago the population was just over 200,000; today it has grown to over 300,000. Community leaders focus on quality and economic development in decisions about housing, open space, education, and infrastructure, making the city a model for other communities its size. The city provides many recreational and cultural opportunities with a large park system and a thriving arts community.

© Stan Rohrer / Courtesy of www.istockphoto.com

Managing Workbooks and Analyzing Data

Organizations typically create workbooks that contain multiple worksheets. In such a workbook, the first worksheet usually summarizes the detailed information in the other worksheets. To make it easier to work with multiple worksheets, there are techniques to enter data into multiple worksheets simultaneously by grouping the worksheets. You can also copy, and then paste information from one worksheet to another. Additional techniques for managing workbooks with multiple worksheets include naming and color coding the sheet tabs so that you can quickly locate the detailed information you are looking for.

In Excel, you can explore options by recalculating formulas that depend on other formulas. For example, you can change the interest rate in a table of loan payments to determine the amount of monthly payments based on differing interest rates.

In this chapter, you will work with workbooks that contain multiple worksheets and analyze data by making projections of future growth.

Project 10A **Ticket Sales**

In Activities 10.01 through 10.10, you will edit an existing Excel workbook for Judith Amaya, the Director of Arts and Parks for Golden Grove. The annual Summer Fair and Arts Festival will be held during the last week in August. During the first week in August, the city is preselling tickets at three locations in the city. The four worksheets of your completed workbook will look similar to Figure 10.1.

For Project 10A, you will need the following file:

e10A_Ticket_Sales

You will save your workbook as
10A_Ticket_Sales_Firstname_Lastname

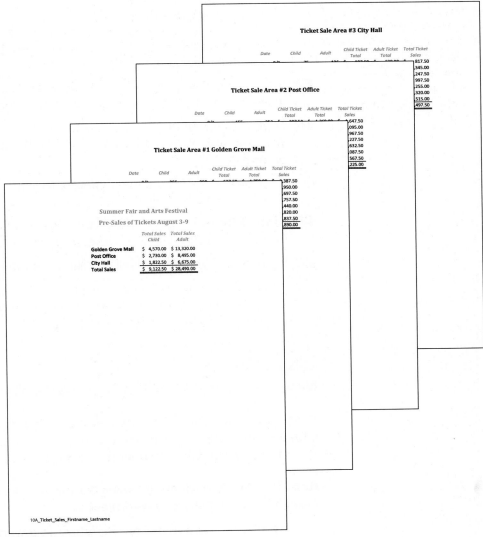

Figure 10.1
Project 10A—Ticket Sales

Objective 1
Create and Save a Workbook from an Existing Workbook

Within a workbook, individual worksheets may contain data for separate topics, locations, or periods of time related to the workbook's data. In such a workbook, it is common practice to have one worksheet that summarizes information from the other worksheets.

Activity 10.01 Creating and Saving a Workbook from an Existing Workbook

Judith has a workbook with worksheets into which she can record the number of tickets sold at the three locations during the first week in August.

1 **Start** Excel. From the **Office** menu ⊙, click **Open**. In the displayed **Open** dialog box, navigate to the student files that accompany this textbook, and then open **e10A_Ticket_Sales**.

> In the displayed e10A_Ticket_Sales workbook, some information has already been entered into the worksheets. For example, on the first worksheet, the dates for the one-week period have been entered, along with information about the ticket prices.

2 From the **Office** menu ⊙, click **Save As**. Navigate to the drive location where you will store your projects for this chapter.

3 On the **Save As** dialog box toolbar, click the **New Folder** button 📷. With the text *New Folder* selected, type **Excel Chapter 10** and then press Enter.

> Windows creates the *Excel Chapter 10* folder and makes it the active folder in the Save As dialog box.

4 In the **File name** box, edit as necessary to indicate, using your own first and last names, **10A_Ticket_Sales_Firstname_Lastname**

5 In the lower right corner of the **Save As** dialog box, click **Save**.

> Excel saves the file in your chapter folder with the new name. The workbook redisplays, and the new name displays in the title bar. Use this technique to create a new workbook from an existing workbook.

Objective 2
Navigate a Workbook and Rename Worksheets

By default, the number of worksheets in a workbook is three. You can add additional worksheets or delete unused worksheets. Using multiple worksheets in a workbook is frequently a logical approach to arranging data.

Activity 10.02 Navigating Among Worksheets, Renaming Worksheets, and Changing the Tab Color of a Worksheet

When you have more than one worksheet in a workbook, you can *navigate* (move) among worksheets by clicking the *sheet tabs*. Sheet tabs identify each worksheet in a workbook and are located along the lower left edge of the workbook window. When you have more worksheets in the workbook than can be displayed in the sheet tab area, use the four sheet tab scrolling buttons to move sheet tabs into and out of view.

Excel names the first worksheet in a workbook *Sheet1* and each additional worksheet in order—*Sheet2*, *Sheet3*, and so on. Most Excel users rename the worksheets with names that are more meaningful. In this activity, you will navigate among three worksheets. You will also rename each worksheet and change the tab color of the sheet tabs.

1 Along the bottom of the Excel window, point to and then click the **Sheet2 tab**. Compare your screen with Figure 10.2.

> The second worksheet in the workbook displays and becomes the active worksheet. *Sheet2* displays in bold.

Figure 10.2

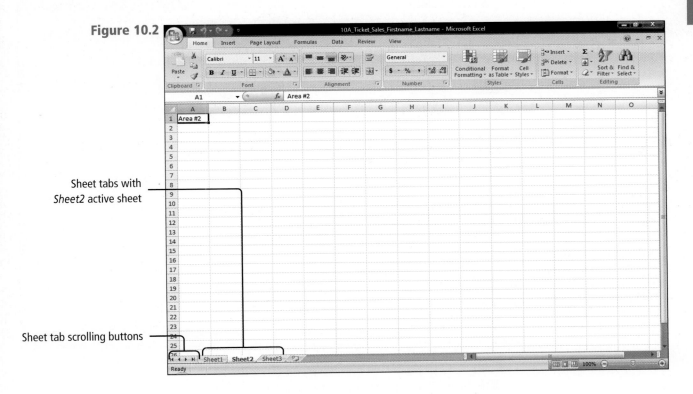

Sheet tabs with *Sheet2* active sheet

Sheet tab scrolling buttons

2 In cell **A1**, notice the text *Area #2*—this worksheet will contain data for Summer Fair tickets purchased at the Area #2 location. Click the **Sheet1 tab**.

> The first worksheet becomes the active worksheet, and cell A1, which is formatted with an orange background, displays *Area #1*.

3 Point to the **Sheet3 tab**, right-click, and then click **Rename**. With *Sheet3* selected, type **City Hall** and then press Enter.

4 Point to the **Sheet1 tab**, and then double-click to select its name. Type **Golden Grove Mall** and then press Enter. Using either of the two methods you just practiced, rename **Sheet2** as **Post Office**

5 Right-click the **Golden Grove Mall sheet tab**. On the shortcut menu, point to **Tab Color** to display the colors associated with the workbook's theme. Under **Theme Colors**, locate and click **Purple, Accent 4, Lighter 40%**.

When the sheet is active, the tab color displays as an underline.

6 Click the **Post Office** sheet tab to make it the active sheet. On the Ribbon's **Home tab**, in the **Cells group**, click the **Format** button, and then from the displayed list, point to **Tab Color**.

7 Under **Theme Colors**, click **Aqua, Accent 5, Lighter 40%**. Using either of the two techniques you just practiced, change the **Tab Color** of the **City Hall** worksheet to **Orange, Accent 6, Lighter 40%**. Compare your screen with Figure 10.3.

Figure 10.3

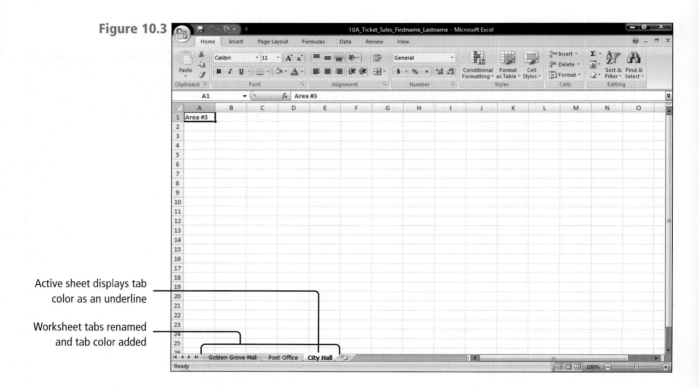

Active sheet displays tab color as an underline

Worksheet tabs renamed and tab color added

8 **Save** the changes to your workbook.

Objective 3
Enter Dates, Clear Contents, and Clear Formats

Dates represent a type of value that you can enter in a cell. When you enter a date, Excel assigns a serial value—a number—to the date. This makes it possible to treat dates like other numbers. For example, if two cells contain dates, you can find the number of days between the two dates by subtracting the older date from the more recent date.

Activity 10.03 Entering and Formatting Dates

In this activity, you will examine the various ways that Excel can format a date that you type into a cell. Date values entered in any of the following formats will be recognized by Excel as a date:

Format	Example
m/d/yy	7/4/09
d-mmm	4-Jul
d-mmm-yy	4-Jul-09
mmm-yy	Jul-09

On your keyboard, ☐ (the hyphen key) and ☐ (the forward slash key) function identically in any of these formats and can be used interchangeably. You can abbreviate the month name to three characters or spell it out. You can enter the year as two digits, four digits, or even leave it off. When left off, the current year is assumed but does not display in the cell.

A two-digit year value of 30 through 99 is interpreted by the Windows operating system as the four-digit years of 1930 through 1999. All other two-digit year values are assumed to be in the 21st century. If you always type year values as four digits, even though only two digits may display in the cell, you can be sure that Excel interprets the year value as you intended. See the table in Figure 10.4 for examples.

How Excel Interprets Dates	
Date Typed As:	**Completed by Excel As:**
7/4/09	7/4/2009
7-4-98	7/4/1998
7/4	4-Jul (current year assumed)
7-4	4-Jul (current year assumed)
July 4	4-Jul (current year assumed)
Jul 4	4-Jul (current year assumed)
Jul/4	4-Jul (current year assumed)
Jul-4	4-Jul (current year assumed)
July 4, 1998	4-Jul-98
July 2009	Jul-09 (first day of month assumed)
July 1998	Jul-98 (first day of month assumed)

Figure 10.4

1 Click the **Golden Grove Mall sheet tab**. Click cell **A5** and notice that the cell indicates *8/3* (August 3). In the **Formula Bar**, notice that the full date of August 3, 2009 displays in the format *8/3/2009*.

2 With cell **A5** selected, on the Ribbon, in the **Number group**, click the **Number Format arrow**. From the bottom of the displayed menu,

click **More Number Formats** to display the **Number tab** of the
Format Cells dialog box. Compare your screen with Figure 10.5.

Under Category, *Date* is selected, and under Type, *3/14* is selected. All
of the dates in Column A were formatted using this format type; that is,
only the month and day display in the cell.

Figure 10.5

Format Cells dialog box

Number tab active

8/3 displays in Sample box

Date category selected

3/14 indicated as Type

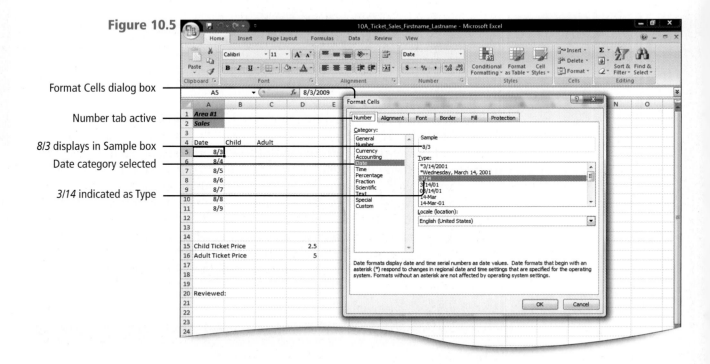

3   In the displayed dialog box, under **Type**, click several other date
types and watch the **Sample** area to see how applying the selected
date format would format your cell. When you are finished, click the
3/14 type, and then at the bottom of the dialog box, click **OK**.

4   Click cell **A21**, type **8/10/2009** and then press Enter.

Cell A21 has no special date formatting applied, and thus displays in
the default date format *8/10/2009*.

Alert!

The date does not display as 8/10/2009?

Settings in your Windows operating system determine the default format for dates.
If your result is different, it is likely that the formatting of the default date was
adjusted on the computer at which you are working.

5   Click cell **A21** again. Hold down Ctrl and press ⟨;⟩ (the semicolon key)
on your keyboard. Press Enter to confirm the entry.

Excel enters the current date, obtained from your computer's internal
calendar, using the default date format. Ctrl + ⟨;⟩ is a quick method to
enter the current date.

6 Click cell **A21** again, type **8/10/09** and then press ⟨Enter⟩.

> Because the year *09* is less than 30, Excel assumes a 21st century date and changes *09* to *2009* to complete the four-digit year. Typing *98* would result in *1998*. For two-digit years that you type that are between 30 and 99, Excel assumes a 20th century date.

7 Click cell **A5**, and then on the **Home tab**, in the **Clipboard group**, click the **Format Painter** button ⟨🖌⟩. Click cell **A21**, and notice that the date format from cell **A5** is copied to cell **A21**. **Save** ⟨💾⟩ your workbook.

Activity 10.04 Clearing Cell Contents and Formats

A cell has contents—a value or a formula—and a cell may also have one or more formats applied, for example bold and italic font styles, fill color, font color, and so on. You can choose to clear the contents of a cell, the formatting of a cell, or both. You can clear—delete—the contents of a selected cell in two ways: Press ⟨Del⟩ or use the Clear Contents command available both from the Editing group on the Ribbon and from a shortcut menu.

Clearing the contents of a cell deletes the value or formula typed there, but it does *not* clear formatting applied to a cell. In this activity, you will clear the contents of a cell and then clear the formatting of a cell that contains a date to see its underlying content.

1 On the **Golden Grove Mall** worksheet, click cell **A1**. On the Ribbon, in the **Editing group**, click the **Clear** button ⟨🧽⟩. From the displayed list, click **Clear Contents**. Click cell **A2**, and then press ⟨Delete⟩.

> You can use either of these two methods to delete the *contents* of a cell. Deleting the contents does not, however, delete the formatting of the cell; you can see that the orange fill color format applied to the two cells still displays.

2 In cell **A1**, type **Area #1** and then on the **Formula Bar**, click the **Enter** button ⟨✓⟩ so that cell **A1** remains the active cell. In the **Editing group**, click the **Clear** button ⟨🧽⟩, and then from the displayed menu, click **Clear Formats**.

> Clearing the formats deletes formatting from the cell—the orange fill color and the bold and italic font styles—but does not delete the cell's contents.

3 Use the same technique to clear the orange fill color from cell **A2**.

4 Click cell **A5**, click the **Clear** button ⟨🧽⟩, and then click **Clear Formats**. In the **Number group**, notice that *General* displays as the number format of the cell.

> The box at the top of the Number group indicates the current Number format of the selected cell. Clearing the date formatting from the cell displays the date's serial number. The date, August 3, 2009, is stored as a serial number that indicates the number of days since January 1, 1900. This date is the 40,028th day since the reference date of January 1, 1900.

5 On the **Quick Access Toolbar**, click the **Undo** button ⟨↺⟩ to restore the date format. **Save** ⟨💾⟩ your workbook, and then compare your screen with Figure 10.6.

Figure 10.6

Date in Formula Bar

Orange fill color and bold italic font style cleared from cell A1

Contents and formats of cell A2 deleted

A5 reformatted as a date

Date indicated as the Number format

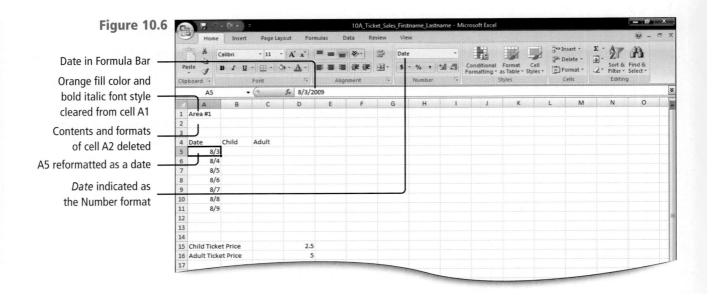

Objective 4
Move, Copy, and Paste Cell Contents

Data in cells can be copied to other cells in the same worksheet, to other sheets in the same workbook, or to sheets in another workbook. Likewise, data can be moved from one place to another. The action of placing cell contents that have been copied or moved to the Office Clipboard to another location is called *paste*.

Activity 10.05 Copying, Pasting, and Moving Cell Contents

The *Office Clipboard* is a temporary storage area maintained by your Windows operating system. When you select one or more cells, and then perform the Copy command or the Cut command, the selected data is placed on the Office Clipboard. From the Office Clipboard storage area, the data is available for pasting into other cells, other worksheets, other workbooks, and even into other Office programs.

1 On the **Golden Grove Mall** sheet, select the range **A20:A21**. Point to the upper edge of the black border surrounding the selected cells until the pointer displays. Drag upward until the ScreenTip displays *A18:A19*, as shown in Figure 10.7, and then release the mouse button to complete the move.

Using this technique, cell contents can be moved from one location to another; this is referred to as *drag and drop*.

Figure 10.7

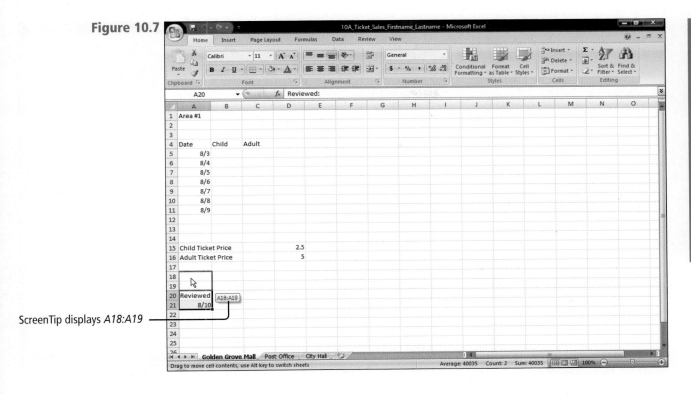

ScreenTip displays *A18:A19*

2 Select the range **A4:D16**.

> A range of cells identical to this one is required for the *Post Office* worksheet and the *City Hall* worksheet.

3 On the **Home tab**, in the **Clipboard group**, click the **Copy** button to place a copy of the selected cells on the Office Clipboard. Alternatively, press Ctrl + C or right-click over the selected range, and then click Copy from the shortcut menu.

> A moving border surrounds the selected range, and a message on the left side of the status bar indicates *Select destination and press ENTER or choose Paste*. These two results confirm that your selected range has been placed on the Office Clipboard.

4 At the bottom of the workbook window, click the **Post Office sheet tab** to make it the active worksheet. Click cell **A4**, and then on the **Home tab**, in the **Clipboard group**, click the **Paste** button. Alternatively, use the keyboard shortcut for Paste, which is Ctrl + V. Compare your screen with Figure 10.8.

> The selected cells from the first worksheet are copied from the Office Clipboard to the second worksheet. When pasting a range of cells, you need only select the cell in the upper left corner of the *paste area*—the target destination for data that has been cut or copied using the Office Clipboard.

Figure 10.8

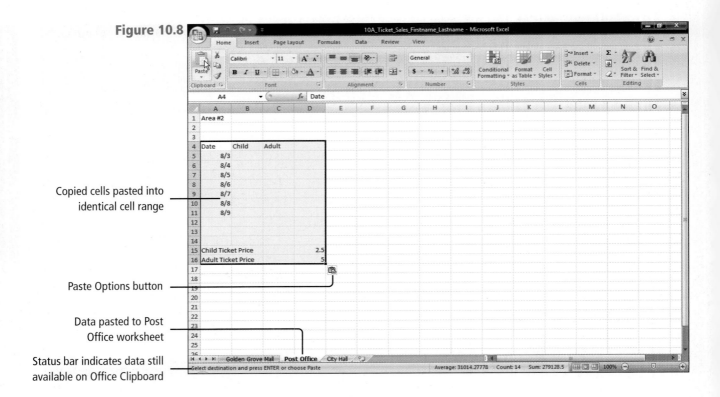

Copied cells pasted into identical cell range

Paste Options button

Data pasted to Post Office worksheet

Status bar indicates data still available on Office Clipboard

---

Note — Pressing Enter to Complete a Paste Action

Pressing ⌷Enter⌷ pastes the text and removes it from the Office Clipboard. Thus, if you want to paste the same text more than one time, click the Paste button so that the copied text remains available on the Office Clipboard.

---

5 In the lower right corner of the paste area, click the **Paste Options** button.

The ***Paste Options button***, which displays just below your pasted selection after you perform the paste operation, displays a list of options that lets you determine how the information is pasted into your worksheet. The list varies depending on the type of content you are pasting and the program you are pasting from.

6 Click any cell to close the list and deselect the paste area. In the status bar, notice that the message still displays, indicating that your selected range remains on the Office Clipboard. Click the **City Hall sheet tab** to make it the active sheet, and then click cell **A4**. In the **Clipboard group**, click the **Paste** button.

7 On the **Home tab**, in the **Clipboard group**, click the **Clipboard Dialog Box Launcher** button ▣, and then compare your screen with Figure 10.9.

The Clipboard task pane displays, and you can view your selection on the Clipboard. Here you can clear your selection from the Clipboard, although it is not necessary to do so.

Figure 10.9

Excel | Chapter 10

Clipboard Dialog Box Launcher button

Clipboard task pane

Your copied range displays

Close button

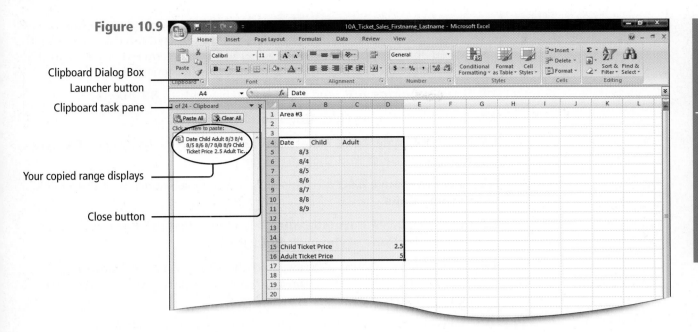

8 In the upper right corner of the **Office Clipboard task pane**, click the **Close** button ☒. Display the **Golden Grove Mall** sheet. Press Esc to cancel the moving border.

> The status bar no longer displays the message.

9 **Save** 🖫 your changes.

Objective 5
Edit and Format Multiple Worksheets at the Same Time

You can enter or edit data on several worksheets at the same time by selecting and grouping multiple worksheets. Data that you enter or edit on the active sheet is reflected in all selected sheets. If you apply color to the sheet tabs, the name of the sheet tab will be underlined in the color you selected. If the sheet tab displays with a background color, the sheet has not been selected.

Activity 10.06 Wrapping Text in a Cell in Several Worksheets at the Same Time

If you want text to appear on multiple lines within a single cell, you can format the cell so that the text wraps automatically, or you can enter a manual line break. In this activity, you will group the worksheets for the three ticket sales locations, and then format additional column titles with wrapped text on all the worksheets at the same time.

1 With the **Golden Grove Mall** worksheet as the active sheet, press Ctrl + Home to make cell **A1** the active cell. Point to the sheet tab, right-click, and then from the displayed menu, click **Select All Sheets**. At the top of your screen, look at the title bar and notice that *[Group]* displays.

All the worksheets are selected, as indicated by *[Group]* in the title bar and the sheet tab names underlined in the selected tab color. Data that you enter or edit on the active sheet will also be entered or edited in the same manner on all the selected sheets in the same cells.

2 Select **columns A:F**, and then set their width to **83 pixels**.

3 Click cell **D4**, type **Child Ticket Total** and then press Tab.

4 In cell **E4**, type **Adult Ticket Total** and then press Tab. In cell **F4**, type **Total Ticket Sales** and then press Enter.

5 Select the range **A4:F4**, right-click over the selection, and then click **Format Cells**.

6 In the displayed **Format Cells** dialog box, click the **Font tab**, and then under **Font style**, click **Bold Italic**.

7 Under **Color**, click the arrow, and then under **Theme Colors**, click **Orange, Accent 6, Darker 25%**. Compare your screen with Figure 10.10.

> Recall that commonly used font formats are also available from the Font group on the Ribbon. However, when applying multiple formats to selected cells, it is efficient to do so from the Format Cells dialog box.

Figure 10.10

[Group] in title bar

Format Cells dialog box, Font tab displayed

Selected range

Bold Italic selected

Font color Orange, Accent 6, Darker 25%

Preview area

Sheet tabs underlined in color

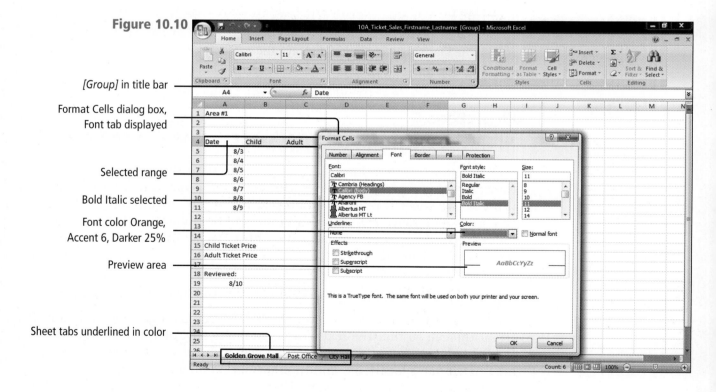

8 In the **Format Cells** dialog box, click the **Alignment tab**.

> Here you can change the alignment of text in the selected range.

9 Under **Text alignment**, click the **Horizontal arrow**, and then from the displayed list, click **Center**.

10 Click the **Vertical arrow**, and then from the displayed list, click **Center**. Under **Text control**, click to select—place a check mark in—the **Wrap text** check box.

> Data in the cell will wrap to fit the column width; a change in column width will automatically adjust the wrapping of the text.

Another Way

To Wrap Text or Start a New Line in a Cell

To wrap text in a cell or range of cells, select the specific cells, and then in the Alignment group, click the Wrap Text button.

To start a new line of text at a specific point in a cell, regardless of column width, double-click the cell, click the location where you want to break the line in the cell, and then press [Alt] + [Enter] to insert a line break.

11 At the bottom of the dialog box, click **OK**, and then compare your screen with Figure 10.11.

> All the formats that you selected in the Format Cells dialog box are applied to the selected range of cells. Those formats that have buttons on the Ribbon are shown as being selected.

Figure 10.11

Center and Middle Align buttons selected

Bold and Italic buttons selected

Dialog Box Launcher button

Wrap Text button selected

All formats selected in Format Cells dialog box applied to range

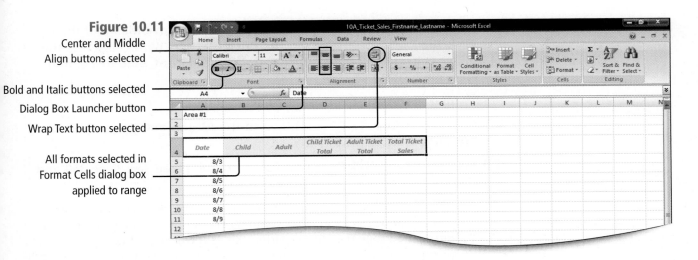

12 In the **Font group**, click the **Dialog Box Launcher** button.

> The Font tab of the Format Cells dialog box displays. The most commonly used settings from this tab are displayed as buttons on the Ribbon.

13 Click **Cancel** to close the dialog box. On the Ribbon, in the **Alignment group**, click the **Dialog Box Launcher** button.

> The Alignment tab of the Format Cells dialog box displays. The most commonly used settings from the Alignment tab display as buttons in the Alignment group on the Ribbon. In this manner, Excel makes frequently used commands quickly available to you on the Ribbon. To perform multiple commands, use either the Ribbon buttons or the Format Cells dialog box. To use commands that are not commonly used and thus not displayed on the Ribbon, use the Format Cells dialog box.

14 Click **Cancel** to close the dialog box. Display the **Post Office** worksheet.

> As soon as you select a single sheet, the grouping of the sheets is canceled and *[Group]* no longer displays in the title bar. Because the sheets were grouped, the same new text and formatting was applied to all of the selected sheets. In this manner, you can make the same changes to all the sheets in a workbook at one time.

15 Display the **City Hall** worksheet, and then verify that the changes have also been made to this worksheet. **Save** 🔲 your workbook.

Activity 10.07 Entering Data and Constructing Formulas on Multiple Worksheets

Recall that formulas are equations that perform calculations on values in your worksheet, and that a formula starts with an equal sign (=). Operators are the symbols with which you specify the type of calculation that you want to perform on the elements of a formula. In this activity, you will enter the number of Child and Adult tickets purchased at each of the three locations during the week of August 3, and then calculate the total sales.

1 Display the **Golden Grove Mall** worksheet as the active sheet. Verify that the sheets are not grouped—*[Group]* does *not* display in the title bar.

2 Click cell **A1**, type **Ticket Sale Area #1 Golden Grove Mall** and then click the **Enter** button ✔ on the **Formula Bar**. With cell **A1** as the active cell, change the **Font** to **Cambria**, the **Font Size** to **14**, and then apply **Bold** **B**.

> Your new typing replaces the contents of the cell.

3 Select the range **A1:F1**, and then in the **Alignment group**, click the **Merge & Center** button.

4 Select the range **B5:C11**, type **255** and then press Enter. Type **350** and then press Enter.

> Although it is not required that you do so, recall that selecting a range in this manner lets you enter columns of data by pressing Enter after each entry, and keeps the entries within the defined range of cells. After you type in the last selected cell in column B, which is B11, pressing Enter will make cell C5 the active cell.

5 Type the remaining number of tickets sold as shown in the following table, pressing Enter after each entry, and then compare your screen with Figure 10.12.

	Child	Adult
8/3	255	350
8/4	350	415
8/5	295	392
8/6	115	294
8/7	214	381
8/8	304	412
8/9	295	420

Figure 10.12

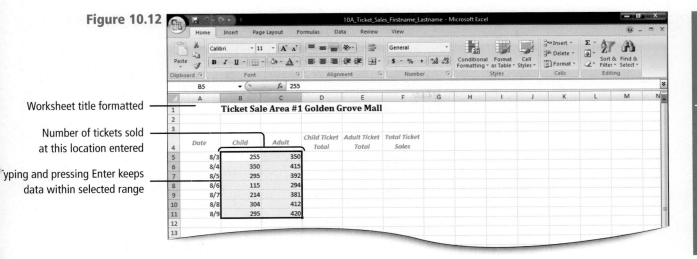

Worksheet title formatted

Number of tickets sold at this location entered

Typing and pressing Enter keeps data within selected range

6 Click cell **A1**, and then in the **Clipboard group**, click the **Format Painter** button. Click the **Post Office sheet tab**, and then click cell **A1** in the active sheet to apply the formatting.

7 In cell **A1**, replace *Area #2* by typing **Ticket Sale Area #2 Post Office** and then pressing Enter.

8 Select the range **B5:C11**, enter the number of tickets purchased at this location as shown in the following table, and then compare your screen with Figure 10.13.

	Child	Adult
8/3	155	252
8/4	210	314
8/5	195	296
8/6	95	198
8/7	87	283
8/8	195	320
8/9	55	36

Figure 10.13

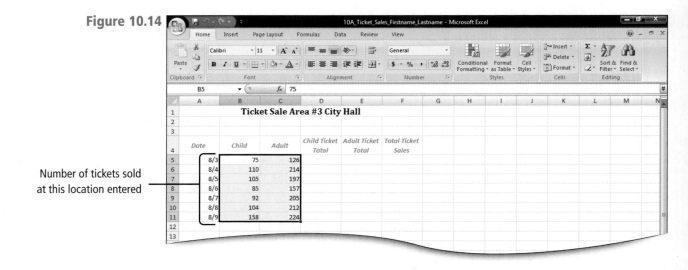

Number of tickets sold at this location entered

| | 10A_Ticket_Sales_Firstname_Lastname - Microsoft Excel |

Ticket Sale Area #2 Post Office

Date	Child	Adult	Child Ticket Total	Adult Ticket Total	Total Ticket Sales
8/3	155	252			
8/4	210	314			
8/5	195	296			
8/6	95	198			
8/7	87	283			
8/8	195	320			
8/9	55	36			

9 Click cell **A1**, right-click, on the displayed Mini toolbar, click the **Format Painter** button, display the **City Hall** worksheet, and then click cell **A1** to copy the format.

10 In cell **A1**, replace *Area #3* by typing **Ticket Sale Area #3 City Hall** and then pressing Enter. Enter the number of tickets sold at this location by selecting the appropriate data range, and then entering the information in the following table. Compare your screen with Figure 10.14.

	Child	Adult
8/3	75	126
8/4	110	214
8/5	105	197
8/6	85	157
8/7	92	205
8/8	104	212
8/9	158	224

Figure 10.14

Ticket Sale Area #3 City Hall

Date	Child	Adult	Child Ticket Total	Adult Ticket Total	Total Ticket Sales
8/3	75	126			
8/4	110	214			
8/5	105	197			
8/6	85	157			
8/7	92	205			
8/8	104	212			
8/9	158	224			

Number of tickets sold at this location entered

11 **Save** 🖫 your changes. Right-click the **Golden Grove Mall sheet tab**, and then from the shortcut menu, click **Select All Sheets**.

The first worksheet becomes the active sheet, and the worksheets are grouped. *[Group]* displays in the title bar, and the sheet tabs are underlined in the tab color to indicate they are selected as part of the group.

Recall that when grouped, any editing or data entry that you perform on the active worksheet is *also* performed on the other selected worksheets.

12 Click cell **D5** and type **=** to begin a formula. Click cell **B5**, type ***** click cell **D15**, and then compare your screen with Figure 10.15.

Recall that the symbols + and – and * and / are used in formulas to perform addition, subtraction, multiplication, and division. This formula will calculate the total amount from the sale of Child tickets on August 3 at the Golden Grove Mall location.

Recall that in the General number format, trailing zeroes do not display.

Figure 10.15

Formula to multiply 255 Child tickets times price of 2.50

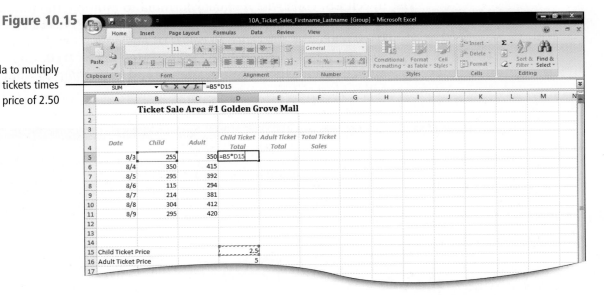

13 Press F4 to make the reference to **Child Ticket Price** in cell **D15** absolute.

Recall that when you copy formulas down to other cells in a column, the cell references change relative to the row number. For the reference to each date in column A, that is the desired result. For the cell reference to the ticket price in cell D15, the cell reference should remain the same for each date.

14 On the **Formula Bar**, click the **Enter** button ✓ to display the formula result of *637.5* and then use the fill handle to copy the formula down for the remaining dates. Compare your screen with Figure 10.16.

Figure 10.16

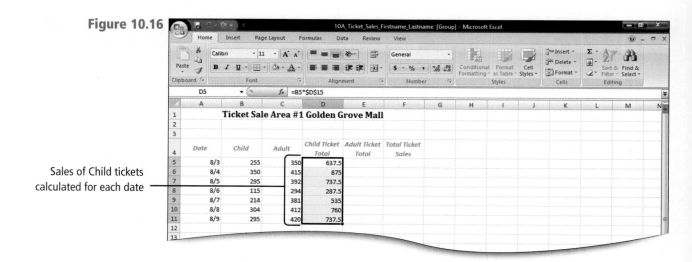

Sales of Child tickets
calculated for each date

---

15 In cell **E5**, construct a similar formula to multiply the number of **Adult** tickets sold on August 3 times the **Adult Ticket Price** in cell **D16**. Make the reference to cell **D16** absolute so that each day's sales are multiplied by the **Adult Ticket Price** in cell **D16**. Copy the formula down for the remaining dates, and then compare your screen with Figure 10.17.

Figure 10.17

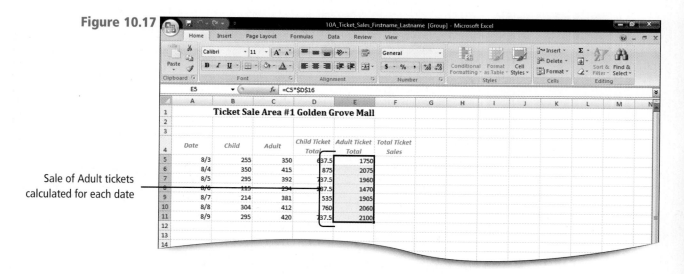

Sale of Adult tickets
calculated for each date

---

16 Click cell **F5**, and then in the **Editing group**, click the **Sum** button Σ . Notice that Excel selects all the numeric values—but not the date values—in the row.

17 To Sum only the values in **D5** and **E5**—the **Child Total** and the **Adult Total**—with your mouse, select the range **D5:E5**, and then compare your screen with Figure 10.18.

> Recall that the Sum function first looks above the selected cell for a range of numbers to sum. If no values display above the selected cell, Excel looks to the left for a range of numbers to sum. You can change the range to which you want to apply the Sum function by simply selecting the desired range.

Figure 10.18

New range selected
for the SUM function

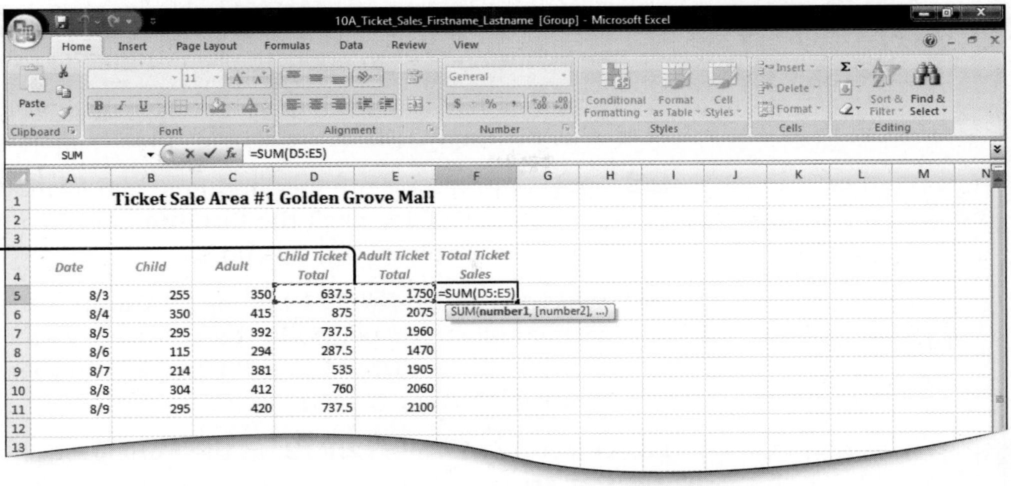

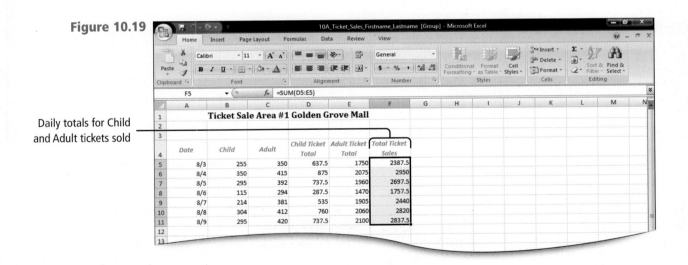

18 On the **Formula Bar**, click the **Enter** button ✔, and then copy the formula down for the remaining dates. Compare your screen with Figure 10.19.

Because your worksheets are grouped, the calculations on the first worksheet are also being performed on the other two worksheets.

Figure 10.19

Daily totals for Child
and Adult tickets sold

19 Click cell **F12**, and then in the **Editing group**, click the **Sum** button Σ ▾. Be sure the range **F5:F11** is selected, and then press Enter.

Excel looks above the selected cell and proposes a range to sum. Your result is *17890*.

20 In cell **A12**, type **Totals** and then on the **Formula Bar**, click the **Enter** button ✔ to confirm the entry and keep **A12** as the active cell. Then apply the **Align Text Right** ≣ format and **Bold** B to the cell.

21 Select the range **B5:E12**, and then in the **Editing group**, click the **Sum** button Σ to apply the Sum function to the range.

Recall that selecting a range in this manner will place the Sum function in the empty cells at the bottom of each column.

22 Apply appropriate number and financial formatting as follows: Select the range **B5:C12**, click the **Comma Style** button, and then click **Decrease Decimal** two times.

23 Select the range **D6:F11** and apply **Comma Style**—leave the two decimal places displayed in these currency amounts. Select the non-adjacent ranges **D5:F5** and **D12:F12**, and then click the **Accounting Number Format** button $\$$.

24 Select the range **B12:F12**, in the **Font group**, click the **Borders button arrow**, and then click **Top and Double Bottom Border** to apply the common format for financial numbers. Click any blank cell to deselect, and then compare your screen with Figure 10.20.

Figure 10.20

Accounting Number Format applied

Comma Style applied

Borders applied and columns totaled

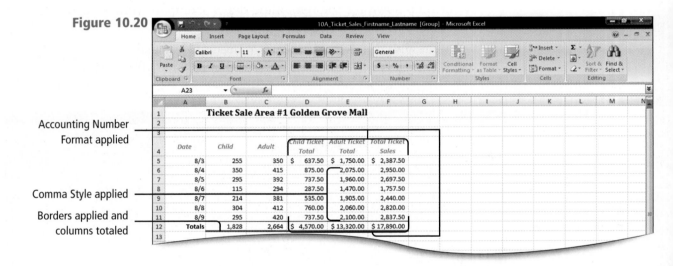

Note — Apply Comma Style First

When combining both the Comma Style and the Accounting Number Format to different ranges within a contiguous group of cells, apply Comma Style first.

25 Select the range **D15:D16**, right-click over the selection, and then on the Mini toolbar, click the **Accounting Number Format** $\$$ button.

26 Display the **Post Office** worksheet to examine the totals, and then compare your screen with Figure 10.21.

Because your worksheets were grouped while making the calculations, all the calculations and formatting on the first worksheet were also being performed on the other two worksheets.

As soon as you select an individual sheet, as you have done here, the grouping is canceled. *[Group]* no longer displays in the title bar.

Figure 10.21

[Group] no longer displays
(sheets are ungrouped)

Ticket Sale Area #2 Post Office

Date	Child	Adult	Child Ticket Total	Adult Ticket Total	Total Ticket Sales
8/3	155	252	$ 387.50	$ 1,260.00	$ 1,647.50
8/4	210	314	525.00	1,570.00	2,095.00
8/5	195	296	487.50	1,480.00	1,967.50
8/6	95	198	237.50	990.00	1,227.50
8/7	87	283	217.50	1,415.00	1,632.50
8/8	195	320	487.50	1,600.00	2,087.50
8/9	55	36	137.50	180.00	317.50
Totals	992	1,699	$ 2,480.00	$ 8,495.00	$ 10,975.00

Totals calculated
for Area #2

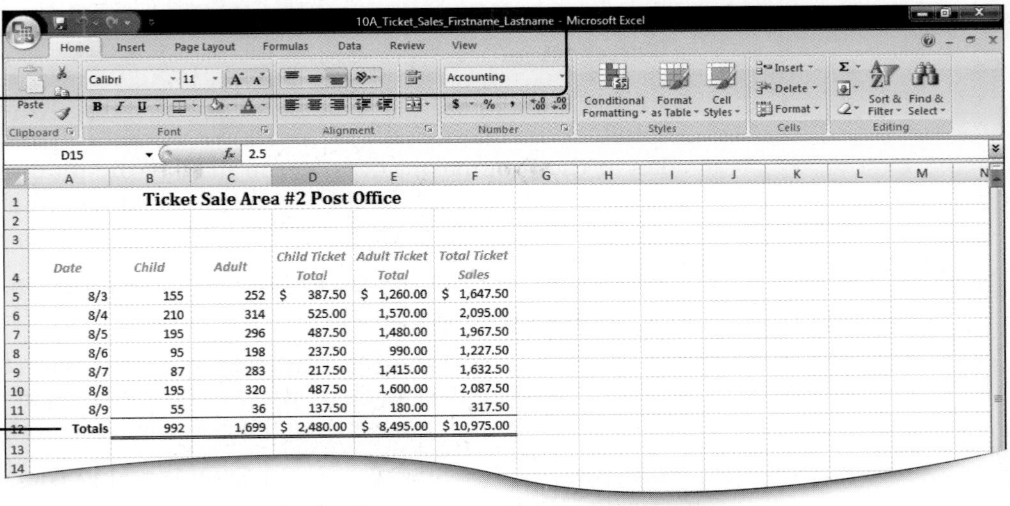

27 Display the **City Hall** worksheet to examine the totals, and then compare your screen with Figure 10.22.

You can see that by grouping sheets and copying formulas, it is easy to make multiple calculations in Excel without typing formulas multiple times.

Figure 10.22

Ticket Sale Area #3 City Hall

Date	Child	Adult	Child Ticket Total	Adult Ticket Total	Total Ticket Sales
8/3	75	126	$ 187.50	$ 630.00	$ 817.50
8/4	110	214	275.00	1,070.00	1,345.00
8/5	105	197	262.50	985.00	1,247.50
8/6	85	157	212.50	785.00	997.50
8/7	92	205	230.00	1,025.00	1,255.00
8/8	104	212	260.00	1,060.00	1,320.00
8/9	158	224	395.00	1,120.00	1,515.00
Totals	729	1,335	$ 1,822.50	$ 6,675.00	$ 8,497.50

Totals calculated
for Area #3

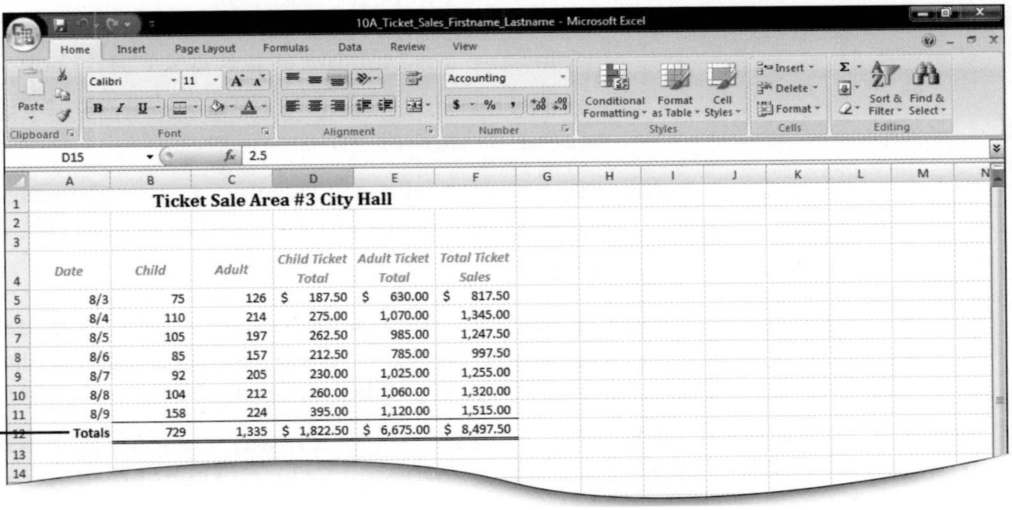

28 **Save** your workbook.

Objective 6
Create a Summary Sheet

A summary sheet is a worksheet where totals from other worksheets are displayed and summarized.

Activity 10.08 Constructing Formulas that Refer to Cells in Another Worksheet

In this activity, you will insert a new worksheet in which you will place the totals from each ticket sale location's worksheet. You will construct formulas in the Summary worksheet to display the total revenue for each of the two types of tickets—Child and Adult—that will update the Summary worksheet whenever changes are made to the other worksheet totals.

1 To the right of the **City Hall** worksheet tab, click the **Insert Worksheet** button 🗐.

> A new worksheet displays with the name *Sheet1* or *Sheet2* or some other number, depending on whether the other worksheets have been renamed and how many times a new worksheet has been inserted.

2 Rename the new worksheet **Summary** and then change the **Tab Color** to **Olive Green, Accent 3, Lighter 40%**.

3 In cell **A4**, type **Golden Grove Mall** In cell **A5**, type **Post Office** and then in cell **A6**, type **City Hall**

4 Select the range **A4:A6**, right-click, and then on the Mini toolbar, change the **Font Size** to **12** and apply **Bold** B . In the **column heading area**, point to the right border of **column A** to display the ⊞ pointer, and then double-click to AutoFit the column.

5 In cell **B3**, type **Total Sales Child** and then in cell **C3**, type **Total Sales Adult**

6 Select the range **B3:C3**, and then right-click over the selection to display the Mini toolbar. Click **Bold** B , click **Italic** I , change the **Font** to **Cambria**, and then change the **Font Color** A ▾ to **Orange, Accent 6, Darker 25%**.

7 With the two cells still selected, in the **Alignment group**, click the **Wrap Text** button 🗐, the **Center** button ≡, and then click the **Middle Align** ≡ button.

8 Click cell **B4**. Type = and then click the **Golden Grove Mall sheet tab**. On the **Golden Grove Mall** worksheet, click cell **D12**, and then press Enter to redisplay the **Summary** worksheet.

9 Click cell **B4** to select it again. Look at the **Formula Bar** and notice that instead of a value, the cell contains a formula that is equal to the value in another cell in another worksheet. Compare your screen with Figure 10.23.

> The value in this cell is equal to the value in cell D12 of the *Golden Grove Mall* worksheet. The Accounting Number Format applied to the referenced cell is carried over. By using a formula of this type, changes in cell D12 on the *Golden Grove Mall* worksheet will be automatically updated in this *Summary* worksheet.

Figure 10.23

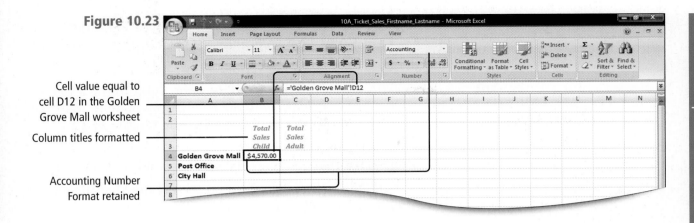

Cell value equal to cell D12 in the Golden Grove Mall worksheet

Column titles formatted

Accounting Number Format retained

10 Click cell **C4**. Type **=** and then click the **Golden Grove Mall sheet tab**. Click cell **E12**, and then press Enter.

11 Use the technique you just practiced to copy the week's total for **Child** and **Adult** ticket sales for the **Post Office worksheet** and the **City Hall worksheet**. Compare your screen with Figure 10.24.

> The formulas in cells B4:C6 display the totals from the other three worksheets. Changes made to any of the other three worksheets—sometimes referred to as *detail worksheets* because the details of the information are contained there—that affect their totals will display on this Summary worksheet. In this manner, the summary worksheet accurately displays the current totals from the other worksheets.

Figure 10.24

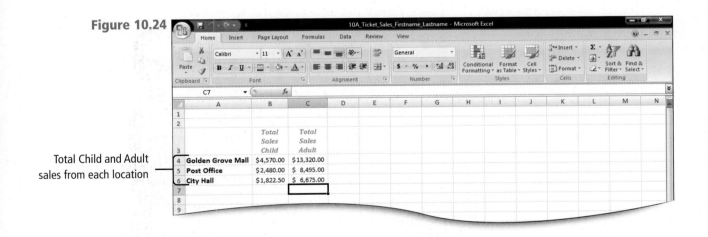

Total Child and Adult sales from each location

12 In cell **A1**, type **Summer Fair and Arts Festival** and then **Merge & Center** the text over the range **A1:C1**. In cell **A2**, type **Pre-Sales of Tickets August 3-9** and then **Merge & Center** the text over the range **A2:C2**.

13 Select the two worksheet titles and change the **Font** to **Cambria**, change the **Font Color** A ▾ to **Orange, Accent 6, Darker 25%**, change the **Font Size** to **14**, and apply **Bold** B .

14 Select **rows 1:2**. From the **row heading area**, point to the lower boundary of either selected row to display the ✛ pointer, increase the row height to **35 pixels**, and then click the **Middle Align** button ≡ .

15 Select **columns B:C**, and then set the column width to **80 pixels**.

16 In cell **A7**, type **Total Sales** press Enter, and then notice that the formatting from the cell above is carried down to the new cell.

17 Select the range **B4:C7**, and then use the **Sum** button Σ ▾ to total the two columns. Compare your screen with Figure 10.25.

> Recall that cell formatting carries over to adjacent cells unless two cells are left blank.

Figure 10.25

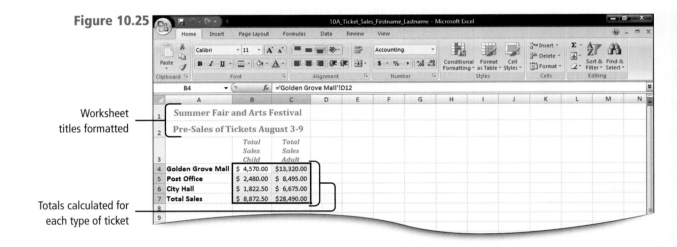

Worksheet titles formatted

Totals calculated for each type of ticket

18 In the **Total Sales Child column**, notice the total for the *Post Office* location is *$2,480.00* and the *Total Sales* is *$8,872.50*.

19 Display the **Post Office** worksheet, click cell **B11**, type **155** and then press Enter. Notice that the formulas in the worksheet recalculate.

20 Display the **Summary** worksheet, and notice that in the **Total Sales Child column**, both the total for the *Post Office* location and the *Total Sales* also recalculated. Compare your screen with Figure 10.26.

> In this manner, a Summary sheet recalculates any changes made in the other worksheets.

Figure 10.26

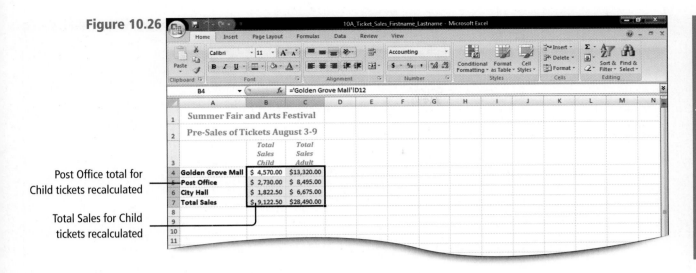

Post Office total for Child tickets recalculated

Total Sales for Child tickets recalculated

	Total Sales Child	Total Sales Adult
Summer Fair and Arts Festival		
Pre-Sales of Tickets August 3-9		
Golden Grove Mall	$ 4,570.00	$13,320.00
Post Office	$ 2,730.00	$ 8,495.00
City Hall	$ 1,822.50	$ 6,675.00
Total Sales	$ 9,122.50	$28,490.00

Cell reference: B4 ='Golden Grove Mall'!D12

21 Select the range **B7:C7**, and then apply a **Top and Double Bottom** border.

22 **Save** your workbook.

Objective 7
Format and Print Multiple Worksheets in a Workbook

Each worksheet within a workbook can have different formatting, for example different headers or footers. If all the worksheets in the workbook will have the same header or footer, you can select all the worksheets and apply formatting common to all of the worksheets; for example, you can set the same footer in all of the worksheets.

Activity 10.09 Moving and Formatting Worksheets in a Workbook

In this activity, you will move the Summary sheet to become the first worksheet in the workbook. Then you will format and prepare your workbook for printing. The four worksheets containing data can be formatted simultaneously.

1 Point to the **Summary sheet tab**, hold down the left mouse button to display a small black triangle—a caret—and then notice that a small paper icon attaches to the mouse pointer.

2 Drag to the left until the caret and mouse pointer are to the left of the **Golden Grove Mall sheet tab**, as shown in Figure 10.27, and then release the left mouse button.

Use this technique to rearrange the order of worksheets within a workbook.

Figure 10.27

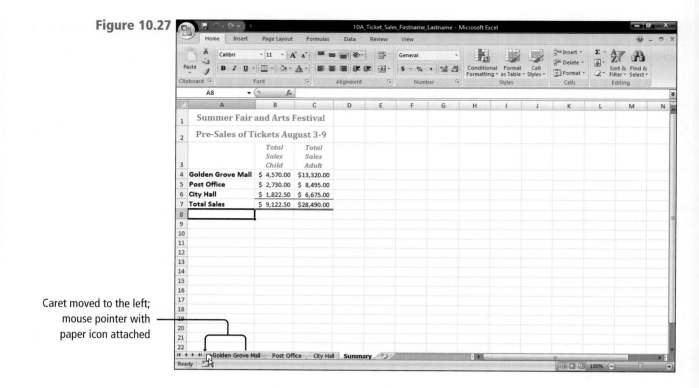

Caret moved to the left; mouse pointer with paper icon attached

3 Be sure the **Summary** worksheet is the active sheet. Then point to its sheet tab, right-click, and then click **Select All Sheets** to display *[Group]* in the title bar. On the Ribbon, click the **Insert tab**, and then in the **Text group**, click the **Header & Footer** button.

4 In the **Navigation group**, click the **Go to Footer** button, click in the **left section** above the word *Footer*, and then in the **Header & Footer Elements group**, click the **File Name** button.

5 Click in a cell above the footer to deselect the **Footer area** and view your file name. On the Ribbon, click the **Page Layout tab**. In the **Page Setup group**, click the **Margins** button, and then at the bottom of the **Margins gallery**, click **Custom Margins**.

6 In the displayed **Page Setup** dialog box, under **Center on page**, select the **Horizontally** check box. Click **OK**, and then on the status bar, click the **Normal** button ⊞ to return to Normal view.

> After displaying worksheets in Page Layout View, dotted lines display to indicate the page breaks when you return to Normal view.

7 Press Ctrl + Home to move to the top of the worksheet. Verify that *[Group]* still displays in the title bar.

> Recall that by selecting all sheets, you can apply the same formatting to all the worksheets at the same time.

8 **Save** 🖫 your changes. From the **Office** menu 🏛, point to the **Print** button, and then from the displayed menu, click **Print Preview**. Alternatively, press Ctrl + F2 to display the Print Preview. Compare your screen with Figure 10.28.

> With all the sheets grouped, you can view all of the sheets in Print Preview. If you do not see *Page 1 of 4* in the status bar, close the Preview, select all the sheets again, and then redisplay Print Preview.

Figure 10.28

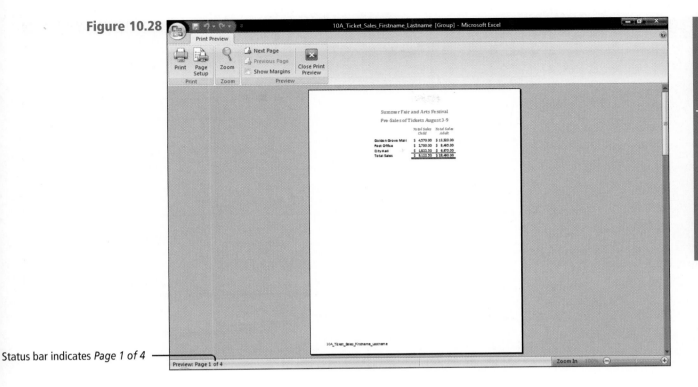

Status bar indicates *Page 1 of 4*

9 On the Ribbon, in the **Preview group**, click the **Next Page** button as necessary and take a moment to view each page of your workbook. After viewing all the worksheets, click the **Close Print Preview** button.

Activity 10.10 Printing All the Worksheets in a Workbook

1 **Save** 🔲 your workbook before printing. Check your *Chapter Assignment Sheet* or *Course Syllabus*, or consult your instructor, to determine if you are to submit your assignments on paper or electronically. To submit electronically, follow the instructions provided by your instructor.

2 Verify that the worksheets in your workbook are still grouped—*[Group]* displays in the title bar. From the **Office** menu 🔘, click the **Print** button. In the displayed **Print** dialog box, under **Print range**, verify that the **All** option button is selected.

3 Under **Print what**, verify that **Active sheet(s)** is selected. Alternatively, if your worksheets are not grouped, you can click *Entire workbook* in this dialog box to print all the worksheets in the workbook. Under **Copies**, verify that the **Number of copies** is **1**. Compare your screen with Figure 10.29.

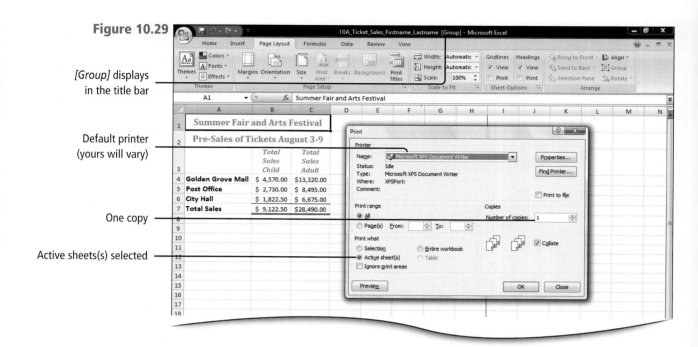

Figure 10.29

[Group] displays in the title bar

Default printer (yours will vary)

One copy

Active sheets(s) selected

4 Click **OK** to print your worksheets. Determine if you are to print formulas for any or all of the worksheets in this workbook. To print formulas, refer to Activity 9.17 in Project 9A.

5 If you printed your formulas, be sure to redisplay the worksheet by pressing Ctrl + `. From the **Office** menu, click **Close**. If you are prompted to save changes, click **No** so that you do not save the changes to the Print layout that you used for printing formulas. **Exit** Excel.

End **You have completed Project 10A** ——————

Project 10B **Growth Projection**

In Activities 10.11 through 10.15, you will assist Mervyn Aghazarian, the City Planner for Golden Grove, in creating a workbook to estimate future population growth based on three different growth rates. Your resulting worksheet and chart will look similar to Figure 10.30.

For Project 10B, you will need the following file:

New blank Excel workbook

You will save your workbook as
10B_Growth_Projection_Firstname_Lastname

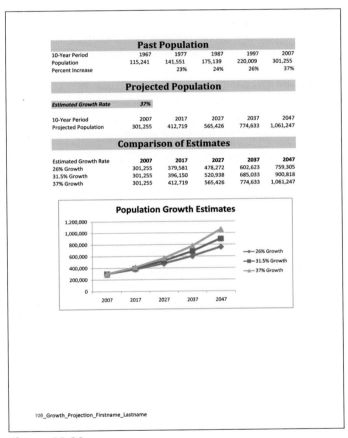

Figure 10.30
Project 10B—Growth Projection

Objective 8
Design a Worksheet for What-If Analysis

Excel recalculates; if you change the value in a cell referenced in a formula, the result of the formula is automatically recalculated. Thus, you can change cell values to see *what* would happen *if* you tried different values. This process of changing the values in cells to see how those changes affect the outcome of formulas in your worksheet is called ***what-if analysis***.

Activity 10.11 Using Parentheses in a Formula

Mr. Aghazarian has the city's population figures for the past five 10-year periods. In each 10-year period, the population has increased. In this activity, you will construct a formula to calculate the ***percentage rate of increase***—the percent by which one number increases over another number—for each 10-year period over the past years. From this information, future population growth can be estimated.

1 **Start** Excel and display a new workbook. From the **Office** menu 🟠, click **Save As**. Navigate to your **Excel Chapter 10** folder, in the **File name** box, name the file **10B_Growth_Projection_Firstname_Lastname** and then click **Save** or press Enter.

2 In cell **A3**, type **Population** and press Enter. In cell **A4**, type **Percent Increase** and press Enter.

3 Point to the right boundary of **column A** to display the ✛ pointer, and then double-click to AutoFit the column to accommodate its longest entry. Alternatively, on the Home tab, in the Cells group, click the Format button, and then click AutoFit Column Width.

4 In cell **A2**, type **10-Year Period** and then press Tab. In cell **B2**, type **1967** and then press Tab.

5 In cell **C2**, type **1977** and then press Tab. Select the range **B2:C2**, drag the fill handle to the right through cell **F2**, and then compare your screen with Figure 10.31.

> By establishing a pattern of 10-year intervals with the first two cells, you can use the fill handle to continue the series. The Auto Fill feature will do this for any pattern that you establish with two or more cells.

Figure 10.31

Pattern used to fill 10-year periods to create column titles

Row titles entered

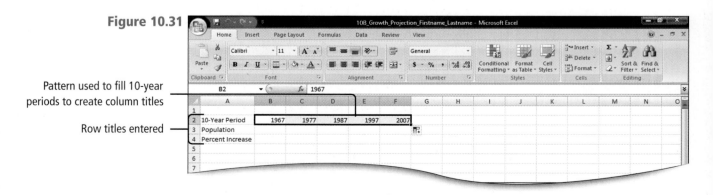

6 Click cell **A1**. Type **Past Population** and press Enter. Select the range **A1:F1**, and then right-click to display the Mini toolbar. Click the **Merge & Center** button ⊞▾, apply **Bold** **B**, change the **Font** to **Cambria**, and then change the **Font Size** to **18**.

7 Beginning in cell **B3**, and then pressing Tab to move across the row, enter the following values for the population in the years listed:

1967	1977	1987	1997	2007
115241	141551	175139	220009	301255

8 Select the range **B3:F3**, right-click, on the Mini toolbar, click **Comma Style** ▾, and then **Decrease Decimal** two times.

9 Click cell **C4**. Being sure to include the parentheses, type **=(c3-b3)/b3** and then press Enter. Click cell **C4**. In the **Number group**, click the **Percent Style** button %, and then examine the formula in the **Formula Bar**.

> The mathematical formula to calculate the percentage rate of population increase from 1967 to 1977 is *rate = amount of increase/base*.
>
> First, determine the *amount of increase* by subtracting the **base**—the starting point represented by the 1967 population—from the 1977 population. Thus, the *amount of increase* = 141,551 − 115,241 or 26,310. Between 1967 and 1977, the population increased by 26,310 people. In the formula, this calculation is represented by *c3-b3*.
>
> Second, calculate the *rate*—what the amount of increase (26,310) represents as a percentage of the base (1967's population of 115,241). Determine this by dividing the amount of increase (26,310) by the base (115,241). Thus, 26,310 divided by 115,241 is equal to 0.22830416 or, when rounded to a percent—23%.

10 In the **Formula Bar**, locate the parentheses enclosing *C3-B3*.

> Excel follows a set of mathematical rules called the **order of operations**, which has four basic parts:
>
> - Expressions within parentheses are processed first.
> - Exponentiation, if present, is performed before multiplication and division.
> - Multiplication and division are performed before addition and subtraction.
> - Consecutive operators with the same level of precedence are calculated from left to right.

11 Click cell **D4**, type **=** and then by typing or using a combination of typing and clicking cells to reference them, construct a formula similar to the one in cell **C4** to calculate the rate of increase in population from 1977 to 1987. Compare your screen with Figure 10.32.

> Recall that the first step is to determine the *amount of increase*—1987 population minus 1977 population—and then to write the calculation so that Excel performs this operation first; that is, place it in parentheses.
>
> The second step is to divide the result of the calculation in parentheses by the *base*—the population for 1977.

Figure 10.32

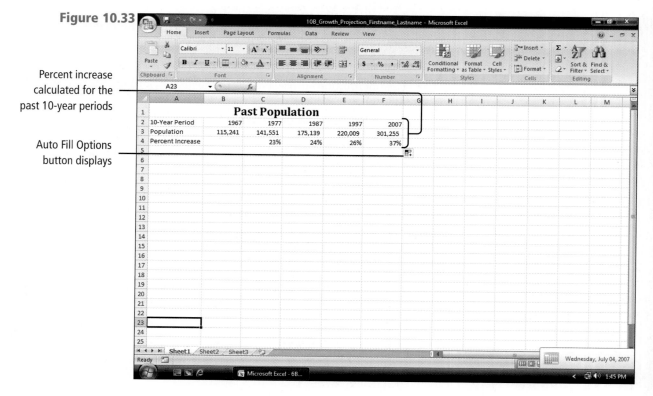

Formula to calculate percent increase from 1977 to 1987

	A	B	C	D	E	F	G	H	I	J	K	L	M
1			Past Population										
2	10-Year Period	1967	1977	1987	1997	2007							
3	Population	115,241	141,551	175,139	220,009	301,255							
4	Percent Increase		23%	=(d3-c3)/c3									
5													
6													
7													
8													

12 Press Enter, and then format cell **D4** with the **Percent Style** %. Your result is *24%*.

13 With cell **D4** selected, drag the fill handle to the right through cell **F4**. Click any empty cell to cancel the selection, **Save** 💾 your workbook, and then compare your screen with Figure 10.33.

Because this formula uses relative cell references—that is, for each year, the formula is the same but the values used are relative to the formula's location—you can copy the formula in this manner. For example, the result for 1987 uses 1977 as the base, the result for 1997 uses 1987 as the base, and the result for 2007 uses 1997 as the base.

The formula results show the percent of increase for each 10-year period between 1967 and 2007. You can see that in each 10-year period, the population has grown as much as 37%—between 1997 and 2007—and as little as 23%—between 1967 and 1977.

Figure 10.33

Percent increase calculated for the past 10-year periods

Auto Fill Options button displays

	A	B	C	D	E	F	G
1			Past Population				
2	10-Year Period	1967	1977	1987	1997	2007	
3	Population	115,241	141,551	175,139	220,009	301,255	
4	Percent Increase		23%	24%	26%	37%	
5							

Use of Parentheses in a Formula

When writing a formula in Excel, use parentheses to communicate the order in which the operations should occur. For example, to average three test scores of 100, 50, and 90 that you scored on three different tests in a class, you would add the test scores and then divide by the number of test scores in the list. If you write this formula as =100+50+90/3, the result would be 180, because Excel would first divide 90 by 3 and then add 100+50+30. Excel would do so because the order of operations states that multiplication and division are calculated *before* addition and subtraction.

The correct way to write this formula is =(100+50+90)/3. Excel will add the three values, and then divide the result by 3, or 240/3 resulting in a correct average of 80. Parentheses play an important role in assuring that you get the correct result in your formulas.

Activity 10.12 Formatting as You Type

You can format numbers as you type them. When you type numbers in a format that Excel recognizes, Excel automatically applies that format to the cell. Recall that once applied, cell formats remain with the cell, even if the cell contents are deleted. In this activity, you will format cells by typing the numbers with percent signs and use Format Painter to copy text (non-numeric) formats.

1 In cell **A6**, type **Projected Population** and then press Enter. Click cell **A1**. On the **Home tab**, in the **Clipboard group**, click the **Format Painter** button, and then click cell **A6**.

> The format of cell A1 is *painted* or applied to cell A6, including the merging and centering of the text across cells A6:F6.

2 In cell **A8**, type **Estimated Growth Rate** and then press Enter. AutoFit **column A** to accommodate the new longer entry.

3 In cell **A10**, type **10-Year Period** and then in cell **A11**, type **Projected Population**

4 In cell **B10**, type **2007** and then press Tab. In cell **C10**, type **2017** and then press Tab.

5 Select the range **B10:C10**, and then drag the fill handle through cell **F10** to extend the pattern of years to *2047*. Compare your screen with Figure 10.34.

Figure 10.34

New title entered and formatted

Row and column titles entered

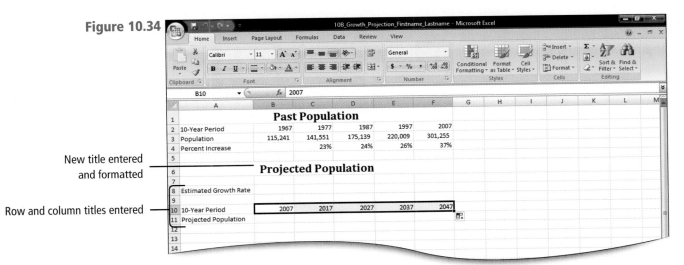

6 Click cell **B11**, and then in the **Number group**, notice that the format indicates *General*. Including the comma, type **301,255**

7 On the **Formula Bar**, click the **Enter** button ✓ to keep the cell active, and then in the **Number group**, notice that the format changed to *Number*. Then, press Delete, and in the **Number group**, notice that the *Number* format is still indicated.

> Recall that deleting the contents of a cell does not delete the cell's formatting.

8 *Without* typing a comma, in cell **B11**, type **301255** and then press Enter.

> The comma is inserted even though you did not type it. When you type a number and include a formatting symbol such as a comma, dollar sign, or percent sign, Excel applies the format to the cell. Thus, if you delete the contents of the cell and type in the cell again, the format you established remains applied to the cell. This is referred to as *format as you type*.

9 Examine the format of the value in cell **B11**, and then compare it to the format in cell **B3** where you used the Comma Style button to format the cell. Notice that the number in cell **B11** is flush with the right edge of the cell, but the number in cell **B3** leaves a small space on the right edge.

> When you type commas as you enter numbers, Excel applies the *Number* format, which does *not* leave a space at the right of the number for a closing parenthesis in the event of a negative number. This is different from the format that is applied when you use the *Comma Style* button on the Ribbon or Mini toolbar, as you did for the numbers entered in row 3. Recall that the Comma Style format applied from either the Ribbon or the Mini toolbar leaves space on the right for a closing parenthesis in the event of a negative number.

10 In cell **B8**, type **26%** and then on the **Formula Bar**, click **Enter** ✓. Then, press Delete and *without* typing a percent sign, type **26**, and then press Enter.

> The percent sign is inserted even though you did not type it—this is another example of the *format as you type* feature.

11 Select the range **A8:B8**, and then apply **Bold** B and **Italic** I.

12 **Save** 🖫 your workbook.

More Knowledge — Percentage Calculations

When you type a percentage into a cell—for example *26%*—the percentage format, without decimal points, displays in both the cell and the Formula Bar. Excel will, however, use the decimal value of *0.26* for actual calculations.

Activity 10.13 Calculating a Value After an Increase

A growing population results in increased use of city services. Thus, city planners in Golden Grove must estimate how much the population will increase in the future. The calculations you made in the previous activity show that the population has increased at varying rates during each

10-year period, ranging from a low of 23% to a high of 37% per 10-year period.

Population data from the state and surrounding areas suggests that future growth will trend closer to that of the recent past. To plan for the future, Mr. Aghazarian wants to prepare three forecasts of the city's population based on the percentage increases in 1997, in 2007, and for a percentage increase halfway between the two, that is, for 26%, 31.5%, and 37%. In this activity, you will calculate the population that would result from a 26% increase.

1 Click cell **C11**. Type **=b11*(100%+b8)** and then on the **Formula Bar**, click the **Enter** button ✓. Compare your screen with Figure 10.35.

This formula calculates what the population will be in the year 2017 assuming an increase of 26% over 2007's population. The mathematical formula to calculate a value after an increase is ***value after increase = base × percent for new value***.

First, establish the *percent for new value*. The **percent for new value = base percent + percent of increase**. The *base percent* of 100% represents the base population and the *percent of increase* in this instance is 26%. Thus, the population will equal 100% of the base year plus 26% of the base year. This can be expressed as 126% or 1.26. In this formula, you will use 100% + the rate in cell B8, which is 26%, to equal 126%.

Second, enter a reference to the cell that contains the *base*—the population in 2007. The base value resides in cell B11—301,255.

Third, calculate the *value after increase*. Because in each future 10-year period the increase will be based on 26%—an absolute value located in cell B8—this cell reference can be formatted as absolute with the use of dollar signs.

Figure 10.35

Absolute reference to cell B8 ⟶

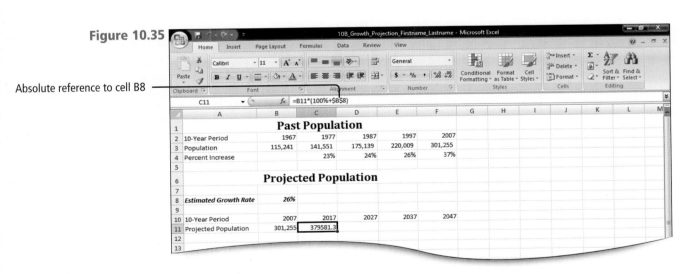

2 With cell **C11** as the active cell, drag the fill handle to copy the formula to the range **D11:F11**.

3 Click cell **B11**, click the **Format Painter** 🖌 button, and then select the range **C11:F11**. Click an empty cell to cancel the selection, and then compare your screen with Figure 10.36.

This formula uses a relative cell address—B11—for the *base*; the population in the previous 10-year period is used in each of the formulas in cells D11:F11 as the *base* value. Because the reference to the *percent of increase* in cell B8 is an absolute reference, each *value after increase* is calculated with the value from cell B8.

The population projected for 2017—*379,581*—is an increase of 26% over the population in 2007. The projected population in 2027—*478,272*—is an increase of 26% over the population in 2017 and so on.

Figure 10.36

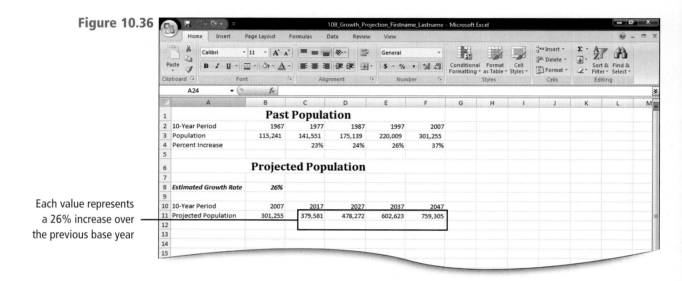

Each value represents a 26% increase over the previous base year

4 Save your workbook.

Workshop

Calculating Percent Increase or Decrease

The basic formula for calculating an increase or decrease can be done in two parts. First determine the percent by which the base value will be increased or decreased, and then add or subtract the results to the base. The formula can be simplified by using (1+amount of increase) or (1−amount of decrease), where 1 represents the whole, rather than 100%. Thus, the formula used in Step 1 of Activity 10.13 could also be written =b11*(1+b8), or =(b11*b8)+b11.

Objective 9
Perform What-If Analysis

If a formula depends on the value in a cell, you can see what effect it will have if you change the value in that cell. Then, you can copy the value computed by the formula and paste it into another part of the worksheet where it can be compared and charted. This can be done for multiple formulas.

Activity 10.14 Performing What-If Analysis and Using Paste Special

Mr. Aghazarian can see that a growth rate of 26% in each 10-year period will result in a population of almost 760,000 people by 2047. The city planners will likely ask him what the population might be if population grows at the highest rate (37%) or at a rate that is halfway between the 1997 and 2007 rates (31.5%).

Because the formulas are constructed to use the growth rate displayed in cell B8, Mr. Aghazarian can answer these questions quickly by entering different percentages into that cell. To keep the results of each set of calculations so they can be compared, you will paste the results of each what-if analysis into another area of the worksheet.

1 In cell **A13**, type **Comparison of Estimates** and then press [Enter]. Click cell **A6**, click **Format Painter** 🖌, and then click cell **A13**.

2 Select the range **A8:B8**, right-click to display the Mini toolbar, click the **Fill Color button arrow** 🎨▾, and then under **Theme Colors**, apply **Olive Green, Accent 3, Lighter 40%**.

3 Click cell **A1**, hold down [Ctrl], and then click cells **A6** and **A13**. In the **Font group**, click the **Fill Color** button 🎨▾ to apply the same fill color to these titles.

> Recall that the Fill Color button retains its most recent color.

4 In the range **A15:A18**, type the following row titles:

Estimated Growth Rate
26% Growth
31.5% Growth
37% Growth

5 Select the range **B10:F10**. On the **Home tab**, in the **Clipboard group**, click the **Copy** 📋 button, click cell **B15**, and then in the **Clipboard group**, click the **Paste** button.

> Recall that when pasting a group of copied cells to a target range, you need only select the first cell of the range.

6 Select the range **B11:F11**, click **Copy** 📋, click cell **B16**, and then click the **Paste** button. Click cell **C16**, and notice on the **Formula Bar** that the *formula* was pasted into the cell. Compare your screen with Figure 10.37.

> This is *not* the desired result. The actual *calculated values*—not the formulas—are needed in the range B16:F16.

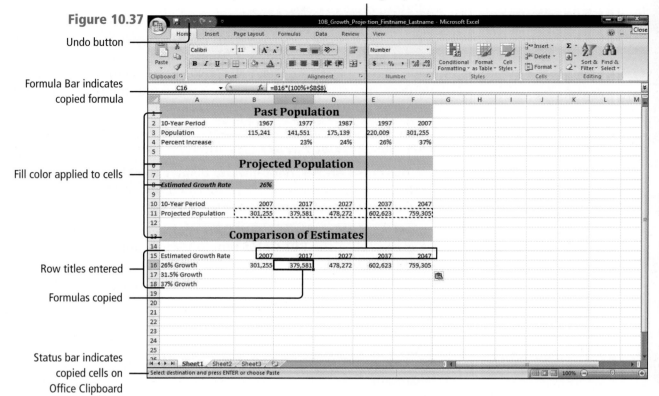

Figure 10.37

Undo button

Formula Bar indicates copied formula

Fill color applied to cells

Row titles entered

Formulas copied

Status bar indicates copied cells on Office Clipboard

Column headings copied

7 On the **Quick Access Toolbar**, click the **Undo** button. With the range **B11:F11** still copied to the Clipboard—as indicated by the message in the status bar and the moving border—in the **Clipboard group**, click the **Paste button arrow**. From the displayed menu, click **Paste Special**.

8 In the displayed **Paste Special** dialog box, under **Paste**, click the **Values and number formats** option button.

> The *Paste Special* dialog box offers various options for the manner in which you can paste the contents of the Office Clipboard. The *Values and number formats* command pastes the *calculated values* that result from the calculation of formulas into other cells—along with the formatting applied to the copied cells.

9 In the displayed **Paste Special** dialog box, click **OK**. Click cell **C16**. Notice on the **Formula Bar** that the cell contains a value, not a formula. Press Esc to cancel the moving border and then compare your screen with Figure 10.38.

> The calculated estimates based on a 26% growth rate are pasted along with their formatting.

Figure 10.38

Formula Bar indicates the value

Calculated value pasted

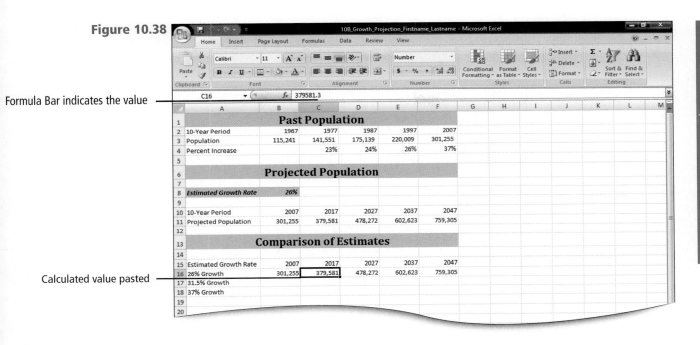

10 Click cell **B8**. Type **31.5** and then watch the values in **C11:F11** recalculate as, on the **Formula Bar**, you click the **Enter** button ✓.

> The value *31.5%* is halfway between 26% and 37%—the growth rates from the two most recent 10-year periods. Although the cell may display 32%, you can see that the underlying value is 31.5%.

11 Select the range **B11:F11**, and then press Ctrl + C, which is the keyboard shortcut for the Copy command. Click cell **B17**. In the **Clipboard group**, click the **Paste button arrow**, and then click **Paste Special**.

12 In the **Paste Special** dialog box, click the **Values and number formats** option button, and then click **OK**.

13 In cell **B8**, type **37** and then press Enter. Notice that the projected values in **C11:F11** are recalculated.

14 Using the skills you just practiced, copy the range **B11:F11**, and then paste the **values and number formats** of the copied range to the range **B18:F18**.

15 Press Esc to cancel the moving border, and then click an empty cell to cancel the selection. In **rows 15:18**, notice that the data and titles are arranged in simple rows and columns in adjacent cells for convenient charting. Compare your screen with Figure 10.39.

> With this information, Mr. Aghazarian can answer several what-if questions about the future population of the city and provide a range of population estimates based on the rates of growth over the past 10-year periods.

Figure 10.39

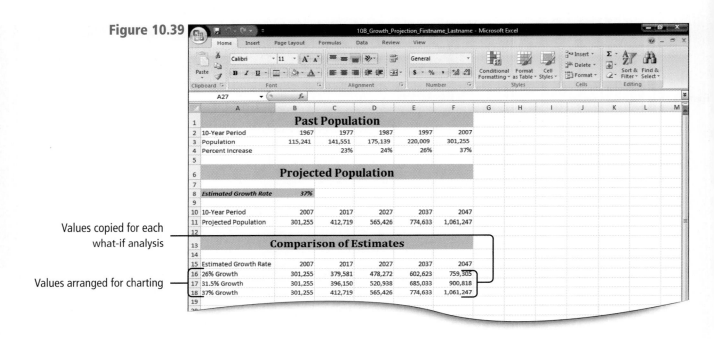

Values copied for each what-if analysis

Values arranged for charting

16 **Save** 💾 your workbook.

Another Way

To Display the Paste Special Dialog Box

Right-click over the target area, and then from the shortcut menu, click Paste Special. In many instances, using this method shortens the distance your mouse must travel in order to select an option from this dialog box.

Objective 10
Compare Data with a Line Chart

A *line chart* displays trends over time. Time is displayed along the bottom axis and the data point values are connected with a line. If you want to compare more than one set of values, each group is connected by a different line. The curves and directions of the lines make trends obvious to the reader.

Activity 10.15 Creating a Line Chart

In this activity, you will chart the values that represent the three different possible rates of population growth for Golden Grove. The 10-year periods will form the categories of time along the bottom of the chart and each set of values corresponding to a different growth rate will be represented by a line.

1 Select the range **B15:F15** and apply **Bold** 🅱.

2 Select the range **A16:F18**. On the **Insert tab**, in the **Charts group**, click the **Line** button. From the displayed gallery of line charts, in the second row, point to the first chart type to display the ScreenTip *Line with Markers* as shown in Figure 10.40.

Figure 10.40

Line with Markers chart type

Data selected for charting

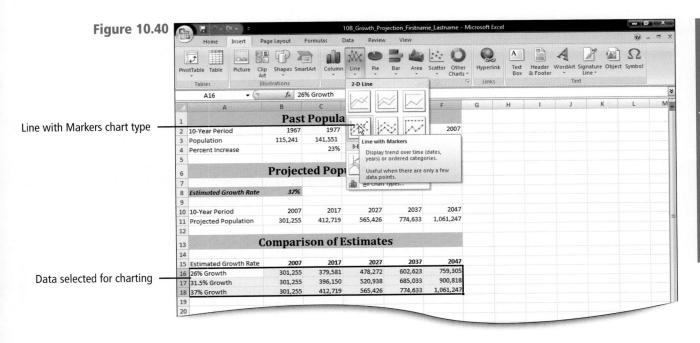

3 Click the **Line with Markers** chart type to create the chart as an embedded chart in the worksheet.

4 By using the ⟨pointer⟩ pointer, move the upper left corner of the chart just inside the upper left corner of cell **A20**. Then, scroll down so that you can view both the data and the chart on your screen. Compare your screen with Figure 10.41.

The chart still requires appropriate time labels along the category axis.

Figure 10.41

Line representing each growth rate

Green border indicates legend

Blue border indicates charted data points

Chart positioned below data

Category axis requires time labels

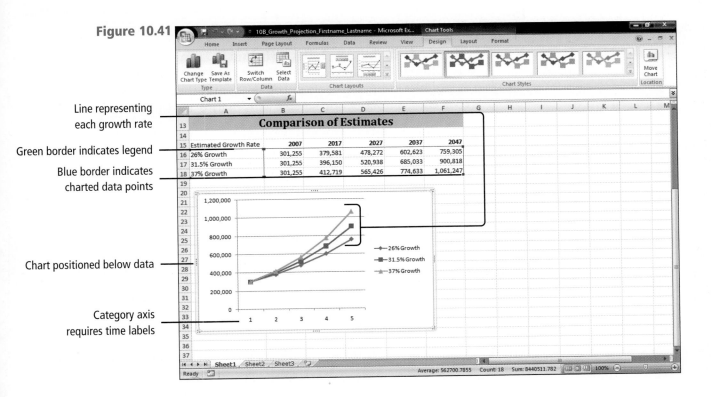

5 Be sure the chart is still selected. In the lower left corner of the chart, point to where the vertical and horizontal axis lines intersect near the *0* until the ScreenTip *Horizontal (Category) Axis* displays. Right-click and click **Select Data**.

6 On the right side of the displayed **Select Data Source** dialog box, under **Horizontal (Category) Axis Labels**, locate the **Edit** button, as shown in Figure 10.42.

Figure 10.42

Select Data Source dialog box

Edit button to edit labels on the category axis

Category (X) axis requires labels to identify each 10-year period

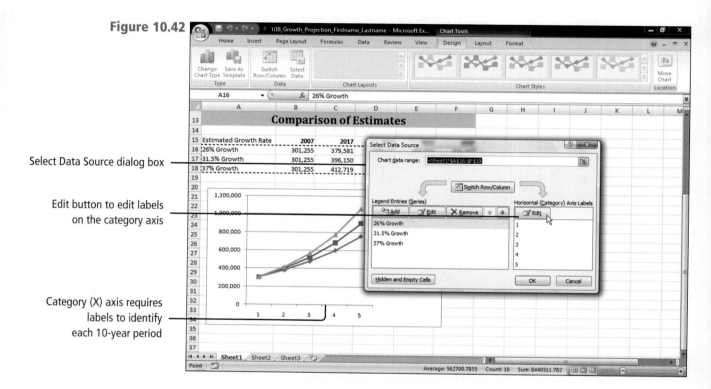

7 In the right column, click the **Edit** button. Drag the title bar of the **Axis Labels** dialog box to the right of the chart as necessary so that it is not blocking your view of the data, and then select the range **B15:F15**. Compare your screen with Figure 10.43.

Figure 10.43

Range of years surrounded by moving border

Axis Labels dialog box

Range selected with absolute references

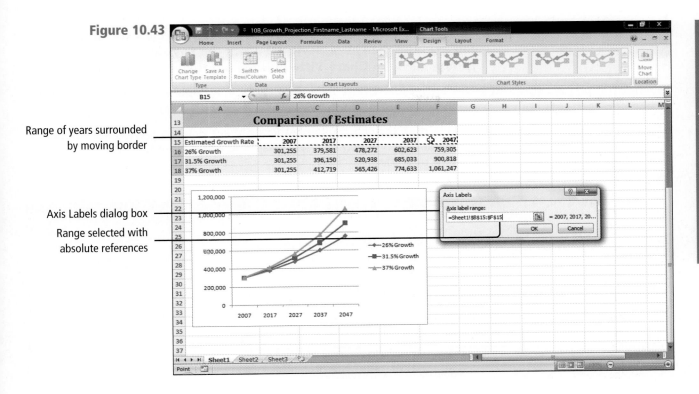

8 In the **Axis Labels** dialog box, click **OK**, and notice that in the right column, the years display as the category labels. Click **OK** to close the **Select Data Source** dialog box. Compare your screen with Figure 10.44.

Figure 10.44

Three rows of data charted as three lines

Years display as category labels

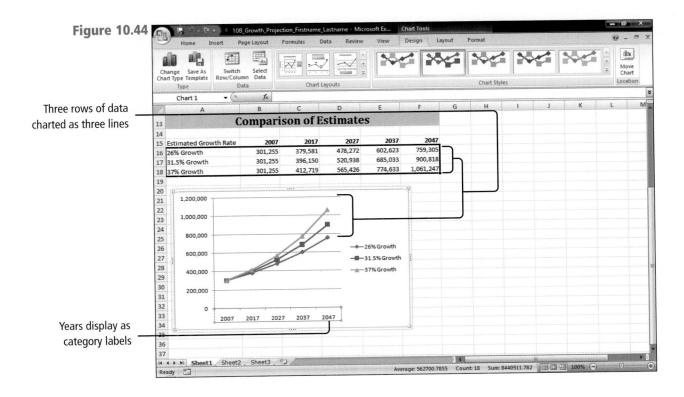

9 On the **Design tab**, in the **Chart Styles group**, click the **More** button ⮟, and then click **Style 10**. Click the **Layout tab**. In the **Labels group**, click the **Chart Title** button, and then click **Above Chart**.

10 Delete the text *Chart Title*, and then type **Population Growth Estimates** as the chart title. Compare your screen with Figure 10.45.

Based on the chart, city planners can see that the population will probably double between now and 2037 and could more than triple between now and 2047.

Figure 10.45

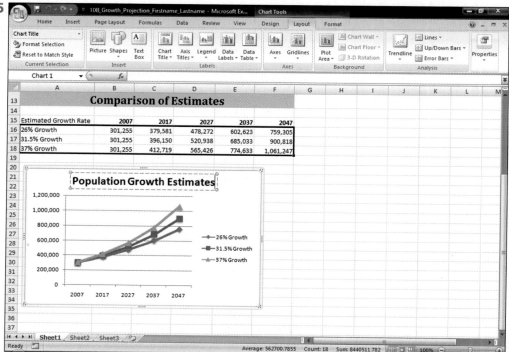

11 Click any cell to deselect the chart. Click the **Insert tab**, and then in the **Text group**, click **Header & Footer** to switch to **Page Layout View** and open the **Header area**.

12 In the **Navigation group**, click the **Go to Footer** button, click just above the word *Footer*, and then in the **Header & Footer Elements group**, click the **File Name** button. Click in a cell just above the footer to exit the **Footer area** and view your file name.

13 Scroll up and to the left as necessary to view your chart. Click the chart to select it, and notice that the chart is not centered under the data in the cells. Position the pointer over the **right resize handle** to display the ⟷ pointer, and then drag to the right so that the right border of the chart is just inside the right border of **column F**.

14 Click any cell to deselect the chart. Click the **Page Layout tab**. In the **Page Setup group**, click the **Margins** button, and then at the bottom of the **Margins gallery**, click **Custom Margins**.

15 In the displayed **Page Setup** dialog box, under **Center on page**, select the **Horizontally** check box. Click **OK** to close the dialog box, and then **Save** 🖫 the changes to your workbook.

16 On the status bar, click the **Normal** button 🔲 to return to Normal view, and then press Ctrl + Home to move to the top of your worksheet.

17 At the lower edge of the window, click to select the **Sheet2 tab**, hold down Ctrl, and then click the **Sheet3 tab** to select the two unused sheets. Right-click over the selected sheet tabs, and then on the displayed shortcut menu, click **Delete**.

18 **Save** 🖫 the changes you have made to your workbook. Check your *Chapter Assignment Sheet* or *Course Syllabus* or consult your instructor to determine if you are to submit your assignments on paper or electronically. To submit electronically, follow the instructions provided by your instructor.

19 Press Ctrl + F2 to display the **Print Preview** to check the placement of your worksheet. In the **Print group**, click the **Print** button. In the displayed **Print** dialog box, click **OK** to print your worksheet. If you are directed to submit printed formulas, refer to Activity 9.17 to do so.

20 If you printed your formulas, be sure to redisplay the worksheet by pressing Ctrl + `. From the **Office** menu ⊙, click **Close**. If the dialog box displays asking if you want to save changes, click **No** so that you do *not* save the changes you made for printing formulas. **Exit** Excel.

End **You have completed Project 10B** ————————

There's More You Can Do!

Close Excel and any other open windows. Display the Start menu, click Computer, and then navigate to the student files that accompany this textbook. In the folder **02_theres_more_you_can_do**, locate and open the folder for this chapter. Open and print the instructions for this project, which are provided to you in Adobe PDF format.

Try IT! 1 — Change the Office Theme in an Excel Workbook

In this Try It! exercise, you will change an Office theme in an Excel workbook.

Content-Based Assessments

Summary

In this chapter, you created and saved a workbook from an existing workbook, renamed worksheets, and color-coded worksheet tabs. You examined and practiced the various ways that Excel formats numbers in a worksheet. You moved, copied, and pasted cell contents using the Office Clipboard. Workbooks frequently contain multiple worksheets, and when they do, a Summary sheet is often included to summarize the data on the individual worksheets. You practiced grouping worksheets to enter and format data simultaneously on multiple worksheets, and then created a summary worksheet to summarize the data.

What-if analysis is used to determine what would happen to one value if another value changes. In this chapter, you used a what-if analysis process to project future trends, and then created a line chart to visually represent those trends.

Key Terms

The 🔘 symbol represents Key Terms found on the Student CD in the 02_theres_more_you_can_do folder for this chapter.

Content-Based Assessments

Matching

Match each term in the second column with its correct definition in the first column. Write the letter of the term on the blank line to the left of the correct definition.

_____ **1.** To move within a document or workbook.

_____ **2.** The labels along the lower border of the worksheet window that identify each worksheet.

_____ **3.** The action of placing cell contents that have been copied or moved to the Office Clipboard to another location.

_____ **4.** A temporary storage area maintained by your Windows operating system.

_____ **5.** A method of moving or copying the content of selected cells in which you point to the selection and then drag it to a new location.

_____ **6.** The target destination for data that has been cut or copied using the Office Clipboard.

_____ **7.** A button that displays in the lower right corner of a pasted selection and that displays a list of options that lets you determine how the information is pasted into your worksheet.

_____ **8.** Within a workbook of multiple worksheets, a worksheet that contains the details of information summarized on a summary worksheet.

_____ **9.** The process of changing the values in cells to see how those changes affect the outcome of formulas in your worksheet.

_____ **10.** The percent by which one number increases over another.

_____ **11.** The mathematical formula to calculate a rate of increase.

_____ **12.** The starting point when you divide the amount of increase by it to calculate the rate of increase.

_____ **13.** The mathematical rules for performing multiple calculations within a formula.

_____ **14.** The Excel feature by which a cell takes on the formatting of the number typed into the cell.

_____ **15.** The formula for calculating the value after an increase by multiplying the original value—the base—by the percent for new value.

A Base

B Detail worksheet

C Drag and drop

D Format as you type

E Navigate

F Office Clipboard

G Order of operations

H Paste

I Paste area

J Paste Options

K Percent rate of increase

L Rate = amount of increase/base

M Sheet tabs

N Value after increase = base × percent for new value

O What-if analysis

Content-Based Assessments

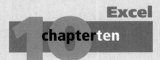

Fill in the Blank

Write the correct answers in the space provided.

1. When a worksheet is active, its tab color displays as an _____.

2. When you enter a date, Excel assigns a _____ value to the date, which makes it possible to treat dates like other numbers for the purpose of calculating the number of days between two dates.

3. A two-digit year value of 30 through 99 is interpreted by the Windows operating system as the four-digit years 1930 through _____.

4. The keyboard shortcut Ctrl + ; enters the _____ _____, which is obtained from your computer's internal calendar.

5. Clearing the contents of a cell does not clear the _____ of a cell—for example, fill color applied to the cell.

6. You can view selections stored on the Office Clipboard by displaying its _____ _____ from the Dialog Box Launcher in the Clipboard group.

7. According to the order of operations for formulas, the first expressions calculated are those within _____.

8. According to the order of operations, _____ and division are performed before addition and subtraction.

9. According to the order of operations, consecutive operators with the same level of _____ are calculated from left to right.

10. The symbol used to indicate the multiplication operation is the _____ symbol.

11. In the formula *percent for new value = base percent + percent of increase*, the base percent is usually _____ %.

12. When pasting a group of copied cells to a target range, you need only select the _____ cell of the target range.

13. The chart type that displays trends over time and that connects data point values with a line is called a _____ chart.

14. In the formula *=(B3-C4)*D3* the mathematical operation that is performed first is _____.

15. When copying the formula *=(B3-B4)*$A$2* to the right, the formula in column C would be _____.

Excel

chapterten

Skills Review

Project 10C — Permit Sales

In this project, you will apply the skills you practiced from the Objectives in Project 10A.

Objectives: 1. *Create and Save a Workbook from an Existing Workbook;* **2.** *Navigate a Workbook and Rename Worksheets;* **3.** *Enter Dates, Clear Contents, and Clear Formats;* **4.** *Move, Copy, and Paste Cell Contents;* **5.** *Edit and Format Multiple Worksheets at the Same Time;* **6.** *Create a Summary Sheet;* **7.** *Format and Print Multiple Worksheets in a Workbook.*

In the following Skills Review, you will edit a workbook for the Golden Grove Parks and Recreation Director to summarize the sales of weekly and daily campground permits for the three city campgrounds in the month of June. The four worksheets of your completed workbook will look similar to those shown in Figure 10.46.

For Project 10C, you will need the following file:

e10C_Permit_Sales

You will save your workbook as
10C_Permit_Sales_Firstname_Lastname

Figure 10.46

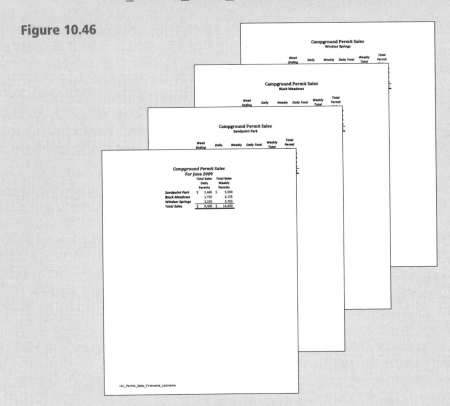

(Project 10C–Permit Sales continues on the next page)

Content-Based Assessments

Excel

chapterten

Skills Review

(Project 10C–Permit Sales continued)

1. **Start** Excel. From the **Office** menu, click **Open**, and then navigate to the student files that accompany this textbook. Locate, select, and then open the file **e10C_Permit_Sales**. **Save** the file in your **Excel Chapter 10** folder as **10C_Permit_Sales_Firstname_Lastname** Take a moment to examine the data in each of the three worksheets.

2. Point to the **Sheet1 tab**, and then double-click to select its name. Type **Sandpoint Park** and then press [Enter] to rename the sheet. Right-click the **Sandpoint Park sheet tab**, point to **Tab Color** to display the colors associated with the workbook's theme. Under **Theme Colors**, click **Purple, Accent 4, Lighter 40%**.

3. Point to the **Sheet2 tab**, right-click, and then click **Rename**. Type **Black Meadows** and then press [Enter] to rename the sheet. On the **Home tab**, in the **Cells group**, click the **Format** button, and then point to **Tab Color**. Under **Theme Colors**, click **Aqua, Accent 5, Lighter 40%**.

4. Using either of the two techniques you just practiced, change the name of the **Sheet3 tab** to **Windsor Springs** and then change the **Tab Color** to **Orange, Accent 6, Lighter 40%**.

5. Display the **Sandpoint Park** worksheet, and then select the range **A13:D14**. On the **Home tab**, in the **Clipboard group**, click the **Copy** button to place a copy of the selected cells on the Office Clipboard.

6. Click the **Black Meadows sheet tab** to make it the active worksheet. Click cell **A13**, and then on the **Home tab**, in the **Clipboard group**, click the **Paste** button. Click the **Windsor Springs sheet tab** to make it the active worksheet, and then click cell **A13**. In the **Clipboard group**, click the **Paste** button. Click the

Sandpoint Park sheet tab to make it the active worksheet, and then press [Esc] to cancel the moving border.

7. Right-click the **Sandpoint Park sheet tab**, and then click **Select All Sheets** to group the sheets—*[Group]* displays in the title bar. Select the range **A5:A8**. On the **Home tab**, in the **Number group**, click the **Number Format arrow**, at the bottom, click **More Number Formats**, under **Category**, click **Date**, and then under **Type**, click **3/14** and click **OK**. The date format for the selected range of cells is changed for all three worksheets.

8. With the worksheets still grouped, click cell **D4**, type **Daily Total** and then press [Tab]. In cell **E4**, type **Weekly Total** and then press [Tab]. In cell **F4**, type **Total Permit Sales** and then press [Enter].

9. Select the range **A4:F4**, right-click, and then click **Format Cells**. Click the **Font tab**, and then under **Font style**, click **Bold Italic**. Click the **Alignment tab**. Under **Text alignment**, click the **Horizontal arrow**, and then click **Center**. Click the **Vertical arrow**, and then click **Center**. Under **Text control**, select the **Wrap text** check box. Click **OK**.

10. With the worksheets still grouped, select the range **A1:F1**, and then in the **Alignment group**, click the **Merge & Center** button. Change the **Font** to **Cambria**, the **Font Size** to **14**, and then apply **Bold**. Select the range **A2:F2**, right-click, and then on the Mini toolbar, click the **Merge & Center** button, change the **Font Size** to **12**, and apply **Bold**.

11. With the worksheets still grouped, click cell **D5** and construct a formula to calculate the total sales of *Daily* permits for the week ending June 6 as follows: type **=** to

(Project 10C–Permit Sales continues on the next page)

(Project 10C–Permit Sales continued)

begin a formula, click cell **B5**, type * click cell **D13**, and then press F4 to make the reference to cell **D13** absolute. On the **Formula Bar**, click the **Enter** button. Your result is *340*. Use the fill handle to copy the formula down for the remaining dates.

12. In cell **E5**, construct a similar formula to multiply the number of *Weekly* permits sold during the week of June 6 in cell **C5** times the *Weekly Permit Price* in cell **D14**. Make the reference to cell **D14** absolute so that each week's sales are multiplied by the *Weekly Permit Price* in cell **D14**. Your result is *585*. Copy the formula down for the remaining dates.

13. Click cell **A9**, and then apply **Align Text Right** and **Bold**. Select the range **B5:E9**, and then in the **Editing group**, click the **Sum** button to sum each column.

14. With the worksheets still grouped, select the range **D5:F9**, and then in the **Editing group**, click the **Sum** button to sum the rows for *Total Permit Sales* for each week.

15. With the worksheets still grouped, select the nonadjacent ranges **B5:C9** and **D6:F8**, and then apply the **Comma Style** with **zero decimal places**. Select the nonadjacent ranges **D5:F5** and **D9:F9**, and then apply **Accounting Number Format** with **zero decimal places**. Select the range **B9:F9**, in the **Font group**, click the **Borders button arrow**, and then click **Top and Double Bottom Border**. Select **columns B:F**, and then set the width to **70 pixels**.

16. Click the **Black Meadows sheet tab**, and then verify that the formulas and formatting that you applied in Steps 7 through 15 were applied to the worksheet—recall that selecting an individual worksheet

ungroups the sheets. Click the **Windsor Springs sheet tab**, and then verify that the formulas and formatting that you applied in Steps 7 through 15 were applied.

17. **Save** your workbook. To the right of the **Windsor Springs** worksheet tab, click the **Insert Worksheet** button. Rename the new worksheet **Summary** and then change the **Tab Color** to **Olive Green, Accent 3, Lighter 40%**. In cell **A4**, type **Sandpoint Park** In cell **A5**, type **Black Meadows** In cell **A6**, type **Windsor Springs** In cell **A7**, type **Total Sales** Select the range **A4:A7**, change the **Font Size** to **12**, and then apply **Bold** and **Italic**. **AutoFit column A**.

18. In cell **B3**, type **Total Sales Daily Permits** and then in cell **C3**, type **Total Sales Weekly Permits** Select the two cells, and then in the **Alignment group**, click the **Wrap Text** button and the **Center** button. In the **Font group**, click **Bold**.

19. Click cell **B4**. Type = and then click the **Sandpoint Park sheet tab**. On the **Sandpoint Park** worksheet, click cell **D9**, and then press Enter to create a formula that references the *Daily Total Sales* for *Sandpoint Park*.

20. Click cell **C4**. Type = and then click the **Sandpoint Park sheet tab**. Click cell **E9**, and then press Enter to create a formula that references the *Weekly Total Sales* for *Sandpoint Park*. Then, use the same technique to copy the totals for *Daily* and *Weekly* permit sales for the **Black Meadows worksheet** and the **Windsor Springs worksheet**.

21. In cell **A1**, type **Campground Permit Sales** and then **Merge & Center** the text over the range **A1:C1**. Change the **Font** to **Cambria**, the **Font Size** to **14**, and apply

(Project 10C–Permit Sales continues on the next page)

(Project 10C–Permit Sales continued)

Bold and **Italic**. In cell **A2**, type **For June 2009** and then use **Format Painter** to apply the format from cell **A1**.

22. Select the range **B4:C7**, click the **Sum** button to total the two columns. Format the range **B5:C6** with **Comma Style** and **zero decimal places**. Format the nonadjacent ranges **B4:C4** and **B7:C7** with the **Accounting Number Format** and **zero decimal places**. Apply a **Top and Double Bottom** border to the range **B7:C7**.

23. Point to the **Summary sheet tab**, hold down the left mouse button to display a small black caret symbol, and then drag to the left until the caret is positioned to the left of the **Sandpoint Park sheet tab**; release the left mouse button to make the Summary sheet the first sheet in the workbook.

24. Be sure the **Summary** worksheet is the active sheet. Then point to its sheet tab, right-click, and click **Select All Sheets** to display *[Group]* in the title bar. Click the **Insert tab**, and then in the **Text group**, click the **Header & Footer** button. In the **Navigation group**, click the **Go to Footer** button, click in the **left section** above the word *Footer*, and then in the **Header & Footer Elements group**, click the **File Name** button.

25. Click in a cell above the footer to deselect the **Footer area** and view your file name. Click the **Page Layout tab**. In the **Page Setup group**, click the **Margins** button, and then at the bottom of the **Margins gallery**, click **Custom Margins**. In the

displayed **Page Setup** dialog box, under **Center on page**, select the **Horizontally** check box. Click **OK**, and then on the status bar, click the **Normal** button. Press Ctrl + Home to move to the top of the worksheet. Verify that *[Group]* still displays in the title bar.

26. **Save** your workbook. Check your *Chapter Assignment Sheet* or *Course Syllabus*, or consult your instructor, to determine if you are to submit your assignments on paper or electronically. To submit electronically, follow the instructions provided by your instructor.

27. From the **Office** menu, point to the **Print arrow**, and then from the displayed menu, click **Print Preview**. At the top of the screen, click the **Next Page** button as necessary to view and check each page of your workbook.

28. Click the **Print** button. Under **Print range**, verify that the **All** option button is selected. Under **Print what**, click **Active sheet(s)** (assuming your worksheets are still grouped) and then under **Copies**, verify that the **Number of copies** is **1**. Click **OK** to print your workbook. Determine if you are to print formulas for any or all of the worksheets in this workbook. To print formulas, refer to Activity 9.17 in Project 9A.

29. If you printed your formulas, be sure to redisplay the worksheet by pressing Ctrl + `. From the **Office** menu, click **Close**. If you are prompted to save changes, click **No. Exit** Excel.

End **You have completed Project 10C**

Excel

chapterten

Skills Review

Project 10D — Property Tax

In this project, you will apply the skills you practiced from the Objectives in Project 10B.

Objectives: 8. *Design a Worksheet for What-If Analysis;* **9.** *Perform What-If Analysis;* **10.** *Compare Data with a Line Chart.*

In the following Skills Review, you will create a worksheet for the Controller of Golden Grove to forecast property tax revenue for the next 10 years. Your completed worksheet will look similar to the one shown in Figure 10.47.

For Project 10D, you will need the following file:

New blank Excel workbook

You will save your workbook as 10D_Property_Tax_Firstname_Lastname

Figure 10.47

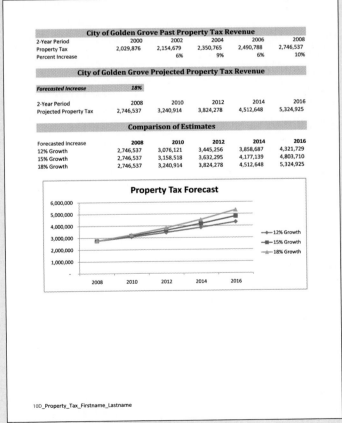

(Project 10D–Property Tax continues on the next page)

Content-Based Assessments

(Project 10D–Property Tax continued)

1. **Start** Excel and display a new workbook. In cell **A1**, type **City of Golden Grove Past Property Tax Revenue** and then press Enter. Adjust the width of **column A** to **155 pixels**. Select the range **A1:F1**, right-click, and then on the Mini toolbar, apply **Bold**, change the **Font** to **Cambria**, change the **Font Size** to **14**, and click the **Merge & Center** button. From the **Office** menu, click **Save As**, navigate to your **Excel Chapter 10** folder, in the **File name** box, name the file **10D_Property_Tax_Firstname_Lastname** and then click **Save**.

2. In cell **A2**, type **2-Year Period** In cell **B2**, type **2000** and then press Tab. In cell **C2**, type **2002** and then press Tab. Select the range **B2:C2**, and then drag the fill handle to the right through cell **F2** to enter years through *2008*.

3. In cell **A3**, type **Property Tax** and then press Enter. In cell **A4**, type **Percent Increase** and then press Enter. Beginning in cell **B3** and pressing Tab to move across the row, enter the following values for property tax revenue in the years listed:

2000	2002	2004	2006	2008
2029876	2154679	2350765	2490788	2746537

4. Select the range **B3:F3**, and then right-click over the selection. On the Mini toolbar, apply the **Comma Style**, and then click **Decrease Decimal** two times to apply **zero decimal places**.

5. Click cell **C4**. Type **=(c3-b3)/b3** and then press Enter to calculate the *Percent Increase* from the year 2000 to the year 2002. Point to cell **C4** and right-click, and then on the Mini toolbar, click the **Percent Style** button. Your result is *6%*.

6. Click cell **D4**, type **=** and then by either typing, or using a combination of typing and clicking cells to reference them, construct a formula similar to the one in cell **C4** to calculate the rate of increase in property tax from 2002 to 2004. Press Enter, and then format cell **D4** with the **Percent Style**. With cell **D4** selected, drag the fill handle to the right through cell **F4** to calculate the property tax *Percent Increase* for each 2-year period.

7. In cell **A6**, type **City of Golden Grove Projected Property Tax Revenue** and then press Enter. Click cell **A1**. On the **Home tab**, in the **Clipboard group**, click the **Format Painter** button, and then click cell **A6**.

8. In cell **A8**, type **Forecasted Increase** and then press Enter. In cell **A10**, type **2-Year Period** and then in cell **A11**, type **Projected Property Tax** In cell **B10**, type **2008** and then press Tab. In cell **C10**, type **2010** and then press Enter. Select the range **B10:C10**, and then drag the fill handle through cell **F10** to extend the pattern of years to **2016**.

9. **Save** the changes you have made to your workbook thus far. In cell **B8**, type **12%** and then press Enter. Select the range **A8:B8**, right-click, and then on the Mini toolbar, click **Bold** and **Italic**.

10. In cell **B11**, type **=** click cell **F3**, and then press Enter to create a formula that references the 2008 Property Tax collected by the city.

11. Click cell **C11**. Type **=b11*(100%+b8)** and then on the **Formula Bar**, click the **Enter** button to create a formula that calculates the city's projected property tax revenue based on a forecasted increase of 12%. With cell **C11** as the active cell, drag the fill handle to copy the formula to **D11:F11**. Click cell **B11**, click the **Format Painter** button, and then select the range **C11:F11** to copy the formatting.

(Project 10D–Property Tax continues on the next page)

Content-Based Assessments

(Project 10D–Property Tax continued)

12. In cell **A13**, type **Comparison of Estimates** and then press Enter. Click **A6**, click the **Format Painter** button, and then click cell **A13**. Select the range **A8:B8**, right-click to display the Mini toolbar, click the **Fill Color button arrow**, and then under **Theme Colors**, click **Aqua, Accent 5, Lighter 40%**. Click cell **A1**, and then hold down Ctrl and click **A6** and **A13**. In the **Font group**, click the **Fill Color** button to apply the same fill color to these titles.

13. In cells **A15:A18**, type the following row titles:
    Forecasted Increase
    12% Growth
    15% Growth
    18% Growth

14. Select the range **B10:F10**. On the **Home tab**, in the **Clipboard group**, click the **Copy** button, click cell **B15**, and then in the **Clipboard group**, click the **Paste** button.

15. Select the range **B11:F11**, and then click **Copy**. Click cell **B16**, and then in the **Clipboard group**, click the **Paste button arrow**. From the displayed menu, click **Paste Special**. In the displayed **Paste Special** dialog box, under **Paste**, click the **Values and number formats** option button. Click **OK** to paste the values in the cells rather than the formulas.

16. Press Esc to cancel the moving border. Click cell **B8**. Type **15** and then press Enter to recalculate the values in cells **C11:F11** for a 15% increase.

17. Select the range **B11:F11**, and then press Ctrl + C to copy the selection. Click cell **B17**. In the **Clipboard group**, click the **Paste button arrow**, and then click **Paste Special**. In the **Paste Special** dialog box, click the **Values and number formats** option button, and then click **OK**.

18. In cell **B8**, change the **Forecasted Increase** to 18 and press Enter. Using the skills you just practiced, copy the values and number formats in the range **B11:F11** to the range **B18:F18**. Press Esc to cancel the moving border.

19. **Save** the changes you have made thus far. Select the range **B15:F15** and apply **Bold**.

20. Select the range **A16:F18**. On the **Insert tab**, in the **Charts group**, click the **Line** button. Click the **Line with Markers** chart type to create the chart as an embedded chart in the worksheet. Drag to position the upper left corner of the chart slightly inside the upper left corner of cell **A20**.

21. Along the lower portion of the chart, point to any of the category axis numbers such as *1* or *2* to display the ScreenTip. *Horizontal (Category) Axis* displays. Then, right-click, and from the displayed short-cut menu, click **Select Data**. On the right side of the displayed **Select Data Source** dialog box, under **Horizontal (Category) Axis Labels**, click the **Edit** button. Drag the title bar of the **Axis Labels** dialog box to the right of the chart as necessary so that it is not blocking your view of the data, and then select the range **B15:F15**. Click **OK** two times so that the years display on the horizontal axis.

22. On the **Design tab**, in the **Chart Styles group**, click the **More** button, and then click **Style 2**. Click the **Layout tab**. In the **Labels group**, click the **Chart Title** button, and then click **Above Chart**. Delete the text *Chart Title*, and then type **Property Tax Forecast**

23. Click any cell to deselect the chart. Click the **Insert tab**, and then in the **Text group**, click **Header & Footer**. In the **Navigation**

(Project 10D–Property Tax continues on the next page)

Skills Review

(Project 10D–Property Tax continued)

group, click the **Go to Footer** button, click just above the word *Footer*, and then in the **Header & Footer Elements group**, click the **File Name** button. Click in a cell just above the footer to exit the **Footer area** and view your file name.

24. Scroll up to view your chart, click an edge of the chart to select it, position the pointer over the right resize handle to display the ↔ pointer, and then drag to the right so that the right border of the chart is just inside the right border of **column F**.

25. Click any cell to deselect the chart. Click the **Page Layout tab**. In the **Page Setup group**, click the **Margins** button, and then at the bottom of the **Margins gallery**, click **Custom Margins**. In the displayed **Page Setup** dialog box, under **Center on page**, select the **Horizontally** check box. Click **OK** to close the dialog box.

26. On the status bar, click the **Normal** button to return to Normal view, and then press `Ctrl` + `Home` to move to the top of your worksheet. At the lower edge of the window, click to select the **Sheet2 tab**, hold down `Ctrl`, and then click the **Sheet3 tab** to

select the two unused sheets. Right-click, and then click **Delete** to delete the unused sheets.

27. **Save** the changes you have made to your workbook. Check your *Chapter Assignment Sheet* or *Course Syllabus* or consult your instructor to determine if you are to submit your assignments on paper or electronically. To submit electronically, follow the instructions provided by your instructor.

28. From the **Office** menu, point to the **Print button arrow**, and then click **Print Preview** to check the placement of your worksheet. In the **Print group**, click the **Print** button. In the displayed **Print** dialog box, click **OK** to print your worksheet. If you are directed to submit printed formulas, refer to Activity 9.17 in Project 9A to do so.

29. If you printed your formulas, be sure to redisplay the worksheet by pressing `Ctrl` + `'`. From the **Office** menu, click **Close**. If the dialog box displays asking if you want to save changes, click **No** so that you do *not* save the changes you made for printing formulas. **Exit** Excel.

End You have completed Project 10D

Content-Based Assessments

Mastering Excel

Project 10E — Operations Costs

In this project, you will apply the skills you practiced from the Objectives in Projects 10A and 10B.

Objectives: 1. *Create and Save a Workbook from an Existing Workbook;* **2.** *Navigate a Workbook and Rename Worksheets;* **3.** *Enter Dates, Clear Contents, and Clear Formats;* **4.** *Move, Copy, and Paste Cell Contents;* **5.** *Edit and Format Multiple Worksheets at the Same Time;* **6.** *Create a Summary Sheet;* **7.** *Format and Print Multiple Worksheets in a Workbook.* **10.** *Compare Data with a Line Chart.*

In the following Mastering Excel assessment, you will edit a workbook that summarizes and charts the operations costs of Golden Grove's Public Works Department. The department's three divisions are Contract Administration, Engineering, and Street Services. Your completed workbook will look similar to Figure 10.48.

For Project 10E, you will need the following file:

e10E_Operations_Costs

You will save your workbook as
10E_Operations_Costs_Firstname_Lastname

Figure 10.48

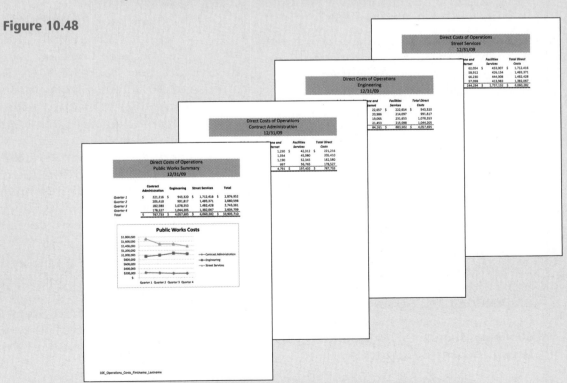

(Project 10E–Operations Costs continues on the next page)

(Project 10E–Operations Costs continued)

1. **Start** Excel and from your student files, open **e10E_Operations_Costs**. **Save** the workbook in your **Excel Chapter 10** folder as **10E_Operations_Costs_Firstname_Lastname**

2. Rename the **Sheet1 tab** as **Contract Administration** and then change its **Tab Color** to **Purple, Accent 4, Lighter 40%**. Rename **Sheet2** as **Engineering** and then change its **Tab Color** to **Aqua, Accent 5, Lighter 40%**. Rename **Sheet3** as **Street Services** and then change its **Tab Color** to **Orange, Accent 6, Lighter 40%**.

3. Point to the **Contract Administration** sheet tab, right-click, and then select all of the sheets so that they are grouped. **Merge and Center** the titles in **A1** and **A2** over **columns A:E**. In cell **A3**, type **12/31/2009** and then apply the **03/14/01** date format to the cell. **Merge and Center** cell **A3** over **columns A:E**, and then change the **Font Size** to **16**. Select the range **A1:A3**, and then apply a **Fill Color** of **Red, Accent 2, Lighter 40%**.

4. With the worksheets still grouped, in **row 5**, apply **Wrap Text** formatting to the column titles, and then apply **Bold** and **Italic**. **Center** the column titles.

5. With the worksheets still grouped, sum the columns and then sum the rows. Beginning with **Comma Style**, apply appropriate financial formatting using **zero decimal places**, and then change the width of **column A** to **110 pixels**. Select cell **A10** and **Clear Formats** so that the text is aligned at the left and not bold.

6. Ungroup the worksheets and verify that the formulas and formatting applied in Steps 3 through 5 were applied to the **Engineering** and **Street Services** sheets. Insert a new worksheet and **Rename** it **Summary** Change the **Tab Color** to **Olive Green, Accent 3, Lighter 40%**.

7. Display the **Contract Administration** worksheet. Select and **Copy** the range **A1:A3**, and then **Paste** the selection to the **Summary** worksheet in cell **A1**. In the **Summary** worksheet, click cell **A2**, and then type **Public Works Summary**

8. Display the **Contract Administration** worksheet. **Copy** the range **A6:A9**, **Paste** the selection to the **Summary** worksheet in cell **A6**, and then in the **Summary** worksheet, adjust the width of **column A** to **110 pixels** and the width of **columns B:E** to **100 pixels**. In cell **A10**, type **Total** and notice that the italic emphasis will carry forward from the cell above.

9. In cell **B5**, type **Contract Administration** In cell **C5**, type **Engineering** In cell **D5**, type **Street Services** In cell **E5**, type **Total Center** and apply **Wrap Text** formatting to the column titles in **row 5**, apply **Bold**, and then apply **Middle Align**.

10. **Save** the changes you have made to your workbook thus far. In the **Summary** worksheet, in cell **B6**, create a formula that references the **Contract Administration** worksheet *Quarter 1 Total Direct Costs* in cell **E6**. Fill the formula down through **B9** to create formulas that reference the remaining quarter's *Total Direct Costs*. Create similar formulas for the **Engineering** and **Street Services** quarterly *Total Direct Costs*. Sum the columns and then sum the rows. Beginning with **Comma Style**, apply appropriate financial formatting using **zero decimal places**.

11. Select the range **A5:D9**, and then insert a line chart using the **Line with Markers** chart type. Position the upper left corner of the chart inside the upper left corner of cell **A12**. Apply **Chart Style 10**, and then add the **Chart Title Public Works Costs** in the **Above Chart** position. From the

(Project 10E–Operations Costs continues on the next page)

Content-Based Assessments

Excel
chapterten

Mastering Excel

(Project 10E–Operations Costs continued)

status bar, click the **Page Layout View** button, widen the chart to display attractively below the data, and then click any cell to deselect the chart. **Move** the **Summary** worksheet so that it is the first sheet in the workbook.

12. Group the worksheets, insert a footer with the **File Name** on the left, and then center the worksheets **Horizontally**. Return to **Normal** view and display the upper portion of the worksheet.

13. **Save** your workbook, and then examine your grouped worksheets in **Print Preview**.

Print or submit electronically as directed. If the worksheets are grouped, all the worksheets will print. If the worksheets are not grouped, click Entire workbook to print all the sheets. Determine if you are to print formulas for any or all of the worksheets in this workbook. To print formulas, refer to Activity 9.17 in Project 9A.

14. If you printed your formulas, be sure to redisplay the worksheet by pressing Ctrl + `. From the **Office** menu, click **Close**. If you are prompted to save changes, click **No**. **Exit** Excel.

 End **You have completed Project 10E**

Content-Based Assessments

Mastering Excel

Project 10F—Venue Revenue

In this project, you will apply the skills you practiced from the Objectives in Projects 10A and 10B.

Objectives: 3. *Enter Dates, Clear Contents, and Clear Formats;* **8.** *Design a Worksheet for What-If Analysis;* **9.** *Perform What-If Analysis;* **10.** *Compare Data with a Line Chart.*

In the following Mastering Excel assessment, you will complete a workbook for the Director of Conventions, Culture, and Leisure, which shows revenue estimates for city-owned venues for conventions, cultural events, and leisure activities and their associated parking structures. Your resulting worksheet and chart will look similar to Figure 10.49.

For Project 10F, you will need the following file:

New blank Excel workbook

**You will save your workbook as
10F_Venue_Revenue_Firstname_Lastname**

Figure 10.49

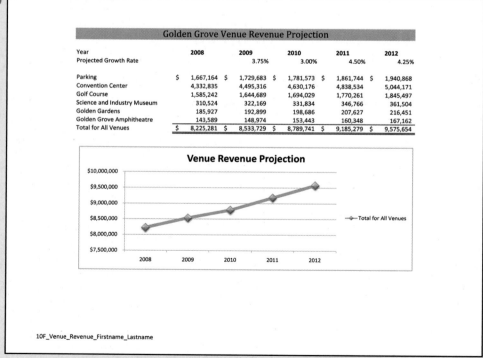

(Project 10F–Venue Revenue continues on the next page)

Content-Based Assessments

Excel

chapterten | **Mastering Excel**

(Project 10F–Venue Revenue continued)

1. **Start** Excel and display a new blank workbook. **Save** the workbook in your **Excel Chapter 10** folder as **10F_Venue_Revenue_Firstname_Lastname**

2. In cell **A1**, type **Golden Grove Venue Revenue Projection** and then **Merge and Center** the title across cells **A1:F1**. Change the **Font** to **Cambria**, the **Font Size** to **16**, and then apply the **Olive Green, Accent 3 Fill Color**. In cell **A3**, type **Year** In the range **B3:F3**, create a pattern of years from 2008 through 2012. Format the years with **Bold** and **Center**.

3. In cell **A4**, type **Projected Growth Rate** In the range **C4:F4**, type the following percentages: **3.75%** and **3.0%** and **4.5%** and **4.25%**

4. Widen **column A** to **200 pixels** and widen columns **B:F** to **100 pixels**. In the range **A6:B11**, enter the following data:

Parking	1667164
Convention Center	4332835
Golf Course	1585242
Science and Industry Museum	310524
Golden Gardens	185927
Golden Grove Amphitheatre	143589

5. In cell **C6**, construct a formula that calculates the year *2009* revenue for *Parking* assuming an increase of 3.75% (the rate in cell C4) over the previous year. That is, multiply the base value in cell **B6** times 100% plus the value in cell **C4**. Place the second expression in parentheses so that addition is performed first, and make the reference to the value in **C4** absolute so that you can copy this formula down column C. In cell **D6**, for the year *2010*, construct a similar formula using the previous year's revenue and the rate in cell **D4**. Construct similar formulas for the years

2011 and *2012* using the previous year's revenue and the projected growth rate for the year indicated. **Copy** the formulas in **row 6** down through **row 11**.

6. In cell **A12**, type **Total for All Venues** and then in **row 12**, sum the values in **columns B:F**. Beginning with **Comma Style**, apply appropriate financial formatting with **zero decimal places**.

7. **Save** the changes you have made to your workbook thus far. Using the data in the range **A12:F12**, insert a line chart using the **Line with Markers** chart type, and then apply **Chart Style 29**. Edit the data source so that the **Horizontal (Category) Axis** uses the years in the range **B3:F3** as the labels. Change the chart title to **Venue Revenue Projection** Position the upper left corner of the chart inside the upper left corner of cell **A14**.

8. Click any cell to deselect the chart. Change the **Orientation** to **Landscape**, and then center the worksheet on the page **Horizontally**. Insert a footer with the **File Name** on the left side. Widen the chart so that it displays attractively under the data. Deselect the chart, return to **Normal** view, display the top of the worksheet, and then delete the unused sheets in the workbook.

9. **Save** your workbook, and then examine your worksheet in **Print Preview**. **Print** or submit electronically as directed. To print formulas, refer to Activity 9.17 in Project 9A.

10. If you printed your formulas, be sure to redisplay the worksheet by pressing [Ctrl] + [`]. From the **Office** menu, click **Close**. If you are prompted to save changes, click **No**. **Exit** Excel.

End **You have completed Project 10F**

Content-Based Assessments

Mastering Excel

Project 10G—Analysis

In this project, you will apply the skills you practiced from all the Objectives in Projects 10A and 10B.

Objectives: 1. *Create and Save a Workbook from an Existing Workbook;* **2.** *Navigate a Workbook and Rename Worksheets;* **3.** *Enter Dates, Clear Contents, and Clear Formats;* **4.** *Move, Copy, and Paste Cell Contents;* **5.** *Edit and Format Multiple Worksheets at the Same Time;* **6.** *Create a Summary Sheet;* **7.** *Format and Print Multiple Worksheets in a Workbook;* **8.** *Design a Worksheet for What-If Analysis;* **9.** *Perform What-If Analysis;* **10.** *Compare Data with a Line Chart.*

In the following Mastering Excel assessment, you will complete a workbook for the Director of Parks and Recreation, which shows departmental expenses for the three departments reporting to the director. Your resulting worksheet and chart will look similar to Figure 10.50.

For Project 10G, you will need the following file:

e10G_Analysis

You will save your workbook as 10G_Analysis_Firstname_Lastname

Figure 10.50

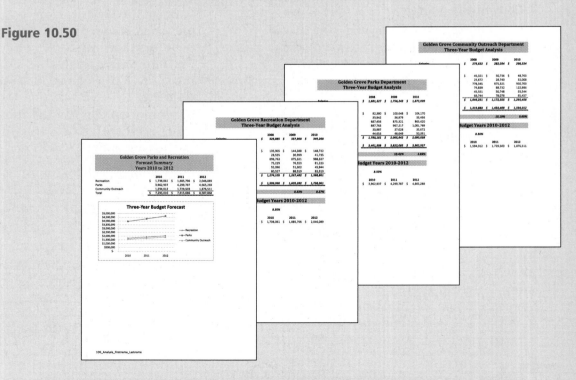

(Project 10G–Analysis continues on the next page)

Excel
chapterten   ## Mastering Excel

(Project 10G–Analysis continued)

1. **Start** Excel, and then from your student files, open the file **e10G_Analysis**. Rename **Sheet1** as **Recreation** and then change the **Tab Color** to **Blue, Accent 1, Lighter 40%**. Rename **Sheet2** as **Parks** and then change the **Tab Color** to **Red, Accent 2, Lighter 40%**. Rename **Sheet3** as **Community Outreach** and then change the **Tab Color** to **Olive Green, Accent 3, Lighter 40%**. **Save** the workbook in your **Excel Chapter 10** folder as **10G_Analysis_Firstname_Lastname**

2. Display the **Recreation** worksheet, and then group the three worksheets. Select the range **A1:A2**, change the **Font** to **Cambria**, the **Font Size** to **16**, apply **Bold**, and then apply a **Fill Color** of **Aqua, Accent 5, Lighter 40%**. **Merge & Center** the two worksheet titles across the ranges **A1:D1** and **A2:D2**. Select the years in the range **B4:D4** and apply **Bold**, and **Center alignment**. Select the **Salaries** data in the range **B5:D5**, apply **Accounting Number Format** with **zero decimal places**, and then select the range **A5:D5** and apply **Bold** and **Italic**. Use **Format Painter** to copy the formatting from cell **A5** to cell **A7** and to cell **A14**.

3. Verify that the worksheets are still grouped, and then in **row 14**, sum each year's data for *Expenses*. Apply **Bold** and **Italic** to the totals. Beginning with **Comma Style** and using **zero decimal places**, apply appropriate financial formatting to the *Expenses* data, *without* a Top and Double Bottom Border. Instead, to the range **B14:D14**, apply only a **Top Border**.

4. Ungroup the worksheets and verify that the formatting and editing changes that you made in Steps 2 and 3 were applied to all three worksheets. On the **Recreation** worksheet, **Copy** the text in cell **A16**, and then **Paste** it to the same location in the

Parks worksheet and **Community Outreach** worksheet.

5. Display the **Recreation** worksheet and press Esc to cancel the moving border. Group the three worksheets. In cell **B16**, construct a formula that adds the *2008 Salaries* in cell **B5** and the *2008 Total Expenses* in cell **B14**. Fill the formula across the remaining two years, and then with the range **B16:D16** still selected, apply a **Bottom Double Border**. Select the range **A16:D16**, and then apply **Bold** and **Italic**.

6. With the worksheets still grouped, in cell **A18**, type **Total Departmental Increase** In cell **C18**, construct a formula that calculates the percent increase of the *Total Departmental Increase* for *2009* from *2008*. Your result is *0.003307521*, an increase of less than 1%. Apply **Percent Style** formatting with **two decimal places** for a result of *0.33%*. Copy the formula to the right for the year 2010; in this year, the percentage increase was more significant—*8.27%*. To the range **A18:D18**, apply **Bold**, **Italic**, and a **Fill Color** using **Aqua, Accent 5, Lighter 40%**.

7. With the worksheets still grouped, in cell **A20**, type **Projected Budget Years 2010 – 2012** and then use **Format Painter** to copy the format from cell **A1** to cell **A20**. In cell **A22**, type **Forecasted Increase** In cell **A24**, type **Year** and in cell **A25**, type **Forecasted Total Budget** Apply **AutoFit** to **column A**. In the range **B24:D24**, enter a pattern of years from 2010 through 2012, and then **Center** and **Bold** the years. In cell **B22**, type **8.5%** which will display as *8.50%*. To the range **A22:B22**, apply **Bold** and **Italic**.

8. With the worksheets still grouped, in cell **B25**, construct a formula that references

(Project 10G–Analysis continues on the next page)

(Project 10G–Analysis continued)

cell **D16**—the *Total Department* expenses for *2010*. In cell **C25**, construct a formula that calculates the *Forecasted Total Budget* for *2011* based on the 8.5% increase in cell **B22**. Be sure to make the reference to cell **B22** absolute. (The result might display as being too wide for the cell.) **Copy** the formula to cell **D25**, and then use **Format Painter** to copy the formatting from cell **B25** to the range **C25:D25**.

9. **Save** the changes you have made thus far. **Insert** a new worksheet, rename the worksheet **Summary** and then change the **Tab Color** to **Orange, Accent 6, Lighter 40%**. In cell **A1**, type **Golden Grove Parks and Recreation** In cell **A2**, type **Forecast Summary** In cell **A3**, type **Years 2010 to 2012** In the range **B5:D5**, enter the years **2010** and **2011** and **2012** Apply **Bold** and **Center** to the years. In the range **A6:A9**, enter the row titles **Recreation** and **Parks** and **Community Outreach** and **Total** Widen **column A** to **230** pixels. Widen columns **B:D** to **95** pixels.

10. **Merge & Center** each of the three worksheet titles across **columns A:D**, and then change the **Font** to **Cambria**, the **Font Size** to **16**, and apply a **Fill Color** of **Aqua, Accent 5, Lighter 40%**.

11. In cell **B6**, enter a formula that references the **Forecasted Total Budget** for **2010** from cell **B25** in the **Recreation** worksheet. Fill the formula across through cell **D6**, and then construct similar formulas for the **Forecasted Total Budget** amounts from the **Parks** worksheet and the **Community Outreach** worksheet. Calculate totals for each year in **row 9**. Beginning with **Comma Style**, apply appropriate financial formatting to the data with **zero decimal places**.

12. **Save** your changes. Using the data in the range **A6:D8**, insert a line chart using the **Line with Markers** chart type. Position the upper left corner of the chart inside the upper left corner of cell **A11**, apply **Chart Style 2**, and then edit the data source so that the **Horizontal (Category) Axis** displays the years in the range **B5:D5**. Insert a chart title in the **Above Chart** position with the text **Three-Year Budget Forecast**

13. Click any cell to deselect the chart. Move the **Summary** worksheet to become the first worksheet in the workbook, and then group the worksheets. Center the worksheets in the workbook **Horizontally** on the page. Insert a footer on the left side with the **File Name**. Ungroup the worksheets. Adjust the width of the chart so that it is slightly inside the right boundary of **column D** to display attractively below the data. Return to **Normal** view, deselect the chart, and display the top of the worksheet.

14. **Save** your workbook, and then examine your worksheets in **Print Preview**. **Print** or submit electronically as directed. If the worksheets are grouped, all the worksheets will print. If the worksheets are not grouped, click **Entire workbook** to print all the sheets. Determine if you are to print formulas for any or all of the worksheets in this workbook. To print formulas, refer to Activity 9.17 in Project 9A.

15. If you printed your formulas, be sure to redisplay the worksheet by pressing Ctrl + `. From the Office menu, click **Close**. If you are prompted to save changes, click No. **Exit** Excel.

End **You have completed Project 10G**

Content-Based Assessments

Mastering Excel

Project 10H — *GO!* Fix It

In this project, you will construct a solution by applying any combination of the skills you practiced from the Objectives in Projects 10A and 10B.

The Golden Grove City Council has maintained the same pool pass fee structure for the past six years. It has asked staff to provide information on attendance and receipts, to see if an increase in fees is warranted. Your task is to review and correct a draft workbook containing this information and to make revenue projections.

For Project 10H, you will need the following file:

e10H_Pool_Passes

**You will save your workbook as
10H_Pool_Passes_Firstname_Lastname**

From the student files that accompany this textbook, open the file **e10H_Pool_Passes**, and then save the file in your chapter folder as **10H_Pool_Passes_Firstname_Lastname**

This workbook contains five errors that you must find and correct. Read and examine the document, and then edit to correct the errors that you find. Types of errors could include:

- Spelling, grammar, and punctuation errors in cells, charts, worksheet tabs, or file names.

- Errors in data entry and workbook layout. Formatting errors in text, numbers, alignment, indents and spacing, tabs, wrapping, merge and center, text direction and orientation, fonts, borders, patterns, protection, AutoFormat, conditional formatting, data sort, filter, and validation.

- Formula and function errors such as incorrect and missing formulas, error indicators and values, relative versus absolute cell referencing, What-If Analysis, Paste Special, function arguments, and Goal Seek.

- Errors in object design, layout, and formatting, for example chart type, location, data source, elements, size, scale, positioning, pictures, and hyperlinks.

- Row and column formatting errors such as height, width, and AutoFit.

- Worksheet, tab design, and formatting errors such as missing or blank worksheets, worksheet tab colors, and locations.

- Page setup errors such as page orientation and scaling, margins and centering, headers and footers, sheet gridlines, and row and column headings.

(Project 10H–*GO!* Fix It continues on the next page)

(Project 10H–*GO!* Fix It continued)

To complete the project you should know:

- In your finished workbook, the grand total in Cell E36 on the Summary worksheet should be $6,193,765.

- It is efficient to work from the last worksheet to the first when looking for errors.

- Formula errors and omissions in a range of cells count as a single error.

- A chart title should be inserted above the chart, entitled *Revenue from Pool Passes 2003–2008* and formatted as Verdana, 18 pt bold.

- All the workbook pages should be centered horizontally.

Save the changes you have made, add the file name to the footers, and then submit as directed.

 You have completed Project 10H ——————————

Outcomes-Based Assessments

Rubric

The following outcomes-based assessments are *open-ended assessments*. That is, there is no specific correct result; your result will depend on your approach to the information provided. Make *Professional Quality* your goal. Use the following scoring rubric to guide you in *how* to approach the problem and then to evaluate *how well* your approach solves the problem.

The *criteria*—Software Mastery, Content, Format and Layout, and Process—represent the knowledge and skills you have gained that you can apply to solving the problem. The *levels of performance*—Professional Quality, Approaching Professional Quality, or Needs Quality Improvements—help you and your instructor evaluate your result.

	Your completed project is of Professional Quality if you:	**Your completed project is Approaching Professional Quality if you:**	**Your completed project Needs Quality Improvements if you:**
1-Software Mastery	Choose and apply the most appropriate skills, tools, and features and identify efficient methods to solve the problem.	Choose and apply some appropriate skills, tools, and features, but not in the most efficient manner.	Choose inappropriate skills, tools, or features, or are inefficient in solving the problem.
2-Content	Construct a solution that is clear and well organized, contains content that is accurate, appropriate to the audience and purpose, and is complete. Provide a solution that contains no errors of spelling, grammar, or style.	Construct a solution in which some components are unclear, poorly organized, inconsistent, or incomplete. Misjudge the needs of the audience. Have some errors in spelling, grammar, or style, but the errors do not detract from comprehension.	Construct a solution that is unclear, incomplete, or poorly organized; contains some inaccurate or inappropriate content; and contains many errors of spelling, grammar, or style. Do not solve the problem.
3-Format and Layout	Format and arrange all elements to communicate information and ideas, clarify function, illustrate relationships, and indicate relative importance.	Apply appropriate format and layout features to some elements, but not others. Overuse features, causing minor distraction.	Apply format and layout that does not communicate information or ideas clearly. Do not use format and layout features to clarify function, illustrate relationships, or indicate relative importance. Use available features excessively, causing distraction.
4-Process	Use an organized approach that integrates planning, development, self-assessment, revision, and reflection.	Demonstrate an organized approach in some areas, but not others; or, use an insufficient process of organization throughout.	Do not use an organized approach to solve the problem.

Excel
chapterten

Problem Solving

Project 10I — Fire Stations

In this project, you will construct a solution by applying any combination of the skills you practiced in the Objectives covered in Projects 10A and 10B.

For Project 10I, you will need the following file:

New blank Excel workbook

You will save your workbook as
10I_Fire_Stations_Firstname_Lastname

The City of Golden Grove has approved a bond measure for the construction of three new fire stations. Using the information provided, create a workbook that the City Controller can present to the City Council that details construction costs covered by the bond measure. Design your workbook so that the data for each fire station is on a separate worksheet. First, group the sheets to apply formatting and type the row and column titles that will be the same across all sheets; this will help you avoid unnecessary typing and formatting. Then, ungroup the sheets, include the fire station location at the top of each worksheet, and type the costs into each sheet. To type the costs, it may be helpful to select the range first so that the movement of the insertion point is confined to the range.

Grand Avenue Fire Station Costs	Land	Design	Construction
Phase 1	13840320	343900	2209384
Phase 2	1102984	230098	3384950
Phase 3	1920384	119739	6937409

South Edison Fire Station Costs	Land	Design	Construction
Phase 1	1866428	459320	1938400
Phase 2	293040	664739	6790474
Phase 3	288730	193804	8498502

Hill Street Fire Station Costs	Land	Design	Construction
Phase 1	394058	484927	1849023
Phase 2	1293846	559680	7593084
Phase 3	129800	583920	5890503

(Project 10I–Fire Stations continues on the next page)

Problem Solving

(Project 10I–Fire Stations continued)

For all of the worksheets, calculate totals for each Phase (rows) and for each type of cost (columns). Insert a worksheet that summarizes, for each fire station, the total costs by type of cost (Land, Design, and Construction). Sum the columns. On each worksheet, use borders, fill colors, and font styles and sizes to create a professional worksheet. Add a footer to each worksheet that includes the file name and center the worksheets on the page. Save the workbook as **10I_Fire_Stations_Firstname_Lastname** and submit it as directed.

End **You have completed Project 10I** ——————————

Outcomes-Based Assessments

Excel
Problem Solving

Project 10J — Water Usage

In this project, you will construct a solution by applying any combination of the skills you practiced in the Objectives covered in Projects 10A and 10B.

For Project 10J, you will need the following file:

New blank Excel workbook

You will save your workbook as 10J_Water_Usage_Firstname_Lastname

Golden Grove is a growing community and the City Council has requested an analysis of future water needs. In this project, you will create a worksheet for the Department of Water and Power that contains data regarding past residential water usage and that forecasts water usage in the future. Create a worksheet with the following data:

Year	2002	2004	2006	2008	2010
Water Use in Acre Feet	62500	68903	73905	76044	80342

Calculate the percent increase in water usage from 2002 to 2004, and then for 2006, 2008, and 2010. Using Project 10B as a guide, add a section to the worksheet to calculate the projected water usage for the years 2010 to 2018 in two-year increments. The 2010 amount is 80,342. Add a comparison of estimates section to the worksheet with three forecasted increases: 4%, 6%, and 9%. Include a worksheet title and use formatting and editing techniques that you practiced in this chapter so that the worksheet looks attractive and professional. Add the file name to the footer. Save the workbook as **10J_Water_Usage_Firstname_Lastname** and submit it as directed.

End You have completed Project 10J

Problem Solving

Project 10K—Schools

In this project, you will construct a solution by applying any combination of the skills you practiced in the Objectives in Projects 10A and 10B.

For Project 10K, you will need the following file:

New blank Excel workbook

**You will save your workbook as
10K_Schools_Firstname_Lastname**

As the city of Golden Grove grows, the school district must plan for additional students that will enroll in the elementary, middle, and high schools. In this project, you will create a workbook that contains enrollment projections for the next four years. First, create three worksheets containing the following information:

Elementary Schools	2008	2009	2010	2011	2012
Projected Increase		2%	3.5%	7%	5%
Wyndham	1350				
Warm Creek	956				
Los Serranos	1175				
Hidden Canyon	1465				
Butterfield	854				

Middle Schools	2008	2009	2010	2011	2012
Projected Increase		4.5%	5.75%	3%	3.5%
Townsend	1194				
Canyon Hills	1575				
Golden Springs	1392				

High Schools	2008	2009	2010	2011	2012
Projected Increase		6%	7.5%	4%	2.75%
Poppy Hills	2276				
Diamond Ranch	3150				

On each sheet, create formulas in the 2009 column that increase the 2008 enrollment by the Projected Increase percent. Create similar formulas for each year, increasing the previous year's enrollment by the Projected Increase percent. Calculate totals by year. Insert a line chart on each sheet with the years on the category horizontal axis. Create a summary sheet that includes the total enrollment by year for each *type* of school—Elementary Schools, Middle Schools, and High Schools—and then calculate totals for each year. Use formatting and editing techniques that you practiced in this chapter so that the workbook looks attractive and professional. Add the file name to the footer. Save the workbook as **10K_Schools_Firstname_Lastname** and submit it as directed.

End You have completed Project 10K ——————

More on your Student CD

The instructions for the following additional end-of-chapter projects are on your student CD in the folder 03_additional_end_of_chapter_projects.

Content-Based Assessments	
Project L Mastering Excel	Apply the skills you practiced in Project A.
Project M Mastering Excel	Apply the skills you practiced in Project B.
Project N Business Running Case	Apply the skills you practiced in Projects A and B while helping an entrepreneur with the daily tasks of running a business.
	In each chapter, this project focuses on applying the skills you have practiced in Projects A and B to a business. The project related to this business runs throughout the textbook. You will see how the Office applications relate to the day-to-day operation of a small business called Nelson Architectural Planning.

Outcomes-Based Assessments	
Project O Problem Solving	Construct a solution by applying any combination of the skills you practiced from Projects A and B.
Project P Problem Solving	Construct a solution by applying any combination of the skills you practiced from Projects A and B.
Project Q You and GO!	Construct a solution that applies to your own life by applying any combination of the skills you practiced from Projects A and B.
Project R GO! with Help	Practice using Microsoft Office's Help Feature.
Project S Group Business Running Case	Work as part of a group to apply the skills you have gained thus far to help the Bell Orchid Hotel Group achieve its business goals.

Multimedia

The following multimedia accompany this textbook:

Companion Web site *www.prenhall.com/go*	An interactive Web site designed to reinforce and test your understanding of the skills in this chapter.
AV-EDDs	In the folder in the front of this book you will find videos that demonstrate the objectives of the A and B projects in this chapter. These may help you understand how to complete the projects in this book.
Video Podcasts	In the folder in the front of this book are videos that can be played on your iPod, MP3 player, or computer. These videos demonstrate how to complete the more challenging objectives in this textbook.

chapter eleven

Using Functions and Tables

OBJECTIVES

At the end of this chapter you will be able to:

1. Use SUM, AVERAGE, MEDIAN, MIN, and MAX Functions
2. Use COUNTIF and IF Functions, and Apply Conditional Formatting
3. Use a Date Function
4. Freeze Panes and Create an Excel Table
5. Format and Print a Large Worksheet

6. Use Financial Functions
7. Use Goal Seek
8. Create a Data Table

OUTCOMES

Mastering these objectives will enable you to:

PROJECT 11A

Track Inventory by Using Math, Logical, and Statistical Functions and by Creating an Excel Table

PROJECT 11B

Make Financial Decisions by Using Financial Functions and What-If Analysis

Adamantine Jewelry, Inc.

Adamantine Jewelry is based in Milan, Italy, one of the world's leading centers for fashion and design. The company's designers take inspiration from nature, cultural artifacts, and antiquities to produce affordable, fashionable jewelry that is sold through major retailers around the world. With a 40-year history, the company is well respected among its retail customers and has recently expanded to online and television retailers. In addition to women's bracelets, necklaces, rings, and earrings, the company also produces sport and fashion watches for men and women.

© Paul Harris and Anne Heslope / Dorling Kindersley

Using Functions and Tables

In this chapter, you will design worksheets that use the library of formulas and procedures provided with Excel to perform specific functions. You will also use more What-If Analysis tools. Using these tools will make your worksheets valuable tools for analyzing data and making financial decisions.

Project 11A Milan Inventory

In Activities 11.01 through 11.13, you will edit a worksheet for Rose Elleni, Vice President of Production, detailing the current inventory of two product types at the Milan production facility. Your completed worksheet will look similar to Figure 11.1.

For Project 11A, you will need the following file:

e011A_Milan_Inventory

You will save your workbook as
11A_Milan_Inventory_Firstname_Lastname

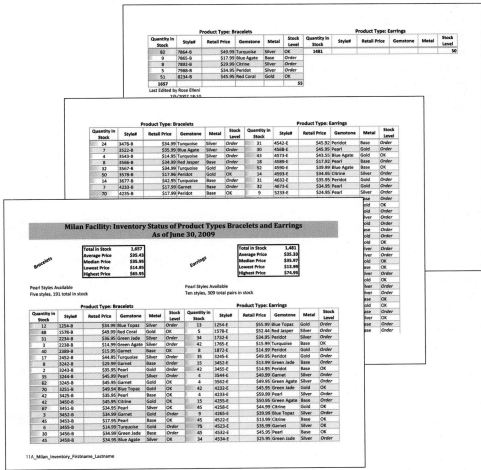

Figure 11.1
Project 11A—Milan Inventory

Objective 1
Use SUM, AVERAGE, MEDIAN, MIN, and MAX Functions

A *function* is a predefined formula—a formula that Excel has already built for you—that performs calculations by using specific values in a particular order or structure.

Activity 11.01 Using the SUM, AVERAGE, and MEDIAN Functions

In this activity, you will use the SUM and AVERAGE functions to gather information about the product inventory.

1 **Start** Excel. From the student files that accompany this text, locate and open **e11A_Milan_Inventory**. From the **Office** menu 🅱, display the **Save As** dialog box, and then navigate to the location where you are storing your projects for this chapter. Create a **New Folder** named **Excel Chapter 11**.

2 In the **File name** box, type **11A_Milan_Inventory_Firstname_Lastname** and then click **Save** or press Enter.

3 Scroll down the worksheet, and notice that the worksheet contains data related to two product types—*Bracelets* and *Earrings*—and then for each product type, information regarding the *Quantity in Stock*, *Style#*, *Retail Price*, *Gemstone*, and *Metal* is included.

4 In cell **A1**, type **Milan Facility: Inventory Status of Product Types Bracelets and Earrings** and in cell **A2** type **As of June 30, 2009 Merge and Center** 🗗▾ each worksheet title across columns **A:L**. Format both titles with **Bold** B, change the **Font** to **Cambria**, change the **Font Size** to **16**, and then apply a **Fill Color** ◇▾ of **Dark Blue, Text 2, Lighter 60%**.

5 In cell **A4**, type **Total in Stock** In cell **A5**, type **Average Price** In cell **A6**, type **Median Price** Click cell **B4**. Click the **Formulas tab**, and then in the **Function Library group**, click the **AutoSum** button. Compare your screen with Figure 11.2.

> The **SUM function** that you have used is a predefined formula that adds all the numbers in a selected range of cells.

Figure 11.2

AutoSum button

Function Library group

Formulas tab selected

SUM function started in cell

Worksheet titles formatted

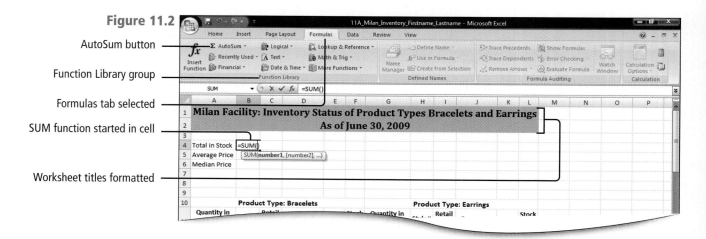

6 With the insertion point blinking in the function, select the range **A12:A66**, dragging down as necessary, and then press Enter. Scroll up to view the top of your worksheet, and notice your result in cell **B4**, *1657*.

7 Click cell **B4**, look at the **Formula Bar**, and then compare your screen with Figure 11.3.

> The values in parentheses are the ***arguments***—the values that an Excel function uses to perform calculations or operations. In this instance, the argument consists of the values in the range A12:A66.

Figure 11.3

SUM function in Formula Bar ⎯⎯⎯

Number of Bracelets in stock ⎯⎯⎯

Argument in parentheses ⎯⎯⎯

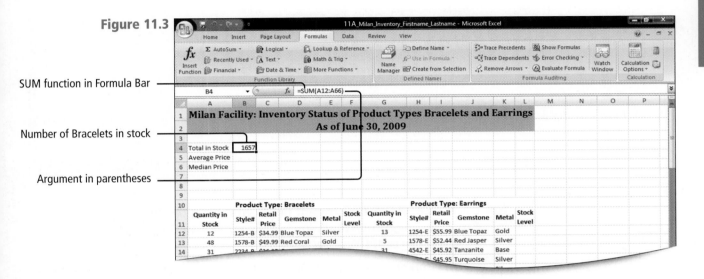

8 Click cell **B5**. In the **Function Library group**, click the **More Functions** button, point to **Statistical**, in the list, point to **AVERAGE**, and then compare your screen with Figure 11.4.

> ***Statistical functions*** are prewritten formulas that analyze a group of measurements.

Figure 11.4

More Functions button —

Statistical category —

List of Statistical functions —

AVERAGE ScreenTip —

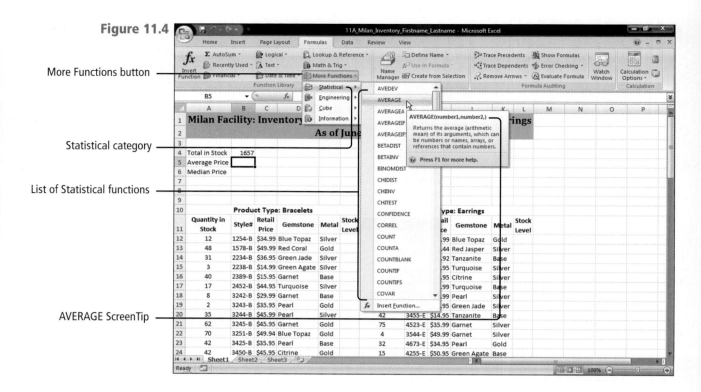

9 Click **AVERAGE**, and then if necessary, drag the title bar of the **Function Arguments** dialog box down and to the right so you can view the **Formula Bar** and cell **B5**.

> The Function Arguments dialog box for the AVERAGE function displays. The *AVERAGE function* is a formula that adds a group of values, and then divides the result by the number of values in the group.

> In the cell, the Formula Bar, and the dialog box, Excel proposes to average the value in cell B4. Recall that Excel functions will propose a range if data is above or to the left of a selected cell. Because you want to average the values in the range C12:C66—and *not* cell B4—you must edit the proposed range.

10 In the **Function Arguments** dialog box, click in the **Number1** box to display the insertion point. Delete the existing text, type **c12:c66** and then compare your screen with Figure 11.5.

> The result displays in the dialog box.

Figure 11.5

Formula Bar displays function and argument

Function Arguments dialog box for AVERAGE function

Range of cells to average

Result displays

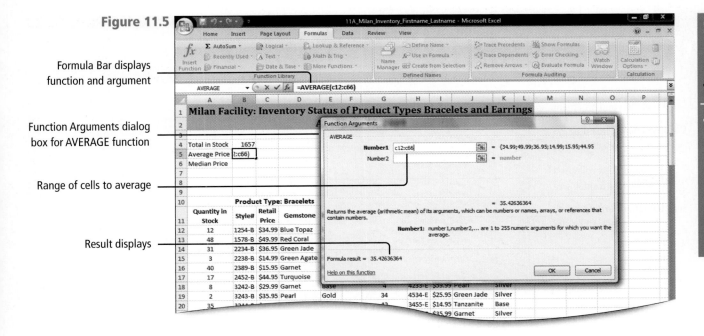

11 In the **Function Arguments** dialog box, click **OK**.

The result indicates that the average Retail Price of all Bracelets is *$35.43*.

12 Click cell **B6**. In the **Function Library group**, click the **More Functions** button, display the list of **Statistical** functions, scroll down as necessary, and then click **MEDIAN**.

The ***MEDIAN function*** is a statistical function commonly used to describe a group of data—you have likely seen it used to describe the price of houses in a particular geographical area. The MEDIAN function finds the *middle value* that has as many values *above* it in the group as are *below* it. It differs from AVERAGE in that the result is not affected as much by a single value that is greatly different from the others.

13 In the **Function Arguments** dialog box, to the right of the **Number1** box, click the **Collapse Dialog** button ▦—the square with the red arrow.

The dialog box collapses to a small size containing only space for the first argument. Now you can see more of your worksheet data.

14 Select the range **C12:C66**, and then compare your screen with Figure 11.6.

Figure 11.6

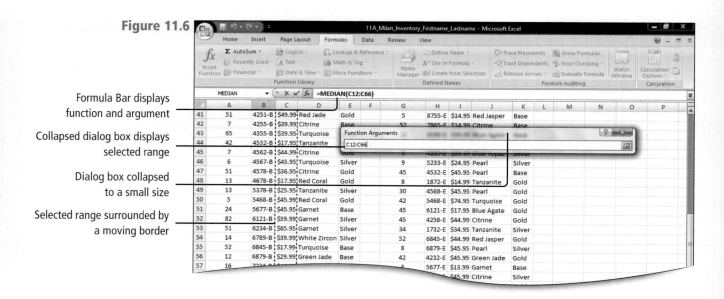

Formula Bar displays function and argument

Collapsed dialog box displays selected range

Dialog box collapsed to a small size

Selected range surrounded by a moving border

15 Press Enter.

The dialog box expands to its original size and the selected range displays as the argument in the Number1 box. When entering arguments into a Function Arguments dialog box, you can either select the range of cells in this manner, or type the range into the argument box.

16 In the lower right corner of the **Function Arguments** dialog box, click **OK**. Save your workbook.

Your result is *$35.95*—in the range of prices, $35.95 is the middle value. Half of all Bracelet products are priced *above* $35.95 and half are priced *below* $35.95.

17 Select the range **A4:A6**, right-click over the selection, and then click **Copy**. Point to cell **G4**, right-click, and then click **Paste**. Press Esc to cancel the moving border.

18 Scroll to the bottom of your worksheet and notice that the **Earrings** product type ends in **row 61**. Then, in cell **H4**, use the technique you just practiced to **SUM** the total number of **Earrings** in stock.

19 In cell **H5**, use the **AVERAGE** function to display the average **Retail Price** of the **Earrings** product type. In cell **H6**, use the **MEDIAN** function to display the median value of the **Retail Price** for **Earrings**.

20 Select cells **B4** and **H4**, apply **Comma Style** with **zero decimal places**, click any cell to deselect, and then compare your screen with Figure 11.7.

Figure 11.7

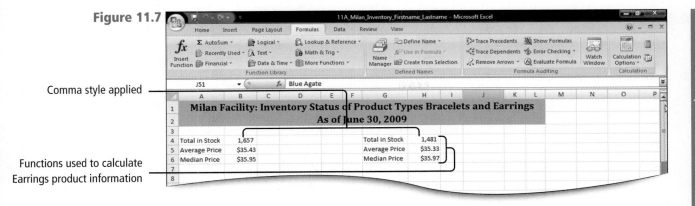

Comma style applied

Functions used to calculate Earrings product information

21 **Save** your workbook.

Activity 11.02 Using the MIN and MAX Functions

The *MIN function* determines the smallest value in a selected range of values. The *MAX function* determines the largest value in a selected range of values.

1 In cell **A7**, type **Lowest Price** and then in cell **A8**, type **Highest Price**

2 Click cell **B7**. On the **Formulas tab**, in the **Function Library group**, click the **More Functions** button, display the list of **Statistical** functions, scroll as necessary, and then click **MIN**.

3 At the right end of the **Number1** box, click the **Collapse Dialog** button, select the range **C12:C66**, and then press Enter. Click **OK**.

The lowest retail price in the Bracelets product group is *$14.95*.

4 In cell **B8**, using a similar technique, insert the **MAX** function to determine the highest **Retail Price** in the **Bracelets** product type.

The highest Retail Price in the Bracelets product type is *$65.95*.

5 Copy the range **A7:A8** and paste it in cell **G7**. Then in cells **H7** and **H8**, use the **MIN** and **MAX** functions to calculate the lowest and highest **Retail Price** for products in the **Earrings** product type. Compare your screen with Figure 11.8.

Figure 11.8

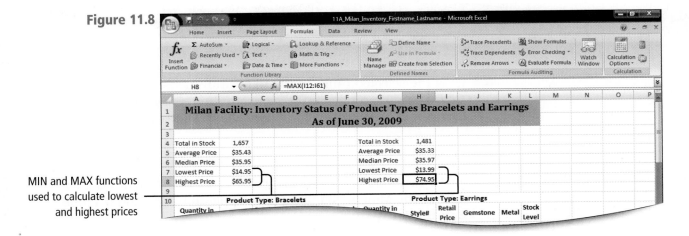

MIN and MAX functions used to calculate lowest and highest prices

6 **Save** 🖫 your workbook.

Activity 11.03 Moving Data, Adding Borders, and Rotating Text

Recall that you can select and move a range of cells containing formulas or functions. Use borders to emphasize a range of cells and to draw the reader's eye to a specific portion of a worksheet. Similarly, use rotated text to draw attention to data on your worksheet.

1 Select the range **A4:B8**. Point to the right edge of the selected range to display the ⬚ pointer, and then compare your screen with Figure 11.9.

Figure 11.9

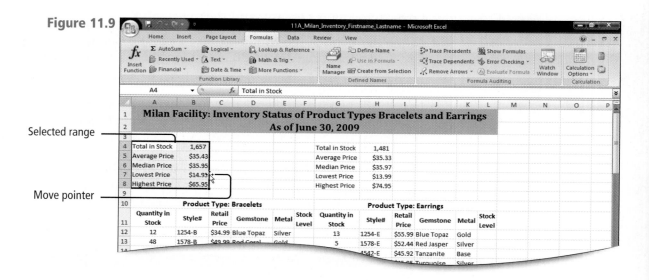

Selected range

Move pointer

2 Drag the selected range to the right until the ScreenTip displays *C4:D8*, and then release the mouse button. Select **columns C:D**, and then apply **AutoFit** to adjust the column widths.

3 By using the same technique, move the range **G4:H8** to the range **I4:J8**. Select **columns I:J**, and then apply **AutoFit**.

4 Select the nonadjacent ranges **C4:D8** and **I4:J8**, right-click to display the Mini toolbar, and then apply **Bold** **B** and a **Thick Box Border** ⬚ ▾.

5 In cell **A6**, type **Bracelets** Select the range **A5:A7**, right-click over the selection, and then click **Format Cells**. In the **Format Cells** dialog box, click the **Alignment tab**. Under **Text control**, select the **Merge cells** check box.

6 In the upper right portion of the dialog box, under **Orientation**, point to the **red diamond**, and then drag the diamond upward until the **Degrees** box indicates **30**. Alternatively, type the number of degrees directly into the Degrees box. Compare your screen with Figure 11.10.

Figure 11.10

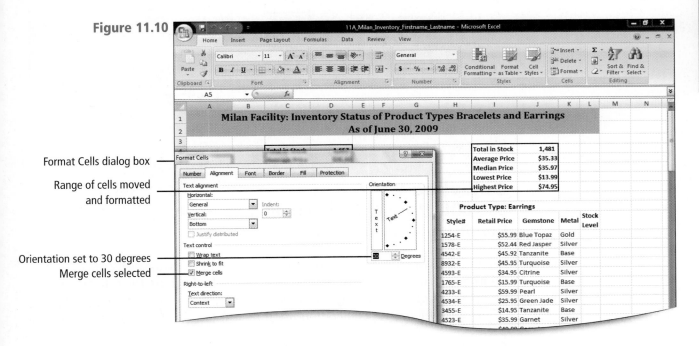

Format Cells dialog box

Range of cells moved and formatted

Orientation set to 30 degrees

Merge cells selected

7 In the lower right corner of the **Format Cells** dialog box, click **OK**. With the merged cell still selected, display the Mini toolbar, change the **Font Size** to **12**, and then apply **Bold** B and **Italic** I.

8 On the **Home tab**, in the **Alignment group**, apply **Center** align- ment and **Middle Align** .

9 In cell **G5**, type **Earrings** Point to the merged cell **A5** and right-click. On the Mini toolbar, click the **Format Painter** button , and then click cell **G5** to copy the formatting. Compare your screen with Figure 11.11.

Figure 11.11

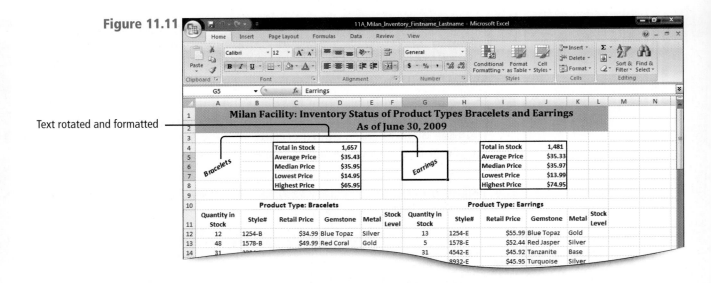

Text rotated and formatted

10 **Save** your workbook.

Objective 2
Use COUNTIF and IF Functions, and Apply Conditional Formatting

Recall that statistical functions analyze a group of measurements. Another group of Excel functions, referred to as *logical functions*, test for specific conditions. Logical functions typically use conditional tests to determine whether specified conditions—called *criteria*—are true or false.

Activity 11.04 Using the COUNTIF Function

The **COUNTIF function** counts the number of cells within a range that meet the given condition—the criteria that you provide. The COUNTIF function has two arguments—the range of cells to check and the criteria.

Adamantine's pearl bracelets and earrings will be featured on an upcoming segment of a TV shopping channel in Italy. In this activity, you will use the COUNTIF function to determine the number of pearl styles currently available in inventory.

1 From the **row heading area**, point to **row 10**, right-click, and then click **Insert**. Press F4 two times to repeat the last action and thus insert three blank rows.

2 Click cell **D4**, look at the **Formula Bar**, and then notice that the arguments of the **SUM** function adjusted and refer to **rows 15:69**.

> The referenced range updates to A15:A69 after you insert the three new rows. In this manner, Excel adjusts the cell references in a formula relative to their new locations.

3 In cell **A10**, type **Pearl Styles Available** and then press Enter. Copy cell **A10**, and then paste it to cell **G10**. Press Esc to cancel the moving border.

4 Click cell **A11**. On the **Formulas tab**, in the **Function Library group**, click the **More Functions** button, and then display the list of **Statistical** functions. Click **COUNTIF**.

> Recall that the COUNTIF function counts the number of cells within a range that meet the given condition.

5 In the **Range** box, click the **Collapse Dialog** button [icon], select the range **D15:D69**, and then press Enter. Click in the **Criteria** box, type **Pearl** and then compare your screen with Figure 11.12.

Figure 11.12

Function displays in Formula Bar

Function Arguments dialog box

Criteria indicated as *Pearl*

Range indicated as *D15:D69*

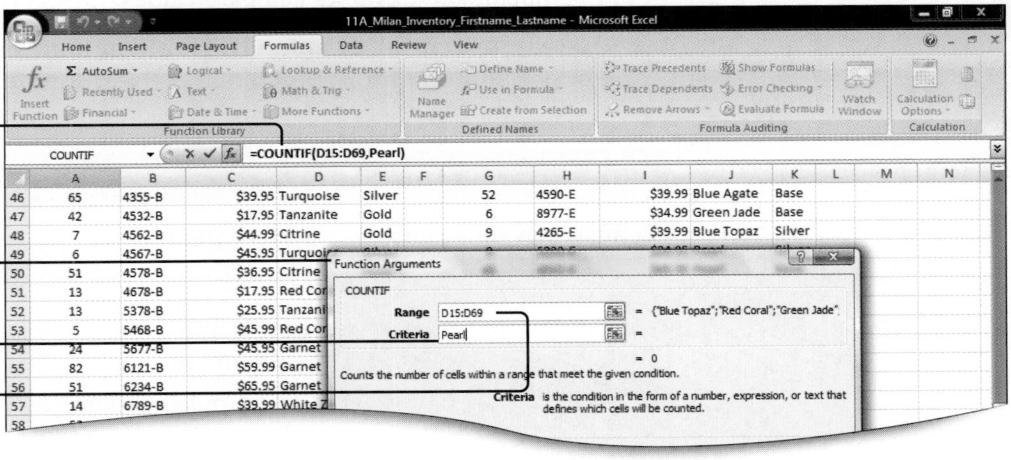

6 In the lower right corner of the **Function Arguments** dialog box, click **OK**.

> Five different styles of Pearl bracelets are available to feature on the TV show.

7 Using the technique you just practiced, in cell **G11**, count the number of **Pearl** styles available in the **Earrings** product type.

> Ten different styles of Pearl earrings are available to feature on the TV show.

8 Select cells **A11** and **G11**, and then on the **Home tab**, in the **Alignment group**, click the **Align Text Left** button [icon].

9 **Save** [icon] your workbook.

Activity 11.05 Using the IF Function and Applying Conditional Formatting

A *logical test* is any value or expression that can be evaluated as being true or false. The *IF function* uses a logical test to check whether a condition is met, and then returns one value if true, and another value if false. For example, *C8=100* is an expression that can be evaluated as true or false. If the value in cell C8 is equal to 100, the expression is true. If the value in cell C8 is not 100, the expression is false.

In this activity, you will use the IF function to determine the inventory stock levels and determine if more products should be ordered.

1 Click cell **F15**. On the **Formulas tab**, in the **Function Library group**, click the **Logical** button, and then in the list, click **IF**. If necessary, drag the title bar of the **Function Arguments** dialog box up so that you can view **row 15** on your screen.

2 With the insertion point in the **Logical_test** box, click cell **A15**, and then type **<40**

> This logical test will look at the value in cell A15, the value of which is *12*, and then determine if the number is less than 40. The expression *<40* includes the < ***comparison operator***, which means *less than*. Comparison operators compare values.

3 Take a moment to examine the table in Figure 11.13 for a list of comparison operator symbols and their definitions.

Comparison Operators

Comparsion Operators	Symbol Definition
=	Equal to
>	Greater than
<	Less than
>=	Greater than or equal to
<=	Less than or equal to
<>	Not equal to

Figure 11.13

4 Press Tab to move the insertion point to the **Value_if_true** box, and then type **Order**

> If the result of the logical test is true—the Quantity in Stock is less than 40—the cell will display the text *Order* indicating that additional product must be ordered.

5 Press Tab to move the insertion point to the **Value_if_false** box, type **OK** and then compare your dialog box with Figure 11.14.

> If the result of the logical test is false—the Quantity in Stock is *not* less than 40—then Excel will display *OK* in the cell.

Figure 11.14

Logical test will determine if value in A15 is less than 40

Value if false (40 or more) will indicate *OK*

Value if true (less than 40) will indicate *Order*

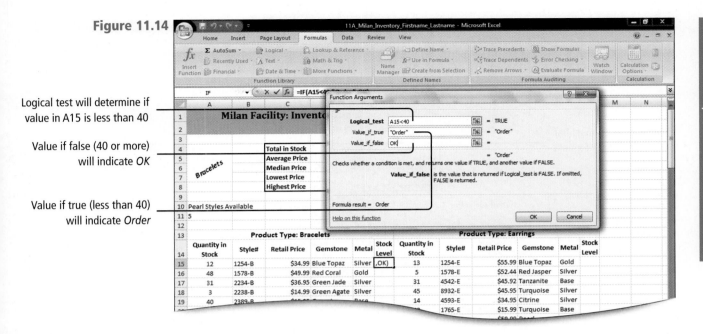

6 Click **OK** to display the result *Order* in cell **F15**. Then, using the fill handle, copy the function down through cell **F69**. Look at cell **A19**, and then look at cell **F19** and notice that the **Stock Level** is indicated as *OK*.

> The comparison operator indicated <40 (less than 40) and thus a value of *exactly* 40 is indicated as OK.

7 Click cell **L15**, and then using the technique you just practiced and a quantity *less than* 40, conduct a logical test on the quantities of **Earrings** in stock. Then, scroll to the upper portion of your worksheet, click cell **L15**, look at the **Formula Bar**, and then compare your screen with Figure 11.15.

Note — Copying Functions

You can also copy the function in cell F15 to cell L15 and the cell references will adjust accordingly.

Figure 11.15

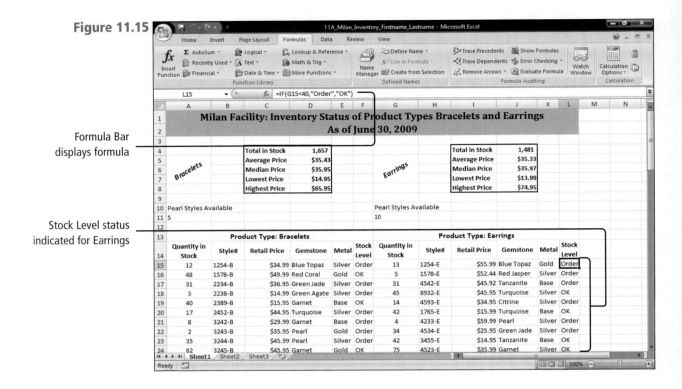

Formula Bar displays formula

Stock Level status indicated for Earrings

---

8 **Save** 📁 your workbook.

Activity 11.06 Applying Conditional Formatting Using Custom Formats and Data Bars

A *conditional format* changes the appearance of a cell range based on a condition—a criteria. If the condition is true, the cell range is formatted based on that condition; if the condition is false, the cell range is *not* formatted based on the condition. In this activity, you will use conditional formatting as another way to draw attention to the Stock Level of products.

1 Select the range **F15:F69**. On the **Home tab**, in the **Styles group**, click the **Conditional Formatting** button. In the list, point to **Highlight Cells Rules**, and then click **Text that Contains**.

2 In the **Text That Contains** dialog box, with the insertion point blinking in the first box, type **Order** In the second box, click the **arrow**, and then in the list, click **Custom Format**.

> The Format Cells dialog box displays. Here you can select any combination of formats to apply to the cell if the condition is true. The custom format that you specify will be applied to any cell in the selected range if it contains the specific text *Order*.

3 In the **Format Cells** dialog box, on the **Font tab**, under **Font style**, click **Bold Italic**. Click the **Color arrow**, and then under **Theme Colors**, click **Dark Blue, Text 2, Darker 25%**. In the lower right corner of the **Format Cells** dialog box, click **OK**. Compare your screen with Figure 11.16.

> Within the selected range, if the cell meets the condition of containing *Order*, the font color will change to Bold Italic, Dark Blue, Text 2 Darker 25%.

Figure 11.16

Text That Contains dialog box

Only cells with the text *Order* will be formatted

Custom Format indicated

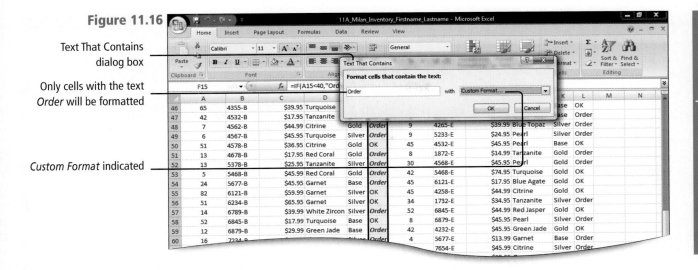

4 In the **Text That Contains** dialog box, click **OK** to apply the conditional formatting.

5 Select the range **A15:A69**. In the **Styles group**, click the **Conditional Formatting** button. In the list, point to **Data Bars**, and then in the **gallery**, click **Orange Data Bar**.

A **data bar** provides a visual cue to the reader about the value of a cell relative to other cells. The length of the data bar represents the value in the cell. A longer bar represents a higher value and a shorter bar represents a lower value. Data bars are useful to quickly identify higher and lower numbers within a large group of data, such as very high or very low levels of inventory.

6 Using the techniques you just practiced, apply the same conditional formatting to the *Stock Level* column for the **Earrings** product type, and then apply the same data bars to indicate the *Quantity of Stock* in inventory. Press [Ctrl] + [Home] to make cell **A1** the active cell, and then compare your screen with Figure 11.17.

Figure 11.17

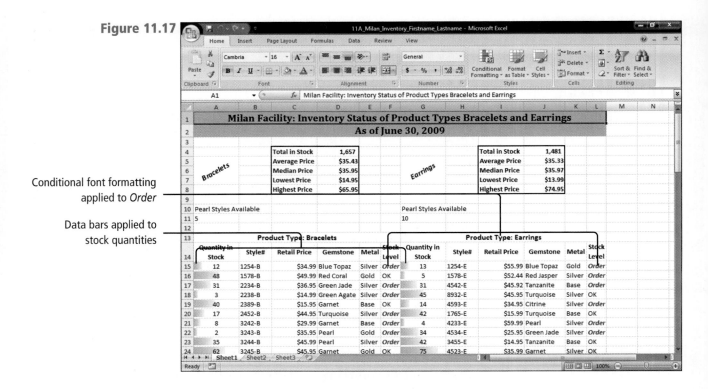

Conditional font formatting applied to *Order*

Data bars applied to stock quantities

7 **Save** 🖫 your workbook.

More Knowledge — Use Format Painter to Copy Conditional Formatting

You can also use Format Painter to apply the same conditional formatting from one range of cells to another.

Activity 11.07 Using Find and Replace

The *Find and Replace* feature searches the cells in a worksheet—or in a selected range—for matches, and then replaces each match with a replacement value of your choice.

Because a quality grade of Tanzanite was not readily available for manufacturing, the pieces listed as having the gemstone Tanzanite were actually set with Peridot. In this activity, you will replace all occurrences of *Tanzanite* with *Peridot*.

1 To the left of the **Formula Bar**, click in the **Name Box**, type **d15:d69,j15:j64** and then press Enter. Alternatively, select the nonadjacent ranges of Gemstones with your mouse.

> The range of cells that contains the gemstone names for both product types is selected. Restrict the find and replace operation to a specific range if there is a possibility that the name occurs elsewhere in the worksheet.

2 On the **Home tab**, in the **Editing group**, click the **Find & Select** button, and then click **Replace**.

3 In the **Find and Replace** dialog box, in the **Find what** box, type **Tanzanite** In the **Replace with** box type **Peridot** and then compare your screen with Figure 11.18.

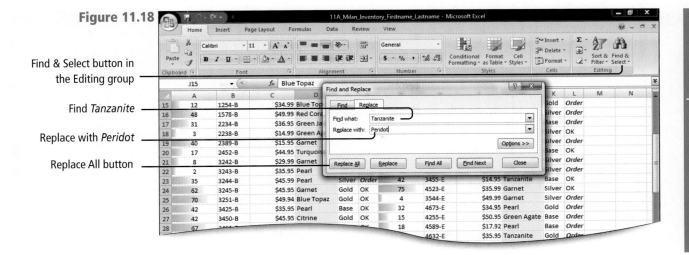

Figure 11.18

Find & Select button in the Editing group

Find *Tanzanite*

Replace with *Peridot*

Replace All button

4 Click the **Replace All** button. In the message box, notice that *12 replacements* were made, and then click **OK**. In the lower right corner of the **Find and Replace** dialog box, click the **Close** button. Click any cell to deselect the ranges.

5 **Save** 🖫 your workbook.

Objective 3
Use a Date Function

Excel can obtain the date and time from the computer's calendar and clock and display this information on your worksheet.

Activity 11.08 Using the NOW Function

The ***NOW function*** retrieves the date and time from your computer's calendar and clock and inserts the information into the selected cell. The result is formatted as a date and time, rather than in the sequential number that Excel uses for dates. This feature is useful to date stamp a worksheet to record when it was last edited.

1 Scroll down to view **row 71**. Click cell **A71**, type **Last Edited by Rose Elleni** and then press Enter.

2 With cell **A72** as the active cell, on the **Formulas tab**, in the **Function Library group**, click the **Date & Time** button. In the list of functions, click **NOW**. Compare your screen with Figure 11.19.

Figure 11.19

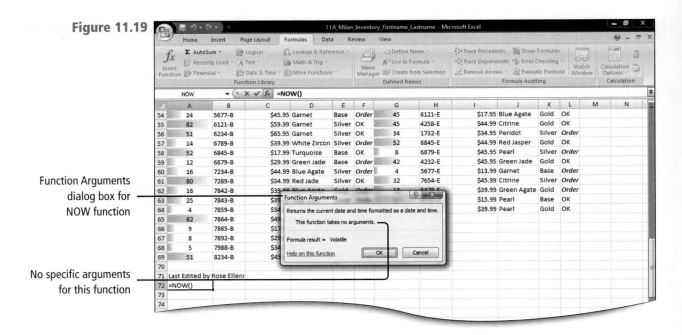

Function Arguments
dialog box for
NOW function

No specific arguments
for this function

3 Take a moment to read the description in the **Function Arguments** dialog box, and notice that this result is *Volatile*.

> The Function Arguments dialog box displays a message indicating that this function does not require an argument. It also states that this function is ***volatile***, meaning the date and time will not remain as entered, but rather the date and time will be updated each time you open this workbook.

4 In the **Function Arguments** dialog box, click **OK** to close the dialog box to display the current date and time in cell **A72**.

5 **Save** 📄 your workbook.

Note — **NOW Function Recalculates When the Workbook Opens**

The NOW function places a sequential number in the cell that corresponds to the date and time at the moment. The NOW function updates this number each time the workbook is opened. If you open a workbook with the NOW function in it and then close the workbook, you will see a message that asks if you want to save the changes. The change to which this message refers is the new date that has been inserted by the NOW function. With the workbook open, you can force the NOW function to update by pressing F9, for example, to update the time.

Objective 4
Freeze Panes and Create an Excel Table

By freezing or splitting panes, you can view two areas of a worksheet and lock rows and columns in one area. When you freeze panes, you select the specific rows or columns that you want to remain visible when scrolling in your worksheet.

To analyze a group of related data, you can convert a range of cells to an ***Excel table***. An Excel table is a series of rows and columns that contains related data that is managed independently from the data in other rows and columns in the worksheet.

Activity 11.09 Freezing and Unfreezing Panes

In a large worksheet, if you scroll down more than 25 rows or scroll beyond column O (the exact row number and column letter varies, depending on your screen resolution), you will no longer see the top rows of your worksheet where identifying information about the data is usually placed. You will likely find it easier to work with your data if you can always view the identifying row or column titles.

The **Freeze Panes** command enables you to select one or more rows or columns and freeze (lock) them into place. The locked rows and columns become separate panes. A **pane** is a portion of a worksheet window bounded by and separated from other portions by vertical or horizontal bars.

1 Press Ctrl + Home to make cell **A1** the active cell. Scroll down until **row 40** displays at the top of your screen, and notice that all of the identifying information in the column titles is out of view.

2 Press Ctrl + Home again, and then select **row 15**. Click the **View tab**, and then in the **Window group**, click the **Freeze Panes** button. In the list, click **Freeze Panes**. Click any cell to deselect the row, and then notice that a line displays along the upper border of **row 15**.

> By selecting row 15, the rows above—rows 1 through 14—are frozen (locked) in place and will not move as you scroll down the worksheet.

3 Watch the row numbers below **row 14**, and then begin to scroll down to bring **row 40** into view again. Compare your screen with Figure 11.20.

> Rows 1:14 remain frozen in place and the remaining rows of data continue to scroll. Use this feature when you have long or wide worksheets.

Figure 11.20

Freeze Panes button in Window group

Freeze Panes command freezes rows 1-14

Row 40 in view

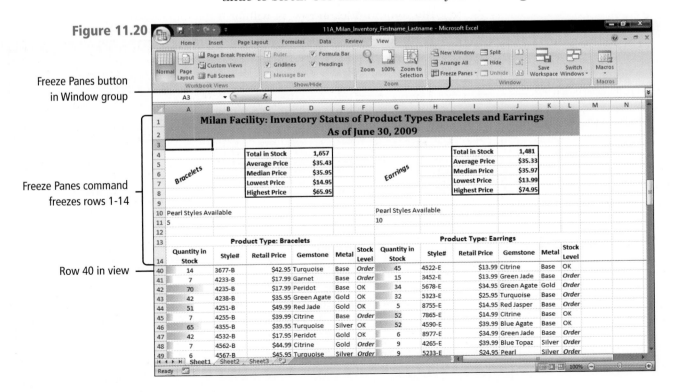

4 In the **Window group**, click the **Freeze Panes** button, and then click **Unfreeze Panes** to unlock all rows and columns.

5 **Save** 🖫 your workbook.

More Knowledge — Freeze Columns or Freeze Both Rows and Columns

You can freeze columns that you want to remain in view on the left. Select the column to the right of the column(s) that you want to remain in view while scrolling to the left, and then click the Freeze Panes command. You can also use the command to freeze both rows and columns; click a *cell* to freeze the rows *above* the cell and the columns to the *left* of the cell.

Activity 11.10 Sorting and Filtering in an Excel Table

Recall that an Excel table is a series of rows and columns with related data that can be managed independently from the data in other rows and columns. For example, in your 11A_Milan_Inventory workbook, you have data for two product types—*Bracelets* and *Earrings*.

To manage several groups of data, you can insert more than one table in the same worksheet. In Activities 11.10 and 11.11, you will create an Excel table for each of the two product types, and then work with each set of data independently of the other.

1 Press [Ctrl] + [Home] to make cell **A1** the active cell. Be sure that you have applied the Unfreeze Panes command—no rows on your worksheet are locked.

2 Select the range **A14:F69**. Click the **Insert tab**, and then in the **Tables group**, click the **Table** button. In the **Create Table** dialog box, if necessary, click to select the **My table has headers** check box, and then compare your screen with Figure 11.21.

The column titles in row 14 will form the table headers.

Figure 11.21

Create Table dialog box

Column titles will form table headers

Range of data selected

Check box selected

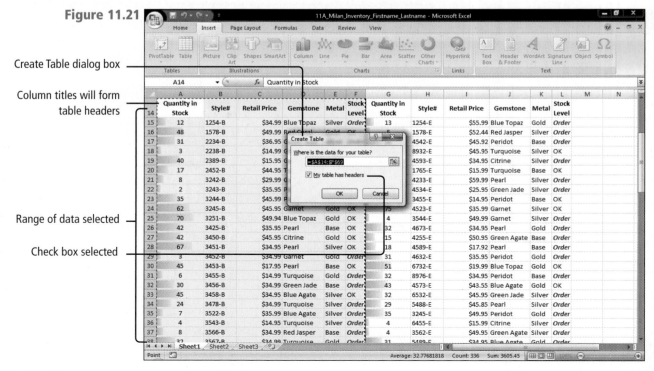

3 In the **Create Table** dialog box, click **OK**. With the range still selected, on the Ribbon notice that the **Table Tools** are active. On the **Design tab**, in the **Table Styles group**, click the **More** button ⬇, and then under **Light**, locate and click **Table Style Light 16**.

4 Press [Ctrl] + [Home] to make cell **A1** the active cell and to cancel the selection, and then compare your screen with Figure 11.22.

> Sorting and filtering arrows display in the table's header row. You can sort tables in ascending or descending order or by color. You can filter tables to show only the data that meets the criteria that you specify, or you can filter by color.

Figure 11.22

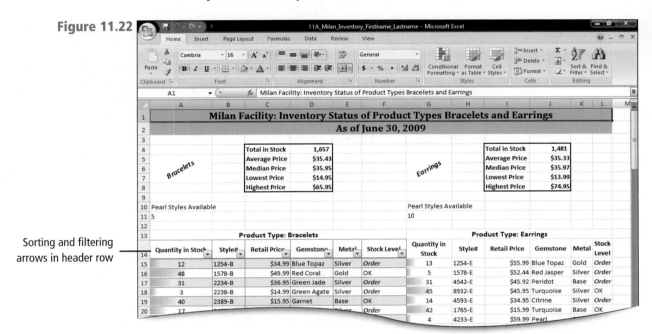

Sorting and filtering arrows in header row

5 In the header row of the table, click the **Retail Price arrow**, and then from the menu, click **Sort Smallest to Largest**. Next to the arrow, notice the small **up arrow** indicating the sort.

> The rows in the table, which includes only columns A:F, are sorted from the lowest retail price to highest retail price. Cells in the same rows in columns G:L are not affected by the sort because the table feature isolates the table cells and treats them independently of other cells outside of the table.

6 In the header row of the table, click the **Gemstone arrow**. From the menu, click **Sort A to Z**. Next to the arrow, notice the small **up arrow** indicating an ascending (A to Z) sort.

> The rows in the table are sorted alphabetically by Gemstone.

7 Click the **Gemstone arrow** again, and then sort from **Z to A**.

> The rows in the table are sorted in reverse alphabetic order by Gemstone name, and the small arrow points downward, indicating a descending (Z to A) sort.

8 Click the **Gemstone arrow** again. On the menu, click the **(Select All)** check box to clear all the check boxes. Click to select only the **Pearl** check box, and then click **OK**. Compare your screen with Figure 11.23.

Only the rows containing *Pearl* in the Gemstone column display, and the remaining rows are hidden from view. A small funnel in the Gemstone arrow indicates that a filter is applied to the data in the table. Additionally, the row numbers display in blue to indicate that some rows are hidden from view. A filter hides the entire row in the worksheet.

Figure 11.23

Funnel indicates that a filter is applied

Blue row numbers indicate some rows are hidden from view

Only bracelets that have *Pearl* as the gemstone display

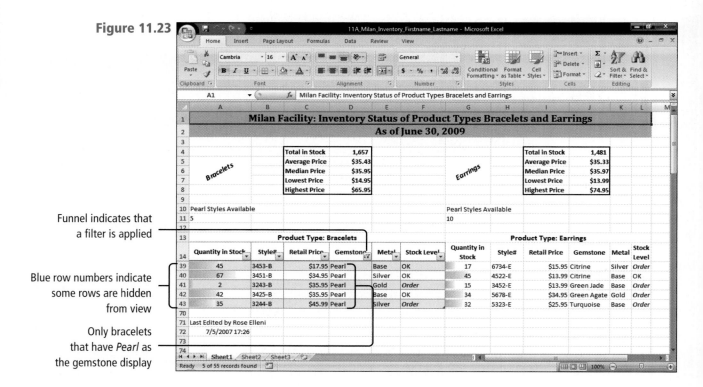

9 Click any cell in the table so that the table is selected. On the Ribbon, click the **Design tab**, and then in the **Table Style Options group**, click to select the **Total Row** check box.

Total displays in cell A70, and in cell F70, the number *5* indicates that five rows are currently displayed.

10 Click cell **A70**, click the **arrow** that displays to the right of cell A70, and then in the list, click **Sum**.

Excel sums only the visible rows in Column A, and indicates that *191* bracelets containing the Gemstone *Pearl* are in stock. In this manner, you can use an Excel table to quickly find information about a group of data.

11 Click cell **A11**, type **Five styles, 191 total in stock** and then press [Enter].

12 In the table header row, click the **Gemstone arrow**, and then on the menu, click **Clear Filter From "Gemstone"**.

All the rows in the table redisplay. The Z to A sort on Gemstone remains in effect.

13 Click the **Metal arrow**, click the **(Select All)** check box to clear all the check boxes, and then click to select the **Gold** check box. Click **OK**. Click the **Gemstone arrow**, click the **(Select All)** check box to clear all the check boxes, and then click the **Red Coral** check box. Click **OK**, and then compare your screen with Figure 11.24.

By applying multiple filters, Rose can quickly determine that among the Bracelets product type, four styles have a Red Coral gemstone in a Gold setting and there are 117 total in stock.

Figure 11.24

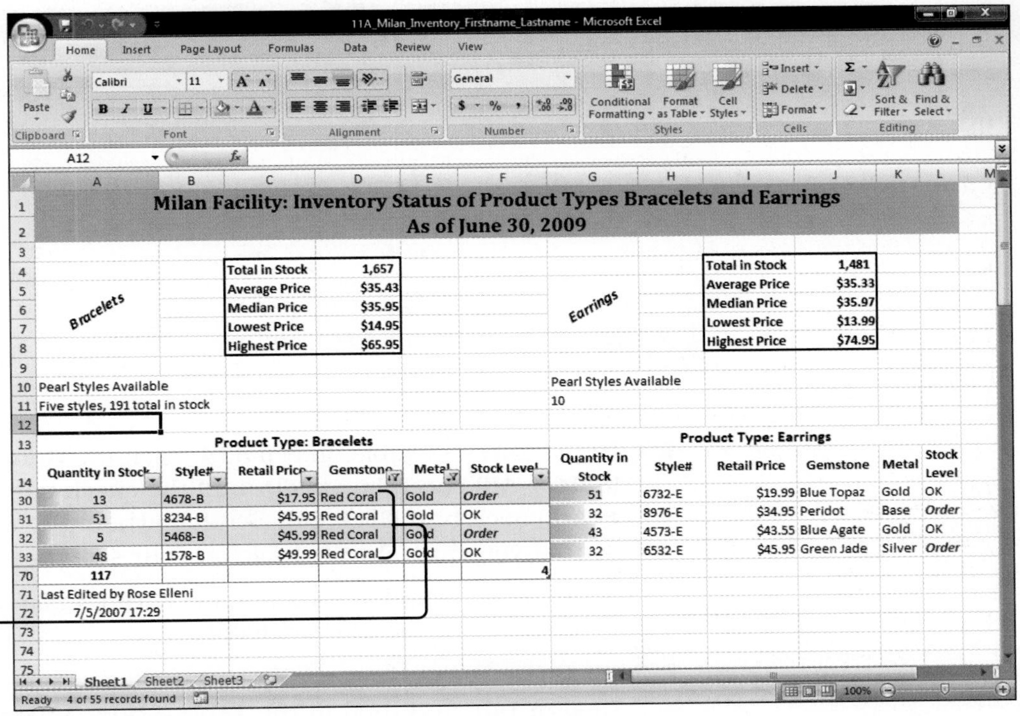

Four bracelet styles have *Red Coral* as *Gemstone* and *Gold* as *Metal*

14 Click the **Gemstone arrow**, and then click **Clear Filter from "Gemstone"**. Use the same technique to remove the filter from the **Metal** column.

15 In the table header row, click the **Style# arrow**, and then click **Sort A to Z**, which will apply an ascending sort to the *Style#* column.

16 **Save** your workbook.

Activity 11.11 Inserting a Second Table in a Worksheet

In this activity, you will format the product information for *Earrings* as a table.

1 Select the range **G14:L64**. On the **Insert tab**, in the **Tables group**, click the **Table** button. Be sure the **My table has headers** check box is selected, and then click **OK**.

2 In the **Table Styles group**, click the **More** button ⬇, and then under **Light**, click **Table Style Light 18**. Press Ctrl + Home, and then compare your screen with Figure 11.25.

Figure 11.25

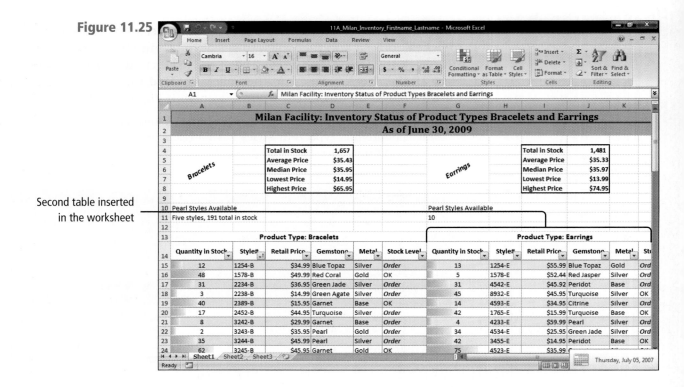

Second table inserted in the worksheet

In the image: Title bar: 11A_Milan_Inventory_Firstname_Lastname - Microsoft Excel

Cell A1 contents: Milan Facility: Inventory Status of Product Types Bracelets and Earrings

Milan Facility: Inventory Status of Product Types Bracelets and Earrings					
As of June 30, 2009					

Bracelets section:

Total in Stock	1,657
Average Price	$35.43
Median Price	$35.95
Lowest Price	$14.95
Highest Price	$65.95

Earrings section:

Total in Stock	1,481
Average Price	$35.33
Median Price	$35.97
Lowest Price	$13.99
Highest Price	$74.95

Pearl Styles Available — Five styles, 191 total in stock
Pearl Styles Available — 10

Product Type: Bracelets

Quantity in Stock	Style#	Retail Price	Gemstone	Metal	Stock Level
12	1254-B	$34.99	Blue Topaz	Silver	Order
48	1578-B	$49.99	Red Coral	Gold	OK
31	2234-B	$36.95	Green Jade	Silver	Order
3	2238-B	$14.99	Green Agate	Silver	Order
40	2389-B	$15.95	Garnet	Base	OK
17	2452-B	$44.95	Turquoise	Silver	Order
8	3242-B	$29.99	Garnet	Base	Order
2	3243-B	$35.95	Pearl	Gold	Order
35	3244-B	$45.99	Pearl	Silver	Order
62	3245-B	$45.95	Garnet	Gold	OK

Product Type: Earrings

Quantity in Stock	Style#	Retail Price	Gemstone	Metal	Sto
13	1254-E	$55.99	Blue Topaz	Gold	Ord
5	1578-E	$52.44	Red Jasper	Silver	Ord
31	4542-E	$45.92	Peridot	Base	Ord
45	8932-E	$45.95	Turquoise	Silver	OK
14	4593-E	$34.95	Citrine	Silver	Ord
42	1765-E	$15.99	Turquoise	Base	OK
4	4233-E	$59.99	Pearl	Silver	Ord
34	4534-E	$25.95	Green Jade	Silver	Ord
42	3455-E	$14.95	Peridot	Base	OK
75	4523-E	$35.99			

Sheet1 / Sheet2 / Sheet3

Thursday, July 05, 2007

---

3 In the **Earrings** table, in cell **J14**, click the **Gemstone arrow**, click the **(Select All)** check box to clear all the check boxes, and then click the **Pearl** check box. Click **OK**. Scroll down and to the right as necessary so that you can view the table on your screen.

In the worksheet, rows within the Earrings table that do not contain *Pearl* as the gemstone are hidden.

4 Click any cell in the **Earrings** table to select the table, click the **Design tab**, and then in the **Table Style Options group**, click to select the **Total Row** check box.

Total displays in cell G65, and in cell L65, the number *10* indicates that ten rows are currently displayed.

5 Click cell **G65**, click the **arrow** that displays to the right of cell G65, and then in the list, click **Sum**. Compare your screen with Figure 11.26.

Excel sums only the visible rows in Column G, and indicates that *309* earrings containing the Gemstone *Pearl* are in stock. Recall that in this manner, you can use an Excel table to quickly find information about a group of data.

Figure 11.26

Excel | Chapter 11

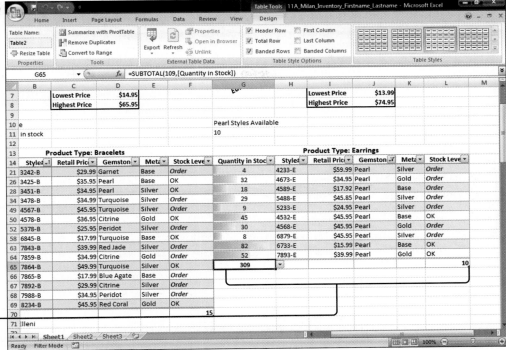

309 total Pearl earrings in stock; 10 Pearl styles

6 Click cell **G11**, type **Ten styles, 309 total pairs in stock** and then press Enter.

7 In the table header row, click the **Gemstone arrow**, and then on the menu, click **Clear Filter From "Gemstone"** to redisplay all the rows in the table.

8 In the table header row of the **Earrings** table, click the **Style# arrow**, and then click **Sort A to Z**, which will apply an ascending sort to the **Style#** column.

9 **Save** 💾 your workbook.

Activity 11.12 Converting a Table to a Range of Data

When you are finished answering questions about the data in a table by sorting, filtering, and totaling, you no longer need the table. You can remove a table by converting it back to a normal range.

1 Click anywhere in the **Bracelets** table to activate the table and display the **Table Tools** on the Ribbon.

2 On the **Design tab**, in the **Tools group**, click the **Convert to Range** button. In the message box, click **Yes**.

The list arrows are removed from the column titles; the color and shading formats applied from the table style remain.

3 Use the technique you just practiced to convert the **Earrings** table to a range, and then compare your screen with Figure 11.27.

Figure 11.27

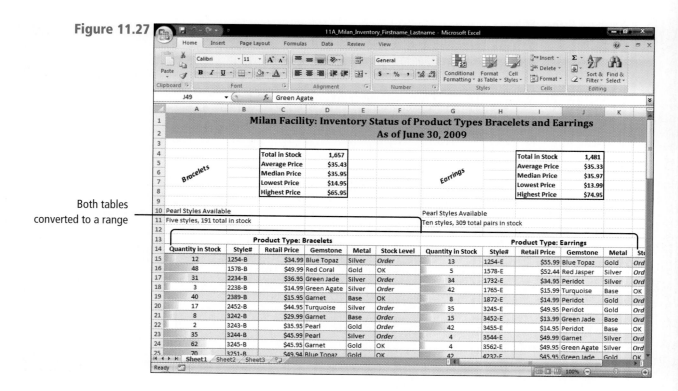

Both tables converted to a range

4 **Save** 💾 your workbook.

More Knowledge — How To Remove Shading Formats From a Table

If you do not want to retain the shading and other formats applied from a table style, apply the *None* table style before converting back to a range.

Objective 5
Format and Print a Large Worksheet

A large worksheet will be too wide, too long—or both—to print on a single page. To make reading multiple printed pages easier, Excel features let you print row and column headings on each page of a worksheet.

Activity 11.13 Printing Large Worksheets

In this activity, you will adjust the column widths, change the Page Layout so that column titles display on every page, and print the worksheet.

1 Select **column C**, hold down Ctrl, select the nonadjacent **column I**, and then set their width to **90 pixels**. Select **column A**, hold down Ctrl and select columns **D**, **G**, and **J**, and then set their width to **80 pixels**.

2 Select **column B**, hold down Ctrl and select **column H**, and then set their width to **70 pixels**.

3 Select **columns E**, **F**, **K**, and **L** and set their width to **55 pixels**. Select the range **A72:B72**, right-click, click **Format Cells**, and then

on the **Alignment tab** of the **Format Cells** dialog box, under **Text control**, select the **Merge cells** check box. Click# **OK**.

> The merged cell is widened so that it can display the result of the NOW function that it contains.

4 Select the column titles in **Row 14**, and then on the **Home tab**, in the **Alignment group**, click the **Wrap Text** button ▣. Look at the column titles in Row 14 and either verify that the full column titles display in each cell, or if necessary, click the **Wrap Text** button again so that the full titles display.

5 Press [Ctrl] + [Home] to display the top of your worksheet.

6 On the **Insert tab**, in the **Text group**, click **Header & Footer** to switch to **Page Layout view**. In the **Navigation group**, click the **Go to Footer** button, click just above the word *Footer*, and then in the **Header & Footer Elements group**, click the **File Name** button. Click a cell just above the footer to deselect the **Footer area** and view your file name.

7 Click the **Page Layout tab**. In the **Page Setup group**, click the **Orientation** button, and then click **Landscape**. In the same group, click the **Print Titles** button. Under **Print titles**, click in the **Rows to repeat at top** box, and then at the right, click the **Collapse Dialog** button 🔲. From the **row heading area**, select **rows 13:14**, and then compare your screen with Figure 11.28.

Figure 11.28

Collapsed dialog box displays the row numbers as an absolute reference

Rows 13 and 14 selected; surrounded by moving border

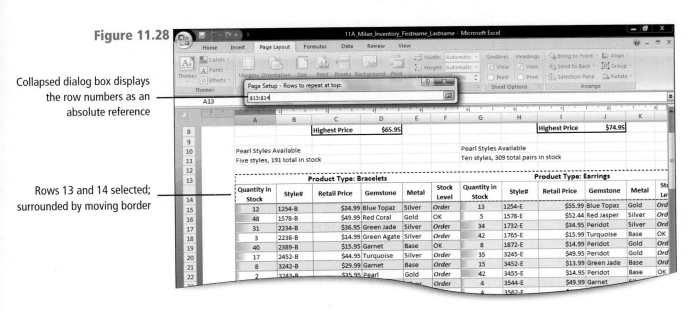

8 Press [Enter], and then in the **Page Setup** dialog box, click the **Margins tab**. Under **Center on page**, select the **Horizontally** check box, and then click **OK**.

9 Delete the unused sheets **Sheet2** and **Sheet3**. On the right edge of the status bar, click the **Normal** button 🔲, and then press [Ctrl] + [Home] to display the top of your worksheet.

10 From the **Office** menu 🔵, point to **Print**, and then click **Print Preview**. On your screen, it is possible that the *Earrings Stock Level*

column does not display. In the **Preview Group**, click **Next Page** several times to determine if the *Stock Level column* displays on separate pages. Close the **Print Preview**.

11 If necessary, on the **Page Layout tab**, in the **Scale to Fit group**, click the **Width button arrow**, and then click **1 page**.

Excel will make the necessary adjustments to fit the worksheet columns to one page.

12 **Save** 🖫 your workbook. To submit electronically, follow the instructions provided by your instructor. To print, from the **Office** menu 🏶, point to the **Print** button, and then click **Print Preview**. In the **Preview group**, click the **Next Page** and **Previous Page** buttons as necessary to view and check each page. Be sure the two header rows and the footer display on each page, and then click the **Print** button. In the **Print** dialog box, under **Print range**, be sure that **All** is selected, and then click **OK**. If you are directed to submit printed formulas, refer to Activity 9.17 in Project 9A to do so.

13 If you printed your formulas, be sure to redisplay the worksheet by pressing Ctrl + `. From the **Office** menu 🏶, click **Close**. If a dialog box displays asking if you want to save changes, click **No** so that you do *not* save the changes you made for printing formulas. **Close** Excel.

More Knowledge — Adjust Scaling for Data that is Slightly Larger than the Printed Page

If your data is just a little too large to fit on a printed page, you can scale the worksheet to make it fit. Scaling reduces the horizontal and vertical size of the printed data to a percentage of its original size or by the number of pages that you specify. To adjust the printed output to a percentage of its actual size, for example to 80%, on the Page Layout tab, in the Scale to Fit group, click the Scale arrows to select a percentage.

End You have completed Project 11A —————————————

Project 11B New Store Loan

In Activities 11.14 through 11.19, you will create a worksheet for Wattana Dithasaro, International Sales Director, that details the loan information to purchase furniture and fixtures for a new Adamantine Jewelry store in Mexico City. Wattana plans to borrow money to pay for the new store furniture and fixtures, and then pay off the loan in monthly payments. She must decide how to arrange the loan to buy the furniture and fixtures she needs and still keep the monthly payment within her budget for new store openings. You will create a worksheet containing payments for combinations of time periods and interest rates so Wattana can identify what range of rates and time periods will meet her requirements. The worksheets of your workbook will look similar to Figure 11.29.

For Project 11B, you will need the following file:

New blank Excel workbook

You will save your workbook as
11B_New_Store_Loan_Firstname_Lastname

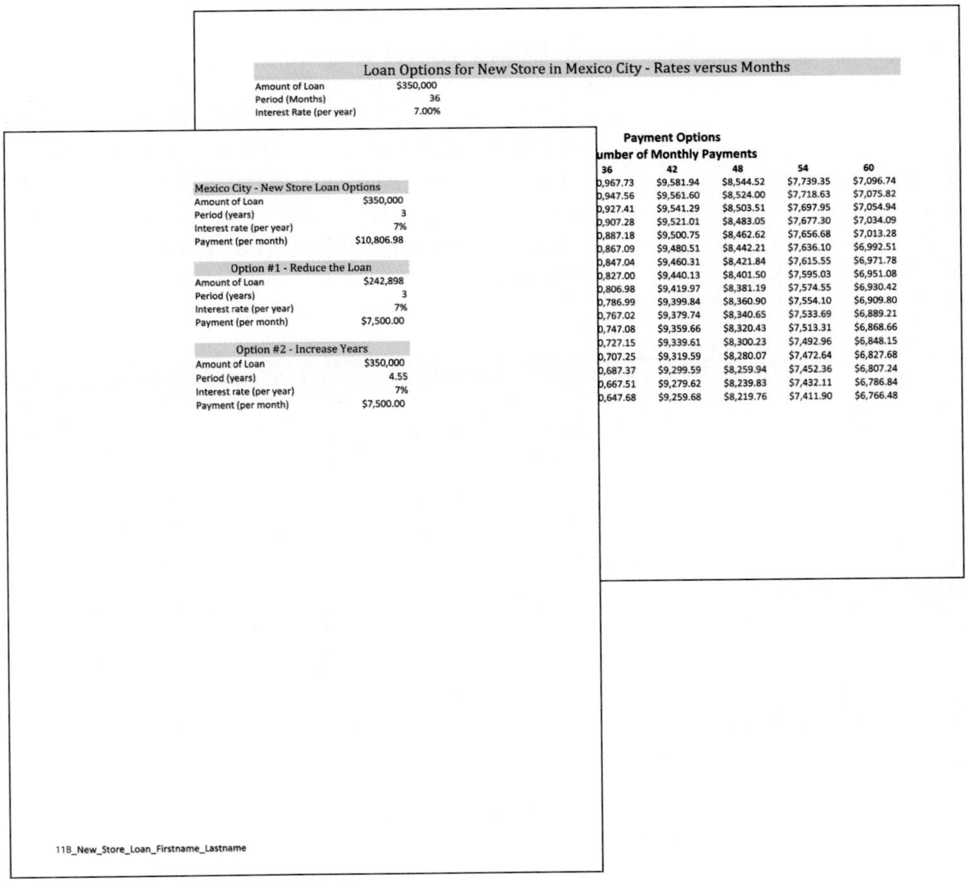

Figure 11.29
Project 11B—New Store Loan

Objective 6
Use Financial Functions

Financial functions perform common business calculations such as calculating a loan payment on a vehicle or calculating how much to save each month to buy something. Financial functions commonly involve a period of time such as months or years.

Activity 11.14 Designing a Loan Worksheet

1 **Start** Excel and display a new blank workbook. From the **Office** menu , display the **Save As** dialog box, navigate to your **Excel Chapter 11** folder, and then in the **File name** box, name the file **11B_New_Store_Loan_Firstname_Lastname**

2 Widen **column A** to **180 pixels** and **column B** to **100 pixels**. In the range **A2:B5**, enter the following row titles and data. Recall that you can format the numbers as you type by typing them with their symbols as shown:

Amount of Loan	$350,000
Period (years)	3
Interest rate (per year)	7%
Payment (per month)	

3 In cell **A1**, type **Mexico City - New Store Loan Options Merge and Center** the title in the range **A1:B1**, add a **Fill Color** of **Olive Green, Accent 3, Lighter 60%**, change the **Font** to **Cambria**, and then change the **Font Size** to **12**. Rename the worksheet tab **New Store Loan** and then **Save** your workbook. Compare your screen with Figure 11.30.

Figure 11.30

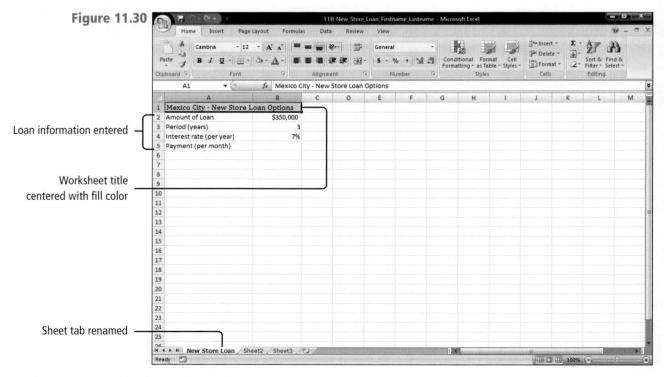

Loan information entered

Worksheet title centered with fill color

Sheet tab renamed

Activity 11.15 Inserting the PMT Financial Function

When you borrow money from a bank or a similar lending institution, the amount charged to you for your use of the borrowed money is called **interest**. Loans are typically made for a period of years, and the interest that must be paid is a percentage of the loan amount that is still owed. In Excel, this percentage is called the **rate**.

The initial amount of the loan is called the **Present value (Pv)**, which is the total amount that a series of future payments is worth now, and is also known as the **principal**. When you borrow money, the loan amount is the *present value* to the lender. The number of time periods—number of payments—is abbreviated **nper**. The value at the end of the time periods is the **Future value (Fv)**—the cash balance you want to attain after the last payment is made. The future value is usually zero for loans.

In this activity, you will calculate the monthly payments that Adamantine Jewelry will have to make to finance the purchase of the furniture and fixtures for the new store in Mexico City, the total cost of which is $350,000. You will calculate the monthly payments, including interest, for a three-year loan at an annual interest rate of 7.0%. To stay within Wattana's budget, the monthly payment must be approximately $7,500.

1 Click cell **B5**. On the **Formulas tab**, in the **Function Library group**, click the **Financial** button. Scroll down the list as necessary, and then click **PMT**.

The Function Arguments dialog box displays. Recall that arguments are the values that an Excel function uses to perform calculations or operations.

2 If necessary, drag the **Function Arguments** dialog box to the right side of your screen so you can view **columns A:B**.

The **PMT function** calculates the payment for a loan based on constant payments and at a constant interest rate. To complete the PMT function, first you must determine the total number of loan payment periods (months), which is 12 months × 3 years, or 36 months.

3 With your insertion point positioned in the **Rate** box, type **b4/12** Alternatively, click cell B4 and then type */12*.

Excel will divide the annual interest rate of 7%, which is 0.070 in decimal notation, located in cell B4 by 12 (months), which will result in a *monthly* interest rate.

When borrowing money, the interest rate and number of periods are quoted in years. The payments on a loan, however, are usually made monthly. Therefore, the number of periods, which is stated in years, and the *annual* interest rate, must be changed to a monthly equivalent in order to calculate the monthly payment amount. You can see that calculations like these can be made as part of the argument in a function.

4 Press Tab to move the insertion point to the **Nper** box. In the lower portion of the dialog box, notice that *Nper is the total number of payments for the loan* (number of periods). Type **b3*12** to have Excel convert the number of years in the loan (3) to the total number of months.

Recall that the PMT function calculates a *monthly* payment. Thus, all values in the function must be expressed in months.

5 Press `Tab` to move to the **Pv** box, and then type **b2**

> Pv represents the present value—the amount of the loan before any payments are made—in this instance $350,000.

6 In cell **B5** and on the **Formula Bar**, notice that the arguments that comprise the PMT function are separated by commas. Notice also, in the **Function Arguments** dialog box, that the value of each argument displays to the right of the argument box. Compare your screen with Figure 11.31.

Figure 11.31

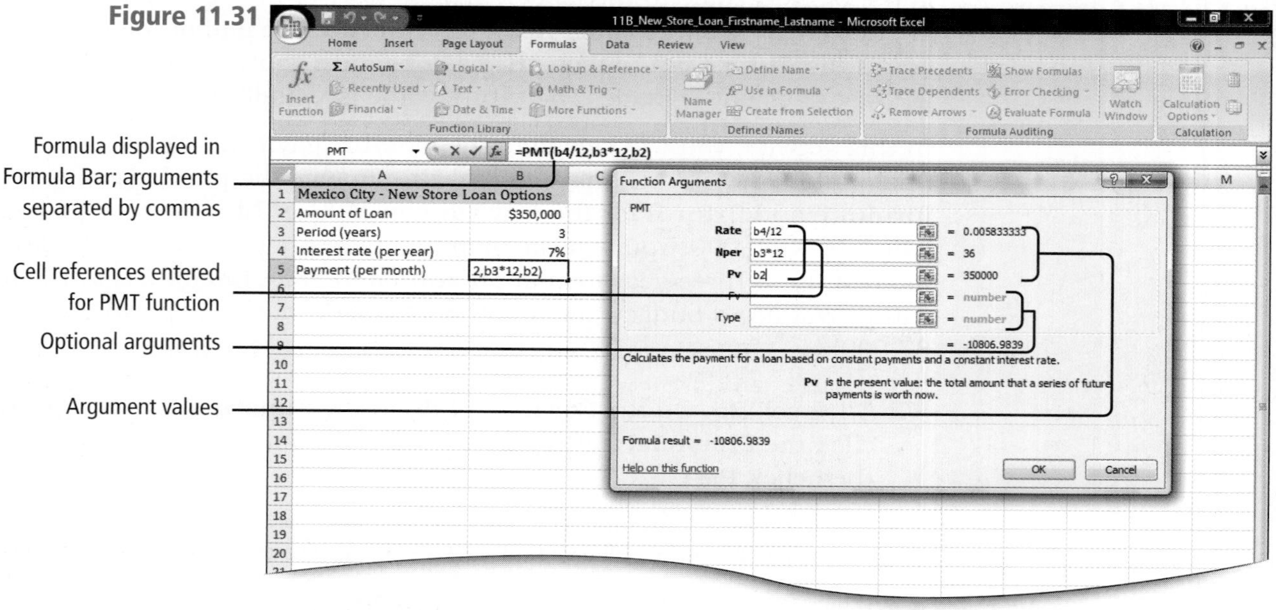

Formula displayed in Formula Bar; arguments separated by commas

Cell references entered for PMT function

Optional arguments

Argument values

Note — Optional Arguments

The PMT function has two arguments not indicated by bold; these are optional. The Future value (Fv) argument assumes that the unpaid portion of the loan should be zero at the end of the last period. The *Type argument* assumes that the payment will be made at the end of each period. These default values are typical of most loans and may be left blank.

---

7 In the dialog box, click **OK**.

> The monthly payment amount, ($10,806.98), displays in cell B5. The amount displays in red and in parentheses to show that it is a negative number, a number that will be *paid out*. This monthly payment of $10,806.98 is over the budget of $7,500 per month that Wattana has in mind.

8 Click in the **Formula Bar**, and then use the arrow keys on the keyboard as necessary to position the insertion point between the equal sign and *PMT*. Type – (minus sign) to insert a minus sign into the formula, and then press `Enter`. **Save** 🖫 your workbook.

> By placing a minus sign in the formula, the monthly payment amount, $10,806.98, displays in cell B5 as a *positive* number, which is more familiar and less distracting to work with.

Objective 7
Use Goal Seek

Goal Seek is a method to find a specific value for a cell by adjusting the value of one other cell. With Goal Seek, you can work backward from the desired outcome to find the input necessary to achieve your goal. If you have a result in mind, you can try different numbers in one of the cells used as an argument in the function until you get close to the answer you want. Goal Seek is one of Excel's What-If Analysis tools.

Activity 11.16 Using Goal Seek to Produce the Desired Result

Wattana knows that her budget cannot exceed $7,500 per month for the new store loan. The amount of $350,000 is necessary to purchase the furniture and fixtures to open the new store. Now she has two options— borrow less money and reduce the amount or quality of the furniture and fixtures in the store, or extend the time to repay the loan. To find out how much she can borrow for three years to stay within the budget, or how much to increase the repayment period, you will use the Goal Seek tool.

1 Click cell **B5**. On the **Data tab**, in the **Data Tools group**, click the **What-If Analysis** button, and then in the list, click **Goal Seek**. In the **Goal Seek** dialog box, in the **Set cell** box, confirm that *B5* displays.

> The cell address in this box is the cell that displays the desired result.

2 Press [Tab]. In the **To value** box, type the payment goal of *7500.00* and press [Tab]. In the **By changing cell** box, type **b2** which is the amount of the loan, and then compare your dialog box with Figure 11.32. Alternatively, you can click cell B2.

> In the By changing cell box, if you click cell B2, Excel will make the cell reference absolute.

Figure 11.32

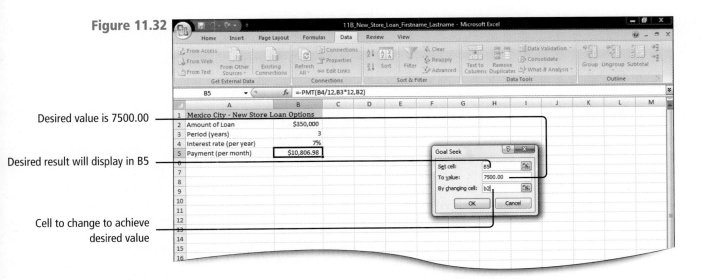

Desired value is 7500.00

Desired result will display in B5

Cell to change to achieve desired value

3 In the **Goal Seek** dialog box, click **OK**. In the **Goal Seek Status** dialog box, click **OK**.

Excel's calculations indicate that to achieve a monthly payment of $7,500.00 using a 3-year loan, Wattana can borrow only *$242,898*—not $350,000.

4 Click cell **A7**. Type **Option #1 - Reduce the Loan** and press Enter. Right-click cell **A7**. On the Mini toolbar, apply a **Fill Color** ▢ of **Olive Green, Accent 3, Lighter 60%**, change the **Font** to **Cambria** and the **Font Size** to **12**. **Merge and Center** ▢ the title across the range **A7:B7**.

5 Select the range **A2:B5**, right-click, and then click **Copy**. Click cell **A8**, right-click, and then click **Paste Special**. In the **Paste Special** dialog box, under **Paste**, click the **Values and number formats** option button, and then click **OK**.

Press Esc to cancel the moving border. **Save** ▢ your workbook, click anywhere to deselect, and then compare your worksheet with Figure 11.33.

Recall that with the Paste Special command, you can copy the *value* in a cell, rather than the formula, and the cell formats are retained—cell B5 contains the PMT function formula, and here you need only the value that *results* from that formula.

Figure 11.33

Values and formats pasted

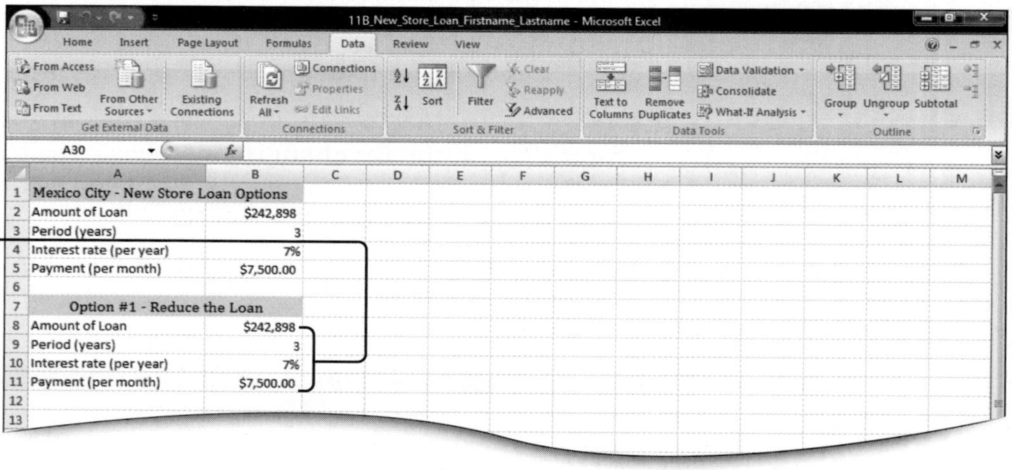

Workshop

Savings Accounts—Using the Future Value Function

Another commonly used financial function, similar to the PMT function, is the Future Value function. The function has three required arguments: Rate, Nper, and Pmt. The Rate argument is the interest rate paid to you by the financial institution; the Nper is the number of periods; and Pmt is the amount you deposit into the account each period. The function also has two optional arguments—Pv and Type. The Pv argument is the amount you start with in the account. Excel assumes this is zero if you do not provide a starting amount. The Type argument assumes that the payment is made at the beginning of the time period.

For example, in the Fv Function Arguments dialog box, enter a rate of 6%/12 (6% annually divided by 12 months), enter 60 (5 years or 60 months) as the number of periods, enter 100 ($100) as the monthly deposit you will make, and enter a present value of 1500 ($1,500 opening deposit in the account). Excel will calculate that at the end of 5 years, you will have $9,000.28 in your savings account.

Activity 11.17 Using Goal Seek to Find an Increased Period

For Wattana's purchase of furniture and fixtures for the new store in Mexico City, an alternative to borrowing less money—which would mean buying fewer items or items of lesser quality—would be to increase the number of years of payments.

1 In cell **B2**, type **350000** and then press Enter to restore the original loan amount. Click cell **B5**. On the **Data tab**, in the **Data Tools group**, click the **What-If Analysis** button, and then click **Goal Seek**.

2 In the **Set cell** box, confirm that **B5** displays. press Tab. In the **To value** box, type **7500.00** and press Tab. In the **By changing cell** box, type **b3** which is the number of years for the loan. Compare your dialog box with Figure 11.34.

Figure 11.34

Value of $350,000 restored

Cell with the number of payment periods indicated as the *change* cell

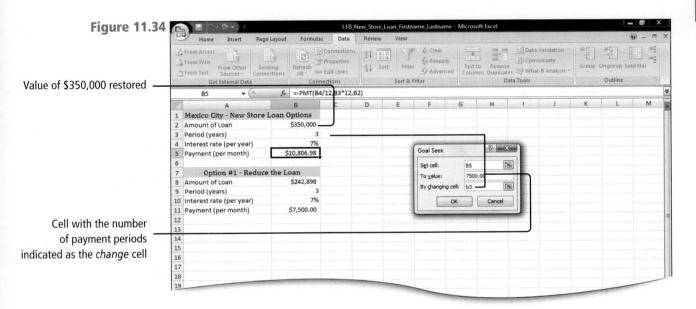

3 Click **OK** two times.

Excel's calculations indicate that by making payments for 4.5 years—4.552648969—a monthly payment of $7,500.00 is achieved.

4 Click **A13**. Type **Option #2 - Increase Years** and then press Enter. Right-click cell **A7**, on the Mini toolbar, click the **Format Painter** button, and then click cell **A13** to copy the formats.

5 Select the range **A2:B5**, right-click, click **Copy**, and then click cell **A14**. Right-click, click **Paste Special**, click the **Values and number formats** option button, and then click **OK**. Press Esc to cancel the moving border.

6 Click cell **B15**, right-click to display the Mini toolbar, and then click the **Decrease Decimal** button until the number of decimal places is two. Click cell **B3**. Type **3** and then press Enter to restore the original value. Compare your worksheet with Figure 11.35.

Figure 11.35

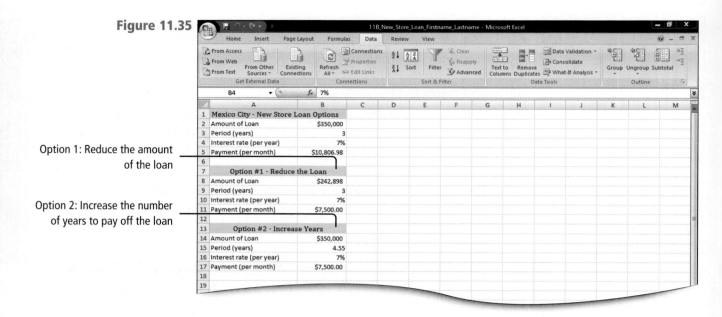

Option 1: Reduce the amount of the loan

Option 2: Increase the number of years to pay off the loan

7 Click the **Insert tab**, and then in the **Text group**, click the **Header & Footer** button to switch to **Page Layout View** and open the **Header area**. In the **Navigation group**, click the **Go to Footer** button, click just above the word *Footer*, and then in the **Header & Footer Elements group**, click the **File Name** button. Click in a cell just above the footer to exit the **Footer area** and view your file name.

8 Click the **Page Layout tab**. In the **Page Setup group**, click the **Margins** button, and then at the bottom of the **Margins gallery**, click **Custom Margins**. In the **Page Setup** dialog box, under **Center on page**, select the **Horizontally** check box. Click **OK**, and then on the status bar, click the **Normal** button ⊞. Press Ctrl + Home to move to the top of the worksheet.

9 **Save** 🖫 your workbook.

Objective 8
Create a Data Table

A **data table** is a range of cells that shows how changing certain values in your formulas affects the results of those formulas. Data tables make it easy to calculate multiple versions in one operation, and then to view and compare the results of all the different variations.

For example, banks may offer loans at different rates for different periods of time, which require different payments. Using a data table, you can calculate the possible values for each argument.

A **one-variable data table** changes the value in only one cell. For example, use a one-variable data table if you want to see how different interest rates affect a monthly payment. A **two-variable data table** changes the values in two cells—for example, you can see how both different interest rates *and* different payment periods will affect a monthly payment.

Activity 11.18 Designing a Two-Variable Data Table

Recall that the PMT function has three required arguments: Present value (Pv), Rate, and Number of periods (Nper). Because Wattana would still like to borrow $350,000 and purchase the fixtures and furniture that she has selected for the new store in Mexico City, in this data table the present value will not change. The two values that will change are the Rate and Number of periods. Possible periods will range from 24 months (2 years) to 60 months (5 years) and the Rate will vary from 8% to 6%.

1 Double-click the **Sheet2 tab**, rename it **Payment Table** and then press Enter. Right-click the **Sheet3 tab** and click **Delete**.

2 With the **Payment Table** worksheet active, widen **column A to 165 pixels**. Widen **column B to 80 pixels**. Select **columns C:I**, and then widen them to **85 pixels**.

3 In the range **A2:B4**, enter the following row titles and data. Recall that you format numbers as you type by typing them with their symbols as shown:

Amount of Loan	$350,000
Period (Months)	36
Interest rate (per year)	7.00%

4 Click cell **C8**. Type **24** and then press Tab. Type **30** and then press Tab.

5 Select the range **C8:D8**. Point to the fill handle, and then drag to the right through cell **I8** to fill in a pattern of months from 24 to 60 in increments of six months.

6 In cell **B9**, type **8.000%** and then press Enter. Type **7.875%** and then press Enter.

The display of both values is rounded to two decimal places.

7 Select the range **B9:B10**. Point to the fill handle, and then drag down through cell **B25** to fill in a pattern of interest rates in increments of .125 from 8.00% down to 6.00%.

8 With the range **B9:B25** still selected, right-click anywhere over the range, and then on the Mini toolbar, click the **Increase Decimal** button 📷 one time. Compare your screen with Figure 11.36.

Row 8 represents the number of monthly payments, and column B represents a range of possible annual interest rates. These two arguments will be used to calculate varying payment arrangements for a loan of $350,000.

Figure 11.36

Varying arguments for months ——

Varying arguments for rates ——

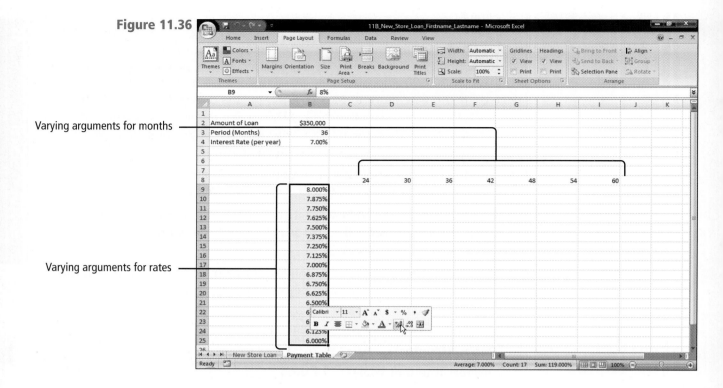

Click cell **A1**. Type **Loan Options for New Store in Mexico City - Rates versus Months** and then press Enter. **Merge and Center** this title across the range **A1:I1**. Change the **Font** to **Cambria**, the **Font Size** to **16**, and then apply a **Fill Color** of **Olive Green, Accent 3, Lighter 60%**.

10 Click cell **C6**. Type **Payment Options** and then press Enter. **Merge and Center** this title across the range **C6:I6**. Change the **Font Size** to **14**, and then apply **Bold B**.

11 Click cell **C7**. Type **Number of Monthly Payments** and then use the **Format Painter** to apply the format of cell **C6** to cell **C7**.

12 Click cell **A9**, type **Rates** and then press Enter. Select the range **A9:A25**. On the **Home tab**, in the **Alignment group**, click the **Merge and Center** button, click the **Align Text Right** button, and then click the **Middle Align** button. Change the **Font Size** to **14**, and then apply **Bold B**. Compare your screen with Figure 11.37.

Figure 11.37

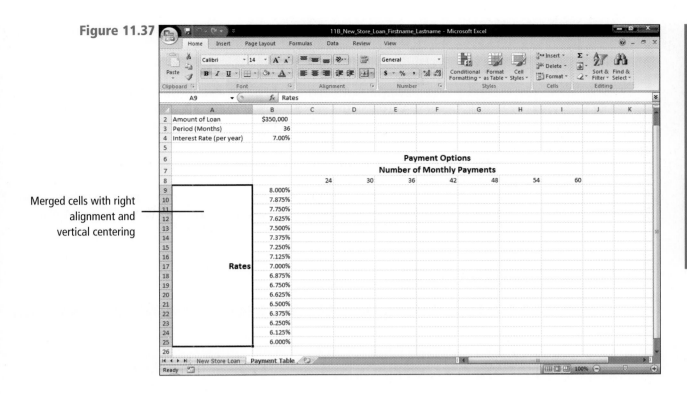

Merged cells with right alignment and vertical centering

	A	B	C	D	E	F	G	H	I	J	K
2	Amount of Loan	$350,000									
3	Period (Months)	36									
4	Interest Rate (per year)	7.00%									
5											
6					Payment Options						
7					Number of Monthly Payments						
8			24	30	36	42	48	54	60		
9		8.000%									
10		7.875%									
11		7.750%									
12		7.625%									
13		7.500%									
14		7.375%									
15		7.250%									
16		7.125%									
17	Rates	7.000%									
18		6.875%									
19		6.750%									
20		6.625%									
21		6.500%									
22		6.375%									
23		6.250%									
24		6.125%									
25		6.000%									
26											

New Store Loan Payment Table

13 Save your workbook.

Activity 11.19 Using a Data Table to Calculate Options

Recall that a data table is a range of cells that shows how changing certain values in your formulas affects the results of those formulas. In this activity, you will create a table of payments for every combination of payment periods, which are represented by the column titles under *Number of Monthly Payments*, and interest rates, which are represented by the row titles to the right of *Rates*. From the resulting table, Wattana can find a combination of payment periods and interest rates that will enable her to go forward with her plan to borrow $350,000 to purchase the necessary furniture and fixtures for the new store in Mexico City.

1 Click cell **B8**, type **=** and notice that in the upper left corner of your screen, in the **Name Box**, *PMT* displays indicating the most recently used function. Click in the **Name Box** to open the **Function Arguments** dialog box for the **PMT** function. Alternatively, use one of the other methods you have practiced to insert the PMT function.

> The PMT function is entered in the upper left corner of your range of data, so that when the data table is completed, the months in row 8 and the rates in column B will be substituted into each cell's formula to fill the table with the range of months and interest rate options that are displayed.

2 In the **Rate** box, type **b4/12** to divide the interest rate per year by 12 and convert it to a monthly interest rate.

3 Press Tab to move the insertion point to the **Nper** box. Type **b3** and then press Tab.

The periods in cell B3 are already stated in months and need not be changed.

4 In the **Pv** box, type **-b2** and then click **OK**.

The payment—$10,806.98—is calculated for the values in cells B2, B3, and B4. This is the same payment that you calculated on the first worksheet. Now it displays as a positive number because you entered the loan amount in cell B2 as a negative number.

5 Select the range **B8:I25**. On the **Data tab**, in the **Data Tools group**, click the **What-If Analysis** button, and then in the list, click **Data Table**. In the **Data Table** dialog box, in the **Row input cell** box, type **b3** and then press Tab. In the **Column input cell** box, type **b4** and then compare your screen with Figure 11.38.

The row of months will be substituted for the value in cell B3, and the column of interest rates will be substituted for the value in cell B4.

Figure 11.38

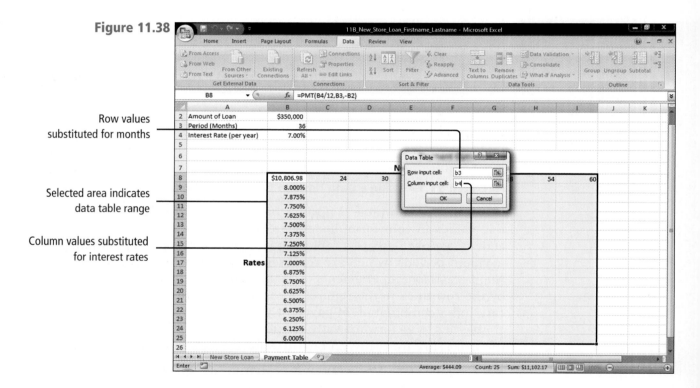

Row values substituted for months

Selected area indicates data table range

Column values substituted for interest rates

6 In the **Data Table** dialog box, click **OK**. Click cell **H21**, and then examine the formula in the **Formula Bar**. Compare your screen with Figure 11.39.

The table is filled with payment options that use the month and interest rate corresponding to the position in the table. Thus, if Wattana chooses a combination of 54 months at an interest rate of 6.5%, the monthly payment will be $7,492.96.

The data table is one of a group of Excel's What-If Analysis tools.

Figure 11.39

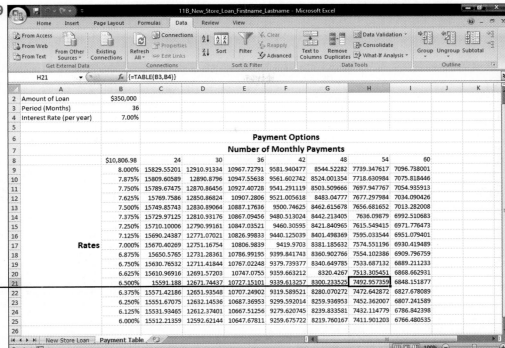

Period of 54 months, at 6.500% interest, results in $7,492.96 payment

7 Right-click cell **B8**, and then on the Mini toolbar, click the **Format Painter** button. Select the range **C9:I25** to apply the same format.

8 Use Ctrl to select the non-adjacent ranges **B9:B25** and **C8:I8**. Right-click over the selection, and then on the Mini toolbar, apply **Bold** B and **Center**. Click anywhere to deselect the range, and then compare your worksheet with Figure 11.40.

By using a data table of payment options, you can see that Wattana must get a loan for at least 54 months (4.5 years) for any of the interest rates between 6.500% and 6.000% in order to purchase the furniture and fixtures she wants and still keep the monthly payment at approximately $7,500.

Figure 11.40

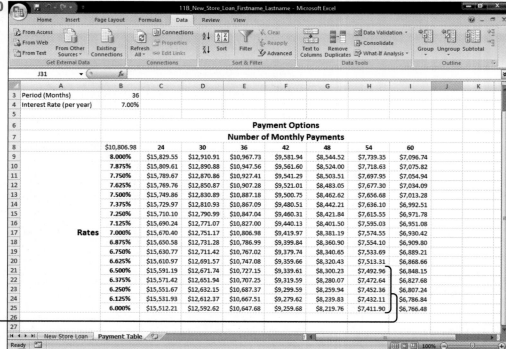

For a 54-month period, loan options in this range will be within the budget

	A	B	C	D	E	F	G	H	I
3	Period (Months)	36							
4	Interest Rate (per year)	7.00%							
5									
6					**Payment Options**				
7					**Number of Monthly Payments**				
8		$10,806.98	24	30	36	42	48	54	60
9		8.000%	$15,829.55	$12,910.91	$10,967.73	$9,581.94	$8,544.52	$7,739.35	$7,096.74
10		7.875%	$15,809.61	$12,890.88	$10,947.56	$9,561.60	$8,524.00	$7,718.63	$7,075.82
11		7.750%	$15,789.67	$12,870.86	$10,927.41	$9,541.29	$8,503.51	$7,697.95	$7,054.94
12		7.625%	$15,769.76	$12,850.87	$10,907.28	$9,521.01	$8,483.05	$7,677.30	$7,034.09
13		7.500%	$15,749.86	$12,830.89	$10,887.18	$9,500.75	$8,462.62	$7,656.68	$7,013.28
14		7.375%	$15,729.97	$12,810.93	$10,867.09	$9,480.51	$8,442.21	$7,636.10	$6,992.51
15		7.250%	$15,710.10	$12,790.99	$10,847.04	$9,460.31	$8,421.84	$7,615.55	$6,971.78
16		7.125%	$15,690.24	$12,771.07	$10,827.00	$9,440.13	$8,401.50	$7,595.03	$6,951.08
17	Rates	7.000%	$15,670.40	$12,751.17	$10,806.98	$9,419.97	$8,381.19	$7,574.55	$6,930.42
18		6.875%	$15,650.58	$12,731.28	$10,786.99	$9,399.84	$8,360.90	$7,554.10	$6,909.80
19		6.750%	$15,630.77	$12,711.42	$10,767.02	$9,379.74	$8,340.65	$7,533.69	$6,889.21
20		6.625%	$15,610.97	$12,691.57	$10,747.08	$9,359.66	$8,320.43	$7,513.31	$6,868.66
21		6.500%	$15,591.19	$12,671.74	$10,727.15	$9,339.61	$8,300.23	$7,492.96	$6,848.15
22		6.375%	$15,571.42	$12,651.94	$10,707.25	$9,319.59	$8,280.07	$7,472.64	$6,827.68
23		6.250%	$15,551.67	$12,632.15	$10,687.37	$9,299.59	$8,259.94	$7,452.36	$6,807.24
24		6.125%	$15,531.93	$12,612.37	$10,667.51	$9,279.62	$8,239.83	$7,432.11	$6,786.84
25		6.000%	$15,512.21	$12,592.62	$10,647.68	$9,259.68	$8,219.76	$7,411.90	$6,766.48
26									
27									

New Store Loan   Payment Table

9 Click the **Insert tab**, and then in the **Text group**, click the **Header & Footer** button to switch to **Page Layout View** and open the **Header area**. In the **Navigation group**, click the **Go to Footer** button, click just above the word *Footer*, then in the **Header & Footer Elements group**, click the **File Name** button. Click in a cell just above the footer to exit the **Footer area** and view your file name.

10 Click the **Page Layout tab**. In the **Page Setup group**, click the **Orientation** button, and then click **Landscape**. Click the **Margins** button, and then at the bottom of the **Margins gallery**, click **Custom Margins**. In the **Page Setup** dialog box, under **Center on page**, select the **Horizontally** check box. Click **OK**, and then on the status bar, click the **Normal** button. Press [Ctrl] + [Home] to move to the top of the worksheet.

11 **Save** 🖫 your workbook. Press [Ctrl] + [F2] to display the worksheet in **Print Preview**. To print, in the **Print group**, click the **Print** button, under **Print what**, click the **Entire workbook** option button, and then click **OK**. To submit electronically, follow your instructor's directions. Determine if you are to print formulas for any or all of the worksheets in this workbook. To print formulas, refer to Activity 9.17 in Project 9A.

12 If you printed your formulas, be sure to redisplay the worksheet by pressing [Ctrl] + [']. From the **Office** menu, click **Close**. If you are prompted to save changes, click **No**. **Close** Excel.

End **You have completed Project 11B**

There's More You Can Do!

Close Excel and any other open windows. Display the Start menu, click Computer, and then navigate to the student files that accompany this textbook. In the folder **02_theres_more_you_can_do**, locate and open the folder for this chapter. Open and print the instructions for this project, which are provided to you in Adobe PDF format.

Try IT! 1—Apply Conditional Formats by Using Color Scales, Icon Sets, and Top/Bottom Rules

In this Try It! exercise, you will use Color Scales, Icon Sets, and Top/Bottom rules to help you visualize data distribution and variation.

Content-Based Assessments

Summary

Predefined formulas, referred to as functions, are available in Excel in various categories including Statistical, Logical, Date & Time, and Financial. Such functions enable you to make complex calculations without having to build the formulas yourself. Conditional formatting enables you to highlight interesting cells based on criteria, emphasize unusual values, and visualize data using Data Bars. The DATE function adds the current date to a workbook. Financial functions, along with the Goal Seek tool and data tables, are useful when making choices among various financing options.

Key Terms

The ◉ symbol represents Key Terms found on the Student CD in the 02_theres_more_you_can_do folder for this chapter.

Content-Based Assessments

Matching

Match each term in the second column with its correct definition in the first column by writing the letter of the term on the blank line in front of the correct definition.

_____ **1.** A predefined formula—a formula that Excel has already built for you—that performs calculations by using specific values in a particular order.

_____ **2.** The values that an Excel function uses to perform calculations or operations.

_____ **3.** A statistical function that adds a group of values, and then divides the result by the number of values in the group.

_____ **4.** A statistical function that determines the smallest value in a group of values.

_____ **5.** An Excel feature which, after typing an = (equal sign) and the beginning letter or letters of a function name, displays a list of function names that match the typed letter(s), and from which you can insert the function by pointing to its name, and then pressing the Tab key or double-clicking.

_____ **6.** Conditions that you specify in a logical function.

_____ **7.** Any value or expression that can be evaluated as being *true* or *false*.

_____ **8.** The symbols < (less than), > (greater than), and = (equal) that evaluate each field value to determine if it is the same, greater than, less than, or in between a range of values as specified by the criteria.

_____ **9.** A cell format consisting of a shaded bar that provides a visual cue to the reader about the value of a cell relative to other cells; the length of the bar represents the value in the cell—a longer bar represents a higher value and a shorter bar represents a lower value.

_____ **10.** A function within the *Date & Time* category that retrieves the date and time from your computer's calendar and clock and inserts the information into the selected cell.

_____ **11.** A series of rows and columns in a worksheet that contains related data, and that is managed independently from the data in other rows and columns in the worksheet.

_____ **12.** A portion of a worksheet window bounded by and separated from other portions by vertical and horizontal bars.

_____ **13.** The amount charged for the use of borrowed money.

_____ **14.** The total amount that a series of future payments is worth now; also known as the principal.

_____ **15.** An Excel function that calculates the payment for a loan based on constant payments and at a constant rate of interest.

A Arguments

B AVERAGE

C Comparison operators

D Criteria

E Data Bar

F Excel table

G Formula AutoComplete

H Function

I Interest

J Logical test

K MIN

L NOW

M Pane

N PMT

O Present value

Content-Based Assessments

Fill in the Blank

Write the correct answer in the space provided.

1. The Excel function that adds all the numbers in a selected range of cells is the _____ function.

2. Prewritten formulas that analyze a group of measurements are _____ functions.

3. A statistical function commonly used to describe a group of data, and which finds the middle value in a group of values that has as many values above it in the group as are below it is the _____ function.

4. The MAX function determines the _____ value in a selected range of values.

5. Prewritten formulas that test for specific conditions, and which typically use conditional tests to determine whether specified conditions, referred to as criteria, are true or false, are _____ functions.

6. To count the number of cells within a range that meets the given condition, use the _____ function.

7. The IF function uses a logical test to check whether a condition is met, and then returns one value if true, and another value if _____.

8. A format that changes the appearance of a cell range—for example, by adding cell shading or font color—based on a condition is a _____ format.

9. The command that searches the cells in a worksheet—or in a selected range—for matches, and then replaces each match with a replacement value of your choice is called _____ _____ _____.

10. The term used to describe an Excel function that is subject to change each time the workbook is reopened; for example, when the NOW function updates itself to the current date and time each time the workbook is opened, is _____.

11. The command that enables you to select one or more rows or columns and freeze (lock) them into place as separate panes is_____ _____.

(Fill in the Blank continues on the next page)

Content-Based Assessments

Fill in the Blank

(Fill in the Blank continued)

12. The group of functions in Excel that performs common business calculations, such as calculating a loan payment on a vehicle, and that commonly involves a period of time such as months or years, are called _____ functions.

13. The value at the end of the time periods in an Excel function is known as the _____ _____.

14. One of Excel's What-If Analysis tools, which provides a method to find a specific value for a cell by adjusting the value of one other cell, is _____ _____.

15. A range of cells that shows how changing certain values in your formulas affects the results of those formulas, and that makes it easy to calculate multiple versions in one operation, is a _____ _____.

Excel

chaptereleven

Skills Review

Project 11C — Pendants

In this project, you will apply the skills you practiced from the Objectives in Project 11A.

Objectives: 1. *Use SUM, AVERAGE, MEDIAN, MIN, and MAX Functions;*
2. *Use COUNTIF and IF Functions, and Apply Conditional Formatting;*
3. *Use a Date Function;* **4.** *Freeze Panes and Create an Excel Table;*
5. *Format and Print a Large Worksheet.*

Adamantine Jewelry creates castings, which it sells to other jewelry makers. In the following Skills Review, you will edit a worksheet for Rose Elleni, Vice President of Production, detailing the current inventory of pendant castings at the Milan production facility. Your completed worksheet will look similar to the one shown in Figure 11.41.

For Project 11C, you will need the following file:

e11C_Pendants

You will save your workbook as
11C_Pendants_Firstname_Lastname

Figure 11.41

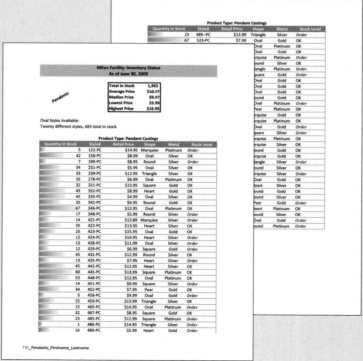

(Project 11C–Pendants continues on the next page)

Content-Based Assessments

(Project 11C–Pendants continued)

1. **Start** Excel. From the student files that accompany this text, locate and open **e11C_Pendants**. **Save** the file in your **Excel Chapter 11** folder as **11C_Pendants_Firstname_Lastname**

2. Click cell **B4**. Click the **Formulas tab**, and then in the **Function Library group**, click the **AutoSum** button. Select the range **A12:A77**, dragging downward as necessary, and then press Enter. Right-click cell **B4**, and then apply **Comma Style** with zero decimal places.

3. Click cell **B5**. In the **Function Library group**, click the **More Functions** button, and then point to **Statistical**. Click **AVERAGE**, and then if necessary, drag the title bar of the **Function Arguments** dialog box down and to the right so you can view the **Formula Bar** and cell **B5**. In the **Function Arguments** dialog box, in the **Number1** box, delete the existing text, and then type **c12:c77** Click **OK** to calculate the average product price.

4. Click cell **B6**. In the **Function Library group**, click the **More Functions** button, display the list of **Statistical** functions, scroll down as necessary, and then click **MEDIAN**. In the **Function Arguments** dialog box, to the right of the **Number1** box, click the **Collapse Dialog** button. Select the range **C12:C77**, and then press Enter. Click **OK** to calculate the median product price.

5. Using either of the techniques that you practiced in Steps 3 and 4, in cell **B7**, insert the **MIN** function for the range **C12:C77**. In cell **B8** insert the **MAX** function for the range **C12:C77**.

6. Select the range **A4:B8**. Point to the right edge of the selected range to display the ⬚ pointer. Drag the selected range to the right until the ScreenTip displays *C4:D8*, and then release the mouse button. Select **columns C:D**, and then apply **AutoFit** to adjust the column widths. Select the range **C4:D8**, and then apply **Bold** and a **Thick Box Border**.

7. In cell **A6**, type **Pendants** Select the range **A5:A7**, right-click over the selection, and then from the shortcut menu, click **Format Cells**. In the **Format Cells** dialog box, click the **Alignment tab**. Under **Text control**, select the **Merge cells** check box. In the upper right portion of the dialog box, under **Orientation**, point to the **red diamond**, and then drag the diamond upward until the **Degrees** box indicates *30*. Click **OK**.

8. With the cell still selected, click the **Home tab**, change the **Font Size** to **12**, and then apply **Bold** and **Italic**. In the **Alignment group**, apply **Center** alignment and **Middle Align**.

9. From the **row heading area**, point to **row 10** and right-click. From the shortcut menu, click **Insert**. Press F4 two times to insert two more rows. In cell **A10** type **Oval Styles Available:** and press Enter.

10. With cell **A11** active, on the **Formulas tab**, in the **Function Library group**, click the **More Functions** button, and then display the list of **Statistical** functions. Click **COUNTIF**. In the **Range** box, click the **Collapse Dialog** button, select the range **D15:D80**, and then press Enter. Click in the **Criteria** box, type **Oval** and then click **OK** to calculate the number of Oval pendant castings that Adamantine Jewelry has in stock.

11. Click cell **F15**. On the **Formulas tab**, in the **Function Library group**, click the **Logical** button, and then in the list, click **IF**. With

(Project 11C–Pendants continues on the next page)

(Project 11C–Pendants continued)

the insertion point in the **Logical_test** box, click cell **A15**. Type **<25** and then press Tab to move the insertion point to the **Value_if_true** box. Type **Order** and then press Tab to move the insertion point to the **Value_if_false** box. Type **OK** and then click **OK** to display the result *Order* in cell **F15**. Then, using the fill handle, copy the function down through cell **F80** to indicate the order status for each Style#.

12. Be sure the range **F15:F80** is selected. On the **Home tab**, in the **Styles group**, click the **Conditional Formatting** button. In the list, point to **Highlight Cells Rules**, and then click **Text that Contains**. In the **Text That Contains** dialog box, with the insertion point blinking in the first box, type **Order** In the second box, click the **arrow**, and then in the list, click **Custom Format**. On the **Font tab**, under **Font style**, click **Bold Italic**. Click the **Color arrow**, and then under **Theme Colors**, click **Dark Blue, Text 2, Darker 25%**. Click **OK**, and then click **OK** again to apply the formatting to the items that need to be ordered.

13. Select the range **A15:A80**. In the **Styles group**, click the **Conditional Formatting** button. In the list, point to **Data Bars**, and then in the **gallery**, click **Blue Data Bar** to visually indicate the quantity in stock for each item.

14. To the left of the **Formula Bar**, in the **Name Box**, type **e15:e80** and then press Enter. On the **Home tab**, in the **Editing group**, click the **Find & Select** button. From the menu, click **Replace** to display the **Find and Replace** dialog box. In the **Find what** box, type **Base** In the **Replace with** box, type **Platinum** Click the **Replace All** button, and then click **OK** to replace 16 occurrences of *Base* with *Platinum*.

Click **OK** to close the message box. **Close** the **Find and Replace** dialog box.

15. Scroll down to view **row 81**. Click cell **A81**, type **Last Edited by Rose Elleni** and then press Enter. With cell **A82** as the active cell, on the **Formulas tab**, in the **Function Library group**, click the **Date & Time** button. In the list of functions, click **NOW**. In the **Function Arguments** dialog box, click **OK** to close the dialog box. Adjust the width of **column A** to **127 pixels** to display the current date and time. Apply **Align Text Left** to cell **A82**.

16. **Save** your changes up to this point. Press Ctrl + Home to make cell **A1** the active cell. Select the range **A14:F80**. Click the **Insert tab**, and then in the **Tables group**, click the **Table** button. In the **Create Table** dialog box, if necessary, select the **My table has headers** check box. Click **OK** to create the table.

17. On the **Design tab**, in the **Table Styles group**, click the **More** button, and then under **Light**, click **Table Style Light 9**.

18. In the header row of the table, click the **Retail Price arrow**, and then from the menu, click **Sort Smallest to Largest** to rearrange the data so that the products display in ascending order with the lowest price item first and the highest price item last.

19. In the header row of the table, click the **Shape arrow**. From the menu, click **Sort A to Z**. Click the **Shape arrow** again. On the menu, click the **(Select All)** check box to clear all the check boxes. Then, click to select only the **Oval** check box, and then click **OK** to display only the **Oval** products.

20. Click any cell in the table so that the table is selected. On the Ribbon, click the **Design tab**, and then in the **Table Style**

(Project 11C–Pendants continues on the next page)

Skills Review

(Project 11C–Pendants continued)

Options group, select the **Total Row** check box. Click cell **A81**, click the **arrow** that displays, and then in the list, click **Sum** to display *683*—the total number of oval shaped pendant castings in stock. Click cell **A11**, type **Twenty different styles, 683 total in stock** and then press Enter.

21. Click any cell in the table. On the Ribbon, click the **Design tab**, and then in the **Table Style Options group**, click the **Total Row** check box to clear it and remove the Total row from the bottom of the table. In the table header row, click the **Shape arrow**, and then on the menu, click **Clear Filter From "Shape"** to redisplay all of the products.

22. In the table header row, click the **Style# arrow**, and then click **Sort A to Z**, which will apply an ascending sort to the **Style#** column. In the **Tools group**, click the **Convert to Range** button. In the message box, click **Yes**.

23. Press Ctrl + Home to display the top of your worksheet. On the **Insert tab**, in the **Text group**, click **Header & Footer** to switch to **Page Layout view**. In the **Navigation group**, click the **Go to Footer** button, click just above the word *Footer*, and then in the **Header & Footer Elements group**, click the **File Name** button. Click a cell just above the footer to deselect the **Footer area** and view your file name.

24. Click the **Page Layout tab**. In the **Page Setup group**, click the **Margins** button, and then at the bottom of the **Margins**

gallery, click **Custom Margins**. In the **Page Setup** dialog box, under **Center on page**, select the **Horizontally** check box. Click **OK**, and then return the worksheet to **Normal** view. Press Ctrl + Home to move to the top of the worksheet. Delete **Sheet2** and **Sheet3**.

25. On the **Page Layout tab**, in the **Page Setup group**, click the **Print Titles** button. Under **Print titles**, click in the **Rows to repeat at top** box, and then at the right, click the **Collapse Dialog** button. From the **row heading area**, select **rows 13:14**, and then press Enter. Click **OK**.

26. **Save** your workbook. To submit electronically, follow the instructions provided by your instructor. To print, from the **Office** menu, point to the **Print** button, and then click **Print Preview**. In the **Preview group**, click the **Next Page** and **Previous Page** buttons as necessary to view and check each page. Be sure the two header rows and the footer display on each page, and then click the **Print** button. In the **Print** dialog box, under **Print range**, be sure that **All** is selected, and then click **OK**. If you are directed to submit printed formulas, refer to Activity 9.17 in Project 9A to do so.

27. If you printed your formulas, be sure to redisplay the worksheet by pressing Ctrl + `. From the **Office** menu, click **Close**. If a dialog box displays asking if you want to save changes, click **No** so that you do *not* save the changes you made for printing formulas. **Close** Excel.

End **You have completed Project 11C**

Content-Based Assessments

Skills Review

Project 11D — Auto Loan

In this project, you will apply the skills you practiced from the Objectives in Project 11B.

Objectives: 6. *Use Financial Functions;* **7.** *Use Goal Seek;* **8.** *Create a Data Table.*

In the following Skills Review, you will create a worksheet for Jennifer Bernard, U.S. Sales Director, that details loan information for purchasing eight automobiles for Adamantine Jewelry sales representatives. The monthly payment for the eight automobiles cannot exceed $3,000. The two worksheets in your workbook will look similar to Figure 11.42.

For Project 11D, you will need the following file:

New blank Excel workbook

You will save your workbook as
11D_Auto_Loan_Firstname_Lastname

Figure 11.42

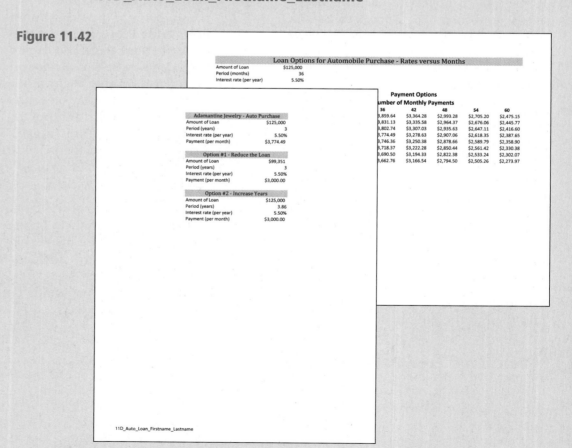

(Project 11D–Auto Loan continues on the next page)

(Project 11D–Auto Loan continued)

1. **Start** Excel and display a new blank workbook. From the **Office** menu, display the **Save As** dialog box, navigate to your **Excel Chapter 11** folder, and then in the **File name** box, type **11D_Auto_Loan_Firstname_Lastname** Click **Save** or press Enter.

2. Widen **column A** to **180 pixels** and **column B** to **100 pixels**. In cell **A1**, type **Adamantine Jewelry – Auto Purchase**

3. **Merge and Center** the worksheet title in the range **A1:B1**, change the **Font** to **Cambria**, the **Font Size** to **12**, and then add a **Fill Color** of **Orange, Accent 6, Lighter 40%**. Rename the worksheet tab as **Auto Loan**

4. In the range **A2:B5**, enter the following row titles and data.

Amount of Loan	$125,000
Period (years)	3
Interest rate (per year)	5.5%
Payment (per month)	

5. Click cell **B5**. On the **Formulas tab**, in the **Function Library group**, click the **Financial** button, and then click **PMT**. Drag the **Function Arguments** dialog box to the right side of your screen so you can view **columns A:B**.

6. In the **Rate** box, type **b4/12** to convert the annual interest rate to a monthly interest rate. Press Tab, and then in the **Nper** box, type **b3*12** to convert the number of years in the loan to the total number of months. Press Tab, and then in the **Pv** box, type **b2** to enter the present value of the loan. Click **OK** to create the function. In the **Formula Bar**, between the equal sign and *PMT*, type – (minus sign) to insert a minus sign into the formula, and then press Enter

   to display the loan payment as a positive number.

7. The result of *$3,774.49* is higher than the monthly payment of $3,000 that Jennifer wants. One option is to reduce the amount of money that she is going to borrow; she can determine the maximum amount that she can borrow and still keep the payment at $3,000 by using Goal Seek. Click cell **B5**. On the **Data tab**, in the **Data Tools group**, click the **What-If Analysis** button, and then in the list, click **Goal Seek**. In the **Goal Seek** dialog box, in the **Set cell** box, confirm that *B5* displays.

8. Press Tab. In the **To value** box, type the payment goal of **3000** and then press Tab. In the **By changing cell** box, type **b2** which is the amount of the loan. Click **OK** two times. For three years at 5.5%, Jennifer can borrow only $99,351 if she maintains a monthly payment of $3,000.

9. Click cell **A7**. Type **Option #1 - Reduce the Loan** and then press Enter. Right-click cell **A1**. On the Mini toolbar, click the **Format Painter** button, and then click cell **A7** to copy the formats.

10. Select the range **A2:B5**, right-click, and then click **Copy**. Click cell **A8**, right-click, and then from the shortcut menu, click **Paste Special**. In the **Paste Special** dialog box, under **Paste**, click the **Values and number formats** option button, and then click **OK**. Press Esc to cancel the moving border.

11. In cell **B2**, type **125000** and then press Enter to restore the original loan amount. Another option that Jennifer can explore with Goal Seek is to increase the number of years over which she finances the automobiles. Click cell **B5**. On the **Data tab**, in the **Data Tools group**, click the **What-If**

(Project 11D–Auto Loan continues on the next page)

Content-Based Assessments

Skills Review

(Project 11D–Auto Loan continued)

Analysis button, and then click **Goal Seek**.

12. In the **Set cell** box, confirm that **B5** displays. Press Tab. In the **To value** box, type **3000** and then press Tab. In the **By changing cell** box, type **b3** which is the number of years for the loan. Click **OK** two times. Extending the loan over 3.86 years will maintain a monthly payment of $3,000 at the current interest rate.

13. Click **A13**. Type **Option #2 - Increase Years** and then press Enter. Use the **Format Painter** to copy the formats from cell **A7** to cell **A13**. Select the range **A2:B5**, right-click, click **Copy**, and then click cell **A14**. Right-click, click **Paste Special**, click the **Values and number formats** option button, and then click **OK**. Press Esc to cancel the moving border.

14. Click cell **B15**, right-click to display the Mini toolbar, and then click the **Decrease Decimal** button until the number of decimal places is two. Click cell **B3**. Type **3** and then press Enter to restore the original value.

15. Display the worksheet in **Page Layout** view, and then insert the **File Name** in the footer. Center the worksheet **Horizontally**, and then return the worksheet to **Normal** view. Press Ctrl + Home to move to the top of the worksheet.

16. **Save** the changes you have made thus far. To determine how variable interest rates and a varying number of payments affect the payment amount, Jennifer will set up a two-variable data table. Double-click the **Sheet2 tab**, rename it **Payment Table** and then press Enter. In cell **A1**, type **Loan Options for Automobile Purchase - Rates versus Months** and then press Enter. **Merge and Center** this title across the range

A1:I1. Change the **Font** to **Cambria**, the **Font Size** to **16**, and apply a **Fill Color** of **Orange, Accent 6, Lighter 40%**.

17. Widen **column A** to **165 pixels**. Widen **column B** to **80 pixels**. Select **columns C:I** and widen them to **85 pixels**. In the range **A2:B4**, enter the following row titles and data.

Amount of Loan	$125,000
Period (months)	36
Interest rate (per year)	5.5%

18. Click cell **C8**. Type **24** and then press Tab. Type **30** and then press Tab. Select the range **C8:D8**. Drag the fill handle to the right through cell **I8** to fill a pattern of months from 24 to 60 in increments of six months.

19. In cell **B9**, type **7.0%** and press Enter. Type **6.5%** and press Enter. Select the range **B9:B10**, and then drag the fill handle down through cell **B16** to fill a pattern of interest rates in increments of .5% from 7.00% down to 3.50%.

20. Click cell **C6**. Type **Payment Options** and then press Enter. **Merge and Center** this title across the range **C6:I6**. Change the **Font Size** to **14** and apply **Bold**. Click cell **C7**. Type **Number of Monthly Payments** and then use the **Format Painter** to apply the format of cell **C6** to cell **C7**.

21. Click cell **A9**, type **Rates** and then press Enter. Select the range **A9:A16**. On the **Home tab**, in the **Alignment group**, click the **Merge and Center** button, click the **Align Text Right** button, and then click the **Middle Align** button. Change the **Font Size** to **14** and apply **Bold**.

(Project 11D–Auto Loan continues on the next page)

(Project 11D–Auto Loan continued)

22. Click cell **B8**. On the **Formulas tab**, in the **Function Library group**, click the **Financial** button, and then click **PMT**. In the **Rate** box, type **b4/12** to divide the interest rate per year by 12 to convert it to a monthly interest rate. press (Tab), and then in the **Nper** box, type **b3** press (Tab). In the **Pv** box, type **-b2** and then click **OK**.

23. Select the range **B8:I16**. On the **Data tab**, in the **Data Tools group**, click the **What-If Analysis** button, and then in the list, click **Data Table**. In the **Data Table** dialog box, in the **Row input cell** box, type **b3** and then press (Tab). In the **Column input cell** box, type **b4** In the **Data Table** dialog box, click **OK** to create the data table.

24. Click cell **B8**, and then right-click to display the Mini toolbar. Click the **Format Painter** button. Select the range **C9:I16** to apply the same format. Select the ranges **B9:B16** and **C8:I8** and apply **Bold** and **Center**. Notice that in cell **G9**, the payment is *$2,993.28*, which is close to Jennifer's goal of a monthly payment of $3,000. At any of the interest rates, she will have to extend the loan over at least 48 months to stay within her goal of $3,000 per month.

25. Display the worksheet in **Page Layout** view, and then insert the **File Name** in the footer. Center the worksheet **Horizontally**, and set the **Orientation** to **Landscape**. Then return the worksheet to **Normal** view. Press (Ctrl) + (Home) to move to the top of the worksheet. Delete **Sheet3** from the workbook.

26. **Save** your workbook. Press (Ctrl) + (F2) to display the worksheet in **Print Preview**. To print, in the **Print group**, click the **Print** button, under **Print what**, click the **Entire workbook** option button, and then click **OK**. To submit electronically, follow your instructor's directions. Determine if you are to print formulas for any or all of the worksheets in this workbook. To print formulas, refer to Activity 9.17 in Project 9A.

27. If you printed your formulas, be sure to redisplay the worksheet by pressing (Ctrl) + (ˈ). From the **Office** menu, click **Close**. If you are prompted to save changes, click **No**. **Close** Excel.

End **You have completed Project 11D**

Excel

chaptereleven

Mastering Excel

Project 11E—Sales

In this project, you will apply the skills you practiced from the Objectives in Projects 11A and 11B.

Objectives: 1. *Use SUM, AVERAGE, MEDIAN, MIN, and MAX Functions;* **2.** *Use COUNTIF and IF Functions, and Apply Conditional Formatting;* **3.** *Use a Date Function;* **4.** *Freeze Panes and Create an Excel Table;* **5.** *Format and Print a Large Worksheet;* **7.** *Use Goal Seek.*

In the following Mastering Excel assessment, you will edit a worksheet for Jennifer Bernard, U.S. Sales Director for Adamantine Jewelry, that calculates the October sales commission and bonuses for the U.S. sales representatives. The sales representatives earn 15% commission and those whose sales exceed $20,000 per month earn a bonus of $750. The worksheet will also provide sales statistics for the month of October and will detail November sales goals. The worksheets of your workbook will look similar to Figure 11.43.

For Project 11E, you will need the following file:

e11E_Sales

You will save your workbook as 11E_Sales_Firstname_Lastname

Figure 11.43

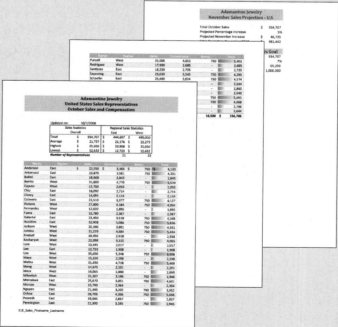

11E_Sales_Firstname_Lastname

(Project 11E–Sales continues on the next page)

Content-Based Assessments

(Project 11E–Sales continued)

1. **Start** Excel, locate and open the file **e11E_Sales**, and then **Save** the file in your **Excel Chapter 11** folder as 11E_Sales_ Firstname_Lastname Rename **Sheet1** as Sales Data In cell **C6**, enter the **NOW** function, and then on the **Home tab**, in the **Number group**, click the **Number Format arrow** and apply the **Short Date** format to the date. In cell **C9**, enter a function that sums the total sales in the range **C16:C58**. In cells **C10**, **C11**, and **C12**, use statistical functions to calculate the average sales, the highest sales, and the lowest sales.

2. In cell **D16**, construct a formula to calculate the commission on sales earned by **Anderson** by using a commission formula of *Sales times 15%*. Format the result with **Comma Style** and **zero decimal places**. Copy the formula down for each sales representative. In cell **E16**, enter an **IF** function and test whether the sales value in cell **C16** is greater than **20000**. If true, display **750** and if false, display **0** Format the result as **Comma Style**, with **zero decimal places**, and then fill the formula down for each sales representative. Those representatives who receive no bonus will display – (a minus sign) in the cell.

3. In cell **F16**, construct a formula to calculate the total compensation by adding the **Commission** and **Bonus** amounts for **Anderson**. The format of Comma Style and zero decimal places will be applied based on the reference to cell D16. Fill the formula down for each sales representative. With the range **F16:F58** still selected, apply **Light Blue Data Bar Conditional Formatting** to the **Total** column. In cell **D13**, enter a **COUNTIF** function to count the number of sales representatives in the **East** region. Enter a similar function in cell **E13** for the **West** region.

4. Select the range **A15:F58**, and then **Insert** a **Table** with headers. Apply **Table Style Medium 7**. In the **Name** column, **Sort** the table **A to Z**. Change the **Table Style Options** to display the **Total Row**.

5. If necessary, scroll up so that you can view **rows 1:18** on your screen. Select **row 16**, click the **View tab**. In the **Window group**, click the **Freeze Panes** button, and then click **Freeze Panes**. Scroll to bring the **Total row** at the bottom of the table closer to **row 15**—it is OK to leave three or four rows visible for visual reference. Recall that you can freeze panes in this manner to keep row titles visible while scrolling down through a large amount of data.

6. Filter the table to display only the sales representatives in the **East** region—the table will be filtered even though not all rows are in view. Click cell **C59**, and then by using the functions available from the **Total row arrow** in the **Sales** column, **Sum** the **Sales** for the **East** region. Right-click over the result, **Copy** the result, right-click over cell **D9**, click **Paste Special**, and then paste the **Values and number formats** to cell **D9**.

7. Using the same technique, and by using the **Total row arrow** in the **Sales** column, calculate the **Average** for the **East** region, and then copy and paste the **value and number format** to cell **D10**. By using the **Total row arrow** in the **Sales** column, calculate the highest and lowest sales amount for the **East** region, and paste the **values and number formats** to cells **D11** and **D12**. You can see that by freezing panes and using the shortcut menus, you can easily copy and paste values from one section of your worksheet to another without unnecessary scrolling.

(Project 11E–Sales continues on the next page)

(Project 11E–Sales continued)

8. Filter the **Sales** data for the **West** region, scroll to view the data and notice that the Freeze Panes command is still in effect. Position the **Total row** close to **row 15**. Then, by using the **Total row arrow** in the **Sales** column in the manner you did in the previous step, make similar calculations and then copy and paste the **Values and number formats** into the range **E9:E12**.

9. Clear the filter to redisplay all of the data in the table, and then in the **Total** row, **Sum** the **Sales**, **Commission**, **Bonus**, and **Total** columns. Select the four totals, right-click, and then apply **Accounting Number Format** with **zero decimal places**. Click the **View tab**, in the **Window group**, click the **Freeze Panes** button, and then click **Unfreeze Panes**. Click inside the table, and then on the **Design tab**, convert the table to a range. To the ranges **C9:E12** and **C16:F16**, apply **Accounting Number Format** with **zero decimal places**.

10. Insert a **Footer** with the **File Name** in the left section, and then **Center** the worksheet **Horizontally**. Click the **Print Titles** button and repeat **row 15** at the top of each page. Return to **Normal** view and display the top of your worksheet.

11. **Save** your work up to this point. **Rename Sheet2 as November Sales Goal** In cell **A1**, type **Adamantine Jewelry** and then adjust the column width of **column A to 220 pixels**. **Merge and Center** the title across **A1:B1**. Change the **Font** to **Cambria**, change the **Font Size** to **14**, and then add a **Fill Color** of **Orange, Accent 6, Lighter 40%**. In cell **A2**, type **November Sales Projection – U.S.** Copy the format from cell **A1** to cell **A2**. In the range **A4:B7**, enter the following data.

Total October Sales	
Projected Percentage Increase	5%
Projected November Increase	
Sales Projection November 2010	

12. Click cell **B4**, type = to begin a formula, click the **Sales Data worksheet** to make it the active sheet, click cell **C9**, and then press Enter to return to the **November Sales Goal** worksheet and reference the **Total October Sales** in cell **B4**. Format the result with **Accounting Number Format** with **zero decimal places**.

13. In cell **B6**, construct a formula to multiply the **Total October Sales** times the **Projected Percentage Increase**, and then format the result the same as cell **B4**. In cell **B7**, construct a formula to add the **Total October Sales** and the **Projected November Increase**.

14. Jennifer's sales goal for the U.S. sales representatives is $1,000,000. Use **Goal Seek** to determine the **Projected Percentage Increase** if the **Sales Projection November 2010** value is **1,000,000**. In cell **A9**, type **Increase Needed to Reach Sales Goal** and then format the cell the same as cell **A1**. **Copy** the range **A4:B7**, and then paste the **Values and number formats** to cell **A10**. In cell **B5**, reset the original value to **5%** and press Enter.

15. Insert a **Footer** in the left section with the **File Name**, and then **Center** the worksheet **Horizontally** on the page. Return to **Normal** view and display the top of the worksheet. Delete **Sheet3** from the workbook.

(Project 11E–Sales continues on the next page)

(Project 11E–Sales continued)

16. Save your workbook. **Print** the **Entire workbook** or submit electronically as directed. If you are directed to submit printed formulas, refer to Activity 9.17 in Project 9A to do so. If you printed your formulas, be sure to redisplay the worksheet by pressing Ctrl + `. From the **Office** menu, click **Close**. If you are prompted to save changes, click **No**. **Close** Excel.

End You have completed Project 11E

Mastering Excel

Project 11F — Retirement

In this project, you will apply the skills you practiced from the Objectives in Projects 11A and 11B.

Objectives: 3. *Use a Date Function;* **6.** *Use Financial Functions;* **8.** *Create a Data Table.*

In the following Mastering Excel project, you will create a data table for Rosetta Caputo, the Chief Financial Officer for Adamantine Jewelry, that she will use to consider investment alternatives for the employee benefits retirement fund. Your workbook will look similar to Figure 11.44.

For Project 11F, you will need the following file:

New blank Excel workbook

You will save your workbook as
11F_Retirement_Firstname_Lastname

Figure 11.44

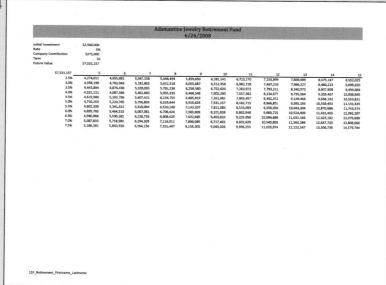

(Project 11F–Retirement continues on the next page)

Content-Based Assessments

(Project 11F–Retirement continued)

1. **Start** Excel and display a new blank workbook. In your **Excel Chapter 11** folder, **Save** the file as **11F_Retirement_Firstname_Lastname** In cell **A1**, type **Adamantine Jewelry Retirement Fund** and then **Merge and Center** the text across **A1:L1**. Change the **Font** to **Cambria**, change the **Font Size** to **16**, and then apply a **Fill Color** of **Red, Accent 2, Lighter 40%**.

2. Copy the formatting from cell **A1** to cell **A2**. Then, in cell **A2**, enter the **NOW** function. On the **Home tab**, in the **Number group**, click the **Number Format arrow**, and then apply the **Short Date** format. In the range **A4:B8**, enter the following row titles and data and then **AutoFit column A**.

Initial Investment	$2,500,000
Rate	5%
Company Contribution	$275,000
Term	10
Future Value	

3. Click cell **B8**. Click the **Formulas tab**, and then insert the **Financial** function *FV* to calculate the future value of the retirement fund based on the data that you entered in Step 2. Complete the arguments as follows: the **Rate** is the value in cell **B5**, and **Nper** is the value in cell **B7**. **Pmt** is the amount of the **Company contribution** in cell **B6**, and **Pv** is the **Initial Investment** in cell **B4**. Click **OK**, and then edit the formula in the **Formula Bar** so that the result displays as a positive number. Format the **Future Value** with **zero decimal places**. Based on the calculations, at the end of ten years, the fund will have a value of *$7,531,157*.

4. In the range **B10:L10**, in one-year increments, use **AutoFill** to enter a series of years from **5** to **15**, indicating the term of the retirement fund. Apply a **Thick Bottom Border** to the range. Beginning in cell **A11**, enter the possible interest rates for the fund beginning with **2.5%** and increasing in increments of .5% up to 7.5%. Format the interest rates with **one decimal place**.

5. In cell **A10** type **=b8** to enter a formula that references cell **B8**. Select the range **A10:L21**, and then create a **Data Table** with a **Row input cell** that references cell **B7** and a **Column input cell** that references **B5**. Format the results in the data table with **Comma Style, zero decimal places**. You can see by the resulting data table, that the higher the interest rate that can be obtained for the investment, the higher the value of the fund will be in future years.

6. Insert a footer in the left section with the **File Name**, exit the **Footer area**, display the **Page Layout tab**, and then **Center** the worksheet **Horizontally** on the page. Change the **Orientation** to **Landscape**. In the **Scale to Fit group**, set the **Width** to **1 page** and the **Height** to **1 page** (or scale to 70%). Return to **Normal** view, display the top of the worksheet, and then delete the extra worksheets from the workbook.

7. **Save** your workbook. **Print** the worksheet, or submit electronically as directed. If you are directed to submit printed formulas, refer to Activity 9.17 in Project 9A to do so.

8. If you printed your formulas, be sure to redisplay the worksheet by pressing Ctrl + `. From the **Office** menu, click **Close**. If you are prompted to save changes, click **No**. **Close** Excel.

End You have completed Project 11F

Mastering Excel

Project 11G — Opals

In this project, you will apply the skills you practiced from all of the Objectives in Projects 11A and 11B.

Objectives: 1. *Use SUM, AVERAGE, MEDIAN, MIN, and MAX Functions;*
2. *Use COUNTIF and IF Functions, and Apply Conditional Formatting;*
3. *Use a Date Function;* **4.** *Freeze Panes and Create an Excel Table;*
5. *Format and Print a Large Worksheet;* **6.** *Use Financial Functions;*
7. *Use Goal Seek;* **8.** *Create a Data Table.*

In the following Mastering Excel assessment, you will edit a worksheet for Adamantine Jewelry's Chief Financial Officer, Rosetta Caputo. Adamantine Jewelry is considering the purchase of Opal Industries—a large distributor of elegant and expensive opal jewelry. The purchase includes the entire current inventory held by Opal Industries. Rosetta wants to compute the value of the Opal Industries inventory and determine which items are still in production and which items are in a warehouse. She must also explore alternatives for financing the purchase. Your completed workbook will look similar to Figure 11.45.

For Project 11G, you will need the following file:

e11G_Opals

You will save your workbook as
11G_Opals_Firstname_Lastname

Figure 11.45

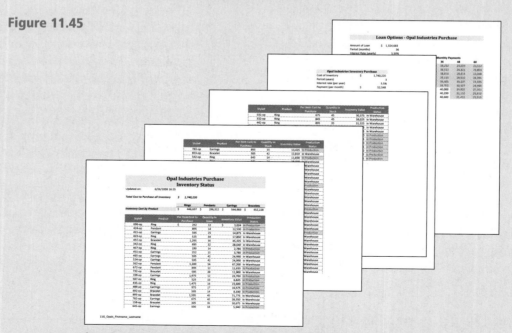

(Project 11G–Opals continues on the next page)

Content-Based Assessments

(Project 11G–Opals continued)

1. **Start** Excel. From the student files that accompany this text, locate and open the file **e11G_Opals**, and then **Save** it in your **Excel Chapter 11** folder as **11G_Opals_ Firstname_Lastname**

2. In cell **B3**, insert the **NOW** function. In cell **E11**, construct a formula to calculate the **Inventory Value** of the first Style# by multiplying the **Per Item Cost to Purchase** times the **Quantity in Stock**, and then copy the formula down through **row 76**. Format the selected range with **Comma Style** and **zero decimal places**.

3. Opal Industries moves stock from the production facility to the warehouse after 20 items are produced. In cell **F11**, enter an **IF** function to test whether the **Quantity in Stock** value in cell **D11** is **greater than or equal to 20**. If true, display **In Warehouse** and if false, display **In Production** Copy the formula down through **row 76**. With the range still selected, use the **Text that Contains** conditional formatting to apply **Green Fill with Dark Green Text** to cells that contain **In Production**

4. Select the range **A10:F76**, and then **Insert** a **Table** with headers. Apply **Table Style Light 9**. Change the **Table Style Options** to display the **Total Row**. Press Ctrl + Home to deselect the table and view **row 1** on your screen. Select **row 11**, click the **View tab**, in the **Window group**, click the **Freeze Panes** button, and then click **Freeze Panes**.

5. Filter the table to display only the **Ring** products, and then scroll so that the **Total row** is closer to the column titles in **row 14**. In the **Total row**, calculate the **Sum** for the **Inventory Value** of Rings. **Copy** the result, and then in cell **C8**,

Paste the **Values and number formats**. Even though some rows are out of view, the calculation is made on the appropriate rows.

6. Repeat Step 5 for the **Pendant**, **Earrings**, and **Bracelet** products in the appropriate cells. Then clear any filters to display all of the data in the table. Click any table cell, click the **Design tab**, remove the **Total Row** from the table, and then convert the table to a range.

7. In cell **C5**, enter a function to calculate the cost to purchase the total inventory, which is the sum of the range **C8:F8**. Your result is *1,740,220*. On the **View tab**, in the **Window group**, click the **Freeze Panes** button, and then click **Unfreeze Panes**. Select cell **C11**, and then hold down Ctrl and select cell **E11**, cell **C5**, and the range **C8:F8**. To the selected cells, apply **Accounting Number Format** with **zero decimal places**. Set the width of **columns C:F** to **100 pixels**.

8. Insert a footer with the **File Name** in the left section, and then **Center** the sheet **Horizontally**. Set the **Print Titles** option to repeat **row 10** at the top of each page. Change the **Orientation** to **Landscape**, return to **Normal** view, and then display the top of your worksheet. **Save** your workbook.

9. **Copy** cell **C5**, display the **Goal** sheet, and then use **Paste Special** to paste the **Values and number formats** to cell **B2** in the **Goal** sheet. In cell **B5**, insert the **PMT** function using the data from the range **B2:B4**. Be sure that you convert the interest rate and period to reflect monthly payments by dividing the interest rate by 12 and multiplying the years by 12. Display the result as a positive number. Apply the

(Project 11G–Opals continues on the next page)

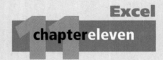

(Project 11G–Opals continued)

Accounting Number Format with zero decimal places to cell **B5**—your result is $52,548.

10. Rosetta prefers that the monthly payment not exceed $40,000. Use **Goal Seek** to determine the amount of money that Adamantine Jewelry can finance to keep the payment at $40,000. The interest rate and period will not change. The result is $1,324,683.07.

11. Copy the range **B2:B5**, and then paste the **Values and number formats** to cell **B8**. In cell **B2**, type **1740220** to restore the original amount.

12. Insert a footer in the left section with the **File Name**, and then **Center** the sheet **Horizontally** on the page. Display the sheet in **Normal** view, and then **Save** your workbook.

13. Copy cell **B8**, display the **Financing** sheet, and then in cell **B3**, paste the value and number format; this will reference the amount that Rosetta has decided to finance as the **Amount of Loan**. In cell **B7**, enter a **PMT** function using the data in the range **B3:B5**. The period is already expressed in months, but the rate is not. Be sure that the result displays as a positive number. To determine how changes in interest rates and number of payments affect the payment amount, Rosetta will set up a two-variable data table. Rosetta is exploring loan programs from 12 to 60 months in duration and at rates of 2.5% to 6.5%.

14. Select the range **B7:G16**, and then create a **Data Table** using the information in cells **B3:B5** in which the **Row input cell** is the **Period** and the **Column input cell** is the **Interest rate**. Format the data with **Comma Style** and **zero decimal** places. Format cell **B7** with **Accounting Number Format** and **zero decimal places**.

15. Select the data table results—the range **C8:G16**. Recall that Rosetta prefers a monthly payment that does not exceed $40,000. Apply **Conditional Formatting** using the **Highlight Cells Rules Less Than** option. In the **Format cells that are LESS THAN** box, type **40000** and use **Light Red Fill with Dark Red Text**. Click any cell to deselect. Rosetta can clearly see which financing rates and terms are acceptable.

16. Insert a footer in the left section with the **File Name**, and then **Center** the sheet **Horizontally** on the page. Display the sheet in **Normal** view and press Ctrl + Home to display the top of the worksheet.

17. **Save** your workbook. **Print** the **Entire workbook**, or submit electronically as directed. If you are directed to submit printed formulas, refer to Activity 9.17 in Project 9A to do so.

18. If you printed your formulas, be sure to redisplay the sheet by pressing Ctrl + `. From the **Office** menu, click **Close**. If you are prompted to save changes, click **No**. **Close** Excel.

End You have completed Project 11G

Content-Based Assessments

Excel
chaptereleven

Mastering Excel

Project 11H—*GO!* Fix It

In this project, you will construct a solution by applying any combination of the skills you practiced from the Objectives in Projects 11A and 11B.

For Project 11H, you will need the following file:

e11H_Ruby_Inventory

You will save your document as
11H_Ruby_Inventory_Firstname_Lastname

From the student files that accompany this textbook, open the file **e11H_Ruby_Inventory**, and then save the file in your chapter folder as **11H_Ruby_Inventory_Firstname_Lastname**

Adamantine Jewelry maintains a large stock of rubies for use in its retail business. In this project, you will edit and complete an Inventory and Reorder List and Loan Information tables.

This document contains five errors that you must find and correct. Read and examine the workbook, and then edit to correct the errors that you find. Types of errors could include:

- Spelling, grammar, and punctuation errors in cells, charts, worksheet tabs, or file names.

- Errors in data entry and workbook layout. Formatting errors in text, numbers, alignment, indents and spacing, tabs, wrapping, merge and center, text direction and orientation, fonts, borders, patterns, protection, AutoFormat, conditional formatting, data sorting, filtering, and validation.

- Formula and function errors such as incorrect and missing formulas, error indicators and values, relative vs. absolute cell referencing, What-If Analysis, Paste Special, function arguments, and Goal Seek.

- Errors in object design, layout, and formatting.

- Row and column formatting errors such as height, width, and AutoFit.

- Worksheet, tab design, and formatting errors such as missing or blank worksheets, worksheet tab colors, and locations.

- Page setup errors such as page orientation and scaling, margins and centering, headers and footers, sheet gridlines, and row and column headings.

(Project 11H–*GO!* Fix It continues on the next page)

(Project 11H–*GO!* Fix It continued)

To complete this project you should know:

- There are no spelling, grammar, punctuation, usage, font, font size, or border errors in the body of the worksheets.

- All the errors in the Inventory & Reorder List are in the top portion of the worksheet.

- There are no errors in the Loan Information sheet, but you must calculate the Payment in cell E13 and then create the data table.

Save the changes you have made, add the file name to the footers, and then submit as directed.

End **You have completed Project 11H** —————————————

Outcomes-Based Assessments

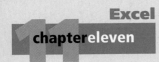

Rubric

The following outcomes-based assessments are *open-ended assessments*. That is, there is no specific correct result; your result will depend on your approach to the information provided. Make *Professional Quality* your goal. Use the following scoring rubric to guide you in *how* to approach the problem, and then to evaluate *how well* your approach solves the problem.

The *criteria*—Software Mastery, Content, Format and Layout, and Process—represent the knowledge and skills you have gained that you can apply to solving the problem. The *levels of performance*—Professional Quality, Approaching Professional Quality, or Needs Quality Improvements—help you and your instructor evaluate your result.

	Your completed project is of Professional Quality if you:	Your completed project is Approaching Professional Quality if you:	Your completed project Needs Quality Improvements if you:
1-Software Mastery	Choose and apply the most appropriate skills, tools, and features and identify efficient methods to solve the problem.	Choose and apply some appropriate skills, tools, and features, but not in the most efficient manner.	Choose inappropriate skills, tools, or features, or are inefficient in solving the problem.
2-Content	Construct a solution that is clear and well organized, contains content that is accurate, appropriate to the audience and purpose, and is complete. Provide a solution that contains no errors of spelling, grammar, or style.	Construct a solution in which some components are unclear, poorly organized, inconsistent, or incomplete. Misjudge the needs of the audience. Have some errors in spelling, grammar, or style, but the errors do not detract from comprehension.	Construct a solution that is unclear, incomplete, or poorly organized; contains some inaccurate or inappropriate content; and contains many errors of spelling, grammar, or style. Do not solve the problem.
3-Format and Layout	Format and arrange all elements to communicate information and ideas, clarify function, illustrate relationships, and indicate relative importance.	Apply appropriate format and layout features to some elements, but not others. Overuse features, causing minor distraction.	Apply format and layout that does not communicate information or ideas clearly. Do not use format and layout features to clarify function, illustrate relationships, or indicate relative importance. Use available features excessively, causing distraction.
4-Process	Use an organized approach that integrates planning, development, self-assessment, revision, and reflection.	Demonstrate an organized approach in some areas, but not others; or, use an insufficient process of organization throughout.	Do not use an organized approach to solve the problem.

Outcomes-Based Assessments

Problem Solving

Project 11I — Capital Equipment

In this project, you will construct a solution by applying any combination of the skills you practiced from the Objectives in Projects 11A and 11B.

For Project 11I, you will need the following file:

New blank Excel workbook

You will save your workbook as
11I_Capital_Equipment_Firstname_Lastname

Adamantine Jewelry plans to renovate the Milan production facility. The renovation consists primarily of the purchase and installation of new capital equipment used in the production of earrings and pendants. The renovation and equipment will cost $1,500,000. Rosetta Caputo, Chief Financial Officer, is exploring financing options for the purchase of the equipment. Create a workbook with two worksheets that Rosetta can use to analyze loan payment information. In the first worksheet, enter a title in cell A1. In cells A2:A5, enter the following row titles: **Amount of Loan, Period (years), Interest Rate (per year)**, and **Payment (per month)**. In cells B2:B4, enter the loan amount, **$1,500,000**; the Period, **10** years; and the Interest rate, **6.5%**. Adjust the column widths as necessary. In B5, use the preceding data to construct a PMT function to calculate the monthly loan payment, converting the interest rate and the period to reflect monthly payments.

Marco Canaperi, the company president, has asked Rosetta to keep the loan payments below $15,000. Use Goal Seek to explore two options for reducing the loan payment, either by reducing the loan or by increasing the number of years. Arrange the worksheet so that the two loan options display similar to Project 11B in the chapter.

In the second worksheet, using your work in Project 11B as a guide, create a data table to calculate payments over 10, 15, 20, and 25 years with varying interest rates from 3.5% to 8.5% in .5% increments. In A2:B4 enter the row titles and the loan information. In C6:C7 enter titles that describe the data table. In C8:F8 enter the yearly increments. In B9:B19 enter the interest rates in .5% increments. In B8 construct the PMT function, and then create the data table. On each worksheet, apply appropriate number formatting, use borders, fill colors, and font styles and sizes to create a professional worksheet. Add a footer to each worksheet that includes the file name, center the worksheets on the page, and delete unused sheets. Save the workbook as **11I_Capital_Equipment_Firstname_Lastname** and submit it as directed.

End You have completed Project 11I

Outcomes-Based Assessments

Problem Solving

Project 11J — Commission

In this project, you will construct a solution by applying any combination of the skills you practiced from the Objectives in Projects 11A and 11B.

For Project 11J, you will need the following file:

e11J_Commission

You will save your workbook as
11J_Commission_Firstname_Lastname

The U.S. Sales Director for Adamantine Jewelry, Jennifer Bernard, wants a report on the December sales and compensation for the U.S. sales representatives. From your student files, open e11J_Commissions. Calculate the Commission (Commission Rate times Sales) for each sales representative, using absolute cell references as necessary. Sales representatives whose sales exceed $20,000 receive a bonus of $750. In the Bonus column, use an IF function to calculate bonuses—the value_if_true is 750 and the value_if_false is 0. Then calculate the total Compensation (Commission + Bonus) for each sales representative. Use Conditional Formatting to apply Data Bars to the Total Compensation column. In the range B8:C12, enter functions to calculate the total sales and commission, the average sales and commission, the median sales and commission, and the highest and lowest sales and commission.

Insert a table using the range of data A16:F59. Sort the table from A to Z on the Name column. Add a Total Row to the table, freeze panes if you want to do so, and then filter the table for each region. Calculate the total Sales and Commissions for each region and enter the amounts in cells F8:G11 being sure to paste the value and number format. Then, total the Sales and Commissions in F12:G12. Convert the table to a range and unfreeze panes if necessary. Use the NOW function to enter the current date in cell B5 and apply the Short Date format. Add the file name to the footer, delete unused sheets, set up for printing appropriately, including printing the table header row on each page. Save the workbook as **11J_Commission_Firstname_Lastname** and submit it as directed.

End **You have completed Project 11J** ———————————

Problem Solving

Project 11K — Truck Purchase

In this project, you will construct a solution by applying any combination of the skills you practiced from the Objectives in Projects 11A and 11B.

For Project 11K, you will need the following file:

New blank Excel workbook

You will save your workbook as 11K_Truck_Purchase_Firstname_Lastname

Rosetta Caputo, Chief Financial Officer for Adamantine Jewelry, is exploring financing options for the purchase of five new delivery trucks for the Milan production facility. The cost of the five trucks is $150,000.

Rosetta wants to look at various loan arrangements by creating a data table. In A1, enter an appropriate title for the worksheet. In A2:A4, enter the following row titles: **Amount of Loan, Period (months), Interest Rate (per year)**. In B2:B4, enter the financing data: **$150,000**; **36**; **4.5%**. In C6 fill the payment periods in six-month increments beginning with 24 and concluding with 60. In the column beginning in cell B7, create a list of varying interest rates from 4.5% to 8% in .5% increments. In B6, construct a PMT function using the data in cells B2:B4 and then create the data table. Use formatting and editing techniques that you practiced in this chapter so that the workbook looks professional and is easy to read. Add the file name to the footer, delete unused sheets, and then arrange for attractive printing. Save the workbook as **11K_Truck_Purchase_Firstname_Lastname** and submit it as directed.

End You have completed Project 11K ————————————

More on your Student CD

The instructions for the following additional end-of-chapter projects are on your student CD in the folder 03_additional_end_of_chapter_projects.

Content-Based Assessments

Project L Mastering Excel — Apply the skills you practiced in Project A.

Project M Mastering Excel — Apply the skills you practiced in Project B.

Project N Business Running Case — Apply the skills you practiced in Projects A and B while helping an entrepreneur with the daily tasks of running a business.

In each chapter, this project focuses on applying the skills you have practiced in Projects A and B to a business. The project related to this business runs throughout the textbook. You will see how the Office applications relate to the day-to-day operation of a small business called Nelson Architectural Planning.

Outcomes-Based Assessments

Project O Problem Solving — Construct a solution by applying any combination of the skills you practiced from Projects A and B.

Project P Problem Solving — Construct a solution by applying any combination of the skills you practiced from Projects A and B.

Project Q You and GO! — Construct a solution that applies to your own life by applying any combination of the skills you practiced from Projects A and B.

Project R GO! with Help — Practice using Microsoft Office's Help Feature.

Project S Group Business Running Case — Work as part of a group to apply the skills you have gained thus far to help the Bell Orchid Hotel Group achieve its business goals.

Multimedia

The following multimedia accompany this textbook:

Companion Web site
www.prenhall.com/go — An interactive Web site designed to reinforce and test your understanding of the skills in this chapter.

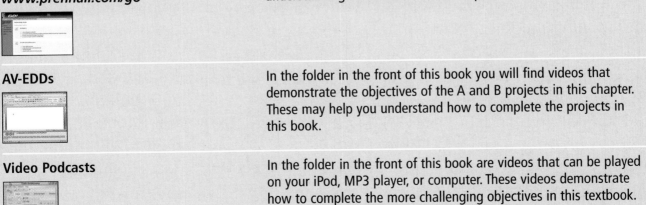

AV-EDDs — In the folder in the front of this book you will find videos that demonstrate the objectives of the A and B projects in this chapter. These may help you understand how to complete the projects in this book.

Video Podcasts — In the folder in the front of this book are videos that can be played on your iPod, MP3 player, or computer. These videos demonstrate how to complete the more challenging objectives in this textbook.

chapter twelve

Getting Started with Access Databases and Tables

OBJECTIVES

At the end of this chapter you will be able to:

1. Start Access and Create a New Blank Database
2. Add Records to a Table
3. Rename Table Fields in Datasheet View
4. Modify the Design of a Table
5. Add a Second Table to a Database
6. Print a Table
7. Create and Use a Query
8. Create and Use a Form
9. Create and Print a Report
10. Close and Save a Database

11. Create a Database by Using a Template
12. Organize Database Objects in the Navigation Pane
13. Create a New Table in a Database Created with a Template
14. View a Report and Print a Table in a Database Created with a Template
15. Use the Access Help System

OUTCOMES

Mastering these objectives will enable you to:

PROJECT 12A
Create a New Blank Database

PROJECT 12B
Create a Database from a Template

Texas Lakes Medical Center

Texas Lakes Medical Center is an urban hospital serving the city of Austin and surrounding Travis County, an area with a population of over one million people. Texas Lakes is renowned for its cardiac care unit, which is rated among the top ten in Texas. The hospital also offers state-of-the-art maternity and diagnostic services, a children's center, a Level II trauma center, and a number of specialized outpatient services. Physicians, nurses, scientists, and researchers from around the world come together at Texas Lakes to provide the highest quality patient care.

© Jeff Perkell / Photolibrary.com

Getting Started with Access Databases and Tables

Do you have a collection of belongings, such as a coin or stamp collection, a box of favorite recipes, or a stack of music CDs? Do you have an address book with the names, addresses, and phone numbers of your friends, business associates, and family members? If you collect something, chances are you have made an attempt to keep track of and organize the items in your collection.

Microsoft Office Access 2007 is a program you can use to organize a collection of related information, such as an inventory list, a list of people in an organization, or the students who are enrolled in classes in a college. Whether you use Access for personal or business purposes, it is a powerful program that enables you to organize, search, sort, retrieve, and present information in an organized manner.

Project 12A Doctor and Patient Contact Information

In Activities 12.01 through 12.14, you will assist June Liu, Chief Administrative Officer at Texas Lakes Medical Center, in creating a new database for tracking the contact information for doctors and patients. Using June's lists of doctors and patients, you will create an Access database to keep track of this information and to prepare a report. Your results will look similar to Figure 12.1.

For Project 12A, you will need the following file:

New blank Access database

You will save your database as
12A_Contact_Information_Firstname_Lastname

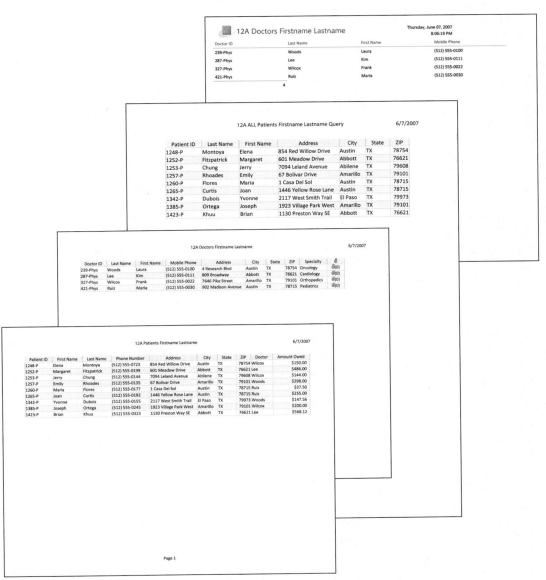

Figure 12.1
Project 12A—Contact Information

Objective 1
Start Access and Create a New Blank Database

A *database* collects and organizes *data*—facts about people, events, things, or ideas—related to a particular topic or purpose. *Information* is data that has been organized in a useful manner.

Many databases start as a simple list on paper, in a Word document, or in an Excel worksheet. As the list grows and the data becomes more difficult to keep track of, it is a good idea to transfer the data to a *database management system* (*DBMS*) such as Access.

The names and addresses of all the doctors and patients at a medical facility are an example of data that could be in a database. A database includes not only the data, but also the tools for organizing the data in a way that is useful to you.

The first step in creating a new database is to plan your database on paper. Determine what information you want to track, and then ask yourself, *What questions should this database be able to answer for me?*

For example, in a Contact Information database for the Texas Lakes Medical Center, the questions to be answered may include:

- How many doctors and patients are there at the Texas Lakes Medical Center?

- Which and how many patients live in Austin?

- Is any doctor or patient listed twice?

- Which and how many patients have a balance owed?

Activity 12.01 Starting Access, Creating and Naming a Folder, and Creating a Database from a New Blank Database

There are two methods to create a new Access database: create a new database by using a *template*—a preformatted database designed for a specific purpose—or create a new *blank database*. A blank database has no data and has no database tools; you create the data and the tools as you need them. In this activity, you will create a new blank database.

Regardless of which method you use, you must name and save the database before you can create any *objects* in the database. Objects are the basic parts of a database; you will create objects to store your data and to work with your data. Think of an Access database as a container for the database objects that you will create.

> **Note — Comparing Your Screen with the Figures in This Textbook**
>
> Your screen will match the figures shown in this textbook if you set your screen resolution to 1024 × 768. At other resolutions, your screen will closely resemble, but not match, the figures shown. To view your screen's resolution, on the Windows desktop, right-click in a blank area, click Personalize, and then click Display Settings.

1 Click the **Start** button 🌐, determine where the **Access** program is located, and then open the program. Take a moment to compare your screen with Figure 12.2 and study the parts of the Microsoft Access window described in the table in Figure 12.3.

From this Access starting point, you can open an existing database, create a new blank database, or create a new database from a template.

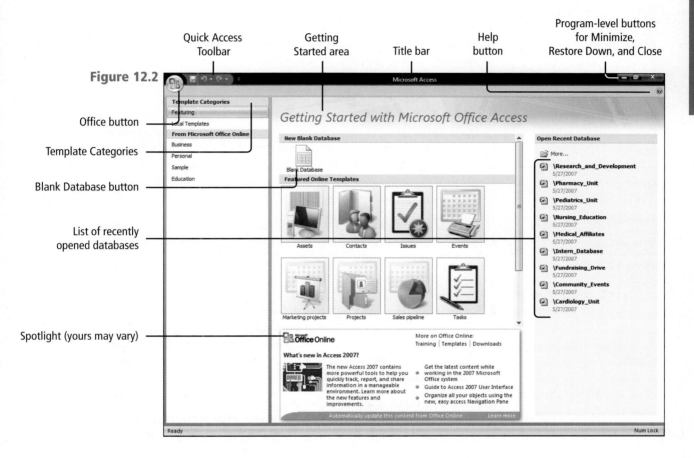

Figure 12.2

Quick Access Toolbar · Getting Started area · Title bar · Help button · Program-level buttons for Minimize, Restore Down, and Close

Office button · Template Categories · Blank Database button · List of recently opened databases · Spotlight (yours may vary)

The Access Getting Started Screen	
Window Part	**Description**
Blank Database button	Starts a new blank database.
Getting Started area	Contains the starting point to begin a New Blank Database or view new information from Microsoft Office Online.
Help button	Displays the Access Help window.
Open Recent Database	Displays a list of the most recently opened databases on the computer at which you are working.
Office button	Displays a menu of commands related to things you can do *with* a database, such as opening, saving, printing, or managing.
Program-level buttons for Minimize, Restore Down, and Close	Minimizes, restores, or closes the Access program.
Quick Access Toolbar	Displays buttons to perform frequently used commands with a single click. Frequently used commands in Access include Save, Undo, and Redo. You can add commands that you use frequently to the Quick Access Toolbar.
Spotlight	Displays the latest online content, such as new templates, articles about Access, and tips from Microsoft's Web site.
Template Categories	Displays a list of available database templates.
Title bar	Displays the program name and the program-level buttons.

Figure 12.3

2 Decide where you will store your Access databases for this textbook—for example, in the *Documents* folder on your hard disk drive or on a removable USB flash drive. Then, in the **Getting Started with Microsoft Office Access** area, under **New Blank Database**, click **Blank Database**.

3 On the right side of your screen, to the right of the **File Name** box, click the **Browse** button. In the **File New Database** dialog box, notice the default location in the **Address bar**, which is your *Documents* folder on your hard disk drive.

> A **dialog box** is a window containing commands or that asks you to make a decision.

4 In the **File New Database** dialog box, navigate to the location where you are storing your projects for this chapter; for example, *Documents* on your hard disk drive or *LEXAR MEDIA (E:)* to store on a USB flash drive—the exact name and drive letter will vary. Then, on the toolbar, click the **New Folder** button. Type **Access Chapter 12** and press Enter. Compare your screen with Figure 12.4.

Figure 12.4

Address bar displays your new folder

File New Database dialog box

New Folder button

Other files or folder at this location may display in Content pane

Location of new folder selected in Folders List

File name box

Save as type box

Browse button

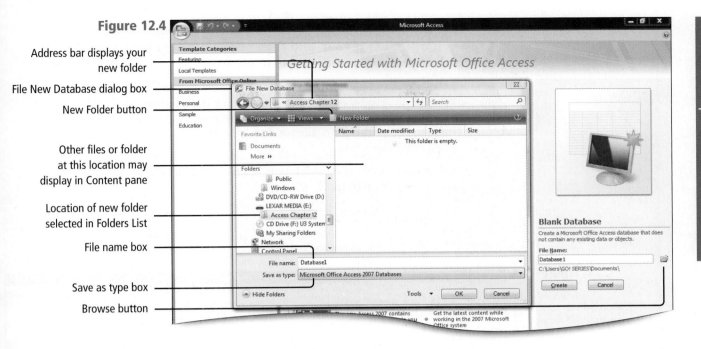

5 In the lower portion of the dialog box, in the **File name** box, select the existing text. Using your first name and last name, type **12A_ Contact_Information_Firstname_Lastname** and then press Enter. Compare your screen with Figure 12.5.

> To facilitate sending your files over the Internet, in this textbook, you will save files using an underscore between words rather than a space.

Figure 12.5

.accdb file extension

File Name box with your database name

Drive and folder where your database is stored

Create button

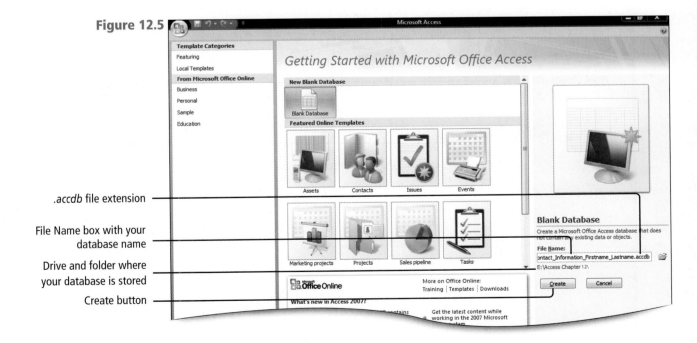

6 In the lower right corner, click the **Create** button, compare your screen with Figure 12.6, and then take a moment to study the screen elements described in the table in Figure 12.7.

Access creates the new database and opens a ***table*** named *Table1*. A table is an Access object that stores your data in columns and rows, similar to an Excel worksheet. Recall that *object* is the term used to refer to the parts of an Access database that you will use to store and work with your data.

Table objects are the foundation of an Access database because tables store the actual data.

Table Tools for working with tables

Title bar with your database name

Object window

Figure 12.6

Ribbon with command groups arranged on tabs

Navigation Pane

Table1 tab

Command group names

Right side of status bar

Left side of status bar

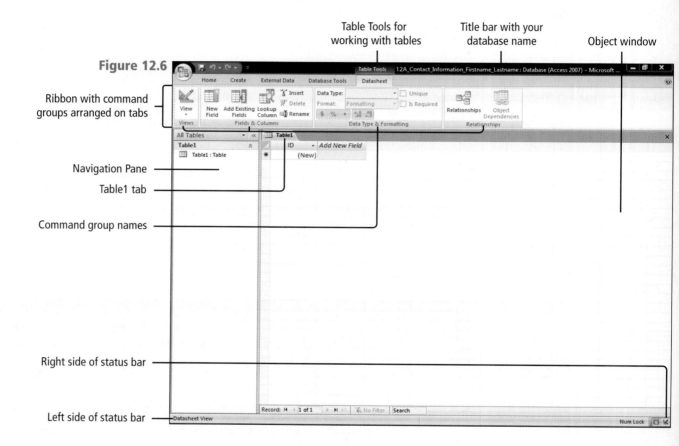

Parts of the Access Window

Window Part	Description
Command group names	Contain groups of related command buttons associated with the selected command tab.
Left side of status bar	Indicates the active view and the status of actions occurring within the database.
Navigation Pane	Displays the database objects; from here you open the database objects to display in the object window at the right.
Object window	Displays the open table object.
Ribbon with command groups arranged on tabs	Groups the commands for performing related database tasks on tabs.
Right side of status bar	Provides buttons to switch between Datasheet view and Design view.
Table Tools for working with tables	Provides tools for working with a table object; Table Tools are available only when a table is displayed.
Table1 tab	Enables you to select the table object.
Title bar with your database name	Displays the name of your database.

Figure 12.7

7 Leave your database open for the next activity.

Objective 2
Add Records to a Table

After you have saved and named the database, the next step is to plan and create the tables in which to enter your data. Recall that tables are the foundation of your database because the actual data is stored there.

Limit the data in each table to one subject. For example, think of all the data at your college; there is likely one table for student information, another table for course information, another table for classroom information, and so on.

Within each table, create as many columns as necessary so that you can break down information into the smallest usable part. For example, instead of a single column for an entire address, create a column for the street address, a column for the city name, a column for the state, and a column for the ZIP or postal code. By breaking your data into small, usable parts, you can find all of the people who live on a particular street, in a particular city, and so on.

In this project, you will create a database with two tables. One table will store the names and contact information for patients at Texas Lakes Medical Center and the other table will store the names and contact information for doctors at Texas Lakes Medical Center.

Activity 12.02 Adding Records to a Table

In a table object, each column represents a ***field***. Fields describe each piece of data stored in the table. Field names display at the top of each column and can be added before or while entering data. Each row in a table represents a ***record***—all of the fields of data pertaining to one person, place, thing, event, or idea. ***Table design*** refers to the number of fields, the names of fields, the type of content within a field—numbers or text—and other characteristics of the fields or records.

Think about buying yourself a new address book. It is not very useful until you fill it with names, addresses, and phone numbers. Likewise, a new database is not useful until you ***populate*** or fill a table with data. You can populate a table with records by typing data directly into the table.

In this activity, you will populate a table that stores contact information for patients at Texas Lakes Medical Center.

1 Notice the new blank table that displays in Datasheet view. Take a moment to study the elements of the table object window as shown in Figure 12.8.

> There are two ways to view a table—in ***Datasheet view*** or in ***Design view***. Datasheet view displays the table data organized in columns and rows similar to an Excel worksheet. Design view displays the underlying design or structure of the table object.

> When you create a new blank database, only one object—a new blank table—is created. Because you have not yet named this table, the Table tab displays a default name of *Table1*. Access creates the first field and names it *ID*. In the ID field, Access assigns a unique sequential number—each number incremented by one—to each record as it is entered into the table.

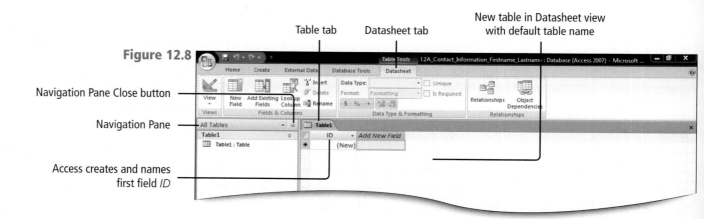

Figure 12.8

Table tab Datasheet tab

New table in Datasheet view with default table name

Navigation Pane Close button

Navigation Pane

Access creates and names first field *ID*

2 In the **Navigation Pane, click the Open/Close** button $\boxed{\ll}$ to collapse the **Navigation Pane** into a narrow bar at the left side of your screen. Notice that you have more screen space in which to work with your table.

3 In the second column, click in the ***cell***—the box formed by the intersection of a row and a column—under *Add New Field*, type **Elena** and then press Tab or Enter.

4 Click in the **ID** field. On the **Datasheet tab**, in the **Data Type & Formatting group**, click the **Data Type arrow**, and then click **Text**.

5 Type **1248-P** and then to the right of *Elena*, click in the **Add New Field** cell. Type **L** and then press ⟨Tab⟩. Compare your screen with Figure 12.9.

> As soon as information is entered, Access assigns the name *Field1* to the field and enters an AutoNumber of 1 in the ID field, which is created automatically by Access.
>
> By default, Access creates this field for all new tables and sets the data type for the field to **AutoNumber**, which sequentially numbers each entry. Changing the ID field data type from *AutoNumber* to *Text* enables you to enter a custom patient number. As you enter data, Access assigns Field names as *Field1*, *Field2*, and so on; you can rename the fields when it is convenient for you to do so.
>
> The pencil icon $\mathscr{I}$ in the **record selector box**—the small box at the left of a record in Datasheet view which, when clicked, selects the entire record—indicates that a new record is being entered or edited.

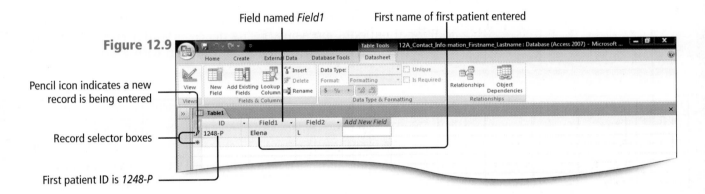

Figure 12.9

Field named *Field1*

First name of first patient entered

Pencil icon indicates a new record is being entered

Record selector boxes

First patient ID is *1248-P*

6 With the insertion point positioned in the fourth column, in the cell under *Add New Field*, type **Montoya** and then press ⟨Tab⟩ or ⟨Enter⟩.

7 Type **(512) 555-0723** and then press ⟨Enter⟩. Type **854 Red Willow Drive** and then press ⟨Tab⟩ to create *Field5*.

> Do not be concerned if the data does not completely display in the column. As you progress in your study of Access, you will adjust the column widths so that you can view all of the data.

8 Type **Austin** and then press ⟨Enter⟩ to create *Field6*. Type **TX** and then press ⟨Enter⟩ to create *Field7*.

9 Type **78754** and then press ⟨Enter⟩ to create *Field8*. Type **Wilcox** and then press ⟨Enter⟩ to create *Field9*. Type **150** and then press ⟨Enter⟩ two times. Compare your screen with Figure 12.10.

> To move across the row, you can press ⟨Tab⟩ or ⟨Enter⟩. Pressing ⟨Tab⟩ two times moves the insertion point to the next row to begin a new record. As soon as you move to the next row, Access saves the record—you do not have to take any specific action to save the record.

Figure 12.10

First record entered and saved ——

First field in row two is active ——

Note — Correct Typing Errors

If you make a mistake while entering data, you can correct the error by using ⟨←Bksp⟩ to remove characters to the left, ⟨Delete⟩ to remove characters to the right, or by selecting the text you want to replace and typing the correct information. Press ⟨Esc⟩ to exit out of a new record.

---

10 Beginning with the record for *Margaret E Fitzpatrick*, and using the technique you just practiced, enter the contact information for three additional patients, pressing ⟨Enter⟩ as necessary after entering the information in *Field10*. Then compare your screen with Figure 12.11.

ID	Field1	Field2	Field3	Field4	Field5	Field6	Field7	Field8	Field9	Field10
1248-P	Elena	L	Montoya	(512) 555-0723	854 Red Willow Drive	Austin	TX	78754	Wilcox	150
1252-P	Margaret	E	Fitzpatrick	(512) 555-0199	601 Meadow Drive	Abbott	TX	76621	Lee	486
1253-P	Jerry	R	Chung	(512) 555-0144	7094 Leland Avenue	Abilene	TX	79608	Wilcox	144
1257-P	Emily	A	Rhoades	(512) 555-0135	67 Bolivar Drive	Amarillo	TX	79101	Woods	298

Figure 12.11

Field 10 out of view (your screen may vary in how many columns are shown) ——

Records for four patients entered ——

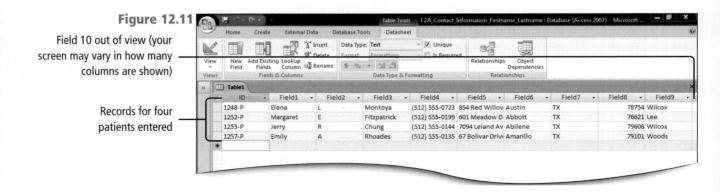

More Knowledge — Format for Typing Telephone Numbers in Access

Access does not require any specific format for typing telephone numbers in a database. The examples in this project use the format used in Microsoft Outlook. Using such a format facilitates easy transfer of Outlook information to and from Access.

Objective 3
Rename Table Fields in Datasheet View

Recall that each column in a table is a *field*, and that field names display at the top of each column of the table. Recall also that each row is a *record*—all of the data pertaining to one person, place, thing, event, or idea—and that each record is broken up into smaller parts—the *fields*. Use meaningful names to name fields; for example, *Amount Owed*.

Activity 12.03 Renaming the Fields in a Table in Datasheet View

1 At the top of the second column, point to the text *Field1* to display the ⬇ pointer and click. Compare your screen with Figure 12.12.

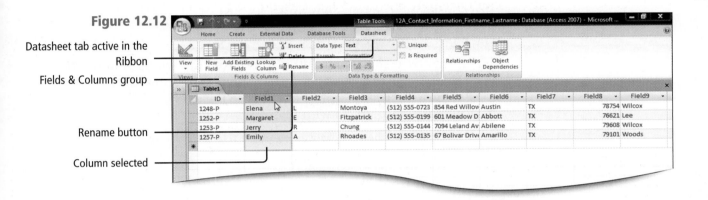

Figure 12.12

Datasheet tab active in the Ribbon

Fields & Columns group

Rename button

Column selected

2 On the Ribbon, notice that **Table Tools** displays above the **Datasheet tab**. In the **Fields & Columns group**, click the **Rename** button, and notice that the text *Field1* is selected.

3 Type **First Name** as the field name, and then press Enter. Point to the text *Field2*, click to select the column, and then in the **Fields & Columns group**, click the **Rename** button. Type **Middle Initial** and then press Enter.

4 Point to the text *Field3* and double-click to select the text. Type **Last Name** and then press Enter. Point to the text *Field4* and then right-click. From the shortcut menu, click **Rename Column**, type **Phone Number** and then press Enter.

5 Using any of the techniques you just practiced, **Rename** the remaining fields as follows, and then compare your screen with Figure 12.13.

Field5	**Address**
Field6	**City**
Field7	**State/Province**
Field8	**ZIP/Postal Code**
Field9	**Doctor**
Field10	**Amount Owed**

Figure 12.13
Fields renamed —

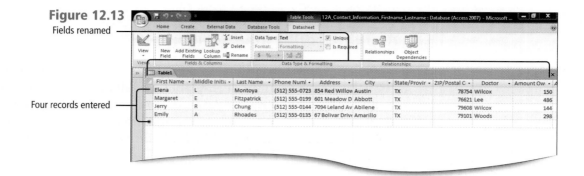

Four records entered —

Activity 12.04 Changing the Data Type of a Field in Datasheet View

Data type is the characteristic that defines the kind of data that you can type in a field, such as numbers, text, or dates. A field in a table can have only one data type. Based on the data you type into a field, Access assigns a data type, but you can change the data type if another type more accurately describes your data.

1 In any of the four records that you have entered, click in the **ID field**. On the Ribbon, on the **Datasheet tab**, in the **Data Type & Formatting group**, notice that in the **Data Type** box, *Text* displays. Compare your screen with Figure 12.14.

> Recall that the ID field was changed from *AutoNumber*, which sequentially numbers each entry, to *Text* so that a custom ID number for patients can be assigned.

Figure 12.14

Data Type box —
Text indicated as Data Type —
ID field —
Data Type & Formatting group —
Datasheet tab is active —

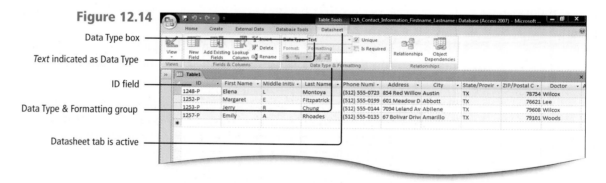

2 In any record, click in the **Last Name** field, and then on the **Datasheet tab**, notice that the **Data Type** indicates *Text*. Click the **Data Type arrow** to display a list of data types as shown in Figure 12.15, and then take a moment to study the table in Figure 12.16 that describes the different data types.

Figure 12.15
Data Type arrow —

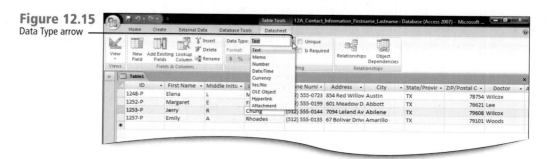

Data Types

Data Types	Description	Example
Text	Text or combinations of text and numbers; also numbers that are not used in calculations. Limited to 255 characters or length set on field, whichever is less. Access does not reserve space for unused portions of the text field. This is the default data type.	An inventory item such as a computer, or a phone number or postal code that is not used in calculations, and that may contain characters other than numbers.
Memo	Lengthy text or combinations of text and numbers up to 65,535 characters or limitations of database size.	Description of a product or information pertaining to a patient.
Number	Numeric data used in mathematical calculations with varying field sizes.	A quantity, such as 500.
Date/Time	Date and time values for the years 100 through 9999.	An order date, such as 11/10/2009 3:30 P.M.
Currency	Monetary values and numeric data that can be used in mathematical calculations involving data with one to four decimal places. Accurate to 15 digits on the left side of the decimal separator and to 4 digits on the right side. Use this data type to store financial data and when you do not want Access to round values.	An item price, such as $8.50.
Yes/No	Contains only one of two values—Yes/No, True/False, or On/Off. Access assigns -1 for all Yes values and 0 for all No values.	Whether an item was ordered—Yes or No.
OLE Object	An object created by programs other than Access that is linked to or embedded in the table. *OLE* is an abbreviation for *object linking and embedding*, a technology for transferring and sharing information among programs.	A graphics file, such as a picture of a product, a sound file, a Word document, or an Excel worksheet stored as a bitmap image.
Hyperlink	Web or e-mail address.	An e-mail address, such as dwalker@txlakemed.org or a Web page, such as *www.txlakemed.org.*
Attachment	Any supported type of file—images, worksheet files, documents, or charts. Similar to e-mail attachments. Preferred over OLE Object.	Same as OLE Object.
AutoNumber	Available in Design view. A unique sequential or random number assigned by Access as each record is entered and that cannot be updated.	An inventory item number, such as 1, 2, 3 or a randomly assigned employee number, such as 3852788.
Lookup Wizard	Available in Design view. Not a data type, but will display on Data Type list. Links to fields in other tables to display a list of data instead of having to manually type in the data.	Link to another field in another table.

Figure 12.16

3 Click the **Data Type arrow** again to close the list without changing the data type. In any record, click in the **Address** field, and notice that the **Data Type** box displays *Text*.

> As described in the table in Figure 12.16, Access assigns a data type of *Text* to combinations of letters and numbers.

4 Scroll to the right as necessary, in any record, click in the **Amount Owed** field, and then in the **Data Type** box, notice that Access assigned a data type of *Number*.

5 Click the **Data Type arrow** to the right of *Number*, and then from the list, click **Currency**. Compare your screen with Figure 12.17.

> Based on your typing of only numbers, Access determined this data type to be *Number*. However, Amount Owed refers to a monetary value, so the data type should be defined as *Currency*. With the Currency data type, Access automatically adds a U.S. dollar sign ($) and two decimal places to all of the fields in the column.

Figure 12.17

Data Type box indicates
Currency

Amount Owed field data
type changed to *Currency*

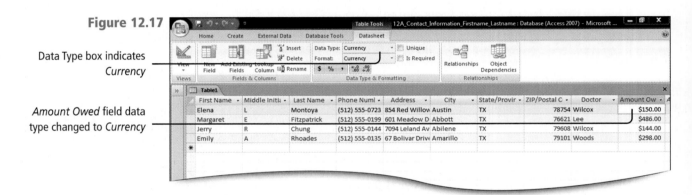

6 Scroll to the left as necessary, and in any record, click in the **ID** field.

> In a database, each record should, in some way, be different from all of the other records. What is important is that the value is unique; no other record in the table will be assigned this value. You are probably familiar with unique values. For example, at your college, no two students have the same Student ID number, although they could have the same name, such as *David Michaels*.

> When records in a database have *no* unique value, for example the last names in your address book, the AutoNumber data type is a useful way to automatically create a unique number so that you have a way to ensure that every record is different from the others.

7 Change the name of the **ID** field to **Patient ID**

8 In the new record row, which is indicated by an asterisk (*) in the record selector box on the left, click in the **Patient ID** field, and then type the records shown in the following list. The data in each field should be typed on one line. When you are finished, compare your screen with Figure 12.18.

> Recall that you need not be concerned if the data does not completely display in the column. Also, as soon as you move to the next row, the record is saved. Correct typing mistakes using ordinary methods you have practiced in this and other programs.

Patient ID	First Name	Middle Initial	Last Name	Phone Number	Address	City	State/ Province	ZIP/Postal Code	Doctor Name	Amount Owed
1260-P	Maria	S	Flores	(512) 555-0177	1 Casa Del Sol	Austin	TX	78715	Ruiz	37.5
1265-P	Joan	M	Curtis	(512) 555-0192	1446 Yellow Rose Lane	Austin	TX	78715	Ruiz	255
1342-P	Yvonne	L	Dubois	(512) 555-0155	2117 West Smith Trail	El Paso	TX	79973	Woods	147.56
1385-P	Joseph	C	Ortega	(512) 555-0245	1923 Village Park West	Amarillo	TX	79101	Wilcox	200
1423-P	Brian	K	Khuu	(512) 555-0323	1130 Preston Way SE	Abbott	TX	76621	Lee	568.12

Figure 12.18

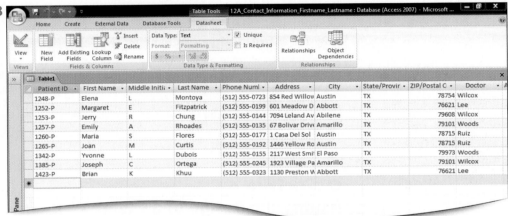

9 On the **Quick Access Toolbar**, click the **Save** button .

The Save As dialog box displays. Recall that a record is saved as soon as you move to another row in the table.

You should give the table a more meaningful name that describes the information it contains. You can use up to 64 characters (letters or numbers), including spaces, to name a table. In the Table Name box, a suggested name of *Table1* displays and is selected—yours may differ depending on the number of tables you have attempted to create in this database.

10 In the **Save As** dialog box, in the **Table Name** box and using your first and last names, type **12A Patients Firstname Lastname** and then click **OK**. Notice that the table tab displays the new table name. Compare your screen with Figure 12.19.

When you save objects within a database, it is not necessary to use underscores. Your name is included as part of the object name so that you and your instructor will be able to identify your printouts and electronic files.

Figure 12.19

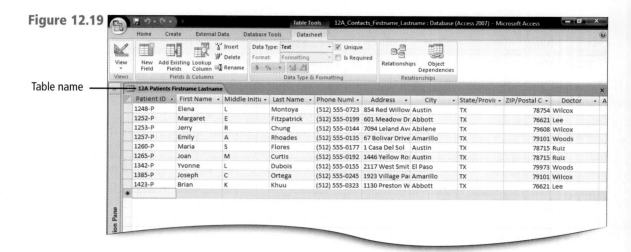

Table name

Objective 4
Modify the Design of a Table

When you create and populate a new table in Datasheet view, the data that you type for the first record determines the number of fields and the data type for each field in the table. This is referred to as the *table design*. Later, you may need to make changes to the design of the table by adding or deleting fields, or changing the order of the fields within a table. You can change a table in Datasheet view, but you may prefer to change the table in Design view where you have additional options.

Activity 12.05 Deleting a Field in Design View

June Liu has decided that a field for the patient's middle initial is not necessary for the 12A Patients table, so you will delete the Middle Initial field in Design view.

1 On the **Datasheet tab**, in the **Views group**, click the **View button arrow**.

There are four common views in Access, but two that you will use often are Datasheet view and Design view. On the displayed list, Design view is represented by a picture of a pencil, a ruler, and a protractor.

Datasheet view displays the table in rows and columns. When one of these icons is on the View button, clicking the View button will display the table in the view represented by the icon.

2 From the list, click **Design View**, and then take a moment to study Figure 12.20.

Design view displays the underlying design—the structure—of the table. Each field name is listed, along with its data type. A column to add a Description—information about the data in the field—is provided.

At the bottom of the Design view window, in the Field Properties area, you can make numerous decisions about how each individual field will look and behave. For example, you can set a specific field size.

Figure 12.20

Delete Rows button on Ribbon

Row selector box

Field Names

Data Type for each field

Field Properties area

Space to add field description

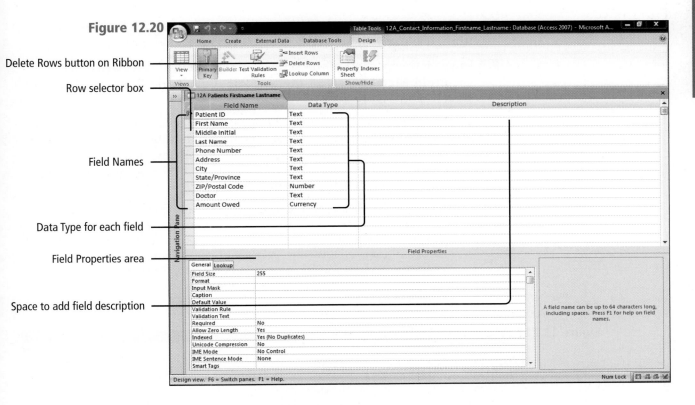

3 In the **Field Name** column, to the left of **Middle Initial**, point to the row selector box to display the → pointer, and then click to select—outline in orange—the entire row.

4 On the **Design tab**, in the **Tools group**, click the **Delete Rows** button, read the message in the message box, and then click **Yes**.

Deleting a field deletes both the field and its data; you cannot undo this action. If you change your mind after deleting the field, you must add the field back into the table and then reenter the data in that field for each record.

More Knowledge — Choosing the Proper View to Make Changes

You can make design changes in Datasheet view or Design view. Design view provides more flexibility in the types of design changes you can make, and you will become familiar with these as you progress in your study of Access.

Activity 12.06 Modifying a Field Size and Description in Design View

More than one person typically enters data into a database table. For example, at your college there are likely many Registration Assistants who enter and modify student and course information daily.

When you design your database, there are things you can do to help yourself and others to enter accurate data. Two ways to ensure accuracy are to restrict what can be typed in a field and to add descriptive information within the database itself.

1 With your table still displayed in **Design** view, in the **Field Name** column, click anywhere in the **State/Province** field name.

2 In the lower portion of the screen, under **Field Properties**, click in the **Field Size** box, select the text *255*, type **2** and then compare your screen with Figure 12.21.

> This action limits the size of the State/Province field to no more than two characters—the size of the two-letter state abbreviations provided by the United States Postal Service. *Field properties* control how the field displays and how data can be entered in the field. You can define properties for each field in the Field Properties area.

> The default field size for a text field is 255 characters. Limiting the field size property to 2 ensures that only two characters can be entered for each state. However, this does not prevent a user from entering two characters that are incorrect. A primary goal of any database is to ensure the accuracy of the data that is entered. Setting the proper data type for the field and limiting the field size are two ways to help to reduce errors.

Figure 12.21

State/Province field selected ——

Field Properties Field Size
changed to 2 ——

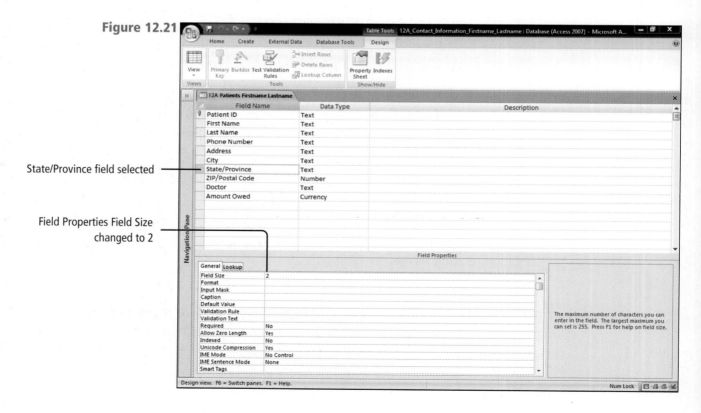

3 In the **State/Province** row, click in the **Description** box, and then type **Two-character state abbreviation**

> Descriptions for fields in a table are optional. Include a description if the field name does not provide an obvious explanation of the field. Information typed in the description area displays in the status bar of the Datasheet view when the field is active, providing additional information to individuals who are entering data.

4 In the **Amount Owed** row, click in the **Description** box, and then type **Outstanding balance**

5 On the **Quick Access Toolbar**, click the **Save** button 🖫, and then in the message box, click **Yes**.

> The message indicates that if more than two characters are currently present in the State/Province field, the data could be lost because the field was not previously restricted to two characters.

Activity 12.07 Setting a Primary Key and Saving a Table

A *primary key* is the field that uniquely identifies a record in a table. For example, in a college registration system, your Student ID number uniquely identifies you—no other student at the college has your exact student number. In the 12A Patients table, the Patient ID uniquely identifies each patient.

When you create a table, Access designates the first field as the primary key field. It is a good database design practice to establish a primary key. Doing so ensures that you do not enter the same record more than once. You can imagine the confusion if another student at your college had the same Student ID number as you do.

1 With your table still displayed in **Design** view, in the **Field Name** column, click to place your insertion point in the **Patient ID** box. To the left of the box, notice the small icon of a key, as shown in Figure 12.22.

> Access automatically designates the first field as the primary key field. However, using the Primary Key button on the Ribbon, you can set any field as the primary key.

Figure 12.22

Primary Key button

Primary Key icon

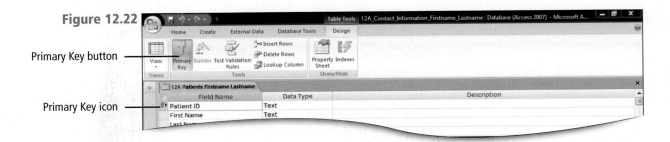

2 On the **Design tab**, in the **Views group**, notice that the **View** button contains a picture of a Datasheet, indicating that clicking the button will return you to Datasheet view. Click the **View** button; and, if prompted, click **Yes** to save the changes you have made to the design of your table.

Objective 5
Add a Second Table to a Database

Access includes a ***table template***—a pre-built table format for common topics such as contacts, issues, and tasks. You can use the table template as it is or customize it to suit your needs. Using a table template is a fast way to add an additional table to your database.

Activity 12.08 Adding a Second Table to a Database

In this activity, you will add a second table to your database. The table will store contact information for the doctors at the medical center. You will use a table template that is specifically designed for contact information.

1 With your **12A Patients** table displayed in Datasheet view, on the Ribbon, click the **Create tab**. In the **Tables group**, click the **Table Templates** button, and then from the list, click **Contacts**. Compare your screen with Figure 12.23.

A new table with predefined fields displays in the object window. Your 12A Patients table is still open—its tab is visible—but is behind the new table. The Contacts Table Template most closely matches the business need to track doctor information.

Figure 12.23

Table Templates button

12A Patients table still open

New Table1 added
with predefined fields

2 On the Ribbon, click the **Datasheet tab** to display the groups of Datasheet commands.

3 In the second column of the table, point to the **Company** field name, click to select the field, and then on the **Datasheet tab**, in the **Fields & Columns group**, click the **Delete** button. Alternatively, right-click on the selected field name, and from the shortcut menu, click Delete Column.

You can delete fields in Design view, as you did in Activity 12.5, or you can delete fields directly in Datasheet view as you have done here.

4 Point to the **E-mail Address** field until the ↓ pointer displays. Drag to the right to select both the **E-mail Address** field and the **Job Title** field. Right-click over the selected field names, and then from the shortcut menu, click **Delete Column**.

5 Using the techniques you have just practiced, delete the following fields: **Business Phone**, **Home Phone**, **Fax Number**, **Country/Region**, **Web Page**, and **Notes**.

> The field displaying a paper clip is the *Attachments* field. Recall that an attachment field can contain a graphics file such as a picture, a sound file, a Word document, or an Excel spreadsheet. In the future, June may use this field to attach a picture and a biography of each doctor, so do not delete it.

6 On the **Datasheet tab**, in the **Views group**, click the **View** button to switch to **Design** view. In the **Save As** dialog box, in the **Table Name** box, using your first name and last name, type **12A Doctors Firstname Lastname** and then click **OK**.

> Changes you have made to the design of the table—deleting fields—are saved, and a more meaningful table name is provided. The table displays in Design view, where the names of each field and the data types assigned to the fields display.

7 Under **Field Name**, click anywhere in the **Attachments** box. On the **Design tab**, in the **Tools group**, click **Insert Rows**. In the newly inserted field name box, type **Specialty** and then press Tab two times. In the **Description** box, type **Medical field specialty** and then compare your screen with Figure 12.24.

Figure 12.24

Table tab with new name

Description for new field

New field added

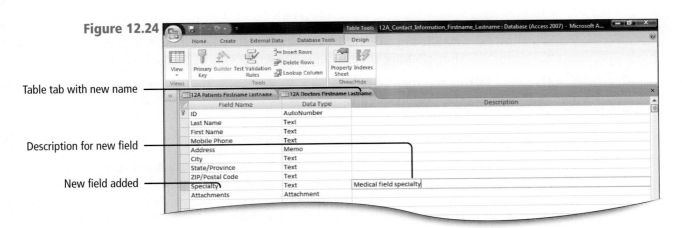

8 Under **Field Name**, click in the **ID** box. Replace the text with **Doctor ID** and then press Tab. In the **Data Type** column, click the arrow, and then from the list, click **Text**.

9 Press Tab to move to the **Description** column, and then type **Physician ID Number**

> Because the Medical Center assigns a unique ID number to each doctor, that ID number will be used as the Primary Key instead of the AutoNumber. Recall that AutoNumber is useful only when no other unique number for a record is available.

10 Under **Field Name**, click in the **State/Province** box. In the lower portion of the screen, under **Field Properties**, change the **Field Size** to **2** and then compare your screen with Figure 12.25.

Figure 12.25

Doctor ID Data Type set to *Text*

Doctor ID field name

Descriptions added for two fields

Description for Doctor ID

State/Province Field Size changed to 2

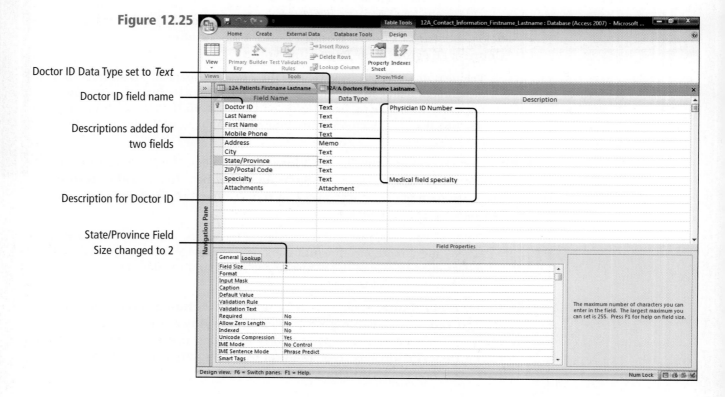

11 On the **Design tab**, in the **Views group**, click the **View** button to switch to Datasheet view—the picture of a datasheet reminds you that clicking the button will switch you to Datasheet view.

12 In the message box, click **Yes** to save the changes you have made to the design of your table.

Activity 12.09 Adding Records to a Second Table

1 With your **12A Doctors** table displayed in **Datasheet** view, beginning in the first record row under **Doctor ID**, enter the following four records. When you have entered all four records, on the **fourth record**—*Doctor ID* of *421-Phys*—click in the **Specialty** field, and then compare your screen with Figure 12.26.

> As you type in the Doctor ID field, *Physician ID Number* displays in the status bar. As you type in the Specialty field, *Medical field specialty* displays in the status bar. This description helps the person who enters the records.

Doctor ID	Last Name	First Name	Mobile Phone	Address	City	State/Province	ZIP/Postal Code	Specialty
239-Phys	Woods	Laura	(512) 555-0100	4 Research Blvd	Austin	TX	78754	Oncology
287-Phys	Lee	Kim	(512) 555-0111	809 Broadway	Abbott	TX	76621	Cardiology
327-Phys	Wilcox	Frank	(512) 555-0022	7646 Pike Street	Amarillo	TX	79101	Orthopedics
421-Phys	Ruiz	Maria	(512) 555-0030	902 Madison Avenue	Austin	TX	78715	Pediatrics

Figure 12.26

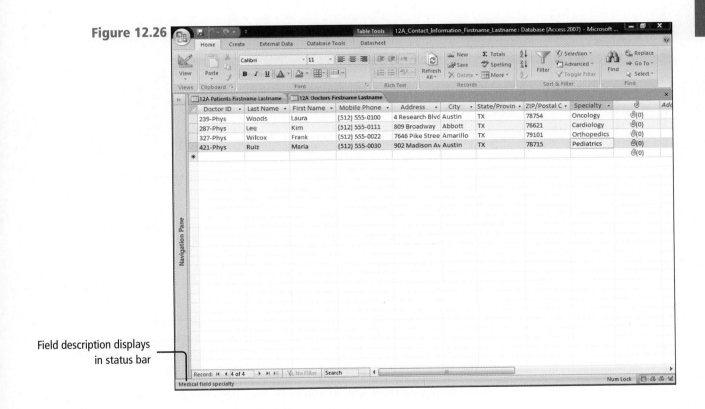

Field description displays in status bar

Objective 6
Print a Table

You can print a table, and although it will not look as professional as a printed report, there are times when you will want to do so. For example, you might need a quick reference or want to proofread the data that has been entered.

Activity 12.10 Adjusting Column Widths and Printing a Table

1 In the object window, click the tab for your **12A Patients** table.

Clicking the tabs along the top of the object window enables you to display open objects so that you can work with them.

All the columns are the same width regardless of the amount of data in the field, the field size that was set, or the length of the field name. If you print the table as currently displayed, some of the data or some of the field names may not fully display unless you adjust the column widths.

2 Change the field name of the **State/Province** field to **State** and change the name of the **ZIP/Postal Code** field to **ZIP**

3 In the field names row, point to the right boundary of the **Address** field to display the ⊹ pointer, and then compare your screen with Figure 12.27.

Figure 12.27

Pointer positioned on right boundary of Address field

Field name changed to *State*
Field name changed to *ZIP*

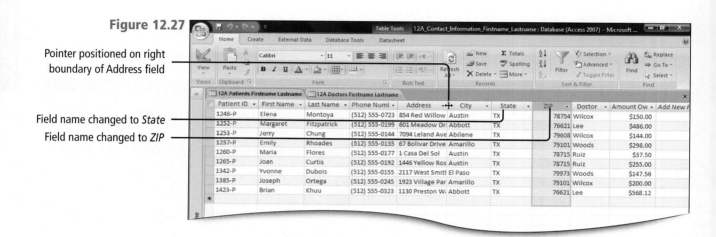

4 With your ⊹ pointer positioned as shown in Figure 12.27, double-click the right boundary of the **Address** field.

The column width of the Address field widens to fully display the longest entry in the field. In this manner, the width of a column can be increased or decreased to fit its contents.

5 In the field names row, point to the right border of the **City** field, and then with the ⊹ pointer, hold down the left mouse button and drag to the left to visually narrow the column width to accommodate only the widest entry in that column.

Adjusting the width of columns does not change the data stored in the table's records. It changes only the display of the data.

Another Way ── **To Adjust Column Widths**

Select multiple columns, and then in the field names row, double-click the right boundary of any selected column to adjust all of the field widths, similar to adjusting field widths in an Excel spreadsheet. Alternatively, select one or more columns and right-click over the selection. From the shortcut menu click Column Width, and then in the Column Width dialog box, click Best Fit.

6 Using any of the techniques you have practiced or as described previously, adjust all of the column widths, and then compare your screen with Figure 12.28.

Figure 12.28

All column widths adjusted to fit longest entry in the column

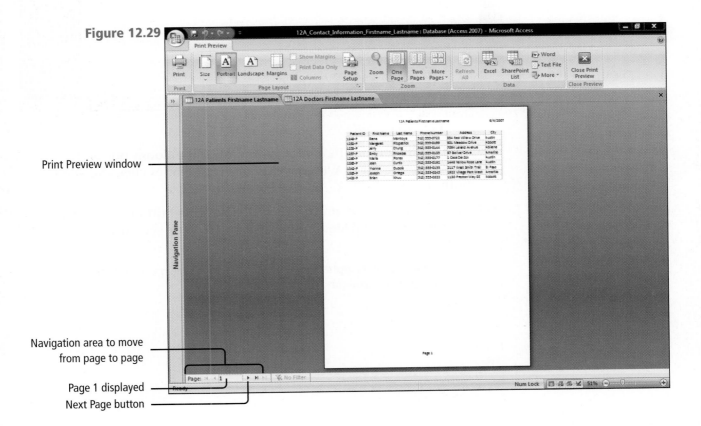

Patient ID	First Name	Last Name	Phone Number	Address	City	State	ZIP	Doctor	Amount Owed	Add New
1248-P	Elena	Montoya	(512) 555-0723	854 Red Willow Drive	Austin	TX	78754	Wilcox	$150.00	
1252-P	Margaret	Fitzpatrick	(512) 555-0199	601 Meadow Drive	Abbott	TX	76621	Lee	$486.00	
1253-P	Jerry	Chung	(512) 555-0144	7094 Leland Avenue	Abilene	TX	79608	Wilcox	$144.00	
1257-P	Emily	Rhoades	(512) 555-0135	67 Bolivar Drive	Amarillo	TX	79101	Woods	$298.00	
1260-P	Maria	Flores	(512) 555-0177	1 Casa Del Sol	Austin	TX	78715	Ruiz	$37.50	
1265-P	Joan	Curtis	(512) 555-0192	1446 Yellow Rose Lane	Austin	TX	78715	Ruiz	$255.00	
1342-P	Yvonne	Dubois	(512) 555-0155	2117 West Smith Trail	El Paso	TX	79973	Woods	$147.56	
1385-P	Joseph	Ortega	(512) 555-0245	1923 Village Park West	Amarillo	TX	79101	Wilcox	$200.00	
1423-P	Brian	Khuu	(512) 555-0323	1130 Preston Way SE	Abbott	TX	76621	Lee	$568.12	

7 On the **Quick Access Toolbar**, click the **Save** button to save the changes you have made to the table's design—changing the column widths.

> If you do not save the table after making design changes, Access reminds you to save when you close the table.

8 In the upper left corner of your screen, click the **Office** button . On the menu, point to **Print**, click **Print Preview**, and then compare your screen with Figure 12.29.

Figure 12.29

Print Preview window

Navigation area to move from page to page

Page 1 displayed

Next Page button

9 In the lower left corner of your screen, in the navigation area, click the **Next Page** ▶ button. Point to the data at the top of the page to display the 🔍 pointer, click one time to zoom in, and then compare your screen with Figure 12.30.

> The second page of the table displays the last four fields, and the display is larger. In the navigation area, the Next Page button is dimmed, indicating that there are no more pages to display. The Previous Page button is darker, indicating that a page exists before the displayed page.

Figure 12.30

Last four fields display on a second page

Previous Page button

Page 2

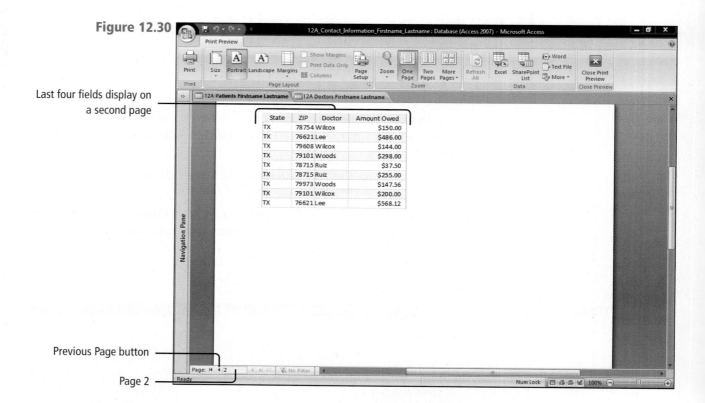

10 On the Ribbon, in the **Zoom group**, click the **Zoom** button to zoom back to Fit to Window view—be sure not to click the Zoom button arrow.

11 In the **Page Layout group**, click the **Margins** button. In the **Margins gallery**, point to **Wide**, and then compare your screen with Figure 12.31.

> The Wide gallery option sets top and bottom margins at 1 inch and left and right margins at .75 inch.

Figure 12.31

Margins button

Wide gallery choice

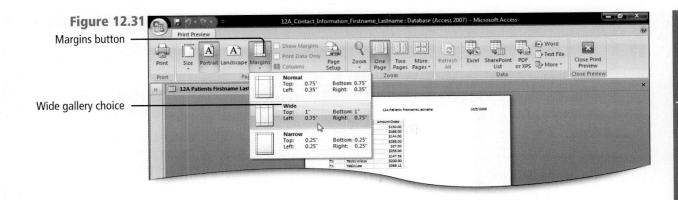

12 Click **Wide**. Then, in the **Page Layout group**, click the **Landscape** button.

> The orientation of the printout changes, and the navigation arrows are inactive because all of the fields and all of the records display on one page. Additionally, the table name and current date display at the top of the page, and the page number displays at the bottom.

> By default, Access prints in ***portrait orientation***—the printed page is taller than it is wide. In ***landscape orientation***, the printed page is wider than it is tall.

> The change in orientation from portrait to landscape is not saved with the table. Each time you print, you must check the margins, page orientation, and other print parameters to ensure that the data will print as you intend.

Note — Headers and Footers in Access Objects

The headers and footers in Access tables and queries are controlled by default settings; you cannot add additional information or edit the information. The object name displays in the center of the header area with the date on the right—that is why adding your own name to the object name is helpful to identify your paper or electronic results. The page number displays in the center of the footer area. The headers and footers in Access reports and forms, however, are more flexible; you can add to and edit the information.

---

13 On the right side of the status bar, just to the right of the **View** buttons, drag the **Zoom** slider to the right—or click the **Zoom In** button—until you have zoomed to approximately **120%**, as shown in Figure 12.32.

> To ***zoom*** means to increase or decrease the viewing area of the screen. Zoom in to look closely at a particular section of a document, and then zoom out to see a whole page on the screen. You can also zoom to view multiple pages on the screen.

Figure 12.32

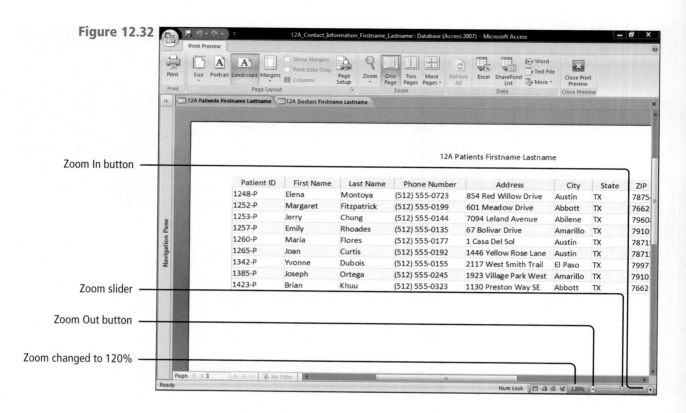

Zoom In button

Zoom slider

Zoom Out button

Zoom changed to 120%

14 Drag the **Zoom** slider to the left—or click the **Zoom Out** button—until you have zoomed to approximately **50%**, as shown in Figure 12.33.

Figure 12.33

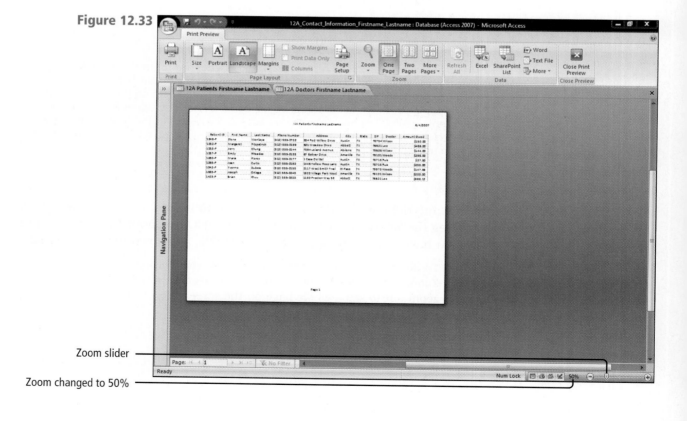

Zoom slider

Zoom changed to 50%

15 Check your *Chapter Assignment Sheet* or *Course Syllabus*, or consult your instructor, to determine whether you are to submit the printed pages that are the results of this project. If you are submitting your work on paper, on the **Print Preview tab**, in the **Print group**, click the **Print** button, and then in the **Print** dialog box, click **OK**.

16 On the Ribbon, in the **Close Preview group**, click the **Close Print Preview** button. If you are submitting your work electronically, follow the directions given by your instructor.

17 At the far right edge of the object window, click the **Close Object** button ☒ to close the **12A Patients** table. If prompted, click Yes to save design changes.

18 With your **12A Doctors** table displayed, **Rename** the **State/Province** field to **State** and the **ZIP/Postal Code** field to **ZIP** Then, adjust all of the column widths to accommodate the longest entry in the column, including the **Attachments** column, which displays a paper clip icon.

19 Display the table in **Print Preview**. Change the **Margins** to **Wide** and the orientation to **Landscape**. Print if you are directed to do so, and then click the **Close Print Preview** button, or submit your work electronically.

20 At the far right of the object window, click the **Close Object** button ☒. Click **Yes** to save the changes you made to the layout—changing the column widths.

> All your database objects—the *12A Patients* table and the *12A Doctors* table—are closed, and the object window is empty.

Objective 7
Create and Use a Query

A **query** is a database object that retrieves specific data from one or more database objects—either tables or other queries—and then, in a single datasheet, displays only the data you specify. Because the word *query* means *to ask a question*, think of a query as a question formed in a manner that Access can interpret.

A **select query** is one type of Access query. A select query, also called a **simple select query**, retrieves (selects) data from one or more tables or queries, displaying the selected data in a datasheet. A select query is used to create subsets of data that can be used to answer specific questions; for example, *Which patients live in Austin, TX?*

Activity 12.11 Using the Simple Query Wizard to Create a Query

The table(s) or query(ies) from which a query gets its data are referred to as the query's **data source**. In the following activity, you will create a simple select query using a **wizard**. A wizard is a feature in Microsoft Office programs that walks you step-by-step through a process.

The process involves choosing the data source, and then indicating the fields you want to include in the query result. The query—the question that you want to ask—is *What are the name, complete mailing address, and Patient ID of every patient in the database?*

1 Click the **Create tab**, and then in the **Other group**, click the **Query Wizard** button. In the **New Query** dialog box, click **Simple Query Wizard**, and then click **OK**. Compare your screen with Figure 12.34.

Figure 12.34

Simple Query Wizard dialog box

Tables/Queries arrow

Add Field button

No database objects display in object window; all are closed

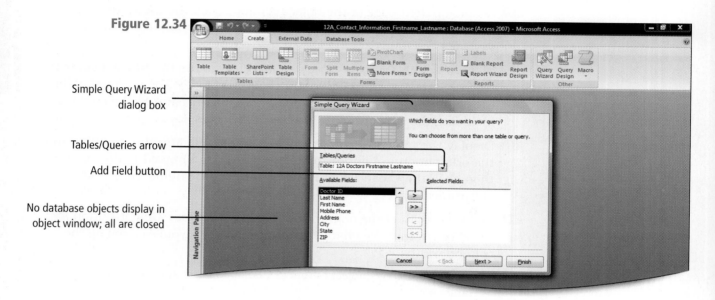

2 Click the **Tables/Queries arrow**, and then click **Table: 12A Patients**.

To create a query, first choose the data source—the table(s) or query(ies) from which to select data. The name and complete mailing address of every patient is stored in the 12A Patients table.

3 Under **Available Fields**, click **Patient ID**, and then click the **Add Field** button ▶ to move the field to the **Selected Fields** list on the right. Using the same technique, add the **Last Name** to the list. Alternatively, double-click the field name to move it to the Selected Fields list. Compare your screen with Figure 12.35.

This is the second step in creating a query—choosing the fields that you want to include in your query results.

Figure 12.35

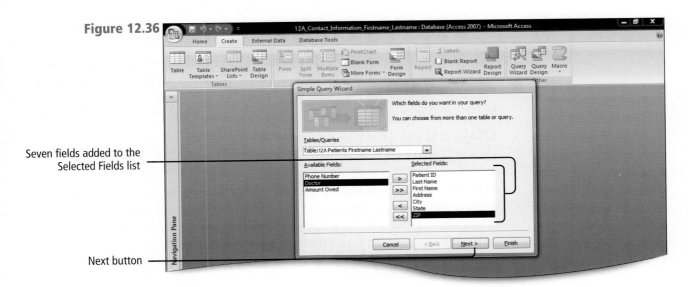

Two fields added to
Selected Fields list

4 Using either the **Add Field** button ▶ or by double-clicking, add the
following fields to the **Selected Fields** list: **First Name**, **Address**,
City, **State**, and **ZIP**. Compare your screen with Figure 12.36.

> Choosing these seven fields will give you the query result that you
> want—it will answer the question, *What are the name, address, and
> Patient ID of every patient in the database?*

Figure 12.36

Seven fields added to the
Selected Fields list

Next button

5 In the lower right corner, click the **Next** button. Be sure that the
option for **Detail (shows every field of every record)** is selected,
and then in the lower right corner, click the **Next** button.

6 In the **Simple Query Wizard** dialog box, click in the **What title do
you want for your query?** box. Edit as necessary so that the query
name, using your own first and last names, is **12A ALL Patients
Firstname Lastname Query** and then compare your screen with
Figure 12.37.

Figure 12.37

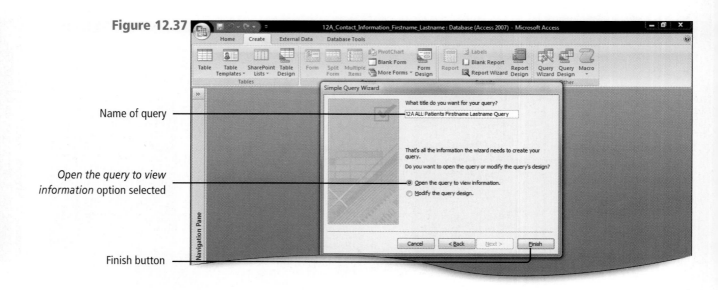

Name of query

Open the query to view information option selected

Finish button

---

7 Click **Finish**.

> Access **runs** the query—performs the actions indicated in your query design by searching the table of records included in the query, finding the records that match the criteria, and then displaying the records in a datasheet—so that you can see the results. A select query *selects*—pulls out and displays—*only* the information from the data source that you requested.

> In the object window, Access displays every patient record in Datasheet view, but displays only the seven fields that you included in the Selected Fields list in the Simple Query Wizard dialog box.

8 Display the query in **Print Preview**. **Print** the query, and then click the **Close Print Preview** button. Or, submit electronically as directed. Leave the query object open.

Objective 8
Create and Use a Form

A *form* is an Access object used to enter data, edit data, or display data from a table or a query. In a form, the fields are laid out in a visually attractive format on the screen, which makes working with the database more pleasant and more efficient.

One type of Access form displays only one record in the database at a time. Such a form is useful not only to the individual who performs the data entry—typing in the actual records—but also to anyone who has the job of viewing information in a database.

For example, when you visit the Records office at your college to obtain a transcript, someone displays your record on a screen. For the viewer, it is much easier to look at one record at a time, using a form, than to look at all of the student records in the database table.

Activity 12.12 Creating a Form

The Form command on the Ribbon creates a form that displays all of the fields from the underlying data source (table) one record at a time. You can use this new form immediately, or you can modify it. Records that you create or edit in a form are automatically added to or updated in the underlying table or tables.

1 In the upper right corner of the object window, click the **Close Object** button ☒ to close the query. Then, at the top of the **Navigation Pane**, click the **Open** button ⧉.

2 In the **Navigation Pane**, notice that a table displays a datasheet icon and a query displays an icon of two overlapping datasheets. Right-click the **12A Patients** table to display a shortcut menu as shown in Figure 12.38.

Figure 12.38

Navigation Pane Close button

12A Patients table
Table icon
Query icon

Navigation Pane expanded

Shortcut menu

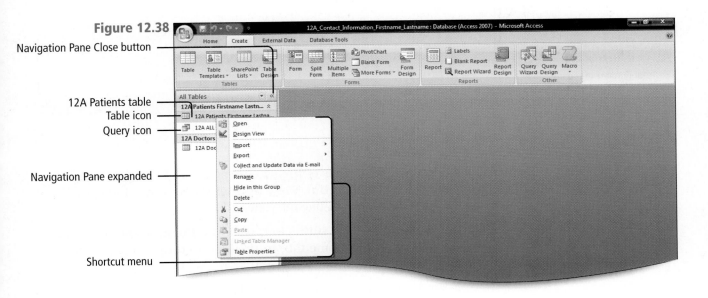

3 From the shortcut menu, click **Open** to display the table in the object window, and then **Close** ⧏ the **Navigation Pane** to maximize your screen space.

4 Notice that there are 10 fields in the table. Click the **Create tab**, and then in the **Forms group**, click the **Form** button. Compare your screen with Figure 12.39.

> Access creates a form based on the currently selected object—the 12A Patients table. Access creates the form in a simple top-to-bottom format, with all of the fields in the record lined up in a single column.
>
> The form displays in Layout view, where you can modify the design of the form. Each field displays the data for the first record in the table— *Elena Montoya*.

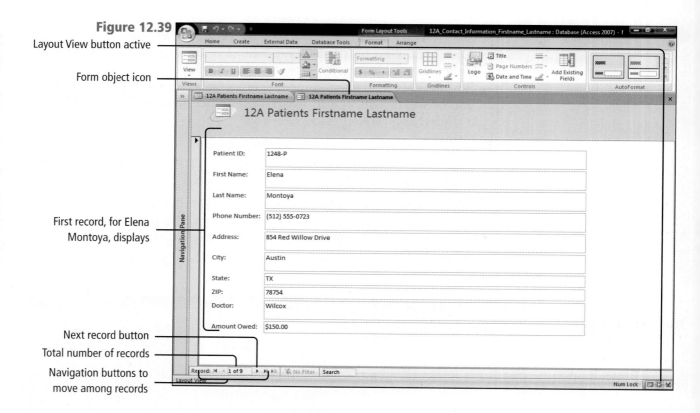

Figure 12.39

Layout View button active

Form object icon

First record, for Elena Montoya, displays

Next record button

Total number of records

Navigation buttons to move among records

5 In the lower right corner of the screen, at the right edge of the status bar, notice that the **Layout View** button ⊞ is active, indicating that the form is displayed in Layout view.

6 At the right edge of the status bar, click the **Form View** button ▣. Alternatively, on the Home tab, in the Views group, click the View button, which displays an icon of a form.

> In Form view, you can view the records, but you cannot change the layout or design of the form.

7 In the navigation area, click the **Next record** button ▸ three times. The fourth record—*Emily Rhoades*—displays.

> Use the navigation buttons to scroll among the records to display any single record.

8 On the **Quick Access Toolbar**, click the **Save** button ▦. In the **Save As** dialog box, accept the default name for the form—*12A Patients Firstname Lastname*—by clicking **OK**. **Close** ✕ the form object.

> The *12A Patients Firstname Lastname* table remains open.

Objective 9
Create and Print a Report

A ***report*** is a database object that displays the fields and records from a table or a query in an easy-to-read format suitable for printing. Create reports to summarize information in a database in a professional-looking manner.

Activity 12.13 Creating and Printing a Report

In this activity, you will create a report that lists mobile phone contact information for doctors at Texas Lakes Medical Center.

1 **Open** » the **Navigation Pane**, and then open your **12A Doctors** table by double-clicking the table name or by right-clicking and clicking Open from the shortcut menu.

2 **Close** « the **Navigation Pane**. Click the **Create tab**, and then in the **Reports group**, click the **Report** button. Compare your screen with Figure 12.40.

> A report displays all of the fields and all of the records in the table in a format suitable for printing. The report displays in Layout view, which means you can make quick changes to the design or layout of the report. Dotted lines indicate how the report would be broken across pages if the report were printed.

Figure 12.40

Report Layout Tools available

Report object tab displays a Report icon

Dotted line indicates page break if printed in current layout

Layout View button active

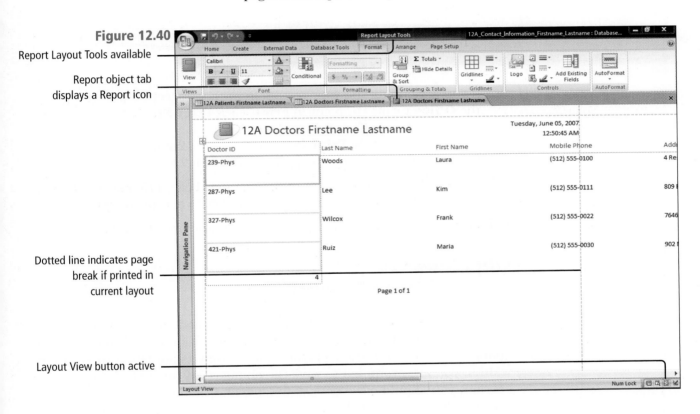

3 Scroll to the right as necessary, point to the **Address** field, right-click, and then from the shortcut menu, click **Delete.**

> The Address field and data are deleted, and the report readjusts to accommodate the deletion.

4 Use the same technique to delete the following fields in the report: **City**, **State**, **ZIP**, **Specialty**, and **Attachments**.

> This report will provide June with a quick list of each doctor and his or her ID and mobile phone number.

5 Click the **Page Setup tab**, and then in the **Page Layout group**, click the **Landscape** button. Scroll to the left, and then compare your screen with Figure 12.41.

Figure 12.41

6 If you are submitting your results from this project on paper, from the **Office** menu ⓐ, point to **Print**, click **Print Preview**, and then in the **Print group**, click **Print**. In the **Print** dialog box, click **OK**, and then click the **Close Print Preview** button. To submit electronically, follow the directions provided by your instructor.

7 **Close** ⊠ the report object. In the message box, click **Yes** to save the report. In the **Save As** dialog box, click **OK** to accept the report name.

8 **Close** ⊠ all of the open objects, leaving the object window empty.

Objective 10
Close and Save a Database

When you close an Access table, any changes made to the records are saved automatically. If you have changed the design of the table, or have changed the layout of the Datasheet view, such as adjusting the column widths, you are prompted to save the changes. At the end of your Access session, you should close your database, and then exit Access. If the Navigation Pane is closed when you close Access, it will be closed when you reopen the database.

Activity 12.14 Closing and Saving a Database

1 Be sure that all of the objects are closed.

2 From the **Office** menu ⓐ, click **Close Database**, and then at the right edge of the Access title bar, click the **Close** button ⊠ to close the Access program. Alternatively, from the Office menu, click Exit Access.

End **You have completed Project 12A** ——————

Project 12B Health Seminars

In Activities 12.15 through 12.21, you will assist June Liu, Chief Administrative Officer, by creating a database to store information about community health seminars presented by Texas Lakes Medical Center. You will use a database template that tracks event information, add seminar information to the database, and then print the results. Your printout will look similar to Figure 12.42.

For Project 12B, you will need the following file:

New Access database using the Events template

You will save your database as
12B_Health_Seminars_Firstname_Lastname

Location	On Site/Off Site	Seating Capacity	Room Arrangement	Visual Equipment
Dogwood Room	On Site	50	Classroom	Computer Projector
Jefferson High School	Off Site	150	Theater	Computer Projector
Sandbox Preschool	Off Site	20	Classroom	White Board
Yellow Rose Room	On Site	20	U-Shape Table	Computer Projector

12B Seminar Locations Firstname Lastname — 6/7/2007

Page 1

Figure 12.42
Project 12B—Health Seminars

Objective 11
Create a Database by Using a Template

Students: Project B uses an Events database template. In the project, you are asked to enter dates in the year 2009 but events for which the date has passed are automatically rejected by the template. Because it is now past April 2009, you can successfully complete these projects by simply using 2010, 2011, or some other future year, instead of 2009. Please clarify with your instructor which year you should use. Other projects affected in this chapter are: D, F, G, M, and N.

A database template contains pre-built tables, queries, forms, and reports to perform a specific task, such as tracking a large number of events. For example, your college may hold events such as athletic contests, plays, lectures, concerts, and club meetings. Using a predefined template, your college Activities Director could quickly create a database to manage these events.

The advantage of using a template to start a new database is that you do not have to create the objects—all you need to do is enter your data and modify the pre-built objects to suit your needs.

The purpose of the database in this project is to track the health seminars offered by Texas Lakes Medical Center. The questions to be answered may include:

- *What seminars will be offered and when will they be offered?*
- *In what Medical Center rooms or community locations will the seminars be held?*
- *Which seminar rooms have a computer projector for PowerPoint presentations?*

Activity 12.15 Creating a New Database Using a Template

1 **Start** Access. On the left, under **Template Categories**, click **Local Templates**. Compare your screen with Figure 12.43.

> Local templates are stored on your computer; they were saved when Access was installed on your computer.

Figure 12.43

Local Templates

Available Local Templates

Events template

2 In the Spotlight area, under **Local Templates**, click **Events**. On the right side of the screen, to the right of the **File Name** box, click the **Browse** button, and then navigate to your **Access Chapter 12** folder.

3 At the bottom of the **File New Database** dialog box, select the text in the **File name** box. Using your own information, type **12B_Health_ Seminars_Firstname_Lastname** and then press Enter.

4 On the right side of the screen, click the **Create** button.

The *12B Health Seminars* database is created, and the database name displays in the title bar. A predesigned *form*—Event List—displays in the object window.

5 Under the Ribbon, on the **Message Bar**, check to see if a **Security Warning** displays. If a security warning does *not* display, skip the rest of this step. If a security warning displays, on the **Message Bar**, click the **Options** button. In the **Microsoft Office Security Options** dialog box, click the **Enable this content** option button, and then click **OK**. Compare your screen with Figure 12.44.

Databases provided by Microsoft are safe to use on your computer.

Figure 12.44

Database name displays in the title bar

Form icon indicates a form object

Multiple items form prenamed as *Event List*

Total line displays by default

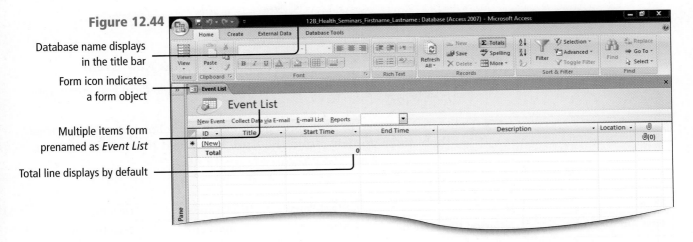

Activity 12.16 Building a Table by Entering Records in a Multiple Items Form

The purpose of a form is to simplify the entry of data into a table—either for you or for others who enter data. In Project 12A, you created a simple form that enabled you to display or enter records in a table one record at a time.

The Events template creates a **Multiple Items form**, a form that enables you to display or enter *multiple* records in a table, but still with an easier and more simplified layout than typing directly into the table itself.

1 Click in the first empty **Title** field. Type **Repetitive Stress Injuries** and then press Tab. In the **Start Time** field, type **3/9/09 7p** and then press Tab.

Access formats the date and time. As you enter dates and times, a small calendar displays to the right of the field, which you can click to select a date instead of typing.

2 In the **End Time** field, type **3/9/09 9p** and then press Tab. In the **Description** field, type **Workplace Health** and then press Tab. In the **Location** field, type **Yellow Rose Room** and then press Tab three times to move to the **Title** field in the new record row. Compare your screen with Figure 12.45.

> Because the seminars have no unique value, Access uses the AutoNumber data type of the ID field to assign a unique, sequential number to each record.

Figure 12.45

First record entered

Access formats date and time

Link bar

AutoNumber creates a unique number

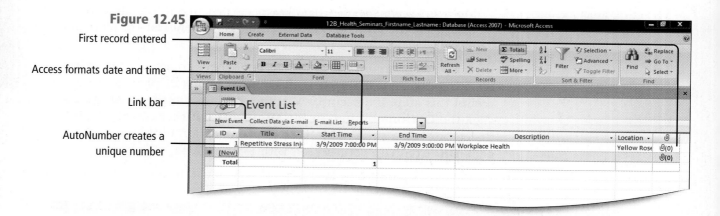

3 In the **Link bar**, just above the field names, click **New Event**.

> A single-record form displays, similar to the simple form you created in Project 12A.

4 Using Tab to move from field to field, enter the following record—press Tab three times to move from the **End Time** field to the **Description** field. Compare your screen with Figure 12.46.

Title	Location	Start Time	End Time	Description
First Aid for Teens	**Jefferson High School**	**3/10/09 4p**	**3/10/09 6p**	**Teen Health**

Figure 12.46

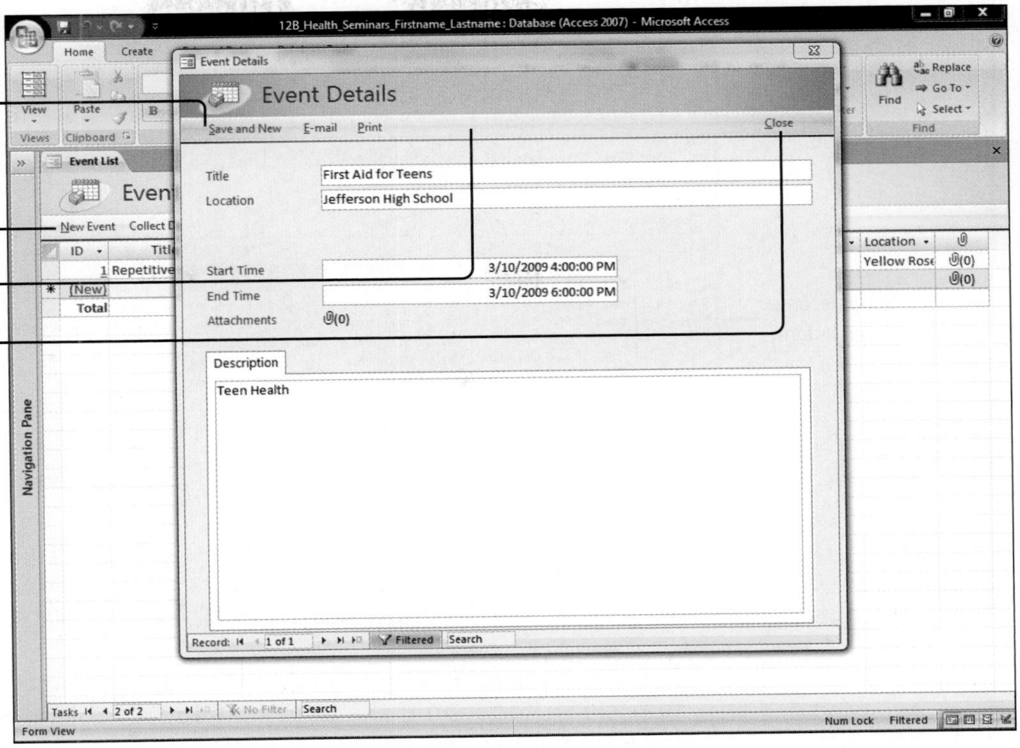
Save and New link
New Event link on Link bar
Single-record form
Close link
12B_Health_Seminars_Firstname_Lastname : Database (Access 2007) - Microsoft Access
Event Details
Save and New
E-mail
Print
Close
Title
First Aid for Teens
Location
Jefferson High School
Start Time
3/10/2009 4:00:00 PM
End Time
3/10/2009 6:00:00 PM
Attachments
Description
Teen Health
Event List
New Event
Navigation Pane

5 In the upper right corner of the single-record form, click **Close**, and notice that the new record displays in the Multiple Items form.

6 Using either the rows on the Multiple Items form or the New Event single-record form, enter the following records, and then compare your screen with Figure 12.47.

ID	Title	Start Time	End Time	Description	Location
3	**Safety on the Job**	**3/18/09 2p**	**3/18/09 4p**	**Workplace Health**	**Yellow Rose Room**
4	**Nutrition for Toddlers**	**3/19/09 1p**	**3/19/09 3p**	**Child Health and Development**	**Sandbox Preschool**
5	**Stay Healthy While You Travel**	**4/6/09 9a**	**4/6/09 11a**	**Life Style and Health**	**Dogwood Room**
6	**Work Smart at Your Computer**	**4/8/09 11a**	**4/8/09 12:30p**	**Workplace Health**	**Dogwood Room**
7	**Be Heart Smart**	**4/14/09 7p**	**4/14/09 9p**	**Life Style and Health**	**Yellow Rose Room**

Alert!

Does a single-record form open?

In the Multiple Items form, pressing Enter three times at the end of a row to begin a new record may display the single-record New Event form. If you prefer to use the Multiple Items form, close the single-record form and continue entering records, using the Tab key to move from field to field.

Figure 12.47

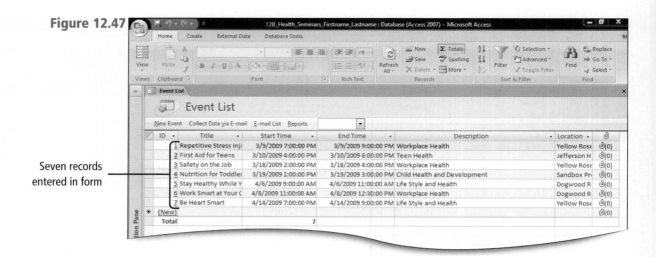

Seven records entered in form

Objective 12
Organize Database Objects in the Navigation Pane

Use the Navigation Pane to organize database objects, to open them, and to perform common tasks like renaming an object. So far, your databases have had only a few objects, but databases can have a large number of tables and other objects. The Navigation Pane is your tool for organizing database objects.

Activity 12.17 Organizing Database Objects in the Navigation Pane

The Navigation Pane groups and displays your database objects and can do so in predefined arrangements. In this activity, you will group your database objects using the *Tables and Views category*, an arrangement that groups objects by the table to which they are related. This grouping is useful because you can easily determine the underlying source table of queries, forms, and reports.

1 **Open** the **Navigation Pane**. At the top of the **Navigation Pane**, click the **Navigation arrow**. From the list, under **Navigate To Category**, click **Tables and Related Views**.

2 Click the **Navigation arrow** to display the list again, and then under **Filter By Group**, point to **All Tables**. Compare your screen with Figure 12.48.

Figure 12.48

All Tables displays

Tables and Related Views selected

All Tables selected

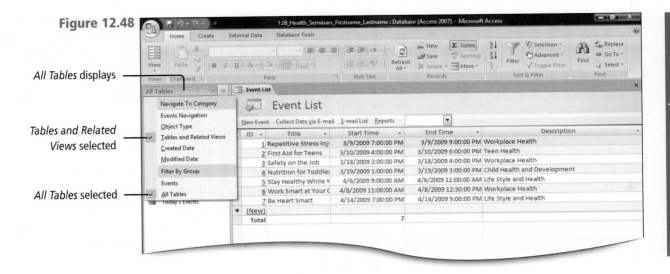

3 Click **All Tables** to close the list, and then confirm that *Events* displays in the blue bar at the top of the **Navigation Pane**. Compare your screen with Figure 12.49.

> The icons to the left of the objects listed in the Navigation Pane indicate that the Events template created a number of objects for you—among them, one table titled *Events*, one query, two forms, and five reports. The Event List Multiple Items form, which is currently displayed in the object window, is included in the Navigation Pane. All of the objects were created using the underlying data source, which is the Events table.

Figure 12.49

One table
One query
Two forms

Five reports

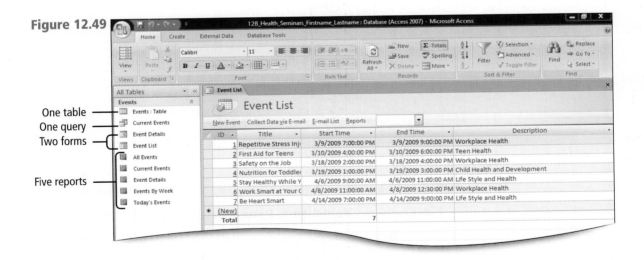

4 In the **Navigation Pane**, point to the **Events** *table*, right-click, and then click **Open**. Alternatively, double-click the table name to open it in the object window.

> The Events table is the active object in the object window. Use the Navigation Pane to open objects for use.

The seven records that you entered using the Multiple Items *form* display in the *table*. Tables are the foundation of your database because your data must be stored in a table. You can enter records directly into a table, or you can use a form to enter records.

5 In the object window, click the **Event List form tab** to bring it into view and make it the active object.

Recall that a form presents a more user-friendly screen for entering records into a table.

6 In the **Navigation Pane**, right-click the *report* named **Current Events**, and then click **Open**. Alternatively, double-click the report name to open it. Compare your screen with Figure 12.50.

An advantage of using a template to begin a database is that many objects, such as attractively formatted reports, are already designed for you.

Figure 12.50

Current Events report preformatted and designed by the template

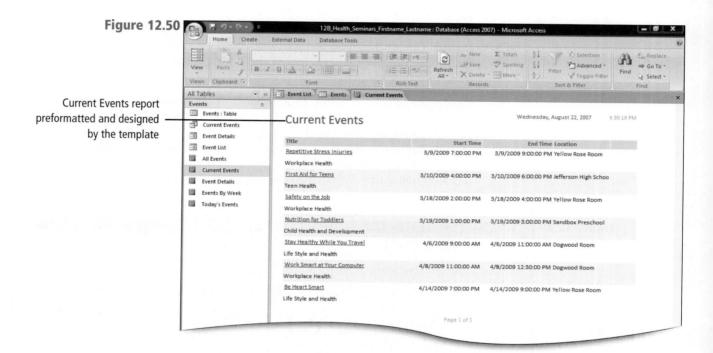

7 In the object window, **Close** ✕ the **Current Events** report.

8 From the **Navigation Pane**, open the **Events By Week** report.

In this predesigned report that came with the database template, the events are displayed by week. After entering records in the form or table, the preformatted reports are updated with the records from the table.

9 **Close** ✕ the **Events By Week** report, and then **Close** ✕ the remaining two open objects. Leave the **Navigation Pane** open.

Objective 13
Create a New Table in a Database Created with a Template

The Events database template created only one table—the *Events* table. Although the database was started from a template and contains many other objects, you can add additional objects as needed.

Create a new table in a database when you begin to see repeated information. For example, in the Events database, both the Yellow Rose Room and the Dogwood Room are listed more than one time.

Activity 12.18 Creating a New Table and Changing Its Design

June has information about the various locations where seminars are held. For example, for the Yellow Rose Room, she has information about the seating arrangements, number of seats, and audio-visual equipment.

In the Events table, three seminars are scheduled in the Yellow Rose Room and two are scheduled in the Dogwood Room. It would not make sense to store information about the rooms multiple times in the same table. It is *not* considered good database design to have duplicate information in a table.

When data in a table becomes repetitive or redundant, it is usually a signal to create a new table to contain the information about the topic. In this activity, you will create a table to track the seminar locations and the equipment and seating arrangements in each location.

1 **Close** « the **Navigation Pane** to maximize your screen space. On the Ribbon, click the **Create tab**, and then in the **Tables group**, click the **Table** button.

2 Click in the cell under **Add New Field**, type **Yellow Rose Room** and then press Tab. Type **On Site** and then press Tab.

3 Type **20** and then press Tab. Type **U-Shape Table** and then press Tab. Type **Computer Projector** and then press Tab three times. Compare your screen with Figure 12.51.

> Access assigns an AutoNumber in the ID field.

Figure 12.51

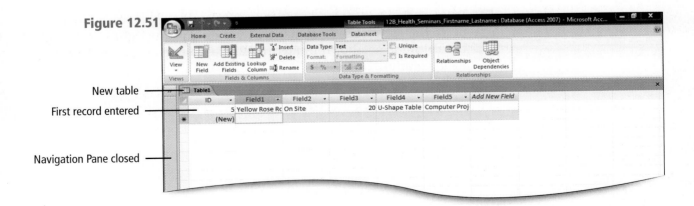

New table

First record entered

Navigation Pane closed

4 Point to the text *Field1*, right-click, and then from the shortcut menu, click **Rename Column**. Type **Location** and then double-click *Field2* to select the text. Type **On Site/Off Site** and then point to and click *Field3*.

5 On the Ribbon, if necessary, click the **Datasheet tab**. In the **Fields & Columns group**, click the **Rename** button, and then type **Seating Capacity** Using any of the techniques you have just practiced, change *Field4* to **Room Arrangement** and *Field5* to **Visual Equipment**

6 In the **Views group**, click the **View** button to switch to **Design** view. In the dialog box, **Save** the table as **12B Seminar Locations Firstname Lastname** and then click **OK**.

7 In **Design** view, in the **Field Name** column, click in the **Location** box. Then, on the **Design tab**, in the **Tools group**, click the **Primary Key** button.

The key icon moves to the left of the Location field. Recall that the Primary Key is a field that contains a unique identifier for each record. In the Seminar Locations table, the Location name is unique; no other record will have the same Location name.

8 Point to the **row selector box** for the **ID** field to display the ➡ pointer, and then click to select the entire row. On the **Design tab**, in the **Tools group**, click the **Delete Rows** button. In the message box, click **Yes**.

Because the Location name will serve as the primary key field, the ID field is no longer needed.

9 On the **Design tab**, in the **Views group**, click the **View** button, which by its icon indicates that you will return to the Datasheet view of the table. In the message box, click **Yes** to save the design changes to the table.

10 Enter the following records in the table:

Location	On Site/ Off Site	Seating Capacity	Room Arrangement	Visual Equipment
Jefferson High School	Off Site	150	Theater	Computer Projector
Dogwood Room	On Site	50	Classroom	Computer Projector
Sandbox Preschool	Off Site	20	Classroom	White Board

11 Point to the field name *Location* to display the ⬇ pointer. Hold down the left mouse button, and then drag to the right to select all of the columns as shown in Figure 12.52—do *not* select the *Add New Field* column.

Figure 12.52

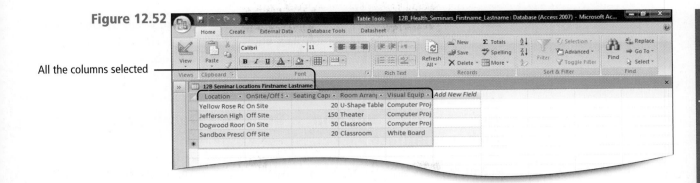

All the columns selected

12 Point to any of the selected field names in the top row, right-click, and then click **Column Width**. In the **Column Width** dialog box, click **Best Fit**. Alternatively, with the columns selected, in the field name row, point to the right boundary of any of the selected columns to display the ✚ pointer, and then double-click to apply Best Fit to all of the selected columns. Notice that the widths of all of the columns are adjusted to accommodate the longest entry in the column.

13 Click in any record to cancel the selection of the columns. **Open** ⟫ the **Navigation Pane**, locate the name of your new table, and then compare your screen with Figure 12.53.

Recall that as it is currently arranged, the Navigation Pane organizes the objects by tables and related views. The Events table is listed first, followed by its related objects, and then the Seminar Locations table is listed. Currently, no other objects were created using the Seminar Locations table.

Figure 12.53

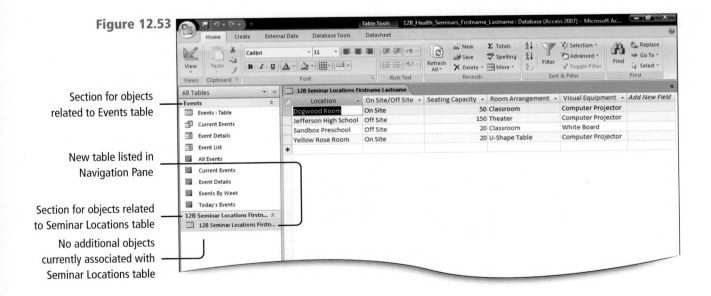

Section for objects related to Events table

New table listed in Navigation Pane

Section for objects related to Seminar Locations table

No additional objects currently associated with Seminar Locations table

14 In the object window, **Close** ☒ the **12B Seminar Locations** table, and then, in the message box, click **Yes** to save the column width layout changes. Leave the **Navigation Pane** open.

Objective 14
View a Report and Print a Table in a Database Created with a Template

Recall that an advantage to starting a new database with a template is that many report objects are already created for you.

Activity 12.19 Viewing a Report

1 From the **Navigation Pane**, open the **All Events** report. Compare your screen with Figure 12.54.

>The All Events pre-built report displays in an attractively arranged format.

Figure 12.54

All Events report

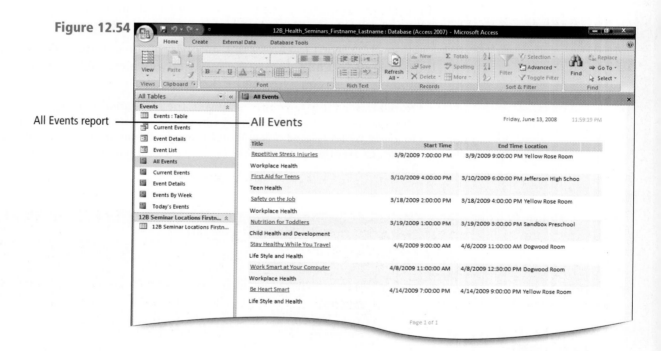

2 **Close** ☒ the **All Events** report.

3 Open the **Event Details** report and compare your screen with Figure 12.55.

>The Event Details pre-built report displays in an attractively arranged format. Each report displays the records in the table in different useful formats.

Figure 12.55

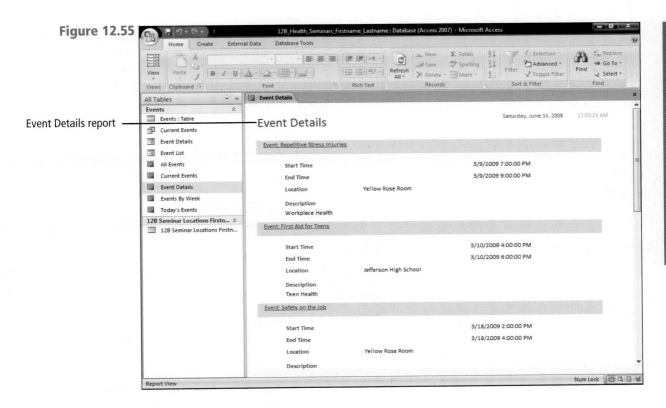

Event Details report

4 **Close** ☒ the **Event Details** report.

Activity 12.20 Printing a Table

Use the Print Preview command to determine if a table will print on one page, or if you need to adjust column widths, margins, or the orientation.

Recall that there will be occasions when you want to print a table for a quick reference or for proofreading. For a more professional-looking format, print a report instead of the table.

1 From the **Navigation Pane**, open the **12B Seminar Locations** table. Display the **Office** menu 🔘, point to the **Print** button, and then click **Print Preview**.

> The table displays in the Print Preview window, showing how it will look when it is printed. The name of the table and the date the table was created display at the top of the page. The navigation area at the bottom of the window displays *1* in the Pages box, and the right-pointing arrow—the Next button—is active.

> Recall that when you are in the Print Preview window, the navigation buttons are used to navigate from one page to the next, rather than from one record to the next.

2 In the navigation area, click the **Next Page** button ▶.

> The second page of the table displays the last field column. Whenever possible, try to print all of the fields horizontally on one page. Of course, if there are many records, more than one page may be needed to print all of the records.

3 On the **Print Preview tab**, in the **Page Layout group**, click the **Margins** button, and then click **Wide**. Notice that this did not move the last field column to the first page. Click the **Landscape** button, and then compare your screen with Figure 12.56. Notice that the entire table will print on one page.

Figure 12.56

Table in landscape orientation

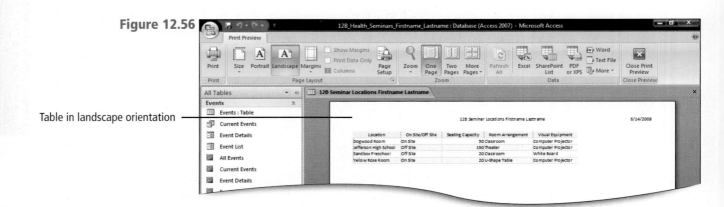

4 To submit your work on paper, on the **Print Preview tab**, in the **Print group**, click the **Print** button. In the **Print** dialog box, click **OK**. In the **Close Preview group**, click the **Close Print Preview** button. To submit your work electronically, follow the directions provided by your instructor.

5 Close ⊠ the **12B Seminar Locations** table, and then **Close** « the **Navigation Pane**.

6 From the **Office** menu ⬚, click **Close Database**. From the **Office** menu ⬚, click **Exit Access**.

Objective 15
Use the Access Help System

Access has a Help feature to assist you when performing a task or to get more information about a particular topic. Activate the Help feature by clicking the Help button or by pressing F1.

Activity 12.21 Using the Access Help System

1 **Start** Access. In the upper right corner of the **Access** window, click the **Microsoft Office Access Help** button ⬚. In the **Access Help** window, click the **Search button arrow**, and then under **Content from this computer**, click **Access Help**.

Help information was stored on your computer when you installed Office. You can also obtain online help from Microsoft.

2 Click in the **Search** box, type **database design** and then press Enter. In the list, click **Database design basics**.

> This information is an informative overview of how to design a database, beginning with writing your ideas on paper. This information can be printed by clicking the Print button.

3 In the upper right corner of the **Access Help** window, click the **Close** button ⊠. On the title bar for the **Getting Started** window, **Close** ⊠ Access.

End **You have completed Project 12B** ——————————

There's More You Can Do!

Display the Start menu, click Computer, and then navigate to the student files that accompany this textbook. In the folder **02_theres_more_you_can_do**, locate and open the folder for this chapter. Open and print the instructions for this project, which are provided to you in Adobe PDF format.

Try IT!—Convert a Database to a Different Format

In this Try It! exercise, you will convert an Access 2007 database to a database that others can view and edit in Access 2002 or Access 2003.

Content-Based Assessments

Access
chapter twelve

Summary

Microsoft Office Access is a database management system that uses various objects—tables, forms, queries, reports—to organize a database. Data is stored in tables in which you establish fields, set the data type and field size, and create a primary key. Data from a database can be reported and printed.

Key Terms

The ☺ symbol represents Key Terms found on the Student CD in the 02_theres_more_you_can_do folder for this chapter.

Content-Based Assessments

Access
chapter**twelve**

Matching

Match each term in the second column with its correct definition in the first column. Write the letter of the term on the blank line in front of the correct definition.

_____ 1. An organized collection of facts about people, events, things, or ideas related to a particular topic or purpose.

_____ 2. Facts about people, events, things, or ideas.

_____ 3. Data that is organized in a useful manner.

_____ 4. The basic parts of a database, which include tables, forms, queries, reports, and macros.

_____ 5. The Access object that stores your data organized in an arrangement of columns and rows.

_____ 6. The area of the Access window that displays and organizes the names of the objects in a database, and from where you open objects for use.

_____ 7. The portion of the Access window that displays open objects.

_____ 8. A category that describes each piece of data stored in a table.

_____ 9. All of the categories of data pertaining to one person, place, thing, event, or idea.

_____ 10. The number of fields, and the type of content within each field, in an Access table.

_____ 11. The Access view that displays an object organized in a format of columns and rows similar to an Excel spreadsheet.

_____ 12. The Access view that displays the underlying structure of an object.

_____ 13. The action of filling a database table with records.

_____ 14. The characteristic that defines the kind of data that can be entered into a field, such as numbers, text, or dates.

_____ 15. An Access feature that sequentially numbers entered records creating a unique number for each field and which is useful for data that has no distinct field that is unique.

A AutoNumber

B Data

C Data type

D Database

E Datasheet view

F Design view

G Field

H Information

I Navigation Pane

J Object window

K Objects

L Populate

M Record

N Table

O Table design

Content-Based Assessments

Fill in the Blank

Write the correct word in the space provided.

1. DBMS is an acronym for _____ _____ _____.

2. A preformatted database designed for a specific purpose is a database _____.

3. A database that has no data and has no database tools, in which you create the data and the tools as you need them, is referred to as a _____ database.

4. Characteristics of a field that control how the field will display and how data can be entered in a field are known as the _____ _____.

5. The field that uniquely identifies a record in a table is the _____ _____.

6. A pre-built table format for common topics such as contacts, issues, and tasks is a _____ _____.

7. A database object that retrieves specific data from one or more tables, and then displays the specified data in Datasheet view is a _____.

8. A type of query that retrieves data from one or more tables and makes it available for use in the format of a datasheet is a _____ query.

9. The table or tables from which a query gets its data is the _____ _____.

10. A feature in Microsoft Office programs that walks you step-by-step through a process is a _____.

11. To search a table of records included in a query, find the records that match the criteria, and then display the records, _____ the query.

12. An Access object with which you can enter new records into a table, edit existing records in a table, or display existing records from a table is a _____.

13. The Access object that displays data in a formatted manner for printing and publication is a _____.

14. The Access form object in which multiple records can be entered into or displayed from a table is a _____ _____ form.

15. An arrangement of objects in the Navigation Pane in which the objects are grouped by the table to which they are related is the _____ _____ _____ category.

Skills Review

Project 12C — Departments

In this project, you will apply the skills you practiced from the Objectives in Project 12A.

Objectives: 1. *Start Access and Create a New Blank Database;* **2.** *Add Records to a Table;* **3.** *Rename Table Fields in Datasheet View;* **4.** *Modify the Design of a Table;* **5.** *Add a Second Table to a Database;* **6.** *Print a Table;* **7.** *Create and Use a Query;* **8.** *Create and Use a Form;* **9.** *Create and Print a Report;* **10.** *Close and Save a Database.*

In the following Skills Review, you will assist Kendall Walker, the CEO of Texas Lakes Medical Center, in creating a database to store information about the Departments and Department Directors at Texas Lakes Medical Center. Your printed results will look similar to those in Figure 12.57.

For Project 12C, you will need the following file:

New blank Access database

You will save your database as
12C_Departments_Firstname_Lastname

Figure 12.57

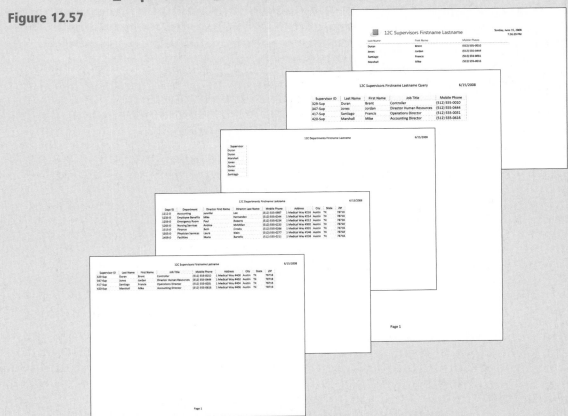

(Project 12C–Departments continues on the next page)

Content-Based Assessments

Access
chaptertwelve

Skills Review

(Project 12C–Departments continued)

1. **Start** Access and create a new **Blank Database**. In the lower right corner, click the **Browse** button, navigate to your **Access Chapter 12** folder. In the **File New Database** dialog box, name the database **12C_Departments_Firstname_Lastname** and then press [Enter]. In the lower right corner, click **Create**.

2. In the **Navigation Pane**, click the **Close** button to collapse the **Navigation Pane** and maximize your screen space. Click in the first **Add New Field** box, type **Accounting** and then click in the **ID** field. To assign custom Department IDs, on the **Datasheet tab**, in the **Data Type & Formatting group**, click the **Data Type arrow**, and then click **Text**. Type **1212-D** and then click in the next **Add New Field** box to the right of *Accounting*. Complete the entry of this record and the next record as follows:

ID	Field1	Field2	Field3	Field4	Field5	Field6	Field7	Field8	Field9	Field10
1212-D	Accounting	Jennifer	R	Lee	(512) 555-0987	1 Medical Way #216	Austin	TX	78718	Duran
1233-D	Employee Benefits	Mike	M	Hernandez	(512) 555-0344	1 Medical Way #214	Austin	TX	78718	Duran

3. Point to the text *ID*, and then click to select the column. On the **Datasheet tab**, in the **Fields & Columns group**, click the **Rename** button. Type **Dept ID** and then press [Tab]. Point to the text *Field1*, right-click, and then click **Rename Column**. Type **Department** and then press [Tab]. Point to the text *Field2* and double-click. With the text selected, type **Director First Name** and then press [Tab]. Using any of these techniques and the information in the following list, **Rename** the fields:

Field3	Director Middle Initial
Field4	Director Last Name
Field5	Mobile Phone
Field6	Address
Field7	City
Field8	State
Field9	ZIP
Field10	Supervisor

(Project 12C–Departments continues on the next page)

Content-Based Assessments

Skills Review

(Project 12C–Departments continued)

4. Enter the following additional records:

Dept ID	Department	Director First Name	Director Middle Initial	Director Last Name	Mobile Phone	Address	City	State	ZIP	Supervisor
1259-D	Emergency Room	Paul	S	Roberts	(512) 555-0234	1 Medical Way #212	Austin	TX	78718	Marshall
1265-D	Nursing Services	Andrea	T	McMillan	(512) 555-0233	1 Medical Way #302	Austin	TX	78718	Jones
1313-D	Finance	Beth	N	Crosby	(512) 555-0266	1 Medical Way #301	Austin	TX	78718	Duran
1355-D	Physician Services	Laura	O	Klein	(512) 555-0277	1 Medical Way #146	Austin	TX	78718	Jones
1459-D	Facilities	Mario	B	Bartello	(512) 555-0211	1 Medical Way #236	Austin	TX	78718	Santiago

5. On the **Datasheet tab**, in the **Views group**, click the **View button arrow**, and then click **Design View**. To save the changes you made to the field names and data types, and to give the table a more meaningful name, **Save** the table—using your own name—as **12C Departments Firstname Lastname** and then click **OK**.

6. In the **Field Name** column, click the **row selector box** to the left of the **Director Middle Initial** field name to select the entire row. On the **Design tab**, in the **Tools group**, click the **Delete Rows** button, read the message in the message box, and then click **Yes**. For this table, Kendall decides that having the Director's middle initial is not necessary.

7. With the table displayed in **Design** view, in the **Field Name** column, click in the **Dept ID** box. To the left of the box, notice the small icon of a key representing the primary key. Recall that the primary key is the field that uniquely identifies each individual record—no two records in the database will have the same Dept ID.

8. In the **Field Name** column, click in the **State** box, and then in the **Field Properties** area, set the **Field Size** to 2 In the **Description** column, click in the **Address** row, and then type **Include the Room number** Recall that these descriptions display in the status bar when entering records using a form, and communicate helpful information to the person entering data.

9. Click the **View** button to switch to **Datasheet** view, and then click **Yes** two times to save the changes you made to the design of the table—deleting a field, adding a description, and changing a field property.

10. With the **12C Departments** table displayed in **Datasheet** view, notice that in the **Supervisor** field, several names are repeated. Thus, it would not make sense to include information about these individuals multiple times in the same table. Recall that when you see repeated information, it is likely that an additional table should be added to the database. On the Ribbon, click the **Create tab**. In the **Tables group**, click the **Table Templates** button, and then from the list, click **Contacts**.

(Project 12C–Departments continues on the next page)

(Project 12C–Departments continued)

11. Click the **Datasheet tab** to display the groups of Datasheet commands. In the second column, point to the text *Company*, click to select the field, and then on the **Datasheet tab**, in the **Fields & Columns group**, click the **Delete** button.

12. **Delete** the **E-mail Address** field. With your mouse, drag to the right to select the **Business Phone** field and **Home Phone** field. Right-click over the field names, and then click **Delete Column**. **Delete** the **Fax Number** field. Then, **Delete** the fields **Country/Region**, **Web Page**, **Notes**, and **Attachments** (the field with the paper clip icon).

13. On the **Datasheet tab**, in the **Views group**, click the **View** button to switch to **Design** view. To save the changes you made to the field arrangement and to give the table a more meaningful name, **Save** the table—using your own name—as **12C Supervisors Firstname Lastname** and then click **OK**.

14. In the **Field Name** column, click the **ID** box, delete the text, and then type **Supervisor ID** Click in the **Data Type** box, click the **Data Type arrow**, and then from the list, click **Text**. Click in the **Description** box, and type **Supervisor's ID number** The medical center assigns a unique ID number to each Supervisor, which you will use as the primary key instead of the AutoNumber.

15. In the **Field Name** column, click in the **State/Province** box, and then in the **Field Properties** area, set the **Field Size** to **2** Click the **View** button to switch to **Datasheet** view, and then click **Yes** to save the changes you have made to the design of your table—changing a field name, adding a description, and changing a field property.

16. With your **12C Supervisors** table displayed in **Datasheet** view, in the new record row which is indicated by an asterisk (*) in the record selector box on the left, click in the **Supervisor ID** field, and then add the following records:

Supervisor ID	Last Name	First Name	Job Title	Mobile Phone	Address	City	State/ Province	ZIP/Postal Code
329-Sup	Duran	Brent	Controller	(512) 555-0010	1 Medical Way #400	Austin	TX	78718
347-Sup	Jones	Jordan	Director Human Resources	(512) 555-0444	1 Medical Way #402	Austin	TX	78718
417-Sup	Santiago	Francis	Operations Director	(512) 555-0031	1 Medical Way #404	Austin	TX	78718
420-Sup	Marshall	Mike	Accounting Director	(512) 555-0616	1 Medical Way #406	Austin	TX	78718

(Project 12C–Departments continues on the next page)

(Project 12C–Departments continued)

17. Change the field name **State/Province** to **State** and **ZIP/Postal Code** to **ZIP** Select all of the columns, and then apply **Best Fit** either by double-clicking the right border of any selected column or by displaying the shortcut menu, clicking Column Width, and then clicking Best Fit. On the **Quick Access Toolbar**, click the **Save** button to save the changes you have made to the layout of the table.

18. From the **Office** menu, point to **Print**, and then click **Print Preview**. In the **Page Layout group**, click the **Margins** button, and then click **Normal**. Click the **Landscape** button. If you are submitting paper results, click the **Print** button, and in the **Print** dialog box, click **OK**. Click the **Close Print Preview** button. To submit electronically, follow the directions provided by your instructor.

19. **Close** the **12C Supervisors** table. In the **12C Departments** table, select all of the columns, and then apply **Best Fit**. On the **Quick Access Toolbar**, click the **Save** button. From the **Office** menu, point to **Print**, and then click **Print Preview**. In the **Page Layout group**, click the **Margins** button, and then click **Normal**. Click the **Landscape** button. If you are submitting paper results, click the **Print** button, and in the **Print** dialog box, click **OK**. Click the **Close Print Preview** button. To submit electronically, follow the directions provided by your instructor.

20. **Close** the **12C Departments** table. Click the **Create tab**, and then in the **Other group**, click the **Query Wizard** button. In the **New Query** dialog box, click **Simple Query Wizard**, and then click **OK**. Click the **Tables/Queries arrow**, and then click **Table: 12C Supervisors**. Under **Available Fields**, click **Supervisor ID**, and then click the **Add Field** button to move the field to the **Selected Fields** list on the right. Add the **Last Name**, **First Name**, **Job Title**, and **Mobile Phone** fields to the **Selected Fields** list in the order specified. Recall that you can also double-click a field name to move it.

This query will answer the question *What are the Supervisor ID, name, job title, and mobile phone number of every Supervisor in the database?* Click the **Next** button. Be sure that the option **Open the query to view information** is selected. Click **Finish**. Display the query in **Print Preview**, use the default margins and orientation, **Print**, and then **Close Print Preview**. Or, submit electronically as directed.

21. **Close** your query. **Open** the **Navigation Pane**, click to select the **12C Supervisors** table. Do not open the table, just select it. **Close** the **Navigation Pane**. On the Ribbon, click the **Create tab**, and then in the **Forms group**, click the **Form** button. The form displays in Layout view, in which you can make changes to the layout of the form. Because no changes are necessary, on the **Home tab**, in the **Views group**, click the **View button arrow**, and then from the list, click **Form View**. From the **Office** menu, click **Save** to save your newly designed form, and then click **OK** to accept the default name. **Close** the form object. Recall that you typically create forms to make data entry easier for the individuals who enter new records into your database.

22. **Open** the **Navigation Pane**, locate the **12C Supervisors** table—recall that a table displays a small icon of a datasheet, a query displays a small icon of two datasheets, and a form displays a small form icon. Open the table either by double-clicking the table name or right-clicking and clicking Open. **Close** the **Navigation Pane**. On the **Create tab**, in the **Reports group**, click the **Report** button.

(Project 12C–Departments continues on the next page)

(Project 12C–Departments continued)

23. Point to the **Supervisor ID** column heading, right-click, and then click **Delete**. **Delete** the **Job Title**, **Address**, **City**, **State**, and **ZIP** fields from the report layout. From the **Office** menu, point to **Print**, and then click **Print Preview**. In the **Page Layout group**, click the **Margins** button, and then click **Wide**. Click the **Landscape** button. If you are submitting paper results, click the **Print** button. Click the **Close Print Preview** button. To submit electronically, follow the instructions provided by your instructor.

24. **Close** your **12C Supervisors** report, and then click **Yes** to save the design changes. In the **Save As** dialog box, click **OK** to save the report with the default name. If necessary, close any remaining objects and **Close** the **Navigation Pane**. From the **Office** menu, click **Close Database**. From the **Office** menu, click **Exit Access**.

End **You have completed Project 12C**

Skills Review

Project 12D — Benefits Fair

In this project, you will apply the skills you practiced from the Objectives in Project 12B.

Objectives: 11. *Create a Database by Using a Template;* **12.** *Organize Database Objects in the Navigation Pane;* **13.** *Create a New Table in a Database Created with a Template;* **14.** *View a Report and Print a Table in a Database Created with a Template.*

In the following Skills Review, you will assist Sharon Fitzgerald, the Human Resources Director at Texas Lakes Medical Center, in creating a database to store information about the Employee Benefits Fair at Texas Lakes Medical Center. Your printed result will look similar to Figure 12.58.

For Project 12D, you will need the following file:

New Access database using the Events template

You will save your database as
12D_Benefits_Fair_Firstname_Lastname

Figure 12.58

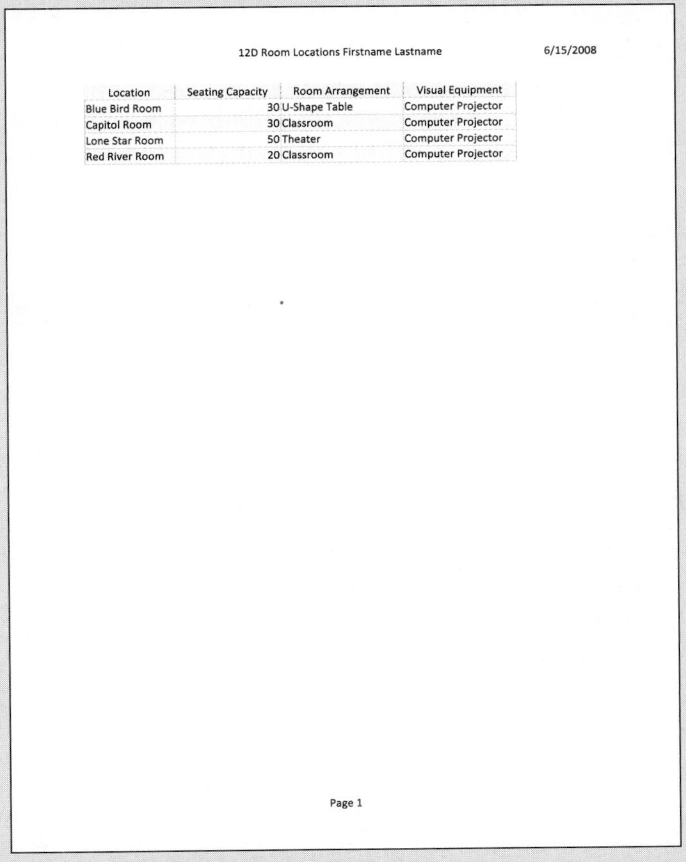

12D Room Locations Firstname Lastname   6/15/2008

Location	Seating Capacity	Room Arrangement	Visual Equipment
Blue Bird Room	30	U-Shape Table	Computer Projector
Capitol Room	30	Classroom	Computer Projector
Lone Star Room	50	Theater	Computer Projector
Red River Room	20	Classroom	Computer Projector

Page 1

(Project 12D–Benefits Fair continues on the next page)

Content-Based Assessments

(Project 12D–Benefits Fair continued)

1. **Start** Access. Under **Template Categories**, click **Local Templates**, and then click **Events**. In the lower right portion of the screen, click the **Browse** button 🗁, navigate to your **Access Chapter 12** folder. **Save** the database as **12D_Benefits_Fair_Firstname_Lastname** and then press [Enter]. In the lower right corner, click the **Create** button. If necessary, to the right of the Security Warning, click Options, click Enable this content, and then click OK.

2. Recall that a template opens with a pre-built Multiple Items form into which you can enter records to build a table. In the **Event List** Multiple Items form, enter the following records, pressing [Tab] to move across the row:

ID	Title	Start Time	End Time	Description	Location
1	Medical Plan	5/1/09 8a	5/1/09 5p	Health Benefits	Lone Star Room
2	Eye Care Plan	5/1/09 9a	5/1/09 3p	Health Benefits	Red River Room
3	Prescription Plan	5/1/09 8a	5/1/09 8p	Health Benefits	Lone Star Room
4	Pension Plan	5/1/09 10a	5/1/09 7:30p	Retirement Benefits	Capitol Room
5	Life Insurance Plan	5/1/09 1p	5/1/09 5p	Life Insurance Benefits	Blue Bird Room
6	Deferred Compensation Plan	5/1/09 10a	5/1/09 3p	Compensation Benefits	Red River Room

3. In the **Link bar**, just above the field names row, click **New Event**, and then enter the following record using the single-record form. Recall that you can also use this form to enter records into a table:

Title	Location	Start Time	End Time	Description
Dental Plan	Blue Bird Room	5/1/09 8a	5/1/09 5p	Health Benefits

4. **Close** the single-record form. **Close** the **Event List** form. **Open** the **Navigation Pane**. At the top of the **Navigation Pane**, click the **Navigation arrow**. Under **Navigate To Category**, click **Tables and Related Views**. Click the **Navigation arrow** again, and then in the **Filter By Group** section, notice that **All Tables** is selected. Recall that this arrangement organizes the database objects by the table to which they are related.

5. On the **Navigation Pane**, right-click the **Events** table, and then click **Open**—or double-click the table name to open it. This is the table that was built from the records you entered into the form. Rather than enter information about the Locations multiple times in this table, you will create another table for the Location information. **Close** the **Events** table, and then **Close** the **Navigation Pane**.

(Project 12D–Benefits Fair continues on the next page)

Content-Based Assessments

(Project 12D–Benefits Fair continued)

6. Click the **Create tab**, and then in the **Tables group**, click the **Table** button. Enter the following records, pressing [Tab] or [Enter] to move across the row. Recall that Access assigns unique numbers; your ID numbers may vary.

ID	Field1	Field2	Field3	Field4
4	Blue Bird Room	30	U-Shape Table	Computer Projector
5	Red River Room	20	Classroom	Computer Projector
6	Capitol Room	30	Classroom	Computer Projector

7. Point to the text *Field1* and click to select the column. On the **Datasheet tab**, in the **Fields & Columns group**, click the **Rename** button, and then type **Location** Point to the text *Field2*, right-click, and then click **Rename Column**. Type **Seating Capacity** Point to the text *Field3* and double-click. With the text selected, type **Room Arrangement** Using any of these techniques, **Rename** *Field4* as **Visual Equipment**

8. Enter one additional record as follows:

ID	Location	Seating Capacity	Room Arrangement	Visual Equipment
7	Lone Star Room	50	Theater	Computer Projector

9. On the **Home tab**, in the **Views group**, click the **View button arrow**, and then click **Design View**. **Save** the table as **12D Room Locations Firstname Lastname** and then click **OK**.

10. In the **Field Name** column, click in the **Location** box, and then on the **Design tab**, click the **Primary Key** button. Point to the row selector box for the **ID** field, and then click to select the entire row. On the **Design tab**, click the **Delete Rows** button, and then click **Yes**. The Location name will serve as the primary key for this table. In the **Views group**, click the **View** button, and then click **Yes** to save the changes you made to the table design.

11. In the field names row, drag across to select all of the fields (columns). Right-click over any field name, click **Column Width**, and then in the **Column Width** dialog box, click **Best Fit**.

12. **Close** the **12D Room Locations** table, and then click **Yes** to save the layout changes you made to the column widths. From the **Navigation Pane**, open the **All Events** report. Open the **Event Details** report. The pre-built reports are arranged in various useful formats. **Close** both reports.

13. From the **Navigation Pane**, open your **12D Room Locations** table. From the **Office** menu, point to **Print**, and then click **Print Preview**. If you are submitting your work on paper, on the **Print Preview tab**, in the **Print group**, click the **Print** button, and then **Close Print Preview**. To submit electronically, follow the directions provided by your instructor.

14. **Close** the **12D Room Locations** table. **Close** the **Navigation Pane**. With all of the database objects closed, from the **Office** menu, click **Close Database**. From the **Office** menu, click **Exit Access**.

End You have completed Project 12D

Mastering Access

Project 12E — Gift Shop

In this project, you will apply skills you practiced from the Objectives in Projects 12A and 12B.

Objectives: 1. *Start Access and Create a New Blank Database;* **2.** *Add Records to a Table;* **3.** *Rename Table Fields in Datasheet View;* **4.** *Modify the Design of a Table;* **5.** *Add a Second Table to a Database;* **6.** *Print a Table;* **7.** *Create and Use a Query;* **8.** *Create and Use a Form;* **9.** *Create and Print a Report;* **10.** *Close and Save a Database;* **12.** *Organize Database Objects in the Navigation Pane.*

In the following Mastering Access project, you will assist Scott Williams, the Gift Shop Manager of Texas Lakes Medical Center, in creating a database to store information about gift items in the shop's inventory. Your printed results will look similar to those shown in Figure 12.59.

For Project 12E, you will need the following file:

New blank Access database

You will save your database as 12E_Gift_Shop_Firstname_Lastname

Figure 12.59

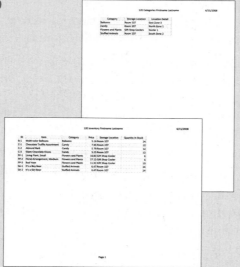

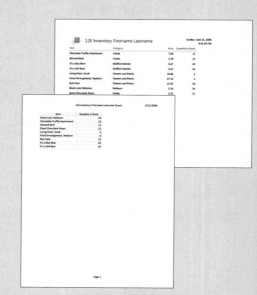

(Project 12E–Gift Shop continues on the next page)

(Project 12E–Gift Shop continued)

1. **Start** Access, create a new **Blank Database**, and then **Save** it in your **Access Chapter 12** folder as **12E_Gift_Shop_Firstname_Lastname**

2. **Close** the **Navigation Pane**. For the **ID** field, change the **Data Type** to **Text**. Enter the following records:

ID	Field1	Field2	Field3	Field4	Field5
C-1	Chocolate Truffle Assortment	Candy	7.95	Room 107	12
C-2	Almond Bark	Candy	5.79	Room 107	12
SA-1	It's a Boy Bear	Stuffed Animals	6.47	Room 107	24
SA-2	It's a Girl Bear	Stuffed Animals	6.47	Room 107	24
FP-1	Living Plant, Small	Flowers and Plants	10.83	Gift Shop Cooler	6
FP-2	Floral Arrangement, Medium	Flowers and Plants	27.15	Gift Shop Cooler	6
FP-3	Bud Vase	Flowers and Plants	11.91	Gift Shop Cooler	10
B-1	Multi-color Balloons	Balloons	5.16	Room 107	24
C-3	Giant Chocolate Kisses	Candy	5.25	Room 107	12

3. **Rename** the fields as follows:

Field1	Item
Field2	Category
Field3	Price
Field4	Storage Location
Field5	Quantity in Stock

4. Select all of the fields (columns), and then apply **Best Fit**. **Save** the table, and name it **12E Inventory Firstname Lastname** Display the table in **Print Preview**, set the margins to **Wide** and the orientation to **Landscape**. If you are submitting printed pages, click **Print**; and then **Close Print Preview**. To submit electronically, follow the directions provided by your instructor. **Close** the table and **Save** any changes.

5. **Create** a second **Table** to record the information about the storage of inventory categories. Add the following records to the new table. Recall that Access will assign unique ID numbers; yours may vary.

ID	Field1	Field2	Field3
3	Candy	Room 107	North Zone 1
4	Stuffed Animals	Room 107	South Zone 2
5	Flowers and Plants	Gift Shop Coolers	Cooler 1
6	Balloons	Room 107	East Zone 3

(Project 12E–Gift Shop continues on the next page)

Content-Based Assessments

(Project 12E–Gift Shop continued)

6. **Rename** *Field1* as **Category Rename** *Field2* as **Storage Location** and **Rename** *Field3* as **Location Detail** Switch to **Design** view, name the table **12E Categories Firstname Lastname** Set the **Category** field as the **Primary Key**—each category of inventory items is unique. **Delete** the **ID** field.

7. Switch to **Datasheet** view, saving the changes. Select all of the fields (columns), and then apply **Best Fit**. View the table in **Print Preview**. If you are submitting printed pages, **Print** the table, and then **Close Print Preview**. To submit electronically, follow the directions provided by your instructor. **Close** the **12E Categories** table, saving the changes to the layout.

8. **Create**, using the **Query Wizard**, a **Simple Query** based on your **12E Inventory** table. Include only the **Item** and **Quantity in Stock** fields in the query result. The query will answer the question *How many of each item do we currently have in stock?* Accept the default name. If you are submitting printed pages, **Print** the query, and then **Close** the query. To submit electronically, follow the directions provided by your instructor.

9. **Create** a **Report** based on your **12E Inventory** table. **Delete** the **ID** field and the **Storage Location** field. Display the report in **Print Preview**, set the margins to **Wide** and the orientation to **Landscape**. If you are submitting printed pages, **Print** the report. To submit electronically, follow the directions provided by your instructor. **Close** the report, **Save** the design changes, and then accept the default name. **Close** any open objects, and then **Close** the **Navigation Pane**. **Close** the **Database**, and then **Exit Access**.

 You have completed Project 12E ————————————————————

Content-Based Assessments

Project 12F — Recruiting Events

In this project, you will apply skills you practiced from the Objectives in Projects 12A and 12B.

Objectives: 2. *Add Records to a Table;* **6.** *Print a Table;* **7.** *Create and Use a Query;* **10.** *Close and Save a Database;* **11.** *Create a Database by Using a Template;* **12.** *Organize Database Objects in the Navigation Pane;* **13.** *Create a New Table in a Database Created with a Template;* **14.** *View a Report and Print a Table in a Database Created with a Template.*

In the following Mastering Access project, you will assist Serge Juco, Vice President of Human Resources, in creating a database to track recruiting events that are scheduled to attract new employees to careers at the medical center. Your printed results will look similar to those shown in Figure 12.60.

For Project 12F, you will need the following file:

New Access database using the Events template

You will save your database as
12F_Recruiting_Events_Firstname_Lastname

Figure 12.60

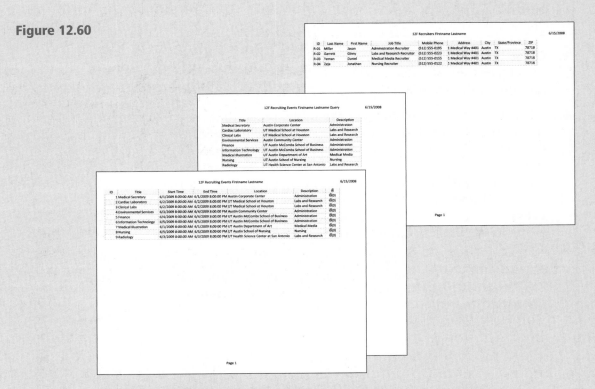

(Project 12F–Recruiting Events continues on the next page)

(Project 12F–Recruiting Events continued)

1. **Start** Access and then from **Local Templates**, create a new database based on the **Events** template. In your **Access Chapter 12** folder, name the new database **12F_Recruiting_Events_ Firstname_Lastname** In the lower right corner, click the Create button. If necessary, to the right of the Security Warning, click Options, click Enable this content, and then click OK.

2. In the **Multiple Items** form, enter the following records to build the Event List table; or, if you prefer, use the New Event single record form, which is available on the Link bar:

ID	Title	Start Time	End Time	Description	Location
1	Medical Secretary	6/1/09 8a	6/1/09 8p	Administration	Austin Corporate Center
2	Cardiac Laboratory	6/2/09 8a	6/2/09 8p	Labs and Research	UT Medical School at Houston
3	Clinical Labs	6/2/09 8a	6/2/09 8p	Labs and Research	UT Medical School at Houston
4	Environmental Services	6/3/09 8a	6/4/09 8p	Administration	Austin Community Center
5	Finance	6/4/09 8a	6/4/09 8p	Administration	UT Austin McCombs School of Business
6	Information Technology	6/5/09 8a	6/5/09 8p	Administration	UT Austin McCombs School of Business
7	Medical Illustration	6/1/09 8a	6/1/09 8p	Medical Media	UT Austin Department of Art
8	Nursing	6/5/09 8a	6/5/09 8p	Nursing	UT Austin School of Nursing
9	Radiology	6/3/09 8a	6/3/09 8p	Labs and Research	UT Health Science Center at San Antonio

3. **Close** the form, and then display the **Navigation Pane**. Using the **Navigation arrow**, organize the objects by **Tables and Related Views**. Point to the **Events** table, right-click, click **Rename**, and then type **12F Recruiting Events Firstname Lastname** and press Enter to rename the table.

4. **Open** the **12F Recruiting Events** table; recall that the table was built by typing records into the Multiple Items form. Leave the Attachments field because Serge may decide to attach job description brochures for each event. The AutoNumber ID serves as the primary key—the unique identifier for each record. **Close** the **Navigation Pane**. Select all of the columns and apply **Best Fit**. Display the table in **Print Preview**, set the margins to **Normal** and the orientation to **Landscape**. If you are submitting paper results, **Print** and then **Close Print Preview.** Or, follow your instructor's directions for electronic submission. **Close** the table, saving the changes to the layout.

5. **Create** a new table using the **Contacts Table Template**. **Delete** the **Company** field. **Delete** the following fields: **E-mail Address, Business Phone, Home Phone, Fax Number, Country/Region, Web Page, Notes**, and **Attachments**. Click in the first **ID** field. From the

(Project 12F–Recruiting Events continues on the next page)

Content-Based Assessments

(Project 12F–Recruiting Events continued)

Datasheet tab, change the **Data Type** of the **ID** field to **Text**, and then enter the following records:

ID	Last Name	First Name	Job Title	Mobile Phone	Address	City	State/Province	ZIP/Postal Code
R-01	Miller	Jason	Administration Recruiter	(512) 555-0195	1 Medical Way #401	Austin	TX	78718
R-02	Garrett	Ginny	Labs and Research Recruiter	(512) 555-0223	1 Medical Way #401	Austin	TX	78718
R-03	Yeman	Daniel	Medical Media Recruiter	(512) 555-0155	1 Medical Way #401	Austin	TX	78718
R-04	Zeja	Jonathan	Nursing Recruiter	(512) 555-0122	1 Medical Way #401	Austin	TX	78718

6. **Close** the table, **Save** the changes, and then name the table **12F Recruiters Firstname Lastname**

7. **Create**, using the **Query Wizard**, a **Simple Query** based on your **12F Recruiting Events** table. Add the appropriate fields to the query to answer the question *What are the title, location, and description of all the recruiting events?* Accept the default name for the query. **Print** and then **Close** the query.

8. From the **Navigation Pane**, open your **12F Recruiters** table. Change the name of the **ZIP/Postal Code** field to **ZIP** Select all the columns in the table and apply **Best Fit**. Display the table in **Print Preview**, set the margins to **Normal** and the orientation to **Landscape**. **Print** the table, and then **Close Print Preview**. Or, submit electronically.

9. **Close** the table, saving the layout changes. From the **Navigation Pane**, open the **All Events** report. Then, open the **Events By Week** report. Recall that one advantage of starting a database from a database template is that many objects, such as attractively arranged reports, are provided.

10. **Close** the reports and any other open objects. **Close** the **Navigation Pane**. From the **Office** menu, first **Close** the **Database**, and then **Exit Access**.

End **You have completed Project 12F**

Access
chaptertwelve

Mastering Access

Project 12G — Facility Expansion

In this project, you will apply all the skills you practiced from the Objectives in Projects 12A and 12B.

Objectives: 1. *Start Access and Create a New Blank Database;* **2.** *Add Records to a Table;* **3.** *Rename Table Fields in Datasheet View;* **4.** *Modify the Design of a Table;* **5.** *Add a Second Table to a Database;* **6.** *Print a Table;* **7.** *Create and Use a Query;* **8.** *Create and Use a Form;* **9.** *Create and Print a Report;* **10.** *Close and Save a Database;* **11.** *Create a Database by Using a Template;* **12.** *Organize Database Objects in the Navigation Pane;* **13.** *Create a New Table in a Database Created with a Template;* **14.** *View a Report and Print a Table in a Database Created with a Template.*

In the following Mastering Access project, you will assist Jerry Lopez, the Budget Director, in creating a database to store information about the facility expansion at Texas Lakes Medical Center and in creating a separate database to store information about public events related to the expansion. Your printed results will look similar to the ones shown in Figure 12.61.

For Project 12G, you will need the following files:

New blank Access database
New Access database using the Events template

You will save your databases as
12G_Facility_Expansion_Firstname_Lastname
12G_Public_Events_Firstname_Lastname

Figure 12.61

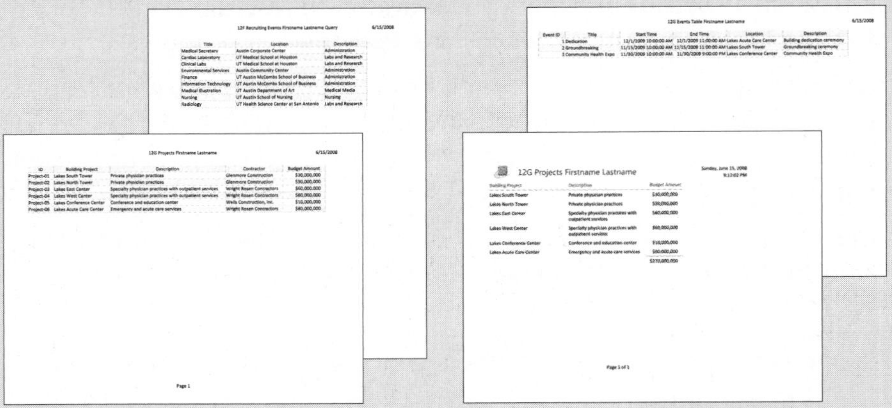

(Project 12G–Facility Expansion continues on the next page)

Content-Based Assessments

Mastering Access

(Project 12G–Facility Expansion continued)

1. **Start** Access, create a new **Blank Database**, and **Save** it in your **Access Chapter 12** folder as 12G_Facility_Expansion_Firstname_Lastname

2. **Close** the **Navigation Pane**. For the **ID** field, change the **Data Type** to **Text**. Enter the following records:

ID	Field1	Field2	Field3	Field4
Project-01	Lakes South Tower	Private physician practices	Glenmore Construction	30,000,000
Project-02	Lakes North Tower	Private physician practices	Glenmore Construction	30,000,000
Project-03	Lakes East Center	Specialty physician practices with outpatient services	Wright Rosen Contractors	60,000,000
Project-04	Lakes West Center	Specialty physician practices with outpatient services	Wright Rosen Contractors	60,000,000
Project-05	Lakes Conference Center	Conference and education center	Wells Construction, Inc.	10,000,000
Project-06	Lakes Acute Care Center	Emergency and acute care services	Wright Rosen Contractors	80,000,000

3. **Rename** the fields as follows:

Field1	Building Project
Field2	Description
Field3	Contractor
Field4	Budget Amount

4. For the **Budget Amount** field, change the **Data Type** to **Currency**. Apply **Best Fit** to all of the columns in the table. **Save** the table as **12G Projects Firstname Lastname** and then in **Print Preview**, set the margins to **Wide** and the orientation to **Landscape**. If you are submitting printed pages, click **Print**; and then **Close Print Preview**. Or, submit electronically as directed by your instructor. **Close** your **12G Projects** table.

5. **Create** a second **Table** to record the information about the contractors for the facility expansion. Add the following records to the new table. Recall that Access will assign unique ID numbers; your numbers may vary.

ID	Field1	Field2	Field3
3	Glenmore Construction	Bob Ballard	(512) 555-0900
4	Wright Rosen Contractors	Lisa Li	(512) 555-0707
5	Wells Construction, Inc.	Frank Levin	(512) 555-0444

(Project 12G–Facility Expansion continues on the next page)

Access

chaptertwelve

Mastering Access

(Project 12G–Facility Expansion continued)

6. **Rename** the fields as follows:

Field1	Contractor
Field2	Project Manager
Field3	Phone Number

7. Switch to **Design** view, name the table **12G Contractors Firstname Lastname** Set the **Contractor** field as the **Primary Key**—each contractor name is unique. **Delete** the **ID** field. Switch to **Datasheet** view and **Save** the changes. Apply **Best Fit** to all of the columns.

8. If you are submitting printed pages, **Print** the table; or submit electronically as directed by your instructor. **Close** the **12G Contractors** table and **Save** the changes to the layout—the column widths.

9. **Create**, using the **Query Wizard**, a **Simple Query** based on your **12G Projects** table. Include only the appropriate fields to answer the question *For each Building Project, what is the Budget Amount?* Accept the default name, display the query in **Print Preview**, **Print**, and then **Close Print Preview**. Or, submit electronically as directed by your instructor. **Close** the query.

10. In the **Navigation Pane**, select your **12G Projects** table. **Create** a **Form**, and then **Close** the **Navigation Pane**. View the created form, and then **Close** the form. **Save** and accept the default name.

11. **Open** the **12G Projects** table from the **Navigation Pane**. With the table open, **Create** a **Report**. Delete the **ID** field and the **Contractor** field. Display the report in **Print Preview**, set the margins to **Wide** and the orientation to **Landscape**. If you are submitting printed pages, **Print** the report, and then **Close Print Preview**. To submit electronically, follow the directions provided by your instructor. **Close** the report, **Save** the changes, and accept the default name. **Close** any open objects and close the **Navigation Pane**. From the **Office** menu, click **Close Database**.

12. From the **Local Templates**, create a new database using the **Events template**. **Save** the database in your **Access Chapter 12** folder and name it **12G_Public_Events_Firstname_Lastname** If necessary, enable the content.

13. To build the **Events** table, enter the following records using either the displayed Multiple Items Event List form or the single-record form, which is available by clicking New Event in the Link bar:

Title	Start Time	End Time	Description	Location
Dedication	12/1/09 10a	12/1/09 11a	Building dedication ceremony	Lakes Acute Care Center
Groundbreaking	11/15/09 10a	11/15/09 11a	Groundbreaking ceremony	Lakes South Tower
Community Health Expo	11/30/09 10a	11/30/09 9p	Community Health Expo	Lakes Conference Center

(Project 12G–Facility Expansion continues on the next page)

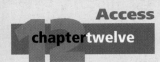

(Project 12G–Facility Expansion continued)

14. **Close** the **Event List** form. **Open** the **Navigation Pane**, and then using the **Navigation arrow**, arrange the **Navigation Pane** by **Tables and Related Views**. From the **Navigation Pane**, point to the **Events** table and right-click. From the shortcut menu, click **Rename**, type **12G Events Table Firstname Lastname** and then press Enter. Then open the table. Recall that the table was created by entering records in the form. Change the field name **ID** to **Event ID** Delete the **Attachments** field. Select all of the columns in the table, apply **Best Fit**, and then display the table in **Print Preview**. Set the margins to **Normal** and the orientation to **Landscape**. **Print**, and then **Close Print Preview**. Or, submit electronically as directed by your instructor. **Close** the table and **Save** the changes to the layout.

15. If necessary, close the Navigation Pane and close any open objects. **Close** the **Database** and **Exit Access**.

End **You have completed Project 12G** ———————————————

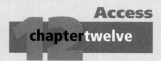

Mastering Access

Project 12H — GO! Fix It

In this project, you will apply the skills you practiced from the Objectives in Projects 12A and 12B.

> **For Project 12H, you will need the following file:**
>
> a12H_fixit_Cardiac_Patients

You will save your database as
12H_Cardiac_Patients_Firstname_Lastname

In this project, you will edit a draft of an Access database that will be used by the Cardiac Unit nursing staff at the Texas Lakes Medical Center. From the student files that accompany this textbook, locate and make a copy of the database **a12H_Cardiac_Patients** in your **Access Chapter 12** folder. Name the copy **12H_Cardiac_Patients_Firstname_Lastname**

This database contains errors that you must find and correct. Examine the database, and then correct the errors that you find. Types of errors could include:

- Spelling, grammar, punctuation, and usage errors such as text case.

- Missing or incorrect data in tables, queries, forms, and reports such as file names, field names, types, descriptions, properties, records, and criteria.

- Table design errors such as primary key.

- Query design errors such as field, table, and show.

- Page setup errors such as margins, orientation, layout, or alignment.

Things you should know to complete this project:

- The primary key in the table should be *Patient ID*.

- Field names in the table should be properly spelled.

- Martin Harris is 68 years old.

- Both Age and Monitor Level should have a Data Type of *Text*.

- The following record is missing: Elizabeth Norton, Patient ID: 2008-0911-056, Room Number: 3006A, Age: 82, Monitor Level: 3, Attending Physician: Obester M, Secondary Physician: Ovitz J, and 2nd Physician Specialty: Gerontology.

Add your first and last names to the name of the table. Print the table in Landscape orientation or submit your database electronically directed.

 End **You have completed Project 12H** —————

Outcomes-Based Assessments

Rubric

The following outcomes-based assessments are *open-ended assessments*. That is, there is no specific correct result; your result will depend on your approach to the information provided. Make *Professional Quality* your goal. Use the following scoring rubric to guide you in *how* to approach the problem and then to evaluate *how well* your approach solves the problem.

The criteria—Software Mastery, Content, Format and Layout, and Process—represent the knowledge and skills you have gained that you can apply to solving the problem. The *levels of performance*—Professional Quality, Approaching Professional Quality, or Needs Quality Improvements—help you and your instructor evaluate your result.

	Your completed project is of Professional Quality if you:	Your completed project is Approaching Professional Quality if you:	Your completed project Needs Quality Improvements if you:
1-Software Mastery	Choose and apply the most appropriate skills, tools, and features and identify efficient methods to solve the problem.	Choose and apply some appropriate skills, tools, and features, but not in the most efficient manner.	Choose inappropriate skills, tools, or features, or are inefficient in solving the problem.
2-Content	Construct a solution that is clear and well organized, contains content that is accurate, appropriate to the audience and purpose, and is complete. Provide a solution that contains no errors of spelling, grammar, or style.	Construct a solution in which some components are unclear, poorly organized, inconsistent, or incomplete. Misjudge the needs of the audience. Have some errors in spelling, grammar, or style, but the errors do not detract from comprehension.	Construct a solution that is unclear, incomplete, or poorly organized; contains some inaccurate or inappropriate content; and contains many errors of spelling, grammar, or style. Do not solve the problem.
3-Format and Layout	Format and arrange all elements to communicate information and ideas, clarify function, illustrate relationships, and indicate relative importance.	Apply appropriate format and layout features to some elements, but not others. Overuse features, causing minor distraction.	Apply format and layout that does not communicate information or ideas clearly. Do not use format and layout features to clarify function, illustrate relationships, or indicate relative importance. Use available features excessively, causing distraction.
4-Process	Use an organized approach that integrates planning, development, self-assessment, revision, and reflection.	Demonstrate an organized approach in some areas, but not others; or, use an insufficient process of organization throughout.	Do not use an organized approach to solve the problem.

Outcomes-Based Assessments

Problem Solving

Project 12I — Public Seminars

In this project, you will construct a solution by applying any combination of the skills you practiced from the Objectives in Projects 12A and 12B.

For Project 12I, you will need the following files:

New Access database using the Events template
a12I_Public_Seminars (Word document)

You will save your database as
12I_Public_Seminars_Firstname_Lastname

Texas Lakes Medical Center has developed a series of public health seminars. The information about the seminars is located in your student files, in the Word document **a12I_Public_Seminars**.

Using the data in the Word document and a new database created from the Events database template, enter the data into the Multiple Items form. Each seminar will begin at 7 p.m. and end at 9 p.m. After entering the records, in the Navigation Pane, point to the name of the table that was created as a result of entering the records into the Multiple Items form, click Rename, and then name the table **12I Seminars Firstname Lastname** Open the table, apply Best Fit to the table's columns, and then display and modify the Print Preview so that that all the columns fully display on a single sheet. Print the table or submit electronically. Save the database with the name **12I_Public_Seminars_Firstname_Lastname** and then close the database.

End **You have completed Project 12I** ———————————

Outcomes-Based Assessments

Problem Solving

Project 12J — Media Contacts

In this project, you will construct a solution by applying any combination of the skills you practiced from the Objectives in Projects 12A and 12B.

For Project 12J, you will need the following files:

New blank Access database
a12J_Media_Contacts (Word document)

You will save your database as
12J_Media_Contacts_Firstname_Lastname

The Public Relations Department at Texas Lakes Medical Center maintains a list of media contacts who receive e-mail notification when press releases regarding the Medical Center are issued. The information about the media contacts is located in your student files, in the Word document **a12J_Media_Contacts**.

Create a new blank database, and then close the default Table1. Create a new table using the Contacts table template, and then use the data in the Word document to enter the records. Delete the unneeded fields from the table. As necessary, rename fields to match those in the Word document. Change the data type of the ID field to Text, and use the IDs provided. Close the table, and save it as **12J Media Contacts Firstname Lastname** Create a report and delete the Media ID column. In Page Setup or Print Preview, use narrow margins and landscape orientation to arrange the report. Print or submit the report electronically. Close the database.

End **You have completed Project 12J** ———————

Outcomes-Based Assessments

Problem Solving

Project 12K — Billing Rates

In this project, you will construct a solution by applying any combination of the skills you practiced from the Objectives in Projects 12A and 12B.

> **For Project 12K, you will need the following files:**
>
> New blank Access database
> a12K_Billing_Rates (Word document)
>
> **You will save your database as**
> **12K_Billing_Rates_Firstname_Lastname**

Physicians at Texas Lakes Medical Center have varying billing rates. The information about the physician names and billing rates is located in your student files, in the Word document **a12K_Billing_Rates**.

Create a new blank database. Create a table with the Physician IDs and billing rates. For the rates, change data type to Currency. Apply Best Fit to the columns, save and name the table **12K Rates Firstname Lastname** and then print the table, or submit electronically as directed. From the table, create a query indicating only the Physician ID and the rate, and print or submit the query electronically. Create a second table using the Contacts table template, enter the names and phone numbers of the physicians, and delete unneeded columns. Apply Best Fit to the columns, save and name the table **12K Physicians Firstname Lastname** Print the table or submit electronically. Save the database with the name **12K_Billing_Rates_Firstname_Lastname** and then close the database.

End You have completed Project 12K ——————

More on your Student CD

The instructions for the following additional end-of-chapter projects are on your student CD in the folder 03_additional_end_of_chapter_projects.

Content-Based Assessments

Project L Mastering Access	Apply the skills you practiced in Project A.
Project M Mastering Access	Apply the skills you practiced in Project B.
Project N Business Running Case	Apply the skills you practiced in Projects A and B while helping an entrepreneur with the daily tasks of running a business.
	In each chapter, this project focuses on applying the skills you have practiced in Projects A and B to a business. The project related to this business runs throughout the textbook. You will see how the Office applications relate to the day-to-day operation of a small business called Nelson Architectural Planning.

Outcomes-Based Assessments

Project O Problem Solving	Construct a solution by applying any combination of the skills you practiced from Projects A and B.
Project P Problem Solving	Construct a solution by applying any combination of the skills you practiced from Projects A and B.
Project Q You and GO!	Construct a solution that applies to your own life by applying any combination of the skills you practiced from Projects A and B.
Project R GO! with Help	Practice using Microsoft Office's Help Feature.
Project S Group Business Running Case	Work as part of a group to apply the skills you have gained thus far to help the Bell Orchid Hotel Group achieve its business goals.

Multimedia

The following multimedia accompany this textbook:

Companion Web site *www.prenhall.com/go*	An interactive Web site designed to reinforce and test your understanding of the skills in this chapter.
AV-EDDs	In the folder in the front of this book you will find videos that demonstrate the objectives of the A and B projects in this chapter. These may help you understand how to complete the projects in this book.
Video Podcasts	In the folder in the front of this book are videos that can be played on your iPod, MP3 player, or computer. These videos demonstrate how to complete the more challenging objectives in this textbook.

chapter thirteen

Sort and Query a Database

OBJECTIVES

At the end of this chapter, you will be able to:

1. Open an Existing Database
2. Create Table Relationships
3. Sort Records in a Table
4. Create a Query in Design View
5. Create a New Query from an Existing Query
6. Sort Query Results
7. Specify Criteria in a Query

8. Create a New Table by Importing an Excel Spreadsheet
9. Specify Numeric Criteria in a Query
10. Use Compound Criteria
11. Create a Query Based on More Than One Table
12. Use Wildcards in a Query
13. Use Calculated Fields in a Query
14. Group Data and Calculate Statistics in a Query

OUTCOMES

Mastering these objectives will enable you to:

PROJECT 13A
Sort and Query a Database

PROJECT 13B
Create a Database Table from an Excel Spreadsheet and Create Complex Queries

Florida Port Community College

Florida Port Community College is located in St. Petersburg, Florida, a coastal port city located near the Florida High-Tech Corridor. With 60 percent of Florida's high-tech companies and a third of the state's manufacturing companies located in the St. Petersburg and Tampa Bay areas, the college partners with businesses to play a vital role in providing a skilled workforce. The curriculum covers many areas, including medical technology, computer science, electronics, aviation and aerospace, and simulation and modeling. The college also serves the community through cultural, athletic, and diversity programs, and provides adult basic education.

© Dennis MacDonald PhotoEdit Inc.

Sort and Query a Database

To convert data into meaningful information, the data must be manipulated in a way that you can answer questions. One question might be: *What are the names and addresses of students who are enrolled in the Business Information Technology program and who have a grade point average of 3.0 or higher?* With such information, you could send information about scholarships or internships to selected students.

Questions can be answered by sorting the data in a table or by creating a query. Queries enable you to isolate specific data in database tables by limiting the fields that display and by setting conditions that limit the records to those that match specified conditions. You can also use a query to create a new field that is calculated using one or more existing fields. In this chapter, you will sort Access database tables, and create and modify queries.

Project 13A **Instructors and Courses**

Florida Port Community College uses sorting techniques and queries to locate information in their databases. In Activities 13.01 through 13.13, you will assist Lydia Barwari, the Dean of Business Information Technology, in locating information about instructors and courses in the Business Information Technology Department. Your completed queries and report will look similar to those in Figure 13.1.

For Project 13A, you will need the following file:

a13A_Instructors_and_Courses

You will save your database as
13A_Instructors_and_Courses_Firstname_Lastname

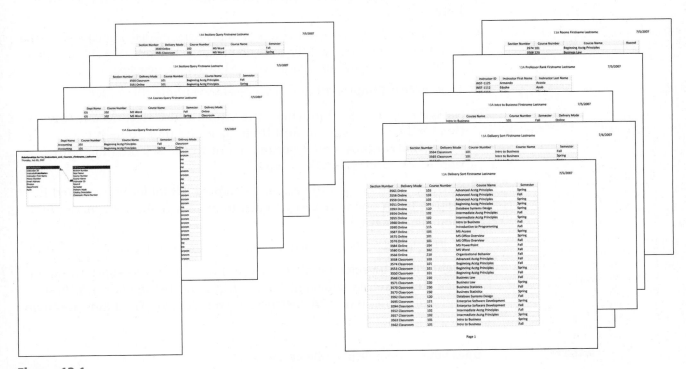

Figure 13.1
Project 13A—Instructors and Courses

Objective 1
Open an Existing Database

There are times when you might want to work with a database and still keep an original copy of the database. Like the other Microsoft Office 2007 applications, you can open a database file and save it with a new name or you can copy the original database to a new storage location and rename it before opening it.

Activity 13.01 Renaming and Opening an Existing Database

1 On the taskbar, click the **Start** button 💮, and then on the **Start menu**, click **Computer**. Navigate to the location where you are saving your projects for this chapter.

2 On the left side of your screen, click **Organize**, and then click **New Folder**.

> A new folder is created, the words *New Folder* display highlighted in the folder's name box, and the insertion point is blinking. Recall that within Windows, highlighted text is replaced by typing new text.

3 Type **Access Chapter 13** and press Enter to rename the folder.

4 Navigate to the location where the student files that accompany this textbook are stored, and then click one time to select **a13A_Instructors_and_Courses**. Point to the selected file name, right-click, and then click **Copy**.

5 Navigate to and open the **Access Chapter 13** folder you created in Step 3. In an open area, right-click to display a shortcut menu, and then click **Paste**.

> The database file is copied to your folder and is selected.

6 Right-click the selected file name, and then from the shortcut menu, click **Rename**. As shown in Figure 13.2, and using your own first and last name, type **13A_Instructors_and_Courses_Firstname_Lastname**

Alert!

Does your system display file extensions?

If the Windows operating system on the computer at which you are working is set to display file extensions, be sure to type the new file name in front of the extension, for example: 13A_Instructors_and_Courses_Firstname_Lastname.accdb

---

Figure 13.2

Access Chapter 13 indicated in the title bar

Your name here

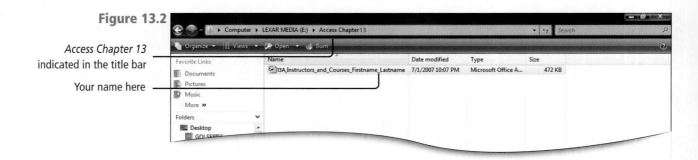

7 Press `Enter` to save the file with the new name. On the title bar, click **Close** ![X] to close the **Computer** window.

Does a Confirm File Rename message display?

If the file you have copied has a Read-only property applied, a message displays to alert you when you attempt to rename the file. In the message box, click Yes to rename the file. Then, right-click the file name, and from the shortcut menu, click Properties. In the Properties dialog box, on the General tab under Attributes, click to clear the Read-only check mark. Click OK to accept the change, and then close the dialog box.

Activity 13.02 Opening an Existing Database and Resolving Security Alerts

The *Message Bar* is the area directly below the Ribbon that displays information such as security alerts when there is potentially unsafe, active content in an Office 2007 document that you open. Settings that determine which alerts display on your Message Bar are set in the Access *Trust Center*, which is an area of the Access program where you can view the security and privacy settings for your Access installation.

You may or may not be able to change the settings in the Trust Center, depending upon decisions made within your organization's computing environment. To display the Trust Center, from the Office menu, in the lower right corner click Access Options, and then click Trust Center.

1 **Start** Access. From the **Office** menu 🔘, click **Open**. In the **Open** dialog box, navigate to your **Access Chapter 13** folder.

2 Click your **13A_Instructors_and_Courses_Firstname_Lastname** database file one time to select it, and then, in the lower right corner, click the **Open** button. Alternatively, double-click the name of the database to open it.

> The database window opens, and the database name displays in the title bar.

3 On the **Message Bar**, check to see if a **Security Warning**, similar to the one shown in Figure 13.3, displays.

Figure 13.3

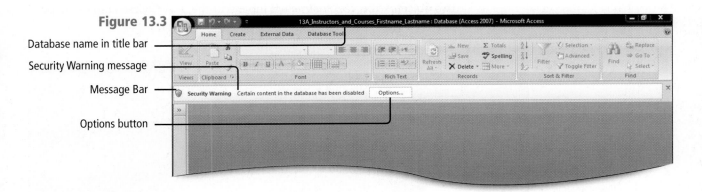

Database name in title bar

Security Warning message

Message Bar

Options button

4 If a security warning displays, on the **Message Bar**, click the **Options** button. In the **Microsoft Office Security Options** dialog box, click the **Enable this content** option button, and then click **OK** or press Enter.

When working with the student files that accompany this textbook, repeat these actions each time you see this security warning. Databases provided with this textbook are safe to use on your computer.

Objective 2
Create Table Relationships

Access databases are *relational databases* because the tables in the database can relate—actually *connect*—to other tables through *common fields*. Common fields are fields that contain the same data in more than one table.

After you have set up a table for each subject in your database, you must provide a way to bring that data back together again when you need to create meaningful information. To do this, place common fields in related tables, and then define table *relationships*. A relationship is an association that you establish between two tables based on common fields. After the relationship is established, you can create a query, a form, or a report that displays information from more than one table.

Activity 13.03 Creating Table Relationships and Enforcing Referential Integrity

In this activity, you will connect a field in one table with a field in another table to create a relationship. The common field between the two tables is Instructor ID; that is, Instructor ID is the field that appears in both tables.

1 Open » the **Navigation Pane**, and at the top, click the **Navigation Pane arrow** . Look at the menu to verify that the objects are organized by **Tables and Related Views**. Click outside of the menu to close it, and then compare your screen with Figure 13.4.

Two objects—the *13A Instructors* table and the *13A Courses* table—display in the Navigation Pane.

Figure 13.4

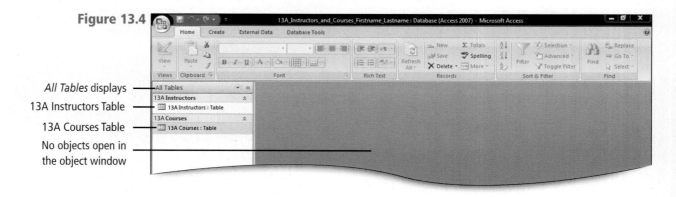

All Tables displays — All Tables

13A Instructors Table — 13A Instructors / 13A Instructors : Table

13A Courses Table — 13A Courses / 13A Courses : Table

No objects open in the object window

2 Double-click the **13A Instructors** table and take a moment to examine its contents. Then, open the **13A Courses** table and examine its contents.

> In the 13A Instructors table, *Instructor ID* is the primary key field, which ensures that each instructor will appear in the table only one time.

> In the 13A Courses table, *Section Number* is the primary key. Each course's record includes the Instructor ID for the instructor who teaches the course.

> Because *one* instructor can teach *many* different courses, *one* Instructor ID number can appear *many* times in the 13A Courses table. The relationship between each instructor and the courses is referred to as a **one-to-many relationship**. This is the most common type of relationship in Access.

3 **Close** ☒ both tables and leave the **Navigation Pane** open. On the Ribbon, click the **Database Tools tab**. In the **Show/Hide group**, click the **Relationships** button to open the Relationships window and to display the **Relationship Tools tab** on the Ribbon.

4 On the **Design tab**, in the **Relationships group**, click the **Show Table** button. In the **Show Table** dialog box, in the list of table objects, click **13A Courses**, and then at the bottom of the dialog box, click **Add**.

Another Way

To Show Tables

If the Show Table dialog box does not display, on the Design tab, in the Query Setup group, click the Show Table button. Alternatively, right-click in the table area, and from the shortcut menu, click Show Table.

5 In the **Show Table** dialog box, double-click **13A Instructors** to add the table to the **Relationships** window, and then click **Close** to close the **Show Table** dialog box.

> Use either technique to add a table to the Relationships window. A **field list**—a list of the field names in a table—for each of the two table objects displays and each table's primary key is identified. Although this database currently has only two tables, larger databases can have many tables.

6 In the **13A Courses** field list, position your mouse pointer over the lower right corner of the field list to display the ⬂ pointer, and then drag down and to the right to increase the height and width of the field list until the names of each field are completely displayed.

> Expanding the field list enables you to see all of the available fields, and removes the vertical scroll bar.

7 Use the ⬂ pointer to resize the **13A Instructors** field list so that all of the field names are visible. One at a time, point to the title bar of each field list and by dragging, position the expanded field lists approximately as shown in Figure 13.5.

> Recall that *one* instructor can teach *many* courses. Arranging the tables in this manner on your screen displays the *one table* on the left side and the *many table* on the right side.

Recall that the primary key in each table is the field that uniquely identifies the record in each table. In the Instructors table, each instructor is uniquely identified by the Instructor ID. In the Courses table, each course section offered is uniquely identified by the Section Number.

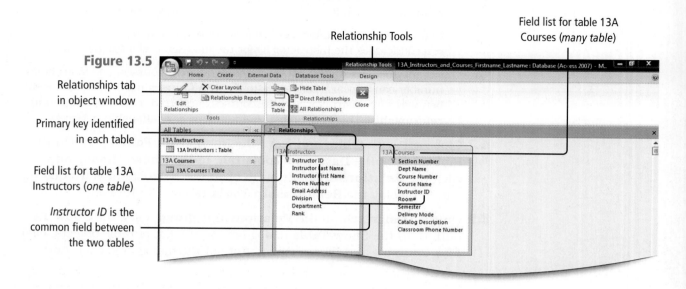

Figure 13.5

Relationships tab in object window

Primary key identified in each table

Field list for table 13A Instructors (*one table*)

Relationship Tools

Field list for table 13A Courses (*many table*)

Instructor ID is the common field between the two tables

Note — Highlighted Field Does Not Matter

As the two field lists in the Relationships window are rearranged, the highlighted field indicates the active field list, which is the list you moved last, and the active field. This is of no consequence for completing the activity.

8. In the **13A Instructors** field list, point to **Instructor ID**, hold down the left mouse button, and then drag to the right to the **13A Courses** field list until your mouse pointer is on top of **Instructor ID** as shown in Figure 13.6. Then release the mouse button.

As you drag, a small graphic displays to indicate that you are dragging a field from one field list to another. The Edit Relationships dialog box displays.

A table relationship works by matching data in two fields—the common field. In these two tables the common field has the same name—Instructor ID. Common fields are not required to have the same names; however, they must have the same data type and field size.

Figure 13.6

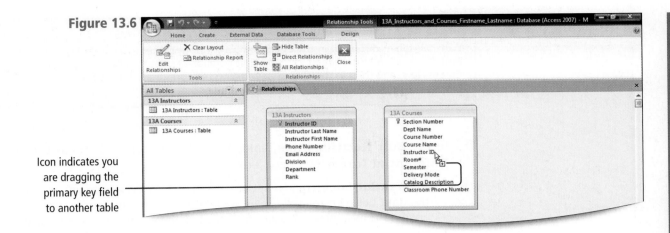

Icon indicates you are dragging the primary key field to another table

9 Point to the title bar of the **Edit Relationships** dialog box, and then drag the dialog box below the two field lists as shown in Figure 13.7.

> Both tables include the Instructor ID field—that is the common field between the two tables. By dragging, you created the one-to-many relationship. In the Instructors table, Instructor ID is the primary key. In the Courses table, Instructor ID is referred to as the **_foreign key_** field. The foreign key is the field that is included in the related table so the field can be joined with the primary key in another table.
>
> The field on the *one* side of the relationship is typically the primary key. Recall that *one* instructor can teach *many* courses. Thus, *one* instructor record in the Instructors table can be related to *many* course records in the Courses table.

Figure 13.7

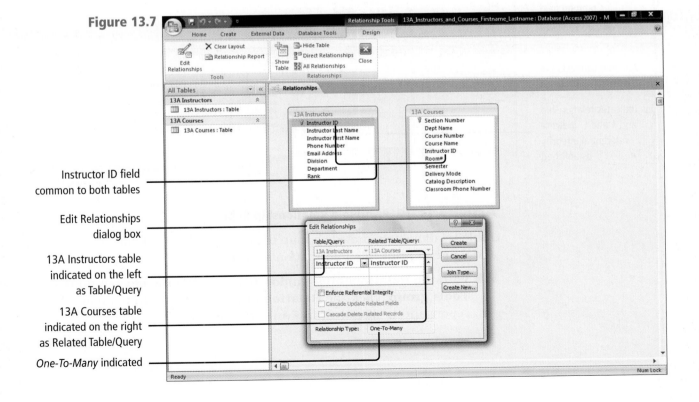

Instructor ID field common to both tables

Edit Relationships dialog box

13A Instructors table indicated on the left as Table/Query

13A Courses table indicated on the right as Related Table/Query

One-To-Many indicated

Another Way

To Create a Table Relationship

With the tables displayed in the Relationships window, rather than dragging one field into another field list, instead, click the Edit Relationships button on the Ribbon, click Create New, and then in the Create New dialog box, designate the Left and Right tables and fields that will create the relationship.

10 In the **Edit Relationships** dialog box, click to select the **Enforce Referential Integrity** check box.

Referential integrity is a set of rules that Access uses to ensure that the data between related tables is valid. Enforcing referential integrity ensures that a course cannot be added to the 13A Courses table with the name of an instructor that is *not* included in the 13A Instructors table, ensuring that you do not have courses listed in the 13A Courses table without a corresponding instructor in the 13A Instructors table. Similarly, you cannot delete an Instructor from the 13A Instructors table if there is a course listed for that instructor in the 13A Courses table.

11 In the upper right corner of the **Edit Relationships** dialog box, click the **Create** button, and then compare your screen with Figure 13.8.

A *join line*—the line joining two tables—displays between the two tables. On the join line, *1* indicates the *one* side of the relationship, and the infinity symbol (∞) indicates the *many* side of the relationship. These symbols display when referential integrity is enforced.

Figure 13.8

Common field in both tables

Join line connects the two common fields

Line indicates relationship and 1 and ∞ indicate referential integrity established

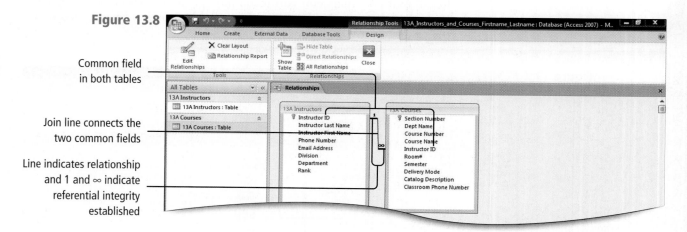

Activity 13.04 Printing a Relationship Report

Table relationships provide a map of how your database tables are related, and you can print this information as a report.

1 With the **Relationships** window open, on the **Design tab**, in the **Tools group**, click the **Relationship Report** button to create the report and to display it in Print Preview.

2 On the **Print Preview tab**, in the **Page Layout group**, click the **Margins** button, and then click **Normal**. Compare your screen with Figure 13.9.

Figure 13.9

Print Preview tab

Database name

Current date (yours will differ)

Field lists with join line

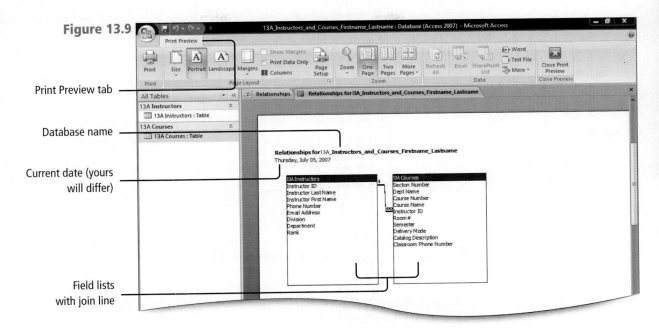

3 If you are submitting your results from this project on paper, on the **Print Preview tab**, in the **Print group**, click the **Print** button. In the **Print** dialog box, click **OK**. In the **Close Preview group**, click the **Close Print Preview** button. To submit electronically, follow the directions provided by your instructor.

4 On the **Quick Access Toolbar**, click the **Save** button 🖫 to save the report. In the **Save As** dialog box, click **OK** to accept the default name.

The report name displays in the Navigation Pane under *Unrelated Objects*. Because the report is just a map of the relationships and not a report containing actual records, it is not associated with either of the tables.

5 In the object window, **Close** ✕ the report, and then **Close** ✕ the **Relationships** window.

6 In the **Navigation Pane**, open the **13A Instructors** table. On the left side of the table, in the first record, point to the **plus sign** (+), and then click one time. If the Field List pane displays on the right side of the screen, click the Close button to remove it from the screen. Compare your screen with Figure 13.10.

Plus signs to the left of a record in a table indicate that *related* records exist in another table. In the first record for *Julie Adeeb*, you can see that related records exist in the Courses table—she is teaching six courses. The plus sign displays because you created a relationship between the two tables using the Instructor ID field—the common field.

Figure 13.10

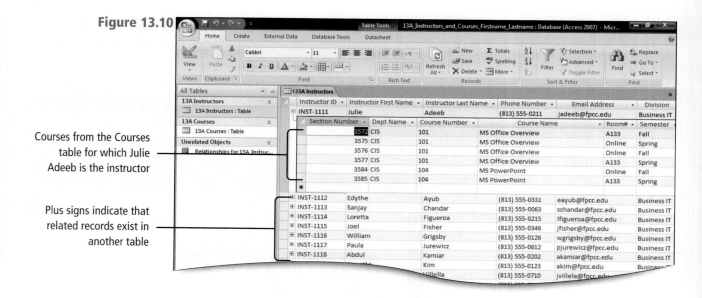

Courses from the Courses table for which Julie Adeeb is the instructor

Plus signs indicate that related records exist in another table

7 **Close** [×] the **13A Instructors** table.

More Knowledge — Other Types of Relationships: One-to-One and Many-to-Many

There are other relationships you can create using the same process in the Relationships window. The type of relationship is determined by the placement of the primary key field. A one-to-one relationship exists between two tables when a record in one table is related to a single record in a second table. In this case, both tables use the same field as the primary key. This is most often used when data is placed in a separate table because access to the information is restricted.

You can also create a many-to-many relationship between tables, where many records in one table can be related to many records in another table. For example, many students can enroll in many courses. To create a many-to-many relationship, you must create a third table that contains the primary key fields from the tables. These primary key fields are then joined to their related fields in the other tables. In effect, you create multiple one-to-one relationships.

Objective 3
Sort Records in a Table

Sorting is the process of arranging data in a specific order based on the value in a field. For example, you could sort the names in your address book alphabetically by each person's last name, or you could sort your CD collection by the date of purchase.

Initially, records in an Access table display in the order in which they are entered into the table. After a primary key is established, the records are displayed in order based on the primary key field.

Activity 13.05 **Sorting Records in a Table in Ascending or Descending Order**

In the following activity, you will determine the courses in the Business Information Technology Division that will be offered each semester by sorting the data. You can sort data in either *ascending order* or *descending order*. Ascending order sorts text alphabetically (A to Z)

and sorts numbers from the lowest number to the highest number. Descending order sorts text in reverse alphabetical order (Z to A) and sorts numbers from the highest number to the lowest number.

1 From the **Navigation Pane**, open the **13A Courses** table, and then **Close** « the **Navigation Pane**. Notice that the records are sorted in ascending order by Section Number, which is the primary key field.

2 In the field names row, click the **Dept Name arrow**, click **Sort A to Z**, and then compare your screen with Figure 13.11.

To sort records in a table, click the arrow to the right of the field name in the column on which you want to sort, and then choose the sort order. After a field is sorted, a small arrow after the field name indicates its sort order. The small arrow after the field name points upward indicating an ascending sort, and in the Ribbon, the Ascending button is selected.

The records display in alphabetical order by Dept Name. Because like names are now grouped together, you can quickly scroll the length of the table to see how many courses are offered by each department.

Figure 13.11

Ascending button selected
Small arrow indicates order in which field is sorted

Records sorted alphabetically by Dept Name

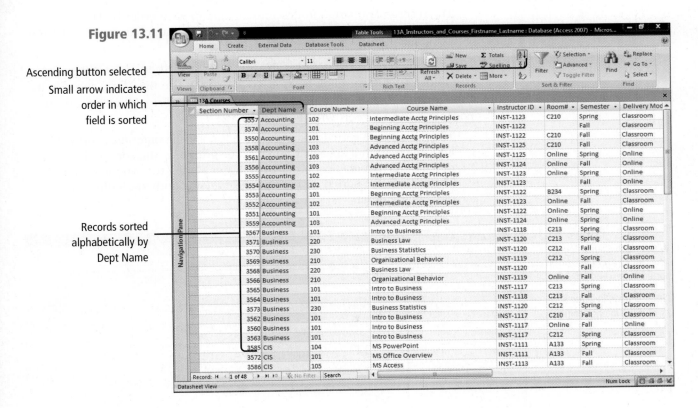

3 In the **Sort & Filter group**, click the **Clear All Sorts** button 🔽 to clear all of the sorts and to return the records to the default sort order, which is by the primary key field—*Section Number.*

4 If necessary, scroll to the right, click the **Semester arrow**, and then click **Sort Z to A**.

The records in the table are sorted by semester in reverse alphabetical order; thus *Spring* courses are listed before *Fall* courses. The small arrow in the Field name points down indicating a descending sort, and in the Ribbon, the Descending button is selected.

Activity 13.06 Sorting Records in a Table on Multiple Fields

To sort a table on two or more fields, first identify the fields that will act as the *outermost sort field* and the *innermost sort field*. The outermost sort field is the first level of sorting, and the innermost sort field is the second level of sorting. For example, you might want to sort first by the last name field, which would be the outermost sort field, and then by the first name field, which would be the innermost sort field. After you identify your outermost and innermost sort fields, sort the innermost field first, and then sort the outermost field.

Lydia Barwari, the Dean, would like to display the course names in alphabetical order by delivery mode, with online classes listed first. Access enables you to sort on two or more fields in a table.

1 On the **Home tab**, in the **Sort & Filter group**, click the **Clear All Sorts** button to clear any sorts from the previous activity. In the **Delivery Mode** field, click any record. In the **Sort & Filter group**, click the **Descending** button .

> The records are sorted in descending alphabetical order by Delivery Mode, with Online courses listed before Classroom courses. The Delivery Mode field is the innermost sort field.

2 Point anywhere in the **Course Name** field, and then right-click. From the shortcut menu, click **Sort A to Z**. Notice the first four records in the **Course Name** column, for *Advanced Acctg Principles*, and then compare your screen with Figure 13.12.

> The records are sorted first by Course Name—the *outermost* sort field— and then within a specific Course Name grouping, the sort continues in descending alphabetical order by Delivery Mode—the *innermost* sort field. The records are sorted on multiple fields using both ascending and descending order.

Figure 13.12

Within each *Course Name*, Online and Classroom sorted in descending order

Small arrows indicate sort order in each column

Course Name column sorted in ascending order

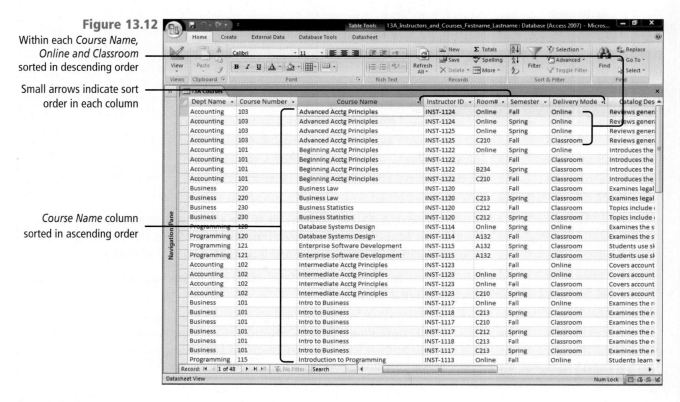

3 In the **Sort & Filter group**, click the **Clear All Sorts** button 🎲. In the object window, **Close** ✕ the table. In the message box, click **No**; you do not need to save any design changes.

Objective 4
Create a Query in Design View

Recall that a **select query** is a database object that retrieves (selects) specific data from one or more tables and then displays the specified data in Datasheet view. A query answers a question such as *Which instructors are teaching CIS courses in the Fall semester?* Unless a query has already been set up to ask this question, you must create a new query.

Database users rarely need to see all of the records in all of the tables. That is why a query is so useful; it creates a subset of records according to your specifications, and then displays only those records.

Activity 13.07 Creating a New Select Query in Design View

Previously, you created a query using the Query Wizard. To create complex queries, use Query Design view instead of the Query Wizard. Recall that the table or tables from which a query selects its data is referred to as the **data source**.

1 On the Ribbon, click the **Create tab**, and then in the **Other group**, click the **Query Design** button. Compare your screen with Figure 13.13.

A new query opens in Design view and the Show Table dialog box displays, which lists all of the tables in the database.

Figure 13.13

Query1 tab

Available tables

Show Table dialog box

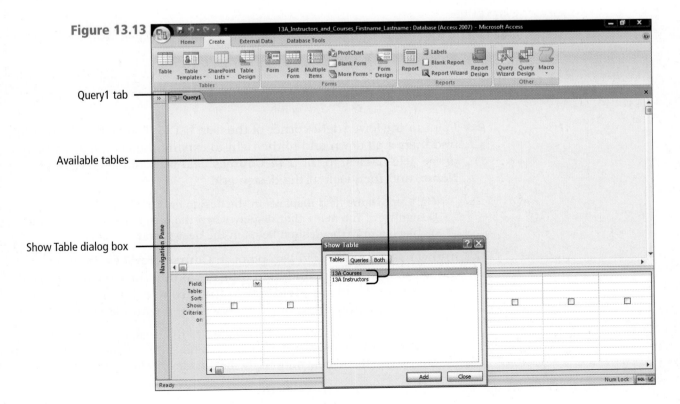

2 In the **Show Table** dialog box, click **13A Courses**, click the **Add** button, and then **Close** the **Show Table** dialog box. Alternatively, double-click a table name to add it to the Query window. Compare your screen with Figure 13.14.

> A field list for the 13A Courses table displays in the upper area of the Query window. The Section Number field is the primary key field.
>
> The Query window has two parts: the **table area** (upper area), which displays the field lists for tables that are used in the query, and the **design grid** (lower area), which displays the design of the query.

Figure 13.14

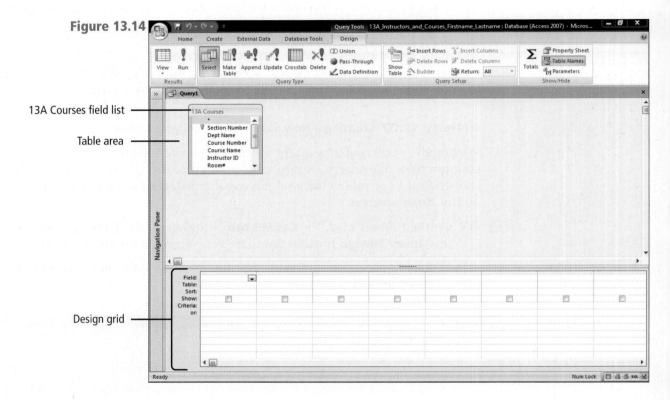

13A Courses field list

Table area

Design grid

3 Point to the lower right corner of the field list to display the ⬚ pointer, and then drag down and to the right to expand the field, displaying all of the field names. In the **13A Courses** field list, double-click **Dept Name**, and then look at the design grid.

> The Dept Name field displays in the design grid in the Field row. In Design view, the fields that display when the query is run can be limited by placing only the desired fields in the design grid.

4 In the **13A Courses** field list, point to **Course Number**, hold down the left mouse button, and then drag down into the design grid until you are pointing to the **Field** row in the second column. Release the mouse button, and then compare your screen with Figure 13.15.

> This is a second way to add field names to the design grid. As you drag the field, a small rectangular shape attaches to the mouse pointer. When you release the mouse button, the field name displays in the Field row.

Figure 13.15

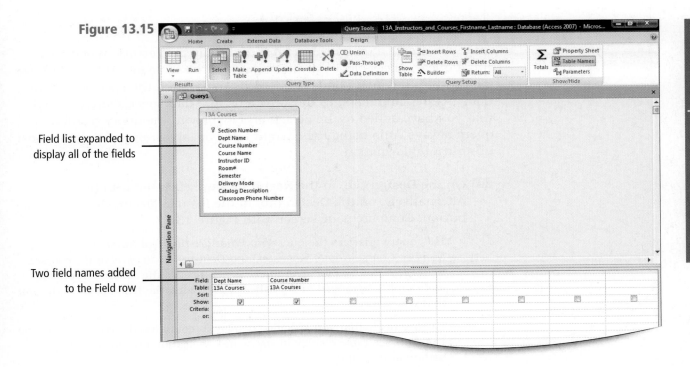

Field list expanded to
display all of the fields

Two field names added
to the Field row

5 In design grid, in the **Field** row, click in the third column, and then click the **arrow** that displays. From the list, click **Course Name** to add the field to the design grid, which is a third way to add a field to the design grid.

6 Using one of the techniques you practiced, add the **Semester** field to the fourth column in the design grid, and then add the **Delivery Mode** field to the fifth column in the design grid. Compare your screen with Figure 13.16.

Figure 13.16

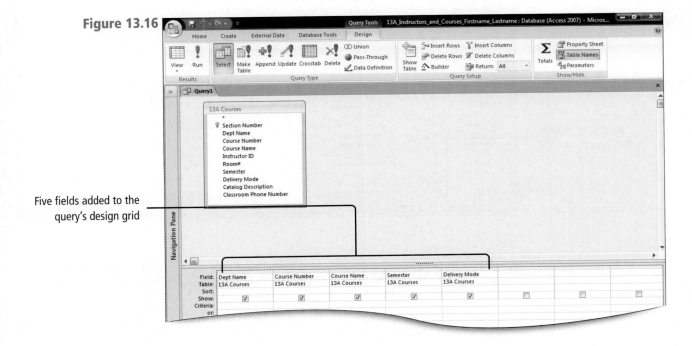

Five fields added to the
query's design grid

Activity 13.08 Running, Saving, Printing, and Closing a Query

After you create a query, you *run* it to display the results. When you run a query, Access looks at the records in the table (or tables) you have included in the query, finds the records that match the specified conditions (if any), and displays those records in a datasheet. Only the fields that you have added to the design grid display in the query results. The query always runs using the current table or tables, presenting the most up-to-date information.

1 On the **Design tab**, in the **Results group**, click the **Run** button. Alternatively, on the Design tab, in the Results group, click the View button. Compare your screen with Figure 13.17.

> This query answers the question, *What are the Dept Name, Course Number, Course Name, Semester, and Delivery Mode of all of the courses in the 13A Courses table?* A query is a subset of the records in one or more tables, arranged in Datasheet view, using the fields and conditions that you specify.
>
> The five fields that you specified display in columns, the records from the 13A Courses table display in rows, and navigation buttons display at the bottom of the window.

Figure 13.17

Five fields specified in query design display

Records in rows

Number of records in the query result (48)

Record navigation buttons

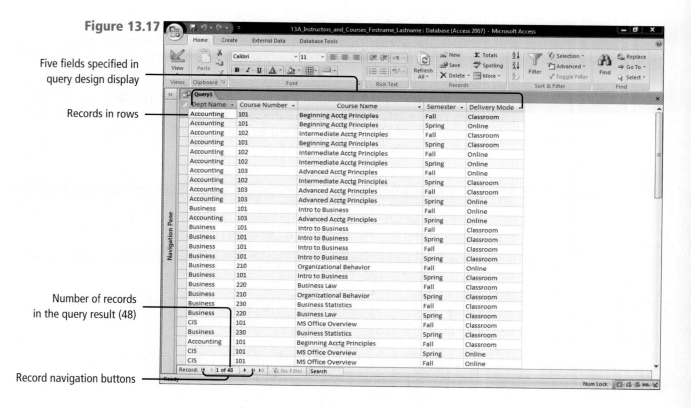

2 On the **Quick Access Toolbar**, click the **Save** button. In the **Save As** dialog box, type **13A Courses Query Firstname Lastname** and then click **OK**.

> Save your queries if you are likely to ask the same question again; doing so will save you the effort of creating the query again to answer the same question.

3 From the **Office** menu 🗐, point to the **Print** button, and then click **Print Preview**. In the **Page Layout group**, click the **Landscape** button. In the **Zoom group**, click the **Two Pages** button to see how the query will print on two pages. If you are printing your assignments on paper, click the **Print** button, and then in the **Print** dialog box, click **OK**. Click the **Close Print Preview** button. To submit electronically, follow the directions provided by your instructor.

Two pages will print. Queries are created to answer questions and to create information from the data in the tables. Queries are typically created as a basis for a report. Query results can also be printed.

4 **Close** ✕ the query. **Open** » the **Navigation Pane**, and then compare your screen with Figure 13.18.

The query is saved and closed. The new query name displays in the Navigation Pane under the table with which it is related—the *13A Courses* table. Only the design of the query is saved. The records still reside in the table object.

Each time you open a query, Access runs it again and displays the results based on the data stored in the related table(s). Thus, the results of a query always reflect the latest information in the related table(s).

Figure 13.18

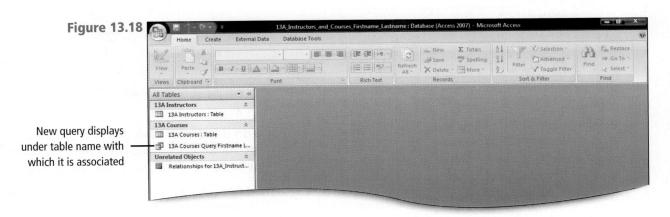

New query displays under table name with which it is associated

Objective 5
Create a New Query from an Existing Query

You can create a new query from scratch or you can open an existing query, save it with new name, and then modify the design to suit your needs. Using an existing query saves you time if your new query will use all or some of the same fields and conditions that are specified in the existing query.

Activity 13.09 Creating a New Query from an Existing Query

1 From the **Navigation Pane**, open your **13A Courses Query** by either double-clicking the name or by right-clicking and clicking Open.

The query runs and opens in Datasheet view, displaying the records from the 13A Courses table as specified in the query design.

2 From the **Office** menu 🔘, click **Save As**. In the **Save As** dialog box, type **13A Sections Query Firstname Lastname** and then click **OK**. On the **Home tab**, in the **Views group**, click the **View** button to switch to **Design** view. Compare your screen with Figure 13.19.

> A new query, based on a copy of the 13A Courses Query, is created and displays in the object window and on the Navigation Pane. The query displays in Design view.

Figure 13.19

New 13*A Sections* query in object window

New query 13*A Sections* displays in Navigation Pane

Selection bar in design grid

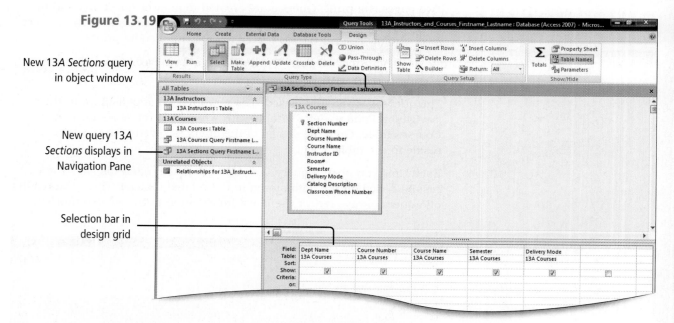

3 **Close** « the **Navigation Pane**. In the design grid, point to the thin gray selection bar above the **Dept Name** field name until the ⬇ pointer displays. Click to select the **Dept Name** column, and then press Delete.

> The Dept Name field is removed from the design grid and the remaining four fields move to the left. This action deletes the field from the query design only—it has no effect on the underlying 13A Courses table.

4 In the gray selection bar, select the **Delivery Mode** column. In the selected column, point to the **selection bar** to display the ⬉ pointer, and then drag to the left until a dark vertical line displays on the left side of the Course Number column. Release the mouse button to position the **Delivery Mode** field in the first column.

> To rearrange fields in the query design, first select the field to move, and then drag it to a new position in the design grid.

5 From the field list, add the **Section Number** field as the fifth column in the design grid. Then, select and move the **Section Number** field to the first column in the design grid. Click outside of the grid to cancel the selection, and then compare your screen with Figure 13.20.

Figure 13.20

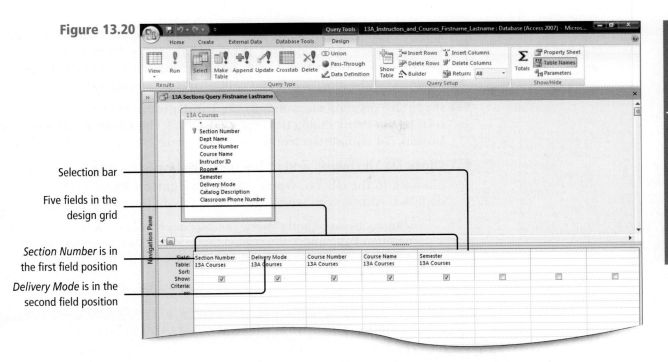

Selection bar

Five fields in the design grid

Section Number is in the first field position

Delivery Mode is in the second field position

6 On the **Design tab**, in the **Results group**, click the **Run** button. Notice the five fields that display, and then compare your screen with Figure 13.21.

This query answers the question, *What are the Section Number, Delivery Mode, Course Number, Course Name, and Semester of every course in the 13A Courses table?* The results of the query are a subset of the records contained in the 13A Courses table.

Figure 13.21

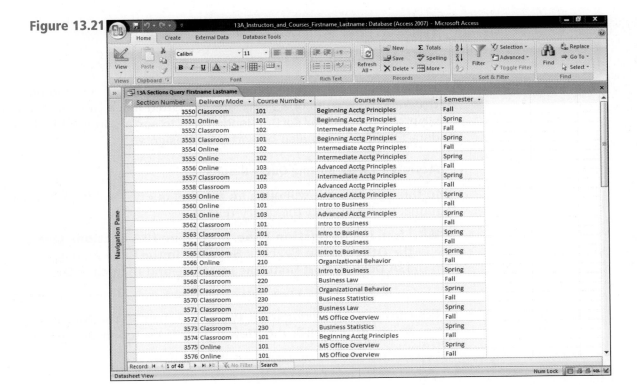

7 From the **Office** menu ⊕, point to the **Print** button, and then click **Print Preview**. On the **Print Preview tab**, in the **Page Layout group**, click **Landscape**. In the **Zoom group**, click the **Two Pages** button to view how your query will print on two pages.

8 If you are printing on paper, in the **Print group**, click the **Print** button. In the **Print** dialog box, click **OK**. Click the **Close Print Preview** button. To submit electronically, follow your instructor's directions.

9 **Close** ☒ the query, and in the message box, click **Yes** to save the changes to the design. **Open** ⯈ the **Navigation Pane**, and then compare your screen with Figure 13.22.

> The query is saved and closed. The new query name displays in the Navigation Pane under the related table. Recall that when you save a query, only the *design* of the query is saved; the records reside in the related table object(s).

Figure 13.22

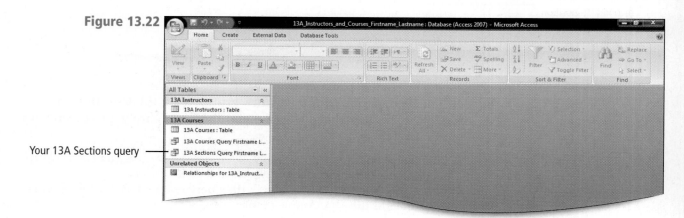

Your 13A Sections query

Objective 6
Sort Query Results

You can sort the results of a query in ascending or descending order. Because the results of a query are formatted like a table in Datasheet view, the process for sorting is identical to sorting in a table; however, data in a query can also be sorted in Design view.

Activity 13.10 Sorting Query Results

In this activity, you will open an existing query, save it with a new name, and then sort the query results.

1 From the **Navigation Pane**, open your **13A Sections Query**. From the **Office** menu ⊕, click **Save As**. In the **Save As** dialog box, type **13A Delivery Sort Firstname Lastname** and then click **OK**.

> Access creates a new query, based on a copy of your 13A Sections Query.

2 **Close** ☒ the **Navigation Pane**, and then on the **Home tab**, in the **Views group**, click the **View** button to switch to **Design** view.

3 In the design grid, in the **Sort** row, click in the **Delivery Mode** field to display the insertion point and an arrow. Click the **Sort arrow**, and then in the list, click **Descending**. Compare your screen with Figure 13.23.

Figure 13.23

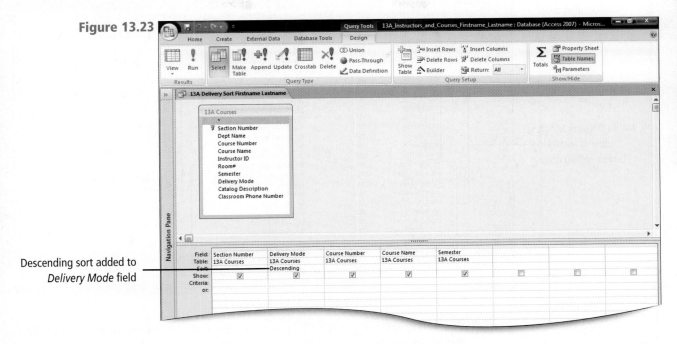

Descending sort added to *Delivery Mode* field

4 In the **Sort** row, under **Course Name**, click to display the **Sort arrow**, click the arrow, and then click **Ascending**.

5 On the **Design tab**, in the **Results group**, click the **Run** button, and then compare your screen with Figure 13.24.

Fields with a Sort designation are sorted from left to right. That is, the sorted field on the left becomes the outermost sort field, and the sorted field on the right becomes the innermost sort field. Thus, the records are sorted first in descending alphabetical order by the Delivery Mode field—the leftmost sort field. Then, within each Delivery Mode field, the Course Names are sorted in ascending alphabetical order.

Figure 13.24

Within Course Name, records sorted in ascending order

Within Delivery Mode, records sorted in descending order

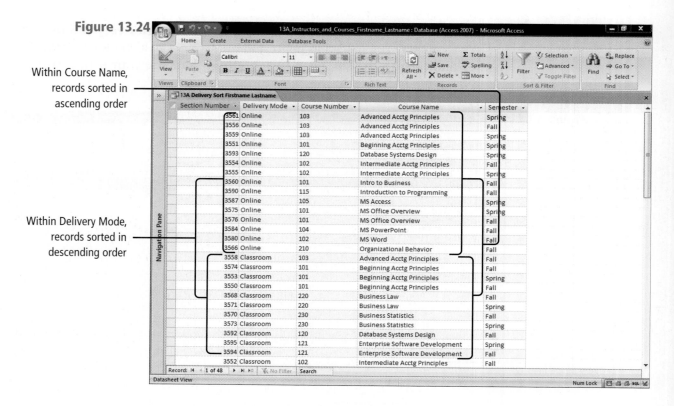

6 From the **Office** menu 🪟, point to the **Print** button, and then click **Print Preview**. On the **Print Preview tab**, in the **Page Layout group**, click **Landscape**.

7 In the **Zoom group**, click the **Two Pages** button to view the layout of the pages. If you are printing on paper, in the **Print group**, click the **Print** button. In the **Print** dialog box, click **OK**. Click the **Close Print Preview** button. To submit electronically, follow your instructor's directions.

8 **Close** ⊠ the query. In the message box, click **Yes** to save the changes to the query design.

More Knowledge — Sorting

If you add a sort order to the *design* of a query, it remains as a permanent part of the query design. If you use the sort buttons in the Datasheet view, it will override the sort order of the query design, and can be saved as part of the query. A sort order designated in Datasheet view will not display in the Sort row of the query design grid.

Objective 7
Specify Criteria in a Query

Queries can locate information in an Access database based on *criteria* that you specify as part of the query. Criteria are conditions that identify the specific records for which you are looking.

Criteria enable you to ask a more specific question; therefore, you will get a more specific result. For example, if you want to find out how many *Business Law* courses will be offered in the Fall and Spring semesters, limit the results to that specific course name, and then only the records that match the specified course name will display.

Activity 13.11 Specifying Text Criteria in a Query

In this activity, you will assist Lydia by creating a query to answer the question, *How many sections of Intro to Business will be offered in the Fall and Spring semesters?*

1 Be sure that all objects are closed and that the **Navigation Pane** is closed. Click the **Create tab**, and then in the **Other group**, click the **Query Design** button.

2 In the **Show Table** dialog box, **Add** the **13A Courses** table to the table area, and then **Close** the **Show Table** dialog box.

3 Expand the field list. Add the following fields to the design grid in the order given: **Course Name**, **Course Number**, **Semester**, and **Delivery Mode**.

4 In the **Criteria** row of the design grid, click in the **Course Name** field, type **Intro to Business** and then press Enter. Compare your screen with Figure 13.25.

Access places quotation marks around the criteria to indicate that this is a ***text string***—a sequence of characters. Use the Criteria row to specify the criteria that will limit the results of the query to your exact specifications.

Figure 13.25

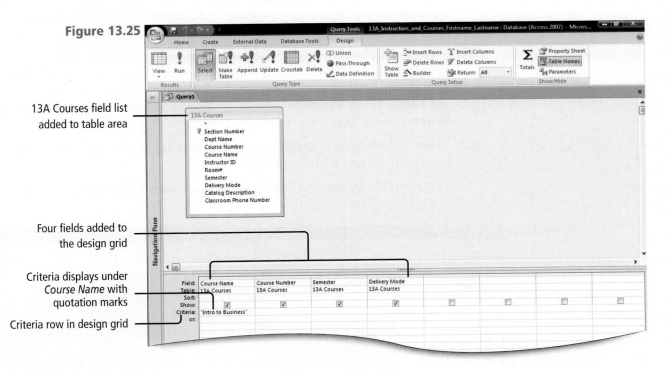

13A Courses field list added to table area

Four fields added to the design grid

Criteria displays under *Course Name* with quotation marks

Criteria row in design grid

5 **Run** the query, and then compare your screen with Figure 13.26.

Six records display that meet the specified criteria—records that have *Intro to Business* in the Course Name field.

Figure 13.26

Query result with records matching Course Name *Intro to Business* criteria

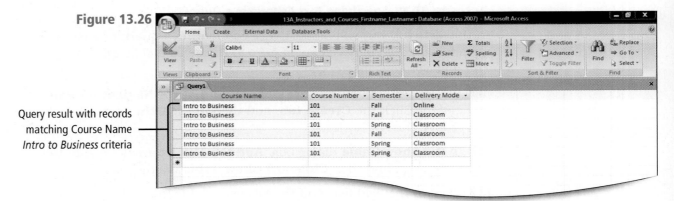

Do your query results differ?

If you mistype the criteria, enter it under the wrong field, or make some other error, the result will display no records. This indicates that there are no records in the table that match the criteria as you entered it. If this occurs, return to the Design view and reexamine the query design. Verify that the criteria is typed on the Criteria row, under the correct field, and that there are no typing errors. Then rerun the query.

6 On the **Quick Access Toolbar**, click the **Save** button. In the **Save As** dialog box, type **13A Intro to Business Firstname Lastname** and then click **OK**.

7 From the **Office** menu, point to **Print**, and then click **Print Preview**. If you are printing your assignments on paper, in the **Print group**, click the **Print** button. In the **Print** dialog box, click **OK**. Click the **Close Print Preview** button. To submit electronically, follow your instructor's directions.

8 **Close** the query, **Open** the **Navigation Pane**, and then compare your screen with Figure 13.27.

Recall that queries in the Navigation Pane display an icon of two overlapping tables.

Figure 13.27

Queries display a distinctive icon of two tables overlapping

Four queries created based on 13A Courses table

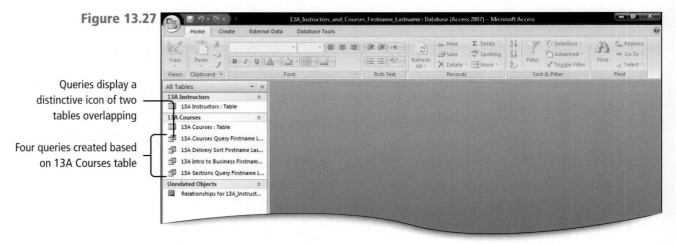

Activity 13.12 Specifying Criteria Using a Field Not Displayed in the Query Results

So far, all of the fields that you included in the query design have also been included in the query results. It is not required to have every field in the query display in the result. In this activity, you will assist Lydia by creating a query to answer the question, *Which instructors have a rank of Professor?*

1 **Close** « the **Navigation Pane**. Click the **Create tab**, and then in the **Other group**, click the **Query Design** button.

2 From the **Show Table** dialog box, **Add** the **13A Instructors** table to the table area, and then **Close** the dialog box. Expand the field list.

3 Add the following fields, in the order given, to the design grid: **Instructor ID**, **Instructor First Name**, **Instructor Last Name**, and **Rank**.

4 In the **Sort** row, click in the **Instructor Last Name** field, click the **arrow**, and then click **Ascending**.

5 In the **Criteria** row, click in the **Rank** field, type **Professor** and then press Enter. Compare your screen with Figure 13.28.

When you press Enter, the insertion point moves to the next criteria box and quotation marks are added around the text string that you entered.

Figure 13.28

Show check boxes
selected for every field

Show row

New criteria

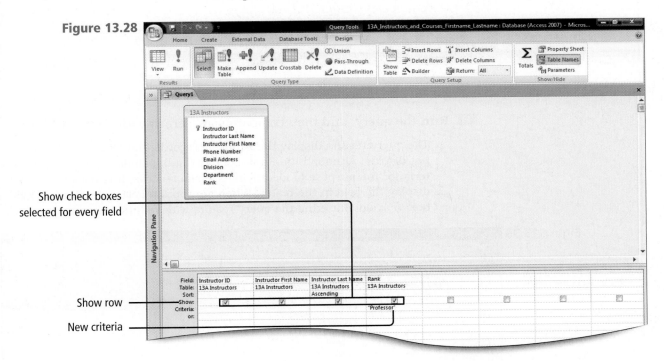

6 In the design grid, in the **Show** row, notice that the check box is selected for every field. **Run** the query to view the result of the query.

Six records meet the criteria. In the Rank column each record displays *Professor*.

7 On the **Home tab**, in the **Views group**, click the **View** button to switch to **Design** view. In the design grid, under **Rank**, in the **Show** row, click to clear the check box, and then compare your screen with Figure 13.29.

> Because it is repetitive and not particularly useful to have *Professor* display for each record in the query results, clear this check box so that the field does not display.

Figure 13.29

Show check box cleared for the Rank field

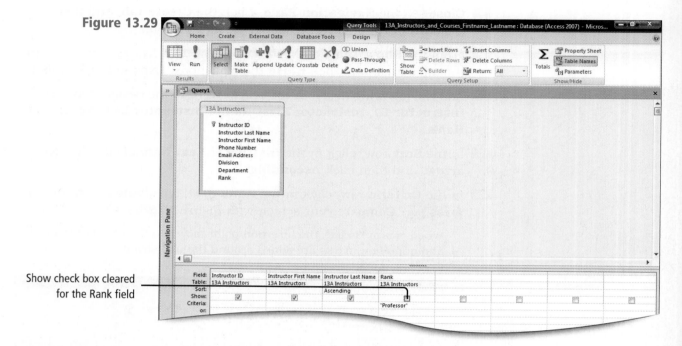

8 **Run** the query, and then compare your screen with Figure 13.30.

> The query results display the same six records, but the *Rank* field does not display. Although the Rank field was still included in the query criteria for the purpose of identifying specific records, it is not necessary to display the field in the result. When appropriate, clear the Show check box to avoid cluttering the query results with redundant data.

Figure 13.30

Rank field not displayed in the result

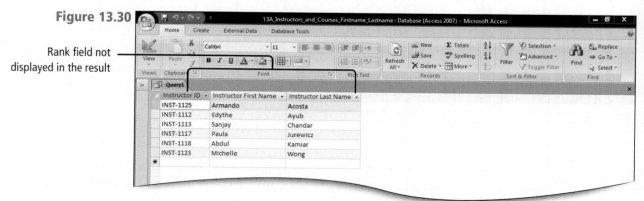

9 On the **Quick Access Toolbar**, click the **Save** button. In the **Save As** dialog box, type **13A Professor Rank Firstname Lastname** and then click **OK**.

10 From the **Office** menu ⊞, point to **Print**, and then click **Print Preview**. If you are printing your assignments on paper, in the **Print group**, click the **Print** button. In the **Print** dialog box, click **OK**. Click the **Close Print Preview** button. To submit electronically, follow your instructor's directions.

11 **Close** ✕ the query, **Open** ≫ the **Navigation Pane**, and then notice that the query is listed under the table with which it is related—the *13A Instructors* table.

Activity 13.13 Using Is Null Criteria to Find Empty Fields

Sometimes you must locate records where data is *missing*. You can locate such records by using ***is null***—empty—as the criteria in a field. Additionally, you can display only the records where a value *has* been entered in a field by using ***is not null*** as the criteria, which will exclude records where the specified field is empty.

In this activity, you will help Lydia design a query to find out *Which course sections have not yet had a classroom assigned?*

1 **Close** ≪ the **Navigation Pane**. Click the **Create tab**, and then in the **Other group**, click the **Query Design** button. **Add** the **13A Courses** table to the table area, and then **Close** the **Show Table** dialog box. Expand the field list.

2 Add the following fields to the design grid in the order given: **Section Number**, **Course Number**, **Course Name**, and **Room#**.

3 On the **Criteria** row, click in the **Room#** field, type **Is Null** and then press Enter. Alternatively, type *is null* and Access will change the criteria to display with capital letters. Compare your screen with Figure 13.31.

The criteria *Is Null* examines the field and looks for records that do *not* have any values entered in the Room# field, enabling you to determine which courses still need an assigned classroom.

Figure 13.31

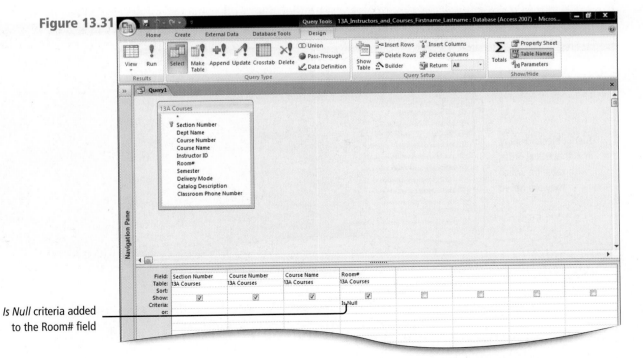

Is Null criteria added to the Room# field

4 On the **Sort** row, click in the **Course Name** field, click the **Sort arrow**, and then click **Ascending**. **Run** the query, and then compare your screen with Figure 13.32.

> Five course sections do not have a Room# assigned—the Room# field is empty. The course names are sorted in ascending (alphabetical) order.

Figure 13.32

Records sorted in ascending order by *Course Name* field

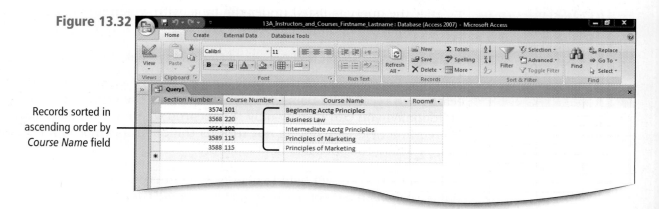

5 **Save** the query as **13A Rooms Firstname Lastname**

6 From the **Office** menu , point to **Print**, and then click **Print Preview**. If you are printing your assignments on paper, in the **Print group**, click the **Print** button. In the **Print** dialog box, click **OK**. Click the **Close Print Preview** button. To submit electronically, follow your instructor's directions.

7 **Close** the query. **Open** the **Navigation Pane**, and then compare your screen with Figure 13.33.

> Each query that you created displays under the table with which it is related. The objects display in alphabetical order.

Figure 13.33

Query objects display, in alphabetical order, with table on which they are based

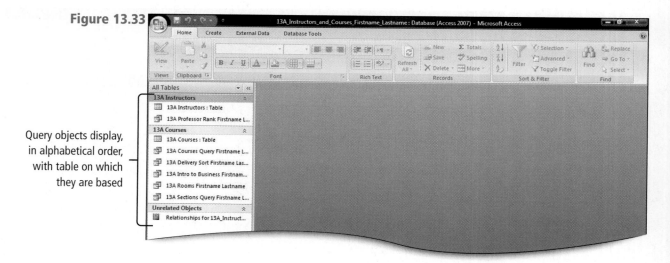

8 **Close** « the **Navigation Pane** and be sure that all objects are closed.

9 From the **Office** menu, click **Close Database**, and then at the right edge of the Access title bar, click the **Close** button  to close the Access program. Alternatively, from the Office menu, click Exit Access.

End **You have completed Project 13A**————————————

Project 13B Athletes and Scholarships

In Activities 13.14 through 13.25, you will assist Marcus Simmons, Athletic Director for Florida Port Community College, in developing and querying his Athletes and Scholarships database. In this database, Mr. Simmons tracks the scholarships awarded to student athletes. Your completed Relationship report and queries will look similar to those in Figure 13.34.

For Project 13B, you will need the following files:

a13B_Athletes_and_Scholarships
a13B_Athletes (Excel file)

You will save your database as
13B_Athletes_and_Scholarships_Firstname_Lastname

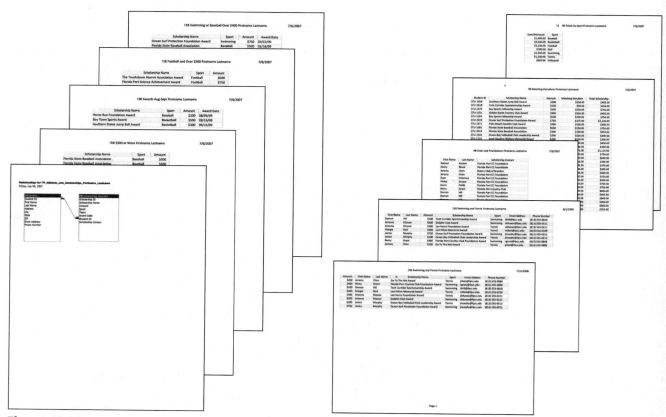

Figure 13.34

Objective 8
Create a New Table by Importing an Excel Spreadsheet

Many users of Microsoft Office track their data in an Excel spreadsheet. The sorting and filtering capabilities of Excel are useful for a simple database where all the information resides in one large Excel spreadsheet.

Excel is limited as a database management tool because it cannot support multiple tables, nor can it *relate* the information so that you can retrieve information from multiple spreadsheets using a query. However, data in an Excel spreadsheet can easily become an Access table by importing the spreadsheet because Excel's format of columns and rows is similar to that of an Access table.

Activity 13.14 Opening an Existing Database and Preparing to Import an Excel Spreadsheet

In this activity, you will open, rename, and save an existing database, and then examine an Excel spreadsheet that Mr. Simmons wants to bring into Access as a new table.

1 On the taskbar, click the **Start** button, and then click **Computer**. Navigate to the student files that accompany this textbook, and then click one time to select **a13B_Athletes_and_Scholarships**.

2 Point to the selected file name, right-click to display a shortcut menu, and then click **Copy**. Navigate to and open the **Access Chapter 13** folder you created in Project 13A. In an open area, right-click to display a shortcut menu, and then click **Paste**.

3 Right-click the selected file name, and then click **Rename**. Using your own first and last name type **13B_Athletes_and_Scholarships_Firstname_Lastname** and then press Enter to save the new file name. **Close** the **Computer** window.

4 **Start** Access. From the **Office** menu, click **Open**. In the **Open** dialog box, navigate to your **Access Chapter 13** folder, and then open the **13B_Athletes_and_Scholarships** database file.

5 On the **Message Bar**, click the **Options** button. In the **Microsoft Office Security Options** dialog box, click the **Enable this content** option button, and then click **OK**.

6 **Open** the **Navigation Pane**, and then open the **13B Scholarships Awarded** table. **Close** the **Navigation Pane**, and then take a moment to examine the data in the table. Compare your screen with Figure 13.35.

In this table, Mr. Simmons tracks the names and amounts of scholarships awarded to student athletes. Students are identified only by their Student ID numbers, and the primary key is the Scholarship ID field.

Figure 13.35

Student ID of student
receiving scholarship

Scholarship Name field

Amount field

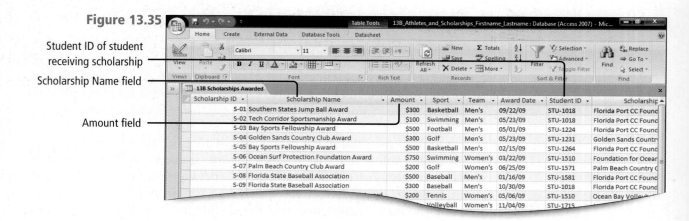

7 **Close** ✕ the table. Click **Start** ⊙, and then locate and open **Microsoft Office Excel 2007**. In Excel, from the **Office** menu ⊙, click **Open**. Navigate to the student files for this textbook, and then open **a13B_Athletes**. Compare your screen with Figure 13.36.

Mr. Simmons created an Excel spreadsheet to store the names, addresses, and other information of all of the student athletes.

Because *one* athlete can receive *many* scholarships, Mr. Simmons can see that using Access, rather than Excel, and having two *related* tables of information, will enable him to track and query this information more efficiently.

Figure 13.36

Excel spreadsheet
containing student
information

Student ID field

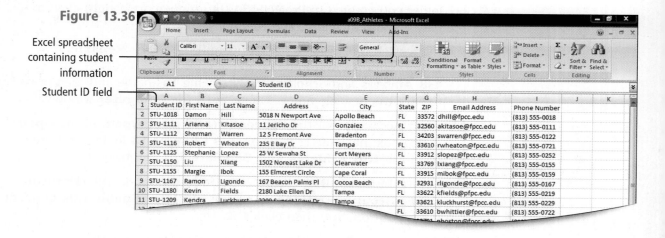

8 In the Excel spreadsheet, notice that in **row 1**, the column titles are similar to the field names in an Access table, and that each row contains the information for one student, representing a record. From the **Office** menu ⊙, in the lower right corner of the menu, click **Exit Excel**.

Activity 13.15 Creating a New Table by Importing an Excel Spreadsheet

In this activity, you will create a new Access table by importing the Excel spreadsheet containing the names and addresses of the student athletes, create a one-to-many relationship between the new table and the 13B Scholarships Awarded table, enforce referential integrity, and then print a Relationship report.

1 **Open** ➤ the **Navigation Pane**. On the Ribbon, click the **External Data tab**, and then in the **Import group**, click the **Excel button**. In the **Get External Data – Excel Spreadsheet** dialog box, to the right of the **File name** box, click **Browse**.

2 In the **File Open** dialog box, navigate to the location where the student files for this textbook are saved, and then click **a13B_Athletes**. In the lower right corner, click **Open**, and then compare your screen with Figure 13.37.

Figure 13.37

Get External Data – Excel Spreadsheet dialog box

Location of Excel file displays here (yours may vary)

Option button selected

Browse button

OK button

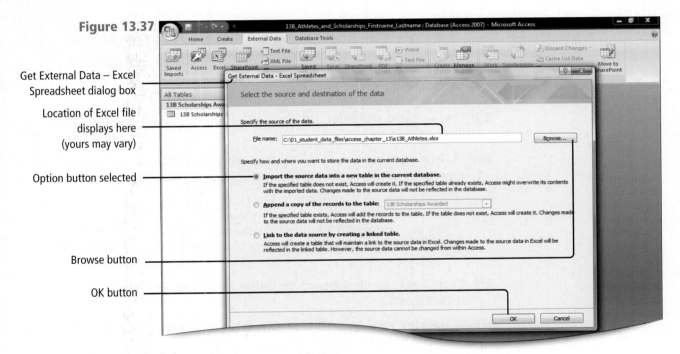

3 Be sure that the **Import the source data into a new table in the current database** option button is selected, and then click **OK**.

The Import Spreadsheet Wizard opens and displays the worksheet data.

4 In the upper left portion of the **Import Spreadsheet Wizard**, click to select the **First Row Contains Column Headings** check box.

The Excel data in the lower portion of the Wizard is framed, indicating that the first row of Excel column titles will become the Access table field names, and the remaining rows will become the individual records for the new Access table.

5 Click **Next**. Notice that the first column is selected, and in the upper portion of the Wizard, the **Field Name** and the **Data Type** display. Click anywhere in the **First Name** column, and then compare your screen with Figure 13.38.

Here you can review and change the field properties for each field (column).

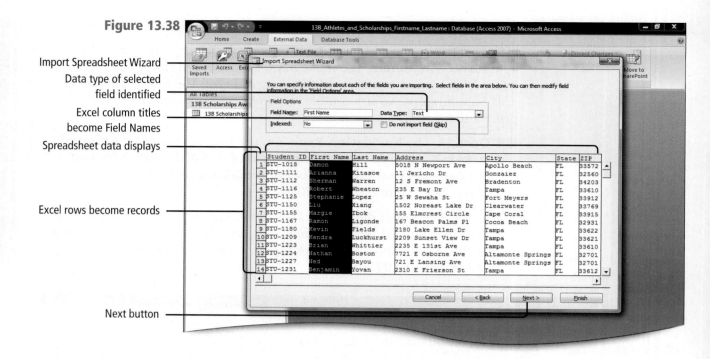

Figure 13.38

Import Spreadsheet Wizard

Data type of selected field identified

Excel column titles become Field Names

Spreadsheet data displays

Excel rows become records

Next button

6 Under **Field Options**, no changes should be made for any of the fields. Click **Next**.

7 In the upper portion of the Wizard, click the **Choose my own primary key** option button, and then be sure that **Student ID** displays.

In the new table, Student ID will be the primary key. No two students have the same Student ID. By default, Access selects the first field as the primary key. If another field should be defined as the primary key, click the arrow next to the option button and then select the desired field name.

8 Click **Next**. In the **Import to Table** box, type **13B Athletes** and then click **Finish**.

9 In the **Get External Data – Excel Spreadsheet Wizard**, click **Close**.

That is all the information the Wizard needs to import the Excel data. In the Navigation Pane, the new table displays.

10 On the Ribbon, click the **Database Tools tab**, and then in the **Show/Hide group**, click the **Relationships** button.

11 On the **Design tab**, in the **Relationships group**, click the **Show Table** button. In the **Show Table** dialog box, **Add** the **13B Athletes** table, and then **Add** the **13B Scholarships Awarded** table to the table area. **Close** the **Show Table** dialog box.

12 Expand the field lists, and then position the field lists so that the **13B Athletes** table is on the left side, allowing approximately 1 inch of space between the two field lists. Compare your screen with Figure 13.39.

Repositioning the field lists is not required, but doing so makes it easier for you to view the field lists and the join line when creating relationships.

Figure 13.39

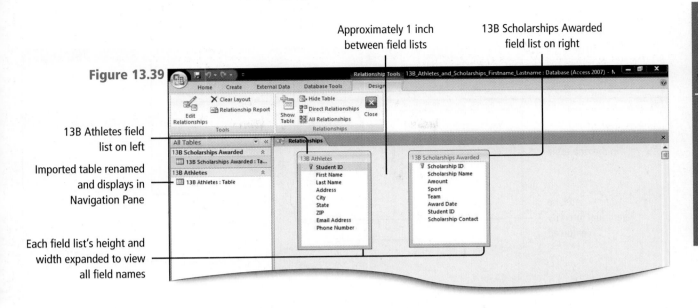

Approximately 1 inch between field lists

13B Scholarships Awarded field list on right

13B Athletes field list on left

Imported table renamed and displays in Navigation Pane

Each field list's height and width expanded to view all field names

13 In the **13B Athletes** field list, point to the **Student ID** field. Hold down the left mouse button, drag into the **13B Scholarships Awarded** field list, position the mouse pointer on top of the **Student ID** field, and then release the mouse button.

14 Point to the title bar of the **Edit Relationships** dialog box, and then drag it below the two field lists.

15 In the **Edit Relationships** dialog box, be sure that the **13B Athletes** table is displayed on the left side, that the **13B Scholarships Awarded** table is displayed on the right side, and that **Student ID** is displayed as the common field for both the *13B Athletes* and the *13B Scholarships Awarded* tables.

> The two tables are related in a one-to-many relationship—*one* athlete can be awarded *many* scholarships. The common field between the two tables is the Student ID field. In the 13B Athletes table, Student ID is the primary key. In the 13B Scholarships Awarded table, Student ID is the foreign key.

16 In the **Edit Relationships** dialog box, select the **Enforce Referential Integrity** check box. Click **Create**, and then compare your screen with Figure 13.40.

> The one-to-many relationship is established, and the *1* and ∞ indicate that referential integrity is enforced. Enforcing referential integrity ensures that a scholarship cannot be awarded to a student whose name is not in the 13B Athletes table. Similarly, you cannot delete a student athlete from the 13B Athletes table if there is a scholarship listed for that student in the 13B Scholarships Awarded table.

Figure 13.40

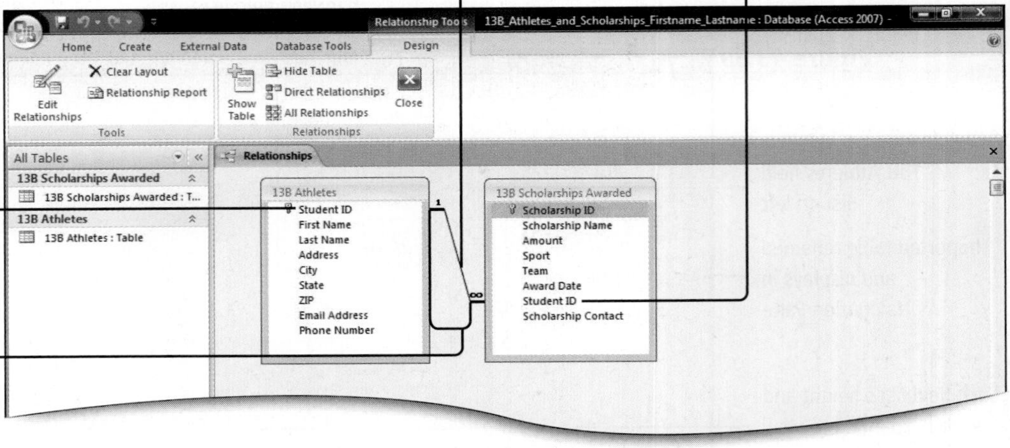

Join line indicates relationship established using *Student ID* as common field

Foreign key field in the *many* table

Primary key field in the *one* table

1 and ∞ indicate referential integrity enforced

17 On the **Design tab**, in the **Tools group**, click the **Relationship Report** button. On the **Print Preview tab**, in the **Page Layout group**, click the **Margins button**, and then click **Normal**. If you are printing your assignments on paper, click the **Print** button, and then click **OK**. Click the **Close Print Preview button**. To submit electronically, follow your instructor's directions.

18 On the **Quick Access Toolbar**, click the **Save** button 🖫 to save the report. With the text in the **Save As** dialog box highlighted, type **13B Relationships Firstname Lastname** and then click **OK**.

19 **Close** ✕ the report and the Relationships window.

20 From the **Navigation Pane**, open the **13B Athletes** table. On the left side of the table, in the first record, click the **plus sign**.

> In the first record—for *Damon Hill*—three related records exist in the 13B Scholarships Awarded table. The related records display because you created a relationship between the two tables using the Student ID field as the common field.

21 **Close** ✕ the **13B Athletes** table, and then **Close** « the **Navigation Pane**.

Objective 9
Specify Numeric Criteria in a Query

Criteria can be set for fields containing numeric data. When you design your table, set the appropriate data type for fields that will contain numbers, currency, or dates so that mathematical calculations can be performed.

Activity 13.16 Specifying Numeric Criteria in a Query

Mr. Simmons wants to know *Which scholarships are in the amount of $300, and for which sport?* In this activity, you will specify criteria in the query so that only the records of scholarships in the amount of $300 will display.

1 On the Ribbon, click the **Create tab**. In the **Other group**, click the **Query Design** button.

2 In the **Show Table** dialog box, **Add** the **13B Scholarships Awarded** table to the table area, and then **Close** the **Show Table** dialog box. Expand the field list.

3 Add the following fields to the design grid in the order given: **Scholarship Name**, **Sport**, and **Amount**.

4 Click in the **Sort** row under **Sport**, click the **Sort arrow**, and then click **Ascending**.

5 On the **Criteria** row, click in the **Amount** field, type **300** and then press Enter. Compare your screen with Figure 13.41.

> When entering currency values as criteria in the design grid, do not type the dollar sign, and include a decimal point only if you are looking for a specific amount that includes cents—for example, 300.50. Access does not insert quotation marks around the criteria because the field's data type contains numeric data.

Figure 13.41

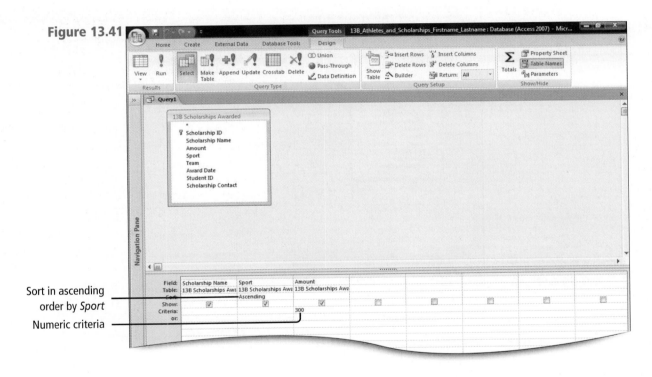

Sort in ascending order by *Sport*

Numeric criteria

6 On the **Design tab**, in the **Results group**, click the **Run** button to view the results. Alternatively, click the View button.

> Five awarded scholarships are in the exact amount of $300. In the navigation area, *1 of 5* displays to indicate the number of records that match the criteria.

7 On the **Home tab**, in the **Views group**, click the **View** button to switch to **Design** view.

Activity 13.17 Using Comparison Operators

Comparison operators are symbols that evaluate each field value to determine if it is the same (=), greater than (>), less than (<), or in between a range of values as specified by the criteria.

If no comparison operator is specified, equal (=) is assumed. For example, in the previous activity, you created a query to display only records where the *Amount* was 300. The comparison operator of = was assumed, and Access displayed only records that had entries equal to 300.

In this activity, you will specify criteria in the query to display records from the 13B Scholarships Awarded table that have scholarships that are *greater* than $300 and then to display scholarships that are *less* than $300.

1 Be sure your query is displayed in **Design view**. On the **Criteria** row, click in the **Amount** field, delete the existing criteria, type **>300** and then press Enter. Compare your screen with Figure 13.42.

Figure 13.42

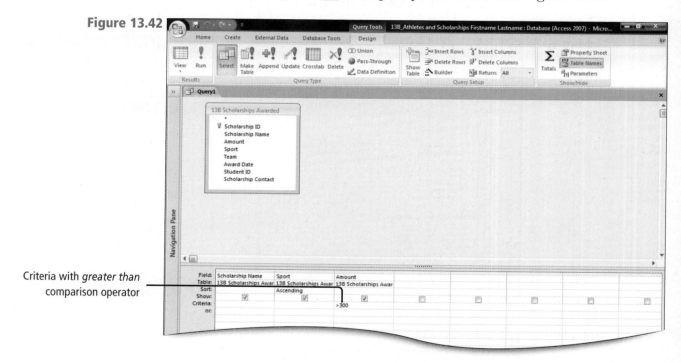

Criteria with *greater than* comparison operator

2 On the **Design tab**, in the **Results group**, click the **Run** button.

Fourteen records match the criteria for an Amount that is greater than $300. The results show the records for which the Amount is *greater than* $300, but do not display amounts that are *equal* to $300.

3 Click the **View** button to switch to **Design view**. On the **Criteria** row, under **Amount**, delete the existing criteria. Type **<300** and then press Enter. On the **Design tab**, in the **Results group**, click the **Run** button.

Eleven records display and each has an Amount less than $300. The results show the records for which the Amount is *less than* $300, but do not include amounts that are *equal to* $300.

4 Switch to **Design** view. On the **Criteria** row, click in the **Amount** field, delete the existing criteria, type **>=300** and then press ⏎.

Note — Pressing Enter After Criteria Is Added

If you press ⏎ or click in another column or row in the query design grid after you have added your criteria, you can see how Access alters the criteria so it can interpret what you have typed. Sometimes, there is no change, such as when you add criteria to a number or currency field. Other times, Access may capitalize a letter or add quotation marks or other symbols to clarify the criteria. Whether or not you press ⏎ after adding criteria does not affect the query results. It is used in this text to help you see how the program behaves.

---

5 **Run** the query, and then compare your screen with Figure 13.43.

Nineteen records display, including the records for scholarships in the exact amount of $300. The records include scholarships *equal to* or *greater than* $300. In this manner, comparison operators can be combined.

This query answers the question, *Which scholarships have been awarded in the amount of $300 or more, and for which sports?*

Figure 13.43

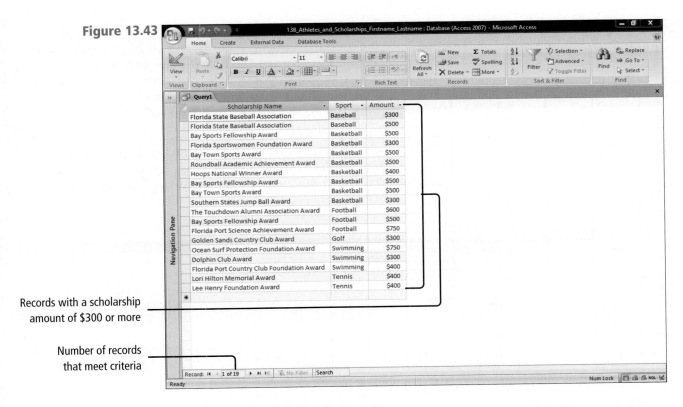

Records with a scholarship amount of $300 or more

Number of records that meet criteria

6 On the **Quick Access Toolbar**, click the **Save** button. In the **Save As** dialog box, type **13B $300 or More Firstname Lastname** and then click **OK**.

7 From the **Office** menu, point to **Print**, and then click **Print Preview**. If you are printing your assignments on paper, in the **Print** group, click the **Print** button. In the **Print** dialog box, click **OK**. Click the **Close Print Preview** button. To submit electronically, follow your instructor's directions.

8 **Close** ✕ the query. **Open** » the **Navigation Pane**, and notice that the new query displays under the table from which it retrieved the records.

Activity 13.18 Using the Between ... And Comparison Operator

The ***Between ... And operator*** is a comparison operator that looks for values within a range. It is particularly useful when you need to locate records that are within a range of dates, for example, scholarships awarded between August 1 and September 30. In this activity, you will create a new query from an existing query, and then add criteria to look for values within a range of dates. The query will answer the question, *Which scholarships were awarded between August 1 and September 30?*

1 From the **Navigation Pane**, open the **13B $300 or More** query. From the **Office** menu 🏠, click **Save As**. In the **Save As** dialog box, type **13B Awards Aug-Sept Firstname Lastname** and then click **OK**.

2 **Close** « the **Navigation Pane**, and then on the **Home** tab, in the **Views group**, click the **View** button to switch to **Design** view. From the **13B Scholarships Awarded** field list, add the **Award Date** as the fourth field in the design grid.

3 On the **Criteria** row, click in the **Amount** field, and then delete the existing criteria so that the query is not restricted by amount. On the **Criteria** row, click in the **Award Date** field, type **Between 08/01/09 And 09/30/09** and then press Enter. Notice that Access places quotation marks around the dates. Compare your screen with Figure 13.44, where the column has been widened to fully display the criteria.

> This criteria instructs Access to look for values in the Award Date field that begin with 08/01/09 and end with 09/30/09. Both the beginning and ending dates will be included in the query results. If you type the operators *Between ... And* using lowercase letters, Access will capitalize the first letter of each operator.

Figure 13.44

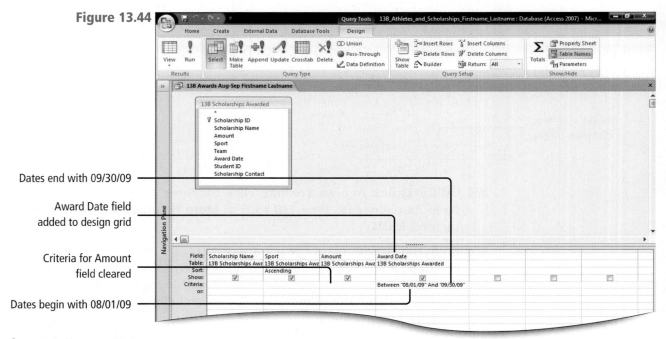

Dates end with 09/30/09

Award Date field added to design grid

Criteria for Amount field cleared

Dates begin with 08/01/09

Note — Widening Columns in the Query Grid

For a better view of your criteria, widen a column in the design grid using the same techniques that are used in a table. In the selection bar at the top of the column, point to the right border and double-click to expand the column and to fully display the contents on the criteria row. You can also drag the right border to the desired width.

4 **Run** the query and notice that three scholarships were awarded between 08/01/09 and 09/30/09.

5 From the **Office** menu 🏢, point to **Print**, and then click **Print Preview**. If you are printing your assignments on paper, in the **Print group**, click the **Print** button. In the **Print** dialog box, click **OK**. Click the **Close Print Preview** button. To submit electronically, follow your instructor's directions.

6 **Close** ⊠ the query. In the message box, click **Yes** to save the changes to the query design. **Open** » the **Navigation Pane**, and notice that the new query displays under the table from which it retrieved records.

Objective 10
Use Compound Criteria

You can specify more than one condition—criteria—in a query; this is called **compound criteria**. Compound criteria enable you to create queries that are quite specific. Two types of compound criteria used in queries are AND and OR, which are **logical operators**. Logical operators enable you to enter criteria for the same field or different fields.

Activity 13.19 Using AND Criteria in a Query

Compound criteria use an AND condition to display records in the query results that meet *both* parts of the specified criteria. In this activity, you will help Mr. Simmons answer the question, *Which scholarships over $500 were awarded for Football?*

1 **Close** « the **Navigation Pane.** On the Ribbon, click the **Create tab**. In the **Other group**, click the **Query Design** button. **Add** the **13B Scholarships Awarded** table to the table area. **Close** the **Show Table** dialog box, and then, expand the field list.

2 Add the following fields to the design grid in the order given: **Scholarship Name**, **Sport**, and **Amount**.

3 On the **Criteria** row, click in the **Sport** field, type **Football** and then press ⎆Tab.

4 On the **Criteria** row, in the **Amount** field, type **>500** and then press ⎆Enter. Compare your screen with Figure 13.45.

> The AND condition is created by placing the criteria for both fields on the same line in the Criteria row. The results will display records that contain *Football* AND an amount greater than *$500*.

Figure 13.45

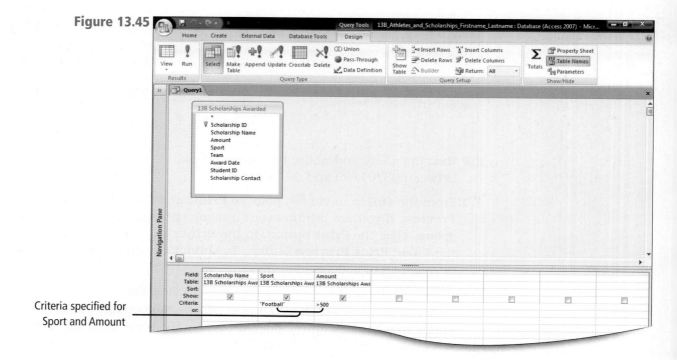

Criteria specified for
Sport and Amount

5 On the **Design tab**, in the **Results group**, click the **Run** button.

Two records display that match both conditions—Football in the Sport field and greater than $500 in the Amount field.

6 **Close** ☒ the query. In the message box, click **Yes** to save changes to the query. In the **Save As** dialog box, type **13B Football and Over $500 Firstname Lastname** and then click **OK** or press Enter.

7 **Open** ≫ the **Navigation Pane**, and then click one time to select the **13B Football and Over $500** query. From the **Office** menu ⊙, point to the **Print** button and click **Print Preview**. If you are printing your assignments on paper, in the **Print group**, click the **Print** button. In the **Print** dialog box, click **OK**. Click the **Close Print Preview** button. To submit electronically, follow your instructor's directions.

8 **Close** ≪ the **Navigation Pane**.

You can print any selected object from the Navigation Pane—the object does not have to be displayed on your screen to print.

Activity 13.20 Using OR Criteria in a Query

Use the OR condition to specify multiple criteria for a single field, or multiple criteria on different fields when you want to display the records that meet either condition. In this activity, you will help Mr. Simmons answer the question, *Which scholarships over $400 were awarded in the sports of Baseball or Swimming?*

1 On the Ribbon, click the **Create tab**. In the **Other group**, click the **Query Design** button.

2 **Add** the **13B Scholarships Awarded** table and then **Close** the dialog box. Expand the field list, and then add the following four fields to the design grid in the order given: **Scholarship Name**, **Sport**, **Amount**, and **Award Date**.

3 On the **Criteria** row, click in the **Sport** field, and then type **Baseball**

4 In the design grid, on the **or** row, click in the **Sport** field, type **Swimming** and then press Enter. **Run** the query.

The query results display seven scholarship records where the Sport is either Baseball *or* Swimming. Use the OR condition to specify multiple criteria for a single field.

5 Switch to **Design** view. Under **Sport**, on the **or** row, delete the text. Under **Sport**, click in the **Criteria** row, and then delete the existing text. Type **Swimming Or Baseball** and then on the **Criteria** row, click in the **Amount** field. Type **>400** and then press Enter. Compare your screen with Figure 13.46.

This is an alternative way to use the OR compound operator in the Sport field. Because criteria has been entered for two different fields, Access will return the records that are Baseball *or* Swimming and that have a scholarship awarded in an amount greater than $400.

Figure 13.46

OR condition for two criteria in the same field

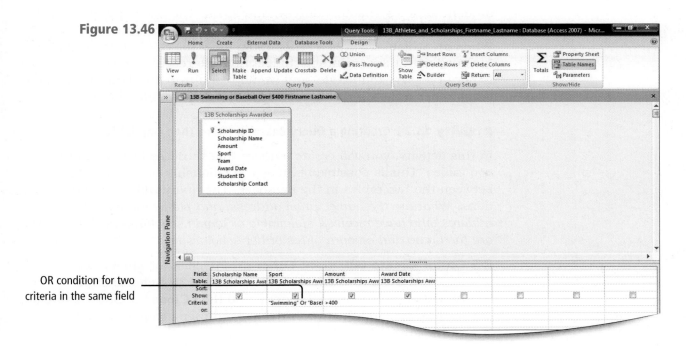

6 **Run** the query to display the two records that match the conditions.

7 **Close** ✕ the query. In the message box, click **Yes** to save changes to the query. In the **Save As** dialog box, type **13B Swimming or Baseball Over $400 Firstname Lastname** and then click **OK** or press Enter.

8 **Open** » the **Navigation Pane** and click one time to select the **13B Swimming or Baseball Over $400** query. From the **Office** menu 🏢, point to **Print**, and then click **Print Preview**. If you are printing your assignments on paper, in the **Print group**, click the **Print** button. In the **Print** dialog box, click **OK**. Click the **Close Print Preview** button. To submit electronically, follow your instructor's directions.

9 **Close** « the **Navigation Pane**.

Objective 11
Create a Query Based on More Than One Table

In a relational database, you can retrieve information from more than one table. Recall that each table in a relational database contains all of the records about a single topic. Tables are joined by relating the primary key field in one table to a foreign key field in another table. This common field creates a relationship, enabling you to include data from more than one table in a query.

For example, the Athletes table contains all of the information about the student athletes—name, address, and so on. The Scholarships Awarded table includes the scholarship name, amount, award date, and so on. When an athlete receives a scholarship, only the Student ID field is included with the scholarship to identify who received the scholarship. It is not necessary to include, and would result in redundant information, if any other athlete data was stored in the Scholarships Awarded table.

Activity 13.21 Creating a Query Based on More Than One Table

In this activity, you will create a query that retrieves information from two tables. This is possible because a relationship has been established between the two tables in the database. The query will answer the questions, *What are the name, email address, and phone number of student athletes who have received swimming or tennis scholarships, and what are the name and amount of his or her scholarship?*

1 On the **Create tab**, in the **Other group**, click the **Query Design** button. **Add** the **13B Athletes** table and the **13B Scholarships Awarded** table to the table area, and then **Close** the **Show Table** dialog box. Expand the two field lists, and then compare your screen with Figure 13.47.

> The join line indicates the one-to-many relationship—*one* athlete can have *many* scholarships. Student ID is the common field in the two tables. In the Athletes table, Student ID is the primary key field; in the Scholarships Awarded table, Student ID is the foreign key field.

Figure 13.47

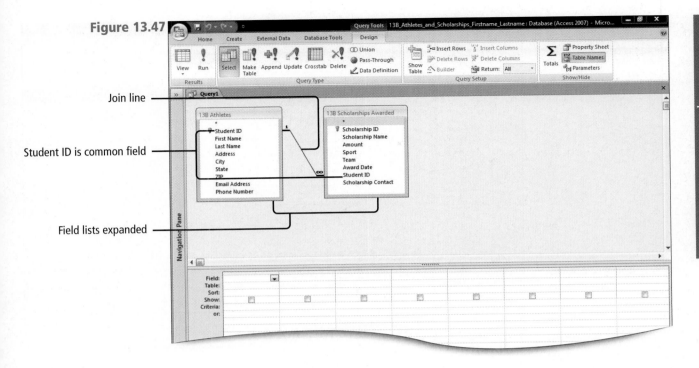

Join line

Student ID is common field

Field lists expanded

☑ From the **13B Athletes** field list, add the following fields to the design grid in the order given: **First Name**, **Last Name**, **Address**, **City**, **State**, and **ZIP**.

☑ On the **Sort** row, click in the **Last Name** field. Click the **Sort arrow**, and then click **Ascending** to sort the records in alphabetical order by last name.

☑ From the **13B Scholarships Awarded** field list, add the following fields to the design grid in the order given: **Scholarship Name**, **Sport**, and **Amount**.

☑ Click in the **Criteria** row, under **Sport**. Type **Swimming** and on the **or** row, under **Sport**, type **Tennis** and then press Enter.

☑ In the design grid, on the second row—the **Table** row—notice that for each field, the table from which the field was added is displayed. Compare your screen with Figure 13.48.

> When extracting data from multiple tables, the information on the Table row is helpful, especially when different tables may include the same field names, such as address, but different data, such as a student's address or a coach's address.

Figure 13.48

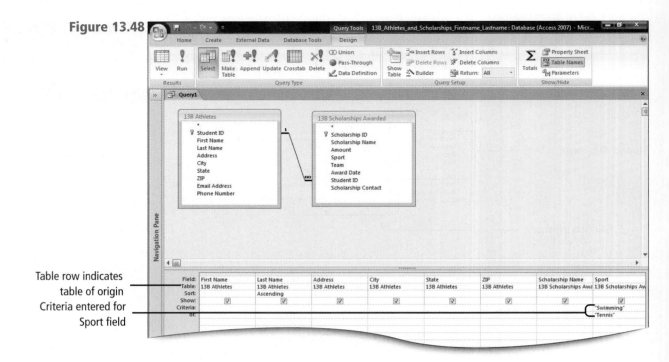

Table row indicates
table of origin
Criteria entered for
Sort field

7 **Run** the query.

> The names and addresses of eight student athletes display. Notice that the First Name and Last Name fields are included in the query results even though the common field—Student ID—was *not* included in the query design. Because Student ID is included in both tables, and a one-to-many relationship was created between the tables, you can display data from both tables in one query.

> Two students—*Arianna Kitasoe* and *Janice Murphy*—received scholarships in both Swimming and Tennis. Recall that *one* student athlete can receive *many* scholarships.

8 Switch to **Design** view. From the **13B Athletes** field list, add **Phone Number** to the design grid. In the **13B Athletes** field list, point to **Email Address**, drag it to the design grid on top of **Amount**, and then release the mouse button.

> The Email Address field is inserted to the left of the Amount field.

9 In the design grid, select, by dragging in the gray selection bar, the **Address**, **City**, **State**, and **ZIP** fields, and then press ⌐Delete⌐.

10 In the design grid, select the **Amount** field, and then drag it to the first field position in the design grid. Click outside of the grid to cancel the selection, and then compare your screen with Figure 13.49.

> The design of the query is modified. Phone Number is added as the last field in the design grid. The Address, City, State, and ZIP fields are deleted. The Amount field is in the first position.

Figure 13.49

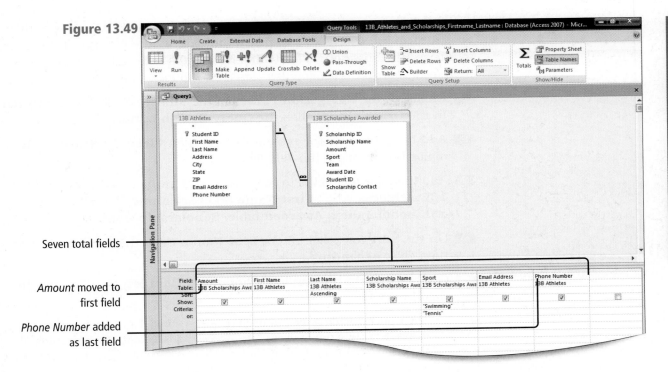

Seven total fields

Amount moved to first field

Phone Number added as last field

Run the query. Select all of the columns in the query results and then apply **Best Fit**—in the field heading row, point to the right boundary of any of the selected columns to display the ⊞ pointer, and then double-click.

On the **Quick Access Toolbar**, click the **Save** button 🔲, type **13B Swimming and Tennis Firstname Lastname** and then click **OK**. Display the query in **Print Preview**, set the **Margins** to **Normal**, and then change the orientation to **Landscape**. If you are submitting your results from this project on paper, **Print** the query and then **Close Print Preview**. To submit electronically, follow the instructions provided by your instructor.

Close ✕ the query, **Open** ≫ the **Navigation Pane**, and notice that your new query—*13B Swimming and Tennis*—displays under *both* tables from which it retrieved records.

In the Tables and Related Views arrangement of the Navigation Pane, any object that references a table displays with that table.

Objective 12
Use Wildcards in a Query

Wildcard characters serve as a placeholder for one or more unknown characters in the criteria. When you are unsure of the particular character or set of characters to include in criteria, use wildcard characters in place of the characters.

Activity 13.22 Using a Wildcard in a Query

Use the asterisk (*) to represent one or more characters. For example, if you use the * wildcard in the criteria Fo*, the results will return Foster,

Forrester, Forrest, Fossil, or any word beginning with *Fo*. In this activity, you will use the asterisk (*) wildcard and specify the criteria in the query to answer the question, *Which student athletes received scholarships from local Rotary Clubs, country clubs, and foundations?*

1 **Close** « the **Navigation Pane**. On the Ribbon, click the **Create tab**. In the **Other group**, click the **Query Design** button.

2 **Add** both tables to the table area, and then **Close** the **Show Table** dialog box. Expand the field lists.

3 Add the following fields to the design grid in the order given: from the **13B Athletes** table, **First Name** and **Last Name**; from the **13B Scholarships Awarded** table, **Scholarship Contact**.

4 On the **Sort** row, click under **Last Name**. Click the **sort arrow**, and then click **Ascending**.

5 On the **Criteria** row, under **Scholarship Contact**, type **Rotary*** and then press Enter.

> The wildcard character * is used as a placeholder to match one or more characters. When you press Enter, Access adds *Like* to the beginning of the criteria. This is used to compare a sequence of characters and test whether or not the text matches a pattern.

6 **Run** the query to display the three student athletes who received scholarships from Rotary Clubs.

7 Switch to the **Design** view. On the **or** row, under **Scholarship Contact**, type ***Country Club** and then press Enter.

> The * can be used at the beginning, middle, or end of the criteria. The position of the * wildcard character determines the location of the unknown characters. Here you will search for records that end in *Country Club*.

8 **Run** the query to display a total of six records.

9 Switch to **Design** view. Under **Scholarship Contact** and under **Like "*Country Club"**, type ***Foundation*** and then press Enter. Compare your screen with Figure 13.50.

> The query will also display records that have the word *Foundation* anywhere—beginning, middle, or end—in the field. Three *OR* criteria have been included for the Scholarship Contact field—the query results will display students who have received scholarships from an organization name that begins with Rotary, that ends in County Club, or that has Foundation anywhere in the middle of the name.

Figure 13.50

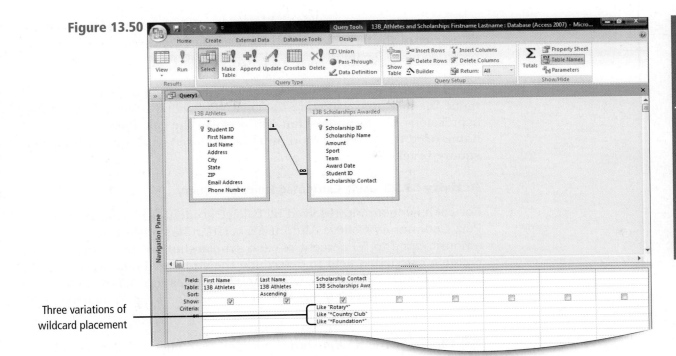

Three variations of wildcard placement

10 **Run** the query to display a total of 28 records.

> Twenty-eight scholarships were awarded from a Country Club, a Rotary Club, or a Foundation.

11 On the **Quick Access Toolbar**, click the **Save** button. Name the query **13B Clubs and Foundations Firstname Lastname** and then display the results in **Print Preview**. If you are submitting paper assignments, **Print** the query results. To submit electronically, follow your instructor's directions. **Close Print Preview**.

12 **Close** ☒ the query results, and then **Open** ≫ the **Navigation Pane**.

> Because the 13B Clubs and Foundations query retrieved data from two tables, it displays below the 13B Scholarships Awarded table and the 13B Athletes table.

More Knowledge — Search for a Single Unknown Character by Using the ? Wildcard

The question mark (?) is a wildcard that is used to search for unknown single characters. For each question mark included in a criteria, any character can be inserted. For example, if you used *b?d* as a criteria, the query might locate bid, bud, bed or any three-character word beginning with *b* and ending with *d*. If *b??d* is entered as the criteria, the results could include bind, bend, bard or any four-character word beginning with *b* and ending with *d*.

Objective 13
Use Calculated Fields in a Query

Queries can create calculated values. For example, Florida Port Community College could multiply two fields together, such as Total Credit Hours and Tuition per Credit Hour to get a Total Tuition Due amount for each student without having to include a specific field for this amount in the table, which reduces the size of the database and provides more flexibility.

There are two steps to produce a calculated field in a query. First, name the field that will store the calculated values. Second, write the expression—the formula—that will perform the calculation. Each field name used in the calculation must be enclosed within its own pair of square brackets.

Activity 13.23 Using Calculated Fields in a Query

For each scholarship received by college student athletes, the Florida Port Community College Alumni Association has agreed to donate an amount equal to 50 percent of each scholarship. In this activity, you will create a calculated field to determine the additional amount each scholarship is worth. The query will answer the question, *What will the value of each scholarship be if the Alumni Association makes a matching 50% donation?*

1 **Close** « the **Navigation Pane**, and then click the **Create tab**. In the **Other group**, click the **Query Design** button.

2 **Add** the **13B Scholarships Awarded** table to the table area, **Close** the **Show Table** dialog box, and then expand the field list. Add the following fields to the design grid in the order given: **Student ID**, **Scholarship Name**, and **Amount**.

3 Click in the **Sort** row under **Student ID**, click the **Sort arrow**, and then click **Ascending**.

4 In the **Field** row, right-click in the first empty column to display a shortcut menu, and then click **Zoom**.

> The Zoom dialog box gives you more working space so that you can see the entire calculation as you type it. The calculation can also be typed directly in the empty Field box in the column.

5 In the **Zoom** dialog box, type **Matching Donation:[Amount]*0.5** and then compare your screen with Figure 13.51.

> The first element, *Matching Donation*, is the new field name where the calculated amounts will display. Following that is a colon (:), which separates the new field name from the expression. *Amount* is enclosed in square brackets because it is an existing field name in the 13B Scholarships Awarded table, containing the numeric data on which the calculation will be performed. Following the square brackets is an asterisk (*), which in math calculations signifies multiplication. Finally, the percentage (0.5 or 50%) displays.

Figure 13.51

Calculated value

New field name

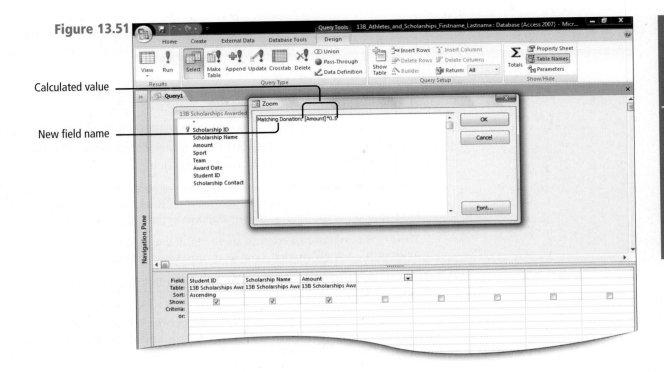

6 In the **Zoom** dialog box, click **OK**, and then **Run** the query. Select all of the columns and apply **Best Fit**. Compare your screen with Figure 13.52.

> The query results display three fields from the 13B Scholarships Awarded table plus a fourth field—*Matching Donation*—in which a calculated amount displays. Each calculated amount equals the amount in the Amount field multiplied by 0.5.

Figure 13.52

New calculated field created (50% of Amount)

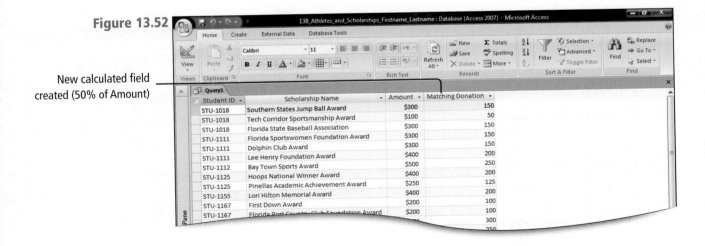

Alert!   **Does your screen differ?**

If your calculations in a query do not work, carefully check the expression you typed. Spelling or syntax errors prevent calculated fields from working properly.

7 Notice the formatting of the **Matching Donation** field—there are no dollar signs, commas, or decimal places; you will adjust this formatting later.

8 Switch to **Design** view. On the **Field** row, in the first empty column, right-click, and then click **Zoom**.

9 In the **Zoom** dialog box, type **Total Scholarship:[Amount]+[Matching Donation]** and then click **OK**. **Run** the query to view the results. Apply **Best Fit** to the **Total Scholarship** field.

Total Scholarship is calculated by adding together the Amount field and the Matching Donation field. Each existing field name—*Amount* and *Matching Donation*—must be enclosed in separate pairs of brackets.

The Total Scholarship column includes dollar signs, commas, and decimal points, which carried over from the Amount field.

10 Switch to **Design** view. On the **Field** row, click in the **Matching Donation** field name.

11 On the **Design tab**, in the **Show/Hide group**, click the **Property Sheet** button. Alternatively, right-click the Matching Donation field name, and then click Properties.

The Property Sheet displays on the right side of your screen, where you can customize fields in a query, for example, the format of numbers in the field. The left column displays the Property name, for example, Description. To the right of the Property name is the Property setting box.

12 In the **Property Sheet**, on the **General tab**, click in the **Format** property setting box, and then click the **arrow** that displays. Compare your screen with Figure 13.53.

A list of formats for the Matching Donation field displays.

Figure 13.53

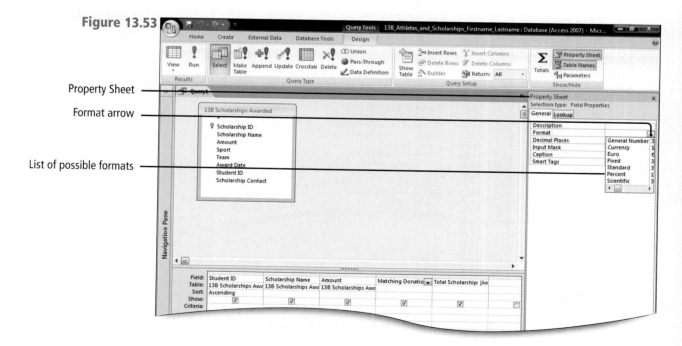

Property Sheet

Format arrow

List of possible formats

13 In the list, click **Currency**, and then **Close** × the **Property Sheet**.

14 **Run** the query. Compare your screen with Figure 13.54.

The Matching Donation column displays with currency formatting—a dollar sign, thousands comma separator, and two decimal places.

Figure 13.54

Currency format applied to all columns

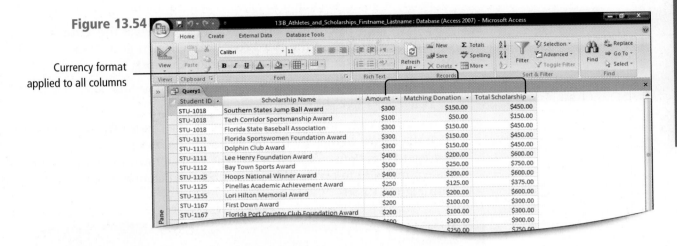

15 On the **Quick Access Toolbar**, click the **Save** 🖫 button. Name the query **13B Matching Donations Firstname Lastname** and then display the query results in **Print Preview**. Change the **Orientation** to **Landscape**. If you are submitting paper assignments, **Print** the query results. **Close Print Preview**. To submit electronically, follow your instructor's directions.

16 **Close** × the query.

Objective 14
Group Data and Calculate Statistics in a Query

In Access queries, you can perform statistical calculations on a group of records. Calculations that are performed on a group of records are called *aggregate functions*.

Activity 13.24 Using the MIN, MAX, AVG and SUM Functions in a Query

In this activity, you will use the minimum, maximum, average, and sum functions in a query to examine the amounts of scholarships awarded. The last query will answer the question, *What is the total dollar amount of scholarships awarded?*

1 On the Ribbon, click the **Create tab**. In the **Other group**, click the **Query Design** button.

2 Add the **13B Scholarships Awarded** table to the table area, **Close** the **Show Table** dialog box, and then expand the field list. Add the **Amount** field to the design grid.

> When you want to summarize a field, include only the field you want to summarize in the query, so that the aggregate function (minimum, maximum, average, sum, and so forth) is applied to that single field.

3 On the **Design tab**, in the **Show/Hide group**, click the **Totals** button to add a **Total** row as the third row in the design grid. Notice that in the design grid, on the **Total** row, under **Amount**, *Group By* displays.

> On the Total row, you select the function, such as Min, Max, Avg, or Sum, that you want to use for the field.

4 In the **Total** row, under **Amount**, click in the **Group By** box, and then click the **arrow** to display the list of functions. Access supports the aggregate functions summarized in the table shown in Figure 13.55. Take a moment to review this table, and then compare your screen with Figure 13.56.

Aggregate Functions

Function Name	What It Does
Sum	Totals the values in a field
Avg	Averages the values in a field
Min	Locates the smallest value in a field
Max	Locates the largest value in a field
Count	Counts the number of records in a field
StDev	Calculates the Standard Deviation on the values in a field
Var	Calculates the Variance on the values in a field
First	Displays the First value in a field
Last	Displays the Last value in a field
Expression	Creates a calculated field that includes an aggregate function
Where	Limits records displayed to those that match a condition specified on the Criteria row

Figure 13.55

Figure 13.56

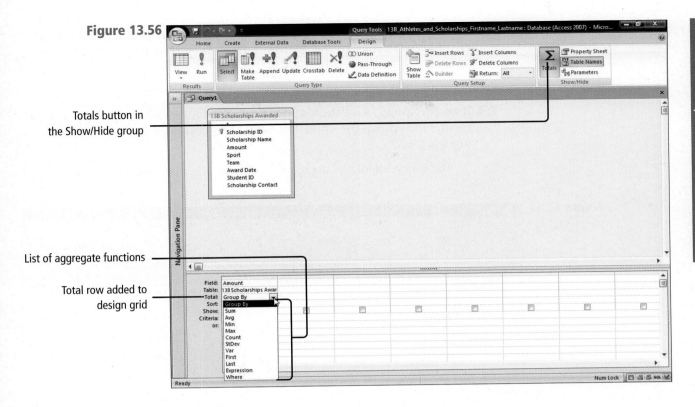

Totals button in the Show/Hide group

List of aggregate functions

Total row added to design grid

5 From the list of functions, click **Min**, and then **Run** the query. Double-click the right boundary of the new column heading to widen the column.

> Access calculates the minimum (smallest) scholarship award—$100.00. The field name, *MinOfAmount* displays for the calculation. This query answers the question, *What is the minimum (smallest) scholarship amount awarded?*

6 Switch to **Design** view. Using the technique you just practiced, select the **Max** function, and then **Run** the query.

> The maximum (largest) scholarship amount is *$750.00*.

7 Switch to **Design** view, select the **Avg** function, and then **Run** the query.

> The average scholarship amount awarded is *$358.33*.

8 Switch to **Design** view. Select the **Sum** function, and then **Run** the query.

> Access sums the Amount field for all of the records and displays a result of *$10,750.00*. The field name, SumOfAmount, displays. This query answers the question, *What is the total dollar amount of all the scholarships awarded?*

Activity 13.25 Grouping Data in a Query

The aggregate functions can also be used to calculate totals by groups of data. For example, if you want to group (summarize) the amount of scholarships awarded to each student, you would include the Student ID field, in addition to the Amount field, and then group all of the records for each student together to calculate a total awarded to each student. Similarly, you can calculate how much money is awarded to each sport.

1 Switch to **Design** view. Add the **Student ID** field to the design grid. On the **Total** row, under **Student ID**, notice that *Group By* displays.

> The design of this query will group—summarize—the records by StudentID and calculate a total Amount for each student.

2 **Run** the query, and then apply **Best Fit** to the fields. Click in any record to remove the selection, and then compare your screen with Figure 13.57.

> The query calculates the total amount of all scholarships for each student.

Figure 13.57

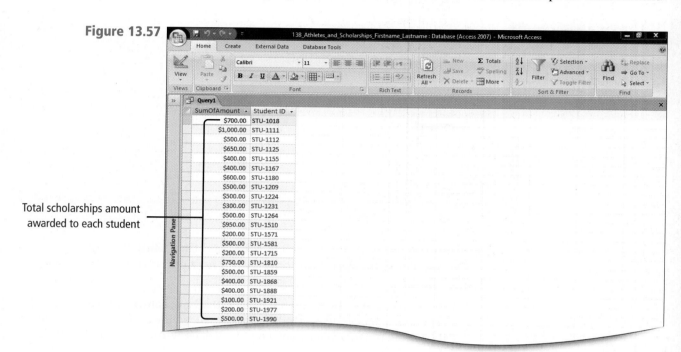

Total scholarships amount awarded to each student

3 Switch to **Design** view. In the design grid, delete the **Student ID** field, and then add the **Sport** field to the design grid. **Run** the query, and then compare your screen with Figure 13.58.

> Access summarizes the data by each sport. Basketball scholarships received the largest total Amount—$3,500.00.

Figure 13.58

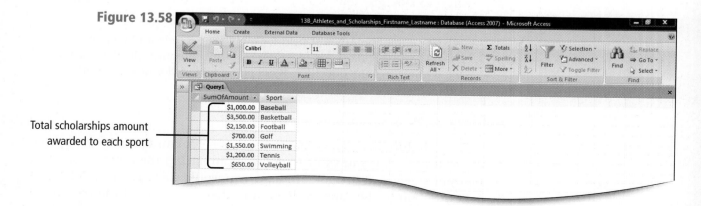

Total scholarships amount awarded to each sport

4 On the **Quick Access Toolbar**, click the **Save** button. Name the query **13B Totals by Sport Firstname Lastname** and then display the query results in **Print Preview**. If you are submitting paper assignments, **Print** the query results, and then **Close Print Preview**. To submit electronically, follow your instructor's directions.

5 **Close** ☒ the query, and then **Open** » the **Navigation Pane** to view the queries you have created.

6 **Close** « the **Navigation Pane**, **Close** the Database, and then **Exit** Access.

End You have completed Project 13B ───────────

There's More You Can Do!

Close Access and any other open windows. Display the Start menu, click Computer, and then navigate to the student files that accompany this textbook. In the folder **02_theres_more_you_can_do**, locate and open the folder for this chapter. Open and print the instructions for this project, which are provided to you in Adobe PDF format.

Try IT! 1—Password Protect Your Database

In this Try It! exercise, you will encrypt and password protect your database to conceal data and prevent unwanted users from opening your database.

Content-Based Assessments

Summary

Importing an Excel spreadsheet is an efficient way to create new tables in an Access database. Sorting data in a table reorders the records based on one or more fields and is a quick way to alphabetize records or to find the highest or lowest amount in a numeric, currency, or date field. Use queries to ask complex questions about the data in a database in a manner that Access can interpret. Save queries so they can be run as needed against current records. Use queries to limit the fields that display, add criteria to restrict the number of records in the query results, create calculated values, and include data from more than one table.

Key Terms

Content-Based Assessments

Matching

Match each term in the second column with its correct definition in the first column. Write the letter of the term on the blank line in front of the correct definition.

_____ **1.** The area directly below the Ribbon that displays information such as security alerts when there is potentially unsafe, active content in an Office 2007 document that you open.

_____ **2.** An area of the Access program where you can view the security and privacy settings for your Access installation.

_____ **3.** A type of database in which the tables in the database can relate or connect to other tables through common fields.

_____ **4.** Fields that contain the same data in more than one table.

_____ **5.** An association that is established between two tables using common fields.

_____ **6.** A relationship between two tables where one record in the first table corresponds to many records in the second table—the most common type of relationship in Access.

_____ **7.** A list of the field names in a table.

_____ **8.** The field that is included in the related table so that it can be joined to the primary key in another table for the purpose of creating a relationship.

_____ **9.** A set of rules that Access uses to ensure that the data between related tables is valid.

_____ **10.** In the Relationships window, the line joining two tables that visually indicates the related field and the type of relationship.

_____ **11.** The process of arranging data in a specific order based on the value in each field.

_____ **12.** A sorting order that arranges text in alphabetical order (A to Z) or numbers from the lowest to highest number.

_____ **13.** A database object that retrieves (selects) specific data from one or more tables and then displays the specified data in Datasheet view.

_____ **14.** When sorting on multiple fields in Datasheet view, the field that will be used for the first level of sorting.

_____ **15.** The table or tables from which a query selects its data.

A Ascending

B Common fields

C Data source

D Field list

E Foreign key

F Join line

G Message Bar

H One-to-many

I Outermost sort field

J Referential integrity

K Relational

L Relationship

M Select query

N Sorting

O Trust Center

Content-Based Assessments

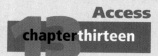
Fill in the Blank

Write the correct answer in the space provided.

1. The upper pane of the Query window, which displays the field lists for tables that are used in the query is the _____ _____.

2. The lower pane of the Query window, which displays the design of the query is the _____ _____.

3. The process in which Access searches the records in the table(s) included in a query design, finds the records that match the specified criteria, and then displays those records in a datasheet is called _____.

4. Conditions that identify the specific records you are looking for are called _____.

5. Each time you open a saved query, Access _____ the query again and displays the results based on the data stored in the associated tables; thus, the results always reflect the latest information in the tables.

6. A sequence of characters, which when used in query criteria, must be matched, is referred to as a _____ _____.

7. A criteria that searches for fields that are empty is called _____ _____.

8. A criteria that searches for fields that are *not* empty is called _____ _____.

9. Symbols that evaluate each field value to determine if it is the same (=), greater than (>), less than (<), or in between a range of values as specified by the criteria are referred to as _____ _____.

10. In a _____ condition, both parts of the query must be met.

11. In a _____ condition, either part of the query must be met.

12. Multiple conditions in a query or filter are called _____ _____.

13. In a query, a character that serves as a placeholder for one or more unknown characters is a _____.

14. Calculations that are performed on a group of records are called _____ _____.

15. To locate the largest value in a group of records, use the _____ function.

Content-Based Assessments

Skills Review

Project 13C—Music Department

In this project, you will apply the skills you practiced from the Objectives in Project 13A.

Objectives: 1. *Open an Existing Database;* **2.** *Create Table Relationships;* **3.** *Sort Records in a Table;* **4.** *Create a Query in Design View;* **5.** *Create a New Query from an Existing Query;* **6.** *Sort Query Results;* **7.** *Specify Criteria in a Query.*

In the following Skills Review, you will assist Pascal Sanchez, Florida Port Community College Music Director, in using his database to answer various questions about the instruments in the Music Department's inventory. Your query results will look similar to those shown in Figure 13.59.

For Project 13C, you will need the following file:

a13C_Music_Department

You will save your database as
13C_Music_Department_Firstname_Lastname

Figure 13.59

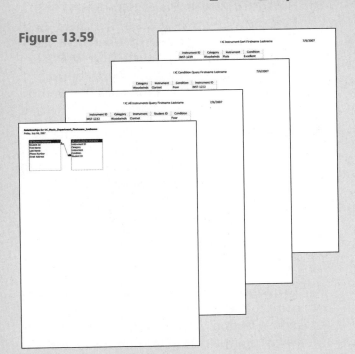

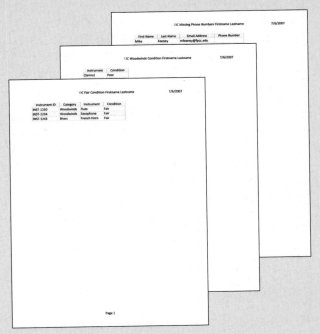

(Project 13C–Music Department continues on the next page)

Content-Based Assessments

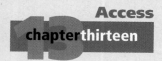
(Project 13C–Music Department continued)

1. Navigate to the location where the student data files for this textbook are saved. Locate **a13C_Music_Department** and click one time to select the file. **Copy** and then **Paste** the file to your **Access Chapter 13** folder. **Rename** the file as 13C_Music_Department_Firstname_Lastname and then **Start** Access. Navigate to your **Access Chapter 13** folder, open **13C_ Music_Department**, and then **Enable this content**.

2. Click the **Database Tools tab**. In the **Show/Hide group**, click the **Relationships** button. On the **Design tab**, in the **Relationships group**, click the **Show Table** button. In the **Show Table** dialog box, click the **13C Student Musicians** table, and then at the bottom of the dialog box, click **Add**. Point to the **13C Instruments Inventory** table, and then double-click to add the table to the Relationships window. **Close** the **Show Table** dialog box. In each table, use the pointer to expand the field lists to display the entire table name and all of the field names.

3. In the **13C Student Musicians** field list, point to **Student ID**, hold down the left mouse button, and then drag to the right to the **13C Instruments Inventory** field list until your mouse pointer is on top of **Student ID**. Release the mouse button, and then drag the **Edit Relationships** dialog box below the two field lists. The relationship between the two tables is a one-to-many relationship; *one* student can play *many* instruments. The common field is Student ID.

4. Click to select the **Enforce Referential Integrity** check box, and then click **Create**. On the **Design tab**, in the **Tools group**, click the **Relationship Report** button. If you are submitting paper

assignments, on the **Print Preview tab**, in the **Print group**, click the **Print** button, and then click **OK**. Click **Close Print Preview**. To submit electronically, follow your instructor's directions. On the **Quick Access Toolbar**, click the **Save** button, and then in the **Save As** dialog box, click **OK** to accept the default name. **Close** all of the open objects.

5. **Open** the **Navigation Pane**, **Open** the **13C Instruments Inventory** table, and then **Close** the **Navigation Pane**. In the **Condition** field, click any record. On the **Home tab**, in the **Sort & Filter group**, click the **Descending** button to sort the records from *Poor* to *Excellent*. Point anywhere in the **Category** field, and then right-click. From the shortcut menu, click **Sort A to Z**. The records are sorted first by *Category*, the outermost sort field, and then within categories, by *Condition*, the innermost sort field. In the **Sort & Filter group**, click the **Clear All Sorts** button. **Close** the table, and then click **No**; you do not need to save the changes to the design.

6. Click the **Create tab**, and then in the **Other group**, click the **Query Design** button. From the **Show Table** dialog box, **Add** the **13C Instruments Inventory** table to the table area, and then **Close** the **Show Table** dialog box. Expand the field list.

7. In the **13C Instruments Inventory** field list, double-click **Instrument ID** to add it to the design grid. In the **13C Instruments Inventory** field list, point to **Category**, hold down the left mouse button, and then drag the field down into the design grid until you are pointing to the **Field** row in the next available column. Release the mouse button. In the **Field** row of the design grid, click in the third column, and then click the

(Project 13C–Music Department continues on the next page)

Content-Based Assessments

(Project 13C–Music Department continued)

arrow that displays. From the list, click **Instrument** to add this field to the design grid.

8. Using any technique, add the **Student ID** and **Condition** fields as the fourth and fifth fields in the design grid. On the **Design tab**, in the **Results group**, click the **Run** button. This query answers the question, *What are the Instrument ID, Category, Instrument, Student ID, and Condition of all of the instruments in the inventory?* On the **Quick Access Toolbar**, click the **Save** button. In the **Save As** dialog box, type **13C All Instruments Query Firstname Lastname** and then click **OK**.

9. If you are submitting paper assignments, from the **Office** menu, point to the **Print** button, click **Print Preview**, and then click the **Print** button. Click the **Close Print Preview** button. To submit electronically, follow your instructor's directions.

10. From the **Office** menu, click **Save As**. In the **Save As** dialog box, type **13C Condition Query Firstname Lastname** and then click **OK**. Recall that you can create a new query based on an existing query.

11. On the **Home tab**, in the **Views group**, click the **View** button to switch to **Design** view. In the design grid, point to the thin gray selection bar above the **Student ID** field until the ⬇ pointer displays. Click to select the **Student ID** column, and then press Delete. From the gray selection bar, select the **Instrument ID** column. Then, point to the selection bar at the top of the selected column to display the ⬉ pointer, and drag to the right to position **Instrument ID** as the fourth (last) column.

12. **Run** the query. The query results display four fields. This query answers the question,

What are the Category, Instrument, Condition, and Instrument ID of every instrument in the inventory? **Close** the query, and then click **Yes**. **Open** the **Navigation Pane** and click one time to select **13C Condition Query**. If you are submitting paper assignments, from the **Office** menu, point to the **Print** button, click **Print Preview**, and then click the **Print** button. Click the **Close Print Preview** button. To submit electronically, follow your instructor's directions.

13. **Open** the **13C All Instruments Query**. **Save** the query as **13C Instrument Sort Firstname Lastname** and then switch to **Design** view. In the design grid, delete the **Student ID** field. In the **Category** field, click in the **Sort** row, click the **Sort arrow**, and then click **Descending**. Under **Condition**, click to display the **Sort arrow**, and then click **Ascending**. **Run** the query. This query answers the question, *Within each category (with Category in descending alphabetical order), what instruments are in the inventory and what is the instrument's condition (with the condition listed in ascending alphabetic order)?* **Print** the query or submit electronically as directed. **Close** the query, and then click **Yes** to save the changes.

14. **Close** any open objects and **Close** the **Navigation Pane**. Click the **Create tab**, and then in the **Other group**, click the **Query Design** button. **Add** the **13C Instruments Inventory** table to the table area, and then expand the field list. Add the following fields to the design grid in the order given: **Instrument ID**, **Category**, **Instrument**, and **Condition**. In the design grid, on the **Criteria** row and under **Condition**, type **Fair** and then press Enter. **Run** the query. This query answers the question, *What are the Instrument ID, Category, and Instruments*

(Project 13C–Music Department continues on the next page)

Content-Based Assessments

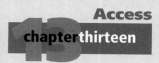
(Project 13C–Music Department continued)

that are in Fair condition? On the **Quick Access Toolbar**, click the **Save** button. Name the query **13C Fair Condition Firstname Lastname** and then **Print** or submit the query electronically. **Close** the query.

15. **Create** a query in **Query Design View**. **Add** the **13C Instruments Inventory** table to the table area, and then expand the field list. Add the following fields to the design grid in the order given: **Category**, **Instrument**, and **Condition**. On the **Criteria** row, under **Category**, type **Woodwinds** and then press Enter. Under **Category**, in the **Show** row, click to clear the **Show** check box, and then **Run** the query. This query answers the question, *What are the conditions of the woodwind instruments in the inventory?* Recall that if all results use the same criteria, such as Woodwinds, it is not necessary to display the data in the query results. **Save** the query with the name **13C Woodwinds Condition Firstname Lastname** and then **Print** or submit the query electronically. **Close** the query.

16. **Create** a query in **Query Design View**. **Add** the **13C Student Musicians** table to the table area, and then add the following fields to the design grid in the order given: **First Name**, **Last Name**, **Email Address**, and **Phone Number**. On the **Criteria** row, under **Phone Number**, type **Is Null** and then press Enter. On the **Sort** row, click in the **Last Name** field, click the **Sort arrow**, and then click **Ascending**. **Run** the query. This query answers the question, *For which student musicians are phone numbers missing?* **Save** the query as **13C Missing Phone Numbers Firstname Lastname** and then **Print** or submit the query electronically. **Close** the query.

17. If necessary, **Close** any open objects and be sure that the Navigation Pane is closed. From the **Office** menu, click **Close Database**, and then at the right side of the Access title bar, click the **Close** button to close the Access program. Alternatively, from the Office menu, click Exit Access.

End You have completed Project 13C ⎯⎯⎯⎯⎯⎯⎯⎯⎯⎯⎯

Content-Based Assessments

Skills Review

Project 13D — Concerts and Sponsors

In this project, you will apply the skills you practiced from the Objectives in Project 13B.

Objectives: 8. *Create a New Table by Importing an Excel Spreadsheet;* **9.** *Specify Numeric Criteria in a Query;* **10.** *Use Compound Criteria;* **11.** *Create a Query Based on More Than One Table;* **12.** *Use Wildcards in a Query;* **13.** *Use Calculated Fields in a Query;* **14.** *Group Data and Calculate Statistics in a Query.*

In the following Skills Review, you will assist Pascal Sanchez, College Music Director, in answering questions about concerts, sponsors, box office receipts, dates, and concert locations. Your query results will look similar to those shown in Figure 13.60.

> **For Project 13D, you will need the following files:**
>
> a13D_Concerts_Sponsors
> a13D_Sponsors (Excel file)
>
> **You will save your database as**
> **13D_Concerts_Sponsors_Firstname_Lastname**

Figure 13.60

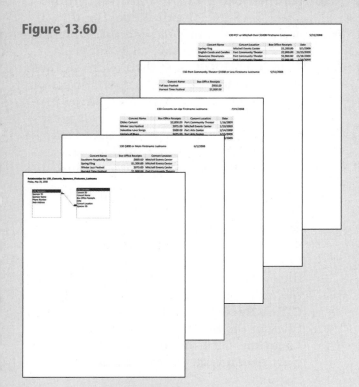

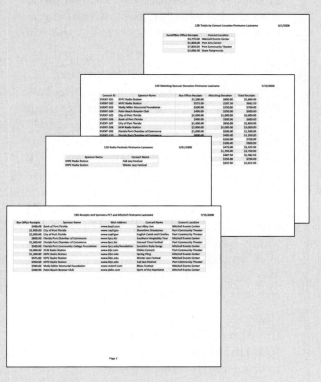

(Project 13D–Concerts and Sponsors continues on the next page)

Content-Based Assessments

(Project 13D–Concerts and Sponsors continued)

1. Navigate to the location where the student files for this textbook are saved. Locate **a13D_Concerts_Sponsors** and click one time to select the file. **Copy** and then **Paste** the file to your **Access Chapter 13** folder. **Rename** the file as **13D_Concerts_Sponsors_Firstname_Lastname** and then **Start** Access. Navigate to your **Access Chapter 13** folder, open **13D_Concerts_Sponsors**, and then **Enable this content**.

2. **Open** the **Navigation Pane**. On the Ribbon, click the **External Data tab**, and then in the **Import group**, click the **Excel** button. In the **Get External Data – Excel Spreadsheet** dialog box, to the right of the **File name** box, click **Browse**. Navigate to the location where the student files for this textbook are saved, and then double-click the **a13D_Sponsors** Excel file. Be sure that the **Import the source data into a new table in the current database** option button is selected, and then click **OK**.

3. In the upper portion of the **Import Spreadsheet Wizard**, click to select the **First Row Contains Column Headings** check box, and then click **Next**. Under **Field Options**, do not make any changes for the fields, and then click **Next**. In the upper portion of the Wizard, click the **Choose my own primary key** option button, and then be sure that **Sponsor ID** displays. Click **Next**. In the **Import to Table** box, type **13D Sponsors** and then click **Finish**. In the Wizard, click **Close**. The imported Excel spreadsheet becomes the second table in the database.

4. Click the **Database Tools tab**, and then in the **Show/Hide group**, click the **Relationships** button. On the **Design tab**, in the **Relationships group**, click the

Show Table button. **Add** the **13D Concerts** table, and then **Add** the **13D Sponsors** table to the table area. **Close** the **Show Table** dialog box. Expand the field lists, and then reposition the field lists so that the **13D Sponsors** field list is on the left side.

5. In the **13D Sponsors** field list, point to the **Sponsor ID** field, hold down the left mouse button, drag into the **13D Concerts** field list, position the mouse pointer on top of the **Sponsor ID** field, and then release the mouse button. In the **Edit Relationships** dialog box, click to select the **Enforce Referential Integrity** check box, and then click the **Create** button. A one-to-many relationship is established; *one* sponsor organization can sponsor *many* concerts.

6. On the **Design tab**, in the **Tools group**, click the **Relationship Report** button. If you are submitting paper assignments, on the **Print Preview tab**, click the **Print** button, click **OK**, and then click the **Close Print Preview** button. To submit electronically, follow your instructor's directions. On the **Quick Access Toolbar**, click the **Save** button, and then click **OK** to accept the default name. **Close** all open objects, and then **Close** the **Navigation Pane**.

7. Click the **Create tab**, and then in the **Other group**, click the **Query Design** button. **Add** the **13D Concerts** table to the table area, **Close** the **Show Table** dialog box, and then expand the field list. Add the following fields to the design grid in the order given: **Concert Name**, **Box Office Receipts**, and **Concert Location**. Click in the **Sort** row under **Concert Location**, click the **Sort arrow**, and then click **Ascending**. On the **Criteria** row,

(Project 13D–Concerts and Sponsors continues on the next page)

Content-Based Assessments

(Project 13D–Concerts and Sponsors continued)

under **Box Office Receipts**, type **800** and then press ⏎. **Run** the query. Only one concert—*Southern Hospitality Tour*—had Box Office Receipts of exactly $800.

8. On the **Home tab**, in the **Views group**, click the **View** button to switch to **Design** view. On the **Criteria** row, under **Box Office Receipts**, delete the existing criteria, type **>800** and then press ⏎. **Run** the query. Eight concerts had Box Office Receipts greater than $800. Switch to **Design** view, change the **Box Office Receipts** criteria to **<800** and then **Run** the query. Eight concerts had Box Office Receipts less than $800. Switch to **Design** view, change **Box Office Receipts** criteria to **>=800** and then **Run** the query. Nine records meet the criteria. This query answers the questions, *Which concerts had Box Office Receipts of $800 or more, what was the amount of the Box Office Receipts, and where was each concert held?* **Save** the query as **13D $800 or More Firstname Lastname Print** or submit electronically as directed.

9. From the **Office** menu, click **Save As**, type **13D Concerts Jan-Apr Firstname Lastname** and then click **OK**. Switch to **Design** view. From the **13D Concerts** field list, add **Date** to the fourth field in the design grid. On the **Criteria** row, under **Box Office Receipts**, delete the existing criteria so that the query is not restricted by receipts. Click in the **Sort** row under **Concert Location**, click the **Sort arrow**, and then click **(not sorted)**. Click in the **Sort** row under **Date**, click the **Sort arrow**, and then click **Ascending**. Click in the **Criteria** row under **Date**, type **Between 01/01/2009 And 04/30/2009** and then press ⏎. **Run** the query; five records meet the criteria. This query

answers the question, *What are the name, box office receipts, location, and date, in chronological order, of concerts held between January 1, 2009, and April 30, 2009?* **Print** or submit electronically as directed. **Close** the query and click **Yes** to save the changes to the design.

10. **Create** a query in **Query Design View**. **Add** the **13D Concerts** table to the table area, and then expand the field list. Add the following fields to the design grid in the order given: **Concert Name**, **Concert Location**, and **Box Office Receipts**. On the **Criteria** row under **Concert Location**, type **Port Community Theater** and then press ⏭. On the **Criteria** row under **Box Office Receipts**, type **<=1000** and then press ⏭. **Run** the query; two records display. This query answers the question, *Which concerts that were held at the Port Community Theater had Box Office Receipts of $1,000 or less?* Switch to **Design** view, and then in the **Concert Location** field, clear the **Show** check box. **Run** the query. Recall that if all the records have the same criteria in one of the fields, it is not necessary to display that field in the query results. **Save** the query as **13D Port Community Theater $1000 or Less Firstname Lastname** and then **Print** or submit the query electronically. **Close** the query.

11. **Create** a query in **Query Design View**. **Add** the **13D Concerts** table to the table area, and then expand the field list. From the **13D Concerts** table, add the following fields to the design grid in the order given: **Concert Name**, **Concert Location**, **Box Office Receipts**, and **Date**. On the **Criteria** row, under **Concert Location**, type **Port Community Theater** On the **or** row, under **Concert Location**, type **Mitchell Events**

(Project 13D–Concerts and Sponsors continues on the next page)

Content-Based Assessments

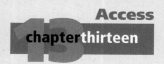

(Project 13D–Concerts and Sponsors continued)

Center and then press Enter. **Run** the query. Twelve records meet the criteria. This query answers the question, *How many concerts were held at either the Port Community Theater or the Mitchell Events Center?*

12. Switch to **Design** view. On the **or** row, under **Concert Location** delete the text. On the **Criteria** row, under **Concert Location**, delete the existing text, type **Port Community Theater Or Mitchell Events Center** and then press Tab. On the **Criteria** row, under **Box Office Receipts**, type **>1000** and then press Tab. **Run** the query. Four records display. This query answers the questions, *Which concerts held at either the Port Community Theater or the Mitchell Events Center had Box Office Receipts of more than $1,000 and on what dates were the concerts held?* **Save** the query as **13D PCT or Mitchell Over $1000 Firstname Lastname** and then **Print** or submit the query electronically. **Close** the query.

13. **Create** a query in **Query Design View**, **Add** both tables to the table area, and then expand the field lists. Reposition the field lists so that **13D Sponsors** is on the left side. From the **13D Sponsors** field list, add the following fields to the design grid in the order given: **Sponsor ID**, **Sponsor Name**, and **Phone Number**. Click in the **Sort** row under **Sponsor Name**, click the **Sort arrow**, and then click **Ascending**. From the **13D Concerts** field list, add the following fields to the design grid in the order give: **Concert Name**, **Concert Location**, **Box Office Receipts**, and **Date**.

14. On the **Criteria** row, under **Concert Location**, type **Port Community Theater** and then click in the **or** row, under **Concert Location**. Type **Mitchell Events**

Center and then press Enter. **Run** the query. Twelve records display. Switch to **Design** view. From the **13D Sponsors** field list, drag **Web Address** to the design grid on top of **Phone Number**, and then release the mouse button to insert the new field to the right of **Sponsor Name**. Select the **Sponsor ID** field and then delete it.

15. In the design grid, select the **Box Office Receipts** field, and then drag it to the first field position in the grid. Delete the **Phone Number** and **Date** fields. **Run** the query. This query answers the question, *What were the box office receipts, sponsor name, sponsor Web address, concert name, and concert location of all concerts held at either the Port Community Theater or the Mitchell Events Center, sorted alphabetically by sponsor name?*

16. Select all of the columns in the query results, and then double-click any column border to apply **Best Fit**. **Save** the query as **13D Receipts and Sponsors PCT and Mitchell Firstname Lastname** and then display the query results in **Print Preview**. Change the orientation to **Landscape**, change the **Margins** to **Normal**, and then **Print** or submit the query electronically. **Close** the query, **Open** the **Navigation Pane**, and then notice that the query displays under *both* tables from which it retrieved records. **Close** the **Navigation Pane**.

17. **Create** a query in **Query Design View**, **Add** both tables to the table area, and then expand the field lists. Reposition the field lists so that **13D Sponsors** is on the left side. From the **13D Sponsors** table, add the **Sponsor Name** field to the design grid. From the **13D Concerts** table, add the **Concert Name** field to the design grid. On

(Project 13D–Concerts and Sponsors continues on the next page)

Content-Based Assessments

(Project 13D–Concerts and Sponsors continued)

the **Criteria** row, under **Sponsor Name**, type **Florida*** and then press Enter. **Run** the query and widen the **Sponsor Name** column to display all of the data. Three sponsors have names that begin with *Florida*.

18. Switch to **Design** view. On the **Criteria** row, under **Sponsor Name**, delete the text. On the **Criteria** row, under **Concert Name**, type ***Festival** and then press Enter. **Run** the query; five Concert Names end with the word *Festival*. Switch to **Design** view. On the **Criteria** row, under **Sponsor Name**, type ***Radio*** and then press Enter. **Run** the query; two records have the word *Radio* somewhere in the Sponsor Name and the word *Festival* at the end of the Concert Name. This query answers the question, *Which radio stations are sponsoring Festival-type concerts?* **Save** the query as **13D Radio Festivals Firstname Lastname** and then **Print** or submit the query electronically. **Close** the query.

19. **Create** a query in **Query Design View**. **Add** both tables to the table area, and then expand the field lists. Reposition the field lists so that **13D Sponsors** is on the left side. From the field lists, add the following fields to the design grid in the order given: **Concert ID**, **Sponsor Name**, and **Box Office Receipts**. Click in the **Sort** row under **Concert ID**, click the **Sort arrow**, and then click **Ascending**. Sponsors have indicated that they will donate an additional amount to the Music Department based on 50 percent of the Box Office Receipts. On the **Field** row, right-click in the first empty column to display a shortcut menu, and then click **Zoom**. In the **Zoom** dialog box, type **Matching Donation:[Box Office Receipts]*0.5** and then click **OK**. **Run** the query to view the new field—*Matching Donation*.

20. Switch to **Design** view. In the **Field** row, in the first empty column, right-click, and then click **Zoom**. In the **Zoom** dialog box, type **Total Receipts:[Box Office Receipts]+ [Matching Donation]** and then click **OK**. In the **Field** row, click in the **Matching Donation** field (fourth column), and then on the **Design tab**, in the **Show/Hide group**, click the **Property Sheet** button. In the **Property Sheet**, click in the **Format** property setting box, click the **arrow**, and then click **Currency**. **Close** the **Property Sheet**.

21. **Run** the query. This query answers the question, *In ascending order by Concert ID, assuming each sponsor makes a matching 50 percent donation based on each concert's Box Office Receipts, what are the Sponsor Name, Box Office Receipts, Matching Donation, and Total Receipts for each concert?* Select all of the columns, and then apply **Best Fit**. **Save** the query as **13D Matching Sponsor Donation Firstname Lastname** and then display the query results in **Print Preview**. Change the orientation to **Landscape**, and then **Print** or submit the query electronically. **Close** the query.

22. **Create** a query in **Query Design View**. **Add** the **13D Concerts** table to the table area, expand the field list, and then add the **Box Office Receipts** field to the design grid. On the **Design tab**, in the **Show/Hide group**, click the **Totals** button, which adds a *Total* row as the third row in the design grid. On the **Total** row, under **Box Office Receipts**, click in the **Group By** box, and then click the **arrow**. In the list of functions, click **Min**, and then **Run** the query. The lowest amount of Box Office Receipts for any concert was *$400.00*.

(Project 13D–Concerts and Sponsors continues on the next page)

Content-Based Assessments

(Project 13D–Concerts and Sponsors continued)

23. Switch to **Design** view. On the **Total** row, under **Box Office Receipts**, select the **Max** function, and then **Run** the query. The highest amount of Box Office Receipts for any concert was *$2,500.00*. Switch to **Design** view. On the **Total** row, under **Box Office Receipts**, select the **Avg** function, and then **Run** the query. The average Box Office Receipts for each concert was *$1,027.94*. Using the same technique, select the **Sum** function and then **Run** the query. The total Box Office Receipts for all the concerts was *$17,475.00*.

24. Apply **Best Fit** to the **SumOfBox Office Receipts** column. Switch to **Design** view. Add the **Sponsor ID** field to the design grid, and then **Run** the query. Concerts sponsored by *SPONSOR-101* had the largest amount of Box Office Receipts— *$4,975.00*.

25. Switch to **Design** view. In the design grid, select and delete the **Sponsor ID** field, and then add the **Concert Location** field to the design grid. **Run** the query. This query answers the question, *What are the total Box Office Receipts for each concert location?* **Save** the query as **13D Totals by Concert Location Firstname Lastname** and then **Print** or submit the query electronically. **Close** the query. From the **Office** menu, click **Close Database**, and then at the right side of the Access title bar, click the **Close** button to close the Access program. Alternatively, from the Office menu, click Exit Access.

End You have completed Project 13D

Content-Based Assessments

Mastering Access

Project 13E — Grants and Organizations

In this project, you will apply the skills you practiced from the Objectives in Projects 13A and 13B.

Objectives: 1. *Open an Existing Database;* **2.** *Create Table Relationships;* **4.** *Create a Query in Design View;* **5.** *Create a new Query from an Existing Query;* **6.** *Sort Query Results;* **7.** *Specify Criteria in a Query;* **8.** *Create a New Table by Importing an Excel Spreadsheet;* **9.** *Specify Numeric Criteria in a Query;* **10.** *Use Compound Criteria;* **11.** *Create a Query Based on More Than One Table;* **12.** *Use Wildcards in a Query;* **14.** *Group Data and Calculate Statistics in a Query.*

In the following Mastering Access project, you will assist Peter Donahue, Director of Grants for the college, in using his database to answer questions about public and private grants awarded to college departments. Your query results will look similar to those shown in Figure 13.61.

For Project 13E, you will need the following files:

a13E_Grants_Organizations
a13E_Organizations (Excel file)

You will save your database as
13E_Grants_Organizations_Firstname_Lastname

Figure 13.61

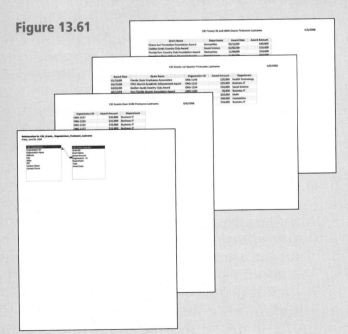

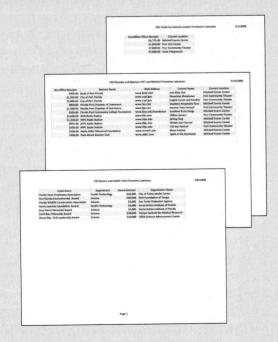

(Project 13E–Grants and Organizations continues on the next page)

(Project 13E–Grants and Organizations continued)

1. Navigate to the location where the student files for this textbook are saved. Locate **a13E_Grants_Organizations** and click one time to select the file. **Copy** and then **Paste** the file to your **Access Chapter 13** folder. **Rename** the file as 13E_Grants_Organizations_Firstname_Lastname and then **Start** Access. Navigate to your **Access Chapter 13** folder, open **13E_Grants_Organizations**, and then **Enable this content**.

2. **Import** the **a13E_Organizations** Excel spreadsheet from the student data files that accompany this textbook into the current database. Use the first row of the spreadsheet as the column headings, and then choose the **Organization ID** field as the primary key. Name the table **13E Organizations**.

3. **Open** the **Navigation Pane**, open the database tables, and then examine their fields and records to become familiar with the data. **Close** the tables, and then **Close** the **Navigation Pane**. Create a one-to-many relationship between the **13E Organizations** table and the **13E Grants Awarded** table based on the **Organization ID** field, and then **Enforce Referential Integrity**; *one* Organization can award *many* Grants. Create a **Relationship Report**, saving it with the default name. **Print** or submit the report electronically as directed, and then **Close** all open objects.

4. **Create** a query in **Query Design** view using both tables to answer the question, *What are the Organization ID and Award Amount for grants greater than $10,000 and to what Departments (in alphabetical order) were the grants awarded?* Display the fields in the order listed in the question. Twelve records meet the criteria.

Apply **Best Fit** to the columns in the query results. **Save** the query as **13E Grants Over $10K Firstname Lastname** and then **Print** or submit the query electronically as directed. Leave the query open.

5. Create a query from the **13E Grants Over $10K** query. **Save As 13E Grants 1st Quarter Firstname Lastname** and then redesign the query to answer the question, *In chronological order by Award Date, which Grants were awarded between 01/01/2009 and 03/31/2009, from which Organization ID, for what amount, and to which Department?* Display the fields in the order listed in the question, display *only* the fields listed in the question, sort *only* on one field, and do *not* restrict the amount. Seven records meet the criteria. Apply **Best Fit** to the columns in the query results. In **Print Preview**, set the orientation to **Landscape**, and then **Print** or submit the query electronically as directed. **Close** the query, saving the design changes.

6. **Create** a query in **Query Design View**. Use the **13E Grants Awarded** table to answer the question, *What are the names of privately funded grants awarded to either the Social Science or Humanities department, on what date were they awarded, and with the largest grants listed first, for what amount?* (Hint: Open the 13E Grants Awarded table to see how the data is stored in the fields.) Display the results in the order listed in the question. Nine records meet the criteria. (Hint: If 11 records display, return to **Design** view and use the OR operator to place the department criteria on one line in the design grid.) Do *not* show the type of grant in the query results. **Save** the query as **13E Private SS and HMN Grants Firstname**

(Project 13E–Grants and Organizations continues on the next page)

Content-Based Assessments

(Project 13E–Grants and Organizations continued)

Lastname and then display the query results in **Print Preview**. Set the orientation to **Landscape**, and then **Print** or submit the query electronically as directed. **Close** the query.

7. **Create** a query in **Query Design View** using both tables to answer the question, *Which grants were awarded to either the Science or Health Technology department, for what amount, and, from which Organization Name (in alphabetical order)?* Seven records meet the criteria. Apply **Best Fit** to the columns in the query results. **Save** the query as **13E Science and Health Tech Firstname Lastname** and then display the query results in **Print Preview**. Set the orientation to **Landscape**, and then **Print** or submit the query electronically as directed. **Close** the query.

8. **Create** a query in **Query Design View** using both tables to answer the question, *Which grants were awarded from organizations that are Foundations, what is the name of the organization, what is the amount of the grant listed in descending order by amount, and what is the name*

and phone number of the organization contact? (Hint: Use a wildcard in the format of **Foundation** to find organization names containing the word *Foundation*.) Fourteen records meet the criteria. Apply **Best Fit** to the columns in the query results. **Save** the query as **13E Foundation Grants Firstname Lastname** and then display the query results in **Print Preview**. Change the orientation to **Landscape**, set the **Margins** to **Normal**, and then **Print** or submit the query electronically as directed. **Close** the query.

9. **Create** a query in **Query Design View**. Using the **13E Grants Awarded** table and the **Sum** aggregate function, answer the question, *Listed from the largest amounts to the smallest, what are the total Award Amounts for each Department?* The *Humanities* Department received *$93,000.00*. Apply **Best Fit** to the columns in the query results. **Save** the query as **13E Totals by Department Firstname Lastname** and then **Print** or submit the query electronically as directed. **Close** the query, **Close** the Database, and then **Exit** Access.

End You have completed Project 13E

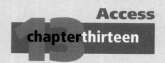
Project 13F — Events and Clients

In this project, you will apply skills you practiced from the Objectives in Projects 13A and 13B.

Objectives: 1. *Open an Existing Database;* **2.** *Create Table Relationships;* **4.** *Create a Query in Design View;* **5.** *Create a New Query from an Existing Query;* **6.** *Sort Query Results;* **7.** *Specify Criteria in a Query;* **8.** *Create a New Table by Importing an Excel Spreadsheet;* **9.** *Specify Numeric Criteria in a Query;* **10.** *Use Compound Criteria;* **11.** *Create a Query Based on More Than One Table;* **12.** *Use Wildcards in a Query;* **13.** *Use Calculated Fields in a Query;* **14.** *Group Data and Calculate Statistics in a Query.*

In the following Mastering Access project, you will assist Peter Steinmetz, Facilities Manager at the college, in using his database to answer questions about facilities that the college rents to community and private organizations. Renting the facilities at times when they are not in use for college activities requires additional funding to maintain and staff the facilities. Your query results will look similar to those shown in Figure 13.62.

For Project 13F, you will need the following files:

a13F_Events_Clients
a13F_Rental_Clients (Excel file)

You will save your database as
13F_Events_Clients_Firstname_Lastname

Figure 13.62

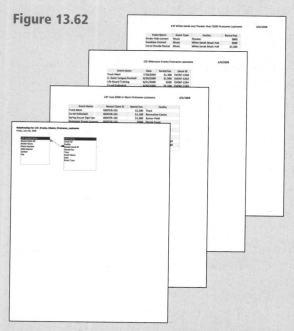

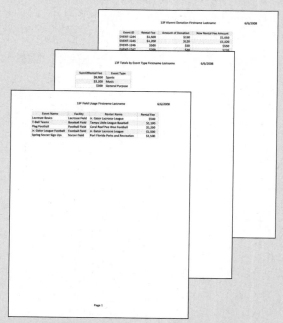

(Project 13F–Events and Clients continues on the next page)

Content-Based Assessments

(Project 13F–Events and Clients continued)

1. Navigate to the location where the student files for this textbook are saved. Locate **a13F_Events_Clients** and click one time to select the file. **Copy** and then **Paste** the file to your **Access Chapter 13** folder. **Rename** the file as 13F_Events_Clients_ Firstname_Lastname and then **Start** Access. Navigate to your **Access Chapter 13** folder, open **13F_Events_Clients**, and then **Enable this content**.

2. **Import** the **a13F_Rental_Clients** Excel spreadsheet from the student data files that accompany this textbook into the current database. Use the first row of the spreadsheet as the column headings, and then choose the **Rental Client ID** field as the primary key. Name the table **13F Rental Clients**

3. **Open** the **Navigation Pane**, open the database tables, and then examine their fields and records to become familiar with the data. **Close** the tables, and then **Close** the **Navigation Pane**. Create a one-to-many relationship between the **13F Rental Clients** table and the **13F Events** table based on the **Rental Client ID** field, and then **Enforce Referential Integrity**; *one* Rental Client can have *many* Events. Create a **Relationship Report**, saving it with the default name. **Print** or submit the report electronically as directed, and then **Close** all open objects, saving changes if prompted.

4. **Create** a query in **Query Design View** using the 13F Events table to answer the question, *What are the Event Name, Rental Client ID, and Rental Fee for events with fees greater than or equal to $500, in ascending order by Rental Client ID, and in which Facility was the event held?* Display the fields in the order listed in the question.

Eleven records meet the criteria. **Save** the query as **13F Fees $500 or More Firstname Lastname** and then **Print** or submit the query electronically as directed. Leave the query open.

5. **Create** a query from the **13F Fees $500 or More** query. **Save** the query as **13F Afternoon Events Firstname Lastname** and then redesign the query to answer the question, *Which Events were held in the Afternoon between 07/01/2009 and 08/31/2009, in chronological order by date, what was the Rental Fee, and what was the Event ID?* (Hint: Open the 13F Events table to see how the data is stored in the fields.) Display the fields in the order listed in the question, but do *not* display the **Time** field in the result. Do *not* restrict the result by Rental Fee. Four records meet the criteria. **Print** or submit the query electronically as directed. **Close** the query, saving design changes.

6. **Create** a query in **Query Design View** using the **13F Events** table to answer the question, *Which Events and Event Types were held in either the White Sands Music Hall or the Theater that had Rental Fees greater than $500?* Three records meet the criteria. Apply **Best Fit** to the columns in the query results. **Save** the query as **13F White Sands and Theater Over $500 Firstname Lastname** and then **Print** or submit the query electronically as directed. **Close** the query.

7. **Create** a query in **Query Design View** using both tables to answer the question, *Which Events were held on one of the sports fields, for which Renter Name, and what was the Rental Fee in order of lowest fee to highest fee?* (Hint: Use a wildcard with the word *Field*.) Five records meet the

(Project 13F–Events and Clients continues on the next page)

(Project 13F–Events and Clients continued)

criteria. Apply **Best Fit** to the columns in the query results. **Save** the query as **13F Field Usage Firstname Lastname** and then **Print** or submit the query electronically as directed. **Close** the query.

8. **Create** a query in **Query Design View**. Using the **13F Events** table and the **Sum** aggregate function, answer the question, *In descending order by total, what are the total Rental Fees for each Event Type?* Change the properties of all appropriate fields to display in **Currency** format with **0** decimal places. For a *Sports* Event Type, Rental Fees totaled *$8,900.* Apply **Best Fit** to the columns in the query results. **Save** the query as **13F Totals by Event Type Firstname Lastname** and then **Print** or submit the query electronically as directed. **Close** the query.

9. The college Alumni Association will donate money to the Building Fund in an amount based on 10 percent of total facility rental fees. **Create** a query in **Query Design View** to answer the question, *In ascending order by Event ID, what will the total of each Rental Fee be if the Alumni Association donates an additional 10 percent of each fee?* (Hint: First compute the amount of the donation and name the new field **Amount of Donation** and then calculate the new rental fee and name the new field **New Rental Fee Amount**) As necessary, change the properties of the new fields to display in **Currency** format with **0** decimal places. For *EVENT-1244,* the *Amount of Donation* is *$150* and the *New Rental Fee Amount* is *$1,650.* Apply **Best Fit** to the columns in the query results. **Save** the query as **13F Alumni Donation Firstname Lastname** and then **Print** or submit the query electronically as directed. **Close** the query, **Close** the Database, and then **Exit** Access.

End You have completed Project 13F

Access

chapterthirteen

Mastering Access

Project 13G—Students and Scholarships

In this project, you will apply the skills you practiced from all the Objectives in Projects 13A and 13B.

Objectives: 1. *Open an Existing Database;* **2.** *Create Table Relationships;* **3.** *Sort Records in a Table;* **4.** *Create a Query in Design View;* **5.** *Create a New Query From an Existing Query;* **6.** *Sort Query Results;* **7.** *Specify Criteria in a Query;* **8.** *Create a New Table by Importing an Excel Spreadsheet;* **9.** *Specify Numeric Criteria in a Query;* **10.** *Use Compound Criteria;* **11.** *Create a Query Based on More Than One Table;* **12.** *Use Wildcards in a Query;* **13.** *Use Calculated Fields in a Query;* **14.** *Group Data and Calculate Statistics in a Query.*

In the following Mastering Access project, you will assist Diane Nguyen, director of academic scholarships, in using her database to answer questions about academic scholarships awarded to students. Your query results will look similar to those shown in Figure 13.63.

For Project 13G, you will need the following files:

a13G_Students_Scholarships
a13G_Students (Excel file)

You will save your database as
13G_Students_Scholarships_Firstname_Lastname

Figure 13.63

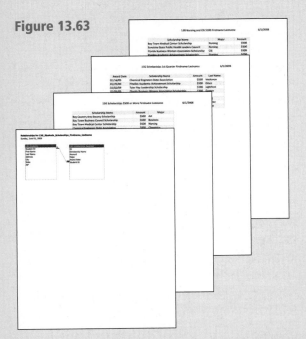

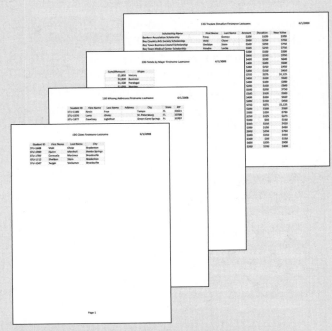

(Project 13G–Students and Scholarships continues on the next page)

(Project 13G–Students and Scholarships continued)

1. Navigate to the location where the student files for this textbook are saved. Locate **a13G_Students_Scholarships** and click one time to select the file. **Copy** and then **Paste** the file to your **Access Chapter 13** folder. **Rename** the file as **13G_Students_Scholarships_Firstname_Lastname** and then **Start** Access. Navigate to your **Access Chapter 13** folder, open **13G_Students_Scholarships**, and then **Enable this content**.

2. **Import** the **a13G_Students** Excel spreadsheet from the student data files that accompany this textbook into the current database. Use the first row of the spreadsheet as the column headings, and choose the **Student ID** field as the primary key. Name the table **13G Students**

3. **Open** the **Navigation Pane**, open the two database tables, and then examine their fields and records to become familiar with the data. **Close** the tables, and then **Close** the **Navigation Pane**. Create a one-to-many relationship between the **13G Students** table and the **13G Scholarships Awarded** table based on the **Student ID** field, and then **Enforce Referential Integrity**; *one* student can have *many* scholarships. Create the **Relationship Report**, and then **Print** or submit the report electronically as directed, saving it with the default name. **Close** all open objects.

4. **Open** the **Navigation Pane**, display the **13G Students** table, and notice the + signs that indicate the relationships you created. **Close** the **Navigation Pane**. Perform a multiple-field sort on the table to sort students in alphabetic order by Last Name within City names that are also in alphabetical order. Remember to sort *first* by the innermost sort field. After examining the sorted table, **Clear All**

Sorts, **Close** the table, and do not save the changes.

5. **Create** a query in **Query Design View** using the **13G Scholarships Awarded** table to answer the question, *In alphabetical order by Scholarship Name, what are the Scholarship Name, Amount, and Major for scholarships greater than or equal to $500?* Display the fields in the order listed in the question. Ten records meet the criteria. **Save** the query as **13G Scholarships $500 or More Firstname Lastname** and then **Print** or submit the query electronically as directed. Leave the query open.

6. Create a query from the **13G Scholarships $500 or More** query. **Save** the query as **13G Scholarships 1st Quarter Firstname Lastname** and then redesign the query to answer the question, *In chronological order by Award Date, which scholarships were awarded between 01/01/2009 and 03/31/2009, for what amount, and what was the last name of the student?* Be sure the fields display in the order listed in the question, display *only* the fields listed in the question, do not restrict the amount, and sort only by date. Eight records meet the criteria. **Print** or submit the query electronically as directed. **Close** the query, saving the design changes.

7. **Create** a query in **Query Design View** using the **13G Scholarships Awarded** table to answer the question, *Which scholarships were awarded for either Nursing or CIS majors for amounts of more than $100, listed in descending order by amount?* Display the fields in the order listed in the question. Four records meet the criteria. (Hint: If five records display, switch to **Design** view and combine the majors on one criteria line using OR.) **Save** the query as **13G Nursing and CIS $100 Firstname Lastname** and then

(Project 13G–Students and Scholarships continues on the next page)

(Project 13G–Students and Scholarships continued)

Print or submit the query electronically as directed. **Close** the query.

8. **Create** a query in **Query Design View**. Use the **13G Students** table and a wild-card to answer the question, *In alphabetical order by Last Name, what are the Student ID, First Name, Last Name, and City of all students in cities that begin with the letter B?* Display the fields in the order listed in the question. Five records meet the criteria. **Save** the query as **13G Cities Firstname Lastname** and then **Print** or submit the query electronically as directed. **Close** the query.

9. **Create** a query in **Query Design View** using the **13G Students** table and all of the table's fields to answer the question, *For which students is the Address missing?* Three students are missing addresses. Apply **Best Fit** to the columns. **Save** the query as **13G Missing Addresses Firstname Lastname** and then **Print** or submit the query electronically as directed. **Close** the query.

10. **Create** a query in **Query Design View**. Use the **13G Scholarships Awarde**d table and the **Sum** aggregate function to answer the question, *In descending order by amount, what is the total scholarship amount for each Major?* Display the fields in the order listed in the question. Use the **Property Sheet** to display the sums in the **Currency** format with **0** decimal places. *History majors received $1,850 in scholarships.*

Apply **Best Fit** to the columns in the query results. **Save** the query as **13G Totals by Major Firstname Lastname** and then **Print** or submit the query electronically as directed. **Close** the query.

11. For each academic scholarship received by students, the Board of Trustees of the college will donate an amount equal to 50 percent of each scholarship. **Create** a query in **Query Design View**. Use both tables and calculated fields to answer the question, *In alphabetical order by scholarship name, and including the first and last name of the scholarship recipient, what will the value of each scholarship be if the Board of Trustees makes a matching 50 percent donation?* (Hint: First compute the amount of the donation, naming the new field **Donation** and then calculate the new scholarship value, naming the new field **New Value**) As necessary, change the properties of all the numeric fields to display in **Currency** format with **0** decimal places. For the *Bankers Association Scholarship*, the *Donation* is *$100* and the *New Value* is *$300*. Apply **Best Fit** to the columns in the query results. **Save** the query as **13G Trustee Donation Firstname Lastname** and then display the query results in **Print Preview**. Set the orientation to **Landscape**, and then **Print** or submit the query electronically as directed. **Close** the query, **Close** the Database, and then **Exit** Access.

End **You have completed Project 13G**

Mastering Access

Project 13H — *GO!* Fix It

In this project, you will apply the skills you practiced from the Objectives in Projects 13A and 13B.

For Project 13H, you will need the following file:

a13H_Division_Social_Science

You will save your document as
13H_Division_Social_Science_Firstname_Lastname

Navigate to the location where the student files for this textbook are saved. Locate **a13H_Division_Social_Science** and click one time to select the file. **Copy** and then **Paste** the file to your **Access Chapter 13** folder. **Rename** the file as **13H_Division_Social_Science_Firstname_Lastname** and then **Start** Access. Navigate to your **Access Chapter 13** folder, open **13H_Division_Social_Science**, and then **Enable this content**.

This database contains **five errors** that you must find and correct. Examine the tables and queries in the database, and then edit to correct the errors that you find. Types of errors could include:

- Missing or incorrect data in tables, queries, forms, and reports such as file names, field names, types, descriptions, properties, records, and criteria.

- Table design errors such as primary key.

- Query design errors such as field, table, show, sort, and criteria.

- Forms design errors such as form header and footer, page header and footer, detail, and layout.

- Reports design errors such as report header and footer, page header and footer, detail, and layout.

- Page setup errors such as margins, orientation, layout, or alignment.

To complete the project, you should know:

- There is no table relationship between the Faculty table and the Course Schedule table. Create the relationship and the report; one faculty member can teach many courses.

- Examine and correct any queries that do not accurately reflect the query name. Add your first name and last name to the query name.

Print the relationship report and the four queries or submit your database as directed.

 End **You have completed Project 13H** ——————

Outcomes-Based Assessments

Rubric

The following outcomes-based assessments are *open-ended assessments*. That is, there is no specific correct result; your result will depend on your approach to the information provided. Make *Professional Quality* your goal. Use the following scoring rubric to guide you in *how* to approach the problem and then to evaluate *how well* your approach solves the problem.

The *criteria*—Software Mastery, Content, Format and Layout, and Process—represent the knowledge and skills you have gained that you can apply to solving the problem. The *levels of performance*—Professional Quality, Approaching Professional Quality, or Needs Quality Improvements—help you and your instructor evaluate your result.

	Your completed project is of Professional Quality if you:	Your completed project is Approaching Professional Quality if you:	Your completed project Needs Quality Improvements if you:
1-Software Mastery	Choose and apply the most appropriate skills, tools, and features and identify efficient methods to solve the problem.	Choose and apply some appropriate skills, tools, and features, but not in the most efficient manner.	Choose inappropriate skills, tools, or features, or are inefficient in solving the problem.
2-Content	Construct a solution that is clear and well organized, contains content that is accurate, appropriate to the audience and purpose, and is complete. Provide a solution that contains no errors of spelling, grammar, or style.	Construct a solution in which some components are unclear, poorly organized, inconsistent, or incomplete. Misjudge the needs of the audience. Have some errors in spelling, grammar, or style, but the errors do not detract from comprehension.	Construct a solution that is unclear, incomplete, or poorly organized; contains some inaccurate or inappropriate content; and contains many errors of spelling, grammar, or style. Do not solve the problem.
3-Format and Layout	Format and arrange all elements to communicate information and ideas, clarify function, illustrate relationships, and indicate relative importance.	Apply appropriate format and layout features to some elements, but not others. Overuse features, causing minor distraction.	Apply format and layout that does not communicate information or ideas clearly. Do not use format and layout features to clarify function, illustrate relationships, or indicate relative importance. Use available features excessively, causing distraction.
4-Process	Use an organized approach that integrates planning, development, self-assessment, revision, and reflection.	Demonstrate an organized approach in some areas, but not others; or, use an insufficient process of organization throughout.	Do not use an organized approach to solve the problem.

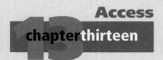

Problem Solving

Project 13I—Student Refunds

In this project, you will construct a solution by applying any combination of the skills you practiced from the Objectives in Projects 13A and 13B.

For Project 13I, you will need the following files:

a13I_Student_Refunds
a13I_Student_Refunds (Word document)

**You will save your database as
13I_Student_Refunds_Firstname_Lastname**

Start Microsoft Word, and then from your student files, open the Word document **a13I_Student_Refunds**. Use the skills you have practiced in this chapter to assist Kathy Knudsen, the Associate Dean of Student Services, in answering questions about student refunds in your database **13I_Student_Refunds_Firstname_Lastname**. Save queries that you create, include your name in the query title, and submit your queries as directed by your instructor. Record your answers to the questions in the Word document.

 End **You have completed Project 13I** ⎯⎯⎯⎯⎯⎯⎯⎯

Outcomes-Based Assessments

Access

chapter thirteen

Problem Solving

Project 13J — Leave

In this project, you will construct a solution by applying any combination of the skills you practiced from the Objectives in Projects 13A and 13B.

For Project 13J, you will need the following files:

a13J_Leave
a13J_Leave (Word document)

You will save your database as
13J_Leave_Firstname_Lastname

Start Microsoft Word, and then from your student files, open the Word document **a13J_Leave**. Use the skills you have practiced in this chapter to assist Gabe Stevens, the Director of Human Resources, in answering questions about employee leave time in your database **13J_Leave_Firstname_Lastname**. Save queries that you create, include your name in the query title, and submit your queries as directed by your instructor. Record your answers to the questions in the Word document.

End **You have completed Project 13J** —————————

Problem Solving

Project 13K — Coaches

In this project, you will construct a solution by applying any combination of the skills you practiced from the Objectives in Projects 13A and 13B.

For Project 13K, you will need the following files:

a13K_Coaches
a13K_Coaches (Word document)

You will save your database as
13K_Coaches_Firstname_Lastname

Start Microsoft Word, and then from your student files, open the Word document **a13K_Coaches**. Use the skills you have practiced in this chapter to assist Marcus Simmons, the Athletic Director, in answering questions about the coaches in your database **13K_Coaches_Firstname_Lastname**. Save queries that you create, include your name in the query title, and submit your queries as directed by your instructor. Record your answers to the questions in the Word document.

End You have completed Project 13K ——————————————

More on your Student CD

The instructions for the following additional end-of-chapter projects are on your student CD in the folder 03_additional_end_of_chapter_projects.

Content-Based Assessments

Project L Mastering Access — Apply the skills you practiced in Project A.

Project M Mastering Access — Apply the skills you practiced in Project B.

Project N Business Running Case — Apply the skills you practiced in Projects A and B while helping an entrepreneur with the daily tasks of running a business.

In each chapter, this project focuses on applying the skills you have practiced in Projects A and B to a business. The project related to this business runs throughout the textbook. You will see how the Office applications relate to the day-to-day operation of a small business called Nelson Architectural Planning.

Outcomes-Based Assessments

Project O Problem Solving — Construct a solution by applying any combination of the skills you practiced from Projects A and B.

Project P Problem Solving — Construct a solution by applying any combination of the skills you practiced from Projects A and B.

Project Q You and GO! — Construct a solution that applies to your own life by applying any combination of the skills you practiced from Projects A and B.

Project R GO! with Help — Practice using Microsoft Office's Help Feature.

Project S Group Business Running Case — Work as part of a group to apply the skills you have gained thus far to help the Bell Orchid Hotel Group achieve its business goals.

Multimedia

The following multimedia accompany this textbook:

Companion Web site
www.prenhall.com/go — An interactive Web site designed to reinforce and test your understanding of the skills in this chapter.

AV-EDDs — In the folder in the front of this book you will find videos that demonstrate the objectives of the A and B projects in this chapter. These may help you understand how to complete the projects in this book.

Video Podcasts — In the folder in the front of this book are videos that can be played on your iPod, MP3 player, or computer. These videos demonstrate how to complete the more challenging objectives in this textbook.

chapterfourteen

Forms, Filters, and Reports

OBJECTIVES

At the end of this chapter you will be able to:

1. Create a Form
2. Use a Form to Add and Delete Records
3. Create a Form by Using the Form Wizard
4. Modify a Form in Design View and in Layout View
5. Filter Records

OUTCOMES

Mastering these objectives will enable you to:

PROJECT 14A
Create Forms to Enter and Display Data in a Database

6. Create a Report by Using the Report Tool
7. Create a Report by Using the Blank Report Tool
8. Create a Report by Using the Report Wizard
9. Modify the Design of a Report
10. Print a Report and Keep Data Together

PROJECT 14B
Create Reports to Display Database Information

Baltimore Area Job Fair

The Baltimore Area Job Fair is a nonprofit organization that brings together employers and job seekers in the Baltimore and Washington, D.C. metropolitan areas. Each year the organization holds a number of targeted job fairs, and the annual Greater Baltimore Job Fair draws over 1,000 employers in more than 70 industries, and registers more than 4,000 candidates. Candidates pay a small registration fee. Employers pay to display and present at the fairs, and to have access to candidate resumes. Candidate resumes and employer postings are managed by a state-of-the-art database system, allowing participants quick and accurate access to job data and candidate qualifications.

© Mark Wilson / Getty Images, Inc.—Liaison

Forms, Filters, and Reports

You can both enter and view information directly in database tables. However, for entering and viewing information, it is usually easier to use an Access form. You can design forms to display one record at a time, with fields placed in the same order to match a paper source document. When the form on the screen matches the layout of information on the paper form, it is easier to enter the new information. Records in a form or table can be filtered to display only a portion of the total records based on matching specific values.

When viewing information, it is usually easier to view only one record at a time instead of all of the records in a table. For example, your college counselor can look at a college transcript in a nicely laid-out form on the screen without seeing the records of other students at the same time.

In Access, reports summarize data in a database in a professional-looking manner that is suitable for printing. The design of a report can be modified so that the final report is laid out in a format that is useful to the person reading it. In this chapter, you will create and modify forms and reports for Access databases.

Project 14A **Candidate Interviews**

Local employers and candidates who are seeking jobs get together at the two-day Greater Baltimore Job Fair. In Activities 14.01 through 14.10, you will assist Janna Sorokin, database manager for the Job Fair, in using an Access database to track the job candidates and the job interviews they have scheduled with employers during the fair event. Your completed database objects will look similar to those in Figure 14.1.

For Project 14A, you will need the following file:

a14A_Candidate_Interviews

You will save your database as
14A_Candidate_Interviews_Firstname_Lastname

14 A Candidates Input Form

Candidate ID#:	22155
First Name	Firstname
Last Name	Lastname
Phone Number	(443) 555-0765
College Major	Business
Internships Completed	Government

10A Candidates Input Form Firstname Lastname

14A Candidates

Candidate ID#:	22155
Candidate First Name:	Firstname
Candidate Last Name:	Lastname
College Major:	Business
Internships Completed:	Government
Phone Number:	(443) 555-0765
Registration Fee:	$10.00
Date Fee Collected:	10/10/2009

Figure 14.1
Project 14A—Candidate Interviews

Objective 1
Create a Form

A *form* is an Access object you can use to enter, edit, or display data from a table or a query. One typical use of a form is to control access to the data. For example, in a college registration system, you could design a form for Registration Assistants who can see and enter the courses scheduled and fees paid by an individual student. However, they cannot see or enter grades or other personal information in the student's record. Think of a form as a window through which others see and access your database.

Some Access forms display only one record at a time; other forms display multiple records at the same time. A form that displays only one record at a time is useful not only to the individual who performs the *data entry*—typing in the actual records—but also to anyone who has the job of viewing information in a database. For example, when you visit the Records office at your college to obtain a transcript, someone displays your record on a screen. For the viewer, it is much easier to look at one record at a time, using a form, than to look at all of the student records in the database.

Activity 14.01 Creating a Form

There are several ways to create a form in Access, but the fastest and easiest way is to use the *Form tool*. With a single mouse click, all of the fields from the underlying data source (table or query) are placed on the form. You can use the new form immediately, or you can modify it in Layout view or in Design view.

The Form tool incorporates all of the information—both the field names and the individual records—from an existing table or query, and then instantly creates the form for you. Records that you edit or create using a form automatically update the underlying table or tables. In this activity, you will create a form, and then use it to add new interview records to the database.

1 Click **Start**, and then on the **Start menu**, click **Computer**. Navigate to the location where you are saving your projects for this chapter. Create a new folder and name it **Access Chapter 14**

2 Navigate to the student files for this textbook. Locate **a14A_Candidate_ Interviews** and click one time to select the file. **Copy** and then **Paste** the file to your **Access Chapter 14** folder. **Rename** the file as **14A_ Candidate_Interviews_Firstname_Lastname** and then **Start** Access. Navigate to your **Access Chapter 14** folder, open **14A_Candidate_ Interviews**, and then **Enable this content**.

3 **Open** >> the **Navigation Pane**. Click the **Database Tools tab**, and then in the **Show/Hide group**, click the **Relationships** button. Compare your screen with Figure 14.2. If your relationships do not display, in the Relationships group, click the All Relationships button.

> At the Job Fair event, *one* candidate can have interviews with *many* organizations. Thus, a one-to-many relationship has been established between the 14A Candidates table and the 14A Interviews table using Candidate ID# as the common field.

Figure 14.2

Join line with symbols indicating one-to-many relationship and referential integrity

Candidate ID# is common field

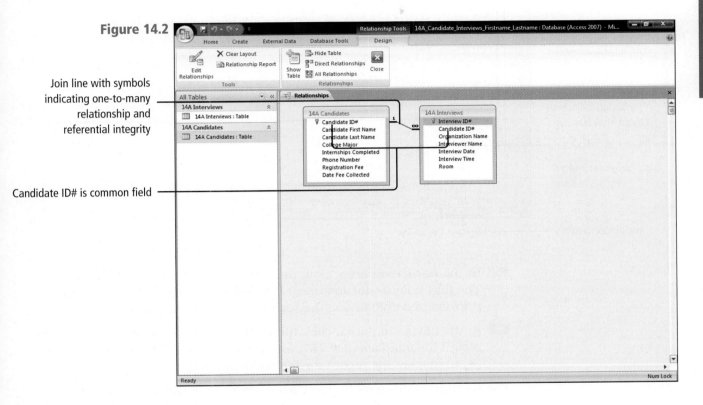

4 In the **Relationships group**, click the **Close** button to close the **Relationships window**. If prompted to save your changes, click No.

5 From the **Navigation Pane**, open the **14A Interviews** table, and notice the seven fields—*Interview ID#*, *Candidate ID#*, *Organization Name*, *Interviewer Name*, *Interview Date*, *Interview Time*, and *Room*. **Close** × the **14A Interviews** table.

6 In the **Navigation Pane**, be sure the **14A Interviews** table is still selected. Click the **Create tab**, and then in the **Forms group**, click the **Form** button. **Close** « the **Navigation Pane**, and then compare your screen with Figure 14.3.

> Access creates the form based on the currently selected object—the 14A Interviews table—and displays the form in *Layout view*. In Layout view, changes can be made to the form while it is displaying data. For example, you can adjust the size of the text boxes to fit the data. You can use Layout view for many of the changes you might need to make to a form.

> Access creates the form in a simple top-to-bottom layout, with all seven fields in the table lined up in a single column. The data for the first record in the table displays in the fields.

Figure 14.3

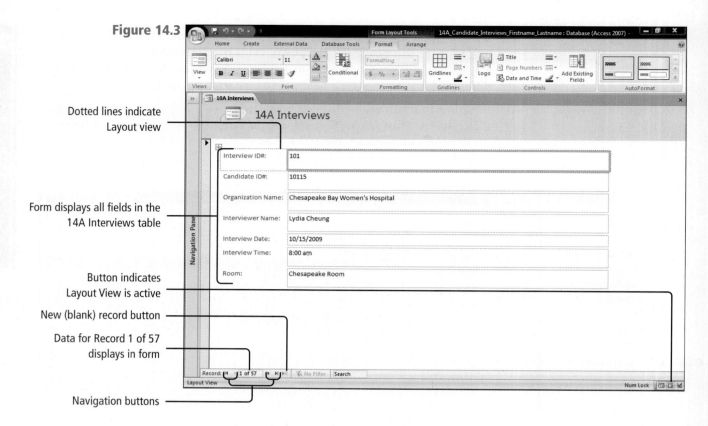

Dotted lines indicate Layout view

Form displays all fields in the 14A Interviews table

Button indicates Layout View is active

New (blank) record button

Data for Record 1 of 57 displays in form

Navigation buttons

7 In the navigation area, click the **Next record** button four times. The fifth record—for *Interview ID# 105*—displays. Use the navigation buttons to scroll among the records to display any single record.

8 In the navigation area, click the **Last record** button to display the record for *Interview ID# 157*, and then click the **First record** button to display the record for *Interview ID# 101*.

9 From the **Office** menu , click **Save** to save this form for future use. In the **Save As** dialog box, name the form **14A Interviews Form** and click **OK**. **Close** the form object.

10 **Open** the **Navigation Pane**, and notice that your new form displays under the table to which it is related—the **14A Interviews table**. Notice also that your new form displays the form icon.

11 In the **Navigation Pane**, select the **14A Candidates** table. Click the **Create tab**, and then in the **Forms group**, click the **Form** button. **Close** the **Navigation Pane**, and then compare your screen with Figure 14.4. Scroll down and notice that *Candidate ID# 10115*, for *Sally Marques*, has five interviews scheduled during the two-day Job Fair event.

If a form's record has related records in another table, the related records display in the form.

Figure 14.4

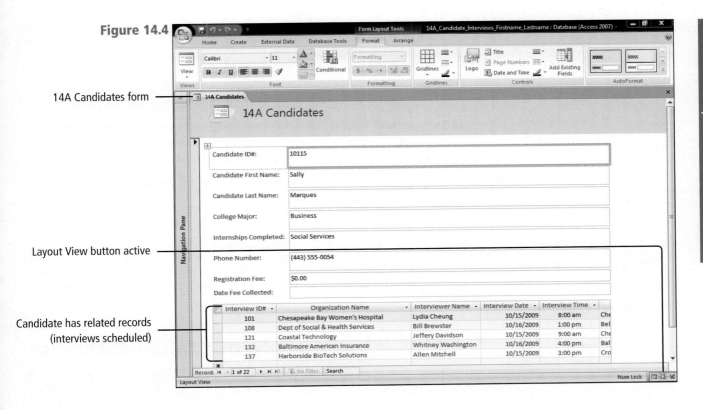

14A Candidates form

Layout View button active

Candidate has related records
(interviews scheduled)

12 **Close** ☒ the **14A Candidates** form. In the message box, click **Yes**.
In the **Save As** dialog box, name the form **14A Candidates Form** and
then click **OK**.

Objective 2
Use a Form to Add and Delete Records

By using a single-record form to add and delete records, you can reduce
the number of data entry errors because the person performing the data
entry is looking at only one record at a time. Recall that your database is
useful only if the information is accurate—just like your personal address
book is useful only if it contains accurate addresses and phone numbers.

Activity 14.02 Adding Records to a Table by Using a Form

Forms are based on, also referred to as *bound* to, the table where the
records are stored. When a record is entered in a form, the new record
is added to the underlying table. The reverse is also true—when a record
is added to a table, the new record can be viewed in the related form. In
this activity, you will add a new record to the 14A Interviews table by
using the form that you just created.

1 **Open** ⟫ the **Navigation Pane**, and then open **14A Interviews
Form**. **Close** ⟪ the **Navigation Pane**. In the navigation area, click the
New (blank) record button ▸▧.

A new blank form displays, indicated in the navigation area by *58 of 58*.
Adding a new record increases the number of records in the underlying
table to 58.

2 In the **Interview ID#** field, type **158** and then press Tab.

> Use the Tab key to move from field to field in a form. This is known as the *tab order*—the order in which the insertion point moves from one field to the next on a form when you press the Tab key. Alternatively, you can press the Enter key if there are no special buttons on the form.
>
> After you start typing, the pencil image displays in the *record selector* bar at the left—the bar used to select an entire record. The pencil image displays when a record is being created or edited.

3 Continue entering the data as shown in the following table, and then compare your screen with Figure 14.5.

Candidate ID#	Organization Name	Interviewer Name	Interview Date	Interview Time	Room
22101	Jefferson Business Consultants	Rob Jones	10/15/2009	4:00 pm	Hudson Room

Figure 14.5

Pencil image in record selector bar

New record entered using the form

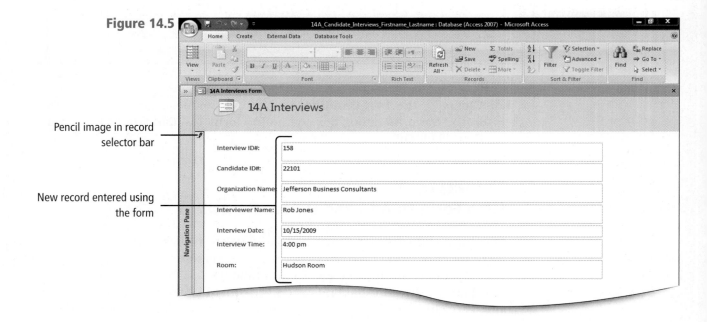

4 In the last field, press Tab to save the record. **Close** ✕ **14A Interviews Form. Open** ≫ the **Navigation Pane**, open **14A Candidates Form**, and then **Close** ≪ the **Navigation Pane**.

5 In the navigation area, click the **New (blank) record** button. In the blank form, and using your own first and last names, fill in the form using the information in the following table:

Candidate ID#	Candidate First Name	Candidate Last Name	College Major	Internships Completed	Phone Number	Registration Fee	Date Fee Collected
22155	Firstname	Lastname	Business	Government	(443) 555-0765	$10.00	10/10/2009

6 **Close** ☒ **14A Candidates Form**, **Open** ≫ the **Navigation Pane**, open the **14A Candidates table**, and then verify that your record as a candidate displays as the last record in the table. **Close** ☒ the table.

Activity 14.03 Deleting Records from a Table by Using a Form

You can delete records from a database table by using a form. In this activity, you will delete Interview ID# 103 because Jennifer Lee has notified Janna that she will be unable to meet with AAA Telecom.

1 From the **Navigation Pane**, open **14A Interviews Form**, click in the **Interview ID#** field, and then on the **Home tab**, in the **Find group**, click the **Find** button. Alternatively, press Ctrl + F to open the Find and Replace dialog box.

2 In the **Look In** box, notice that *Interview ID#* is displayed because you clicked in this field before opening the Find and Replace dialog box. In the **Find What** box, type **103** and then click **Find Next**. Compare your screen with Figure 14.6 and confirm that the record for **Interview ID# 103** displays.

Figure 14.6

Record for *Interview ID# 103* displays

Find and Replace dialog box

Find What box—type what you want to find here

Look In box indicates Access will search the *Interview ID#* field

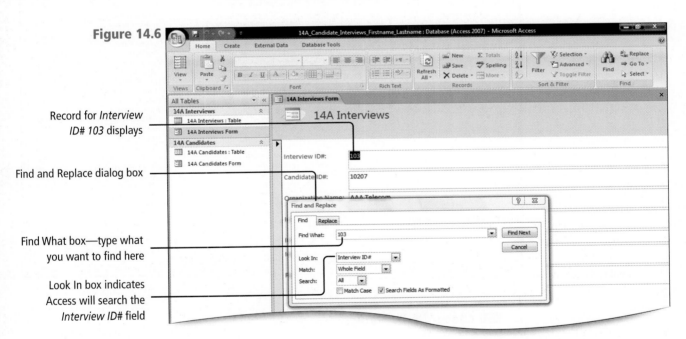

3 **Close** ☒ the **Find and Replace** dialog box.

4 On the **Home tab**, in the **Records group**, click the **Delete button arrow**. In the list, click **Delete Record** to delete the record for Interview ID# 103.

The record is removed from the screen, and a message displays alerting you that you are about to delete *1 record*. If you click Yes to delete the record, you cannot use the Undo button to reverse the action. If you delete a record by mistake, you must re-create the record by reentering the data.

5 In the message box, click **Yes** to delete the record. In the navigation area, notice that the number of records in the table is *57*. **Close** ✕ the form object.

6 In the **Navigation Pane**, open the **14A Interviews table**.

7 Examine the table to verify that the record for *Interview ID# 103* no longer exists. By default, tables are sorted in ascending order by their primary key field, which in this table is the **Interview ID#** field. Scroll down to verify that the new record you added for **Interview ID# 158** is stored in the table, and then compare your screen with Figure 14.7.

> Adding and deleting records in 14A Interviews Form updates the records stored in the 14A Interviews table.

Figure 14.7

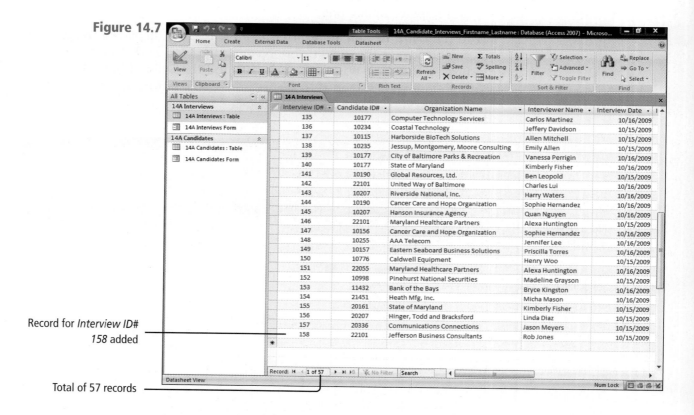

Record for *Interview ID# 158* added

Total of 57 records

8 **Close** ✕ the table.

Activity 14.04 Printing a Form

Like other Access objects, forms can be printed. Clicking the Print button while a form is displayed causes *all* of the records to print on separate pages in the form layout.

1 In the **Navigation Pane**, open **14A Candidates Form**. Press [Ctrl] + [F] to display the **Find and Replace** dialog box. In the **Find What** box, type **22155** In the **Look In** box, be sure that *Candidate ID#* is indicated, and then click **Find Next** to display the record with your name. **Close** ✕ the dialog box.

2 From the **Office** menu 🔘, click **Print**. In the **Print** dialog box, under **Print Range**, click the **Selected Record(s)** option button. In the lower left corner of the dialog box, click **Setup**.

3 In the **Page Setup** dialog box, click the **Columns tab**. Under **Column Size**, in the **Width** box, delete the existing text, type **7"** and then compare your screen with Figure 14.8.

> The width of the column is changed so that the form will print on one page. Forms are usually not printed, so the width of the column may be greater than the width of the paper on which you are printing.

Figure 14.8

Column Width set to 7"

Selected Record(s) option button selected

Your record displays

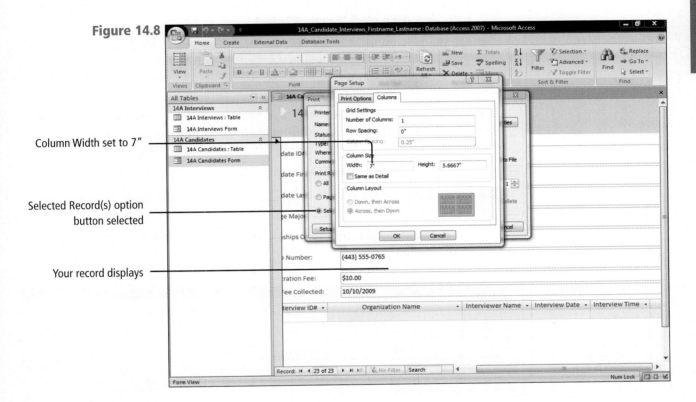

4 Click **OK** two times to print only your record in the form layout, or submit electronically as directed.

5 **Close** ✖ **14A Candidates Form**, saving changes to the design.

Objective 3
Create a Form by Using the Form Wizard

The Form tool creates an instant form in a simple top-to-bottom layout with all the fields lined up in a single column. The Form Wizard, on the other hand, creates a form quickly, but gives you more flexibility in the design, layout, and number of fields.

The design of the form should be planned for the individuals who use the form—either for entering new records or viewing records. For example, when your college counselor displays information to answer a question, it is easier for her or him to view the information spread out in a logical pattern across the screen rather than in one long column.

Activity 14.05 Creating a Form by Using the Form Wizard

By using the Form Wizard to create your form, you control how the form looks by selecting the fields to include, the style to apply, and the layout. When candidates register to attend the Job Fair and view job openings from exhibiting employers, they fill out a paper form. To make it easier to enter candidates into the database, you will create an Access form that matches the layout of the paper form. This will make it easier for the person entering the data into the database.

1 In the **Navigation Pane**, click to select the **14A Candidates table**. On the **Create tab**, in the **Forms group**, click the **More Forms** button, and then click **Form Wizard**.

> The Form Wizard walks you step by step through the process of creating a form by asking questions. In the first Form Wizard page, you select the fields you want on the form. The fields can come from more than one table or query.

2 Under **Tables/Queries**, in the text box, click the **arrow** to display a list of available tables and queries from which you can create the form.

> There are two tables from which you can create a new form.

3 Click **Table: 14A Candidates**, and then compare your screen with Figure 14.9.

> The field names from the 14A Candidates table display in the Available Fields list.

Figure 14.9

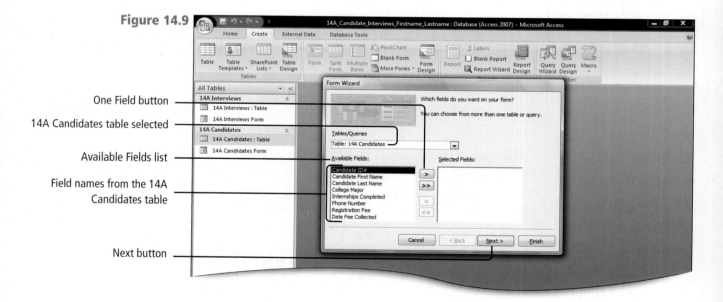

One Field button

14A Candidates table selected

Available Fields list

Field names from the 14A Candidates table

Next button

4 Using the **One Field** button ⊳, move the following fields to the **Selected Fields** list: **Candidate First Name**, **Candidate Last Name**, **College Major**, **Internships Completed**, and **Phone Number**. Alternatively, double-click a field name to move it to the Selected Fields list.

5 Click **Next**. Be sure **Columnar** is selected as the layout, and then click **Next**.

> Here you select the style for your form. The style controls the font, font size, font color, and background.

6 Click several of the styles to see the formatting. Scroll as necessary, click **Trek**, and then click **Next**. Under **What title do you want for your form?**, name the form **14A Candidates Input Form** and then click **Finish** to close the Wizard and create the form. Compare your screen with Figure 14.10. Leave the new form open for the next activity.

> The form is saved and added to the Navigation Pane under its related table.

Figure 14.10

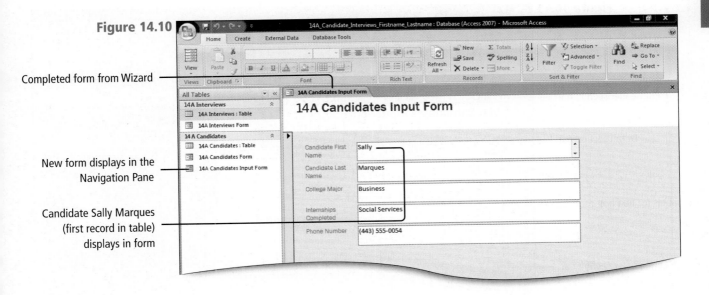

Completed form from Wizard

New form displays in the Navigation Pane

Candidate Sally Marques (first record in table) displays in form

Objective 4
Modify a Form in Design View and in Layout View

After you create a form, you can make changes to it. For example, you can resize the fields on the form for easier viewing or more efficient data entry.

Activity 14.06 Modifying a Form in Design View

Design view presents a detailed view of the structure of your form. Because the form is not actually running when displayed in Design view, you cannot see the underlying data. However, some tasks, such as resizing sections, must be completed in Design view.

1 **Close** « the **Navigation Pane** and be sure your **14A Candidates Input Form** displays. On the right side of the status bar, click the **Design View** button . Alternatively, in the Views group, click the View button arrow, and then click Design View. Compare your screen with Figure 14.11.

This form is divided into three sections—***Form Header***, ***Detail***, and ***Form Footer***—each designated by a ***section bar***. ***Controls*** are objects on a form that display data, perform actions, and let you view and work with information; controls make the form easier to use for the person entering or viewing data.

The most commonly used control is the ***text box control***, which typically displays data from the underlying table. A text box control is a ***bound control***—its source data comes from a table or query. Access places a ***label control*** to the left of a text box control, which contains descriptive information that displays on the form, usually the field name. A control that does not have a source of data, for example a label that displays the title of the form, is an ***unbound control***.

Figure 14.11

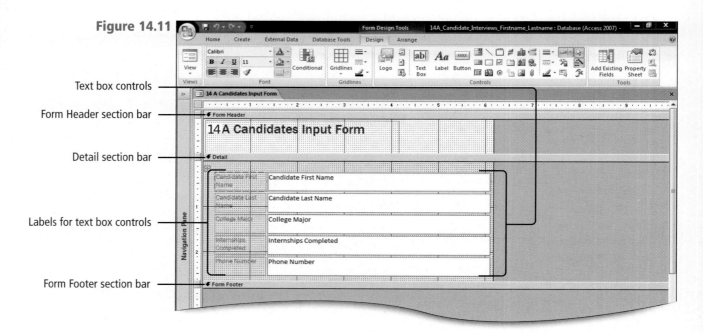

- Text box controls
- Form Header section bar
- Detail section bar
- Labels for text box controls
- Form Footer section bar

Alert!

Does the Field List pane display?

If the Field List pane displays on the right, in the upper right corner, click its Close button.

2 Point to the upper edge of the **Detail section bar** to display the ⬌ pointer, and then drag downward approximately **0.5 inch**. Compare your screen with Figure 14.12.

> The height of Form Header section increases—do not be concerned if your expanded Form Header area does not match Figure 14.12 exactly; you will adjust it later. The background grid is dotted and divided into one-inch squares by horizontal and vertical grid lines to help you place and align controls on the form precisely. You can also use the vertical and horizontal rulers to guide the placement of a control on the form.

Figure 14.12

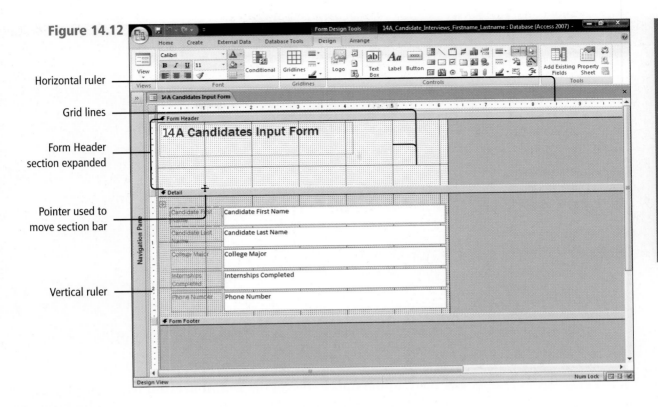

Horizontal ruler

Grid lines

Form Header section expanded

Pointer used to move section bar

Vertical ruler

Alert!

Are the rulers missing?

If the horizontal and vertical rulers do not display, on the Arrange tab, in the Show/Hide group, click the Ruler button.

---

3 In the **Form Header section**, click anywhere in the title *14A Candidates Input Form* to select it. On the **Design tab**, in the **Font group**, click the **Font Size arrow** and then click **18**. Click the **Bold** button **B** to add bold emphasis to the text. Click the **Font Color button arrow**, and then under **Access Theme Colors**, in the second row, click the ninth color—**Access Theme 9**.

The label is selected as displayed by the orange border surrounding it. The border displays small boxes called *sizing handles*, which are used to resize the control.

4 On the right side of the selected label control, point to the **middle sizing handle** to display the ↔ pointer—or point to one of the other sizing handles to display a resize pointer—and then double-click to adjust the size of the label control. Compare your screen with Figure 14.13.

The size of the label resizes to fit the text as it has been reformatted.

Figure 14.13

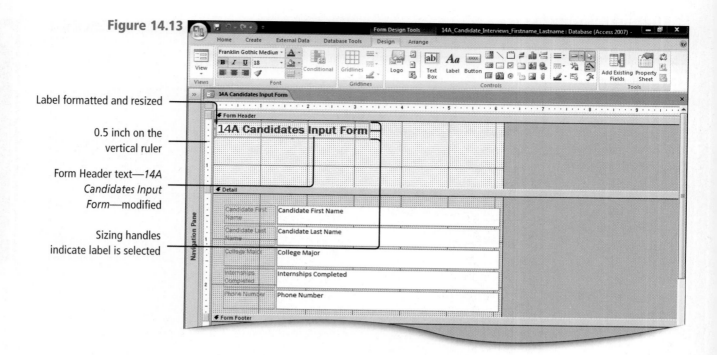

Label formatted and resized

0.5 inch on the vertical ruler

Form Header text—*14A Candidates Input Form*—modified

Sizing handles indicate label is selected

---

5 Point to the upper edge of the **Detail section bar** to display the ⊕ pointer, and then drag upward until the bar is at **0.5 inch on the vertical ruler**—allowing approximately two rows of dots between the lower edge of the **label control** border and the upper edge of the **Detail section bar**.

6 At the bottom of the form, point to the lower edge of the **Form Footer section bar** to display the ⊕ pointer, and then drag downward approximately **0.5 inch** to increase the height of the Form Footer section.

7 On the **Design tab**, in the **Controls group**, click the **Label** button. Position the plus sign of the ⁺A pointer in the **Form Footer** section at approximately **0.25 inch on the horizontal ruler** and even with the lower edge of the Form Footer section bar. Drag to the right to **5 inches on the horizontal ruler**, and then downward approximately **0.25 inch**. If you are not satisfied with the result, click Undo and begin again.

8 Using your own name, type **14A Candidates Input Form Firstname Lastname** and then press Enter. Point to a sizing handle to display one of the resize pointers, and then double-click to fit the control to the text you typed. On the right side of the status bar, click the **Form View** button ▦. Compare your screen with Figure 14.14.

> Form Footer text displays on the screen at the bottom of the form, and prints only on the last page if all of the forms are printed as a group.

Figure 14.14

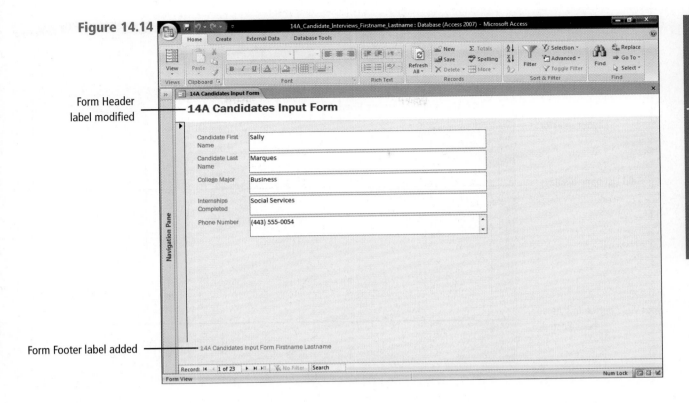

Form Header label modified

Navigation Pane

Form Footer label added

9 On the **Quick Access Toolbar**, click the **Save** button 🖫 to save the changes you have made to the design of your form. Leave the **14A Candidates Input Form** open for the next activity.

Activity 14.07 Adding, Resizing, and Moving Controls in Layout View

Use the Layout view to change the form's ***control layout***—the grouped arrangement of controls on a form in Layout view. Use Layout view to make quick changes to the form's design by adding or moving controls.

1 At the right side of the status bar, click the **Layout View** button 🔲.

> On the Ribbon, the Format tab is active. A dotted line surrounds the first control—label and text box—and the white text box control is surrounded by a solid orange border. Above and to the left of the first field name—Candidate First Name—the ***layout selector*** displays, with which you can select and move the entire group of controls in Layout view.

2 In the **Controls group**, click the **Add Existing Fields** button to display the **Field List** pane. Compare your screen with Figure 14.15.

Figure 14.15

First label control and text box control selected

Layout selector

Field List pane displays

Layout View button in status bar selected

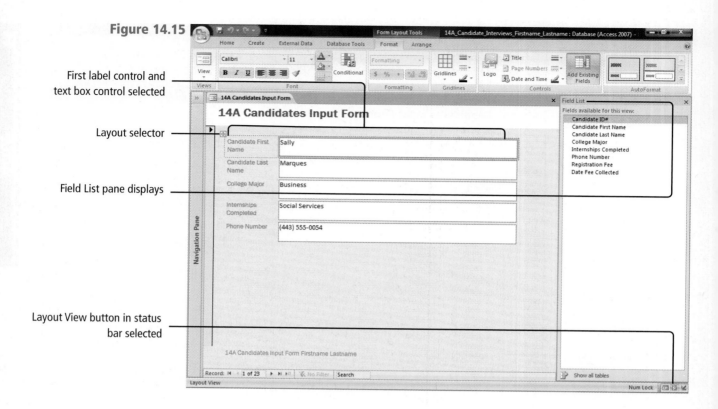

3 In the **Field List** pane, point to **Candidate ID#**, hold down the left mouse button, and then drag to the left until the pointer is in the upper portion of the *Candidate First Name* label control and a thick orange line displays above the control. Release the mouse button, and then compare your screen with Figure 14.16. If you are not satisfied with the result, click Undo and begin again.

The Candidate ID# controls are added to the form. Add a bound text box to a form by dragging a field from the Field List pane.

Figure 14.16

Candidate ID# text box control added to the form

Candidate ID# label control

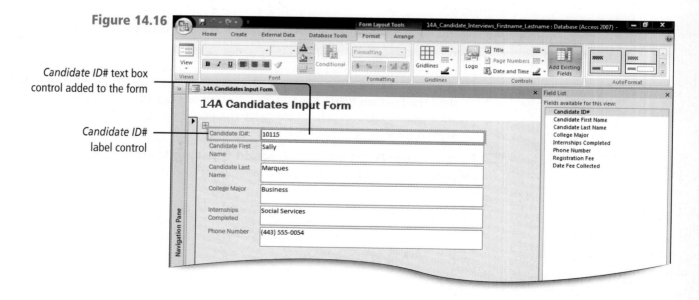

4 **Close** ✕ the **Field List** pane. Click the **Candidate ID# text box control**, which currently displays *10115*, to surround it with an orange border. Point to the right edge of the **text box control** until the ↔ pointer displays, and then drag to the left until all of the text box controls align under the *m* in the form title above. Compare your screen with Figure 14.17.

> All six text box controls are resized simultaneously. By decreasing the width of the text box controls, you have more space in which to rearrange the form controls. In Layout view, because you can see your data, you can determine visually that the space you have allotted is adequate to display all of the data in every field.

Figure 14.17

Right edges of text box controls align under *m* in form title

Horizontal resize pointer

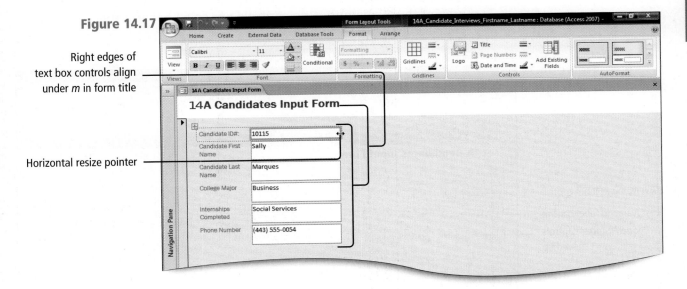

5 Click the **Phone Number text box control**, which currently displays *(443) 555-0054*. Point to the **text box control** until the pointer displays, and then drag upward until a thick orange line displays above the **College Major controls** as shown in Figure 14.18.

Figure 14.18

Move pointer

Orange line indicates where the control will be placed

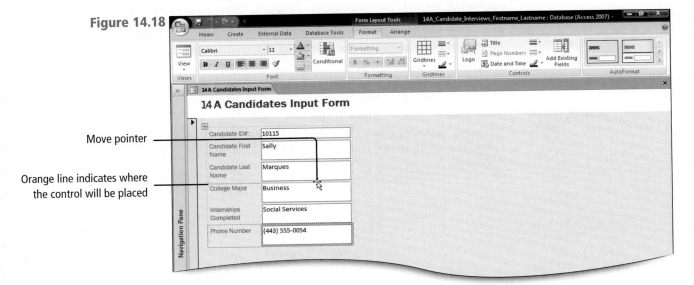

6 Release the mouse button to place the **Phone Number controls** above the **College Major controls**.

7 Click the **Candidate First Name label control** to select it. Click to the left of the word *First* to place the insertion point in the label control, and then press ⌫Bksp as necessary to delete the text *Candidate* so that the label displays *First Name*.

> With the insertion point placed in the label, you can edit the label. The form label text does not have to match the field name in the source table.

8 Using the technique you just practiced, edit the **Candidate Last Name label control** to display only *Last Name*. Click in a shaded area of the form so that no controls are selected, and then compare your screen with Figure 14.19.

Figure 14.19

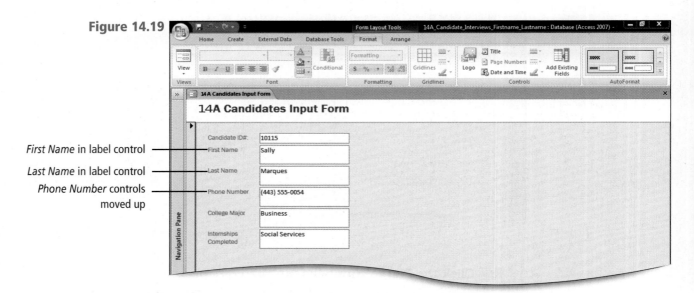

First Name in label control
Last Name in label control
Phone Number controls moved up

9 **Save** 🖫 the changes you have made to the design of your form.

Activity 14.08 Formatting and Aligning Controls in Layout View

1 With the form still displayed in Layout view, hold down ⇧Shift and then click each of the **text box controls**.

Alert!   **Do your controls change order when selecting?**

If, when selecting all the controls, the controls change order, click Undo and select the controls again. Be careful not to drag the mouse when you are selecting multiple controls.

---

2 With the six text box controls selected, on the **Format tab**, in the **Font group**, click the **Fill/Back Color button arrow**. Under **Access Theme Colors**, in the second row, click the fourth color— **Access Theme 4**. Click the **Font Size button arrow**, and then click **12**.

> The text box controls have a background color of blue, and the font size is increased.

3 Click in a shaded area of the screen to deselect all of the text box controls. Hold down ⇧Shift, and then click each of the six **label controls**. Change the **Font Size** to **12**, change the **Font Color**—*not* the Fill/Back Color—to **Access Theme 9**, and then apply **Bold** **B**. Click in a shaded area to deselect the label controls, and then compare your screen with Figure 14.20.

Figure 14.20

Text box controls formatted with Font Size 12 and Access Theme 4 fill color

Label controls formatted with Font Size 12, Font Color Access Theme 9, and Bold

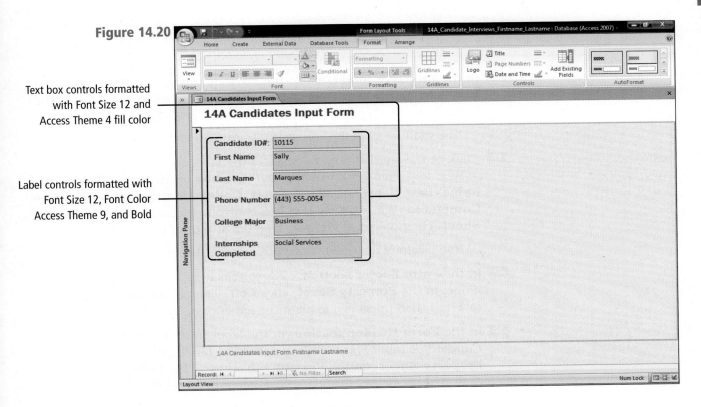

4 Click the **Internships Completed label control**. On the Ribbon, click the **Arrange tab**, and then in the **Tools group**, click the **Property Sheet** button. Compare your screen with Figure 14.21.

> The *Property Sheet* for the selected label control displays. Each control has an associated Property Sheet where precise changes to the properties—characteristics—of selected controls can be made.

Figure 14.21

Arrange tab selected

Property Sheet for label

Property Sheet
button in Tools group

Label control selected

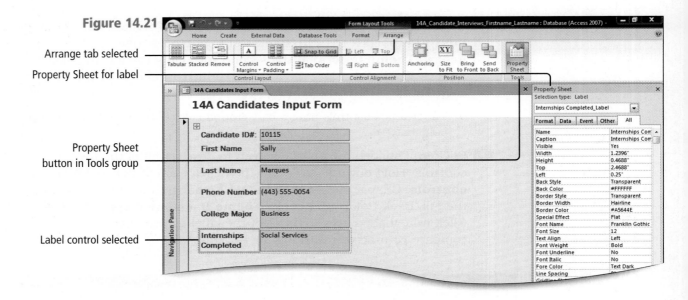

5 In the **Property Sheet**, select the **Format tab**. In the **Width** property box, point to the word **Width**, and then click to select its value to the right. Type **2** to replace the value, and then press Enter.

The width of all of the label controls changes to 2 inches.

6 Click in the shaded area to deselect the label control. Hold down ⇧ Shift, and then click to select the **text box controls** for **First Name**, **Last Name**, **Phone Number**, **College Major**, and **Internships Completed**. With the five text box controls selected, in the **Property Sheet**, click the word **Height**, type **0.3** and then press Enter.

The height of the selected text box controls decreases.

7 In the **Form Footer section**, click to select the label control with your name. In the **Property Sheet**, click **Left**. Change the property setting to **1** and then press Enter to align the left edge of the label at 1 inch.

8 In the **Form Header section**, in the label control that displays *14A Candidates Input Form*, click to select the label control. In the **Property Sheet**, on the **Format tab**, change the **Left** property to **1** and then press Enter. Compare your screen with Figure 14.22.

Recall that each control has an associated Property Sheet on which you can change the properties—characteristics—of the control. Because this is a label control that was added to the form, Access assigns it a number. The number on your Property Sheet may differ from the figures in this textbook. The left edges of the Form Header and Form Footer label controls align at 1 inch. In this manner, you can place a control in a specific location on the form.

Figure 14.22

Width of label controls changed to 2 inches

Form Header label control left aligned at 1 inch

Height of five text box controls modified to 0.3 inch

Label number

Form Footer label control left aligned at 1 inch

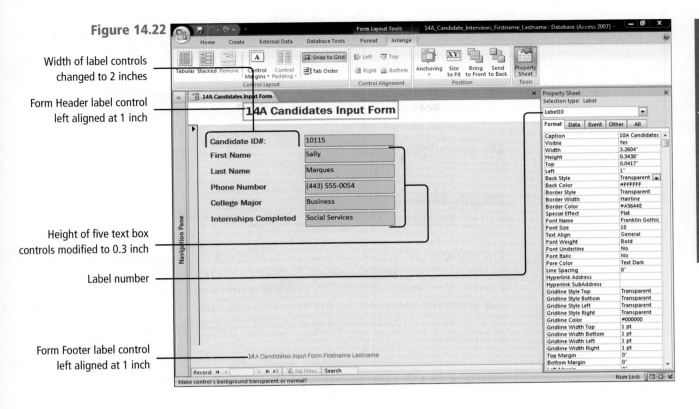

9 **Close** × the **Property Sheet**. On the right side of the status bar, click the **Form View** button. Compare your screen with Figure 14.23.

The form displays in Form view. Using these techniques, you can make a form attractive and easy to use for those who view and enter records on a screen.

Figure 14.23

Form displays in Form view

Form View button on status bar

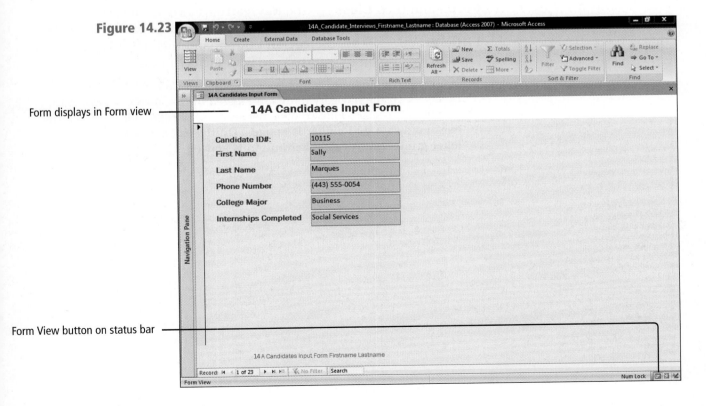

10 **Save** 🔲 the changes you have made to your form's design. In the navigation area, click the **Last record** button 🔘 to display the record containing your name.

11 From the **Office** menu 🔘, click **Print**. In the **Print** dialog box, under **Print Range**, click the **Selected Record(s)** option button. Click **OK** to print, or submit electronically as directed.

12 **Close** ❎ the form.

Objective 5
Filter Records

Filtering records in a form is the process of displaying only a portion of the total records—a *subset*—based on matching specific values. Filters are commonly used to provide a quick answer, and the result is not generally saved for future use. For example, by filtering records in a form, you can quickly display a subset of records for students majoring in Business.

Activity 14.09 Filtering Data by Selection on One Field

Several interviewers at the Baltimore Job Fair would like to see records for candidates who are majoring in Business. Use the *Filter By Selection* command—which retrieves only the records that contain the value in the selected field—to temporarily remove the records that do *not* contain the value in the selected field.

1 **Open** 🔘 the **Navigation Pane**, open **14A Candidates Input Form**, and then **Close** 🔘 the **Navigation Pane**. In the first record, click the **College Major label control**. On the **Home tab**, in the **Sort & Filter group**, click the **Selection** button, and then click **Equals "Business"**. Compare your screen with Figure 14.24.

> Ten records match the contents of the selected College Major field—*Business*. In the navigation area, a *Filtered* button displays next to the number of records. *Filtered* also displays on the right side of the status bar to indicate that a filter is applied. On the Home tab, in the Sort & Filter group, the Toggle Filter button is active.

Figure 14.24

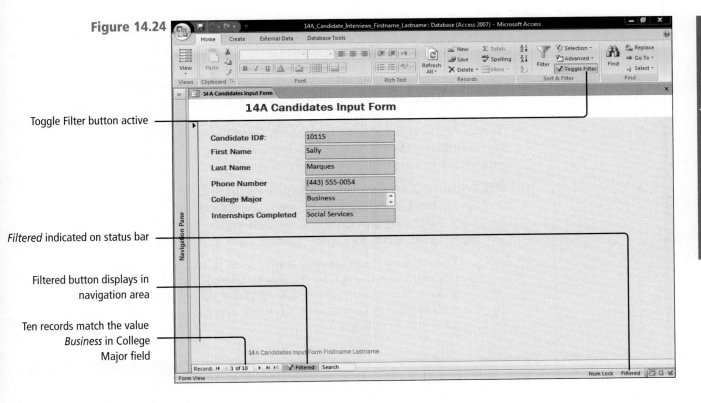

Toggle Filter button active

Filtered indicated on status bar

Filtered button displays in navigation area

Ten records match the value *Business* in College Major field

2 On the **Home tab**, in the **Sort & Filter group**, click the **Toggle Filter** button to remove the filter and display all 23 records. Alternatively, click the Filtered button in the navigation area to remove a filter. Notice the **Unfiltered** button in the navigation area.

3 Be sure that the first record—for *Sally Marques*—displays, and then click in the **College Major text box control** to display up and down arrows. On the **Home tab**, in the **Sort & Filter group**, click the **Toggle Filter** button to reapply the filter. In the navigation area, click the **Last record** button to display the last of the ten records that match *Business*.

The record for *Candidate ID# 22155* displays—the record with your name.

4 In the **Sort & Filter group**, click the **Toggle Filter** button to remove the filter and display all of the records. In the navigation area, click the **Next record** button to move to **Record 2**. In the **Phone Number** field, select the text *(410)* including the parentheses, which is the Area Code. On the **Home tab**, in the **Sort & Filter group**, click the **Selection** button, and then click **Begins with "(410)"**.

A new filter is applied that displays fourteen records in which the *Phone Number* contains the (410) Area Code.

5 On the **Home tab**, in the **Sort & Filter group**, click the **Toggle Filter** button to remove the filter and display all of the records.

Activity 14.10 Using Filter By Form

Use the *Filter By Form* command to filter the records in a form based on one or more fields, or based on more than one value in the *same* field. The Filter By Form command offers greater flexibility than the Filter by Selection command when you want an answer to a question that requires matching multiple values. In this activity, you will help Janna Sorokin determine how many candidates have a major of *Communications* or *Graphic Arts* because several interviewers are interested in candidates with one of these two backgrounds.

1 With the **14A Candidates Input Form** still open, on the **Home tab**, in the **Sort & Filter group**, click the **Advanced** button. In the list, click **Filter By Form**. Click the **Advanced** button again, and then click **Clear Grid**. Compare your screen with Figure 14.25.

> The Filter by Form window displays; all of the field names are included, but without any data. In the empty text box controls for each field, type a value or choose from a list of available values. The *Look for* and *Or* tabs display at the bottom. The Clear Grid command removes data from all of the form fields.

Figure 14.25

Filter by Form ⎯

Data is cleared ⎯

Look for and *Or* tabs ⎯

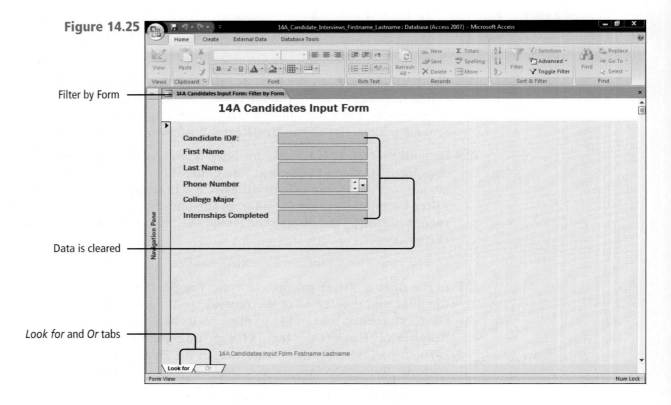

2 Click the **College Major text box control**. At the right edge of the text box, click the larger **down arrow**, and then in the list, click **Communications**. In the **Sort & Filter group**, click the **Toggle Filter** button, and then compare your screen with Figure 14.26.

> As displayed in the navigation area, six candidate records include a College Major of *Communications*.

Figure 14.26

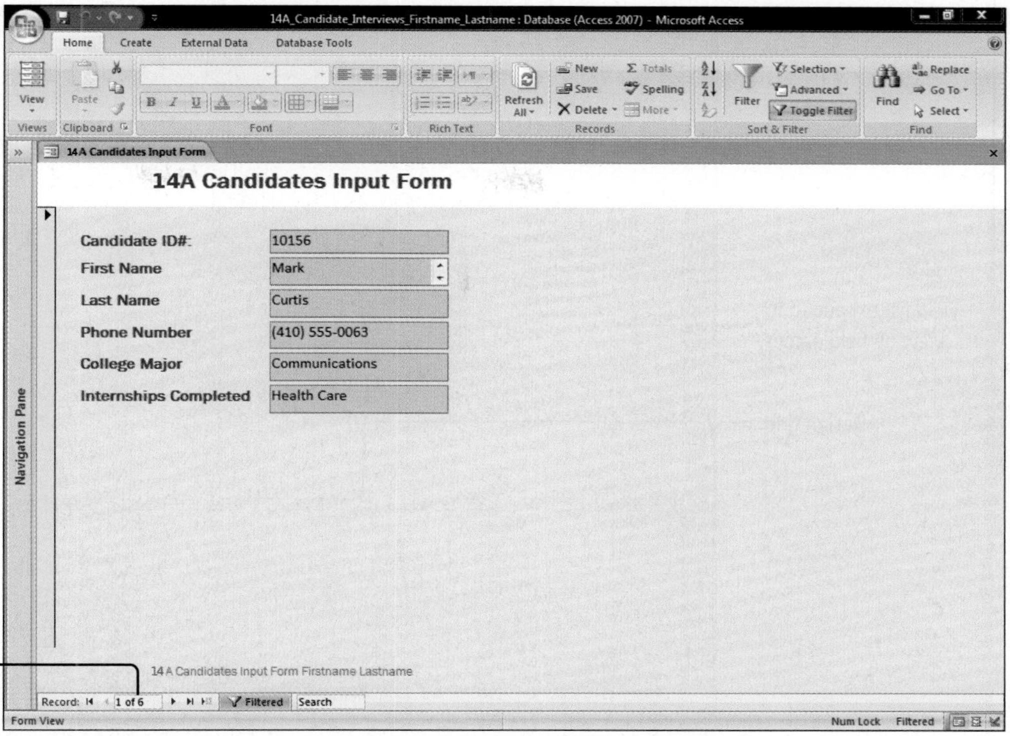

6 records have a College
Major of *Communications*

Note — Toggle Filter Button

On the Home tab, the Toggle Filter button is used to apply or remove a filter. If no filter has been created, the button is not active—it is dimmed. After a filter is created, this button becomes active. Because it is a toggle button used to apply or remove filters, the ScreenTip that displays for this button alternates between Apply Filter—when a filter has been created but is not currently applied—and Remove Filter—when a filter has been applied.

3 Click in the **College Major text box control**. In the **Sort & Filter group**, click the **Filter** button. From the shortcut menu, select the **Graphic Arts** check box, and then click **OK**.

> As displayed in the navigation area, eight candidate records have a College Major in either Communications *or* Graphic Arts. You have created an **OR condition**; that is, only records where one of two values—Communications *or* Graphic Arts—is present in the selected field are displayed.

4 If necessary, click in the **College Major text box control**. In the **Sort & Filter group**, click the **Advanced** button, and then click **Clear All Filters**. Click the **Advanced** button, and then from the list, click **Advanced Filter/Sort**. Use the ⬉ pointer to expand the field list, and then compare your screen with Figure 14.27.

> The Advanced Filter design grid displays. The design grid is similar to the Query Design grid.

Figure 14.27

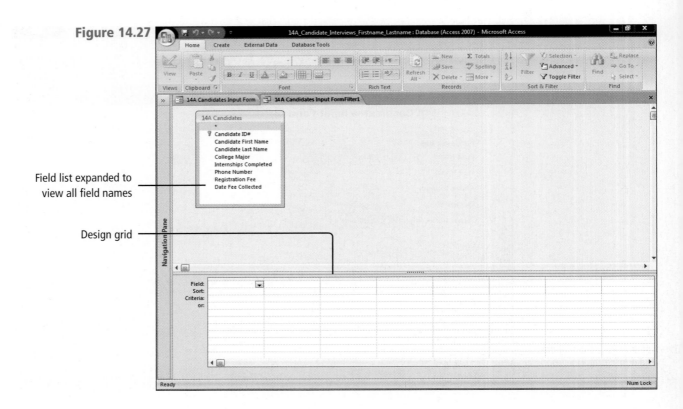

Field list expanded to view all field names

Design grid

5 From the **14A Candidates** field list, add the **College Major** field and **Internships Completed** field to the design grid. In the **Criteria** row, in the **College Major** field, type **Business,** and then press Enter. In the **Criteria** row, in the **Internships Completed** field, type **Finance** and then press Enter. In the **Sort & Filter group**, click the **Toggle Filter** button, and then compare your screen with Figure 14.28.

As displayed in the navigation area, three records match the criteria. You have created an *AND condition*; that is, only records where both values—Business *and* Finance—are present in the selected fields display. There are three Business majors who have completed an internship in Finance.

Figure 14.28

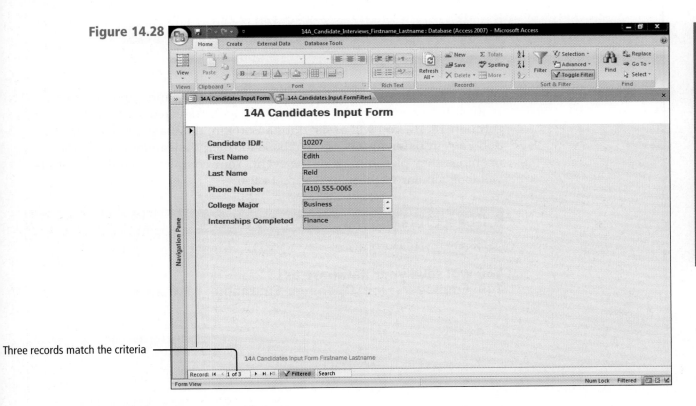

Three records match the criteria ——

[6] In the **Sort & Filter group**, click the **Toggle Filter** button to remove the filter from the records. **Close** ☒ all open objects. From the **Office** menu ⊕, **Close** the Database, and then **Exit** Access.

End **You have completed Project 14A** ————————

Project 14B Employers and Job Openings

At the Job Fair event, employers post job openings and candidates can request interviews for jobs in which they are interested. In Activities 14.11 through 14.16, you will assist Janna Sorokin, database manager for the Job Fair, in using an Access database to track the employers and the job openings they plan to post at the event. Your completed database objects will look similar to those in Figure 14.29.

For Project 14B, you will need the following file:

a14B_Employers_Job_Openings

You will save your database as
14B_Employers_Job_Openings_Firstname_Lastname

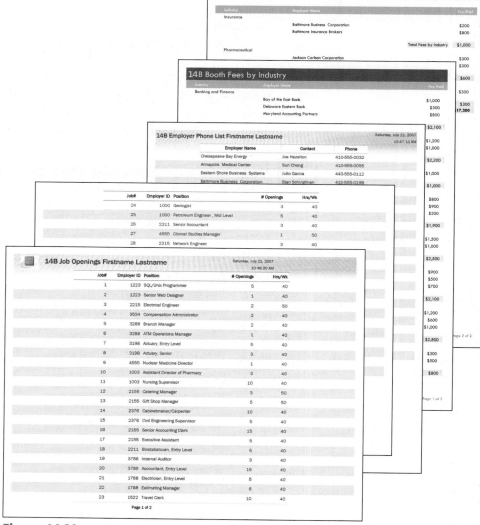

Figure 14.29
Project 14B—Employers and Job Openings

Objective 6
Create a Report Using the Report Tool

A *report* is a database object that summarizes the fields and records from a table, or from a query, in an easy-to-read format suitable for printing. The report consists of information extracted from tables or queries and also the report's design items, such as labels, headings, and graphics. The tables or queries that provide the underlying data for a report are referred to as the report's *record source*.

Access provides three tools to create a report: the Report tool, the Blank Report tool, and the Report Wizard. After you create a report, you can modify the report in Layout view or in Design view.

Activity 14.11 Creating and Modifying a Report Using the Report Tool and Layout View

The *Report tool*, which is the fastest way to create a report, generates a report immediately by displaying all of the fields and records from the record source that you select. You can use the Report tool to quickly look at the underlying data in an easy-to-read format, after which you can save the report and modify it in Layout view or in Design view.

In this activity, you will use the Report tool to create a report for Janna Sorokin that lists all of the employers who are participating in the Job Fair, modify the report in Layout view, and then print the report.

1 Navigate to the location where the student files for this textbook are saved. Locate **a14B_Employers_Job_Openings** and click one time to select the file. **Copy** and then **Paste** the file to your **Access Chapter 14** folder. **Rename** the file as **14B_Employers_Job_Openings_Firstname_Lastname** and then **Start** Access. Navigate to your **Access Chapter 14** folder, open **14B_Employers_Job_Openings**, and then **Enable this content**.

2 Click the **Database Tools tab**, and then in the **Show/Hide group**, click the **Relationships** button. Compare your screen with Figure 14.30. If your relationships do not display, in the Relationships group, click the All Relationships button.

At the Job Fair event, *one* employer can have *many* job openings. Thus, a one-to-many relationship has been established between the 14B Employers table and the 14B Job Openings table using Employer ID# as the common field.

Figure 14.30

Join line with symbols
indicating a one-to-many
relationship

Employer ID is common field

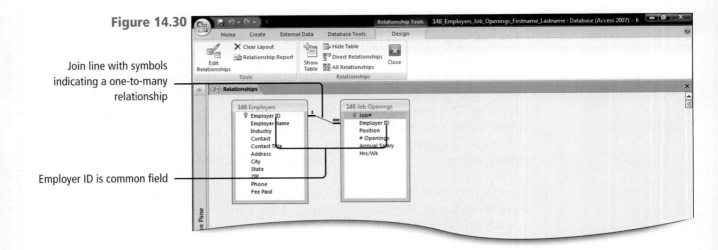

3 In the **Relationships group**, click the **Close** button to close the **Relationships** window. If prompted to save your changes, click No.

4 Open ⏵ the **Navigation Pane**, click to select the **14B Job Openings** table. Click the **Create tab**, and then in the **Reports group**, point to the **Report** button and read its ScreenTip. Click the **Report** button, and then **Close** ⏴ the **Navigation Pane**. Compare your screen with Figure 14.31.

Access creates the 14B Job Openings report and displays it in Layout view. The report includes all of the fields and all of the records in the table. In Layout view, you can see the margins and page breaks in the report.

Figure 14.31

All fields from table
display in report

Dotted lines indicate margins

All records from table display
in report

Report displays in Layout view

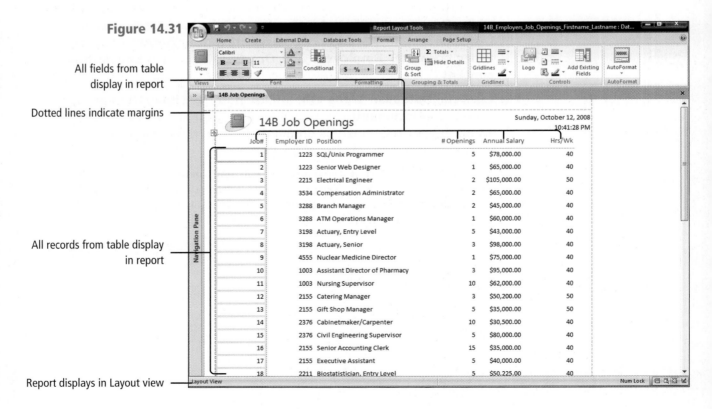

5 Click the **Annual Salary** field name, which surrounds the field name with an orange border and selects the entire column. Right-click over the selected field name, and then from the shortcut menu, click **Delete** to delete the Annual Salary field from the report.

6 Click the **# Openings** field name to select the entire column. On the **Format tab**, in the **Grouping & Totals group**, click the **Totals** button. In the list, click **Sum**. Scroll down to display the last line of the report, and notice that Access summed the numbers in the # *Openings* field, and that the total number of job openings is *182*.

> Use Layout view to make quick changes to a report created with the Report tool. The Report tool is not intended to create a perfectly formatted formal report, but rather it is a way to quickly summarize the data in a table or query in an easy-to-read format suitable for printing and reading.

7 Click the **Page Setup tab**, and then in the **Page Layout group**, click the **Landscape** button.

8 Click the **Format tab**, and then in the **AutoFormat group**, click the **AutoFormat** button. From the gallery of formats, locate, and then click the **Trek** AutoFormat. The name of the format displays as you point to a format.

> AutoFormat enables you to apply a predefined format to a report, which is another way to give a professional look to a report created quickly with the Report tool. Apply AutoFormat before performing other editing to the text of your report.

9 At the top of the report, in the **Report Header** section, click the text *14B Job Openings*, and then click again to position the insertion point in the title. Alternatively, double-click the title. Add your first name and last name to the end of the title. On the **Format tab**, in the **Font group**, change the **Font Size** to **16**.

10 Click any field in the report. In the upper left corner of the report, click the **layout selector**, and then drag it to the right until the pointer is positioned approximately below the *O* in the word *Openings*. Compare your screen with Figure 14.32.

> Using the layout selector, you can move the entire layout of the label controls and text box controls to easily center the records on the page visually.

Figure 14.32

Report Header Font Size changed to 16 pt.

Layout selector button

Your name displays in Report Header

Trek AutoFormat applied

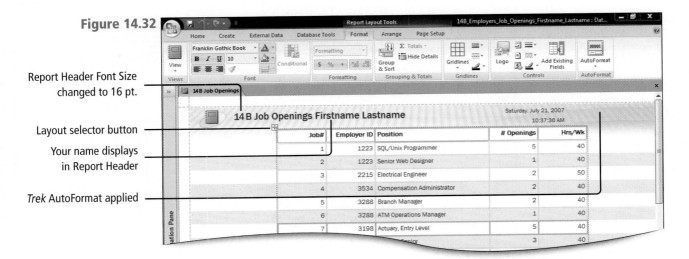

11 At the right side of the status bar, click the **Print Preview** button 🔍. On the **Print Preview tab**, in the **Zoom group**, click the **Two Pages** button to view the two pages of your report.

12 To print your report, on the **Print Preview tab**, in the **Print group**, click **Print**, and then click the **Close Print Preview** button. Or, submit electronically as directed.

13 **Close** ⊠ the **14B Job Openings** report. In the message box, click **Yes** to save changes to the design of the report. In the **Save As** dialog box, click **OK** to accept the default name—*14B Job Openings.*

Objective 7
Create a Report Using the Blank Report Tool

Use the ***Blank Report tool*** to create a report from scratch. This is an efficient way to create a report, especially if you plan to include only a few fields in your report.

Activity 14.12 Creating a Report Using the Blank Report Tool

In this activity, you will build a report that lists only the Employer Name, Contact, and Phone fields, which Janna will use as a quick reference for phoning various employers to verify the details of their Job Fair participation.

1 On the **Create tab**, in the **Reports group**, click the **Blank Report** button.

> A blank report displays in Layout View, and the Field List pane displays.

2 In the **Field List** pane, if necessary, click **Show all tables**, and then click the **plus sign (+)** next to the **14B Employers table**. Compare your screen with Figure 14.33.

> The fields in the 14B Employers table display.

Figure 14.33

Field List pane

Field list for the 14B Employers table expanded

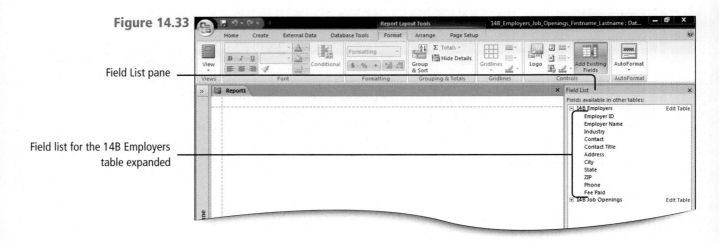

3 Point to the **Employer Name** field, right-click, and then click **Add Field to View**.

The Employer Name field and its associated records display as the first column of the report. Build the report field by field, in the order that you want the fields to display using this method.

4 From the **Field List** pane, drag the **Contact** field into the blank report—anywhere to the right of *Employer Name*. Double-click the **Phone** field to add it as the third field in the report. Compare your screen with Figure 14.34.

Use any of the techniques you just practiced to add fields to a blank report.

Figure 14.34

Three fields added to the report

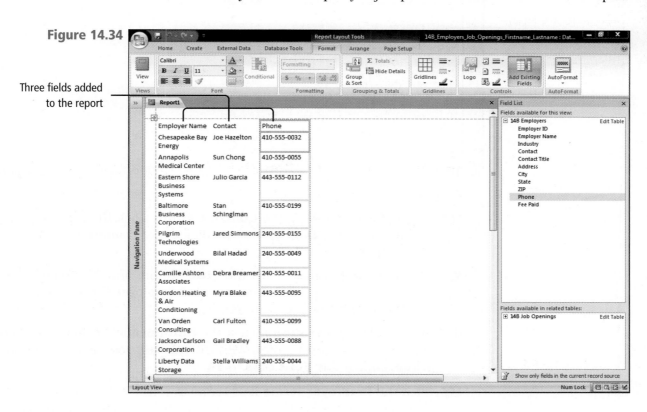

5 **Close** [×] the **Field List** pane. Click the **Employer Name** field name to select the column. Point to the right edge of the orange border to display the [↔] pointer, and then drag to the right until the name for *Gordon Heating & Air Conditioning* displays on one line and there is a small amount of space between the name and the next column.

6 Using the technique you just practiced, widen the **Contact** field so that all the names display on one line and some space is allowed between the end of the longest name and the beginning of the next column. Compare your screen with Figure 14.35.

Figure 14.35

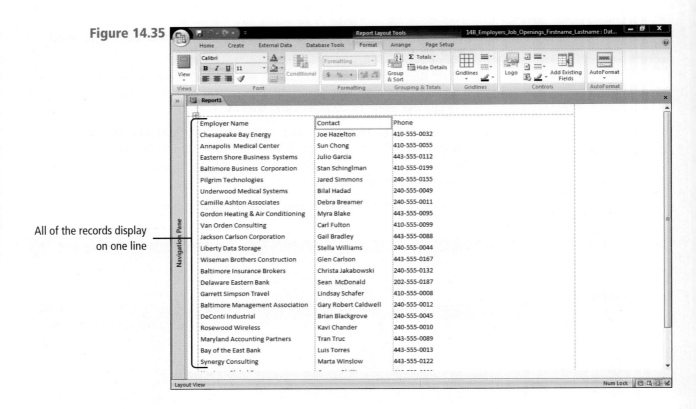

All of the records display on one line

7 On the **Format tab**, in the **Controls group**, click the **Date & Time** button. In the **Date and Time** dialog box, examine the options, and then click **OK**.

8 In the **Controls group**, click the **Title** button, and then using your own first name and last name, type **14B Employer Phone List Firstname Lastname** and then press Enter.

9 In the **AutoFormat group**, click the **AutoFormat** button, and then apply the **Trek** AutoFormat. With the title still selected, in the **Font group**, change the **Font Size** to **14**.

10 Click the **Employer Name** field name to select it. Hold down Shift, click the **Contact** field name, and then click the **Phone** field name to select all three columns. On the **Format tab**, in the **Font group**, click the **Center** button.

11 In the upper left corner of the report, click the **layout selector**, and then drag it to the right until the pointer is positioned approximately below the *P* in the word *Phone* in the title—or to whatever position appears to center the group of controls horizontally between the dotted margin lines. Compare your screen with Figure 14.36.

Figure 14.36

Field names formatted and centered over data

Report title added

Trek AutoFormat applied

Layout visually centered horizontally on the page

Date and Time inserted (yours will vary)

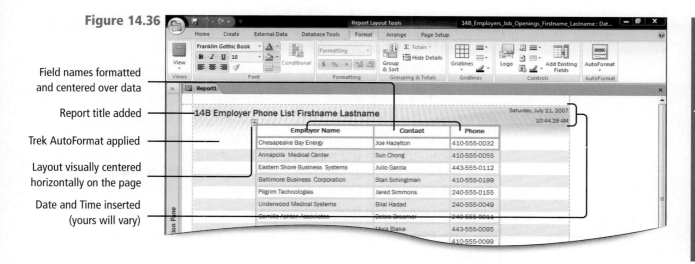

12. On the status bar, click the **Print Preview** button. On the **Print Preview tab**, in the **Print group**, click **Print** to print the report. In the **Close Preview group**, click the **Close Print Preview** button. Or, submit electronically as directed.

13. **Close** the report. In the message box, click **Yes** to save the changes to the design of the report. In the **Save As** dialog box, type **14B Employer Phone List** and then click **OK**.

14. **Open** the **Navigation Pane**. Notice that the reports display below the table with which they are related. Notice also that report objects display a small green notebook icon. **Close** the **Navigation Pane**.

Objective 8
Create a Report by Using the Report Wizard

Use the **Report Wizard** when you need flexibility and want to control the report content and design. The Report Wizard enables you to specify how the data is grouped and sorted, and you can use fields from more than one table or query, provided you have specified the relationships between the tables and queries beforehand.

The Report Wizard is similar to the Form Wizard; it creates a report by asking you a series of questions and then designs the report based on your answers.

Activity 14.13 Creating a Report by Using the Report Wizard

The Greater Baltimore Area Job Fair database includes data regarding employment information such as industry sectors, employers, job openings, and annual salaries. Based on the data that has been collected, Janna would like to have a report that shows groupings by industry, employer, and the total fees paid by employers for renting a booth at the Job Fair.

1 Click the **Create tab**, and in the **Reports group**, click the **Report Wizard** button.

On the first Report Wizard page, you select the tables or queries from which you want to extract information, and then select the fields to include in the report. You can also select more than one table or query.

2 Click the **Tables/Queries arrow**, and then click **Table: 14B Employers**. Using either the **One Field** button $\boxed{>}$ or by double-clicking the field name, move the following fields to the **Selected Fields** list in the order given: **Industry**, **Employer Name**, and **Fee Paid** (scroll down as necessary to find the *Fee Paid* field). Click **Next**.

On the second Report Wizard page, you can add grouping levels.

3 With **Industry** selected, click the **One Field** button $\boxed{>}$, and then compare your screen with Figure 14.37.

Grouping data helps to organize and summarize the data in your report. Grouping data in a report places all of the records that have the same data in a field together as a group—in this instance, each *Industry* will display as a group.

Figure 14.37

Report will be grouped by Industry

Employer Name and Fee Paid will display left to right

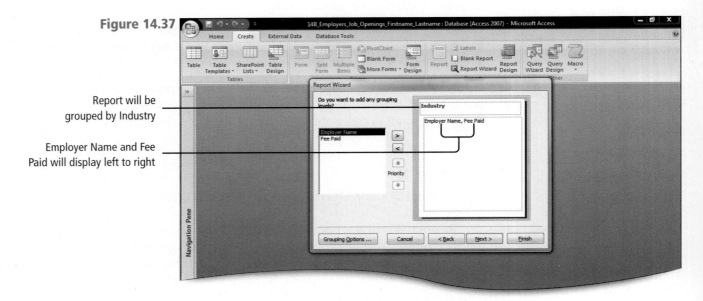

4 Click **Next**. Click the **1** box **arrow**, and then click **Employer Name**. Compare your screen with Figure 14.38.

Here you decide how to sort and summarize the information. You can sort on up to four fields. The Summary Options button displays because the data is grouped and contains numerical or currency data. The records in the report will be sorted alphabetically by Employer Name within the grouping option specified, which is *Industry*. Sorting records in a report presents a more organized report.

Figure 14.38

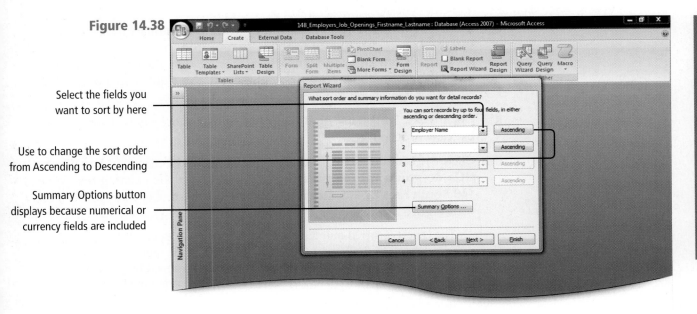

Select the fields you want to sort by here

Use to change the sort order from Ascending to Descending

Summary Options button displays because numerical or currency fields are included

5 In the Report Wizard, click **Summary Options**, and then compare your screen with Figure 14.39.

The Summary Options dialog box displays where you can choose to display only summary information or to display both details—each record— and the summary information. The Fee Paid field can be summarized by selecting one of four options—Sum, Avg, Min, or Max.

Figure 14.39

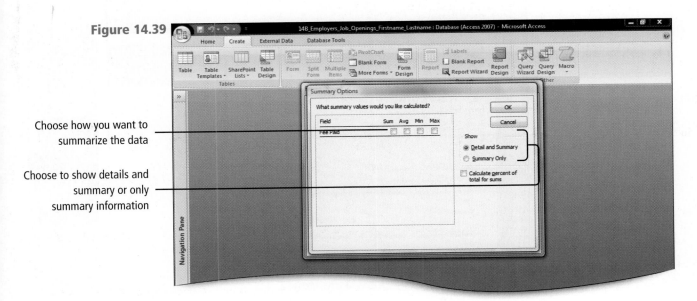

Choose how you want to summarize the data

Choose to show details and summary or only summary information

6 To the right of **Fee Paid**, select the **Sum** check box. Under **Show**, be sure that the **Detail and Summary** option button is selected, click **OK**, and then click **Next**.

Here you select the layout and the page orientation. The box on the left displays a preview of the selected layout.

7 Click each **Layout** option button, noticing the changes in the preview box, and then click the **Stepped** option button to select it as the layout for your report. Under **Orientation**, be sure that **Portrait** is selected, and at the bottom be sure that the **Adjust the field width so all fields fit on a page** check box is selected.

8 Click **Next**. In the list of styles, click one or more styles to view the preview on the right.

9 Click the **Median** style, and then click the **Next** button. In the **What title do you want for your report?** box, select the existing text, type **14B Booth Fees by Industry** and then click **Finish**. Compare your screen with Figure 14.40.

> The report is saved and displays in Print Preview. Each of the specifications you defined in the Report Wizard is reflected in the report, although some data is not completely visible. The records are grouped by Industry, and then within each Industry, the Employer Names are alphabetized.
>
> In a manner similar to an Excel spreadsheet, numeric data that does not fit into the space may display as a series of # signs. Within each Industry grouping, the Fee Paid is summarized—the word *Sum* displays at the end of the grouping.

Figure 14.40

Report displays in Print Preview

Data grouped by Industry

Records sorted by Employer Name

Summary information included

Fees summed by Industry

indicates data too wide for field

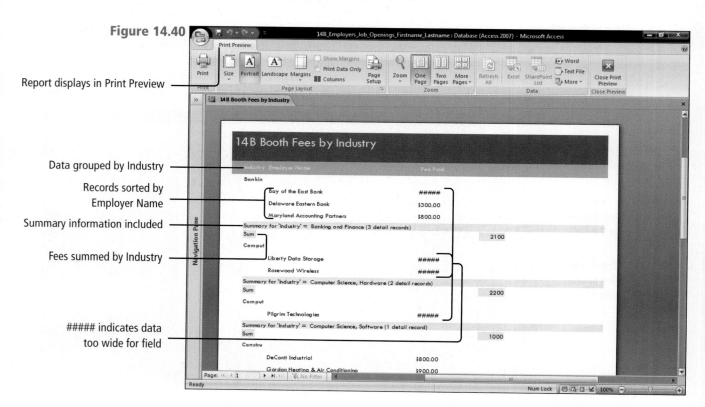

10 In the **Zoom group**, click the **Two Pages** button and notice that the report will print on two pages.

11 On the status bar, click the **Layout View** button 🖽 to switch to Layout view.

Objective 9
Modify the Design of a Report

After a report is created, you can modify its design by using tools and techniques similar to those you used to modify the design of a form. You can change the format of controls, add controls, remove controls, or change the placement of controls in the report. Most report modifications can be made in Layout view.

Activity 14.14 Modifying a Report in Layout View

In your *14B Booth Fees by Industry* report, under the *Industry* heading, several of the industry names are truncated—not fully displayed. Likewise, some of the amounts under Fee Paid are not fully displayed and display as # signs. You can modify the controls on a report to accommodate the data that displays.

1 Be sure that your **14B Booth Fees by Industry** report displays in Layout view.

2 In the upper left corner of the report, click to select the **Industry label control** to select the column. Point to the right edge of the selected label control to display the ↔ pointer, and then drag to the right until the right edge is aligned under the *I* in *Industry* in the Report Header above. Compare your screen with Figure 14.41.

Figure 14.41

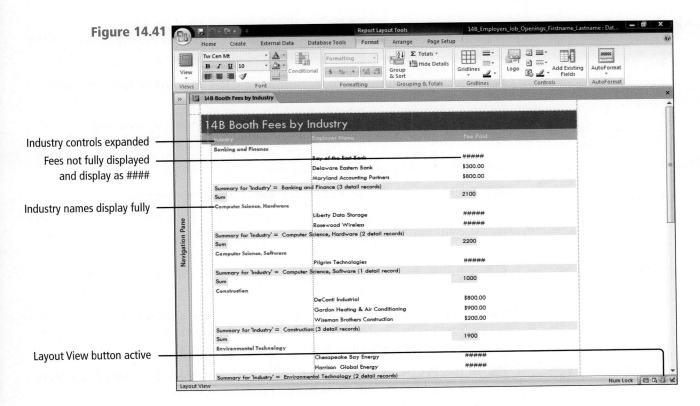

Industry controls expanded

Fees not fully displayed and display as ####

Industry names display fully

Layout View button active

3 Click to select the **Fee Paid label control**, and then drag its right edge to the right just slightly inside the dashed margin. Then drag the left side of the control to the right to shorten the control and leave a small amount of space to the left of the dollar signs ($) in the fees. Compare your screen with Figure 14.42.

The # signs are removed and the fee amounts display fully.

Figure 14.42

Right side of control moved to right margin

Left side of control shortened

Fees fully display

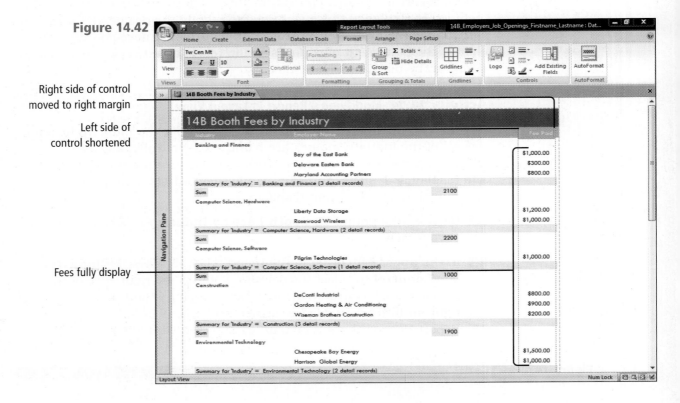

4 Within each Industry grouping, notice the **Summary for 'Industry'** information.

Access includes a summary line that details what is being summarized (in this case, summed) and how many records are included in the summary total. Now that Janna has viewed the report, she has decided this information is not necessary and can be removed.

5 Click any one of the **Summary for 'Industry' controls**.

The control that you clicked is surrounded by an orange border, and all of the controls are surrounded by paler borders to indicate that all are selected.

6 Right-click any of the selected controls, and then from the shortcut menu, click **Delete**. Alternatively, press [Delete].

7 In the **Fee Paid** field, click any one of the fee amounts to select all of the text box controls. Right-click any of the selected controls, and then from the shortcut menu, click **Properties**.

8 In the **Property Sheet**, on the **Format tab**, click the **Decimal Places** property name, and then in the property settings box, click the **arrow**. Compare your screen with Figure 14.43.

Figure 14.43

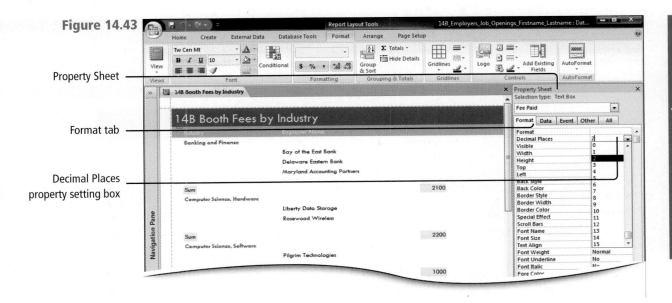

Property Sheet

Format tab

Decimal Places
property setting box

9 In the list, click **0**, and then **Close** ☒ the **Property Sheet**.

The fees display with no decimal places.

10 In the **Banking and Finance grouping** of the report, to the right of the word *Sum*, click **2100** to select all of the calculated controls. Point to any of the selected controls, right-click, and then from the shortcut menu, click **Properties**.

These amounts would be more relevant if they included currency formatting to indicate that they are the sum of the fees paid within each industry grouping.

The summary controls are examples of ***calculated controls***—controls that contain an expression—often a formula—that uses one or more fields from the underlying table or query.

11 In the **Property Sheet**, on the **Format tab**, click **Format**, and then click the **arrow** that displays in the property setting box.

12 In the list of formats, click **Currency**. Click the **Decimal Places** property box, click the **arrow** that displays in the property setting box, and then click **0**. **Close** ☒ the **Property Sheet**.

13 With the ↔ pointer, drag the right edge of any of the selected controls to the right, just inside the right dotted margin line. After you release the mouse button, adjust as necessary so that the summed amounts display directly under the fees above. Then, decrease the width of the controls by dragging the left edge of the control to the right with just enough space to accommodate the data. Compare your screen with Figure 14.44.

Figure 14.44

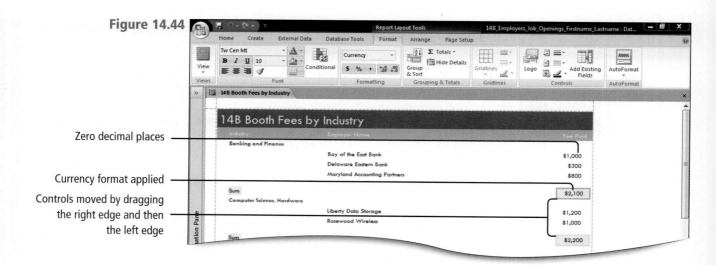

Zero decimal places

Currency format applied

Controls moved by dragging the right edge and then the left edge

14 On the left side of the report, click one of the **Sum label controls** to select all of the controls, and then click again to place the insertion point inside the selected control. Alternatively, double-click to place the insertion point inside the control.

15 Delete the text, type **Total Fees by Industry** and then press Enter. Notice that the label control is on the left side of the page, but the Fee Paid to which it refers is on the right.

> The new text more clearly states what is being summed; however, the label control would be more useful if it were positioned next to the summary value.

16 Use the ↔ pointer to lengthen the right side of the **Total Fees by Industry label control** so that it is slightly to the left of the total amount, and then shorten the left side so that the control accommodates the text with no extra space. Compare your screen with Figure 14.45.

Figure 14.45

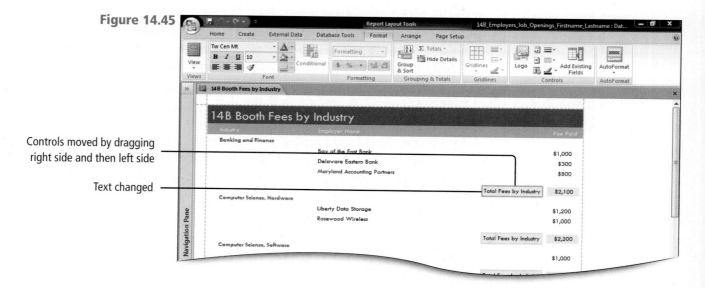

Controls moved by dragging right side and then left side

Text changed

17 At the top of your report, click to select the **Industry label control**. Hold down ⇧ Shift, then click the **Employer Name label control**, and then click the **Fee Paid label control** to select all three fields. In the **Font group**, click the **Bold** button **B**.

18 Scroll down to view the end of the report. Click to select the sum **17300**, which is the Grand Total for all fees paid. Display the **Property Sheet** for this calculated control and change its format to **Currency** with **0 Decimal Places**. **Close** ☒ the **Property Sheet**, and then adjust each side of the selected control to position it below the other fees as shown in Figure 14.46.

19 By adjusting the right and left sides of the control, move the text **Grand Total** label control to the immediate left of **$17,300**. Compare your screen with Figure 14.46.

The *Grand Total* amount displays in the **Report Footer** section at the end of the data. The current date and the page number information display at the bottom of the page in the **Page Footer** section.

The report footer displays one time at the end of the data, and displays items such as report totals. It displays *only* if the data has been summarized. A page footer displays at the bottom of every page of the report.

Figure 14.46

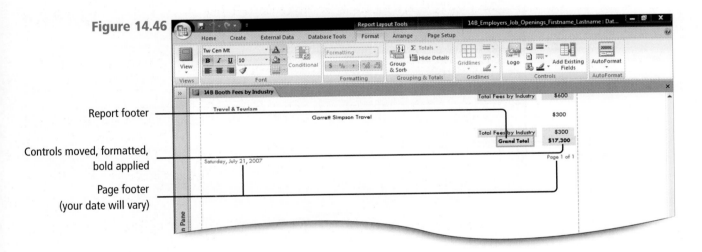

Report footer

Controls moved, formatted, bold applied

Page footer (your date will vary)

20 **Save** 🖫 the changes you have made to the report.

Activity 14.15 Modifying a Report in Design View

Design view gives you a more detailed view of the structure of your report. You can see the header and footer sections for the report, for the page, and for groups. In Design view, your report is not actually running, so you cannot see the underlying data while you are working. However, some tasks, such as adding labels and images, are accomplished in Design view. In this activity, you will add a label to the Page Footer section of your *14B Booth Fees by Industry* report and insert identifying information there.

1 Be sure that your **14B Booth Fees by Industry** report is displayed in Layout view. Press Ctrl + Home to display the top of the report. On the status bar, click the **Design View** button. Compare your screen with Figure 14.47.

The Design view for a report is similar to the Design view for a form. The layout of the report can be modified in this view, and the dotted grid pattern can be used to align controls. This report contains a **Report Header**, a **Page Header**, a **Group Header**, which in this instance is the *Industry* grouping, a **Detail** section that displays the data, a **Group Footer** (Industry), a **Page Footer**, and a **Report Footer**.

The Report Header displays information at the top of the *first page* of a report. The Page Header displays information at the top of *every page* of a report. The Group Header and Group Footer display the field label by which the data has been grouped—*Industry* in this instance. If you do not group data in a report, the Group Header does not display. Similarly, if you do not summarize data, the Group Footer does not display.

Figure 14.47

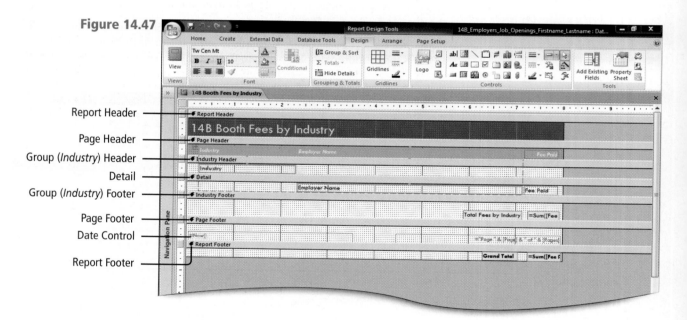

Report Header —
Page Header —
Group (*Industry*) Header —
Detail —
Group (*Industry*) Footer —
Page Footer —
Date Control —
Report Footer —

2 Locate the **Page Footer** section of the report and examine the two controls in this section.

The **date control** on the left side, displayed as *=Now( )*, inserts the current date each time the report is opened. The **page number control** on the right side, displayed as *="Page" & [Page] & " of " & [Pages]*, inserts the page number, for example Page 1 of 2, in the report when the report is displayed in Print Preview or when printed. Both of these are examples of programming code that is used by Access to create controls in a report.

3 In the **Page Footer** section, click the **date control**. Shorten this control by dragging the right middle sizing handle to the left to **1.75 inches** on the **horizontal ruler**.

The Page Footer displays information at the bottom of *every page* in the report, including the page number and the current date inserted by those controls.

4 In the **Page Footer** section, click the **page number control**. Shorten this control by dragging the left middle sizing handle to the right to **5.5 inches** on the **horizontal ruler**.

5 On the **Design tab**, in the **Controls group**, click the **Label** button $\boxed{Aa}$. In the **Page Footer** section, position the middle of the $\boxed{+}$ portion of the $\boxed{{}^{+}A}$ pointer vertically in the middle of the section and horizontally at **2 inches** on the **horizontal ruler**. Click one time. Using your own first name and last name, type **14B Booth Fees by Industry Firstname Lastname** and then press $\boxed{\text{Enter}}$.

6 With the control selected, hold down $\boxed{\text{Ctrl}}$, and then press $\boxed{\uparrow}$ or $\boxed{\downarrow}$ to align the bottom edge even with the other two controls in the section. Do not be concerned if this control overlaps the page number control. Compare your screen with Figure 14.48.

> As you type, the label expands to accommodate the text. An Error Checking Options button displays to the left of the label because Access detects a potential problem. In this instance, the control you added is a new unassociated label. If you click the Error Checking Options button, a list of options display, one of which is to associate—attach—the new label to a text box control so that the two controls can be treated as one unit for the purpose of moving the controls. This label control should not be attached to a text box control, so you can ignore the Error Checking Options button. A green triangle displays in the upper left corner of the affected control to indicate there might be a potential problem with the control.

Figure 14.48

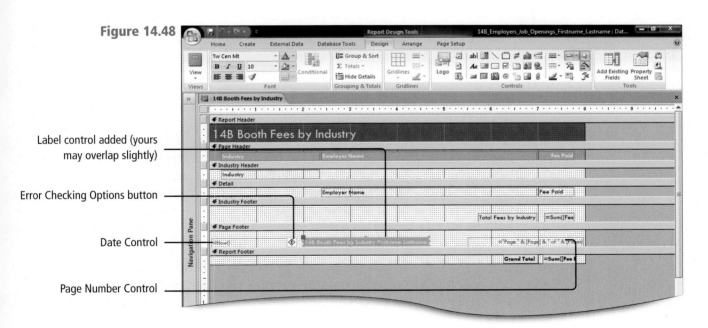

Label control added (yours may overlap slightly)

Error Checking Options button

Date Control

Page Number Control

7 With the label control selected, on the **Design tab**, in the **Font group**, click the **Font Color button arrow**, and then under **Access Theme Colors**, on the second row, click **Access Theme 1**.

8 Save ⊟ the report. On the status bar, click the **Report View** button ▣. Scroll down to the bottom of the report, and then compare your screen with Figure 14.49.

> The new label displays with your name and the new font color.

Figure 14.49

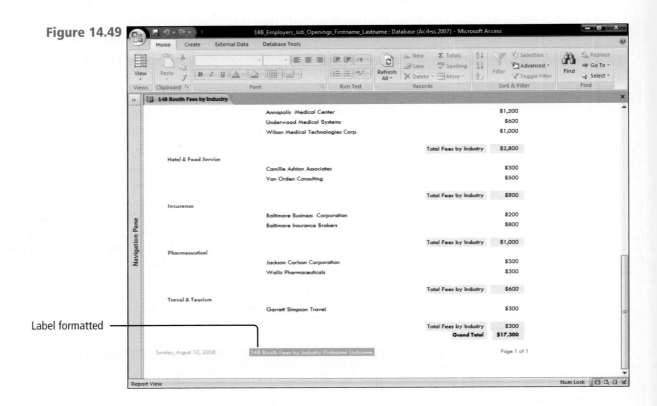

Label formatted

Objective 10
Print a Report and Keep Data Together

Before you print a report, examine the preview of the report to ensure that all of the labels and data are fully displayed, and to make sure that all of the data is properly grouped. Sometimes a page break occurs in the middle of a group of data, leaving the labels on one page and the data or totals on another page.

Activity 14.16 Keeping Data Together and Printing a Report

It is possible to keep the data in a group together so it does not break across a page unless, of course, the data itself exceeds the length of a page.

1 From the **Office** 🗐 menu, point to the **Print** button, and then click **Print Preview**. On the **Print Preview tab**, in the **Zoom group**, click the **One Page** button.

2 In the **Zoom group**, click the **Zoom button arrow**, and then click **Zoom 100%**. Scroll down to the bottom of the report to see where the first page ends, and then at the bottom of the screen, click the **Next Page** button ▸. Scroll up to display the top of **Page 2**. Alternatively, in the Zoom group, click the Two Pages button to see a reduced view of the pages side by side.

This report will print on two pages. The data in the *Insurance* group is split between pages 1 and 2.

3 On the **Print Preview tab**, in the **Close Preview group**, click the **Close Print Preview** button. On the status bar, click the **Layout View** button.

4 On the **Format tab**, in the **Grouping & Totals group**, point to the **Group & Sort** button, and then read its ScreenTip. Then click the **Group & Sort** button.

At the bottom of the screen, the *Group, Sort, and Total pane* displays, where you can control how information is sorted and grouped. This pane gives you the most flexibility when you want to add or modify groups, sort orders, or totals options on a report. Layout view is the preferred view in which to accomplish such tasks, because you can see how your changes affect the display of the data.

5 In the **Group, Sort, and Total** pane, on the **Group on Industry bar**, click **More**. To the right of **do not keep group together on one page**, click the **arrow**, and then point to **keep whole group together on one page**. Compare your screen with Figure 14.50.

Figure 14.50

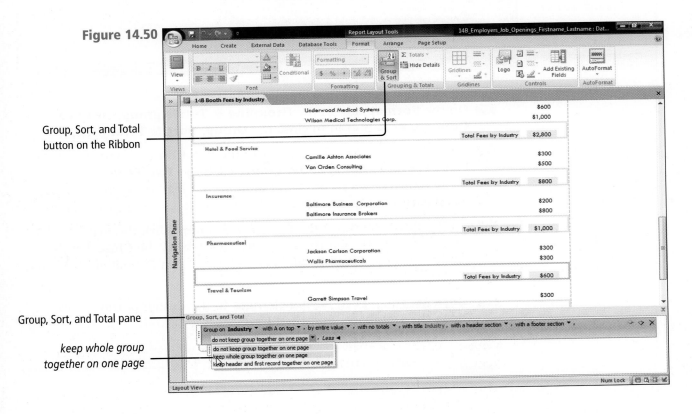

Group, Sort, and Total button on the Ribbon

Group, Sort, and Total pane

keep whole group together on one page

6 Click **keep whole group together on one page**. On the **Group on Industry bar**, click the **with A on top arrow**, and then click **with A on top**, which indicates this field is sorting in ascending order. Compare your screen with Figure 14.51.

The *keep whole group together on one page* command keeps each employer group together, from the name in the group header through the summary in the group footer.

Figure 14.51

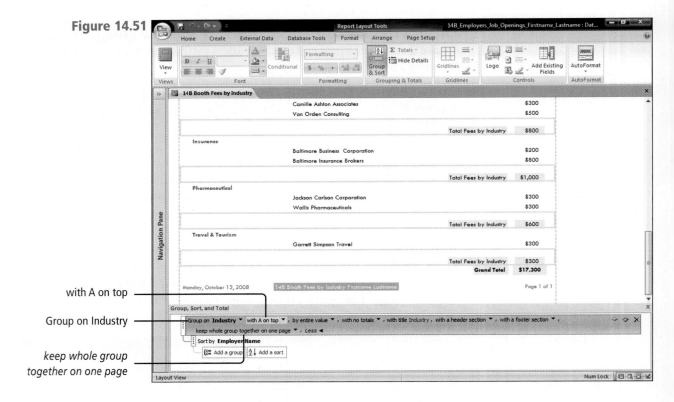

with A on top

Group on Industry

keep whole group
together on one page

7 On the **Format tab**, in the **Grouping & Totals group**, click the **Group & Sort** button to close the **Group, Sort & Total** pane.

8 From the **Office** menu, point to the **Print** button, and then click **Print Preview**. In the **Zoom group**, click the **Two Pages** button. Verify that the two records and total for the *Insurance* group display together at the top of page 2.

9 On the **Print Preview tab**, in the **Print group**, click the **Print** button to print the report. On the **Print Preview tab**, in the **Close Preview group**, click the **Close Print Preview** button. Or, submit electronically as directed.

10 **Close** ☒ the report, saving changes to the design of the report. **Close** the Database, and then **Exit** Access.

End **You have completed Project 14B** ———————

There's More You Can Do!

Close Access and any other open windows. Display the Start menu, click Computer, and then navigate to the student files that accompany this textbook. In the folder **02_theres_more_you_can_do**, locate and open the folder for this chapter. Open and print the instructions for this project, which are provided to you in Adobe PDF format.

Try IT! 1—Insert a Logo into a Form or a Report

In this Try It! exercise, you will insert a logo into an Access form.

Content-Based Assessments

Summary

A form is a tool for either entering or viewing information in a database. Although you can both enter and view database information in the database table itself, using a form is easier because it can display one record at a time. The Form tool creates an instant form based on the fields in the table. Using the Form Wizard, you can create a customized form. When created, a form can be modified in Layout View or in Design View.

Reports in Access summarize the data in a database in a professional-looking manner suitable for printing. The Report tool, the Blank Report tool, and the Report Wizard assist in report creation. The design of a report can be modified so that the final report is laid out in a format that is useful for the person reading it.

Key Terms

Content-Based Assessments

Matching

Match each term in the second column with its correct definition in the first column by writing the letter of the term on the blank line in front of the correct definition.

_____ **1.** An Access object with which you can enter, edit, or display data from a table or a query; a window for displaying and collecting information.

_____ **2.** The action of typing a record into a database.

_____ **3.** The Access tool that creates a form with a single mouse click, and that includes all the fields from the underlying data source (table or query).

_____ **4.** The Access view in which you can make changes to a form or to a report while the form is running, and in which the data from the underlying record source displays.

_____ **5.** The term used to describe objects and controls that are based on data that is stored in tables.

_____ **6.** The order in which the insertion point moves from one field to the next in a form when you press the Tab key.

_____ **7.** The bar on the left side of a form with which you can select the entire record.

_____ **8.** The detailed structured view of a form or report, and the view in which some tasks must be performed; only the controls, and not the data, are visible in this view.

A Bound

B Controls

C Data entry

D Design view

E Detail section

F Form

G Form Footer

H Form Header

I Form tool

J Label

K Layout view

L Record selector

M Section bar

N Tab order

O Text box control

_____ **9.** Information, such as a form's title, which displays at the top of the screen in Form view, and that is printed at the top of the first page when records are printed as forms.

_____ **10.** The section of a form or report that displays the records from the underlying table or query.

_____ **11.** Information at the bottom of the screen in Form view that is printed after the last Detail section on the last page.

_____ **12.** In Design view, a bar in a form or report that identifies and separates one section from another; used to select the section and to change the size of the adjacent section.

_____ **13.** Objects on a form or report that display data, perform actions, and let you view and work with information.

_____ **14.** The graphical object on a form or report that displays the data from the underlying table or query.

_____ **15.** A control on a form or report that contains descriptive information, typically a field name.

Content-Based Assessments

Fill in the Blank

Write the correct answer in the space provided.

1. A control that does not have a source of data is a _____ control.

2. The small boxes around the edge of a control indicating the control is selected and that can be adjusted to resize the selected control are _____ handles.

3. The grouped arrangement of controls on a form or report is referred to as the _____ layout.

4. A small symbol that displays in the upper left corner of a selected control layout, and with which you can move the entire group of controls is the _____ _____.

5. A list of characteristics for controls on a form or report in which you can make precision changes to each control is the _____ Sheet.

6. The process of displaying only a portion of the total records (a subset) based on matching specific values is called _____.

7. An Access command that retrieves only the records that contain the value in the selected field is called _____ _____ _____.

8. An Access command that filters the records in a form based on one or more fields, or based on more than one value in the same field is called _____ _____ _____.

9. A condition in which only records where one of two values is present in the selected field is the _____ condition.

10. A condition in which only records where both specified values are present in the selected fields is a _____ condition.

11. A database object that summarizes the fields and records from a table, or from a query, in an easy-to-read format suitable for printing is a _____.

12. The tables or queries that provide the underlying data for a report are referred to as the _____ _____.

13. The Access feature that creates a report with one mouse click, and which displays all the fields and records from the record source that you choose is the _____ _____.

14. An Access feature with which you can create a report from scratch by adding the fields you want in the order you want them to appear is the _____ _____ _____.

15. A control whose source of data is an expression—typically a formula—rather than a field is called a _____ control.

Content-Based Assessments

Access

chapter fourteen

Skills Review

Project 14C — Counseling Sessions

In this project, you will apply the skills you practiced from the Objectives in Project 14A.

Objectives: 1. *Create a Form;* **2.** *Use a Form to Add and Delete Records;* **3.** *Create a Form by Using the Form Wizard;* **4.** *Modify a Form in Design View and in Layout View;* **5.** *Filter Records.*

At the Job Fair, various professional organizations schedule personal one-on-one counseling sessions with interested candidates to give them advice about opportunities in the fields they represent. Janna Sorokin, the database manager, has a database in which she is tracking the counseling sessions that have been scheduled thus far. Your completed database objects will look similar to those in Figure 14.52.

For Project 14C, you will need the following file:

a14C_Counseling_Sessions

You will save your database as
14C_Counseling_Sessions_Firstname_Lastname

Figure 14.52

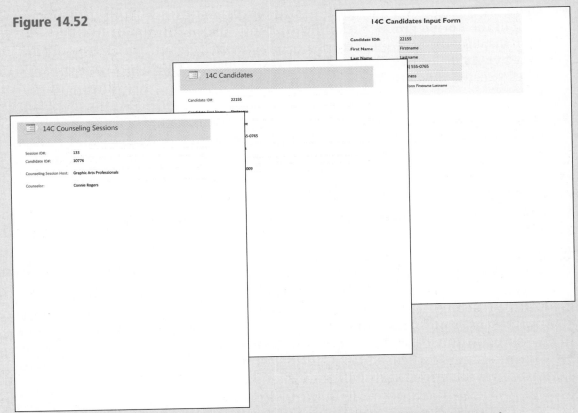

(Project 14C–Counseling Sessions continues on the next page)

Content-Based Assessments

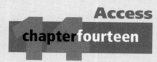
Skills Review

(Project 14C—Counseling Sessions continued)

1. Navigate to the location where the student files for this textbook are saved. Locate **a14C_ Counseling_Sessions** and click one time to select the file. **Copy** and then **Paste** the file to your **Access Chapter 14** folder. **Rename** the file as **14C_Counseling_Sessions_Firstname_ Lastname** and then **Start** Access. Navigate to your **Access Chapter 14** folder, open **14C_Counseling_Sessions**, and then **Enable this content**.

2. Click the **Database Tools tab**, and then in the **Show/Hide group**, click the **Relationships** button. If your relationships do not display, in the Relationships group, click the All Relationships button. Notice the one-to-many relationship between the 14C Candidates table and the 14C Counseling Sessions table using Candidate ID# as the common field. *One* candidate can attend *many* counseling sessions. **Close** the Relationships window. If prompted, do not save your changes.

3. **Open** the **Navigation Pane** and select the **14C Counseling Sessions** table. Click the **Create tab**, and then in the **Forms group**, click the **Form** button. **Close** the **Navigation Pane**. Click the **Next record** button four times to display the record for *Session ID# 105*. Click the **Last record** button to display the record for *Session ID# 132*, and then click the **First record** button to display the record for *Session ID# 101*. Recall that you can view records one at a time using a form. **Save** ⊟ the form. In the **Save As** dialog box, name the form **14C Counseling Sessions Form** and then click **OK**. As additional candidates schedule sessions, you can use this form to enter the data into the 14C Counseling Sessions table. **Close** the form.

4. **Open** the **Navigation Pane** and select the **14C Candidates** table. Click the **Create tab**, and then in the **Forms group**, click the **Form** button. **Close** the **Navigation Pane**. Notice that the form displays the scheduled sessions for the first candidate's record. **Save** ⊟ the form. In the **Save As** dialog box, name the form **14C Candidates Form** and then click **OK**. As new candidates register, this form can be used to enter the data into the Candidates table. **Close** the form.

5. **Open** the **Navigation Pane**, and then open **14C Counseling Sessions Form**. **Close** the **Navigation Pane**. Click the **New (blank) record** button. In the **Session ID#** field, type **133** and then press Tab. Continue entering the data as shown in the following table:

Candidate ID#	Counseling Session Host	Counselor
10776	Graphic Arts Professionals	Connie Rogers

6. **Close 14C Counseling Sessions Form** and then **Open** the **Navigation Pane**. Open the **14C Counseling Sessions** table, and then verify that the record you just entered in the form displays as the last record in the table. **Close** the table. From the **Navigation Pane**, open the **14C Counseling Sessions Form**, and then **Close** the **Navigation Pane**. From the **Office** menu, click **Print**. In the **Print** dialog box, under **Print Range**, click the **Selected Record(s)** option button, and then click **Setup**. In the **Page Setup** dialog box, click the **Columns tab**. Under **Column Size**, change the **Width** to **7** and then click **OK** two times to print the single record, or submit electronically as directed.

(Project 14C—Counseling Sessions continues on the next page)

Content-Based Assessments

Skills Review

(Project 14C–Counseling Sessions continued)

7. **Open** the **Navigation Pane**, open **14C Candidates Form**, and then **Close** the **Navigation Pane**. Click the **New (blank) record** button. Using your own first and last names, fill in the form using the data in the following table:

Candidate ID#	Candidate Firstname	Candidate Lastname	Phone Number	Professional Interest	Registration Fee	Date Fee Collected
22155	Firstname	Lastname	(443) 555-0765	Business	$15.00	10/10/2009

8. **Close 14C Candidates Form**. **Open** the **Navigation Pane**, open the **14C Candidates** table, and then verify that your record as a candidate displays as the last record in the table. **Close** the table.

9. From the **Navigation Pane**, open **14C Counseling Sessions Form**. **Close** the **Navigation Pane**. Click in the **Session ID#** field, and then on the **Home tab**, in the **Find group**, click the **Find** button. In the **Find and Replace** dialog box, in the **Look In** box, notice that *Session ID#* is displayed. In the **Find What** box, type **106** and then click **Find Next**. Confirm that the record for **Session ID# 106** displays. **Close** the **Find and Replace** dialog box.

10. On the **Home tab**, in the **Records group**, click the **Delete button arrow**, and then click **Delete Record**. In the message box, click **Yes** to delete the record, and notice that the number of records in the table decreased to *32*. **Close** the form.

11. **Open** the **Navigation Pane**, open the **14C Counseling Sessions** table. In the table, notice that the record for *Session ID# 106* no longer displays. **Close** the table.

12. From the **Navigation Pane**, open **14C Candidates Form**. **Close** the **Navigation Pane**. Press [Ctrl] + [F] to display the **Find and Replace** dialog box. In the **Find What** box, type **22155** and then in the **Look In** box, be sure that *Candidate ID#* is displayed. Click **Find Next** to display the record with your name. **Close** the **Find and Replace** dialog box.

13. From the **Office** menu, click **Print**. In the **Print** dialog box, under **Print Range**, click the **Selected Record(s)** option button. Click the **Setup** button, click the **Columns tab**, and then under **Column Size**, in the **Width** box, delete the existing text and type **7"** Click **OK** two times to print only your record in the form layout, or submit electronically as directed. **Close** the form.

14. **Open** the **Navigation Pane**, and then select the **14C Candidates** table. Click the **Create tab**. In the **Forms group**, click the **More Forms** button, and then click **Form Wizard**. Click the **Tables/Queries arrow**, and then click **Table: 14C Candidates**. Move the following fields to the **Selected Fields** list in the order given: **Candidate First Name**, **Candidate Last Name**, **Professional Interest**, and **Phone Number**. Click **Next**. Be sure **Columnar** is selected, and then click **Next**. Click **Solstice**, click **Next**, name the form **14C Candidates Input Form** and then click **Finish** to close the wizard and create the form.

(Project 14C–Counseling Sessions continues on the next page)

Content-Based Assessments

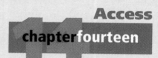
Skills Review

(Project 14C–Counseling Sessions continued)

15. **Close** the **Navigation Pane** and be sure your **14C Candidates Input Form** displays. Switch to **Design** view. If necessary close the Field List pane. Point to the upper edge of the **Detail section bar** to display the ⊹ pointer, and then drag downward approximately **0.5 inch**. In the **Form Header section**, click in the title *14C Candidates Input Form* to select the label control. On the **Design tab**, in the **Font group**, click the **Font Size arrow**, and then click **18**. Click the **Bold** button. Click the **Font Color arrow**, and then under **Access Theme Colors**, click **Access Theme 9**.

16. In the **label control** for the title, point to any **sizing handle** and double-click to apply Best Fit. Point to the upper edge of the **Detail section bar**, and then by using the ⊹ pointer, drag upward until the bar is at **0.5 inch on the vertical ruler**.

17. Drag the lower edge of the **Form Footer section bar** downward approximately **0.5 inch**. On the **Design tab**, in the **Controls group**, click the **Label** button. Position the plus sign of the pointer in the **Form Footer** section at approximately **0.25 inch on the horizontal ruler** and even with the bottom edge of the **Form Footer section bar**. Drag to the right to **5 inches on the horizontal ruler**, and then downward approximately **0.25 inch**. Using your own name, type **14C Candidates Input Form Firstname Lastname** and then press Enter. Double-click a sizing handle to apply Best Fit to the label control. Switch to **Form** view. **Save** 🖫 the changes you have made thus far.

18. Switch to **Layout** view. On the **Format tab**, in the **Controls group**, click the **Add Existing Fields** button to display the **Field List** pane. In the **Field List** pane, point to **Candidate ID#**, and then drag to position the pointer above the **Candidate First Name** controls. Release the mouse button. **Close** the **Field List** pane. Click the **text box control** for **Candidate ID#**, which currently displays *10115*, to surround it with an orange border. Point to the right edge of the **text box control**, and then drag to the left until all of the right edges of the text box controls align under the *m* in the form title above.

19. Click the **text box control** for **Phone Number**, which currently displays *(443) 555-0054*. With the control selected, drag upward with the 🔩 pointer until a thick orange line displays above **Professional Interest**. Release the mouse button to place the **Phone Number controls** above the **Professional Interest controls**. Click the **Candidate First Name label control** to select it, and then click again to place the insertion point in the control. In the label control, delete the word *Candidate* so that the label control displays *First Name*. Edit the **Candidate Last Name** label so that the label control displays *Last Name*. **Save** 🖫 the changes you have made to the form.

20. Click in a shaded area of the form to deselect controls. Hold down Shift, and then click to select each of the five **text box controls**. On the **Format tab**, in the **Font group**, click the **Fill/Back Color button arrow**. Under **Access Theme Colors**, click **Access Theme 3**. Click the **Font Size button arrow**, and then click **12**. Click in a shaded area of the screen to deselect all of the controls. Using the technique you just practiced, select the five **label controls**, change the **Font Size** to **11**, change the **Font Color** to **Access Theme 9**, and then apply **Bold**.

21. Click the **Professional Interest label control**, right-click, and then click **Properties**. In the **Property Sheet**, on the **Format tab**, click **Width**, type **1.75** and then press Enter. Click in a

(Project 14C–Counseling Sessions continues on the next page)

Content-Based Assessments

(Project 14C–Counseling Sessions continued)

shaded area to deselect the label control. Holding down ⌖Shift, select the **First Name**, **Last Name**, **Phone Number**, and **Professional Interest text box controls**, which have a blue background color applied. In the **Property Sheet**, change the **Height** to **0.3** and then press ⏎.

22. In the **Form Footer** section, click to select the **label control** with your name. In the **Property Sheet**, change the **Left** property to **1** and then press ⏎. In the **Form Header** section, click anywhere in the **label control** that displays *14C Candidates Input Form*. In the **Property Sheet**, change the **Left** property to **1** and then press ⏎. **Close** the **Property Sheet**.

23. Switch to **Form** view. Click the **Last record** button to display the record containing your name. From the **Office** menu, click **Print**. Under **Print Range**, click the **Selected Record(s)** option button. Click **OK** to print, or submit electronically as directed. **Close** the form, and then click **Yes** to save the changes you have made.

24. **Open** the **Navigation Pane**, and then open **14C Candidates Input Form**. **Close** the **Navigation Pane**. In the first record, click the **Professional Interest text box control**, which displays *Business*. On the **Home tab**, in the **Sort & Filter group**, click the **Selection** button, and then in the list, click **Equals "Business"**. Ten records display *Business* in the Professional Interest field. On the **Home tab**, in the **Sort & Filter group**, click the **Toggle Filter** button to remove the filter and display all 22 records. In the navigation area, notice the **Unfiltered** button.

25. Be sure that the first record displays, and then click to place the insertion point in the **Professional Interest text box control**. On the **Home tab**, in the **Sort & Filter group**, click the **Toggle Filter** button to reapply the filter. In the navigation area, click the **Last record** button to display the tenth record that matches *Business*, which is your record. In the **Sort & Filter group**, click the **Toggle Filter** button to display all of the records. In the navigation area, click the **Next record** button one time to move to **Record 2**. In the **Phone Number** field, select the area code text *(443)* including the parentheses. On the **Home tab**, in the **Sort & Filter group**, click the **Selection** button, and then click **Begins With "(443)"**. Nine records contain this area code. On the **Home tab**, in the **Sort & Filter group**, click the **Toggle Filter** button to remove the filter and display all 22 records.

26. With **14C Candidates Input Form** still open, on the **Home tab**, in the **Sort & Filter group**, click the **Advanced** button, and then click **Filter By Form**. Click the **Advanced** button again, and then click **Clear Grid**. Click the **Professional Interest** text box control, click the large **arrow** at the right edge of the control, and then click **Nursing**. In the **Sort & Filter group**, click the **Toggle Filter** button. Four candidates have a professional interest in *Nursing*. Click in the **Professional Interest text box control** again. In the **Sort & Filter group**, click the **Filter** button. Select the **Biology** check box, and then click **OK**. Five records meet the OR condition; that is, five candidates have a Professional Interest of either Nursing *or* Biology.

27. Click the **Toggle Filter** button to remove all filters. **Close** the form, **Close** the Database, and then **Exit** Access.

End **You have completed Project 14C** ——————————————————————————

Content-Based Assessments

Skills Review

Project 14D — Workshops and Rooms

In this project, you will apply the skills you practiced from the Objectives in Project 14B.

Objectives: 6. *Create a Report by Using the Report Tool;* **7**. *Create a Report by Using the Blank Report Tool;* **8**. *Create a Report by Using the Report Wizard;* **9**. *Modify the Design of a Report;* **10**. *Print a Report and Keep Data Together.*

In the following Skills Review, you will create, modify, and print reports for Janna Sorokin regarding details about the Workshop rooms for the Job Fair. Your completed database objects will look similar to Figure 14.53.

For Project 14D, you will need the following file:

a14D_Workshops_Rooms

You will save your database as
14D_Workshops_Rooms_Firstname_Lastname

Figure 14.53

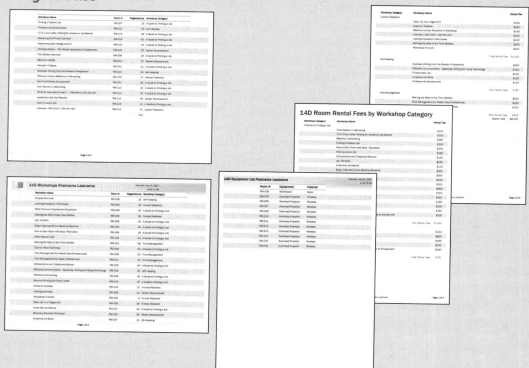

(Project 14D–Workshops and Rooms continues on the next page)

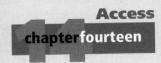

(Project 14D–Workshops and Rooms continued)

1. Navigate to the location where the student files for this textbook are saved. Locate **a14D_Workshops_Rooms** and click one time to select the file. **Copy** and then **Paste** the file to your **Access Chapter 14** folder. **Rename** the file as 14D_Workshops_Rooms_Firstname_Lastname and then **Start** Access. Navigate to your **Access Chapter 14** folder, open **14D_Workshops_Rooms**, and then **Enable this content**. Click the **Database Tools tab**, and then in the **Show/ Hide group**, click the **Relationships** button to view the relationship between the 14D Rooms table and the 14D Workshops table; *one* room can have *many* workshops. If your relationships do not display, in the Relationships group, click the All Relationships button. **Close** the Relationships window, and do *not* save changes if prompted.

2. **Open** the **Navigation Pane**, and then select the **14D Workshops** table. Click the **Create tab**, and then in the **Reports group**, click the **Report** button. **Close** the **Navigation Pane**. Click to select the field name **Workshop #**, right-click the selected name, and then click **Delete**. Click the **Rental Fee** field name, and then delete the field. Click the **Registrations** field name. On the **Format tab**, in the **Grouping & Totals group**, click the **Totals** button, and then click **Sum**. Scroll to the bottom of the report; the total number of registrations for the various workshops is *988*.

3. Click the **Page Setup tab**, and then in the **Page Layout group**, click the **Landscape** button. Click the **Format tab**, and then in the **AutoFormat group**, click the **AutoFormat button arrow**. Locate, and then click **Trek** AutoFormat. In the **Report Header** at the top of the screen, double-click the header text *14D*

Workshops to position the insertion point in the label control. Add your first name and last name to the end of the header text, and then on the **Format tab**, in the **Font group**, change the **Font Size** to **16**.

4. Click the **Workshop Name** field name, point to the right edge of the **label control** to display the ↔ pointer, and then drag to the right until each workshop name displays on one line. Click the **Room #** field name, point to the right edge of the **label control** to display the ↔ pointer, and then drag to the left to set the column width to accommodate the longest entry with a small amount of space to the right. Click any record in the report. In the upper left corner of the report, click the **layout selector** and then drag it to the right until the pointer is positioned approximately below the *D* in *14D* of the Report Header.

5. On the status bar, click the **Print Preview** button. On the **Print Preview tab**, in the **Zoom group**, click the **Two Pages** button to view the two pages of your report. To print your report, on the **Print Preview tab**, in the **Print group**, click **Print** and then click the **Close Print Preview** button. Or, submit electronically as directed. **Close** the **14D Workshops** report. In the displayed message box, click **Yes** to save changes to the design of the report. In the **Save As** dialog box, name the report **14D Workshop Attendance Report** and then click **OK**.

6. Click the **Create tab**, and then in the **Reports group**, click the **Blank Report** button. In the **Field List** pane, click **Show all tables**, and then click the **plus sign (+)** next to the **14D Rooms** table. Point to the **Room #** field, right-click, and then click **Add Field to View**. In the **Field List**

(Project 14D–Workshops and Rooms continues on the next page)

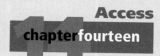

(Project 14D–Workshops and Rooms continued)

pane, drag the **Equipment** field into the blank report—anywhere to the right of **Room #**. Double-click the **Internet** field to add it as the third field in the report, and then **Close** the **Field List** pane.

7. Click the **Equipment** field name, point to the right edge of the orange border to display the ⟷ pointer, and then drag to the right until the text *Overhead Projector* displays on one line and there is a small amount of space between the name and the next column. On the **Format tab**, in the **Controls group**, click the **Date & Time** button. In the **Date and Time** dialog box, click **OK**. In the **Controls group**, click the **Title** button. Using your own name, type **14D Equipment List Firstname Lastname** and then press Enter. In the **AutoFormat group**, click the **AutoFormat button arrow**, and then apply the **Trek** AutoFormat. With the title selected, in the **Font group**, change the **Font Size** to **14**.

8. Click the **Room #** field name. Holding down ⇧ Shift, click the **Equipment** and **Internet** field names. With the three field names selected, change the **Font Size** to **12**. Using the **layout selector** button, move the group of controls until the pointer is positioned approximately below the *t* in the word *List*—or to whatever position appears to be horizontally centered between the margins. On the status bar, click the **Print Preview** button, and then **Print** the report, or submit electronically as directed. **Close Print Preview**, and then **Close** the report. In the message box, click **Yes** to save the changes to the design of the report. In the **Save As** dialog box, type **14D Equipment List Firstname Lastname** and then click **OK**.

9. Click the **Create tab**, and then in the **Reports group**, click the **Report Wizard**

button. Click the **Tables/Queries arrow**, and then click **Table: 14D Workshops**. Use the **One Field** button to move the following fields to the **Selected Fields** list in the order given: **Workshop Category**, **Workshop Name**, and **Rental Fee**. Click **Next**. With **Workshop Category** selected, click the **One Field** button to group the report by this field. Click **Next**. Click the **1** box **arrow**, and then click **Workshop Name** to sort by the name of the workshop. Click the **Summary Options** button. To the right of **Rental Fee**, select the **Sum** check box. Under **Show**, be sure the **Detail and Summary** option button is selected, and then click **OK**.

10. Click **Next**. Under **Layout**, be sure that the **Stepped** option button is selected. Under **Orientation**, be sure that **Portrait** is selected, and at the bottom be sure that the **Adjust the field width so all fields fit on a page** check box is selected. Click **Next**. In the list of styles, click the **Trek** style, and then click **Next**. In the **What title do you want for your report?** text box, name the report **14D Room Rental Fees by Workshop Category** and then click **Finish**. In the **Zoom group**, click the **Two Pages** button, and then examine the report as currently formatted. On the status bar, click the **Layout View** button.

11. Select the **Workshop Category label control**, and then widen the right side of the controls to align under the *t* in *Rental* in the Report Header above. Widen the right side of the **Rental Fee label control** to just slightly inside the dashed margin. Then drag the left side of the control to the right to shorten the control and leave a small amount of space to accommodate the data.

(Project 14D–Workshops and Rooms continues on the next page)

(Project 14D–Workshops and Rooms continued)

12. Scroll down to display the summary information for the workshop categories of *A Guide to Finding a Job* and *Career Advancement*. Within each **Workshop Category group**, notice the **Summary for 'Workshop Category'** information. Click any one of the **Summary for 'Workshop Category' controls**. Right-click the selected control, and then from the shortcut menu, click **Delete**.

13. Click any of the **Rental Fee text box controls**—the last field. Right-click any of the selected controls, and then from the shortcut menu, click **Properties**. In the **Property Sheet**, click the **Format tab**. Click in the **Decimal Places** property setting box, and then click the **arrow** that displays to the right of *Auto*. In the list, click **0**. **Close** the **Property Sheet**.

14. In any of the **Workshop Category groupings** of the report, to the right of the word *Sum*, click the dollar amount to select these controls. Point to any of the selected controls, right-click, and then from the shortcut menu, click **Properties**. Change the number of **Decimal Places** to **0**, and then **Close** the **Property Sheet**.

15. Using the ↔ pointer in the selected control, move the right edge and then the left edge of the control to position the summed amounts directly under the Rental Fees field—the last field—with just enough space to accommodate the data. On the left side of the report, click one of the **Sum label controls** to select these controls, and then click again to place the insertion point inside the selected control. Alternatively, double-click to place the insertion point inside the control. **Delete** the text, type **Total Rental Fees** and then press Enter. Move the controls to the immediate left of the summed amounts.

16. At the top of the report, click the **Workshop Category label control**. Holding down ⇧ Shift, click the **Workshop Name label control**, and then click the **Rental Fee label control**. On the **Format tab**, in the **Font group**, click the **Italic** button. Scroll down to display the end of the report. Click to select the sum **$6400.00**, which is the Grand Total for all the rental fees. Display the **Property Sheet** for this control and change its format to **0 Decimal Places**. **Close** the **Property Sheet**, and then adjust each side of the control to position it below the other fees. In the **Font group**, click the **Bold** button. By adjusting the right and left sides of the label control, move the text *Grand Total* to the immediate left of **$6,400**, and then apply **Bold**. **Save** 🔲 the changes you have made to your report.

17. Press Ctrl + Home to display the top of the report, and then on the status bar, click the **Design View** button. Drag the upper edge of the **Page Header section bar** downward approximately **0.5 inch**. Click the **Report Header** *14D Room Rental Fees by Workshop Category*, and then change the **Font Size** to **26**. Double-click a sizing handle to apply Best Fit. Drag the **Page Header section bar** upward slightly to approximately **0.5 inch on the vertical ruler**.

18. In the **Page Footer** section, click to select the **date control**. Shorten this control by dragging the right sizing handle to the left to **1.75 inches on the horizontal ruler**. Click the **page number control** and shorten this control by dragging the left sizing handle to the right to **5.5 inches on the horizontal ruler**.

19. On the **Design tab**, in the **Controls group**, click the **Label** button, and then in the **Page Footer** section, position the plus sign portion of the pointer vertically in the

(Project 14D–Workshops and Rooms continues on the next page)

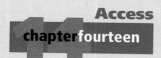

(Project 14D–Workshops and Rooms continued)

middle of the section and horizontally at **2 inches on the horizontal ruler**. Click one time, and then using your own name, type **14D Rental Fees by Category Firstname Lastname** and then press [Enter]. If necessary, hold down [Ctrl] and then press [↑] to align the top edge of the control even with the top edges of the other two controls. Do not be concerned if this control overlaps the page number control. With the label control selected, on the **Design tab**, in the **Font group**, click the **Font Color button arrow**, and then under **Access Theme Colors**, click **Access Theme 9**.

20. **Save** 🖫 the report, and then on the status bar, click the **Print Preview** button. If necessary, in the **Zoom group**, click the **Two Pages** button to view how your report is currently laid out. Notice that the bottom of **Page 1** does not break at the end of a category. **Close Print Preview**.

21. On the status bar, click the **Layout View** button. On the **Format tab**, in the

Grouping & Totals group, click the **Group & Sort** button. In the **Group, Sort, and Total pane**, on the **Group on Workshop Category bar**, click the **More** button, click the **do not keep group together on one page arrow**, and then click **keep whole group together on one page**. Click the **with A on top arrow**, and then click **with A on top**, which indicates this field is sorting in ascending order. In the **Grouping & Totals group**, click the **Group & Sort** button to close the **Group, Sort & Total pane**.

22. On the status bar, click the **Print Preview** button. Notice that the categories are kept together on the printed pages. **Print** the report, or submit electronically as directed. **Close** the report and click **Yes** to save the changes to the design of your report. **Close** the Database, and then **Exit** Access.

End **You have completed Project 14D** ————————————

Access

chapter**fourteen**

Mastering Access

Project 14E — Raffle Sponsors

In this project, you will apply skills you practiced from the Objectives in Projects 14A and 14B.

Objectives: 1. *Create a Form;* **2**. *Use a Form to Add and Delete Records;* **6**.*Create a Report by Using the Report Tool;* **7**. *Create a Report by Using the Blank Report Tool;* **10**. *Print a Report and Keep Data Together.*

In the following Mastering Access project, you will assist Janna Sorokin, database manager for the Greater Baltimore Area Job Fair, in using a database to track raffle items and sponsors for the fair event. Your completed form and report will look similar to Figure 14.54.

For Project 14E, you will need the following file:

a14E_Raffle_Sponsors

You will save your database as 14E_Raffle_Sponsors_Firstname_Lastname

Figure 14.54

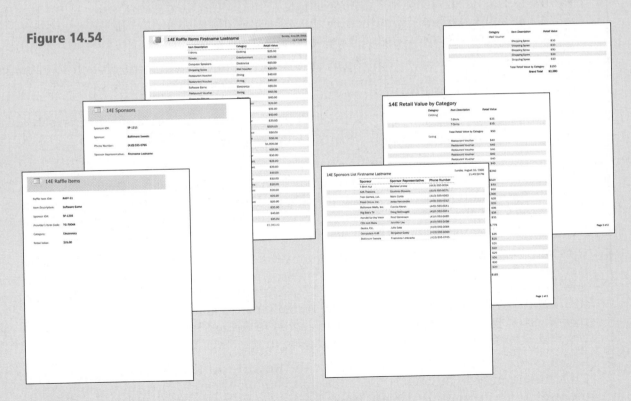

(Project 14E–Raffle Sponsors continues on the next page)

Content-Based Assessments

(Project 14E–Raffle Sponsors continued)

1. Navigate to the location where the student files for this textbook are saved. Locate **a14E_Raffle_Sponsors** and click one time to select the file. **Copy** and then **Paste** the file to your **Access Chapter 14** folder. **Rename** the file as **14E_Raffle_Sponsors_Firstname_Lastname** and then **Start** Access. Navigate to your **Access Chapter 14** folder, open **14E_Raffle_Sponsors**, and then **Enable this content**. Click the **Database Tools tab** and view the relationship between the 14E Sponsors table and the 14E Raffle Items table. *One* sponsor can provide *many* raffle items during the Job Fair event. If your relationships do not display, in the Relationships group, click the All Relationships button. **Close** the Relationships window, and do *not* save changes if prompted.

2. Based on the **14E Raffle Items** table, use the **Form** tool to create a form. Switch to **Form** view and scroll through the records. Add a new record as follows:

Raffle Item ID#	Item Description	Sponsor ID#	Provider's Item Code	Category	Retail Value
RAFF-31	**Software Game**	**SP-1203**	**TG-79044**	**Electronics**	**35**

3. After adding the record, display the **Print** dialog box, click the **Selected Record(s)** option button, click the **Setup** button, click the **Columns tab**, and then under **Column Size**, in the **Width** box, type **7"** Click **OK** two times to print only this record in the form layout, or submit electronically as directed. **Close** the form, saving it as **14E Raffle Items Form**

4. Based on the **14E Sponsors** table, use the **Form** tool to create a form. Switch to **Form** view, and then using your own first and last names, add a new record as follows:

Sponsor ID#	Sponsor	Phone Number	Sponsor Representative
SP-1211	**Baltimore Sweets**	**(410) 555-0765**	**Firstname Lastname**

5. After adding the record, display the **Print** dialog box, click the **Selected Record(s)** option button, click the **Setup** button, click the **Columns tab**, and then under **Column Size**, in the **Width** box, type **7"** Click **OK** two times to print only this record in the form layout, or submit electronically as directed. **Close** the form, saving it as **14E Sponsors Form**

6. Open the **14E Sponsors** table, verify that your record as a sponsor representative displays as the last record in the table, and then **Close** the table. Open **14E Raffle Items Form**. Use the **Find and Replace** dialog box to locate the record for **RAFF-02**, **Delete** the record for **RAFF-02**, and then **Close** the form. Open the **14E Raffle Items** table. Examine the table and verify that the record for *RAFF-02* no longer displays. Then scroll to **Record 30** and verify that the new record you added for **Sponsor ID# SP-1203** is included in the table. **Close** the table.

7. Based on the **14E Raffle Items** table, use the **Report** tool to create a new report. Apply the **Trek** AutoFormat to the report, recalling that you should apply the AutoFormat first, and then edit other formatting. **Delete** the following fields: **Raffle Item ID#**, **Sponsor ID#**, and **Provider's Item Code**.

(Project 14E–Raffle Sponsors continues on the next page)

(Project 14E–Raffle Sponsors continued)

8. At the bottom of the report, notice that the Report tool summed the **Retail Value** field; the total is *$2,380.00*. Add your name to the end of the Report Header text, and then change the **Font Size** to **16**. Shorten the right side of the **Category** field leaving a small amount of space between the columns. Use the **layout selector** to visually center the layout horizontally between the margins. **Print** the report, or submit electronically as directed. **Close** the report, saving it as **14E Retail Value List**

9. Based on the **14E Sponsors** table, create a **Blank Report**. Add the following fields in the order given: **Sponsor**, **Sponsor Representative**, and **Phone Number**. Apply the **Trek** AutoFormat to the report. Widen the **Sponsor** field until all of the names display on one line. Add the **Date & Time** and **Title** controls, and then type **14E Sponsors List Firstname Lastname** as the report title.

10. Change the title's **Font Size** to **14**. Select the three field names, and then change the **Font Size** to **12**. Visually center the layout horizontally between the margins. **Print** the report; or, submit electronically as directed. **Close** the report, saving it as **14E Sponsors List**

11. Based on the **14E Raffle Items** table, create a report by using the **Report Wizard**, and then add the following fields in the order listed: **Category**, **Item Description**, and **Retail Value**. **Group** the report by **Category**, **Sort** by **Item Description** in **Ascending** order, and **Sum** the **Retail Value** field. Select the **Stepped** option, **Portrait** orientation, and **Trek** style. For the report title, type **14E Retail Value by Category** and then in **Print Preview**, click the **Two Pages** button to examine how the records break across the two pages.

12. Switch to **Layout** view. Widen the right side of the **Category controls** to accommodate the longest category name. Shorten the right side of the **Item Description controls** to accommodate the longest line, leaving a small amount of space between the columns. Select the three field names and apply **Italic**. Visually center the layout horizontally between the margins.

13. Select, and then **Delete** the **Summary for 'Category' controls.** Select any value in the **Retail Value** field, and then from the **Property Sheet**, change the **Decimal Places** to **0**. In the **Clothing** grouping of the report, to the right of the word *Sum*, click **$50.00** to select the calculated controls. Change the number of **Decimal Places** to **0**, change the **Font Color** to **Access Theme 10**, and then align the total under the values above.

14. Select one of the **Sum label controls**, change the text to Total Retail Value by Category and then align this control to the immediate left of the amount. Change the **Font Color** of the label control to **Access Theme 10**.

15. At the bottom of the report, select the Grand Total **$2,380.00**, change the number of **Decimal Places** to **0**, apply **Bold**, and then change the **Font Color** to **Access Theme 10**. Position the total directly below the other totals. For the **label control** that displays *Grand Total*, apply **Bold** and then change the **Font Color** to **Access Theme 10**. Position this label to the immediate left of the total amount, and then **Save** the changes you have made.

(Project 14E–Raffle Sponsors continues on the next page)

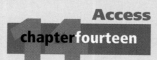

Mastering Access

(Project 14E–Raffle Sponsors continued)

16. Switch to **Design** view. In the **Page Footer** section, shorten the **date control** by moving its right edge to **1.75 inches on the horizontal ruler**. Shorten the **page number control** by moving its left edge to **5.5 inches on the horizontal ruler**. In the **Page Footer** section, create a **Label**, positioning the pointer at **2 inches on the horizontal ruler** and in the vertical center of the section. Click one time, and then using your own name, type **14E Retail Values by Category Firstname Lastname** and then press Enter. Double-click a sizing handle to apply Best Fit. With the label control selected, change the **Font Color** to **Access Theme 9**.

17. Display the report in **Print Preview** in the **Two Pages** arrangement, noticing the bottom of **Page 1**, and then **Close Print Preview**. Switch to **Layout** view. On the **Format tab**, in the **Grouping & Totals group**, click the **Group & Sort** button. From the **Group, Sort, and Total** pane, select **keep whole group together on one page** and sort **with A on top**. **Close** the pane, display the report in **Print Preview**, and then verify that the entire *Mall Voucher* group displays at the top of **Page 2**.

18. **Print** the report, or submit electronically as directed. **Close** the report, saving your changes, **Close** the Database, and then **Exit** Access.

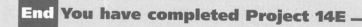

End **You have completed Project 14E** _____

Content-Based Assessments

Mastering Access

Project 14F— Contractors and Facility Services

In this project, you will apply skills you practiced from the Objectives in Projects 14A and 14B.

Objectives: 1. *Create a Form;* **2**. *Use a Form to Add and Delete Records;* **6**. *Create a Report by Using the Report Tool;* **7**. *Create a Report by Using the Blank Report Tool;* **8**. *Create a Report by Using the Report Wizard;* **9**. *Modify the Design of a Report;* **10**. *Print a Report and Keep Data Together.*

In the following Mastering Access project, you will assist Janna Sorokin, database manager for the Greater Baltimore Area Job Fair, in using a database to track facility and staff services for the fair event. Your completed objects will look similar to Figure 14.55.

For Project 14F, you will need the following file:

a14F_Contractors_Facility_Services

You will save your database as 14F_Contractors_Facility_Services_Firstname_Lastname

Figure 14.55

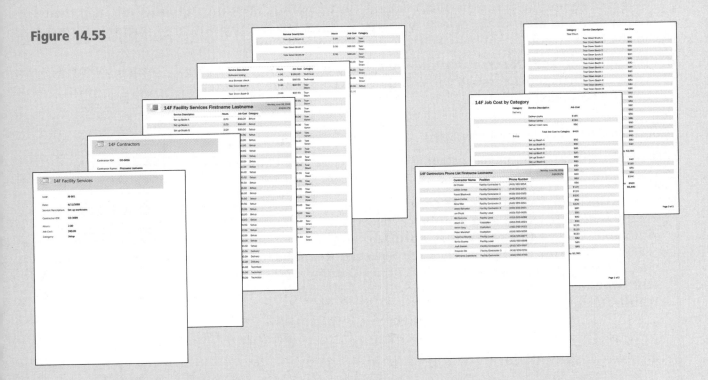

(Project 14F–Contractors and Facility Services continues on the next page)

Content-Based Assessments

(Project 14F–Contractors and Facility Services continued)

1. Navigate to the location where the student files for this textbook are saved. Locate **a14F_Contractors_Facility_Services** and click one time to select the file. **Copy** and then **Paste** the file to your **Access Chapter 14** folder. **Rename** the file as **14F_Contractors_Facility_Services_Firstname_Lastname** and then **Start** Access. Navigate to your **Access Chapter 14** folder, open **14F_Contractors_Facility_Services**, and then **Enable this content**. Click the **Database Tools tab** and view the relationship between the 14F Contractors table and the 14F Facility Services table. *One* contractor can provide *many* facility services during the Job Fair event. If your relationships do not display, in the Relationships group, click the All Relationships button. **Close** the Relationships window, and do *not* save changes if prompted.

2. Based on the **14F Facility Services** table, use the **Form** tool to create a form. Switch to **Form** view, and then scroll through some of the 60 records. Add a new record as follows:

Job#	Date	Service Description	Contractor ID#	Hours	Job Cost	Category
JB-061	4/11/2009	Set up workroom	CO-3009	2	$80.00	Setup

3. **Close** the form, saving it as **14F Facility Services Form** and then **Open** the **Navigation Pane**. Open the **14F Facility Services** table, scroll to the bottom, and verify that the new record for Job# JB-061 displays. **Close** the table, and then open **14F Facility Services Form**. In the navigation area, click the **Last Record** button. Display the **Print** dialog box, click the **Selected Record(s)** option button, click the **Setup** button, click the **Columns tab**, and then under **Column Size**, in the **Width** box, type **7"** Click **OK** two times to print only this record in the form layout, or submit electronically as directed. **Close** the form.

4. Based on the **14F Contractors table**, use the **Form** tool to create a form. Switch to **Form** view, and then scroll through some of the 15 records. Add a new record as follows, using your own first and last names:

Contractor ID#	Contractor Name	Position	Phone Number
CO-3016	Firstname Lastname	Facility Contractor 1	(410) 555-0765

5. **Close** the form, saving it as **14F Contractors Form** and then open the **14F Contractors** table. Verify that your record as a contractor displays as the last record in the table, and then **Close** the table. Open **14F Contractors Form**. In the navigation area, click the **Last Record** button. Display the **Print** dialog box, click the **Selected Record(s)** option button, click the **Setup** button, click the **Columns tab**, and then under **Column Size**, in the **Width** box, type **7"** Click **OK** two times to print only this record in the form layout, or submit electronically as directed. **Close** the form.

(Project 14F–Contractors and Facility Services continues on the next page)

(Project 14F–Contractors and Facility Services continued)

6. Open **14F Facility Services Form**. Use the **Find and Replace** dialog box to locate the record for **JB-003**, **Delete** the record for **JB-003**, and then **Close** the form. Open the **14F Facility Services** table. Examine the table and verify that the record for *JB-003* no longer displays. Then, scroll to the end of the table and verify that the new record you added for *JB-061* is included in the table. **Close** the table.

7. Based on the **14F Facility Services** table, use the **Report** tool to create a new report. Apply the **Trek** AutoFormat to the report. **Delete** the following fields: **Job#**, **Date**, and **Contractor ID#**. At the bottom of the **Job Cost** column, notice that the total job cost is *$5,440.00*.

8. Add your name to the end of the Report Header text. Shorten the right side of the **Service Description** field leaving a small amount of space between the columns (longest line is toward the bottom). Shorten the right side of the **Category** field to accommodate the data. Use the **layout selector** to visually center the controls horizontally between the margins.

9. Display the report in **Print Preview**, and then **Print** the report, or submit electronically as directed. **Close** the report, saving it as **14F Job Cost List Firstname Lastname**

10. Based on the **14F Contractors** table, create a **Blank Report**. Add the following fields to the report in the order given: **Contractor Name**, **Position**, and **Phone Number**. Widen the **Position** field until all of the positions display on one line. Click the **Date & Time** and **Title** buttons. For the title, type **14F Contractors Phone List Firstname Lastname** and then with the title still selected, apply the **Trek** AutoFormat, and then change the title's **Font Size** to **14**.

11. Select the three field names, and then change the **Font Size** to **12**. Visually center the controls horizontally on the page. Display the report in **Print Preview**, and then **Print** the report, or submit electronically as directed. **Close** the report, saving it as **14F Contractors Phone List Firstname Lastname**

12. Based on the **14F Facility Services** table, create a report by using the **Report Wizard**. Select the following fields in the order given: **Category**, **Service Description**, and **Job Cost**. Group the report by **Category**, **Sort** by **Service Description** in **Ascending** order, and **Sum** the **Job Cost** field. Select the **Stepped** option, **Portrait** orientation, and **Trek** style. For the report title, type **14F Job Cost by Category**

13. With the report displayed in **Print Preview**, click the **Two Pages** button and examine your report. Switch to **Layout** view. Widen the right side of the **Category control** to accommodate the longest category name, which is *Technical*. Shorten the right side of the **Service Description control** to accommodate the longest line, and leave a small amount of space between the columns (the longest line is at the bottom of the list). Select the three field names, and then apply **Italic**. Visually center the layout horizontally between the margins.

14. Select, and then **Delete** the **Summary for 'Category' controls**. Select any value in the **Job Cost** field, right-click, click **Properties**, and then change the number of **Decimal Places** to **0**. In the **Delivery** grouping of the report, to the right of the word *Sum*, click the value displayed as ##### or $400.00 to select the calculated controls. Change the number of **Decimal Places** to **0**, change the **Font Color** to **Access Theme 10**, and then align the total under the values above.

(Project 14F–Contractors and Facility Services continues on the next page)

Content-Based Assessments

(Project 14F–Contractors and Facility Services continued)

15. Select one of the **Sum label controls**, place the insertion point inside the control, delete the text, type **Total Job Cost by Category** and then press Enter. Align this control to the immediate left of the amount, and then change its **Font Color** to **Access Theme 10**. Be sure you have aligned the amount properly so that each Category's amount displays completely.

16. At the bottom of the report, select the Grand Total sum that displays as #####, change the number of **Decimal Places** to **0**, apply **Bold**, and then change the **Font Color** to **Access Theme 10**. Position the total directly below the other totals. If necessary, drag the left edge of the control to the left so that the entire grand total amount displays. Apply the same formatting—**Bold**, and **Font Color** of **Access Theme 10**—to the label control that displays *Grand Total*, and then position this label to the immediate left of the total amount. **Save** the changes you have made.

17. Switch to **Design** view. In the **Page Footer** section, shorten the **date control** by moving its right edge to **1.75 inches on the horizontal ruler**. Shorten the **page number control** by moving its left edge to **5.5 inches on the horizontal ruler**. In the **Page Footer** section, create a **Label**, positioning the pointer at **2 inches on the horizontal ruler** and in the vertical center of the section. Using your own name, type **14F Job Cost by Category Firstname Lastname** and then press Enter. Double-click a sizing handle to apply Best Fit. With the label control selected, change the **Font Color** to **Access Theme 9**.

18. Display the report in **Print Preview** in the **Two Pages** arrangement. Notice how the groups flow from the bottom of **Page 1** to the top of **Page 2**, and then **Close Print Preview**. Switch to **Layout** view. On the **Format tab**, in the **Grouping & Totals group**, click the **Group & Sort** button. From the **Group, Sort, and Total** pane, select **keep whole group together on one page** and **with A on top**.

19. Display the report in **Print Preview** in the **Two Pages** arrangement, and then verify that the entire *Tear Down* group displays on **Page 2**. **Print** the report, **Close Print Preview,** or submit electronically as directed.

20. **Close** the report, saving your changes. **Close** the Database, and then **Exit** Access.

End **You have completed Project 14F** _____

Content-Based Assessments

Mastering Access

Project 14G—Career Bookstore

In this project, you will apply all the skills you practiced from the Objectives in Projects 14A and 14B.

Objectives: 1. *Create a Form;* **2**. *Use a Form to Add and Delete Records;* **3**. *Create a Form by Using the Form Wizard;* **4**. *Modify a Form in Design View and in Layout View;* **5**. *Filter Records;* **6**. *Create a Report by Using the Report Tool;* **7**. *Create a Report by Using the Blank Report Tool;* **8**. *Create a Report by Using the Report Wizard;* **9**. *Modify the Design of a Report;* **10**. *Print a Report and Keep Data Together.*

In the following Mastering Access project, you will assist Janna Sorokin, database manager for the Greater Baltimore Area Job Fair, in using a database to track publishers and book titles for the books that are for sale at the Career Bookstore during the Job Fair event. Your completed objects will look similar to Figure 14.56.

For Project 14G, you will need the following file:

a14G_Career_Bookstore

You will save your database as
14G_Career_Bookstore_Firstname_Lastname

Figure 14.56

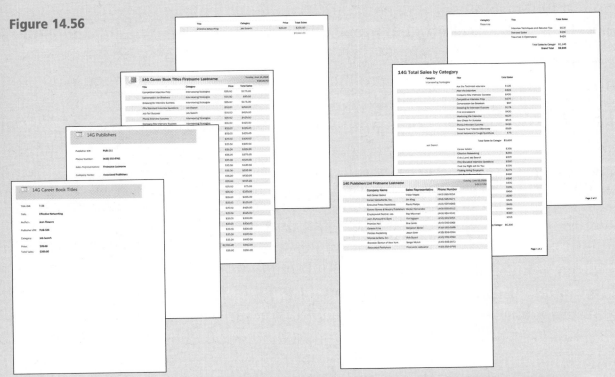

(Project 14G–Career Bookstore continues on the next page)

Content-Based Assessments

(Project 14G–Career Bookstore continued)

1. Navigate to the location where the student files for this textbook are saved. Locate **a14G_Career_Bookstore** and click one time to select the file. **Copy** and then **Paste** the file to your **Access Chapter 14** folder. **Rename** the file as 14G_Career_Bookstore_Firstname_Lastname and then **Start** Access. Navigate to your **Access Chapter 14** folder, open **14G_Career_Bookstore**, and then **Enable this content**. Click the **Database Tools tab** and view the relationship between the 14G Publishers table and the 14G Career Book Titles table. *One* publisher can publish *many* career books. If your relationships do not display, in the Relationships group, click the All Relationships button. **Close** the Relationships window, and do *not* save changes if prompted.

2. Based on the **14G Career Book Titles** table, use the **Form** tool to create a form. Switch to **Form** view, and then scroll through the 32 records to view the data. Add a new record as follows:

Title ID #	Title	Author	Publisher ID#	Category	Price	Total Sales
T-33	Effective Networking	Jean Flowers	PUB-100	Job Search	20	200

3. **Close** the form, saving it as **14G Career Book Titles Form** and then **Open** the **Navigation Pane**. Open the **14G Career Book Titles** table, scroll to the bottom, and verify that the new record for Title ID# T-33 displays. **Close** the table, and then open **14G Career Book Titles Form**. In the navigation area, click the **Last Record** button. Display the **Print** dialog box, click the **Selected Record(s)** option button, click the **Setup** button, click the **Columns tab**, and then under **Column Size**, in the **Width** box, type **7"** Click **OK** two times to print only this record in the form layout, or submit electronically as directed. **Close** the form.

4. Based on the **14G Publishers** table, use the **Form** tool to create a form. Switch to **Form** view, and then scroll through the 11 records to view the data. Using your own first and last name, add a new record as follows:

Publisher ID#	Phone Number	Sales Representative	Company Name	Title
PUB-111	(410) 555-0765	Firstname Lastname	Associated Publishers	Sales Associate

5. **Close** the form, saving it as **14G Publishers Form** and then open the **14G Publishers** table. Verify that your record as a Sales Associate displays as the last record in the table. **Close** the table, and then open **14G Publishers Form**. In the navigation area, click the **Last Record** button. Display the **Print** dialog box, click the **Selected Record(s)** option button, click the **Setup** button, click the **Columns tab**, and then under **Column Size**, in the **Width** box, type **7"** Click **OK** two times to print only this record in the form layout, or submit electronically as directed. **Close** the form.

6. Open **14G Career Book Titles Form**. Use the **Find and Replace** dialog box to locate the record for **T-05**, **Delete** the record for **T-05**, and then **Close** the form. Open the **14G Career Book Titles** table. Examine the table and verify that the record for *T-05* no longer displays. **Close** the table.

(Project 14G–Career Bookstore continues on the next page)

Content-Based Assessments

Mastering Access

(Project 14G–Career Bookstore continued)

7. Based on the **14G Career Book Titles** table, use the **Report** tool to create a new report. Apply the **Trek** AutoFormat to the report. **Delete** the following fields: **Title ID#**, **Author**, and **Publisher ID#**. At the bottom of the report, notice that the Report tool summed the **Total Sales** field; the total is *$9,945.00*.

8. Add your name to the end of the Report Header text, and then change the **Font Size** to **16**. Shorten the right side of the **Category** field leaving a small amount of space between the columns. Use the **layout selector** button to visually center the layout horizontally between the margins. **Print** the report, or submit electronically as directed. **Close** the report, saving it as **14G Total Sales**

9. Based on the **14G Publishers** table, create a **Blank Report**. Add the following fields to the report in the order given: **Company Name**, **Sales Representative**, and **Phone Number**. Widen the **Company Name** field until all of the names display on one line. Click the **Date & Time** and **Title** buttons. For the title, type **14G Publishers List Firstname Lastname** and then apply the **Trek** AutoFormat. Change the title's **Font Size** to **14**. Select the three field names and change the **Font Size** to **12**. Use the **layout selector** to visually center the layout horizontally between the margins. **Print** the report; or, submit electronically as directed. **Close** the report, saving it as **14G Publishers List**

10. Based on the **14G Career Book Titles** table, create a report by using the **Report Wizard**, and add the following fields in the order listed: **Category**, **Title**, and **Total Sales**. **Group** the report by **Category**, **Sort** by **Title** in **Ascending** order, and then **Sum** the **Total Sales** field. Select the **Stepped** option, **Portrait** orientation, and **Trek** style. For the report title, type **14G Total Sales by Category** and then in **Print Preview**, click the **Two Pages** button to examine how the records break across the two pages.

11. Switch to **Layout** view. Widen the right side of the **Category controls** to accommodate the longest category name. Shorten the right side of the **Title controls** to accommodate the longest line and leave a small amount of space between the columns. Select the three field names and apply **Italic**. Visually center the layout horizontally between the margins.

12. Select, and then delete the **Summary for 'Category' controls**. Select any value in the **Total Sales** field, right-click, click **Properties**, and then change the **Decimal Places** to **0**. In the **Interviewing Strategies** grouping of the report, to the right of the word *Sum*, click **$3,600.00** to select these controls. Change the number of **Decimal Places** to **0**, change the **Font Color** to **Access Theme 10**, and then align the total under the values above.

13. Select one of the **Sum label controls**. Change the text to **Total Sales by Category** and then align this control to the immediate left of the amount. Change the label control's **Font Color** to **Access Theme 10**.

14. At the bottom of the report, select the calculated control that displays *$9,945.00*, which is the Grand Total. Change the number of **Decimal Places** to **0**, apply **Bold**, and then change the **Font Color** to **Access Theme 10**. Position the Grand Total directly below the other totals. Select the **label control** that displays *Grand Total*. Apply **Bold**, change the **Font Color** to **Access Theme 10**, and then position this label to the immediate left of the Grand Total amount. **Save** the changes you have made to your report.

(Project 14G–Career Bookstore continues on the next page)

Content-Based Assessments

(Project 14G–Career Bookstore continued)

15. Switch to **Design** view. In the **Page Footer** section, shorten the **date control** by moving its right edge to **1.75 inches on the horizontal ruler**. Shorten the **page number control** by moving its left edge to **5.5 inches on the horizontal ruler**. In the **Page Footer** section, create a label, and then position the pointer at **2 inches on the horizontal ruler** and in the vertical center of the section. Click one time, and then using your own name, type **14G Total Sales by Category Firstname Lastname** and then press Enter. Double-click a sizing handle to apply Best Fit. With the label control selected, change the **Font Color** to **Access Theme 9**.

16. Display the report in **Print Preview** in the **Two Pages** arrangement, notice the flow between the bottom of **Page 1** and the top of **Page 2**, and then **Close Print Preview**. Switch to **Layout** view. On **the Format tab**, in the **Grouping & Totals group**, click the **Group & Sort** button. From the **Group, Sort, and Total** pane, **keep whole group together on one page** and sort **with A on top**. **Close** the pane, and then display the report in **Print Preview** in the **Two Pages** arrangement. Verify that the entire *Resumes* group displays at the top of **Page 2**. **Print** the report, or submit electronically as directed. **Close** the report, saving the changes to the report.

17. Open **14G Publishers Form**. In the first record, click the **Title text box control**. In the **Sort & Filter group**, click the **Selection** button, and then click **Equals "Sales Representative"**. Six records contain the title *Sales Representative*. In the **Sort & Filter group**, click the **Toggle Filter** button to remove the filter and display all 12 records. Be sure the first record displays, and then click to place the insertion point in the **Title text box control**. Click the **Toggle Filter** button to reapply the filter, and then in the navigation area, click the **Last record** button to display the sixth record in the filtered group. In the **Phone Number text box control**, select the Area Code text *(443)*. Click the **Selection** button, and then click **Begins with "(443)"**. Four *Sales Representatives* have a phone number with an area code of *443*. Click the **Toggle Filter** button to remove the filter and display all of the records.

18. **Close** the form, **Close** the Database, and then **Exit** Access.

End **You have completed Project 14G** ———————————————

Content-Based Assessments

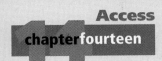
Mastering Access

Project 14H — *GO!* Fix It

In this project, you will apply the skills you practiced from the Objectives in Projects 14A and 14B.

For Project 14H, you will need the following file:

a14H_Resume_Workshops

You will save your workbook as
14H_Resume_Workshops_Firstname_Lastname

From the student files that accompany this textbook, locate and make a copy of the database **a14H_Resume_Workshops** in your chapter folder. Name the copy **14H_Resume_Workshops_Firstname_Lastname**

This database contains five errors that you must find and correct. Read and examine the database, and then edit to correct the errors that you find. Types of errors could include:

- Missing or incorrect data in tables, queries, forms, and reports, such as filenames, field names, types, descriptions, properties, records, and criteria.
- Table design errors, such as primary key.
- Forms design errors, such as form header and footer, page header and footer, detail, and layout.
- Reports design errors, such as report header and footer, page header and footer, detail, and layout.
- Page setup errors, such as margins, orientation, layout, or alignment.

To complete the project you should check for the following:

- In the Workshop Schedule Report, the items in the first column should display on one line. After adjusting the report, add your first name and last name to the report title.
- In the Workshops and Participants report, the columns are not fully visible and the format is not attractive. Adjust accordingly and use the Trek AutoFormat. After adjusting the report, add your first and last names to the report title.
- Examine the Participant Input form and adjust the field widths and heights to accommodate the data. Add your name to the title.
- Add a title to the Participant Fees report and include your name.
- Examine the Participant Fees report for accurate calculations; the report should indicate the total Workshop Fees and an appropriate label.

Print each database object that you correct, or submit your database electronically as directed.

End You have completed Project 14H

Outcomes-Based Assessments

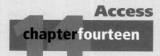
Rubric

The following outcomes-based assessments are *open-ended assessments*. That is, there is no specific correct result; your result will depend on your approach to the information provided. Make *Professional Quality* your goal. Use the following scoring rubric to guide you in *how* to approach the problem and then to evaluate *how well* your approach solves the problem.

The *criteria*—Software Mastery, Content, Format and Layout, and Process—represent the knowledge and skills you have gained that you can apply to solving the problem. The *levels of performance*—Professional Quality, Approaching Professional Quality, or Needs Quality Improvements—help you and your instructor evaluate your result.

	Your completed project is of Professional Quality if you:	Your completed project is Approaching Professional Quality if you:	Your completed project Needs Quality Improvements if you:
1-Software Mastery	Choose and apply the most appropriate skills, tools, and features and identify efficient methods to solve the problem.	Choose and apply some appropriate skills, tools, and features, but not in the most efficient manner.	Choose inappropriate skills, tools, or features, or are inefficient in solving the problem.
2-Content	Construct a solution that is clear and well organized, contains content that is accurate, appropriate to the audience and purpose, and is complete. Provide a solution that contains no errors of spelling, grammar, or style.	Construct a solution in which some components are unclear, poorly organized, inconsistent, or incomplete. Misjudge the needs of the audience. Have some errors in spelling, grammar, or style, but the errors do not detract from comprehension.	Construct a solution that is unclear, incomplete, or poorly organized; contains some inaccurate or inappropriate content; and contains many errors of spelling, grammar, or style. Do not solve the problem.
3-Format and Layout	Format and arrange all elements to communicate information and ideas, clarify function, illustrate relationships, and indicate relative importance.	Apply appropriate format and layout features to some elements, but not others. Overuse features, causing minor distraction.	Apply format and layout that does not communicate information or ideas clearly. Do not use format and layout features to clarify function, illustrate relationships, or indicate relative importance. Use available features excessively, causing distraction.
4-Process	Use an organized approach that integrates planning, development, self-assessment, revision, and reflection.	Demonstrate an organized approach in some areas, but not others; or, use an insufficient process of organization throughout.	Do not use an organized approach to solve the problem.

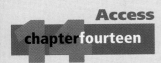

Problem Solving

Project 14I — Candidates and Offers

In this project, you will construct a solution by applying any combination of the Objectives found in Projects 14A and 14B.

For Project 14I, you will need the following file:

a14I_Candidates_Offers

You will save your database as
14I_Candidates_Offers_Firstname_Lastname

Copy the student file **a14I_Candidates_Offers** to your **Access Chapter 14** folder. Rename it as **14I_Candidates_Offers_Firstname_Lastname**

Michael Dawson, Executive Director of the Baltimore Area Job Fair, would like one form and two reports created from the Job Fair database. Mr. Dawson wants a report listing the Organization Name and Offer Amount of each job offered to a candidate as a result of the Job Fair.

Create and save the report as **14I Offers Firstname Lastname** and then print the report or submit it electronically as directed. Mr. Dawson also wants a report of the names, college majors, and phone numbers of the candidates. Save the report as **14I Candidates Firstname Lastname** and then print the report, or submit electronically as directed. Using the skills you have practiced in this chapter, create an attractive, easy-to-follow form that can be used to update candidate records. Using your own information, add a new record as **Candidate ID# 22102**. Save the form as **14I Candidate Update Firstname Lastname**

End **You have completed Project 14I** ————————————————

Outcomes-Based Assessments

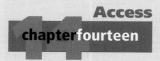
Problem Solving

Project 14J — Applicants and Job Openings

In this project, you will construct a solution by applying any combination of the Objectives found in Projects 14A and 14B.

For Project 14J, you will need the following file:

a14J_Applicants_Job_Openings

You will save your database as
14J_Applicants_Job_Openings_Firstname_Lastname

Copy the file **a14J_Applicants_Job_Openings** to your **Access Chapter 14** folder and rename it **14J_Applicants_Job_Openings_Firstname_Lastname**

Janice Strickland, Employer Coordinator, wants to know which types of positions have the most openings so she can highlight them on the Job Fair Web site.

Sort the records in the table so that you can provide Janice with the appropriate information, print the table in the sorted order, save the table as **14J Table Sort Firstname Lastname** or submit electronically, and save the changes to the table's design.

Janice also needs an input form for Job Fair applicants so she can update the database if needed. Save the form as **14J Applicant Input Form Firstname Lastname** and using your own information, add a new record as **Applicant ID# 4600** and then print the form page with your information, or submit electronically.

Janice needs a report with applicant contact information so she can send updates about new job openings. Create an attractive, easy-to-read applicant contact information report. Include a Report Header with **14J Applicant Contact Information Firstname Lastname** and then save and print the report, or submit electronically.

End **You have completed Project 14J** ——————

Outcomes-Based Assessments

Problem Solving

Project 14K—Candidates and Activities

In this project, you will construct a solution by applying any combination of the Objectives found in Projects 14A and 14B.

For Project 14K, you will need the following file:

a14K_Candidates_Activities

**You will save your database as
14K_Candidates_Activities_Firstname_Lastname**

Copy the file **a14K_Candidates_Activities** to your **Access Chapter 14** folder and rename it **14K_Candidates_Activities_Firstname_Lastname**

Janice Strickland, Employer Coordinator, wants a report that shows the room where each activity is being held so that she can give the Activity Coordinators their room assignments. Create an attractive, easy-to-read report that shows the Meeting Room for each activity. Include your name in the report heading, save the report as **14K Activity Meeting Rooms Firstname Lastname** and then print the report, or submit electronically.

Then, create a Candidate Input Form to add information for new candidates. Using your own information, add a new record as **STU-2049** to the form. Save the form as **14K Candidate Input Form Firstname Lastname** and then print the STU-2049 record from the form, or submit electronically.

End You have completed Project 14K ——————

More on your Student CD

The instructions for the following additional end-of-chapter projects are on your student CD in the folder 03_additional_end_of_chapter_projects.

Content-Based Assessments

Project L Mastering Access

Apply the skills you practiced in Project A.

Project M Mastering Access

Apply the skills you practiced in Project B.

Project N Business Running Case

Apply the skills you practiced in Projects A and B while helping an entrepreneur with the daily tasks of running a business.

In each chapter, this project focuses on applying the skills you have practiced in Projects A and B to a business. The project related to this business runs throughout the textbook. You will see how the Office programs relate to the day-to-day operation of a small business called Nelson Architectural Planning.

Outcomes-Based Assessments

Project O Problem Solving

Construct a solution by applying any combination of the skills you practiced from Projects A and B.

Project P Problem Solving

Construct a solution by applying any combination of the skills you practiced from Projects A and B.

Project Q You and GO!

Construct a solution that applies to your own life by applying any combination of the skills you practiced from Projects A and B.

Project R GO! with Help

Practice using Microsoft Office's Help Feature.

Project S Group Business Running Case

Work as part of a group to apply the skills you have gained thus far to help the Bell Orchid Hotel Group achieve its business goals.

Multimedia

The following multimedia accompany this textbook:

Companion Web site
www.prenhall.com/go

An interactive Web site designed to reinforce and test your understanding of the skills in this chapter.

AV-EDDs

In the folder in the front of this book you will find videos that demonstrate the objectives of the A and B projects in this chapter. These may help you understand how to complete the projects in this book.

Video Podcasts

In the folder in the front of this book are videos that can be played on your iPod, MP3 player, or computer. These videos demonstrate how to complete the more challenging objectives in this textbook.

chapter eighteen

Using Access Data with Other Office Programs

OBJECTIVES

At the end of this project you will be able to:

OUTCOMES

Mastering these objectives will enable you to:

1. Export Access Data to Excel
2. Create a Formula in Excel
3. Create a Chart in Excel
4. Copy Access Data into a Word Document
5. Copy Excel Data into a Word Document
6. Insert an Excel Chart into a PowerPoint Presentation

PROJECT 18A

Use Access Data with Other Office Programs

Introduction

An Access database may be the source of information you want to use to create content for a variety of other kinds of documents. For example, you may want to create an Excel worksheet to show numerical information, create a table within a Word document to list information, or create an Excel chart to include as part of a PowerPoint presentation.

You are preparing information in a Word document and in a PowerPoint presentation for a meeting. You will complete your materials for the meeting with some additional data from an Access database and an Excel worksheet.

Project 18A **Meeting Slides**

In Activities 18.01 through 18.6, you will prepare for a meeting by updating a Word document and creating a PowerPoint presentation using information gathered from Excel and Access. Your completed project will look similar to Figure 18.1.

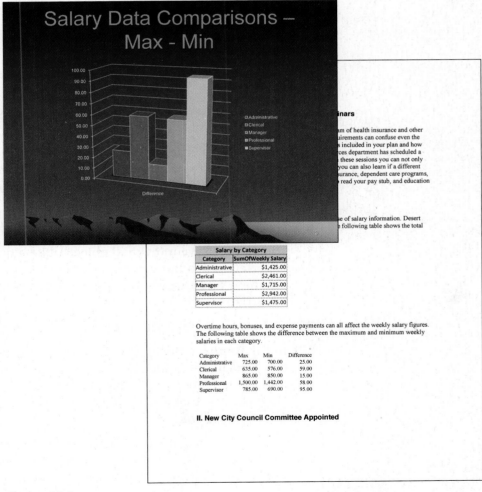

Figure 18.1
Project 18A—Meeting Information

Objective 1
Export Access Data to Excel

Activity 18.01 Exporting Access Data to Excel

Access includes a tool to export data from an Access database to an Excel workbook.

1 **Start** Access. From the folder that contains your project files, open the Access database **ip18A_Dept_Data**.

An Access database can have many different objects that organize the database information and that output data for different uses. The different types of Access objects are available in the Navigation Pane on the left side of the screen. Clicking the down arrow on the Navigation Pane changes what is displayed or selects a different object type. Selecting an object type from the list displays the objects of that type in the Navigation Pane.

Alert!

Did you get a security alert?

If you see a Security Alert Warning at the top of the screen, click the Options button. In the Microsoft Office Security Options dialog box, click the Enable this content option button and click OK.

2 In the **Navigation Pane**, if necessary, click **Queries** to review the list of query objects.

A query uses criteria to select, sort, or manipulate only those records in the database that meet the criteria. Queries are useful for reports and for searching for data to meet specific conditions, such as a date or a value.

3 Double-click the **Weekly Salary Query** to display the selected data.

You cannot save individual objects, like a query, as a file. Data is exported instead. Information can be maintained in an Access database and can be available for use by other programs through exporting.

4 Click the **External Data tab**, and in the **Export group**, click **Excel**.

5 In the **Export - Excel Spreadsheet** dialog box, use the **Browse** button to navigate to the folder that contains your project files. In the **File Save** dialog box, in the **File name** box, type **18A_Meeting_Data_ Firstname_Lastname** and make sure the **Save as type** box displays **Excel Workbook**.

Access includes different file types to choose from to create the exported data file. An Excel file type is a good choice when you plan to use the information with other Office programs.

6 Click the **Save** button, and then in the **Export - Excel Spreadsheet** dialog box, click **OK**. At the next prompt to

Save Export Steps, leave the Save export steps check box unchecked, and then click **Close**.

This saves the data from the Access query as a new Excel workbook.

7 **Close** the Query window, and leave Access open.

Objective 2
Create a Formula in Excel

Activity 18.02 Creating a Formula for Calculation in Excel

One of Excel's most powerful and valuable features is the ability to perform mathematical calculations. Although Excel has many automatic functions for calculating, you may need to create your own formulas. In this activity, you will create a formula to calculate the difference between numbers.

1 **Start** Excel. From the folder that contains your project files, open the Excel workbook **18A_Meeting_Data_Firstname_Lastname** that you saved in the previous export activity.

Excel refers to columns by letters and to rows by numbers. The intersection of a row and a column—a cell—is always named using the column letter first and then the row number, for example, A2. Clicking in a cell location enables you to enter or edit information in that cell.

2 Click cell **B1**, and then type **Max** to change the column heading. Press Tab to complete the entry. In cell **C1**, type **Min** to change the column heading. Press Tab. In cell **D1**, type **Difference** as a new column heading. Press Enter to complete the last cell entry.

You want Excel to calculate the difference between the Max and Min salary values in columns B and C. Excel formulas always begin with an = sign and use the cell reference (such as A2), not the actual value displayed in a cell.

3 In cell **D2**, type the formula **=B2-C2** and then press Enter.

Cell D2 displays the calculated value. You want to use the same calculation for the other items. The Auto Fill feature in Excel lets you duplicate the difference formula for the rest of the rows. The cell references will change relative to the new cell location for the formula, using the cells in the new row.

The Fill handle is a solid box at the lower right corner of a selected cell. When the mouse pointer is on the fill handle, it changes to a ⊞.

4 Click cell **D2**, and drag the **fill handle** at the lower right corner of the cell to cell **D6**, and then release the mouse button.

This copies the formula to the other selected cells in the Difference column and changes the cell references for each row's calculation. The calculated value is displayed in each cell.

5 Select columns **A:D**. On the **Home tab**, in the **Cells group**, click **Format**, and then in the displayed gallery, click **AutoFit Column Width**. Click outside the selection to cancel the selection. Compare your screen with Figure 18.2.

Figure 18.2

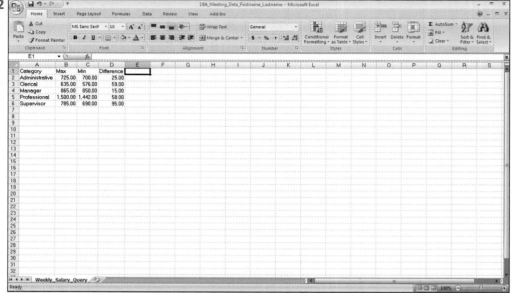

6 **Save** your workbook and leave it open for the next activity.

Objective 3
Create a Chart in Excel

Activity 18.03 Creating a Chart in Excel

To create a chart quickly, you can use the default settings in Excel. You can also select specific cells of data from the worksheet to include in the chart. Press and hold the Ctrl key when selecting multiple nonadjacent ranges.

1 Select cells **A1:A6**. Press and hold the Ctrl key, and then select cells **D1:D6**. You should have two nonadjacent areas of shaded selected cells.

Because you include the cells showing column headings in your selection, these labels will also display on your chart.

2 Click the **Insert tab**, and then in the **Charts group**, click **Column**. In the displayed gallery, click the first choice in the gallery.

This creates a chart with the default choices, a column chart on the current sheet, with a legend, and adds the Design contextual tab to the Ribbon. The Chart Area is the background area of the chart object that has no other chart content. When you use the mouse to point to the Chart Area, a ScreenTip displays that shows the name *Chart Area*.

3 Move the insertion point into the **Chart Area**, right-click, and then click **Select Data**. In the **Select Data Source** dialog box, click the **Switch Row/Column** button, and then click **OK**.

This creates a data set and legend items based on each row instead of each column. When you create charts, you will select rows or columns based on how you need to present the data.

Excel displays the chart along with the other information on the worksheet. You can move and position the chart on the sheet by clicking on the colored outer border on the chart, and then dragging the chart to a new position. You can also resize the chart using its sizing handles.

4 At the lower right corner of the chart object, drag the sizing handle to the right and down a bit, making the chart larger and easier to read. Point to the top border of the chart to display the ⊕ pointer, hold down the left mouse button, and then drag the upper left corner of the chart just inside the upper left corner of cell **A8** so it is under the cells containing the data.

5 On the **Design contextual tab**, in the **Chart Styles group**, click the **More** button. In the displayed gallery, move your mouse pointer over the chart styles and click **Style 11** to format the chart. Compare your screen with Figure 18.3.

Figure 18.3

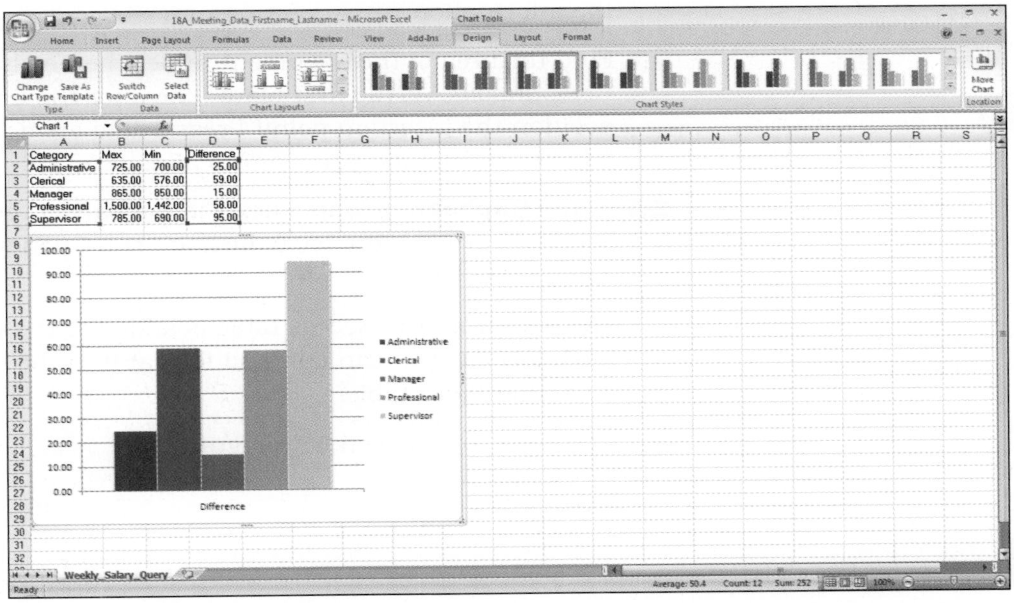

6 **Save** your workbook and leave it open.

Objective 4
Copy Access Data into a Word Document

Activity 18.04 Copying Access Data to a Word Document

Copy and paste are Windows tools. In this activity, you will use them to add data from an Access database to a Word document.

1 **Start** Word. Open the Word document **ip18A_Meeting_Topics** from the folder that contains your project files. **Save** the document as 18A_Meeting_Topics_Firstname_Lastname

2 On the taskbar, click the button to return to the Access database **ip18A_Dept_Data**, or open the file from the folder that contains your project files if you have closed it.

3 In the **Navigation Pane** in the **Queries** list, double-click to open the **Salary by Category** query.

You can copy data from Access, and then use it in another Office program.

4 Click the **Home tab**. In the **Find group**, click the **Select arrow**, and then click **Select All**. In the **Clipboard group**, click **Copy**, and then on the Windows taskbar, click the button to return to your open Word document.

Be sure to locate the correct position in the document before pasting the information.

5 Find the area of the document under the heading *II. Salary Data Comparisons.* At the first blank line after the first paragraph, click to position the insertion point. Press [Enter] to create another blank line for the information you want to add.

6 In the **Clipboard group**, click the top part of the **Paste** button. If you accidentally click the Paste button arrow, you will need to click Paste again.

The data from the Access table is added to the Word document in a table format. You can edit and format it in the same way as you can any other Word table.

Compare your screen with Figure 18.4.

Figure 18.4

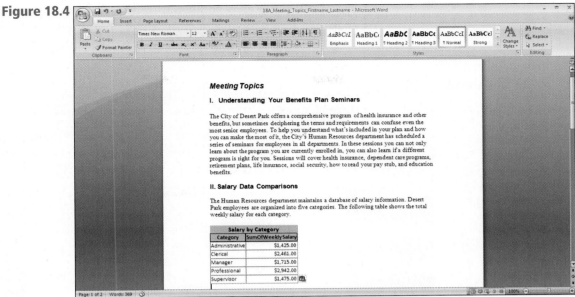

7 **Save** the document and leave it open for the next activity. **Close** Access.

Your Windows taskbar should now show buttons for your Excel workbook and your Word document.

Objective 5
Copy Excel Data into a Word Document

Activity 18.05 Copying Excel Data to a Word Document

You can also use copy and paste with Excel to get information to use in other Office programs. You can select only the cells that contain the information you want to use.

1 On the Windows taskbar, click the button to return to your Excel workbook **18A_Meeting_Data_Firstname_Lastname**.

2 Click and drag, starting in cell **A1** and ending with cell **D6**. In the **Clipboard group**, click **Copy**, and then on the Windows taskbar, click the button to return to your Word document.

3 Find the text paragraph after the *Salary by Category* table. Click in the first blank line after the paragraph to position the insertion point. Press Enter to create a new blank line for the data you will add.

4 In the **Clipboard group**, click the top part of the **Paste** button. The information from the cells in Excel is added to the Word document as a table. Compare your screen with Figure 18.5.

Tables in Word are easy to format and work with in your document. You can use Excel for performing any calculations, and then copy your results to paste as a table into your Word document.

Figure 18.5

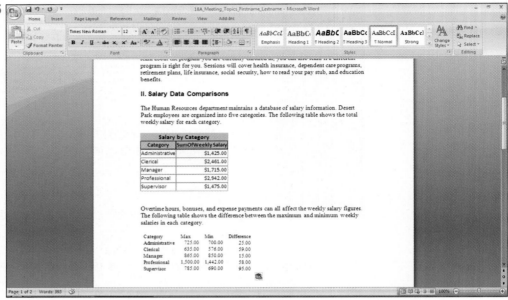

5 **Save** your document and **Close** Word. Leave the Excel workbook open to use in the next activity.

Objective 6
Insert an Excel Chart into a PowerPoint Presentation

Activity 18.06 Adding an Excel Chart to a PowerPoint Presentation

The last step in your preparation for the meeting is to add the chart you created in Excel to your PowerPoint slides.

1 **Start** PowerPoint. **Open** the file **ip18A_Meeting_Slides** from the folder that contains your project files. **Save** the file as **18A_Meeting_Slides_Firstname_Lastname**

PowerPoint presentations can convey ideas with visual impact. The Excel chart created from the Access data will add more visual content to the presentation. Because each of the Office programs has tools that are more specialized for the ideas you want to convey, you may need to create the information in one program and then copy it into another program.

2 Click **Slide 3**, where you will add your chart.

3 On the Windows taskbar, click the button to return to your Excel workbook **18A_Meeting_Data_Firstname_Lastname**. In the **Chart Area**, click to select the chart.

In the Office programs, a chart is a graphic object. When you want to select a chart, click the Chart Area to display the sizing handles on the corners and borders of the chart object.

4 In the **Clipboard group**, click **Copy**, and then on the Windows taskbar, click the button to return to your PowerPoint presentation.

5 In the **Clipboard group**, click the top of the **Paste** button.

The chart will be placed on the slide, but it may be sized and positioned differently than you want it to be in your presentation. You can size and position the chart on the slide just as you did in the Excel workbook.

6 Use the sizing handle in the lower right corner of the chart to make the chart about .75 inches wider and .75 inches longer. Point to the top border of the chart to display the ⊕ pointer, hold down the left mouse button, and then position the chart on the slide so that it is centered on the slide and below the title.

You may decide to edit the appearance of the chart. An Excel chart pasted into another Office program will have Excel contextual tabs available for editing the chart. The ribbon will change to show these contextual tabs when editing the chart.

7 On the **PowerPoint** slide, if necessary, click in the **Chart Area**. The Ribbon will show the Chart Tools contextual tabs. Click the **Design tab**, and in the **Type group**, click **Change Chart Type**. The **Change Chart Type** dialog box displays.

Chart types display to the left, and subtypes of these categories display to the right.

8 In the **Change Chart Type** dialog box, click the **3-D Clustered Column** subtype—the fourth item in the first row—and then click **OK**. The chart columns now have a different look to them.

9 Click outside of the chart to cancel the chart selection and remove the Excel contextual tabs.

Compare your screen with Figure 18.6.

Figure 18.6

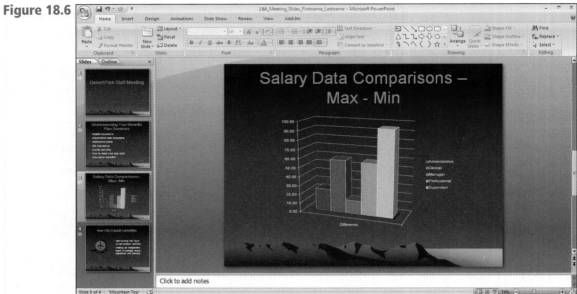

10 **Save** and **Close** the PowerPoint presentation and **Exit** PowerPoint, and then **Close** the Excel workbook and **Exit** Excel.

End You have completed this integration project ——

Glossary

Absolute cell reference A cell reference that refers to cells by their fixed position in a worksheet; an absolute cell reference remains the same when the formula is copied.

Accounting Number format The Excel number format that applies a thousand comma separator where appropriate, inserts a fixed U.S. dollar sign aligned at the left edge of the cell, applies two decimal places, and leaves a small amount of space at the right edge of the cell to accommodate a parenthesis for negative numbers.

Active cell The cell, surrounded by a black border, ready to receive data or be affected by the next Excel command.

Active window The window in which the mouse pointer movements, commands, or text entry occur when two or more windows are open.

Adaptive A feature where menus adapt to the way you work by displaying the commands you most frequently use.

Address bar Displays the path of the current file or folder; also, in Internet Explorer, displays the address of the active Web page.

Adjacent ranges Cell ranges that are next to each other.

Adjustment handle A handle on a selected object that can be used to drag parts of an object into various positions.

Adware Spyware that tracks a user's Internet browsing and installs malicious cookies.

Aggregate functions Calculations that are performed on a group of records.

Alignment The placement of paragraph text relative to the left and right margins

American Psychological Association (APA) style One of two commonly used styles for formatting research papers.

Anchor A symbol that indicates to which paragraph an object is attached.

AND condition A condition in which only records where both specified values are present in the selected fields.

Animated banner A series of rotating or changing text and images embedded within the Web page.

Animation effects Effects used to introduce individual slide elements so that the slide can progress one element at a time.

Antispyware software A program that protects a computer from malicious software designed to threaten privacy and confidentiality.

Antivirus software A program that protects a computer from malicious codes such as viruses, worms, and Trojan horses.

Application software Programs with which you accomplish tasks such as word processing, photo editing, or sending email, and use the computer in a productive manner.

Appointment A calendar activity occurring at a specific time and day that does not require inviting other people.

Appointment area A one-day view of the current day's calendar entries.

Archive To back up files and store them somewhere other than the main hard drive.

Arguments The values that an Excel function uses to perform calculations or operations.

Arithmetic logic unit (ALU) Part of the CPU that performs all the arithmetic and logic functions for the computer; handles addition, subtraction, multiplication, and division, and also makes logical and comparison decisions.

Arithmetic operator The symbols +, −, *, /, %, and ^ used to denote addition, subtraction (negation), multiplication, division, percentage, and exponentiation in an Excel formula.

Arrow keys The keys at the lower right section of the keyboard, used to move the insertion point within the program window.

Ascending order A sorting order that arranges text in alphabetical order (A to Z) or numbers from the lowest to highest number.

Aspect ratio The relationship of an object's height to its width; if locked, changing either the height or width will resize the object proportionally.

Audio port A port that connects audio equipment to the sound card of a computer to facilitate the exchange of data.

Auto fill An Excel feature that extends values into adjacent cells based on the values of selected cells.

AutoComplete (Excel) A feature that speeds your typing and lessens the likelihood of errors; if the first few characters you type in a cell match an existing entry in the column, Excel fills in the remaining characters for you.

AutoComplete (Word) A feature that assists in your typing by suggesting words or phrases.

AutoCorrect (Excel) A feature that assists in your typing by automatically correcting and formatting some text as you type; for example Excel compares your typing to a list of commonly mistyped words and when it finds a match, it substitutes the correct word.

AutoCorrect (Word) A feature that corrects common typing and spelling errors as you type, for example changing *teh* to *the*.

AutoFormat As You Type A Word feature that anticipates formatting based on what you type.

AutoNumber An Access feature that sequentially numbers entered records creating a unique number for each record; useful for data that has no distinct field that could be considered unique.

AutoSum Another term for the Sum function.

AutoText A Word feature with which you can create short-cuts to quickly insert long phrases with just a few key-strokes.

AVERAGE function A pre-written formula that adds a group of values and then divides the result by the number of values in the group.

Background style A slide background fill variation that combines theme colors in different intensities.

Backup tape drive A storage device used to save data to tapes resembling audiocassettes.

Banner area The screen area that displays important cal-endar information including *Day*, *Week*, and *Month* view buttons.

Base The starting point when you divide the amount of increase by it to calculate the rate of increase.

Between. . . And operator A comparison operator that looks for values within a range.

Bibliography A term used to describe a list of referenced works in a report or research paper, also referred to as Works Cited, Sources, or References, depending upon the report style.

Black slide A slide that displays at the end of a slide pre-sentation indicating the end of the slide show.

Blank database A database that has no data and has no database tools; you create the data and the tools as you need them.

Blank form In Outlook, a lined page added to the printout of the Card print style that you can use to manually list new contacts.

Blank Report tool An Access feature with which you can create a report from scratch by adding the fields you want in the order you want them to appear.

Bluetooth Wireless technology that uses radio waves to transmit data over short distances, and often used with mobile devices.

Body font A font that is applied to all slide text except titles.

Boot The process of starting up a computer.

Boot process See Boot.

Bound The term used to describe objects and controls that are based on data that is stored in tables.

Building block Pre-formatted content that you can add to your document, such as cover pages, pull quotes, and letterheads.

Bulleted levels Outline levels identified by a symbol.

Bulleted list A list of items with each item introduced by a symbol such as a small circle or check mark—useful when the items in the list can be displayed in any order.

Bullets Text symbols such as small circles or check marks used to introduce items in a list.

Burn The process of recording data to optical media such as a CD or DVD.

Bus topology A networking configuration in which all devices are connected to a central high-speed cable called the bus or backbone.

Calculated controls Controls whose source of data is an expression—typically a formula—rather than a field.

Card Style In Outlook, a print style which displays the name and address information alphabetically by last name.

Category axis The area along the bottom of a chart that identifies the categories of data; also referred to as the x-axis.

Category labels The labels that display along the bottom of a chart to identify the categories of data; Excel uses the row titles as the category names.

Cathode-ray tube (CRT) A picture tube device used in a monitor, similar to a television.

CD burner An optical storage device capable of reading data from and writing data to a CD.

CD drive A storage device used to read and, possibly, write data to CD.

CD-R Another name for a CD-ROM disc.

CD-ROM The acronym for Compact Disc-Read Only Memory; an optical storage device used to permanently store data and from which you can read and open files.

CD-RW A compact disc that can be reused to read and save files.

Cell (Access) The box formed by the intersection of a row and a column in a datasheet.

Cell (Excel) The small box formed by the intersection of a column and a row.

Cell address Another name for a cell reference.

Cell content Anything typed into a cell.

Cell reference The identification of a specific cell by its intersecting column letter and row number.

Center alignment Text centered between the left and right margin.

Central processing unit (CPU) The part of the computer responsible for controlling all the commands and tasks the computer performs, acting as the brain of the computer.

Chart (Excel) The graphic representation of data in a worksheet; data presented as a chart is usually easier to understand than a table of numbers.

Chart A graphic representation of numeric data.

Chart layout The combination of chart elements that can be displayed in a chart such as a title, legend, labels for the columns, and the table of charted cells.

Chart Layouts gallery A group of predesigned chart layouts that you can apply to an Excel chart.

Chart sheet A workbook sheet that contains only a chart and is useful when you want to view a chart separately from the worksheet data.

Chart style The overall visual look of a chart in terms of its graphic effects, colors, and backgrounds; for example, you can have flat or beveled columns, colors that are solid or transparent, and backgrounds that are dark or light.

Chart Styles gallery A group of predesigned chart styles that you can apply to an Excel chart.

Chart types Various chart formats used in a way that is meaningful to the reader; common examples are column charts, pie charts, and line charts.

Citation A list of information about a reference source, usually including the name of the author, the full title of the work, the year of publication, Web address, and other publication information.

Click To press the left (or primary) mouse button once.

Click and type pointer The text select (I-beam) pointer with various attached shapes that indicate which formatting will be applied when you double-click—such as a left-aligned, centered, or right-aligned.

Client In a client/server network, this is the computer most people interact with to request information from the server and to perform many of the tasks that can be accomplished with a computer.

Client/server network A network consisting of client and server computers; often used in businesses.

Clip art Graphic images included with the Microsoft Office program or obtained from other sources.

Clip art (PowerPoint) Images included with Microsoft Office or downloaded from the Web that can make your presentation more interesting and visually appealing; drawings, movies, sounds, or photographic images that are included with Microsoft Office or downloaded from the Web.

Clipboard A temporary storage area in Windows that stores the most recently copied item.

Clock speed A measurement of how quickly a CPU processes data, an indication of a CPU's processing power.

Close button The button in a title bar that closes a window or a program.

Collapse button A small minus (−) button to the left of a folder that you click to hide the items in that folder.

Collect and paste The process of collecting a group of graphics or selected text blocks, and then pasting them into a document at any time; the Office Clipboard holds up to 24 items, and the Office Clipboard task pane displays a preview of each item.

Color scales Visual guides that help you understand data distribution and variation.

Column A vertical group of cells in a worksheet.

Column chart A chart in which the data is arranged in columns and which is useful for showing data changes over a period of time or for illustrating comparisons among items.

Column heading The letter that displays at the top of a vertical group of cells in a worksheet; beginning with the first letter of the alphabet, a unique letter or combination of letters identifies each column.

Comma style The Excel number format that inserts thousand comma separators where appropriate, applies two decimal places, and leaves space at the right to accommodate a parenthesis for negative numbers.

Comment A note that can be added to a Word document from the Review tab; comments are not generally printed.

Comments area In Outlook, the area in the lower half of the Appointments form and Task form where you can enter information not otherwise specified in the form.

Common fields Fields that contain the same data in more than one table.

Communication or organizational software A program such as Microsoft Outlook, used to send and retrieve email and manage day-to-day tasks.

Comparison operators Symbols that evaluate each field value to determine if it is the same (=), greater than (>), less than (<), or in between a range of values as specified by the criteria.

Complimentary closing A parting farewell in a business letter.

Compound criteria Multiple conditions in a query or filter.

Compress A process to reduce the size of a file.

Computer A programmable electronic device that can input, process, output, and store data.

Computer fluent The term used to describe a person who understands the capabilities and limitations of computers and knows how to use computer technology to accomplish tasks.

Conditional format A format that changes the appearance of a cell range—for example by adding cell shading or font color—based on a condition; if the condition is true the cell range is formatted based on that condition, and if the condition is false the cell range is *not* formatted based on the condition.

Connectivity port A port that enables a computer to be connected to other devices or systems, such as networks, modems, and the Internet.

Constant value Numbers, text, dates, or times of day that you type into a cell.

Contact A person or organization about whom you can save information such as street and e-mail addresses, telephone and fax numbers, Web page addresses, birthdays, and pictures.

Context-sensitive command A command associated with activities in which you are engaged; often activated by right-clicking a screen item.

Contextual tabs Tabs that are added to the Ribbon when a specific object, such as a chart, is selected, and that contain commands relevant to the selected object.

Contextual tools Sets of commands added to the Ribbon when a specific object is selected and which enable you to perform specific commands related to the selected object; contextual tools display only when needed and no longer display after the object is deselected.

Control Objects on a form or report that display data, perform actions, and let you view and work with information.

Control keys Special keys, such as Ctrl, Alt, or Esc, used to increase keyboard functionality or provide shortcuts.

Control layout The grouped arrangement of controls on a form or report.

Control unit The part of the CPU responsible for obtaining instructions from the computer's memory; the control unit interprets the instructions and executes them, thereby coordinating the activities of all the other computer components.

Cookie A small text file containing information that identifies a visitor to a Web site.

Copy A command that duplicates a selection and places it on the Clipboard.

Copyright Laws that protect the rights of authors of original works, including text, art, photographs, and music.

COUNTIF function A statistical function that counts the number of cells within a range that meet the given condition—the criteria that you provide.

CPU See Central processing unit.

Criteria (Access) Conditions that identify the specific records you are looking for.

Criteria (Excel) Conditions that you specify in a logical function.

Crosshair pointer The pointer that indicates that you can draw a shape.

CRT See Cathode-ray tube.

Curly quote A decorative quotation mark, with curved lines instead of the straight lines found in straight quotes.

Custom animation list A list that indicates the animation effect applied to slide items.

Cut (PowerPoint) A command that removes selected text or graphics from your presentation and moves the selection to the Clipboard.

Cut (Word) The command to remove selected text from a document and move it to the Office Clipboard.

Daily Style In Outlook, a print style that prints the appointments for the currently displayed day.

Daily Task List In Outlook, an abbreviated list of current tasks stored in the Tasks folder.

Data Words, numbers, sounds, or pictures that represent facts about people, events, things, or ideas.

Data (Access) Facts about people, events, things, or ideas.

Data (Excel) Text or numbers in a cell.

Data bar A cell format consisting of a shaded bar that provides a visual cue to the reader about the value of a cell relative to other cells; the length of the bar represents the value in the cell—a longer bar represents a higher value and a shorter bar represents a lower value.

Data entry The action of typing the record data into a database.

Data marker A column, bar, area, dot, pie slice, or other symbol in a chart that represents a single data point; related data points form a data series.

Data point A value that originates in a worksheet cell and that is represented in a chart by a data marker.

Data series Related data points represented by data markers; each data series has a unique color or pattern represented in the chart legend.

Data source (Word) A list of variable information, such as names and addresses, that is merged with a main document to create customized form letters or labels.

Data source The table or tables from which a query selects its data.

Data table A range of cells that shows how changing certain values in your formulas affects the results of those formulas, and which makes it easy to calculate multiple versions in one operation.

Data type The characteristic that defines the kind of data that can be entered into a field, such as numbers, text, or dates.

Database An organized collection of facts about people, events, things, or ideas related to a particular topic or purpose.

Database software Programs, such as Microsoft Access, used to store and organize large amounts of data and perform complex tasks such as sorting and querying to generate specialized reports.

Datasheet view The Access view that displays an object organized in a format of columns and rows similar to an Excel spreadsheet.

Date control A control on a form or report that inserts the current date each time the form or report is opened.

Date line The first line in a business letter.

Date Navigator In Outlook, a one-month view of the calendar that you can use to display specific days in a month.

DBMS An acronym for database management system.

Dedicated server A computer that is assigned to handle one specific task on a network.

Denial of service (DoS) An attack caused when a large number of computers attempt to access a Web site at the same time, effectively overloading it and causing it to shut down.

Descending order A sorting order that arranges text in reverse alphabetical (Z to A) order or numbers from the highest to the lowest number.

Deselect The action of canceling a selection.

Design grid The lower pane of the Query window, which displays the design of the query.

Design view The detailed structured view of a form or report, and the view in which some tasks must be performed; only the controls, and not the data, are visible in this view.

Desktop The basic screen from which Windows and programs are run, and which consists of program icons, a taskbar, a Start button, and a mouse pointer.

Desktop computer A class of microcomputer, such as a PC or a Mac.

Detail section The section of a form or report that displays the records from the underlying table or query.

Dialog box A box that asks you to make a decision about an individual object or topic.

Dialog Box Launcher A small icon that displays to the right of some group names on the Ribbon, and which opens a related dialog box or task pane providing additional options and commands related to that group.

Digital camera A type of camera that saves photographs in a digital format rather than on film.

Digital Video Interface (DVI) port A port used to connect an LCD monitor to a computer in order to use a pure digital signal.

Digital video recorder A device used to record video in digital format directly to a hard drive, without the need for videotape.

Display screen See Monitor.

Displayed value The data that displays in a cell.

Document Information Panel The area of the screen just below the Ribbon that displays document properties.

Document properties The detailed information about a document that can help you identify or organize your files, including author name, title, and keywords.

Document window The Word window that displays the active document.

Dot leader A series of dots preceding a tab.

Dot matrix An impact printer, useful for printing multi-page forms.

Dot pitch The diagonal distance between adjacent pixels, measured in millimeters and that is used to determine image quality for monitors.

Dots per inch (dpi) A measurement of printer resolution.

Double-click The action of clicking the left mouse button twice in rapid succession while keeping the mouse still.

Downloading The action of requesting and copying a file or program from a remote server, such as a Web server, and saving it on your local computer or storage device.

Draft view A simplified view of a document that does not show graphics, margins, headers, or footers.

Drag The action of moving something from one location on the screen to another; the action of dragging includes releasing the mouse button at the desired time or location.

Drag and drop The action of moving a selection by dragging it to a new location.

Drag and drop (Excel) A method of moving or copying the content of selected cells in which you point to the selection and then drag it to a new location.

Drag and drop (Word) A technique by which you can move selected text from one location in a document to another—best used with text that will be moved a short distance, such as on the same screen.

Dragging The technique of holding down the left mouse button and moving over an area of text in order to select it.

Drawing canvas A work area for creating and editing complex figures created using the drawing tools.

Drawing object A graphic object, including shapes, diagrams, lines, and circles.

Drive An area of storage that is formatted with the Windows file system and that has a drive letter such as C.

Dual-boot A system with two different operating systems installed, giving the user the option to boot the computer using either one.

Dual-core A CPU that includes two microprocessors on a single integrated circuit. See also Multicore.

DVD drive A storage device used to read and, possibly, write data to DVD.

DVI port See Digital Video Interface (DVI) port.

E-Mail Account A unique address that you can use to receive and send e-mail.

Edit (Word) The action of making changes to the text or format of a document.

Edit (Excel) The action of making changes in a worksheet or workbook.

Edit mode A Windows mode that enables you to change the name of a file or folder, and works the same in all Windows programs.

Editing (PowerPoint) The process of adding, deleting, or changing the contents of a slide.

Effect options Animation options that include changing the direction of an effect and playing a sound when an animation takes place.

Em dash The word processing name for a long dash in a sentence, and which marks a break in thought, similar to a comma but stronger.

Embedded chart A chart that displays as an object within a worksheet.

Embedded computers Components of larger products, devices that perform pre-defined tasks using specially programmed processors.

Enclosure An additional document included with a letter.

Endnotes In a report or research paper, references placed at the end of the chapter containing the reference.

Enhanced ScreenTip A ScreenTip for a button that has more information than just the name, sometimes including a link to the topic in the Help system.

Entrance effects Animations that bring a slide element onto the screen.

Ethernet port A port, slightly larger than a telephone jack, that can transmit data at speeds up to 1,000 megabits per second (Mbps) and is usually used to connect to a cable modem or a network.

Excel table A series of rows and columns in a worksheet that contains related data, and that is managed independently from the data in other rows and columns in the worksheet.

Expand button A small plus (+) button to the left of a folder that you click to display the items in that folder.

Expand Formula Bar button An Excel window element with which you can increases the height of the Formula Bar for the purpose of displaying lengthy cell content.

Expand horizontal scroll bar button A button with which you can increase the width of the horizontal scroll bar.

Favorites Center An area in Internet Explorer that lets you manage your favorites list, the history list, and the feeds list.

Field A category that describes each piece of data stored in a table.

Field list A list of the field names in a table.

Field properties Characteristics of a field that control how the field will display and how the data can be entered in the field.

File Data that you save and store on a drive, such as a Word document or a PowerPoint presentation.

File extension The characters to the right of the period in a file name, and that tell the computer the program to use to open the file; extensions can be displayed or hidden.

Fill color (Excel) The background color a cell.

Fill color The inside color of text or an object.

Fill handle The small black square in the lower right corner of a selected cell.

Filter By Form An Access command that filters the records in a form based on one or more fields, or based on more than one value in the same field.

Filter By Selection An Access command that retrieves only the records that contain the value in the selected field.

Filtering The process of displaying only a portion of the total records (a subset) based on matching a specific value.

Financial functions Prewritten formulas that perform common business calculations such as calculating a loan payment on a vehicle or calculating how much to save each month to buy something; financial functions commonly involve a period of time such as months or years.

Find and Replace (Excel) A command that searches the cells in a worksheet—or in a selected range—for matches and then replaces each match with a replacement value of your choice.

Firewall See Personal firewall.

FireWire port A port used to send data at rates up to 800 megabits per second (Mbps), frequently used for digital cameras or digital video recorders.

Flash drive A small, portable, digital storage device that connects to a computer's USB port; also called a thumb drive, jump drive, or USB drive.

Flash memory Portable, nonvolatile memory, that uses electronic, solid-state circuitry.

Flat panel See Liquid crystal display.

Flat screen A type of screen used in CRT monitors, and which differs from flat panel monitors.

Floating object An object or graphic that can be moved independently of the surrounding text.

Floppy disk drive (or floppy drive) The original storage device for a microcomputer, which enables portable, permanent storage on floppy disks.

Folder A storage area, represented on the screen by a picture of a paper file folder, used to store files or other folders.

Font A set of characters with the same design and shape.

Font size The size of characters in a font measured in points; there are 72 points in an inch, with 10 or 11 points being a typical font size.

Font style Formatting emphasis such as bold, italic, and underline.

Font theme A theme that determines the font applied to two types of slide text—headings and body.

Footer (PowerPoint) Text that displays at the bottom of every slide or that prints at the bottom of a sheet of slide handouts or notes pages.

Footer (Word) A reserved area for text and graphics that displays at the bottom of each page in a document or section of a document.

Footers (Excel) Text, graphics, or page numbers that print at the bottom of every page of a worksheet.

Footnotes In a report or research paper, references placed at the bottom of a report page containing the source of the reference.

Foreign key The field that is included in the related table so that it can be joined to the primary key in another table for the purpose of creating a relationship.

Form A window for displaying and collecting information.

Form (Access) An Access object with which you can enter new records into a table, edit existing records in a table, or display existing records from a table.

Form footer Information at the bottom of the screen in Form view that is printed after the last detail section on the last page.

Form header Information, such as a form's title, which displays at the top of the screen in Form view, and that is printed at the top of the first page when records are printed as forms

Form tool The Access tool that creates a form with a single mouse click, and that includes all the fields from the underlying data source (table or query).

Format as you type The Excel feature by which a cell takes on the formatting of the number typed into the cell.

Format Painter (Excel) An Excel feature with which you can copy the formatting of a specific cell to other cells.

Format Painter (PowerPoint) A feature that copies formatting from one selection of text to another, thus ensuring formatting consistency in your presentation.

Format Painter (Word) A Word tool with which you can copy the formatting of specific text, or of a paragraph, to text in another location in the document.

Formatting (Excel) The process of specifying the appearance of cells and the overall layout of a worksheet; accomplished through various commands on the Ribbon, many of which are also available using short-cut menus or keyboard shortcuts.

Formatting (PowerPoint) Changing the appearance of the text, layout, and design of a slide.

Formatting marks Characters that display on the screen, but do not print, indicating where the Enter key, the Spacebar, and the Tab key were pressed; also called nonprinting characters.

Formatting text The process of establishing the overall appearance of text in a document.

Formula An equation that performs mathematical calculations on values in a worksheet.

Formula AutoComplete An Excel feature which, after typing an = (equal sign) and the beginning letter or letters of a function name, displays a list of function names that match the typed letter(s), and from which you can insert the function by pointing to its name and pressing the Tab key or double-clicking.

Formula Bar An element in the Excel window that displays the value or formula contained in the active cell; here you can also enter or edit values or formulas.

Frames Separate areas of content placed closely together so they will display as one unified Web page with or without any visible demarcation lines between them.

Freeze Panes A command that enables you to select one or more rows or columns and freeze (lock) them into place; the locked rows and columns become separate panes.

Full Screen Reading view A view that displays easy-to-read pages that fit on the screen.

Function A predefined formula—a formula that Excel has already built for you—that performs calculations by using specific values in a particular order.

Function key The keys, numbered F1 through F12, located above the numeric keys on a keyboard that have different functions depending upon the software program in use.

Future value The value at the end of time periods in an Excel function; the cash balance you want to attain after the last payment is made—usually zero for loans.

Fv The abbreviation for *future value* in various Excel functions.

Gallery An Office 2007 feature that displays a list of potential results; it shows the results of commands rather than just the command name.

General format The default format that Excel applies to numbers; the general format has no specific characteristics—whatever you type in the cell will display, with the exception that trailing zeros to the right of a decimal point will not display.

Gigabyte (GB) Approximately one billion bytes; a unit of measure for memory and storage space.

Gigahertz (GHz) One billion hertz; hertz is the unit of measure for processor speed.

Goal Seek One of Excel's What-If Analysis tools that provides a method to find a specific value for a cell by adjusting the value of one other cell.

Gradient fill A color combination in which one color fades into another.

Graphic A picture, clip art image, chart, or drawing object.

Graphical user interface (GUI) A computer interface with which you interact with the computer through the use of graphics and point-and-click technology; GUIs show documents as they will look in their final form.

Group A set of command buttons related to the Ribbon tab that is currently selected.

Group footer Displays the field label by which the summarized data has been grouped.

Group header Information printed at the beginning of each new group of records, for example the group name.

Group, Sort, and Total pane A pane that opens at the bottom of your screen in which you can control how information is sorted and grouped in a report; provides the most flexibility for adding or modifying groups, sort orders, or totals options on a report.

GUI See Graphical user interface.

Guides Vertical and horizontal lines that display in the rulers to give you a visual indication of where the crosshair pointer is positioned so that you can draw a shape.

Handheld computers See Personal digital assistant.

Hanging indent An indent style in which the first line of a paragraph extends to the left of the remaining lines, and that is commonly used for bibliographic entries.

Hard copy Data or information retrieved from a computer and printed.

Hard drive A large disk drive inside your computer, also referred to as a Local Disk.

Hardware The physical components of the computer and any equipment connected to it.

Header (PowerPoint) Text that displays at the top of every slide or that prints at the top of a sheet of slide handouts or notes pages.

Header (Word) A reserved area for text and graphics that displays at the top of each page in a document or section of a document.

Headers (Excel) Text, graphics, or page numbers that print at the top of every page of a worksheet.

Headings font The font that is applied to slide titles.

Help button A button at the far right of the Ribbon tabs that you click to display the program's Help window.

History A feature of Internet Explorer that tracks recently visited Web pages and sites.

Home page The Web page that displays every time you start Internet Explorer.

Horizontal scroll bar The bar at the bottom of a window that enables you to move left and right to view information that extends beyond the left and right edges of the screen.

Horizontal window split box A small box with which you can split the document into two horizontal views of the same document.

Hyperlink Text that you click to go to another location in a document, another document, or a Web site; the text is a different color (usually blue) than the surrounding text, and commonly underlined.

Hyperlinks Text, buttons, pictures, or other objects displayed on Web pages that, when clicked, access other Web pages or display other sections of the active page.

Hyperthreading Technology that allows a CPU to emulate multiple processors, improving processing power and speed.

Icon A graphic representation of an object that you can click to open that object.

Icon set A collection of icons such as arrows, flags, bars, or circles that annotate and classify data into three to five categories separated by a threshold value.

IF function A logical function that uses a logical test to check whether a condition is met, and then returns one value if true, and another value if false.

Impact A type of printer that resembles a typewriter; a key and ink ribbon are used to imprint a character on paper.

Inbox In Outlook, the folder that stores e-mail.

Indenting A format for text in which lines of text are moved relative to the left and right margins, for example, moving the beginning of the first line of a paragraph to the right or left of the rest of the paragraph.

Information Data that has been organized in a useful manner.

Information processing cycle The cycle composed of the four basic computer functions: input, process, output, and storage.

Ink-jet Type of printer that uses a special nozzle and ink cartridges to distribute liquid ink on the surface of the paper.

Inline object An object or graphic inserted in a document that acts like a character in a sentence.

Innermost sort field When sorting on multiple fields in datasheet view, the field that will be used for the second level of sorting.

Input The act of entering data into a computer.

Input devices Computer hardware used to enter data and instructions into a computer; examples include the keyboard, mouse, stylus, scanner, microphone, and digital camera.

Insert mode The mode in which text moves to the right to make space for new keystrokes.

Insert Worksheet button Located on the row of sheet tabs, a sheet tab that, when clicked, inserts an additional worksheet into the workbook.

Insertion point A blinking vertical line that indicates where text or graphics will be inserted.

Inside address The address block under the date in a business letter.

Interest The amount charged for the use of borrowed money.

Internet control key Usually found at the top of a keyboard, this type of key can be used for various Internet-related activities including opening a Web browser and sending email.

Internet Explorer 7.0 A software program that allows you to view the contents of the World Wide Web.

Internet Service Provider (ISP) A company that provides an Internet connection through a regular telephone line, a special high-speed telephone line, or a cable.

IrDA port A port enabling data transmission through the use of infrared light waves; the devices sharing data require a clear line of site with no visual obstructions.

Is Not Null A criteria that searches for fields that are not empty.

Is Null A criteria that searches for fields that are empty.

Items An element of information in Outlook, such as a message, a contact name, a task, or an appointment.

Join line In the Relationships window, the line joining two tables that visually indicates the related field and the type of relationship.

Joysticks Input devices used to control actions and movement within computer games.

Justified alignment Text aligned on both the left and right margins.

Key logger A software program or hardware device that records every keystroke made on the computer.

Keyboard The hardware device used to input typed data and commands into a computer.

Keyboard shortcut A combination of keys on the keyboard that perform a command.

Label control A control on a form or report that contains descriptive information, typically a field name.

LAN See Local area network.

Landscape orientation A page orientation in which the printed page is wider than it is tall.

Laser A type of printer that uses a drum, static electricity, and a laser to distribute dry ink or toner on the surface of the paper.

Layout (PowerPoint) The placement and arrangement of the text and graphic elements on a slide.

Layout selector A small symbol that displays in the upper left corner of a selected control layout, and with which you can move the entire group of controls.

Layout view The Access view in which you can make changes to a form or to a report while the form is running—the data from the underlying record source displays.

LCD See Liquid crystal display.

Leader characters Characters that form a solid, dotted, or dashed line that fills the space preceding a tab stop.

Left aligned The cell format in which characters align at the left edge of the cell; this is the default for text entries and is an example of formatting information stored in a cell.

Left alignment Text aligned at the left margin, leaving the right margin uneven.

Left pane In the My Computer window, a pane at the left that displays information and commonly used tools.

Legend A chart element that identifies the patterns or colors that are assigned to the categories in the chart.

Line chart A chart type that displays trends over time; time displays along the bottom axis and the data point values are connected with a line.

Line spacing The distance between lines of text in a paragraph.

Link Select pointer The mouse pointer displaying as a pointing hand as you point to an item that links to another Web page.

Linux An open-source operating system based on the UNIX operating system developed for mainframe computers.

Liquid crystal display (LCD) Technology used in flat panel monitors, resulting in thinner and lighter monitors.

Live Preview A technology that shows the result of applying an editing or formatting change as you move your pointer over the results presented in a gallery.

Local area network (LAN) A network in which the nodes are located within a small geographic area.

Local Disk A large disk drive inside your computer, also referred to as a hard disk.

Logical functions Pre-written formulas that test for specific conditions, and which typically use conditional tests to determine whether specified conditions, referred to as criteria, are true or false.

Logical operators (Access) The criteria of AND and OR used to enter criteria for the same field or different fields; AND requires that both conditions be met and OR requires that either condition be met.

Logical test Any value or expression that can be evaluated as being true or false.

Mac OS The operating system designed specifically for Apple's Mac computers.

Magnetic A type of storage process using magnetized film to store data; used by media such as floppy disks or Zip disks.

Mail merge A Word feature that joins a main document and a data source to create customized letters or labels.

Main document The document that contains the text or formatting that remains constant in a mail merge.

Mainframe A large computer capable of performing more than one task at the same time and supporting many users simultaneously.

Manual column break An artificial end to a column to balance columns or to provide space for the insertion of other objects.

Manual line break The action of ending a line, before the normal end of the line, without creating a new paragraph; this is useful, for example, if your paragraph style includes space before or after paragraphs and you want to begin a new line without the space.

Margins The space between the text and the top, bottom, left, and right edges of the paper.

MAX function A statistical function that determines the largest value in a group of values.

Maximize To increase the size of a window to fill the screen.

MEDIAN function A statistical function commonly used to describe a group of data, and which finds the middle value in a group of values that has as many values above it in the group as are below it.

Megabyte (MB) Approximately one million bytes; a unit of measure for memory and storage space.

Megahertz (MHz) One million hertz; hertz is the unit of measure for processor speed.

Memo Style In Outlook, a print style that prints a single item on a single page and provides detailed information about that item.

Menu A list of commands within a category.

Menu bar The bar beneath the title bar that lists the names of menu categories.

Message Bar The area directly below the Ribbon that displays information such as security alerts when there is potentially unsafe, active content in an Office 2007 document that you open.

Message header In Outlook, the basic information about an e-mail message such as the sender's name, the date sent, and the subject.

MFD See Multifunction device.

Microcomputer The computer most users are familiar with, ranging in size from large desktop systems to handheld devices.

Microphones Input devices used to digitally record sound.

Microprocessor chip See Central processing unit.

Microsoft Exchange Server An e-mail based communications server for businesses and organizations.

Microsoft Windows The operating system found on most microcomputers.

MIDI port Musical Instrument Digital Interface port used to connect electronic musical instruments to a system.

MIN function A statistical function that determines the smallest value in a group of values.

Mini toolbar A small toolbar containing frequently used formatting commands, and sometimes accompanied by a shortcut menu of other frequently used commands, which displays as a result of right-clicking a selection or of selecting text.

Mini toolbar (Excel) A small toolbar containing frequently used formatting commands and which displays as a result of right-clicking or selecting cells; the toolbar fades when you move the mouse away and dismisses itself when you click outside of the toolbar.

Minimize Removing the window from the screen without closing it; minimized windows can be reopened by clicking the associated button in the taskbar.

Mobile devices Lightweight, portable computing devices such as PDAs, smartphones, and handheld computers.

Modem port A port that connects to a standard telephone line, usually used to connect to the Internet or a local network, with a maximum speed of 56 kilobits per second (Kbps).

Modern Language Association (MLA) style One of two commonly used styles for formatting research papers.

Monitor (or display screen) A common output device that displays text, graphics, and video.

Monitor port A port used to connect a monitor to a computer's graphic processing unit, located on the motherboard or video card.

Motherboard A large printed circuit board located in the system unit to which all other boards are connected; the motherboard contains the central processing unit (CPU), the memory (RAM) chips, and expansion card slots.

Mouse An input device used to enter commands and user responses into a computer.

Mouse pointer The arrow, I-beam, or other symbol that shows the location or position of the mouse on your screen; also called the pointer.

Multicore A CPU that includes more than two microprocessors on a single integrated circuit. See also Dual-core.

Multifunction device (MFD) A device that has more than one purpose, often combining input and output capabilities.

Multimedia control key Usually found at the top of a keyboard, this type of key can be used to control or mute speaker volume.

Multimedia projectors Output devices used to display information on a screen for viewing by an audience.

Multiple items form A form in which multiple records can be entered into or displayed from a table.

Multitask The action of performing more than one task at the same time.

Name Box An element of the Excel window that displays the name of the selected cell, table, chart, or object.

Navigate To move within a document or workbook.

Navigation Pane (Access) The area of the Access window that displays and organizes the names of the objects in a database; from here you open objects for use.

Navigation Pane (Outlook) The area on the left side of the Outlook window that provides quick access to Outlook's components.

Network A group of two or more computers (or nodes) connected to share information and resources.

Network topology The layout and structure of a computer network.

Node Any object connected to a network—may be a computer or a peripheral device.

Non-breaking hyphen A special type of hyphen that will not break at the end of a line and is useful for telephone numbers in which you normally do not want the number to be placed on two separate lines by the word wrap feature.

Non-breaking space A special type of space inserted between two words that results in treating the two words as one, and thus forcing both words to wrap even if the second word would normally wrap to the next line.

Nonadjacent ranges Cell ranges that are not next to each other.

Nonimpact A type of printer that does not actually touch the paper.

Nonprinting characters Characters that display on the screen, but do not print, indicating where the Enter key, the Spacebar, and the Tab key were pressed; also called formatting marks.

Nonvolatile Permanent storage, as in read only memory (ROM); data remains even when power is shut down.

Normal view (PowerPoint) The view in which the PowerPoint window is divided into three areas: the Slides/Outline pane, the Slide pane, and the Notes pane.

Normal view (Excel) A screen view that maximizes the number of cells visible on your screen and keeps the column letters and row numbers close to the columns and rows.

Notebook computer Also known as a laptop, this microcomputer is smaller than a desktop and designed to be portable.

Notes area In Outlook, a blank area of the Contact form that can be used for any information about the contact that is not otherwise specified in the form.

Notes pages Printouts that contain the slide image in the top half of the page and speaker's notes in the lower half of the page.

Notification area The area on the right side of the taskbar that keeps you informed about processes that are occurring in the background, such as antivirus software, network connections, and other utility programs; also displays the time.

NOW function A function within the *Date & Time* category that retrieves the date and time from your computer's calendar and clock and inserts the information into the selected cell.

Nper The abbreviation for *number of time periods* in various Excel functions.

Number format A specific way in which Excel displays numbers in a cell.

Numbered lists A list of items with each item introduced by a consecutive number to indicate definite steps, a sequence of actions, or chronological order.

Numeric keypad A bank of keys on a keyboard with which you can input numbers, it is located on the right side of a keyboard and is similar to an adding machine or calculator.

Object window The portion of the Access window that displays open objects.

Objects The basic parts of a database, which includes tables, forms, queries, reports, and macros.

Office button The large button to the left of the Quick Access Toolbar that displays a list of commands related to things you can do *with* a workbook, such as opening, saving, printing, or sharing.

Office Clipboard A temporary storage area maintained by your Microsoft Office program.

Office Clipboard (Word) A temporary storage area that holds text or graphics that has been cut or copied, and that can subsequently be placed in another location in the document or in another Office program.

Offline Your status when you are not connected to a network or to the public Internet.

OLE An abbreviation for *object linking and embedding*, a technology for transferring and sharing information among applications.

One-to-many relationship A relationship between two tables where one record in the first table corresponds to many records in the second table—the most common type of relationship in Access.

One-variable data table A data table that changes the value in only one cell.

Online Your status when you are connected to your organization's network or to the public Internet.

Open-source Software whose code is made available for developers to modify and use as they wish, usually available at no cost.

Operating system A set of instructions that coordinates the activities of your computer; Microsoft Windows XP is an operating system.

Operating system (OS) System software that controls the way in which a computer system functions, including the management of hardware, peripherals, and software; Microsoft Windows XP is an operating system.

Operators The symbols with which you can specify the type of calculation you want to perform in an Excel formula.

Optical A type of storage process using a laser to read and write data; used by media such as CDs and DVDs.

OR condition A condition in which only records where one of two values is present in the selected field.

Order of operations The mathematical rules for performing multiple calculations within a formula.

OS See Operating system.

Outermost sort field When sorting on multiple fields in datasheet view, the field that will be used for the first level of sorting.

Outline view A document view that shows headings and subheadings, which can be expanded or collapsed.

Outlook Today In Outlook, a summary view of your schedule, tasks, and e-mail for the current day.

Output To retrieve data or information from a computer.

Output devices Computer hardware used to retrieve processed data and information from a computer; examples include the monitor, printer, and speakers.

P2P network See Peer-to-peer network.

Page footer Information printed at the end of every page in a report; used to print page numbers or other information that you want to appear at the bottom of every report page.

Page header (Access) Information printed at the top of every page of a report.

Page Layout view A screen view in which you can use the rulers to measure the width and height of data, set margins for printing, hide or display the numbered row headings and the lettered column headings, and change the page orientation; this view is useful for preparing your worksheet for printing.

Page number control A control on a form or report that inserts the page numbers of the pages when displayed in Print Preview or when printed.

Page orientation (Excel) The position of your printed worksheet on paper—either portrait or landscape.

Paint A Windows program in which graphics are created or edited.

Pane A portion of a worksheet window bounded by and separated from other portions by vertical and horizontal bars.

Parallel port A port used to connect a printer to a computer, and which sends data in groups of bits at speeds of up to 500 kilobits per second (Kbps).

Parenthetical reference In the MLA report style, references placed in parenthesis within the report text that include the last name of the author or authors, and the page number in the referenced source.

Paste The action of placing text or objects that have been copied or moved from one location to another location.

Paste (Excel) The action of placing cell contents that have been copied or moved to the Office Clipboard to another location.

Paste area The target destination for data that has been cut or copied using the Office Clipboard.

Paste Options button (Excel) A button that displays in the lower right corner of a pasted selection and that displays a list of options that lets you determine how the information is pasted into your worksheet; the list varies depending on the type of content you are pasting and the program you are pasting from.

Paste Special A dialog box that offers various options for the manner in which you can paste the contents of the Office Clipboard into one or more cells; for example, you can paste the calculated result of a formula rather than the actual formula.

PDA See Personal digital assistant.

Peer-to-peer (P2P) network A network in which each node can communicate directly with every other node, and which is often used for home and small business networks.

Percent for new value = base percent + percent of increase The formula for calculating a percentage by which a value increases by adding the base percentage—usually 100%—to the percent increase.

Percent rate of increase The percent by which one number increases over another.

Peripheral A hardware device connected to a computer, but not located within the system unit, such as a monitor, printer, or mouse.

Permanent memory Memory used by storage devices to retain data and information.

Personal digital assistant (PDA) Also known as a hand-held computer, a small device that enables a user to carry digital information.

Personal firewall A software program or hardware device designed to prevent unauthorized access to a computer.

Personal information manager In Outlook, a feature that enables you to electronically store and manage information about contacts, appointments, and tasks.

Phishing Email that masquerades as an authentic entity such as a bank or credit card company, requesting confidential information.

Picture element A point of light measured in dots per square inch on a screen; sixty-four pixels equals 8.43 characters, which is the average number of digits that will fit in a cell using the default font.

Pie chart A type of chart that shows the relationship of each part to a whole.

Pixel An abbreviated name for picture element.

Placeholder A slide element that reserves a portion of a slide and serves as a container for text, graphics, and other slide elements.

PMT function An Excel function that calculates the payment for a loan based on constant payments and at a constant rate of interest.

Point (noun) A measurement of the size of a font; there are 72 points in an inch, with 10–12 points being the most commonly used font size.

Point (verb) The action of moving the mouse pointer over something on the screen.

Point and click method The technique of constructing a formula by pointing to and then clicking cells; this method is convenient when the referenced cells are not adjacent to one another.

Pointer See mouse pointer.

Pointing Positioning the tip of the pointer in the center of an icon or other screen object.

Pop-up blocker A command on the Tools menu that stops or allows pop-ups to display as you browse the Internet.

Pop-ups Small windows that display on your screen without you actually requesting them as your browse the Internet.

Populate The action of filling a database table with records.

Port An interface through which external devices are connected to the computer.

Portals Home pages that act as launching sites to other Web pages, for example containing links to access frequently visited sites, up-to-the-minute news, weather reports, and maps and directories.

Portrait orientation A page orientation in which the printed page is taller than it is wide.

Present value The total amount that a series of future payments is worth now; also known as the principal.

Presentation graphics software A program used to effectively present information to an audience.

Presentation software A program used to create dynamic slideshows and generate speaker notes and audience handouts.

Primary key The field that uniquely identifies a record in a table—for example, a Student ID number at a college.

Principal Another term for present value.

Print Layout view A view of a document that looks like a sheet of paper, and which displays margins, headers, footers, and graphics.

Print Preview A feature that displays information as it will print based on the options that you select.

Print styles A combination of paper and page settings that determines the way items print.

Printer An output device used to generate hard copy.

Process The term used to describe the action of a computer when it converts data into information.

Program A set of instructions used by a computer to perform certain tasks.

Program tab A tab on the Ribbon that replaces the standard set of tabs when you switch to certain authoring modes or views, such as Print Preview.

Program-level buttons Buttons at the far right of the title bar that minimize, restore, or close the program.

Property sheet A list of characteristics—properties —for controls on a form or report in which you can make precision changes to each property associated with the control.

Protocol A set of rules for transferring data over the Internet.

Pt. An abbreviation for point.

Pv The abbreviation for *present value* in various Excel functions.

Query A database object that retrieves specific data from one or more tables and then displays the specified data in datasheet view.

Quick Access Toolbar A small toolbar in the upper left corner of the program window that displays buttons to perform frequently used commands with a single click.

Quick Launch toolbar An area to the right of the Start button that contains shortcut icons for commonly used programs.

RAM See Random access memory.

Random Access Memory (RAM) A computer's temporary storage space or short-term memory and stored on chips located on the motherboard; measured in megabytes (MB) and gigabytes (GB).

Range Two or more selected cells on a worksheet that are adjacent or nonadjacent; because the range is treated as a single unit, you can make the same change, or combination of changes, to more than one cell at a time.

Range finder An Excel feature that outlines cells in color to indicate which cells are used in a formula; useful for verifying which cells are referenced in a formula or for quickly positioning the insertion point within the cell to perform editing directly in the cell.

Rate In the Excel PMT function, the term used to indicate the interest rate for a loan.

Rate = amount of increase/base The mathematical formula to calculate a rate of increase.

RE Commonly used to mean *in regard to* or *regarding*.

Read Only Memory (ROM) A set of memory chips located on the motherboard that stores data and instructions that cannot be changed or erased; it holds all the instructions the computer needs to start up.

Reading Pane In Outlook, a window in which you can preview an e-mail message without actually opening it.

Recognizer A purple dotted underscore beneath a date or address indicating that the information could be placed into another Microsoft Office application program such as Outlook.

Record All of the categories of data pertaining to one person, place, thing, event, or idea.

Record selector The bar on the left side of a form with which you can select the entire record.

Record selector box The small box at the left of a record in datasheet view which, when clicked, selects the entire record.

Record source The tables or queries that provide the underlying data for a report.

Recycle Bin A storage area for files that have been deleted; files can be recovered from the Recycle Bin or permanently removed.

References Within a report or research paper, a notation to indicate information that has been taken from another source; also in APA style, the title on the page that lists the sources used in the document.

Referential integrity A set of rules that Access uses to ensure that the data between related tables is valid.

Refresh rate The speed at which the pixels are reilluminated, measured in cycles per second and expressed as hertz (Hz).

Relational database A type of database in which the tables in the database can relate or connect to other tables through common fields.

Relationship An association that is established between two tables using common fields.

Relative cell reference In a formula, the address of a cell based on the relative position of the cell that contains the formula and the cell referred to.

Reminder A small dialog box that displays in the middle of the Outlook screen that is used to remind you of a pending appointment or task.

Report A database object that summarizes the fields and records from a table, or from a query, in an easy-to-read format suitable for printing.

Report footer Information printed once at the end of a report; use to print report totals or other summary information for the entire report.

Report header Information printed once at the beginning of a report; used for logos, titles, and dates.

Report tool The Access feature that creates a report with one mouse click, and which displays all the fields and records from the record source that you choose—a quick way to look at the underlying data.

Report Wizard An Access feature with which you can create a report by answering a series of questions; Access designs the report based on your answers.

Resolution The measurement used to assess the clarity of an image on a monitor; determined by pixel density.

Restore Using the Restore Down button to return a window to the size it was before it was maximized.

Restore point A record created by Windows XP for all of a computer's system settings.

Ribbon (Outlook) The area along the top of an Outlook form that contains frequently needed commands.

Ribbon The user interface in Office 2007 that groups the commands for performing related tasks on tabs across the upper portion of the program window.

Rich Text Format A universal document format that can be read by nearly all word processing programs, and that retains most text and paragraph formatting.

Right alignment Text aligned on the right margin, leaving the left margin uneven.

Right-click The action of clicking the right mouse button.

Ring (or token-ring) topology A networking configuration in which all devices are set up in a circular layout; data flows in a circular fashion, in one direction only.

ROM See Read only memory.

Root folder The first folder from which all other folders branch.

Rotate handle A handle on a selected image that can be dragged to rotate the image to any angle.

Rounding A procedure in which you determine which digit at the right of the number will be the last digit displayed and then increase it by one if the next digit to its right is 5, 6, 7, 8, or 9.

Row A horizontal group of cells in a worksheet.

Row headings The numbers along the left side of an Excel worksheet that designate the row numbers.

Ruler (Word) Displays the location of paragraph margins, indents, and tab stops for the selected paragraph.

Run The process in which Access searches the records in the table(s) included in a query design, finds the records that match the specified criteria, and then displays those records in a datasheet; only the fields that have been included in the query design display.

S-video port A port used to connect ancillary video equipment, such as a television or projector to a computer.

Salutation The greeting line of a business letter.

Sans serif font A font with no lines or extensions on the ends of characters.

Scanners Input devices used to convert hard copy documents or images into digital files.

Screen (or window) In a graphical user interface, the rectangular box that contains the program displayed on the monitor.

ScreenTip A small box that displays useful information when you perform various mouse actions such as pointing to screen elements or dragging.

Scroll box The box in the vertical and horizontal scroll bars that can be dragged to reposition the document on the screen.

Scroll box (Excel) The box in the vertical and horizontal scroll bars that can be dragged to reposition the worksheet on the screen.

Scroll wheel A feature on some mouse pointing devices; rolling the wheel enables you to quickly move a page up or down within a window.

Scrolling The action of moving a pane or window vertically (up or down) or horizontally (side to side) to bring unseen areas into view.

Search Engines Software programs that search for keywords in files and documents or other Web sites found on the Internet.

Section bar A gray bar in a form or report that identifies and separates one section from another; used to select the section and to change the size of the adjacent section.

Sectors Wedge-shaped sections of a hard disk drive, each measured from the center point to the outer edge.

Select (Excel) Highlighting, by clicking or dragging with your mouse, one or more cells so that the selected cells can be edited, formatted, copied, or moved; selected cells are indicated by a dark border.

Select All box A box in the upper left corner of the worksheet grid that selects all the cells in a worksheet.

Select Query A database object that retrieves (selects) specific data from one or more tables and then displays the specified data in datasheet view.

Selecting text Highlighting text so that it can be formatted, deleted, copied, or moved.

Separator character A character used to identify column placement in text; usually a tab or a comma.

Serial port A type of port that sends data one bit at a time at speeds of up to 115 kilobits per second (Kbps).

Series A group of things that come one after another in succession; for example, January, February, March, and so on.

Serif A font design that includes small line extensions on the ends of the letters to guide the eye in reading from left to right.

Server In a client/server network, the computer that manages shared network resources and provides access to the client computer when requested.

Shape Style A combination of formatting effects that includes 3-D, glow, and bevel effects and shadows.

Shapes Drawing objects including lines, arrows, stars and banners, and ovals and rectangles that are used to help convey a message by showing process and by containing text.

Sheet tab The labels along the lower border of the workbook window that identify each worksheet.

Sheet tab scrolling buttons Buttons to the left of the sheet tabs used to display Excel sheet tabs that are not in view; used when there are more sheet tabs than will display in the space provided.

Shortcut menu A context-sensitive menu that displays commands and options relevant to the selected object.

Simple select query Another name for a select query.

Sizing handle A small square or circle in the corners and the middle of the sides of a graphic that can be used to increase or decrease the size of the graphic.

Sizing handles (Access) The small boxes around the edge of a control indicating the control is selected and that can be adjusted to resize the selected control.

Slide handouts Printed images of more than one slide on a sheet of paper.

Slide Sorter View A view useful for rearranging slides in which all of the slides in the presentation display as thumbnails.

Small caps A font effect, usually used in titles, that changes lowercase text into capital (uppercase) letters using a reduced font size.

SmartArt graphic A designer-quality visual representation of your information that you can create by choosing from among many different layouts to effectively community your message or ideas.

SmartArt Styles Combinations of formatting effects that are applied to diagrams.

Smartphones Cell phones with additional computing capabilities or the ability to access the Internet.

Soft copy Data or information displayed on a monitor.

Software patches Quick software fixes provided to resolve an error found in program code until a software update can be issued.

Software updates Small, downloadable software modules that repair errors identified in commercial program code.

Sorting The process of arranging data in a specific order based on the value in each field.

Sources A term used to describe a list of referenced works in a report or research paper, also referred to as Works Cited, Bibliography, or References, depending upon the report style.

Spam Junk or unsolicited email.

Speakers Output devices that allow the user to hear any auditory signals the computer sends.

Spin box A small box with an upward- and downward-pointing arrow that lets you move rapidly through a set of values by clicking.

Spin box arrows The upward- and downward-pointing arrows in a spin box.

Split bar The gray bar that indicates the location of the border between two Word windows.

Sponsored links Web sites that pay to be prominently displayed as results at a search engine site.

Spotlight The area in the opening Access program screen that displays content from Microsoft's Web site.

Spreadsheet Another name for a worksheet.

Spreadsheet software A program with which you perform calculations and numerical analyses.

Spyware Software designed to capture personal and confidential information that resides on a computer and then send it elsewhere.

Star topology A flexible and frequently used network configuration for businesses, in which nodes connect to a central communication device known as a switch.

Start button The button on the left side of the taskbar that is used to start programs, change system settings, find Windows help, or shut down the computer.

Statistical functions Pre-written formulas that analyze a group of measurements.

Status area Another name for the notification area on the right side of the taskbar.

Status bar The area along the lower edge of the program window that displays, on the left side, the current mode, page number, and document information, and on the right side, displays buttons to control how the window looks.

Status bar (Word) A horizontal bar at the bottom of the document window that displays, on the left side, the page and line number, word count, and the Proof button. On the right side, displays buttons to control the look of the window. The status bar can be customized to include other information.

Storage To retain data or information for future use.

Straight quote A quotation mark that uses straight, rather than curved, lines.

Style A set of formatting characteristics—such as line spacing, space after paragraphs, font, and font style—that can be applied to text, paragraphs, tables, or lists.

Styles Formats for paragraphs stored in one shortcut command.

Stylus An input device used to write on a tablet computer or PDA.

Subject line The line following the subject line in a business letter that states the purpose of the letter.

Submenu A second-level menu activated by selecting a menu option.

Subpoint Secondary-level information in a SmartArt graphic.

Subset A portion of the total records available.

Suite A collection of application software programs developed by the same manufacturer, bundled together and sold at a price that is usually less than the cost of purchasing each program individually.

SUM function A predefined formula that adds all the numbers in a selected range of cells.

Supercomputer A large, powerful computer typically devoted to specialized tasks.

Synonyms Words with the same meaning as a selected word.

System software The set of programs that enables a computer's hardware devices and program software to work together; it includes the operating system and utility programs.

System tray Another name for the notification area on the right side of the taskbar.

System unit The tower, box, or console that contains the critical hardware and electrical components of a computer.

Tab order The order in which the insertion point moves from one field to the next in a form when you press the Tab key.

Tab stop Specific locations on a line of text, marked on the Word ruler, to which you can move the insertion point by pressing the [Tab] key; used to align and indent text.

Table A format for information that organizes and presents text and data in columns and rows.

Table (Access) The Access object that stores your data organized in an arrangement of columns and rows.

Table area The upper pane of the Query window, which displays the field lists for tables that are used in the query.

Table design The number of fields, and the type of content within each field, in an Access table.

Table Style In Outlook, a format that lists the contents of a folder on a single page and provides limited information about each item.

Table style (Excel) A predefined set of formatting characteristics, including font, alignment, and cell shading.

Table style (PowerPoint) Formatting applied to an entire table so that it is consistent with the presentation theme.

Table template A pre-built table format for common topics such as contacts, issues, and tasks.

Tables and Views category An arrangement of objects in the Navigation Pane in which the objects are grouped by the table to which they are related.

Tablet computer A portable computer that features a screen that swivels and can be written on using advanced handwriting recognition software.

Tabs A feature of Internet Explorer 7.0 that allows multiple Web pages to be displayed at the same time without opening multiple browsers.

Task A personal or work-related activity that you want to track until it is complete.

Task Pane In Outlook, a pane, usually below the appointment area, that can be used to schedule tasks.

Task pane A window within a Microsoft Office application that allows you to enter options for completing a command.

Taskbar The area of the screen that displays the Start button and the name of any open documents.

Template The horizontal placement of text within a placeholder.

Template (Access) A pre-formatted database designed for a specific purpose.

Text box A movable, resizable container for text or graphics.

Text box control The graphical object on a form or report that displays the data from the underlying table or query; a text box control is known as a bound control because its source data comes from a table or a query.

Text format A universal document format that retains text and paragraph marks, but does not support any text or paragraph formatting.

Text string A sequence of characters, which when used in query criteria, much be matched.

Text wrapping The manner in which text displays around an object.

Theme A predefined set of colors, fonts, lines, and fill effects that look good together and that can be applied to your entire document or to specific items

Theme (Excel) A predefined set of colors, fonts, lines, and fill effects that look good together and that can be applied to your entire workbook or to specific items— for example to a chart or table.

Thesaurus A research tool that provides a list of synonyms.

Three-color scale Compares a range of cells by using a gradation of three colors; the shades represent higher, middle, or lower values.

Thumb drive A small storage device that plugs into a computer USB port; also called a USB drive or a flash drive.

Thumbnail A miniature representation of the contents of a picture file.

Thumbnails (PowerPoint) Miniature images of each slide.

Title bar The bar at the top edge of the program window that indicates the name of the current workbook and the program name.

To-Do Bar A pane, usually along the right edge of the Outlook window, which provides quick access to daily tasks.

To-Do List pane In Outlook, a pane that displays an area to type a new task and a flag for each task.

Toggle button A button that can be turned on by clicking it once, and then turned off by clicking it again.

Toggle key A keyboard key that switches on or off each time it is pressed.

Token-ring topology See Ring topology.

Toolbars Rows of buttons, usually located under a menu bar, from which you can perform commands using a single click.

Top-level point The main text points in a SmartArt graphic.

Top/Bottom Rules A set of rules that enable you to apply conditional formatting to the highest and lowest values in a range of cells; for example, you can identify the top 5 selling products or the top 25 salaries in a personnel analysis.

Topology See Network topology.

Track Changes A Word tool that provides a visual indication of deletions, insertions, and formatting changes in a document.

Tracks Concentric circles on a hard disk drive.

Transitions The manner in which a slide appears or disappears during an onscreen slide show.

Trojan horse A program that appears to be useful or desirable, but acts maliciously in the background after installation.

Trust Center (Access) An area of the Access program where you can view the security and privacy settings for your Access installation.

Two-color scale Compares a range of cells by using a gradation of two colors.

Two-variable data table A data table that changes the values in two cells.

Type argument An optional argument in the PMT function that assumes that the payment will be made at the end of each time period.

Unbound control A term used to describe a control that does not have a source of data.

Underlying formula The formula entered in a cell and visible only on the Formula Bar.

Underlying value The data that displays in the Formula Bar.

Uniform Resource Locator (URL) The unique address used to locate a Web page or Web site.

Universal serial bus (USB) port A versatile port used to connect a wide array of peripheral devices to a computer.

USB drive A small storage device that plugs into a computer USB port; also called a thumb drive or a flash drive.

User interface The features of a computer operating system that enable you to interact with the computer.

Utility program A component of system software, typically a small program used to perform routine maintenance and housekeeping tasks for the computer.

Value Another name for constant value.

Value after increase = base x percent for new value Formula for calculating the value after an increase by multiplying the original value—the base—by the percent for new value (see the *Percent for new value* formula).

Value axis A numerical scale on the left side of a chart that shows the range of numbers for the data points; also referred to as the Y-axis.

Vertical scroll bar The bar at the right side of a window that enables you to move up and down to view information that extends beyond the top and bottom of the screen.

Vertical window split box A small box on the vertical scroll bar with which you can split the window into two vertical views of the same document.

View options (Word) Area on the right side of the status bar that contains buttons for viewing the document in Print Layout, Full Screen Reading, Web Layout, Master Document Tools, or Draft views, and also displays controls to Zoom Out and Zoom In.

View options Buttons on the right side of the status bar for viewing in normal, page layout view, or page break preview; also displays controls for zoom out and zoom in.

Views Ways to look at similar information in different formats and arrangements

Virus Malicious code or program, usually installed on a computer without the user's knowledge or permission.

Volatile Temporary storage, as in random access memory (RAM); data is erased when power is shut down.

Volatile (Excel) A term used to describe an Excel function that is subject to change each time the workbook is reopened; for example, the NOW function updates itself to the current date and time each time the workbook is opened.

WAN See Wide area network.

Web browser Software that enables you to use the Web and navigate from page to page and site to site.

Web Layout view A document view that shows how the document would look if viewed with a Web browser.

Web page A document on the World Wide Web that displays as a screen with associated links, frames, pictures, and other features of interest.

Web site A group of related Web pages published to a specific location on the World Wide Web.

What-if analysis The process of changing the values in cells to see how those changes affect the outcome of formulas in your worksheet.

Wide area network (WAN) A network composed of local area networks connected over long distances.

Wildcard A character, such as an asterisk, that can be used to match any number of characters in a file search.

Wildcard character In a query, a character that serves as a placeholder for one or more unknown characters in your criteria.

Window A box or screen that displays information or a program.

Windows See Microsoft Windows.

Wireless network A network that connects using radio waves instead of wires or cable.

Wizard A feature in Microsoft Office programs that walks you step by step through a process.

Word document window Displays the active document.

Word processing software A program used to create and edit written documents such as papers, letters, and resumes.

WordArt A feature that applies combinations of decorative formatting to text, including shadows, reflections, and 3-D effects, as well as changing the line and fill color of text.

Wordpad A simple word processing program that comes with Windows XP.

Wordwrap The feature that moves text from the right edge of a paragraph to the beginning of the next line as necessary to fit within the margins.

Work week A calendar option that shows only the weekdays, Monday through Friday.

Workbook An Excel file that contains one or more worksheets.

Workbook-level buttons Buttons at the far right of the Ribbon tabs used to minimize or restore a displayed workbook.

Works Cited A term used to describe a list of referenced works placed at the end of a research paper or report when using the MLA Style.

Worksheet The primary document that you use in Excel to store and work with data, and which is formatted as a pattern of uniformly spaced horizontal and vertical lines.

Worksheet grid The area of the Excel window that displays the columns and rows that intersect to form the cells of the worksheet.

Worm A program that is able to replicate and spread from computer to computer without human interaction.

Writer's identification The name and title of the author of a letter, placed near the bottom of the letter, under the complimentary closing.

X-axis Another name for the category axis.

Y-axis Another name for the value axis.

Zip drive A magnetic storage device used to save and retrieve data on Zip disks.

Zombie A computer that is controlled remotely and can be used to help spread viruses, spyware, and spam.

Zoom The action of increasing or decreasing the viewing area of the screen.

Index

 The CD symbol represents Index entries found on the CD (see CD file name for page numbers).

SmartArt Styles gallery (PowerPoint 2007), 875
Soft Edges feature fades (pictures), 155
sorting
   query results, 622–624
   records, 612–615
   tables in worksheets, 466–469
Source Manager dialog box (Word 2007), 118–119
spacing
   documents (Word 2007)
     between sentences, 11
     lines, 78–79
     MLA (Modern Language Association), 102
     paragraphs, 80–81
   lists, 97
speaker's notes (presentations), adding, 787–788
Special format (Excel 2007), 305
spell correction (PowerPoint 2007), 785
spelling
   Excel 2007, 288–289
   PowerPoint 2007, 784–785
   Word 2007, 37–39, 39–43
spelling and grammar checking feature (Word 2007), 37–39, 39–43
Spelling dialog box (Excel 2007), 288–289
spin boxes
   arrows, 80
   definition, 46, 80
split bar (Word 2007), 33
Split button (Word 2007), 33
splitting windows (Word 2007), 33–35
Spotlight (Access 2007), 523–524
spreadsheets. *See* worksheets
starting
   Access 2007, 522–523
   Excel 2007, 276–279
   PowerPoint 2007, 774–775
   slideshows, 777
   Word 2007, 4–5, 982–983
statistical functions, 449
status bar
   Access 2007, 526–527
   Excel 2007, 276–277, 301
   PowerPoint 2007, 775
   Word 2007, 4–5, 29
StDev function, 656
storing documents in folders (Word 2007), 9–13
straight quotes, compared to smart quotes, 176
strings of words, selecting, 17
Style dialog box (Word 2007), 113
styles
   documents (Word 2007)
     definition, 6
     footnotes, 113–115
     Normal, 8
     pictures, 154–156
     Table Styles, 184–187
   presentations (PowerPoint 2007)
     charts, 931–935
     fonts, 790–791
     pictures, 853–854
     shapes, 853–854
     slide backgrounds, 908–909
     SmartArt graphics, 875–876
subject line (letters), definition, 6
Subject-Verb Agreement error, spelling and grammar checking (Word 2007), 42
subpoints, 242
subsets (records), 712

SUM function, 297–302, 390, 448–453, 655–657
summary controls, 730–733
Summary Options button (Access 2007), 726
Summary Options dialog box (Access 2007), 727
summary sheets (Excel 2007), 393–397
suppressing page numbers in documents (Word 2007), 104
Symbol dialog box (Word 2007), 99–100, 110
Symbol gallery (Word 2007), 110
symbols
   displaying cell values, 294
   documents
     anchor, 149
     inserting, 109–111
   em dash, 110
   as numbers for footnotes, 112
Symbols group, inserting symbols into documents (Word 2007), 109–111
synonyms, definition, 786

T

Tab Alignment button (Word 2007), 159
tab order (forms), 696
tab stops (documents), 157–160
   dot leaders, 161–162
   formatting, 160–162
   inserting text, 162–163
   leader characters, 161
   moving, 164
   removing, 160–162
   selecting tab stop marks, 164
table area (Query window), 616
Table design, definition, 528
Table gallery (Word 2007), 172
Table Properties dialog box (Word 2007), 185–186
Table Styles (Word 2007), 184–187
Table Styles gallery (PowerPoint 2007), 929
table templates (Access 2007), 540
Table Templates button, 540
Table Tools, 172
   Access 2007, 526–527
tables
   databases (Access 2007), 526–527
     adding, 540–542
     adding records, 528–530, 542–543, 695–695
     adding records with forms, 695–697
     cells, 528
     columns, 527, 543–549
     creating by entering records into Multiple Items form, 559–561
     creating by importing worksheets, 635–638
     creating queries based on multiple tables, 646–649
     creating relationships, 606–610
     creating with new designs, 565–568
     data, 527
     Datasheet view, 528
     deleting records with forms, 697–698
     Design view, 528
     fields. See fields (database tables)
     foreign key, 609
     join lines, 610
     moving across rows, 529
     names, 536
     populating with data, 528
     previewing, 569
     primary key, 539–540, 566
     printing, 543–549, 569–570

SINGLE PC LICENSE AGREEMENT AND LIMITED WARRANTY

READ THIS LICENSE CAREFULLY BEFORE OPENING THIS PACKAGE. BY OPENING THIS PACKAGE, YOU ARE AGREEING TO THE TERMS AND CONDITIONS OF THIS LICENSE. IF YOU DO NOT AGREE, DO NOT OPEN THE PACKAGE. PROMPTLY RETURN THE UNOPENED PACKAGE AND ALL ACCOMPANYING ITEMS TO THE PLACE YOU OBTAINED THEM. *THESE TERMS APPLY TO ALL LICENSED SOFTWARE ON THE DISK EXCEPT THAT THE TERMS FOR USE OF ANY SHAREWARE OR FREEWARE ON THE DISKETTES ARE AS SET FORTH IN THE ELECTRONIC LICENSE LOCATED ON THE DISK:*

1. GRANT OF LICENSE and OWNERSHIP: The enclosed computer programs ("Software") are licensed, not sold, to you by Prentice-Hall, Inc. ("We" or the "Company") and in consideration of your purchase or adoption of the accompanying Company textbooks and/or other materials, and your agreement to these terms. We reserve any rights not granted to you. You own only the disk(s) but we and/or our licensors own the Software itself. This license allows you to use and display your copy of the Software on a single computer (i.e., with a single CPU) at a single location for academic use only, so long as you comply with the terms of this Agreement. You may make one copy for back up, or transfer your copy to another CPU, provided that the Software is usable on only one computer.

2. RESTRICTIONS: You may not transfer or distribute the Software or documentation to anyone else. Except for backup, you may not copy the documentation or the Software. You may not network the Software or otherwise use it on more than one computer or computer terminal at the same time. You may not reverse engineer, disassemble, decompile, modify, adapt, translate, or create derivative works based on the Software or the Documentation. You may be held legally responsible for any copying or copyright infringement which is caused by your failure to abide by the terms of these restrictions.

3. TERMINATION: This license is effective until terminated. This license will terminate automatically without notice from the Company if you fail to comply with any provisions or limitations of this license. Upon termination, you shall destroy the Documentation and all copies of the Software. All provisions of this Agreement as to limitation and disclaimer of warranties, limitation of liability, remedies or damages, and our ownership rights shall survive termination.

4. DISCLAIMER OF WARRANTY: THE COMPANY AND ITS LICENSORS MAKE NO WARRANTIES ABOUT THE SOFTWARE, WHICH IS PROVIDED "AS-IS." IF THE DISK IS DEFECTIVE IN MATERIALS OR WORKMANSHIP, YOUR ONLY REMEDY IS TO RETURN IT TO THE COMPANY WITHIN 30 DAYS FOR REPLACEMENT UNLESS THE COMPANY DETERMINES IN GOOD FAITH THAT THE DISK HAS BEEN MISUSED OR IMPROPERLY INSTALLED, REPAIRED, ALTERED OR DAMAGED. THE COMPANY DISCLAIMS ALL WARRANTIES, EXPRESS OR IMPLIED, INCLUDING WITHOUT LIMITATION, THE IMPLIED WARRANTIES OF MERCHANTABILITY AND FITNESS FOR A PARTICULAR PURPOSE. THE COMPANY DOES NOT WARRANT, GUARANTEE OR MAKE ANY REPRESENTATION REGARDING THE ACCURACY, RELIABILITY, CURRENTNESS, USE, OR RESULTS OF USE, OF THE SOFTWARE.

5. LIMITATION OF REMEDIES AND DAMAGES: IN NO EVENT, SHALL THE COMPANY OR ITS EMPLOYEES, AGENTS, LICENSORS OR CONTRACTORS BE LIABLE FOR ANY INCIDENTAL, INDIRECT, SPECIAL OR CONSEQUENTIAL DAMAGES ARISING OUT OF OR IN CONNECTION WITH THIS LICENSE OR THE SOFTWARE, INCLUDING, WITHOUT LIMITATION, LOSS OF USE, LOSS OF DATA, LOSS OF INCOME OR PROFIT, OR OTHER LOSSES SUSTAINED AS A RESULT OF INJURY TO ANY PERSON, OR LOSS OF OR DAMAGE TO PROPERTY, OR CLAIMS OF THIRD PARTIES, EVEN IF THE COMPANY OR AN AUTHORIZED REPRESENTATIVE OF THE COMPANY HAS BEEN ADVISED OF THE POSSIBILITY OF SUCH DAMAGES. SOME JURISDICTIONS DO NOT ALLOW THE LIMITATION OF DAMAGES IN CERTAIN CIRCUMSTANCES, SO THE ABOVE LIMITATIONS MAY NOT ALWAYS APPLY.

6. GENERAL: THIS AGREEMENT SHALL BE CONSTRUED IN ACCORDANCE WITH THE LAWS OF THE UNITED STATES OF AMERICA AND THE STATE OF NEW YORK, APPLICABLE TO CONTRACTS MADE IN NEW YORK, AND SHALL BENEFIT THE COMPANY, ITS AFFILIATES AND ASSIGNEES. This Agreement is the complete and exclusive statement of the agreement between you and the Company and supersedes all proposals, prior agreements, oral or written, and any other communications between you and the company or any of its representatives relating to the subject matter. If you are a U.S. Government user, this Software is licensed with "restricted rights" as set forth in subparagraphs (a)-(d) of the Commercial Computer-Restricted Rights clause at FAR 52.227-19 or in subparagraphs (c)(1)(ii) of the Rights in Technical Data and Computer Software clause at DFARS 252.227-7013, and similar clauses, as applicable.

Should you have any questions concerning this agreement or if you wish to contact the Company for any reason, please contact in writing:

Multimedia Production
Higher Education Division
Prentice-Hall, Inc.
1 Lake Street
Upper Saddle River NJ 07458